W9-AQV-838

ROBERT ALTHANN S.J.

# ELENCHUS OF BIBLICA

# 1997

EDITRICE PONTIFICIO ISTITUTO BIBLICO
ROMA 2001

# ELENCHUS OF BIBLICAL BIBLIOGRAPHY

—————— 13 ——————

ROBERT ALTHANN S.J.

# ELENCHUS OF BIBLICA

## 1997

WITHDRAWN

EDITRICE PONTIFICIO ISTITUTO BIBLICO
ROMA 2001

ISBN: 88-7653-614-0

EDITRICE PONTIFICIO ISTITUTO BIBLICO
Piazza della Pilotta, 35 - 00187 Roma, Italia

# *Urbes editionis* — Cities of publication

| | | | |
|---|---|---|---|
| AA | Ann Arbor | Lp | Leipzig |
| Amst | Amsterdam | LVL | Louisville KY |
| B | Berlin | Lv(N) | Leuven (L-Neuve) |
| Ba/BA | Basel/Buenos Aires | M/Mi | Madrid/Milano |
| Barc | Barcelona | Mkn/Mp | Maryknoll/Minneapolis |
| Bo/Bru | Bologna/Brussel | Mü/Müns('r) | München/Münster |
| C | Cambridge, England | N | Napoli |
| CasM | Casale Monferrato | ND | NotreDame IN |
| Ch | Chicago | Neuk | Neukirchen/Verlag |
| CinB | Cinisello Balsamo | NHv/Nv | New Haven/Nashville |
| CM | Cambridge, Mass. | NY | New York |
| ColMn | Collegeville MN | Ox | Oxford |
| Da:Wiss | Darmstadt, WissBuchg | P/Pd | Paris/Paderborn |
| DG | Downers Grove | Ph | Philadelphia |
| Dü | Düsseldorf | R/Rg | Roma/Regensburg |
| E | Edinburgh | S/Sdr | Salamanca/Santander |
| ENJ | EnglewoodCliffs NJ | SF | San Francisco |
| F | Firenze | Shf | Sheffield |
| Fra | Frankfurt/M | Sto | Stockholm |
| FrB/FrS | Freiburg-Br/Schweiz | Stu | Stuttgart |
| Gö | Göttingen | T/TA | Torino/Tel Aviv |
| GR | Grand Rapids MI | Tü | Tübingen |
| Gü | Gütersloh | U/W | Uppsala/Wien |
| Ha | Hamburg | WL | Winona Lake IN |
| Heid | Heidelberg | Wmr | Warminster |
| Hmw | Harmondsworth | Wsb | Wiesbaden |
| J | Jerusalem | Wsh | Washington D.C. |
| K | København | Wsz | Warszawa |
| L/Lei | London/Leiden | Wu/Wü | Wuppertal/Würzburg |
| LA | Los Angeles | Z | Zürich |

**Punctuation**: To separate a subtitle from its title, we use a COLON (:). The *semicolon* (;) serves to separate items that in other respects belong together. Hence, at the end of an entry a *semicolon* indicates a link with the following entry. This link may consist in the two entries having the same author or in the case of multiauthor works having the same book title; the author will be mentioned in the first entry of such a group, the common book title in the last entry, that is the one which concludes with a fullstop [period] (.).

**Abbreviations**: These follow S.M. Schwertner, **IATG**[2] (De Gruyter; Berlin 1992) as far as possible. A list of other abbreviations appears below.

**Names**: Those beginning with 'van' are listed under this particle.

**Price of books**: This is sometimes rounded off ($10 for $9.95).

# Index systematicus — Contents

The present volume contains all the 1997 material of the Elenchus. Thanks are due to the Catholic Biblical Association of America which has once again granted a welcome subsidy towards defraying the cost of publication. I should also like to thank the staff of the Editrice Pontificio Istituto Biblico which assures the publication of the Elenchus.

The materials for this volume were gathered from the libraries of the Pontifical Biblical Institute, the Pontifical Gregorian University and the University of Innsbruck. I thank the staff of these libraries for their patience and willingness to help. The Department of Biblical Studies at the University of Innsbruck has again provided invaluable assistance in supplying abundant bibliographical information. In return we are continuing to supply book reviews which may be accessed through BILDI on the internet.

As mentioned in the last volume, we are planning to make the material of the Elenchus available on compact disk in association with the library of the Pontifical Biblical Institute.

**Acronyms: Periodica** - Series (small).
*8 fig.* = ISSN; *10 fig.* = ISBN.

A: in Arabic.
**AcBib**: Acta Pontificii Instituti Biblici; R.
Acta Patristica et Byzantina; Pretoria.
**ActBib**: Actualidad Bibliográfica; Barc.
Ad Gentes; Bo.
**AETSC**: Annales de l'Ecole Théologique Saint-Cyprien; Yaoundé, Cameroun.
**AfR**: Archiv für Religionsgeschichte; Stu.
**AHIg**: Anuario de historia de la iglesia; Pamplona.
**AJPS**: Asian Journal of Pentecostal Studies;
**AJSR**: Association for Jewish Studies Review; Waltham, MA.
**Ä&L**: Ägypten und Levante; Wien.
Alei Etzion; Alon Shvut.
Al-Mushir [**Urdu**]; Rawalpindi.
Alpha Omega; R.
Alternativas; Managua.
**AltOrF**: Altorientalische Forschungen; B.
AnáMnesis; México.
**AncB**: Anchor Bible; NY.
Ancient Philosophy; Pittsburgh.
Anime e corpi; Brezzo di Bedero, Va.
Annali Chieresi; Chieri.
Annals of Theology [**P.**]; Krákow.
**AnnTh**: Annales Theologici; R.
**AnScR**: Annali di Scienze Religiose; Mi.
Antologia Vieusseux; F.
Archaeology in the Biblical World; Shafter, CA.
**ARET**: Archivi reali di Ebla, testi; R.

**ARGU**: Arbeiten zur Religion und Geschichte des Urchristentums; Fra.
**ARJ**: The Annual of Rabbinic Judaism; Lei.
**ASJ**: Acta Sumerologica; Kyoto, Japan.
**ATT**: Archivo teologico torinese; Leumann (Torino).
**AtT**: Atualidade teológica; Rio de Janeiro.
Atualização; Belo Horizonte.
**AulOr**: Aula Orientalis (S: Supplement); Barc.
Auriensia; Ourense, Spain [I, 1998].
**BAIAS**: Bulletin of the Anglo-Israel Archaeological Society; L.
Barnabiti Studi; R.
Bazmavep; Venise.
**BBR**: Bulletin for Biblical Research; WL.
**BCSMS**: Bulletin of the Canadian Society for Mesopotamian Studies; Toronto.
**BEgS**: Bulletin of the Egyptological Seminar; NY.
**Bib(L)**: Bíblica; Lisboa.
**Bibl.Interp.**      (**Bibl.Interp.**): Biblical Interpretation; Lei.
**Biblioteca EstB**: Biblioteca de Estudios Bíblicos; S.
**BnS**: La bibbia nella storia; Bo.
Bobolanum [**P.**]; Wsz.
Bogoslovni      Vestnik      [**S.**]; Ljubljana.
**BolT**:      Boletín      teológico; Buenos Aires.
**BoSm**: Bogoslovska Smotra; Zagreb.
**BRT**: The Baptist Review of Theology / La revue baptiste de théologie; Gormely, Ontario.
**BSÉG**: Bulletin de la Société d'Égyptologie; Genève.
**BSLP**: Bulletin de la Société de Linguistique de Paris; P.
**BuBbgB**:      Bulletin      de bibliographie biblique; Lausanne.

Bulletin of Ecumenical Theology; Enugu, Nigeria.

Bulletin of Judaeo-Greek Studies; C.

Bulletin of Research of Christian Culture; Okayama, Japan.

**BurH**: Buried History; Melbourne.

**BWM**:    Bibelwissenschaftliche Monographien; Gießen.

**CAH**: Cambridge Ancient History[2]; Cambridge Univ.

Cahiers de l'Atelier; P.

Cahiers Ratisbonne; J.

**CahPhRel**: Cahiers de l'Ecole des Sciences philosophiques et religieuses; Bru.

**CAL.N**: Comprehensive Aramaic Lexicon, Newsletter; Cincinatti.

**CamArch**:    Cambridge Archaeological Journal; C.

Carthaginensia; Murcia.

Catalyst; Goroka, Papua New Guinea.

Catechisti parrocchiali; R.

Cathedra; Bogotá.

Cathedra [**H.**]; J.

Centro pro unione, Bulletin; R.

Chemins    de    Dialogue; Marseille.

Choisir; Genève.

Chongshin Review; Seoul.

Christian Thought; Seoul.

Chronology and Catastrophism Workshop; Luton.

Cias; Buenos Aires.

C: in Chinese.

**CLEC**: Common Life in the Early Church;

**CLehre**: Die Christenlehre; B.

**CMAO**: Contributi e Materiali di Archeologia Orientale; R.

Colloquium; Brisbane.

Comunidades; S.

**ConAss**:    Convivium    Assisiense; Assisi.

Confer; M.

Contacts; Courbevoie.

Contagion; Rocky Mount.

Convergência; São Paulo.

**CoSe**: Consacrazione e Servizio; R.

**CredOg**: Credereoggi; Padova.

**CritRR**:    Critical    Review    of Books in Religion; Atlanta.

Crkva u Svijetu; Split.

Croire aujourd'hui; P.

Crux: Vancouver.

**CTrB**: Cahiers de traduction biblique; Pierrefitte, France.

**CuesT**: Cuestiones Teológicas; Medellin.

Cuestion Social, La; Mexico.

**CurResB**:    Currents    in    Research: Biblical Studies; Shf.

Daphnis; Amst.

**D**: Director dissertationis.

Diadokhē [ΔΙΑΔΟΧΗ]. Revista de Estudios de Filosofía Platónica y Cristiana; Santiago de Chile.

Didascalia; Rosario, ARG.

Direction; Fresno, CA.

**DiscEg**: Discussions in Egyptology; Oxf.

**DissA**: Dissertation Abstracts International; AA/L. -A [= US *etc.*]: 0419-4209 [C = Europe. 0307-6075].

**DosP**: Les Dossiers de la Bible; P.

**DQ**: Documenta Q; Leuven.

**DSBP**: Dizionario di spiritualità biblico-patristica; R.

**DSD**: Dead Sea Discoveries; Lei.

**E**: Editor, Herausgeber, a cura di.

**Eccl(R)**: Ecclesia; R.

**EfMex**: Efemérides Mexicana; Tlalpan.

**EgArch**: Egyptian Archaeology, Bulletin of the Egypt Exploration Society; L.

**ETJ**:    Ephrem's    Theological Journal; Satna, India.

Emmanuel; St. Meinrads, IN.

**ERSY**: Erasmus of Rotterdam Society Yearbook; Lexington.

**EscrVedat**: Escritos del Vedat; Valencia.

Esprit; P.

Ethics & Medicine; Carlisle.

ETSI Journal; Igbaja, Nigeria.

**EurJT**: European Journal of Theology; Carlisle.

Evangel; E.
Evangelizzare; Bo.
EvV: Evangelio y Vida; León.
Exchange; Lei.
Faith & Mission; Wake Forest, NC.
Feminist Theology; Shf.
F: Festschrift.
FgNT: Filologia Neotestamentaria; Córdoba.
Filosofia oggi; Genova.
Firmana; Fermo.
Florensia; S. Giovanni in Fiore (CS).
FolTh: Folia theologica; Budapest.
Forum. Sonoma, CA.
Forum Religion; Stu.
Franciscanum; Bogotá.
Freiburger Universitätsblätter; FrB.
Fundamentum; Basel.
Furrow; Maynooth.
Gema; Yogyakarta.
Georgica; Konstanz.
G: in Greek.
Gnosis; SF.
Graphè; Lille.
Hagiographica; F.
Hamdard Islamicus; Karachi.
HBO: Hallesche Beiträge zur Orientwissenschaft; Halle.
Hekima Review; Nairobi.
Henoch; T.
H: in Hebrew.
History of European Ideas; Oxf.
HIL: Das Heilige Land; Köln.
Holy Land; J.
Horeb; Pozzo di Gotto (ME).
Horizons; Villanova, PA.
HorWi: Horizonty Wiary; Kraków.
Ho Theológos; Palermo.
IAJS: Index of Articles on Jewish Studies; J.
Ichthys ΙΧΘΥΣ; Aarhus.
Igreja e Missão; Valadares, Cucujaes.
IHR: International History Review; Burnaby, Canada.
IJCT: International Journal of the Classical Tradition; New Brunswick, NJ.

INTAMS.R: INTAMS [International Academy for Marital Spirituality] review; Sint-Genesius-Rode, Belgium.
Inter Fratres; Fabriano (AN).
Interpretation(F). Journal of Political Philosophy; Flushing.
Iran; L.
Isidorianum; Sevilla.
IslChr: Islamochristiana; R.
ITBT: Interpretatie; Zoetermeer.
Iter; Caracas.
Itin(M): Itinerarium; Messina.
JAAT: Journal of Asian and Asian American Theology; Claremont, Calif.
JAB: Journal for the Aramaic Bible; Shf.
JAGNES: Journal of the Association of Graduates in Near Eastern Studies; Berkeley, CA.
Jahrbuch Politische Theologie; Mü.
Japan Mission Journal; Tokyo.
JBTSA: Journal of Black Theology in South Africa; Atteridgeville.
JEarlyC: Journal of Early Christian Studies; Baltimore.
Jeevadhara; Alleppey, Kerala.
JEGTFF: Jahrbuch der Europäischen Gesellschaft für theologische Forschung von Frauen; Mainz.
JHiC: Journal of Higher Criticism; Montclair, NJ.
Jian Dao; Hong Kong.
J: in Japanese.
JIntH: Journal of interdisciplinary history; CM.
JJTP: Journal of Jewish Thought & Philosophy; Ba.
JKTh: Jahrbuch für kontextuelle Theologien; Fra.
JNSL: Journal of Northwest Semitic Languages; Stellenbosch.
Jota; Lv.
Journal of Ancient History; Moscow.
Journal of Institutional and

Theoretical Economics; Tü.

Journal of Medieval History; Amsterdam.

Journal of Psychology and Judaism; NY.

**JPentec**: Journal of Pentecostal Theology; Shf (S: Supplement).

**JPersp**: Jerusalem Perspective; J.

**JProgJud**: Journal of Progressive Judaism; Shf.

**JPURS**: Jnanadeepa, Pune Journal of Religious Studies; Pune.

**JRadRef**: Journal from the Radical Reformation; Morrow, GA.

**JRTR**: Jahrbuch für Religionswissenschaft und Theologie der Religionen; FrB.

**JSem**: Journal for Semitics; Pretoria.

**JSQ**: Jewish Studies Quarterly; Tü.

**JSSEA**: Journal of the Society for the Study of Egyptian Antiquities; Toronto.

**JTrTL**: Journal of Translation and Textlinguistics; Dallas.

**Jud.**: Judaism; NY.

Kairos(G); Guatemala.

**KaKe**: Katorikku-Kenkyu [**J.**]; Tokyo.

Kerux; Escondido, CA.

**K**: in Korean.

Kwansei-Gakuin-Daigaku; Japan.

Landas. Journal of Loyola School of Theology; Manila.

Laós; Catania.

Living Light; Wsh.

**LSDC**: La Sapienza della Croce; R.

Luther-Bulletin; Amst.

Luther Digest; Crestwood, Miss.

**M.**: Memorial.

**MAI**: Masters Abstracts International; AA: 0898-9095.

**MastJ**: Master's Seminary Journal; Sun Valley, CA.

Mayéutica; Marcilla (Navarra).

**MEAH**: Miscellánea de Estudios Árabes y Hebraicos (**MEAH.A**: Árabe-Islam. **MEAH.H**: Hebreo); Granada.

**MESA.B**: Middle East Studies Association Bulletin; Muncie, IN.

Mid-Stream; Indianapolis.

Miles Immaculatae; R.

**MillSt**: Milltown Studies; Dublin.

**MissTod**: Mission Today; Shillong, India.

Mitteilungen für Anthropologie und Religionsgeschichte; Saarbrücken.

Mondo della Bibbia, Il; T.

Moralia; M.

MST Review; Manila.

**NAC**: New American Commentary; Nv.

**NAOTS**: Newsletter on African Old Testament Scholarship; Stavanger [0808-2413].

**NEA(BA)**: Near Eastern Archaeology [BA]; Boston.

Neukirchener Theologische Zeitschrift; Neuk.

**NewTR**: New Theology Review; Ch.

**NHMS**: Nag Hammadi and Manichaean Studies; Lei.

**NIBC**: New International Biblical Commentary; Peabody.

Nicolaus; Bari.

**NIntB**: The New Interpreter's Bible; Nv.

**NotesTrans**: Notes on Translation; Dallas.

**NTGu**: New Testament Guides; Shf.

**NTTRU**: New Testament Textual Research Update; Ashfield NSW, Australia.

Nuova Umanità; R.

Obnovljeni Život; Zagreb.

Ḥokhma; Lausanne.

Omnis Terra; R.

**OrBibChr**: Orbis biblicus et christianus; Glückstadt.

**OrExp**: Orient-Express, Notes et Nouvelles d'Archéologie Orientale; P.

Orient; Tokyo.
Orientamenti pedagogici; R.
P: in Polish.
Pacifica. Australian Theological Studies; Melbourne.
Paginas; Lima.
PaiC.: Paideia Cristiana; Rosario, ARG.
Paléorient; P.
Palestjinskji Sbornik [R.]; Moskva.
Parabola; NY.
Pensiero politico, Il; F.
Phase; Barc.
Philosophiques; Montréal.
Physis; F.
PoeT: Poetics Today; Durham, NC.
PoST: Poznańskie studia teologiczne; Poznán (83-86360-18-6).
PredOT: Prediking van het Oude Testament; Baarn.
Presbyteri; Trento.
Presbyterion; St. Louis.
PresPast: Presenza Pastorale, R.
Prism; St. Paul, MN.
ProcGLM: Proceedings of the Eastern Great Lakes and Midwest Bible Societies; Buffalo.
ProEc: Pro ecclesia; Northfield, MN.
Prooftexts; Baltimore.
Proverbium; Burlington, VT.
Proyección; Granada.
ProySal: Proyecto Centro Salesiano de Estudios; BA.
Prudentia [.S]; Auckland, NZ.
PzB: Protokolle zur Bibel; Klosterneuburg.
Quaderni di azione sociale; R.
Quaderni di scienze religiose; Loreto.
Qumran Chronicle; Kraków.
QVC: Qüestions de Vida Cristiana; Barc.
R: in Russian.
R: recensio, book-review.
Ragion Pratica; Genova.
RANL: Rendiconti dell'Accademia Nazionale dei Lincei; R.

RASM: Revue africaine des sciences de la mission; Kinshasa.
RBBras: Revista Bíblica Brasileira; Fortaleza.
Reason and the Faith, The; Kwangju.
Recollectio; R.
Reformation, The; Oxf (Tyndale Soc.).
Religion; L.
Religious Research; Wsh.
RelT: Religion and Theology; Pretoria.
RenSt: Renaissance Studies; Oxf.
ResB: Reseña Bíblica; Estella.
RevCT: Revista de cultura teológica; São Paulo.
Revista católica; Santiago de Chile.
Revue d'éthique et de théologie morale; P.
RGRW: Religions in the Graeco-Roman World; Lei.
Ribla: Revista de interpretação biblica latino-americana; Petrópolis.
RICAO: Revue de l'Institut Catholique de l'Afrique de l'Ouest; Abidjan.
Rivista di archeologia; R.
Roczniki Teologiczne; Lublin
Romania; P.
RRT: Reviews in Religion and Theology; L.
R&T: Religion and theology = Religie en teologie; Pretoria.
S: Slovenian.
SAAA: Studies on the Apocryphal Acts of the Apostles; Kampen.
SAA Bulletin: State Archives of Assyria Bulletin; Padova.
SAAS: State Archives of Assyria, Studies; Helsinki.
Saeculum Christianum; Wsz.
San Juan de la Cruz; Sevilla.
SaThZ: Salzburger Theologische Zeitschrift; Salzburg.
SBL.SCSt: Society of Biblical Literature, Septuagint and Cognate Studies; Atlanta.

Science and Christian Belief;
Carlisle.
Scriptura; Stellenbosch.
Scrittura e civiltà; F.
SdT: Studi di Teologia; R.
SEAP: Studi di Egittologia e di
Antichità Puniche; Pisa.
Search; Dublin.
Sedes Sapientiae; Chéméré-le-
Roi.
Segni e comprensione; Lecce.
SeK: Skrif en Kerk; Pretoria.
Semeia; Atlanta.
Semiotica; Amst.
Sen.: Sendros; Costa Rica.
Servitium; CasM.
SetRel: Sette e Religioni; Bo.
Sevartham; Ranchi.
Sève; P.
Sewanee Theological Review;
Sewanee, TN.
Shofar; West Lafayette, IN.
SIDIC: Service International
de Documentation Judéo-
Chrétienne; R.
Sinhak Jonmang; Kwangju, S.
Korea.
Soleriana; Montevideo.
Soundings; Nv.
Sources; FrS.
Spiritual Life; Wsh.
Spiritus; P.
SPJMS: South Pacific Journal
of Mission Studies; North
Turramurra NSW.
SRATK: Studia nad Rodzina,
Akademia Teologii Katolik-
kiej; Wsz, 1429-2416.
Stauros. Bolletino trimestrale
sulla teologia della Croce;
Pescara.
StEL: Studi epigrafici e lin-
guistici; Verona.
St Mark's Review; Canberra.
StSp(K): Studies in Spiri-
tuality; Kampen.
Studi emigrazione; R.
Studia Textus Novi Testamenti;
Osaka.
Studies in World Christianity;
E.
Studi Fatti Ricerche; Mi.
Stulos. Theological Journal;
Bandung, Indonesia.

StWC: Studies in World Chri-
stianity; E.
SUBB: Studia Universitatis
Babeş-Bolyai; Cluj-Napoca,
Romania.
Synaxis; Catania.
Tanima; Kochi, Kerala.
TCNN: Theological College of
Northern Nigeria; Bukuru.
Teocomunicaçâo; Porto
Alegre, Brasil.
Teologia Iusi; Caracas.
Ter Herkenning; 's-Graven-
hage.
Tertium Millennium; R.
TEuph: Transeuphratène; P.
TGr.T Tesi Gregoriana, Serie
Teologia; R.
Theologica & Historica; Ca-
gliari.
Theologika; Lima.
Théologiques; Montréal.
Theologischer; Siegburg.
Theology for Our Times; Ban-
galore.
Theotokos; R.
ThirdM: Third Millennium:
Pune, India.
T&K: Texte und Kontexte;
Stu.
TrinJ: Trinity Journal; Deer-
field, IL.
TTE: The Theological Educa-
tor; New Orleans.
T: Translator.
Tychique; Lyon.
Umat Baru; Yogyakarta, Indo-
nesia.
Una Voce-Korrespondenz;
Köln.
Vie Chrétienne; P.
Vie, La: des communautés reli-
gieuses; Montréal.
Vita Sociale; F.
Vivarium; Catanzaro.
VivH: Vivens Homo; F.
VO: Vicino Oriente; R.
VTW: Voices from the Third
World; Bangalore.
Vox Patrum; Lublin.
VoxScr: Vox Scripturae; São
Paulo.
WaW: Word and World; St.
Paul, Minn.

Way, The; L.
WBC: Word Biblical Commentary; Waco.
West African Journal of Ecclesial Studies; Ibadan, Nigeria.
WUB: Welt und Umwelt der Bibel; Stu.
Yonsei Journal of Theology;

Seoul.
ZAC: Zeitschrift für antikes Christentum;
ZAR: Zeitschrift für altorientalische und biblische Rechtsgeschichte; Wsb.
ZME: Zeitschrift für medizinische Ethik; Salzburg.

# I. Bibliographica

## A1 Opera collecta .1 Festschriften, memorials

1 AHLSTROEM, Gösta W.: The pitcher is broken. EHolloway, Steven W.; Handy, Lowell K.: JSOT.S 190: 1995, ⇒11/1,1. RCBQ 59 (1997) 195-196 (*Betlyon, John W.*).

2 ALBERIGO, Giuseppe: Cristianesimo nella storia. EMelloni, Alberto: 1996, ⇒12,1. RStPat 44 (1997) 213-215 (*Sartori, Luigi*).

3 ALDRED, Cyril: Chief of seers: Egyptian studies in memory of... EGoring, Elizabeth; Reeves, Carl Nicholas; Ruffle, John: Studies in Egyptology: L 1997, Kegan P xx; 313 pp. 1 port., fig. 0-7103-0449-8.

4 ASHTON, John: Understanding, studying and reading: New Testament essays in honour of... ERowland, Christopher; Fletcher-Louis, Crispin H.T.: JSNT.S 153: Shf 1997, JSOT 267 pp. £37.50/$62. 1-85075-828-X.

5 ASTOUR, Michael C.: Crossing boundaries and linking horizons: studies in honor of... on his 80th birthday. EYoung, Gordon Douglas; Chavalas, Mark William; Averbeck, Richard E.; collab. *Danti, Kevin L.*: Bethesda, MD 1997, CDL xxiii; 689 pp. Bibl. $55. 1-883053-32-3.

6 AVIRAM, Joseph: Archaeological, historical and geographical studies. EBiran, Avraham: ErIs 25: 1996, ⇒12,2 [Hebrew, English]. ROLZ 92 (1997) 525-531 (*Pfeifer, Gerhard*).

7 BAARDA, Tjitze: Sayings of Jesus: canonical and non-canonical: essays in honour of ... EPetersen, William L.; Jonge, Henk Jan de; Vos, Johan Sijko: NT.S 89: Lei 1997, Brill xxvi; 344 pp. Bibl. *f*176. 90-04-10380-5. REThL 73 (1997) 456-458 (*Neirynck, F.*).

8 BAUMGARTEN, Joseph M.: Legal texts and legal issues: proceedings of the second meeting of the International Organization for Qumran Studies, C 1995, EBernstein, Moshe J.; García Martínez, Florentino; Kampen, John Irwin: StTDJ 23: Lei 1997, Brill xxv; 539 pp. Published in honour of ... Bibl. by García Martínez, Florentino XIX-XXV; an appreciation by Schwartz, Daniel R. XV-XVIII. *f*247/$152. 90-04-10829-7.

9 BECK, Eleonore: Rosen in der Wüste: ein Mosaik zu Jesaja 40-55. EMiller, Gabriele: Ostfildern 1996, Schwaben 295 pp. [StZ 215,428s—Dorner, Stephan].

10 BEKER, Johan Christiaan: Biblical theology. EOllenburger, Ben C., (*al*), 1995, ⇒11/1,6. RCBQ 59 (1997) 196-198 (*Bernas, Casimir*).

11 BETTI, Umberto: La 'Dei Verbum' trent'anni dopo. 1995, ⇒11/2,20. RLASBF 47 (1997) 623-626 (*Chrupcała, Lesław Daniel*).

12 BEUKEN, Willem A.M.: Studies in the book of Isaiah. EVan Ruiten, Jacques T.A.G.M.; Vervenne, Marc: BEThL 132: Lv 1997, Peeters xx; 540 pp. FB3000. 90-6831-926-4 [ETR 73,311].

13 BLENKINSOPP, Joseph: Priests, prophets and scribes: essays on the formation and heritage of second temple Judaism in honour of... ᴱUlrich, Eugene, (al), JSOT.S 149: 1992, ⇒8,19a. ᴿVT 47 (1997) 569-570 (Emerton, John A.E.); JJS 48 (1997) 356-357 (Knoppers, Gary N.).

14 BOARDMAN, John: The archaeology of Greek colonisation. 1994, ⇒11/2,22. ᴿAJA 101 (1997) 601-602 (Hoffman, Gail L.);

15 Greek offerings: essays on Greek art in honour of... ᴱPalagia, Olga: Oxbow Monograph 89: Oxf 1997, Oxbow vi; 214 pp. Bibl. 1-900188-44-9.

16 BOLLE, Kees W.: The persistence of religions: essays in honor of... ᴱDenning-Bolle, Sara J.; Gerow, Edwin: Other realities 9: Malibu 1996, Undena xxi; 444 pp. Bibl. 0-89003-500-1.

17 BREKELMANS, C.H.W.: Deuteronomy and Deuteronomic literature. ᴱVervenne, Marc; Lust, Johan: BEThL 133: Lv 1997, Peeters xi; 637 pp. FB3000. 90-6831-936-1 [ETR 73,311].

18 BURGMANN, Hans: Mogilany 1993: papers on the Dead Sea Scrolls. ᴱKapera, Zdzislaw J.: Qumranica Mogilanensia 13: 1996, ⇒12,12. ᴿDSD 4 (1997) 362-364 (Abegg, Martin G.).

19 CASCIARO, José María: Biblia, exegesis y cultura. ᴱAranda, G.: 1994, ⇒10,22a; 12,14. ᴿOCP 63/1 (1997) 234-235 (Farrugia, E.G.).

20 COATS, George W.: A biblical itinerary: in search of method, form and content: essays in honor of... ᴱCarpenter, Eugene E.: JSOT.S 240: Shf 1997, Academic 194 pp. £30/$49.50. 1-85075-653-8.

21 COUROYER, Bernard: Études égyptologiques et bibliques: à la mémoire du Père ... ᴱSigrist, Marcel: CRB 36: P 1997, Gabalda 125 pp. FF140. 2-85021-090-0.

22 DASSMANN, Ernst: Stimuli: Exegese und ihre Hermeneutik in Antike und Christentum: Festschrift für... ᴱSchöllgen, Georg; Scholten, Clemens: JAC.E 23: 1996, ⇒12,19. ᴿNRTh 119 (1997) 107-108 (Ska, J.L.); Sal. 59 (1997) 560-561.

23 DOTHAN, Moshe: Studies in the archaeology and history of ancient Israel in honor of... ᴱHeltzer, Michael, (al), 1993, ᴿJNES 56 (1997) 137-138 (Rast, Walter E.).

24 FREEDMAN, David Noel: Fortunate the eyes that see. ᴱBeck, Astrid B., (al), 1995, ⇒11/1,10. ᴿCBQ 59 (1997) 406-408 (Green, Barbara); AUSS 35 (1997) 249-251 (Hasel, Michael G.).

25 FRIEDLANDER, Albert H.: "Das Leben leise wieder lernen": jüdisches und christliches Selbstverständnis nach der Schoah: Festschrift für... zum 70.ten. ᴱStegemann, Ekkehard W.; Marcus, Marcel: Stu 1997, Kohlhammer 287 pp. 3-17-014843-5.

26 GABRIELI, Francesco: In memoria di Francesco Gabrieli. RSO 71, Suppl. 2: R 1997, Bardi 229 pp.

27 GEORGI, Dieter: Religious propaganda and missionary competition in the New Testament world. ᴱBormann, Lukas; Tredici, Kelly del; Standhartinger, Angela: NT.S 74: 1994, ⇒10,40; 12,30. ᴿTTK 68/1 (1997) 73-74 (Sandnes, Karl Olav).

28 GERHARDSSON, Birger: Matteus och hans läsare—förr och nu. Matteussymposiet i Lund den 27-28 sept 1996: en hyllning till professor... som fyllde 70 år den 26 september 1996. ᴱOlsson, Birger; Byrskog, Samuel; Übelacker, Walter: Religio 48: Lund 1997, Lunds universitet 114 pp. 0280-5723 [RB 105,298—Langlamet, F.].

29 GERSTENBERGER, Erhard S.: "Ihr Völker alle, klatscht in die Hände!": Festschrift für... zum 65. Geburtstag. ᴱKessler, Rainer;

**Ulrich, Kerstin; Schwantes, Milton:** Exegese in unserer Zeit 3: Müns 1997, Lit vii; 428 pp. 3-8258-2937-5.

30 **Giordano, Card. Michele:** Sicut flumen pax tua: studi in onore del... ᴱAscione, Antonio; Gioia, Mario: N 1997, D'Auria 901 pp. 88-7092-131-X.

31 **Goldenberg, Gideon:** Gideon Goldenberg Festschrift: ᴱBar Asher, M.: Massorot 9-11: J 1997, Centre for Jewish Languages, Hebrew University xlvii; 577 pp. Eng. sum. [JJS 49,371s— Morgenstern, Matthew]. **H.**

32 **Gottlieb, Gunther:** Contra qui ferat arma deos?: vier Augsburger Vorträge zur Religionsgeschichte der römischen Kaiserzeit. ᴱBarceló, **Pedro:** Schriften der philosophischen Fakultäten der Universität Augsburg 53: Mü 1997, Vögel 111 pp. 3-89650-020-1 [RQ 93,140s— Klein, Richard].

33 **Graesser, Erich:** Eschatologie und Schöpfung. ᴱEvang, Martin; Merklein, Helmut M.; Wolter, Michael: BZNW 89: B 1997, de Gruyter xi; 451 pp. Port. 3-11-015545-1.

34 **Greenberg, Moshe:** Tehillah le-Moshe: biblical and Judaic studies in honor of... ᴱCogan, Mordechai; Tigay, Jeffrey H.; Eichler, Barry L.: Bibl. xxiii-xxxviii; Moshe Greenberg: an appreciation ixxxi. WL 1997, Eisenbrauns xliii; 349 (Eng.); 257 (Heb.) pp. $59.50. 1-57506-027-2.

35 **Greenfield, Jonas C.:** Solving riddles and untying knots: biblical, epigraphic, and Semitic studies in honor of... ᴱZevit, Ziony; Gitin, Seymour; Sokoloff, Michael: 1995, ⇒11/1,11. ᴿZAW 109 (1997) 159-160 (Köckert, M.).

36 **Hahn, Ferdinand:** Die Verwurzelung des Christentums im Judentum. ᴱBreytenbach, Cilliers: 1996, ⇒12,34. ᴿThLZ 122 (1997) 991-993 (Broer, Ingo).

37 **Haran, Menaham:** Texts, temples, and traditions: a tribute to... ᴱFox, Michael V.: 1996, ⇒12,35. ᴿCBQ 59 (1997) 193-194 (Murphy, Roland E.); LASBF 47 (1997) 570-571 (Cortese, Enzo).

38 **Harl, Marguerite:** KATA TOUS O': selon les Septante: trente études sur la Bible grecque des Septante: 1995, ⇒11/1,13. ᴿRHR 214 (1997) 487-490 (Schenker, Adrien).

39 **Hartman, Lars:** Texts and contexts: biblical texts in their textual and situational contexts: essays in honour... ᴱFornberg, T., Hellholm, D.: 1995, ⇒11/1,14; 12,37. ᴿJThS 48 (1997) 212-214 (Hickling, C.J.A.).

40 **Hayes, John H.:** History and interpretation: essays in honour of... JSOT.S 173: 1993, ⇒9,62. ᴿVT 47 (1997) 557-560 (Emerton, John A.E.).

41 **Hofius, Otfried:** Jesus Christus als die Mitte der Schrift: Studien zur Hermeneutik des Evangeliums. ᴱLandmesser, Christof; Eckstein, Hans-Joachim; Lichtenberger, Hermann: BZNW 86: B 1997, de Gruyter xii; 1000 pp. DM298. 3-11-015388-2.

42 **Houwink ten Cate, Philo H.J.:** Studio historiae ardens: ancient Near Eastern studies. ᴱRoos, Johan de; Van den Hout, Theo P.J.: 1995, ⇒11/2,84. ᴿAfO 44-45 (1997-98) 531-532 (Jursa, Michael).

43 **Hyldahl, Niels:** Tro og historie: festskrift til... i anledning af 65 års fødselsdagen den 30. december 1995. ᴱFatum, Lone; Müller, Mogens: Forum for bibelsk eksegese 7: K 1996, Museum Tusculanum Press 320 pp. Bibl. 87-7289-364-8.

44 JANKUHN, Herbert: Haus und Hof in ur- und frühgeschichtlicher Zeit: Bericht über zwei Kolloquien der Kommission für die Altertumskunde Mittel- und Nordeuropas vom 24. bis 26. Mai 1990 und 20. bis 22. November 1991 (34. und 35. Arbeitstagung): Gedenkschrift für... EBeck, Heinrich; Steuer, Heiko: AAWG.PH 218: Gö 1997, Vandenhoeck & R 595 pp. Port. 3-525-82386-X.

45 JAVIERRE ORTAS, Antonio María: Super fundamentum apostolorum: Studi in onore di S.Em. il Cardinale ... EAmato, Angelo; Maffei, Giuseppe: BSRel 125: R 1997, LAS 768 pp. Port. 88-213-0349-7.

46 KAMPHAUS, Franz: 'Den Armen eine frohe Botschaft': Festschrift für Bischof ... zum 65. Geburtstag. EHainz, Josef; Jüngling, Hans-Winfried; Sebott, Reinhold: Fra 1997, Knecht xii; 435 pp. DM78. 3-7820-0751-4 [ThRv 94,625ss—Wieh, Hermann].

47 KERTELGE, Karl: Ekklesiologie des Neuen Testaments. EKampling, Rainer; Söding, Thomas: 1996, ⇒12,48. ROrdKor 38 (1997) 371-372 (Giesen, Heinz).

48 KNIERIM, Rolf: Problems in biblical theology: essays in honor of ... ESun, Henry T.C.; Eades, Keith L.; collab. Robinson, James M.; Moller, Garth I.: GR 1997, Eerdmans xvi; 403 pp. $49. 0-8028-3803-0. REThL 73 (1997) 415-417 (Lust, J.).

49 KROTKOFF, Georg: Humanism, culture, and language in the Near East: studies in honor of ... EAfsaruddin, Asma; Zahniser, A.H. Mathias: WL 1997, Eisenbrauns xxiii; 440 pp. Port. $49.50. 1-57506-020-5.

50 KUDASIEWICZ, Jósef: W posludze Slowa Panskiego: ksiega pamiatkowa poswiecona Ks. Prof. Dr. Hab. ... z okazji 70-lecia urodzin. EBielecki, Stanislaw; Ordon, H.; Witczyk, H.: Kielce 1997, "Jednosc" 484 pp. Port. 83-85-957-1. P.

51 KUENG, Hans: Dialogo con ...: con la lezione di congedo di ... EJens, Walter; Kuschel, Karl-Josef: Giornale di teologia 253: Brescia 1997, Queriniana 125 pp. Bibl. 88-399-0753-X.

52 LACH, Jan: Milosc jest z Boga: Wokól zagadnien biblijno-moralnych: Studium ofiarowane ... [Love is from God: studies in biblical theology and ethics offered to Rev. Prof. ...]. Wsz 1997, Wydawnictwo Akademii Teologii Katolickiej 463 pp. Bibl. 83-7072-083-8.

53 LAUER, Jean-Philippe: Études sur l'Ancien Empire et la nécropole de Saqqâra: dédiées à ... EBerger, Catherine; Mathieu, Bernard: Orientalia Monspeliensia 9: Montpellier 1997, Université Paul Valéry 2 vols. Bibl. 2-84269-047-8.

54 LEGASSE, Simon: L'Evangile exploré. EMarchadour, Alain: LeDiv 166: 1996, ⇒12,51. RBLE 98 (1997) 278-282 (Debergé, P.); RevBib 59 (1997) 242-243 (Levoratti, A.J.).

55 LIPINSKA, Jadwiga: Essays in honour of Prof. Dr. ... Warsaw Egyptological Studies 1: Wsz 1997, "PRO-EGIPT" National Museum in Warsaw x; 446 pp. Bibl.; 63 pl. 83-7100-091-X.

56 LOHFINK, Norbert: Biblische Theologie und gesellschaftlicher Wandel. EBraulik, Georg; Groß, Walter; McEvenue, Sean: 1993, ⇒9,212; 12,52. RBZ 41 (1997) 295-297 (Scharbert, Josef); VM 39/1 (1997) 237-238 (Ribera-Mariné, R.).

57 LOEHRER, Magnus; TRAGAN, Pius-Ramon: Patrimonium fidei: traditionsgeschichtliches Verstehen am Ende?: Festschrift für ... und

... ᴱPerroni, Marinella; Salmann, Elmar: St Ans 124: R 1997, Pontificio Ateneo S. Anselmo 788 pp. Bibl. L120.000. 88-8139-083-3.

58 Lukonin, Vladimir G.: Mesopotamia and Iran in the Persian period: conquest and imperialism 539 - 331 BC. ᴱCurtis, John E.: L 1997, British Museum 86 pp. Proceedings of a seminar in memory of ...; funded by a gift from Raymond and Beverly Sackler. 0-7141-1142-2.

59 Maier, Gerhard: Dein Wort ist die Wahrheit: Festschrift für ...: Beiträge zu einer schriftgemäßen Theologie. ᴱHahn, Eberhard; Hille, Rolf; Neudorfer, Heinz-Werner: TVGMS 424: Wu 1997, Brockhaus 366 pp. Ausgewählte Bibliographie von Eißler, Tobias; Morstein, Torsten 357-363. 3-417-29424-X.

60 Mara, Maria Grazia: Studi sul cristianesimo. 1995, ⇒11/2,119. ᴿStMon 39 (1997) 403-404 (Olivar, A.).

61 McKenzie, Steven L.: The Chronicler as historian. ᴱGraham, M. Patrick; Hoglund, Kenneth G.; Dillard, Raymond B.: JSOT.S 238: Shf 1997, Academic 336 pp. £40 / $60. 1-85075-651-1. ᴿEThL 73 (1997) 158-159 (Lust, J.).

62 Meeks, Wayne A.: The social world of the first christians: essays in honor of ... ᴱWhite, Michael; Yarbrough, O. Larry: 1995, ⇒11/1,20. ᴿCBQ 59 (1997) 200-202 (Osiek, Carolyn).

63 Menzies, Robert P.: Pentecostalism in context: essays in honor of ... ᴱMa, Wonsuk; Menzies, William W.: JPentec.S 11: Shf 1997, Academic 373 pp. Port. £16 / $22. 1-85075-803-4.

64 Metzger, Bruce M.: The text of the New Testament in contemporary research. ᴱEhrman, Bart D.; Holmes, Michael W.: StD 46: 1995, ⇒11/2,126; 12,59. ᴿEvQ 69/1 (1997) 65-67 (Head, Peter M.); CBQ 59 (1997) 190-191 (Hurtado, Larry W.).

65 Meyendorff, John: New perspectives on historical theology. ᴱBradley, Nassif: 1996, ⇒12,62. ᴿOrChrP 63 (1997) 583-585 (Farrugia, E.G.).

66 Michel, Diethelm: 'Jedes Ding hat seine Zeit...': Studien zur israelitischen und altorientalischen Weisheit. ᴱDiesel, Anja A., (al), BZAW 241: 1996, ⇒12,64. ᴿRETR 72 (1997) 462-463 (Römer, Thomas).

67 Milgrom, Jacob: Pomegranates and golden bells. ᴱWright, David P., (al.), 1995, ⇒11/1,21. ᴿZAW 109 (1997) 152-153 (Köckert, M.).

68 Moltmann, Jürgen: How I have changed: reflections on thirty years of theology. L 1997, SCM x; 130 pp. 0-334-02707-1.

69 Murphy, Roland E.: Wisdom, you are my sister: studies in honor of ... on the occasion of his eightieth birthday. ᴱBarré, Michael L.: CBQ.MS 29: Wsh 1997, Cath. Biblical Assoc. of America viii; 289 pp. $13. 0-915170-28-0;

70 Master of the sacred page: essays and articles in honour of ... on the occasion of his eightieth birthday. ᴱEgan, Keith J.; Morrison, Craig E.; Wastag, Michael J.: Wsh 1997, Carmelite Institute vi; 401 pp. Bibl. $20. 0-9656910-0-4.

71 Orbe, Antonio: Homenaje a ... en sus ochenta años. Epimeleia 6,11-12: BA 1997, Departamento de Filosofía Universidad Argentina John F. Kennedy 350 pp. Bibl.

72 Popham, Mervyn: Minotaur and centaur: studies in the archaeology of Crete and Euboea presented to ... ᴱEverly, Doniert, (al.), 1996, ⇒12,72. ᴿAJA 101 (1997) 599-600 (Watrous, L. Vance).

73 POSCHARSKY, Peter: Vom Orient bis an den Rhein: Begegnungen mit der christlichen Archäologie: ... zum 65. Geburtstag. <sup>E</sup>Lange, Ulrike; Sörries, Reiner: Christliche Archäologie III: Dettelbach 1997, Röll 275 pp. 3-927-522-47-3 [DBAT 29,317—Diebner, B.J.].

74 RAVANELLI, Virginio: Entrarono a Cafarnao: lettura interdisciplinare di Mc 1: studi in onore di ... <sup>E</sup>Adinolfi, Marco; Kaswalder, Pietro: SBFA 44: J 1997, Franciscan Printing Press 309 pp. $25. <sup>R</sup>CDios 210 (1997) 920-922 (*Gutiérrez, J.*).

75 ROELLIG, Wolfgang: Ana šadô Labnani lu allik: Beiträge zu altorientalischen und mittelmeerischen Kulturen: Festschrift für ... <sup>E</sup>Pongratz-Leisten, Beate, (*al.*), AOAT 247: Neuk 1997, Neuk xxxv; 472 pp. 3-7666-0074-5.

76 RUIZ DE LA PENA, Juan Luis: Coram Deo: memorial prof. ... <sup>E</sup>González de Cardedal, Olegario; Fernández Sangrador, Jorge Juan: BSal.E 189: S 1997, Universidad Pontificia 598 pp. PTA4.300. 84-7299-396-5 [RB 105,299—Langlamet, F.].

77 SANDERS, James A.: The quest for context and meaning: studies in biblical intertextuality in honor of ... <sup>E</sup>Evans, Craig A.; Talmon, Shemaryahu: Bibl.Interp. 28: Lei 1997, Brill xxxix; 671 pp. Bibl. ƒ280 / $175. 90-04-10835-1.

78 SARNA, Nahum M.: Minḥah le-Naḥum: biblical and other studies presented to ... in honour of his 70th birthday. <sup>E</sup>Brettler, Marc; Fishbane, Michael: JSOT.S 154: 1993, ⇒9,135; 12,78. <sup>R</sup>BZ 41 (1997) 291-292 (*Scharbert, Josef*).

79 SCHOTTROFF, Willy: Gott an den Rändern. <sup>E</sup>Bail, Ulrike; Jost, Renate: 1996, ⇒12,81. <sup>R</sup>ThLZ 122 (1997) 323-324 (*Pilhofer, Peter*).

80 SCHREINER, Josef: Der eine Gott Israels: gesammelte Schriften zur Theologie des Alten Testaments, 3: zum 75. Geburtstag des Autors. <sup>E</sup>Zenger, Erich: Wü 1997, Echter 332 pp. DM68. 3-429-01903-6 [OrdKor 38,512].

81 SCHWAGER, Raymund: Vom Fluch und Segen der Sündenböcke: <sup>E</sup>Niewiadomski, Józef; Palaver, Wolfgang: Beiträge zur mimetischen Theorie: Müns 1997, Lit 264 pp. DM49.80. 3-8258-3112-4. <sup>R</sup>BiLi 70/1 (1997) 74-75 (*Bodenhofer, Gerhard*).

82 SCROGGS, Robin: Putting body and soul together: essays in honor of... <sup>E</sup>Wiles, Virginia; Brown, Alexandra; Snyder, Graydon F.: Valley Forge 1997, Trinity xxiv; 360 pp. $30 / $20. 1-56338-209-1 / -206-7 [ThD 45,87—Heiser, W. Charles].

83 SHEA, William H.: To understand the scriptures: essays in honor of ... <sup>E</sup>Merling, David: Berrien Springs, Michigan 1997, Institute of Archaeology xxx; 330 pp. Bibl. 0-9642060-2-1.

84 SHEVOROSHKIN, Vitalij V.: Indo-European, Nostratic, and beyond: Festschrift for ... <sup>E</sup>Hegedüs, Irén; Michalove, Peter A.; Manaster Ramer, Alexis: Journal of Indo-European Studies, Monograph 22: Wsh 1997, Institute for the Study of Man viii, 348 pp. 0-941694-59-3.

85 SILBERMAN, Lou H.: The echoes of many texts: reflections on Jewish and Christian traditions: essays in honor of ... <sup>E</sup>Dever, William G.; Wright, J. Edward: BJSt 313: Atlanta 1997, Scholars xii; 250 pp. $30. 0-7885-0417-7 [RB 105,296—Langlamet, F.].

86 SIMPSON, William Kelly: Studies in honor of ... <sup>E</sup>Manuelian, Peter Der: Boston 1996, Museum of Fine Arts xxxi; 428 + x; 450 pp. $225. 0-87846-390-9 [BiOr 56,597—Berlev, Oleg].

87 SLENCZKA, R.: In der Wahrheit bleiben: Dogma—Schriftauslegung—Kirche. <sup>E</sup>Seitz, Manfred; Lehmkühler, Karsten:

Gö 1996, Vandenhoeck & R 205 pp. 3-525-58163-7 [EE 72,576—Alemany, José J.].

88 SLOYAN, Gerard Stephen: Open Catholicism: the tradition at its best: essays in honor of ... EEfroymson, David Patrick; Raines, John C.: ColMn 1997, Liturgical vii; 224 pp. Bibl. $20. 0-8146-5879-2.

89 SOARES-PRABHU, George: The dharma of Jesus: interdisciplinary essays in memory of ... ED'Sa, Francis X.: Pune 1997, Institute for the Study of Religion x; 482 pp. Rs230/$17; Rs215/$15 [JPJRS 1,165-168].

90 SPYCKET, Agnès: Collectanea orientalia: histoire, arts de l'espace et industrie de la terre. 1996, ⇒12,83. RAfO 44-45 (1997-98) 529-530 (Jursa, Michael).

91 STECK, Odil Hannes: Rezeption und Auslegung im Alten Testament und in seinem Umfeld: ein Symposion aus Anlass des 60. Geburtstags von ... EKratz, Reinhard Gregor; Krüger, Thomas: OBO 153: FrS 1997, Universitätsverlag 139 pp. FS39. 3-525-53789-1.

92 STUHLMACHER, Peter: Evangelium, Schriftauslegung, Kirche: Festschrift für ... zum 65. Geburtstag. EÅdna, J.; Hafemann, S.J.; Hofius, O.; collab. Feine, G.: Gö 1997 Vandenhoeck & R x; 460 pp. Bibl. 419-438. Port. DM125. 3-525-53643-7 [ThLZ 122,997].

93 SWEET, John Philip McMurdo: A vision for the church: studies in early Christian ecclesiology in honour of ... EBockmuehl, Markus N.A.; Thompson, Michael B.: E 1997, Clark xiv; 248 pp. Bibl. £22.50. 0-567-08573-2 / 9-1.

94 TALMON, Shemaryahu: 'Shaʿarei Talmon': studies in the bible, Qumran and the ancient Near East. 1992, ⇒8,181. RIEJ 48 (1997) 287-290 (Ahituv, Shmuel).

95 TE VELDE, Herman: Essays on ancient Egypt in honour of ... EVan Dijk, Jacobus: Egyptological Memoirs 1: Groningen 1997, STYX xiii; 400 pp. Bibl. 90-5693-014-1.

96 TOMIC, Celestin: SPE gaudentes: u nadi radosni zbornik u povodu 80. rodendana ... EMaracic, Ljudevit: Zagreb 1997, Provincijalat hrvatskih franjevaca konventualaca 411 pp.

97 TUCKER, Gene M.: Old Testament interpretation. 1995, ⇒11/1,36. RCBQ 59 (1997) 198-199 (O'Brien, Julia M.).

98 ULLRICH, Lothar: Unterwegs zum einen Glauben: Festschrift für ... zum 65. Geburtstag. EBeinert, Wolfgang; Feiereis, Konrad; Röhrig, Hermann-Josef: EThSt 74: Lp 1997, Benno 672 pp. 3-7462-1216-2.

99 VAN BEEK, Gus W.: Retrieving the past. ESeger, Joe D.: 1996, ⇒12,96. RRB 104 (1997) 421-422 (Langlamet, F.); CBQ 59 (1997) 811-813 (Campbell, Edward F.).

100 VAN DER WOUDE, Adam S.: The scriptures and the scrolls. EGarcía Martínez, F.: VT.S 49: 1992, ⇒8,198. RBiOr 54 (1997) 183-185 (Smend, Rudolf); TJT 13 (1997) 258-259 (McCready, W.O.).

101 VOORDECKERS, Edmond: La spiritualité de l'univers byzantin dans le verbe et l'image: hommages offerts à ... à l'occasion de son éméritat. EDemoen, Kristoffel; Vereecken, Jeannine: IP 30: Steenbrvgis 1997, Abbatia Sancti Petri 392 pp. 2-503-50559-7.

102 WAGNER, Siegfried: Von Gott reden. EVieweger, Dieter: 1995, ⇒11/1,37. RThLZ 122 (1997) 230-232 (Reventlow, Henning Graf).

103 WEISS, Joseph G.: Hasidism reappraised. ERapoport-Albert, Ada:
L 1997, The Littman Library of Jewish Civilization xxiv; 514 pp.
Proc. of the International Conf. of the Institute of Jewish Studies in
memory of ... 21-23 June 1988; Bibl. 1-874774-35-8.
104 WHYBRAY, R. Norman: Of prophets' vision and the wisdom of
sages. EMcKay, Heather A.; Clines, David J.A.: 1993, ⇒9,170;
10,138. RBZ 41 (1997) 292-295 (Scharbert, Josef).
105 WICKERT, Ulrich: Die Weltlichkeit des Glaubens in der alten Kirche: Festschrift für ... zum siebzigsten Geburtstag. EWyrwa, Dietmar; collab. Schäublin, Christoph; Aland, Barbara: BZNW 85: B
1997, De Gruyter x; 480 pp. 3-11-015441-2.
106 WOSCHITZ, Karl Matthäus: Gott-Bild: gebrochen durch die Moderne?: für ... ELarcher, Gerhard: Graz 1997, Styria 440 pp. Bibl.
3-222-12544-9.
107 YOUNG, Dwight W.: Go to the land I will show you. EColeson,
Joseph E.; Matthews, Victor H.: 1996, ⇒12,107. REThL 73 (1997)
145-146 (Lust, J.); CBQ 59 (1997) 410-412 (McLaughlin, John L.).


A1.2 **Miscellanea** unius auctoris

108 **Althann, Robert** Studies in Northwest Semitic. BibOr 45: R 1997,
Pont. Istituto Biblico xii; 205 pp. Bibl. L36.000. 88-7653-348-6.
109 **Bammel, Ernst** Judaica et Paulina: Kleine Schriften II. Afterword
Pilhofer, Peter: WUNT 91: Tü 1997, Mohr x; 384 pp. DM198. 3-
16-146541-5.
110 **Barrett, Charles K.** Jesus and the word. 1995, ⇒11/2,229. RThLZ
122 (1997) 256-257 (Lohse, Eduard).
111 **Bauer, Johannes Baptist** Studien zu Bibeltext und Väterexegese.
EFelber, Anneliese: SBAB 23: Stu 1997, Katholisches Bibelwerk 288
pp. DM79. 3-460-06231-2 [NTS 43,620].
112 **Beckwith, Roger T.** Calendar and chronology, Jewish and christian:
biblical, intertestamental and patristic studies. AGJU 33: 1996,
⇒12,112. RJJS 48 (1997) 376-377 (Stern, Sacha).
113 **Best, Ernest** Interpreting Christ. 1993, ⇒9,183. REvQ 69 (1997)
352-354 (Towner, Philip H.).
114 **Bird, Phyllis A.** Missing persons and mistaken identities: women
and gender in ancient Israel. Overtures to Biblical Theology: Mp
1997, Fortress x; 291 pp. $19. 0-8006-3128-5.
115 **Bonora, Antonio; Priotto, Michelangelo** Libri sapienziali e altri
scritti. LOGOS, Corso di studi biblici 4: Leumann (Torino) 1997,
Elle Di Ci 480 pp. L60.000. 88-01-10473-1.
116 **Bori, Pier Cesare** L'estasi del profeta ed altri saggi tra ebraismo e
cristianesimo dalle origini sino al 'Mosè' di FREUD. Bo 1989, Mulino 256 pp. RBeO 39 (1997) 124-126 (Jucci, Elio).
117 **Braulik, Georg** Studien zum Buch Deuteronomium. SBAB 24: Stu
1997, Katholisches Bibelwerk 285 pp. DM79. 3-460-06241-X.
118 **Cazelles, Henri** Études d'histoire religieuse et de philologie biblique. 1996, ⇒12,120. RRICP 64 (1997) 295-297 (Briend, Jacques).
119 **Collins, John Joseph** Seers, sybils [sic] and sages in Hellenistic-
Roman Judaism. JSJ.S 54: Lei 1997, Brill xi; 438 pp. f210. 90-04-
10752-5.
120 **Columbus, Christopher** The book of prophecies. ERusconi, Roberto; TSullivan, Blair: Repertorium Columbanum 3: Berkeley 1997,

Univ. of California Press xiv; 419 pp. $45. 0-520-20047-0 [ThD 45,62—Heiser, W. Charles].

121 **Coman, Constantin** Die Bibel in der Kirche: Abhandlungen mit biblischem Hintergrund. Bukarest 1997, 189 pp. [OrthFor 13/1,75s—Basarab, Mircea] [in Rumanian].

122 **Dautzenberg, Gerhard** Studien zur Theologie der Jesustradition. SBAB 19: 1995, ⇒11/2,247. ᴿBZ 41 (1997) 128-130 *(Kosch, Daniel)*.

123 **Fitzmyer, Joseph A.** The Semitic background of the New Testament: combined edition of Essays on the Semitic background of the New Testament and A wandering Aramean: collected Aramaic essays. Biblical Resource: GR 1997, Eerdmans xxi + 524; iv + 300 pp. $35. 0-8028-4344-1 [LouvSt 23,78—Verheyden, Joseph].

124 **Freedman, David Noel** Divine commitment and human obligation: selected writings of ... I History and religion; II Poetry and orthography. ᴱ*Huddlestun, John R.*: GR 1997, Eerdmans xxix + 545; xx + 269 pp. $45 + $30. 0-8028-3815-4 [CBQ 59,819].

125 **Fridrichsen, Anton** Exegetical writings: a selection. ᵀᴱ*Caragounis, Chrys C.; Fornberg, Tord*: WUNT 2/76: 1994, ⇒10,173. ᴿEvQ 69/1 (1997) 91-93 *(Starr, James)*.

126 **Fritz, Volkmar O.** Studien zur Literatur und Geschichte des alten Israel. SBAB 22: Stu 1997, Katholisches Bibelwerk 296 pp. DM79. 3-460-06221-5.

127 **Gese, Hartmut** Alttestamentliche Studien. 1991, ⇒7,204a. ᴿJSSt 42 (1997) 143-145 *(Barton, John)*.

128 **Goldberg, Arnold** Gesammelte Studien, 1: Mystik und Theologie des rabbinischen Judentums. ᴱ*Schlüter, Margarete; Schäfer, Peter*: TSAJ 61: Tü 1997, Mohr xxiii; 457 pp. DM278. 3-16-146633-0.

129 **Graf, David** Rome and the Arabian frontier: from the Nabataeans to the Saracens. CStS 594: Aldershot 1997, Ashgate 348 pp. $94. 0-86078-658-7 [MESA.B 33,192—Schick, Robert E.].

130 **Grafinger, Christine Maria** Beiträge zur Geschichte der Biblioteca Vaticana. Studi e documenti sulla formazione della Biblioteca Apostolica Vaticana 3, StT 373: Città del Vaticano 1997, Biblioteca Apostolica Vaticana xii; 235 pp. 88-210-0668-9.

131 **Güterbock, Hans Gustav** Perspectives on Hittite civilization: selected writings of ... ᴱ*Hoffner, Harry A., Jr.;* collab. *Diamond, Irving L.*: AS 26: Ch 1997, The Oriental Institute of the University of Chicago xi; 274 pp. 1-885923-04-X.

132 **Hartman, Lars O.** Text-centered New Testament studies: text-theoretical essays on early Jewish and early christian literature. ᴱ*Hellholm, David*: WUNT 102: Tü 1997, Mohr viii; 316 pp. DM178. 3-16-146836-8.

133 **Häussling, Angelus A.** Christliche Identität aus der Liturgie: theologische und historische Studien zum Gottesdienst der Kirche. ᴱ*Klöckener, Martin*: LWQF 79: Müns 1997, Aschendorff xii; 407 pp. Bibl. 3-402-04058-1.

134 **Hengel, Martin** Judaica et Hellenistica: kleine Schriften I. WUNT 90: 1996, ⇒12,128. ᴿQumran Chronicle 7 (1997) 255-258 *(Kapera, Zdzisław J.)*.

135 **Henry, Carl F.H.** Gods of this age or God of the ages?. Nv 1994, Broadman and H 323 pp. $16. ᴿAUSS 35 (1997) 279-280 *(Kharbteng, Boxter)*.

136 **Hooker, Morna D.** Beginnings: keys that open the gospels. The 1996 Diocese of British Columbia John Albert Hall Lectures at the Centre for Studies in Religion and Society in the Univ. of Victoria. L 1997, SCM xiv; 98 pp. £8. 0-334-02710-1 [RRT 1998/1,90].

137 **Irsigler, Hubert** Vom Adamssohn zum Immanuel: Gastvorträge Pretoria 1996. ATSAT 58: St. Ottilien 1997, EOS viii; 158 pp. Bibl. 3-88096-558-7.

138 **Jenni, Ernst** Studien zur Sprachwelt des Alten Testaments. E*Huwyler, Beat; Seybold, Klaus:* Stu 1997, Kohlhammer 224 pp. DM79 / FS72 / SCH577. 3-17-014779-X [NThAR 1997,192].

139 **Jones, Gareth Lloyd** The bones of Joseph: from the ancient texts to the modern church: studies in the scriptures. GR 1997, Eerdmans ix; 197 pp. 0-8028-3842-1.

140 **Kasemaa, K.** Semitistikat ja poeetikat [Aus Semitistik und Poetik]. Dissertationes Theologicae Universitatis Tartuensis 3: Tartu 1997, Tartu Ülikooli Kirjastus 130 pp [ZAW 110,301—Kaiser, Otto].

141 **Klagsbald, Victor** A l'ombre de Dieu: dix essais sur la symbolique dans l'art juif. Lv 1997, Peeters xi; 150 pp. Préf. *Idel, Moshe.* [JQR 88,356s—Shatzmiller, Joseph].

142 **Lanne, Emmanuel** Tradition et communion des églises: recueil d'études. BEThL 129: Lv 1997, Peeters xxv; 704 pp. 90-6831-892-6.

143 **Lewis, David M.** Selected papers in Greek and Near Eastern history. E*Rhodes, Peter J.:* C 1997, CUP xii; 418 pp. Bibl. 0-521-46564-8.

144 **Lubsczyk, Hans** Die Einheit der Heiligen Schrift: gesammelte Aufsätze. E*Hentschel, Georg; Rücker, Heribert:* Lp [2]1997, Benno 246 pp. 3-7462-1235-9 [NThAR 1999,179].

145 **Marín Heredia, Francisco** Torrente temas bíblicos. 1994, ⇒10,13324; 12,10581. R*Ben.* 44/1 (1997) 225-226 *(Ranzato, A.).*

146 **Martyn, J. Louis** Theological issues in the letters of Paul. Studies of the NT and Its World: E 1997, Clark xviii; 334 pp. £25. 0-567-08592-9 [RRT 1998/1,71—Goodacre, Mark].

147 **Mazar, Benjamin** Biblical Israel: state and people. E*Ahituv, Shmuel:* 1992, ⇒8,283...10,10999. R*JNES* 56 (1997) 147-8 *(Holloway, S.W.).*

148 **McKane, William** A late harvest: reflections on the Old Testament. 1995, ⇒11/1,56; 12,139. R*VT* 47 (1997) 561-563 *(Emerton, John A.E.);* CBQ 59 (1997) 741-742 *(Lemke, Werner E.).*

149 **Michel, Diethelm** Studien zur Überlieferungsgeschichte alttestamentlicher Texte. E*Wagner, Andreas; Müller, Achim:* TB 93: Gü 1997, Kaiser viii; 237 pp. 3-579-01819-1.

150 **Morla Asensio, Víctor** Libri sapienziali e altri scritti. Introduzione allo studio della Bibbia 5: Brescia 1997, Paideia 430 pp. L67.000. 88-394-0538-0;

151 Libros Sapienciales y otros escritos. Introducción al estudio de la Biblia 5: 1994, ⇒10,3214; 11/1,1886. R*RivBib* 45 (1997) 230-232 *(Prato, Gian Luigi).*

152 (*a*) **Muffs, Yochanan** Love and joy: law, language, and religion in ancient Israel. 1992, R*JAOS* 117 (1997) 721-723 *(Eichler, Barry L.);* (*b*) **Munk, Eliyahu** The just lives by his faith, Habakuk 2,4: essays on topics which challenge our faith in Torah and its exponents. J 1996, n.p. (8) 274 pp.

153 **Paulsen, Henning** Zur Literatur und Geschichte des frühen Christentums: gesammelte Aufsätze. E*Eisen, Ute E.:* WUNT 99: Tü 1997, Mohr x; 504 pp. DM248. 3-16-146513-X [OrdKor 39,256].

154 **Pearson, Birger A.** The emergence of the christian religion: essays on early christianity. Ph 1997, Trinity xiv; 241 pp. $19. 1-56338-218-0.

155 **Peretto, Elio** Saggi di patristica e di filologia biblica. Scripta Pontificiae Facultatis Theologicae "Marianum" 24: R 1997, Marianum (4) iii; 764 pp. Bibl. L80.000. 88-87016-50-X. RVetChr 34 (1997) 389-390 *(Aulisa, Immacolata)*.

156 **Rad, Gerhard von** La acción de Dios en Israel: ensayos sobre el Antiguo Testamento. ESteck, Odil Hannes; TMínguez, Dionisio: 1996, ⇒12,144. REE 72 (1997) 744-746 *(López, Mariola)*.

157 **Robert, René** Quelques croix de l'exégèse néotestamentaire. 1993, ⇒11/2,317. RRSR 85/1 (1997) 155-157 *(Léon-Dufour, Xavier)*.

158 **Saperstein, Marc** 'Your voice like a ram's horn': themes and texts in traditional Jewish teaching. Kiev Library: Cincinnati 1996, Hebrew Union College Press xix; 522 pp. $50 [HR 38,414—Sommer, Benjamin D.].

159 **Sarfatti, Gad B.** In the language of my people: essays on Hebrew. Studies in language 1: J 1997, Academy of the Hebrew Language (10) 339 pp. 965-481-009-3.

160 **Schillebeeckx, Edward** The language of faith. 1995, ⇒11/2,324. NewTR 10/1 (1997) 116-118 *(Dowd, John)*.

161 **Scholem, Gershom Gerhard** On the possibility of Jewish mysticism in our time & other essays. EShapira, Avraham; TChipman, Jonathan: Ph 1997, Jewish Publication Society of America xix; 244 pp. 0-8276-0579-X.

162 **Smend, Rudolf** Bibel, Theologie, Universität. KVR 1582: Gö 1997, Vandenhoeck & R 263 pp. DM26.80. 3-525-33602-0 [EuA 73/4, 333].

163 **Swanson, Reuben J.** New Testament Greek manuscripts. 1995-1996, 4 vols. ⇒12,152. RNT 39 (1997) 286-289 *(Elliott, J.K.)*.

164 **Thiede, Carsten Peter** Rekindling the word: in search of gospel truth. 1995, ⇒11/2,336. RJThS 48 (1997) 221-227 *(Chapa, Juan)*; DSD 4/1 (1997) 132-135 *(Evans, Craig A.)*.

165 **Ukpong, Justin S.** New Testament essays. Lagos 1995, Campbell 140 pp. RThPh 72 (1997) 574-575 *(Beutler, J.)*.

166 **Wagner, Siegfried** Ausgewählte Aufsätze zum Alten Testament. EMathias, Dietmar: BZAW 240: 1996, ⇒12,156. RThLZ 122 (1997) 996-997 *(Reventlow, Henning Graf)*.

167 **Walter, Nikolaus** Praeparatio Evangelica: Studien zur Umwelt, Exegese und Hermeneutik des Neuen Testaments. EKraus, Wolfgang; Wilk, Florian: WUNT 98: Tü 1997, Mohr x; 442 pp. DM178. 3-16-146717-5 [JSJ 28,368].

168 ETWilson, Nigel Guy AELIANUS: varia historia: historical miscellany. LCL 486: CM 1997, Harvard University Press (6) 514 pp. 0-674-99535-X.

A1.3 *Plurium compilationes* **biblicae**

169 EAichele, George; **Pippin, Tina** The monstrous and unspeakable: the bible as fantastic literature. Playing the texts 1: Shf 1997, Academic 246 pp. Bibl. 1-85075-692-9/-821-2 [NThAR 1999,221].

170 ᴱArnal, William E.; Desjardins, Michel Whose historical Jesus?.
SCJud 7: Waterloo, Ontario 1997, Wilfid Laurier Univ. Press 337
pp. $28. 0-88920-295-8.

171 Barbi, Augusto, (al.), Cercare Dio. PSV 35: Bo 1997, EDB 291
pp.

172 ᴱBeal, Timothy Kandler; Gunn, David M. Reading Bibles, writing
bodies: identity and the Book. Biblical limits: L 1997, Routledge
xvi; 292 pp. $19. 0-415-12664-9.

173 Beauchamp, Paul, (al.), Il tempo. PSV 36: Bo 1997, EDB 359 pp.

174 ᴱBeese, Dieter Tatverdächtigter David—biblische Geschichten aus
polizeilicher Sicht. Bielefeld 1997, Luther 140 pp. DM19.80 [LM
38,43—Eggebrecht, Jürgen].

175 ᴱBird, Phyllis A. Reading the bible as women: perspectives from
Africa, Asia, and Latin America. Semeia 78: Atlanta 1997, Scholars
vi; 165 pp. $20 [NThAR 1999,2].

176 ᴱBissoli, C. Un anno con la parola di Dio: vademecum per 'l'anno
della Bibbia'. Ufficio catechistico nazionale settore apostolato biblico. Leumann 1997, Elle Di Ci 208 pp. L16.000 [RivBib 45,256].

177 ᴱᵀBlowers, Paul M. The bible in Greek christian antiquity. The
Bible through the ages 1: Notre Dame, IN 1997, University of Notre
Dame xi; 468 pp. $60 / $40. 0-268-00701-2 / -2-0.

178 ᴱBohlen, Reinhold Dominikus von BRENTANO: Publizist, Aufklä-
rungstheologe, Bibelübersetzer. Trier 1997, Paulinus 307 pp. 3-
7902-0176-6.

179 ᴱBrenner, Athalya A feminist companion to the Hebrew Bible in the
NT. 1996, ⇒12,170. ʀCBQ 59 (1997) 796-798 (Laffey, Alice L.).

180 ᴱBrenner, Athalya; Fontaine, Carole R. A feminist companion to
reading the Bible: approaches, methods and strategies. Shf 1997,
Academic 654 pp. $39.50. 1-85075-674-0.

181 ᴱBroyles, Craig C.; Evans, Craig A. Writing and reading the scroll
of Isaiah: studies of an interpretive tradition I-II. VT.S 70/1-2; Formation and interpretation of OT literature 1/1-2: Lei 1997, Brill xx;
474; vii, 829 pp. ƒ275/$172. 90-04-10936-6 / -11026-7.

182 ᴱChalcraft, D.J. Social-scientific Old Testament criticism: a Sheffield reader. BiSe 47: Shf 1997, Academic 400 pp. £15. 1-85075-
813-1.

183 Chilton, Bruce David; Evans, Craig A. Jesus in context: temple,
purity, and restoration. AGJU 39: Lei 1997, Brill xi; 572 pp. Bibl.
ƒ310. 90-04-10746-0.

184 ᴱClines, David J.A. The poetical books. BiSe 41: Shf 1997, Academic 370 pp. £15 / $20. 1-85075-787-9.

185 ᴱCohen, Shaye J.D.; Frerichs, Ernest S. Diaspora in antiquity.
BJSt 288: 1993, ⇒10,239c. ʀREJ 156 (1997) 206-208 (Hadas-Lebel,
Mireille).

186 ᴱCurtis, Adrian H.W.; Römer, Thomas The book of Jeremiah and
its reception: le livre de Jérémie et sa réception. BEThL 128: Lv
1997, Peeters 331 pp. FB2.400. 90-6831-815-2.

187 ᴱDeurloo, Karel; Hoekema, Alle Van masker tot aangezicht: opstel-
len over bijbelse theologische en kerkelijke confrontaties. Baarn
1997, Ten Have 159 pp. ƒ30. 90-259-4743-3 [ITBT 6/4,33—
Engelen, Jan C.M.].

188 ᴱDohmen, Christoph; Söding, Thomas 'Eine Bibel—zwei Testamente': Positionen biblischer Theologie. 1995, ⇒11/2,361. ʀThRv

93 (1997) 121-123 *(Niebuhr, Karl-Wilhelm)*; CBQ 59 (1997) 604-606 *(Dozeman, Thomas B.)*; ThLZ 122 (1997) 1100-1104 *(Labahn, Antje; Labahn, Michael)*.

189 EDuhaime, Jean; Mainville, Odette La voce del Dio vivente: interpretazioni e letture attuali della bibbia. TValentino, Carlo: Nuove vie dell'esegesi: R 1997, Borla 351 pp. L45.000. 88-263-1135-8.

190 EEsler, Philip Modelling early christianity. 1995, ⇒11/2,363. RStudies in World Christianity 3 (1997) 254-256 *(Northcott, Michael)*; TJT 13 (1997) 270-272 *(Oakman, Douglas E.)*; AThR 79 (1997) 598-599 *(Jervis, Ann)*.

191 EEvans, Craig A.; Sanders, James A. Early christian interpretation of the scriptures of Israel: investigations and proposals. JSNT.S 148; Studies in Scripture in Early Judaism and Christianity 5: Shf 1997, Academic 476 pp. 1-85075-679-1.

192 EExum, J. Cheryl The historical books. BiSe 40: Shf 1997, Academic 383 pp. £15. 1-85075-786-0.

193 EFerreira, Joel Antônio Comunidades e massa a partir da Bíblia. Estudos Bíblicos 55: Petrópolis 1997, Vozes 124 pp [REB 57,1008].

194 EFewell, Danna Nolan Bible and ethics of reading. Semeia 77: Atlanta 1997, Scholars iv; 290 pp. $20 [NThAR 1999,43].

195 EFocant, C. La loi dans l'un et l'autre testament. LeDiv 168: P 1997, Cerf 326 pp. FF200. 2-204-05644-8 [ETR 73,308].

196 EFrishman, Judith; Van Rompay, Lucas The book of Genesis in Jewish and oriental christian interpretation: a collection of essays. Traditio Exegetica Graeca 5: Lv 1997, Peeters x; 290 pp. 90-6831-920-5 [LTP 54,216].

197 EGaiser, Frederick J. The quest for Jesus and the christian faith. Word & World.S 3: St. Paul, Minn. 1997, Word & World x; 214 pp. 0-9632389-2-2 [NThAR 1998,271].

198 EGarmus, Ludovico Criança na Bíblia. 1997, ⇒10,13763 [REB 57,1008].

199 EGitay, Yehoshua Prophecy and prophets: the diversity of contemporary issues in scholarship. SBL.Semeia Studies 33: Atlanta, GA 1997, Scholars viii; 174 pp. $40 / $25. 0-7885-0317-0 / 6-2.

200 EGrabbe, Lester L. Can a 'History of Israel' be written?. JSOT.S 245: European Seminar in Historical Methodology 1: Shf 1997, Academic 201 pp. £40/$66. 0-85075-669-4. RET 109 (1997-98) 129-131 *(Rodd, C.S.)*.

201 EGroß, Walter Jeremia und die 'deuteronomistische Bewegung'. BBB 98: 1995, ⇒11/1,86; 12,3462. RCBQ 59 (1997) 804-805 *(Diamond, A.R. Pete)*.

202 EHaase, Wolfgang ANRW 2.34/3: B 1997, De Gruyter xi; 1945-2772 pp. DM628. 3-11-015700-4.

203 EHallo, William W.; Younger, K. Lawson Jr. The context of scripture, 1: canonical compositions from the biblical world. Lei 1997, Brill xxviii; 599 pp. ƒ175/$109.50. 90-04-09629-9. RRExp 94 (1997) 607-608 *(Block, Daniel I.)*; RBBras 14 (1997) 293-295.

204 EHorsley, Richard A. Paul and empire: religion and power in Roman imperial society. Harrisburg, PA 1997, Trinity xi; 257 pp. $19. 1-56338-217-2.

205 Huizing, Klaas; Körtner, Ulrich H.J.; Müller, Peter Lesen und Leben: drei Essays zur Grundlegung einer Lesetheologie. Bielefeld 1997, Luther 135 pp. 3-7858-0392-3.

206 ᴱKaiser, Otto Weisheitstexte...: Mythen und Epen II. Collab. *Hekker, Karl*: TUAT 3/4: 1994, ⇒11/2,374. ᴿOrdKor 38 (1997) 232-233 *(Heinemann, Franz Karl)*.

207 ᴱKeck, Leander E.; Petersen, David L.; Long, Thomas G. General and Old Testament articles: Genesis, Exodus, Leviticus. NIntB 1: 1994, ⇒10,1575... 12,1246. ᴿJES 34/1 (1997) 140-141 *(Levine, Amy-Jill)*; RBBras 14 (1997) 308-309;

208 Introduction to apocalyptic literature; Daniel; (Twelve Prophets). NIntB 7: 1996, ⇒12,186. ᴿVJTR 61 (1997) 438-439 *(Meagher, P.M.)*;

209 Introduction to wisdom literature, the book of Proverbs, the book of Ecclesiastes, the Song of Songs, the book of Wisdom, the book of Sirach. NIntB 5: Nv 1997, Abingdon 875 pp. $55. 0-687-27818-X.

210 ᴱKingsbury, Jack Dean Gospel interpretation: narrative-critical & social-scientific approaches. Harrisburg, PA 1997, Trinity xii; 307 pp. $24. 1-56338-214-8.

211 ᴱKinoti, Hannah W.; Wakiggo, John M. The bible in African christianity: essays in biblical theology. African Christianity: Nairobi 1997, Acton vii; 209 pp. 9966-888-36-5 [EThL 74,159*].

212 ᴱKraus, Wolfgang Christen und Juden: Perspektiven einer Annäherung. Gü 1997, Gü'er 202 pp. DM39. 3-579-02093-5 [GuL 71,237].

213 ᴱLongenecker, Richard N. Patterns of discipleship in the New Testament. 1996, ⇒12,188. ᴿScrB 27 (1997) 85-86 *(Stafford, Barbara)*; EvQ 69 (1997) 347-348 *(Agan, C.J.)*.

214 ᴱLundin, Roger Disciplining hermeneutics: interpretation in christian perspective. GR 1997, Eerdmans viii; 177 pp. $18. 0-8028-0858-1.

215 ᴱLux, Rüdiger, *(al.)*, Mitteilungen und Beiträge, 10-11. Forschungsstelle Judentum a.d. Theol. Fak. Leipzig. Leipzig 1997, Thomas 92 pp. DM14. 3-86174-047-8 [BoL 1998,12—Grabbe, Lester L.].

216 ᴱMarrocu, Giuseppe L'obbedienza e la disobbedienza nella bibbia. Studio biblico teologico aquilano 17: L'Aquila 1997, ISSRA xv; 223 pp.

217 ᴱO'Callaghan, José La formación del Nuevo Testamento. ResB 13 (1997) 1-72.

218 ᴱPathrapankal, Joseph Text and context in biblical interpretation. 1993, ⇒9,292c; 11/2,8100. ᴿBiBh 23 (1997) 199-200 *(George, M. Gabriel)*.

219 Perdue, Leo G., *(al.)*, Families in ancient Israel. The family, religion, and culture: Louisville, KY 1997, Westminster xv; 285 pp. $20. 0-664-25567-1.

220 ᴱPorter, Stanley E.; Evans, Craig A. New Testament backgrounds. BiSe 43: Shf 1997, Academic 335 pp. £15/$20. 1-85075-796-8.

221 ᴱPorter, Stanley E.; Tombs, David Approaches to New Testament study. JSNT.S 120: 1995, ⇒11/2,381; 12,198. ᴿTrinJ 18 (1997) 124-127 *(Nelson, Peter K.)*.

222 ᴱReventlow, Henning Graf Eschatology in the bible and in Jewish and christian tradition. JSOT.S 243: Shf 1997, Academic 267 pp. £40/$66. 0-85075-664-3;

223 Theologische Probleme der Septuaginta und der hellenistischen Hermeneutik. Veröffentlichungen der Wissenschaftlichen Gesellschaft für Theologie 11: Gü 1997, Gü'er 138 pp. Bibl. 3-579-01813-2.

224 ᴱReventlow, Henning Graf; Farmer, William R. Biblical studies and the shifting of paradigms 1850-1914. JSOT.S 192: 1995, ⇒11/2,383; 12,201. ᴿTJT 13/2 (1997) 261-262 *(Kloppenborg, J.S.)*.

225 ᴱSarrazin, Bernard La bible parodiée: paraphrases et parodies. P 1993, Cerf 235 pp. FF152/EUR23,17. 2-204-04711-2. ᴿRSR 71 (1997) 523-524 *(Brottier, Laurence)*.

226 ᴱSchottroff, Luise; Wacker, Marie-Theres Von der Wurzel getragen: christlich-feministische Exegese in Auseinandersetzung mit Antijudaismus. Bibl.Interp. 17: 1996, ⇒12,204. ᴿThLZ 122 (1997) 653-654 *(Ego, Beate)*; KuI 12/1 (1997) 91-92 *(Kirchberg, Julie)*.

227 ᴱScott, James M. Exile: Old Testament, Jewish, and christian conceptions. JSJ.S 56: Lei 1997, Brill 384 pp. *f*210. 90-04-10676-6.

228 ᴱSegovia, Fernando F.; Tolbert, Mary Ann Reading from this place, 1: social location and biblical interpretation in the United States. 1995, ⇒11/1,112. ᴿCBQ 59 (1997) 615-617 *(Bergant, Dianne)*.

229 ᴱSellin, Gerhard; Vouga, François Logos und Buchstabe: Mündlichkeit und Schriftlichkeit im Judentum und Christentum der Antike. TANZ 20: Tü 1997, Francke 269 pp. DM86. 3-7720-1871-8 [RB 105,158].

230 ᴱShillington, V. George Jesus and his parables: interpreting the parables of Jesus today. Foreword *Freyne, Seán:* E 1997, Clark xvi; 199 pp. £13. 0-567-08596-1. ᴿET 109 (1997-98) 193-194 *(Rodd, C.S.)*.

231 ᴱSimms, Karl Translating sensitive texts: linguistic aspects. Approaches to Translation Studies 14: Amst 1997, Rodopi viii; 333 pp. Bibl. 90-420-0270-0.

232 ᴱSmith-Christopher, Daniel Text and experience. BiSe 35: 1995, ⇒11/2,533. ᴿCBQ 59 (1997) 813-814 *(Bowe, Barbara E.)*.

233 ᴱSoukup, Paul A.; Hodgson, Robert From one medium to another: communicating the bible through multimedia. Kansas City 1997, Sheed & W (4) 382 pp. Bibl. $25. 1-55612-968-8.

234 ᴱTuckett, Christopher M. The scriptures in the gospels. BEThL 131: Lv 1997, Peeters xxiv; 721 pp. FB2400. 90-6831-932-9 [ETR 73,310].

## A1.4 *Plurium compilationes* theologicae

235 ᴱAlbertz, Rainer Religion und Gesellschaft: Studien zu ihrer Wechselbeziehung in den Kulturen des antiken Vorderen Orients. Collab. *Otto, Susanne:* AOAT 248: Müns 1997, Ugarit-Verlag viii; 220 pp. Veröffentlichungen des Arbeitskreises zur Erforschung der Religions- und Kulturgeschichte des antiken Vorderen Orients (AZERKAVO), 1. 3-927120-54-5.

236 ᴱAssmann, Jan; Sundermeier, Theo; Wrogemann, Henning Schuld, Gewissen und Person: Studien zur Geschichte des inneren Menschen. Studien zum Verstehen fremder Religionen 9: Gü 1997, Gü'er. 3-579-01791-8.

237 ᴱBørresen, Kari Elisabeth The image of God: gender models in Judaeo-Christian tradition. Mp 1995, Augsburg 320 pp. $25. 0-8006-2951-5. ᴿThTo 54/1 (1997) 102-106 *(May, Melanie A.)*; ChH 66 (1997) 875-876 *(Barstow, Anne Llewelyn)*; JR 77 (1997) 483-485 *(Pitkin, Barbara)*.

238 EBousquet, François; Doré, Joseph La théologie dans l'histoire. Sciences théologiques et religieuses 6: P 1997, Beauchesne 265 pp. 2-7010-1353-4 [EThL 74,423*].

239 ECoakley, Sarah Religion and the body. Cambridge Studies in Religious Traditions 8: C 1997, CUP xvii; 312 pp. 0-521-36669-0.

240 ECunliffe-Jones, Hubert A history of christian doctrine. E 1997, Clark xiv; 601 pp. 0-567-08580-5.

241 EDi Berardino, Angelo; Studer, Basil History of Theology 1: the patristic period. TO'Connell, Matthew J.: ColMn 1997, Liturgical xxi; 632 pp. $100 [BTB 28,86—Sloyan, Gerard S.].

242 EFerguson, Everett Encyclopedia of early christianity. Hamden, Conn 21997, Garland 2 vols; xxvii; 1213 pp. $150. 0-8153-1663-1 [JEarlyC 5,316].

243 EFord, David F. The modern theologians: an introduction to christian theology in the twentieth century. Oxf 21997, Blackwell xviii; 772 pp. 0-631-19591-2.

244 EFowl, Stephen E. The theological interpretation of scripture: classic and contemporary readings. Blackwell Readings in Modern Theology: Oxf 1997, Blackwell xxx; 409 pp. $65/£16. 1-55786-835-2. RRRT (1997/3) 44-46 (Jones, Gareth).

245 EGevers, Lieve; Kenis, Leo De faculteit Godgeleerdheid in de K.U. Leuven, 1969-1995. ANL 39: Lv 1997, Peeters xviii; 542 pp. 90-6831-910-8 [EThL 74,102*].

246 EHartlieb, Elisabeth; Methuen, Charlotte Sources and resources of feminist theologies. JEGTFF 5: 1997.

247 EHebler, Makarios Neunter Internationaler Regula-Benedicti-Kongreß. RBS 19: St. Ottilien 1997, Eos xiii; 269 pp. R (Sant'Anselmo) 9.-14. September 1996. 3-88096-293-6.

248 EJoncheray, Jean Approches scientifiques des faits religieux. Sciences théologiques et religieuses 7: P 1997, Beauchesne 298 pp. FF180. 2-7010-1363-1 [RTL 29,127].

249 EKing, Karen L. Women and goddess traditions: in antiquity and today. Introd. Torjesen, Karen Jo: Studies in Antiquity & Christianity: Mp 1997, Fortress xiv; 450 pp. $45. 0-8006-2919-1.

250 EKunnumpuram, Kurien; D'Lima, Errol; Parappally, Jacob The church in India: in search of a new identity. Bangalore 1997, NBCLC 408 pp.

251 ELucas, Ernest Christian healing: what can we believe?. L 1997, SPCK 202 pp. £13. 1-901443-00-0 [Ethics & Medicine 14,92s—Short, David].

252 EMathon, Gérard; Baudry, G.-H. Catholicisme: hier, aujourd'hui, demain, 15/69-70. P 1997, Letouzey et A. 1-256; 257-512 pp [RSR 86,323ss—Vallin, Pierre].

253 EMerks, Karl-Wilhelm; Schreurs, Nico De passie van een grensganger: theologie aan de vooravond van het derde millennium. Baarn 1997, Ten Have 320 pp. ƒ40. 90-259-4740-9 [ITBT 6/4,34—Engelen, Jan].

254 EMödl, Ludwig Ein sperriges Zeichen: praktisch-theologische Überlegungen zur Theologie des Kreuzes. Mü 1997, Don-Bosco 190 pp. DM39 [GuL 71,156ss—Steinmetz, Franz-Josef].

255 EMüller, Hans Peter Das Evangelium und die Weltreligionen: theologische und philosophische Herausforderungen. Stu 1997, Kohlhammer 120 pp. 3-17-014983-0.

256  EPorter, Stanley E.; Hayes, Michael A.; Tombs, David Images of
     Christ: ancient and modern. Roehampton Institute London Papers 2:
     Shf 1997, Academic 406 pp. £57.50/$95; £17/$28. 1-85075-658-9 /
     1-85075-812-3.
257  ERainer, Michael J.; Janßen, Hans-Gerd Bilderverbot. Jahrbuch
     Politische Theologie 2 (1997).
258  ERobbins, Thomas; Palmer, Susan J. Millennium, messiahs, and
     mayhem: contemporary apocalyptic movements. NY 1997,
     Routledge ix; 334 pp. 0-415-91649-6.
259  ESchifferle, Alois Pfarrei in der Postmoderne?: Gemeindebildung in
     nachchristlicher Zeit. FrB 1997, Herder 446 pp. DM88. 3-451-
     26242-8.
260  EStoffer, Dale Rupert The Lord's Supper: believers' church per-
     spectives. Scottdale, PA 1997, Herald 334 pp. $25. 0-8361-3119-3.
261  ESugirtharajah, R.S. Voices from the margin: interpreting the Bible
     in the third world. ²1995 <1991>. ⇒11/1,129. RCBQ 59 (1997)
     814-816 (Okoye, James C.).
262  ETerrin, Aldo Natale Liturgia e incarnazione: caro salutis cardo.
     Contributi 14: Padova 1997, Messagero 399 pp. L36.000. 88-250-
     0640-3 [RTL 29,131].
263  ETVaage, Leif E. Subversive scriptures: revolutionary readings of
     the christian bible in Latin America. Valley Forge, PA 1997, Trinity
     x; 213 pp. $19. 1-56338-200-8.
264  EWard, Graham The postmodern God: a theological reader. Black-
     well Readings in Modern Theology: Oxf 1997, Blackwell xlvii; 368
     pp. 0-631-20141-6.

### A1.5  Plurium compilationes philologicae vel archaeologicae

265  EAufrecht, Walter E. Urbanism in antiquity: from Mesopotamia to
     Crete. JSOT.S 244: Shf 1997, JSOT 291 pp. 1-85075-666-X.
266  EBakker, Egbert J. Grammar as interpretation: Greek literature in
     its linguistic contexts. Mn.S 171: Lei 1997, Brill vii; 262 pp. 90-04-
     10730-4.
267  EBartl, Karin; Bernbeck, Reinhard; Heinz, Marlies Zwischen
     Euphrat und Indus: aktuelle Forschungsprobleme in der vorderasiati-
     schen Archäologie. Hildesheim 1995, Olms x; 408 pp. Num. ill.
     DM94. 3-487-10043-6. RAfO 44-45 (1997-98) 481-486 (Stiehler-
     Alegria, G.).
268  EBartlett, John R. Archaeology and biblical interpretation. Biblical
     Studies, Archaeology: L 1997, Routledge xv; 176 pp. $60/$19. 0-
     415-14114-1.
269  EBen-Tor, Amnon; Bonfil, Ruhama; Paris, Alan Hazor V: an ac-
     count of the fifth season of excavation, 1968. J 1997, Israel Explora-
     tion Society xvi; 390 pp. The James A. De Rothschild Expedition at
     Hazor. $90. 965-221-033-1.
270  ECapasso, M. Bicentenario della morte di Antonio PIAGGIO.
     Papyrologica Lupiensia 5: Galatina (LE) 1997, Congedo 262 pp.
     [RivBib 47,374ss—Passoni Dell'Acqua, Anna].
271  ECartledge, P.; Garnsey, P.; Gruen, E. Hellenistic constructs: es-
     says in culture, history and historiography. Hellenistic Culture and
     Society 26: Berkeley 1997, University of California Press vii; 319
     pp. £40/$50. 0-520-20676-2 [ClR 48,380ss—Davidson, James].

272 ᴱColeman, John E.; Walz, Clark A. Greeks and barbarians: essays on the interactions between Greeks and non-Greeks in antiquity and the consequences for Eurocentrism. Bethesda, MD 1997, CDL xviii; 310 pp. Occasional Publications of the Department of Near Eastern Studies and the Program of Jewish Studies, Cornell University 4. $42. 1-883053-44-7.

273 ᴱCollon, Dominique 7000 years of seals. L 1997, British Museum 240 pp. 0-7141-1143-0.

274 ᴱDavies, W. Vivian; Schofield, Louise Egypt, the Aegean and the Levant. 1995, ⇒11/2,461. ᴿWO 28 (1997) 191-193 *(Gamer-Wallert, Ingrid)*.

275 ᴱEdwards, Douglas R.; McCollough, C. Thomas Archaeology and the Galilee: texts and contexts in the Graeco-Roman and Byzantine periods. SFSHJ 143: Atlanta 1997, Scholars vii; 187 pp. $95. 0-7885-0333-2 [JJS 49,360ss—Schwartz, Joshua].

276 ᴱEvans, Craig A.; Flint, Peter W. Eschatology, messianism, and the Dead Sea Scrolls. SDSSRL 1: GR 1997, Eerdmans xii; 176 pp. $20. 0-8028-4230-5 [ETR 73,307].

277 ᴱFagan, Brian M. Eyewitness to discovery: first-person accounts of more than fifty of the world's greatest archaeological discoveries. NY 1997, OUP 493 pp. 8 col. pl.; 55 fig. $40. 0-19-508141-2 [AJA 101,632].

278 Fantham, Elaine, *(al.)*, Women in the classical world. 1994, ⇒11/2,465. ᴿGn. 69 (1997) 645-647 *(Schmitt-Pantel, Pauline)*.

279 ᴱForte, Maurizio; Siliotti, Alberto Virtual archaeology: re-creating ancient worlds. NY 1997, Abrams 288 pp. 660 col. fig.; 9 fig; 15 plans. $49.50. 0-8109-3943-6 [AJA 101,818].

280 ᴱGoodman-Thau, Eveline Vom Jenseits: jüdisches Denken in der europäischen Geistesgeschichte. B 1997, Akademie 249 pp. DM98. 3-05-002719-3 [ThLZ 125,381s—Becker, Hans-Jürgen] [Zech 9,9].

281 ᴱHabinek, Thomas N.; Schiesaro, Alessandro The Roman cultural revolution. C 1997, CUP xxi; 238 pp. Bibl. 0-521-58092-7.

282 ᴱHandy, Lowell K. The age of Solomon: scholarship at the turn of the millennium. Studies in the History and Culture of the Ancient Near East 11: Leiden 1997, Brill xx; 539 pp. ƒ195. 90-04-10476-3 [NThAR 1998,98].

283 ᴱHetzron, Robert The Semitic languages. L 1997, Routledge xx; 572 pp. £125 [BSOAS 63,102—Ullendorff, Edward].

284 ᴱIzreʾel, Shlomo; Drory, Rina Language and culture in the Near East. Israel Oriental Studies 15: 1995, ⇒11/2,5773. ᴿAfO 44-45 (1997-98) 532-533 *(Hunger, H.)*.

285 ᴱJones, P.; Sidwell, K. The world of Rome: an introduction to Roman culture. C 1997 CUP xvii; 399 pp. £45/£16. 0-521-38421-4/-600-4 [ClR 48,417ss—Barker, Peter].

286 ᴱKjær-Hansen, Kai Tod eines Messias: Messiasgestalten und Messiaserwartungen im Judentum. Neuhausen/Stuttgart 1996, Hänssler 3-7751-2450-0.

287 ᴱKlein, Josef; Fix, Ulla Textbeziehungen: linguistische und literaturwissenschaftliche Beiträge zur Intertextualität. Stauffenburg-Linguistik: Tü 1997, Stauffenburg 402 pp. 3-86057-705-0.

288 ᴱKoloski-Ostrow, Ann Olga; Lyons, Claire L. Naked truths: women, sexuality and gender in classical art and archaeology. L 1997, Routledge xv; 315 pp. Bibl.; 60 fig. $75. 0-415-15995-4.

289 ᴱLindner, Manfred Petra und das Königreich der Nabatäer: Lebensraum, Geschichte und Kultur eines arabischen Volkes der Antike. Mü 1997, Delp 336 pp. 3-7689-0116-5.

290 ᴱMarkkanen, Raija; Schröder, Hartmut Hedging and discourse: approaches to the analysis of a pragmatic phenomenon in academic texts. Research in Text Theory 24; Untersuchungen zur Texttheorie 24: B 1997, De Gruyter viii; 280 pp. 3-11-015591-5.

291 ᴱMikasa, Takahito Cult and ritual in the ancient Near East. Bulletin of the Middle Eastern Culture Center in Japan 6: Wsb 1992, Harrassowitz vii; 158 pp. DM68. ᴿOLZ 92 (1997) 692-694 (Cancik-Kirschbaum, Eva).

292 ᴱMolyneaux, Brian Leigh The cultural life of images: visual representation in archaeology. L 1997, Routledge xvii; 274 pp. 99 fig. $70. 0-415-10675-3 [AJA 102,619s—Davis, Whitney].

293 ᴱMossman, Judith PLUTARCH and his intellectual world: essays on PLUTARCH. L 1997, Duckworth xii; 249 pp. 0-7156-2778-3.

294 ᴱMost, Glenn W. Collecting fragments; Fragmente sammeln. Aporemata 1: Gö 1997, Vandenhoeck & R x; 338 pp. 3-525-25900-X.

295 ᴱMoxnes, Halvor Constructing early christian families: family as social reality and metaphor. L 1997, Routledge xvi; 267 pp. £45 / £15. 0-415-14638-0 / 39-9 [NThAR 1997,291].

296 ᴱNielsen, Thomas Heine Yet more studies in the ancient Greek polis. Historia, Einzelschriften 117: Stu 1997, Steiner 262 pp. 3-515-07222-5.

297 ᴱOlmo Lete, Gregorio del Mitología y religión del Oriente Antiguo. 1993-1995. 2 vols. ⇒11/2,474. ᴿBiOr 54 (1997) 306 (Soggin, J.A.).

298 Porten, Bezalel The Elephantine papyri in English: three millennia of cross-cultural continuity and change. DMOA 22: 1996, ⇒12,009. ᴿArOr 65 (1997) 396-398 (Segert, Stanislav).

299 ᴱPorter, Stanley E.; Evans, Craig A. The scrolls and the scriptures: Qumran fifty years after. JSPE.S 26; Roehampton Institute London papers 3: Shf 1997, Academic 414 pp. £47.50. 1-85075-845-X.

300 ᴱQuirke, Stephen G.J. The temple in ancient Egypt: new discoveries and recent research. London 1997, British Museum x; 241 pp. £30. 0-7141-0993-2.

301 ᴱRoberts, Deborah H.; Dunn, Francis M.; Fowler, Don Classical closure: reading the end in Greek and Latin literature. Princeton, NJ 1997, Princeton University Press xvi; 311 pp. Bibl. 0-691-04452-X.

302 ᴱRunia, David T. The Studia Philonica Annual: studies in Hellenistic Judaism 8; BJSt 309: Atlanta, GA 1996, Scholars viii; 228 pp. $35. 0-7885-0311-1. ᴿAbr-n. 34 (1996-97) 122-124 (Martin, M.J.).

303 ᴱSallmann, K. Die Literatur des Umbruchs, von der römischen zur christlichen Literatur. Handbuch der lateinischen Literatur der Antike 4. Mü 1997, Beck xxxii; 651 pp. DM238. 3-406-39020-X [JRS 89,246s—Powell, J.G.F.].

304 ᴱSasson, Jack M. Civilizations of the ancient Near East. 1995, 4 vols, ⇒11/2,476. ᴿOLZ 92 (1997) 329-334 (Klengel, Horst); AJA 101 (1997) 149-153 (Morris, Sarah P.).

305 ᴱSellin, Gerhard; Vouga, François Logos und Buchstabe: Mündlichkeit und Schriftlichkeit im Judentum und Christentum der Antike. TANZ 20: Tü 1997, Francke 269 pp. 3-7720-1871-8.

306 ᴱShanks, Hershel Archaeology's publication problem. 1996, ⇒12,240. ᴿArOr 65 (1997) 399-400 (Segert, Stanislav).

307 ᴱShipley, Graham; Salmon, John Human landscapes in classical antiquity: environment and culture. 1996, ⇒12,241. ᴿAJA 101 (1997) 789-790 *(Cartledge, Paul).*

308 ᴱSigrist, Christian; Neu, Rainer Die Entstehung des Königtums. Ethnologische Texte zum Alten Testament 2: Neuk 1997, Neuk 210 pp. 3-7887-1419-0 [NThAR 1997,290].

309 ᴱTubb, Kathryn Walker Antiquities, trade or betrayed: legal, ethical and conservation issues. L 1995, Archetype xxi; 263 pp. 35 col. pl. $35. 1-873132-70-0. ᴿAJA 101 (1997) 403-404 *(Wright, J.C.).*

310 ᴱWagner, Andreas Studien zur hebräischen Grammatik. OBO 156: Gö 1997, Vandenhoeck & R viii; 199 pp. FS62. 3-525-53792-1.

311 ᴱWeber, Thomas; Wenning, Robert Petra: antike Felsstadt zwischen arabischer Tradition und griechischer Norm. Zaberns Bildbände zur Archäologie, Sonderhefte der Antiken Welt: Mainz 1997, Zabern iv; 172 pp. 188 ill. 3-8053-1983-5/6-X [EuA 73,330].

A2.1 **Acta** *congressuum* **biblica**

312 ᴱAlexander, Philip S.; Samely, Alexander Artefact and text: the re-creation of Jewish literature in medieval Hebrew texts. BJRL 75/3: 1993, ⇒10,303c. ᴿJSSt 44 (1997) 424-426 *(Schlüter, Margarete).*

313 Atti del Convegno Nazionale 'Tradurre la Bibbia'. Settimello 1997, BIBLIA 182 pp. Facoltà Valdese, Roma 29-30 aprile 1995.

314 ᴱAusín, Santiago De la ruina a la afirmación: el entorno del reino de Israel en el siglo VIII a.C. Estella 1997, Verbo Divino 262 pp. Pts2.900 [Proyección 45,323—Sicre, J.L.].

315 ᴱBeaude, Pierre-Marie La bible en littérature. P 1997, Cerf 366 pp. Actes du colloque international de Metz. FF150. 2-204-05751-7 [FV 97/2,88—Vahanian, Gabriel].

316 ᴱBenyik, György Biblikus Konferencia (1996: Szeged): Gyermekségtörténet és mariológia [Storia d'infanzia e mariologia]. Szeged 1997, JATEPress 271 pp;

317 Szegedi Biblikus Konferencia: A messiási kérdés [Conferenza biblica di Szeged: la questione messianica], Szeged 1995, szeptember 4-7. Szeged 1997, JATEPress 132 pp.

318 ᴱBorgen, Peder; Giversen, Søren The New Testament and Hellenistic Judaism. Peabody, MA 1997 <1995>, Hendrickson 293 pp. $20. 1-565-63261-3 [BTB 27,120].

319 ᴱBron, H.; Lipschitz, O. דוד מלך ישראל חי וקיים?: הרצאות בכנס בוגרט החוג למקרא של האוניברסיטה העברטת, ירושלים [David King of Israel alive and enduring?]. J 1997, Simor 213 pp. Papers read at the meeting of the graduates, Bible Dept, Hebrew Univ. $25. 965-242-010-0 [RB 105,308]. H.

320 ᴱCarroll, John T.; Green, Joel B. The death of Jesus in early Christianity. 1995. ⇒11/2,491. ᴿNT 39 (1997) 194-196 *(Doble, P.);* RTR 56/2 (1997) 97-98 *(Gibson, Richard);* CBQ 59 (1997) 798-800 *(Gallagher, Eugene V.);* JBL 116 (1997) 361-363 *(Crossan, John Dominic);* TrinJ 18 (1997) 102-105 *(deSilva, David A.).*

321 ᴱCharlesworth, James H.; Johns, Loren L. Hillel and Jesus: comparative studies of two major religious leaders. Mp 1997, Fortress xxxi; 486 pp. $50. 0-8006-2564-1.

322 ᴱColafemmina, Cesare Dagli dei a Dio: parole sacre e parole profetiche sulle sponde del Mediterraneo. Cassano Murge (Ba) 1997, Mes-

saggi xv; 190 pp. Atti del Convegno Internazionale di Studi promosso dall'Associazione "Biblia" Bari, 13-15 settembre 1991. L30.000.

323 ᴱEmerton, J.A. Congress volume: Cambridge 1995. VT.S 66: Lei 1997, Brill 419 pp.;

324 Congress volume: Paris 1992. VT.S 61: 1995, ⇒11/1,135; 12,256. ᴿCBQ 59 (1997) 192-193 *(Graham, M. Patrick)*; Synaxis 15/1 (1997) 359-364 *(Minissale, Antonino)*.

325 ᴱFrerichs, Ernest S., *(al.)*, Exodus—the Egyptian evidence. Winona Lake 1997, Eisenbrauns 112 pp. Papers presented at a conference held at Brown University in 1992. $30. 1-57506-025-6 [NThAR 1998,98].

326 ᴱGreenspoon, Leonard; Munnich, Olivier VIII Congress of the International Organization for Septuagint and Cognate Studies: Paris 1992. SCSt 41: 1995, ⇒11/1,136. ᴿCBQ 59 (1997) 415-416 *(Cox, Claude)*.

327 Heiligenthal, Roman, *(al.)*, Verfälschter Jesus?: Christentum und Christusbilder. Herrenalber Protokolle 97: Karlsruhe ²1997, Evangelische Akademie Baden 81 pp. Beiträge einer Tagung der Evangelischen Akademie Baden 2-4 April 1993, Bad Herrenalb. 3-89674-097-0 [NThAR 1999,221].

328 ᴱKieffer, René J.J.; Bergman, Jan La main de Dieu: die Hand Gottes. WUNT 94: Tü 1997, Mohr xiv; 212 pp. DM148. 3-16-146715-9.

329 ᴱLipschitz, Ora David King of Israel alive and enduring?. 1997, ⇒319.

330 ᴱLongenecker, Richard N. The road from Damascus: the impact of Paul's conversion on his life, thought, and ministry. McMaster New Testament Studies: GR 1997, Eerdmans xv; 253 pp. H.H. Bingham Colloquium in New Testament (2: 1996: McMaster Divinity College). £17. 0-8028-4191-0.

331 ᴱMoreschini, Claudio; Menestrina, Giovanni Motivi letterari ed esegetici in GEROLAMO: atti del convegno tenuto a Trento il 5-7 dicembre 1995. Religione e cultura 9: Brescia 1997, Morcelliana 300 pp. Istituto di Scienze Religiose in Trento. 88-372-1633-5.

332 Musulmanes y cristianos 'quien decís que soy yo?'. M 1997, Darek Nyumba 226 pp. Tercer congreso internacional a distancia organizado por Crislam [IslChr 24,276—Lacunza Balda, Justo].

333 ᴱOlsson, Birger Kristna tolkningar av gamla testamentet. Sto 1997, Verbum 198 pp. Lund-konferanse i Höör 1996. 91-526-2547-8. [NTT 99,262s—Skeggestad, Marit].

334 La parola di Dio sorgente di vita. 1997. Dichiaraizaione finale della V Assemblea Plenaria della Federazione Biblica Cattolica, Hong-Kong 2-12 luglio 1996 [PaVi 42/3,52-57.

335 ᴱPenna, Romano Qumran e le origini cristiane. RStB 9/2: Bo 1997, Dehoniane 293 pp. Atti del VI Convegno di Studi Neotestamentari (L'Aquila, 14-17.9.1995).

336 ᴱPorter, Stanley E.; Olbricht, Thomas H. The rhetorical analysis of scripture: essays from the 1995 London Conference. Journal for the Study of the New Testament, Suppl. 146: Sheffield 1997, Academic 504 pp. 1-85075-671-6.

337 ᴱPrato, Gian Luigi 'Un tempo per nascere e un tempo per morire': cronologie normative e razionalità della storia nell'antico Israel.

RStB 9/1: Bo 1997, Dehoniane 218 pp. Atti del IX Convegno di Studi Veterotestamentari (L'Aquila, 11-13.9.1995).
338 Septuaginta: libri sacri della diaspora giudaica e dei cristiani. Atti della II giornata di studio, 13 maggio 1997. Annali di Scienze Religiose 2 (1997) 141-207.
339 EShanks, Hershel; Meinhardt, Jack Aspects of monotheism: how God is one: symposium at the Smithsonian Institution, October 19, 1996. Wsh 1997, Biblical Archaeology Society 131 pp. 1-880317-19-2/-50-8.
340 ETaylor, Bernard A. IX Congress of the International Organization for Septuagint and Cognate Studies. SCSt 45: Atlanta 1997, Scholars xiv; 452 pp. $50. 0-7885-0419-3 [RB 105,317].
341 ETurner, John D.; McGuire, Anne The Nag Hammadi library after fifty years. NHMS 44: Lei 1997, Brill xviii; 531 pp. Proceedings of the 1995 Society of Biblical Literature Commemoration. f300. 90-04-10824-6. RRThPh 129 (1997) 284-285 (Borel, Jean).
342 EVan Wolde, Ellen Narrative syntax and the Hebrew bible: papers of the Tilburg conference 1996. Bibl.Interp. 29: Lei 1997, Brill x; 269 pp. f153/$90. 90-04-10787-8.

A2.3 Acta congressuum theologica

343 EAhn, Gregor; Dietrich, Manfried Engel und Dämonen: theologische, anthropologische und religionsgeschichtliche Aspekte des Guten und Bösen: Akten des gemeinsamen Symposiums der Theologischen Fakultät der Universität Tartu und der Deutschen Religionsgeschichtlichen Studiengesellschaft am 7. und 8. April 1995 zu Tartu. FARG 29: Müns 1997, Ugarit-Verlag xv; 192 pp. 3-927120-31-6.
344 As origens da vida: diálogo entre ciência e teologia. Lisboa 1997, Rei dos Livros 327 pp. Semanas de Studos Teológicos. 972-510-653-9.
345 EBellelli, Gloria M.; Bianchi, Ugo Orientalia Sacra Urbis Romae: Dolichena et Heliopolitana: receuil d'études archéologiques et historico-religieuses sur les cultes cosmopolites d'origine commagénienne et syrienne. Studia archaeologica 84: R 1997, Bretschneider 616 pp. Bibl. 88-7062-933-2.
346 EBoespflug, François; Dunand, Françoise Le comparatisme en histoire des religions. Patrimoines: P 1997, Cerf 455 pp. Actes du Colloque international de Centre de Recherches d'Histoire des Religions, Strasbourg (18-20 septembre 1996). FF240. 2-204-05788-6 [RB 105,309].
347 EBurkert, Walter; Stolz, Fritz Hymnen der alten Welt im Kulturvergleich. OBO 131: 1994, ⇒11/2,555. ROLZ 92 (1997) 467-469 (Reck, Christiane).
348 ECastello, Gaetano Abramo nostro padre nella fede: atti degli incontri tra culture e religioni del Mediterraneo (Napoli 1995). N 1997, Donnaregina 86 pp. L7.000 [RdT 40,945—Villano, Francesco].
349 ECocchini, Francesca Il dono e la sua ombra: ricerche sul Peri euches di ORIGENE. SEAug 57: R 1997, Institutum Patristicum Augustinianum 195 pp. Atti del I Convegno del Gruppo Italiano di Ricerca su "Origene e la Tradizione Alessandrina" (1996: Chieti). 88-7961-040-6. RASEs 14 (1997) 553-554 (Pieri, F.).

350 <sup>E</sup>Kehl-Bodrogi, Krisztina; Kellner-Heinkele, Barbara; Otter-Beaujean, Anke Syncretistic religious communities in the Near East: collected papers of the International Symposium "Alevism in Turkey and comparable syncretistic religious communities in the Near East in the past and present", Berlin, 14-17 April 1995. SHR 76: Lei 1997, Brill xvii; 255 pp. 90-04-10861-0.

351 <sup>E</sup>Livingstone, Elizabeth A. Studia Patristica vols. XXIX-XXXIII: papers presented at the Twelfth International Conference on Patristic Studies held in Oxford 1995. Lv 1997, Peeters 5 vols. 90-6831-.

352 <sup>E</sup>Schäfer, Peter; Kippenberg, Hans Gerhard Envisioning magic: a Princeton seminar and symposium. Numen.SHR 75: Lei 1997, Brill xi; 281 pp. 90-04-10777-0.

353 <sup>E</sup>Scheible, Heinz MELANCHTON in seinen Schülern. Wolffenbütteler Forschungen 73: Wsb 1997, Harrassowitz 587 pp. 3-447-03926-4 [DBAT 29,326—Diebner, B.J.].

354 El seguimiento de Cristo. M 1997, PPC 445 pp [RevAg 41,857—Sánchez-Gey Venegas, Juana].

355 <sup>E</sup>Triacca, A.M.; Pistoia, A. Liturgie et culture: conférences Saint-Serge, XLIII<sup>e</sup> Semaine d'Études liturgiques, Paris, 25-28 juin 1996. BEL.S 90: R 1997, Liturgiche 220 pp. 88-86655-20-7 [EThL 74,444*].

## A2.5 *Acta* philologica *et* historica

356 <sup>E</sup>Alcock, Susan E. The early Roman Empire in the East. Oxbow Monograph 95: Oxf 1997, Oxbow x; 212 pp. £24. 1-900188-52-X.

357 <sup>E</sup>Bérard, François; Di Vita-Évrard, Ginette L'épigraphie dans les "Mélanges d'archéologie et d'histoire" (1881-1970). Collab. *Chausson, François*: R 1997, École Française de Rome 89 pp. Congresso internazionale di epigrafia greca e latina. 2-7283-0379-7.

358 <sup>E</sup>Bodel, John; Tracy, Stephen Greek and Latin inscriptions in the USA: a checklist. R 1997, American Academy in Rome xx; (2) 249 pp. Congresso Internazionale di Epigrafia Greca e Latina, Roma. 1-879549-05-0.

359 <sup>E</sup>Bouzek, Jan; Ondřejová, Iva Roman portraits: artistic and literary. Mainz 1997, Von Zabern 130 pp. Acts of the Third International Conference on the Roman portraits held in Prague and in the Bechyně Castle from 25 to 29 September 1989; 30 pl. DM135. 3-8053-2335-2 [AJA 103,161s—Brilliant, Richard].

360 Les enjeux de la traduction: l'expérience des missions chrétiennes: Actes des sessions 1995 et 1996 sw l'AFOM et du CREDIC. Lyon 1997, 359 pp. [Mémoire Spiritaine 7,155—Buis, Pierre].

361 <sup>E</sup>Fernández, Leandro Félix; Ortega Arjonilla, Emilio Estudios sobre traducción e interpretación. Jornadas Internacionales de Traducción e Interpretación de la Universidad de Málaga 1: Málaga 1997, Universidad de Málaga 589 pp. Actas: Málaga, 22-24 de abril de 1996. 84-7785-174-3.

362 Flashar, Hellmut, (*al.*), Médicine et morale dans l'Antiquité. Entretiens 43: Genève 1997, Fondation Hardt viii; 415 pp. Entretiens sur l'antiquité classique (1996: Vandoeuvres); dix exposés suivis de discussions. FS70.

363 ᴱFreedman, David Noel, (al.), Studies in Hebrew and Aramaic orthography. 1992, ⇒8,9354... 11/2,5715. ᴿJNES 56 (1997) 142-144 *(Pardee, Dennis)*.

364 ᴱHansen, Mogens Herman The polis as an urban centre and as a political community: symposium August, 29-31 1996. Det Kongelige Danske Videnskabernes Selskab. Historisk-filosofiske Meddelelser 75; Acts of the Copenhagen Polis Centre 4: K 1997, Munksgaard 547 pp. 87-7304-291-9.

365 ᴱHägg, Robin The role of religion in the early Greek polis. Acta Instituti Atheniensis Regni Sueciae 14: Sto 1996, Åström 176 pp. Proceedings of the 3rd international seminar of ancient Greek cult organized by the Swedish Institute at Athens, Oct. 1992; 39 fig. 91-7916-033-6 [Kernos 12,305—Jost, Madeleine].

366 ᴱHoffman, Michael C.; Rotroff, Susan I. The romanization of Athens: proceedings of an international conference held at Lincoln, Nebraska (April 1996). Oxbow Monograph 94: Oxf 1997, Oxbow xiii; 208 pp. 1-900188-51-1.

367 ᴱKramer, Bärbel, (al.), Akten des 21. Internationalen Papyrologenkongresses, Berlin 13.-19.8.1995. APF.B 3: Stu 1997, Teubner 2 vols. DM475. 3-8154-7535-X [CÉg. 73,379s—Nachtergael, G.].

368 ᴱMoggi, Mauro; Cordiano, Giuseppe Schiavi e dipendenti nell'ambito dell''oikos' e della 'familia'. Pisa 1997, ETS 463 pp. Atti del XXII congresso del Groupe International de Recherche sur l'Esclavage Antique, Pontignano, 1995 [At. 88,317ss—Giglioni, G.B.].

369 ᴱMuraoka, Takamitsu; Elwolde, J.F. The Hebrew of the Dead Sea Scrolls and Ben Sira. StTDJ 26: Lei 1997, Brill vii; (2) 222 pp. Proceedings of a symposium held at Leiden University 11-14 December 1995. ƒ130. 90-04-10820-3 [JSJ 28,367].

370 La Rome impériale: démographie et logistique. CEFR 230: R 1997, Ecole Française de Rome 241 pp. Actes de la table ronde (Rome, 25 mars 1994). L70.000. 2-7283-0370-3 [JRS 89,234—Rathbone, D.].

## A2.7 *Acta* orientalistica

371 ᴱCharpin, D.; Joannès, F. La circulation des biens, des personnes et des idées dans le Proche-Orient ancien. 1991, ⇒8,683; 10,1369. ᴿJNES 56 (1997) 231-233 *(Biggs, Robert D.)*.

372 ᴱFitschen, Klaus; Staats, Reinhart Grundbegriffe christlicher Ästhetik: Beiträge des V. Makarios-Symposiums Preetz 1995. GOF.S 36: Wsb 1997, Harrassowitz 172 pp. 3-447-03855-1.

373 ᴱFragner, B.G., (al.), Proceedings of the Second European Conference of Iranian Studies, Bamberg 30.9.-4.10.1991. ISMEO SOR 73: R 1995, Societas Iranologica Europea ix; 779 pp. 52 pl. ᴿAMI 29 (1997) 505-507 *(Reck, Christiane)*.

374 ᴱHeintz, Jean-Georges Oracles et prophéties dans l'antiquité. Travaux du centre de recherches sur le Proche-Orient et la Grèce antiques 15: P 1997, De Boccard 542 pp. Actes du Colloque de Strasbourg, 15-17 juin 1995 [Or. 68,173ss—Bonnet, Corinne].

375 ᴱMalul, Meir Mutual influences of peoples and cultures in the ancient Near East. Haifa 1996, Hecht Museum 179 pp. Conference, Haifa 1994. $20. ᴿWO 28 (1997) 214-216 *(Haase, Richard)*.

376 ᴱParpola, Simo; Whiting, Robert M. Assyria 1995: proceedings of the 10th anniversary symposium of the Neo-Assyrian Text Corpus

Project: Helsinki, September 7-11, 1995. Helsinki 1997, The Neo-Assyrian Text Corpus Project x; 389 pp. $50. 951-45-7703-5.

377 ᴱSérandour, Arnaud Des sumériens aux romains d'orient la perception géographique du monde: espaces et territoires au Proche-Orient ancien: actes de la table ronde du 16 novembre 1996 organisée par l'URA 1062 "Études sémitiques". Antiquités sémitiques 22: P 1997, Maisonneuve 209 pp. 2-7200-1110-X.

378 ᴱStaehelin, Elisabeth; Jaeger, Bertrand Ägypten-Bilder: Akten des "Symposions zur Ägypten-Rezeption" Augst bei Basel, vom 9-11. September 1993. Collab. *Hofmeier, Thomas; Schneider, Thomas*: OBO 150: Gö 1997, Vandenhoeck & R 383 pp. DM161. 3-525-53786-7.

379 ᴱWaetzoldt, Hartmut; Hauptmann, Harald Assyrien im Wandel der Zeiten: XXXIXe Rencontre Assyriologique Internationale, Heidelberg 6.-10. Juli 1992. Heidelberger Studien zum Alten Orient 6: Heidelberg 1997, Orientverlag xvii; 397 pp. 61 pl. DM148. 3-927552-25-9.

## A2.9 *Acta* archaeologica

380 ᴱAndersen, Helle Damgaard, (*al.*), Urbanization in the Mediterranean in the ninth to sixth centuries B.C. Acta Hyperborea 7: K 1997, Museum Tusculanum Press 467 pp. Meeting, Copenhagen 1994; 9 pl.; 76 fig.; 20 plans. $66. 87-7289-412-1 [AJA 103,558s—Snodgrass, A.M.].

381 ᴱBarham, Anthony J.; Macphail, Richard I. Archaeological sediments and soils: analysis, interpretation, and managment. L 1995, Institute of Archaeology, University College xv; 239 pp. 10th Anniversary Conference of the Association for Environmental Archaeology, London 1989; 49 fig., 15 pl. £18.50/$29.50. 0-905-5853-31-8. ᴿAJA 101 (1997) 593 *(Timpson, Michael E.)*.

ᶠBaumgarten, Joseph M. Legal texts... proc. of the 2nd meeting of the International Organization for Qumran Studies 1995 ⇒8.

382 ᴱBéarat, H., (*al.*), Roman wall painting: materials, techniques, analysis and conservation. FrS 1997, Inst. of Mineralogy and Petrography, Univ. of Fribourg 378 pp. Proceedings of the International Workshop, Fribourg, 7-9 March 1996; 20 col pl.; 108 fig. 2-97001-320-7 [AJA 103,575s—Ling, Roger].

383 ᴱBeavis, John; Barker, Katherine Science and site: evaluation and conservation. Occasional Paper 1: Poole 1995, Bournemouth University School of Conservation Science ix; 247 pp. Proceedings of the archaeological science conference, Bournemouth, Sept. 1993; 116 fig.; 9 tables; 2 pl. £22.50/$36. 1-85899-011-4. ᴿAJA 101 (1997) 592-593 *(Timpson, Michael E.)*.

384 ᴱBiran, Avraham; Aviram, Joseph Biblical archaeology today, 1990: proceedings of the second international congress on biblical archaeology. 1993, ⇒9,554. ᴿJNES 56 (1997) 279-281 *(Joffe, A.H.)*.

385 ᴱBorrell, Augustí; Fuente, Alfonso de la; Puig, Armand La Bíblia i el Mediterrani: actes del Congrès de Barcelona 18-22 de setembre de 1995. Scripta Bíblica 1-2: Barc 1997, Associació Bíblica de Catalunya 2 vols. 84-7826-857-X [NTS 44,623].

386 ᴱCastel, Corinne; al-Maqdissi, Michel; Villeneuve, François Les maisons dans la Syrie antique du IIIᵉ millénaire aux débuts de l'is-

lam: pratiques et représentations de l'espace domestique. BAHI 150: Beyrouth 1997, Institut Français d'Archéologie du Proche-Orient iv; xvii; 332 pp. (franç.); xii pp. (arabe). Actes du Colloque International, Damas 27-30 juin 1992. 2-7053-0567-X [RB 105,634].

387 Çilingiroğlu, Altan; French, D.H. Anatolian Iron Ages 3. L 1994, British Institute of Archaeology at Ankara xxxviii; 314 pp. Proceedings of the third Anatolian Iron Ages Colloquium, Van 1990; 27 pl.; 27 fig. £30/$54. 1-898249-05-9. RAJA 101 (1997) 787-788 *(Sagona, Antonio)*.

388 ECumberpatch, C.G.; Blinkhorn, P.W. Not so much a pot, more a way of life: current approaches to artefact analysis in archaeology. Monograph 83: Oxf 1997, Oxbow vi; 162 pp. 42 fig. 40 tables. £24. 1-900-188-38-4 [Antiquity 73,940—James, N.].

389 EDurand, Jean-Marie Mari, Ébla et les hourrites: dix ans de travaux: première partie. Amurru 1: 1996, ⇒12,306. RRB 104 (1997) 420-421 *(Langlamet, F.)*; AfO 44-45 (1997-98) 363-365 *(Eidem, Jesper)*.

390 EFunk, Bernd Hellenismus: Beiträge zur Erforschung von Akkulturation und politischer Ordnung in den Staaten des hellenistischen Zeitalters. Tü 1996, Mohr 798 pp. Akten des internationalen Hellenismus-Kolloquiums, 1994, Berlin. DM298. RBBras 14 (1997) 452-453.

391 EGenière, J. de la Héra: images, espaces, cultes. Collection du Centre Jean Bérard 15: N 1997, Centre Jean Bérard 270 pp. Actes du Colloque International du Centre de Recherches Archéologiques de l'Université de Lille III et de l'Association P.R.A.C. Lille, 29-30 novembre 1993. 2-903189-54-4.

392 EGillis, C.; Risberg, C.; Sjöberg, B. Trade and production in premonetary Greece: production and the craftsman  Studies in Mediterranean Archaeology and Literature Pocket book 143: Jonsered 1997, Åströms 281 pp. Proceedings of the 4th and 5th international workshops, Athens 1994 and 1995; 80 fig., tables. 91-7081-164-4 [BiOr 56,746—Crielaard, Jan Paul].

393 EGitin, Seymour Recent excavations in Israel: a view to the west: reports on Kabri, Nami, Miqne-Ekron, and Ashkelon. Archaeological Institute of America, Colloquia and Conference Papers 1: Dubuque 1995, Kendall H xiii; 122 pp. Archaeological Institute of America 1992. $28. 0-7872-0486-2. RAfO 44-45 (1997-98) 510-516 *(Weippert, Helga)*; JAOS 117 (1997) 606-608 *(Knapp, A. Bernard)*.

394 EGundlach, Rolf; Raedler, Christine Selbstverständnis und Realität. AAT 36,1; Beiträge zur (alt)ägyptischen Königsideologie 1: Wsb 1997, Harrassowitz. Akten des Symposiums zur Ägyptischen Königsideologie in Mainz, 15.-17.6.1995. 3-447-03965-5.

395 EGundlach, Rolf; Rochholz, Matthias Ägyptische Tempel. Akten der Ägyptologischen Tempeltagungen 1990, 1992. 1994, ⇒10,470. RCEg 72 (1997) 279-291 *(Laboury, Dimitri)*.

396 EHägg, Robin The function of the "Minoan Villa": proceedings of the Eighth International Symposium at the Swedish Institute at Athens, 6-8 June 1992. Acta Instituti Atheniensis Regni Sveciae, 4 46; Skrifter Utgivna av Svenska Institutet i Athen, 4 46: Sto 1997, Almqvist & W 245 pp. 91-7916-034-4.

397 EKarageorghis, V.; Laffineur, R.; Vandenabeele, F. Four thousand years of images on Cypriote pottery: proceedings of the

third international conference of Cypriote studies Nicosia, 3-4 May 1996. Bru 1997, Leventis Foundation. 9963-560-31-8 [IEJ 48,159].
398 EKarageorghis, Vassos; Michaelides, Demetrios Cyprus and the sea. Nicosia 1995, University of Cyprus 292 pp. Proceedings of the International Symposium, Nicosia 25-26.6.1993. RRSFen 25/1 (1997) 109-114 (Medas, Stefano).
399 ELaffineur, Robert; Betancourt, Philip P. TEXNH: Craftsmen, craftswomen and craftsmanship in the Aegean Bronze Age. Aegaeum 16: Liège 1997, Univ. de Liège xi; 548 pp.; 2 vols. Proceedings of the 6th International Aegean Conference/6e Rencontre égéenne internationale, Ph, Temple (18-21 April 1996). FB6.000. D-1997-0480-16 [AJA 103,552ss—Gillis, Carole].
400 Mito e storia in Magna Grecia: atti del trentaseiesimo Convegno di studi sulla Magna Grecia, Taranto, 4-7 ottobre 1996. Taranto 1997, Istituto per la storia e l'archeologia della Magna Grecia 584 pp.
401 EO'Mahony, Anthony The christian heritage in the Holy Land. L 1995, Scorpion C 320 pp. Conference, Jerusalem, 1994. RIslChr 23 (1997) 291-292 (Lane, Andrew J.).
402 EOakley, John H.; Coulson, William D.E.; Palagia, Olga Athenian potters and painters: the conference proceedings. Oxbow Monograph 67: Oxf 1997, Oxbow 539 pp. 1-900188-12-0.
403 EOren, Eliezer D. The Hyksos: new historical and archaeological perspectives. University Museum Monographs 98: Ph 1997, Univ. Museum, Univ. of Pennsylvania xxvi; 434 pp. 188 fig. 23 pl. 16 tables. Seminar, Univ. of Pennsylvania Museum of Archaeology and Anthropology, Jan.-April 1992 [JARCE 36,169—Riggins, Thomas].
404 EPrior, Michael; Taylor, William Christians in the Holy Land. L 1994, World of Islam Festival Trust xviii; 235 pp. Conference, 1993, London. RIslChr 23 (1997) 293-295 (Lane, Andrew J.).
405 ERittershofer, Karl-Friedrich Demographie der Bronzezeit: Paläodemographie—Möglichkeiten und Grenzen. Internationale Archäologie 36: Leidorf 1997, Espelkamp xii; 328 pp. West- u. Süddeutscher Verband für Altertumsforschung Jahrestagungen vom 24.-25. Mai 1989, Fra—Kolloquium der Arbeitsgemeinschaft Bronzezeit; fig; tables. DM98. 3-89646-308-X [AJA 103,557s—Chamberlain, A.].
406 EWilhelm, Gernot Die orientalische Stadt: Kontinuität, Wandel, Bruch: 1. Internationales Colloquium der Deutschen Orient-Gesellschaft, 9.-10. Mai 1996 in Halle/Saale. Colloquien der Deutschen Orient-Gesellschaft 1; Saarbrücken 1997, Saarbrücker Verlag xiii; 409 pp. DM139. 3-930843-24-2. RAfO 44-45 (1997-98) 468-472 (Hirsch, H.).
407 EWörrle, Michael; Zanker, Paul Stadbild und Bürgerbild im Hellenismus. Mü 1995, Beck 273 pp. Kolloquium Mü 1993; 153 fig. DM198. 3-406-39036-6. RAJA 101 (1997) 418-419 (Reger, G.L.).

A3.1 *Opera consultationis*—Reference works *plurium* infra

408 DBS 12/71: Sichem-Songe. EBriend, Jacques; Cothenet, Edouard: P 1997, Letouzey & A. 1281-1544 col. FF345 [RB 104,470].
409 D.S.: EDerville, A., (al.), 1932-1995, 17 vols, ⇒11/2,763; 12,329. RStMed 38 (1997) 1020-1021 (Lamarche, Paul).

410  DSBP 15: Elezione—vocazione, predestinazione. EPanimolle, Salvatore A.. R 1997, Borla 367 pp. L37.000. 88-263-1121-8.
411  DSBP 16: Escatologia. EPanimolle, Salvatore A.: R 1997, Borla 316 pp. L37.000. 88-263-1163-3.
412  DSBP 17: L'Esodo nella bibbia. EPanimolle, Salvatore A.: R 1997, Borla 237 pp. L37.000. 88-263-1164-1.
413  DSBP 18: L'Esodo nei padri della chiesa. EPanimolle, Salvatore A.: R 1997, Borla 184 pp. L37.000. 88-263-1165-X.
414  LThK 6: Kirchengeschichte bis Maximianus. EKasper, Walter, (al.), FrB ³1997, Herder 14 pp., 1508 Sp. 3-451-22006-7.
415  TDOT 7: כ-לאיץ EBotterweck, G.J.; Ringgren, Helmer; Fabry, Heinz-Josef: 1995, ⇒11/2,771. RCart. 13 (1997) 215-217 (Álvarez Barredo, M.); AUSS 35 (1997) 254-255 (Hasel, Michael G.).
416  TDOT 8: lākad-mōr. EBotterweck, G.J.; Ringgren, H.; Fabry, Heinz-Josef; TStott, Douglas W.: GR 1997, Eerdmans xxiv; 560 pp. $45. 0-8028-2332-7 [BoL 1998,2—Whybray, R.N.] [not infra].
417  ThWAT 8/4: ša'ar-šātāh. EFabry, H.J.; Ringgren, H.: 1994, ⇒10,519...12,333. RNRTh 119 (1997) 109-110 (Ska, J.L.).
418  ThWAT 10/4: Register/Literaturbeiträge. EFabry, Heinz-Josef; Ringgren, Helmer: Stu 1997, Kohlhammer 193-256 pp. DM64. 3-17-015433-8 [BoL 1998,8—Whybray, R.N.].
419  TRE 27: Politik/Politologie-Publizistik/Presse. EMüller, Gerhard: B 1997, De Gruyter 807 pp. 3-11-015435-8.
420  TRE 28: Pürstinger-Religionsphilosophie. EMüller, Gerhard: B 1997, De Gruyter 804 pp. 3-11-015580-X.

A3.3 Opera consultationis biblica non excerpta infra—not subindexed

421  EBalz, Horst; Schneider, Gerhard Dizionario esegetico del Nuovo Testamento, 1. 1995, ⇒11/2,776. RStPat 44/1 (1997) 208-209 (Leonardi, Giovanni).
422  ECoenen, Lothar; Haacker, Klaus Theologisches Begriffslexikon zum Neuen Testament, 1: A-H. Wu ²1997 <1971>, Brockhaus 1015 pp. 3-417-24841-8 [NThAR 1997,196].
423  EFilippi, Alfio Le chiavi della Bibbia: vocabulario della Bibbia di Gerusalemme. 1996, ⇒12,346. RProtest. 52 (1997) 194-195 (Tron, Claudio); CivCatt 148 IV (1997) 634-635 (Scaiola, D.).
424  Gérard, André Marie Diccionario de la Biblia. 1995, EstFr 98/1 (1997) 383-385 (Cortès, E.).
425  EGörg, Manfred; Lang, Bernhard Neues Bibel-Lexikon: Obadja - Qudschu. Lief. 11. Solothurn 1997, Benziger 1-224 pp. 3-545-23061-9/-2-7.
426  Grande enciclopedia illustrata della bibbia. EPrato, Gian Luigi, (al.), TPiazzoni, Ambrogio M.; Occhipinti, Pino: CasM 1997, Piemme 3 vols.
427  Haag, Herbert Dizionario biblico. EMaggioni, Bruno. Dizionari tascabili: Assisi 1997, Cittadella xi; 624 pp. 88-308-0629-3.
428  EJenni, Ernst; Westermann, Claus Theological Lexicon of the Old Testament. TBiddle, Mark E.: Peabody 1997, Hendrickson 3 vols. xlviii; 1638 pp. $120. 1-56563-133-1 [ThD 45,93—Heiser, W.C.].
429  EKee, Howard C., (al.), The Cambridge companion to the bible. C 1997, CUP 616 pp. £35. 0-521-34369-0 [NTS 43,521].

430 <sup>E</sup>Martin, Ralph P.; Davids, Peter H. Dictionary of the later New Testament & its development. Downers Grove 1997, InterVarsity xxx; 1288 pp. $40. 0-8308-1779-4 [BiTod 36,135—Senior, Donald].

431 Mertens, Heinrich A. Handbuch der Bibelkunde: literarische, historische, archäologische, religionsgeschichtliche, kulturkundliche, geographische Aspekte des Alten und Neuen Testamentes. Dü ²1997 <1984>, Patmos xiv; 862 pp. DM29.80 [ZAW 110,472—Rösel, M.].

432 Spicq, Celas Theological lexicon of the NT. 1994, 3 vols, ⇒10,9318... 12,7917. <sup>R</sup>RTR 56/1 (1997) 40-41 *(Bird, Anthony E.)*; AUSS 35 (1997) 298-299 *(Badenas, Roberto)*.

433 <sup>E</sup>Strecker, Georg; Schnelle, Udo Neuer Wettstein: Texte zum Neuen Testament aus Griechentum und Hellenismus 2/1: Texte zur Briefliteratur und zur Johannesapokalypse. 1996, ⇒12,5754. <sup>R</sup>ThPQ 145 (1997) 421-423 *(Niemand, Christoph*; BZ 41 (1997) 89-95 *(Klauck, Hans-Josef)* [also on earlier vols].

434 TUAT 6: Texte aus der Umwelt des Alten Testaments: Weisheitstexte, Mythen und Epen, IV. <sup>E</sup>Dietrich, M.; Loretz, O.: Gü 1997, Gü'er 1089-1369 pp. 3-579-00083-7. <sup>R</sup>RBBras 14 (1997) 290-291.

435 <sup>E</sup>Van der Toorn, Karel; Becking, Bob; Van der Horst, Pieter W. Dictionary of deities and demons in the bible. 1995, ⇒11/2,800; 12,359. <sup>R</sup>Annales Theologici 11 (1997) 536-538 *(Estrada, Bernardo)*; CBQ 59 (1997) 560-561 *(Fulco, William J.)*.

436 <sup>E</sup>VanGemeren, Willem A. New international dictionary of Old Testament theology & exegesis. GR 1997, Zondervan 5 vols. $200. 0-310-48170-8 [ThD 44,374—Heiser, W. Charles].

A3.5 *Opera consultationis* theologica *non excerpta infra*

437 <sup>E</sup>Bowker, John The Oxford dictionary of world religions. NY 1997, OUP xxiv; 1111 pp. $55. 0-19-213965-7 [ThD 45,84—Heiser, W.].

438 <sup>E</sup>Cross, Frank Leslie; Livingstone, Elizabeth A. The Oxford dictionary of the christian church. Oxf ³1997, OUP xxxvii; 1786 pp. $125/£70. 0-19-211655-X.

439 García Gual, C. Diccionario de mitos. Barc ²1997, Planeta 382 pp. [EstAg 33,423—Antolín, J.].

440 <sup>E</sup>Gunton, Colin E. The Cambridge companion to christian doctrine. C 1997, CUP xix; 307 pp. £13. 0-521-47695-X.

441 <sup>E</sup>Hainz, Josef; Sand, Alexander Münchener theologisches Wörterbuch zum Neuen Testament. Dü 1997, Patmos 484 pp. 3-491-77014-9 [NThAR 1997,261].

442 <sup>E</sup>Hinnells, John R. The Penguin dictionary of religions. L 1997, Penguin xxxvii; 760 pp. £11/$17. 0-14-051261-6 [BoL 1998,9—Dearey, P.].

443 <sup>E</sup>Latourelle, René; Fisichella, Rino Dictionary of fundamental theology. 1995, ⇒12,6692. <sup>R</sup>AUSS 35 (1997) 286-288 *(Hasel, F.)*.

444 Montero, S. Diccionario de adivinos, magos y astrólogos de la Antigüedad. M 1997, Trotta 323 pp [Proyección 45,324—Sicre, J.L.].

445 Sierra Bravo, Restituto Diccionario social de los Padres de la Iglesia. M 1997, Edibesa 384 pp [TE 42,281—Ramón, Lucía].

446 <sup>E</sup>Stuhlmueller, Carroll; Bergant, Dianne The Collegeville pastoral dictionary of biblical theology. 1996, ⇒12,371. <sup>R</sup>DoLi 47/3 (1997) 186-188 *(O'Leary, Anthony)*; CBQ 59 (1997) 595-596 *(Cahill, M.)*.

A3.6 *Opera consultationis* generalia

447 **Crystal, David** The Cambridge encyclopedia of language. C $^2$1997, CUP viii; 480 pp. 0-521-550505.
448 Enciclopedia del cristianesimo: storia e attualità di 2000 anni di speranza. Novara 1997, Istituto Geografico de Agostini 703 pp. 88-415-4454-6.
449 Encyclopaedia Judaica. J 1997, Judaica Multimedia. *f*841.50. 965-07-0665-B. CD-ROM edition [JSJ 31,73—García Martínez, Florentino].
450 $^E$**Gilman, Sander L.; Zipes, Jack** The Yale companion to Jewish writing and thought in German culture, 1096-1996. NHv 1997, Yale University Press xxxiv; 864 pp. £35 [JJS 49,390ss—Albanis, Elisabeth].
451 **RAC** 17: Reallexikon für Antike und Christentum: Iao-indictio feriarum. 1994, ⇒11/2,768. $^R$VigChr 51 (1997) 334-336 *(Van Winden, J.C.M.)*.
452 **RLA** 8/1-4: Reallexikon der Assyriologie. $^E$**Edzard, Dietz Otto**: 1993-1994. ⇒9,601; 11/2,769. $^R$BiOr 54 (1997) 708-710 *(Hallo, William W.)*.
453 $^E$**Silverman, David P.** Ancient Egypt. NY 1997, OUP 256 pp. Bibl. $35. 0-19-521270-3.
454 $^E$**Vauchez, André** Dictionnaire encyclopédique du Moyen Âge. Collab. *Vincent, Catherine*: P 1997, Cerf xxxi; 1692 pp.; 2 vols. 2-204-05865-3 [AnBoll 116,430ss—Godding, Robert].

A4.0 **Bibliographiae,** computers **biblicae**

455 *Adamo, David Tuesday* Doing Old Testament research in Africa. NAOTS 3 (1997) 8-11.
456 *Alkier, Stefan; Cornils, Anja* Bibliographie Mündlichkeit-Schriftlichkeit. Logos. $^E$Sellin, Gerhard. TANZ 20: 1997, ⇒305. 235-265.
457 La bibbia e il messale. Città del Vaticano 1997, Vaticana; Unitelm CD-ROM, versione 1.21. L225.000 [Ang. 75,284ss—Stancati, T.].
458 Bible [bibliography]. QS 67 (1997) 387-414.
459 The Bible in English: a full-text database for literary, linguistic, and biblical studies. CD-ROM. 1996, ⇒12,380. Reformation 2 (1997) 345-351 *(Westbrook, Vivienne)*.
460 Bible study software: Cyber Bible study for 1997. BArR 23/3 (1997) 54-56, 60-64.
461 BibleWorks 3.5. Big Fork, Montana, Hermeneutika. $^R$AUSS 35 (1997) 310-312 *(Klingbeil, Gerald)*.
462 Bulletin de bibliographie biblique. $^E$**Kaestli, Jean-Daniel**: Lausanne 1997, Institut des sciences bibliques de l'Université de Lausanne. 3 issues a year.
463 Elenchus Bibliographicus 1997. EThL 73. $^E$**Brito, E.**, (*al.*),: Lv 1997, Peeters 707* pp. FB2.000. 0013-9513.
464 Era uma vez...1. O menino Jesus, 1997; 2. a aldeia da música, 1998. CD-ROM cassete. 1997-98 [Bib(L) 7/7,180ss—Morgado, Lopes].

465 Gamma Unitype: ancient/biblical/scholarly volume [Version 1.7, July 1995]. 1995, ⇒10,9694; 11/2,7005. ᴿSJTh 50 (1997) 384-388 *(Good, Deirdre J.)*.

466 *Gibert, Pierre; Abadie, Philippe; Carrière, Jean-Marie* Bulletin d'exégèse de l'Ancien Testament. RSR 85 (1997) 277-292, 427-450.

467 **IZBG** 44: ᴱ**Lang, Bernhard:** Dü 1997-1998, Patmos xv; 475 pp.

468 *Kawale, Winston R.* New data base: Bible in Africa research project. NAOTS 3 (1997) 3-4.

469 Logos Bible atlas for Microsoft Windows. Wsh, Logos Research Systems. 5 Disk. oder 1 CD-ROM, Systemvoraussetzungen: Windows 3.1 oder höher, 2 MB Arbeitsspeicher, 8 MB freier Festplatte, Maus (zu beziehen über: ÖKB). OS900. ᴿBiLi 70 (1997) 328 *(Schreiber, Hannes)*.

470 *Luciani, Didier* Chronique d'écriture sainte. VieCon 69 (1997) 325-338.

471 *Mertins, Michael* Literatur zur Biblischen Theologie 1988-1996. JBTh 12 (1997) 353-406.

472 *Muutuki, Joseph* Library resources for Old Testament research in Nairobi. NAOTS 3 (1997) 5-7.

473 **NTAb** 41: ᴱ**Harrington, Daniel J.**: CM 1997, Weston Jesuit School of Theology 637 pp. $33/$36. 0028-6877.

474 **OTA** 20: ᴱ**Begg, Christopher T.**: Wsh 1997, Catholic Biblical Association 623 pp. $26. 0364-8591.

475 *Piech, Stanisław* Dysertacje o tematyce biblijnej i liturgicznej na wydziale teologicznym Uniwersytetu Jagiellońskiego w latach 1945-1954 [De dissertationibus biblicis et liturgicis in facultate theologica Universitatis Jagellonicae in annis 1945-1954]. RBL 50 (1997) 266-276. **P.**

476 *Sampathkumar, P.A.* Books and articles published by Fr. L. LEGRAND. ITS 34/1-3 (1997) V-XVI.

477 **Sassoon, Rosemary; Gaur, Albertine** Signs, symbols and icons: pre-history to the computer age. Exeter 1997, Intellect 191 pp. 1-871516-73-0.

478 ᴱ**Sheehan, William J.**: Bibliothecae Apostolicae Vaticanae incunabula. StT 380-383: Città del Vaticano 1997, Biblioteca Apostolica Vaticana 4 vols. Bibl. 88-210-0676-X.

479 **ThD** 44: ᴱ*Heiser, W. Charles*: Book survey. Duluth, MN 1997, Theology Digest. 55-95; 155-195; 253-294; 351-390. 0040-5728.

480 Universitätsbibliothek Tübingen: Der Zeitschriften Inhaltsdienst Theologie (ZID): eine Datenbank der Universitätsbibliothek Tübingen. 1996, ⇒12,400. ᴿThLZ 122 (1997) 232-233 *(Schanz, Martin)*.

481 **ZAW** 109: Zeitschriften und Bücherschau. ᴱ*Waschke, Ernst-Joachim; Köckert, Matthias*: B 1997, De Gruyter. DM276. 95-167; 275-325; 442-479. 0044-2526/97.

482 **ZID**: Tü 1997, Universitätsbibliothek, Theologische Abt. Monthly. 0340-8361.

483 **ZNW** 88: ᴱ*Grässer, Erich*: B 1997, De Gruyter. 149-156; 327-333.

A4.3 *Bibliographiae diversae*

484 **Camarero Maria, Lorenzo** Revelaciones solemnes de Jesús: derás cristológico en Jn 7-8 (fiesta de las tendas). Diss. Madrid, 1993,

$^D$*Muñoz Léon, D.*: Monografías 4: M 1997, Claretianas 482 pp.
PTA4.327. 84-7966-140-2 [EThL 74,316*].

485 **Chidester, David; Tobler, Judy; Wratten, Darrel** Christianity in
South Africa: an annotated bibliography. Bibliographies and Indexes
in Religious Studies 43: Westport, Conn. 1997, Greenwood ix; 487
pp. £76. 0-313-30473-4 [JRA 29,508s—Hodgson, Janet].

486 *Deller, K.; Klengel, H.; Schuster, A.* Keilschriftbibliographie 56
(1996) (mit Nachträgen aus früheren Jahren). Or. 66 (1997) 1*-108*.

487 $^E$**Dimarogonas, Andrew D.** Synopsis: an annual index of Greek studies I: 1992. Amst 1997, Harwood v; 311 pp. £81/$125. 90-5702-
541-8 [CBQ 59,818].

488 *Durand, G.-M. de* Bulletin de Patrologie. RSPhTh 81 (1997) 85-
119.

489 Excerpta e dissertationibus in sacra theologia. Pamplona 1995, Servi-
cio de Publicaciones de la Universidad de Navarra 378 pp. [Laur.
40,538—Gonzalez, Manuel].

490 **Keller, Adalbert** Translationes patristicae graecae et latinae:
Bibliographie der Übersetzungen altchristlicher Quellen, 1: A-H. Stu
1997, Hiersemann xxxiv; 454 pp. [AHC 31,193—Nadig, Peter].

491 **Mikkelsen, Gunner B.** Bibliographia Manichaica: a comprehensive
bibliography of Manichaeism through 1996. Fontium Manichaeorum
Subsidia 1: Turnhout 1997, Brepols xlvi; 314 pp. EUR74. 2-503-
50653-4 [VigChr 53,442s—Schipper, H.G.].

492 $^E$**Nappo, Tommaso; Noto, Paolo** Indice biografico italiano. Introd.
*Furlani, Silvio:* Mü $^2$1997, Saur 3 vols. 3-598-33168-1.

493 **Wollmann, Ninette-Eileen** Bibliographie zur kirchlichen Zeitgeschichte. Collab. *Lüder, Andreas:* KZG 10 (1997) 412-555.


## II. Introductio


B1.1  *Introduction tota vel VT*—**Whole Bible or OT**

494 **Ackermann, Sonja** Christliche Apologetik und heidnische Philosophie im Streit um das Alte Testament. Diss. Bonn 1996, $^D$*Hossfeld,
F.-L.:* SBB 36: Stu 1997, Katholisches Bibelwerk 193 pp. DM79. 3-
460-00361-5 [RTL 29,121].

495 *Aleixandre, Dolores* Imágenes bíblicas para el acompañamiento. Sal-
Ter 85 (1997) 641-657.

496 **Alonso Schökel, Luis,** (*al.*), La bibbia nel suo contesto. Introduzione allo Studio della Bibbia 1: 1994, ⇒10,710; 11/2,1076.
$^R$RivBib 45 (1997) 469-471 *(Fabris, Rinaldo);*

497 Lezioni sulla Bibbia. 1996, ⇒12,414. $^R$RdT 38 (1997) 849-851
*(Franco, Ettore);*

498 *Alonso Schökel, Luis* Las diez y una noches. SalTer 87 (1997) 867-
876.

499 *Anandaraj, Francis S.* Old Testament introductions. VJTR 61 (1997)
54-57.

500 **Artola Arbiza, Antonio M.; Sánchez Caro, José M.** Bibbia e parola di Dio. Introduzione allo Studio della Bibbia 2: 1994, ⇒10,711.
$^R$RivBib 45 (1997) 471-474 *(Fabris, Rinaldo).*

501 *Barbaglio, Giuseppe* Testimonianza biblica. Servitium 111 (1997) 40-53.
502 **Barclay, William** Introducing the Bible. Foreword *Barclay, Ronnie*; E*Rogerson, John*: Nv 1997, Abingdon 189 pp. $10. 0-687-36590-2.
503 E**Benetti, Santos** La bibbia tematica: Antico Testamento. 1996, ⇒12,418. RLetteratura Liturgica 84 (1997) 547-8 *(Troía, Pasquale)*.
504 **Boitani, Piero** Ri-Scritture. Incontri 5: Bo 1997, Il Mulino 244 pp. Bibl. 88-15-06132-0.
505 *Bradshaw, Christopher J.* John BALE and the use of English Bible imagery. Reformation 2 (1997) 173-189.
506 **Cappelletto, Gianni** Il cammino con Israele: introduzione all'Antico Testamento. Strumenti di scienze religiose: Padova 1997, Messagero 399 pp. L29.000. 88-250-0629-2 [RTL 29,123].
507 E**Carey, George** The bible for everyday life. 1996, ⇒12,424. ROTEs 10 (1997) 553-555 *(Domeris, W.R.)*.
508 E**Carstens, P.; Lundager Jensen, H.J.** Loesninger og tolkninger af det Gamle Testmente. Tekst og teologi, 1. Fredriksberg 1997, Anis 258 pp. 87-7457-198-2 [NTT 98,180].
509 **Christensen, Duane L.** Bible 101: God's story in human history. Richland Hills, TX 1997, BIBAL xv; 247 pp. $20. 0-941073-42-8 [ThD 45,166—Heiser, W. Charles].
510 E**Clark, Douglas R.; Brunt, John C.** Introducing the Bible. Lanham 1997, University Press of America 2 vols. $69. 0-7618-.
511 **Cohn-Sherbok, Dan** The Hebrew Bible. L 1996, Cassell xiii; 257 pp. 0-304-33702-1/3-X.
512 **Crenshaw, James L.** Old Testament story and faith: a literary and theological introduction. 1992, ⇒9,822. RVJTR 61 (1997) 278-279 *(Meagher, P.M.)*.
513 E**Dalla Vecchia, F.; Nepi, A.; Corti, G.L.** Introduzione generale allo studio della Bibbia. 1996, ⇒12,429. RCivCatt 148 IV (1997) 315-316 *(Scaiola, D.)*.
514 *Daoust, Joseph* L'Ancien Testament corrigé. EeV 107/20 (1997) 451-452.
515 E**Denecke, Axel** Die Bibel hat viele Gesichter: Annäherungen an die Heilige Schrift. Stu 1997, Radius 140 pp. 3-87173-121-8 [NThAR 1998,97].
516 *Deurloo, Karel* Gezegend. ITBT 5/7 (1997) 29-30.
517 **Dohmen, Christoph** Vom Umgang mit dem Alten Testament. 1995, ⇒12,431. RThLZ 122 (1997) 242-243 *(Conrad, Joachim)*.
518 **Duggan, Michael** The consuming fire: a christian introduction to the OT. 1991, ⇒8,1020c...10,721*. RTJT 13/1 (1997) 89-90 *(Davies, Gordon F.)*.
519 **Elliger, Katharina** Paare in der Bibel: was damals alles möglich war. 1996, ⇒12,433. RBiLi 70 (1997) 80-82 *(Gillmayr-Bucher, S.)*.
520 E**Fabris, R.** Introduzione generale alla Bibbia. Logos 1: 1994, ⇒10,722...12,177. RQuaderni di Scienze Religiose 6 (1997) 95-7 *(Fattorini, Gino)*.
521 **Frankenfeld, Kurt** Genealogie der Bibel: ein biblischer Stammbaum. Fra 1997, Haag und Herchen 384 pp. 3-86137-589-3.
522 *Freedman, David Noel* The continuing revolution in biblical research. Divine Commitment 1. 1997 <1963>, ⇒124. 133-138;
523 The law and the prophets. Divine Commitment 1. 1997 <1963>, ⇒124. 139-151.

524 **Gibert, Pierre** Así se escribió la Biblia: introducción al Antiguo y Nuevo Testamento. M 1997, Narcea 166 pp. 84-271-2071-0 [TeCa 67,141—Barrado Fernández, P.].

525 **Girard, Marc** Les symboles dans la Bible. RFTP 26: 1991, ⇒8,1162... 12,440. RSal. 59 (1997) 558-559;

526 Os símbolos na Bíblia. TLemos, Benôni: São Paulo 1997, Paulus 800 pp. [REB 57,1020].

527 **Gitau, Samson**, (al.), Contextualized Old Testament programmes?. NAOTS 2 (1997) 3-7.

528 **Gordon, Cyrus Herzl; Rendsburg, Gary A.** The bible and the ancient Near East. NY ⁴1997 [1965], Norton 345 pp. bibl. $32.50 / $15. 0-393-03942-0 / 0-393-31689-0 [NThAR 1998,99].

529 **Greaves, Sheldon Wilde** The power of the word in the ancient Near East. Diss. Univ. of California, Berkeley; DKilmer, Anne D. 1996. 195 pp. [DAI-A 57/09, p. 3982; AAC 962294].

530 **Grelot, Pierre** Sentido cristiano del Antiguo Testamento. Biblioteca Manual Desclée 2: Bilbao ²1995, Desclée de Brouwer 525 pp. RCDios 210 (1997) 635-636 (Gutiérrez, J.).

531 EHolt, Else Kragelund; **Nielsen, Kirsten** Bibelkundskab: introduktion til det Gamle Testamente. Aarhus 1997, Universitetsforlag 317 pp. [SJOT 12,146—Ejarnœs, Bodil].

532 Holter, Knut Gammeltestamentlig forskning mellom Sahara og Zambezi. Teologi og Kirke 68 (1997) 135-146 [EThL 74,170*].

533 Hong, Joseph Chapter and verse divisions in the bible: their origins, and their use in today's common language translations. PPBT 48 (1997) 401-410.

534 **Jagersma, H.** De bijbel lezen hoe kun je dat?. Kampen 1997, Kok 111 pp. f20. 90-242-9323-5 [ITBT 6/7,32—Van Leeuwen, Th.M.].

535 **Janowski, Bernd** Stellvertretung: alttestamentliche Studien zu einem theologischen Grundbegriff. SBS 165: Stu 1997, Katholisches Bibelwerk 158 pp. DM41.80. 3-460-04651-1.

536 **Kaiser, Otto** Die poetischen und weisheitlichen Werke. Grundriß der Einleitung in die ... Schriften des ATs. 1994, ⇒10,735; 11/2,1104. ROrdKor 38 (1997) 233-234 (Heinemann, Franz Karl).

537 Kee, Howard Clark Introduction. The Cambridge companion. 1997, ⇒429. 1-31.

538 **Kissling, Paul J.** Reliable characters in the primary history: profiles of Moses, Joshua, Elijah and Elisha. JSOT.S 224: 1996, ⇒12,451. RCBQ 59 (1997) 547-548 (McKenzie, Steven L.).

539 **Kostulias, Ray** I witness: dramatic monologues from Hebrew scriptures. Cleveland 1997, United Church 70 pp. $11 [BiTod 36,131—Bergant, Dianne].

540 **LaSor, William S.; Hubbard, David A.; Bush, Frederic W.** Old Testament survey. 1996, ⇒12,456. RVJTR 61 (1997) 277-278 (Meagher, P.M.).

541 **MacArthur, John** The MacArthur study bible. Nv 1997, Word xxxii; 2201 pp. also CD-Rom $40. $40. 0-8499-1222-9 [ThD 45,80—Heiser, W. Charles].

542 **Maeijer, Floor** Beeldige teksten; een bijbels ABC van symbolen. Baarn 1997, Gooi en S 165 pp. f34.90. 90-304-0900-2 [Streven 64,1050].

543 **Magonet, Jonathan** The subversive bible. L 1997, SCM (8) 151 pp. £12.50. 0-334-02671-7. RTheology 798 (1997) 450-451 (Dell, K.J.).

544 **Marchadour, Alain** Les mots de la bible. P 1997, Bayard 135 pp. FF95 [EeV 107,443].

545 [E]**Marconot, J.-M.** Le héros et l'héroïne bibliques dans la culture. Recherche biblique interdisciplinaire: Montpellier 1997, UPV-Montpellier III 314 pp. 2-84269-066-4 [ETR 73,309].

546 **Marín Heredia, Francisco** La Bíblia, palabra profética. El Mundo de la Biblia. 1992, ⇒11/2,2080. [R]EstB 55 (1997) 542-543 *(Asenjo, J.)*.

547 **Mas, D.** La palabra de Dios: la biblia en aforismos. Barc 1997, EDHASA 191 pp. [RelCult 44,220—Bardón, Eliseo].

548 **Mason, Rex** Propaganda and subversion in the Old Testament. L 1997, SPCK ix; 194 pp. £13. 0-281-05015-5.

549 **Matthews, Victor H.; Moyer, James C.** The Old Testament: text and context. Peabody 1997, Hendrickson ix; 308 pp. $30. 1-56563-168-4.

550 **Mesters, Carlos** Dios, ¿dónde estás?: una introducción práctica a la Biblia. Estudios Bíblicos 12: Estella [2]1997, Verbo Divino 259 pp. 84-7151-828-7.

551 *Meyers, Eric M.; Rogerson, John W.* The Old Testament world. The Cambridge companion. 1997, ⇒429. [E]Kee, H. 32-287.

552 **Müller, Mogens** Det Gamle Testamente som kristen bog. Fredriksberg 1997, Anis 92 pp. DKK98. 87-7457-200-8 [TTK 68/3,240].

553 **Nobile, Marco** Introduzione all'Antico Testamento. 1995, ⇒11/2,1118. [R]EstB 55 (1997) 541-542 *(Precedo, M.J.)*.

554 O Deus pelas costas: teologia narrativa da bíblia, 2: teologia negativa: o exílio, épocas persa e helenística. RBBras 14/1-3 (1997) 7-262.

555 **Ravasi, Gianfranco** Il racconto del cielo: le storie, le idee, i personaggi dell'Antico Testamento. Oscar Saggi: Mi 1995, Mondadori 317 pp. Bibl. 88-04-40310-1.

556 *Rogerson, J.W.* Recent continental Old Testament literature. ET 108 (1997) 363-365.

557 **Rosenstiehl, M.; Zuber, H.** Raconter la bible. Foi Vivante 385: P 1997, Cerf 112 pp. 2-204-05683-9 [ETR 73,310].

558 **Salas, Antonio** Introducción a la Biblia. México 1997, Dabar 10 vols. [EfMex 16,264s—Serraima Cirici, Enrique].

559 **Travis, Stephen** Comenzar con el Antiguo Testamento. Bilbao 1997, Mensajero 64 pp. [SalTer 87,438].

560 **Tullock, John H.** The Old Testament story. Upper Saddle River, NJ [4]1997, Prentice-Hall xv; 394 pp. 0-13-266347-3.

561 **Vaux, Roland de** Ancient Israel: its life and institutions. Biblical Resource: GR 1997 <1961>, Eerdmans xxiv; 592 pp. $30. 0-8028-4278-X.

562 **Walsh, Richard G.** Reading the bible: an introduction. Notre Dame 1997, Cross Cultural ix; 608 pp. $30. 0-940121-43-3 [NThAR 1998,268].

563 **Willman, Jarkko** Ideal och verklighet: Hilma GRANQVISTS studier av 'Kvinnorna i gamla testamentet' åren 1921-1925. Religionsvetenskapliga skrifter 35: Åbo 1997, Åbo Akademi 105 pp. 952-12-0033-2 [NThAR 1998,99].

564 [E]**Zenger, Erich** Einleitung in das Alte Testament. 1995 [[2]1996], ⇒11/2,1147; 12,487. [R]Cart. 13 (1997) 214 *(Sanz Valdivieso, R.)*; ThRv 93 (1997) 281-286 *(Kaiser, Otto)*; CBQ 59 (1997) 565-566

*(Boadt, Lawrence)*; Anton. 72/1 (1997) 129-131 *(Nobile, Marco)*; TThZ
106 (1997) 39-59, 232-240 *(Mosis, Rudolf)*;
565 Lebendige Welt der Bibel: Entdeckungsreise in das Alte Testament.
FrB 1997, Herder 204 pp. DM68. 3-451-26123-5.
566 *Zenger, Erich* Entstehung und Aufbau des Alten Testaments. Lebendige Welt. 1997, ⇒565. [E]Zenger, Erich. 126-140.
567 **Zenger, Erich** Il primo Testamento: la Bibbia ebraica e i cristiani.
Giornale di teologia 248: Brescia 1997, Queriniana 237 pp. L32.000.
88-399-0748-3. [R]StPat 44/3 (1997) 204-205 *(Segalla, Giuseppe)*.

## B1.2 'Invitations' to Bible or OT

568 **Adams, Douglas** The prostitute in the family tree: discovering
humor and irony in the bible. LVL 1997, Westminster 127 pp. $12.
0-664-25693-7.
569 *Alonso Schökel, Luis* Itinerarios de libros del AT. ResB 12 (1997) 5-
12 [AcBib 10/4,388].
570 **Auneau, Joseph,** *(al.)*, Abans de l'exili. Llegir l'Antic Testament:
una iniciació 1. Saurí 133: Montserrat 1997, Abadia de Montserrat
164 pp. [Qüestions de Vida Cristiana 187,191].
571 **Bach, Daniel** L'Ancien Testament dans tous ses états: dix textes
clefs pour nous le rendre familier. Lausanne 1997. Du Moulin 100
pp. FF58 [RHPhR 77,247].
572 **Barton, Stephen** Invitation to the bible. L 1997, SPCK 166 pp. £9
[Theol. 101,213s—West, Maxine].
573 *Bignardi, Paola* Lampada ai miei passi è la tua parola... la parola e
la vita. Presenza Pastorale 67 (1997) 807-816.
574 *Bozzini, Ida* Pensare la fede e leggere la parola. Presenza Pastorale
67 (1997) 849-853.
575 **Brown, Raymond E.** 101 preguntas y respuestas sobre la Biblia.
1996, ⇒12,496. [R]EE 72 (1997) 549-550 *(Ruiz Cañamares, J.A.)*.
576 **Brueggemann, Walter** The bible and postmodern imagination: texts
under negotiation. 1993, ⇒9,867... 12,497. [R]Bibl.Interp. 5 (1997)
216-217 *(Gorringe, Tim)*.
577 **Buzzetti, Carlo** 4x1: un unico brano biblico e vari 'fare'. 1994,
⇒10,771. [R]CivCatt 148 I (1997) 206-207 *(Scaiola, D.)*;
578 **Bibbia per noi:** leggere, attualizzare, comunicare. Guide per la prassi
ecclesiale 18: Brescia 1997, Queriniana 156 pp. L16.000. 88-399-
1858-2 [Asp. 46,308—Di Bianco, Nicola].
579 **Carlucci, Zaccaria** Scorrendo la bibbia: una rapida panoramica e
considerazioni per agevolarne la lettura. Bibbia e preghiera 31: R
1997, ADP 102 pp. L12.000. 88-7357-172-7.
580 *Chica Arellano, Fernando* Uso pastoral de la biblia. RelCult 43
(1997) 935-948.
581 **Cipriani, Settimio** Primo incontro con la bibbia: i libri dell'Antico
Testamento. 1996, ⇒12,499. [R]RCI 78/5 (1997) 392-393 *(Ghidelli,
Carlo)*; CivCatt 148 IV (1997) 628-630 *(Scaiola, D.)*.
582 **Courthial, Pierre** Le jour des petits recommencements: essai sur
l'actualité de la parole. 1996, ⇒12,502. [R]FV 96/3 (1997) 71-73
*(Martin, Alain G.)*.
583 *Cremonesi, Cecilia* Giovani universitari e parola di Dio: per una proposta originale. Presenza Pastorale 67 (1997) 841-847.

584 **Dieterle, Christiane; Maire, Charles Daniel; Massini, Alain** Il était une fois... la bible: de l'Ancien au Nouveau Testament, parcourir les textes et leur histoire. Lyon 1997, Réveil 96 pp. 2-902916-30-9 [RHPhR 77/2,248].

585 **Fanin, Luciano** Come leggere 'il libro': lineamenti di introduzione biblica. 1993, ⇒9,827... 11/2,1161. RBen. 44/1 (1997) 223-224 *(Ranzato, Agostino)*.

586 **Ferlo, Roger** Opening the bible. The church's teaching: CM 1997, Cowley. $12 [AThR 80,140ss—Hawkins, Peter S.).

587 **Fortosis, Stephen** Great men and women of the bible. Mumbai 1997, St Pauls 138 pp. Rs45. 81-7109-305-1 [VJTR 64,323—Meagher, P.M.].

588 **Giavini, Giovanni** Verso la bibbia e in ascolto del suo messaggio. Mi 1997, Àncora 200 pp. 88-7610-613-8 [NThAR 1999,178].

589 *Henning, I.J.* Kommunikasiehelderheid van de bybelkunde- en/of bybelonderrigonderwyser. Scriptura 60 (1997) 71-80 [ZID 23,278].

590 **Holladay, William L.** Long ago God spoke: how christians may hear the Old Testament today. 1995, ⇒11/2,1175. RTS 58 (1997) 149-150 *(Humphrey, Hugh M.)*; CBQ 59 (1997) 121-122 *(Pilch, John J.)*; CritRR 10 (1997) 181-183 *(Gnuse, Robert)*.

591 **Konings, Johan** Descobrir a bíblia a partir da liturgia. São Paulo 1997, Loyola 302 pp. 85-15-01609-5 [PerTeol 29,437].

592 *Le Dorze, Marcel* Au Japon on lit toute la Bible en 100 semaines. Mission de l'Église 117 (1997) 66-71.

593 *Lenne, Francine* Parole donnée. FV 96/1 (1997) 1-5.

594 **Maiberger, Paul** Le grandi figure dell'Antico Testamento. 1995, ⇒11/2,1190. RCivCatt 148 II (1997) 93-94 *(Scaiola, D.)*.

595 *Marcaletti, Francesco* Giovani, parola e vita. Presenza Pastorale 67 (1997) 837-839.

596 *Miller, Patrick* Popularizing the bible. ThTo 53 (1997) 435-438.

597 **Monforte, Josemaría** Conocer la biblia: iniciación a la sagrada escritura. Biblioteca de iniciación teológica 3: M ²1997, Rialp 175 pp. 84-321-3129-6 [ScrTh 29,675].

598 *Nebout, Michel* Des outils pour entrer dans la bible. Cahiers de l'Atelier 476 (1997) 101-106 [Matt 25,31-46].

599 **Poulain, Gaston; Dujardin, Jean** Lire l'Ancien Testament: contribution à une lecture catholique de l'Ancien Testament pour permettre le dialogue entre juifs et chrétiens. Documents des églises: P 1997, Cerf 44 pp. 2-204-05898-X.

600 *Ranzato, Viviana* Condiscepoli di un unico maestro: i ragazzi e la parola di Dio. Presenza Pastorale 67 (1997) 827-835.

601 **Sánchez, Manuel** Conoce la biblia. Mérida, Venezuela 1997, 160 pp. [Carmelus 45,181—Velasco, Balbino].

602 *Sevin, Marc* La lecture croyante de la Bible. Cahiers de l'Atelier 473 (1997) 64-70.

603 *Silvestre, Giuseppe* La lettura popolare della bibbia speranza di liberazione per l'Africa e l'America Latina e cammino per l'ecumenismo. Vivarium 5 (1997) 397-413.

604 **Staubli, Thomas** Begleiter durch das erste Testament. Dü 1997, Patmos 379 pp. 3-491-77015-7 [NThAR 1997,291].

605 **Tabuyo Ortega, María** La biblia contada a todas las gentes. M 1997, 1998, Anaya [SalTer 86,765ss—Tabuyo, María].

606 **Travis, Stephen** The bible in time: a chronological exploration of
    130 passages. Nv 1997, Abingdon 280 pp. $12 [BiTod 37,55—
    Bergant, Dianne].
607 **Vigée, Claude; Malka, Victor** Treize inconnus de la bible. 1996,
    ⇒12,526. ᴿFV 96 (1997) 79-80 *(Giniewski, Paul)*.
608 *Zenger, Erich* Spuren des Alten Testaments in der Alltagswelt. Le-
    bendige Welt. 1997, ⇒565. ᴱZenger, Erich. 10-21.

B1.3 *Paedagogia biblica*—Bible-teaching techniques

609 **Baldermann, Ingo** Einführung in die biblische Didaktik. 1996,
    ⇒12,533. ᴿThRv 93 (1997) 331-332 *(Dormeyer, Detlev)*.
610 **Becker, Ulrich; Johannsen, Friedrich; Noormann, Harry** Neute-
    stamentliches Arbeitsbuch für Religionspädagogen. Urban-Ta-
    schenbücher 439: Stu ²1997, Kohlhammer 296 pp. 3-17-014095-7.
611 *Beeching, Paul Q.* Gospels in the classroom: where the bible's just a
    good book. BiRe 13/3 (1997) 40-43, 54.
612 *Betori, Giuseppe* Dalla bibbia alla catechesi in Italia nel dopo Conci-
    lio. Firmana 15 (1997) 37-56.
613 *Degenaar, Johan* Religious discourse, power and the public.
    Neotest. 31 (1997) 39-58.
614 **Emeis, Dieter** Bibelarbeit praktisch—Methoden—Impulse. Biblische
    Bücher 3: FrB 1994, Herder 144 pp. DM19.80. 3-451-23480-7.
    ᴿThRv 93 (1997) 57-58 *(Dormeyer, Detlev)*.
615 **Fitzmyer, Joseph A.** Catecismo cristológico: respuestas del Nuevo
    Testamento. Nueva Alianza 146: S ³1997, Sígueme 173 pp.
    Ptas1.400. 84-301-0945-5 [Proyección 45,73].
616 **Getty-Sullivan, Mary Ann** God speaks to us in feeding stories. Ill.
    *Antkowski, Marygrace Dulski.* ColMn 1997, Liturgical 63 pp. $18.
617 *Holland, Martin* Was nützt der Gemeinde eine wissenschaftliche
    Ausbildung?. TVGMS 424: 1997, ⇒59. ᶠMᴀɪᴇʀ G., 261-272.
618 **Irure, Martín; Larrañeta, Jesús M.** Catequesis bíblicas para jóve-
    nes y adultos. M 1997, CCS 387 pp. [Mayéutica 23,556—Alonso,
    Gonzalo].
619 *Kee, Howard Clark* The formation of the christian community. The
    Cambridge companion 1997, ⇒429. ᴱKee, Howard Clark. 441-583.
620 *Koerrenz, Ralf* Hermeneutik des Lernens: der anthropologische
    Wirklichkeitsbezug der biblischen Überlieferung. JBTh 12 (1997)
    221-242.
621 *Lombaard, Christo J.S.* Developing Old Testament diploma courses
    at TEEC(SA). NAOTS 2 (1997) 9-12.
622 **Matsumura, Koichi** A guide book approach to the Old Testament on
    stamps. Hokkaido 1993, Japan Philatelic Society 621 pp. ᴿCoTh
    67/4 (1997) 221-224 *(Chrostowski, Waldemar)*.
623 *Mijoga, Hilary B.* Hidden and public ways of doing contextual bible
    study in southern Africa: South Africa and Malawi as case studies.
    Religion in Malawi 7 (1997) 41-44 [ZID 24,402].
624 *Nipkow, Karl Ernst* Konfirmanden—Kirche—Jesus Christus: zum
    heimlichen Lehrplan in der Konfirmandenzeit. BZNW 86: 1997,
    ⇒41. ᶠHᴏꜰɪᴜs Ö., 907-930.
625 La novità del vangelo: itinerari di catechesi per adulti. Bo 1997,
    EDB 184 pp. Ufficio Catechistico in Verona: Équipe per la Catechesi
    degli Adulti. L21.000 [RivBib 45,507].

626 *Pacomio, Luciano* L'insegnamento della sacra scrittura nei seminari oggi e in prospettiva futura. Seminarium 37 (1997) 21-33.
627 **Plescan, G.** Vivere la bibbia: simulazioni bibliche. Pref. *Bachelet, G.*: R 1997, Soc. Biblica Britannica e For. 143 pp. L40.000 [Protest. 53,369—Tomassone, Letizia].
628 ᴱ**Porter, David** The word on the box. Carlisle 1997, Paternoster vii; 109 pp. Compiled from the 1995 London lectures on contemporary christianity. 0-85364-794-1 [RB 105,157].
629 **Printz, Markus** Grundlinien einer bibelorientierten Gemeindepädagogik. 1996, ⇒12,567. ᴿJETh 11 (1997) 348-351 *(Faix, W.)*.
630 *Rothgangel, Martin* Empirische Überlegungen zur gegenwärtigen Behandlung der Passionsgeschichte im evangelischen Religionsunterricht. Christen und Juden. 1997, ⇒212. ᴱKraus, Wolfgang. 119-141.
631 **Solari, Gabriella** Produzione e circolazione del libro evangelico nell'Italia dell'Ottocento: la casa editrice Claudiana e i circuiti popolari della stampa religiosa. Studi e tese 5: R 1997, Manziana 200 pp. L40.000 [Protest. 54,404ss—Spini, Giorgio].
632 ᴱ**Soukup, Paul A.; Hodgson, Robert** From one medium to another: communicating the bible through multimedia. Kansas City, MO 1997, Sheed & W (4) 382 pp. Bibl. $25. 1-55612-968-8.
633 **Stutschinsky, Abrascha** La bibbia raccontata ai bambini secondo la sacra scrittura e l'aggadà ebraica. Padova 1997, Messagero 608 pp. L35.000 [Studi Fatti Ricerche 78,14].
634 *Thompson, John L. & Marianne M.* Teaching the bible to your children: the risks and the rewards. Word and World 17/3 (1997) 295-300 [ZID 23,415].
635 **Wrege, Hans-Theo** Religion, Bibel, Bildung: Untersuchungen zur Fachwissenschaft und Fachdidaktik der Evangelischen Religion. Beiträge zur Erziehungswissenschaft und biblischen Bildung 1: Fra 1997, Lang 205 pp. 3-631-49949-3.

## B2.1 Hermeneutica

636 *Alonso Schökel, Luis* Hermenéutica a la luz del lenguaje y la literatura. Hermenéutica. 1997 <1963>, ⇒658. 183-203;
637 Tres notas de hermenéutica. EstB 55 (1997) 73-87.
638 **Alonso Schökel, Luis; Bravo Aragon, J.M.** Appunti di ermeneutica. 1994, ⇒10,831; 11/2,1261. ᴿLat. 63 (1997) 317-8 *(Deiana, G.)*.
639 *Amador, J.D.H.* The word made flesh: epistemology, ontology and postmodern rhetorics. Rhetorical analysis. JSNT.S 146: 1997, ⇒336. ᴱPorter, Stanley E., 53-65.
640 *Anderson, Bernhard W.* The bible within the bible. BiRe 13/1 (1997) 17, 48;
641 The bible: word of God in human words. BiRe 13/3 (1997) 22, 56.
642 *Androutsopoulos, Jannis K.* Intertextualität in jugendkulturellen Textsorten. Textbeziehungen. 1997, ⇒287. ᴱKlein, Josef, 339-372.
643 *Angelini, Giuseppe* La questione biblica tra ricerca teologica e ministero pastorale. Teol(Br) 22 (1997) 319-328.
644 **Arens, Eduardo; Díaz Mateos, Manuel** El escándalo de la palabra: ¿interpretación de la biblia en crisis?. CEP 182: Lima 1997, Centro de Espiritualidad Ignaciana 128 pp. [NThAR 1998,365].

645  *Barban, Alessandro* La teologia tra fede, intellectus e storia: la meto-
dologia teologica di Magnus LOEHRER. StAns 124: 1997, ⇒57.
FLOEHRER M. — TRAGAN P. 629-666.

646  *Bartlett, John R.* What has archaeology to do with the Bible—or vice
versa?. Archaeology and biblical interpretation. 1997, ⇒268.
EBartlett, John R., 1-19.

647  *Bartolomei, Maria Cristina* La ragione teologica tra storia e simbolo:
riflessioni a partire da Mysterium Salutis. StAns 124: 1997, ⇒57.
FLOEHRER M. — TRAGAN P., 667-696.

648  *Beuchot, Mauricio* La hermenéutica en S. AGUSTIN y en la actualidad. RevAg 38 (1997) 139-156.

649  *Bilezikian, Gilbert* Hermeneutical bungeejumping: subordination in
the Godhead. JETS 40 (1997) 57-68.

650  **Blanchard, Robert** Paroles, symboles et paraboles: principes de lecture des textes bibliques: principes d'interprétation de leurs parties
symboliques. P 1997, L'Ange Vert [EeV 107,443].

651  **Blennberger, Erik** Bibelsyn—tillkomst, tolkning och giltighet
[Views of the bible—origin, interpretation and validity]. Diss.
Uppsala 1997 [StTh 51,81].

652  **Boer, Theo de** Pleidooi voor interpretatie. Amst 1997, Boom 195
pp. ƒ39. 90-5352-322-7 [ITBT 7/7,34—Spijkerboer, Anne Marijke].

653  *Bonhoeffer, Dietrich* Selections from the cost of discipleship. Interpretation of scripture. 1997, ⇒244. EFowl, S., 285-293.

654  *Boon, Rudolf* Vergezichten in bijbelse hermeneutiek. ITBT 5/1
(1997) 20-22.

655  *Brant, Jo-Ann A.* Hammering out a response from one Mennonite's
perspective. Semeia 77 (1997) 285-290.

656  *Burrus, Virginia* Resistance by the book?: some questions in response. Semeia 79 (1997) 93-96.

657  *Cañellas, Gabriel* El fundamentalismo judío. BiFe 23 (1997) 161-
188.

658  ECaparrós, José Domínguez Hermenéutica: compilación de textos,
introducción y bibliografía. Lecturas: M 1997, Arco 259 pp. 84-
7635-280-8.

659  **Carpenter, Joel A.** Revive us again: the reawakening of American
fundamentalism. NY 1997, OUP xiv; 335 pp. $30 [TS 59,339s—
Fackre, Gabriel].

660  *Carroll, Robert P.* Clio and canons: in search of a cultural poetics of
the Hebrew Bible. Bibl.Interp. 5 (1997) 300-323.

661  *Carson, Don A.* Is the doctrine of "claritas scripturae" still relevant
today?. TVGMS 424: 1997, ⇒59. FMAIER G., 97-111.

662  **Chalier, Catherine** L'inspiration du philosophe, 'l'amour de la sagesse' et sa source prophétique. P 1996, Albin M 187 pp. REeV 107
(1997) 62 *(Gire, Pierre)*.

663  *Charry, Ellen T.* Cure of body and soul: interpretation as art and
science. Disciplining hermeneutics. 1997, ⇒214. ELundin, Roger,
85-95.

664  EChiarini, Paolo; Zimmermann, Hans Dieter Schrift Sinne: Exegese, Interpretation, Dekonstruktion 3. Forum Guardini 3: B 1994,
Guardini Stiftung 198 pp. DM24. 3-9803395-3-X. RThLZ 122
(1997) 124-126 *(Micskey, K.N.)*.

665  *Childs, Brevard S.* Interpreting the bible amid cultural change. ThTo
54 (1997) 200-211.

666 *Chirico, Leonardo De* L'evangelismo tra crisi della modernità e sfida della postmodernità. Studi di Teologia 9/1 (1997) 3-52.
667 *Citrini, Tullio* La sacra scrittura e la teologia. Seminarium 37 (1997) 34-47.
668 **Clines, David J.A.** The bible and the modern world. BiSe 51: Shf 1997, Academic 116 pp. Bibl. £9.50. 1-85075-841-7.
669 *Cowen, Gerald* Evangelicals and the hermeneutical jungle. Faith & Mission 14/2 (1997) 46-55.
670 *D'Ors, Pablo J.* Fenomenología y teología del escribir. StAns 124: 1997, ⇒57. ᶠLOEHRER M. — TRAGAN P., 209-244.
671 *Dalferth, Ingolf U.* Die Mitte ist außen: Anmerkungen zum Wirklichkeitsbezug evangelischer Schriftauslegung. BZNW 86: 1997, ⇒41. ᶠHOFIUS O., 173-198.
672 **Davies, Philip R.** Whose bible is it anyway?. JSOT.S 204: Shf 1995, Academic 150 pp. £27/£10. 1-58075-569-8/-749-6. ᴿCBQ 59 (1997) 536-537 *(Pilch, John J.)*; ET 109 (1997-98) 15-16 *(Knights, Chris)*.
673 *Delzant, Antoine* Lire la bible en régime chrétien. La Bible en littérature. 1997, ⇒315. ᴱBeaude, Pierre-Marie, 327-341.
674 *Diekmeyer, Gerhard* Staunend Gott in seinem Wort verstehen lernen: der Beitrag Hermann CREMERS zu einer biblischen Hermeneutik. TVGMS 424: 1997, ⇒59. ᶠMAIER G., 41-49.
675 *Dillmann, Rainer* Autor-Text-Leser: Grundfragen der Pragmatik und ihre Relevanz für die Interpretation biblischer Texte. ThGl 87 (1997) 81-96.
676 *Dohmen, Christoph* Neue Interessen bei der Bibelauslegung?: ein Literaturbericht. BiLi 70 (1997) 44-47.
677 **Dohmen, Christoph; Stemberger, Günter** Hermeneutik der jüdischen Bibel und des Alten Testaments. KStTh 1/2. 1996, ⇒12,604. ᴿZKTh 119 (1997) 72-75 *(Vonach, Andreas)*; ThPQ 145 (1997) 299-300 *(Hubmann, Franz D.)*; KuI 12 (1997) 184-185 *(Rendtorff, Rolf)*.
678 *Donaldson, Mara E.* Bordercrossing: fall and fantasy in Blade Runner and Thelma and Louise. The monstrous. 1997, ⇒169. ᴱAichele, George, 19-42.
679 **Eden, Kathy** Hermeneutics and the rhetorical tradition: chapters in the ancient legacy and its humanist reception. NHv 1997, Yale University Press 119 pp. [Rhetorica 16,230—Miller, Richard A].
680 **Farmer, Ronald L.** Beyond the impasse: the promise of a process hermeneutic. SABH 13: Macon, Georgia 1997, Mercer University Press xvi; 269 pp. $20. 0-86554-558-8 [RB 105,635].
681 *Fiedler, Sabine* Intertextualität in der Plansprache (dargestellt an publizistischen und literarischen Texten im Esperanto). Textbeziehungen. 1997, ⇒287. ᴱKlein, Josef, 383-402.
682 ᴱFinan, Thomas; Twomey, Vincent Scriptural interpretation in the Fathers: letter and spirit. 1995, ⇒11/2,504; 12,179. ᴿJRH 21/2 (1997) 229-231 *(Harris, B.F.)*.
683 Fontaine, Carole R. Editor's preface to Claus WESTERMANN's 'Beauty in the Hebrew Bible'. A feminist companion. 1997, ⇒180. ᴱBrenner, Athalya. 582-583.
ᴱFowl, Stephen E. The theological interpretation of scripture. ⇒244.
684 *Fraas, Claudia* Bedeutungskonstitution im Diskurs—Intertextualität über variierende Wiederaufnahme diskursiv zentraler Konzepte: eine

exemplarische Analyse. Textbeziehungen. 1997, ⇒287. EKlein, Josef, 219-234.
685 *Frank, Évelyne* La joie des écritures. NRTh 119 (1997) 172-192.
686 **Frankovic, Joseph** Reading the Book: a popular essay on christian biblical hermeneutics. Tulsa, OK 1997, HaKesher 52 pp. [JPersp 55,32—Wright, Archie].
687 *Freedman, David Noel* On method in biblical studies: the Old Testament. Divine Commitment 1. 1997 <1963>, ⇒124. 152-160.
688 *Fuchs, Ottmar* Kriterien gegen den Mißbrauch der Bibel. JBTh 12 (1997) 243-274.
689 *Gerdmar, Anders* Exegesis, postmodernism, and Auschwitz—on human dignity and the ethics of interpretation. StTh 51/2 (1997) 113-143.
690 *Giroud, Jean-Claude* Lire les écritures. SémBib 87 (1997) 48-60.
691 *Glebe-Moller, Jens* Whereof one cannot speak, thereof one must be silent [*Wittgenstein, Ludwig*]. RStTh 51/2 (1997) 156-167.
692 **Goldingay, John** Models for interpretation of Scripture. 1995, ⇒11/2,1298. ThLZ 122 (1997) 127-130 *(Schmeller, Thomas)*; VJTR 61 (1997) 498-499 *(Meagher, P.M.)*; JBL 116 (1997) 721-722 *(Green, Joel B.)*.
693 *Görg, Manfred* "Menschenwort" und "Gotteswort": die biblische Ursprache als Gegenstand biblischer Theologie. MThZ 48 (1997) 239-253.
694 EGreen, Joel B. Hearing the New Testament: strategies for interpretation. 1995, ⇒11/2,372. RHeyJ 38 (1997) 191-192 *(King, N.)*.
695 **Haack, Susan** Evidence and inquiry: towards reconstruction in epistemology. Oxf 1997, Blackwell x; 259 pp. Bibl. 0-631-19679-X.
696 **Hahn, Eberhard** Johann Christian Konrad VON HOFMANNS Programm theologischer Erneuerung: dargestellt anhand seines Werkes "Der Schriftbeweis". TVGMS 424: 1997, ⇒59. FMAIER G., 65-82.
697 **Hauerwas, Stanley** Unleashing the scripture: freeing the Bible from captivity to America. 1993, ⇒10,785; 11/2,1170. RSJTh 50 (1997) 253-254 *(Hart, Trevor)*.
698 *Hendel, Ronald S.* The plain sense of scripture. BiRe 13/6 (1997) 17, 47.
699 *Hendel, Ronald S.; Sternberg, Shlomo* The bible code—cracked and crumbling. BiRe 13/4 (1997) 22-25.
700 *Hermisson, Hans-Jürgen* Jesus Christus als externe Mitte des Alten Testaments: ein unzeitgemäßes Votum zur Theologie des Alten Testaments. BZNW 86: 1997, ⇒41. FHOFIUS O., 199-233.
701 *Hille, Rolf* Was ist schriftgemäß?. TVGMS 424: 1997, ⇒59. FMAIER G., 13-40.
702 *Hornig, Gottfried* Textinterpretation und Hermeneutik des Einverständnisses: kritische Anmerkungen zu den Theorien von Hans-Georg GADAMER und Peter STUHLMACHER. BZNW 89: 1997, ⇒33. FGRAESSER E., 123-137.
703 **Huizing, Klaas** *Homo legens*: vom Ursprung der Theologie im Lesen. TBT 75: B 1996, De Gruyter 243 pp. DM168. RLM 36/4 (1997) 59 *(Asendorf, Ulrich)*.
704 *Human, D.J.* Interpreting the bible in the "new" South Africa: remarks on some problems and challenges. HTS 53 (1997) 570-579.
705 **Hurley, Robert J.** Hermeneutics and catechesis: biblical interpretation in the 'Come to the Father' catechetical series. Lanham 1997,

University Press of America 295 pp. $62/$41. 0-7618-0873-6/ 0-7618-0874-4 [BiTod 36,260—Bergant, Dianne].

706 *Hübner, Hans* Ein neuer textus receptus und sein Problem: Synchronie als Abwertung der Geschichte?. BZNW 86: 1997, ⇒41. ᶠHoғɪus O., 235-247.

707 *Jennings, Willie James* Baptizing a social reading: theology, hermeneutics, and postmodernity. Disciplining hermeneutics. 1997, ⇒214. ᴱLundin, Roger, 117-127.

708 *Kanyoro, Musimbi R.* Biblical hermeneutics: ancient Palestine and the contemporary world. RExp 94 (1997) 363-378.

709 *Karavidopoulos, Ioannis D.* The interpretation of the New Testament in the Orthodox Church. BZNW 86: 1997, ⇒41. ᶠHoғɪus O., 249-262.

710 *Keel, Othmar* Leben aus dem Wort Gottes?: vom Anspruch und vom Umgang mit den Schriften des Alten und des Neuen Testaments. Pfarrei. 1997, ⇒259. ᴱSchifferle, Alois, 95-109.

711 *Kerman, Judith B.* A teshuva on sacred clowning from Reb Kugel. The monstrous. 1997, ⇒169. ᴱAichele, George, 61-74.

712 *Kingsbury, Jack Dean* Introduction. Gospel interpretation. 1997, ⇒210. ᴱKingsbury, Jack Dean, 1-5.

713 *Ko Ha Fong, Maria* Die Bibel im asiatischen Kontext lesen. BiKi 52 (1997) 63-73.

714 *Kosch, Daniel* Kontextuelle Bibellektüren: eine Einführung. BiKi 52 (1997) 54-62.

715 *Körtner, Ulrich H.J.* Theologie in dürftiger Zeit: die Aufgabe der Theologie und das Problem einer biblischen Hermeneutik im gegenwärtigen Kontext von Kirche und Gesellschaft. JBTh 12 (1997) 153-179.

716 *Kramer, Jennifer* Cold comfort: Stephen W. Hawking and the bible. The monstrous. 1997, ⇒169. ᴱAichele, George, 102-134.

717 *Landy, Francis* Do we want our children to read this book?. Semeia 77 (1997) 157-176.

718 *Laurenzi, Maria Cristina* Come intendere un pensiero biblico?. Prot. 52 (1997) 219-234.

719 *Lawrence, Fred* The seriousness of play: Gadamer's hermeneutics as a resource for christian mission. From one medium. 1997, ⇒233. ᴱSoukup, Paul A., 109-136.

720 *Lincoln, Andrew T.* Postmodern biblical interpretation: a response. TJT 13 (1997) 235-244.

721 *Lindbeck, George* The gospel's uniqueness: election and untranslatability, 1. MoTh 13 (1997) 423-450.

722 *Lindemann, Andreas* "Es steht geschrieben": Überlegungen zur christlichen Hermeneutik der jüdischen Bibel. ThGl 87 (1997) 39-54.

723 *Lubac, Henri de* Spiritual understanding. Early christian interpretation. 1997, ⇒191. 3-25.

724 *Lundin, Roger* Introduction to |Disciplining hermeneutics|. Disciplining hermeneutics. 1997, ⇒214. ᴱLundin, Roger, 1-21.

725 *Lyon, David* Sliding in all directions?: social hermeneutics from suspicion to retrieval. Disciplining hermeneutics. 1997, ⇒214. ᴱLundin, Roger, 99-115.

726 *Marshall, Donald* Truth, universality, and interpretation. Disciplining hermeneutics. 1997, ⇒214. ᴱLundin, Roger, 69-84.

727 *Matlock, R. Barry* Biblical criticism and the rhetoric of inquiry. Bibl.Interp. 5 (1997) 133-159.

728 *McKnight, Edgar V.* Der hermeneutische Gewinn der neuen literarischen Zugänge in der neutestamentlichen Bibelinterpretation. BZ 41 (1997) 161-173.

729 *Melugin, Roy F.* Scripture and the formation of christian identity. JSOT.S 240: 1997, ⇒20. [F]COATS G., 167-182.

730 *Melugin, Roy F.* Scripture and the Sitz im Leben of the interpreter. 1997, ⇒29. [F]GERSTENBERGER S., 226-237.

731 **Mesters, Carlos** God, where are you?. [T]*Drury, John; McDonagh, F.*: 1995, ⇒11/2,1191. [R]OTEs 10 (1997) 558-561 *(Vorster, J.H.)*.

732 **Meyer, Ben F.** Reality and illusion in New Testament scholarship: a primer in critical realist hermeneutics. 1994, ⇒11/2,1323. [R]CBQ 58 (1996) 165-166 *(Bernas, Casimir)*.

733 *Meyers, Carol* Gender and God in the Hebrew Bible—some reflections. 1997, ⇒29. [F]GERSTENBERGER S., 256-268.

734 *Mies, Françoise* L'herméneutique du témoignage en philosophie: littérature, mythe et bible. RSPhTh 81 (1997) 3-20.

735 *Molinaro, Aniceto* L'apparizione dell'eterno: riflessioni sulla storicità. StAns 124: 1997, ⇒57. [F]LOEHRER M. — TRAGAN P., 35-58.

736 **Montague, George T.** Understanding the bible: a basic introduction to biblical interpretation. Mahwah, NJ 1997, Paulist vi; 239 pp. $20. 0-8091-3744-5 [ThD 46,84—Heiser, W. Charles].

737 **Mosconi, Luis** Hacia una lectura fiel de la Biblia. Pastoral Bíblica: México 1995, Dabar 238 pp. [R]EfMex 15 (1997) 288-289 *(Landgrave Gándara, Daniel)*.

738 *Mullins, Phil* Media ecology and the new literacy: notes on an electronic hermeneutic. From one medium. 1997, ⇒233. [E]Soukup, Paul A., 301-333.

739 *Okure, Teresa* Von Bogota nach Hongkong—von Emmaus nach Sychar: Gedanken zu Lk 24 und Joh 4 aus afrikanischer Perspektive. BiKi 52 (1997) 74-79.

740 *Olbricht, Erika Mae* Constructing the dead author: postmodernism's rhetoric of death. The rhetorical analysis. JSNT.S 146: 1997, ⇒336. [E]Porter, Stanley E., 66-78.

741 **Ott, Heinrich** Die kreative Kontinuität im Dialog: Bemerkungen zur Hermeneutik der christlichen Überlieferung. StAns 124: 1997, ⇒57. [F]LOEHRER M. — TRAGAN P., 59-80.

742 **Pable, Martin** Catholics and fundamentalists: understanding the difference. Ch [2]1997, ACTA 94 pp. $6 [BiTod 36,261—Bergant, Dianne].

743 *Pannenberg, Wolfhart* Die Bedeutung des Alten Testaments für den christlichen Glauben. JBTh 12 (1997) 181-192.

744 **Patte, Daniel** Ethics of biblical interpretation. 1995, ⇒11/2,1331. [R]JBL 116 (1997) 325-327 *(Fowler, Robert M.)*.

745 *Paulsen, Henning* Aufgaben und Probleme einer Geschichte der frühchristlichen Literatur. Zur Literatur. WUNT 99: 1997 <1995>, ⇒153. [E]Eisen, Ute E., 396-411.

746 *Pippin, Tina; Aichele, George* Introduction: imagining God. The monstrous. 1997, ⇒169. [E]Aichele, George, 11-18.

747 **Polk, Timothy Houston** The biblical KIERKEGAARD: reading by the rule of faith. Macon 1997, Mercer University Press xiv; 232 pp. $22. 0-86554-539-1 [RRT 1998/1,91].

748 <sup>E</sup>**Porter, Stanley E.; Evans, Craig A.** New Testament text and language. BiSe 44: Shf 1997, Academic 311 pp. £15/$20. 1-85075-795-X [BTB 27,120];

749 New Testament interpretation and methods. BiSe 45: Shf 1997, Academic 321 pp. £15/$20. 1-85075-794-1.

750 *Pui-lan, Kwok* Overlapping communities and multicultural hermeneutics. A feminist companion. 1997, ⇒180. <sup>E</sup>Brenner, Athalya, 203-215 [Matt 15,21-28; Mark 7,25-30].

751 *Punt, Jeremy* Biblical studies in South Africa?: the case for hermeneutics. Scriptura 60 (1997) 15-30.

752 **Raguse, Hartmut** Der Raum des Textes: Elemente einer transdisziplinären theologischen Hermeneutik. 1994, ⇒11/2,1335. <sup>R</sup>ThZ 53 (1997) 275-277 *(Frey, Jörg)*.

753 *Raja, R.J.* Biblical fundamentalism: an enquiry. ITS 34/1-3 (1997) 124-137.

754 <sup>F</sup>**Rogerson, John** The Bible in human society. <sup>E</sup>**Carroll R., M. D.**, JSOT.S 200: 1995, ⇒11/1,23. <sup>R</sup>JThS 48 (1997) 137-139 *(Houston, Walter J.)*; CBQ 59 (1997) 408-409 *(Seeman, Chris)*.

755 **Russotto, Mario** La parola di Dio nel grembo del silenzio. Presenza Pastorale 67 (1997) 785-793.

756 *Sánchez Caro, José Manuel* Hermenéutica bíblica y teología: reflexiones metodológicas. ScrTh 29 (1997) 841-875.

757 *Saccon, Allessandra* Dio, linguaggio e realtà: ermeneutica teologica e filosofia nel pensiero di Gerhard EBELING. StPat 44 (1997) 85-97.

758 *Salmann, Elmar* Tradition als Nachlese: eine theologische Phänomenologie der Lektüre. StAns 124: 1997, ⇒57. <sup>F</sup>LOEHRER M. — TRAGAN P., 159-184.

759 **Sandy, D. Brent; Giese, Ronald L.** Cracking Old Testament codes: a guide to interpreting the literary genres of the Old Testament. 1995, ⇒11/2,1341. <sup>R</sup>BS 154 (1997) 376-377 *(Taylor, Richard A.)*.

760 **Scalise, Charles J.** Hermeneutics as theological prolegomena: a canonical approach. 1995, ⇒11/2,1343. <sup>R</sup>RRT (1997/1) 32-33 *(Vanhoozer, Kevin)*; ProEc 6 (1997) 509-510 *(Burnett, Richard E.)*.

761 **Scalise, Charles J.** From scripture to theology: a canonical journey into hermeneutics. DG 1996, InterVarsity 150 pp. $13 [CTJ 34,453—Pomykala, Kenneth E.].

762 **Schmidt, Werner H.** Vielfalt und Einheit alttestamentlichen Glaubens: Studien zu Hermeneutik und Methodik: Pentateuch und Prophetie. <sup>E</sup>*Graupner, A.; Delkurt, H.; Ernst, A.B.:* Neuk 1995, Neuk 2 vols; viii; 257; viii; 290 pp. DM68+78. 3-7887-1546-4/7-2. <sup>R</sup>ThLZ 122 (1997) 229-230 *(Wagner, Siegfried)*.

763 *Schütz, Christian* Was bedeutet das Lehrer-Schüler-Verhältnis für die Theologie?. StAns 124: 1997, ⇒57. <sup>F</sup>LOEHRER M. — TRAGAN P., 603-627.

764 *Seitz, Manfred* Geistliche Schriftlesung: Bibellektüre des Glaubens. 1997, ⇒92. <sup>F</sup>STUHLMACHER P., 382-393.

765 *Shin, Kuk W.* Hermeneutics encounters critical theory. ATA Journal 5/1 (1997) 3-67 [ZID 23,439].

766 <sup>E</sup>**Silva, Moisés, (al.),** Foundations of contemporary interpretation. Leicester 1997, Apollos 688 pp. 0-85111-769-4.

767 *Silva, Moisés* Recent developments in New Testament hermeneutics. From one medium. 1997, ⇒233. <sup>E</sup>Soukup, Paul A., 41-49.

768  *Smend, Rudolf* Hat die Bibel wirklich recht?. Bibel, Theologie. KVR
     1582: 1997 <1965>, ⇒162. 41-45.
769  *Smith, Abraham* "I saw the book talk": a cultural studies approach to
     the ethics of an African American biblical hermeneutics. Semeia 77
     (1997) 115-138.
770  *Snyman, Gerrie* On opening windows and doors of Old Testament
     studies in South Africa. OTEs 10 (1997) 474-493.
771  *Sorg, Theo* Sind wir schon evangelisch?: TVGMS 424: 1997, ⇒59.
     FMAIER G., 237-248.
772  **Stein, Robert H.** Playing by the rules. 1994, ⇒11/2,1349. RFaith &
     Mission 14/2 (1997) 90-91 *(Riddle, Jeffrey T.)*.
773  *Steins, Georg* Eine Bibel—viele Zugänge und Leseweisen. Lebendige
     Welt. 1997, ⇒565. EZenger, Erich, 141-151.
774  *Stone, Ken* The hermeneutics of abomination: on gay men, Canaani-
     tes, and biblical interpretation. BTB 27 (1997) 36-41.
775  *Streete, Gail Corrington* Outrageous (speech) acts and everyday (per-
     formative) rebellions: a response of resistance. Semeia 79 (1997) 97-
     105.
776  **Stylianopoulos, Theodore G.** The New Testament: an Orthodox
     perspective 1: scripture, tradition, hermeneutics. Brookline, MA
     1997, Holy Cross Orthodox Press 271 pp. $17. 1-885652-13-5 [NTS
     44,625].
777  *Sullivan, Lisa M.* "I responded, 'I will not ...'": christianity as cata-
     lyst for resistance in the Passio Perpetuae et Felicitatis. Semeia 79
     (1997) 63-74.
778  **Tate, W. Randolph** Biblical interpretation: an integrated approach.
     Peabody ²1997 <1991>, Hendrickson xxvi; 276 pp. $25. 1-56563-
     252-4 [ThD 45,93—Heiser, W. Charles].
779  **Torrance, Thomas F.** Divine meaning: studies in patristic herme-
     neutics. 1995, ⇒11/2,1355. RThomist 61/1 (1997) 146-150 *(Dris-
     coll, Jeremy)*.
780  *Troschina, Natalia* Stilistisches Koordinatensystem und Intertex-
     tualität im öffentlichen Medienkurs Rußlands. Textbeziehungen.
     1997, ⇒287. EKlein, Josef. 167-176.
781  *Vadakumpadan, Paul* Gospel-culture encounter: reflections on the
     Church's teaching. IMR 19/1 (1997) 69-76.
782  *Van Buren, Paul* The gospel according to the scriptures. Open catho-
     licism. 1997, ⇒88. FSLOYAN G., 26-39.
783  *Van Cangh, Jean-Marie* Tolérance et interprétation pluraliste de la
     Bible. Perspectives actuelles sur la tolérance. E**Doré, Joseph**: P
     1997, Publications de l'Académie internationale des Sciences reli-
     gieuses 151-166.
784  *Vanhoozer, Kevin J.* Il mondo messo bene in scena?: teologia, cul-
     tura ed ermeneutica. TChirico, L. De: Studi di Teologia 9/1 (1997)
     53-88;
785  The spirit of understanding: special revelation and general hermeneu-
     tics. Disciplining hermeneutics. 1997, ⇒214. ELundin, Roger, 131-
     165.
786  *Veeser, H. Aram* Christianity, wild turkey, and syphilis. Bibl.Interp.
     5 (1997) 465-481.
787  *Vikström, Björn* Bibelläsaren: skapad av texten eller textens skapare?.
     SvTK 73/4 (1997) 155-166.
788  **Walker, Graham B.** Tradition and context: the dance of empower-
     ment. RExp 94 (1997) 379-390.

789 *Walsh, Richard* Ancient biblical worlds and recent magical realism: affirming and denying reality. The monstrous. 1997, ⇒169. ᴱAichele, George, 135-147.

790 **Watson, Francis** Text, church and world: biblical interpretation in theological perspective. GR 1994, Eerdmans viii; 366 pp. $35. ᴿCBQ 58 (1996) 366-368 *(Neufeld, Dietmar)*.

791 *Weder, Hans* Einverständnis: eine Überlegung zu Peter Sᴛᴜʜʟᴍᴀᴄʜᴇʀs hermeneutischem Ansatz. 1997, ⇒92. ᶠSᴛᴜʜʟᴍᴀᴄʜᴇʀ P., 403-418;

792 Die Externität der Mitte: Überlegungen zum hermeneutischen Problem des Kriteriums der Sachkritik am Neuen Testament. BZNW 86: 1997, ⇒41. ᶠHoꜰɪᴜs O., 291-320.

793 *Weise, Günter* Zur Spezifik der Intertextualität in literarischen Texten. Textbeziehungen. 1997, ⇒287. ᴱKlein, Josef, 39-48.

794 *West, Gerald* Finding a place among the posts for post-colonial criticism in biblical studies in South Africa. OTEs 10 (1997) 322-342;

795 On the eve of an African biblical studies: trajectories and trends. JTSA 99 (1997) 99-115.

796 *Westermann, Claus* Beauty in the Hebrew Bible. A feminist companion. 1997, ⇒180. ᴱBrenner, Athalya, 584-602.

797 *Westphal, Merold* Post-Kantian reflections on the importance of hermeneutics. Disciplining hermeneutics. 1997, ⇒214. ᴱLundin, Roger, 57-66.

798 *Willard, Dallas* Hermeneutical occasionalism. Disciplining hermeneutics. 1997, ⇒214. ᴱLundin, Roger, 167-172.

799 *Wilson, R. McL.* Of words and meanings. New Testament text. BiSe 44: 1997 <1989>, ⇒748. ᴱPorter, S., 107-113.

800 *Wimbush, Vincent L.* The bible and African Americans: an outline of an interpretative history. Theological interpretation. 1997, ⇒244. 70-86;

801 Introduction: interpreting resistance, resisting interpretations. Semeia 79 (1997) 1-10;

802 Religious and theological studies as religious criticism: a future for biblical studies. 1997, ⇒82. ᶠSᴄʀoɢɢs R., 294-310.

803 *Wolterstorff, Nicholas* The importance of hermeneutics for a christian worldview. Disciplining hermeneutics. 1997, ⇒214. ᴱLundin, Roger, 25-47.

804 *Worley, Lloyd* Impaling, Dracula, and the Bible. The monstrous. 1997, ⇒169. ᴱAichele, George, 168-180.

805 **Zemka, Sue** Victorian testaments: the bible, christology, and literary authority in early nineteenth-century British culture. Stanford, CA 1997, Stanford University Press ii; 279 pp. $45 [AThR 81,156s— Wallace, Catherine M.].

806 ᴱ**Zuck, Roy B.** Rightly divided: readings in biblical hermeneutics. GR 1996, Kregel 320 pp. $15. ᴿCBTJ 13/2 (1997) 69-70 *(McLain, Charles E.)*.

807 **Zumstein, Jean** Rettet die Bibel!: Plädoyer für die Erneuerung des Lesens. Z 1997, Theolog. Verl. 93 pp. 3-290-17138-8.

### B2.4 *Analysis* **narrationis** *biblicae*

808 *Anbar, Moshé* Formule d'introduction du discours direct au milieu du discours à Mari et dans la bible. VT 47 (1997) 530-536 [Gen 15; 16; 21; 30; 46; Exod 32; Num 32].

809 *Bird, Phyllis A.* The harlot as heroine: narrative art and social pre-supposition in three Old Testament texts. Missing persons. 1997 <1989>, ⇒114. 197-218 [Gen 38,1-26; Josh 2,1-24; 1 Kgs 3,16-27].

810 **Boer, Roland** Novel histories: the fiction of biblical criticism. Playing the Texts 2: Shf 1997, Academic 221 pp. Bibl. £45. 0-85075-836-0.

811 **Emmott, Catherine** Narrative comprehension: a discourse perspective. Oxf 1997, Clarendon xiv; 320 pp. 0-19-823649-2.

812 **Exum, J. Cheryl** Tragedy and biblical narrative: arrows of the Almighty. 1996 <1992>, ⇒8,1213...12,683. ᴿOTEs 10 (1997) 353-356 *(West, Gerald O.).*

813 *Ginsburg, Michal Peled* Framing narrative. PoeT 18 (1997) 571-588.

814 **Healy, Joseph; Sybertz, Donald** Towards an African narrative theology. Nairobi 1996, Paulines 400 pp. African Christian Studies 13/4 (1997) 86-91 *(Magesa, Laurenti).*

815 ᴱHeijst, **Annelies van** Het verhaal van God: essays over narratieve theologie. Baarn 1997, Gooi & S 136 pp. ƒ32.50. 90-304-0859-6 [ITBT 5/5,34].

816 *Jahn, Manfred* Frames, preferences, and the reading of third-person narratives: towards a cognitive narratology. Sum. 441. PoeT 18 (1997) 441-468.

817 *Kafalenos, Emma* Functions after PROPP: words to talk about how we read narrative. Sum. 469. PoeT 18 (1997) 469-494.

818 *Klerk, Johannes C. de* Situating biblical narrative studies in literary theory and literary approaches. R & T 4 (1997) 190-207.

819 *Koenen, Klaus* Prolepsen in alttestamentlichen Erzählungen: eine Skizze. VT 47 (1997) 456-477.

820 *Lenchak, Timothy* The bible and new evangelization: outsiders and insiders in Old Testament short stories. Word remembered word proclaimed: selected papers from symposia celebrating the SVD centennial in North America. Studia Instituti Missiologici Societatis Verbi Divini 65: ᴱBevans, **Stephen; Schroeder, Roger**: Nettetal 1997, Steyler 3-8050-0398-6. 57-75.

821 **Loughlin, Gerard** Telling God's story: bible, church and narrative theology. 1996, ⇒12,687. Theol. 100 (1997) 46-47 *(Ward, Graham)*; JThS 48 (1997) 366-368 *(Kerr, Fergus)*; Teol. 34 (1997) 548-550 *(Buckley, James L.).*

822 **Minette de Tillesse, C.** 'Tu me verras de dos': théologie narrative de la bible. 1995, REB 12. ⇒11/2,1387. NRTh 119 (1997) 108-109 *(Ska, J.L.)*; ThLZ 122 (1997) 246-248 *(Reventlow, Henning Graf)*; RSR 85 (1997) 443-444 *(Gibert, Pierre).*

823 **Parker, Simon Bruce** Stories in scripture and inscriptions: comparative studies on narratives in Northwest Semitic inscriptions and the Hebrew Bible. NY 1997, OUP xi; 195 pp. Bibl. 0-19-511620-8.

824 **Prickett, Stephen** Origins of narrative: the romantic appropriation of the bible. 1996, ⇒12,696. ᴿSal. 59 (1997) 548-550 *(Abbà, Giuseppe)*; TS 58 (1997) 553-554 *(Pfordresher, John)*; AThR 79 (1997) 624-625 *(Gregory, Alan P.R.).*

825 *Revell, E.J.* The repetition of introductions to speech as a feature of Biblical Hebrew. VT 47 (1997) 91-110.

826 **Revell, Ernest John** The designation of the individual: expressive usage in biblical narrative. 1996, ⇒12,469. ᴿBiOr 54 (1997) 452-454

*(Verheij, Arian)*; OTEs 10 (1997) 562-565 *(Nel, Philip J.)*; JNSL 23/2 (1997) 247-250; *(van der Merwe, C.H.J.)*; CBQ 59 (1997) 553-554 *(Winther-Nielsen, Nicolai)*.

827 **Tertel, Hans Jürgen** Text and transmission: an empirical model for the literary devlopment of Old Testament narratives. BZAW 221: 1994, ⇒10,926...12,699. <sup>R</sup>CBQ 58 (1996) 138-139 *(Fleming, D.E.)*.

828 *Vanoni, Gottfried* Prosa, Alttestamentliche. TRE 27 (1997) 517-521.

829 *Walsh, Richard* Who is the narrator?. Sum. 495. PoeT 18 (1997) 495-513.

830 **Watts, James W.** Psalm and story: inset hymns in Hebrew narrative. JSOT.S 139: 1992, ⇒8,1228...11/2,2224. <sup>R</sup>BZ 41 (1997) 103-104 *(Gerstenberger, Erhard S.)*.

831 **Weitzman, Steven** Song and story in biblical narrative: the history of a literary convention in ancient Israel. Diss. Harvard, <sup>D</sup>*Kugel, James*: Indiana Studies in Biblical Literature: Bloomington, IND 1997, Indiana University Press xiv; 209 pp. $30. 0-253-33236-2.

832 *Zgorzelski, Andrzej* The systemic equivalent as a genological factor. Sum. 515. PoeT 18 (1997) 515-532.

833 *Price, Robert M.* Implied reader response and the evolution of genres: transitional stages between the ancient novels and the apocryphal act. HTS 53 (1997) 909-938.

## B3.1 *Interpretatio ecclesiastica* Bible and Church

834 *Alonso Schökel, Luis Dei Verbum* 12 in due tappe. Som., sum. 32. VivH 8 (1997) 23-32.

835 *Angelini, Giuseppe* La questione biblica tra ricerca teologica e ministero pastorale. Teol(Br) 22 (1997) 319-328.

836 **Ariarajah, Seevaratnam Wesley** Die Bibel und die Andersgläubigen. 1994, ⇒11/2,1403. <sup>R</sup>ThRv 93 (1997) 69-74 *(Schoen, Ulrich)*.

837 *Artola Arbiza, Antonio M<sup>a</sup>* El Nuevo Testamento como palabra de Dios. ResB 13 (1997) 51-59.

838 *Binz, Stephen J.* The bible as focal symbol for the church. BiTod 35 (1997) 177-182.

839 *Cipriani, Settimio* L'interpretazione della Bibbia nella chiesa. Hermeneutica [Urbino] (1997) 195-213.

840 **Dinter, Paul E.** Beyond naive belief: the bible and adult catholic faith. 1994, ⇒11/2,1092. <sup>R</sup>TJT 13/1 (1997) 144-145 *(Donovan, D.)*.

841 *Dirscherl, Erwin* Pluralität ja—Fundamentalismus nein!: vom Umgang mit der Bibel in "postmodernen" Zeiten. BiLi 70 (1997) 208-212.

842 *Feldkämper, Ludger* Bewegende Vielfalt: die Katholische Bibelföderation. BiKi 52 (1997) 80-83.

843 *Fischer, Irmtraud* Frauen und feministische Exegese im Dokument der Päpstlichen Bibelkommission "Die Interpretation der Bibel in der Kirche". BiLi 70 (1997) 53-56.

844 *Fisichella, Rino* La parola di Dio nella vita della Chiesa. Som. 286. RCI 78/4 (1997) 286-299.

845 **Fitzmyer, Joseph A.** A bíblia na igreja. <sup>T</sup>*Lambert, Bárbara Theoto*: Bíblica Loyola 21: São Paulo 1997, Loyola 112 pp. 85-15-01584-6 [PerTeol 29,437].

846  *Gacege, Peter D. Njoroge* Initiating biblical apostolate in a parish. AMECEA Documentation Service 467 (1997) 12-14 [ThIK 18/2,16].
847  *Ghiberti, Giiuseppe* Il rinnovamento biblico in Italia: la recezione nella comunità ecclesiale. Firmana 15 (1997) 15-36.
848  *Heidemanns, Katja* Eine "postkoloniale Kehrtwendung"?: Anmerkungen zum Dokument der Päpstlichen Bibelkommission aus missionswissenschaftlicher Sicht. BiLi 70 (1997) 57-61.
849  *Holman, Jan* Heeft de katholieke kerk een boodschap aan het Oude Testament?. De passie van een grensganger. 73-91 [EThL 74,171*].
850  *L'Hour, Jean* Pour une lecture "catholique" de la bible. Bibl.Interp. 5 (1997) 113-132.
851  *La Potterie, Ignace de* La interpretación de la Escritura en el mismo Espíritu en que fu escrita (DV 12,3), 2. VE 13 (1997) 99-128;
852  Dei verbum: costituzione dogmatica sulla divina rivelazione. Interviewer *Stenico, T.:* Il Concilio Vaticano II: carisma e profezia. Libreria Vaticana 1997, 293-321 [AcBIB 10/3,267].
853  *McGrath, Alister E.* The genesis of doctrine: a study in the foundation of doctrinal criticism. GR 1997, Eerdmans x; 266 pp. Bibl. 0-8028-4316-6.
854  *Meunier, Bernard* La généalogie du dogme et l'hérésie. LV(L) 46/1 (1997) 29-36.
855  *Montsarrat, Violaine; Montsarrat, Jean-Pierre* La communauté croyante et l'exégèse. LV(L) 46/1 (1997) 21-28.
856  **Mora Paz, Cesar** ¿Para qué la biblia?: la sagrada escritura en la vida de la iglesia. México 1994, Comisión Episcopal de Pastoral Bíblica 468 pp. [R]EfMex 15 (1997) 410-411 *(Muñoz Tónix, Reyes).*
857  *Negro, Dino* Il primato della parola nella vita della chiesa. Presenza Pastorale 67 (1997) 795-805.
858  *Noël, Damien* Regard d'un exégète [*Populorum Progressio*]. Spiritus 38 (1997) 306-313.
859  **O'Collins, Gerald; Kendall, Daniel** The bible for theology: ten principles for the theological use of scripture. Mahwah 1997, Paulist iii; 208 pp. $15. 0-8091-3743-7.
860  La palabra de Dios—fuente de vida: declaración final de la V Asamblea Plenaria de la Federación Bíblica Católica (FBC) Hong Kong, 2-12 julio 1996. NuMu 53 (1997) 63-74.
861  **Pelikan, Jaroslav** The reformation of the bible: the bible of the Reformation. 1996, ⇒12,730. [R]Theol. 100/3 (1997) 223-224 *(Trueman, Carl R.)*; ChH 66 (1997) 812-813 *(Kammerling, Joy).*
862  **Ratzinger, Card. Joseph** Le sel de la terre: le christianisme et l'église catholique au seuil du IIIe millénaire: entretiens avec Peter Seewald. [T]*Casanova, Nicole*: P 1997, Flammarion 278 pp. 2-08-067433-1.
863  *Rebic, Adalbert* Aktualnost i mjerodavnost Biblije na pragu treceg tisucljeca: uz dokument Papinske biblijske komisije "Tumacenje Biblije u Crkvi" (1993). BoSm 67 (1997) 141-170. **Croatian.**
864  *Scheffbuch, Rolf* Schriftgemäße Möglichkeiten und Grenzen des kirchlichen Leitungsamtes. TVGMS 424: 1997, ⇒59. [F]Maier G., 249-259.
865  Schlußdokument der Katholischen Bibelföderation von Hongkong. BiKi 52 (1997) 84-90.
866  *Scholtissek, Klaus* Relecture—zu einem neu entdeckten Programmwort der Schriftauslegung (mit Blick auf das Johannesevangelium). BiLi 70 (1997) 309-315.

867 *Schreiner, Josef* Das Alte Testament auf dem Tisch des Wortes im II. Vatikanischen Konzil. F SCHREINER, J., 1997 <1996>, ⇒80. 219-239.
868 *Studer, Basil* The bible as read in the church. History of Theology, 1. 1997, ⇒241. E Di Berardino, A., 353-373.
869 *Terribile, Manuela* Comunità e scrittura: per un'educazione alla fede. Presenza Pastorale 67 (1997) 855-857.
870 *Umoren, Anthony Iffen* The origin and use of the bible in the church: a bible guide for catholics. Gwagwalada, Abuja 1997, Vinria xvii; 107 pp. 978-33234-1-5 [NThAR 1998,333].
871 *Vanhoye, Albert* Catholicism and the bible: an interview with Albert Vanhoye. Interviewer *Williamson, Peter*: First Things 74 (1997) 35-40 [AcBIB 10/3,270].
872 *Westermann, Claus* La benedizione nella bibbia e nell'azione della chiesa. T *Montaldi, Gianluca*: Nuovi Saggi Queriniana 77: Brescia 1997, Queriniana 176 pp. L25.000. 88-399-0977-X.
873 *Zenger, Erich* Die konstitutive Bedeutung der Bibel Israels für christliche Identität. Edith Stein Jahrbuch 3 (1997) 262-277.

### B3.2 *Homiletica*—The Bible in preaching

874 **Bartow, Charles L.** God's human speech: a practical theology of proclamation. GR 1997, Eerdmans xiv; 190 pp. £13. 0-8028-4335-2 [RRT 1998/1,88].
875 **Brueggemann, Walter** Cadences of home: preaching among exiles. LVL 1997, Westminster 159 pp. $16. 0-664-25749-6 [BiTod 36,259—Bergant, Dianne].
876 *Brueggemann, Walter* Overhearing the good news. Cadences. 1997, ⇒875. 78-98;
877 Rhetoric and community. Cadences. 1997, ⇒875. 57-77.
878 Testimony as a decentered mode of preaching. Cadences. 1997, ⇒875. 38-56.
879 **Camery-Hoggatt, Jerry** Speaking of God: reading and preaching the word of God. 1995, ⇒11/2,1530. R RTR 56/2 (1997) 96-97 *(Salier, Bill)*.
880 **Campbell, Charles L.** Preaching Jesus: new directions for homiletics in Hans FREI's postliberal theology. GR 1997, Eerdmans xiv; 289 pp. £19. 0-8028-4156-2 [RRT 1998/1,89].
881 *Campbell, Charles L.* Principalities, powers, and preaching: learning from William STRINGFELLOW. Interp. 51 (1997) 384-401.
882 **Carroll, John T. & James R.** Preaching the hard sayings of Jesus. Peabody, MASS 1996, Hendrickson xiv; 174 pp. $15. 1-56563-230-3. R SEÅ 62 (1997) 171-172 *(Ekenberg, Anders)*.
883 E Cothenet, Edouard Les premières lectures du dimanche du temps ordinaire. CEv 100: P 1997, Cerf 67 pp. F33. 0222-9714.
884 *Farris, Stephen* Limping away with a blessing: biblical studies and preaching at the end of the second millennium. Interp. 51 (1997) 358-370.
885 **Gadecki, Stanislaw** "Niech Slowo moje pada jak rosa": homilie, rozwazania i przemyslenia biblijne. Gniezno 1997, Gaudentinum 2 vols. 83-85654-73-9. P.

886 <sup></sup>EHolmgren, Fredrick C.; Schaalman, Herman E. Preaching biblical texts. 1995, ⇒11/2,1551. RNew Theology Review 10/3 (1997)
103-105 *(Waznack, Robert P.)*.

887 Josuttis, Manfred Gesetz und Evangelium in der Predigtarbeit.
Homiletische Studien 2: Gü 1995 Gü'er 197 pp. DM68  3-579-
02070-6. RThLZ 122 (1997) 292-294 *(Gräb, Wilhelm)*; LM 36/8
(1997) 42 *(Denecke, Axel)*; LuThK 21 (1997) 223-225 *(Schwarz, A.)*.

888 EKorenhof, Mieke Mit Eva predigen. 1996, ⇒12,749. LM 36/4
(1997) 61 *(Kempin, Susanna)*.

889 *Krimmer, Heiko* Schriftgemäß predigen—aber wie?. TVGMS 424:
1997, ⇒59. FMAIER G., 273-278.

890 *Mathewson, Steven D.* Guidelines for understanding and proclaiming
Old Testament narratives. BS 154 (1997) 410-435.

891 *Mindling, Joseph A.* Preaching the cross of Christ during Lent. New
Theology Review 10/1 (1997) 86-91.

892 *Mohler, R. Albert* In season and out of season: the centrality of scripture in preaching. Faith & Mission 14/2 (1997) 78-87.

893 *Ortkemper, Franz-Josef* Arbeitslosigkeit—Herausforderung für Christen: eine Predigt. BiKi 52 (1997) 138-140.

894 Pilch, John J. The cultural world of Jesus, Sunday by Sunday, cycle
C. ColMn 1997, Liturgical 171 pp. £10 [DoLi 48/1,62s McCarthy,
Flor].

895 *Redhardt, Jürgen* NIEMOELLER als Prediger über alttestamentliche
Texte. 1997, ⇒29. FGERSTENBERGER S., 417-426.

896 Stock, Klemens Jezus Dobrocią Bożą: szkice homilii na roc C [Gesù
la bontà di Dio]. Kraków 1997, WAM 182 pp. AcBib 10,395]. P.

897 *Stollberg, Dietrich* Ein 'unmöglicher' Text?: zur Predigt über sch-
wierige biblische Texte. PTh 86 (1997) 284-294.

898 *Theißen, Gerd* Über homiletische Killerparolen oder die Chancen
protestantischer Predigt heute. Praktische Theologie 32 (1997) 179-
202.

899 ETheissen, Gerd Le défi homiletique: l'exégèse au service de la prédication. 1994, ⇒11/2,1578. RBen. 44 (1997) 470-471 *(De Piccoli,
Sergio)*.

900 *Zink-Sawyer, Beverly* "The word purely preached and heard": the lis-
teners and the homiletical endeavor. Interp. 51 (1997) 342-357.

## B3.3 Inerrantia, inspiratio

901 *Becker, Wolfgang* Die Autorität der Heiligen Schrift in der evangeli-
stischen Verkündigung: zu einer These von Wolfgang BUB am Beispiel des Evangelisten Wilhelm BUSCH. TVGMS 424: 1997, ⇒59.
FMAIER G., 279-295.

902 *Beutel, Albrecht* Scriptura ita loquitur, cur non nos?: Sprache des
Glaubens bei LUTHER [The language of faith according to Luther].
Adapted by *Rossol, Heinz D.* Luther Digest 5 (1997) 5-7.

903 *Bird, Phyllis A.* Biblical authority in the light of feminist critique.
Missing persons. 1997 <1994>, ⇒114. 248-264.

904 Bloesch, Donald Holy Scripture: revelation, inspiration, and interpretation. 1994, ⇒11/2,1086; 12,421. RJR 77 (1997) 636-638
*(Bell, Richard H.)*.

905 *Botas, Mario* Entre l'Écriture et le dogme: la parole de Dieu. LV(L)
46/1 (1997) 59-70.

906 *Büchner, Dirk* Inspiration and the texts of the bible. HTS 53 (1997) 393-406.

907 *Chédozeau, Bernard* La lecture de la *Bible* chez et par les catholiques: lecture de croyance et/ou lecture de savoir?. XVIIᵉ Siècle 49 (1997) 9-17 [EThL 74,165*].

908 *Chilton, Bruce* Biblical authority, canonical criticism, and generative exegesis. Bibl.Interp. 28: 1997, ⇒77. ᶠSᴀɴᴅᴇʀs J., 343-355.

909 *Duquoc, Christian* Un compromis précaire: énoncés dogmatiques et exégèse. LV(L) 46/1 (1997) 71-81.

910 *Freedman, David Noel* Religious freedom and the Old Testament. Divine Commitment 1. 1997 <1966>, ⇒124. 211-217.

911 **Goldingay, John** Models for scripture. 1994, ⇒11/2,1599; 12,769. ᴿCBQ 58 (1996) (1997) 547-549 *(Forestell, J. Terence).*

912 *Kvalbein, Hans* Die Inspirationslehre und die Autorität der Heiligen Schrift. TVGMS 424: 1997, ⇒59. ᶠMᴀɪᴇʀ G., 51-64.

913 **Laghi, Card. Pio; Gilbert, Maurice; Vanhoye, Albert** Chiesa e sacra scrittura: un secolo di magistero ecclesiastico e studi biblici. 1994, ⇒10,977... 12,722. ᴿEstB 55 (1997) 405-406 *(Precedo, M.J.).*

914 *Laplanche, François* Le sens mystique des écritures. XVIIᵉ Siècle 49 (1997) 31-41 [EThL 74,165*].

915 *Marshall, Howard I.* "To find out what God is saying": reflections on the authorizing of scripture. Disciplining hermeneutics. 1997, ⇒214. ᴱLundin, Roger, 49-55.

916 *Marshall, I. Howard* Is the principle 'in accordance with scripture' in accordance with scripture?. TVGMS 424: 1997, ⇒59. ᶠMᴀɪᴇʀ G., 83-95.

917 **Martin, François** Pour une théologie de la lettre: l'inspiration des Écritures. CFi 196: 1996, ⇒12,778. ᴿCart. 13 (1997) 211-212 *(Marín Heredia, F.).*

918 *Martin, François* Jésus et la vérité des Écritures. LV(L) 46/1 (1997) 47-57.

919 *Mildenberger, Friedrich* Inspiration und trinitarische Hermeneutik: Schriftverstehen am Ende des metaphysischen Zeitalters. 1997, ⇒92. ᶠSᴛᴜʜʟᴍᴀᴄʜᴇʀ P., 310-324.

920 ᴱ**Moo, Douglas** Biblical authority and conservative perspectives. Biblical Forum 1: GR 1997, Kregel 240 pp. $12. 0-8254-3348-7 [TD 44,157].

921 *Moule, C.F.D.* A note on the authority of scripture. ET 108 (1997) 142.

922 *Nodet, Étienne* De l'Inspiration de l'Écriture. RB 104 (1997) 237-274.

923 *Pannenberg, Wolfhart* On the inspiration of scripture. ThTo 54 (1997) 212-215.

924 ᴱ**Pannenberg, Wolfhart; Schneider, Theodor** Verbindliches Zeugnis II: Schriftauslegung—Lehramt-Rezeption. Dialog der Kirchen 9: FrB 1995, Herder 333 pp. DM60. 3-451-23625-7. ᴿJETh 11 (1997) 249-251 *(Meier, Ralph).*

925 *Peretto, Elio* L'autorità della scrittura nel dibattito del Concilio di Aquileia dell'anno 381. 1997 <1981>, ⇒155. Saggi. 263-283.

926 *Raja, R.J.* Biblical fundamentalism: an enquiry. ITS 34 (1997) 124-137.

927 *Spieckermann, Hermann* Die Verbindlichkeit des Alten Testaments: unzeitgemäße Betrachtungen zu einem ungeliebten Thema. JBTh 12 (1997) 25-51.
928 *Swarat, Uwe* Schriftgemäßheit—für Freikirchen (k)ein Problem?. TVGMS 424: 1997, ⇒59. [F]MAIER G., 297-313.
929 *Vergani, Valentina* 'The "words" of God': il ruolo delle citazioni bibliche nel *Journal* di George FOX. Acme 50/3 (1997) 211-231.
930 *Walsh, Brian J.* Reimaging biblical authority. CscR 26/2 (1997) 206-220 [ZID 23,191].
931 **Wenz, Armin** Das Wort Gottes—Gericht und Rettung: Untersuchungen zur Autorität der Heiligen Schrift. FSÖTh 75: 1996, ⇒12,784. [R]JETh 11 (1997) 261-264 *(Felber, Stefan)*.
932 **Wolterstorff, Nicholas** Divine discourse: philosophical reflections on the claim that God speaks. 1995, ⇒11/2,1613. [R]SJTh 50/1 (1997) 97-110 *(Thiselton, Anthony C.)*.

### B3.4 Traditio

933 **Backus, Irena Dorota** Das Prinzip "sola scriptura" und die Kirchenväter in den Disputationen von Baden (1526) und Bern (1528). [T]*Zillenbiller, Anette*: Z 1997, Theologischer Verlag 158 pp. Bibl. 3-290-10996-8.
934 [E]**Cremascoli, Giuseppe; Leonardi, Claudio** La Bibbia nel Medioevo. 1996, ⇒12,787. [R]VP 80 (1997) 388-389 *(Mambretti, Renato)*; ASEs 14/1 (1997) 255-259 *(Savigni, Raffaele)*.
935 *Evdokimov, Michel* Tradition. UnChr 128 (1997) 3-23.
936 *Fisichella, Rino* Tradizione e scrittura: parola viva e parola scritta. Presenza Pastorale 67 (1997) 775-784.
937 **Fitzmyer, Joseph A.** Escritura, a alma da teología. [T]*Lambert, Bárbara Theoto*: São Paulo 1997, Loyola 116 pp. 85-15-01585-4 [PerTeol 29,437].
938 **Gaboriau, Florent** L'Écriture seule?. Théologie Nouvelle: P 1997, FAC 269 pp. FF129. 2-903422-63-X. [R]RSR 71 (1997) 528-530 *(Vibrac, Dominique)*; DoC 50 (1997) 292-294 *(Vibrac, Dominique)*.
939 **Jolly, Karen Louise** Tradition & diversity: christianity in a world ·context to 1500. Sources & studies in world history: Armonk, N.Y. 1997, Sharpe xiv; 569 pp. 1-56324-467-5.
940 **Navarro Lecanda, A.M.** 'Evangelii traditio': tradición como evangelización a la luz de Dei Verbum I-II. Vitoria-Gasteiz 1997, ESET 2 vols. [Did(L) 28,222s—Teixeira, João António Pinheiro].
    **Stylianopoulos, T.** Scripture, tradition, hermeneutics ⇒776.

### B3.5 Canon

941 **Barton, John** Holy writings, sacred text: the canon in early christianity. LVL 1997, Westminster xiii; 210 pp. Bibl. $18. 0-664-25778-X.
942 The spirit and the letter: studies in the biblical canon. L 1997, SPCK xiii; 210 pp. £17.50. 0-281-05011-2. [R]ET 108 (1996-97) 289-290 *(Rodd, C.S.)*.
943 *Basset, Jean-Claude* Faut-il réviser le canon des écritures?: les apocryphes et la foi. BCPE 49/2-3 (1997) 35-43.

944 *Bauer, Johannes B.* Aspekte des Kanonproblems. Studien zu Bibel-text. <sup>E</sup>**Felber, Anneliese**: 1997 <1983>, ⇒111. 9-29.

945 *Baum, Armin D.* Der neutestamentliche Kanon bei EUSEBIOS (*Hist. Eccl.* III,25,1-7) im Kontext seiner literaturgeschichtlichen Arbeit. Zsfg. 348. EThL 73 (1997) 307-348.

946 *Baum, Armin Daniel* Literarische Echtheit als Kanonkriterium in der alten Kirche. ZNW 88 (1997) 97-110.

947 *Betz, Hans Dieter* Canone N.T. Conc(I) 33/3 (1997) 61-77; Conc(P) 271,50-65; Conc(GB) 1997/3,35-46; (D33,322-333).

948 **Blanchard, Y.-M.** Aux sources du canon: le témoignage d'IRENEE. CFi 175: 1993, ⇒9,1259... 12,794. NT 39 (1997) 304-309 *(Amphoux, C.)*.

949 *Brooke, George J.* 'The canon within the canon' at Qumran and in the New Testament. The scrolls and the scriptures. JSPE.S 26: 1997, ⇒299. <sup>E</sup>Porter, S., 242-266 [Mk 12,1-12; Lk 7,22-23; Phil 2,6-11].

950 *Budde, Achim* Der Abschluß des alttestamentlichen Kanons und seine Bedeutung für die kanonische Schriftauslegung. BN 87 (1997) 39-55.

951 *Collins, John J.* Before the canon: scriptures in Second Temple Judaism. Seers. JSJ.S 54: 1997 <1995>, ⇒119. 3-21.

952 *Edwards, Mark* Authorship and canonicity: some patristic evidence. JSOT.S 153: 1997, ⇒4. <sup>F</sup>ASHTON J., 174-179.

953 *Freedman, David Noel* Canon of the Old Testament. Divine Commitment 1. 1997 <1976>, ⇒124. 267-278;

954 The formation of the canon of the Old Testament: the selection and identification of the torah as the supreme authority of the postexilic community. Divine Commitment 1. 1997 <1990>, ⇒124. 470-484;

955 Toward a common bible?. Divine Commitment 1. 1997 <1965>, ⇒124. 200-210.

956 **Halbertal, Moshe** People of the book: canon, meaning, and authority. CM 1997, Harvard University Press x; (2) 185 pp. $19. 0-674-66112-5.

957 **Harnack, Adolf von** MARCION: das Evangelium vom fremden Gott: eine Monographie zur Geschichte der Grundlegung der katholischen Kirche. Bibliothek klassischer Texte: Da:Wiss <sup>2</sup>1996, 3-534-01837-0.

958 *Herms, Eilert* Was haben wir an der Bibel?: Versuch einer Theologie des christlichen Kanons. JBTh 12 (1997) 99-152.

959 *Knights, Chris* Whose Bible is it really?. ET 109 (1997) 15-16.

960 **McDonald, L.M.** The formation of the christian biblical canon. <sup>2</sup>1995, ⇒11/2,1650; 12,810. <sup>R</sup>NRTh 119 (1997) 272-274 *(Ska, J.-L.)*; EThL 73 (1997) 187-188 *(Verheyden, J.)*; SEÅ 62 (1997) 151-153 *(Ekenberg, Anders)*; RBBras 14 (1997) 359-361.

961 *McDonald, Lee Martin* The First Testament: its origin, adaptability, and stability. 1997, ⇒77. <sup>F</sup>SANDERS J., 287-326.

962 **Metzger, Bruce Manning** Il canone del Nuovo Testamento: origine, sviluppo e significato. Introduzione allo studio della Bibbia, Suppl 3: Brescia 1997, Paideia 286 pp. L56.000. 88-394-0551-8.

963 **Noble, P.R.** The canonical approach. 1996, ⇒12,814. <sup>R</sup>CBQ 59 (1997) 551-552 *(Gnuse, Robert)*.

964 *Ohme, Heinz* Der Kanon-Begriff der Synode von Nizäa (325). Studia Patristica 29. 1997, ⇒351. <sup>E</sup>Livingstone, Elizabeth A., 310-315.

965 *Paulsen, Henning* Die Bedeutung des Montanismus für die Herausbildung des Kanons. 1997 <1978>;

966 Sola Scriptura und das Kanonproblem. Zur Literatur. WUNT 99: 1997 <1991>, ⇒153. EEisen, Ute E., 310-343/344-361.

967 *Pickering, Stuart R.* The formation of the New Testament: some general issues. NTTRU 5 (1997) 1-18;

968 Literature, scripture and canon. NTTRU 5 (1997) 61-78;

969 The New Testament as a stable collection of writings. NTTRU 5 (1997) 101-118.

970 EPokorný, Petr Bibelauslegung als Theologie. WUNT 100: Tü 1997, Mohr ix; 372 pp. DM198. 3-16-146766-3.

971 EPorter, Stanley E. Handbook to exegesis of the New Testament. NTTS 25: Lei 1997, Brill xiii; 638 pp. ƒ280. 90-04-099921-2.

972 **Rendtorff, Rolf** Canon and theology: overtures to an OT theology. 1994, ⇒7,252...12,818. RJSSt 42 (1997) 145-146 *(Sanders, J.A.)*.

973 *Roth, Wolfgang* To invert or not to invert: the Pharisaic canon in the gospels. Early christian interpretation. JSNT.S 148: 1997, ⇒191. EEvans, Craig A., 59-78.

974 *Saldarini, Anthony J.* The uses and abuses of heresy. BiRe 13/6 (1997) 16, 47.

975 *Sanders, James A.* The exile and canon formation. Exile. JSJ.S 56: 1997, ⇒227. EScott, James M., 37-61.

976 *Ska, Jean Louis* Il canone ebraico e il canone cristiano dell'Antico Testamento. CivCatt 148 III (1997) 213-225.

977 *Souček, Josef B.* Einheit des Kanons—Einheit der Kirche. Bibelauslegung. EPokorný, Petr: WUNT 100: 1997 <1968>, ⇒970. 99-108.

978 *Stanton, Graham N.* The fourfold gospel. NTS 43 (1997) 317-346.

979 *Stuhlmacher, Peter* Der Kanon und seine Auslegung. BZNW 86: 1997, ⇒41. FHOFIUS O., 263-290.

980 **Trobisch, David** Die Endredaktion des Neuen Testaments: eine Untersuchung zur Entstehung der christlichen Bibel. NTOA 31: 1996, ⇒12,826. RLASBF 47 (1997) 599-603 *(Chrupcała, Lesław Daniel)*.

981 *Ulrich, Eugene* The community of Israel and the composition of the scriptures. Bibl.Interp. 28: 1997 ⇒77. FSANDERS J., 327-342.

982 *Vonach, Andreas* Die sogenannte "Kanon- oder Ptahotepformel": Anmerkungen zu Tradition und Kontext einer markanten Wendung. PzB 6 (1997) 73-80 [Deut 4,2; 13,1].

983 *Wall, Robert W.* Canonical criticism. Handbook. NTTS 25: 1997, ⇒971. EPorter, Stanley E., 291-312.

984 *Walter, Nikolaus* 'Bücher: so nicht der heiligen Schrifft gleich gehalten...'?: KARLSTADT, LUTHER—und die Folgen. Praeparatio evangelica. EKraus, Wolfgang. WUNT 98: 1997 <1992>, ⇒167. 341-369.

B4.1 *Interpretatio humanistica* The Bible—man; health, toil, age

985 **Alonso Schökel, Luis** Familia y sociedad: cien máximas bíblicas. Eseñamos a orar: Bilbao 1997, Mensajero 118 pp. 84-271-2098-2;

986 El hombre: cien máximas bíblicas. Enseñamos a orar: Bilbao 1997, Mensajero 118 pp. 84-271-2097-4;

987 I nomi dell'amore: simboli matrimoniali nella bibbia. CasM 1997, Piemme 303 pp. Bibl. 88-384-2949-9.

988 *Alves, Isidro Manuel* Gesù e il malato. Com(I) 154-155 (1997) 16-20.

989 *Barker, Margaret* Food in scripture. Way 37 (1997) 17-24.
990 *Bayer, Oswald* "die größte Lust zu haben / allein an deinem Wort": vom Lebensverhältnis zur Bibel. BZNW 86: 1997, ⇒41. [F]HOFIUS O., 793-804.
991 **Bendor, Sônî'a** The social structure of ancient Israel: the institution of the family (Beit 'Ab) from the settlement to the end of the monarchy. Jerusalem Biblical Studies 7: 1996, ⇒12,827. [R]Anthropos 92 (1997) 589 *(Lang, Bernhard)*; Henoch 19/1 (1997) 115-116 *(Soggin, J. Alberto)*; LASBF 47 (1997) 573-575 *(Cortese, Enzo)*.
992 *Briend, Jacques* Bad und Schönheitspflege in biblischer Zeit. Welt und Umwelt der Bibel 3 (1997) 54-55.
993 *Chmiel, Jerzy* Siedem spojrzeń na płciowość w biblii [Sept regards sur la sexualité dans la bible]. RBL 50 (1997) 28-35. **P**.
994 **Goodman, Naomi; Marcus, Robert; Woolhandler, Susan** Recepten uit de tijd van de bijbel. [T]*Van de Velde-Oosterom, C.*: Lei 1996, Groen. *f*30. [R]Phoe. 43 (1997) 168-169 *(Folmer, Margaretha)*.
995 **Hart, Maarten t'** Wie God verlaat heeft niets te vrezen: de Schrift betwist. Amst 1997, Arbeiderspers 176 pp. 90-295-2079-5 [Streven 64,858].
996 **Heß, Irmgard** Mann und Frau in der Bibel. Münster-Schwarzach 1997, Vier Türme. DM19.80 [BiLi 73,78—Koch, Christiane].
997 **Leaman, Oliver** Evil and suffering in Jewish philosophy. CSRT 6: 1995, ⇒11/2,1685. [R]TS 58 (1997) 183-184 *(Keenan, James F.)*.
998 *Marín i Torner, Joan Ramon* La mort prematura en l'Antic Testament. Qüestions de Vida Cristiana 188 (1997) 57-69.
999 *McLoughlin, David* Healthy eating for all!: the challenge of Jesus' ministry. Month 30 (1997) 92-93.
1000 **Ohler, Annemarie** Väter wie die Bibel sie sieht. 1996, ⇒12,842. [R]BiKi 52 (1997) 97-99 *(Baur, Wolfgang)*.
1001 **Ossanna, Tullio Faustino** Immagini di famiglia nel vangelo. Borgonuovo di Pontecchio Marconi (BO) 1997, Immacolata 102 pp. [R]Miles Immaculatae 33/2 (1997) 539 *(Galy, Silvia)*.
1002 **Pastore, Corrado; Wyssenbach, Jean Pierre** La familia en la biblia. Caracas 1997, Iter 32 pp;
1003 La vida en la biblia. Caracas 1997, Iter 32 pp.
1004 *Pilch, John J.* Family violence in cross-cultural perspective: an approach for feminist interpreters of the bible. A feminist companion. 1997, ⇒180. [E]Brenner, Athalya. 306-323;
1005 The meaning of hair. BiTod 35 (1997) 229-233.
1006 **Prior, Michael Patrick** The Bible and colonialism: a moral critique. BiSe 48: Shf 1997, Academic 342 pp. £17. 1-85075-815-8.
1007 *Puig i Tàrrech, Armand* Els drets humans i la Bíblia. Sum. 287. RCatT 22 (1997) 263-287.
1008 *Quesnel, Michel* Bad und Schönheitsplege in neutestamentlicher Zeit. Welt und Umwelt der Bibel 3 (1997) 56.
1009 **Schwartz, Marco** Los amores en la Biblia. Historia: M 1997, Temas de Hoy 303 pp. 84-7880-745-4.
1010 **Seifert, Elke** Tochter und Vater im Alten Testament: eine ideologiekritische Untersuchung zur Verfügungsgewalt von Vätern über ihre Töchter. Neukirchener Theologische Diss. und Habilitationen 9: Neuk 1997, Neuk xiv; 336 pp. 3-7887-1609-6 [NThAR 1997,291].

1011  **Sinopoulos, P.A.** Η Οικογένεια ως μονάδα εργασίας του λαού
      της Παλαιάς Διαθήκης [The family as a unity of work in the
      people of the Old Testament]. Athens 1997, E.K.K.E.  [R]DBM
      16/1 (1997) 89-90 *(Agourides, S.)*. **G.**

1012  *Tadmor, Hayim* "And if given the strength—eighty years": the
      terms for longevity in Akkadian, Biblical Hebrew, and Mishnaic
      Hebrew. 1997, ⇒34. [M]GREENBERG M., 93*-97*. **H.** [Ps 90,10].

1013  **Tucci, Lorenzo** I vangeli rifatti da bambini distratti. Pratola Pe-
      ligna 1997, 125 pp. Edizione extra commerciale. [MF 97,366].

1014  *Ukpong, Justin S.* Lepra: intocables en el evangelio y en nuestros
      días. Conc(GB) 1997/5,63-70;  Conc(F) 273,87-95;  Conc(I)
      33,980-991; (D33,639-647); Conc(E) 273 (1997) 905-914.

1015  **Van der Toorn, Karel** Family religion in Babylonia, Syria, and
      Israel: continuity and change in the forms of religious life. Studies
      in the History and Culture of the Ancient Near East 7: 1996,
      ⇒12,849. [R]OLZ 92 (1997) 694-698 *(Heltzer, Michael)*; Mes. 32
      (1997) 368-372 *(Piantelli, M.)*; JBL 116 (1997) 529-530 *(Blen-
      kinsopp, Joseph)*.

1016  **Van der Zee, William R.** Someday there'll be no tomorrow.
      North Andover, MA 1997, Genesis 151 pp. $17. 1-886670-05-6
      [ThD 44,390—Heiser, W. Charles].

1017  *Vander Stichele, Caroline* Waar is de wereld?: de bijbel en de
      krant. ITBT 5/8 (1997) 22-23.

1018  **Zuck, Roy B.** Precious in his sight: childhood and children in the
      Bible. 1996, ⇒12,852. [R]BS 154 (1997) 485-486 *(McLaughlin, L.)*.

B4.2  *Femina, familia;* **Woman in the Bible** [⇒B4.1; H8.8s]

1019  **Bach, Alice** Women, seduction, and betrayal in biblical narrative.
      C 1997, CUP xiv; 296 pp. Bibl. 0-521-47532-5/60-0 [NThAR
      1998,97].

1020  *Bezuidenhout, L.C.* Voorstellings van Batseba: intertekstualiteit in
      literêre kuns, beeldende kuns en werklikheid. HTS 53 (1997) 529-
      542 [2 Sam 11,2-27].

1021  *Bird, Phyllis A.* Images of women in the Old Testament. <1974>;

1022  Israelite religion and the faith of Israel's daughters: reflections on
      gender and religious definition. <1991>;

1023  The place of women in the Israelite cultus. <1987>;

1024  Women (Old Testament). <1992>. Missing persons. 1997,
      ⇒114. 13-51/103-120/81-102/52-66.

1025  *Bosetti, Elena* La donna nel progetto di Dio. TS(I) (1997/1) 8-11.

1026  **Brakeman, Lyn** Spiritual lemons: biblical women, irreverent
      laughter, and righteous rage. Ph 1997, Innisfree 126 pp. 1-880913-
      22-4.

1027  **Bronner, Leila Leah** From Eve to Esther: rabbinic reconstructions
      of biblical women. 1994, ⇒10,1126...12,858. [R]CBQ 58 (1996)
      341-342 *(Bergant, Dianne)*.

1028  *Crüsemann, Frank* Das Alte Testament—eine Wurzel der Gewalt
      gegen Frauen?. JK 58 (1997) 268-273.

1029  **Drewermann, Eugen** L'évangile des femmes. [T]*Bagot, Jean-Pierre*
      P 1996, Seuil 222 pp. [SR 26,400—Barry, Catherine];

1030  El mensaje de las mujeres: la ciencia del amor. 1996, ⇒12,862.
      [R]Iter 8/2 (1997) 159-161 *(Frades, Eduardo)*.

1031 *Eskenazi, Tamara C.* Out from the shadows: biblical women in the post-exilic era. Historical Books. 1997 <1992>, ⇒192. EExum, J. Cheryl, 349-366.

1032 **Exum, J. Cheryl** Fragmented women: feminist (sub)versions of biblical narratives. JSOT.S 163: 1993, ⇒9,1320... 11/2,1723. RTJT 13/1 (1997) 90-91 *(Isaac, Jacqueline R.)*;

1033 Plotted, shot and painted: cultural representations of biblical women. JSOT.S 215: 1996, ⇒12,864. RScrB 27 (1997) 80-82 *(O'Kane, Martin)*.

1034 *Exum, J.C.* Rizpah. Word and World 17 (1997) 260-268 [ZID 23,415].

1035 **Fletcher, Elizabeth** Women in the bible: a historical approach. Melbourne 1997, Harper Collins 160 pp. $AUS20. 1-8637-1683-1 [Pacifica 11,239s—Macdonald, Marie].

1036 **France, Richard Thomas** Women in the church's ministry: a test-case for biblical interpretation. GR 1997, Eerdmans 96 pp. 0-8028-4172-4.

1037 *Heuberger, Rachel* Die Stellung der Frau im Judentum: Tradition und Moderne. Edith Stein Jahrbuch 3 (1997) 190-200.

1038 **Hyman, Naomi Mara** Biblical women in the midrash: a source-book. Northvale, NJ 1997 Aronson xlii; 194 pp. Bibl. 0-7657-6030-4.

1039 *Koch, Christiane* "Und Debora war richtend Israel in jener Zeit ..." (Ri 4,4): Leitungsverantwortung im Ersten Testament am Beispiel der Prophetin Debora. Entschluss 52/2 (1997) 33-35.

1040 **Nowell, Irene** Women in the Old Testament. ColMn 1997, Liturgical v; 208 pp. Bibl. 0-8146-2411-1.

1041 **Oñate Ojeda, Juan-Angel** La mujer en la Biblia. Valentina 39: Valencia 1997, Facultad de Teología San Vicente Ferrer vii; 268 pp. Bibl. 84-921032-6-4.

1042 *Schäfer-Lichtenberger, Christia* Beobachtungen zur Rechtsstellung der Frau in der alttestamentlichen Überlieferung. WuD 24 (1997) 95-120.

1043 **Streete, Gail C.** The strange woman: power and sex in the bible. LVL 1997, Westminster x; 219 pp. Bibl. $19. 0-664-25622-8.

1044 **Van der Lingen, Anton** Vrouwen rond de koningen van oud-Israël. Zoetermeer 1997, Boekencentrum 161 pp. ƒ32.50. 90-239-0963-1 [RB 105,479].

1045 *Willi-Plein, Ina* Michal und die Anfänge des Königtums in Israel. Congress volume 1995. VT.S 66. 1997, ⇒323. EEmerton, J.A., 401-419.

### B4.4 *Exegesis litteraria*—The Bible itself as literature

1046 **Alter, Robert** The world of biblical literature. 1992, ⇒8,1512... 10,1172. RSJTh 50 (1997) 502-504 *(Guest, P. Deryn)*.

1047 **Amit, Yairah** Covert polemics in biblical narrative. Bibl.Interp. 25: Lei 1997, Brill 240 pp. c.ƒ120/$77.50. 90-04-10153-5.

1048 *Boer, Roland* National allegory in the Hebrew Bible. JSOT 74 (1997) 95-116 [2 Sam 12,1-12; 1 Kgs 13].

1049 *Cramer, Thomas* Der Buchstabe als Medium des gesprochenen Wortes: über einige Probleme der Mündlichkeits-Schriftlichkeitsdebatte am Beispiel mittelalterlicher Lyrik;

1050 *Frede, Dorothea* Mündlichkeit und Schriftlichkeit: von PLATON zu PLOTIN. Logos. TANZ 20: 1997, ⇒229. ᴱSellin, Gerhard, 127-152/33-54.

1051 **Frye, Northrop** Il potere delle parole: nuovi studi su bibbia e letteratura. F 1994, Nuova Italia 355 pp. L35.000. ᴿCivCatt 148 I (1997) 309-311 *(Scaiola, D.)*.

1052 *Hess, Richard S.* Getting personal: what names in the bible teach us. BiRe 13/6 (1997) 30-37.

1053 *Jasper, David* Reflections on the London conference on the rhetorical analysis of scripture. Rhetorical analysis. JSNT.S 146: 1997, ⇒336. ᴱPorter, Stanley E., 476-482.

1054 **Kirsch, Jonathan** The harlot by the side of the road: forbidden tales of the bible. L 1997, Rider x; 378 pp. 0-7126-7209-5 [NThAR 1998,98] [Gen 19,30-38; 34; 38; Ex 2,22; Judg 12; 19; 2 Sam 13].

1055 *Klerk, Johannes C. de* The "literariness" of the New Testament gospels. R & T 4 (1997) 208-219.

1056 **Kreitzer, Larry J.** The New Testament in fiction and film: on reversing the hermeneutical flow. 1993, ⇒9,1366; 11/2,1803. SBET 15/1 (1997) 76-77 *(Nolan, Steve)*.

1057 *Kullmann, Wolfgang* Der Übergang von der Mündlichkeit zur Schriftlichkeit im frühgriechischen Epos;

1058 *Löhr, Winrich A.* Mündlichkeit und Schriftlichkeit im Christentum des 2. Jahrhunderts;

1059 *Marks, Herbert* Schrift und Mikra. Logos. TANZ 20: 1997, ⇒229. ᴱSellin, Gerhard, 55-75/211-230/103-126/.

1060 **Miles, Jack** Dieu—une biographie. ᵀ*Dauzat, Emmanuel:* 1996, ⇒12,894. ᴿHokhma 64 (1997) 73-76 *(Desplanque, Christophe)*; BCLF 584 (1997) 1419;

1061 'Gott': eine Biographie. 1996, ⇒12,895. ᴿEK (1997/2) 112-113 *(Andric, Zoran)*.

1062 *Olbricht, Thomas H.* The flowering of rhetorical criticism in America;

1063 *Porter, Stanley E.* Introduction: the London papers in perspective. Rhetorical analysis. JSNT.S 146: 1997, ⇒336. ᴱPorter, S., 79-102/17-21.

1064 ᴱ*Regt, Lénart J. de;* **Waard, J. de; Fokkelman, J.P.** Literary structure and rhetorical strategies in the Hebrew Bible. 1996, ⇒12,200. ᴿCTrB 28 (1997) 18-19 *(Schneider, Théo)*.

1065 *Robbins, Vernon K.* The present and future of rhetorical analysis. Rhetorical analysis. JSNT.S 146: 1997, ⇒336. ᴱPorter, S., 24-52.

1066 *Sarrazin, Bernard* Première table ronde: exégèse biblique et analyse littéraire. La Bible en littérature. 1997, ⇒315. ᴱBeaude, Pierre-Marie, 343-352.

1067 *Sellin, Gerhard* Das lebendige Wort und der tote Buchstabe: Aspekte von Mündlichkeit und Schriftlichkeit in christlicher und jüdischer Theologie. Logos. TANZ 20: 1997, ⇒229. ᴱSellin, G., 11-31.

1068 *Stefano, Piero* La Bibbia come classico. RCI 78/1 (1997) 65-68.

1069 *Verrier, Jean* Deuxième table ronde: la lecture comme réception du texte biblique. La Bible en littérature. 1997, ⇒315. ᴱBeaude, Pierre-Marie, 353-363.

1070 **Walker, Robert Martin** Politically correct Old Testament stories. Kansas City 1997, Andrews and M x; 86 pp. 0-8362-3198-8 [NThAR 1998,99].

1071 **Wangerin, Walter** Das Buch von Gott: die Bibel als Roman. T*Schrödter, Wolfgang; Thomson, J. Guthrie*: Wu 1997, Brockhaus 959 pp. DM49.80. 3-417-24673-3. RBiKi 52 (1997) 207-208 *(Trutwin, Werner)*.

1072 *Willi-Plein, Ina* Spuren der Unterscheidung von mündlichem und schriftlichem Wort im Alten Testament. Logos. TANZ 20: 1997, ⇒229. ESellin, G., 77-89.

1073 **Wills, Lawrence M.** The Jewish novel in the ancient world. 1995, 11/2,6801; 12,8062. RCBQ 59 (1997) 142-143 *(Frizzell, Lawrence)*; AJS Review 22/1 (1997) 110-112 *(Greenspoon, Leonard J.)*; JBL 115 (1996) 531-532 *(Walsh, Jerome T.)*.

### B4.5 Influxus biblicus in litteraturam profanam, *generalia*

1074 *Atherton, Mark* The image of the temple in the *Psychomachia* and late Anglo-Saxon literature. BJRL 79/3 (1997) 263-285.

1075 **Fernández Marcos, Natalio; Fernández Tejero, Emilia** Biblia y humanismo: textos, talantes y controversias del siglo XVI español. Monografías 69: M 1997, Fundación Universitaria Española 293 pp. 84-7392-389-8 [CDios 211,661—Gutiérrez, J.].

1076 **Frye, Northrop** Poderosas palabras: la biblia y nuestras metáforas. T*López de Lamadrid, Claudio*: Ensayo 35: Barc 1996, Muchnik 420 pp. 84-7669-230-7. RActBib 34 (1997) 201-202 *(Boada, J.)*.

1077 **Goatly, Andrew** The language of metaphors. L 1997, Routledge xvi; 360 pp. 0-415-12876-5.

1078 **Goedegebuure, Jaap** De veelvervige rok: de bijbel in de moderne literatuur, 2. Amst 1997, Amst. Univ. Press 146 pp. 90-5356-238-9 [Str. 64,956].

1079 **González de Cardedal, Olegario** Cuatro poetas desde la otra ladera: UNAMUNO, JEAN PAUL, MACHADO, Oscar WILDE: prolegómenos para una cristología. 1996, ⇒12,907. REstB 55 (1997) 365-370 *(Pego Puigbo, Armando)*.

1080 *Hooker, Roger H.* Some christian reflections on the contemporary Hindi novel. Sum. 289. VJTR 61 (1997) 289-306.

1081 **Howlett, D.R.** British books in biblical style. Dublin 1997, Four Courts xi; 625 pp. 1-85182-182-1;

1082 The Celtic Latin tradition of biblical style. 1996, ⇒12,910. JEH 48 (1997) 532-533 *(Wieland, Gernot)*.

1083 **Irblich, Cornelia** Apokalyptische Bibelechos in ausgewählten amerikanischen Romanen seit Stephan CRANE. Mainzer Studien zur Amerikanistik 34: Fra 1996, Lang. 3-361-49823-3 [ThZ 55,372—Raguse, Hartmut].

1084 **Josipovici, Gabriel** El libro de Dios: una respuesta a la Biblia. 1995, ⇒11/2,1177; 12,505. RIter 8/2 (1997) 156-158 *(Frades, Eduardo)*; ScrTh 29/1 (1997) 284-285 *(Balaguer, V.)*.

1085 *Las Heras, Isabel J.* Temas y expresiones bíblicas en las crónicas del ciclo de ALFONSO III. Sum. res. 587. HispSac 49 (1997) 587-600.

1086  *Martyn, J. Louis* From Paul to Flannery O'CONNOR with the power of grace. Theological issues. 1997 <1981>, ⇒146. 279-297.

1087  *Mayer, Désirée* Dire, redire ou contredire: éclats du corpus sacré dans la littérature hébraïque moderne. La Bible en littérature. 1997, ⇒315. ᴱBeaude, Pierre-Marie, 139-160.

1088  **Muir, Lynette R.** The biblical drama of medieval Europe. 1995, ⇒11/2,1839; 12,914. ᴿSpec. 72 (1997) 865-867 *(Knight, Alan E.)*.

1089  *Muñoz García de Iturrospe, Teresa* Ecos bíblicos en autores latinos cristianos: la representación del mar. La Bíblia i el Mediterrani. 1997, ⇒385. ᴱBorrell, d'Agustí, 53-66.

1090  *Nytrová, Olga; Balabán, Milan* Ohlasy Starého Zákona v české literatuře 19. a 20 století [Echoes of the Old Testament in the Czech literature of the XIXth and XXth century]. Praha 1997, OIKOTMENH 240 pp. [CV 40,73s—Pokorný, Petr].

1091  *Ostrowiecki, Hélène* La bible des libertins. XVIIᵉ Siècle 49 (1997) 43-55 [EThL 74,165*].

1092  *Panier, Louis* Du texte biblique à l'énonciation littéraire et à son sujet. La Bible en littérature. 1997, ⇒315. ᴱBeaude, P.-M., 313-326.

1093  *Renaud-Chamska, Isabelle* Écriture poétique, Écritures bibliques. RICP 61 (1997) 5-16.

1094  **Sanchez-Silva, José-María** La adolescencia de Jesús nunca contada. M 1997, Planeta 188 pp. [Mayéutica 24,298—Alonso, Gonzalo].

1095  **Stäuble, Antonio** Le sirene eterne: studi sull'eredità classica e biblica nella letteratura italiana. Memoria del tempo, Studi e testi medievali e rinascimentali 6: Ravenna 1996, Longo 206 pp. ᴿAevum 71 (1997) 889-892 *(Motta, Uberto)*.

1096  **Thompson, John J.** The *Cursor mundi*: poem, texts and contexts. MAeM 19: Oxf 1997, Society for the Study of Medieval Languages and Literature xi; 193 pp. £11/$25. 0-907570-12-7 [[MAe 66,378].

1097  *Tosaus, José Pedro* Longinos: de la biblia al Cantar de Mio Cid. La Bíblia i el Mediterrani. 1997, ⇒385. ᴱBorrell, d'Agustí, 87-100.

1098  ᴱ**Vallecalle, Jean Claude** Littérature et religion au Moyen Âge et à la Renaissance. XI-XVI Littérature: Lyon 1997, Presses Universitaires de Lyon 220 pp. [RSLR 35/1,215ss—Ardissino, Erminia].

B4.6 *Singuli auctores*—**Bible influence on individual authors**

1099  *Balasch, Manuel* Moments precristians en la filosofia de PLATO. La Bíblia i el Mediterrani. 1997, ⇒385. ᴱBorrell, d'Agustí, 255-261.

1100  *Baude, Jeanne-Marie* André FRENAUD: regard d'un poète athée sur le Christ aux Oliviers;

1101  *Bonnet, Henri* Gérard de NERVAL et la bible: la quête d'une nouvelle alliance;

1102  *Boschian-Campaner, Catherine* Les références bibliques dans l'œuvre de Barbey d'AUREVILLY. La Bible en littérature. 1997, ⇒315. ᴱBeaude, P.-M., 175-189/13-28/55-71.

1103 <sup>E</sup>**Bucks, René** A Bíblia e a ética: a relação entre filosofia e a sagrada escritura na obra de Emmanuel LEVINAS. Fé e Realidade 35: São Paulo 1997, Loyola 220 pp. 85-15-01500-5 [PerTeol 29,282].

1104 *Chmiel, Jerzy* Biblijmy teatr godziny słowa Danuty MICHAŁOWSKIEJ [De arte recitandi Sacrae Scripturae in theatro Danutae Michałowska]. RBL 50 (1997) 144-147. **P.**

1105 *Couffignal, Robert* Une référence biblique dans l'œuvre de Marcel PROUST "Avec le geste d'Abraham" [Gen 22];

1106 *Deprez, Bérengère* Ferveur et scepticisme: présence et directions des sources bibliques dans l'œuvre narrative de Marguerite YOURCENAR;

1107 *Dufetel, Jacques* Bible et mythe symboliste: Lilith de Rémy de GOURMONT;

1108 *Engel, Vincent* De la nuit au crépuscule, au loin d'Élie WIESEL: minutes et impasses d'un procès biblique. La Bible en littérature. 1997, ⇒315. <sup>E</sup>Beaude, P.-M., 87-94/95-104/29-40/115-137.

1109 **Frades Gaspar, Eduardo** El uso de la Biblia en los escritos de Fray Bartolomé de LAS CASAS. Diss. Univ. Javeriana de Bogotá. <sup>D</sup>*Baena, Gustavo:* Santa Rosa de Lima 2: Caracas 1997, Instituto Universitario Seminario Interdiocesano Santa Rosa de Lima 554 pp. 980-07-44259-X.

1110 *Frank, Évelyne* Jean GROSJEAN, Noël PIERRE-EMMANUEL et la bible [Gen 2-3];

1111 *Halpern-Guedj, Betty* Edmond FLEG et les sources midrachiques: la mort de Moïse [Deut 34]. La Bible en littérature. 1997, ⇒315. <sup>E</sup>Beaude, P.-M., 191-206/105-113.

1112 *Koenen, Hans* Vincent van GOGH: zijn bijbel en de leer van Boeddha. Streven 64 (1997) 483-496.

1113 **Kuschel, Karl-Josef** Im Spiegel der Dichter: Mensch, Gott und Jesus in der Literatur des 20. Jahrhunderts. Dü 1997, Patmos 420 pp. DM49.80. 3-491-72378-7. <sup>R</sup>EK (1997) 748-749 *(Hurth, E.).*

1114 *Law-Viljoen, Bronwyn* Midrash, myth, and prophecy: George ELIOT's reinterpretation of biblical stories. JLT 11 (1997) 80-92 [EThL 74,161*].

1115 <sup>E</sup>**Moraglia, F.; Tripodi, A.M.** ROSMINI tra vangelo e cultura. R 1997, Città Nuova 71 pp. <sup>R</sup>RRFC 91 (1997) 644-646 *(Facco, Maria Luisa).*

1116 *Morisco, Gabriella* La bibbia secondo Emily DICKINSON: una versione non autorizzata. VS 76 (1997) 53-71.

1117 *Peloso, Silvano* O paradigma bíblico como modelo universalista de leitura em António VIEIRA. Brot. 145 (1997) 557-565.

1118 *Salmona, Bruno* La sacra scrittura come fonte di ROSMINI. RRFC 91/3-4 (1997) 301-371.

1119 *Salvatierra Ossorio, Aurora* De Sefarad a Sión: los poemas del mar de Yehudah HA-LEVI. La Bíblia i el Mediterrani. 1997, ⇒385. <sup>E</sup>Borrell, d'Agustí, 389-396.

1120 *Sarrazin, Bernard* Allusion ou illousion: les paradoxes de la référence biblique dans l'œuvre de Villiers de LISLE-ADAM, croyant et mécréant. La Bible en littérature. 1997, ⇒315. <sup>E</sup>Beaude, P.-M., 41-54.

1121 *Sicher, Efraim* George ELIOT's rescripting of scripture: the "ethics of reading" in Silas Marner. Semeia 77 (1997) 243-270.

1122  *Simard, Micheline* L'anti-évangile d'une Québécoise: l'euguélionne de Louky BERSIANIK. La Bible en littérature. 1997, ⇒315. ᴱBeaude, P.-M., 225-242.

1123  **Ventura, Maria Concetta** Prosa narrativa cristiana: i grandi scrittori narrano la loro fede. Narrativa cristiana: R 1997, Dehoniane 167 pp. 88-396-0709-9.

1124  *Viotto, Piero* La figura di Gesù in MARITAIN. RCI 78 (1997) 448-463.

1125  *Vray, Jean-Bernard* La bible revue et détournée par Michel TOURNIER;

1126  *Watthee-Delmotte, Myriam* De LOTH à Jean-Baptiste: le jeu des allusions bibliques dans le récit: dans les années profondes de Pierre Jean JOUVE. La Bible en littérature. 1997, ⇒315. ᴱBeaude, P.-M., 207-223/161-173.

### в4.7 *Interpretatio* psychiatrica

1127  *Bosch i Veciana, Antoni* Hermenèutica i lectura psicoanalítica de textos religiosos: reflexió des del punt de vista de l'hermenèutica Heideggeriana. Sum. 305. RCatT 22 (1997) 289-305.

1128  *Boyarin, Daniel* 'An imaginary and desirable converse': *Moses and monotheism* as family romance [Freud, Sigmund]. Reading bibles. 1997, ⇒172. ᴱBeal, Timothy K., 184-204.

1129  **Caballero Arencibia, Agustín** Psicoanálisis y biblia. Biblioteca Salmanticensis, Estudios 161: 1994, ⇒10,1250; 11/2,1916. ᴿActBib 34 (1997) 23-25 *(Patuel i Puig, Jaume)*.

1130  *Castro, Secundino* Hermenéutica bíblica y psicología profunda: una propuesta de E. DREWERMANN. REsp 56 (1997) 413-421 [EThL 74,168*].

1131  **Drewermann, Eugen** Psicologia del profondo e esegesi 2: la verità delle opere e delle parole: miracolo, visione, profezia, apocalisse, storia, parabola. BTCon 87: 1996, ⇒924. ᴿCivCatt 148 III (1997) 154-163 *(Rossi, Giacomo)*;

1132  Näher zu Gott—nah bei den Menschen: ein Gespräch mit Gwendoline Jarczyk. ᵀStüer, *Colette*: 1996, ⇒12,925. ᴿActBib 34 (1997) 56-57 *(Boada, J.)*;

1133  Psicologia del profondo e esegesi 1: sogno, mito, fiaba, saga e legenda. BTCon 86: 1996, ⇒12,923. ᴿREsp 224 (1997) 413-421 *(Castro, Secundino)*; EE 72 (1997) 347-352 *(Castro, S.)*; CivCatt 148 III (1997) 154-163 *(Rossi, Giacomo)*;

1134  Dios inmediato: conversaciones con Gwendoline Jarczyk. ᵀVidal, *José Manuel*: Estructuras y Processos, Religión: M 1997, Trotta 166 pp. 84-8164-139-1. ᴿActBib 34 (1997) 25-26 *(Patuel, Jaume)*.

1135  **Drosnin, Michaël** La bible: le code secret. ᵀYnchboat, *Arthur G.H.*: P 1997, Laffont 279 pp. FF129/EUR19,67. 2-221-08538-8.

1136  **Grelot, Pierre** Réponse à Eugen DREWERMANN. 1994, ⇒10,1256; 11/2,1930. ᴿEstB 55 (1997) 136-137 *(Ródenas, A.)*.

1137  *Hennig, Gerhard* "Christus solus noster Episcopus, pfarherr, Seelsorger...": Überlegungen zum Verhältnis von Seelsorge und Psychotherapie. BZNW 86: 1997, ⇒41. ᶠHOFIUS O., 805-821.

1138  *Jobling, David* Transference and tact in biblical studies. Reading bibles. 1997 <1993>, ⇒172. ᴱBeal, Timothy K., 208-218.

1139  *Kings, Steven* JUNG's hermeneutics of scripture. JR 77 (1997) 233-251.
1140  **Leiner, Martin** Psychologie und Exegese: Grundfragen einer textpsychologischen Exegese des Neuen Testaments. 1995, ⇒12,932. ᴿThLZ 122 (1997) 916-918 *(Pratscher, Wilhelm)*.
1141  *Leiner, Martin* Die drei Hauptprobleme der Verwendung psychologischer Theorien in der Exegese. ThZ 53 (1997) 289-303.
1142  **Lüdemann, Gerd** The unholy in holy scripture: the dark side of the bible. ᵀ*Bowden, John*: L 1997, SCM xii; 167 pp. £9.95/$14 [Theology 797,379].
1143  *Marchadour, Alain* Rencontre entre psychanalyse et bible. BLE.S 4 (1997) 25-36.
1144  *Pilch, John J.* Psychological and psychoanalytical approaches to interpreting the bible in social-scientific context. BTB 27 (1997) 112-116.
1145  *Vandermeersch, Patrick* Psychanalyse et interprétation de textes religieux. Compte-rendu du cours interdisciplinaire (3-7 fév. 1997) à Groningue. RCatT 22 (1997) 157-162.

B5  **Methodus exegeticus** [⇒F2.1]

1146  **Adam, A.K.M.** What is postmodern biblical criticism?. 1995, ⇒11/2,1965. New Theology Review 10/1 (1997) 113-114 *(McDonald, Patricia M.)*.
1147  *Artus, Olivier; Baudoz, Jean-François* L'évolution de la pratique exégétique dans les trente dernières années: nouveaux champs de recherche et principaux débats actuels. RICP 62 (1997) 177-198.
1148  *Baena B., Gustavo* El método histórico-critico. ThX 47/2 (1997) 155-179.
1149  *Barton, Stephen C.* Social-scientific criticism. Handbook. NTTS 25: 1997, ⇒971. ᴱPorter, Stanley E., 277-289.
1150  ᴱ**Bodine, Walter R.** Discourse analysis of biblical literature. 1995, ⇒11/2,1980. ᴿJSSt 44 (1997) 377-379 *(Watson, Wilfred G.E.)*.
1151  *Butler, Trent* Narrative form criticism: dead or alive?. JSOT.S 240: 1997, ⇒20. ᶠCoats G., 39-59.
1152  *Casarella, Peter J.; Young, Robin Darling* Spirit and history: the intelligence of scripture. Com(US) 24 (1997) 843-845.
1153  ᴱ**Castelli, Eslizabeth** The postmodern bible. 1995, ⇒11/2,359; 12,948. Bibl.Interp. 5 (1997) 216-219 *(Gorringe, Tim)*; Interp. 51 (1997) 426-428 *(Schneiders, Sandra M.)*.
1154  *Catchpole, David R.* Source, form and redaction criticism of the New Testament. Handbook. NTTS 25: 1997, ⇒971. ᴱPorter, S., 167-188.
1155  *Childs, Brevard S.* The genre of the biblical commentary as problem and challenge. 1997, ⇒34. ᴹGreenberg M. 185-192.
1156  ᴱ**Counet, Patrick Chatelion; Eynikel, Erik** Is het grote verhaal verloren?: het scheppen van bijbelse verhalen. Kampen 1997, Kok 102 pp. ƒ24.50. 90-242-9273-5 [ITBT 6/3,32—Abma, Richtsje].
1157  *Cziglányi, Zsolt* Egzetgetikai módszerek a hívő megértés mérlegén [Exegetical methods on the balance of believer understanding]. Gyermekségtörténet. 1997, ⇒316. ᴱBenyik, György: Sum., Zsfg., Rias. 133-139. **Hungarian.**

1158  **Deist, Ferdinand** Ervaring, rede en metode in skrifuitleg: 'n wetenskaps-historiese ondersoek na skrifuitleg in die Ned Geref Kerk 1840-1990. Pretoria 1994, RGN viii; 535 pp. R89. 0-7969-1636-7 [OTEs 11,645—Lombaard, C.J.S.].

1159  *Deist, Ferdinand* Inside a commentary: reflections on the writing of bible commentaries. OTEs 10 (1997) 369-386.

1160  *Deurloo, Karel* Christus onder de heidenen. PrakTh 24 (1997) 425-429.

1161  *Fontaine, Carole R.* Response to BRENNER's 'identifying the speaker-in-the-text'. A feminist companion. 1997, ⇒180. ᴱBrenner, Athalya, 151-153.

1162  *Gagey, Henri-Jérôme; Souletie, Jean-Louis* Encore une fois, exégèse et dogmatique. La théologie dans l'histoire. 1997, ⇒238. ᴱBousquet, F., 17-56 [EThL 74,166*].

1163  **Gosse, Bernard** Structuration des grands ensembles bibliques et intertextualité à l'époque perse: de la rédaction sacerdotale du livre d'Isaïe à la contestation de la Sagesse. BZAW 246: B 1997, De Gruyter xiv; 197 pp. DM148. 3-11-015395-5.

1164  **Graves, Mike** The sermon as symphony: preaching the literary forms of the New Testament. Valley Forge 1997, Judson xix; 289 pp. $18. 0-8170-1257-5 [NThAR 1998,100].

1165  *Hahn, Ferdinand* Die Bedeutung der historisch-kritischen Methode für die evangelische und die katholische Exegese: eine problemgeschichtliche Skizze. MThZ 48 (1997) 231-237.

1166  *Hartmann, Lars* Some reflections on the problem of the literary genre of the gospels. Text-centered NT studies. WUNT 102: 1997 <1978>, ⇒132. ᴱHellholm, David, 3-23.

1167  *Hasitschka, Martin* Wörtlicher und geistlicher Sinn der Schrift. BiLi 70 (1997) 152-155.

1168  *Heinemann, Wolfgang* Zur Eingrenzung des Intertextualitätsbegriffs aus textlinguistischer Sicht. Textbeziehungen. 1997, ⇒287. ᴱKlein, Josef, 21-37.

1169  *Heintz, Jean-Georges* Des textes sémitiques anciens à la Bible hébraïque: un comparatisme légitime?. Le comparatisme. 1997, ⇒346. ᴱBoespflug, François. 127-156.

1170  ᴱ*Hengel, Martin; Löhr, H.* Schriftauslegung im antiken Judentum und im Urchristentum. WUNT 73: 1994, ⇒10,322*; 12,257. ᴿCDios 210/1 (1997) 343-344 *(Gutiérrez, J.)*; ThLZ 122 (1997) 1019-1023 *(Hübner, Hans)*.

1171  **Hirshman, Marc G.** A rivalry of genius: Jewish and christian biblical interpretation in late antiquity. 1996, ⇒956. ᴿCritRR 10 (1997) 150-152 *(Visotzky, Burton L.)*.

1172  *Hoeres, Walter* Menschliche, allzu menschliche Betrachtungen: Scheingefechte heutiger Exegese. Theologisches 27 (1997) 215-221.

1173  *Jonge, H.J. de* De historisch-kritische exegese. PrakTh 24 (1997) 446-456.

1174  *Jonker, L.C.* Bridging the gap between bible readers and 'professional' exegetes. OTEs 10 (1997) 69-83.

1175  *Kratz, Reinhard G.* Redaktionsgeschichte/Redaktionskritik: Altes Testament. TRE 28 (1997) 367-378.

1176  *La Potterie, Ignace de* Le sens spiritual de l'Ecriture (d'après le cardinal H. de LUBAC). Fidélité et ouverture 114 (1997) 12-20 [AcBib 10/4,393].

1177 **Lescow, Theodor** Das Stufenschema: Untersuchungen zur Struktur alttestamentlicher Texte. BZAW 211: 1992, ⇒8,1201... 11/2,1369. <sup>R</sup>ThRv 93 (1997) 279-281 *(Schweizer, Harald)*.

1178 *Lindbeck, George* The story-shaped church: critical exegesis and theological interpretation. Teological interpretation. 1997, ⇒244. <sup>E</sup>Fowl, S., 39-52.

1179 *Linnemann, Eta* Evangelical and historical-critical theology. Faith & Mission 14/2 (1997) 3-27.

1180 *Martini, Card. Carlo Maria* 'Ci spiegava le scritture' (Lc 24,32). PaVi 42/4 (1997) 53-62.

1181 *Merk, Otto* Redaktionsgeschichte/Redaktionskritik: Neues Testament. TRE 28. 1997, ⇒420. 378-384.

1182 *Mijoga, Hilary B.* Hidden and public ways of doing contextual bible study in Southern Africa: South Africa and Malawi as case studies. Religion in Malawi 7 (1997) 41-44.

1183 *Moore, Stephen D.* History after theory?: biblical studies and the new historicism. Bibl.Interp. 5 (1997) 289-299.

1184 *Müller, Hans-Peter* Theologie und Religionsgeschichte im Blick auf die Grenzen historisch-kritischen Textumgangs. ZThK 94 (1997) 317-335.

1185 *Niemand, Christoph* Zum Anfang: am Ende?: Gedanken zum Thema. StAns 124: 1997, ⇒57. <sup>F</sup>Loehrer M. — Tragan P., 29-32.

1186 <sup>E</sup>**Patlagean, Éveline: Le Boulluec, Alain** Les retours aux Écritures: fondamentalismes présents et passés. 1993, ⇒9,293... 12,266. <sup>R</sup>Annales 52/1 (1997) 221-222 *(Lemaitre, Nicole)*.

1187 *Paulsen, Henning* Sozialgeschichtliche Auslegung des Neuen Testaments <1993>;

1188 Traditionsgeschichtliche Methode und religionsgeschichtliche Schule <1978>. Zur Literatur. WUNT 99: 1997, ⇒153. <sup>E</sup>Eisen, Ute E., 462-467/426-461.

1189 *Pearson, Birger A.* Some personal observations on scholarly method. The emergence. 1997, ⇒154. 214-225.

1190 *Pearson, Brook W.R.* New Testament literary criticism;

1191 *Pearson, Brook W.R.; Porter, Stanley E.* The genres of the New Testament;

1192 *Pippin, Tina* Ideological criticisms, liberation criticisms, and womanist and feminist criticisms. Handbook. NTTS 25: 1997, ⇒971. <sup>E</sup>Porter, Stanley E., 241-266/131-165/267-275.

1193 *Pokorný, Petr* Exegese als Zeugnis. Bibelauslegung. WUNT 100: 1997, <sup>E</sup>Pokorný, Petr, 3-11.

1194 *Porter, Stanley E.* The basic tools of exegesis of the New Testament: a bibliographical essay;

1195 *Porter, Stanley E.; Clarke, Kent D.* What is exegesis?: an analysis of various definitions. Handbook. NTTS 25: 1997, ⇒971. <sup>E</sup>Porter, Stanley E., 23-41/3-21.

1196 **Preus, Jonathan** Reading the bible through Christ: an introduction to exegesis and interpretation. Jos 1997, Theological College of Northern Nigeria 155 pp. 978-2023-06-X [NThAR 1998,333].

1197 *Reed, Jeffrey T.* Discourse analysis. Handbook. NTTS 25: 1997, ⇒971. <sup>E</sup>Porter, Stanley E., 189-217.

1198 *Rese, Martin* Intertextualität: ein Beispiel für Sinn und Unsinn 'neuer' Methoden. The scriptures in the gospels. BEThL 131: 1997, ⇒234. <sup>E</sup>Tuckett, Christopher M., 431-439.

1199 *Rodríguez Carmona, Antonio* Historia de las formas. ResB 13 (1997) 15-22.

1200 *Rofé, Alexander* From tradition to criticism: Jewish sources as an aid to the critical study of the Hebrew Bible. Congress volume 1995. VT.S 66: 1997, ⇒323. <sup>E</sup>Emerton, J.A., 235-247.

1201 *Roux, Jurie le* Our historical heritage. OTEs 10 (1997) 401-423.

1202 **Schirrmacher, Thomas** Die Vielfalt biblischer Sprache: über 100 alt- und neutestamentliche Stilarten, Ausdrucksweisen, Redeweisen und Gliederungsformen: eine Auswahl mit Beispieltexten alphabetisch geordnet. Biblia et Symbiotica 15: Bonn 1997, Verl. für Kultur und Wiss. 98 pp. 3-926105-83-6.

1203 **Sion, Avi** Judaic logic: a formal analysis of biblical, talmudic and rabbinic logic. Geneva 1997, Slatkine 262 pp. 2-05-101544-9 [NThAR 1998,269].

1204 *Souček, Josef B.* Die Entmythologisierung in der tschechischen Theologie. Bibelauslegung. WUNT 100: 1997 <1955>, ⇒970. 51-68.

1205 *Stamps, Dennis L.* Rhetorical and narratological criticism. Handbook. NTTS 25: 1997, ⇒971. <sup>E</sup>Porter, Stanley E., 219-239.

1206 **Steck, Odil Hannes** Old Testament exegesis: a guide to the methodology. <sup>T</sup>*Nogalski, James D.*: SBL Resources for Biblical Study 33: 1995, ⇒11/2,2048. <sup>R</sup>HebStud 38 (1997) 91-94 *(Nel, Philip J.)*.

1207 *Steinmetz, David C.* The superiority of pre-critical exegesis. Theological interpretation. 1997, ⇒244. <sup>E</sup>Fowl, S., 26-38.

1208 *Stone, Lawson G.* Redaction criticism: whence, whither, and why?: or, going beyond source and form criticism without leaving them behind. JSOT.S 240: 1997, ⇒20. <sup>F</sup>COATS G., 77-90.

1209 **Strecker, G.; Schnelle, U.** Introducción a la exégesis del Nuevo Testamento. Biblioteca de Estudios Bíblicos minor 1: S 1997, Sígueme 217 pp. 84-301-1296-0. <sup>R</sup>RET 57 (1997) 496-497 *(Barrado Fernández, P.)*.

1210 **Strecker, Georg** History of New Testament literature. <sup>T</sup>*Katter, Calvin; Mollenhauer, Hans-Joachim*: Harrisburg, Pennsylvania 1997, Trinity xiv; 238 pp. $24. 1-563-38203-2.

1211 *Studer, Basil* The characteristics of theological work;
1212 A rational knowledge of the bible;
1213 A search for a synthesis of biblical thought. History of Theology, 1. 1997, ⇒241. <sup>E</sup>Di Berardino, A., 334-352/374-386/387-408.

1214 *Turiot, Cécile* Pour une lecture délibérément figurative. La théologie dans l'histoire. 1997, ⇒238. <sup>E</sup>Bousquet, F., 93-105 [EThL 74,167*].

1215 *Vaccaro, Andrea* Dio parla in modo oscuro?: spunti filosofici e teologici sulle oscurità della Bibbia. Sapienza 50/2 (1997) 163-171.

1216 *Vanhoye, Albert* L'esegesi biblica e la fede. Seminarium 37 (1997) 48-55.

1217 *Washington, Harold C.* Violence and the construction of gender in the Hebrew Bible: a new historicist approach. Bibl.Interp. 5 (1997) 324-363.

1218 *Yeago, David S.* The New Testament and the Nicene dogma: a contribution to the recovery of theological exegesis. Theological interpretation. 1997, ⇒244. <sup>E</sup>Fowl, S., 87-100.

1219 **Young, Frances Margaret** Biblical exegesis and the formation of christian culture. C 1997, CUP xiv; 325 pp. The Speaker's lectures delivered in the University of Oxford in 1992 and 1993. £37.50. 0-521-58153-2.

1220 *Zorn, Jean-François* La contextualisation: un concept théologique?. RHPhR 77 (1997) 171-189.

## III. Critica Textus, Versiones

### D1 Textual Criticism

1221 *Adair, Jimmy R.* TC—a journal of biblical textual criticism: a model for successfull [sic] electronic publishing. JNSL 23/2 (1997) 235-242.

1222 **Dupont-Roc, Roselyne; Mercier, Philippe** Les manuscrits de la bible et la critique textuelle. CEv 102: P 1997, Cerf 66 pp. FF35. 0222-9714.

1223 **Person, Raymond Franklin, Jr.** The Kings—Isaiah and Kings—Jeremiah recensions. BZAW 252: B 1997, De Gruyter viii; 127 pp. DM98. 3-11-015457-9.

1224 **Siamakis, Constantine** Transmission of the text of the Holy Bible = Ε ΠΑΡΑΔΟΣΙΣ ΤΟΥ ΚΕΙΜΕΝΟΥ ΤΕΣ ΑΓΙΑΣ ΓΡΑΦΕΣ. ᵀ*Hendry, Andrew;* ᴱ*Gerostergios, Asterios*: Belmont 1997, Institute for Byzantine and Modern Greek Studies 54 pp. $6. 1-884729-26-6 [ThD 45,91—Heiser, W. Charles].

### D2.1 *Biblia hebraica.* **Hebrew text**

1225 **Azcárraga Servert, María Josefa de** Masorah Parva: la Masora Parva del Códice de Profetas de el Cairo: índice analítico. TECC 61: M 1997, Consejo Superior de Investigaciones Científicas xvi; 704 pp. 84-00-07648-6.

1226 *Bonilla A., Plutarco* ¿Mayusculas or minusculas?. RevBib 59 (1997) 33-43 [Isa 65,11-16].

1227 ᴱ**Cohen, Menachem** Miqra'ot gedolot ha-keter sefer yehoshua'—sefer shofetim. Miqra'ot Gedolot 'Haketer': Joshua—Judges: 1992, ⟹9,2587; 10,2474. ᴿJJS 48/1 (1997) 148-149 *(Lawee, Eric)*.

1228 *Freedman, David Noel* The earliest Bible < 1983 >;

1229 The symmetry of the Hebrew Bible < 1992 >. Divine Commitment 1. 1997, ⟹124. 341-349/496-520.

1230 *Gunn, David M.* What does the bible say?: a question of text and canon. Reading bibles. 1997, ⟹172. ᴱBeal, T., 242-261 [1 Sam 17].

1231 *Leiman, Sid Z.* Masorah and halakhah: a study in conflict. 1997, ⟹34. ᴹGREENBERG M., 291-306.

1232 *Lemmelijn, Bénédicte* What are we looking for in doing Old Testament text-critical research?. JNSL 23/2 (1997) 69-80.

1233 *Levoratti, A.J.* Las parábolas como ficciones poéticas: comentario de libros. RevBib 59/1 (1997) 45-61.

1234 **Metzger, Thérèse** Die Bibel von Meschullam. 1994, ⟹11/2,2513. BSOAS 60 (1997) 543-545 *(Zwiep, Irene E.)*.

1235  *Miller, Peter N.* Aux origines de la *Polyglotte* parisienne: *philolgia sacra*, contre-réforme et raison d'état. XVII<sup>e</sup> Siècle 49 (1997) 57-66 [EThL 74,165*].

1236  *Ognibeni, Bruno* Les listes marginales de la ʾ*oḵlah* de Halle. Res., sum. 371. Sef. 57 (1997) 97-126, 333-371.

1237  *Sanders, James A.* The task of text criticism. 1997, ⇒48. <sup>F</sup>Knierim R., 315-327.

1238  *Sanders, James A.; Beck, Astrid* The Leningrad Codex: rediscovering the oldest complete Hebrew Bible. BiRe 13/4 (1997) 32-41, 46.

1239  **Tov, Emanuel** Textual criticism of the Hebrew Bible. 1992, ⇒8,1761... 12,1010. <sup>R</sup>TJT 13/1 (1997) 94-95 *(Cox, Claude E.)*; ATG 60 (1997) 542-549 *(Torres, A.)*.

1240  *Tov, Emanuel* The scribes of the texts found in the Judean desert. Bibl.Interp. 28: 1997, ⇒77. <sup>F</sup>Sanders J., 131-152.

1241  **Tov, Emanuel** Der Text der Hebräischen Bibel: Handbuch der Textkritik. <sup>T</sup>*Fabry, Heinz-Josef*, (al.), Stu 1997 <1992>, Kohlhammer xxxiv; 376 pp. DM69. 3-17-013503-1 [RB 105,317].

1242  **Van der Kooij, Arie** Zum Verhältnis von Textkritik und Literarkritik: Überlegungen anhand einer Beispiele. Congress volume 1995. VT.S 66: 1997, ⇒323. <sup>E</sup>Emerton, J.A., 185-202 [Josh 20; 1 Sam 17; Jer 33].

1243  **Würthwein, Ernst** The text of the Old Testament. <sup>2</sup>1995, ⇒11/2,2529. <sup>R</sup>HebStud 38 (1997) 94-97 *(Pisano, Stephen)*.

## D2.2 Targum

1244  *Chilton, Bruce D.* Salvific exile in the Isaiah targum. Exile. JSJ.S 56: 1997, ⇒227. <sup>E</sup>Scott, James M., 239-247.

1245  *Kaufman, Stephen A.* On methodology in the study of the targums and their chronology. New Testament text. BiSe 44: 1997 <1985>, ⇒748. <sup>E</sup>Porter, S., 267-274.

1246  **Klein, Michael L.** Targumic manauscripts in the Cambridge Genizah collections. 1992, ⇒8,1769... 10,1407. <sup>R</sup>JNES 56 (1997) 210-211 *(Menn, Esther M.)*.

1247  *Klein, Michael L.* The Masorah to Onqelos: a reflection of targumic consciousness. HUCA 68 (1997) 63-75.

1248  **Posen, Rafael B.** The consistency of the Targum Onkelos' translation. Diss. Bar Ilan; <sup>D</sup>*Kasher, R.*: 1997, 385 pp. [RTL 29,581].

1249  *Shapiro, Marc* On Targum and tradition: J.J. Weinberg, Paul Kahle and Exodus 4:22 /22:4/. Henoch 19/2 (1997) 215-232.

1250  *Wilcox, Max* The promise of the 'seed' in the New Testament and the Targumim. New Testament text. BiSe 44: 1997 <1979>, ⇒748. <sup>E</sup>Porter, S., 275-293.

## D3.1 *Textus graecus*—Greek NT

1251  **Aland, Kurt** Konstantin von Tischendorf (1815-1874): neutestamentliche Textforschung damals und heute. SSAW 133/2: 1993, ⇒9,1465; 10,1416. <sup>R</sup>JThS 48 (1997) 228-231 *(Birdsall, J.N.)*;

1252 Kurzgefasste Liste der griechischen Handschriften des Neuen Testaments. ANTT 1: [2]1994 <1963>, ⇒10,1414. [R]NT 39 (1997) 85-87 *(Elliott, J.K.)*.

1253 [E]**Aland, Kurt; Rosenbaum, Hans-Udo** Kirchenväter-Papyri: Teil 1 Beschreibungen. Repertorium der griechischen christlichen Papyri. PTS 42: 1995, ⇒11/2,g053, 12,10801. [R]ThLZ 122 (1997) 157-158 *(Chadwick, Henry)*.

1254 **Blount, Brian K.** Cultural interpretation: reorienting NT criticism. 1995, ⇒11/2,1268. [R]ThTo 54/1 (1997) 98-102 *(Patte, Daniel)*; CBQ 59 (1997) 762-763 *(Malbon, Elizabeth Struthers)*.

1255 **Clarke, Kent D.** Textual optimism: a critique of the United Bible Societies' Greek New Testament. JSNT.S 138: Shf 1997, Academic 350 pp. Diss., £47.50/$70. 1-85075-649-X. Fil.Neotest. 10 (1997) 157-158 *(Black, David Alan)*.

1256 *Delobel, Joël* Focus on the 'Western' text in recent studies. EThL 73 (1997) 401-410.

1257 **Ehrman, Bart D.** The orthodox corruption of scripture: the effects of early christological controversies on the text of the NT. 1993, ⇒9,1569... 12,1033. [R]ChH 66/1 (1997) 81-83 *(Countryman, Louis William)*; SJTh 50 (1997) 506-507 *(Parker, D.C.)*.

1258 **Elliott, J.K.** Essays and studies in New Testament textual criticism. Estudios de Filología Neotestamentaria 3: 1992, ⇒8,239; 9,1521. [R]EstB 55 (1997) 123-124 *(Ibarzábal, S.)*.

1259 *Elliott, James Keith* The influence of the apocrypha on manuscripts of the New Testament. Sum. rés. 265. Apocrypha 8 (1997) 265-271.

1260 **Elliott, Keith** Manuscripts and the text of the New Testament: an introduction for English readers. 1995, ⇒11/2,2563; 12,1036. [R]NT 39 (1997) 89-90 *(Rodgers, Peter R.)*; CritRR 10 (1997) 175-176 *(Mullen, Roderic L.)*.

1261 *Epp, Eldon Jay* The International Greek New Testament Project: motivation and history. NT 39 (1997) 1-20.

1262 *Epp, Eldon Jay* Textual criticism in the exegesis of the New Testament, with an excursus on canon. Handbook. NTTS 25: 1997, ⇒971. [E]Porter, Stanley E., 45-97.

1263 **Greenlee, J. Harold** Introduction to New Testament textual criticism. [2]1995, ⇒11/2,2567. [R]TJT 13/2 (1997) 273-274 *(Racine, Jean-François)*.

1264 *Head, P.M.; :Warren, M.* Re-inking the pen: evidence from P.Oxy. 657 (P13) concerning unintentional scribal errors. NTS 43 (1997) 466-473.

1265 *Larson, Stan* The 26th edition of the Nestle-Aland Novum Testamentum graece: a limited examination of its apparatus <1981>;

1266 *MacKenzie, R. Sheldon* The Latin column in Codex Bezae <1980>. New Testament text. BiSe 44: 1997, ⇒748. [E]Porter, S., 92-104/52-65.

1267 **Metzger, Bruce M.** A textual commentary on the Greek New Testament. The Greek New Testament 4: [2]1994, ⇒10,1432; 11/2,2568. [R]ThRv 93 (1997) 20-23 *(Elliott, J.K.)*; SEÅ 62 (1997) 167-168 *(Kieffer, Rene)*.

1268 **Mullen, Roderic L.** The New Testament text of CYRIL of Jerusalem. SBL NT in the Greek Fathers 7: Atlanta, GA 1997, Scholars xiv; 431 pp. $39.95. 0-7885-0339-1.

1269 **O'Callaghan, José** Los primeros testimonios del Nuevo Testamento: papirologia neotestamentaria. 1995, ⇒11/2,2569; 12,1048. REstB 55 (1997) 409-413 *(Sánchez de Toca, M.)*; RTL 28 (1997) 537-538 *(Gryson, R.)*; RBBras 14 (1997) 358-359;

1270 Introducció a la crítica textual del Nou Testament. Collectio Paràbola 10: Barc 1997, Claret 128 pp. 84-8297-210-3. RFil.Neotest. 10 (1997) 158-162 *(Elliott, J.K.)*.

1271 EParker, D.C.; Amphoux, C.-B. Codex Bezae. NTTS 22: 1996, ⇒12,265. RThLZ 122 (1997) 674-675 *(Elliott, J.K.)*; VigChr 51 (1997) 327-328 *(Klijn, A.F.J.)*.

1272 *Parker, David* A 'dictation theory' of Codex Bezae. New Testament text. BiSe 44: 1997 <1982>, ⇒748. EPorter, S., 66-80.

1273 **Parker, David C.** The living text of the gospels. C 1997, CUP xvi; 224 pp. £35. 0-521-59062-0. RET 109 (1997-98) 65-67 *(Rodd, C.S.)*.

1274 **Passoni Dell'Acqua, A.** Il testo del NT. 1994, ⇒11/2,2571; 12,1054. RAmicizia Ebraico-Cristiana 32 (1997) 148-150 *(Carrara, Paolo)*.

1275 *Pickering, Stuart R.* Literary theory and the New Testament text. NTTRU 5 (1997) 81-98.

1276 *Ramaroson, Léonard* Mise en oeuvre de l'"électisme intégral": à propos de Jn 8,57 et de Lc 9,54-56. ScEs 49 (1997) 181-185.

1277 *Segalle, Giuseppe* Ridatare i vengeli?: novità e conferme. StPat 44 (1997) 99-112.

1278 *Skeat, T.C.* The oldest manuscript of the four gospels?. NTS 43 (1997) 1-34.

1279 **Swanson, Reuben J.** NT Greek manuscripts: variant readings arranged...against Codex Vaticanus. 1995-1996, 4 vols. ⇒12,152. RNT 39 (1997) 286-289 *(Elliott, J.K.)*.

1280 **Thiede, Carsten Peter; d'Ancona, Matthew** Témoin de Jésus: le papyrus d'Oxford et l'origine des évangiles. 1996, ⇒12,1063. RHokhma 66 (1997) 88-91 *(Decorvet, Jean)*.


D3.2 *Versiones graecae*—VT, Septuaginta etc.

1281 *Betz, Otto* Die Septuaginta: das Verhältnis von Übersetzung und Deutung. TVGMS 424: 1997, ⇒59. FMAIER G., 189-204.

1282 *Büchner, Dirk* Jewish commentaries and the Septuagint. JJS 48 (1997) 250-261.

1283 *Brottier, Laurence* L'obscurcissement du soleil en plein jour: quelques réflexions des pères commentateurs de la Septante des prophètes. VigChr 51 (1997) 339-358.

1284 *Chmiel, Jerzy* Biblią aleksandryjską po polsku? [La Bible d'Alexandrie en polonais?]. ACra (1997) 113-115. P.

1285 **Cimosa, Mario** Guida allo studio della Bibbia greca (LXX): storia—lingua—testi. 1995, ⇒11/2,2583; 12,1066. RBib. 78 (1997) 107-108 *(Harl, Marguerite)*; RivBib 45 (1997) 100-101 *(Rizzi, Giovanni)*; RHPhR 77 (1997) 193-194 *(Le Moigne, Philippe)*.

1286 *Cook, J.* The Septuagint between Judaism and Christianity. OTEs 10 (1997) 213-225;

1287 Aspects of the relationship between the Septuagint versions of Proverbs and Job. IX Congress IOSCS. SCSt 45: 1997, ⇒340. ETaylor, Bernard A., 309-328.

1288 **Dogniez, Cécile** Bibliography of the Septuagint / Bibliographie de la Septante (1970-1993). VT.S 60: 1995, ⇒11/2,2586; 12,1069. RJAOS 117 (1997) 373-374 *(Gentry, Peter J.)*.

1289 *Goldenberg, Robert* The Septuagint ban on cursing the gods. JSJ 28 (1997) 381-389 [Exod 22,27].

1290 *Greenspoon, L.* 'It's all Greek to me': Septuagint studies since 1968. CurResB 5 (1997) 147-174.

1291 **Heath, Dale E.** The Orthodox Septuagint. Lake City, Fla. 1997, Heath xi; 156 pp. Plus separate 'afterword' (10 pp.); sequel to *The scripture of St. Paul* [NThAR 1997,290].

1292 *Lamarche, Paul* The Septuagint: bible of the earliest christians. The bible in Greek christian antiquity. 1997 <c.1984>, ⇒177. ETBlowers, Paul M., 15-33,

1293 *Lust, J.* Tools for Septuagint studies. EThL 73 (1997) 215-221.

1294 *Martone, Corrado* I LXX e le attestazioni testuali ebraiche di Qumran. AnScR 2 (1997) 159-174.

1295 *Mélèze-Modrzejewski, Joseph, (al.),* Septuagina: libri sacri della diaspora giudaica e dei cristiani. AnScR 2 (1997) 141-173.

1296 *Modrzejewski, Joseph Mélèze* La Septante comme 'nomos': comment la torah est devenue une 'loi civique' pour les juifs de'Égypte. AnScR 2 (1997) 143-158.

1297 **Müller, Mogens** The first bible of the church: a plea for the Septuagint. JSOT.S 206: 1996, ⇒12,1075. RCritRR 10 (1997) 198-200 *(Powery, Emerson B.)*.

1298 *Norton, Gerard J.* Collecting data for a new edition of the fragments of the Hexapla. IX Congress IOSCS. SCSt 45: 1997, ⇒340. ETaylor, Bernard A., 251-262.

1299 *Passoni Dell'Acqua, Anna* Il testo biblico di Filone e i LXX. AnScR 2 (1997) 175-196.

1300 *Pietersma, Albert* A new English translation of the Septuagint. IX Congress IOSCS. SCSt 45: 1997, ⇒340. ETaylor, B.A., 177-187.

1301 *Raurell, Frederic* Il binomio 'santità' (ἁγιωσύνη) e 'gloria' (δόχα) di Dio nei LXX. Sum. 244. RCatT 22 (1997) 231-244.

1302 *Rofé, Alexander* The methods of late biblical scribes as evidenced by the Septuagint compared with the other textual witnesses. 1997, ⇒34. MGREENBERG M., 259-270.

1303 Septuaginta: libri sacri della diaspora giudaica e dei cristiani. Atti della II giornata di studio, 13 maggio 1997. AnScR 2 (1997) 141-207.

1304 **Tov, Emanuel** The text-critical use of the Septuagint in biblical research. Jerusalem Biblical Studies 8: J ²1997, Simor xxxv; 289 pp. $47. 965-242-008-9.

1305 *Trebolle Barrera, Julio* Mestizaje textual de la biblia en el Mediterráneo. La Bíblia i el Mediterrani. 1997, ⇒385. EBorrell, d'A., 11-40.

1306 *Troiani, Lucio* Gli autori giudaico-ellenistici e la Settanta. AnScR 2 (1997) 197-207.

1307 *Vian, Giovanni Maria* Le versioni greche della Scrittura nella polemica tra giudei e cristiani. Sum. 3. ASEs 14/1 (1997) 39-54.

## D4 Versiones orientales

1308 <sup>E</sup>**Avishur, Yitzhak** The oldest translation of the Early Prophets into Judaeo-Arabic: the text of Bodleian Manuscript Poc. 349 with an introduction and notes. Publications of the Hebr. Univ. Language Traditions Project 19: J 1995, Magnes 342 pp. 965-350-019-8 [JSSt 44,143s—Khan, Geoffrey].

1309 **Baarda, Tjitze** Essays on the Diatesseron. 1994, ⇒11/2,2604. <sup>R</sup>JThS 48 (1997) 657-659 *(Birdsall, J. Neville)*.

1310 *Bauer, Johannes B.* 'Westliche' Lesearten des Neuen Testaments im arabischen Sondergut des MAKARIOS/SYMEON. Studien zu Bibeltext. 1997 <1981>, ⇒111. 94-106.

1311 *Brock, Sebastian P.* What's in a word? an intriguing choice in the Syriac Diatessaron. JSOT.S 153: 1997, ⇒4. <sup>F</sup>ASHTON J., 180-187.

1312 *Cowe, S.P.* The theological mission of the holy translators. Saint Nersess theological review 1/1 (1996) 13-23.

1313 **Desreumaux, Alain** Codex sinaiticus Zosimi rescriptus: description codicologique des feuillets araméens melkites des manuscrits Schoyen 35, 36 et 37 (Londres - Oslo) comprenant l'édition de nouveaux passages des Évangiles et des Catéchèses de CYRILLE. Histoire du texte biblique 3: Lausanne 1997, Zèbre 207 pp. 2-9700088-3-1.

1314 **Dirksen, Piet B.** La Peshitta dell'Antico Testamento. 1993, ⇒9,1599...11/2,2606. <sup>R</sup>Protest. 52 (1997) 76-77 *(Costabel, B.)*.

1315 <sup>E</sup>**Dirksen, Piet B.; Van der Kooij, Arie** The Peshitta as a translation: papers read at the II Peshitta Symposium, held at Leiden, 19-21 August 1993. MPIL 8: 1995, ⇒11/1,76. <sup>R</sup>BiOr 54 (1997) 742-746 *(Wevers, John W<sup>M</sup>)*.

1316 **Joosse, Nanne Pieter** The Sermon on the Mount in the Arabic Diatessaron. Diss., <sup>D</sup>*Baarda, Tjitze*: Amst 1997, Centrale Huisdrukkerij VU. 90-901-0131-4 [NT 41,297ss—Sepmeijer, F.].

1317 *Joosten, Jan* La tradition syriaque des évangiles et la question du "substrat araméen". RHPhR 77 (1997) 257-272.

1318 **Kiraz, George Anton** Comparative edition of the Syriac gospels. NTTS 21/1-4: 1996, ⇒12,1090. <sup>R</sup>ThLZ 122 (1997) 913-915 *(Šuermann, Harald)*; Muséon 110 (1997) 471-472 *(Schmidt, A.B.)*.

1319 <sup>E</sup>**Müller-Kessler, Christa; Sokoloff, Michael** The christian Palestinian Aramaic Old Testament and Apocrypha versions from the early period. A Corpus of Christian Palestinian Aramaic 1: Groningen 1997, Styx (6) 324 pp. 90-5693-007-9.

1320 **Petersen, William, L.** TATIAN's Diatessaron: its creation, dissemination, significance, and history in scholarship. SVigChr 25: 1994, ⇒11/2,2612. <sup>R</sup>JThS 48 (1997) 649-657 *(Birdsall, J. Neville)*; CBQ 58 (1996) 166-168 *(Holmes, Michael W.)*.

1321 **Polliack, Meira** The Karaite tradition of Arabic Bible translation: a linguistic and exegetical study of Karaite translations of the pentateuch from the tenth and eleventh centuries C.E.. Études sur le judaïsme médiéval 17: Lei 1997, Brill xx; 338 pp. 90-04-10267-1.

1322 <sup>E</sup>**Prinzing, Günter; Schmidt, Andrea** Das Lemberger Evangeliar: eine wiederentdeckte armenische Bilderhandschrift des 12. Jahrhunderts. Sprachen und Kulturen des christlichen Orients 2: Wsb 1997, Reichert 186 pp. 29 pl; ill.; 3-88226-903-0 [NThAR 1998,336].

1323 **Schüssler, Karlheinz** Biblia Coptica: die koptischen Bibeltexte 2: das sahidische Alte und Neue Testament: sa 21-48. Wsb 1996, Harrassowitz Lieferung 2. DM88. 3-447-03782-2.

## D5.0 Versiones latinae

1324 *Catastini, Alessandro* Testo antiocheno e Vetus Latina: su alcune pubblicazioni recenti. Henoch 19/1 (1997) 81-93.

1325 *Cortesi, Mariarosa* Lorenzo VALLA, GEROLAMO e la Vulgata. Motivi letterari. 1997, ⇒331. EMoreschini, C., 269-289.

1326 **Dutton, Paul Edward; Kessler, Herbert L.** The poetry and paintings of the first bible of CHARLES the Bald. Recentiores: Ann Arbor 1997, Univ. of Michigan Press xii; 137 pp. $65. 0-472-10815-8 [ThD 46,66—Heiser, W. Charles].

1327 **Farr, Carol** The Book of Kells: its function and audience. British Library Studies in Medieval Culture: L 1997, British Library 196 pp. 8 col. pl.; 30 ill. [ChH 68,438—Fleming, Martha H.].

1328 EGameson, **Richard** The early medieval bible: its production, decoration, and use. 1994, ⇒10,1482... 12,1100. RStT 16/1 (1997) 95-97 *(Firth, Francis)*; ChH 66/1 (1997) 98-99 *(Countryman, Louis William)*.

1329 EGryson, **Roger** Esaias: Is 30,15-35,5; 35,5-39,8. VL 12/1: 1993-1994. Fasc. 9-10; Pars II, Fasc. 1-2. ⇒12,3322. RGn. 69 (1997) 74-75 *(Doignon, Jean)*;

1330 Esaias: Is 40,1-41,20. VL 12/2: 1993-1994. Fasc. 1-2. ⇒10,3448. RGn. 69/1 (1997) 74-75 *(Doignon, Jean)*.

1331 *Lozares, Angel Ibisate* Impresos complutenses del siglo XVI en la biblioteca del Seminario Diocesano de Vitoria: notas a "La Imprenta en Alcalá de Henares (1502-1600)" de Julián MARTIN Abad. ScrVict 44 (1997) 305-330.

1332 **Marsden, Richard** The text of the Old Testament in Anglo-Saxon England. CSASE 15: 1995, ⇒11/2,2645; 12,1103. RChH 66 (1997) 792-793 *(Madigan, Kevin)*.

1333 *Morano, Ciríaca* El influjo de las primeras traducciones latinas de la biblia en la cultura mediterránea. La Bíblia i el Mediterrani. 1997, EBorrell, d'Agustí. 39-52.

1334 *Tkacz, Catherine Brown* OVID, JEROME and the Vulgate. StPatr 33: 1997, ⇒351. ELivingstone, Elizabeth A., 378-382.

1335 Travaux du Centre de recherches sur la Bibel latine, Louvain-la-Neuve. BVLI 41 (1997) 25-30.

1336 Vetus Latina: Arbeitsbericht der Stiftung 41. Vetus Latina: Bericht des Instituts 30: FrB 1997, Herder 39 pp.

## D6 Versiones modernae .1 *romanicae,* romance

1337 *Alonso Schökel, Luis* José Maria VALVERDE y las traducciones biblico-litúrgicas. RF 1184 (1997) 647-653.

1338 **Alonso Schökel, Luis** Nuevo Testamento. Biblia del peregrino 3. 1996, ⇒12,1114. RThLZ 122 (1997) 1125-1126 *(Nagel, Walter)*.

1339 **Babut, Jean-Marc** Lire la bible en traduction. LiBi 113: P 1997, Cerf 167 pp. FF90. 2-20-405680-4 [EeV 107,119].

1340  *Barbieri, Edoardo* Panorama delle traduzioni bibliche in volgare prima del concilio di Trento 1. FolTh 8 (1997) 169-197.

1341  Bible pastorale. Turnhout ²1997, Brepols 1852 pp. Version établie par les moines de Maredsous. 2-503-50599-6.

1342  **Buzzetti, Carlo** Come scegliere le traduzioni della Bibbia. Leumann 1997, Elle Di Ci 72 pp. L8.000. 88-01-00760-4 [RivBib 45,255].

1343  Conferenza Episcopale Italiana. La Sacra Bibbia: Nuovo Testamento. Città del Vaticano 1997, Vaticana 654 pp. 88-209-2368-8 [RTL 29,130].

1344  *Leonardi, Lino* Volgarizzare la Bibbia nell'Italia medievale: notizie di una ricerca in corso (con appunti sull'*Apocalisse*). 'Tradurre la Bibbia', 1997, ⇒313. 85-135.

1345  *Leoni, Aron di Leone* New information on Yom Tob ATIAS (alias Alvaro Vargas), co-publisher of the Ferrara Bible. Res., sum. 276. Sef. 57 (1997) 271-276.

1346  Novo Testamento. Petrópolis 1997, Vozes 528 pp. Conf. Nacional dos Bispos do Brasil [REB 57,1007].

1347  Nuevo Testamento y Salmos. M 1997, Sociedad Bíblica 556 pp. [SalTer 87,440].

1348  EO'Callaghan, José Nuevo Testamento griego-español. BAC 574: M 1997, BAC xx; 1486 pp. 84-7914-271-5. RActBib 34 (1997) 36-37 *(Solé, Salvador)*; CDios 210 (1997) 639-641 *(Gutiérrez, J.)*.

1349  **Pérez Alonso, Mª** Isabel Contribución al estudio de los hebraísmos léxicos semánticos y morfosintácticos en la biblia medieval romanceada [Contribution to the study of lexical, semantic and morfosyntactic Hebraisms in *Biblia medieval romanceada*]. Sum. res. 11. MEAH.H 46 (1997) 11-22.

1350  ESchwartz, Marco Los relatos más bellos de la biblia. Pref. **Miret Magdalena, Enrique** Clásicos: M 1997, Temas de Hoy li; 169 pp. 84-7880-892-2.

1351  EScío de S. Miguel, Felipe Bíblia Americana San Jerónimo. Valencia 1994, Edicep 1861 pp. Revisada. REfMex 15/1 (1997) 112-113 *(Serraima Cirici, Enrique)*.

1352  *Selbach, Vanessa* La bible illustrée au XVIIᵉ siècle. XVIIᵉ Siècle 49 (1997) 69-92 [EThL 74,165*].


D6.2  *Versiones anglicae*—**English Bible Translations**

1353  **Allen, Ward S.; Jacobs, Edward C.** The coming of the King James gospels: a collation of the translators' work-in-progress. 1995, ⇒11/2,2678. RChH 66 (1997) 824-825 *(Danner,Dan G.)*.

1354  *Boitani, Piero* La Bibbia di San Giacomo e altre storie inglesi e americane: la King James Bible. 'Tradurre la Bibbia', 1997, ⇒313. 137-164.

1355  *Bradshaw, Christopher J.* John BALE and the use of English bible imagery. Reformation 2 (1997) 173-189.

1356  ECarroll, Robert P.; Prickett, Stephen The Bible: Authorized King James Version: introduction and notes. The world's classics: Oxf 1997, OUP. $16. 0-19-283099-6. RDSD 4 (1997) 354-356 *(Brooke, George J.)*.

1357  *Harris, J.W.* Inclusive language and the names of God in the latest English bible translations. PPBT 48 (1997) 207-217.

1358 *Hooker, Morna D.* TYNDALE's 'heretical' translation. Reformation 2 (1997) 127-142.

1359 *Hunter, C. Bruce* JEFFERSON's bible: cutting and pasting the good book. BiRe 13/1 (1997) 38-41, 46.

1360 *Jannetta, Mervyn* Good news from Stuttgart: a previously unrecorded copy of the 1526 Worms edition of William TYNDALE's New Testament translation. Reformation 2 (1997) 1-5.

1361 EKohlenberger III, Jōhn R. The parallel Apocrypha: Greek text, King James Version, Douay Old Testament, The Holy Bible by Ronald KNOX, Today's English Version, New Revised Standard Version, New American Bible, New Jerusalem Bible. NY 1997, OUP lix; 1188 pp. 0-19-528444-5.

1362 Lenker, Ursula Die Westsächsische Evangelienversion und die Perikopenordnungen im angelsächsischen England. Diss. MUS Texte und Untersuchungen zur Englischen Philologie 20: Mü 1997, Fink 548 pp. 3-7705-3185-X. RLJ 47/3-4 (1997) 236-237 *(Heinz, Andreas)*; RBen 107/3-4 (1997) 392-394 *(Bogaert, P.-M.)*.

1363 Lindberg, Conrad The earlier version of the Wycliffite Bible. Acta Universitatis Stockholmiensis. Stockholm Studies in English 87: Stockholm 1997, Almqvist & W 376 pp. Bibl.; edited from MS Christ Church 145. 91-22-01745-3.

1364 *Newman, B.M.* Features of poetry in the CEV;

1365 Focus on translators [CEV]. PPBT 48 (1997) 218-221/236-243.

1366 The New Testament and Psalms: an inclusive version. EGold, Victor R., *(al.)*, 1995, ⇒11/2,2684. RChM 111/1 (1997) 58-61 *(O'Brien, Peter)*.

1367 Remley, Paul G. Old English biblical verse: studies in Genesis, Exodus and Daniel. CSASE 16: 1996, ⇒12,1139. RKHÅ 97 (1997) 202-203 *(Härdelin, Alf)*.

1368 ERhodes, Erroll R.; Lupas, Liana The translators to the reader: the original preface of the King James Version of 1611 revisited. NY 1997, American Bible Society 85 pp.

1369 Sheeley, Steven M.; Nash, Robert N. The bible in English translation: an essential guide. Nv 1997, Abingdon 116 pp. $13. 0-687-00153-6 [RRT 1998/2,92].

1370 *Summerson, Henry* An English bible and other books belonging to HENRY IV. BJRL 79/1 (1997) 109-115.

1371 *Van Kampen, Kimberly* The bible in print in England before TYNDALE. Reformation 2 (1997) 111-126.

1372 *Westbrook, Vivienne* Richard TAVERNER revising TYNDALE. Reformation 2 (1997) 191-205.

1373 EWinter, David The way in New Testament: New Revised Standard Version. Introd., notes. Oxf 1997, OUP xviii; 313 pp. 0-19-107026-2 [NThAR 1999,225].

## D6.3 *Versiones germanicae*—Deutsche Bibelübersetzungen

1374 Dolcetti Corazza, Vittoria La bibbia gotica e i Bahuvrihi. Bibliotheca Germanica 5: Alessandria 1997, dell'Orso 148 pp. Bibl. 88-7694-300-5.

1375 Gute Nachricht Bibel: Altes und Neues Testament mit den Spätschriften des Alten Testaments (Deuterokanonische Schriften—

Apokryphen). Stu 1997, Deutsche Bibelgesellschaft 13; 1062; 439 pp. Rev. Fassung 1997 der 'Bibel in heutigem Deutsch'. 3-438-01642-7/2-3.

1376 **Hartmann, Martin; Jahr, Hannelore** Lutherbibel mit Bildern von Marc CHAGALL. Stu 1997, Deutsche Bibelgesellschaft 1308 + 46 pp. 72 pl. [LM 37/9,43—Jeziorowski, Jürgen].

1377 **Himmighöfer, Traudel** Die Zürcher Bibel bis zum Tode ZWINGLIS (1531). VIEG 154: 1995, ⇒11/2,2705. ᴿSCJ 28/1 (1997) 370-371 *(Wandel, Lee Palmer)*.

1378 ᴱ**Joerg, Urs; Hoffmann, David Marc** Die Bibel in der Schweiz: Ursprung und Geschichte. Basel 1997, Schweizerischen Bibelgesellschaft 352 pp. FS128. 3-7965-1004-3 [Bijdr. 58,358];

1379 La bible en Suisse: origines et histoire. Basel 1997, Schwabe 352 pp. publ. par la Société biblique suisse; 192 pl. FS128. 3-7965-1005-1 [ThLZ 124,378s—Kohler, Herbert].

1380 *Knoller, Alois* Die Kontroverse um Dominikus VON BRENTANOS Übersetzung des Neuen Testaments 1790-1794. Dominikus VON BRENTANO. 1997, ⇒178. ᴱBohlen, Reinhold, 121-204.

1381 **Köster, Uwe** Studien zu den katholischen deutschen Bibelübersetzungen im 16., 17. und 18. Jahrhundert. 1995, ⇒11/2,2706. ᴿThLZ 122 (1997) 1107-1108 *(Döring, Brigitte)*.

1382 ᵀ**Schade, Karl-Emil** Das Ole Testament: översett ut de uurtext. Ed. Arbeidskring 'Plattdüütsch in de Kark' in Nordelbien. Neumünster ³1997 <1995>, Wachholtz 936 pp. 3-529-04958-1 [DBAT 29,—Diebner, B.J.].

1383 *Schilling, Johannes* Martin LUTHERs deutsche Bibel. Zsfg. 45. Luther-Bulletin 6 (1997) 23-45.

1384 ᵀ**Weber, Emil** S Nöi Teschtamänt züritüütsch. Z 1997, Jordan 521 pp. 3-906561-34-8 [NThAR 1999,46].

1385 ᵀ**Wille, Friedrich** De Plattduitsche Baibel: et Aule Testament, de laten boiker, et Naie Testament. Einbeck 1997, Scheele 824 pp. [DBAT 29,262—Diebner, B.J.] [Acts 1,18-19].

### D6.4 Versiones nordicae *et variae*

1386 Sveto pismo Stare in Nove zaveze. Ljubljana 1997, Svetopisemska družba Slovenije 1952 pp. Slovenski standardni prevod iz izvirnih jezikov [Slovenian Bible—Slovenian Standard Version]. 961-6138-17-0.

1387 **Benyik, György** Ungarische Bibelübersetzungen. Szeged 1997, JATEPress 48 pp.

1388 **Den Hollander, A.A.** De nederlandse bijbelvertalingen 1522-1545 [Dutch translations of the Bible 1522-1545]. BBN 33: Nieuwkoop 1997, De Graaf xiv; 563 pp. ƒ250. 90-6004-430-4 [RHPhR 77,248].

1389 **Kades, Tharwat** Die arabischen Bibelübersetzungen im 19. Jahrhundert. SIGC 104: Fra 1997, Lang xiii; 238 pp. Bibl. 3-631-31865-0.

1390 **Koole, J.A.** Het Oude Testament in de NBG-vertaling 1951. 1996, ⇒12,1168. ᴿKeTh 48/2 (1997) 159 *(Woude, A.S. van der)*.

1391 ᴱ**Kronsteiner, Otto** Die Methodbibel 10: Handschriftenverzeichnis zu Band 1-9. Kritische Ausgaben altbulgarischer Texte: Salzburg

1997, Institut für Slawistik der Universität Salzburg 97 pp. [NT-hAR 1998,299].

1392 *Kucala, Marian* Modyfikacje frazeologii biblijnej [Modifications of biblical phraseology]. RoczHum 45/1 (1997) 49-59 Sum. [IAJS 45,225]. **P.**

1393 **Neudecker, Hannah** The Turkish bible translation by Yahya bin ʾIshak, also called Ḥaki (1659). Lei 1994, Oosters ix; 404 pp. RJQR 87 (1997) 378-379 *(Dankoff, Robert).*

1394 *Newman, Barclay* Revising the Malay bible. PPBT 48 (1997) 433-442.

1395 T**Romaniuk, Kazimierz** Pismo Swiete: Starego i Nowego Testamentu "Biblia Warszwsko-Praska". Wsz 1997, Towarzystwo Biblijne w Polsce 2400 pp. 83-85260-15-3.

1396 **Stachowski, Marek** Studien zum Wortschatz der jakutischen Übersetzung des Neuen Testaments. Kraków 1995, Enigma. RFolOr 33 (1997) 227-229 *(Pomorska, Marzanna).*

1397 Sveto pismo Stare in Nove zaveze. Ljubljana 1997, Svetopisemska družba Slovenije 1952 pp. Slovenski standardni prevod iz izvirnih jezikov [Slovenian Bible—Slovenian Standard Version]. 961-6138-17-0.

1398 Ukrainian Bible Society. New Testament... Kyiv (Ukraine) 1997, Bible Society 542 pp. 966-7136-04-3. **Ukrainian.**

1399 T**Wierød, Ole** Det nye Testamente. 1997, Alios 281 pp. DK150. RIXΘΥΣ 24/2 (1997) 81-85 *(Søvndal, Steen Frøjk).*

D7 *Problema vertentis*—Bible translation techniques

1400 *Ablondi, Alberto* La traposizione del linguaggio biblico in altre culture. 'Tradurre la Bibbia', 1997, ⇒313. 35-44.

1401 *Adair, James R.* "Literal" and "free" translations: a proposal for a more descriptive terminology. JNSL 23/1 (1997) 181-209 [Exod 3; 1 Sam 3].

1402 *Alonso Schökel, Luis* El factor estilístico en la traducción. Lecciones de teoría y prática de la traducción. Málaga 1997, Universidad 13-24.

1403 **Askani, Hans-Christoph** Das Problem der Übersetzung dargestellt an Franz ROSENZWEIG: die Methoden und Prinzipien der Rosenzweigschen und BUBER-Rosenzweigschen Übersetzungen. HUTh 35: Tü 1997, Mohr xvi; 388 pp. Bibl. 3-16-146624-17.

1404 *Bird, Phyllis A.* Translating sexist language as a theological and cultural problem. Missing persons. 1997 <1988>, ⇒114. 239-247.

1405 *Buzzetti, Carlo* Traduzioni bibliche: note tra teoria, prassi ed esempi. 'Tradurre la Bibbia', 1997, ⇒313. 45-73.

1406 *Cattrysse, Patrick* Audiovisual translation and new media. From one medium. 1997, ⇒233. ESoukup, Paul A., 67-88.

1407 *Clark, David J.* Macaronic scripture translation;
1408 Minority language status and attitudes towards bible translation. TPBT 48 (1997) 143-150/336-345.

1409 *Davenport, Glorianna* Stories as dynamic adaptive environments. From one medium. 1997, ⇒233. ESoukup, Paul A. 293-299.

1410 *De Benedetti, Paolo* Alcune considerazioni sulle versioni bibliche nella tradizione ebraica: uso liturgico, criteri letterari, risultati. 'Tradurre la Bibbia', 1997, ⇒313. 165-182.

1411 *Ellingworth, Paul* Text and translation: model and reality. Translating sensitive texts. 1997, ⇒231. ᴱSimms, Karl, 197-205.

1412 *Evans, J. Barrie* Does blood cry out?: considerations in generating the cognitive environment. JNSL 23/2 (1997) 129-141 [Gen 4,10].

1413 *Freedman, David Noel* Editing the editors: translation and elucidation of the text of the bible. Divine Commitment 1, 1997 <1993>, ⇒124. 521-545.

1414 *Goethals, Gregor* Multimedia images: Pʟᴀᴛᴏ's cave revisited. From one medium. 1997, ⇒233. ᴱSoukup, Paul A., 229-247.

1415 *González, Jennifer* Installation art: sacred places in secular spaces. From one medium. 1997, ⇒233. ᴱSoukup, Paul A., 181-195.

1416 *Gueunier, Nicole* Une traduction biblique peut-elle encore aujourd'hui être "littéraire"?. La Bible en littérature. 1997, ⇒315. ᴱBeaude, Pierre-Marie, 259-269.

1417 *Hermanson, Eric A.* The transliteration of New Testament proper names into Zulu. TPBT 48 (1997) 138-143.

1418 *Keen, Elizabeth* Telling the story in dance;

1419 *Lambert, José* Problems and challenges of translation in an age of new media and competing models. From one medium. 1997, ⇒233. ᴱSoukup, Paul A., 151-180/51-65.

1420 **Lederer, Marianne** La traduction aujourd'hui: le modèle interprétatif. P 1994, Hachette 224 pp. ᴿTPTR 48 (1997) 153-155 *(Lind, Sarah)*.

1421 *Loader, Jayne* Film language and communication: from Cecil B. Dᴇ Mɪʟʟᴇ to Martin Sᴄᴏʀᴄᴇsᴇ. From one medium. 1997, ⇒233. ᴱSoukup, Paul A., 197-213.

1422 *Loba Mkole, Jean-Claude* Les femmes congolaises et la traduction de la bible. RASM 7 (1997) 223-234.

1423 *Marín Heredia, F.* Traducción como problema. Carthaginensia 13 (1997) 39-50.

1424 *Mundhenk, N.A.* Translating 'Holy Spirit'. PPBT 48 (1997) 201-207.

1425 *Natoli, Salvatore* Traducibilità e intraducibilità di un testo. 'Tradurre la Bibbia', 1997, ⇒313. 17-33.

1426 **Nichols, Anthony Howard** Translating the bible: a critical analysis of E.A. Nɪᴅᴀ's theory of dynamic equivalence and its impact upon recent bible translations. Diss. Sheffield 1997, ᴰRogerson, J.W., Sum. TynB 50,159ss.

1427 *Nida, Eugene A.* Translating a text with a long and sensitive tradition. Translating sensitive texts. 1997, ⇒231. ᴱSimms, Karl, 189-196.

1428 *Paul, Toomas* Über die Entmythologisierung mancher anthropologischer Termini in den modernen Bibelübersetzungen. Engel und Dämonen. FARG 29: 1997, ⇒343. ᴱAhn, Gregor, 137-144.

1429 *Péter-Contesse, René* Traduction biblique et inculturation. Liturgie et culture. BEL.S 90: 1997, ⇒355. 181-194 [EThL 74,160*].

1430 *Pettus, Reg* Programming issues in multimedia design;

1431 *Shreve, Gregory M.* From sciptural to virtual: bible translation, hypercommunication, and virtual reality;

1432 *Soukup, Paul A.* Understanding audience understanding. From one medium. 1997, ⇒233. ᴱSoukup, P.A., 249-257/263-290/91-107.

1433 *Stähli, Hans-Peter* 'Gut deutsch geredet': Probleme der Bibel-übersetzung. WuD 24 (1997) 209-236.
1434 *Wendland, Ernst R.* A review of "relevance theory" in relation to bible translation in South-Central Africa, part II. JNSL 23/1 (1997) 83-108.
1435 *Werner, J. Ritter* Musical *Mimesis* for modern media. From one medium. 1997, ⇒233. ᴱSoukup, P.A., 221-227.

D8 *Concordantiae, lexica specialia*—Specialized dictionaries, synopses

1436 Concordância fiel do Novo Testamento 2: Portugês grego. São José dos Campos 1997, Fiel 849 pp. [RBBras 15,440].
1437 ᴱCross, Frank Leslie; Livingstone, Elizabeth A. The Oxford dictionary of the christian church. Oxf ³1997, OUP xxxvii; 1786 pp. $125/£70. 0-19-211655-X.
1438 Kiraz, George A. A computer-generated concordance to the Syriac NT. 1993, ⇒9,1601...11/2,2609. ᴿJAOS 117 (1997) 727-729 *(Sokoloff, Michael)*; ThLZ 122 (1997) 1122-1124 *(Juckel, Andreas)*.
1439 Kohlenberger, John R.; Goodrick, Edward W.; Swanson, James M. The Greek English concordance to the New Testament: with the New International Version. GR 1997, Zondervan xviii; 1131 pp. $40. 0-310-40220-4 [ThD 44,368—Heiser, W. Charles].
1440 Lasserre, Guy Synopse des lois du pentateuque. 1994, ⇒10,2283; 11/1,702. ᴿRBBras 14 (1997) 310-311.
1441 ᴱMcDarby, Nancy The Collegeville bible handbook. ColMn 1997, Liturgical 352 pp. $20.
1442 *Muraoka, Takamitsu* A new index to Hatch and Redpath. Sum. 276. EThL 73 (1997) 257-276.
1443 Orel, Vladimir E.; Stolbova, Olga V. Hamito-Semitic etymological dictionary: materials for a reconstruction. HO 18: 1995, ⇒11/2,6604; 12,8004. ᴿBASOR 60 (1997) 365-367 *(Kaye, A.S.)*.
1444 *Petersen, William L.* From JUSTIN to PEPYS: the history of the harmonized gospel tradition. StPat 30. 1997, ⇒351. ᴱLivingstone, Elizabeth A., 71-96.
1445 Pickering, D. Bibel Quiz: Fragen und Antworten. Stu 1997 Katholisches Bibelwerk 29 pp. [Diak. 29,354—Bee-Schroedter, Heike].
1446 Reuter, Rainer Synopse zu den Briefen des Neuen Testaments. Synopsis of the New Testament letters I: Kol., Eph;, II Thess. ARGU 5: Fra 1997, Lang 774 pp. £72. 3-63131-456-6 [NT 40,396—Elliott, J.K.].
1447 Rousseau, John J.; Arav, Rami Jesus and his world: an archaeological and cultural dictionary. 1995, ⇒11/2,799; 12,358. ᴿRExp 94 (1997) 138-139 *(Drinkard, Joel F. Jr.)*; EvQ 69 (1997) 348-349 *(Marshall, I. Howard)*.
1448 *Schweizer, Harald* Nochmals zu: KONKORDANZEN: zwei Fragen an ᴠᴀɴ Wɪᴇʀɪɴɢᴇɴ—BN 82 (1996) 21-26. ⇒12,3404. BN 86 (1997) 63-65.
1449 *Segal, Alan F.* Electronic echoes: using computer concordances for Bible study. BArR 23/6 (1997) 58-60, 74-75.
1450 Thoumieu, Marc Dizionario d'iconografia romanica. Ill. *Deney, F. Noël;* phot. *Zodiaque.* Mi 1997, Jaca 390 pp. 88-16-60206-6.
1451 *Tov, Emanuel* The accordance search program for the MT, LXX, and the CATSS database. BIOSCS 30 (1997) 36-44.

## IV. Exegesis generalis VT vel cum NT

### D9 Commentaries on the whole Bible or OT

1452   EAlonso Schökel, Luis Antiguo Testamento, poesia. Biblia del peregríno. Bilbao 1997, Mensajero 1150 pp. Edición de studio 2.

1453   EBischoff, Bernhard; Lapidge, Michael Biblical commentaries from the Canterbury school of THEODORE and HADRIAN. CSASE 10: 1994, ⇒10,14273*; 12,10982. RJEH 48/1 (1997) 145-148 *(Ward, Benedicta)*; HeyJ 38 (1997) 69-70 *(Stevenson, Jane)*; Spec. 72 (1997) 435-437 *(Matter, E. Ann)*; KHÅ 97 (1997) 197-198 *(Härdelin, Alf)*.

1454   EBrown, Raymond E.; Fitzmyer, Joseph A.; Murphy, Roland E. Nuovo grande commentario biblico. *EDalla Vecchia, Flavio; Segalla, Giuseppe; Vironda, Marco;* Pres. *Martini, Card. Carlo Maria*: Brescia 1997, Queriniana xlvi; 1938 pp. 88-399-0054-3. RHenoch 19 (1997) 379 *(Soggin, J. Alberto)*; EThL 73 (1997) 445-446 *(Neirynck, F.)*.

1455   McGrath, Alister E. The NIV Bible companion: a basic commentary on the Old and New Testaments. GR 1997, Zondervan 448 pp. Bibl. 0-310-20547-6 [NThAR 1998,98].

1456   ERavasi, Gianfranco Isaia—Geremia—Lamentazioni—Baruc. La bibbia per la famiglia 7: Mi 1997, Paoline 396 pp.

1457   Trapp, John A commentary on the Old and New Testaments. Eureka, Calif. 1997 <1856-1868>, Tanski 5 vols. $310 [CTJ 33,484s—Muller, Richard A.].

## V. Libri historici VT

### E1.1 Pentateuchus, Torah *Textus, commentarii*

1458   Boorer, Suzanne The promise of the land as oath. 1992, ⇒9,1729... 12,1235. RRStR 23/1 (1997) 22-31 *(Carr, David M.)*; BiOr 54 (1997) 168-171 *(Van Seters, John)*.

1459   EBorbone, Pier G. The Pentateuch. The Old Testament in Syriac: pt. 5. Concordance 1. Lei 1997, Brill xxvi; 976 pp. ƒ425/$250. 90-04-10664-2.

1460   Crüsemann, Frank Die Tora. 1992, ⇒8,2544*; 9,1730. RRStR 23/1 (1997) 22-31 *(Carr, David M.)*.

1461   TFox, Everett The five books of Moses...a new translation. The Schocken Bible 1: 1995, ⇒11/1,144; 12,1240. RAThR 79 (1997) 595-596 *(Wiggins, Steve A.)*.

1462   Georgeot, J.-M. La Tora. De Saint-Marc jusqu'à Tertullien 2.2: n.p. 1997, n.p. 288 pp.

1463   *Katz, Ben Zion* Judah HAHASID: three controversial commentaries. JBQ 25/1 (1997) 23-30.

1464 **Maori, Yeshayahu** The peshitta version of the pentateuch and early Jewish exegesis. 1995, ⇒11/1,148. <sup>R</sup>JJS 48 (1997) 383-384 *(Papoutsakis, Manolis)*; AJSR 22 (1997) 250-252 *(Lund, J.A.)*. **H.**

1465 <sup>TE</sup>**Pelcovitz, Raphael** ʿÔvadyā Ben-Yaʿaqov (Sforno): commentary on the Torah. Artscroll Mesorah: Brooklyn 1997, Mesorah xvi; 1027 pp. Transl., notes. 0-89906-268-7 [NThAR 2000,122].

1466 **Polliak, Meira** The Karaite tradition of Arabic bible translation: a linguistic and exegetical study of Karaite translations of the pentateuch from the tenth and eleventh centuries C.E. EJM 17: Lei 1997, Brill xx; 338 pp. [Tarb. 67/3,x—Blau, Joshua].

1467 Pentateuco: traducción y notas. Sagrada biblia. Pamplona 1997, EUNSA 934 pp. [EstTrin 32,438s—Vázquez Allegue, Jaime].

## ε1.2 *Pentateuchus* Introductio: Fontes JEDP

1468 **Ackermann, Dirck** August KLOSTERMANN und der Pentateuch: ein forschungsgeschichtlicher Beitrag zum Pentateuchproblem. Neukirchener Theologische Dissertationen und Habilitationen 14: Neuk 1997, Neuk ix; 251 pp. 3-7887-1639-8.

1469 *Cortese, Enzo* Tappe della formazione del sistema espiatorio "sacerdotale". RB 104 (1997) 338-353 [Num 28; 29; Lev 23].

1470 *Dempster, Stephen* An "extraordinary fact": torah and temple and the contours of the Hebrew canon. TynB 48 (1997) 23-56, 191-218.

1471 *Freedman, David Noel* Pentateuch. Divine Commitment 1. 1997 <1962>, ⇒124. 99-132.

1472 *Fritz, Volkmar* Das Geschichtsverständnis der Priesterschrift. Studien zur Literatur. 1997 <1987>, ⇒126. 67-81;

1473 Die Konzeption der priesterschriftlichen Sinaierzählung und die Frage nach ihrem Verfasser. Studien zur Literatur. 1997 <1977>, ⇒126. 83-94.

1474 **Gleßmer, Uwe** Einleitung in die Targume zum Pentateuch. TSAJ 48: 1995, ⇒11/1,155. <sup>R</sup>JJS 48/1 (1997) 160-162 *(Hayward, Robert)*; ThLZ 122/6 (1997) 549-552 *(Bartelmus, Rüdiger)*.

1475 *Gosse, Bernard* Les premiers chapitres du livre de l'Exode et l'unification de la rédaction du Pentateuque. BN 86 (1997) 31-35.

1476 **Hiebert, Theodore** The Yahwist's landscape: nature and religion in early Israel. 1996, ⇒12,1266. <sup>R</sup>ThTo 54/1 (1997) 138-139 *(Lemke, Werner E.)*; JThS 48 (1997) 555-559 *(Dell, Katharine J.)*; CBQ 59 (1997) 541-542 *(Wiggins, Steve A.)*.

1477 **Kugel, James L.** The Bible as it was. CMA 1997, Harvard University Press xvii (2); 680 pp. Bibl. $35. 0-674-06940-4.

1478 **Levin, Christoph** Der Jahwist. FRLANT 157: 1993, ⇒9,1747... 12,1274. <sup>R</sup>RStR 23/1 (1997) 22-31 *(Carr, David M.)*.

1479 *Lohfink, Norbert* Arbeitswoche und Sabbat in der Priesterlichen Geschichtserzählung. BiKi 52 (1997) 110-118.

1480 **Lopes Cardozo, Nathan T.** The written and oral torah. Northvale 1997, Aronson xviii; 284 pp. Bibl. 0-7657-5989-6 [NThAR 1998,269 ].

1481 *Minette de Tillesse, Caetano* Sacerdotal—'P'. RBB 14/1-3 (1997) 31-40.

1482 **Mullen, Everett Theodore, Jr.** Ethnic myths and pentateuchal foundations: a new approach to the formation of the pentateuch.

SBL Semeia Studies 35: Atlanta, GA 1997, Scholars xi; 350 pp. Bibl. $35. 0-7885-0382-0.

1483 *Otto, Eckart* Forschung zur Priesterschrift. ThR 62 (1997) 1-50.

1484 **Owczarek, Susanne** Die Vorstellung vom Wohnen Gottes inmitten seines Volkes in der Priesterschrift: zur Heiligtumstheologie der priesterlichen Grundschrift. Diss. Erlangen-Nürnberg 1996-1997, ᴰ*Schmitt, H.-Ch.* [ThLZ 122,761].

1485 *Rendtorff, Rolf* Directions in pentateuchal studies. CurResB 5 (1997) 43-65.

1486 *Sacchi, Paolo* Il pentateuco, il deuteronomista e SPINOZA. Nuova Umanità 19 (1997) 571-589.

1487 **Schmidt, Ludwig** Studien zur Priesterschrift. BZAW 214: 1993, ⇒9,1754... 11/1,164. ᴿBZ 41 (1997) 112-114 *(Scharbert, Josef)*.

1488 **Van Seters, John** Prologue to history: the Yahwist as historian in Genesis. 1992, ⇒8,1977...11/1,170. ᴿRStR 23/1 (1997) 22-31 *(Carr, David M.)*; JNES 56 (1997) 149-150 *(Holloway, S.W.)*.

1489 *Van Seters, John* The deuteronomistic redaction of the pentateuch: the case against it. BEThL 133: 1997, ⇒17. ᶠBREKELMANS C., 301-319.

1490 **Whybray, R. Norman** Introduction to the Pentateuch. 1995, ⇒11/1,171; 12,1294. ᴿKerux 12/3 (1997) 35-49 *(Irons, Misty)*; RSR 85 (1997) 278-279 *(Gibert, Pierre)*.

1491 **Wynn-Williams, Damian J.** The state of the pentateuch: a comparison of the approaches of M. NOTH and E. BLUM. BZAW 249: B 1997, De Gruyter xi; 263 pp. Bibl. DM168. 3-11-015397-1.

1492 *Zenger, Erich* Priesterschrift. TRE 27. 1997, ⇒419. 435-446.

## E1.3 *Pentateuchus,* themata

1493 *Ausloos, Hans Les extrêmes se touchent...* proto-Deuteronomic and simili-Deuteronomistic elements in Genesis-Numbers, BEThL 133: 1997, ⇒17. ᶠBREKELMANS C., 341-366.

1494 *Böhl, Felix* On the interpretation of names in the targums of the pentateuch and in midrash. JSQ 4/2 (1997) 145-168.

1495 *Cohen, Naomi G.* The names of the separate books of the pentateuch in PHILO's writings. StPhilo 9 (1997) 54-78.

1496 *Dulk, Maarten den* TER LINDEN: een bijbels-theologische tussenstand. PrakTh 24 (1997) 501-514.

1497 **Jaroslavskij, Emeljan** La Bibbia per i credenti e non credenti. Studi e documenti: Mi 1997, Teti 300 pp.

1498 *Kamesar, Adam* The literary genres of the pentateuch as seen from the Greek perspective: the testimony of PHILO of Alexandria. StPhilo 9 (1997) 143-189.

1499 **Longhi, Mauro** La dottrina del pentateuco sulla creazione in S. IRENEO. Diss. Athenaeum Sanctae Crucis, ᴰ*Galván, Joseph Maria*: Roma 1997, 379 pp.

1500 **Murphy, Roland Edmund** Responses to 101 questions on the biblical torah: reflections on the pentateuch. 1996, ⇒12,1303. ᴿScrTh 29 (1997) 928-929 *(Jarne, J.)*.

1501 **Pröbstl, Volker** Nehemia 9, Psalm 106 und Ps 136 und die Rezeption des Pentateuchs. Diss. Erlangen 1997, ᴰ*Schmidt, L.* [ThLZ 122,761].

E1.4 **Genesis;** *textus, commentarii*

1502 **Armstrong, Karen** Εν Αρχή, Μια νέα ερμηνεία του Βιβλίου της Γενέσεως [In the beginning: a new interpretation of the book of Genesis]. ᵀ*Mpekridake, Dem.:* 1996, Philistor [DBM 18,136—Agourides, S.].

1503 *Brottier, Laurence* Remarques sur trois témoins des sermons *Sur la Genèse* de Jean CHRYSOSTOME: (*Monacensis Gr.* 352, *Sinaiticus Gr.* 376, *Parisinus Gr.* 775). Sum. RHT 27 (1997) 223-237.

1504 ᴱ**Croatto, J. Severino** Exilio y sobrevivencia: traiciones contraculturales en el pentateuco (comentario de Génesis 4:1-12:9). BA 1997, Lumen 463 pp. 950-724-663-0. ᴿRevBib 59 (1997) 238-241 *(Ricciardi, Alberto)*.

1505 **Donnet-Guez, B.** Légendes et commentaires sur la Genèse. La Varenne 1996, Vera Pax 247 pp. 2-9508095-1-0.

1506 *Gorman, Michael* The commentary on Genesis of CLAUDIUS of Turin and biblical studies under LOUIS the Pious. Spec. 72 (1997) 279-329;

1507 A critique of BISCHOFF's theory of Irish exegesis: the commentary on Genesis in Munich Clm 6302 (Wendepunkte 2). Journal of Medieval Latin 7 (1997) 178-233;

1508 The Visigothic commentary on Genesis in Autun 27 (S.29). RechAug 30 (1997) 167-239.

1509 **Gunkel, Hermann** Genesis. ᵀ*Biddle, Mark E.;* Foreword *Nicholson, Ernest W.*: Mercer Library of Biblical Studies: Macon 1997, Mercer Univ. Press 478 pp. $60. 0-86554-517-0.

1510 *Haar Romeny, R.B. ter* EUSEBIUS of Emesa's commentary on Genesis and the origins of the Antiochene school. The book of Genesis. 1997, ⇒196. ᴱFrishman, Judith, 125-142;

1511 A Syrian in Greek dress: the use of Greek, Hebrew and Syriac biblical texts in EUSEBIUS of Emesa's Commentary on Genesis. Traditio exegetica graeca 6: Lovanii 1997, Peeters xii; 484 pp. Bibl. FB2.400. 90-6831-958-2.

1512 **Halevi, Shira** The life story of Adam and Havah: a new targum of Genesis 1:26-5:5. Northvale, NJ 1997, Aronson ix; 315 pp. Bibl. 0-7657-5962-4.

1513 **Hamilton, Victor P.** The book of Genesis: chapters 18-50. NIC.OT: 1995, ⇒11/1,196; 12,1318. ᴿScrB 27 (1997) 35-37 *(Corley, Jeremy)*; OTEs 10 (1997) 358-359 *(Van Tonder, C.A.P.)*; CBQ 59 (1997) 540-541 *(Hendel, Ronald S.)*; HebStud 38 (1997) 110-113 *(Moberly, Walter R.W.L.)*; RBBras 14 (1997) 314-315.

1514 *Kruisheer, Dirk* Reconstructing JACOB of Edessa's scholia;

1515 *Mathews, Edward G. Jr.* The Armenian commentary on Genesis attributed to EPHREM the Syrian. The book of Genesis. 1997, ⇒196. ᴱFrishman, Judith, 187-196/143-161.

1516 **Mathews, Kenneth A.** Genesis 1-11. NAC 1A: 1995, ⇒12,1327. ᴿHebStud 38 (1997) 108-110 *(Nicol, George G.)*.

1517 *May, Gerhard* MARCIONS Genesisauslegung und die "Antithesen". BZNW 85: 1997, ⇒105. ᶠWICKERT U., 189-198.

1518 Genesis, 1 Mikra᾽ot gedolot 'haketer': a revised and augmented scientific ed. of 'Mikra᾽ot gedolot' based on the Aleppo Codex and early medieval mss. Ramat-Gan 1997, Bar-Ilan University Press 46, 250 pp. 965-266-202-1f [NThAR 1999,253]. **H.**

1519 *Molenberg, Corrie* Išoʿ bar NUN and ISHOʿDAD of Merv on the book of Genesis: a study of their interrelationship. The book of Genesis. 1997, ⇒196. ᴱFrishman, Judith, 197-228.
1520 *Nestingen, James Arne* LUTHER in front of the text: the Genesis commentary. Adapted by *Maschke, Timothy H.*: Luther Digest 5 (1997) 21-23.
1521 **Petit, Françoise** La chaîne sur la Genèse: chapîtres 1 à 3. 1991, ⇒7,1728... 10,1626. ᴿJThS 48 (1997) 284-286 *(Parvis, P.M.)*.
1522 *Rogerson, J.W.* Genesis 1-11. CurResB 5 (1997) 67-90.
1523 ᵀ**Rottzoll, Dirk U.** Abraham IBN ESRAS Kommentar zur Urgeschichte: mit einem Anhang: RASCHBAMSS Kommentar zum ersten Kapitel der Urgeschichte. SJ 15: 1996, ⇒12,1333. ᴿThLZ 122 (1997) 251-252 *(Schreiner, Stefan)*;
1524 Rabbinischer Kommentar zum Buch Genesis. 1994, ⇒10,1629; 11/1,210. ᴿETR 72/1 (1997) 134-135 *(Bauks, Michaela)*.
1525 **Rösel, Martin** Übersetzung als Vollendung der Auslegung: Studien zur Genesis Septuaginta. Diss. BZAW 223: 1994, ⇒10,1551... 12,1334. ᴿETR 72/3 (1997) 456-458 *(Bauks, Michaela)*; ThRv 93 (1997) 216-217 *(Schenker,Adrian)*; BiOr 54 (1997) 456-459 *(Van der Kooij, Arie)*.
1526 *Salvesen, Alison* Hexaplaric readings in ISHOʿDAD of Merv's commentary on Genesis. The book of Genesis. 1997, ⇒196. ᴱFrishman, Judith, 229-252.
1527 ᴱ**Savoca, Gaetano** Traduzione interlineare della Genesi sul testo della BHS. ᵀ*Di Marco, A. Salvatore*: 1995, ⇒11/1,213; 12,1336. ᴿRivBib 45 (1997) 87-88 *(Scippa, Vincenzo)*.
1528 **Seebaß, Horst** Genesis 1: Urgeschichte (1,1-11,26). 1996, ⇒12,1408. ᴿHenoch 19 (1997) 233-236 *(Soggin, J.A.)*;
1529 Genesis II: Vätergeschichte 1 (11,27-22,24). Neuk 1997, Neuk v; 222 pp. 3-7887-1526-X [EThL 74,192*].
1530 **Soggin, J. Alberto** Das Buch Genesis: Kommentar. Da:Wiss 1997, xv; 604 pp. DM178. 3-534-12276-3. ᴿRBBras 14 (1997) 312-313.
1531 **Van Wolde, Ellen** Words become worlds: semantic studies of Genesis 1-11. 1994, ⇒10,1692; 12,1361. ᴿJBL 115 (1996) 333-335 *(Mainelli, Helen Kenik)*.
1532 *Weber, Dorothea Communis loquendi consuetudo*: zur Struktur von AUGUSTINUS, *De Genesi contra Manichaeos*. StPatr 33: 1997, ⇒351. ᴱLivingstone, E.A., 274-279.
1533 *Weitenberg, J.J.S.* EUSEBIUS of Emesa and Armenian translations. The book of Genesis. 1997, ⇒196. ᴱFrishman, Judith, 163-170.
1534 **Wenham, Gordon J.** Genesis 16-50. WBC 2: 1994, ⇒10,1635; 12,1340. ᴿJThS 48 (1997) 147-150 *(Houston, Walter J.)*; VT 47 (1997) 572-573 *(Harland, P.J.)*.

ᴇ1.5 *Genesis*, **topics**

1535 **Armstrong, Karen** In the beginning: a new interpretation of Genesis. 1996, ⇒12,1342. ᴿDoLi 47 (1997) 314-315 *(McCarthy, Carmel)*.
1536 *Brottier, Laurence* Les huit sermons *Sur la Genèse* de Jean CHRYSOSTOME: les apports d'une nouvelle édition. StPatr 29: 1997, ⇒351. ᴱLivingstone, Elizabeth A., 439-450.

1537 **Carr, David McClain** Reading the fractures of Genesis: historical and literary approaches. 1996, ⇒12,1345. RZAW 109 (1997) 299-300 *(Schmitt, H.-C.)*; JThS 48 (1997) 549-551 *(Lipton, Diana)*.

1538 *Craven, Toni* Women in Genesis. BiTod 35 (1997) 32-39.

1539 **Feuillet, André** Histoire du salut de l'humanité d'après les premiers chapitres de la Genèse. 1995, ⇒11/1,224. RDivinitas 40/2 (1997) 179-181 *(Vibrac, Dominique)*.

1540 *Freedman, David Noel* Notes on Genesis. Divine Commitment 1. 1997 <1953>, ⇒124. 3-7.

1541 *Frishman, Judith* Themes on Genesis 1-5 in early East-Syrian exegesis. The book of Genesis. 1997, ⇒196. EFrishman, Judith, 171-186.

1542 **Gelander, Shamai** The good Creator: literature and theology in Genesis 1-11. SFSHJ 147: Atlanta, GA 1997 Scholars v; 140 pp. 0-7885-0343-X.

1543 *Glaser, Ida J.* Qur'anic challenges for Genesis. JSOT 75 (1997) 3-19.

1544 EGomez-Acebo, Isabel Relectura del Génesis. Bilbao 1997, DDB 266 pp. 84-330-1247-97 [Mayéutica 24,250—Lozano, Renée].

1545 THayward, C.T.R. JEROME's *Hebrew questions on Genesis*. 1995, ⇒11/1,225; 12,1350. RJSSt 42 (1997) 160-162 *(VanderKam, James C.)*.

1546 **Hess, Richard S.** Studies in the personal names of Genesis 1-11. AOAT 234: 1993, ⇒9,5715. RBiOr 54/3-4 (1997) 435-437 *(Blum, Erhard)*.

1547 EHess, Richard S.; Tsumura, David Toshio Studied inscriptions from before the Flood—ancient Near Eastern, literary, and linguistic approaches to Genesis 1-11. 1994, ⇒10,1727. RAUSS 35 (1997) 280-282 *(Dybdahl, Jon L.)*.

1548 *Hopkins, David C.* The first stories of Genesis and the rhythm of the generations. BJSt 313: 1997, ⇒85. FSILBERMAN L., 25-41.

1549 **Houziaux, Alain** Le tohu-bohu, le serpent et le bon Dieu. Préf. *Tournier, Michel:* P 1997, Presses de la Renaissance 197 pp. FF99. 2-85616-682-2 [RHPhR 77,250].

1550 **Jalevi, Shira** The life story of Adam and Havah: a new targum of Genesis 1:26-5:5. Northvale, NJ 1997 Aronson ix; 315 pp. 0-7657-5962-4 [NThAR 1997,258].

1551 **Jędrzejewski, Sylwester** U korzeni zła: Rdz 1-11 w interpretacij apokaliptyki żydowskiej. Lublin 1997, KUL 192 pp. 83-228-0485-7. RRBL 50 (1997) 226-227 *(Kondracki, Andrzej)*.

1552 *Lenchak, Timothy A.* Israel's refugee ancestors. BiTod 35 (1997) 11-15.

1553 *MacKeown, James* The theme of land in Genesis 1-11 and its significance for the Abraham narrative. IBSt 19 (1997) 51-64, 133-144.

1554 *O'Loughlin, Thomas* ISIDORE's use of GREGORY the Great in the exegesis of Genesis. RBen 107 (1997) 263-269.

1555 **Pelikan, Jaroslav** What has Athens to do with Jerusalem?: Timaeus and Genesis in counterpoint. The Jerome Lectures 21: Ann Arbor, MI 1997, University of Michigan Press xvi; 139 pp. Bibl. 0-472-10807-7.

1556 *Pfeffer, Georg* Brüder, Väter, Gatten: Verwandschaft in der Genesis. Anthr. 91 (1996) 153-167.

1557 **Pitzele, Peter** Our fathers' wells: a personal encounter with the myths of Genesis. 1995, ⇒11/1,289; 12,1449. ᴿCrossCur 47/2 (1997) 256-259 *(Ostriker, Alicia)*.

1558 **Rosenblatt, Naomi H.** Wrestling with angels: what Genesis teaches us about our spiritual identity: sexuality and personal relationships. Delta 1997 <1995>, NY xxiv; 388 pp. [Synaxis 16/1,318—Minissale, Antonino].

1559 *Rummel, Stan* The ninth day: to say "creation" in Genesis 1:1-11:26. ꟳKɴɪᴇʀɪᴍ R., 1997, ⇒48. 295-314.

1560 **Steinberg, Naomi** Kinship and marriage in Genesis: a household economic perspective. 1993, ⇒9,1799; 11/1,1799. ᴿTJT 13/1 (1997) 92-93 *(Isaac, Jacqueline R.)*.

1561 **Stephenson, Virginia** Genesis, awakening from the dream. Lakewood, Co. ²1997 Acropolis viii; 105 pp. 1-889051-18-7 [NThAR 1998,99].

ᴇ1.6 **Creatio**, *Genesis 1s*

1562 *Albrecht, Ralf* Das Ende der neueren Urkundenhypothese—zur Einheit der Schöpfungsgeschichte der Genesis. TVGMS 424: 1997, ⇒59. ꟳMᴀɪᴇʀ G., 133-146.

1563 Der Allmächtige: Annäherung an ein umstrittenes Gottesprädikat. BTSP 13: Gö 1997, Vandenhoeck & R 152 pp. 3-525-61352-0.

1564 *Altner, Günter* Schöpfung als Prozeß—Gott im Geschehen der Welt. Der Allmächtige. 1997, ⇒1563. 68-96.

1565 ᴱ**Amand de Mendieta, Emmanuel; Rudberg, Stig Y.** Bᴀsɪʟɪᴜs Caesariensis: Homilien zum Hexaemeron: homiliae in Hexaemeron. GCS N.F. 2: B 1997, Akademie xix; (2) 235 pp. $55. 3-05-0020002-4.

1566 *Amit, Yairah* Creation and the calendar of holiness. 1997, ⇒34. ᴹGʀᴇᴇɴʙᴇʀɢ M., 13*-29*. **H.**

1567 *Angerstorfer, Andreas* Ebenbild eines Gottes in babylonischen und assyrischen Keilschrifttexten. BN 88 (1997) 47-58 [Gen 1,26-27].

1568 *Argarate, Pablo* El hombre creado a la imagen y semejanza de Dios en San Mᴀxɪᴍᴏ el Confesor. Communio 30/2-3 (1997) 189-219 [Gen 1,26-27].

1569 **Arteaga Natividad, Rodolfo** La creación en los comentarios de San Aɢᴜsᴛɪɴ al Génesis. 1994, ⇒10,1658; 11/1,238. ᴿIsidorianum 6 (1997) 264-266 *(Leal Lobón, Manuel)*; Augustinus 42 (1997) 142-143 *(Calvo Madrid, Teodoro)*.

1570 *Bach, Alice* Out of the garden and into the mall: Eve's journey from Eden to MTV. From one medium. 1997, ⇒233. ᴱŠoukup, Paul A., 215-220.

1571 **Bauks, Michaela** Die Welt am Anfang: zum Verhältnis von Vorwelt und Weltentstehung in Gen 1 und in der altorientalischen Literatur. WMANT 74: Neuk 1997, Neuk xii; 362 pp. DM138. 3-7887-1619-3 [ETR 72/3 (1997) 496].

1572 *Beauchamp, Paul* 'E fu sera e fu mattina' (Gen 1,1-2,4a). PSV 36 (1997) 25-36.

1573 *Bird, Phyllis A.* 'Male and female He created them': Genesis 1:27b in the context of the priestly account of creation. Missing persons. 1997 <1981>, ⇒114. 123-154.

1574 **Brown, William P.** Structure, role, and ideology in the Hebrew and Greek texts of Genesis 1:1-2:3. SBL.DS 132: 1993, ⇒9,1810 ... 11/1,246. RJBL 116 (1997) 530-532 *(Endres, John C.)*.

1575 **Carmichael, Calum M.** The story of creation: its origin and its interpretation in PHILO and the fourth Gospel. 1996, ⇒12,1373. RJJS 48 (1997) 368-369 *(Mendelson, Alan)*.

1576 *Carreira das Neves, Joaquim* Hermenêuticas fundamentalistas e esotéricas das origens bíblicas;

1577 *Carvalho, Maria Manuela de* Teologia da criação. As origens da vida. 1997, ⇒344. 161-196/197-211.

1578 **Clifford, Richard J.** Creation accounts in the ancient Near East and in the bible. CBQ.MS 26: 1994, ⇒10,1721*. RBibl.Interp. 5 (1997) 283-284 *(Davila, James R.)*; RivBib 45 (1997) 355-356 *(Minissale, Antonino)*; JQR 87 (1997) 412-415 *(Hurowitz, Victor Avigdor)*.

1579 Genesi 2 e la storia della sua interpretazione. ASEs 13/2: Bo 1997, EDB 457-742 pp. L46.000 [RivBib 45,255].

1580 *Goff, Matthew* Alliteration and the sacred: a study of 'be fertile and increase'. HeyJ 38 (1997) 413-425 [Gen 1,22].

1581 **Görg, Manfred** Nilgans und Heiliger Geist: Bilder der Schöpfung in Israel und Ägypten. Dü 1997, Patmos 170 pp. 3-491-77023-8.

1582 *Gultom, Parlaungan* A taxonomy of approaches of five representative scholars of the creation stories in the Old Testament in the light of Genesis 1-2. Stulos 5 (1997) 1-16 [EThL 74,192*].

1583 EGunton, Colin E. The doctrine of creation. E 1997, Clark vi; 180 pp. £19. 0-567-08588-0 [RRT 1998/1,89].

1584 **Heller, Karin** Et couple il les créa. LiBi 112: P 1997, Cerf 203 pp. FF100. 2-204-05667-7 [FV 97/2,—Arnold, Matthieu].

1585 *Hirth, Volkmar* Zu Tradition und Redaktion in Gen 2,10-14. ZAW 109 (1997) 612-613.

1586 *Hoping, Helmut* Creatio ex nihilo: von der Bedeutung einer schwierigen Unterscheidung für den Begriff des Monotheismus. JBTh 12 (1997) 291-307.

1587 *Jenni, Ernst* Erwägungen zu Gen 1,1 'am Anfang'. Studien zur Sprachwelt. 1997 <1989>, ⇒138. 141-149.

1588 **Laffey, Alice L.** Appreciating God's creation through scripture. Illumination Books: NY 1997, Paulist vi; 76 pp. 0-8091-3714-3.

1589 **Lobay, Roman** The homilies on the Hexaemeron and the biblical exegesis of St. BASIL the Great. Toronto 1997, 93 pp. Diss. excerpt Pont. Institutum Orientale.

1590 **Löning, Karl; Zenger, Erich** Als Anfang schuf Gott: biblische Schöpfungstheologien. Dü 1997, Patmos 254 pp. DM34.80 [BiLi 71,373—Roloff, Jürgen].

1591 **Louyot, Yves** L'homme clefs en mains: relecture pédagogique des sept jours de la Genèse. 1995 <1890>, ⇒11/1,262. RRTL 28 (1997) 112-113 *(Wénin, André)*.

1592 **Maranesi, Pietro** Verbum inspiratum, chiave ermeneutica dell'Hexaëmeron di San BONAVENTURA. BSC 51: 1996, ⇒12,1390. RCFr 67/1-2 (1997) 301-303 *(Blanco, Francisco C.)*; AFH 90 (1997) 358-361 *(Faes de Mottoni, B.)*.

1593 *Martínez de Pisón Liébanas, Ramón* Vocación esencial del ser humano (Gen 1-2). RelCult 43/1 (1997) 91-105.

1594 **Martínez de Pisón, Ramón** Création et liberté: essai d'anthropologie chrétienne. Brèches Théologiques 25: Montréal 1997, Médiaspaul 192 pp. [SR 27,97—Perron, Louis].

1595 [T]**Martin, Christopher F.J.** Robert GROSSETESTE: on the six days of creation: a translation of the *Hexaëmeron*. ABMA 6/2: 1996, ⇒12,1391. [R]RThPh 129 (1997) 288-289 *(Borel, Jean)*.

1596 *Martínez Camino, Juan A.* El hombre, social 'a imagen de Dios'. EE 72 (1997) 469-488 [Gen 1,26-27].

1597 *Minette de Tillesse, Caetano* Hino da criação (Gn 1,1-2,4a). RBB 14/1-3 (1997) 41-64.

1598 **Moss, Harry Walter** The book of the few: a secular interpretation of biblical creation. San Luis Obispo 1997, New Times 67 pp. [NThAR 1998,269].

1599 *Müller, Hans-Peter* Eine griechische Parallele zu Motiven von Genesis i-ii. VT 47 (1997) 478-486.

1600 *Olafsson, Gudmundur* Genesis 2—a special 'creation'?: an introductory study of an old problem. 1997, ⇒83. [F]SHEA W., 1-6.

1601 **Rappel, Simone** 'Macht euch die Erde untertan': die ökologische Krise als Folge des Christentums?. ASE 39: 1996, ⇒12,1399. [R]BiLi 70/1 (1997) 73 *(Praetorius, Ina)*; ThLZ 122 (1997) 593-595 *(Römelt, Josef)* [Gen 1,26-28].

1602 *Rizzi, Armido* Esegesi e teologia biblica della *creatio ex nihilo*. Sum. 7. FilTeo 11/1 (1997) 38-48.

1603 *Romero Pose, Eugenio* La utilización del Gen en BEATO de Liébana: el cristocentrismo de la creación. [M]RUIZ de la Peña, J., BSal.E 189: 1997, ⇒76. 97-110 [RB 105,299—Langlamet, F.].

1604 **Rüterswörden, Udo** Dominium terrae: Studien zur Genese einer alttestamentlichen Vorstellung. BZAW 215: 1993, ⇒9,1863... 12,1401. [R]BZ 41 (1997) 124-125 *(Scharbert, Josef)* [Gen 1,28].

1605 *Ruzer, Serge* Reflections of Genesis 1-2 in the Old Syriac gospels. The book of Genesis. 1997, ⇒196. [E]Frishman, Judith, 91-102.

1606 *Samonà, Leonardo* A partire dal nulla: alterità e alleanza nella *creatio ex nihilo*. Sum. 7. FilTeo 11/1 (1997) 7-26.

1607 **Samuelson, Norbert M.** Judaism and the doctrine of creation. 1994, ⇒10,1684; 11/2,3716. [R]JJS 48/1 (1997) 197-199 *(Solomon, Norman)*; Teol. 34 (1997) 404-406 *(Batnitzky, Leora)*.

1608 *Sattler, Dorothea* "Im Anfang ...". Erwägungen zur Hermeneutik protologischer Aussagen. ThG 40 (1997) 82-93.

1609 **Scholten, Clemens** Antike Naturphilosophie und christliche Kosmologie in der Schrift *De opificio mundi* des Johannes PHILOPONOS. PTS 45: 1996, ⇒12,1405. [R]JThS 48 (1997) 296-298 *(Chadwick, Henry)*.

1610 *Soggin, Alberto* The equality of humankind from the perspective of the creation stories in Genesis 1:26-30 and 2:9, 15, 18-24. JNSL 23/2 (1997) 21-33.

1611 *Stadelmann, Luís* Dominion over animals [Gen 1,26-30];

1612 Adam's rib [Gen 2,21-22]. Month 30 (1997) 364-365/66-67.

1613 *Sulowski, Julian* Dwie mądrości—z Bogiem lub bez Boga?—czy Adam i Ewa 'byli nadzy'? [Two wisdoms: with God and without God: were Adam and Eve 'naked'?]. 1997, ⇒52. [F]ŁACH J., 367-400 [Gen 2,25]. P.

1614 **Van Soest, H.J.** 'Welk is het voortreffelijkste schepsel op aarde'?: de interpretatie van een omstreden bijbelse voorstelling in het 19e en 20e eeuwse Nederland. 1996, ⇒12,1416. <sup>R</sup>BMGN 112/4 (1997) 554-555 *(Schutte, G.J.)* [Gen 1,26-27].

1615 **Van Wolde, Ellen** Stories of the beginning: Genesis 1-11 and other creation stories. <sup>T</sup>*Bowden, John:* Harrisburg 1997, Morehouse xi; 273 pp. $19. 0-8192-1714-X [ThD 45,95—Heiser, W. Charles].

1616 *Vogels, Walter* Man and woman: their dignity, mutuality and fidelity in marriage: a biblical perspective (Gn 1-3). BiBh 23 (1997) 205-227.

1617 **VonDehsen, Christian D.** The imago dei in Genesis 1:26-27. LuthQ 11/3 (1997) 259-270.

1618 *Willi-Plein, Ina* Am Anfang einer Geschichte der Zeit. ThZ 53 (1997) 152-164 [Gen 1,1-2,4].

1619 **Winkler, Ulrich** Vom Wert der Welt: das Verständnis der Dinge in der Bibel und bei BONAVENTURA: ein Beitrag zu einer ökologischen Schöpfungstheologie. Salzburger theologische Studien 5: Innsbruck 1997, Tyrolia 512 pp. Bibl. SCH680. 3-7022-2076-3.

### E1.7 *Genesis 1s:* Bible and myth [⇒M3.8]

1620 *Barié, Paul* "Am Anfang war das Wasser": die Bedeutung des Wassers in den Weltschöpfungsmythen. Symb. 13 (1997) 19-34.

1621 *Bergant, Dianne* The medium is the message. BiTod 35 (1997) 5-9.

1622 *Deifelt, Wanda* The death of the goddess and the rise of humanity: a comparison of two stories. 1997, ⇒29. <sup>F</sup>GERSTENBERGER S., 6-19.

1623 **Diakonoff, Igor M.** Archaic myths of the orient and the occident. 1995, ⇒11/1,285; 12,1437. <sup>R</sup>BiOr 54/1-2 (1997) 61-62 *(Belier, Wouter W.)*; JAOS 117 (1997) 361-362 *(Foster, Benjamin R.)*.

1624 *Dietz, Günter* Okeanos und Proteus, Poseidon und Skamander: Urstrom, Meer und Fluß bei Homer. Symb. 13 (1997) 35-58.

1625 *Huxley, Margaret* The shape of the cosmos according to cuneiform sources. JRAS 7/2 (1997) 189-198.

1626 <sup>E</sup>**Kaiser, Otto** TUAT III: Mythen und Epen IV: Weisheitstexte, Mythen und Epen: Lfg. 6. Gü 1997, Gü'er 1090-1369 pp. 3-579-00082-9.

1627 *Lambert, W.G.* The Assyrian recension of Enuma Eliš. Assyrien im Wandel. 1997, ⇒379. <sup>E</sup>Waetzoldt, Hartmut, 77-79.

1628 *Martins Ramos, José Augusto* Mitos das origens no Próximo Oriente Antigo. As Origens. 1997, ⇒344. 65-97.

1629 *Neves, Joaquim Carreira das* Hermenêuticas fundamentalistas e esotéricas das origens bíblicas. As Origens. 1997, ⇒344. 161-196.

1630 **Rohl, David M.** A test of time 1: the bible: from myth to history. 1995, ⇒11/1,290; 12,8833. <sup>R</sup>BiOr 54 (1997) 166-168 *(Van Haarlem, Willem M.)* PEQ 129 (1997) 172-174 *(Kitchen, K.A.)*.

1631 *Soggin, J. Alberto* pîšôn e gîhôn: osservazioni su due fiumi mitici nell'ʿeden. <sup>F</sup>BREKELMANS C., BEThL 133: 1997, ⇒17. 587-589 [Gen 2,11; 2,13].

1632 *Strijdom, Johan* Teologieë as gevaarlike mensemaaksels: Burton MACK se evaluasie van vroeg-Christelike mites. HTS 53 (1997) 609-622 [ZID 24,127].

1633 *Vaz, Armindo dos Santos* A bíblia e as origens. As Origens. 1997, ⇒344. 99-159.

1634   *Weissert, Elnathan* Creating a political climate: literary allusions to
       Enuma Eliš in Sennacherib's account of the battle of Halule. Assy-
       rien im Wandel. 1997, ⇒379. [E]Waetzoldt, Hartmut, 191-202.

E1.8   *Gen 1s, Jos 10,13...:* **The Bible, the Church and science**

1635   *Araújo Jorge, Maria Manuel* Epistemologia do diálogo ciência e
       religão. As origens. 1997, ⇒344. 267-300.
1636   *Archer, Luís* As origens da vida. As origens. 1997, ⇒344. 41-64.
1637   **Beauchamp, André** Devant la création: regards de science, regards
       de foi. Vivre sa foi: Montréal 1997, Fides 145 pp. [SR 27,96—
       Simard, Noël].
1638   **Boyd, Robert** Boyd's handbook of practical apologetics. GR 1997,
       Kregel 251 pp. [R]Faith & Mission 14/1 (1996) 125-6 *(Bush, L.R.)*.
1639   *Carroll, William E.* GALILEO, science and the bible. Acta Philo-
       sophica 6/1 (1997) 5-37.
1640   *Despland, Michel* Des sciences aux sciences religieuses: le
       programme d'André-Marie AMPERE (1834-1843). RHPhR 77
       (1997) 67-79.
1641   **Druet, Paul** Saisir la vie entre bible et science. Troyes 1997, Fates
       232 pp. Préf. Jacques Delaporte [SR 26,513—Beauchamp, André].
1642   **Fantoli, Annibale** GALILEO: for Copernicanism and for the
       church. 1994. [R]Zygon 32/2 (1997) 272-275 *(Schmitz-Moorman,
       Karl)*.
1643   *Gomes Barbosa, Adérito* Diálogo: ciência-religão: perspectivas
       pedagógico-pastorais. As origens. 1997, ⇒344. 301-327.
1644   *Lachièze-Rey, Marc* A formação das estruturas;
1645   O big-bang. As origens. 1997, ⇒344. 33-40/25-31.
1646   **Laplanche, François** Bible, sciences et pouvoirs au XVIIe siècle.
       Istituto Italiano per gli Studi Filosofici. Lezioni della Scuola di
       Studi Superiori in Napoli 19: N 1997, Bibliopolis 145 pp.
       L25.000. 88-7088-295-0.
1647   *Pilch, John J.* Reading the sky. BiTod 35 (1997) 376-381.
1648   *Pinheiro, Jorge* EEINSTEIN e os caminhos da criação: a cosmogo-
       nia judaica e o conceita espaço-tempo em Gênesis um. Vox Scriptu-
       rae 7/1 (1997) 25-36 [ZID 23,415].
1649   **Poupard, Card. Paul** La nuova immagine del mondo. 1996,
       ⇒12,1481. [R]AnnTh 11 (1997) 281-285 *(Vitoria, María Angeles)*.
1650   **Saget, Henri** La science et la foi. 1996, ⇒12,1483. [R]EeV 107/3
       (1997) 67-68 *(Millet, Jean)*.
1651   *Santos Vaz, Armindo dos* A Bíblia e as origens. As origens. 1997,
       ⇒344. 99-159.
1652   *Scholten, Clemens* Weshalb wird die Schöpfungsgeschichte zum
       naturwissenschaftlichen Bereich?: Hexaemeronauslegung von
       BASILIUS von Cäsarea zu Johannes PHILIPONOS. ThQ 177
       (1997) 1-15.
1653   **Schroeder, Gerald L.** The science of God: the convergence of
       scientific and biblical wisdom. NY 1997, Free xii; 226 pp. $25. 0-
       684-83736-6 [ThD 45,188—Heiser, W. Charles].
1654   **Schwarz, Hans** Schöpfungsglaube im Horizont moderner Natur-
       wissenschaft. 1996, ⇒12,1484. [R]LM 36/5 (1997) 42 *(Clicqué, Guy
       M.)*; JETh 11 (1997) 253-255 *(Junker, Reinhard)*.

1655 *Segre, Michael* Light on the GALILEO case?. Isis 88 (1997) 484-504.
1656 **Tassot, Dominique** La bible au risque de la science: de GALILEE au P. LAGRANGE. Préf. Chenu, Pierre. P 1997, De Guibert 366 pp. FF170. 2-86839-460-4 [FV 97/2,98s—Vahanian, Gabriel].
1657 **Wilkinson, David; Frost, Rob** Thinking clearly about God and science. 1996, ⇒12,1487. RTheol. 100 (1997) 67-68 *(Barber, G.A.).*
1658 **Wright, M.R.** Cosmology in antiquity. 1995, ⇒11/1,302. RCIR 47/1 (1997) 185-187 *(Cuomo, Serafina).*

E1.9 Peccatum originale, **the sin of Eden,** *Genesis 2-3*

1659 *Auffarth, Christoph* Langeweile im Himmel?: das Paradies als Wunsch-Raum und seine Engelsbewohner. Symb. 13 (1997) 125-146.
1660 **Barth, Heinz-Lothar** Unzeitgemäße Betrachtungen zu Satan, Sünde und Sühne. Theologisches 27 (1997) 297-301, 340-343.
1661 **Basset, Lytta** Le pardon originel: de l'abîme du mal au pouvoir de pardonner. 1995 <1994>, ⇒11/1,308; 12,1494. RIstina 42/1 (1997) 91-92 *(Dupuy, B.);* Cart. 13 (1997) 228-229 *(Oliver Alcón, F.).*
1662 **Béresniak, Daniel** Le mythe du péché originel. Âge du Verseau: Monaco 1997, Rocher 154 pp. FF110 [VS 724,598—Arnould, Jacques].
1663 *Benjamin, Don C.* Stories of Adam and Eve. FKNIERIM R., 1997, ⇒48. 38-58.
1664 *Bird, Phyllis A.* Genesis 1-3 as a source for a contemporary theology of sexuality <1987>;
1665 Genesis 3 in modern biblical scholarship <1994>. Missing persons. 1997, ⇒114. 155-173/174-193.
1666 **Blocher, Henri** Original sin: illuminating the riddle. New Studies in Biblical Theology 5: Nottingham 1997, Apollos 158 pp. Bibl. £11. 0-85111-514-4.
1667 **Bonhoeffer, Dietrich** Creation and fall: a theological exposition of Genesis 1-3. ERüter, Martin; Tödt, Ilse; TBax, Douglas S.: Dietrich Bonhoeffer works 5: Mp 1997, Fortress xiv; 207 pp. $30. 0-8006-8303-X [ThD 45,262—Heiser, W. Charles].
1668 *Bonner, Gerald* The figure of Eve in AUGUSTINE's theology. StPatr 33: 1997, ⇒351. ELivingstone, E.A., 22-34.
1669 *Botha, P.J.* Original sin and sexism: St. EPHREM's attitude towards Eve. StPatr 33: 1997, ⇒351. ELivingstone, E.A., 483-489.
1670 **Cerbelaud, Dominique** Le diable. Tout simplement 20: P 1997, Atelier 108 pp. FF85. 2-7082-3306-8. RLV(L) 235 (1997) 82-83 *(Duquoc, Christian).*
1671 **Cioran, Émile** La caduta nel tempo. TTurolla, Tea: Mi 1996, Adelphi [Aquinas 42,619ss—Manganaro, Patrizia].
1672 **Claret, Bernd J.** 'Geheimnis des Bösen': zur Diskussion um den Teufel. Innsbruck 1997, Tyrolia 436 pp. [Alpha Omega 1,504s—Furlong, Jude].
1673 *Collins, Jack* A syntactical note (Genesis 3:15): is the woman's seed singular or plural?. TynB 48 (1997) 139-148 [Gen 3,15].

1674 *Cornelius, Izak* Some pages from the reception history of Genesis 3: the visual arts. JNSL 23/2 (1997) 221-234.

1675 **Dattler, Frederico** Diabo e demônios na Bíblia. São Paulo 1997, Recado 48 pp. [REB 58,772].

1676 *De Carlo, G.* Adamo: tra disobbedienza e autodivinizzazione: obbedienza-disobbedienza nella preistoria della salvezza. L'obbedienza. 1997, ⇒216. [E]Marrocu, Giuseppe, 1-42.

1677 **Delumeau, Jean** History of paradise: the garden of Eden in myth and tradition. 1995, ⇒12,317. [R]CHR 83 (1997) 728-729 *(Ryan, James D.)*.

1678 **Drewermann, Eugen** Le mal 2: approche psychanalytique du récit yahviste des origines. 1996, ⇒12,1506. [R]RSR 85 (1997) 280-282 *(Gibert, Pierre)*; SR 26 (1997) 228-230 *(Barry, Catherine)*.

1679 *Dunand, Jean-Paul* L'homme créé: sa bonté originelle, sa faute historique. Hokhma 65, 67 (1997-1998) 24-42; 1-17.

1680 *Fewell, Danna Nolan; Gunn, David M.* Shifting the blame: God in the garden. Reading bibles. 1997 <1993>, ⇒172. [E]Beal, Timothy K., 16-33.

1681 *Hauke, Manfred* Das Paradies in der Theologie der Gegenwart. AnnTh 11 (1997) 429-457.

1682 *Hesse, Otmar* Vom Paradies der Kirche und vom Paradies im Herzen: zur Deutung der Paradiesesgeschichte bei MAKARIOS/SYMEON und MARKOS Eremites. Grundbegriffe. 1997, ⇒372. [E]Fitschen, K., 23-26.

1683 *Jędrzejewski, Sylwester* Dialogicznosc przymierza a początek grzechu [De dialogo foederis et initio peccati]. RBL 50 (1997) 276-282. **P.**

1684 *Kelly, Joseph F.* The devil in AUGUSTINE's Genesis commentaries;

1685 *Laporte, Jean* From impure blood to original sin [Origenes] [Lev 12,1-8]. StPatr 33: 1997, ⇒351. [E]Livingstone, Elizabeth A., 119-124/438-444.

1686 **Laurentin, René** Der Teufel: Mythos oder Realität?. 1996, ⇒12,1524. [R]ThGl 87 (1997) 674-675 *(Beinert, Wolfgang)*.

1687 *Layton, Scott C.* Remarks on the Canaanite origin of Eve. CBQ 59 (1997) 22-32.

1688 Legged snakes identified: but could they ride bicycles?. BArR 23/4 (1997) 17 [Gen 3,14].

1689 *Mahlke, Adelheid* Beobachtungen zum Verhältnis von Frau und Mann in Gen 1-3. LuThK 21/1 (1997) 18-33.

1690 *Marchadour, Alain* Gn 2-3: premières postérités d'un texte de commencement. La Bible en littérature. 1997, ⇒315. [E]Beaude, Pierre-Marie. 271-292.

1691 *Margain, Jean; Schattner-Rieser, Ursula* Un fragment de pentateuque samaritain. Sum. 113. Sem. 45 (1996) 113-118 [Gen 3,15-18; 3,22-4,1].

1692 *Martelet, Gustave* Le péché originel chez Teilhard de CHARDIN et Maurice ZUNDEL. Rés. 47. Choisir (1997/1) 47-51.

1693 *Michel, Diethelm* Ihr werdet sein wie Gott: Gedanken zur Sündenfallgeschichte in Genesis 3. Studien zur Überlieferungsgeschichte. TB 93: 1997 <1988>, ⇒149. 93-114.

1694 **Pagels, Elaine** Adam, Eve, and the serpent. 1988, ⇒4,2203... 8,2254. [R]Gn. 69 (1997) 661-662 *(Habermehl, Peter)*;

1695  The origin of Satan. 1995, ⇒11/1,334; 12,1535. ᴿTJT 13/1 (1997) 111-112 *(Meagher, John C.)*;

1696  As origens de Satanás: um estudo sobre o poder que as forças irracionais exercem na sociedade moderna. 1996, ⇒12,1536. AtT 1/1 (1997) 97-99 *(Cavalcanti, Tereza)*;

1697  L'origine de Satan. P 1997, Bayard 272 pp. [Choisir (juin 1998) 38—Hug, Joseph].

1698  **Panier, Louis** Le péché originel: naissance de l'homme sauvé. 1996, ⇒12,1538. StPav 44/2 (1997) 253-254 *(Segalla, Giuseppe)*; BLE 98 (1997) 304-306 *(Maldamé, J.M.)*; Telema 23/4 (1997) couverture *(Kaji-Ngulu, Beda)*.

1699  *Penchansky, David* God the monster: fantasy in the garden of Eden. The monstrous. 1997, ⇒169. ᴱAichele, George, 43-60.

1700  *Pettorelli, Jean-Pierre* Péché originel ou amour conjugal?: note sur le sens des images d'Adam et Ève sur les sarcophages chrétiens de l'antiquité tardive. RechAug 30 (1997) 279-334.

1701  *Pinker, Aron* Satanic verses. JBQ 25 (1997) 90-100, 225-233.

1702  *Rosito, M.G.* La caduta delle origini. CiVi 52 (1997) 327-330.

1703  *Rottzoll, Dirk U.* Die Schöpfungs- und Fallerzählung in Gen 2 f. Teil 1: die Fallerzählung (Gen 3). ZAW 109 (1997) 481-499.

1704  *Sancassano, Marialucia* Il mistero del serpente: retrospettiva di studi e interpretazioni moderne. At. 85 (1997) 355-390.

1705  *Savasta, Carmelo* Gen 3,1-19 (IV). BeO 39/4 (1997) 193-206.

1706  **Sayés, José Antonio** El demonio, ¿realidad o mito?. M 1997, San Pablo 217 pp. [Carthaginensia 14,258].

1707  **Schüngel-Straumann, Helen** Die Frau am Anfang—Eva und die Folgen. Müns ²1997, Lit.

1708  **Schwager, Raymund** Erbsünde und Heilsdrama: im Kontext von Evolution, Gentechnologie und Apokalyptik. Müns 1997, LIT 216 pp. DM35. 3-8258-3115-9. ᴿThGl 87 (1997) 662-664 *(Hoping, Helmut)*.

1709  *Stein, Bradley L.* Who the devil is Beelzebul?. BiRe 13/1 (1997) 42-45, 48.

1710  *Stilwell, Peter* Pecado original emquestão. As origens. 1997, ⇒344. 213-229.

1711  **Suchocki, Marjorie Hewitt** The fall to violence: original sin in relational theology. 1994, ⇒11/1,341; 12,1555. ᴿTJT 13 (1997) 347-348 *(Young, Pamela Dickey)*.

1712  *Vogels, Walter* "Her man with her" (Gn 3:6b). EeT(O) 28/2 (1997) 147-160 [Gen 3,6].

1713  *Wiesel, Elie* Supporting roles: the serpent. BiRe 13/6 (1997) 18-19 [Gen 2-3].

## E2.1  Cain and Abel; *gigantes, longaevi; Genesis 4s*

1714  *Basset, Lytta* Abel notre frère, vanité et miroir. MoBi 105 (1997) 16-19.

1715  *Benzoni, Giovanni* Abele e Caino: fratelli per sangue, fratricidi per scelta. Servitium 31/2 (1997) 97-102.

1716  *Brandscheidt, Renate* Kain und Abel: die Sündenfallerzählung des Jahwisten in Gen 4,1-16. TThZ 106 (1997) 1-21.

1717  *Brocke, Edna; Stegemann, Ekkehard W.* "Soll ich meines Bruders Hüter sein?": Bibelarbeit über Gen 4,1-16. 1997, ⇒25. ᶠFRIEDLANDER A., 35-45.

1718  *Calloud, Jean* Caïn et Abel.: l'homme et son frère. SémBib 88 (1997) 3-25.

1719  *Cerbelaud, Dominique* Caïn et Abel: le renversement. RSR 85 (1997) 167-175;

1720  Les interprétations des Pères de l'Église. MoBi 105 (1997) 43-45.

1721  *Chalier, Catherine* Le partage de l'existence. MoBi 105 (1997) 29-31 [Gen 4].

1722  *Fouts, David M.* A defense of the hyperbolic interpretation of large numbers in the Old Testament. JETS 40 (1997) 377-387.

1723  *Gilbert, Pierre* Le premier meurtre de l'humanité. MoBi 105 (1997) 7-11.

1724  **Glenthøj, Johannes Bartholdy** Cain and Abel in Syriac and Greek writers (4th-6th centuries). CSCO 567; CSCO.S 95: Lv 1997, Peeters xxvi; 326 pp. Bibl. FB3.200. 90-6831-909-4.

1725  *Kabasele Mukenge, André* Relecture de Gn 4,1-16 dans le contexte africain. RAT 21 (1997) 149-170 [ThIK 21/1,28].

1726  *Kraus, Wolgang* Zum Begriff der Deszendenz: ein selektiver Überblick. Anthr. 92 (1997) 139-163.

1727  *Kuntzmann, Raymond* Frères dans le Proche Orient ancien. MoBi 105 (1997) 21-24.

1728  *Lestringant, Frank* L'errance de Caïn: D'AUBIGNE, DU BARTAS, HUGO, BAUDELAIRE. RSHum 245 (1997) 13-32.

1729  *Marx, Alfred* L'épreuve des sacrifices. MoBi 105 (1997) 12-16.

1730  **Matthes, Karl-Horst** Schöpfung und Sündenfall: von Kain und Abel bis Lamech: umgestaltete Überlieferungen. Theologie 13: Müns 1997, LIT 87 pp. 3-8258-2655-4 [NThAR 2000,92].

1731  *Neusch, Marcel* Du sacrifice d'Abel à celui du Christ. MoBi 105 (1997) 46-48.

1732  *Romilly, Jacqueline de* Frères ennemis dans la Grèce antique. MoBi 105 (1997) 25-27.

1733  *Sirat, René-Samuel* 'Si vous voyez mon fils aîné'. MoBi 105 (1997) 32-34.

1734  *Smeets, Jean Robert* L'arme et le signe de Caïn dans les traductions de la bible en vers ancien français. Romania 459-460 (1997) 552-562 [IAJS 45,164].

1735  *Tigay, Jeffrey H.* "He begot a son in his likeness after his image" (Genesis 5:3). 1997, ⇒34. ᴹGREENBERG M., 139-147.

1736  *Van der Kooij, Arie* Peshitta Genesis 6: "Songs of God"—angels or judges?. JNSL 23/1 (1997) 43-51.

1737  *Wenham, J.W.* Large numbers in the Hebrew bible. JBQ 25 (1997) 260-267.


E2.2 *Diluvium,* the Flood; Gilgameš (Atraḫasis); Genesis 6...

1738  *Avitabile, Bruno* Babel: la ville et la tour: violence, parole et constructions langagières. SémBib 85 (1997) 9-34.

1739  **Cohn, Norman** Noah's flood: the Genesis story in western thought. 1996, ⇒12,1584. ᴿCHR 83 (1997) 726-728 *(Di Lella, Alexander A.).*

1740 *DiCicco, Mario* God remembered Noah. BiTod 35 (1997) 16-21.
1741 *Emelianov, V.V.* Woman of the righteous man who survived the Flood (The Sumerian Flood Story, VI 256-260). St. Petersburg Journal of Oriental Studies 9 (1997) 266-279 [Akkadica 108,31]. **Russian.**
1742 *Fritz, Volkmar* 'Solange die Erde steht'—vom Sinn der jahwistischen Fluterzählung in Gen 6-8. Studien zur Literatur. 1997 <1982>, ⇒126. 33-50.
1743 *Klein, Jacob* The origin and development of languages on earth: the Sumerian versus the biblical view. 1997, ⇒34. <sup>M</sup>GREENBERG M., 77*-92*. **H.**
1744 *Koltun-Fromm, Naomi* APHRAHAT and the rabbis on Noah's righteousness in light of the Jewish-Christian polemic. The book of Genesis. 1997, ⇒196. <sup>E</sup>Frishman, Judith, 57-71.
1745 **Louyot, Yves** La longue 'marche' de Noé. 1996, ⇒12,1591. <sup>R</sup>EeV 107/4 (1997) 91-92 *(Valleix, S').*
1746 <sup>E</sup>**Maier, John R.** Gilgamesh: a reader. Wauconda, Illinois 1997, Bolchazy-Carducci xi; 491 pp. Bibl. 0-86516-339-1.
1747 *Merrill, Eugene H.* The peoples of the Old Testament according to Genesis 10. BS 154 (1997) 3-22.
1748 **Müller, Klaus** Tora für die Völker: die noachidischen Gebote und Ansätze zur ihrer Rezeption im Christentum. SKI 15: 1994, ⇒10,1989... 12,1596. <sup>R</sup>Jud. 53 (1997) 190-191 *(Wipfler, Judith)* [Gen 9,1-7].
1749 <sup>E</sup>**Parpola, Simo** The standard Babylonian epic of Gilgamesh: cuneiform text, transliteration, glossary, indices and sign list. Collab. *Luukko, Mikko; Fabritius, Kalle:* State Archives of Assyria Studies Cuneiform texts 1: Helsinki 1997, The Neo-Assyrian Text Corpus Project xxviii; 165 pp. $25. 951-45-7760-4.
1750 *Reimer, Haroldo* (Über)Leben im gemeinsamen Haus: eine Bibelarbeit zu Genesis 6-9. 1997, ⇒29. <sup>F</sup>GERSTENBERGER S., 20-27.
1751 <sup>T</sup>**Silva Castillo, Jorge** Gilgamesh, o la angustia por la muerte (poema bibilonio). <sup>2</sup>1995, ⇒11/1,369. <sup>R</sup>JAOS 117/2 (1997) 378-379 *(Rubio Pardo, José Gonzalo).*
1752 *Steck, Odil Hannes* Der Mensch und die Todesstrafe: Exegetisches zur Übersetzung der Präposition Beth in Gen 9,6a. ThZ 53 (1997) 118-130.
1753 *Van der Kooij, Arie* The story of Genesis 11:1-9 and the culture of ancient Mesopotamia. BiOr 53 (1996) 28-38.
1754 *Zipor, Moshe A.* The flood chronology: too many an accident. DSD 4 (1997) 207-210.

## E2.3 Patriarchae, Abraham; *Genesis 12s*

1755 *Brugger, Laurence* Le sein d'Abraham et la fête des Tabernacles. CAr 45 (1997) 69-82.
1756 <sup>TE</sup>**Châtillon, Jean; Duchet-Suchaux, Monique** RICHARD de Saint-Victor: les douze patriarches ou Beniamin minor. Introd., notes *Longère, Jean:* SC 419: P 1997, Cerf 374 pp. Edition bilingue latin-français. FF199. 2-204-05610-3 [BCLF 585-6,1732].
1757 *Cimosa, M.* L'obbedienza de Abramo: l'uomo accetta di essere realizzato da Dio. L'obbedienza. 1997, ⇒216. <sup>E</sup>Marrocu, Giuseppe, 43-58.

1758  **Clerc, D.** Jacob: les aléas d'une bénédiction: Genèse chapitres 25-
35. Genève 1992, Labor et F 176 pp. Dossier pour l'animation
biblique. <sup>R</sup>OTEs 10 (1997) 343-344 *(Snyman, Gerrie)*.

1759  *Czakó, István* Abramo come paradigma del credente nel libro 'Ti-
more e tremore' di Søren KIERKEGAARD. FolTh 8 (1997) 199-
226.

1760  *Dulaey, M.* L'exégèse patristique de Gn 13 et la mosaïque de la
séparation d'Abraham et de Lot à Santa Maria Maggiore (Rome).
StPatr 33: 1997, ⇒351. <sup>E</sup>Livingstone, Elizabeth A., 3-7.

1761  *Eichler, Barry L.* On reading Genesis 12:10-20. 1997, ⇒34.
<sup>M</sup>GREENBERG M., 23-38.

1762  **Habel, Norman C.** The land is mine: six biblical land ideologies.
1995, ⇒11/1,393; 12,1617. <sup>R</sup>JBL 116 (1997) 332-343 *(Lemke,
Werner E.)*.

1763  *Handy, Lowell K.* Biblical Bronze Age memories: the Abraham
cycle as usable past. BR 42 (1997) 43-57.

1764  **Janssen, Wim** Hij zei: Abraham, ga: een voettocht in de kantijn
van Genesis. Zoetermeer 1997, Meinema 152 pp. f34.50. 90-211-
3664-3 [ITBT 5/8,36].

1765  **Kuschel, Karl-Josef** Abraham: sign of hope for Jews, christians
and muslims. 1995, ⇒11/2,4245; 12,9081. <sup>R</sup>JR 77 (1997) 121-122
*(Peters, F.E.)*;

1766  La controversia su Abramo: ciò che divide—e ciò che unisce ebrei,
cristiani e musulmani. 1996, ⇒12,9082. Amicizia Ebraico-Cristiana 32 (1997) 150-156 *(Stefani, Piero)*; RSEc 15 (1997) 132-133
*(Morandini, Simone)*; LASBF 47 (1997) 630-633 *(Cortese, Enzo)*.

1767  *Lanne, Emmanuel* La *'xenitesa"* d'Abraham dans l'œuvre
d'IRENEE: aux origines du thème monastique de la *'peregrinatio'*.
Tradition. BEThL 129: 1997 <1974>, ⇒142. 50-68.

1768  *Martin, George* The tomb of our father Abraham. Catholic Near
East 23/2 (1997) 6-11.

1769  **Massignon, Louis** Les trois prières d'Abraham. Patrimoines: P
1997, Cerf 196 pp. FF140. 2-204-05568-9 [Ibla 61/1,102ss—
Mayaud, Charles].

1770  **Matthes, Karl-Horst** Abraham, Isaak und Jakob geraten in die Geschichte der Väter: eine Studie. Theologie 3: Müns 1997, LIT viii;
314 pp. 3-8258-2655-4 [NThAR 1997,192].

1771  *Mello, Alberto* Abramo, l'uomo del mattino. PSV 36 (1997) 37-45.

1772  **Nauerth, Thomas** Untersuchungen zur Komposition der Jakober-
zählungen: auf der Suche nach der Endgestalt des Genesisbuches.
BEAT 27: Fra 1997, Lang 318 pp. 3-631-30220-7.

1773  *Nocquet, Dany* Abraham ou le 'père adopté': où se cache
l'historicité d'Abraham?. CBFV 36 (1997) 35-53.

1774  *Ravasi, Gianfranco* Abraham et le peuple de Dieu pèlerin. Com(I)
153 (1997) 17-26; Communio[E] 19 (1997) 188-196; Com(F) 22/4
(1997) 66-75; IKaZ 26 (1997) 196-204.

1775  **Remaud, Michel** À cause des pères: le "Mérite des Pères" dans la
tradition juive. Coll. REJ 22: Lv 1997, Peeters 367 pp. Bibl.
FB2.400. 2-87723-356-1.

1776  <sup>E</sup>**Römer, T.** Abraham: nouvelle jeunesse d'un ancêtre. Essais bibliques 28: Genève 1997, Labor et F 149 pp. FF98. 2-8309-0870-8
[ETR 73,310].

1777  **Schorn, Ulrike** Ruben und das System der zwölf Stämme Israels:
redaktionsgeschichtliche Untersuchungen zur Bedeutung des Erst-

geborenen Jakobs. BZAW 248: B 1997, De Gruyter xiv; 302 pp. Diss. Nürnberg 1996. DM168. 3-11-015396-3 [NThAR 1998,99].

1778 *Ska, Jean Louis* L'appel d'Abraham et l'acte de naissance d'Israël: Genèse 12,1-4a. BEThL 133: 1997, ⇒17. [F]BREKELMANS C., 367-389.

1779 *Stoffregen Pedersen, Kirsten* The Amharic andemta commentary on the Abraham stories Genesis 11:24-25:14. The book of Genesis. 1997, ⇒196. [E]Frishman, Judith, 253-261.

1780 *Strange, John* Geography and tradition in the patriarchal narratives. SJOT 11 (1997) 210-222.

1781 **Vogels, Walter** Abrahán y su leyenda: Génesis 12,1-25,11. [T]*Monge, J. Luis:* Bilbao 1997, DDB 223 pp. [Mayéutica 24,254— Doyle, John];

1782 *Abraham et sa légende:* Genèse 12,1-25,11. LiBi 110: 1996, ⇒12,1635. [R]EeV 107 (1997) 272-273 *(Monloubou, Louis)*; REJ 156 (1997) 389-392 *(Couteau, Elisabeth)*.

## E2.4 Melchisedech, Sodoma; *Genesis 14...19*

1783 **Fields, Weston W.** Sodom and Gomorrah: history and motif in biblical narrative. JSOT.S 231: Shf 1997, Academic 228 pp. £40/$60. 1-85075-633-3.

1784 *Manzi, Franco* La figura qumranica di Melchisedek: possibili origini di una tradizione letteraria del primo secolo cristiano?. StPatr 33: 1997, ⇒351. [E]Livingstone, Elizabeth A., 61-70.

1785 *Mutius, Hans-Georg von* Die Bedeutung von וַיְחַלֵּק in Genesis 14,15 im Licht der komparativen Semistik und der aramäischen Qumranschrift Genesis Apokryphon XXII,8ff. BN 90 (1997) 8-12.

1786 *Rainbow, Paul* Melchizedek as a messiah at Qumran. BBR 7 (1997) 179-194 [Isa 52,7; 61,1-2].

## E2.5 The Covenant (alliance, Bund): *Foedus, Genesis 15...*

1787 *Beckman, Gary* New joins to Hittite treaties. ZA 87 (1997) 96-100.

1788 *Behrens, Achim* Gen 15,6 und das Vorverständnis des Paulus. ZAW 109 (1997) 327-341 [Rom 4; Gal 3].

1789 **Chebel, Malek** Histoire de la circoncision: des origines à nos jours. Le nadir: P 1997, Balland 253 pp. Bibl. 2-7158-1149-7.

1790 **Edel, Elmar** Der Vertrag zwischen Ramses II. von Ägypten und Hattusili III. von Hatti. WVDOG 95: B 1997, Mann xvi; 109, 71* pp. DM98. 3-7861-1944-9.

1791 *Freedman, David Noel* Divine commitment and human obligation: the covenant theme. Divine Commitment 1. 1997 <1964>, ⇒124. 168-178.

1792 *Gräbe, Petrus J.* Alttestamentliche Voraussetzungen für das Verständnis des Bundesmotivs im Neuen Testament I: Fragestellung und Bedeutung des Wortes berît; II: Forschungsgeschichtlicher Überblick, Fazit und Ausblick. HTS 53 (1997) 209-226, 227-256 [ZID 23,443].

1793 **Hagelia, Hallvard** Numbering the stars: a phraseological analysis of Genesis 15. CB.OT 39: 1994, ⇒10,2041... 12,1657. [R]BiOr 54 (1997) 171-172 *(Van Seters, John)*.

1794   *Haran, Menahem* The berît 'covenant': its nature and ceremonial background. 1997, ⇒34. <sup>M</sup>GREENBERG M., 203-219.

1795   *Heintz, Jean-Georges* Alliance humaine—alliance divine: documents d'époque babylonienne ancienne & Bible hébraique—une esquisse. BN 86 (1997) 66-76 [Exod 24,7].

1796   *Michel, Diethelm* Beschneidung und Kindertaufe. Studien zur Überlieferungsgeschichte. TB 93: 1997 <1994>, ⇒149. 115-124 [Gen 17].

1797   **Rendtorff, Rolf** Die "Bundesformel". SBS 160: 1995, ⇒11/1,425; 12,1654. <sup>R</sup>ThLZ 122 (1997) 139-140 *(Kratz, Reinhard G.)*.

1798   **Alexander, Thomas Desmond** Abraham in the Negev: a source-critical investigation of Genesis 20:1-22:19. Carlisle 1997, Paternoster ix; 172 pp. Bibl. 0-85364-792-5.

1799   *Benjamin, Don C.* Stories of Hagar. BiTod 35 (1997) 27-31 [Gen 16,1-16].

1800   *Boespflug, François* Autour de l'hospitalité d'Abraham dans la bible et le Coran, et de son écho dans l'art juif et l'art chrétien du Moyen Âge (XIIIe-XVIe siècle): essai d'iconographie comparée. Le comparatisme. 1997, ⇒346. <sup>E</sup>Boespflug, François, 315-343 [Gen 18,1-15].

1801   *Di Pinto, Luigi* Abramo e lo straniero (Genesi 18,1-16): 1: un'introduzione all'ospitalità; 2: l'ospitalità celebrata. RdT 38 (1997) 597-620, 735-769.

1802   *Dulaey, Martine* Le salut de Lot: Gen 19 dans l'Église ancienne. ASEs 14 (1997) 327-353.

1803   *Jericke, Detlef* Die Geburt Isaaks—Gen 21,1-8. BN 88 (1997) 31-38.

1804   *Kuntzmann, Raymond* Abraham victime du comparatisme?: comparaison et raison exégétique. Le comparatisme. 1997, ⇒346. <sup>E</sup>Boespflug, François, 177-194 [Gen 18,1-15].

1805   *Mbuwayesango, Dora R.* Childlessness and woman-to-woman relationships in Genesis and African patriarcal society: Sarah and Hagar from a Zimbabwean woman's perspective (Gen 16:1-16; 21:8-21). Semeia 78 (1997) 27-36.

1806   *Smith, Carol* Challenged by the text: interpreting two stories of incest in the Hebrew Bible. A feminist companion. 1997, ⇒180. <sup>E</sup>Brenner, Athalya, 114-135 [Gen 19,30-38; 2 Sam 13,1-22].

1807   *Thompson, John L.* Hagar, victim or villain?: three sixteenth-century views. CBQ 59 (1997) 213-233 [Gen 16].

E2.6  **The 'Aqedâ; Isaac, Genesis 22...**

1808   **Berman, Louis Arthur** The Akedah: the binding of Isaac. Northvale, NJ 1997 Aronson xx; 259 pp. Bibl. $30. 1-56821-899-0.

1809   *Chrostowski, Waldemar* 'Weź swego jedynego syna, którego miłïjesz' (Rdz 22,2): cierpienie dziecka jako próba wiary rodziców ['Prends ton fils unique que tu aimes' [Gen 22,2]: la souffrance de l'enfant comme l'épreuve de la foi des parents]. AtK 128 (1997) 222-232.

1810   *Garcia-Lopez, Félix* Étude littéraire et théologique de Gn 22,1-19. RICP 62 (1997) 199-217.

1811 *Gossai, Hemchand* Divine vulnerability and human marginality in the Akedah: exploring a tension. HBT 19/1 (1997) 1-23.
1812 **Grishaver, Joel Lurie** The bonding of Isaac: stories and essays about gender and Jewish spirituality. LA 1997, Alef 254 pp. Bibl. 1-88128-320-8 [NThAR 1998,268].
1813 *Heijne,, Camilla von* Aqedat Isak: Judisk tolkning av Genesis 22:1-19. SEÅ 62 (1997) 57-86.
1814 ᴱ**Manns, Frédéric** The sacrifice of Isaac in the three monotheistic religions. ASBF 41: 1995, ⇒11/1,448; 12,1670. ᴿNRTh 119 (1997) 265-266 *(Ska, J.-L.)*.
1815 *Mendl, Hans* Vom Gott, der ins Dunkle führt: eine exemplarische empirische Untersuchung zu Gen 22 (Die Opferung Isaaks). RPäB 39 (1997) 65-92.
1816 *Michel, Diethelm* Überlieferung und Deutung in der Erzählung von Isaaks Opferung (Gen 22). Studien zur Überlieferungsgeschichte. TB 93: 1997 <1977>, ⇒149. 89-92.
1817 *Müller, Hans-Peter* Genesis 22 und das mlk-Opfer: Erinnerung an einen religionsgeschichtlichen Tatbestand. BZ 41 (1997) 237-246.
1818 *Rosenak, Michael* The Akedah—and what to remember. 1997, ⇒34. ᴹGʀᴇᴇɴʙᴇʀɢ M., 307-325.
1819 *Schwantes, Milton* 'Do not extend your hand against the child': observations on Genesis 21 and 22. Subversive scriptures. 1997, ⇒263. ᴱVaage, L., 101-123.
1820 *Van Rompay, Lucas* Antiochene biblical interpretation: Greek and Syriac [ *Ephrem Sirus; Eusebius Emesa]*. The book of Genesis. 1997, ⇒196. ᴱFrishman, Judith, 103-123 [Gen 22; 49].
1821 *VanderKam, James C.* The Aqedah, Jubilees, and Pseudojubilees. Bibl.Interp. 28: 1997, ⇒77. ᶠSᴀɴᴅᴇʀs J., 241-261.

1822 *Fewell, Danna Nolan; Phillips, Gary A.* Drawn to excess, or reading beyond betrothal. Semeia 77 (1997) 23-58 [Gen 24; John 4].
1823 *Monferrer Sala, Juan Pedro* Una traducción árabe de Génesis 24,2-3 [An Arabic translation of Gn 24,2-3]. Sum. res. 23. MEAH.H 46 (1997) 23-35.

E2.7 **Jacob** and Esau: ladder dream; *Jacob, somnium, Gen 25...*

1824 *Abraham, Jed H.* Esau's wives. JBQ 25 (1997) 251-259.
1825 **Heck, Christian** L'échelle céleste dans l'art du moyen âge: un image de la quête du ciel. Idées et Recherches: P 1997, Flammarion 366 pp. FF295 [RSPhTh 81/3,557].
1826 *Jarschel, Haidi* Sexualisierte Geschichte und Theologie des Volkes in Genesis 25-36. 1997, ⇒29. ᶠGᴇʀsᴛᴇɴʙᴇʀɢᴇʀ S., 28-48.
1827 *Russell, D.S.* Earth and heaven: bridging the gap. ET 109 (1997) 7-9 [Gen 28,12].
1828 *Spina, Frank Anthony* The "face of God": Esau in canonical context. Bibl.Interp. 28: 1997, ⇒77. ᶠSᴀɴᴅᴇʀs J., 3-25.
1829 *Viviano, Pauline A.* Bestower of blessing. BiTod 35 (1997) 22-26.
1830 **Wahl, Harald Martin** Die Jakobserzählungen: Studien zu ihrer mündlichen Überlieferung, Verschriftung und Historizität. Diss. Mainz 1994-5, ᴰMichel, D.: BZAW 258: B 1997, De Gruyter xi; 376 pp. DM198 3-11-015758-6.

E2.8  Jacob's wrestling; the Angels; *Gen 31-36 & 38*

1831  *Ahn, Gregor* Grenzgängerkonzepte in der Religionsgeschichte: von Engeln, Dämonen, Götterboten und anderen Mittlerwesen. Engel und Dämonen. FARG 29: 1997, ⇒343. EAhn, Gregor, 1-48.

1832  *Ahn, Gregor; Dietrich, Manfried* Einführung. Engel und Dämonen. FARG 29: 1997, ⇒343. EAhn, Gregor, ix-xv.

1833  *Alonso Schökel, Luis* Gn 35,28-29: muerte de Isaac y reconciliación fraterna. EstB 55 (1997) 287-295.

1834  *Bauer, Johannes B.* Jakobs Kampf mit dem Dämon (Gen 32,23-33). Studien zu Bibeltext. 1997 <1989>, ⇒111. 137-143.

1835  *Beach, Eleanor Ferris* An iconographic approach to Genesis 38. A feminist companion. 1997ₓ ⇒180. EBrenner, Athalya, 285-305.

1836  *Boecker, Hans Jochen* Überlegungen zur "Geschichte Tamars" (Gen 38). 1997, ⇒29. FGERSTENBERGER S., 49-68.

1837  *Freedman, David Noel* Dinah and Shechem, Tamar and Amnon. Divine Commitment 1. 1997 <1990>, ⇒124. 485-495 [Gen 34; 2 Sam 13].

1838  *Kogut, Simcha* Midrashic derivations regarding the transformation of the names Jacob and Israel according to traditional Jewish exegesis: semantic and syntactic aspects. 1997,⇒34. MGREENBERG M., 219*-233* [Gen 32,29; Hos 12,4]. **H.**

1839  *Koiva, Mare* Angels and demons in the contemporary personal experiences changing of mythological beings and experiences;

1840  *Kulmar, Tarmo* Die dämonische Gestalt *supay* in der Inka-Religion. Engel und Dämonen. FARG 29: 1997, ⇒343. EAhn, Gregor, 91-102/103-110.

1841  **Lang, Judith** The angels of God: understanding the bible. L 1997, New City 240 pp. Bibl. $13. 1-56548-101-1 [NThAR 1998,268].

1842  *Le Saux, Madeleine* Les archanges Gabriel, Michel et Raphaël. DosB 70 (1997) 19-21.

1843  *Lepajoe, Marju* Über PLOTINS Daimon. Engel und Dämonen. FARG 29: 1997, ⇒343. EAhn, Gregor, 111-120.

1844  **Mach, Michael** Entwicklungsstadien des jüdischen Engelglaubens in vorrabbinischer Zeit. TSAJ 34: 1992, ⇒8,2424... 11/2,3794. RJNES 56 (1997) 211-212 *(Tomasino, Anthony J.)*.

1845  **McKenna, Megan** Angeli: se non ci fossero bisognerebbe inventarli. CinB 1997, San Paolo [Anime e Corpi 36,524].

1846  **Menn, Esther Marie** Judah and Tamar (Genesis 38) in ancient Jewish exegesis: studies in literary form and hermeneutics. JSJ.S 51: Lei 1997, Brill xvi; 412 pp. Diss. 1995; Bibl. ƒ244/$143.50. 90-04-10630-8.

1847  *Müllers, Josefine* An der Hand des Engels: der Engel in bildender Kunst und Literatur. Symb. 13 (1997) 147-180.

1848  *Neufeld, Ernest* The rape of Dinah. JBQ 25 (1997) 220-224 [Gen 34].

1849  *Noegel, Scott B.* Sex, sticks, and the trickster in Gen. 30:31-43. JANES 25 (1997) 7-17.

1850  **Panteghini, Giacomo** Angeli e demoni: il ritorno dell'invisibile. Problemi & Proposte: Padova 1997, Messagero 203 pp. 88-250-0592-X [PerTeol 30,296—Ruiz de Gopegui, Juan A.].

1851 *Paradise, Jonathan* What did Laban demand of Jacob?: a new reading of Genesis 31:50 and Exodus 21:10. 1997, ⇒34. <sup>M</sup>GREENBERG M., 91-98.

1852 **Salm, Eva** Juda und Tamar: eine exegetische Studie, zu Gen 38. FzB 76: 1996, ⇒12,1713. <sup>R</sup>JBL 116 (1997) 532-534 *(Szpek, H.)*.

1853 *Schäfer-Bossert, Stefanie* Sex and crime in Genesis 38: eine exegetische Auseinandersetzung mit der "Schuld der Tamar". 1997, ⇒29. <sup>F</sup>GERSTENBERGER S., 69-94.

1854 *Schroeder, Joy A.* The rape of Dinah: LUTHER's interpretation of a biblical narrative. Sum. 775. <sup>R</sup>SCJ 28 (1997) 775-791 [Gen 34].

1855 *Soupa, Anne* La vogue des anges. DosB 70 (1997) 24-26 [Dan 9,20-25].

1856 **Spieckermann, Hermann** Der Gotteskampf: Jakob und der Engel in Bibel und Kunst. Collab. *Dähn, Susanne:* Z 1997, Theologischer Verlag 115 pp. 3-290-17152-3 [Gen 32,22-32].

1857 *Steffen, Uwe* Zwei Aspekte der Engelvorstellung. Symb. 13 (1997) 105-115.

1858 *Valk, Ülo* On the stability of some demonic guises in Estonian folk religion: the black man. Engel und Dämonen. FARG 29: 1997, ⇒343. <sup>E</sup>Ahn, Gregor, 171-179.

## E2.9 Joseph; Jacob's blessings; *Genesis 37; 39-50*

1859 *Bammel, Ernst* Das Judentum als eine Religion Ägyptens. Judaica et Paulina. WUNT 91: 1997 <1988>, ⇒109. 115-121.

1860 *Blumenthal, Elke* Thomas MANNs Joseph und die ägyptische Literatur. Ägypten-Bilder. OBO 150: 1997, ⇒378. <sup>E</sup>Staehelin, Elisabeth. 313-332.

1861 **Bohak, Gideon** Joseph and Aseneth and the Jewish temple in Heliopolis. Diss. Princeton. SBL Early Judaism and Its Literature 10: Atlanta, GA 1996, Scholars xv; 141 pp. $13.95. 0-7885-0179-8. <sup>R</sup>JSJ 28 (1997) 353-356 *(Piñero, Antonio)*.

1862 <sup>E</sup>**Catastini, A.** Storia di Giuseppe (Genesi 37-50). 1994, ⇒10,2110. <sup>R</sup>At. 85/1 (1997) 329-331 *(Jucci, Elio)*.

1863 *Elgvin, Torleif* 4Q474—a Joseph apocryphon?. RdQ 18 (1997) 97-108.

1864 **Endo, Yoshinobu** The verbal system of classical Hebrew in the Joseph story: an approach from discourse analysis. SSN 32: Assen 1996, Van Gorcum xiii; 351 pp. ƒ79.50/$42. 90-232-3093-0. <sup>R</sup>RHPhR 77 (1997) 191-192 *(Joosten, J.)*; CBQ 59 (1997) 346-347 *(Gianto, Agustinus)*; OTEs 10 (1997) 351-353 *(Naudé, J.A.)*; HebStud 38 (1997) 113-116 *(Rosenbaum, Michael)*; LASBF 46 (1996) 434-441 *(Niccacci, Alviero)*.

1865 *Hezser, Catherine* 'Joseph and Aseneth' in the context of ancient Greek erotic novels. FJB 24 (1997) 1-40.

1866 *Hirth, Volkmar* Jakobs Segen über Ephraim and Manasse (Gen. 48,15 f.) als Beispiel frühisraelitischer familiärer Frömmigkeit. BN 86 (1997) 44-48.

1867 *Hubbard, Moyer* Honey for Aseneth: interpreting a religious symbol. JSPE 16 (1997) 97-110 [Gen 41,45].

1868 *Koenen, Klaus* Zur Bedeutung von Gen 37,15-17 im Kontext der Josephs-Erzählung und von B 21-28 in dem der ägyptischen Sinuhe-Erzählung. BN 86 (1997) 51-56.

1869  *Lhote, Marie-Josèphe* L'histoire de Joseph et ses frères traitée successivement par Hugo von HOFMANNSTHAL et par Thomas MANN. La Bible en littérature. 1997, ⇒315. ᴱBeaude, Pierre-Marie, 73-86.

1870  **Longacre, Robert E.** Joseph, a study in divine providence: a text theoretical and textlinguistic analysis of Genesis 37 and 39-48. 1989, ⇒5,2334... 8,2443*. ᴿJNES 56 (1997) 155-156 *(Miller, C.)*.

1871  *Mathes, Marianne* Brunnen und Brunnenheld in Thomas MANNS Josephsroman. Symb. 13 (1997) 97-104.

1872  *Minette de Tillesse, Caetano* Na Diáspora: história de José (Gên 37-50). RBB 14/1-3 (1997) 149-154;

1873  Na Diáspora: José no Egito e Ester. RBB 14/1-3 (1997) 174-177.

1874  *O'Brien, Mark A.* The contribution of Judah's speech, Genesis 44:18-34, to the characterization of Joseph. CBQ 59 (1997) 429-447.

1875  *Rabenau, Konrad von Inductio in tentationem*—Joseph in Ägypten. Ägypten-Bilder. OBO 150: 1997, ⇒378. ᴱStaehelin, E., 35-50.

1876  **Standhartinger, Angela** Das Frauenbild im Judentum der hellenistischen Zeit: ein Beitrag anhand von 'Joseph und Aseneth'. Diss. Fra. AGJU 26: 1995, ⇒11/2,6800. ᴿBiOr 54 (1997) 192-195 *(Tromp, J.)*; JSJ 28 (1997) 350-353 *(Piñero, Antonio)*.

1877  **Szwarc, Urszula** Przesłanie Rdz 39 i Pwt 33: studium literacko-egzegetyczno-historyczne [Le message de Gn 49 et Dt 33: étude littéraire, exégétique et historique]. 1997, Diss.-Habil. Lublin. **P**.

## ᴇ3.1  Exodus event and theme; *textus, commentarii*

1878  **Bräumer, Hansjörg** Das zweite Buch Mose: Kap. 1 bis 18. WStB.AT: 1996, ⇒12,1754. ᴿJETh 11 (1997) 180-182 *(Hilbrands, Walter)*.

1879  **Childs, Brevard S.** Il libro dell'Esodo: commentario critico-teologico. ᵀ*Ferroni, Andrea*: 1995, ⇒11/1,526; 12,1756. ᴿProtest. 52 (1997) 73-75 *(Tron, Claudio)*; Gr. 78 (1997) 555-556 *(Prato, Gian Luigi)*; CivCatt 148 I (1997) 517-519 *(Prato, G.L.)*.

1880  *Haar Romeny, R.B. ter* Early Antiochene commentaries on Exodus. StPatr 33: 1997, ⇒351. ᴱLivingstone, Elizabeth A., 114-119.

1881  **Houtman, Cornelis** Exodus II: een praktische bijbelverklaring [15-40]. Kampen 1997, Kok 248 pp. [ITBT 6/3,31—Wöhle, Andreas];

1882  Exodus 2: Chapters 7:14-19:25. Hist. Comment. on the OT: 1996, ⇒12,1757. ᴿETR 72 (1997) 128 *(Macchi, Jean-Daniel)*.

1883  **Jacob, Benno** Das Buch Exodus ᴱ*Mayer, Shlomo* <ed>; Collab. *Hahn, Joachim; Jürgensen, Almuth*: Stu 1997, Calwer xxv; 1098 pp. Leo Baeck Institut. Bibl. 3-7668-3515-7.

1884  **Janzen, J. Gerald** Exodus. Westminster Bible companion: LVL 1997, Westminster xii; 275 pp. $18. 0-664-25255-9.

1885  ᴱᵀ**Lockshin, Martin L.** RASHBAM's commentary on Exodus: an annotated translation. Ill. *Lockshin, Channa*: BJSt 310: Atlanta 1997, Scholars 452 pp. $39.95. 0-7885-0225-5 [JSJ 28,367].

1886  *Ortega-Monasterio, M.ᵃ Teresa* Some Masoretic notes of Mss. L and Or 4445 compared with the Spanish tradition. Sum., res. 133. Sef. 57/1 (1997) 127-133.

1887 [E]*Patton, Corrine* Selections from Nicholas of Lyra's Commentary on Exodus. Theological interpretation. 1997, ⇒244. [E]Fowl, S., 114-128.

1888 [E]**Vervenne, Marc** Studies in the book of Exodus. BEThL 126: 1996, ⇒12,1794. [R]RB 104 (1997) 427-428 *(Langlamet, F.)*; ThLZ 122 (1997) 900-902 *(Utzschneider, Helmut)*; EThL 73 (1997) 419-420 *(Schoors, A.)*.

1889 **Anati, Emmanuel** Esodo tra mito e storia: archeologia, esegesi e geografia storica. Studi Camuni 18: Capo di Ponte Valcamonica (BS) 1997, Centro 304 pp. Bibl. L56.000. 88-86621-10-8.

1890 **Auzou, Georges** Dalla servitù al servizio: il libro dell'Esodo. Lettura pastorale della Bibbia 25: Bo 1997, EDB 314 pp. L38.000. 88-10-20516-2 [RivBib 45,383].

1891 *Barbi, Augusto* L'esodo nell'opera lucana. DSBP 17 (1997) 149-166.

1892 *Bazzi, Carlo* Il valore permanente dell'Esodo. PaVi 42/4 (1997) 4-12.

1893 *Bianchi, F.* Obbedienza e disobbedienza nel libro dell'Esodo: il caso delle 'mormorazioni'. L'obbedienza. 1997, ⇒216. [E]Marrocu, Giuseppe, 59-80.

1894 *Blenkinsopp, Joseph* Structure and meaning in the Sinai-Horeb narrative. JSOT.S 240: 1997, ⇒20. [F]Coats G., 109-125 [Exod 19-34].

1895 *Bonato, Antonio* Passi scelti di Esodo nell'interpretazione di Ambrogio: dalla rivelazione del roveto (c. 3,5ss) all'alleanza del Sinai (cc. 19-20.24). DSBP 18 (1997) 135-184.

1896 *Carbone, Sandro* La teologia e la spiritualità dell'esodo nella letteratura paolina. DSBP 17 (1997) 135-148;

1897 Teologia e spiritualità dell'esodo nell'Apocalisse;

1898 *Carcione, Filippo* Teologia e spiritualità dell'esodo in Ireneo. DSBP 18 (1997) 221-237/35-52.

1899 *Cardellini, Innocenzo* Esodo ...!: quando?: come?. RivBib 45 (1997) 129-142.

1900 *Covito, Antonio* Le figure dell'esodo nei Padri antiocheni;

1901 *Danieli, Maria Ignazia* La teologia e la spiritualità dell'esodo negli scritti di Origene e dei primi padri monastici (III-V secolo). DSBP 18 (1997) 109-134/53-76.

1902 *Davies, Graham I.* K[D] in Exodus: an assessment of E. Blum's proposal. BEThL 133: 1997, ⇒17. [F]Brekelmans C., 407-420.

1903 *Dell'Orto, Giuseppe* Soggiorno e schiavitù degli ebrei in Egitto. PaVi 42/1 (1997) 10-15.

1904 *Dever, William G.* Is there any archaeological evidence for the Exodus?. Exodus. 1997, ⇒325. [E]Frerichs, Ernest S., 67-86.

1905 *Drobner, Hubertus R.* L'esodo secondo gli apologeti greci. [T]*Frasseto, Anna Livia*;

1906 *Drobner, Hubertus R.* L'esodo secondo i Padri asiatici e palestinesi nella tradizione esegetica alessandrina. [T]*Porcedda, William*: DSBP 18 (1997) 23-34/77-108.

1907 *Fabris, Rinaldo* L'esodo nella Lettera agli Ebrei. DSBP 17 (1997) 211-220.

1908 **Facey, A.** Esodo: chiamati all'alleanza. Bo 1997, EDB 60 pp. L8.000 [RivBib 45,383].

1909  **Fontana, Raniero** Sinai e Sion: luogo della sapienza agli uomini. Diss. extract Pontificia Universitas Urbaniana, ᴰ*Federici, Tommaso:* R 1997, 114 pp.

1910  *Frymer-Kensky, Tikva* Forgotten heroines of the Exodus: the exclusion of women from Moses' vision. BiRe 13/6 (1997) 38-44.

1911  *Groll, Sarah I.* The historical background to the Exodus: Papyrus Anastasi VII. CRB 36: 1997, ⇒21. ᴹCouroyer B., 109-114.

1912  **Hoffmeier, James Karl** Israel in Egypt: the evidence for the authenticity of the Exodus tradition. NY 1997, OUP xix; 244 pp. $35. 0-19-509715-7.

1913  *Kaswalder, Pietro* Archeologia dell'Esodo. PaVi 42 1, 2, 3 (1997) 46-49, 42-45, 38-41.

1914  **Knohl, Israel** The sanctuary of silence: the priestly torah and the holiness school. 1995, ⇒11/1,545; 12,1778. ᴿCBQ 59 (1997) 740-741 *(Gnuse, Robert).*

1915  *Malamat, Abraham* The Exodus: Egyptian analogies. Exodus. 1997, ⇒325. ᴱFrerichs, Ernest S., 15-26.

1916  **Oswald, Wolfgang** Gottesberg—Wüste Sinai—Berg Sinai: eine Untersuchung zur Literargeschichte der vorderen Sinaiperikope Ex 19-24 und ihrem historischen Hintergrund. Diss. ᴰ*Krüger, T.:* Z 1996-1997 [ThLZ 122,765] [Exod 19-24].

1917  *Panimolle, Salvatore A:* L'esodo, 'evangelo di Dio';

1918  L'esodo nei primi due vangeli sinottici. DSBP 17 (1997) 9-23/104-134;

1919  L'esodo nei primi scritti dei Padri. DSBP 18 (1997) 9-22;

1920  L'esodo nel quarto vangelo. DSBP 17 (1997) 167-210.

1921  *Perani, Mauro* Lettura giudaica-rabbinica dell'Esodo. PaVi 42/1-4 (1997) 50-53/46-48/41-43/42-44.

1922  *Petit, F.* La chaîne grecque sur l'Exode: description générale et problèmes spécifiques. StPatr 33: 1997, ⇒351. ᴱLivingstone, Elizabeth A., 97-101.

1923  *Polak, Frank H.* Water, rock, and wood: structure and thought pattern in the Exodus narrative. JANES 25 (1997) 19-42.

1924  *Priotto, Michelangelo* Un verbo significativo: uscire. PaVi 42/1 (1997) 34-38.

1925  *Raem, Heinz-Albert* Ökumene als Wüstenwanderung: das Buch Exodus als Wegbeschreibung zur Einheit der Christen: eine ökumenische Meditation. 1997, ᶠUllrich L., ⇒98, 34-43.

1926  *Rendtorff, Rolf* Die Herausführungsformel in ihrem literarischen und theologischen Kontext. BEThL 133: 1997, ⇒17. ᶠBrekelmans C., 501-527.

1927  *Rota Scalabrini, Patrizio* Il Dio dell'Esodo. PaVi 42/2 (1997) 4-9.

1928  *Scognamiglio, Rosario* Lettura origeniana dell'Esodo. PaVi 42/1-4 (1997) 54-56/49-51/44-47/43-46.

1929  **Smith, Mark S.** The pilgrimage pattern in Exodus. Collab. *Bloch-Smith, Elizabeth M.:* JSOT.S 239: Shf 1997, Academic 355 pp. Bibl. £44/$66. 1-85075-652-X.

1930  *Spreafico, Ambrogio* Il triplice esodo nell'Antico Testamento;

1931  *Stefani, Piero* La spiritualità dell'esodo negli scritti giudaici dell'epoca del secondo tempio. DSBP 17 (1997) 24-87/88-103.

1932  *Ward, William A.* Summary and conclusions;

1933  *Weinstein, James* Exodus and archaeological reality. Exodus. 1997, ⇒325. ᴱFrerichs, Ernest S., 105-112/87-103.

E3.2 **Moyses**—Pharaoh, Goshen—*Exodus 1...*

1934 *Alexandre, Jean* Moïse, les femmes, la liberté, la Réforme. Moïse hébreu Moïse égyptien. 1997, ⇒1964. [E]Malet, N.-M., 61-66.

1935 **Assmann, Jan** Moses the Egyptian: the memory of Egypt in western monotheism. CM 1997, Harvard University Press x; (2) 276 pp. $30. 0-674-58738-3.

1936 **Auld, A. Graeme** Kings without privilege: David and Moses in the story of the bible's kings. 1994, ⇒10,2583... 12,2404. [R]SJTh 50 (1997) 256-258 *(Johnstone, William)*; CBQ 59 (1997) 107-108 *(Kennedy, James M.)*.

1937 *Ayoun, Richard* Archéologie et histoire. Moïse hébreu Moïse égyptien. 1997, ⇒1964. [E]Malet, N.-M., 175-184.

1938 *Beauchamp, Paul* Moïse à la place de Dieu. Croire aujourd'hui 21 (1997) 34-35;

1939 Moïse dans le péché des siens. Croire aujourd'hui 22 (1997) 30-31.

1940 *Bernheim, Gilles* La logique du faire. Moïse hébreu Moïse égyptien. 1997, ⇒1964. [E]Malet, N.-M., 79-84.

1941 **Blasi-Cappellini, Emanuele** Le due anime dell'ebraismo: il dilemma ebraico: Mosé. Coll. Thesis: Ancona 1996, Nuove Ricerche 160 pp. Bibl.

1942 **Blum, Erhard** Studien zur Komposition des Pentateuch. BZAW 189: 1990, ⇒6,2527...8,2487. [R]RStR 23 (1997) 22-31 *(Carr, David M.)*.

1943 *Boubakeur, Dalil* Moïse dans l'Islam. Moïse hébreu Moïse égyptien. 1997, ⇒1964. [E]Malet, N.-M., 67-78.

1944 *Boyer, Frédéric* Quand Israël rencontre Pharaon. MoBi 102 (1997) 29-30.

1945 *Briend, Jacques* Pharaon, figure de l'autorité politique. MoBi 102 (1997) 33-35.

1946 *Castello, Gaetano* Mosè: crisi della missione: Es 5,1-6,1. PaVi 42/2 (1997) 15-18.

1947 *Charlier, Pascal* Les pierres du pharaon: étude lexicographique sur les obnâyim d'Exode 1,16. Analecta Bruxellensia 2 (1997) 146-151 [ZID 24,344].

1948 **Chouraqui, André** Moisés: viaje a los confines de un misterio realizado y de una utopía realizable. [T]*Simons, Edison*: Barc 1997, Herder 404 pp. [Mayéutica 23,498s—Mediavilla, Rafael].

1949 *Chouraqui, André* Moïse fondateur et fédérateur des religions abrahamiques. Moïse hébreu Moïse égyptien. 1997, ⇒1964. [E]Malet, N.-M., 43-50.

1950 **Chouraqui, André** Mosè. Genova 1997, Marietti 400 pp. L39.000 [Presbyteri 32/1,78].

1951 *Clark, Malcolm* Biblical and early islamic Moses. JSOT.S 240: 1997, ⇒20. [F]COATS G., 20-38.

1952 **Courtney, Richard** The birth of God: the Moses play and monotheism in ancient Israel. AmUSt 26/26: NY 1997, Lang xv; (2) 235 pp. Bibl. 0-8294-3055-2.

1953 *Dalla Vecchia, Flavio* La missione di Mosè. PaVi 42/2 (1997) 10-14.

1954 *Derda, Tomasz* Did the Jews use the name of Moses in antiquity?. ZPE 115 (1997) 257-260.

1955  *Desroches-Noblecourt, Christiane* Raisonnances bibliques chez une égyptologue;

1956  *Durand, Jean-Paul* Entrer en dialogue: promouvoir un dialogue interreligieux en éthique et en théologie morale;

1957  *Durand, Jean-Paul* La loi et la vie: éléments d'un passage. Moïse hébreu Moïse égyptien. 1997, ⇒1964. EMalet, N.-M., 133-148/17-41/85-95.

1958  *Ferrari, Pier Luigi* Nascita di Mosè (Es 2,1-10). PaVi 42/1 (1997) 18-22.

1959  *Hughes, Paul E.* Moses' birth story: a biblical matrix for prophetic messianism. Eschatology, messianism. SDSSRL 1: 1997, ⇒276. EEvans, Craig A., 10-22.

1960  *Jagersma, H.* 'Toen stond er een nieuwe koning op' Exodus 1:8-14. ITBT 5/5 (1997) 7-8.

1961  *Kattan, Naïm* Moïse, le guide. Moïse hébreu Moïse égyptien. 1997, ⇒1964. EMalet, N.-M., 111-121.

1962  *Kellenberger, Edgar* Der geplagte Mose: Plädoyer für ein nicht-moralisierendes Verständnis von ʿanaw und πραεῖς. PzB 6 (1997) 81-86 [Num 12,3; Matt 5,5].

1963  **MacQuarrie, John** Mediators between human and divine: from Moses to Muhammad. 1996, ⇒12,1810. RHorizons 24 (1997) 330-331 *(Carpenter, David)*.

1964  EMalet, Nicole-Maya Moïse hébreu Moïse égyptien. Revue d'éthique et de théologie morale: le supplément 201: P 1997, Cerf 224 pp. FF120. 0750-1455.

1965  *Malet, Nicole-Maya* Le monothéisme: premiers pas vers la raison. Hommage à Marthe Robert;

1966  Ouverture: inconnue, c'est-à-dire oubliée;

1967  Raisonnances de la figure de Moïse pour tout un chacun. Moïse hébreu Moïse égyptien. 1997, ⇒1964. EMalet, N.-M., 187-190/7-15/3-4.

1968  EMartín-Lunas, Teodoro H. San GREGORIO de Nisa: vida de Moisés. 1993, ⇒9,2280... 10,2169. REstB 55 (1997) 423-426 *(Urbán, A.)*.

1969  *Mazzinghi, Luca* La fuga di Mosè e la risposta di Dio al grido di Israele (Es 2,11-25). PaVi 42/1 (1997) 23-27.

1970  **Nohrnberg, James** Like unto Moses: the constituting of an inter-ruption. ISBL: 1995, ⇒11/1,576; 12,1815. RJR 77 (1997) 455-457 *(Rosenblatt, Jason P.)*.

1971  **Paul, Robert A.** Moses and civilization: the meaning behind FREUD's myth. 1996, ⇒12,1816. RJR 77 (1997) 509-510 *(Jaffe, Samuel P.)*.

1972  *Pelckmans, Paul* De navolging van Mozes. Str. 64/1 (1997) 38-47.

1973  *Rendtorff, Rolf* Some reflections on the canonical Moses: Moses and Abraham. JSOT.S 240: 1997, ⇒20. FCOATS G., 11-19.

1974  *Safouan, Mustapha* Moïse hébreu, Moïse égyptien;

1975  *Seddik, Youssef* Moïse dé-réalisé dans le Coran;

1976  *Sitruk, Joseph* Moïse. Moïse hébreu Moïse égyptien. 1997, ⇒1964. EMalet, N.-M., 51-60/123-126/191-196.

1977  *Smend, Rudolf* Mose als geschichtliche Gestalt. Bibel, Theologie. KVR 1582: 1997 <1995>, ⇒162. 5-20.

1978  ETrigg, Joseph W. Selections from GREGORY of Nyssa's Life of Moses. Theological interpretation. 1997, ⇒244. EFowl, S., 103-113.

1979 **Van Seters, John** The life of Moses: the Yahwist as historian in Exodus-Numbers. 1994, ⇒10,2177... 12,1823. <sup>R</sup>RStR 23/1 (1997) 22-31 *(Carr, David M.)*; Protest. 52 (1997) 326-327 *(Soggin, J.A.)*; SR 26 (1997) 227-228 *(Vogels, Walter)*.

1980 *Venema, G.J.* Mozes in analyse. ITBT 5/7 (1997) 27-28.

1981 *Williams, Margaret H.* Jewish use of Moses as a personal name in Graeco-Roman antiquity—a note. ZPE 113 (1997) 274.

1982 *Zivie, Alain* Ramsès II et l'Exode: une idée reçue?. MoBi 102 (1997) 30-32.

### E3.3 Nomen divinum, Tetragrammaton; *Exodus 3,14...*Plagues

1983 *Adler, William* Exodus 6:23 and the high priest from the tribe of Judah. JThS 48 (1997) 24-47.
Der Allmächtige: Annäherung an ein umstrittenes Gottesprädikat ⇒1563.

1984 **Berge, Kare** Reading sources in a text: coherence and literary criticism in the call of Moses: models—methods—micro-analysis. ATSAT 54: St. Ottilien 1997, EOS ix; 223 pp. 3-88096-554-4.

1985 *Brueggemann, Walter* Exodus 3: summons to holy transformation. Theological interpretation. 1997, ⇒244. <sup>E</sup>Fowl, S., 155-171.

1986 *Crüsemann, Marlene* Gottesname: Jahwe/JHWH. Antijudaismus im NT. <sup>E</sup>Henze, Dagmar, KT 149: 1997, ⇒κ8. 31-32.

1987 *Freedman, David Noel* The name of the God of Moses. Divine Commitment 1. 1997 <1960>, ⇒124. 82-87.

1988 *Fretheim, Terence E.* Exodus 3: a theological interpretation. Theological interpretation. 1997, ⇒244. <sup>E</sup>Fowl, S., 143-154.

1989 *Fritz, Volkmar* Jahwe und El in den vorpriesterschriftlichen Geschichtswerken. Studien zur Literatur. 1997 <1994>, ⇒126. 51-66.

1990 **Gnuse, Robert Karl** No other gods: emergent monotheism in Israel. JSOT.S 241: Shf 1997, Academic 392 pp. $78. 1-87075-657-0.

1991 *Goedicke, Hans* The tetragram in Egyptian?. JSSEA 24 (1994) 24-26.

1992 *Haggenmüller, Odo* Die Heiligung des Namens. EuA 73 (1997) 185-195.

1993 *Joubert, Justin* Moïse mystique;

1994 *Martelet, Gustave* Révélation de l'Horeb et amour de l'autre [Exod 3]. Moïse hébreu Moïse égyptien. 1997, ⇒1964. <sup>E</sup>Malet, N.-M., 201-208/197-200.

1995 **Mettinger, Tryggve N.D.** Buscando a Dios: significado y mensaje de los nombres divinos en la biblia. 1994, ⇒10,2195... 12,1840. <sup>R</sup>RF 181 (1997) 321-322 *(Tamayo-Acosta, Juan José)*.

1996 *Michel, Diethelm* Nur ich bin Jahwe: Erwägungen zur sogenannten Selbstvorstellungsformel. Studien zur Überlieferungsgeschichte. TB 93: 1997 <1973>, ⇒149. 1-12 [1 Kgs 20,13; Isaiah 43,11; 45,5; 42,8].

1997 **Moor, Johannes Cornelis de** The rise of Yahwism: the roots of Israelite monotheism. BEThL 91: Lv <sup>2</sup>1997, Peeters xiv; 445 pp. FB1.400. 90-6831-901-9.

1998   *Ochs, Peter* Three postcritical encounters with the burning bush. Theological interpretation. 1997, ⇒244. ᴱFowl, S., 129-142 [Exod 3].

1999   *Orel, Vladimir* The words on the doorpost. ZAW 109 (1997) 614-617 [Exod 3,14; Deut 6,4].

2000   *Pierro, Matteo* "JHWH": il tetragramma nel Nuovo Testamento. RivBib 45 (1997) 183-186.

2001   *Robinson, Bernard P.* Moses at the burning bush. JSOT 75 (1997) 107-122 [Exod 3].

2002   **Ruck-Schröder, Adelheid** ONOMA: eine exegetisch-theologische Untersuchung zur Bedeutung der Namensaussagen im Neuen Testament. Diss. Berlin 1997-98; ᴰ*Von der Osten-Sacken, P.* [RTL 29,588].

2003   **Scriba, Albrecht** Die Geschichte des Motivkomplexes Theophanie. FRLANT 167: 1995, ⇒11/1,598; 12,1843. ᴿJThS 48 (1997) 209-212 *(Bockmuehl, M.)*; JBL 116 (1997) 550-552 *(Stuckenbruck, Loren)*.

2004   **Tournier, Michel** Eléazar ou la source et le buisson. 1996, ⇒12,1847. ᴿStr. 64/1 (1997) 38-47 *(Pelckmans, Paul)*.

2005   *Trabacchin, Gianni* La rilettura sacerdotale della vocazione di Mosè: Es 6,2-8. PaVi 42/2 (1997) 19-24.

2006   **Van Nieuwpoort, Ad** De kleine Mensengod: de bijbel kan ons nog meer vertellen. Amst 1997, Prometheus 176 pp. ƒ29.90. 90-5333-532-3. ᴿITBT 5/5 (1997) 31 *(Nienhuis, J.R.)*.

2007   *Voghera, Pierluigi* Un roveto di fuoco (Es 3,1-6). PaVi 42/1 (1997) 29-33.

2008   *Vries, Sytze de* 'God, laat ons staan als Mozes hier...': kanttekeningen bij een liedtekst van Karel DEURLOO. ITBT 5/1 (1997) 12-14 [Exod 3].

2009   *Waldman, Nahum M.* Divine names. JBQ 25 (1997) 162-168.

2010   *Wiggins, Steve A.* A rejoinder to J. Glen TAYLOR. ⇒12,1846. JSOT 73 (1997) 109-112.

2011   **Wilson, Marvin T.** YHWH in the bible: divine titles, names & attributes. Celina, Texas 1997, Pilgrim iv; 114 pp. 1-9660979-0-4f [NThAR 2000,123].

2012   *Doglio, Claudio* Il racconto delle 'piaghe': Es 7,8-11,10. PaVi 42/2 (1997) 25-31.

2013   *Ghidelli, Carlo* L'indurimento del cuore del faraone. PaVi 42/2 (1997) 32-37.

2014   **Lemmelijn, Bénédicte** Het verhaal van de 'Plagen in Egypte' (Exodus 7,14-11,10): een onderzoek naar het onstaan en de compositie van de Pentateuchtraditie [Le récit des 'Plaies d'Égypte' (Ex 7,14-11,10): recherche sur la formation et la composition de la tradition du pentateuque. Diss. Leuven 1997; ᴰ*Vervenne, M.*: 2 vols; lvi; 629; 172 pp [RTL 29,578].

2015   *Rashkow, Ilona N.* Oedipus wrecks: Moses and God's rod. Reading bibles. 1997, ⇒172. ᴱBeal, Timothy K., 72-84.

2016   *Richard, Pablo* Las plagas en la biblia: Éxodo y Apocalipsis. Conc(I) 33,958-969; Conc(GB) 1997/5,45-54; Conc(F) 273,65-75; (D33,624-632); Conc(E) 273 (1997) 885-894.

2017   *Schwantes, Milton* "Lass mein Volk aus Ägypten ausziehen": Bemerkungen über Exodus 3. 1997, ⇒29. ᶠGERSTENBERGER S., 95-109.

E3.4 Pascha, sanguis, sacrificium: **Passover, blood, sacrifice, *Ex 11*..**

2018  *Álvarez Baredo, M.* La narración de la pascua en Ex 12,1-28: niveles de formación. Carthaginensia 13 (1997) 1-18.

2019  **Ahuis, Ferdinand** Exodus 11,1-13,16 und die Bedeutung der Trägergruppen für das Verständnis des Passa. FRLANT 168: 1996, ⇒12,1853. ᴿBib. 78 (1997) 266-268 *(Grünwaldt, Klaus)*; ThLZ 122 (1997) 794-795 *(Dohmen, Christoph)*.

2020  *Benzi, Guido* Es 15: il Canto del Mare. PaVi 42/4 (1997) 21-27.

2021  *Boschi, Bernardo Gianluigi* Il valore emblematico della Pasqua a Elefantina. RStB 9/1 (1997) 99-117.

2022  *Bosetti, Elena* Miriam: la profetessa dell'Esodo. TS(I) (1997 maggio-giugno) 11-14 [Exod 15,21].

2023  *Büchner, Dirk* On the relationship between MEKILTA de Rabbi Ishmael and Septuagint Exodus 12-23. IX Congress IOSCS. SCSt 45: 1997, ⇒340. ᴱTaylor, Bernard A., 403-420.

2024  *Carpenter, Eugene* Exodus 18: its structure, style, motifs and function in the book of Exodus. JSOT.S 240: 1997, ⇒20. ᶠCOATS G., 91-108.

2025  *Chilton, Bruce* The hungry knife: towards a sense of sacrifice. Jesus in context. AGAJ 39: 1997 <1995>, ⇒183. 91-108.

2026  **Chiodi, Silvia Maria** Offerte "funebri" nella Lagas presargonica. Materiali per il vocabolario sumerico 5,1-2: R 1997, Università degli Studi di Roma "La Sapienza". Dipart. di Studi Orientali 2 vols.

2027  *Dell'Orto, Giuseppe* La cena pasquale ebraica (Haggadah di Pesah). PaVi 42/3 (1997) 34-37;

2028  L'Israele di Dio (Es 19,1-8). PaVi 42/5 (1997) 4-10;

2029  L'origine della pasqua. PaVi 42/3 (1997) 4-9.

2030  *Di Palma, Gaetano* La teofani del Sinai (Es 19,9-25). PaVi 42/5 (1997) 11-15.

2031  *Ferrari, Pierluigi* Dalla schiavitù faraonica al servizio pasquale. PaVi 42/3 (1997) 28-33.

2032  *Freedman, David Noel* Temple without hands. Divine Commitment 1. 1997 <1981>, ⇒124. 330-340 [Exod 15,17].

2033  *Fritz, Volkmar* 'Bis an die Hörner des Altars': Erwägungen zur Praxis des Brandopfers in Israel. Studien zur Literatur. 1997 <1993>, ⇒126. 227-237.

2034  *Gallazzi, Sandro* 'Worthless is the fat of whole burnt offerings': a critique of the sacrifice of the second temple. Subversive scriptures. 1997, ⇒263. ᴱVaage, L., 124-141.

2035  *Loza Vera, José* Exode 13,17-14,31 et la bataille de Qadesh. CRB 36: 1997, ⇒21. ᴹCOUROYER B., 29-42.

2036  *Manzi, Franco* Il 'memoriale' di Es 12,1-14: lettura sacramentale. PaVi 42/3 (1997) 10-16.

2037  *Marx, Alfred* La place du sacrifice dans l'ancien Israël [Girard, René]. Congress volume 1995. VT.S 66: 1997, ⇒323. ᴱEmerton, J.A., 203-217.

2038  *Milani, Marcello* Il passaggio del mare (Es 14). PaVi 42/4 (1997) 13-19.

2039  *Nepi, Antonio* Massa e Meriba: la crisi della fede. PaVi 42/4 (1997) 28-34 [Exod 17,1-7].

2040  **Plunket, Rodney** 'Between Elim and Sinai': a theological interpretation of Exodus sixteen shaped by its canonical context. Diss. Durham 1997; D*Moberly, R.W.L.*

2041  *Priotto, Michelangelo* Dalla pasqua egiziana alla pasqua di Giosia: storia di un cammino. PaVi 42/3 (1997) 23-27 [Exod 12,29-42; 2 Kgs 23,21-23].

2042  *Rayner, John D.* Die Kinder des Seder. 1997, ⇒25. FFRIEDLANDER A., 153-163.

2043  *Ribichini, Sergio* Sacrifici umani a Tiro?: la testimonianza di Q. Curzio RUFO. AOAT 247: 1997, ⇒75. FROELLIG W., 355-361.

2044  **Rooze, Egbert** Amalek geweldig verslagen: een bijbelstheologisch onderzoek naar de vijandschap Israël-Amalek. 1995, ⇒12,1889. RITBT 5/1 (1997) 23-25 *(Betlem, Henk)* [Exod 17,8-16].

2045  **Saßmann, Christiane Karin** Die Opferbereitschaft Israels: anthropologische und theologische Voraussetzungen des Opferkultes. EHS.T 529: 1995, ⇒12,7146. RThLZ 122 (1997) 26-27 *(Seebass, Horst).*

2046  *Schenker, Adrian* Once again, the expiatory sacrifices. JBL 116 (1997) 697-699.

2047  **Schuil, A.** Amalek: onderzoek naar oorsprong en ontwikkeling van Amaleks rol in het Oude Testament. Diss. Rijksuniversiteit Utrecht 1997; D*Becking, B.*: Zoetermeer 1997, Boekencentrum [Ex 17,8-16].

2048  **Ska, Jean Louis** Le passage de la mer: étude de la construction, du style et de la symbolique d'Ex 14,1-31. AnBib 109: R ²1997 <1986>, Ed. Pont. Ist. Biblico 204 pp. L46.000/EUR23,75. 88-7653-109-2.

2049  *Trabacchin, Gianni* La decima piaga e l'uscita dall'Egitto: Es 12,29-42. PaVi 42/3 (1997) 17-22.

2050  *Vervenne, Marc* Le récit de la mer (Exode xiii 17-xiv 31) reflète-t-il une rédaction de type deutéronomique?: quelques remarques sur le problème de l'identification des éléments deutéronomiques contenus dans le Tétrateuque. Congress volume 1995. VT.S 66: 1997, ⇒323. EEmerton, J.A., 365-380.

2051  *Weimar, Peter* Exodus 12,24-27a: ein Zusatz nachdeuteronomistischer Provenienz aus der Hand der Pentateuchredaktion. BEThL 133: 1997, ⇒17. FBREKELMANS C., 421-448.

E3.5 **Decalogus,** *Ex 20 = Dt 5; Ex 21ss;* **Ancient Near East Law**

2052  **García López, Félix** O decálogo. Cadernos Bíblicos 58: Lisboa 1997, Difusora Bíblica 60 pp. [Bib(L) 7/7,188—Negreiros, Fernando de].

2053  **Harrelson, Walter J.** The ten commandments and human rights. Macon, GA ²1997, Mercer University Press ix; (2) 195 pp. $20. 0-86554-542-1.

2054  *Johnston, Robert M.* The ten commandments and ethical dilemmas. 1997, ⇒83. FSHEA W., 265-271.

2055  *Loza Vera, José* ORIGEN y significación del Decálogo (Ex 20,1-17; Dt 5,4-22). AnáMnesis 7/2 (1997) 5-36.

2056 ᵀSpaeth, Paul J. St. BONAVENTURE's Collations on the Ten Commandments. Works of Saint Bonaventure 6: 1995, ⇒11/1,656. ᴿCFr 67/1-2 (1997) 293-294 *(Maranesi, Pietro)*.

2057 *Stefani, Piero* Il decalogo, legge di Dio per Israele e per le genti. PaVi 42/5 (1997) 16-20.

2058 *Wénin, André* Le Décalogue: approche contextuelle, théologie et anthropologie. La loi. LeDiv 168: 1997, ⇒195. ᴱFocant, Camille, 9-43.

2059 *Arand, Charles P.* LUTHER on the God behind the first commandment. Adapted by *Menschke, Timothy H.*: Luther Digest 5 (1997) 28-33.

2060 ᴱBaptist-Hlawatsch, Gabriele ULRICH von Pottenstein: Dekalog-Auslegung: Text und Quellen: das erste Gebot. 1995, ⇒11/1,660. ᴿThLZ 122 (1997) 348-349 *(Haustein, Jens)*; MAe 66/1 (1997) 165-166 *(Harris, Nigel)* [Exod 20,3; Deut 5,7].

2061 *Burba, Klaus* Das 1. Gebot: meine Existenzform in einer pluralistischen Gesellschaft. Luther 68/1 (1997) 11-17.

2062 ᴱDietrich, Walter; Klopfenstein, Martin A. Ein Gott allein? JHWH-Verehrung und biblischer Monotheismus im Kontext der israelitischen und altorientalischen Religionsgeschichte. OBO 139: 1994, ⇒10,476*. ᴿAcOr 58 (1997) 199-201 *(Barstad, H.M.)*; ThLZ 122 (1997) 1109-1112 *(Weippert, Manfred)* [Exod 20,3].

2063 **Rechenmacher, Hans** "Ausser mir gibt es keinen Gott!": eine sprach- und literaturwissenschaftliche Studie zur Ausschliesslichkeitsformel. ATSAT 49: St. Ottilien 1997, EOS x; 241 pp. Bibl. 3-88096-549-8.

2064 *Schmidt, Werner H.* "Monotheismus" und Erstes Gebot. ThLZ 122 (1997) 1081-1092.

2065 *Smend, Rudolf* "Ich bin der Herr, dein Gott" (Exodus 20,2a). Bibel, Theologie. KVR 1582: 1997, ⇒162, 35-40.

2066 *Amiet, Pierre* Anthropomorphisme et aniconisme dans l'antiquité orientale. RB 104 (1997) 321-337.

2067 **Kochan, Lionel** Beyond the graven image: a Jewish view. NY 1997, New York Univ. Press vi; 223 pp. $45. 0-8147-4700-0 [ThD 45,78—Heiser, W. Charles].

2068 *Kohn, Mathias* 'Du sollst dir kein Bildnis machen': Deutungen und Bedeutungen des alttestamentlichen 'Bildverbots'. 1997, ⇒106. ᶠWOSCHITZ K., 57-69.

2069 **Mettinger, Tryggve N.D.** No graven image?: Israelite aniconism in its ancient Near Eastern context. CB.OT 42: 1995, ⇒11/1,672; 12,1944. ᴿBArR 23/3 (1997) 46-51, 68 *(Hurowitz, Victor)*; BiOr 54 (1997) 310-311 *(Wright, G.H.R.)*; IEJ 48 (1997) 150-153 *(Patrich, Joseph)*; StEL 14 (1997) 125-128 *(Merlo, Paolo)*; CBQ 58 (1996) 719-720 *(Wiggins, Steve A.)*.

2070 *Plattig, Michael* Bilderverbot und Bilderfülle—zwei Wege mit demselben Ziel?. Edith Stein Jahrbuch 3 (1997) 278-292.

2071 ᴱRainer, Michael J.; Janßen, Hans-Gerd Bilderverbot. Jahrbuch Politische Theologie 2 (1997).

2072 *Scognamiglio, Rosario* 'Un Dio geloso' (Es 20,5): l'inizio del decalogo nel commento di ORIGENE. PaVi 42/5 (1997) 46-48.

2073 ᴱVan der Toorn, Karel The image and the book: iconic cults, aniconism, and the rise of book religion in Israel and the ancient Near

East. Contributions to Biblical Exegesis and Theology 21: Lv 1997
Peeters 271 pp. Bibl. FB1.240. 90-6831-983-3.
2074 *Eder, Asher* The Sabbath commandment: its two versions. JBQ 25
(1997) 188-191 [Exod 20,8-11; Deut 5,12-15; Isaiah 6,3].
2075 **McKay, Heather A.** Sabbath and synagogue: the question of sabbath worship in ancient Judaism. 1994, ⇒10,7307... 12,6774. ᴿJSJ
28/3 (1997) 342-343 *(Tomson, Peter J.)*.
2076 *Schüngel-Straumann, Helen* Das Geschenk des Sabbat im Alten
Testament. BiKi 52 (1997) 119-123.
2077 *Grajewski, Jan* 'Czcij ojca swego i matkę twoją': w listach Nowego Testamentu ['Honour your father mother' in the NT epistles].
1997, ⇒52. ᶠLACH J., 139-74. **P.**

2078 **Ausloos, Hans** Deuteronomi(sti)sche elementen in Genesis-Nume-
ri: een onderzoek naar criteria voor identificatie op basis van een li-
teraire analyse van de epiloog van het 'Verbondsboek' (Exodus
23,20-33)> [Éléments deutéronomiques/stes dans Genèse-
Nombres: recherche de critères d'identification sur base d'une analyse littéraire de l'épilogue du 'Code de l'Alliance' (Ex 23,20-33)].
Diss. Leuven 1997; ᴰ*Vervenne, M.:* lxv; 566+21 pp. [RTL
29,576].
2079 *Bord, Lucien-Jean* L'adoption dans la bible et dans le droit cunéi-
forme. ZAR 3 (1997) 174-194.
2080 *Greengus, Samuel* The selling of slaves: laws missing from the
Hebrew Bible?. ZAR 3 (1997) 1-11.
2081 **Houtman, Cornelis** Das Bundesbuch: ein Kommentar. DMOA 24:
Lei 1997, Brill xv; 351 pp. 90-04-10859-9.
2082 *Hübner, Ulrich* Bemerkungen zum Pfandrecht: das judäische Ostrakon von Meṣad Hašavyāhū, alttestamentliches und griechisches
Pfandrecht sowie ein Graffito aus Marissa. UF 29 (1997) 215-225
[Exod 22,25-26; Deut 24,12-13].
2083 **Levinson, Bernard Malcolm** Deuteronomy and the hermeneutics
of legal innovation. NY 1997, OUP xiv; 205 pp. Bibl. $40. 0-19-
511280-6 [Exod 20,22-23,33; Deut 12-26].
2084 *Moorhead, John* Cooking a kid in its mother's milk: patristic exegesis of an Old Testament command. Aug. 37 (1997) 261-271
[Exod 23,19].
2085 **Rothenbusch, Ralf** Zum Verhältnis kasuistischer Rechtssätze in
Israel (Ex 21,2-11.18-22,16) und im Alten Orient. Diss. Fr/B
1997; ᴰ*Ruppert* [BZ 42,316].
2086 *Scaiola, Donatella* Il diritto del povero (Es 22,20-26). PaVi 42/5
(1997) 22-26.

2087 *Albertz, Rainer* Die Theologisierung des Rechts im Alten Israel.
Religion und Gesellschaft. AOAT 248: 1997, ⇒235. ᴱAlbertz, Rainer, 115-132.
2088 *Bovati, Pietro* Pena e perdono nelle procedure giuridiche
dell'Antico Testamento. CivCatt 148 IV (1997) 225-239.
2089 **Brin, Gershon** Studies in biblical law: from the Hebrew Bible to
the Dead Sea Scrolls. ᵀ*Chipman, Jonathan:* JSOT.S 176: 1994,
⇒10,163*... 12,1987. ᴿRdQ 18/1 (1997) 154-155 *(García Martínez, Florentino)*.
2090 *Camps, Guiu bhrjš wbqsjr tšbt* (Ex 34,21b): échantillon d'un ancien calendrier?: essai d'approche aux origines du droit Israélien

antérieur à la consolidation de la royauté. StAns 124: 1997, ⇒57. FLOEHRER M. — TRAGAN P., 247-265.

2091 **Drosnin, Michael** The Bible code. NY 1997, Simon & S 264 pp. 0-684-81079-4. RWThJ 59 (1997) 329-331 *(Hammond, G.C.)*.

2092 **Limbeck, Meinrad** Das Gesetz im Alten und Neuen Testament. Da:Wiss 1997, xii; 253 pp. DM58. 3-534-02442-7. RFrRu 4 (1997) 290-292 *(Bodendorfer, Gerhard)*.

2093 *Loza Vera, José* El don de la ley (Ex 19-24 y 32-34). EfMex 15 (1997) 199-246.

2094 **Matthews, Victor Harold; Benjamin, Don C.** Old Testament parallels: laws and stories from the ancient Near East. NY ²1997, Paulist xiv; 384 pp. Bibl. $20. 0-8091-3731-3.

2095 *Nieuviarts, Jacques* La propriété dans la bible. Sum. 136. BLE 98 (1997) 123-136.

2096 *Otto, Eckart* Recht/Rechtswesen im Alten Orient und im Alten Testament. TRE 28. 1997, ⇒420. 197-209.

2097 **Rosenblatt, Jason P.** Torah and law in *Paradise Lost*. 1994, ⇒10,1239; 12,921. RJQR 87 (1997) 367-368 *(Blau, Rivkah T.)*.

2098 **Schenker, Adrian** Un chemin de bonheur et un miroir de l'humain: une clé de lecture pour les lois bibliques. Connaître la Bible 1: Bru 1997, Lumen Vitae 64 pp. 2-87324-084-9.

2099 *Schwartz, Baruch J.* What really happened at mount Sinai?: four biblical answers to one question. BiRe 13/5 (1997) 20-30, 46.

2100 **Stahl, Nanette** Law and liminality in the bible. JSOT.S 202: 1995, ⇒11/1,707. RCBQ 59 (1997) 752-753 *(Kaltner, John)*.

2101 **Synek, Eva M.** 'Dieses Gesetz ist gut, heilig, es zwingt nicht...': zum Gesetzesbegriff der Apostolischen Konstitutionen. KuR 21: Wien 1997, Plöchl xiii; 129 pp. ÖS300. 3-901407-08-1 [PzB 8,75s—Felber, Anneliese].

2102 *Welch, John W.* A biblical law bibliography—1997 supplement. ZAR 3 (1997) 207-246.

2103 *Wittes, Benjamin* Of bible codes and idols. First Things 78 (1997) 12-14.

2104 EBehrends, Okko; Sellert, Wolfgang Nomos und Gesetz: Ursprünge und Wirkungen des griechischen Gesetzesdenkens. AAWG.PH 209: Gö 1995, Akademie der Wissenschaften 261 pp. Symposium der Kommission 'Die Funktion des Gesetzes in Geschichte und Gegenwart', 6. DM124. 3-525-82597-8. RHZ 265 (1997) 744-746 *(Thür, Gerhard)*.

2105 EFoxhall, Lin; Lewis, Andrew D.E. Greek law in its political setting. 1996, ⇒12,2012. RHZ 265 (1997) 746-748 *(Ruschenbusch, Eberhard)*.

2106 *Haase, Richard* Grenzüberschreitungen im sogenannten mittelassyrischen Rechtsbuch. ZAR 3 (1997) 202-206 [Deut 27,17; 29,14].

2107 *Haase, Richard* Talion und spiegelnde Strafe in den keilschriftlichen Rechtscorpora. ZAR 3 (1997) 195-201.

2108 **Hoffner, Harry Angier** The laws of the Hittites: a critical edition DMOA 23: Lei 1997, Brill xx; 363 pp. Bibl. ƒ192/$120.50. 90-04-10874-2.

2109 EJakob-Rost, Liane; Fales, Frederick Mario Neuassyrische Rechtsurkunden I. WVDOG 94: 1996, ⇒12,2019. RAfO 44-45 (1997-98) 387-393 *(Radner, Karen)*.

2110  **Jas, Remko** Neo-Assyrian judicial procedures. State Archives of Assyria Studies 5: 1996, ⇒12,2020. ᴿMes. 32 (1997) 349-352 *(Gentili, P.)*; AfO 44-45 (1997-98) 379-387 *(Radner, Karen)*.

2111  *Jursa, Michael* "Als König Abi-Ešuh gerechte Ordnung hergestellt hat": eine bemerkenswerte altbabylonische Prozessurkunde. RA 91 (1997) 135-145.

2112  *Neumann, Hans* Gläubiger oder Schuldner?: Anmerkungen zu einem neuassyrischen Privatbrief. AOAT 247: 1997, ⇒75. ꟳRoᴇʟʟɪɢ W., 281-293.

2113  *Olivier, Johannes P.J.* Restitution as economic redress: the fine print of the Old Babylonian *mešarum*-edict of Ammiṣaduqa. ZAR 3 (1997) 12-25 [Lev 25; Deut 15; Neh 5; Jer 34].

2114  *Otto, Eckart* Recht/Rechtswesen im Alten Orient und im Alten Testament. TRE 28. 1997, ⇒420. 197-209.

2115  **Radner, K.** Die neuassyrischen Privatrechtsurkunden als Quelle für Mensch und Umwelt. SAAS 6: Helsinki 1997, The Neo-Assyrian Text Corpus Project xlii; 428 pp. 951-45-7783-3 [Mes. 33,373s—D'Agostino, F.].

2116  **Roth, Martha Tobi** Law collections from Mesopotamia and Asia Minor. 1995, ⇒11/1,716. ᴿJSSt 44 (1997) 361-368 *(Pardee, D.)*.

2117  *Westbrook, Raymond* A matter of life and death [Codex Eshnunna]. JANES 25 (1997) 61-70.

2118  *Whitley, James* Cretan laws and Cretan literacy. AJA 101 (1997) 635-661.

2119  *Wilcke, Claus* Nanaja-šamḫats Rechtsstreit um ihre Freiheit. AOAT 247: 1997, ⇒75. ꟳRoᴇʟʟɪɢ W., 413-429.

2120  *Wunsch, Cornelia* Und die Richter berieten... Streitfälle aus der Zeit Neriglissars und Nabonids. Sum. 59. AfO 44-45 (1997) 59-100.

2121  *Zaccagnini, C.* On the juridical terminology of Neo-Assyrian and Aramaic contracts. Assyrien im Wandel. 1997, ⇒379. ᴱWaetzoldt, Hartmut, 203-208.

### ᴇ3.6 Cultus, *Exodus 24-40*

2122  *Ahituv, Shmuel* The countenance of YHWH. 1997, ⇒34. ᴹGʀᴇᴇɴʙᴇʀɢ M., 3*-11* [Ex 33,14] H.

2123  *Bakon, Shimon* Creation, tabernacle and sabbath. JBQ 25 (1997) 79-85.

2124  *Begg, Christopher T.* The destruction of the golden calf revisited (Exod 32,20 / Deut 9,21). BEThL 133: 1997, ⇒17. ꟳBʀᴇᴋᴇʟᴍᴀɴs C., 469-479.

2125  *Bettenzoli, Giuseppe* Sviluppo e ambientazione delle feste. RStB 9/1 (1997) 75-97.

2126  **Carstens, Pernille** Drikoffer og libation i tempel og på alter [Offering and libation in temple and upon altar]. Diss. Aarhus 1997 [StTh 51,80].

2127  *Castello, Gaetano* Il santuario del popolo in cammino (Es 26). PaVi 42/6 (1997) 4-8.

2128  *Cavedo, Romeo* Aronne e il sacerdozio levitico (Es 28-29). PaVi 42/6 (1997) 10-13.

2129   **Chong Kyoon Shin, Samuel** Centralization and singularization: official cult and royal politics in ancient Israel. Diss. Richmond 1996-1997 [RTL 29,577].

2130   *Cohen, Jeffrey M.* The dilemma of the sanctuary. JBQ 25 (1997) 185-187 [Isa 6,3].

2131   *Cooper, Alan M.; Goldstein, Bernard R.* At the entrance to the tent: more cultic resonances in biblical narrative. JBL 116 (1997) 201-215 [Exod 33,7-11].

2132   *De Zan, Renato* Il cultuale e l'economico nella bibbia. RivLi 84 (1997) 209-219.

2133   *Dell'Orto, Giuseppe* Il peccato 'originale' di Israele (Es 32,1-6). PaVi 42/6 (1997) 18-23.

2134   *Di Palma, Gaetano* L'intercessione di Mosè (Es 32). PaVi 42/6 (1997) 25-28.

2135   *Enstrom, Phyllis; Dyk, Peet J. van* What happened to the ark?. Religion and Theology 4/1 (1997) 50-60 [ZID 23,318].

2136   *Fernández Sangrador, Jorge Juan* Los trece atributos (middôt) de Dios: un comentario a Éxodo 34,6-7. 1997, ⇒76. MRUIZ DE LA PENA J., 67-83 [Exod 34,6-7].

2137   **Gleis, Matthias** Die Bamah. Diss. Tü 1996, DNiehr, H., BZAW 251: B 1997, De Gruyter ix; 291 pp. DM251. 3-11-015690-3.

2138   **Heger, Paul** The development of the incense cult in Israel. Diss. Toronto 1996, DFox, Harry: BZAW 245: B 1997, De Gruyter ix; 314 pp. DM188. 3-11-015367-X.

2139   *Johnstone, William* From the Mountain to Kadesh, with special reference to Exodus 32,30-34,29. BEThL 133: 1997, ⇒17. FBREKELMANS C., 449-467.

2140   *Kaufman, David Jay* The Dead Sea Scrolls and the Oniad high priesthood. Qumran Chronicle 7/1-2 (1997) 51-63;

2141   From Tennes to Leontopolis: a political and literary-historical study of the high priesthood in Hellenistic Palestine (350-159 BCE). Qumran Chronicle 7/1-2 (1997) 117-122.

2142   *Kitz, Anne Marie* The plural form of אוּרִים and תֻּמִּים. JBL 116 (1997) 401-410 [Exod 28,30].

2143   *Knohl, Israel* Two aspects of the "tent of meeting". 1997, MGREENBERG M., ⇒34. 73-79 [Exod 33,6-11; 15,22; Num 11,16-17; 12,4-10; 3,10; Dt 31,14-15].

2144   *Kovacs, Judith L.* Concealment and Gnostic exegesis: CLEMENT of Alexandria's interpretation of the tabernacle. StPatr 31: 1997, ⇒351. ELivingstone, Elizabeth A., 414-437 [Ex 25-27].

2145   **Lascelle, Ruth Specter** A dwelling place for God: a verse-by-verse description from Exodus 25-30 of the ancient Hebrew tabernacle with new covenant applications. Arlington, Wash. ²1997, Bedrock iv; 281 pp. 0-9654519-2-5.

2146   *Malul, Meir kpj* (Ex 33,22) and bḥpnjw (Prov 30,4): hand or skirt?. ZAW 109 (1997) 356-368.

2147   *Mello, Alberto* Il volto di Dio (Es 33,18-34,9). PaVi 42/6 (1997) 29-33.

2148   *Neudecker, Reinhard* "Das ganze Volk sah die Stimmen ...": haggadische Auslegung und Pfingstbericht. Sum. 349. Bib. 78 (1997) 329-349 [Exod 28,18; Acts 2,1-13].

2149   *Passaro, Angelo* La celebrazione dell'alleanza (Es 24). PaVi 42/5 (1997) 27-33.

2150  *Podella, Thomas* Reinheit: Altes Testament. TRE 28. 1997, ⇒420. 477-483.
2151  *Ravasi, Gianfranco* Là è il mio nome: lo spazio e il sacro nella teologia biblica. RCI 78/2 (1997) 123-131.
2152  **Rubenstein, Jeffrey L.** The history of Sukkot in the Second Temple and rabbinic periods. BJSt 302: 1995, ⇒11/1,734; 12,2055. ᴿJSSt 44 (1997) 411-412 *(McKay, Heather A.)*; AJS Review 22/1 (1997) 116-121 *(Yuter, Alan J.)*.
2153  **Sans, Isidro María** Autorretrato de Dios. Teología 28: Bilbao 1997, Universidad de Deusto 162 pp. 84-7485-528-4 [Exod 34,6].
2154  *Schenker, Adrian* Besonderes und allgemeines Priestertum im Alten Bund: Ex 19,6 und Jes 61,6 im Vergleich. Pfarrei. 1997, ⇒259. ᴱSchifferle, Alois, 111-116.
2155  **Shorter, Bani** Susceptible to the sacred: the psychological experience of ritual. L 1996, Routledge xii; 135 pp. 0-415-12620-7.
2156  *Stefani, Piero* Il sabato (Es 31,12-17). PaVi 42/6 (1997) 14-17.
2157  *Strübind, Kim* Was heißt "rein" und "unrein" in der Bibel?: eine theologische Annäherung an die Speisegebote und das kultische Denken im Alten Testament. Zeitschrift für Theologie und Gemeinde 2 (1997) 25-58.
2158  **Vicent Saera, Rafael** La fiesta judía de las Cabañas (Sukkot): interpretaciones midrásicas en la Biblia y en el judaísmo antiguo. 1995, ⇒11/2,3213. ᴿCBQ 59 (1997) 563-564 *(Bernas, Casimir)*.
2159  *Wagner, Andreas* Segnen im Alltag des Alten Israel. Deutsches Pfarrerblatt 97 (1997) 509-510.
2160  *Werman, Cana* Levi and Levites in the Second Temple period. DSD 4 (1997) 211-225.

### ᴇ3.7 Leviticus

2161  *Bakare, Sebastian* An African perspective on the Jubilee celebration. ER 49 (1997) 470-475.
2162  **Barros, Marcelo** A dança do novo tempo: o novo milênio, o jubileu bíblico e uma espiritualidade ecumênica. São Leopoldo 1997, Sinodal 92 pp. 85-233-0452-5 [PerTeol 29,439].
2163  **Bryan, David** Cosmos, chaos and the kosher mentality. JSPE.S 12: 1995, ⇒11/2,3170. ᴿCBQ 59 (1997) 338-339 *(Kugler, R.A.)*.
2164  **Budd, Philip J.** Leviticus. NCBC: 1996, ⇒12,2075. ᴿBS 154 (1997) 237-238 *(Merrill, Eugene H.)*.
2165  *Cardellini, Innocenzo* Ritmi del tempo e normatività religiosa fino agli achemenidi (sabato—anno sabbatico—anno giubilare). RStB 9/1 (1997) 57-74.
2166  **Chirichigno, Gregory C.** Debt slavery in Israel and the ancient Near East. JSOT.S 141: 1993, ⇒9,2466... 12,2076. ᴿBZ 41 (1997) 306-308 *(Kessler, Rainer)*.
2167  **Cortese, Enzo; Kaswalder, Pietro** Il fascino del sacro: alla riscoperta del libro del Levitico. Narrare la Bibbia 3: 1996, ⇒12,2078. ᴿLASBF 47 (1997) 571-573 *(Chrupcała, Lesław Daniel)*.
2168  **Gerstenberger, Erhard S.** Das dritte Buch Mose: Leviticus. ATD 6: 1993, ⇒9,2437...12,2085. ᴿBZ 41 (1997) 115-118 *(Grünwaldt, Klaus)*.

2169  **Gorman, Frank H.** Divine presence and community: a commentary on the book of Leviticus. International Theological Commentary: GR 1997, Eerdmans xi; 163 pp. Bibl. $18. 0-8028-0110-2.

2170  *Grabbe, Lester L.* The book of Leviticus. CurResB 5 (1997) 91-110.

2171  *Kugler, Robert A.* Holiness, purity, the body, and society: the evidence for theological conflict in Leviticus. JSOT 76 (1997) 3-27.

2172  **Lane, David J.** The Peshitta of Leviticus. MPIL 6: 1994, ⇒10,2322... 12,2096. ᴿBiOr 54 (1997) 190-192 *(Owens, Robert)*; JSSt 44 (1997) 419-420 *(Salvesen, Alison)*.

2173  **Lobato, Juan Bautista** El jubileo en la Sagrada Escritura. M 1997, BAC 126 pp. [StLeg 39,326—Trobajo, Antonio].

2174  *Marcus, Marcel* Die revolutionäre Botschaft des Buches Leviticus. 1997, ⇒25. ᶠFᴿɪᴇᴅʟᴀɴᴅᴇʀ A., 141-148.

2175  *Menezes, Rui de* The biblical jubilee year: origin and significance. VJTR 61 (1997) 651-668.

2176  ᴱᵀ**Pérez Fernández, Miguel** Midrás Sifra I: el comentario rabínico al Levítico. Introd. *Stemberger, Günter*: Biblioteca Midrásica 19: Estella 1997, Verbo Divino 346 pp. Edición bilingüe; texto hebreo de base: Ms. Vaticano Assemani 66. Bibl. 84-8169-178-X.

2177  **Riehl, Christian** Levitikus & Numeri. Bibel 2000, 2. Stu 1997, Katholisches Bibelwerk 172 pp. DM68. 3-460-02002-4 [OrdKor 39,255].

2178  ᴱ**Ucko, Hans** The jubilee challenge: utopia or possibility?: Jewish and christian insights. Geneva 1997, WCC viii; 198 pp. £10. 2-8254-1231-7 [RRT 1998/2,92].

2179  **Wells, Jo Bailey** A holy nation; Israel's call to holiness in canonical perspective. Diss. Durham 1997; ᴰ*Moberly, R.W.L.*: 260 pp. [RTL 29,580].

2180  **Wevers, John William** Notes on the Greek text of Leviticus. SBL.SCS 44: Atlanta, GA 1997, Scholars xxxix; 519 pp. $50. 0-7885-0324-3. ᴿEThL 73 (1997) 151-152 *(Vervenne, M.)*.

2181  *Schenker, Adrian* Keine Versöhnung ohne Anerkennung der Haftung für verursachten Schaden: die Rolle von Haftung und Intentionalität in den Opfern ḥaṭṭat und ʾašam (Lev 4-5). ZAR 3 (1997) 164-173.

2182  *Rogl, Christine; Schlor, Ingrid* Ein unediertes Blatt zum Leviticus/Numeri-Codex sa 11. Enchoria 24 (1997-1998) 78-89 [Lev 5,2-18].

2183  *Klingbeil, Gerald A.* Ritual time in Leviticus 8 with special reference to the seven day period in the Old Testament. ZAW 109 (1997) 500-513.

2184  *Wiesel, Elie* Nadav und Avihu. 1997, ⇒25. ᶠFᴿɪᴇᴅʟᴀɴᴅᴇʀ A., 267-277 [Lev 10,1-7].

2185  *Klawans, Jonathan* The impurity of immorality in ancient Judaism. JJS 48 (1997) 1-16 [Lev 11-15; Num 19].

2186  *Ego, Beate* Reinheit und Schöpfung: zur Begründung der Speisegebote im Buch Leviticus. ZAR 3 (1997) 131-144 [Lev 11,41-47; 20,22-26].

2187  **Deiana, Giovanni** Il giorno dell'espiazione: il *kippur* nella tradizione biblica. RivBib.S 30: 1994, ⇒10,2338; 12,2125. ᴿRivBib 45 (1997) 96-100 *(Cardellini, Innocenzo)* [Lev 16].

2188 *Joosten, Jan* "Tu" et "vous" dans le code de sainteté (Lév. 17-26). RevSR 71 (1997) 3-8.

2189 **Ruwe, Andreas** 'Heiligkeitsgesetz' und 'Priesterschrift': theologie-geschichtliche und rechtssystematische Untersuchungen zu Leviti-cus 17-26*. Diss. Bethel 1997; [D]*Winkler, K.* [RTL 29,580].·

2190 *Büchner, Dirk* Inside and outside the camp: the Halakhic back-ground to changes in the Septuagint Leviticus, with reference to two Qumran manuscripts. JNSL 23/2 (1997) 151-162 [Lev 17,3-4].

2191 **Carmichael, Calum M.** Law, legend and incest in the bible: Levi-ticus 18-20. Ithaca 1997, Cornell xi; 209 pp. $35. 0-8014-3388-6 [NThAR 1998,98].

2192 *Meacham, Tirzah* The missing daugther: Leviticus 18 and 20. ZAW 109 (1997) 254-259.

2193 *Freedman, David Noel* The Hebrew Old Testament and the mi-nistry today: an exegetical study of Leviticus 19:18b. Divine Com-mitment 1. 1997 <1964>, ⇒124.

2194 **Massmann, Ludwig** Der Ruf in die Entscheidung: Studien zur Entstehung und Vorgeschichte, dem Wirklichkeitsverständnis und der kanonischen Stellung von Lev 20. Diss. Heidelberg 1997; [D]*Weippert, M.*

2195 *Milgrom, Jacob* The firstfruits festivals of grain and the composi-tion of Leviticus 23:9-21. 1997, ⇒34. [M]GREENBERG M., 81-89.

2196 *Hutton, Rodney R.* Narrative in Leviticus: the case of the blasphe-ming son (Lev 24,10-23). ZAR 3 (1997) 145-163.

2197 *Milgrom, Jacob* Jubilee: a rallying cry for today's oppressed. BiRe 13/2 (1997) 16, 48 [Lev 25,23-24].

2198 **Fager, Jeffrey A.** Land tenure and the biblical jubilee: uncovering Hebrew ethics through the sociology of knowledge. 1993, ⇒9,2467... 11/1,747. [R]TJT 13/1 (1997) 91-92 *(Kessler, John)* [Lev 25].

2199 *Milgrom, Jacob* Leviticus 26 and Ezekiel. Bibl.Interp. 28: 1997, ⇒77. [F]SANDERS J., 57-62.

### E3.8 *Numeri;* Numbers, Balaam

2200 [T]**Börner-Klein, Dagmar** Rabbinische Texte 3: der Midrasch Sifre zu Numeri. II. Reihe:_ Tannaitische Midrashim: Stu 1997, Kohl-hammer xiv; 796 pp. Übersetzung (Teil I) und Erklärung (Teil II: zur Redaktionsgeschichte)) [E]*Mayer, G.*: DM440. 3-17-013634-8. [R]FJB 24 (1997) 162-167 *(Reichman, Ronen)*.

2201 [T]**Clarke, Ernest G.** Targum Pseudo-Jonathan: Numbers: translated with apparatus and notes. The Aramaic Bible 4: 1995, ⇒11/1,781. [R]CBQ 59 (1997) 742-743 *(Golomb, David M.)*.

2202 **Davies, Eryl W.** Numbers. NCeB. 1995, ⇒11/1,782; 12,2140. [R]VJTR 61 (1997) 207-208 *(Meagher, P.M.)*; JThS 48 (1997) 551-553 *(Wenham, G.J.)*; CBQ 59 (1997) 534-536 *(Patrick, Dale)*; HebStud 38 (1997) 116-118 *(Gorman, Frank H.)*; AUSS 35 (1997) 110-111 *(Cairus, Aecio E.)*.

2203 *Derby, Josiah* The daughters of Zelophehad revisited. JBQ 25 (1997) 169-171.

2204 [ET]**Doutreleau, Louis** ORIGENEè: homélies sur les Nombres 1: Homélies I-X. SC 415: 1996, ⇒12,2143. [R]JEarlyC 5 (1997) 608-609 *(Trigg, Joseph W.)*.

2205 *Holcombe, A.D.* Biblical numerology confirms the spiritual validity of its contents. JRPR 20/1 (1997) 101ff [ThD Index February 1997,7].

2206 **Levine, Baruch A.** Numbers 1-20. AncB 4A: 1993, ⇒9,2479... 12,2144. ᴿBZ 41 (1997) 121-122 *(Seebass, Horst)*.

2207 ᵀMcNamara, Martin Targum Neofiti 1: Numbers. The Aramaic Bible 4: 1995, ⇒11/1,788. ᴿCBQ 59 (1997) 742-743 *(Golomb, David M.)*.

2208 *Milgrom, Jacob* Encroaching on the sacred: purity and polity in Numbers 1-10. Interp. 51 (1997) 241-253.

2209 **Olson, Dennis T.** Numbers. 1996, ⇒12,2147. ᴿCBQ 59 (1997) 746-747 *(Vogels, Walter A.)*.

2210 *Reynolds, Carol Bechtel* Life after grace: preaching from the book of Numbers. Interp. 51 (1997) 267-279.

**Riehl, Christian** Levitikus & Numeri ⇒2177.

2211 *Voitila, Anssi* The translator of the Greek Numbers. IX Congress IOSCS. SBL.SCSt 45: 1997, ⇒340. ᴱTaylor, Bernard A., 109-121.

2212 **Wenham, Gordon J.** Numbers. OTGu: Shf 1997, Academic 130 pp. £8/$13. 1-85075-801-8.

2213 *Nihan, Christophe* Nombres 5/11-31 et l'enfantement de la justice divine au sein de la communauté. ETR 72 (1997) 429-436.

2214 *Elwolde, John* Distinguishing the linguistic and the exegetical: the case of Numbers in the Bible and 11QTᵃ. The scrolls and the scriptures. JSPE.S 26: 1997, ⇒299. ᴱPorter, Stanley E., 129-141 [Num 9,3; 19,19; 19,14].

2215 *Römer, Thomas C.* Nombres 11-12 et la question d'une rédaction deutéronomique dans le Pentateuque. BEThL 133: 1997, ⇒17. ᶠBREKELMANS C., 481-498.

2216 *Assmann, Jan* Exodus und Amarna: der Mythos der "Aussätzigen" als verdrängte Erinnerung der Aton-Religion. Ägypten-Bilder. OBO 150: 1997, ⇒378. ᴱStaehelin, Elisabeth, 11-34 [Num 12].

2217 **Artus, Olivier** Études sur le livre des Nombres: récit, histoire et loi en Nombres 13,1-20,13. Diss., OBO 157: Gö 1997, Vandenhoeck & R ix; 298 pp. FS69. 3-525-53793-X.

2218 *Mutius, Hans-Georg von* Das Verständnis der Verbform נשאתי in Numeri 16,15 im Licht des Targums Neofiti 1. BN 87 (1997) 34-38.

2219 *Hentschel, Georg* 'Alle sind heilig—die ganze Gemeinde': zur Auseinandersetzung um das alttestamentliche Priestertum in Num 16. 1997, ⇒98. ᶠULLRICH L., 12-33.

2220 **Teng Kok, Johnson Lim** The sin of Moses and the staff of God: a narrative approach. Studies on Semitics 34: Assen 1997, Van Gorcum 200 pp. $64/f120. 90-232-3261-5 [Num 20,1-13].

2221 *Lim, Johnson* A fresh perspective on a familiar problem [*Rashi*]. Henoch 19/2 (1997) 161-174 [Num 20,24; 27,14].

2222 *Seebass, Horst* Edom und seine Umgehung nach Numeri xx-xxi: zu Numeri xxi 10-13. VT 47 (1997) 255-262.

2223 *Lutzky, Harriet C.* The name "Cozbi" (Numbers xxv 15,18). VT 47 (1997) 546-549.

2224 *Olson, Dennis T.* Negotiating boundaries: the old and new generations and the theology of Numbers. Interp. 51 (1997) 229-240 [Num 25].

2225  *Barré, Michael L.* The portrait of Balaam in Numbers 22-24. Interp. 51 (1997) 254-266.
2226  *Desplanque, Christophe* Mystère divin et ambiguïté humaine dans l'histoire de Balaam: Nombres 22-24. Hokhma 64 (1997) 1-16.
2227  *Sabar, Yona* The story of Balaam and his she-ass in four neo-Aramaic dialects: a comparative study of the translations. 1997, ⇒49. FKROTKOFF G., 301-317 [Num 22,2-41].
2228  *Van Seters, John* From faithful prophet to villain: observations on the tradition history of the Balaam story. JSOT.S 240: 1997, ⇒20. FCOATS G., 126-132 [Num 22-24; 31,8; 31,16; Deut 1-3; 23,4-6; Neh 13,2].


E3.9 **Liber Deuteronomii**

2229  **Clifford, Richard** Deuteronomio. TDi *Giovambattista, F.*: LoB.AT 6: 1995, ⇒11/1,820. RRivBib 45 (1997) 353-355 *(Minissale, Antonino).*
2230  T**Cortès, Enric; Martinez, Teresa** Sifre Deuteronomio: comentario tannaítico al libro del Deuteronomio 2: Pisqa. Barc 1997, Facultat de Teologia de Catalunya 161-357 pp. Introd. y notas; Bibl. 84-86065-47-X.
2231  **Garcia López, Félix** O livro do Deuteronómio. Cadernos Bíblicos 56: Lisboa 1997, Difusora Bíblica 68 pp. [Bib(L) 7/7,188— Negreiros, Fernando de].
2232  **Labuschagne, C.J.** Deuteronomium III. PredOT: Baarn 1997, Callenbach 392 pp. ƒ109.50. 90-266-0886-1 [Str. 65,568— Beentjes, Panc].
2233  **Lohfink, Norbert** Studien zum Deuteronomium und zur deuteronomistischen Literatur 3. SBAB.AT 20: 1995, ⇒11/1,54; 12,2191. RThLZ 122 (1997) 24-26 *(Perlitt, Lothar).*
2234  T**McNamara, Martin** Targum Neofiti 1: Deuteronomy: apparatus and notes. The Aramaic Bible 5A: ColMn 1997, Liturgical xiii; 198 pp. $80. 0-8146-5484-3 [ThD 44,354—Heiser, W. Charles].
2235  **Sabar, Yona** The book of Deuteronomy in Neo-Aramaic in the dialect of the Jewish community of Zakho, including selected texts in other Neo-Aramaic dialects and a glossary. Hebrew University Language Traditions Project 18: J 1994, Magnes xli; 159 pp. 965-350-004-0. RJSSt 42 (1997) 169-171 *(Fassberg, Steven E.).* H.
2236  **Tigay, Jeffrey H.** Deuteronomy. JPS Commentary on the torah 5. 1996, ⇒12,2169. RJBL 116 (1997) 727-729 *(Eslinger, Lyle).*
2237  **Wahl, Otto** Der Deuteronomium-Text der Sacra Parallela. NAWG.PH 1997,3: Gö 1997, Vandenhoeck & R 48 pp.
2238  **Wevers, John William** Notes on the Greek text of Deuteronomy. SCSt 39: 1995, ⇒11/1,826. RBib. 78 (1997) 103-107 *(Harl, Marguerite)*; CBQ 59 (1997) 363-364 *(Davila, James R.)*; HebStud 38 (1997) 120-123 *(Fernández Marcos, N.).*


2239  *Braulik, Georg* Die Entstehung der Rechtfertigungslehre in den Bearbeitungsschichten des Buches Deuteronomium: ein Beitrag zur Klärung der Voraussetzungen paulinischer Theologie;

2240 Die Funktion von Siebenergruppierungen im Endtext des Deuteronomiums. Studien zu Dt. SBAB 24: 1997 <1989>, ⇒117. 11-27/63-79;

2241 Die Völkervernichtung und die Rückkehr Israels ins Verheissungsland: hermeneutische Bemerkungen zum Buch Deuteronomium. BEThL 133: 1997, ⇒17. FBREKELMANS C., 3-38;

2242 "Weisheit" im Buch Deuteronomium. Studien zu Dt. SBAB 24: 1997 <1989>, ⇒117. 225-271.

2243 **Cryer, Frederick** Divination in ancient Israel and its Near Eastern environment: a socio-historical investigation. JSOT.S 142: 1994, ⇒10,2602; 12,2437. RJThS 48 (1997) 153-154 (Curtis, Adrian H.W.); JQR 87 (1997) 416-420 (Hurowitz, Victor Avigdor); JBL 116 (1997) 725-727 (Sweek, Joel).

2244 *De Luca, Gesualdo* Il cammino dell'uomo nella legge a partire dal Deuteronomio. Vivarium 5 (1997) 383-395.

2245 *Duncan, Julie A.* Excerpted texts of Deuteronomy at Qumran. RdQ 18 (1997) 43-62.

2246 **Eynikel, Erik** The reform of King Josiah and the composition of the deuteronomistic history. OTS 33: 1996, ⇒12,2184. REThL 73 (1997) 156-158 (Lust, J.); CBQ 59 (1997) 731-732 (Knoppers, Gary N.); JBL 116 (1997) 536-539 (Sweeney, Marvin A.); ABR 45 (1997) 72-74 (O'Brien, Mark A.).

2247 *Fransen, Paul-Irénée* La discipline de l'Église dans un commentaire anonyme au Deutéronome écrit à Lyon au IXe siècle. ZSRG.K 83 (1997) 52-66.

2248 *Fry, Euan* The Lord your God'—problems with second person pronouns in Deuteronomy. PPBT 48 (1997) 243-245.

2249 **Graf, Fritz** Magic in the ancient world. TPhilip, Franklin: CM 1997, Harvard University Press vi; 313 pp. Bibl. $35. 0-674-54151-0.

2250 **Joseph, Joy V.** 'Re-lecturing' of Deuteronomy (chapter 12-26) in the post-exilic period. Diss. Mü 1997; DBaltzer, K.: B 1997, Logos 343 pp. 3-931216-48-9.

2251 **Keller, Martin** Untersuchungen zur deuteronomisch-deuteronomistischen Namenstheologie. BBB 105: 1996, ⇒12,2188. RThLZ 122 (1997) 437-438 (Lohfink, Norbert); CBQ 59 (1997) 351-352 (Gnuse, Robert).

2252 **Krinetzki, Günter** Rechtsprechung und Amt im Deuteronomium: zur Exegese der Gesetze Dtn 16,18-20; 17,8-18,22. 1994, ⇒10,2427. RCBQ 59 (1997) 126-127 (Toews, Wesley).

2253 **Loretz, Oswald** Des Gottes Einzigkeit: ein altorientalisches Argumentationsmodell zum 'Schma Jisrael'. Da:Wiss 1997, x; 204 pp. DM68. 3-534-13276-9.

2254 *Mello, Alberto* La ricerca di Dio nel Deuteronomio. PSV 35 (1997) 11-22.

2255 *Nelson, Richard D.* herem and the Deuteronomic social conscience. BEThL 133: 1997, ⇒17. FBREKELMANS C., 39-54.

2256 **Olson, Dennis T.** Deuteronomy and the death of Moses. 1994, ⇒10,2450... 12,2198. RCBQ 58 (1996) 327-329 (Laberge, Léo).

2257 *Otto, Eckart* Das Deuteronomium als archimedischer Punkt der Pentateuchkritik: auf dem Wege zu einer Neubegründung der de Wette'schen Hypothese. BEThL 133: 1997, ⇒17. FBREKELMANS C., 321-339.

2258  **Sonnet, Jean-Pierre** The book within the book: writing in Deuteronomy. Diss. Indiana; <sup>D</sup>*Ackerman, J.S.*: Bibl.Interp. 14: Lei 1997, Brill xv; 299 pp. Bibl. ƒ150/$88.50. 90-04-10866-1.

2259  *Suzuki, Yoshihide* "The place which Yahweh your God will choose" in Deuteronomy. 1997, ⇒48. <sup>F</sup>KNIERIM R., 338-352.

2260  <sup>E</sup>**Veijola, Timo** Das Deuteronomium und seine Querbeziehungen. SESJ 62: 1996, ⇒12,209. <sup>R</sup>EThL 73/1 (1997) 153-154 *(Lust, J.)*.

2261  *Vermeylen, Jacques* Un programme pour la restauration d'Israël: quelques aspects de la loi dans le Deutéronome. La loi dans l'un et l'autre Testament. LeDiv 168: 1997, ⇒195. <sup>E</sup>Focant, C., 45-80.

2262  *Wevers, John William* The LXX translator of Deuteronomy. IX Congress IOSCS. SCSt 45: 1997, ⇒340. <sup>E</sup>Taylor, B.A., 57-89.

2263  **Wilson, Ian** Out of the midst of the fire: divine presence in Deuteronomy. SBL.DS 151: 1995, ⇒11/1,866. <sup>R</sup>JThS 48 (1997) 150-152 *(McConville, J.G.)*; CBQ 59 (1997) 364-366 *(Nagel, Elizabeth M.)*; HebStud 38 (1997) 118-120 *(Mayes, A.D.H.)*.

2264  *Glatt-Gilad, David A.* The re-interpretation of the Edomite-Israelite encounter in Deuteronomy ii. VT 47 (1997) 441-455.

2265  *Braulik, Georg* Literarkritik und die Einrahmung von Gemälden: zur literarkritischen und redaktionsgeschichtlichen Analyse von Dtn 4,1-6,3 und 29,1-30,10 durch D. KNAPP. Studien zu Dt. SBAB 24: 1997 <1989>, ⇒117. 29-61.

2266  *Kreuzer, Siegfried* Die Mächtigkeitsformel im Deuteronomium: Gestaltung, Vorgeschichte und Entwicklung. ZAW 109 (1997) 188-207 [Deut 5,15; 26,8].

2267  **Vergote, Antoine** Tu aimeras le Seigneur ton Dieu: l'identité chrétienne. Théologies: P 1997, Cerf 254 pp. FF140/CAN$19. 2-204-05607-3 [EeT(O) 29,155] [Deut 6,5].

2268  *Cox, Claude E.* The textual criticism of the Armenian bible: an example: Deuteronomy 6. Saint Nersess theological review 2/1 (1997) 1-31.

2269  **Morrow, William S.** Scribing the center: organization and redaction in Deuteronomy 14:1-17:13. SBL.MS 49: 1995, ⇒11/1,887; 12,2220. <sup>R</sup>HebStud 38 (1997) 123-125 *(Hope, Leslie J.)*; ThLZ 122 (1997) 135-137 *(Rüterswörden, Udo)*.

2270  *Oosthuizen, Martin J.* Deuteronomy 15:1-18 in socio-rhetorical perspective. ZAR 3 (1997) 64-91.

2271  **Hamilton, Jeffries M.** Social justice and Deuteronomy: the case of Deuteronomy 15. 1992, ⇒8,2706; 10,2424. <sup>R</sup>JBL 116 (1997) 335-336 *(Evans, Carl D.)*.

2272  **Carrière, Jean-Marie** Théorie du politique dans le Deutéronome: analyse des unités, des structures et des concepts de Dt 16,18-18,22. Diss. Institut Catholique de Paris 1997; <sup>D</sup>*Briend, J.*: 444+21 pp.; 2 vols.

2273  *Schmidt, Werner H.* Das Prophetengesetz Dtn 18,9-22 im Kontext erzählender Literatur. BEThL 133: 1997, ⇒17. <sup>F</sup>BREKELMANS C., 55-69.

2274  *Braulik, Georg* Weitere Beobachtungen zur Beziehung zwischen dem Heiligkeitsgesetz und Deuteronomium 19-25. Studien zu Dt. SBAB 24: 1997 <1996>, ⇒117. 183-223.

2275  *Jenni, Ernst* Dtn 19,16: *sará* 'Falschheit'. Studien zur Sprachwelt. 1997 <1981>, ⇒138. <sup>E</sup>Huwyler, Beat. 106-116.

2276 *Braulik, Georg* Die dekalogische Redaktion der deuteronomischen Gesetze: ihre Abhängigkeit von Levitikus 19 am Beispiel von Deuteronomium 22,1-12; 24,10-22; 25,13-16. Studien zu Dt. SBAB 24: 1997 <1995>, ⇒117. 147-182.

2277 *Du Preez, Ron* Does Levirate law promote polygamy?. 1997, ⇒83. FSHEA W., 273-289 [Deut 25,5-10].

2278 *Wilson, P. Eddy* Deuteronomy xxv 11-12—one for the books. VT 47 (1997) 220-235.

2279 *Krausz, Neville* Arami oved avi: Deuteronomy 26:5. JBQ 25 (1997) 31-34.

2280 *Steiner, Richard C.* The "Aramean" of Deuteronomy 26:5: peshat and derash. 1997, ⇒34. MGREENBERG M., 127-138.

2281 *Head, Peter M.* The curse of covenant reversal: Deuteronomy 28:58-68 and Israel's exile. Churchman 111/3 (1997) 218-226 [ZID 23,440].

2282 **Lenchak, Timothy A.** "Choose life!": a rhetorical-critical investigation of Deuteronomy 28,69-30,20. AnBib 129: 1993, ⇒9,2559... 11/1,900. RBZ 41 (1997) 122-124 *(Schäfer-Lichtenberger, Christa)*.

2283 **Steymans, Hans Ulrich** Deuteronomium 28 und die *Adê* zur Thronfolgeregelung Asarhaddons: Segen und Fluch im Alten Orient und in Israel. OBO 145: 1995, ⇒11/1,902; 12,2228. RBib. 78 (1997) 271-275 *(Dion, Paul-Eugène)*; CBQ 59 (1997) 756-757 *(Clements, Ronald E.)*; AfO 44-45 (1997-98) 396-399 *(Lambert, W.G.)*; JBL 116 (1997) 729-730 *(Moore, Michael S.)*; BiOr 54 (1997) 739-742 *(Becking, Bob)*.

2284 *Talstra, Eep* Deuteronomy 31: confusion or conclusion?: the story of Moses' threefold succession;

2285 *García López, Félix* Deuteronomio 31, el Pentateuco y la Historia Deuteronomista;

2286 *Labuschagne, Casper J.* The setting of the song of Moses in Deuteronomy. BEThL 133: 1997, ⇒17. FBREKELMANS C., 87-110/71-85/111-129 [Dt 32].

2287 *Stevens, David E.* Does Deuteronomy 32:8 refer to 'sons of God' or 'sons of Israel'?. BS 154 (1997) 131-141.

2288 *Nigosian, Solomon A.* Linguistic patterns of Deuteronomy 32. Sum. 224. Bib. 78 (1997) 206-224.

2289 **Sanders, Paul** The provenance of Deuteronomy 32. OTS 37: 1996, ⇒12,2231. RETR 72 (1997) 459-460 *(Macchi, Jean-Daniel)*; EThL 73 (1997) 155-156 *(Lust, J.)*; CBQ 59 (1997) 751-752 *(Kugler, Robert A.)*.

2290 **Beyerle, Stefan** Der Mosesegen im Deuteronomium: eine text-, kompositions- und formkritische Studie zu Deuteronomium 33. BZAW 250: B 1997, De Gruyter x; 345 pp. DM178. 3-11-015062-X [RB 104,470].

2291 *Freedman, David Noel* The poetic structure of the framework of Deuteronomy 33. Divine Commitment 2. 1997 <1980>, ⇒124. 88-107.

2292 **Kushelevsky, Rella** Moses and the angel of death. 1995, ⇒11/1,909. RJSSt 44 (1997) 409-411 *(Bauckham, Richard)* [Dt 34].

2293 *Lohfink, Norbert* Moses' death, torah and the liturgy. ThD 44/1 (1997) 3-12 [Dt 34].

E4.1 *Origo Israelis in Canaan: Deuteronomista;* **Liber Josue**

2294 **Bieberstein, Klaus** Josua—Jordan—Jericho: Archäologie, Geschichte und Theologie der Landnahmeerzählung Josua 1-6. Diss. ᴰ*Groß, Walter*: OBO 143: 1995, ⇒11/1,948. ᴿBASOR 60 (1997) 345-346 *(Otto, Eckart)*; ETR 72 (1997) 460-461 *(Römer, Thomas)*; RB 104 (1997) 142-143 *(Steymans, H.U.)*; Levant 29 (1997) 262-264 *(Strange, John)*.

2295 *Ceresko, Anthony R.* Potsherds and pioneers: recent research on the origins of Israel. ITS 34/1-3 (1997) 5-22.

2296 *Dever, William G.* Archaeology and the emergence of early Israel. Archaeology and biblical interpretation. 1997, ⇒268. ᴱBartlett, John R., 20-50.

2297 *Frevel, Christian* Die Entstehung Israels und die neuartige Dorfkultur zu Beginn der Eisenzeit. Lebendige Welt. 1997, ⇒565. ᴱZenger, Erich, 81-93.

2298 *Fritz, Volkmar* Die Landnahme der israelitischen Stämme in Kanaan. Studien zur Literatur. 1997 <1990>, ⇒126. 143-164;

2299 Die Entstehung Israels im 12. und 11. Jahrhundert v. Chr. Biblische Enzyklopädie 2: 1996, ⇒12,2244. ᴿKeTh 48 (1997) 162-163 *(Van der Woude, A.S.)*; ThLZ 122 (1997) 657-658 *(Lemche, Niels Peter)*; JETh 11 (1997) 189-191 *(Gugler, Werner)*.

2300 *Houtman, Cees* Zwei Sichtweisen von Israel als Minderheit inmitten der Bewohner Kanaans: ein Diskussionsbeitrag zum Verhältnis von J und DtrG. BEThL 133: 1997, ⇒17. ᶠBREKELMANS C., 213-231.

2301 *Hurvitz, Avi* The historical quest for "ancient Israel" and the linguistic evidence of the Hebrew Bible: some methodological observations. VT 47 (1997) 301-315.

2302 **Jerick, Detlef** Die Landnahme im Negev: protoisraelitische Gruppen im Süden Palästinas: eine archäologische und exegetische Studie. ADPV 20: Wsb 1997, Harrassowitz xxi; 400 pp. DM148. 3-447-03895-0 [RB 105,312].

2303 *Kitchen, K.A.* The physical text of Merenptah's victory hymn (the 'Israel stela'). JSSEA 24 (1994) 71-76.

2304 **Lemche, Niels Peter** Die Vorgeschichte Israels. Biblische Enzyklopädie 1: 1996, ⇒12,2247. ᴿJETh 11 (1997) 193-195 *(Gugler, Werner)*; ThLZ 122 (1997) 1112-1113 *(Hübner, Ulrich)*.

2305 *Lohfink, Norbert* Landeroberung und Heimkehr: Hermeneutisches zum heutigen Umgang mit dem Josuabuch. JBTh 12 (1997) 3-24.

2306 *Menezes, Rui de* Societes in transition: Israel and the tribes of North East India. ITS 34/1-3 (1997) 23-55.

2307 *Niccacci, Alviero* La stèle d'Israel grammaire et stratégie de communication. CRB 36: 1997, ⇒21. ᶠCOUROYER B., 43-107.

2308 **Noël, Damien** Les origines d'Israël. CEv 99: P 1997, Cerf 67 pp. 0222-9714.

2309 *Whitelam, Keith W.* The identity of early Israel: the realignment and transformation of Late Bronze-Iron Age Palestine. Historical Books. 1997 <1994>, ⇒192. ᴱExum, J. Cheryl, 14-45.

2310 *Wood, Bryant G.* The role of Shechem in the conquest of Canaan. 1997, ⇒83. ᶠSHEA W., 245-256.

2311 *Yurco, Frank J.* Merenptah's Canaanite campaign and Israel's origins. Exodus. 1997, ⇒325. ᴱFrerichs, Ernest S., 27-55.

2312 *Ausloos, Hans* The need for linguistic criteria in characterising biblical pericopes as Deuteronomistic: a critical note to Erhard BLUM's methodology. JNSL 23/2 (1997) 47-56.

2313 *Collins, Terence* Deuteronomist influence on the prophetical books. The book of Jeremiah. BEThL 128: 1997, ⇒186. ᴱCurtis, Adrian H.W., 15-26.

2314 **Doorly, W.D.** Obsession with justice: the story of the deuteronomists. 1994, ⇒10,2459... 12,2257. ᴿVJTR 61 (1997) 279-280 *(Anandaraj, Francis S.).*

2315 *Freedman, David Noel* The Deuteronomic History. Divine Commitment 1. 1997 <1976>, ⇒124. 279-285.

2316 **Harvey, John Edward** Retelling the tetrateuch: the deuteronomistic historians use of tetrateuchal narratives. Diss. St. Michael's, Toronto 1997; ᴰ*Peckham, B.*, 239 pp. [RTL 29,578].

2317 *Houtman, Cees* Zwei Sichtweisen von Israel als Minderheit inmitten der Bewohner Kanaans: ein Diskussionsbeitrag zum Verhältnis von J und DtrG. BEThL 133: 1997, ⇒17. ᶠBREKELMANS C., 213-231.

2318 *Koch, Klaus* The language of prophecy: thoughts on the macrosyntax of the *debar YHWH* and its semantic implications in the deuteronomistic history. ᶠKNIERIM R., 1997, ⇒48. 210-221.

2319 *Kreuzer, Siegfried* Die Verwendung der Mächtigkeitsformel außerhalb des Deuteronomiums: literarische und theologische Linien zu Jer, Ez, dtrG und P. ZAW 109 (1997) 369-384 [Exod 6,6; 7,3].

2320 *Lohfink, Norbert* Geschichtstypologisch orientierte Textstrukturen in den Büchern Deuteronomium und Josua. BEThL 133: 1997, ⇒17. ᶠBREKELMANS C., 133-160.

2321 ᴱMcKenzie, **Steven L.; Graham, M. Patrick** The history of Israel's traditions: the heritage of Martin NOTH. JSOT.S 182: 1994, ⇒10,325*. ᴿThLZ 122 (1997) 541-543 *(Seebass, Horst).*

2322 **Nielsen, Flemming A.J.** The tragedy in history: HERODOTUS and the Deuteronomistic History. JSOT.S 251; Copenhagen International Seminar 4: Shf 1997 Academic 192 pp. £27.50/$45. 1-85075-688-0 [JThS 50,183ss—Murray, D.F.].

2323 ᴱPury, **Albert de; Römer, Thomas; Macchi, Jean-Daniel** Israël construit son histoire: l'historiographie deutéronomiste... MoBi 34: 1996, ⇒12,199. ᴿFV 96/1 (1997) 73-74 *(Montsarrat, Jean-Pierre & Violaine)*; CBQ 59 (1997) 602-604 *(Hoppe, Leslie J.)*; RSR 85 (1997) 286-287 *(Gibert, Pierre).*

2324 *Römer, Thomas* Historiographie et identité: rôles et fonctions de 'l'historiographie deutéronomiste'. CBFV 36 (1997) 3-18.

2325 *Schmitt, Hans-Christoph* Die Josephsgeschichte und das deuteronomistische Geschichtswerk: Genesis 38 und 48-50. BEThL 133: 1997, ⇒17. ᶠBREKELMANS C., 391-405;

2326 Das spätdeuteronomistische Geschichtswerk Genesis I-2 Regum XXV und seine theologische Intention. Congress volume 1995. VT.S 66: 1997, ⇒323. ᴱEmerton, J.A., 261-279.

2327 *Schreiner, Josef* Geschichtsdeutung im Alten Testament: zu Anlaß und Zielsetzung, Sinngebung und Verfahrensweise des deuteronomistischen Geschichtswerkes. ᶠSCHREINER J., 1997 <1996>, ⇒80. 100-112.

2328  **Ahituv, Shmuel** Joshua. 1995, ⇒11/1,937. RCBQ 59 (1997) 722-723 *(Sperling, S. David)*. **H.**

2329  **Bieberstein, Klaus** Lukian und Theodotion im Josuabuch. 1994, ⇒10,2473; 11/1,947. RCBQ 58 (1996) 701-702 *(Greenspoon, Leonard J.)*.

2330  **Curtis, Adrian H.W.** Joshua. OTGu: 1994, ⇒12,2273. RBiOr 54 (1997) 437-438 *(Van der Meer, M.N.)*.

2331  **Fritz, Volkmar** Das Buch Josua. HAT 1/7: 1994, ⇒10,2467... 12,2274. RCBQ 59 (1997) 347-348 *(Younger, K. Lawson)*.

2332  **Navarro Puerto, Mercedes** Los libros de Josué, Jueces y Rut. 1995, ⇒11/1,945; 12,2280. RScrTh 29/2 (1997) 675-676 *(Jarne, J.)*; EfMex 15 (1997) 411-412 *(Muñoz Tónix, Reyes)*; Augustinus 42 (1997) 425-426 *(Robles, Gabriel)*.

2333  **Nelson, Richard Donald** Joshua: à commentary. OTL: LVL 1997, Westminster xviii; 310 pp. Bibl. $40. 0-664-21941-1.

2334  *Anbar, Moshé* Addendum à Josué et l'alliance de Sichem (Josué 24:1-28). BN 86 (1997) 5-6.

2335  *Blum, Erhard* Der kompositionelle Knoten am Übergang von Josua zu Richter: ein Entflechtungsvorschlag. BEThL 133: 1997, ⇒17. FBREKELMANS C., 181-212.

2336  *Coats, George W.* The book of Joshua: heroic saga or conquest theme? <1987>;

2337  *Flanagan, James W.* Chiefs in Israel <1981>. Historical Books. 1997 , ⇒192. EExum, J. Cheryl, 46-62/142-166.

2338  *Frymer-Kensky, Tikav* Reading Rahab. 1997, ⇒34. MGREENBERG M., 57-67 [Josh 2].

2339  *Hawk, L. Daniel* The problem with pagans. Reading bibles. 1997, ⇒172. EBeal, Timothy K., 153-163.

2340  *Hess, Richard S.* West Semitic texts and the book of Joshua. BBR 7 (1997) 63-76.

2341  **Johnson, James Turner** The Holy War idea in Western and Islamic traditions. University Park, PA 1997 Pennsylvania State University Press ix; 185 pp. Bibl. $45. 0-271-01632-9.

2342  *Jost, Renate* Achsas Quellen: feministisch-sozialgeschichtliche Überlegungen zu Josua 15,15/Ri 1,12-15. 1997, ⇒29. FGERSTENBERGER E.S., 110-125.

2343  *Merling, David* The book of Joshua: its structure and meaning. 1997, ⇒83. FSHEA W., 7-27.

2344  **Mitchell, Gordon** Together in the land: a reading of the book of Joshua. JSOT.S 134: 1993, ⇒10,2470... 12,2290. RABR 45 (1997) 70-72 *(O'Brien, Mark A.)*.

2345  *Noort, Ed* The traditions of Ebal and Gerizim: theological positions in the book of Joshua. BEThL 133: 1997, ⇒17. FBREKELMANS C., 161-180.

2346  **Partner, Peter** God of battles: holy wars of christianity and Islam. L 1997, Harper Collins xxvii; 364 pp. 0-00-255567-0.

2347  *Rowlett, Lori* Inclusion, exclusion and marginality in the book of Joshua. Historical Books. 1997 <1992>, ⇒192. EExum, J. Cheryl, 63-71.

2348  **Rowlett, Lori L.** Joshua and the rhetoric of violence: a new historicist analysis. JSOT.S 226: 1996, ⇒12,2292. RBTB 27 (1997) 28-29 *(Hobbs, T.R.)*.

2349  Sánchez, Pierre Le serment amphictionique (Aeschn. Legat. [2]
      115): un faux du IVᵉ siècle?. Hist. 46 (1997) 158-171.
2350  Sipilä, Seppo John CHRYSOSTOM and the book of Joshua. IX
      Congress IOSCS. SCSt 45: 1997, ⇒340. ᴱTaylor, Bernard A.,
      329-354.
2351  Wangerin, Walter Jericho. Word and World 17/3 (1997) 245-250
      [ZID 23,415] [Josh 2].


                  E4.2  Liber Judicum: Richter, Judges


2352  Amit, Yairah The book of Judges: the art of editing. 1992,
      ⇒8,2776. ᴿBZ 41/1 (1997) 99-100 (Maier, Johann). H.
2353  ᴱBrenner, Athalya A feminist companion to Judges. 1994,
      ⇒11/1,980. ᴿCBQ 59 (1997) 110-112 (Green, Barbara).
2354  Dumbrell, W.J. 'In those days there was no king in Israel; every
      man did what was right in his own eyes': the purpose of the book
      of Judges reconsidered. Historical Books. 1997 <1983>, ⇒192.
      ᴱExum, J. Cheryl, 72-82.
2355  Easterly, Ellis A case of mistaken identity: the judges in Judges
      don't judge. BiRe 13/2 (1997) 40-43, 47.
2356  Exum, J. Cheryl Was sagt das Richterbuch den Frauen?. SBS 169:
      Stu 1997, Katholisches Bibelwerk 76 pp. Bibl. 3-460-04691-0.
2357  Guest, Pauline Deryn Dangerous liaisons in the book of Judges.
      SJOT 11 (1997) 241-269.
2358  Lanoir, Corinne Le livre des Juges, l'histoire et les femmes. CBFV
      36 (1997) 55-71.
2359  MacKay, Donald B. Ethnicity and Israelite religion: the anthro-
      pology of social boundaries in Judges. Diss. Toronto 1997;
      ᴰClarke, Ernest: 303 pp. 0-612-27686-4. microfiche [NThAR
      1999,179].
2360  O'Connell, Robert H. The rhetoric of the book of Judges. VT.S
      63: 1996, ⇒12,2303. ᴿJBL 116 (1997) 345-346 (Melugin, Roy F.).
2361  Smelik, Willem F. The targum of Judges. OTS 36: 1995,
      ⇒11/1,983. ᴿJJS 48 (1997) 381-383 (Saldarini, Anthony J.).
2362  Sweeney, Marvin A. Davidic polemics in the book of Judges. VT
      47 (1997) 517-529.
2363  ᴱYee, Gale A. Judges and method: new approaches in biblical stu-
      dies. 1995, ⇒11/1,984. ᴿCBQ 59 (1997) 617-618 (Long, Burke
      O.); HebStud 38 (1997) 125-129 (Hauser, Alan J.).

2364  Wessels, J.P.H. Persuasions in Judges 2.20-3.6: a celebration of
      differences. The rhetorical analysis. JSNT.S 146: 1997, ⇒336.
      ᴱPorter, Stanley E., 120-136.
2365  Asen, Bernhard A. Deborah, Barak and bees: apis mellifera, apicul-
      ture and Judges 4 and 5. ZAW 109 (1997) 514-533.
2366  Layton, Scott C. Yaᶜel in Judges 4: an onomastic rejoinder. ZAW
      109 (1997) 93-94.
2367  Bosetti, Elena Debora: la profetessa giudice. TS(I) (1997 luglio-
      agosto) 7-10 [Judg 5,7].
2368  Fritz, Volkmar Das Debora-Lied Ri 5 als Geschichtsquelle. Studien
      zur Literatur. 1997 <1996>, ⇒126. 165-185.
2369  Block, Daniel I. Will the real Gideon please stand up?: narrative
      style and intention in Judges 6-9. JETS 40 (1997) 353-366.

2370 *Tafferner, Andrea* Politische Verantwortung und Macht: ein Bi-
belspiel zur Jotam-Fabel (Ri 9,7-15). Entschluss 52/11 (1997) 10-
13.

2371 *Liss, Hanna* Die Fabel des Yotam in Ri 9,8-15—Versuch einer
strukturellen Deutung. BN 89 (1997) 12-18.

2372 *Fritz, Volkmar* Abimelech und Sichem in Jdc. IX [Ri 9]. Studien
zur Literatur. 1997 <1982>, ⇒126. 187-203.

2373 *Claassens, Julie* Theme and function in the Jephthah narrative.
JNSL 23/2 (1997) 203-219 [Judg 10,6-18; 11; 12,1-7].

2374 *Willis, Timothy M.* The nature of Jephthah's authority. CBQ 59
(1997) 33-44 [Judg 10,17-11,11].

2375 *Boer, Esther de* Het geloof der 'vaderen': Richteren 11:30-40.
ITBT 5/8 (1997) 26-27.

2376 *Mehlman, Israel* Jephthah's daughter. JBQ 25/2 (1997) 73-78
[Judg 11,34-40].

2377 *Reis, Pamela Tamarkin* Spoiled child: a fresh look at Jephthah's
daughter. Prooftexts 17 (1997) 279-298 [Judg 11].

2378 *Tropper, Josef* Die šibbolæt-Falle (Richter 12,6). ZAH 10 (1997)
198-200 [Judg 12,6].

2379 **Bauske, Bernd** (S[c])hibboleth!: eine Untersuchung zur Wiedergabe der Schibboleth-Episode (Richter 12,6) in der spanischen Bi-
beltradition: mit einer Nachbemerkung zur Wiedergabe in Druck-
ausgaben in den nichtkastilischen Sprachen Spaniens und im Papia-
mentu sowie einem Verzeichnis. Stu 1997, Württemberg. Landes-
bibliothek 104 pp. 3-88282-046-2.

2380 *Bommel, Jan P.* Simson en Delila. ITBT 5/2 (1997) 27-28 [Judg
13-16; Jer 13,12; John 2,1-11].

2381 *Smith, Carol* Samson and Delilah: a parable of power?. JSOT 76
(1997) 45-57 [Judg 13-16].

2382 *Bowman, Richard G.; Swanson, Richard W.* Samson and the son of
God or dead heroes and dead goats: ethical readings of narrative
violence in Judges and Matthew. Semeia 77 (1997) 59-73 [Judg 13-
16].

2383 *Mobley, Gregory* The wild man in the bible and the ancient Near
East. JBL 116 (1997) 217-233 [Judg 13-16].

2384 *Exum, J. Cheryl* Harvesting the biblical narrator's scanty plot of
ground: a holistic approach to Judges 16:4-22. 1997, ⇒34.
ᴹGREENBERG M., 39-46.

2385 *Yoo, Yani* Han-laden women: Korean "comfort women" and
women in Judges 19-21. Semeia 78 (1997) 37-46.


E4.3 **Liber Ruth,** '*V Rotuli*', the Five Scrolls

2386 *Bauckham, Richard* The book of Ruth and the possibility of a feminist canonical hermeneutic. Bibl.Interp. 5 (1997) 29-45.

2387 ᴱ**Bengtsson, Per Å.** Two Arabic versions of the book of Ruth. Studia Orientalia Lundensia 6: 1995, ⇒11/1,1025. ᴿJRAS 7 (1997)
434-436 *(Holes, Clive)*.

2388 *Benjamin, Don C.* Stories of Naomi and Ruth. 1997, ⇒70.
ᶠMURPHY R., Master, 131-154.

2389 *Berlin, Adele* On the use of traditional Jewish exegesis in the modern literary study of the bible. 1997, ⇒34. ᴹGREENBERG M.,
173-183.

2390 *Berquist, Jon L.* Role dedifferentiation in the book of Ruth. Historical Books. 1997 <1993>, ⇒192. ᴱExum, J.C., 83-96.

2391 **Bush, Frederic William** Ruth, Esther. WBC 9: 1996, ⇒12,2326. ᴿRTR 56 (1997) 151-152 *(Goldsworthy, Graeme)*.

2392 **Caspi, Michael Maswari** The book of Ruth: an annotated bibliography. 1994, ⇒10,2520. ᴿHebSt 38 (1997) 172-175 *(Hubbard, Robert L.)*.

2393 *Chu, Julie Li-Chuan* Returning home: the inspiration of the role differentiation in the book of Ruth for Taiwanese women. Semeia 78 (1997) 47-53.

2394 **Costa, Michi** La historia de la abuela Ruth. Bilbao 1997, Desclée de B 180 pp. [Proyecció 44,335].

2395 **Fischer, James A.** Cantico dei Cantici, Rut, Lamentazioni, Qohelet, Ester. La Bibbia per tutti 24: Brescia 1997, Queriniana 150 pp. 88-399-2124-9.

2396 *Frickel, Josef* Hɪᴘᴘᴏʟʏᴛѕ von Rom Kommentar zum Buch Ruth. StPatr 30: 1997, ⇒351. ᴱLivingstone, Elizabeth A., 12-18.

2397 **Hamlin, E. John** Ruth: surely there is a future. 1996, ⇒12,2333. ᴿHebSt 38 (1997) 175-177 *(Keown, Gerald L.)*.

2398 *Honig, Bonnie* Ruth, the model emigrée: mourning and the symbolic politics of immigration. Political Theory 25/1 (1997) 112-136.

2399 *Martel, Gérard de* Le sermon de Jacques de Vɪᴛʀʏ sur le livre de Ruth. Summarium 132. EL 111/2 (1997) 132-146.

2400 **Masini, Mario** "Lectio divina" del libro di Rut. 1994, ⇒10,2530 ... 12,2337. ᴿRdT 38 (1997) 274-275 *(Di Palma, Gaetano)*.

2401 *Minette de Tillesse, Caetano* Na Diáspora: Tamar, a Cananéia e Rute, a Moabita. RBB 14/1-3 (1997) 154-157.

2402 *Moore, Michael S.* Two textual anomalies in Ruth. ᴿCBQ 59 (1997) 234-243 [Ruth 1,21; 2,6-7].

2403 **Nielsen, Kirsten** Ruth: a commentary. OTL: LVL 1997, Westminster xiv; 106 pp. $20. 0-664-22092-4 [ThD 44,375—Heiser, W.].

2404 *Stachowiak, Lech* Historia oddziaływania Księgi Rut w judaizmie i Nowym Testamencie [Zur Wirkungsgeschichte des Buches Rut im Judaismus und im Neuen Testament]. Zsfg. 355. WST 10 (1997) 351-355.

2405 **Van Wolde, Ellen** Ruth en Noömi: twee vreemdgangers. Ten Have 1996, Baarn 163 pp. 90-259-4495-7.

2406 *Van Wolde, Ellen* Intertextuality: Ruth in dialogue with Tamar. A feminist companion. 1997, ⇒180. ᴱBrenner, Athalya, 426-451.

2407 **Van Wolde, Ellen** Ruth and Naomi. L 1997, SCM x; 150 pp. £13. 0-334-02694-6 [RRT 1998/1,38—Gillingham, Susan].

2408 *Van Wolde, Ellen* Texts in dialogue with texts: Intertextuality in the Ruth and Tamar narratives. Bibl.Interp. 5 (1997) 1-28.

2409 *Howell, James C.* Ruth 1:1-18. Interp. 51 (1997) 281-284.

2410 *Hubbard, Robert L.* Ganzheitsdenken in the book of Ruth. 1997, ⇒48. ᶠKɴɪᴇʀɪᴍ R., 192-209 [Ruth 1,08; 2,12; 3,10; 4,14].

2411 *Martel, Gérard de* Le sermon de Gʀᴀᴇᴄᴜʟᴜѕ sur Ruth 1,22 pour la fête de l'Assomption de la Vierge Marie. AFH 90 (1997) 487-503;

2412 Un sermon anonyme sur Ruth 1,22 pour la nativité de la Vierge Marie (Cambridge, Gonville and Caius College 358/585). MS 59 (1997) 1-18.

2413  *Fischer, Irmtraud* Der Männerstammbaum im Frauenbuch: Überlegungen zum Schluss des Rutbuches (4,18-22). 1997, ⇒29. [F]GERSTENBERGER E.S., 195-213.

E4.4  1-2 Samuel

2414  **Dietrich, Walter; Naumann, Thomas** Die Samuelbücher. EdF 287: 1995, ⇒11/1,1052. [R]Anton. 72 (1997) 699-700 *(Nobile, M.)*.
2415  [T]**Grillet, Bernard; Lestienne, Michel;** Collab. *Massonnet, Jean & Anita*: La Bible d'Alexandrie 9,1: premier livre des Règnes. P 1997, Cerf 458 pp. Introd. et notes par Michel Lestienne. 2-204-05545-X.
2416  *Preston, Thomas R.* The heroism of Saul: patterns of meaning in the narrative of the early kingship. Historical Books. 1997 <1982>, ⇒192. [E]Exum, J.C., 122-141.
2417  *Rendtorff, Rolf* Samuel the prophet: a link between Moses and the kings. Bibl.Interp. 28: 1997, ⇒77. [F]SANDERS J., 27-36.
2418  **Sicre Diaz, José Luis** Il primo libro di Samuele. Guide spirituali all'Antico Testamento: R 1997, Città N 190 pp. 88-311-3744-1.
      *Taylor, Bernard A.* The Lucianic text and the MT in 1 Reigns. IX Congress IOSCS. SCSt 45: 1997, ⇒340. [E]Taylor, Bernard A., 1-18.
2419  [E]**Van Liere, Franciscus A.** Expositio hystorica in librum Regum. Andreas de Sancto Victore: Opera. CChr.ILL 91: Turnhout 1997, Brepols 54 pp. 4 microfiches. 2-503-03534-2 [NThAR 1997,290].

2420  *Brettler, Marc* The composition of 1 Samuel 1-2. JBL 116 (1997) 601-612.
2421  *Spina, Frank Anthony* Eli's seat: the transition from priest to prophet in 1 Samuel 1-4. Historical Books. 1997 <1994>, ⇒192. [E]Exum, J.C., 98-106.
2422  **Fokkelman, J.P.** Vow and desire (1 Sam 1-12). SSN 31: 1993, ⇒9,2684... 12,2368. [R]OLZ 92 (1997) 74-78 *(Stoebe, Hans Joachim)*.
2423  *Melano Couch, Beatriz* Liberazione: una visione biblica (1 Sam 1,1-2,11). Conc(I) 33/2 (1997) 47-55; D33/2,153-159.
2424  *Joosten, Jan* Workshop: meaning and use of the tenses in 1 Samuel 1;
2425  *Van der Merwe, Christo H.J.* Workshop: text linguistics and the structure of 1 Samuel 1. Narrative syntax. 1997, ⇒342. [E]Van Wolde, Ellen, 72-83/157-165.
2426  *Raurell, Frederic* La sfida della sterilità feconda: un testo modesto ed un'idea forte (1 Sam 2,5b in alcune biografie di FRANCESCO d'Assisi). Laur. 38/1-2 (1997) 177-217.
2427  *Tov, Emanuel* Different editions of the song of Hannah and of its narrative framework. 1997, ⇒34. [M]GREENBERG M., 149-170 [1 Sam 2].
2428  *Ruffin, Michael L.* 1 Samuel 3:1-20. Interp. 51 (1997) 175-178.
2429  *Colautti, Federico M.* Ratas o tumores?: problemas de crítica textual en 1 SA 6,4. Henoch 19/1 (1997) 17-38 [1 Sam 6,11; 6,4].
2430  *Coggins, Richard* On kings and disguises. Historical Books. 1997 <1991>, ⇒192. [E]Exum, J.C., 249-255 [1 Sam 28; 1 Kgs 20; 22; 14; 2 Chr 35,22].

E4.5 *1 Sam 7...Initia potestatis regiae*, **Origins of kingship**

2431 *Carneiro, Robert L.* Eine Theorie zur Entstehung des Staates;
2432 *Clastres, Pierre* Die Gesellschaft gegen den Staat;
2433 *Evans-Pritchard, Edward E.* Nuer-Propheten. Die Entstehung des Königtums. 1997, ⇒308. ᴱSigrist, C., 113-124/47-60/61-66.
2434 *Fantoni, Vittorio* Camminando con Saul. Sum. 3. Adventus 10 (1997) 3-6.
2435 *Hoebel, Edward Adamson* Die Aschanti: der Triumph des öffentlichen Rechts in einer konstitutionellen Monarchie. Die Entstehung des Königtums. 1997, ⇒308. ᴱSigrist, C., 143-150.
2436 *Hoffmeier, James K.* The king as God's son in Egypt and Israel. JSSEA 24 (1994) 28-38.
2437 *Johnson, Kent L.* Saul and the mayor of Casterbridge: a study in shared experience. Word and World 17/3 (1997) 251-259 [ZID 23,415].
2438 *Leach, Edmund R.* Gumsa und Shan;
2439 *Mair, Lucy* Die Entstehung des Königtums in Ostafrika;
2440 *Mair, Lucy* Königsherrschaft und Ritual;
2441 *Neu, Rainer* Die Entstehung des israelitischen Königtums im Lichte der Ethnosoziologie. Die Entstehung des Königtums. 1997, ⇒308. ᴱSigrist, C., 196-207/101-112/168-182/12-20.
2442 *Ntreh, Benjamin Abotchie* How kings were made in ancient Israel and Judah: from history to tradition. BiBh 23 (1997) 71-89.
2443 *Roberts, Simon* Ordnung und Konflikt. Die Entstehung des Königtums. 1997, ⇒308. ᴱSigrist, C., 151-164.
2444 **Sembrano, Lucio** La regalità di Dio: metafora ebraica e contesto culturale del Vicino Oriente antico. RivBib.S 32: Bo 1997, Dehoniane 247 pp. L37.000. 88-10-30220-6 [NThAR 1998,269].
2445 *Werder, Peter von* Politische Organisation in westafrikanischen Königsherrschaften. Die Entstehung des Königtums. 1997, ⇒308. ᴱSigrist, C., 128-137.

2446 *Eslinger, Lyle* Viewpoints and point of view in 1 Samuel 8-12. Historical Books. 1997 <1983>, ⇒192. ᴱExum, J.C., 107-121.
2447 *Kammerer, Stefan* Die mißratenen Söhne Samuels. BN 88 (1997) 75-88 [1 Sam 8].
2448 *Fritz, Volkmar* Die Deutungen des Königtums Sauls in den Überlieferungen von seiner Entstehung in 1 Sam 9-11. Studien zur Literatur. 1997 <1976>, ⇒126. 205-225.
2449 *Fenton, Terry L.* Deuteronomistic advocacy of the *nābîʾ*: 1 Samuel ix 9: and questions of Israelite prophecy. VT 47 (1997) 23-42.
2450 *Catastini, Alessandro* Dell'importanza dell'errore significativo nella tradizione di testi contemporanei: a proposito di S. Venturini, in "Rivista biblica" 44 (1996), pp. 397-425. Henoch 19/2 (1997) 243-245 [1 Sam 10,27-11,01.

E4.6 *1 Sam 16...2 Sam: Accessio Davidis*. **David's Rise**

2451 *Barrick, W. Boyd* Saul's demise, David's lament, and Custer's last stand. JSOT 73 (1997) 25-41 [1 Sam 31,1-6; 2 Sam 1,19].

EBron, H.; Lipschitz, O. הרצאות בכנס: דוד מלך ישראל חי וקיים?: [David King בוגרט החוג למקרא של האוניברסיטה העברטת, ירושלים of Israel alive and enduring?] ⇒319.

2452  *Dietrich, Walter* דָוִד, דּוֹד und בֵּיתדּוֹד. ThZ 53 (1997) 17-32.
2453  *Evans, Craig A.* David in the Dead Sea scrolls. The scrolls and the scriptures. JSPE.S 26: 1997, ⇒299. EPorter, Stanley E., 183-197.
2454  *Freedman, David Noel* The age of David and Solomon. Divine Commitment 1. 1997 <1979>, ⇒124. 286-313;
2455  The spelling of the name 'David' in the Hebrew Bible. Divine Commitment 2. 1997 <1983>, 108-122.
2456  *Gunn, David M.* Reflections on David. A feminist companion. 1997, ⇒180. EBrenner, Athalya, 548-566.
2457  **Isabelle de la Source, Soeur** Un roi (Ruth - 1 et 2 Samuel - 1 Rois, ch. 1 à 11). Lire la Bible avec les Pères 4: P 1997, Médiaspaul 173 pp. FF90. 2-7122-0637-1.
2458  *Kitchen, Kenneth Anderson* A possible mention of David in the late tenth century BCE, and deity *Dod as dead as the Dodo?. JSOT 76 (1997) 29-44.
2459  *Lipschitz, Ora* Polémique à propos de la 'maison de David'—à la suite de la découverte de l'inscription de Tel Dan;
2460  *Mazar, Amihaï* L'époque du 'Royaume Uni': [point de] vue archéologique. David. 1997, ⇒319. 9-77/79-115 [RB 105,290—Langlamet, F.]. H.
2461  **Noll, K.L.** The faces of David. Diss. Union Theol. Sem. in Virginia, 1996; DMcBride, S.D.: JSOT.S 242: Shf 1997, Academic 204 pp. 1-85075-659-7.
2462  **Pomykala, Kenneth E.** The Davidic dynasty tradition in early Judaism. 1995, ⇒11/1,1111; 12,2426. RJSSt 44 (1997) 398-401 *(Brooke, George J.)*; JBL 115 (1996) 529-530 *(Langston, Scott)*.
2463  *Rofé, Alexander* L'état davidique—révolution et guerre civile. David. 1997, ⇒319. 203-208 [RB 105,290—Langlamet, F.]. H.
2464  *Rottenecker, Susanne* Homosexualität in der Davidserzählung?;
2465  *Schroer, Silvia; Staubli, Thomas* Gibt es eine vorurteilslose Exegese?: Antwort auf die Kritik von Susanne Rottenecker. BiKi 52 (1997) 34-36/36-37.
2466  **Tshidibi Bambila, Donatien Aimé** La rétribution négative dans l'histoire monarchique d'Israël. Diss. Angelicum; DAgius, J.: R 1997 [RTL 29,580].

2467  *Campbell, Antony F.* Structure analysis and the art of exegesis (1 Samuel 16:14-18:30). 1997, ⇒48. FKNIERIM R., 76-103.
2468  *Wong, G.C.I.* Who loved whom?: a note on 1 Samuel xvi 21. VT 47 (1997) 554-556.
2469  *Olmsted, Hugh M.* Maksim GREK's 'David and Goliath' and the Skaryna Bible. Harvard Ukrainian Studies 19 (1997) 451-475 [IAJS 45,228] [1 Sam 17].
2470  *Anbar, Moshé* La critique biblique à la lumière des archives royales de Mari II: 1 S 18,21b. Bib. 78 (1997) 247-251.
2471  *Stein, Peter* "Und man berichtete Saul...". Text- und literarkritische Untersuchungen zu 1. Samuelis 24 und 26. BN 90 (1997) 46-66.
2472  *Reis, Pamela Tamarkin* Cupidity and stupidity: woman's agency and the 'rape' of Tamar. JANES 25 (1997) 43-60 [1 Sam 25; 2 Sam 13].

2473 *Reis, Pamela Tamarkin* Eating the blood: Saul and the witch of Endor. JSOT 73 (1997) 3-23 [Lev 19,26; 1 Sam 28].

2474 **Schmidt, Brian B.** Israel's beneficent dead: ancestor cult and necromancy in ancient Israelite religion and tradition. 1994, ⇒10,10730; 12,8979. ᴿETR 72 (1997) 133-134 *(Römer, Thomas)*; JQR 88 (1997) 91-93 *(Pope, Marvin)* [1 Sam 28].

2475 *Orel, V.; Frolov, S.* Exegetica 1-2. Sum. 121. Journal of Ancient History 223 (1997) 111-121 [1 Sam 28].

2476 **Kleiner, Michael** Saul in En-Dor Wahrsagung oder Totenbeschwörung?: eine synchrone und diachrone Untersuchung zu 1 Sam 28. EThSt 66: 1995, ⇒11/1,1125. ᴿThLZ 122 (1997) 797-798 *(Stolz, Fritz)*; CBQ 59 (1997) 738-739 *(Moore, Michael S.)*.

2477 *Chinitz, Jacob* Two sinners. JBQ 25 (1997) 108-113 [2 Sam 12; 1 Kgs 21].

2478 *Gelio, Roberto* Il settennato hebronita del regno di Davide. Lat. 63 (1997) 5-31.

2479 *Jensen, Hans J.L.* Desire, rivalry and collective violence in the Succession Narrative. Historical Books. 1997 <1992>, ⇒192. ᴱExum, J.C., 184-203.

2480 **Keys, Gillian** The wages of sin: a reappraisal of the 'Succession Narrative'. JSOT.S 221: 1996, ⇒12,2442. ᴿIBSt 19/1 (1997) 46-48 *(McConville, Gordon)*.

2481 *Mendecki, Norbert* Jak Dawid został królem? [Quomodo David factus est rex?]. RBL 50 (1997) 200-202. P.

2482 *Perdue, Leo G.* 'Is there anyone left of the house of Saul...?': ambiguity and the characterization of David in the Succession Narrative. Historical Books. 1997 <1984>, ⇒192. ᴱExum, J.C., 167-183.

2483 **Stoebe, Hans-Joachim** Das zweite Buch Samuelis. KAT 8/2: 1994, ⇒10,2545; 11/1,1053. ᴿBib. 78 (1997) 409-412 *(Pisano, Stephen)*.

2484 *George, Mark K.* Assuming the body of the heir apparent: David's lament. Reading bibles. 1997, ⇒172. ᴱBeal, Timothy K. 164-174 [2 Sam 1,17-27].

2485 *Jenni, Ernst* 'Schlagen' in 2.Sam 2,31 und in den historischen Büchern. Studien zur Sprachwelt. 1997 <1993>, ⇒138. 189-195.

2486 *Freedman, David Noel* On the death of Abiner. Divine Commitment 2. 1997 <1987>, ⇒124. 227-231 [2 Sam 3,33-34].

2487 *Haelewyck, Jean-Claude* L'assassinat d'Ishbaal (2 Samuel iv 1-12). VT 47 (1997) 145-153.

2488 **Gelio, Roberto** L'ingresso di Davide in Gerusalemme capitale: studio letterario, storico e teologico su II Sam 5,6-8; 6,1-23. Studi sulla Bibbia e il suo ambiente 3: CinB 1997, San Paolo 211 pp. L28.000. 88-215-3404-9 [RdT 38,142].

2489 *Derby, Josiah* David's conquest of Jerusalem. JBQ 25 (1997) 35-39 [[2 Sam 5,6-8; 1 Chr 11,6].

2490 *Evans, Craig A.* A note on Targum 2 Samuel 5.8 and Jesus' ministry to the 'maimed, halt nad blind'. JSPE 15 (1997) 79-82 [Isa 35,6; [Micah 4,6-8; Lk 14,15-24; 16,19-31]].

2491 **Eslinger, Lyle** House of God or house of David: the rhetoric of 2 Samuel 7. JSOT.S 164: 1994, ⇒11/1,1139. ᴿTJT 13/2 (1997) 257-258 *(Bergen, Wesley J.)*.

2492 *Stoebe, Hans Joachim* Erlebte Gegenwart—verheissene Zukunft: Gedanken zu II Samuelis 7 und Genesis 15. ThZ 53 (1997) 131-141.

2493 *Laato, Antti* Second Samuel 7 and ancient Near Eastern royal ideology. CBQ 59 (1997) 244-269.

2494 *Nicol, George G.* The alleged rape of Bathsheba: some observations on ambiguity in biblical narrative. JSOT 73 (1997) 43-54 [2 Sam 11].

    *Bezuidenhout, L.C.* Voorstellings van Batseba ⇒1020.

2495 **Müllner, Ilse** Gewalt im Hause Davids: die Erzählung von Tamar und Amnon (2 Sam 13,1-22). Diss.-Habil. Münster, 1997; D*Zenger, E.*: Herders Biblische Studien 13: FrB 1997, Herder ix; 432 pp. Bibl. DM98. 3-451-26404-8.

2496 *Reis, Pamela Tamarkin* Cupidity and stupidity: woman's agency and the 'rape' of Tamar. JANES 25 (1997) 43-60 [1 Sam 25; 2 Sam 13].

2497 **Lyke, Larry L.** King David with the wise woman of Tekoa: the resonance of tradition in parabolic narrative. Diss. Harvard 1996; D*Levenson, J.D.*: JSOT.S 225: Shf 1997, Academic 211 pp. 1-85075-826-3 [2 Sam 14].

2498 *Costen, James H.* Running with the right message: II Samuel 18:9-33. JITC 24 (1996-97) 215-221 [ZID 23,406].

2499 *Wiggins, Steve A.* Between heaven and earth: Absalom's dilemma. JNSL 23/1 (1997) 73-81 [2 Sam 18,9].

2500 *Winters, Alicia* The subversive memory of a woman: 2 Samuel 21:1-14. Subversive scriptures. 1997, ⇒263. E*Vaage, L.*, 142-154.

2501 *West, Gerald* Reading on the boundaries: reading 2 Samuel 21:1-14 with Rizpah. Scriptura 63 (1997) 527-537.

2502 *Grant, J. Jeremy M.* 2 Samuel 23:1-7. Interp. 51 (1997) 415-418.

### E4.7 *Libri Regum:* Solomon, Temple: 1 Kings...

2503 **Buis, Pierre** Le livre des Rois. Sources Bibliques: P 1997, Gabalda 312 pp. FF590. 2-85021-103-6 [RB 105,309].

2504 **Fernández Marcos, Natalio; Busto Saiz, J.R.** 1-2 Reyes. El texto antioqueno de la Biblia griega 2. TECC 53: 1992, ⇒8,2908; 11/1,1151. R*BZ* 41 (1997) 107-110 *(Aejmelaeus, Anneli).*

2505 E**Grossfeld, Bernard** A bilingual concordance to the targum of the prophets 8: Kings 3: ת - y. Lei 1997, Brill 373 pp. ƒ190/$118. 90-04-10750-9;

2506 A bilingual concordance to the targum of the prophets 6: Kings: 1. ז - א. Lei 1997, Brill vi; 338 pp. ƒ190/$118. 90-04-10493-3;

2507 A bilingual concordance to the targum of the prophets 7: Kings 2: ס - ת. Lei 1997, Brill 375 pp. ƒ190/$118. 90-04-10749-5.

2508 **House, Paul R.** 1, 2 Kings. NAC 8: 1995, ⇒11/1,1152. R*HebStud* 38 (1997) 131-134 *(Penchansky, David).*

2509 **Provan, Iain W.** 1 & 2 Kings. OTGu: Shf 1997, Academic 125 pp. £7/$10. 1-85075-802-6 [ET 108,344].

2510 *Taylor, Bernard A.* The Lucianic text and the MT in 1 Reigns. IX Congress IOSCS. SCSt 45: 1997, ⇒340. E*Taylor, B.A.*, 1-18.

2511 **Walsh, Jerome T.** 1 Kings. 1996, ⇒12,2465. R*CBQ* 59 (1997) 361-362 *(McKenzie, Steven L.)*; BTB 27 (1997) 119 *(Craghan, John F.).*

2512 *Deliyannis, Deborah Mauskopf* A biblical model for serial biography: the book of Kings and the Roman Liber Pontificalis. RBen 107 (1997) 15-23.

2513 *Linville, James* Rethinking the 'exilic' book of Kings. JSOT 75 (1997) 21-42.

2514 *Stipp, Hermann-Josef* Traditionsgeschichtliche Beobachtungen zu den Kriegserzählungen der Königsbücher. RB 104 (1997) 481-511 [1 Kgs 20; 22; 2 Kgs 3; 5; 6,8-7,17].

2515 **Volgger, David** Verbindliche Tora am einzigen Tempel: zu Motiv und Ort der Komposition von 1.2 Kön. Diss. habil. Wü 1997/98; ᴰ*Seidl* [BZ 42,319].

2516 *Dreher, Carlos A.* Solomon and the workers. Subversive scriptures. 1997, ⇒263. ᴱVaage, L., 25-38.

2517 *Glatt-Gilad, David A.* The deuteronomistic critique of Solomon: a response to Marvin A. SWEENEY ⇒11/1,1166. JBL 116 (1997) 700-703.

2518 *Handy, Lowell K.* On the dating and dates of Solomon's reign;

2519 *Jobling, David* The value of Solomon's age for the biblical reader;

2520 *Knauf, Ernst Axel* Le roi est mort, vive le roi!: a biblical argument for the historicity of Solomon. The age of Solomon. 1997, ⇒282. ᴱHandy, L.K., 96-105/470-492/81-95.

2521 **Knoppers, Gary N.** The reign of Solomon and the rise of Jeroboam. Two nations under God: the deuteronomistic history of Solomon and the dual monarchies 1. HSM 52: 1993, ⇒9,2807... 12,2478. ᴿBiOr 54 (1997) 439-442 *(Van Keulen, Percy)*; JAOS 117 (1997) 727 *(Soggin, J.A.)*.

2522 *Knoppers, Gary N.* Solomon's fall and Deuteronomy [1 Kgs 11,1-4];

2523 *Lasine, Stuart* Solomon and the wizard of Oz: power and inversibility in a verbal palace. The age of Solomon. 1997, ⇒282. ᴱHandy, L.K., 392-410/375-391 [1 Chr 22-2 Chr 9].

2524 *Lasine, Stuart* The ups and downs of monarchical justice: Solomon and Jehoram in an intertextual world. Historical Books. 1997 <1993>, ⇒192. ᴱExum, J. Cheryl, 216-232.

2525 *Lemche, Niels Peter* On doing sociology with "Solomon". The age of Solomon. 1997, ⇒282. ᴱHandy, L.K., 312-335.

2526 *Mayer, Reinhold; Rühle, Inken* Salomo als Prototyp eines Weisen?: die Weisheit Salomos—einmal anders. BiKi 52 (1997) 193-199.

2527 *Millard, Alan* Assessing Solomon: history or legend?;

2528 King Solomon in his ancient context;

2529 *Miller, J. Maxwell* Response to MILLARD;

2530 Separating the Solomon of history from the Solomon of legend;

2531 *Naʾaman, Nadav* Sources and composition in the history of Solomon;

2532 *Niemann, Hermann Michael* The socio-political shadow cast by the biblical Solomon. The age of Solomon. 1997, ⇒282. ᴱHandy, L.K., 25-29/30-53/54-56/1-24/57-80/252-299.

2533 *Parker, K.I.* Solomon as philosopher king?: the nexus of law and wisdom in 1 Kings 1-11;

2534 *Pyper, Hugh S.* Judging the wisdom of Solomon: the two-way effect of intertextuality. Historical Books. 1997 <1992>, ⇒192. ᴱExum, J. Cheryl, 233-248/204-215.

2535  **Rappe, Claude** Σολομών, ο Βασιλιάς των Γυναικών [Solomon, the king of women]. 1996, ⇒12,2479. ᴿDBM 16/1 (1997) 81-84 *(Agourides, S.)*. G.

2536  **Särkiö, Pekka** Die Weisheit und Macht Salomos in der israelitischen Historiographie: eine traditions- und redaktionskritische Untersuchung über 1 Kön 3-5 und 9-11. SESJ 60: 1994, ⇒10,2658. ᴿZAW 109 (1997) 315-316 *(Köckert, M.)*.

2537  *Shimoff, Sandra R.* The Hellenization of Solomon in rabbinic texts;

2538  *Throntveit, Mark A.* The idealization of Solomon as the glorification of God in the Chronicler's royal speeches and royal prayers;

2539  *Viviano, Pauline A.* Glory lost: the reign of Solomon in the deuteronomistic history. The age of Solomon. 1997, ⇒282. ᴱHandy, L.K., 457-469/411-427/336-347.

2540  *Ulrich, Kerstin* 1. Könige 3,16-28: "anders" gelesen. 1997, ⇒29. ᶠGᴇʀsᴛᴇɴʙᴇʀɢᴇʀ E.S., 126-133.

2541  *Rand, Herbert* Pronunciation: a key to meaning: 1 Kings 3:16-28. JBQ 25 (1997) 246-250.

2542  *Görg, Manfred* Elihoref—oder: ein Name, der keiner war?. BN 89 (1997) 5-11 [1 Kgs 4,3].

2543  *Fritz, Volkmar* Die Verwaltungsgebiete Salomos nach 1. Kön 4,7-19. Studien zur Literatur. 1997 <1995>, ⇒126. 251-263.

2544  *Zwickel, Wolfgang* Der vermißte Stamm Sebulon in 1 Könige IV 7-19. VT 47 (1997) 387-389.

2545  *Williams, P.J.* tmr in 1 Kings ix 18. VT 47 (1997) 262-265.

2546  **Lassner, Jacob** Demonizing the Queen of Sheba. 1994, ⇒9,2798... 12,2485. ᴿJSSt 42 (1997) 187-188 *(Hawting, G.R.)* [1 Kgs 10,1-13].

2547  *Kitchen, Kenneth A.* Sheba and Arabia. The age of Solomon. 1997, ⇒282. ᴱHandy, L.K., 126-153 [1 Kgs 10,1-13].

2548  **Boer, Roland** Jᴀᴍᴇsᴏɴ and Jeroboam. 1996, ⇒12,2511. ᴿCBQ 59 (1997) 726-727 *(Penchansky, David)* [1 Kgs 11-14; 2 Chr 10-13].

### Templum

2549  *Baines, John* Temples as symbols, guarantors, and participants in Egyptian civilization. The temple in ancient Egypt. 1997, ⇒300. ᴱQuirke, S., 216-241.

2550  **Bissoli, Giovanni** Il tempio nella letteratura giudaica e neotestamentaria. SBFA 37: 1995, ⇒11/1,1188. ᴿRevBib 59 (1997) 63-64 *(Ricciardi, Alberto)*; CBQ 59 (1997) 147-149 *(Marrow, Stanley B.)*.

2551  *Bonnet, Charles; Valbelle, Dominique* The Middle Kingdom temple of Hathor at Serabit el-Khadim;

2552  *Bryan, Betsy M.* The statue program for the mortuary temple of Amenhotep III. The temple in ancient Egypt. 1997, ⇒300. ᴱQuirke, S., 82-89/57-81.

2553  *Cansdale, Lena* Jᴜʟɪᴀɴ and the rebuilding of the Jerusalem temple. Abr-n. 34 (1996-1997) 18-29.

2554  *Chilton, Bruce* The temple in the Isaiah targum. Jesus in context. AGAJ 39: 1997, ⇒183. 251-262.

2555  TE*Connolly, Sean* BEDE: on the temple. Introd. *O'Reilly, Jennifer.*
      Translated Texts for Historians 21: Liverpool 1995, Liverpool
      University Press lv; 142 pp. RDR 115 (1997) 155-156 *(McIntyre,*
      *T.);* ChH 66 (1997) 324 *(Chaney, William A.);* Francia 24/1 (1997)
      198-200 *(Padberg, Lutz E. von).*

2556  *Davies, Sue; Smith, H.S.* Sacred animal temples at Saqqara. The
      temple in ancient Egypt. 1997, ⇒300. EQuirke, S., 112-131.

2557  **Edersheim, Alfred** Der Tempel: Mittelpunkt des geistlichen Le-
      bens zur Zeit Jesu. Wu 1997, Brockhaus 253 pp. DM49.80 [EuA
      73/4,321].

2558  *Eliav, Yaron Z* HADRIAN's actions in the Jerusalem Temple
      Mount according to Cassius-Dio and Xiphilini Manus. JSQ 4
      (1997) 125-144.

2559  *Elior, Rachel* From earthly temple to heavenly shrines: prayer and
      sacred song in the hekhalot literature and its relation to temple tra-
      ditions. JSQ 4 (1997) 217-267.

2560  *Favard-Meeks, Christine* The temple of Behbeit el-Hagara. The
      temple in ancient Egypt. 1997, ⇒300. EQuirke, S., 102-111.

2561  *Fritz, Volkmar* Der Tempel Salomos im Licht der neueren For-
      schung <1980>;

2562  Zur Erwähnung des Tempels in einem Ostrakon von Arad
      <1974>. Studien zur Literatur. 1997, ⇒126. 239-249/279-283.

2563  *Hayward, Robert* The chant of the Seraphim and the worship of the
      second temple. PIBA 20 (1997) 62-80 [Isa 6,1-4].

2564  **Hayward, Robert C.** The Jewish temple: a non-biblical source-
      book. 1996, ⇒12,2498. RJJS 48 (1997) 357-358 *(Grabbe, L.L.).*

2565  *Holloway, Steven W.* Porch lights in neo-Assyrian temples. RA 90
      (1996) 27-32.

2566  **Kaufman, Asher Selig** The temple of Jerusalem, part I: Tractate
      Middot; part II (1): Tractate Middot: variant readings for chapters
      1 and 2 presented in novel form as a transcript of manuscripts and
      early printed texts. J 1991-1997, Har Year'ah 102 + 146 pp. [JJS
      49,365s—Schwartz, Joshua]. H.

2567  *Kowalski, Aleksy* Tempio di Dio in Cristo nella 'vita di Mosè' di
      GREGORIO di Nissa. Ricerche Teologiche 8/2 (1997) 401-408.

2568  *Lenhardt, Pierre* La tradition d'Israël sur la présence divine (sheki-
      nah) dans le temple and dans le monde éclaire la foi chrétienne en
      l'incarnation. Sum., som. 160-161. Cahiers Ratisbonne 2 (1997)
      137-161.

2569  *Malek, Jaromir* The temples at Memphis: problems highlighted by
      the EES survey. The temple in ancient Egypt. 1997, ⇒300.
      EQuirke, S., 90-101.

2570  *Niehr, Herbert* In search of Yhwh's cult statue in the first temple.
      The image. 1997, ⇒2073. EVan der Toorn, Karel, 73-95.

2571  *Posener-Kriéger, Paule* News from Abusir. The temple in ancient
      Egypt. 1997, ⇒300. EQuirke, S., 17-23.

2572  *Quaegebeur, Jan* Excavating the forgotten temple of Shenhur
      (Upper Egypt). The temple in ancient Egypt. 1997, ⇒300.
      EQuirke, S., 159-167.

2573  *Rosenfeld, Ben Zion* Sage and temple in rabbinic thought after the
      destruction of the second temple. JSJ 28 (1997) 437-464.

2574  *Schart, Aaron* Die Entgrenzung des heiligen Raumes: Tempelkon-
      zept und Tempelkritik in der biblischen Tradition. PTh 86 (1997)
      348-359.

2575  *Schmid, Hartmut* Der Tempelbaubericht—mehr als ein Baubericht:
Beobachtungen zu 1. Könige 6 und 7. TVGMS 424: 1997, ⇒59.
FMAIER G., 147-164.

2576  **Schmidt, Francis** La pensée du temple: de Jérusalem à Qoumrân.
1994, ⇒10,2668... 12,2505. RRHPhR 77/2 (1997) 234-236
*(Grappe, Ch.)*.

2577  *Schwartz, Daniel R.* The Jews of Egypt between the temple of
Onias, the temple of Jerusalem, and heaven. Sum. v. Zion 62/1
(1997) 5-22. H.

2578  *Stadelmann, Rainer* The development of the pyramid temple in the
fourth dynasty. The temple in ancient Egypt. 1997, ⇒300.
EQuirke, S., 1-16.

2579  *Traunecker, Claude* Lessons from the Upper Egyptian temple of el-
Qal'a. The temple in ancient Egypt. 1997, ⇒300. EQuirke, S.,
168-178.

2580  *Van Seters, John* The Chronicler's account of Solomon's temple-
building: a continuity theme. JSOT.S 238: 1997, ⇒61.
FMCKENZIE S., 283-300 [1 Kgs 6-7; 2 Chr 3-4];

2581  Solomon's temple: fact and ideology in biblical and Near Eastern
historiography. CBQ 59 (1997) 45-57.

2582  **Zwickel, Wolfgang** Der Tempelkult in Kanaan und Israel. FAT
10: 1994, ⇒10,2671... 12,2510. RZAW 109 (1997) 166-167 *(Kök-
kert, M.)*; ETR 72 (1997) 605-607 *(Hüllstrung, Wolfgang)*; Protest. 52 (1997) 327-328 *(Soggin, J.A.)*; JBL 116 (1997) 329-330
*(Dearman, J. Andrew)*.

## 1 Regum 12ss

2583  **Knoppers, Gary N.** The reign of Jeroboam, the fall of Israel and
the reign of Josiah. Two nations under God: the deuteronomistic
history of Solomon and the dual monarchies 2. HSM 53: 1994,
⇒10,2637... 12,2514. RBiOr 54 (1997) 439-442 *(Van Keulen,
Percy)*; JAOS 117 (1997) 727 *(Soggin, J.A.)*.

2584  *Ussishkin, David* Jezreel, Samaria and Megiddo: royal centres of
Omri and Ahab. Congress volume 1995. VT.S 66: 1997, ⇒323.
EEmerton, J.A., 351-364.

2585  *Schenker, Adrian* Jéroboam et la division du royaume dans le texte
massorétique et la Septante ancienne. IX Congress IOSCS. SCSt
45: 1997, ⇒340. ETaylor, B.A., 171-176 [1 Kgs 11; 12,24; 14].

2586  *Shaw, Charles S.* The sins of Rehoboam: the purpose of 3 Kingdoms 12.24a-z. JSOT 73 (1997) 55-64.

2587  **Talshir, Zipora** The alternative story of the division of the kingdom: 3 Kingdoms 12:24a-z. JBS 6: 1993, ⇒9,2802... 12,2488.
RLASBF 47 (1997) 575-576 *(Cortese, Enzo)*.

2588  *Luciani, Ferdinando* L'interpretazione di 1 Re 13,11-32 nel Targum di Jonathan. Aevum 71/1 (1997) 3-10.

2589  *Herr, Bertram* Der wahre Prophet bezeugt seine Botschaft mit dem
Tod: ein Versuch zu 1 Kön 13. BZ 41 (1997) 69-78.

2590  *Emerton, J.A.* The house of Baal in 1 Kings xvi 32. VT 47 (1997)
293-300.

E4.8 *1 Regum 17-22: Elias,* **Elijah**

2591 **Àlvarez Barredo, Miguel** Las narraciones Elías y Eliseo en los libros de los Reyes: formación y teología. 1996, ⇒12,2521. ᴿCDios 210/1 (1997) 345-346 *(Gutiérrez, J.).*

2592 *Banse, Holger* Elia e Gesù. Studi Fatti Ricerche 79 (1997) 3-6.

2593 *Bartolini, Elena* 'Alzati, va' in Zarepta di Sidone': Elia accolto da una vedova. Horeb 18/3 (1997) 28-33 [1 Kgs 17].

2594 *Blum, Erhard* Der Prophet und das Verderben Israels: eine ganzheitliche, historisch-kritische Lektüre von 1 Regum xvii-xix. VT 47 (1997) 277-292.

2595 *Conners, Quinn R.* Elijah and Elisha: a psychologist's perspective. 1997, ⇒70. ᶠMᴜʀᴘʜʏ R., Master, 235-242.

2596 *Cousin, Hugues* Les données du Nouveau Testament. CEv.S 100 (1997) 15-21.

2597 **Crüsemann, Frank** Elia—die Entdeckung der Einheit Gottes: eine Lektüre der Erzählungen über Elia und seine Zeit (1Kön 17-2Kön 2). Kaiser-Taschenbücher 154: Mü 1997, Kaiser 175 pp. DM29.80. 3-579-05154-7 [Mal 3].

2598 *Déclais, Jean-Louis* Élie dans la tradition de l'Islam. CEv.S 100 (1997) 113-121.

2599 *Gese, Hartmut* Zur Bedeutung Elias für die biblische Theologie. 1997, ⇒92. ᶠSᴛᴜʜʟᴍᴀᴄʜᴇʀ P., 126-150.

2600 *Gruson, Philippe; Poirot, Éliane* Élie dans les liturgies. CEv.S 100 (1997) 107-112.

2601 *Herr, Larry G.* Polysemy of *rûaḥ* in 1 Kings 22:19-25. 1997, ⇒83. ᶠSʜᴇᴀ W., 29-31.

2602 *Ketterer, Éliane* Élie dans la tradition juive. CEv.S 100 (1997) 22-62.

2603 ᴱ**Kevers, Paul** Elia: profeet van vuur, mens als wij. Lv 1997, Vlaamse Bijbelstichting 208 pp. FB740. 90-334-3771-6 [Str. 64,950].

2604 *Koops, Rob* Where does a soldier get cold beer on a hot day? (1 Kings 20). PPBT 48 (1997) 445-448.

2605 *Lawrie, Douglas* Telling of(f) prophets: narrative strategy in 1 Kings 18:1-19:18. JNSL 23/2 (1997) 163-180.

2606 *Lévêque, Jean* Élie dans l'Ancien Testament. CEv.S 100 (1997) 5-14.

2607 *McMahon, Patrick* Pater et dux: Elijah in medieval mythology. 1997, ⇒70. ᶠMᴜʀᴘʜʏ R., Master, 283-299.

2608 *Moberly, Walter* To speak for God: the story of Micaiah ben Imlah. Anvil 14/4 (1997) 243-253 [1 Kgs 22].

2609 *Morrison, Craig E.* Handing on the mantle: the transmission of the Elijah cycle in the biblical versions. 1997, ⇒70. ᶠMᴜʀᴘʜʏ R., Master, 109-129.

2610 **Öhler, Markus** Elia im Neuen Testament: Untersuchungen zur Bedeutung des alttestamentlichen Propheten im frühen Christentum. Diss. Wien 1995; ᴰ*Niederwimmer, K.*: BZNW 88: B 1997, De Gruyter xvii; 374 pp. DM228/DM188. 3-11-015547-8.

2611 *Poirot, Éliane* Élie chez les Pères de l'église. CEv.S 100 (1997) 63-106.

2612 **Poirot, Soeur Éliane** Élie, archétype du moine. SpOr 65: 1995, ⇒11/1,1252; 12,2525. RContacts 49 (1997) 190-191 *(Minet, Jacques)*.

2613 *Sarna, Nahum M.* Naboth's vineyard revisited (1 Kings 21). 1997, ⇒34. MGreenberg M., 119-126.

2614 *Sion, Danièle* L'attente du prophète au XVIIIe. CEv.S 100 (1997) 122-128.

2615 *Thiel, Winfried* Character and function of divine sayings in the Elijah and Elisha traditions. TReventlow, Henning Graf: Eschatology in the Bible. JSOT.S 243: 1997, 189-199.

2616 **White, Marsha C.** The Elijah legends and Jehu's coup. Diss. Harvard 1994; DMachinist, P.B.: BJSt 311: Atlanta, 1997, Scholars vi; 116 pp. $23. 0-7885-0334-0 [EThL 74,205*].

E4.9 **2 Reg 1...***Elisaeus, Elisha...* Ezechias, Josias

2617 *Athmann, Peter J.* Die religionspolitschen Ziele der Jehu-Revolution. Zeitschrift für Theologie und Gemeinde 2 (1997) 59-82.

2618 **Gugler, Werner** Jehu und seine Revolution: Voraussetzungen, Verlauf, Folgen. Kampen 1996, Kok 315 pp. 90-390-0134-0.

2619 **Slabbert, M.J.; Breytenbach, A.P.** Die Elisa-siklus teen die agtergrond van die Babiloniese ballingskap. HTS 53 (1997) 257-275 [ZID 23,443].

2620 *Van Midden, Piet* Elisa. ITBT 5/5 (1997) 4-6.

2621 *Getui, Mary* Wash and be clean. ER 49 (1997) 465-469 [2 Kgs 5,1-19].

2622 *Ngan, Lai L.* 2 Kings 5. RExp 94 (1997) 589-597.

2623 *Frevel, Christian* Geschichten von Unheil, Heil und Heilung: Elischa und Damaskus. Welt und Umwelt der Bibel 3 (1997) 40-43 [2 Kgs 5].

2624 *Holloway, Steven W.* Antiochian temporal interpolations in 2 Kgs 6,24-7,20. Bib. 78 (1997) 543-547.

2625 *Smelik, Klaas A.* De grote daden van Hazaël: de actualiteit van 2 Kon 8:13. Analecta Bruxellensia 2 (1997) 152-162 [ZID 24,344].

2626 *Gacek, Stanisław* Analiza literacka perykopy 2 Krl 9,1-10,36 [Literary analysis of 2 Kings 9.1-10.36]. 1997, ⇒52. FLach J., 111-127. **P.**

2627 *Schulte, Hannelis* Die Rettung des Prinzen Joaš: zur Exegese von II Reg 11,1-3. ZAW 109 (1997) 549-556 [2 Chr 22,11].

2628 **Dutcher-Walls, Patricia N.** Narrative art, political rhetoric: the case of Athaliah and Joash. JSOT.S 209: 1996, ⇒12,2535. RCBQ 59 (1997) 343-344 *(Mullen, E. Theodore)* [2 Kgs 11].

2629 *Smelik, Klaas A.D.* The new altar of King Ahaz (2 Kings 16): Deuteronomistic re-interpretation of a cult reform;

2630 *Becking, Bob* From apostasy to destruction: a Josianic view on the fall of Samaria (2 Kings 17,21-23). BEThL 133: 1997, ⇒17. FBrekelmans C., 263-278/279-297.

2631 **Van Keulen, Percy S.F.** Manasseh through the eyes of the deuteronomists: the Manasseh account (2 Kings 21:1-18) and the final chapters of the deuteronomistic history. OTS 38: 1996, ⇒12,2541. REThL 73 (1997) 423-425 *(Lust, J.)*.

2632 *Eynikel, Erik* The portrait of Manasseh and the Deuteronomistic History. BEThL 133: 1997, ⇒17. FBREKELMANS C., 233-261 [2 Kgs 21].

2633 *Toloni, Giancarlo* "Per non entrare nel tempio" (2 Re 23,11aB): storia dell'interpretazione di un sintagma. EstB 55 (1997) 143-169;

2634 La locuzione מִבֹּא בֵית־יְהֹוָה nelle versioni antiche. RivBib 45 (1997) 387-407 [2 Kgs 23,11].

2635 *Schmid, Konrad* Manasse und der Untergang Judas: "Golaorientierte" Theologie in den Königsbüchern?. Sum. 99. Bib. 78 (1997) 87-99 [2 Kgs 23,26-27; 21,3-16; 24,3-4].

### E5.2 *Chronicorum libri*—The books of Chronicles

2636 *Balentine, Samuel E.* "You can't pray a lie": truth and fiction in the prayers of Chronicles;

2637 *Barnes, William H.* Non-synoptic chronological references in the books of Chronicles;

2638 *Ben Zvi, Ehud* The Chronicler as a historian: building texts. JSOT.S 238: 1997, ⇒61. FMCKENZIE S., 246-267/106-131/132-149.

2639 *De Vries, Simon J.* Festival ideology in Chronicles. 1997, ⇒48. FKNIERIM R., 104-124.

2640 **Dörrfuß, Ernst Michael** Mose in den Chronikbüchern. 1994, ⇒10,2162... 12,2555. RThLZ 122 (1997) 435-436 *(Willi, Thomas)*; JBL 116 (1997) 336-338 *(Sweeney, Marvin A.)*; CBQ 58 (1996) 705-707 *(Knoppers, Gary N.)*.

2641 *Fernández Marcos, Natalio* The Old Latin of Chronicles between the Greek and the Hebrew. IX Congress IOSCS. SCSt 45: 1997, ⇒340. ETaylor, B.A., 123-136.

2642 *Freedman, David Noel* The Chronicler's purpose. Divine Commitment 1, 1997 <1961>, ⇒124. 88-93.

2643 **Henning-Hess, Heike** Kult als Norm?: die Rezeption der vorexilischen Geschichte Israels in den Chronikbüchern aufgrund ihrer Darstellung von Priestern und Leviten, Kult und Königtum. Diss. Heidelberg 1997; DRendtorff, R. [RTL 29,578].

2644 *Hoglund, Kenneth G.* The Chronicler as historian: a comparativist perspective. JSOT.S 238: 1997, ⇒61. FMCKENZIE S., 19-29.

2645 *Japhet, Sara* The historical reliability of Chronicles: the history of the problem and its place in biblical research. Historical Books. 1997 <1985>, ⇒192. EExum, J. Cheryl, 258-281.

2646 **Japhet, Sara** The ideology of the book of Chronicles and its place in biblical thought. BEAT 9: Fra ²1997, Lang viii; 553 pp. 3-631-31508-2.

2647 **Johnstone, William** 1 and 2 Chronicles: 1. 1 Chronicles 1-2 Chronicles 9—Israel's place among the nations; 2. 2 Chronicles 10-36—guilt and atonement. JSOT.S 253-254: Shf 1997, JSOT 411 + 300 pp. £42.50 + £42.50. 1-85075-693-7/4-5.

2648 **Kalimi, Isaac** Zur Geschichtsschreibung des Chronisten: literarisch-historiographische Abweichungen der Chronik von ihren Paralleltexten in den Samuel- und Königsbüchern. BZAW 226: 1995, ⇒11/1,1308. RThLZ 122 (1997) 795-797 *(Willi, Thomas)*; JAOS 117 (1997) 153-154 *(Van Seters, John)*; JSSt 44 (1997) 394-396 *(Dirksen, Piet B.)*.

2649 *Kalimi, Isaac* Paronomasie im Buch der Chronik: ein Beitrag zur literarischen Forschung an der Arbeitsweise des Chronisten. BZ 41 (1997) 78-88;

2650 *Kalimi, Isaac* Was the Chronicler a historian?. JSOT.S 238: 1997, ⇒61. ᶠMcKENZIE S., 73-89.

2651 **Kelly, Brian E.** Retribution and eschatology in Chronicles. JSOT.S 211: 1996, ⇒12,2564. ᴿBiOr 54 (1997) 177-180 *(Dirksen, P.B.)*; CBQ 59 (1997) 546-547 *(Schniedewind, William M.)*; RBBras 14 (1997) 344-346.

2652 *Klein, Ralph W.* How many in a thousand?;

2653 *Knoppers, Gary N.* History and historiography: the royal reforms. JSOT.S 238: 1997, ⇒61. ᶠMcKENZIE S., 270-282/178-203.

2654 *Koorevaar, Hendrik J.* Die Chronik als intendierter Abschluß des alttestamentlichen Kanons. JETh 11 (1997) 42-76.

2655 *McDermott, John J.* Multipurpose genealogies. BiTod 35 (1997) 382-386.

2656 *Minette de Tillesse, Caetano* 1-2 Crônicas. RBB 14/1-3 (1997) 126-134.

2657 *Murray, Donald F.* Dynasty, people, and the future: the message of Chronicles <1993>. Historical Books. 1997, ⇒192. ᴱExum, J. Cheryl, 282-302.

2658 *Rainey, Anson F.* The Chronicler and his sources—historical and geographical;

2659 *Schniedewind, William M.* Prophets and prophecy in the books of Chronicles. JSOT.S 238: 1997, ⇒61. ᶠMcKENZIE S., 30-72/204-224.

2660 **Steins, Georg** Die Chronik als kanonisches Abschlußphänomen: Studien zur Entstehung und Theologie von 1/2 Chronik. BBB 93: 1995, ⇒11/1,1314. ᴿCBQ 59 (1997) 754-755 *(Smith-Christopher, Daniel L.)*.

2661 *Steins, Georg* Zur Datierung der Chronik: ein neuer methodischer Ansatz. ZAW 109 (1997) 84-92.

2662 **Thompson, J.A.** 1,2 Chronicles. NAC 9: 1995, ⇒11/1,1303. ᴿHebSt 38 (1997) 180-182 *(McKenzie, Steven L.)*.

2663 *Throntveit, Mark A.* The Chronicler's speeches and historical reconstruction;

2664 *Wright, John W.* The fight for peace: narrative and history in the battle accounts in Chronicles. JSOT.S 238: 1997, ⇒61. ᶠMcKENZIE S., 225-245/150-177.

2665 *Braun, Roddy L.* 1 Chronicles 1-9 and the reconstruction of the history of Israel: thoughts on the use of genealogical data in Chronicles in the reconstruction of the history of Israel. JSOT.S 238: 1997, ⇒61. ᶠMcKENZIE S., 92-105.

2666 *Bail, Ulrike* Mit schielendem Blick: Bemerkungen zu 1 Chronik 7,21b-24. 1997, ⇒29. ᶠGERSTENBERGER E.S., 214-225.

2667 *Abadie, Philippe* David, innocent ou coupable?: nouveau regard sur 1 Chroniques 21. CBFV 36 (1997) 73-83.

2668 *Dirksen, Piet B.* Prophecy and temple music: 1 Chron. 25:1-7. Henoch 19/3 (1997) 259-265 [1 Sam 10,5].

2669 *Fritz, Volkmar* Die sog. Liste der Festungen Rehabeams in 2. Chr 11,5-12—ein Dokument aus der Zeit Joschijas?. Studien zur Literatur. 1997 <1981>, ⇒126. 265-278.

2670 *Snyman, Gerrie* 'Tis a vice to know him': readers' response-ability and responsibility in 2 Chronicles 14-16. Semeia 77 (1997) 91-113.

2671 *Mathys, Hans-Peter* Philologia sacra: das Beispiel der Chronikbücher. ThZ 53 (1997) 64-73 [2 Chr 24,26; 28,09; 17,7; 1 Chr 25,4; 27,30].

2672 *Bianchi, F.; Rossoni, G.* L'armée d'Ozias (2 Ch 26, 11-15) entre fiction et réalité: une esquisse philologique et historique. TEuph 13 (1997) 21-37.

2673 **Fries, Joachim** 'Im Dienst am Hause des Herrn': literaturwissenschaftliche Untersuchungen zu 2 Chr 29-31: Teil 1; zur Hiskijatradition in Chronik: Teil 2: computergestützte Konkordanzarbeit. Diss. Wü 1997/98; <sup>D</sup>*Seidl* [BZ 42,319].

## E5.4 *Esdrae libri*—Ezra, Nehemiah

2674 **Böhler, Dieter** Die heilige Stadt in Esdras a alpha und Esra-Nehemia: zwei Konzeptionen der Wiederherstellung Israels. Diss. Fribourg; <sup>D</sup>*Schenker, A.*: QBO 158: FrS 1997, Univ.-Verl. xiii; 435 pp. 3-7278-1147-1.

2675 *Dequeker, Luc* Nehemiah and the restoration of the temple after the exile. BEThL 133: 1997, ⇒17. <sup>F</sup>BREKELMANS C., 547-567.

2676 **Jobsen, A.** Ezra en Nehemia: een praktische bijbelverklaring. Tekst en Toelichting: Kampen 1997, Kok 180 pp. ƒ40. 90-242-9163-1 [Bijdr. 58,238].

2677 *Kraemer, David* On the relationship of the books of Ezra and Nehemiah. Historical Books. 1997, ⇒192. <sup>E</sup>Exum, J. Cheryl, 303-321.

2678 *Minette de Tillesse, Caetano* Esdras-Neemias. RBB 14/1-3 (1997) 117-125.

2679 **Orde, Klaus vom** Die Bücher Esra und Nehemia erklärt. WStB: Wu 1997, Brockhaus 319 pp. Bibl. 3-417-25331-4.

2680 *Schaper, Joachim* The temple treasury committee in the times of Nehemiah and Ezra. VT 47 (1997) 200-206.

2681 **Schelling, Piet** Ezra/Nehemia. Verklaring van een Bijbelgedeelte: Kampen 1997, Kok 165 pp. ƒ27.50. 90-242-7775-2 [ITBT 5/7,33].

2682 **Schniedewind, William M.** The word of God in transition: from prophet to exegete in the Second Temple period. JSOT.S 197: 1995, ⇒11/2,2086. <sup>R</sup>JBL 116 (1997) 338-341 *(Glazier-McDonald, Beth)*.

2683 *Tollefson, Kenneth D.; Williamson, H.G.M.* Nehemiah as cultural revitalization: an anthropological perspective. Historical Books. 1997, ⇒192. <sup>E</sup>Exum, J. Cheryl, 322-348.

2684 *Van Grol, Harm W.M.* Schuld und Scham: die Verwurzelung von Esra 9,6-7 in der Tradition. EstB 55 (1997) 29-52.

2685 *Croatto, José Severino* The debt in Nehemiah's social reform: a study of Nehemiah 5:1-19. Subversive scriptures. 1997, ⇒263. <sup>E</sup>Vaage, L., 39-59.

2686 *Gross, Carl D.* Is there any interest in Nehemiah 5?. SJOT 11 (1997) 270-278 [Neh 5,6-11].

2687 *Rendtorff, Rolf* Nehemiah 9: an important witness of theological reflection. 1997, ⇒34. <sup>M</sup>GREENBERG M., 111-117.

2688   *Gitay, Yehoshua* A designed anti-rhetorical speech: Ezra and the question of mixed marriage. JNSL 23/2 (1997) 57-68 [Neh 10,10-11].

2689   *Pichon, Christophe* La prohibition des mariages mixtes par Néhémie (xiii 23-31). VT 47 (1997) 168-199.

2690   ᴱᵀ**Drint, Adriana** The Mount Sinai Arabic version of IV Ezra. CSCO 563-64; CSCO.A 48-49: Lv 1997, Peeters 2 vols. 90-6831-839-X.

2691   *Janz, Timothy* The second book of Ezra and the "καιγε group". IX Congress IOSCS. SCSt 45: 1997, ⇒340. ᴱTaylor, B.A., 153-170.

2692   *Strickert, Fred* 2 Esdras 1.11 and the destruction of Bethsaida. JSPE 16 (1997) 111-122 [Matt 11,20-24; Lk 10,13-15].

### ᴇ5.5  Libri Tobiae, Judith, Esther

2693   **Craghan, John** Ester, Giuditta, Tobia, Giona. LoB.AT 11: 1995, ⇒11/1,1344; 12,2602. ᴿRivBib 45 (1997) 89-90 *(Minissale, A.).*

2694   **Nowell, Irene** I libri di Giona, Tobia, Giuditta. La bibbia per tutti 25: Brescia 1997, Queriniana 125 pp. 88-399-2125-7.

2695   ᴱ**Connolly, Seán** BEDA Venerabilis: in librum patris Tobiae allegorica expositio; super Canticum Habacuc allegorica expositio: on Tobit and on the Canticle of Habakkuk. Dublin 1997, Four Courts 141 pp. Bibl. 1-85182-283-6 [Hab 3].

2696   **Doré, Daniel** Le livre de Tobit ou le secret du roi. CEv 101: P 1997, Cerf 67 pp. FF35. 0222-9714.

2697   *Minette de Tillesse, Caetano* Na Diáspora: Tobias. RBB 14/1-3 (1997) 161-163.

2698   **Rabenau, Merten** Studien zum Buch Tobit. BZAW 220: 1994, ⇒10,2818; 12,2607. ᴿThRv 93 (1997) 386-388 *(Schüngel-Straumann, Helen)*; JBL 116 (1997) 348-350 *(Nickelsburg, G.W.E.).*

2699   **Arzt, Peter; Ernst, Michael** *(al.),* Sprachlicher Schlüssel zu Judit. Sprachlicher Schlüssel zu den deuterokanonischen Schriften [Apokryphen] des Alten Testaments] 2: Salzburg 1997, Institut für Neutestamentliche Bibelwissenschaft 195 pp. 3-901636-02-1.

2700   *Marböck, Johannes* Judit in der Vorauer Handschrift 276: literarische Spiegelungen einer biblischen Frauengestalt im Mittelalter. 1997, ⇒106. ᶠWOSCHITZ K., 370-383.

2701   *Minette de Tillesse, Caetano* Na Diáspora: Judite. RBB 14/1-3 (1997) 163-168.

2702   *Virgulin, Stefano* La valenza del tempo nel racconto di Giuditta. PSV 36 (1997) 85-94.

2703   **Beal, Timothy Kandler** The book of hiding: gender, ethnicity, annihiliation, and Esther. L 1997, Routledge xiv; 152 pp. £40 £14 0-415-16779-5 0-415-16780-9 [RRT 1998/1, 88].

2704   *Boyd-Taylor, Cameron* Esther's great adventure: reading the LXX version of the book of Esther in light of its assimilation to the conventions of the Greek romantic novel. BIOSCS 30 (1997) 81-113.

   **Bush, Frederic William** Ruth, Esther ⇒2391.

2705 **Craig, Kenneth M.** Reading Esther. 1995, ⇒11/1,1366; 12,2617. RCBQ 59 (1997) 342 *(Laffey, Alice L.)*; HebSt 38 (1997) 177-180 *(Cotter, David)*.

2706 **Day, Linda** Three faces of a queen: characterization in the book of Esther. JSOT.S 186: 1995, ⇒11/1,1367. RCBQ 59 (1997) 114-115 *(Crawford, Sidnie White)*; JBL 116 (1997) 341-342 *(Crawford, Sidnie White)*.

2707 **Dorothy, Charles V.** The book of Esther: structure, genre and textual integrity. JSOT.S 187: Shf 1997, Academic 384 pp. £50/$75. 1-85075-518-3.

2708 *Firth, David G.* The book of Esther: a neglected paradigm for dealing with the state. OTEs 10 (1997) 18-26.

**Fischer, James A.** Cantico... Ester ⇒2395.

2709 *Fleishman, Joseph* Why was Haman successful at winning King Ahasuerus' approval to exterminate the Jews in the Persian empire?. HUCA 68 (1997) 35*-49*. H.

2710 *Fontaine, Carole R.* More queenly proverb performance: the queen of Sheba in targum Esther Sheni. CBQ.MS 29: 1997, ⇒69. FMURPHY R., 216-233.

2711 *Goodnick, Benjamin* The book of Esther and its motifs. JBQ 25 (1997) 101-107.

2712 *Jobes, Karen H.* The alpha-text of Esther: its character and relationship to the Masoretic text. IX Congress IOSCS. SCSt 45: 1997, ⇒340. ETaylor, B.A., 369-379.

2713 *Klein, Lillian R.* Esther's lot. CurResB 5 (1997) 111-145.

2714 **Levenson, Jon D.** Esther: a commentary. OTL: LVL 1997, Westminster xvi; 142 pp. $22. 0-664-22093-2 [ThD 44,375—Heiser, W. Charles].

2715 *Manns, Frédéric* Introduction au Targum Sheni d'Esther (MS Urbinati 1). Sum. 453. LASBF 47 (1997) 117-128.

2716 **Méroz, Christianne** Esther en exile: pour une spiritualité de la différence. 1995, ⇒11/1,1375. REstB 55 (1997) 269-270 *(Barrado, P.)*.

2717 *Minette de Tillesse, Caetano* Na Diáspora: Ester. RBB 14/1-3 (1997) 168-174.

2718 **Omanson, R.L.; Noss, Ph.A.** The book of Esther: the Hebrew and Greek texts. UBS Handbook: NY 1997, UBS 387 pp. [Sal. 61,623s—Buzzetti, Carlo].

2719 **Pontrémoli, Rafael Hiya** Meam Loez: livre d'Ester. TBenveniste, Albert; Préf. Goetschel, Roland: Les dix paroles: P 1997, Verdier 413 pp. FF125. 2-86432-269-2 [BCLF 602,2271].

2720 **Rodriguez, Angel Manuel** Esther. 1995, ⇒11/1,1379. RAUSS 35 (1997) 297-298 *(Doukhan, Jacques)*.

2721 **Segal, Eliezer** The Babylonian Esther Midrash. BJSt 291: 1994, 3 vols, ⇒10,2829; 11/1,1381. RJQR 88 (1997) 113-120 *(Tabory, Joseph)*; SR 26 (1997) 230-232 *(Fox, Harry)*.

2722 **Siebert-Hommes, J.C.** Esther. Verklaring van de Hebreeuwse Bijbel: Baarn 1997, Callenbach 179 pp. ƒ35. 90-266-0367-3 [Str. 65,855—Beentjes, Panc].

2723 *Siquans, Agnethe* Die Rolle Esters im Esterbuch im Verhältnis zu Mordechai: Fürbitterin und Vorbild ihres Volkes. BN 86 (1997) 77-89.

2724  *Troyer, Kristin de* On crowns and diadems from kings, queens, horses and men. IX Congress IOSCS. SCSt 45: 1997, ⇒340. <sup>E</sup>Taylor, B.A., 355-367.

2725  **Troyer, Kristin de** Het einde van de Alpha-tekst van Ester: vertaal- en verhaaltechniek van MT 8,1-17, LXX 8,1-17 en AT 7,14-41. Diss. Leiden; <sup>D</sup>*Van der Kooij, A.*: Lv 1997, Peeters ix; 361 pp. FB1.600. 90-6831-987-6 [RTL 29,123].

2726  *Wechsler, Michael G.* Shadow and fulfillment in the book of Esther. BS 154 (1997) 275-284.

E5.8  *Machabaeorum libri,* 1-2[3-4] Maccabees

2727  *Amalyan, Hayk M.* The critical text of 1-3 Maccabees. Saint Nersess theological review 2/1 (1997) 33-38.

2728  **Dobbeler, Stephanie von** Die Bücher 1/2 Makkabäer. Neuer Stuttgarter Kommentar, AT 11: Stu 1997, Katholisches Bibelwerk 271 pp. 3-460-07111-7.

2729  *Gruen, Erich S.* Fact and fiction: Jewish legends in a Hellenistic context [2 Macc.]. Hellenistic constructs. 1997, ⇒271. <sup>E</sup>Cartledge, P., 72-88.

2730  *Minette de Tillesse, Caetano* Macabeus. RBB 14/1-3 (1997) 204-209.

2731  *Passoni Dell'Acqua, Anna* Il III libro dei Maccabei e l'amministrazione tolemaica. 21. Papyrologenkongress, 2. 1997, ⇒367. <sup>E</sup>Kramer, Bärbel, 786-794.

2732  **Van Henten, Jan Wilem** The Maccabean martyrs as saviours of the Jewish people: a study of 2 and 4 Maccabees. JSJ.S 57: Lei 1997, Brill xi; 346 pp. Diss. Leiden 1986. ƒ195/$115. 90-04-10976-5 [NThAR 1998,99].

# VI. Libri didactici VT

E6.1  *Poesis metrica,* Biblical and Semitic versification

2733  **Alonso Schökel, Luis** Antologia della poesia biblica. 1995. <sup>R</sup>CivCatt 148 II (1997) 205-207 *(Scaiola, D.)*.

2734  *Barré, Michael L.* "Terminative" terms in Hebrew acrostics. CBQ.MS 29: 1997, ⇒69. <sup>F</sup>Murphy R., 207-215.

2735  *Berlin, Adele* On reading biblical poetry: the role of metaphor. Congress volume 1995. VT.S 66: 1997, ⇒323. <sup>E</sup>Emerton, J.A., 25-36.

2736  **Cross, Frank Moore, Jr.; Freedman, David Noel** Studies in ancient Yahwistic poetry. The Biblical Resource Series: GR 1997, Eerdmans xiii; 130 pp. $27.50. 0-8028-4159-7.

2737  *Freedman, David Noel* Acrostic poems in the Hebrew Bible: alphabetic and otherwise <1986>;

2738  Another look at Biblical Hebrew poetry <1987>;

2739  Deliberate deviation from an established pattern of repetition in Hebrew poetry as a rhetorical device <1986>;

2740 Prose particles in the poetry of the primary history <1985>. Divine Commitment 2, 1997, ⇒124. 183-204/213-26/205-12/171-82.

2741 *Houston, Walter J.* Misunderstanding or midrash?: the prose appropriation of poetic material in the Hebrew Bible. ZAW 109 (1997) 342-355, 534-548 [Exod 14,1-15,18; Josh 10,12-14; Judg 4-5].

2742 **Lord, A.B.** The singer resumes the tale. ELord, M.L.: Myth and Poetics. 1995, ⇒11/1,1410. RClR 47 (1997) 9-11 *(Hainsworth, J.B.).*

2743 *Malul, Meir* Janus parallelism in Biblical Hebrew: two more cases (Canticles 4,9.12). BZ 41 (1997) 246-249.

2744 *Minkopp, Harvey* As simple as ABC: what acrostics in the bible can demonstrate. BiRe 13/2 (1997) 27-31, 46-47.

2745 *Niccacci, Alviero* Analysing Biblical Hebrew poetry. JSOT 74 (1997) 77-93.

2746 **O'Connor, Michael Patrick** Hebrew verse structure. Second printing with afterword. WL 1997, Eisenbrauns xvii; 661 pp. 0-931464-02-1.

2747 *Watson, W.G.E.* New examples of the split couplet in Ugaritic. UF 29 (1997) 715-721.

2748 **Watson, Wilfred G.E.** Traditional techniques in classical Hebrew verse. JSOT.S 170: 1994, ⇒10,230c; 12,2662. RJAOS 117 (1997) 369 *(Revell, E.J.).*

2749 *Watson, Wilfred G.E.* The "split couplet" in Ugaritic verse. SEL 14 (1997) 29-42.

2750 *West, M.L.* Akkadian poetry: metre and performance. Iraq 59 (1997) 175-187.

2751 *Westermann, Claus* Die Beobachtungsgedichte im Alten Testament. CBQ.MS 29: 1997, ⇒69. FMURPHY R., 234-247.

### E6.2 Psalmi, textus

2752 Psaltir. Biblija 1499 goda i biblija v sinodal'nom perevode 4. Moskva 1997, Isdat. Otd. Moskovskogo Patriarchata 343 pp. 5-87389-012-9 [NThAR 2000,61]. **Russian.**

2753 EBlum-Cuny, **Pascale** Blaise de VIGNERE: le psaultier de David torné en prose mesurée ou vers libres 2. 1996, ⇒12,2667. RBHR 59 (1997) 746-748 *(Crescenzo, Richard).*

2754 **Bosson, Nathalie** Wörterverzeichnis: zu Gawdat GABRAS Ausgabe des Psalters im Mesokemischen (Oxyrhynchitischen / Mittelägyptischen) Dialekt des Koptischen (Mudil-Kodex). Collab. *Kasser, Rodolphe*: CSCO 568; CSCO.S 96: Lv 1997, Peeters xvii; 338 pp. 90-6831-911-6.

2755 *Cimosa, Mario* Il salterio greco (LXX) e il Nuovo Testamento. BSRel 125: 1997, ⇒45. FJAVIERRE ORTAS A., 45-67.

2756 EDefaux, **Gérard** Clément MAROT: cinquante pseaumes de David mis en françoys selon la vérité hébraïque: édition critique sur le texte de l'édition publiée en 1543 à Genève par Jean Gérard: introduction, variantes et notes. 1995, ⇒12,2669. RSCJ 28 (1997) 1371-1373 *(Higman, Francis).*

2757 **Flint, Peter W.** The Dead Sea Psalms scrolls and the book of Psalms. Diss. Notre Dame 1993, DUlrich, E.: StTDJ 17: Lei 1997, Brill xxiii; 323 pp. ƒ162/$101.50. 90-04-10341-4.

2758  **Ingebrand, Sven** Swenske songer 1536: vår första bevarade evangeliska psalmbok. Uppsala Studies in Faiths and Ideologies 7: Uppsala 1997, 216 pp [SvTK 76,112ss—Westin, Gunnar T.].

2759  *Kedar, Benjamin* Sebastian MUENSTERs lateinische Psalmenübersetzung. ThZ 53 (1997) 44-52.

2760  **Leri, Clara** Sull'arpa a dieci corde: traduzioni letterarie dei Salmi (1641-1780). BLI, Studi e Testi 47: F 1994, Olschki 201 pp [RSLR 35/1,222ss—Stroppa, Sabrina].

2761  ᴱ**Mares, Franz W.** Psalterii Sinaitici pars nova: (monasterii s. Catharinae codex slav. 2/N). DÖAW.PH.Schriften der Balkan-Kommission, Philologische Abt. 38: W 1997, Verlag der ÖAW xxiii; 201 pp. Bibl. 3-7001-2661-1.

2762  **Noel, William** The Harley psalter. 1995, ᴿHZ 264/1 (1997) 186-187 *(Fried, Johannes)*.

2763  *Olofsson, Staffan* The Kaige group and the Septuagint book of Psalms. IX Congress IOSCS. SCSt 45: 1997, ⇒340. ᴱTaylor, B.A., 189-230.

2764  **Ramello, Laura** Il salterio italiano nella tradizione manoscritta: individuazione e costituzione dello stemma delle versioni toscane; edizione critica della versione veneta. Studi e testi 2: Alessandria 1997, Dell'Orso 491 pp. 88-7694-288-2 [NThAR 1999,44].

2765  *Schenker, Adrian* Gewollt dunkle Wiedergaben in LXX?: zu den scheinbar unverständlichen Übersetzungen im Psalter der LXX am Beispiel von Ps 28 (29),6. Theologische Probleme. 1997, ⇒223. ᴱReventlow, Henning Graf, 63-71.

2766  *Sinclair, Keith Val* La version messine des prières du prône et le psautier de Metz en français. RBen 107 (1997) 149-162.

2767  ᵀ**Slavitt, David R.** Sixty-one psalms of David. 1996, ⇒12,2677. ᴿHebStud 38 (1997) 155-157 *(Brueggemann, Walter)*.

2768  *Wilcox, Max* The translation of the *Targum of Psalms*: a report. ByF 24 (1997) 153-157.

### ᴇ6.3 Psalmi, introductio

2769  *Auwers, J.-M.* Tendances actuelles des études psalmiques: à propos de quelques ouvrages récents sur le Psautier. RTL 28 (1997) 79-97.

2770  **Avishur, Yitzhak** Studies in Hebrew and Ugaritic psalms. 1994, ⇒10,2926. ᴿBiOr 54 (1997) 443-445 *(Korpel, Mario C.A.)*; JAOS 117 (1997) 725-726 *(Pope, Marvin H.)*; HebStud 38 (1997) 152-155 *(Meier, Samuel A.)*.

2771  **Collin, Matthieu** El libro de los Salmos. ᵀ*Darrical, Nicolás*: CuaBi 92: Estella 1997, Verbo Divino 64 pp. 84-8169-149-6.

2772  **Declaisse-Walford, Nancy L.** Reading from the beginning: the shaping of the Hebrew Psalter. Diss. Baylor 1995; Macon, GA 1997, Mercer ix; 143 pp. Bibl. $30. 0-86554-567-7.

2773  **García Trapiello, Jesús** Introducción al estudio de los salmos. Horizonte dos mil 10: S 1997, San Esteban 229 pp. Pta1.950. 84-8260-044-3 [Mayéutica 24,532—Lozano, Renée].

2774  **Glynn, Paul** Psalms: songs for the way home. Alexandria N.S.W. 1997, Dwyer viii; 177 pp. 0-85574-366-2.

2775  *Heine, Ronald E.* The form of GREGORY of Nyssa's treatise *On the inscriptions of the Psalms*. StPatr 32: 1997, ⇒351. ᴱLivingstone, Elizabeth A., 130-135.

2776 *Koffi, Ettien N.* Que faut-il faire des suscriptions des psaumes?. Cahiers de traduction biblique 28 (1997) 4-10.

2777 **Levine, Herbert J.** Sing unto God a new song: a contemporary reading of the Psalms. Indiana Studies in Biblical Literature: 1995, ⇒11/1,1441; 12,2682. RAJS Review 22/1 (1997) 105-106 *(Grossberg, Daniel).*

2778 **Millard, Matthias** Die Komposition des Psalters: ein formgeschichtlicher Ansatz. FAT 9: 1994, ⇒10,2901*... 12,2684. StPat 44/1 (1997) 202-203 *(Lorenzin, Tiziano)*; CBQ 59 (1997) 129-131 *(Craghan, John F.)*; JBL 116 (1997) 539-541 *(Miller, Patrick D.).*

2779 *Nielsen, Kirsten* Sigmund MOWINCKEL—and beyond. SJOT 11 (1997) 200-209.

2780 **Oduyoye, Modupe** The psalms of Satan. Ibadan 1997, Sefer 65 pp. 978-31195-9-1 [NThAR 1998,334].

2781 **Prévost, Jean-Pierre** A short dictionary of the Psalms. TMisrahi, *Mary*: ColMn 1997, Liturgical xiv; 90 pp. Bibl. 0-8146-2370-0.

2782 **Raguer Suner, Hilari** Introduzione ai salmi. Itinerari biblici: R 1997, Borla 298 pp. L30.000. 88-263-1185-4.

2783 *Reynard, J.* La magnanimité de David dans l'*In Inscriptiones Psalmorum* de GREGOIRE de Nysse. StPatr 32: 1997, ⇒351. ELivingstone, Elizabeth A., 208-212.

2784 **Rizzi, A.** Grido e canto dei poveri: iniziazione ai salmi. Sotto il Monte (BG) 1997, Servitium 152 pp. L15.000. [Horeb 24/3,97—Rotella, Caterina].

2785 *Seybold, Klaus; Raeder, Siegfried; Schröer, Henning* Psalmen/Psalmenbuch. TRE 27. 1997, ⇒419. 610-637.

2786 *Soupa, Anne* Le livre des Psaumes. DosB 68 (1997) 3-5.

2787 **Whybray, R. Norman** Reading the psalms as a book. JSOT.S 222: 1996, ⇒12,2693. RRTL 28 (1997) 92 *(Auwers, J.-M.).*

## E6.4 Psalmi, commentarii

2788 EBaker-Smith, Dominic ERASMUS: expositions of the Psalms: Enarratio in primum Psalmum, 'Beatus vir'; commentarius in Psalmum 2, 'Quare fremuerunt gentes'; paraphrasis in tertium Psalmum, 'Domine quid multiplicati'; In Psalmum quartum concio. THeath, *Michael J.*, Collected works of Erasmus 63: Toronto 1997, University of Toronto Press lxxii; 305 pp. $100. 0-8020-4308-9.

2789 EBarratt, Alexandra The Seven Psalms: a commentary on the penitential psalms. THull, *Eleanor*: EETS 307: 1995, ⇒11/1,1457. RJThS 48 (1997) 311-314 *(Carruthers, Leo).*

2790 **Blaumeister, Hubertus** Martin LUTHERs Kreuzestheologie: Schlüssel zu seiner Deutung von Mensch und Wirklichkeit: eine Untersuchung anhand der Operationes in Psalmos. KKTS 60: 1995, ⇒11/1,1458; 12,2697. RÖR 46 (1997) 539-540 *(Dörfel, Donata)*; RHPhR 77 (1997) 355-356 *(Lienhard, M.).*

2791 **Booij, Thijs** Psalmen (81-110). De Prediking van het Oude Testament 3: 1994, ⇒10,2906. RRTL 28 (1997) 85-86 *(Auwers, J.-M.)*; BiOr 54 (1997) 180-182 *(Prinsloo, Willem S.).*

2792 **Brinkman, J.M.** Psalmen II: een praktische bijbelverklaring. Tekst en Toelichting: Kampen 1997, Kok 164 pp. ƒ35. 90-242-9181-X [Bijdr. 58,357].

2793  <sup>T</sup>Cattani, Luigi David KIMCHI: commento ai Salmi: Sal 51-100.
      R 1995, Città Nuova 517 pp. L70.000. <sup>R</sup>CivCatt 148 II (1997)
      301-303 *(Scaiola, D.)*.
2794  **Chahwan, Ayoub** Le commentaire des psaumes 33-60 d'Ibn
      ATTAYIBb: reflet de l'exégèse syriaque orientale. Diss. Pont.
      Univ. Gregoriana 1997, excerpt; <sup>D</sup>*Samir, Khalil*: R 119 pp.
2795  **Clifford, Richard J.** Il libro dei Salmi. La Bibbia per tutti 22-23:
      Brescia 1997, Queriniana 199 pp. 88-399-2122-2.
2796  **De Simone, G.P.** CASSIODORO e l'Expositio Psalmorum. 1993,
      ⇒11/2,1587. <sup>R</sup>RdT 38 (1997) 857 *(Parisi, Serafino)*.
2797  <sup>E</sup>**Doignon, Jean** In psalmos I-XVI. Sancti HILARII Pictaviensis
      episcopi tractatus super psalmos: instructio psalmorum. CChr.SL
      61: Turnhout 1997, Brepols cxv; 364 pp. Sancti Hilarii Picta-
      viensis episcopi opera 1,1. FB7.250. 2-503-00611-6/2-4 [RB
      105,310].
2798  **Eaton, John H.** Psalms of the way and the kingdom. JSOT.S 199:
      1995, ⇒11/1,1465. <sup>R</sup>CBQ 59 (1997) 345 *(Matties, Gordon H.)*.
2799  **Fiedrowicz, Michael** Psalmus vox totius Christi: Studien zu
      AUGUSTINS 'Enarrationes in Psalmos'. Diss.-Habil. Bochum
      1997; FrB 1997, Herder 490 pp. 3-451-26406-4 [NThAR 1999,3].
2800  **Gesigora, Gerd** Ein humanistischer Psalmenexeget des 16. Jahr-
      hunderts: Jacopo SADOLETO (1477-1547): paradigmatische Stu-
      dien zur Hermeneutik und Psalmenexegese des 16. Jahrhunderts.
      EHS.T 556: Fra 1997, Lang 499 pp. 3-631-49361-4.
2801  **Girard, Marc** Les psaumes redécouverts 2-3: 51-100; 101-150.
      1994. ⇒11/1,1467; 12,2701. <sup>R</sup>RTL 28 (1997) 86-91 *(Auwers, J.-
      M.)*;
2802  Les psaumes redécouverts 1: 1-50. <sup>2</sup>1996 <1984>. ⇒65,2642...
      12,2702. <sup>R</sup>RTL 28 (1997) 86-91 *(Auwers, J.-M.)*; RivBib 45
      (1997) 229-230 *(Meynet, Roland)*.
2803  **Hossfeld, Frank-Lothar; Zenger, Erich** Psalm 1-50. NEB.AT
      29: 1993, ⇒10,2910. <sup>R</sup>RTL 28 (1997) 80-84 *(Auwers, J.-M.)*.
2804  **Mays, James Luther** Psalms. 1994, ⇒10,2915; 11/1,1470. <sup>R</sup>RTL
      28 (1997) 84-85 *(Auwers, J.-M.)*; CBQ 58 (1996) 124-125 *(Nasuti,
      Harry P.)*.
2805  <sup>TE</sup>**Raspanti, Antonino** Pico della MIRANDOLA: expositiones in
      Psalmos. <sup>T</sup>*Raspanti, Giacomo*: Studi Pichiani 4: F 1997, Olschki
      286 pp. Bibl. 88-222-4464-8.
2806  **Ravasi, Gianfranco** Il libro dei Salmi: commento e attualizza-
      zione. Lettura pastorale della Bibbia 12, 14, 17: Bo 1997, EDB 3
      vols.
2807  Santo Agostinho: comentário aos salmos (Enarrationes in psalmos):
      Salmos 1-50, 51-100. Patristica 9/1-2: São Paulo 1997 Paulus
      922+1202 pp. Trad. pelas monjas Beneditinas do Mosteiro de
      Maria Mãe de Cristo.    85-349-0750-1 [RBBras 15,573].
2808  **Schneider, Dieter** Psalm 51-100. WStB.AT: 1996, ⇒12,2713.
      <sup>R</sup>JETh 11 (1997) 184-185 *(Möller, Karl)*.
2809  **Seybold, Klaus** Die Psalmen. HAT I 15: 1996. ⇒12,2714. <sup>R</sup>ThZ
      53 (1997) 268-269 *(Kellenberger, Edgar)*.
2810  <sup>T</sup>**Stroobant de Saint-Éloy, Jean-Éric** THOMAS d'Aquin: com-
      mentaire sur les psaumes. 1996, ⇒12,2715. <sup>R</sup>Ang. 74 (1997) 473-
      476 *(González Fuente, A.)*; Sedes Sapientiae 62 (1997) 97-107
      *(Stroobant de Saint-Éloy, Jean-Éric)*; VS 722 (1997) 178-180
      *(Wéber, E.-H.)*.

2811 *Ta-Shma, Israel M.* Open bible criticism in an anonymous commentary on the book of Psalms. Sum. viii. Tarbiz 66 (1997) 403-415. H.

2812 **Zenger, Erich** Die Nacht wird leuchten wie der Tag: Psalmenauslegungen. Akzente: FrB 1997, Herder 496 pp. rev. ed. 3-451-26379-3.

## E6.5 Psalmi, themata

2813 **Bader, Günter** Psalterium affectuum palaestra: prolegomena zu einer Theologie des Psalters. HUTh 33: 1996, ⇒12,2719. RThLZ 122 (1997) 645-646 *(Mildenberger, Friedrich).*

2814 **Barbiero, Gianni** Das Reich Jhwhs und seines Gesalbten: eine synchrone Lektüre des hebräischen ersten Psalmenbuches (Ps 1-41). Diss. habil. St. Georgen 1997/98; DLohfink, Norbert [BZ 42,316].

2815 **Barth, Christoph** Die Errettung vom Tode: Leben und Tod in den Klage- und Dankliedern des Alten Testaments. EJanowski, Bernd: Stu 1997 <1947, 1987>, Kohlhammer 177 pp. DM44. 3-17-014780-3 [ThRv 94,713—Mechtenberg, Theo].

2816 FBeyerlin, Walter Neue Wege der Psalmenforschung: ESeybold, Klaus; Zenger, Erich: 1994, ⇒10,15; 12,7. RStPat 44/1 (1997) 203-206 *(Lorenzin, Tiziano).*

2817 **Bouzard, Walter C., Jr.** We have heard with our ears, O God: sources of the communal laments in the Psalms. Diss. DMiller, Patrick D.: SBL.DS 159: Atlanta 1997, Scholars x; 229 pp. Bibl. $35. 0-7885-0354-5.

2818 **Box, Reginald** Make music to our God: how we sing the Psalms. 1996, ⇒12,2726. RTheol. 100 (1997) 74-75 *(Fenton, Barry D.).*

2819 **Brueggemann, Walter** Abiding astonishment: psalms, modernity, and the making of history. 1991, ⇒7,2771... 10,2927. RVJTR 61 (1997) 563-564 *(Mangai, Poulose).*

2820 *Brueggemann, Walter* The costly loss of lament. Poetical Books. 1997 <1986>, ⇒184. EClines, David J.A., 84-97.

2821 *Collins, Terence* Decoding the psalms: a structural approach to the psalter. Poetical Books. 1997 <1987>, ⇒184. EClines, David J.A., 98-116.

2822 **Diego Lobejón, María Wenceslada de** Los salmos en la literatura española. Literatura 37: Valladolid 1997, Univ. de Valladolid 184 pp. 84-7762-689-8 [NThAR 2000,92].

2823 *Dysinger, Luke* The significance of psalmody in the mystical theology of EVAGRIUS of Pontus. StPatr 30: 1997, ⇒351. ELivingstone, Elizabeth A., 176-182.

2824 **Fløysvik, Ingvar** When God becomes my enemy: the theology of the complaint psalms. St. Louis, Mo. 1997, Concordia 206 pp. Bibl. 0-570-04263-1 [NThAR 1999,44].

2825 EGigliucci, Roberto Salmi penitenziali. TPetrarca, Francesco: Minima 57: R 1997, Salerno 83 pp. Bibl. 88-8402-206-1.

2826 **Green, Barbara Gail** Like a tree planted: an exploration of the psalms and parables through metaphor. Connections: ColMn 1997, Liturgical 160 pp. Bibl. $15. 0-8146-5869-5. RCritRR 10 (1997) 148-150 *(Brueggemann, Walter).*

2827 **Hauge, Martin Ravndal** Between Sheol and temple: motif structure and function in the I-Psalms. JSOT.S 178>: 1995,

⇒11,1/1507; 12,2747. ᴿETR 72 (1997) 130-131 *(Hüllstrung, Wolfgang)*; ThLZ 122 (1997) 243-245 *(Miller, Patrick D.)*; JSSt 42 (1997) 147-150 *(Gillingham, Susan)*.

2828 *Jenni, Ernst* Zu den doxologischen Schlussformeln des Psalters. Studien zur Sprachwelt. 1997 <1984>, ⇒138. 117-124.

2829 **Keel, Othmar** The symbolism of the biblical world: ancient Near Eastern iconography and the book of Psalms. ᵀ*Hallett, Timothy J.*: WL 1997, Eisenbrauns 422 pp. 1-57506-014-0 [EThL 74,223*].

2830 **Kuczynski, Michael P.** Prophetic songs: the Psalms as moral discourse in late medieval England. 1995, ⇒11/1,1516. ᴿSpec. 72/1 (1997) 193-195 *(Besserman, Lawrence)*; MAe 66/1 (1997) 123-124 *(Hudson, Anne)*.

2831 *Łach, Józef* Teologia życia w Biblii w świetle Psałterza [Biblical theology of life in Psalms]. 1997, ⇒52. ᶠŁACH J., 219-232. **P.**

2832 *Manicardi, Luciano* 'Dall'aurora io ti cerco' (Salmi). PSV 35 (1997) 23-37.

2833 *Mayer, Suzanne* Songs of the city of God: MERTON, social justice, and the psalms. Spiritual Life 43/3 (1997) 159-165.

2834 *McNamara, Martin* The Bible in academe and in ecclesia: Antiochene and early Irish exegesis of messianic psalms. Milltown Studies 39 (1997) 112-129.

2835 *Michel, Diethelm* Studien zu den sogenannten Thronbesteigungspsalmen. Studien zur Überlieferungsgeschichte. TB 93: 1997 <1956>, ⇒149. 125-153 [Ps 93].

2836 **Mitchell, David Campbell** The message of the psalter: an eschatological programme in the book of Psalms. Diss. Edinburgh 1995, ᴰ*Provon, I.W.*: JSOT.S 252: Shf 1997, Academic 428 pp. £40/$66. 0-85075-689-9.

2837 **Oduyoye, Modupe** The alphabetical psalms: systematic instruction for a life of faith and trust. Ibadan 1995, Sefer 59 pp. [NAOTS 7,13—Holter, Knut];

2838 Le-mah sabach-tha-niy: lament and entreaty in the Psalms. Ibadan 1995, Sefer 99 pp. [NAOTS 7,13—Holter, Knut];

2839 The psalms of Satan. Ibadan 1997, Sefer 65 pp. [NAOTS 7,13—Holter, Knut].

2840 *Popović, Anto* Molitve protiv nepraijateljâ: analiza 'osvetničkih' Psalama kroz prizmu Psalma 58 [The prayers against the enemies: an analysis of the 'imprecatory psalms' from the viewpoint of Psalm 58]. 1997, ⇒96. ᶠTOMICA C., Sum. 364. 343-364. **Croatian.**

2841 **Reid, Stephen Breck** Listening in: a multicultural reading of the Psalms. Nv 1997, Abingdon 108 pp. RRT 1998/2,91. $20. 0-687-01194-0.

2842 **Schaper, Joachim** Eschatology in the Greek Psalter. WUNT 2/76: 1995, ⇒11/1,1526; 12,2764. ᴿJSJ 28/1 (1997) 123-124 *(Van der Horst, P.W.)*; RevSR 71/2 (1997) 257-258 *(Bons, Eberhard)*; BiOr 54 (1997) 185-190 *(Pietersma, Albert)*; CBQ 59 (1997) 357-359 *(Wright, John W.)*; JBL 116 (1997) 350-352 *(Peters, M.K.H.)*.

2843 **Schroer, Silvia** "Im Schatten deiner Flügel": religionsgeschichtliche und feministische Blicke auf die Metaphorik der Flügel Gottes in den Psalmen, in Ex 19,4; Dtn 32,11 und in Mal 3,20. 1997, ⇒29. ᶠGERSTENBERGER E.S., 296-316.

2844 *Shepherd, John* The place of the imprecatory psalms in the canon of scripture. ChM 111/1 (1997) 27-47 [ZID 23/6,191].

2845 *Stadelmann, Luís I.J.* 'Nome' nos salmos. PerTeol 29 (1997) 97-9.
2846 *Stricher, Joseph* Casse-lui les dents! DosB 68 (1997) 19-21.
2847 *Stutz, Pierre* Der geglückte Tag: Psalmenrede und heutiges Psalmensprechen. KatBl 122 (1997) 294-298.
2848 *Van Riessen, R.D.* In u schuil ik: Psalmen in de moderne Nederlandse poëzie. GThT 97/3 (1997) 107-117.
2849 *Wilson, Gerald H.* The Qumran Psalms Scroll (11QPsa) and the canonical psalter: comparison of editorial shaping. CBQ 59 (1997) 448-464;
2850 The use of royal psalms at the 'seams' of the Hebrew psalter. Poetical Books. 1997 <1986>, ⇒184. EClines, David J.A., 73-83.
2851 **Zenger, Erich** A God of vengeance?... the psalms of divine wrath. 1996, ⇒12,2779. RCBQ 59 (1997) 366-67 *(Brueggemann, Walter)*.
2852 *Zenger, Erich* Der jüdische Psalter—ein anti-imperiales Buch?. Religion und Gesellschaft. AOAT 248: 1997, ⇒235. EAlbertz, Rainer, 95-108.

E6.6 *Psalmi: oratio, liturgia*—Psalms as prayer

2853 *Barros Souza, Marcelo de* The powerful prayer of lament and the resistance of the people of God: a particular approach to the book of Psalms. Subversive scriptures. 1997, ⇒263. EVaage, L., 155-172.
2854 *Barthélemy, Dominique* L'appropriation juive et chrétienne du psautier. Vie Spirituelle 77 (1997) 207-219.
2855 **Bianchi, Enzo** Pregare i Salmi. Mi 1997, Gribaudi 111 pp. 88-7152-442-X.
2856 *Bosch, R.A.* De psalm als gezang in de christelijke eredienst: beschrijving van een actueel spanningsveld. GThT 97/3 (1997) 117-126.
2857 (*a*) **Brueggemann, Walter** The Psalms and the life of faith. EMiller, Patrick D.: 1995, ⇒11/1,41. RDialog 36/1 (1997) 72-73 *(Brusic, Robert)*; (*b*) *Brueggemann, Walter* Psalms and the life of faith: a suggested typology of function. Poetical Books. 1997 <1986>, ⇒184. EClines, David J.A., 35-66.
2858 *Curtis, Edward M.* Ancient psalms and modern worship. BS 154 (1997) 285-296.
2859 **Della Torre, L.** Il canto di lode: chiavi interpretative di salmi e cantici: Lodi e Vespri. Mi 1997, Paoline 2 vols. L24.000 + 12.000 [RPLi 207,89s—Lodi, Enzo].
2860 *Felten, Gustavo* Orando los salmos. La Revista Católica 97/2 (1997) 135-140.
2861 *Goldingay, John* The dynamic cycle of praise and prayer in the Psalms. Poetical Books. 1997 <1981>, ⇒184. EClines, David J.A., 67-72.
2862 *Gruson, Philippe* Les familles de psaumes. DosB 68 (1997) 8-10.
2863 *Hill, Robert C.* The spirituality of CHRYSOSTOM's *Commentary on the Psalms.* JEarlyC 5 (1997) 569-579.
2864 ELardon, Sabine JEAN de Sponde: méditations sur les pseaumes. 1996, ⇒12,2790. RSCJ 28 (1997) 1383-1384 *(Gosselin, Edward)*.
2865 *Mackiewicz, Marie-Claude* Prier les psaumes. DosB 68 (1997) 13-14.

2866 **Möller, Håkan** Den wallinska psalmen. Bibliotheca theologiæ practicæ, Kyrkovetenskapliga studier 56: Sto 1997, Akademisk [TTK 69,235s—Akslen, Laila].

2867 *Phillips, Jack Simon* Joy and lament in Melkite catholic liturgy. BiTod 35 (1997) 241-246.

2868 Die Psalmen: mit Meisterwerken des Mittelalters und der Renaissance. Stu 1997, Belser 208 pp. DM98. 3-7630-5635-1 [OrdKor 39,237s—Heinemann, Franz Karl].

2869 *Taft, Robert F.* The origins and development of the Byzantine communion psalmody I. Studi sull'Oriente Cristiano 1 (1997) 108-134.

2870 *Witvliet, John D.* The spirituality of the Psalter: metrical psalms in liturgy and life in CALVIN's Geneva. CTJ 32 (1997) 273-297.

E6.7 *Psalmi: versiculi—***Psalms by number and verse**

2871 *Bauer, Uwe F.* Antijüdische Deutungen des ersten Psalms bei LUTHER und im Neueren Deutschen Protestantismus. CV 39/2-3 (1997) 101-119.

2872 *Willis, John T.* A cry of defiance—Psalm 2. Poetical Books. 1997 < 1990 >, ⇒184. ᴱClines, David J.A., 117-134.

2873 *Autané, Maurice* Tu es mon fils: le psaume 2. DosB 68 (1997) 25-26.

2874 *Lund, Oystein* From the mouth of babes and infants you have established strength. SJOT 11 (1997) 78-99 [Ps 8,3].

2875 *Anoz, José* El único comentario agustiniano completo del salmo octavo. Augustinus 42 (1997) 229-252.

2876 *Irsigler, Hubert* Die Frage nach dem Menschen in Psalm 8: zu Bedeutung und Horizont eines kontroversen Menschenbildes im Alten Testament: Prof. Dr. Wolfgang Richter zum 70. Geburtstag. Vom Adamssohn. ATSAT 58: 1997, ⇒137. 1-48.

2877 *Harrelson, Walter* Psalm 8 on the power and mystery of speech. 1997, ⇒34. ᴹGREENBERG M., 69-72.

2878 *Auffret, Pierre* L'étude structurelle des psaumes: réponses et compléments III (méthodologie et Pss. 13, 26 et 27). ScEs 49 (1997) 149-174.

2879 **Aparicio Rodríguez, Ángel** Tú eres mi bien: análsis exegético y teológico del Salmo 16. 1993, ⇒9,3100. CRM 78/1-2 (1997) 172-173 *(García Paredes, José Cristo Rey).*

2880 *Kim, Eui W.* An exegetical study of psalm 16: my inheritance from Yahweh. Chongshin Review 2/2 (1997) 71-89 [ZID 23,439].

2881 *Heimpel, Wolfgang* My-Father-is-my-rock. Nouvelles Assyriologiques Brèves et utilitaires 1 (1997) 1-2 [Ps 18,2].

2882 *Heller, Jan* Hindin Morgenröte (Ps 22,1). CV 39/2-3 (1997) 120-127.

2883 *Vall, Gregory* Psalm 22:17b: "the old guess". JBL 116 (1997) 45-56.

2884 ᴱ**Poorthuis, Marcel** Mijn God, mijn God, waarom hebt gij mij verlaten: een interdisciplinaire bundel over psalm 22. Collab. *Beentjes, Panc*: Baarn 1997, Ten Have 192 pp. 90-259-4711-5 [NThAR 1997,290].

2885 *Davis, Ellen F.* Exploding the limits: form and function in Psalm 22. Poetical Books. 1997 < 1992 >, ⇒184. ᴱClines, David J.A., 135-146.

2886 *Scippa, Vincenzo* Il buon pastore e l'anfitrione: il salmo 23 alla luce dei nuovi approcci esegetici. 1997, ⇒30. <sup>F</sup>GIORDANO M., 43-69.

2887 *Kim, Jung W.* A rhetorical approach to psalm 23. Chongshin Review 2/2 (1997) 90-108 [ZID 23,439].

2888 *Smith, Mark S.* Setting and rhetoric in Psalm 23. Poetical Books. 1997 <1988>, ⇒184. <sup>E</sup>Clines, David J.A., 147-152.

2889 *Reifsnyder, Richard W.* Psalm 24. Interp. 51 (1997) 284-288.

2890 *Freedman, David Noel* Patterns in Psalms 25 and 34. Divine Commitment 2. 1997 <1992>, ⇒124. 258-269.

*Schenker, Adrian* Gewollt dunkle Wiedergaben in LXX?... Ps 28 (29),6 ⇒2765.

2891 *Wagner, Andreas* Zum Textproblem von Ps 29,9: Überlegungen zum Plural der Nomina collectiva und der Pflanzennamen im biblischen Hebräisch und ihre Bedeutung für das Verständnis von Ps 29,9. ZAH 10 (1997) 177-197.

2892 *Freedman, David Noel* Psalm 29: a structural analysis. Divine Commitment 2. 1997 <1973>, ⇒124. 70-87.

2893 **Bons, Eberhard** Psalm 31—Rettung als Paradigma: eine synchronleserorientierte Analyse. FTS 48: 1994, ⇒10,3003; 12,2835. SJOT 11 (1997) 306-307 *(Jeppesen, Knud)*.

2894 **Witczyk, Henryk** 'Pokorny Wołał, I Pan Go Wysłuchał' (Ps 34,7a): model komunikacji diafanicznej w psalmach ['Quand un malheureux crie, l'Éternel entend' (Ps 34,7a): le modèle de la communication diaphonique dans les Psaumes <French>]. Lublin 1997, Katolickiego Uniwersytetu Lubelskiego 480 pp. Diss.-Habil. Lublin; Sum. 465-469; som. PalCl 76,905-910.

2895 *Botha, P.J.* The social setting and strategy of Psalm 34. OTEs 10 (1997) 178-197.

2896 <sup>T</sup>**Crouzel, Henri; Brésard, Luc** ORIGENE: homélies sur les psaumes 36 à 38. SC 411: 1995, ⇒11/1,1610; 12,2840. <sup>R</sup>VigChr 51/1 (1997) 94-95 *(Van Winden, J.C.M.)*; REAug 43/1 (1997) 206-207 *(Bottier, Laurence)*; Aug. 37/1 (1997) 249-251 *(Studer, Basil)*.

2897 *Kselman, John* Psalm 36. CBQ.MS 29: 1997, ⇒69. <sup>F</sup>MURPHY R., 3-17.

2898 *Noret, Jacques* Un verset scripturaire contesté et par là remarquable: Ps. 37,21c (LXX). 1997, ⇒101. <sup>F</sup>VOORDECKERS E., 211-29.

2899 *Irsigler, Hubert* Die Suche nach Gerechtigkeit in den Psalmen 37, 49 und 73. Vom Adamssohn. ATSAT 58: 1997, ⇒137. 71-100.

2900 *Lohfink, Norbert* Die Besänftigung des Messias: Gedanken zu Psalm 37. 'Den Armen eine frohe Botschaft'. 1997, ⇒46. <sup>F</sup>KAMPHAUS F., 75-87 [ThRv 94,625].

2901 *Kselman, John A.* Two notes on Psalm 37. Bib. 78 (1997) 252-254.

2902 *Vannier, Marie-Anne* La prière de saint AUGUSTIN: à l'écoute du psaume 41. VS 722 (1997) 53-61 [Lk 4,1-13].

2903 *Augustin, Saint* Les soupirs de l'église: discours de saint AUGUSTIN sur le psaume XLI: sermon au peuple. VS 722 (1997) 63-82 [Lk 4,1-13].

2904 *Kessler, Martin* Response to ALONSO SCHOEKEL. Poetical Books. 1997 <1976>, ⇒184. <sup>E</sup>Clines, David J.A., 24-27 [Ps 42-43].

2905  *Vesco, Jean-Luc* Où est ton Dieu?: la réponse du psaume 42-43. VS 722 (1997) 23-28 [Lk 4,1-13]..

2906  *Alonso Schökel, Luis* The poetic structure of Psalm 42-43 <1972, 1976>;

2907  *Ridderbos, Nic. H.* Response to ALONSO SCHOEKEL. Poetical Books. 1997 <1976>, ⇒184. ᴱClines, David J.A., 16-23/28-34.

2908  **Grünbeck, Elisabeth** Christologische Schriftargumentation... des 44. (45.) Psalms. SVigChr 26: 1994, ⇒10,3013... 12,2847. JEarlyC 5/1 (1997) 144-146 *(Norris, Frederick W.)*.

2909  *Bauer, Johannes B.* Zions Flüsse: Ps 45(46),5. Studien zu Bibeltext. 1997 <1977>, ⇒111. 151-183.

2910  *du Preez, Jannie* Interpreting Psalm 47—some notes on its composition, exegesis and significance for the church's mission at the turn of the century. Sum. 308. Missionalia 25/3 (1997) 308-323.

2911  *Meynet, Roland* Analyse rhétorique du Psaume 51: hommage critique à Marc Girard. RivBib 45 (1997) 187-226.

2912  **Brush, Jack Edmund** Gotteserkenntnis und Selbsterkenntnis: LUTHERs Verständnis des 51. Psalms. HUTh 36: Tü 1997, Mohr xv; 248 pp. Diss.-Habil. Z 1993-94. 3-16-146626-8 [EThL 74,180*].

2913  *Jenni, Ernst* Pleonastische Ausdrücke für Vergleichbarkeit (Ps 55,14; 58,5). Studien zur Sprachwelt. 1997 <1994>, ⇒138. 206-211.

2914  *Auffret, Pierre* L'étude structurelle des psaumes: réponses et compléments II (Pss. 61, 77, 82, 100, 138, 147). ScEs 49 (1997) 39-61.

2915  ᴱᵀMüller, Hildegund Eine Psalmenpredigt über die Auferstehung: Augustinus: enarratio in Psalmum 65. DÖAW.PH 653; VKCLK 15: W 1997, Verlag der ÖAW 138 pp. Einleitung, Text, Übersetzung und Kommentar. 3-7001-2700-6.

2916  *Bauer, Johannes B.* Exegesegeschichte und Textkritik Ps 68(69),32 <1990>;

2917  Psalm 70(71),15: quoniam non cognovi litteraturam <1982>. Studien zu Bibeltext. 1997, ⇒111. 184-188/189-204.

2918  *Broyles, Craig C.* The redeeming king: Psalm 72's contribution to the messianic ideal. Eschatology, messianism. SDSSRL 1: 1997, ⇒276. ᴱEvans, Craig A., 23-40.

2919  ᵀSmet, Joachim F. AYGUANI's commentary on Psalm 72. 1997, ⇒70. ᶠMURPHY R., Master, 353-387.

2920  *Mackiewicz, Marie-Claude* Comme une brute épaisse: le psaume 73. DosB 68 (1997) 6-7.

2921  *Allen, Leslie C.* Psalm 73: pilgrimage from doubt to faith. BBR 7 (1997) 1-9.

2922  *Auffret, Pierre* Souviens-toi de ton assemblée!: étude structurelle du psaume 74. FolOr 33 (1997) 21-31;

2923  C'est Dieu qui juge: étude structurelle du psaume 75. ZAW 109 (1997) 385-394.

2924  **Weber, Beat** Psalm 77 und sein Umfeld: eine poetologische Studie. BBB 103: 1995, ⇒11/1,1635; 12,2866. ᴿBib. 78 (1997) 108-111 *(Berry, Donald K.)*.

2925  *Stevenson, Gregory M.* Communal imagery and the individual lament: Exodus typology in Psalm 77. RestQ 39/4 (1997) 215-229.

2926  **McLain, Charles E.** An investigation of psalm 78 as political accession justification for the Davidic dynasty. Diss. Westminster

Theological Seminary 1996; ᴰ*Longman, Tremper III*: 335 pp. [DAI-A 57/06, p. 2529; AAC 9634683].

2927　*Zakovitch, Yaïr* 'Il choisit la tribu de Juda...il choisit David son serviteur': le psaume 78: sources, structure, signification, but. David. 1997, ⇒319. ᴱBron, H., 117-202 [RB 105,290— Langlamet, F.]. **H.**

2928　*Prinsloo, G.T.M.* Shepherd, vine-grower, father—divine metaphor and existential reality in a community lament (Psalm 80). OTEs 10 (1997) 279-302.

2929　*Hieke, Thomas* Psalm 80 and its neighbors in the psalter: the context of the psalter as a background for interpreting psalms. BN 86 (1997) 36-43;

2930　**Hieke, Thomas** Psalm 80—Praxis eines Methodenprogramms: eine literaturwissenschaftliche Untersuchung mit einem gattungskritischen Beitrag zum Klagelied des Volkes. Diss. Bamberg, 1996; ᴰ*Irsigler, H.*: ATSAT 55: St. Ottilien 1997, EOS xi; 496 pp. 3-88096-555-2.

2931　*Benedetto, Robert* Psalm 84. Interp. 51 (1997) 57-61.

2932　*Renaud, Bernard* Un oracle prophétique (2 S 7) invalidé?: une approche du psaume 89. Oracles. 1997, ⇒374. ᴱHeintz, J.-G., 215-229.

2933　**Koenen, Klaus** Jahwe wird kommen, zu herrschen über die Erde: Ps 90-110 als Komposition. BBB 101: 1995, ⇒11/1,1648. ᴿThZ 53 (1997) 269-271 *(Weber, Beat)*; JBL 116 (1997) 543-544 *(Limburg, James)*.

2934　*Manicardi, Luciano* 'Insegnaci a contare i nostri giorni' (Sal 90). PSV 36 (1997) 47-71.

2935　*Seybold, Klaus* Zu den Zeitvorstellungen in Psalm 90. ThZ 53 (1997) 97-108.

2936　*Irsigler, Hubert* Psalm 90: der vergängliche Mensch vor dem ewigen Gott. Vom Adamssohn. ATSAT 58: 1997, ⇒137. 49-69.

2937　*Weiss, Meir* "A psalm, a song for the sabbath day". 1997, ⇒34. ᴹGREENBERG M., 45*-51*. **H.**

2938　**Howard, David M., Jr.** The structure of Psalms 93-100. Biblical and Judaic Studies 5: WL 1997, Eisenbrauns xvi; 231 pp. $35. 1-57506-009-4.

2939　*Jeremias, Jörg* Die Erde "wankt". 1997, ⇒29. ᶠGERSTENBERGER E.S., 166-180 [Ps 93,2; 46; 75; 82,5].

2940　*Conti, Martino* Dio difensore della causa degli oppressi secondo il salmo 94. Sum. 3. Anton. 72 (1997) 3-37.

2941　*Rimaud, Didier* Jésus le roi de Béthléem. Vie Chrétienne 425 (1997) 29-32 [Ps 95].

2942　*Görg, Manfred* Den "Gott-König" preisen?: Gedanken zu Ps 96. Entschluss 52/11 (1997) 6-9.

2943　*Gosse, Bernard* Le psaume 98 et la rédaction d'ensemble du livre d'Isaie. BN 86 (1997) 29-30.

2944　*Auffret, Pierre* Au milieu de ma maison: étude structurelle du psaume 101. SJOT 11 (1997) 124-137.

2945　**Brunert, Gunhild** Ps 102 im Kontext des vierten Psalmenbuches. SBS 30: 1996, ⇒12,2879. ᴿBib. 78 (1997) 112-115 *(Brueggemann, Walter)*; JBL 116 (1997) 734-735 *(Malchow, Bruce V.)*.

2946　*Warzecha, Julian* Błogosławić czy wielbić pana?: w sprawie przekładu [Benedicere an laudare Dominum?: quomodo traducendum est?]. RBL 50 (1997) 283-287 [Ps 103,1-2] **P.**

2947  *Le Saux, Madeleine* Le Dieu de tendresse et de fidélité: le psaume
103. DosB 68 (1997) 11-12.
2948  **Ravalomanana, Charlotte** Création et providence: étude exégétique du psaume 104. Diss. Montpellier 1997; <sup>D</sup>*Bourguet, D.*: 337
pp. [RTL 29,579].
2949  *Jarick, John* The four corners of Psalm 107. CBQ 59 (1997) 270-
287.
2950  *Roffey, John W.* Beyond reality: poetic discourse and psalm 107.
JSOT.S 240: 1997, ⇒20. <sup>F</sup>Coats G., 60-76.
2951  **Van der Velden, Frank** Psalm 109 und die Aussagen zur
Feindschädigung in den Psalmen. Diss. Bonn, 1995, <sup>D</sup>*Hossfeld,
F.-L.*: SBB 37: Stu 1997, Katholisches Bibelwerk viii; 192 pp.
DM79. 3-460-00371-5.
2952  *Lohfink, Norbert* Drei Arten, von Armut zu sprechen: illustriert an
Psalm 109. ThPh 72 (1997) 321-336.
2953  *Pardee, Dennis* La structure du Psaume 111—réponse à P. Auffret.
JNES 56 (1997) 197-200.
2954  *Auffret, Pierre* Grandes sont les oeuvres de YHWH: étude structurelle du Psaume 111. JNES 56 (1997) 183-196.
2955  *Scoralick, Ruth* Psalm 111—Bauplan und Gedankengang. Sum.
205. Bib. 78 (1997) 190-205.
2956  *Auffret, Pierre* 'Je marcherai à la face de YHWH': étude structurelle du Psaume 116 (suite). ⇒65,2771. OTEs 10 (1997) 161-177.
2957  **Berder, Michel** "La pierre rejetée par les bâtisseurs": Psaume
118,22-23 et son emploi dans les traditions juives et dans le
Nouveau Testament. EtB 31: 1996, ⇒12,2891. <sup>R</sup>EeV 107/4 (1997)
90-91 *(Monloubou, Louis)*.
2958  **Jenni, Ernst** 'Vom Herrn ist dies gewirkt': Ps. 118,23. Studien zur
Sprachwelt. 1997 <1979>, ⇒138. 82-90.
2959  **Toschi, Stefano** La meraviglia: il salmo 118 dal punto di vista
dell'handicap. Scrigni 9: Terlizzi (Bari) 1997, Insieme 127 pp. 88-
85379-30-3.
2960  <sup>E</sup>**Clerici, Agostino** Ambrosius: expositio de Psalmo CXVIII: le
meraviglie della parola: dal commento al salmo 118. Pref. di
*Maggioni, Bruno*: La parola e le parole 62: Mi 1997, Paoline 153
pp. 88-315-1358-3.
2961  *Passerini, Iginio* La fonte del commento al salmo CXVIII di
Ambrogio. ScC 125 (1997) 921-942 [EThL 74,178*].
2962  **Whybray, R.N.** Psalm 119: profile of a psalmist. CBQ.MS 29:
1997, ⇒69. <sup>F</sup>Murphy R., 31-43.
2963  **Oduyoye, Modupe** The longest psalm: the prayers of a student of
moral instruction. Ibadan 1994, Sefer 118 pp. [NAOTS 7,13—
Holter, Knut].
2964  *Vesco, Jean-Luc* Les psaumes des montées. Vie Spirituelle 724
(1997) 431-449.
2965  <sup>TE</sup>**Orazzo, Antonio** Ilario di Poitiers: i salmi delle ascensioni:
cantico del pelegrino. 1996, ⇒12,2709. <sup>R</sup>RdT 38 (1997) 265-267
*(Marafioti, Domenico)*; Aug. 37 (1997) 503-504 *(Cioffi, Antonio)*;
CivCatt 148 I (1997) 617-618 *(Cattaneo, E.)*.
2966  **Cuënot, Michel** Jérusalem joie pour toute la terre: psaumes des
montées. 1996, ⇒12,2902. <sup>R</sup>Sources 23/1 (1997) 46-47 *(Schenker,
Adrian)*.
2967  *Goulder, M.D.* The song of ascents and Nehemiah. JSOT 75
(1997) 43-58.

2968 *Klingbeil, Gerald A.* 'Sun' and 'moon' in Psalm 121:6. 1997, ⇒83. ᶠSHEA W., 33-43.

2969 *Plank, Karl A.* Ascent to darker hills: psalm 121 and its poetic revision. JLT 11/2 (1997) 152-167 [ZID 23,273].

2970 *Alomía, Merling* The psalm of the 'blessed hope': comments on Psalm 126. 1997, ⇒83. ᶠSHEA W., 45-56.

2971 *Loretz, Oswald* Syllabische und alphabetische Keilschrifttexte zu Psalm 127. AOAT 247: 1997, ⇒75. ᶠROELLIG W., 229-251.

2972 *Kiourtzian, Georges* Le psaume 131 et son usage funéraire dans la Grèce, les Balkans et la Cappadoce à la haute époque byzantine. CAr 45 (1997) 31-39.

2973 *Felten, Gustavo* Orando los Salmos: Salmo 131 (130). La Revista Católica 97/1 (1997) 45-49.

2974 *Auffret, Pierre* Rendez grace au Seigneur!: étude structurelle du psaume 136. BN 86 (1997) 7-13.

2975 *Bar-Efrat, Shimon* Love of Zion: a literary interpretation of Psalm 137. 1997, ⇒34. ᴹGREENBERG M., 3-11.

2976 *Auffret, M. Pierre* Souviens-toi YHWH!: étude structurelle du Psaume 137: réponses et compléments. BZ 41 (1997) 250-252.

2977 *Costen, James H.* Viewing life from high places: psalm 139:1-18, Luke 19:1-10. JITC 24 (1996-1997) 183-188 [ZID 23,406].

2978 *Mazor, Yair* When aesthetics is harnessed to psychological characterization: "ars poetica" in Psalm 139. ZAW 109 (1997) 260-271.

2979 *Auffret, Pierre* O Dieu, connais mon coer: étude structurelle du Psaume cxxxix. VT 47 (1997) 1-22.

2980 *Gronewald, Michael* HESIOD, XENOPHON, Psalmen und Alexanderapophthegma in Berliner Papyri. ZPE 115 (1997) 117-120 [Ps 145-146].

2981 *Zenger, Erich* "Daß alles Fleisch den Namen seiner Heiligung segne" (Ps 145,21): die Komposition Ps 145-150 als Anstoß zu einer christlich-jüdischen Psalmenhermeneutik. BZ 41 (1997) 1-27.

2982 **Sedlmeier, Franz** Jerusalem—Jahwes Bau: Untersuchungen zu Komposition und Theologie von Psalm 147. FzB 79: 1996, ⇒12,2914. ᴿThLZ 122 (1997) 898-899 *(Gerstenberger, E.S.).*

2983 *Daris, Sergio* Psalmus 148,7-8. Aeg. 77 (1997) 3-6.

2984 *Schiemenz, Günter Paulus* Der 148. Psalm im Athos-Kloster Philotheou. Georgica 20 (1997) 111-127.

2985 *Prinsloo, Willem S.* Psalm 149: praise Yahweh with tambourine and two-edged sword. ZAW 109 (1997) 395-407.

2986 *Zenger, Erich* Die Provokation des 149. Psalms: von der Unverzichtbarkeit der kanonischen Psalmenauslegung. 1997, ⇒29. ᶠGERSTENBERGER E.S., 181-194.

2987 *Smith, Mark S.* How to write a poem: the case of Psalm 151A (11QPsª28.3-12). The Hebrew of the DSS. StTDJ 26: 1997, ⇒369. ᴱMuraoka, Takamitsu, 182-208.

2988 *Van Rooy, Harry F.* Psalm 154:14 and the relation between the Hebrew and Syriac versions of Psalm 154. JBL 116 (1997) 321-324.

2989 *Eshel, Hannan & Esther* קנד מזמור ,המלך יונתן של לשלומו התפילה ישעיה לפשר והפשר י [4Q448, Psalm 154 and 4QpIsaª]. Sum. VI. Tarb. 67/1 (1997) 121-130.

E7.1 Job, *textus, commentarii*

2990  **Alshekh, Moses** A celestial challenge: the book of Iyyov: the commentary of Rabbi Moshe ALSHICH on the book of Job (Chelkath Mechokek). Alshich Tanach: J 1996, Feldheim 2 vols: v.1, chapters 1-20, v.2, chapters 21-42. 0-87306-745-2.

2991  Centre d'Analyse et de Documentation Patristiques. Le livre de Job chez les Pères. Cahiers de Biblia Patristica 5: 1996, ⇒12,2918. ᴿBLE 98/1 (1997) 82-83 *(Vigne, D.)*; JThS 48 (1997) 683-687 *(Hagedorn, Dieter)*; ThPh 72 (1997) 584-585 *(Sieben, H.J.)*; StPat 44/3 (1997) 208-210 *(Corsato, Celestino)*; VetChr 34 (1997) 390-391 *(Veronese, Maria)*; EE 72 (1997) 747-748 *(Raczkiewicz, M.)*.

2992  *Ciccarese, Maria Pia* Sulle orme di GEROLAMO: la 'Expositio in Iob' del presbitero FILIPPO. Motivi letterari. 1997, ⇒331. ᴱMoreschini, C., 247-268.

2993  ᴱ**Dailey, Thomas F.** The book of Job. Bibliographies for biblical research, OT 13: Lewiston, NY 1997, Mellen xviii; 148 pp. 0-7734-2437-7.

2994  *Freedman, David Noel.*Orthographic peculiarities in the book of Job. Divine Commitment 2. 1997 <1969>, ⇒124. 44-60.

2995  **Guinan, Michael** Giobbe. La Bibbia per tutti. Queriniana 19: Brescia] 1997, Queriniana 123 pp. 88-399-2119-2.

2996  ᴱ**Hagedorn, Ursula & Dieter** Fragmente zu Hiob 9,1-22,30. Die älteren griechischen Katenen zum Buch Hiob 2. PTS 48: B 1997, De Gruyter viii; 395 pp. 3-11-015762-4.

2997  **Kutz, Karl V.** The Old Greek of Job: a study in early biblical exegesis. Diss. Wisconsin-Madison 1997; ᴰFox, Michael V.: abs. BIOSCS 30,24s.

2998  *Röll, Walter* Die Edition der ältesten erhaltenen Hiob-Übersetzung eines deutschen Juden [15th cent. Yiddish Bible trans.]. Chloe 25 (1997) 621-636 [IAJS 45,230].

2999  *Sacks, Robert D.* The book of Job: translation and commentary. Interpretation(F) 24-25 (1997) 135-169; 251-286; 3-36; 155-179.

3000  *Weitzman, Michael* Hebrew and Syriac texts of the book of Job. Congress volume 1995. VT.S 66: 1997, ⇒323. ᴱEmerton, J.A., 381-399.

3001  **Wolfers, David** Deep things out of darkness: the book of Job: essays and a new English translation. 1995, ⇒11/1,1703. ᴿCBQ 59 (1997) 144-145 *(Lasine, Stuart)*; RB 104 (1997) 416-419 *(Tournay, R.J.)*; TTK 68 (1997) 238-239 *(Stordalen, Terje)*; HebSt 38 (1997) 169-172 *(Hartley, John E.)*; AUSS 35 (1997) 306-308 *(Caesar, Lael)*; AJSR 22 (1997) 243-248 *(Noegel, Scot B.)*.

E7.2 *Job: themata*, Topics... *Versiculi*, Verse numbers

3002  *Baltzer, Klaus; Krüger, Thomas* Die Erfahrung Hiobs: "konnektive" und "distributive" Gerechtigkeit nach dem Hiob-Buch. 1997, ⇒48. ᶠKNIERIM R., 27-37.

3003  ᴱ**Beuken, Willem A.M.** The book of Job. BEThL 114: 1994, ⇒10,305... 12,2933. ᴿZKTh 119 (1997) 99-100 *(Oesch, Josef M.)*; RivBib 45 (1997) 90-92 *(Prato, Gian Luigi)*.

3004 *Boorer, Suzanne* The dark side of God?: a dialogue with JUNG's interpretation of the book of Job. Pacifica 10 (1997) 277-297.

3005 **Borgonovo, Gianantonio** La notte e il suo sole: luce e tenebre nel libro di Giobbe: analisi simbolica. AnBib 135: 1995, ⇒11/1,1708. ᴿEstB 55 (1997) 544-545 *(Precedo, M.J.)*; CBQ 59 (1997) 532-533 *(Vall, Gregory)*.

3006 *Brenner, Athalya* Job the pious?: the characterization of Job in the narrative framework of the book. Poetical Books. 1997 <1989>, ⇒184. ᴱClines, David J.A., 298-313.

3007 **Cazier, Pierre** Le cri de Job: approche biblique, mythologique et littéraire du problème de la souffrance du juste. 1996, ⇒12,2940. ᴿGraphè 6 (1997) 178-180 *(Sys, Jacques)*.

3008 *Cazier, Pierre* Lectures du livre de Job chez AMBROISE, AUGUSTIN et GREGOIRE le Grand. Graphè 6 (1997) 81-111.

3009 **Chardonnens, Denis** L'homme sous le regard de la Providence: providence de Dieu et condition humaine selon l'exposition littérale sur le livre de Job de THOMAS d'Aquin. Diss. Freiburg/Br; ᴰTorrell, J.P.: BiblThom 50: P 1997, Vrin 319 pp. FF198. 2-7116-1327-5.

3010 **Cheney, Michael** Dust, wind and agony: character, speech and genre in Job. CB.OT 36: 1994, ⇒10,3090; 11/1,1710. ᴿTTK 68/3 (1997) 237-238 *(Stordalen, Terje)*.

3011 *Cooper, Alan* The sense of the book of Job. Prooftexts 17 (1997) 227-244.

3012 **Déclais, Jean-Louis** Les premiers musulmans face à la tradition biblique: trois récits sur Job. 1996, ⇒12,2945. ᴿIslChr 23 (1997) 274-277 *(Cottini, Valentino)*; StIsl 86 (1997) 172-174 *(Gilliot, Claude)*.

3013 **Dell, Katharine** Shaking a fist at God: struggling with the mystery of undeserved suffering. Liguori, MO ²1997 <1995>, Triumph x; 113 pp. $9. 0-7648-0030-2 [ThD 44,358—Heiser, W. Charles].

3014 *Delmaire, Jean-Marie* Les principaux courants de l'exégèse juive sur Job;

3015 *Deremble, Jean-Paul* Jalons iconographiques du thème de Job: des premiers siècles au début de la Renaissance. Graphè 6 (1997) 59-79/135-155.

3016 **Foucher, Daniel** Job et le mystère du mal. Réponses aux questions 2: La Chapelle Montligeon ²1997, Montligeon 144 pp. 2-908129-40-X [NThAR 2000,32].

3017 **Hoffman, Yair** A blemished perfection: the book of Job in context. JSOT.S 213: 1996, ⇒12,2955. ᴿCBQ 59 (1997) 735-736 *(Lasine, Stuart)*.

3018 **Israel, Martin** The way of growth. L 1997, Mowbray viii; 152 pp. £10 [RRT 1998/1,55—Platten, Stephen].

3019 **Kiš, A.Z.** Knjiga o Jobu u hrvatskoglgolskoj književnosti. Zagreb 1997, Hrvatsko filološko društvo 198 pp. [Bogoslovni Vestnik 58,370ss—Bizjak, Jurij]. **Croatian.**

3020 *Knauf, E.A.* Le monde de Job: l'univers achéménide se reflétant dans la littérature biblique. TEuph 13 (1997) 188.

3021 *Lasine, Stuart* Bird's-eye and worm's-eye views of justice in the book of Job. Poetical Books. 1997 <1988>, ⇒184. ᴱClines, David J.A., 274-297.

3022 *Lévêque, Jean* Le thème du juste souffrant en Mésopotamie et la problématique du livre de Job. Graphè 6 (1997) 11-33.

3023  *McCann, J. Clinton* Wisdom's dilemma: the book of Job, the final form of the book of Psalms, and the entire bible. CBQ.MS 29: 1997, ⇒69. FMURPHY R., 18-30.

3024  *Mettinger, Tryggve N.D.* The enigma of Job: the deconstruction of God in intertextual perspective. JNSL 23/2 (1997) 1-19.

3025  *Minette de Tillesse, Caetano* Jó. RBB 14/1-3 (1997) 70-78.

3026  *Moster, Julius B.* The punishment of Job's friends. JBQ 25 (1997) 211-219.

3027  *Müller, Hans-Peter* Die Theodizee und das Buch Hiob. Sum. 156. NZSTh 39 (1997) 140-156.

3028  *Nebout, Michel* Un empêcheur de 'penser en rond': le livre de Job. Cahiers de l'Atelier 472 (1997) 96-102.

3029  *Richard, Pablo* ¡Grito violencia y nadie me responde! Conc(E) 273 (1997) 895-903.

3030  **Rudolph, Conrad** Violence and daily life: reading, art, and polemics in the Cîteaux "Moralia in Job". Princeton 1997, Princeton University Press xii; 147 pp. 59 pl. $39.50 [Spec. 74,827s— Sazama, Kristin M.].

3031  *Santacroce, Daniela* La straordinaria modernità del libro di Giobbe. Studium 93/1 (1997) 103-106.

3032  **Sitzler, Dorothea** 'Vorwurf gegen Gott': ein religiöses Motiv im Alten Orient (Ägypten und Mesopotamien). StOR 32: Wsb 1995, Harrassowitz xvi; 249 pp. ÖS934. 3-447-03602-8. RThLZ 122 (1997) 891-893 *(Blumenthal, Elke)*; JBL 116 (1997) 327-329 *(Crenshaw, James L.)*; WO 28 (1997) 181-185 *(Quack, Joachim Friedrich)*.

3033  **Susman, Margarete** Das Buch Hiob und das Schicksal des jüdischen Volkes. Pref. *Goldschmidt, Hermann Levin*: 1996 <1946>, ⇒12,2983. RSoziologische Revue 20 (1997) 307-309 *(Rammstedt, Angela)*.

3034  *Szpek, Heidi M.* An observation on the Peshiṭta's translation of *šdy* in Job. VT 47 (1997) 550-553.

3035  *Tamez, Elsa* Giobbe: 'Grido contro la violenza, ma non ho risposta'. Conc(GB) 1997/5,55-62; Conc(F) 273,77-85; (D33,632-639); Conc(I) 33/5,970-979.

3036  *Tayara, Kamal* Job dans le Coran. Graphè 6 (1997) 113-134.

3037  **Terrien, Samuel** The iconography of Job through the centuries: artists as biblical interpreters. 1996, ⇒12,2984. RJTHe 36 (1997) 278-279 *(Ulanov, Barry)*.

3038  **Thomason, Bill** God on trial: the book of Job and human suffering. ColMn 1997, Liturgical vii; 101 pp. $10. 0-8146-2424-3 [NThAR 1997,259].

3039  **Van der Lugt, Pieter** Rhetorical criticism and the poetry of the book of Job. OTS 32: 1995, ⇒11/1,1735; 12,2986. RJBL 116 (1997) 342-344 *(Crenshaw, James L.)*.

3040  **Van Wolde, Ellen** Mr and Mrs Job. L 1997, SCM viii; 152 pp. £13. 0-334-02712-8 [RRT 1998/2,92].

3041  *Vaydat, Pierre* KANT et Carl Gustave JUNG lecteurs du 'livre de Job'. Graphè 6 (1997) 157-173.

3042  *Waters, Larry J.* Reflections on suffering from the book of Job. BS 154 (1997) 436-451.

3043  *Welland, Malcolm* Active imagination in JUNG's *Answer to Job*. Sum., Rés. 297. SR 26 (1997) 297-308.

3044 EZuck, Roy B. Sitting with Job. 1992, ⇒8,3371... 10,3137. RVT 47 (1997) 575-576 (Dell, Katharine J.).

3045 Guillaume, Philippe Job le nudiste ou la genèse de la sagesse. BN 88 (1997) 19-26 [Job 1,21].

3046 Webster, Edwin C. Strophic patterns in Job 3-28. Poetical Books. 1997 <1983>, ⇒184. EClines, David J.A., 232-259.

3047 Althann, Robert Job 3 after the discussion between Mitchell DAHOOD and James BARR. Studies in NWS. BibOr 45: 1997, ⇒108. 121-153.

3048 Weinfeld, Moshe 'Partition, partition; wall, wall, listen': 'leaking' the divine secret to someone behind the curtain. Sum. 222. AfO 44-45 (1997) 222-225 [Job 4,12-17; 15,4-5. 8-14; Jer 23,18-24].

3049 ESiniscalco, Paolo GREGORIUS I: commento morale a Giobbe, 2: IX-XVIII. Opere di Gregorio Magno: R 1994, Città Nuova 729 pp. L100.000. RCivCatt 148 I (1997) 402-403 (Cremascoli, G.).

3050 Bastiaens, Jean Charles The language of suffering in Job 16-19 and in the suffering servant passages in Deutero-Isaiah. BEThL 132: 1997, ⇒12. FBEUKEN W., 421-432.

3051 ESiniscalco, Paolo GREGORIUS I: commento morale a Giobbe: XIX-XXII. Opere di Gregorio Magno 3. R 1997, Città Nuova 617 pp. 88-311-9408-9 [NThAR 1998,99].

3052 Witte, Markus Vom Leiden zur Lehre: der dritte Redegang (Hiob 21-27) und die Redaktionsgeschichte des Hiobbuches. BZAW 230: 1994, ⇒11/1,1765; 12,2999. RZKTh 119 (1997) 100-102 (Oesch, Josef M.);

3053 Philologische Notizen zu Hiob 21-27. BZAW 234: 1995, ⇒11/1,1764; 12,2998. RZKTh 119 (1997) 100-102 (Oesch, Josef M.).

3054 Borgonovo, Gianantonio Due o tre cicli di discorsi tra Giobbe e i tre amici?: una proposta per leggere Gb 22-27. RAnScR 2 (1997) 211-235.

3055 Japhet, Sara Tradition and innovation in the commentary of Rabbi Samuel ben Meir (RASHBAM) on Job: the hymn to wisdom (Job 28). 1997, ⇒34. MGREENBERG M., 115*-142*. H.

3056 Webster, Edwin C. Strophic patterns in Job 29-42. Poetical Books. 1997 <1984>, ⇒184. EClines, David J.A., 260-273.

3057 Dolbeau, François Une citation non reconnue de Job 31,11 (LXX), dans un sermon d'UGUSTIN. REAug 43 (1997) 309-311.

3058 Viviers, Hendrik Elihu (Job 32-37), garrulous but poor rhetor?: why is he ignored?. The rhetorical analysis. JSNT.S 146: 1997, ⇒336. EPorter, Stanley E., 137-153.

3059 Wahl, Harald-Martin Der gerechte Schöpfer... Hiob 32-37. BZAW 207: 1993, ⇒9,3245... 12,3006. RBZ 41 (1997) 114-115 (Scharbert, Josef).

3060 Cohen, Matty Fauves et songe nocturne dans le premier discours d'Eliphaz. Graphè 6 (1997) 35-58 [Job 32].

3061 Viviers, H. How does God fare in the divine speeches (Job 38:1-42:6)?. OTEs 10 (1997) 109-124.

3062 Ritter-Müller, Petra Kennst du die Welt?: eine sprachwissen-schaftliche und exegetische Studie zur ersten Gottesrede im Buch Ijob (Ijob 38 und 39). Diss. Salzburg 1997; DReiterer, F.; Wehrle, J. [RTL 29,579].

3063  *Caquot, André* Behémot. Sum. 49. Sem. 45 (1996) 49-64 [Job
      40,15-24].


e7.3 *Canticum Canticorum*, Song of Songs, Hohelied, *textus, comm.*

3064  **Arminjon, Blaise** La cantata del amor: lectura seguida del Cantar
      de los Cantares. Bilbao 1997, DDB 371 pp. [Mayéutica 24,249—
      Avitia, Juan Carlos].
3065  *Bauer, Johannes B.* Apponiana. Studien zu Bibeltext. 1997
      <1995>, ⇒111. 60-72.
3066  [E]**Bekhor, Shlomo** Cantico dei Cantici: testo originale ebraico con
      traduzione a fronte, commenti esplicativi tratti dal Talmud e dalla
      tradizione rabbinica. [T]*Levi, Mosè; Hadad, Avigail;* Collab. *Tchili-
      bon, Giuseppe*: Mi 1997, DLI 188 pp. 88-86674-07-4.
3067  **Ben-Chorin, Schalom,** *(al.),* Das Hohelied der Liebe: ein einziger
      Blick deiner Augen. 1996, ⇒12,3012. BiLi 70/2 (1997) 158-159
      *(Silber, Ursula).*
3068  **Bühlmann, Walter** Das Hohelied. Neuer Stuttgarter Kommentar,
      AT 15: Stu 1997, Katholisches Bibelwerk 120 pp. Bibl. DM29. 3-
      460-07151-6.
3069  [E]**Dove, Mary** Glossa ordinaria pars 22: in Canticum Canticorum.
      CChr.CM 170: Turnhout 1997, Brepols 455 pp. Bibl. 2-503-
      04701-7.
3070  **Dünzl, Franz** Braut und Bräutigam: die Auslegung des Canticum
      durch GREGOR von Nyssa. BGBE 32: 1993, ⇒9,3259... 12,3018.
      [R]CrSt 18/1 (1997) 175-177 *(Maraval, Pierre).*
3071  **Faessler, Marc; Carrillo, Francine** L'alliance du désir: le Canti-
      que des cantiques revisité. 1995, ⇒11/1,1788. VieCon 69/5 (1997)
      325-326 *(Luciani, Didier).*
3072  [E]**Guérard, Marie-Gabrielle** NIL d'Ancyre: commentaire sur le
      Cantique des Cantiques 1. SC 403: 1994, ⇒10,3166... 12,3023.
      [R]OCP 63/1 (1997) 257-258 *(Ruggieri, V.).*
3073  **Keel, Othmar** Le Cantique des cantiques: introduction et commen-
      taire. [T]*Müller-Trufaut, Suzanne*: LeDiv commentaires 6: FrS 1997,
      Éd. universitaires 312 pp. FF200. 2-8271-0788-0 [BCLF 598-
      599,1564].
3074  **Luzzatto, Amos** Una lettura ebraica del Cantico dei Cantici. Schu-
      lim Vogelmann 61: F 1997, Giuntina 87 pp. L12.000. 88-8057-
      041-2.
3075  [E]**Pablo Maroto, Daniel; Rodríguez, José Vicente** Santa TERESA
      de Jesús: meditaciones sobre los Cantares: exclamaciones. M [2]1997
      <1994>, Espiritualidad 152 pp. [San Juan de la Cruz 21,152s—
      Maqueda Gil, Antonio].
3076  **Ravasi, Gianfranco** Il Cantico dei cantici: commento e attualizza-
      zione. 1992, ⇒8,3417... 10,3176. [R]RTL 28 (1997) 113-114
      *(Auwers, J.-M.).*
3077  *Ruffinatto, Aldo* Un chiuso giardino e una fonte sigillata: il "Can-
      tico dei Cantici" tra interpreti, poeti e inquisitori nella Spagna della
      seconda metà del cinquecento. RSLR 33 (1997) 503-541.
3078  [ET]*Soldano, Carmen; Gioia, Mario* Commento spirituale al Cantico
      dei Cantici: un testo inedito del XVI secolo [*Gagliardi, Achille*].
      1997, ⇒30. [F]GIORDANO M., 805-837.

3079 *Sonnet, J.-P.* Le Cantique, entre érotique et mystique: sanctuaire de la parole échangée. NRTh 119 (1997) 481-502.

3080 *Taradach, Madeleine* Lectures allégoriques des essences et fruits odoriférants dans le Targum du Cantique (TgCt 4,12-15) et le commentaire sur le Cantique de GREGOIRE de Nysse. La Bíblia i el Mediterrani. 1997, ⇒385. EBorrell, d'Agustí. 225-231.

3081 EVerdeyen, Paul GUILLELMUS a Sancto Theodorico: expositio super Cantica canticorum. Guillelmi a Sancto Theodorico Opera omnia 2. CChr.CM 87: Turnhout 1997, Brepols [EThL 74,180*].

3082 TEVrégille, Bernard de; Neyrand, Louis APPONIUS: commentaire sur le Cantique des cantiques [Edition bilingue latin-français] (*a*) 1: livres I-III. SC 420: P 1997, Cerf 386 pp. FF261. 2-204-05527-1 [RHPhR 77,247];

3083 (*b*) 2: livres IV-VIII. SC 421: P 1997, Cerf 345 pp. FF250. 2-204-05709-6 [RHPhR 77,247].

3084 *Weems, Renita J.* The Song of Songs. NIntB 5. 1997, ⇒209. 361-434.

## E7.4 **Canticum,** *themata, versiculi*

3085 **Andiñach, Pablo R.** Cantar de los cantares: el fuego y la ternura. BA 1997, Lumen 155 pp. [RevBib 60,222ss—Mendoza, Claudia].

3086 **Ayo, Nicholas** Sacred marriage: the wisdom of the Song of Songs. NY 1997, Continuum 272 pp. $30. 0-8264-1030-8 [ThD 45,60—Heiser, W. Charles].

3087 *Brenner, Athalya* 'My' Song of Songs. A feminist companion. 1997, ⇒180. EBrenner, Athalya, 567-579.

3088 *Carrera, Nicolás de la* Ha llegado la hora del *Cantar de los cantares*. RF 236 (1997) 511-523.

3089 *De Benedetti, Paolo* Per una lettura del Cantico dei cantici. Hum(B) 52 (1997) 557-566.

3090 *Egan, Keith J.* A Carmelite master of the Song of Songs. 1997, ⇒70. FMURPHY R., Master, 91-108.

3091 *Garbini, Giovanni* Il *Cantico dei cantici* nel quadro della poesia dell'antico Oriente. Res., sum. 68. Sef. 57/1 (1997) 51-68.

3092 *Häusl, Maria; Silber, Ursula* "Schön bist du, meine Freundin": das Hohe Lied der Frauen. BiLi 70 (1997) 136-142.

3093 *Holman, Jan* Pleidooi voor een onderaards Hooglied: resultaten van een cultureel-antropologische lezing. TTh 37 (1997) 113-131.

3094 **Jiménez Hernández, Emiliano** Cantar de los cantares: resonancias bíblicas. Tripode 14: Bilbao 1997, EGA 286 pp. 84-7726-163-6.

3095 **Jinbachian, Manuel M.** The genre of love poetry in the Song of Songs and the pre-Islamic Arabian odes. TPBT 48 (1997) 123-137.

3096 *Keul, Hildegund* "Eia, Liebe, nun laß dich wecken!": das Hohelied und die Anrufung des weiblichen Begehrens in MECHTILD von Magdeburgs "Fließendem Licht der Gottheit". BiLi 70 (1997) 105-114.

3097 *Krahmer, Shawn Madison* The bride as friend in BERNARD of Clairvaux's *Sermones super Cantica*. ABenR 48/1 (1997) 69-87.

3098 *Laga, Carl* Entering the library of JACOBUS Monachus: the *Exemplar* of Jacobus' quotations from the *Commentary on the Song of Songs* by GREGORY of Nyssa. 1997, ⇒101. FVOORDECKERS E., 151-161.

3099  *Minette de Tillesse, Caetano* Cântico. RBB 14/1-3 (1997) 183-188.
3100  *Morfino, Mauro Maria* L'esegesi origeniana del *Cantico dei Cantici*: contributo alla storia dell'esegesi. Theologica & Historica 6 (1997) 11-57.
3101  *Paul, Shalom M.* A lover's garden of verse: literal and metaphorical imagery in ancient Near Eastern love poetry. 1997, ⇒34. ᴹGREENBERG M., 99-110.
3102  *Placida, Roberta* La presenza di ORIGENE nelle Omelie sul Cantico dei cantici di GREGORIO di Nissa. VetChr 34 (1997) 33-49.
3103  *Polaski, Donald C.* What will ye see in the Shulammite?: women, power and panopticism in the Song of Songs. Bibl.Interp. 5 (1997) 64-81.
3104  *Seidl, Theodor* Von PALESTRINA bis PENDERECKI: Vertonungen des Hoheliedes aus fünf Jahrhunderten: ein Überblick. BiLi 70 (1997) 128-136.
3105  *Seiler, Jörg* Weiden und doch ruhen—die 33. Hoheliedpredigt BERNHARDS von Clairvaux. BiLi 70 (1997) 114-119.
3106  *Staubli, Thomas* Von der Heimführung des Hoheliedes aus der babylonischen Gefangenschaft der Allegorese: nebst Anregungen zur Integration biblischer und postbiblischer Liebeslieder in den Gottesdienst. BiLi 70 (1997) 91-99.
3107  *Tanner, J. Paul* The history of interpretation of the Song of Songs. BS 154 (1997) 23-46.
3108  *Tanner, J. Paul* The message of the Song of Songs. BS 154 (1997) 142-161.
3109  *Van Dijk-Hemmes, Fokkelien* The imagination of power and the power of imagination: an intertextual analysis of two biblical love songs: the Song of Songs and Hosea 2. Poetical Books. 1997 <1989>, ⇒184. ᴱClines, David J.A., 173-186.
3110  ᵀVerdeyen, Paul; Fassetta, BERNARD de Clairvaux: sermons sur le Cantique 1: 1-15. SC 414: 1996, ⇒12,3051. ᴿGr. 78 (1997) 573-575 *(Zaffi, Maria Cecilia)*.
3111  *Warzecha, Julian* Miłość oblubieńcza w Pieśni nad Pieśniami [Nuptial love in the Song of Songs]. 1997, ⇒52. ᶠŁACH J., 409-426. P.
3112  *Webster, Edwin C.* Pattern in the Song of Songs. Poetical Books. 1997 <1982>, ⇒184. ᴱClines, David J.A., 154-172.

3113  *Edmée, Sr.* 'Love' or 'breasts' at Song of Songs 1:2 and 4?: the pre-Masoretic evidence. StPatr 30: 1997, ⇒351. ᴱLivingstone, Elizabeth A., 8-11.
3114  *Cerrato, J.A.* HIPPOLYTUS': *On the Song of Songs* and the new prophecy. StPatr 31: 1997, ⇒351. ᴱLivingstone, Elizabeth A., 268-273.
3115  *Scoralick, Ruth* "... Umduftet von Myrrhe und Weihrauch" (Hld 3,6): die Poesie der Textverbindungen in Hld 3,6-5,1. BiLi 70 (1997) 99-104.
3116  *Barbiero, Gianni* Die "Wagen meines edlen Volkes" (Hld 6,12): eine strukturelle Analyse. Sum. 189. Bib. 78 (1997) 174-189.
3117  *Watson, Wilfred G.E.* Love and death once more (Song of Songs viii 6). VT 47 (1997) 385-387.

E7.5 *Libri sapientiales*—Wisdom literature

3118 **Bergant, Dianne** Israel's wisdom literature: a liberation-critical reading. A Liberation-critical reading of the OT. Mp 1997, Fortress 194 pp. $19. 0-8006-2875-6 [BiTod 36,128].

3119 **Blenkinsopp, Joseph** Sage, priest, prophet: religious and intellectual leadership in ancient Israel. 1995, ⇒11/1,1842. <sup>R</sup>JThS 48 (1997) 157-161 *(Whybray, R.N.)*; ThLZ 122 (1997) 241-242 *(Krüger, Thomas)*; JSSt 44 (1997) 379-380 *(Dell, Katharine J.)*; JJS 48 (1997) 354-356 *(Knoppers, Gary N.)*; CBQ 59 (1997) 336-337 *(Hostetter, Edwin C.)*; HebStud 38 (1997) 100-103 *(Schramm, Brooks)*.

3120 **Blenkinsopp, Joseph** Wisdom and law in the OT. 1995, ⇒11/1,1843. <sup>R</sup>NRTh 119 (1997) 267-268 *(Sonnet, J.-P.)*.

3121 **Brown, William P.** Character in crisis: a fresh approach to the wisdom literature of the OT. 1996, ⇒12,3058. <sup>R</sup>CBQ 59 (1997) 112-114 *(Murphy, Roland E.)*; RTR 56 (1997) 92-93 *(Hill, Michael)*; HBT 19/1 (1997) 86-87 *(Morgan, Donn F.)*; HebSt 38 (1997) 162-165 *(Carasik, Michael)*; Interp. 51 (1997) 423-426 *(Crenshaw, James L.)*.

3122 *Burns, Camilla* Woman wisdom: the tree of life. BiTod 35 (1997) 141-146.

3123 **Ceresko, Anthony R.** Psalmists and sages. ITS.S: 1994, ⇒10,166; 12,2645. <sup>R</sup>TJT 13/1 (1997) 88-89 *(Delsnyder, Robert)*.

3124 *Clifford, Richard J.* Introduction to wisdom literature. NIntB 5. 1997, ⇒209. 1-16.

3125 *Collins, John J.* Cosmos and salvation: Jewish wisdom and apocalyptic in the Hellenistic age <1977>;

3126 The root of immortality: death in the context of Jewish wisdom <1978>;

3127 Wisdom, apocalypticism and generic compatibility <1993>. Seers. JSJ.S 54: 1997, ⇒119. 317-338/351-367/385-404;

3128 Wisdom reconsidered, in light of the scrolls. DSD 4 (1997) 265-281.

3129 **Collins, John Joseph** Jewish wisdom in the Hellenistic age. OTL: LVL 1997, Westminster xii; 275 pp. Bibl. $35. 0-664-22109-2.

3130 *Dell, Katharine J.* On the development of wisdom in Israel. Congress volume 1995. VT.S 66: 1997, ⇒323. <sup>E</sup>Emerton, J.A., 135-151.

3131 *Dell, Katharine J.* Wisdom literature makes a comeback: pursuing the good life. BiRe 13/4 (1997) 26-31, 46.

3132 *Dempsey, Carol* The gift of wisdom and the natural world. BiTod 35 (1997) 147-151.

3133 *Di Palma, Gaetano* Il lavoro umano in Qohelet e Siracide. 1997, ⇒30. <sup>F</sup>GIORDANO M., 71-79.

3134 <sup>F</sup>EMERTON J., Wisdom in ancient Israel. <sup>E</sup>Day, John; Gordon, Robert P.; Williamson, H.G.M., 1995, ⇒11/1,9; 12,22. <sup>R</sup>EvQ 69 (1997) 159-160 *(Johnstone, William)*; CBQ 59 (1997) 187-188 *(Burns, Camilla)*.

3135 **Enns, Peter** Poetry and wisdom. IBR Bibliographies 3: GR 1997, Baker 173 pp. $13. 0-8010-2161-8 [BoL 1998,6—Grabbe, L.L.].

3136 *Fischer-Elfert, Hans-W.* Persönliche Frömmigkeit und Bürokratie: zu einer neuen Edition der Lehre des Ani. WO 28 (1997) 18-30.

3137   *Gilbert, Maurice* La loi, chemin de sagesse. La loi. LeDiv 168:
       1997, ⇒195. ᴱFocant, Camille, 93-109.
3138   *Gosse, B.* L'universalisme de la sagesse face au sacerdoce de Jéru-
       salem au retour de l'exil (Le don de "mon Esprit" et de "mes Paro-
       les" en Is 59, 21 et Pr 1, 23). TEuph 13 (1997) 39-45.
3139   **Heaton, E.W.** The school tradition of the OT. 1994, ⇒10,730...
       12,3065. ᴿJBL 115 (1996) (1997) 518-520 *(Bergant, Dianne)*.
3140   *Kaiser, Otto* Einfache Sittlichkeit und theonome Ethik in der altte-
       stamentlichen Weisheit. Sum. 139. NZSTh 39 (1997) 115-139.
3141   **Krüger, Thomas** Kritische Weisheit: Studien zur weisheitlichen
       Traditionskritik im Alten Testament. Z 1997, Pano viii; 240 pp. 3-
       9520323-7-9 [NThAR 1998,269].
3142   *Kugel, James* Wisdom and the anthological temper. Prooftexts 17/1
       (1997) 9-32.
3143   *Loader, J.A.* Speakers calling for order. OTEs 10 (1997) 424-438.
3144   **Ponguta, Silvestre** Escritos sapienciales: una presentación.
       Cuadernos bíblicos 8: Caracas 1997, ABS ii; 104 pp. Bibl. 980-
       345-102-2.
3145   *Rota Scalabrini, Patrizio* Una figura biblica della prudenza. Com(I)
       156 (1997) 23-31.
3146   *Scheffler, Eben* Archaeology and wisdom. OTEs 10 (1997) 459-
       473 [Ps 1,3; Qoh 12,11].
3147   **Shupak, Nili** Where can wisdom be found?. OBO 130: 1993,
       ⇒9,3328...12,3093. ᴿHebSt 38 (1997) 158-162 *(Hoffmeier, J.K.)*.
3148   *Taussig, Hal* Wisdom/Sophia, Hellenistic queens, and women's
       lives. Women and goddess traditions. 1997, ⇒249. ᴱKing, K.,
       264-280.
3149   ᴱ**Trublet, Jacques** La sagesse biblique: de l'Ancien au Nouveau
       Testament. LeDiv 160: 1995, ⇒11/1,117. ᴿCart. 13 (1997) 217-
       218 *(Sanz Valdivieso, R.)*; CBQ 59 (1997) 416-418 *(Ceresko, Ant-
       hony R.)*; RSR 85 (1997) 428-429 *(Gibert, Pierre)*; ScEs 49 (1997)
       366-368 *(Langevin, Paul-Émile)*.
3150   **Van Ek, Gerrit** Mens en maatschappij tussen chaos en kosmos:
       een onderzoek naar fundamenten voor sociale kritiek in de wijs-
       heidsliteratuur in het oude Nabije Oosten en met name in oud Isrä-
       el. Diss. Utrecht; Utrecht 1997, Maatschappij ix; 251 pp. [RTL
       29,582].
3151   *Van Leeuwen, Raymond C.* Scribal wisdom and a biblical proverb
       at Qumran. DSD 4 (1997) 255-264 [Ps 37,23-24].
3152   **Witherington III, Ben** Jesus the sage: the pilgrimage of wisdom.
       1994, ⇒12,4081. ᴿCart. 13 (1997) 218-219 *(Sanz Valdivieso, R.)*;
       CBQ 58 (1996) 175-176 *(Meier, John P.)*.

ᴇ7.6 **Proverbiorum liber,** *themata, versiculi*

3153   (*a*) **Alster, Bendt** Proverbs of ancient Sumer: the world's earliest
       proverb collections. Bethesda 1997, CDL Press 2 vols. 1-883053-
       20-X/X1; (*b*) **Berman, Louis A.** Proverb wit & wisdom: a
       treasury of proverbs, parodies, quips, quotes, cliches, catchwords,
       epigrams and aphorisms. NY 1997, Putnam xxi; 522 pp. 0-399-
       52273-5; (*c*) **Boadt, Lawrence E.** Proverbi: con introduzione alla
       letteratura sapienziale. La Bibbia per tutti, Queriniana 18: Brescia
       1997, Queriniana 150 pp. 88-399-2118-4.
3154   *Clifford, Richard J.* Observations on the text and versions of Pro-
       verbs. CBQ.MS 29: 1997, ⇒69. ᶠMURPHY R., 47-61.

3155 *Gerstenberger, Erhard S.* Proverbia. TRE 27. 1997, ⇒419. 583-590.

3156 **Jones, Cody L.** The complete guide to the book of Proverbs: King Solomon reveals the secrets to long life, riches, and honor. Commerce, MI 1995, Quinten 566 pp. Bibl. 0-9638944-7-1/6-3 [[NThAR 1999,179].

3157 **Lelièvre, André; Maillot, Alphonse** Commentaire des Proverbes 2: chapitres 19-31. LeDiv: Commentaires 4: 1996, ⇒12,3103. RTelema 23/1-2 (1997) 84-85 *(Kaji-Ngulu, Beda)*; NRTh 119 (1997) 270-271 *(Sonnet, J.-P.)*.

3158 *Van Leeuwen, Raymond C.* The book of Proverbs. NIntB 5. 1997, ⇒209. 17-264.

3159 **Whybray, R. Norman** The composition of the book of Proverbs. JSOT.S 168: 1994, ⇒10,3255... 12,3127. RHebSt 38 (1997) 165-166 *(Morgan, Donn F.)*;

3160 Proverbs. NCeB: 1994, ⇒10,3245; 12,3105. RBib. 78 (1997) 115-120 *(Scoralick, Ruth)*; ThRv 93 (1997) 218-223 *(Scherer, Andreas)*; RTR 56/1 (1997) 42-43 *(Goldsworthy, Graeme)*;

3161 The book of Proverbs: a survey of modern study. 1995, ⇒11/1,1904. RNRTh 119 (1997) 268-270 *(Sonnet, J.-P.)*.

3162 **Bruin, W.M. de** Vergeefse moeite als oordeel van God: een onderzoek naar de 'Wirkungslosigkeitssprüche' in het Oude Testament [Peine perdue comme jugement de Dieu: étude des 'proverbes d'inefficacité' dans l'Ancien Testament]. Diss. Utrecht, Rijksuniv. 1997; DVan Leeuwen, C.: 225 pp. [RTL 29,577].

3163 *Camp, Claudia V.* Woman wisdom and the strange woman: where is power to be found?. Reading bibles. 1997, ⇒172. EBeal, Timothy K., 85-112.

3164 *Cook, Johann* Contrasting as a translation technique in the LXX of Proverbs. 1997, ⇒77. FSANDERS J., 403-414.

3165 *Cook, Johann* The law in Septuagint Proverbs. JNSL 23/1 (1997) 211-223.

3166 **Cook, Johann** The Septuagint of Proverbs: Jewish and /or Hellenistic Proverbs?: concerning the Hellenistic colouring of LXX Proverbs. VT.S 69: Lei 1997, Brill xxi; 391 pp. Bibl. ƒ215/$126.50. 90-04-10879-3.

3167 *Fontaine, Carole* Proverb performance in the Hebrew Bible. Poetical Books. 1997 <1985>, ⇒184. EClines, David J.A., 316-332.

3168 *Fox, Michael V.* What the book of Proverbs is about. Congress volume 1995. VT.S 66: 1997, ⇒323. EEmerton, J.A., 153-167;

3169 Who can learn?: a dispute in ancient pedagogy. CBQ.MS 29: 1997, ⇒69. FMURPHY R., 62-77.

3170 **Hausmann, Jutta** Studien zum Menschenbild der älteren Weisheit: (Spr 10ff.). FAT 7: 1995, ⇒11/1,1958; 12,3112. RZKTh 119/1 (1997) 98-99 *(Oesch, Josef M.)*; JSSt 44 (1997) 393-394 *(Whybray, R.N.)*; CrSt 18/2 (1997) 441-443 & Synaxis 15/1 (1997) 368-372 *(Minissale, Antonino)*.

3171 *Hölderlin, Friedrich* Parallelo tra i *Proverbi* de Salomone e *Le opere ed i giorni* di ESIODO. TColombi, Giulio: Humanitas 52/2 (1997) 297-306.

3172 *Lang, Bernhard* Lady Wisdom: a polytheistic and psychological interpretation of a biblical goddess. A feminist companion. 1997, ⇒180. EBrenner, Athalya, 400-423.

3173  *Marböck, Johannes* Erfahrungen mit dem Menschsein: am Beispiel der Spruchliteratur des Alten Testamentes. ThPQ 145 (1997) 53-63.

3174  **Mazza, Attilio** I mille proverbi della Bibbia. Pref. *Orsatti, Mauro*. I tesori: Bergamo 1997, Burgo 340 pp. Bibl.

3175  ENussbaum, S. African proverbs: collections, studies, bibliographies. Colorado Springs 1996, Global Mapping. CD #3 in the 20:21 Library. Version 1.0 for Windows [NAOTS 6,9s—Kimilike, Peter L.].

3176  *Owan, Kris J.N.* African proverbial wisdom & biblical proverbial wisdom: wholesome bedfellows and more. BiBh 23 (1997) 151-173.

3177  **Snell, Daniel C.** Twice-told proverbs and the composition of the book of Proverbs. 1993, ⇒9,3358... 12,3121. RJNES 56 (1997) 309-310 *(Grabbe, Lester L.)*.

3178  *Van Heerden, Willie* Proverbial wisdom, metaphor and inculturation. OTEs 10 (1997) 512-527.

3179  **Washington, Harold C.** Wealth and poverty in the instruction of Amenemope and the Hebrew Proverbs. SBL.DS 142: 1994, ⇒12,3124. RJSSt 42 (1997) 150-151 *(Golka, Friedemann W.)*; EThL 73 (1997) 432-433 *(Schoors, A.)*.

3180  **Wehrle, Josef** Sprichwort und Weisheit. AOtt 38: 1993, ⇒8,3510... 12,3125. RJSSt 42 (1997) 151-152 *(Golka, Friedemann W.)*; JBL 116 (1997) 545-546 *(Washington, Harold C.)*.

3181  *Camp, Claudia V.* The strange woman of Proverbs: a study in the feminization and divinization of evil in biblical thought. Women and goddess traditions. 1997 <1991>, ⇒249. EKing, K., 310-329 [Prov 1-9].

3182  **Maier, Christl Margarethe** Die "fremde Frau": eine exegetische und sozialgeschichtliche Studie zu Proverbien 1-9. OBO 144: 1995, ⇒11/1,1936; 12,3131. REThL 73 (1997) 164-165 *(Lust, J.)*; ThLZ 122 (1997) 658-659 *(Schroer, Silvia)*; AcOr 58 (1997) 198-199 *(Groth, Bente)*.

3183  *Yee, Gale A.* 'I have perfumed my bed with myrrh': the foreign woman (*'iššā zārâ*) in Proverbs 1-9. Poetical Books. 1997 <1989>, ⇒184. EClines, David J.A., 333-348.

3184  *Moss, Alan* Wisdom as parental teaching in Proverbs 1-9. HeyJ 38 (1997) 426-439.

3185  *Müller, Achim* Formgeschichte und Textgrammatik am Beispiel der alttestamentlichen "Lehrrede" in Prov 1-9. Studien zur hebräischen Grammatik. OBO 156: 1997, ⇒310. EWagner, Andreas, 83-100.

3186  *Newsom, Carol A.* Woman and the discourse of patriarchal wisdom. Reading bibles. 1997 <1989>, ⇒172. EBeal, Timothy K., 116-131 [Prov 1-9].

3187  **Harris, Scott L.** Proverbs 1-9: a study of inner-biblical interpretation. SBL.DS 150: 1995, ⇒11/1,1938. RHebSt 38 (1997) 167-169 *(Whybray, R.N.)*.

3188  *Fox, Michael V.* Ideas of wisdom in Proverbs 1-9. JBL 116 (1997) 613-633.

3189  **Estes, Daniel J.** Hear, my son: teaching and learning in Proverbs 1-9. New Studies in Biblical Theology: GR 1997, Eerdmans 174 pp. Bibl. $20. 0-567-4404-9.

3190 *Perdue, Leo G.* Wisdom theology and social history in Proverbs 1-9. CBQ.MS 29: 1997, ⇒69. [F]MURPHY R., 78-101.

3191 *Freedman, David Noel* Proverbs 2 and 31: a study in structural complementarity. 1997, ⇒34. [M]GREENBERG M., 47-55.

3192 *Maier, Christl* "Begehre nicht ihre Schönheit in deinem Herzen" (Prov 6,25): eine Aktualisierung des Ehebruchsverbots aus persischer Zeit. Bibl.Interp. 5 (1997) 46-63.

3193 *Rogers, Cleon L. III* The meaning and significance of the Hebrew word *amwn* in Proverbs 8,30. ZAW 109 (1997) 208-221.

3194 *Alberi, Mary* The mystery of the incarnation and wisdom's house (Prov. 9:1) in ALCUIN's *Disputatio de vera philosophia*. JThS 48 (1997) 505-516.

3195 *Byargeon, Rick W.* The structure and significance of Prov 9:7-12. JETS 40 (1997) 367-375.

3196 **Scoralick, Ruth** Einzelspruch und Sammlung: Komposition im Buch der Sprichwörter, Kapitel 10-15. Diss. [D]*Jüngling, Hans-Winfried*: BZAW 232: 1995, ⇒11/1,1953. [R]ZKTh 119 (1997) 97-98 *(Oesch, Josef M.)*; CBQ 59 (1997) 139-140 *(Gladson, Jerry A.)*; JBL 115 (1996) 525-526 *(Snell, Daniel C.)*.

3197 *Scherer, Andreas* Is the selfish man wise?: considerations of context in Proverbs 10.1-22.16 with special regard to surety, bribery and friendship. JSOT 76 (1997) 59-70.

3198 *D'Alario, Vittoria* Progetti dell'uomo e disegno di Dio: il problema della teodicea in Pr 16,1-9. 1997, ⇒30. [F]GIORDANO M., 13-28.

3199 *Scherer, Andreas* Vielfalt und Ordnung: Komposition in den biblischen Proverbien und in den aramäischen Ahiqarsprüchen. BN 90 (1997) 28-45 [Prov 22,17-24,22].

3200 *Niccacci, Alviero* Proverbi 23,12-25. Sum. 451. LASBF 47 (1997) 33-56.

3201 *Sembrano, Lucio* Si il tuo nemico ha fame, dagli... da mangiare: l'amore per il nemico nell'etica sapienziale di Pr 25,21s. 1997, ⇒30. [F]GIORDANO M., 29-41.

3202 *Van Leeuwen, Raymond C.* The background to Proverbs 30:4aA. CBQ.MS 29: 1997, ⇒69. [F]MURPHY R., 102-121.

3203 *Masenya, Madipoane* Proverbs 31:10-31 in a South African context: a reading for the liberation of African (Northern Sotho) women. Semeia 78 (1997) 55-68.

3204 *Rendsburg, Gary A.* Double polysemy in Proverbs 31:19. 1997, ⇒49. [F]KROTKOFF G., 267-274.

3205 *Crenshaw, James L.* The missing voice. JSOT.S 240: 1997, ⇒20. [F]COATS G., 133-143 [Prov 31].

E7.7 *Ecclesiastes*—**Qohelet;** *textus, themata, versiculi*

3206 **Bardski, Krzysztof** Il 'Commentarius in Ecclesiasten' di S. GIROLAMO: dall'intenzione del testo alle tradizioni interpretative. Diss. Pont. Institutum Biblicum 1997; [D]*Gilbert, Maurice*: Extr. R 1997, 92 pp. [AcBib 10,346s].

3207 *(a)* **Doré, Daniel** Eclesiastés y Eclesiástico o Qohélet y Sirácida. Pref. *Gruson, Philippe*: CuaBi 91: Estella 1997, Verbo Divino 64 pp. 84-8169-148-8; *(b)* **Dosi, Remo** L'Ecclesiaste: l'uomo che pensa sotto il peso della vita. Bussolengo (VR) 1996. BIBLOS 192 pp.

**Fischer, James A.** Cantico... Qohelet ⇒2395.

3208 EHall, S.G. [GREGORY of Nyssa:] homilies on Ecclesiastes: an English version with supporting studies. 1993, ⇒9,383a. RRHPhR 77/1 (1997) 112-114 *(Nys, F.)*.

3209 **Lohfink, Norbert** Qohelet. L'Antico Testamento commentato: Brescia 1997, Morcelliana 149 pp. Bibl. 88-372-1646-7.

3210 *Minette de Tillesse, Caetano* Coélet. RBB 14/1-3 (1997) 178-182.

3211 *Salters, Robert B.* Textual criticism and Qoheleth. JNSL 23/1 (1997) 53-71.

3212 **Schoors, Antoon** The preacher sought to find pleasing words: a study of the language of Qoheleth, I: grammar. OLA 41: 1992, ⇒8,3560; 10,3298. RJNES 56 (1997) 150-154 *(Clemens, D.M.)*.

3213 *Schoors, Antoon* Qohelet in the context of wisdom. Colloquium Biblicum Lovaniense XLVI (1997). EThL 73 (1997) 520-526.

3214 ESchwienhorst-Schönberger, Ludger Das Buch Kohelet: Studien zur Struktur, Geschichte, Rezeption und Theologie. BZAW 254: B 1997, De Gruyter 389 pp. 3-11-015757-8.

3215 *Schwienhorst-Schönberger, Ludger* Kohelet: Stand und Perspektiven der Forschung. Das Buch Kohelet. BZAW 254: 1997, ⇒3214. 5-38.

3216 **Seow, Choon-Leong** Ecclesiastes: a new translation with introduction and commentary. AncB 18C: NY 1997, Doubleday xxiv; 419 pp. $40. 0-385-41114-6.

3217 *Towner, W. Sibley* The book of Ecclesiastes. NIntB 5. 1997, ⇒209. 265-360.

3218 **Vílchez Líndez, J.** Eclesiastés o Qohelet. Nueva Biblia Española. Sapienciales 3: 1994, ⇒10,3284... 12,3154. RRivBib 45 (1997) 479-482 *(Prato, Gian Luigi)*.

3219 TVinel, Françoise GREGOIRE de Nysse: homélies sur l'Ecclésiaste. SC 416: 1996, ⇒12,3177. RVetChr 34 (1997) 161-5 *(Micunco, Giuseppe)*; JThS 48 (1997) 689-90 *(Meredith, Anthony)*.

3220 *Backhaus, Franz Josef* Widersprüche und Spannungen im Buch Qohelet: zu einem neueren Versuch, Spannungen und Widersprüche literarkritisch zu lösen;

3221 *Bohlen, Reinhold* Kohelet im Kontext hellenistischer Kultur. Das Buch Kohelet. BZAW 254: 1997, ⇒3214. 123-154/249-273.

3222 *Bohlen, Reinhold* Kritische Individualität und wache Skepsis: auf dem Weg zu einer religiösen Grunderfahrung im Buch Kohelet. TThZ 106 (1997) 22-38.

3223 *Bons, Eberhard* Das Buch Kohelet in jüdischer und christlicher Interpretation. Das Buch Kohelet. BZAW 254: 1997, ⇒3214. 327-361.

3224 *Carrière, Jean-Marie* "Tout est vanité": l'un des concepts de Qohélet. EstB 55 (1997) 297-311, 463-477.

3225 *Christianson, Eric S.* Qoheleth and the existential legacy of the Holocaust. HeyJ 38 (1997) 35-50.

3226 *D'Alario, Vittoria* Dall'uomo a Dio: l'itinerario della sapienza nella ricerca di Qohelet. PSV 35 (1997) 39-50.

3227 *Dobe, Timothy S. Qoheleth and the Lao Tzu*: an experiment with wisdom. ChFe 40/2 (1997) 129-148.

3228 **Fischer, Alexander A.** Skepsis oder Furcht Gottes?: Studien zur Komposition und Theologie des Buches Kohelet. Diss. Marburg, 1996; DKaiser, O.: BZAW 247: B 1997, De Gruyter x; 289 pp. 3-11-015458-7.

3229 *Harrison, C. Robert* Qoheleth among the sociologists. Bibl.Interp. 5 (1997) 160-180.

3230 *Hossfeld, Frank-Lothar* Die theologische Relevanz des Buches Kohelet. Das Buch Kohelet. BZAW 254: 1997, ⇒3214. 377-389.

3231 *Jong, Stephan de* A book on labour: the structuring principles and the main theme of the book of Qohelet. Poetical Books. 1997 <1992>, ⇒184. <sup>E</sup>Clines, David J.A., 222-230.

3232 *Jong, Stephan de* God in the book of Qohelet: a reappraisal of Qohelet's place in Old Testament theology. VT 47 (1997) 154-167.

3233 *Krüger, Thomas* Das Gute und die Güter: Erwägungen zur Bedeutung von טוב und טובה im Qoheletbuch. ThZ 53 (1997) 53-63.

3234 *Krüger, Thomas* Die Rezeption der Tora im Buch Kohelet;

3235 *Kutschera, Franz* Kohelet: Leben im Angesicht des Todes. Das Buch Kohelet. BZAW 254: 1997, ⇒3214. 303-325/363-376.

3236 **Lavatori, Renzo; Sole, Luciano** Qohelet, l'uomo dal cuore libero. Lettura pastorale della bibbia 2: Bo 1997, Dehoniane 142 pp. L19.000. 88-10-20148-5 [EThL 74,427—Lust, J.].

3237 *Lavoie, Jean-Jacques* Qohélet: une critique moderne de la Bible. 1995, ⇒11/1,1996. <sup>R</sup>RivBib 45 (1997) 356-361 *(Bianchi, F.)*.

3238 *Leanza, Sandro* A proposito di una recente edizione del presunto "Commentario all'Ecclesiaste" di EVAGRIO Pontico. RSLR 33 (1997) 365-398 [⇒9,3385... 12,3152].

3239 *Levine, Étan* The humor in Qohelet. ZAW 109 (1997) 71-83.

3240 *Lohfink, Norbert* Das Koheletbuch: Strukturen und Struktur. Das Buch Kohelet. BZAW 254: 1997, ⇒3214. 39-121.

3241 *Moreno García, Abdón; Boira Sales, José* Concepción Jeronimiana de los sentidos bíblicos en el comentario a Qohélet. EstB 55 (1997) 239-262.

3242 *Moreno García, Abdón; Boira Sales, José* Fuentes y contenido teológico del Comentario a Qohélet de S. JERONIMO. ASEs 14 (1997) 443-475.

3243 *Moyise, Steve* Is life futile?: Paul and Ecclesiastes. ET 108 (1997) 178-179.

3244 *Müller, Hans-Peter* Travestien und geistige Landschaften: zum Hintergrund einiger Motive bei Kohelet und im Hohenlied. ZAW 109 (1997) 557-574.

3245 **Nieto Renteria, Francisco** 'Pero yo alabo la alegría' (Ecl. 8,15): el gozo en el libro de Qohelet. Diss. Pont. Univ. Gregoriana 1997; <sup>D</sup>*Bretón, Santiago:* 245 pp. [RTL 29,579].

3246 *Okorie, A.M.* ¡Vanidad de vanidades!: todo es vanidad: el verdicto del Eclesiastés. RevBib 59/3 (1997) 129-133.

3247 *Reitman, James S.* The structure and unity of Ecclesiastes. BS 154 (1997) 297-319; *Rose, Martin* Querdenken mit und über Qohelet. ThZ 53 (1997) 83-96 [Dt 23,22; Qoh 4,17; 5,1-6].

3248 *Rudman, Dominic* Qohelet's use of לפני. JNSL 23/2 (1997) 143-150;

3249 Woman as divine agent in Ecclesiastes. JBL 116 (1997) 411-427.

3250 *Sacchi, Paolo* Il problema del tempo in Qohelet. PSV 36 (1997) 73-83.

3251 *Schelling, Piet* Roeach in Prediker. ITBT 5/5 (1997) 28-30.

3252 *Shead, Andrew G.* Reading Ecclesiastes "epilogically". TynB 48 (1997) 67-91.

3253 *Sneed, Mark* Qoheleth as 'deconstructionist': 'it is I, the Lord, your Redeemer ... who turns sages back and makes their knowledge nonsense' (Is 44:24-25). OTEs 10 (1997) 303-311.

3254 *Uehlinger, Christoph* Qohelet im Horizont mesopotamischer, levantinischer und ägyptischer Weisheitsliteratur der persischen und hellenistischen Zeit. Das Buch Kohelet. BZAW 254: 1997, ⇒3214. 155-247.

3255 *Vinel, Françoise* Accumulation de ὅτι dans l'Ecclésiaste: brouillage du sens ou force rhétorique?. IX Congress IOSCS. SCSt 45: 1997, ⇒340. ETaylor, Bernard A., 391-401.

3256 **Vinel, Françoise** Que rest-t-il des *Homélies sur l'Ecclésiaste* de GREGOIRE de Nysse dans les *Chaînes sur l'Ecclésiaste*?. StPatr 32: 1997, ⇒351. ELivingstone, Elizabeth A., 220-225.

3257 *Vogel, Dan* Koheleth and the modern times. JBQ 25 (1997) 143-9.

3258 *Whybray, R.N.* Qoheleth, preacher of joy. Poetical Books. 1997 <1982>, ⇒184. EClines, David J.A., 188-198.

3259 *Schwienhorst-Schönberger, Ludger* "Zum Lachen sprach ich: Wie dumm! und zur Freude: Was bringt sie ein?" (Koh 2,2). US 52 (1997) 294-303.

3260 *Görg, Manfred* Zu einer bekannten Paronomasie in Koh 2,8. BN 90 (1997) 5-7.

3261 *Schwienhorst-Schönberger, Ludger* Leben in der Gegenwart: Kohelet 3,1-9. BiLi 70 (1997) 285-289.

3262 *Marböck, Johannes* Kohelet und Sirach: eine vielschichtige Beziehung. Das Buch Kohelet. BZAW 254: 1997, ⇒3214. 275-301 [Sir 39,12-35; Qoh 3,11].

3263 *Lux, Rüdiger* "Denn es ist kein Mensch so gerecht auf Erden, daß er nur Gutes tue ..." Recht und Gerechtigkeit aus der Sicht des Predigers Salomo. ZThK 94 (1997) 263-287 [Qoh 3,16-22; 5,7-8; 7,15-29; 8,1-20; 9,1-10].

3264 *Wright, Addison G.* The poor but wise youth and the old but foolish king (Qoh 4:13-16). CBQ.MS 29: 1997, ⇒69. FMURPHY R., 142-154.

3265 *Rudman, Dominic* A contextual reading of Ecclesiastes 4:13-16. JBL 116 (1997) 57-73.

3266 *Lavoie, Jean-Jacques* Critique cultuelle et doute existentiel: étude de Qo 4,17-5,6. SR 26 (1997) 147-167.

3267 *Zschoch, Hellmut* Martin LUTHERs Argumentation mit Eccl 7,21 in der Auseinandersetzung mit Jacobus LATOMUS [Martin Luther's argument with Eccl. 7:21 in the controversy with Jacobus Latomus]. Adapted by *Posset, Franz*: Luther Digest 5 (1997) 24-6.

3268 *Backhaus, F.J.* Qohelet und der sogenannte Tun-Ergehen-Zusammenhang. BN 89 (1997) 30-61 [Qoh 8,10-15].

3269 **Pahk, Johan Yeong-Sik** Il canto della gioia in Dio: l'itinerario sapienziale espresso dall'unitá letteraria in Qohelet 8,16-9,10 e il parallelo di Gilgames Me. iii. 1996, ⇒12,3186. RBoSm 67/1 (1997) 106-107 *(Rebić, Adalbert)*.

3270 *Rudman, Dominic* The translation and interpretation of Eccl 8:17A. JNSL 23/1 (1997) 109-116.

3271 *Lavoie, Jean-Jacques* La philosophie politique de Qohélet 9,13-16. ScEs 49 (1997) 314-328.

3272 *Krüger, Thomas* "Wertvoller als Weisheit und Ehre ist wenig Torheit" (Kohelet 10,1). BN 89 (1997) 62-75.

3273 *Seow, C.L.* "Beyond them, my son, be warned": the epilogue of Qohelet revisited. CBQ.MS 29: 1997, ⇒69. FMURPHY R., 125-141 [Qoh 12,9-14].

3274 *Fox, Michael V.* Aging and death in Qohelet 12. Poetical Books. 1997, <1988>, ⇒184. ᴱClines, David J.A., 199-221.

## E7.8 *Liber Sapientiae—*Wisdom of Solomon

3275 **Gilbert, Maurice** La sapienza di Salomone. 1995, ⇒11/1,2027. ᴿCivCatt 148 III (1997) 94-95 *(Scaiola, D.)*.
3276 **Grabbe, Lester L.** Wisdom of Solomon. Guides to Apocrypha & Pseudepigrapha: Shf 1997, Academic 106 pp. £8/$12.50. 1-85075-762-3.
3277 *Kolarcik, Michael* The book of Wisdom. NIntB 5. 1997, ⇒209. 435-600.
3278 *Minette de Tillesse, Caetano* Sabedoria. RBB 14/1-3 (1997) 210-213.
3279 **Schenker, Adrian** Il libro della Sapienza. Guide spirituali all'Antico Testamento: R 1996, Città Nuova 131 pp. 88-311-3743-3.
3280 *Scoralick, Ruth* Ein Literaturüberblick zum Buch der Weisheit Salomos. BiKi 52 (1997) 200-203.

3281 **Cheon, Samuel** The Exodus story in the Wisdom of Solomon: a study in biblical interpretation. JSP.S 23: Shf 1997, Academic 169 pp. Bibl. £27.50/$45. 0-85075-670-8.
3282 *Della Corte, Ernesto* Il libro della Sapienza: parola di Dio e parola dell'uomo. 1997, ⇒30. ᶠGiordano M., 81-102.
3283 *Engel, Helmut* Ein alttestamentliches Buch aus der Zeit Jesu. BiKi 52 (1997) 158-165.
3284 *Leemans, Johan* Athanasius and the book of Wisdom. Sum. 368. EThL 73 (1997) 349-368.
3285 *Miranda, Peter* Das Schicksal der Gerechten in der biblischen Tradition. BiKi 52 (1997) 187-190.
3286 *Poniży, Bogdan* Etniczność tradycji a problem religijnego uniwersalizmu w Księdze Mądrości [Ethnicity of tradition and religious universalism in the Wisdom of Solomon]. 1997, ⇒52. ᶠLach J., 303-324. P.
3287 *Schroer, Silvia* Vom Text zum Kontext: Versuche der Situierung des Buches der Weisheit in der religiösen Zeitgeschichte und ihre feministische Relevanz. BiKi 52 (1997) 174-180.

3288 *Neher, Martin* Der Weg zur Unsterblichkeit in der Sapientia Salomonis. Engel und Dämonen. FARG 29: 1997, ⇒343. ᴱAhn, Gregor, 121-136 [Wis 1,11-15].
3289 *Schmitt, Armin* Skepsis, Bedrängnis und Hoffnung in Weish 1,16-2,24: "und danach werden wir sein, als wären wir nie gewesen" (Weish 2,2). BiKi 52 (1997) 166-173.
3290 *Beentjes, Pancratius C.* Wisdom of Solomon 3,1-4,19 and the book of Isaiah. BEThL 132: 1997, ⇒12. ᶠBeuken W., 413-420.
3291 **Enns, Peter** Exodus retold: ancient exegesis of the departure from Egypt in Wis 10:15-21 and 19:1-9. Diss. Harvard, 1994; ᴰ*Kugel, J.L.*: HSM 57: Atlanta 1997, Scholars ix; 204 pp. $30. 0-7885-0403-7 [RB 105,310].
3292 *Strotmann, Angelika* Die Pädagogik Gottes: Überlegungen zum strafenden und wohltätigen Handeln Gottes in Weish 11-19. BiKi 52 (1997) 181-186.

3293  *Weitzman, Michael* Two curious passages in the Peshitta of Wisdom. IOSCS. SCSt 45: 1997, ⇒340. [E]Taylor, Bernard A., 137-151 [Wis 11,13-15; 17,4-15; Lam 3,1].

3294  *Mazzinghi, Luca* La barca della provvidenza: Sap 14,1-10 e la figura di Iside. Som., sum. 89. VivH 8 (1997) 61-90.

3295  *Gilbert, Maurice* The last pages of the Wisdom of Solomon. PIBA 20 (1997) 48-61 [Wis 16-19].

3296  **Dumoulin, P.** Entre la manne... Sg 16,15-17,1a. AnBib 132: 1994, ⇒10,3325... 12,3206. [R]CivCatt 148 I (1997) 403-404 *(Scaiola, D.)*.

3297  **Mazzinghi, Luca** Notte di paura e di luce: esegesi di Sap 17,1-18,4. AnBib 134: 1995, ⇒11/1,2042; 12,3208. [R]NRTh 119 (1997) 105-106 *(Ska, J.L.)*; Henoch 19/1 (1997) 119-121 *(Sacchi, Paolo)*.

## E7.9 *Ecclesiasticus, Siracides;* Wisdom of Jesus Sirach

3298  [E]**Beentjes, Pancratius C.** The book of Ben Sira in modern research: proceedings of the first International Ben Sira Conference, 28-31 July 1996 Soesterberg, Netherlands. BZAW 255: B 1997, De Gruyter x; 233 pp. DM152. 3-11-015673-3.

3299  **Beentjes, Pancratius C.** The book of Ben Sira in Hebrew: a text edition of all extant Hebrew manuscripts and synopsis of all parallel Hebrew Ben Sira texts. VT.S 68: Lei 1997, Brill viii; 183 pp. ƒ135. 90-04-10767-3.

3300  *Beentjes, Pancratius C.* Reading the Hebrew Ben Sira manuscripts synoptically: a new hypothesis. The book of Ben Sira in modern research. BZAW 255: 1997, ⇒3298. 95-111.

3301  *Böhmisch, Franz* Die Textformen des Sirachbuches und ihre Zielgruppen. PzB 6 (1997) 87-122.

3302  *Calduch-Benages, Nuria* Il libro di Sirach: saggio di bibliografia recente (1984-1994). EL 111 (1997) 419-433; *Ceresko, Anthony R.* The liberative strategy of Ben Sira: the sage as prophet. TJT 13 (1997) 169-185.

3303  *Crenshaw, James L.* The book of Sirach. NIntB 5. 1997, ⇒209. 601-867.

**Doré, Daniel** Eclesiastés y Eclesiástico ⇒3207.

3304  *Fassberg, S.E.* On the syntax of dependent clauses in Ben Sira. The Hebrew of the DSS. StTDJ 26: 1997, ⇒369. [E]Muraoka, Takamitsu, 56-71.

3305  *Gilbert, Maurice* The Hebrew texts of Ben Sira a hundred years after their discovery. PIBA 20 (1997) 9-23.

3306  *Hurvitz, Avi* The linguistic status of Ben Sira as a link between Biblical and Mishnaic Hebrew: lexicographical aspects. The Hebrew of the DSS. StTDJ 26: 1997, ⇒369. [E]Muraoka, Takamitsu, 72-86.

3307  **Legrand, Thierry** Le Siracide: problèmes textuels et théologiques de la recension. Diss. Strasbourg 1997; [D]*Philonenko, M.*: 774 pp. [EThL 74,233*].

3308  *Martone, Corrado* Ben Sira manuscripts from Qumran and Masada. The book of Ben Sira in modern research. BZAW 255: 1997, ⇒3298. 81-94.

3309  *Minette de Tillesse, Caetano* Sirácida. RBB 14/1-3 (1997) 189-193.

3310  **Minissale, Antonino** La versione greca del Siracide. AnBib 133: 1995, ⇒11/1,2043; 12,3211. [R]RdT 38 (1997) 125-127 *(Prato, Gian Luigi)*; Bib 78 (1997) 120-121 *(Raurell, Frederic)*.

3311 *Müller, Augustin R.* Eine neue Textausgabe von Jesus Sirach. BN 89 (1997) 19-21.
3312 *Reif, Stefan C.* The discovery of the Cambridge Genizah fragments of Ben Sira: scholars and texts;
3313 *Reiterer, Friedrich Vinzenz* Review of recent research on the book of Ben Sira (1980-1996). The book of Ben Sira in modern research. BZAW 255: 1997, ⇒3298. 1-22/23-60.
3314 *Rizzi, Giovanni* La versione greca del Siracide. RivBib 45 (1997) 347-351.
3315 *Romero, Elena* Una versión judeoespañola de *Los relatos de Ben-Sira* según un manuscrito de la Guenizá de El Cairo. Res., sum. 428. Sef. 57 (1997) 399-428.
3316 ᴱ**Thiele, Walter** Sirach (Ecclesiasticus). Vetus Latina 11/2. 1992-1996. Fasc. 4-6. ⇒12,3212. ᴿJThS 48 (1997) 565-567 *(Elliott, J.K.).*
3317 *Thiele, Walter* Die lateinischen Siratexte als Zeugnis der griechischen Sirachüberlieferung. 1997, ⇒92. ᶠSТUНLМАСНЕК P., 394-402.

3318 *Böhmisch, Franz* "Haec omnia liber vitae": zur Theologie der erweiterten Textformen des Sirachbuches. SNTU.A 22 (1997) 160-180.
3319 *Calduch i Benages, Núria* Elements d'inculturació hellenista en el llibre de Ben Sira: els viatges. La Bíblia i el Mediterrani. 1997, ⇒385. ᴱBorrell, d'Agustí, 113-121;
3320 Ben Sira y el canon de las escrituras. Gr. 78 (1997) 357-370.
3321 *Camp, Claudia V.* Honor and shame in Ben Sira: anthropological and theological reflections. The book of Ben Sira in modern research. BZAW 255: 1997, ⇒3298. 171-187;
3322 Honor, shame, and the hermeneutics of Ben Sira's Ms C. CBQ.MS 29: 1997, ⇒69. ᶠМURРНY R., 157-171.
3323 *Chmiel, Jerzy* Etyczne pouczenia hebrajskich dodatków Księgi Syracha (11 i 51) [Ethical teaching of some Hebrew additions to Ben Sira (11 and 51) (translation and commentary)]. 1997, ⇒52. ᶠŁАСН J., 77-80. **P**;
3324 Księga Syracha zwornik judaizmu palestyńskiego i hellenistycznego: uwagi hermeneutyczne [Le livre de Ben Sira ou Siracide clef de voûte du judaïsme palestinien et hellénistique: remarques herméneutiques]. Rés. 55. WST 10 (1997) 51-55.
3325 *Corley, Jeremy* Rediscovering Sirach. ScrB 27 (1997) 2-7.
3326 *Crenshaw, James L.* The primacy of listening in Ben Sira's pedagogy. CBQ.MS 29: 1997, ⇒69. ᶠМURРНY R., 172-187.
3327 *Di Lella, Alexander A.* Wisdom in Ben Sira. BiTod 35 (1997) 136-140.
3328 *Harrington, Daniel J.* Two early Jewish approaches to wisdom: Sirach and Qumran sapiential work A. JSPE 16 (1997) 25-38.
3329 *Jüngling, Hans-Winfried* Der Bauplan des Buches Jesus Sirach. 'Den Armen eine frohe Botschaft'. 1997, ⇒46. ᶠКАМРНАUS F., 89-105 [ThRv 94,625].
3330 *Kaddari, Menahem Zevi* The syntax of כִּי in the language of Ben Sira. The Hebrew of the DSS. StTDJ 26: 1997, ⇒369. ᴱMuraoka, Takamitsu, 87-91.

3331  *Kaiser, Otto* Der Tod als Schicksal und Aufgabe bei Ben Sira. Engel und Dämonen. FARG 29: 1997, ⇒343. ᴱAhn, Gregor, 75-89.

3332  *Liesen, Jan* First-person passages in the book of Ben Sira. PIBA 20 (1997) 24-47.

3333  **Marböck, Johannes** Gottes Weisheit unter uns: zur Theologie des Buches Sirach. 1995, ⇒11/1,55; 12,3223. ᴿRivBib 45 (1997) 477-479 *(Prato, Gian Luigi)*.

3334  *Marböck, Johannes* Structure and redaction history of the book of Ben Sira: review and prospects. The book of Ben Sira in modern research. BZAW 255: 1997, ⇒3298. 61-79.

3335  *Minissale, Antonino* A descriptive feature of the Greek Sirach: the effect instead of the cause. IX Congress IOSCS. SCSt 45: 1997, ⇒340. ᴱTaylor, Bernard A., 421-429.

3336  **Petraglio, Renzo** Il libro... Ben Sira. 1993, ⇒9,3447... 11/1,2045. ᴿREB 57 (1997) 480-482 *(Garmus, Ludovico)*.

3337  **Schrader, Lutz** Leiden und Gerechtigkeit: Studien zur Theologie und Textgeschichte des Sirachbuches. BET 27: Fra 1994, Lang 327 pp. DM89. 3-631-47279-X. ᴿBijdr. 58 (1997) 210-212 *(Beentjes, P.C.)*.

3338  *Van Peursen, W.Th.* Periphrastic tenses in Ben Sira. The Hebrew of the DSS. StTDJ 26: 1997, ⇒369. ᴱMuraoka, Takamitsu, 158-173.

3339  **Wagner, Christian** Die Septuaginta-Hapaxlegomena im Buch Jesus Sirach: Untersuchungen zu Wortwahl und Wortbildung unter besonderer Berücksichtigung des textkritischen und übersetzungstechnischen Aspekts. Diss. Regensburg 1997; ᴰ*Schmitt* [BZ 42,318].

3340  **Wischmeyer, Oda** Die Kultur des Buches Jesus Sirach. BZNW 77: 1995, ⇒11/1,2061. ᴿJBL 115 (1996) (1997) 344-345 *(Lang, B.)*.

3341  *Wright, Benjamin G. III* "Fear the Lord and honor the priest": Ben Sira as defender of the Jerusalem priesthood. The book of Ben Sira in modern research. BZAW 255: 1997, ⇒3298. 189-222.

3342  *Di Lella, Alexander A.* Fear of the Lord as wisdom: Ben Sira 1,11-30. The book of Ben Sira in modern research. BZAW 255: 1997, ⇒3298. 113-133.

3343  *Calduch-Benages, Nuria* Traducir-interpretar: la versión siríaca de Sirácida 1. EstB 55 (1997) 313-340;

3344  Trial motif in the book of Ben Sira with special reference to Sir 2,1-6. The book of Ben Sira in modern research. BZAW 255: 1997, ⇒3298. 135-151.

3345  *Di Lella, Alexander A.* Fear of the Lord and belief and hope in the Lord amid trials: Sirach 2:1-18. CBQ.MS 29: 1997, ⇒69. ᶠMᴜʀᴘʜʏ R., 188-204.

3346  **Calduch Benages, Nuria** En el crisol de la prueba: estudio exegético de Sir 2. Asociación Bíblica Española 32: Estella 1997, Verbo Divino xviii; 370 pp. 84-8169-193-3.

3347  *Pezhumkattil, Abraham* Wisdom—seeking: a way to moral perfection: a study on Sir 6:18-37. BiBh 23 (1997) 129-150.

3348  *Gilbert, Maurice* Wisdom of the poor: Ben Sira 10,19-11,6. The book of Ben Sira in modern research. BZAW 255: 1997, ⇒3298. 153-169.

3349 *Crenshaw, James L.* The restraint of reason, the humility of prayer. BJSt 313: 1997, ⇒85. [F]SILBERMAN L., 81-97 [Prov 30,1-14; Sir 22,27-23,6; 36,1-22.

3350 *Zakovitch, Yair* "Was it not at his hand the sun stopped?" (Ben Sira 46:6): a chapter in literary archaeology. 1997, ⇒34. [M]GREENBERG M., 107*-114* [Josh 10,12-14] H.

3351 *Petraglio, Renzo* Le Siracide et l'Ancien Testament: relecture et tendances. Apocrypha 8 (1997) 287-301 [Sir 46,13-20].

3352 **Hildesheim, Ralph** Bis daß ein Prophet...: Untersuchungen zum Prophetenverständnis des Ben Sira in Sir 48,1-49,16. TThSt 58: 1996, ⇒12,3245. [R]ThLZ 122 (1997) 896-898 *(Sauer, Georg)*.

3353 *Fleischer, Ezra* Additional fragments of the "rhymed Ben Sira". 1997, ⇒34. [M]GREENBERG M., 205*-217* [Ps 136; Sir 51,21-35]. H.

## VII. Libri prophetici VT

### E8.1 Prophetismus

3354 **Aberbach, David** Imperialism and biblical prophecy, 750-500 BCE. 1993, ⇒9,3454; 10,3342. [R]TJT 13/1 (1997) 87-88 *(Delsnyder, Robert)*.

3355 **Abrego de Lacy, José Maria** I libri profetici. 1996, ⇒12,3247. Protest. 52/1 (1997) 75 *(Tron, Claudio)*.

3356 **Aguiar Retes, Carlos** El ayuno agradable a YHWH: la crítica de los profetas y la posición de Jesús. Diss. Pont. Univ. Gregoriana; [D]*Simian-Yofre, Horacio*: R 1997, 81 pp. Excerpt.

3357 **Aune, David Edward** La profezia nel primo cristianesimo e il mondo mediterraneo antico. BSSTB 10: 1996, ⇒12,3249. [R]StPat 44/1 (1997) 191-194 *(Leonardi, Giovanni)*; Anton. 72 (1997) 701-703 *(Nobile, Marco)*; LASBF 47 (1997) 614-617 *(Chrupcała, Lesław Daniel)*.

3358 *Bammel, Ernst* Prophetie und Deutung. Judaica et Paulina. WUNT 91: 1997 <1989>, ⇒109. 215-221.

3359 *Bauer, Uwe F.* Israel und die Völker in der Hebräischen Bibel: Anmerkungen zu einigen neueren Beiträgen und Positionen. KuI 12/2 (1997) 148-160.

3360 *Bird, Phyllis A.* Poor man or poor woman?: gendering the poor in prophetic texts. Missing persons. 1997 <1996>, ⇒114. 67-78.

3361 **Blenkinsopp, Joseph** A history of prophecy in Israel. LVL [2]1997, Westminster xiii; 291 pp. $26 [CBQ 59,817];

3362 Storia della profezia in Israele. Brescia 1997, Queriniana 314 pp. L46.000. 88-399-2022-6 [RivBib 45,505].

3363 *Boadt, Lawrence* The poetry of prophetic persuasion: preserving the prophet's persona. CBQ 59 (1997) 1-21.

3364 **Bosshard-Nepustil, Erich** Rezeptionen von Jesaia 1-39 im Zwölfprophetenbuch: Untersuchungen zur literarischen Verbindung von Prophetenbüchern in babylonischer und persischer Zeit. Diss. [D]*Steck, O.H.*: OBO 154: Gö 1997, Vandenhoeck & R xiii; 521 pp. DM164. 3-525-53790-5.

3365  **Brauer, Bernd** Das Bild der Unheilsprophetie Israels in der frühen soziologisch orientierten Forschung. Diss. Münster 1996-1997; <sup>D</sup>*Müller, H.-P.* [ThLZ 122,764].

3366  **Brenneman, James E.** Canons in conflict: negotiating texts in true and false prophecy. NY 1997, OUP xvii; 228 pp. Bibl. $45. 0-19-510909-0 [NThAR 1998,97].

3367  <sup>E</sup>**Brenner, Athalya** A feminist companion to the latter prophets. 1995, ⇒11/1,68. <sup>R</sup>CBQ 59 (1997) 110-112 *(Green, Barbara)*.

3368  **Callahan, Tim** Bible prophecy: failure or fulfillment?. Altadena, Calif. 1997, Millennium xii; 274 pp. 0-9655047-0-0 [NThAR 1998,98].

3369  **Carlebach, Joseph** Jesajas, Jirmija, Jecheskel. Basel 1994, Morascha 135 pp. <sup>R</sup>FrRu 4 (1997) 282-284 *(Franz-Klauser, Olivia)*; REJ 156 (1997) 247-249 *(Hayoun, Maurice-Ruben)*.

3370  *Carroll, Robert P.* Deportation and diasporic discourses in the prophetic literature. Exile. JSJ.S 56: 1997, ⇒227. <sup>E</sup>Scott, James M., 63-85.

3371  *Champeaux, Jacqueline* De la parole à l'écriture: essai sur le langage des oracles. Oracles. 1997, ⇒374. <sup>E</sup>Heintz, J.-G., 405-438.

3372  **Chenu, Bruno** L'urgence prophétique: Dieu au défi de l'histoire. P 1997, Bayard 290 pp. F120. 2-227-43652-2 [RTL 28,291].

3373  **Clements, Ronald E.** Old Testament prophecy: from oracles to canon. 1996, CBQ 59 (1997) 409-410 *(Nogalski, James D.)*; HebStud 38 (1997) 134-136 *(Schniedewind, William)*.

3374  *Clements, Ronald E.* Max WEBER, charisma and biblical prophecy. Prophecy and prophets. 1997, ⇒199. <sup>E</sup>Gitay, Yehoshua, 89-108.

3375  *Clements, Ronald Ernest* Introduction: the interpretation of Old Testament prophecy, 1965-1995. Old Testament prophecy: from oracles to canon. 1996, ⇒12,3263. 1-19.

3376  **Collins, Terence** The mantle of Elijah: the redaction criticism of the prophetical books. BiSer 20: 1993, ⇒9,3466... 12,3264. <sup>R</sup>BZ 41 (1997) 119-121 *(Becker, Joachim)*.

3377  **Cook, Stephen L.** Prophecy & apocalypticism. 1995, ⇒11/1,2106. <sup>R</sup>JR 77 (1997) 655-656 *(Petersen, David L.)*.

3378  *Cortese, Enzo* Per una teologia dello Spirito nel tardo profetismo. Sum. 451. LASBF 47 (1997) 9-32.

3379  **Darsey, James** The prophetic tradition and radical rhetoric in America. NY 1997, New York University Press 279 pp. $35 [ThTo 55,474s—Brueggemann, Walter].

3380  **Dassmann, Ernst** Frühchristliche Prophetenexegese. 1996, ⇒12,3266. <sup>R</sup>AHIg 6 (1997) 514-515 *(Viciano, A.)*.

3381  *Dautzenberg, Gerhard* Propheten/Prophetie: Neues Testament und Alte Kirche. TRE 27. 1997, ⇒419. 503-511.

3382  *Durand, Jean-Marie* Les prophéties des textes de Mari. Oracles. 1997, ⇒374. <sup>E</sup>Heintz, J.-G., 115-134.

3383  **Eaton, John** Mysterious messengers: a course on Hebrew prophecy from Amos onwards. L 1997, SCM x; 214 pp. £13. 0-334-02706-3 [RRT 1998/1, 89].

3384  *Fahd, T.* De l'oracle à la prophétie en Arabie. Oracles. 1997, ⇒374. <sup>E</sup>Heintz, J.-G., 231-258.

3385  *Freedman, David Noel* Between God and man: prophets in ancient Israel. Prophecy and prophets. 1997, ⇒199. <sup>E</sup>Gitay, Yehoshua, 57-87;

3386  Discourse on prophetic discourse < 1983 > ;
3387  Headings in the books of the eighth-century prophets < 1987 >.
      Divine Commitment 1, 1997, ⇒124. 350-366/367-382.
3388  *Giordani, G.* Il profetismo: ascolto, disobbedienza e ordinamento
      della storia: esempi di obbedienza e disobbedienza nella predica-
      zione profetica. L'obbedienza. 1997, ⇒216. ᴱMarrocu, Giuseppe,
      81-92.
3389  *Gitay, Zefira* Prophet and prophecy: an artist dilemma. Prophecy
      and prophets. 1997, ⇒199. ᴱGitay, Yehoshua, 149-163.
3390  *González Lamadrid, Antonio* Verdaderos y falsos profetas. NuMu
      53 (1997) 81-88.
3391  ᴱ**Gordon, Robert P.** 'The place is too small for us': the Israelite
      prophets in recent scholarship. 1995, ⇒11/1,83. ᴿCBQ 59 (1997)
      802-804 *(Nash, Kathleen S.).*
3392  *Gosling, F.A.* W. Robertson SMITH: a paradigm for exegesis?.
      SJOT 11 (1997) 223-231.
3393  **Griffin, William Paul** The God of the prophets: an analysis of
      divine action. JSOT.S 249: Shf 1997, Academic 328 pp. Bibl. 1-
      85075-677-5.
3394  **Hayes, Katherine M.** 'The earth mourns': earth as actor in a pro-
      phetic metaphor. Diss. Washington 1997; ᴰ*Gropp, D.*: microfilm:
      Ann Arbor [RTL 29,578].
3395  **Heijkoop, Hendrik Leendert** L'avenir selon les prophéties de la
      bible. Vevey 1997, Bibles et Traités Chrétiens. 191 pp. 2-88458--
      035-2 [NThAR 1998,365].
      ᴱ**Heintz, Jean-Georges** Oracles et prophéties dans l'antiquité
      ⇒374.
3396  *Heintz, Jean-Georges* La 'fin' des prophètes bibliques?: nouvelles
      théories et documents sémitiques anciens. Oracles. 1997, ⇒374.
      ᴱHeintz, J.-G., 195-214.
3397  *Hoffman, Yair* Prophecy and soothsaying. 1997, ⇒34.
      ᴹGREENBERG M., 221-243 [Dt 13,2-6; 18,9-22; Jer 18,7-10; 1;
      26; 28].
3398  **Huffmon, Herbert B.** The expansion of prophecy in the Mari archi-
      ves: new texts, new readings, new information. Prophecy and pro-
      phets. 1997, ⇒199. ᴱGitay, Yehoshua, 7-22.
3399  *Jeremias, Jörg* "Wahre" und "falsche" Prophetie im Alten Testa-
      ment: Entwicklungslinien eines Grundsatzkonfliktes. ThBeitr 28
      (1997) 343-349.
3400  *Koch, Klaus* Propheten/Prophetie: in Israel und seiner Umwelt.
      TRE 27. 1997, ⇒419. 477-499.
3401  **Koenen, Klaus** Heil den Gerechten—Unheil den Sündern! ... zur
      Theologie der Prophetenbücher. BZAW 229: 1994, ⇒10,3361
      ...12,3281. ᴿJBL 115 (1996) 526-529 *(Sweeney, Marvin A.).*
3402  *Kratz, Reinhard G.* Die Redaktion der Prophetenbücher. OBO 153:
      1997, ᶠSTECK O., 9-27.
3403  *Lemaire, André* Oracles, politique et littérature dans les royaumes
      araméens et transjordaniens (IXᵉ-VIIIᵉ s. av. n.è.). Oracles. 1997,
      ⇒374. ᴱHeintz, J.-G., 171-193.
3404  *Levison, John R.* Did the spirit withdraw from Israel?: an eva-
      luation of the earliest Jewish data. NTS 43 (1997) 35-57.
3405  **Marcus, David** From Balaam to Jonah: anti-prophetic satire in the
      Hebrew Bible. BJSt 30: 1995, ⇒11/1,2134; 12,3289. ᴿAJS Review
      22/1 (1997) 103-105 *(Noegel, Scott B.).*

3406 *Muthunayagam, D.J.* Poetic images in prophetic traditions. ATA Journal 5/1 (1997) 68-80 [ZID 23,439];
3407 Exilic and post exilic prophets and economic issues. ITS 34/1-3 (1997) 89-109 [= VFTW 20/1 (1997) 56-77].
3408 *Naᵓaman, Nadav* Prophetic stories as sources for the histories of Jehoshaphat and the Omrides. Sum. 173. Bib. 78 (1997) 153-173 [1 Kgs 17,1-22,38; 2 Kgs 1,2-10,28].
3409 **Parpola, Simo** Assyrian prophecies. Collab. *Reade, Julian*: State Archives of Assyria 9: Helsinki 1997, Helsinki University Press cxxi; 84 pp. 13 pl.; $43/$32. 951-570-167-8/6-X [RB 105,638].
3410 *Petersen, David L.* Rethinking the nature of prophetic literature. Prophecy and prophets. 1997, ⇒199. ᴱGitay, Yehoshua, 23-40.
3411 **Pindur, Gabriela** Rola patriarchów w przepowiadaniu prorockim [Le rôle des patriarches dans la prédication des prophètes]. Diss. Lublin 1997; ᴰ*Homerski, J.*: xxvi; 219 pp. [RTL 29,579]. **P.**
3412 **Prévost, Jean-Pierre** Pour lire les prophètes. 1995, ⇒11/1,2146; 12,3296. ᴿScrTh 29/2 (1997) 679-680 *(Ausín, S.)*;
3413 How to read the prophets. ᵀ*Bowden, John*: NY 1997, Continuum iv; 140 pp. $20. 0-8264-0943-1 [ThD 44,377—Heiser, W.C.].
3414 *Rendtorff, Rolf* Kontinuität und Diskontinuität in der alttestamentlichen Prophetie. ZAW 109 (1997) 169-187.
3415 *Reventlow, Henning Graf* The eschatologization of the prophetic books: a comparative study. Eschatology in the bible. JSOT.S 243: 1997, ⇒222. ᴱReventlow, Henning Graf, 169-188.
3416 *Rodríguez, Juan Carlos* Cuando duele la vida y la palabra. NuMu 53 (1997) 75-80.
3417 **Rofé, Alexander** Introduzione alla letteratura profetica. StBi 111: 1995, ⇒11/1,2151; 12,3301. ᴿGr. 78 (1997) 155-156 *(Conroy, Charles)*; RivBib 45 (1997) 482-484 *(Marconcini, Benito)*;
3418 Introduction to the prophetic literature. BiSe 21: Shf 1997, Academic 118 pp. 1-85075-805-0.
3419 ᴱ**Rusconi, Roberto** The book of prophecies edited by Christopher Coʟᴜᴍʙᴜs. ᵀ*Sullivan, Blair*: Repertorium Columbianum 3: Berkeley 1997, University of California Press xiv; 419 pp. $45 [SCJ 29,922ss—Barnes, Robin B.].
3420 *Safrai, Chana* Propheten/Prophetie: im Judentum. TRE 27. 1997, ⇒419. 499-503.
3421 **Simon, Uriel** Reading prophetic narratives. ᵀ*Schramm, Lenn J.*: ISBL: Bloomington 1997, Indiana University Press xx; 363 pp. Bibl. $45. 0-253-33227-3.
3422 *Sivatte, Rafael de* Monseñor Roᴍᴇʀo, los profetas de Israel y los ídolos: la religión, las potencias extranjeras, las armas, el poder. RLAT 14 (1997) 173-192.
3423 **Speyr, Adrienne von** The mission of the prophets. ᵀ*Kipp, David*; Foreword *Balthasar, Hans Urs von*: SF 1997, Ignatius 125 pp. $10. 0-89870-593-2 [ThD 44,384—Heiser, W. Charles].
3424 *Steck, Odil Hannes* Beobachtungen zur Sachbewegung vorexilischer Gerichtsprophetie. 1997, ⇒48. ᶠKɴɪᴇʀɪᴍ R., 328-337.
3425 *Strydom, J.G.* Where have all the prophets gone?: the new South Africa. OTEs 10 (1997) 494-511.
3426 **Surmar, Bohumil** Die Unterscheidung zwischen den wahren und falschen Propheten: eine Untersuchung aufgrund der Lehre des Rabbi Mᴀɪᴍoɴɪᴅᴇs auf dem Hintergrund der rabbinischen

Lehren, der griechischen und arabischen Philosophie und der Prophetologie des Islam. EHS.T 615: Bern 1997, Lang 272 pp. DM74. 3-906759-25-3 [ThLZ 125,397ss—Schreiner, Stefan].

3427 <sup>E</sup>**Taithe, Bertrand; Thornton, Tim** Prophecy: the power of inspired language in history 1300-2000. Themes in History: Gloucestershire 1997, Sutton viii; 216 pp. 0-7509-1332-0.

3428 *Tucker, Gene M.* Sin and "judgment" in the prophets. 1997, ⇒48. <sup>F</sup>KNIERIM R., 373-388.

3429 *Uehlinger, Christoph* Figurative policy, Propaganda und Prophetie. Congress volume 1995. VT.S 66: 1997, ⇒323. <sup>E</sup>Emerton, J.A., 297-349.

3430 <sup>E</sup>**Valerio, Adriana** Donna potere e profezia. La dracma 6: N 1995, D'Auria M. 300 pp. L49.000. 88-7092-109-3. <sup>R</sup>RdT 38 (1997) 136-139 *(Luzenberger, Alda de)*; CrSt 18/1 (1997) 239-242 *(Fontana, Paolo)*.

3431 **Van Dam, Cornelis** The Urim and Thummim: a means of revelation in ancient Israel. Diss. Kampen, 1986. WL 1997, Eisenbrauns xxiii; 296 pp. $34.50. 0-931464-83-8.

3432 <sup>F</sup>WATTS J., Forming prophetic literature. <sup>E</sup>**Watts, James W.; House, Paul R.**: JSOT.S 235: 1996, ⇒12,105. <sup>R</sup>ScrB 27 (1997) 82-83 *(O'Kane, Martin)*.

3433 **Weems, Renita J.** Battered love: marriage, sex, and violence in the Hebrew prophets. 1995, ⇒11/1,,2167. <sup>R</sup>JThS 48 (1997) 563-5 *(Dell, Katharine J.)*; CBQ 59 (1997) 362-363 *(Batto, Bernard F.)*.

3434 **Weems, Renita J.** Amor maltratado: matrimonio, sexo y violencia en los profetas hebreos. Bilbao 1997, Desclée de B 185 pp. 84-330-1249-5 [EE 73,514s—Aleixandre, Dolores].

3435 *Weippert, Manfred* 'Das Frühere, siehe, ist eingetroffen...': über Selbstzitate im altorientalischen Prophetenspruch. Oracles. 1997, ⇒374. <sup>E</sup>Heintz, J.-G., 147-169.

3436 **Wünsche, M.** Der Ausgang der urchristlichen Prophetie in der frühkatholischen Kirche: Untersuchung zu den Apostolischen Vätern, den Apologeten, IRENAEUS von Lyon und den antimontanistischen Anonymus. Stu 1997, Calwer 316 pp. <sup>R</sup>EstAg 32 (1997) 567-568 *(Luis, P. de)*.

3437 *Zincone, Sergio* Le omelie di Giovanni CRISOSTOMO 'De prophetiarum obscuritate'. StPatr 32: 1997, ⇒351. <sup>E</sup>Livingstone, Elizabeth A., 393-409.

3438 **Zucker, David J.** Israel's prophets. 1994, ⇒10,3376... 12,3315. <sup>R</sup>ScrTh 29/2 (1997) 678-679 *(Ausín, S.)*.

### E8.2 Proto-Isaias, *textus, commentarii*

3439 Bibliography of Isaiah;

3440 *Gelston, Anthony* Was the Peshitta of Isaiah of Christian origin?. Writing and reading... Isaiah. VT.S 70/2: 1997, ⇒181. <sup>E</sup>Broyles, Craig C., 717-771/563-582.

3441 <sup>E</sup>**Goshen-Gottstein, Moshe H.** The book of Isaiah. 1995, ⇒11/1,2177. <sup>R</sup>CBQ 59 (1997) 348-350 *(Althann, Robert)*.

3442 <sup>E</sup>**Greene-McCreight, Kathryn** Selections from John CALVIN's sermons on Isaiah. Theological interpretation. 1997, ⇒244. <sup>E</sup>Fowl, E., 186-198.

3443 <sup>E</sup>Gryson, Roger Esaias 1-39; 40,1-54,17. Die Reste der altlateini-
schen Bibel nach Petrus Sabatier 12: I, II Fasc. 1-7. 1987-1996,
⇒12,3322. <sup>R</sup>CBQ 59 (1997) 561-562 *(Cody, Aelred)*.

3444 **Kustár, Zoltán** 'Durch seine Wunden sind wir geheilt'—das Bild
der Krankheit und Züchtigung Israels im Jesajabuch: eine motiv-,
kompositions- und redaktionsgeschichtliche Untersuchung. Diss.
Halle-Wittenberg 1997; iii; 245 pp. [NThAR 1999,3].

3445 *LaRocca-Pitts, Beth* Isaiah and the future of Israel. BiTod 35
(1997) 204-209.

3446 *Linafelt, Tod* Speech and silence in the servant passages: towards a
final-form reading of the book of Isaiah. Theological interpretation.
1997, ⇒244. <sup>E</sup>Fowl, E., 199-209 [Isa 52-53].

3447 **Lohfink, Norbert; Zenger, Erich** Der Gott Israels und die Völker:
Untersuchungen zum Jesajabuch und zu den Psalmen. SBS 154:
1994, ⇒10,3402; 12,3327. <sup>R</sup>ThRv 93 (1997) 215-216 *(Schenker,
Adrian)*.

3448 **Marconcini, Benito** El libro de Isaías (1-39). 1995, 11/1,2185;
12,3329. <sup>R</sup>EfMex 15 (1997) 286-287 *(López López, Rafael)*; Augustinus 42 (1997) 424-425 *(Robles, Gabriel)*.

3449 Isaiah Mikra'ot gedolot 'haketer': a revised and augmented scientific ed. of 'Mikra'ot gedolot' based on the Aleppo Codex and early
medieval mss.      Ramat-Gan 1996, Bar-Ilan University Press 14,
406 pp. 965-266-180-7f [NThAR 1999,253]. H.

3450 *Porter, Stanley E.; Pearson, Brook W.R.* Isaiah through Greek
eyes: the Septuagint of Isaiah. Writing and reading... Isaiah. VT.S
70/2: 1997, ⇒181. <sup>E</sup>Broyles, Craig C., 531-546.

3451 *Raurell, Frederic* Isaïas-LXX i Isaïas-Qumran. RCatT 22 (1997)
395-407.

3452 *Rendtorff, Rolf* The book of Isaiah—a complex unity: synchronic
and diachronic reading. Prophecy and prophets. 1997, ⇒199.
<sup>E</sup>Gitay, Yehoshua, 109-128.

3453 <sup>E</sup>*Russell Christman, Angela* Selections from THEODORET of
Cyrus's Commentary on Isaiah. Theological interpretation. 1997,
⇒244. <sup>E</sup>Fowl, E., 173-185 [Isa 52-53].

3454 **Sawyer, John F.A.** The fifth gospel: Isaiah in the history of christianity. 1996, ⇒12,3337. <sup>R</sup>Theol. 100 (1997) 55-56 *(Houlden,
Leslie)*; Religion 27 (1997) 217-218 *(Blenkinsopp, Joseph)*; AThR
79 (1997) 626-627 *(Soulen, R. Kendall)*.

3455 **Seitz, Christopher R.** Isaiah 1-39. 1993, ⇒9,3518... 12,3338.
<sup>R</sup>BiOr 54 (1997) 445-446 *(Haak, Robert D.)*; AsbTJ 52 (1997) 99-
100 *(Oswalt, John N.)*.

3456 *Simian-Yofre, Horacio* Isaías: introducción y comentario. Comentario al Antiguo Testamento, 2. M 1997, Casa de la Biblia. 23-103
[AcBib 10/4,394].

3457 *Stoll, Claus-Dieter* Umstrittene Verfasserschaft am Beispiel des
Jesaja-Buches. TVGMS 424: 1997, ⇒59. <sup>F</sup>MAIER G., 165-187.

3458 **Sweeney, Marvin Alan** Isaiah 1-39: with an introduction to prophetic literature. FOTL 16: 1996, ⇒12,3346. <sup>R</sup>ScrB 27 (1997) 37-
39 *(Greenhalgh, Stephen)*; Anton. 72/1 (1997) 131-132 *(Nobile,
Marco)*; ThLZ 122 (1997) 545-546 *(Coggins, Richard)*; Bib. 78
(1997) 275-278 *(Carr, David)*; EThL 73 (1997) 160-161 *(Lust, J.)*;
VJTR 61 (1997) 131-132 *(Meagher, P.M.)*.

3459 *Tov, Emanuel* The text of Isaiah at Qumran. Writing and reading...
Isaiah. VT.S 70/2: 1997, ⇒181. <sup>E</sup>Broyles, Craig C., 491-511.

3460 **Waard, Jan de** A handbook on Isaiah. Textual Criticism and the Translator 1: WL 1997, Eisenbrauns xviii; 228 pp. Bibl. $29.50. 1-57506-023-X.

3461 **Wildberger, Hans** Isaiah 13-27: a continental commentary. <sup>T</sup>*Trapp, Thomas H.*: Continental commentaries: Mp 1997, Fortress x; 624 pp. $65. 0-8006-9509-7 [ThD 45,194—Heiser, W.C.].

### E8.3 Isaias 1-39, themata, versiculi

3462 *Barton, John* Ethics in the book of Isaiah. Writing and reading... Isaiah. VT.S 70/2: 1997, ⇒181. <sup>E</sup>Broyles, Craig C., 67-77.

3463 **Becker, Uwe** Jesaja—von der Botschaft zum Buch. FRLANT 178: Gö 1997, Vandenhoeck & R 346 pp. Diss.-Habil. Gö 1996; Bibl. DM148. 3-525-53862-6.

<sup>F</sup>BEUKEN W., Studies in the book of Isaiah ⇒12.

3464 *Brooke, George J.* Isaiah in the Pesharim and other Qumran texts;

3465 *Chilton, Bruce D.* Two in one: renderings of the book of Isaiah in Targum Jonathan. Writing and reading... Isaiah. VT.S 70/2: 1997, ⇒181. <sup>E</sup>Broyles, Craig C., 609-632/547-562.

3466 *Clements, Ronald E.* Zion as symbol and political reality: a central Isaianic quest. BEThL 132: 1997, ⇒12. <sup>F</sup>BEUKEN W., 3-17;

3467 "Arise, shine; for your light has come": a basic theme of the Isaianic tradition. Writing and reading... Isaiah. VT.S 70/2: 1997, ⇒181. <sup>E</sup>Broyles, Craig C., 441-454 [Isa 60,1-22].

3468 *Conrad, Edgar W.* Reading Isaiah and the Twelve as prophetic books. Writing and reading... Isaiah. VT.S 70/2: 1997, ⇒181. <sup>E</sup>Broyles, Craig C., 3-17.

3469 *Evans, Craig A.* The function of Isaiah in the New Testament. Writing and reading... Isaiah. VT.S 70/2: 1997, ⇒181. <sup>E</sup>Broyles, Craig C., 651-691.

3470 *Gitay, Yehoshua* Back to historical Isaiah: reflections on the act of reading. BEThL 132: 1997, ⇒12. <sup>F</sup>BEUKEN W., 63-72;

3471 Why metaphors?: a study of the texture of Isaiah. Writing and reading...Isaiah. VT.S 70/2: 1997, ⇒181. <sup>E</sup>Broyles, C.C., 57-65.

3472 *Hohnjec, Nikola* Teologija svjetlosti u proroka Izaije [Die Theologie des Lichtes im Jesajabuch]. 1997, ⇒96. <sup>F</sup>TOMICA C.; Zsfg. 144. 128-144. **Croatian.**

3473 **Kizhakkeyil, Sebastian** Prophet Isaiah and Zion. Diss. Pont. Athenaeum Antonianum 1997; <sup>D</sup>*Niccacci, A.*: Thesis ad Doctoratum 355: J 1997, xiv; 338 pp; pars publ. ix; 80 pp. [LASBF 47,646-648].

3474 *Knibb, Michael A.* Isaianic traditions in the Apocrypha and Pseudepigrapha;

3475 *Melugin, Roy F.* The book of Isaiah and the construction of meaning. Writing and reading... Isaiah. VT.S 70/2: 1997, ⇒181. <sup>E</sup>Broyles, Craig C., 633-650/39-55.

3476 **Pfaff, Heide-Marie** Die Entwicklung des Restgedankens in Jesaja 1-39. EHS.T 561: 1996, ⇒12,3356. <sup>R</sup>ThLZ 122 (1997) 659-660 *(Höffken, Peter).*

3477 *Porton, Gary G.* Isaiah and the kings: the rabbis on the prophet Isaiah. Writing and reading... Isaiah. VT.S 70/2: 1997, ⇒181. <sup>E</sup>Broyles, Craig C., 693-716.

3478  *Roberts, J.J.M.* Blindfolding the prophet: political resistance to First Isaiah's oracles in the light of ancient Near Eastern attitudes toward oracles. Oracles. 1997, ⇒374. [E]Heintz, J.-G., 135-146.

3479  *Schmitt, John J.* The city as woman in Isaiah 1-39. Writing and reading... Isaiah. VT.S 70/2: 1997, ⇒181. [E]Broyles, C., 95-119.

3480  *Schoors, Antoon* Historical information in Isaiah 1-39. BEThL 132: 1997, ⇒12. [F]BEUKEN W., 75-93.

3481  *Sterk, Jan P.* Re-creating Isaiah's poetry. TPBT 48 (1997) 301-08.

3482  *Tucker, Gene M.* The futile quest for the historical prophet. JSOT.S 240: 1997, ⇒20. [F]COATS G., 144-152.

3483  *Van der Kooij, Arie* Isaiah in the Septuagint. Writing and reading... Isaiah. VT.S 70/2: 1997, ⇒181. [E]Broyles, C., 513-529;

3484  Zur Theologie des Jesajabuches in der Septuaginta. Theologische Probleme. 1997, ⇒223. [E]Reventlow, Henning Graf, 9-25.

3485  *Virgulin, Stefano* La ricerca di Dio in Isaia. PSV 35 (1997) 51-60.

3486  *Wodecki, Bernard* Jerozolima—Syjon w tekstach Proto-Izajasza. 1997, ⇒52. [F]LACH J., 427-442. **P.**

3487  *Blum, Erhard* Jesajas prophetisches Testament: Beobachtungen zu Jes 1-11. ZAW 109 (1997) 12-29.

3488  *Williamson, Hugh G.M.* Relocating Isaiah 1:2-9. Writing and reading...Isaiah. VT.S 70/2: 1997, ⇒181. [E]Broyles, C.C., 263-277.

3489  *Kessler, Rainer* "Söhne habe ich grossgezogen und emporgebracht...": Gott als Mutter in Jes 1,2. 1997, ⇒29. [F]GERSTENBERGER E.S., 134-147.

3490  *Holmgren, Fredrick C.* Isaiah 2:1-5. Interp. 51 (1997) 61-64.

3491  *Limburg, James* Swords to plowshares: text and contexts. Writing and reading... Isaiah. VT.S 70/2: 1997, ⇒181. [E]Broyles, Craig C., 279-293 [Isa 2,1-5].

3492  *Willis, John T.* Isaiah 2:2-5 and the Psalms of Zion. Writing and reading...Isaiah. VT.S 70/2: 1997, ⇒181. [E]Broyles, C., 295-316.

3493  *Irsigler, Hubert* Speech acts and intention in the 'Song of the Vineyard' Isaiah 5:1-7. OTEs 10 (1997) 39-68.

3494  *Loretz, Oswald* Zitat der ersten Hälfte einer Weinberg-Parabel in Jes 5,1-7. UF 29 (1997) 489-510.

3495  **Lloyd-Jones, D. Martin** A nation under wrath: studies in Isaiah 5. GR 1997, Baker 190 pp. $14. 0-85476-720-7 [BS 156,113s—Zuck, Roy B.].

3496  *Zarras, Konstantinos* Seraphim (Isaïah 6,1-7) and cherubim (Ezekiel 1,5-10 and 10,1): the origin and the relation between the two, as it comes out of the calling-oracles of both prophets. DBM 16/2 (1997) 16-30. **G.**

3497  *Brueggemann, Walter* Planned people/planned book?. Writing and reading... Isaiah. VT.S 70/2: 1997, ⇒181. [E]Broyles, Craig C., 19-37 [Isa 6,1-8; 40,1-11].

3498  *Stuhlman, Daniel D.* A variant text from the Isaiah Scroll. JBQ 25 (1997) 177-184 [Isa 6,3].

3499  *Carroll, Robert P.* Blindsight and the vision thing: blindness and insight in the book of Isaiah. Writing and reading... Isaiah. VT.S 70/2: 1997, ⇒181. [E]Broyles, Craig C., 79-93 [Isa 6,9].

3500  *Williamson, H.G.M.* Isaiah 6,13 and 1,29-31. BEThL 132: 1997, ⇒12. [F]BEUKEN W., 119-128.

3501  **Hartenstein, Friedhelm** Die Unzugänglichkeit Gottes im Heiligtum: Jesaja 6 und der Wohnort JHWHs in der Jerusalemer Kulttradition. Diss. Mü 1995-96; <sup>D</sup>*Jeremias, J.*: WMANT 75: Neuk 1997, Neuk x; 274 pp. DM98. 3-7887-1640-1.

3502 *Lind, Millard C.* Political implications of Isaiah 6. Writing and reading...Isaiah. VT.S 70/2: 1997, ⇒181. <sup>E</sup>Broyles, C., 317-338.

3503 *Irsigler, Hubert* Der Aufstieg des Immanuel: Jes 7,1-17 und die Rezeption des Immanuelworts in Jes 7-11. Vom Adamssohn. ATSAT 58: 1997, ⇒137. 101-152.

3504 *Rumianek, Ryszard* Proroctwo mesjańskie o Emmanuelu Iz 7,14 [La profezia dell'Emmanuele—Is 7,14]. Rias. 291. WST 10 (1997) 285-291. **P.**

3505 *Karlić, Ivan* Mesijanska nada u Iz 7,14 [La speranza messianica in Isa 7,14]. 1997, ⇒96. <sup>F</sup>TOMICA C., Rias. 106. 79-107. **Croatian.**

3506 **Jodar Estrella, Pedro** El texto del oráculo de Enmanuel: elementos de lingüística textual en el estudio de un texto bíblico. Diss. Pempelune 1997; <sup>D</sup>*Varo, F.*, 418 pp. [Isa 7,14] [RTL 29,575].

3507 *Alonso Schökel, Luis* La promessa dell'Emmanuele. La bibbia per la famiglia 7. 1997, ⇒1456. <sup>E</sup>Ravasi, G., 27-29 [Isa 7,14]

3508 *Loretz, Oswald* Eine assyrische Parallele zum Topos "Adlerflügel" in Jes 8,8b: philologische und kolometrische Anmerkungen zu Jes 8,5-10. UF 29 (1997) 467-487.

3509 *Van der Woude, Adam Simon* Jesaja 8,19-23a als literarische Einheit. BEThL 132: 1997, ⇒12. <sup>F</sup>BEUKEN W., 129-136.

3510 *Roberts, J.J.M.* Whose child is this?: reflections on the speaking voice in Isaiah 9:5. HThR 90 (1997) 115-129.

3511 *Zenger, Erich* Die Verheissung Jesaja 11,1-10: universal oder partikular?;

3512 *Van Wieringen, Archibald L.H.M.* Isaiah 12,1-6: a domain and communication analysis. BEThL 132: 1997, ⇒12. <sup>F</sup>BEUKEN W., 137-147/149-172.

3513 **Zapff, Burkard M.** Schriftgelehrte Prophetie—Jes 13. fzb 74: 1995, ⇒11/1,2226. <sup>R</sup>ATG 60 (1997) 399-400 *(Sicre, J.L.)*.

3514 *Jensen, Joseph* Helel ben Shaḥar (Isaiah 14:12-15) in bible and tradition. Writing and reading... Isaiah. VT.S 70/2: 1997, ⇒181. <sup>E</sup>Broyles, Craig C., 339-356.

3515 *Willis, John T.* An interpretation of Isaiah 22.15-25 and its function in the New Testament. Early christian interpretation. JSNT.S 148: 1997, ⇒191. <sup>E</sup>Evans, Craig A., 334-351 [Mt 16,13-23].

3516 **Scholl, Reinhard** Die Elenden in Gottes Thronrat: stilistisch-kompositorische Untersuchungen zu Jes 24-27. Diss. Greifswald 1997; <sup>D</sup>*Zobel, H.-J.*

3517 **Baranowski, Michal** La teologia di Sion nel libro di Isaia: studio esegetico-teologico: con particolare riferimento a Is 25,6-8; 28,14-22; 54,11-17; 60. Diss. Pont. Univ. Gregoriana 1997; <sup>D</sup>*Simian-Yofre, Horacio*: R 1997, 125 pp. extr.

3518 *Doyle, Brian* A literary analysis of Isaiah 25,10a. BEThL 132: 1997, ⇒12. <sup>F</sup>BEUKEN W., 173-193.

3519 *Day, John* The dependence of Isaiah 26:13-27:11 on Hosea 13:4-14:10 and its relevance to some theories of the redaction of the "Isaiah Apocalypse".Writing and reading... Isaiah. VT.S 70/2: 1997, ⇒181. <sup>E</sup>Broyles, Craig C., 357-368.

3520 *Van Grol, Harm W.M.* Isaiah 27,10-11: God and his own people. BEThL 132: 1997, ⇒12. <sup>F</sup>BEUKEN W., 195-209.

3521 *Wong, G.C.I.* Faith and works in Isaiah xxx 15. VT 47 (1997) 236-246.

3522 *Beuken, Willem A.M.* Isaiah 30: a prophetic oracle transmitted in two successive paradigms. Writing and reading... Isaiah. VT.S 70/2: 1997, ⇒181. EBroyles, Craig C., 369-397.

3523 **Mathews, Claire R.** Defending Zion: Edom's desolation and Jacob's restoration (Isaiah 34-35) in context. Diss. D*Seitz, Christopher*: BZAW 236: 1995, ⇒11/1,2245. RBiOr 54 (1997) 446-447 *(Höffken, Peter)*; ThLZ 122 (1997) 798-800 *(Fechter, Friedrich)*; CBQ 59 (1997) 355-356 *(Miscall, Peter D.)*; OTEs 10 (1997) 360-362 *(Gitay, Yehoshua)*; JBL 116 (1997) 546-548 *(White, Hugh C.)*.

3524 *Vermeylen, Jacques* Hypothèses sur l'origine d'Isaïe 36-39. BEThL 132: 1997, ⇒12. FBEUKEN W., 95-118.

3525 **Barthel, Jörg** Prophetenwort und Geschichte: die Jesajaüberlieferung in Jes 6-8 und 28-31. FAT 19: Tü 1997, Mohr xiv; 522 pp. Bibl. DM198. 3-16-146746-9.

3526 *Grzybek, Stanisław* Bóg Izajasza w Świetle jego wizji (Iz 6,1-13) [Deus visionis Isaianae (Is 6,1-13)]. RBL 50 (1997) 175-87. **P.**

3527 **Jones, Brian C.** Howling over Moab: irony and rhetoric in Isaiah 15-16. SBL.DS 157: 1996, ⇒12,3381. RЕThL 73 (1997) 427-428 *(Lust, J.)*.

E8.4 **Deutero-Isaias 40-52:** *commentarii, themata, versiculi*

3528 **Barstad, Hans M.** The Babylonian captivity of the book of Isaiah: 'exilic' Judah and the provenance of Isaiah 40-55. Institute for comparative research in human culture, Serie B.,Skrifter 102: Oslo 1997, Novus 120 pp Bibl. NOK149. 82-7099-289-5 [RTL 29,121]. FBECK E., Rosen... zu Jesaja 40-55 ⇒9.

3529 **Brassey, Paul D.** Metaphor and the incomparable God in Isaiah 40-55. Diss. Harvard 1997 [HThR 90,438].

3530 *Candido, Dioniso* I predicati participiali di JHWH nel Deutero-Isaia. Synaxis 15/1 (1997) 177-217.

3531 *Dijkstra, Meindert* Lawsuit, debate and wisdom discourse in Second Isaiah. BEThL 132: 1997, ⇒12. FBEUKEN W., 251-271.

3532 *Gianto, Augustinus* Un messaggio di speranza contro ogni crisi di fede. La biblia per la famiglia 7. 1997, ⇒1456. ERavasi, G., 126-129.

3533 *Goldingay, John* Isaiah 40-55 in the 1990s: among other things, deconstructing, mystifying, intertextual, socio-critical, and hearer-involving. Bibl.Interp. 5 (1997) 225-246.

3534 E*Gruson, Philippe* Le deuxième Isaïe et ses disciples (Is 40-66). DosB 66 (1997) 1-31.

3535 **Hanson, Paul D.** Isaiah 40-66. 1995, ⇒11/1,2252. RHebStud 38 (1997) 139-140 *(Nielsen, Kirsten)*; ThLZ 122 (1997) 23-24 *(Höffken, Peter)*.

3536 *Hermisson, Hans-Jürgen* "Die Frau Zion". BEThL 132: 1997, ⇒12. FBEUKEN W., 19-39.

3537 *Holladay, William L.* Was Trito-Isaiah Deutero-Isaiah after all?. Writing and reading... Isaiah. VT.S 70/2: 1997, ⇒181. EBroyles, Craig C., 193-217.

3538 **Koole, Jan L.** Isaiah 40-48. Isaiah III/1. Historical Commentary on the OT: Lv 1997, Peeters xxv; 611 pp. 90-390-0173-1.

3539 *Kuntz, J. Kenneth* The form, location, and function of rhetorical questions in Deutero-Isaiah. Writing and reading... Isaiah. VT.S 70/2: 1997, ⇒181. ᴱBroyles, Craig C., 121-141.

3540 **Labahn, Antje** Wort Gottes und Schuld Israels: Motive deuteronomistischer Theologie im Deuterojesaja Buch und deren Bedeutung für das Verhältnis von Jes 40-55 zum Deuteronomismus. Diss. Gö 1997; ᴰ*Perlitt, L.*, 348 pp. [RTL 29,578].

3541 *Leene, Henk* History and eschatology in Deutero-Isaiah;

3542 *McEvenue, Sean* Who was Second Isaiah?. BEThL 132: 1997, ⇒12. ᶠBᴇᴜᴋᴇɴ W., 223-249/213-222;

3543 ¿Quién fue el segundo Isaías?. RevBib 60 (1997) 1-12.

3544 *Melugin, Roy F.* Israel and the nations in Isaiah 40-55. ᶠKɴɪᴇʀɪᴍ R., 1997, ⇒48. 249-264.

3545 *Mettinger, Tryggve N.D.* In search of the hidden structure: YHWH as king in Isaiah 40-55. Writing and reading... Isaiah. VT.S 70/2: 1997, ⇒181. ᴱBroyles, Craig C., 143-154.

3546 *Michel, Diethelm* Das Rätsel Deuterojesaja. Studien zur Überlieferungsgeschichte. TB 93: 1997 <1977>, ⇒149. 199-218.

3547 *Minette de Tillesse, Caetano* Dêutero-Isaías. RBB 14/1-3 (1997) 79-99.

3548 **Rosenbaum, Michael** Word-order variation in Isaiah 40-55. Studies on Semitics 35: Assen 1997, Van Gorcum 248 pp. $64/ƒ120. 90-232-3262-3.

3549 *Scott, Timothy* Hope for redemption. BiTod 35 (1997) 222-228.

3550 *Snodgrass, Klyne R.* Streams of tradition emerging from Isaiah 40.1-5 and their adaptation in the New Testament. NT Backgrounds. 1997 <1980>, ⇒F1.1. ᴱEvans, Craig A., 149-168.

3551 *Sweeney, Marvin A.* The reconceptualization of the Davidic covenant in Isaiah. BEThL 132: 1997, ⇒12. ᶠBᴇᴜᴋᴇɴ W., 41-61.

3552 **Willey, Patricia Tull** Remember the former things: the recollection of previous texts in Second Isaiah. Diss. Emory, 1996; ᴰ*Newsom, C.A.*: SBL.DS 161: Atlanta 1997, Scholars xi; 297 pp. Bibl. $40. 0-7885-0364-2.

3553 **Williamson, H.G.M.** The book called Isaiah: Deutero-Isaiah's role in composition and redaction. 1994, ⇒10,3397... 12,3350. ᴿJBL 116 (1997) 347-348 *(Irwin, William H.)*.

3554 *Freedman, David Noel* The structure of Isaiah 40:1-11. Divine Commitment 2. 1997 <1987>, ⇒124. 232-257.

3555 *Merendino, Rosario Pius* Is 40,3-5: osservazioni sul testo. RivBib 45 (1997) 3-30.

3556 *Charlesworth, James H.* Intertextuality: Isaiah 40:3 and *Serek Ha-Yahad*;

3557 *Davidson, Robert* The imagery of Isaiah 40:6-8 in tradition and interpretation. 1997, ⇒77. ᶠSᴀɴᴅᴇʀs J., 197-224/37-55.

3558 **Holter, Knut** Second Isaiah's idol-fabrication passages. BeitBExT 28: 1995, ⇒11/1,2265. ᴿCBQ 59 (1997) 542-543 *(Dick, Michael B.)*; TTK 68 (1997) 309-310 *(Tångberg, Arvid)* [Isa 40,19—46,7].

3559 *Van Leeuwen, Kees* An old crux: *hamesukkan teruma* in Isaiah 40,20;

3560 *Teugels, Lieve* Consolation and composition in a rabbinic homily on Isaiah 40 (Pesiqta' de Rav Kahana' 16). BEThL 132: 1997, ⇒12. ᶠBᴇᴜᴋᴇɴ W., 273-287/433-446.

3561 *Dempsey, Deirdre Ann* ונרעה and ונאמר in Isa 41:26; w'r' in Isa 41:28. BN 86 (1997) 18-23.

3562 *Prinsloo, Willem S.* Isaiah 42,10-12: "Sing to the Lord a new song..."     BEThL 132: 1997, ⇒12. ᶠBEUKEN W., 289-301.

3563 *Carroll, Robert P.* Razed temple and shattered vessels: continuities and discontinuities in the discourses of exile in the Hebrew Bible: an appreciation of the work of Peter R. Ackroyd on the occasion of his eightieth birthday. JSOT 75 (1997) 93-106 [Ex 3,1-6; 19; Num 8,4; Isa 43,2].

3564 *Van Winkle, D.W.* Proselytes in Isaiah xl-lv?: a study of Isaiah xliv 1-5. VT 47 (1997) 341-359.

3565 *Fokkelman, Jan P.* The Cyrus oracle (Isaiah 44,24-45,7) from the perspectives of syntax, versification and structure. BEThL 132: 1997, ⇒12. ᶠBEUKEN W., 303-323.

3566 *Broyles, Craig C.* The citations of Yahweh in Isaiah 44:26-28. Writing and reading... Isaiah. VT.S 70/2: 1997, ⇒181. ᴱBroyles, Craig C., 399-421 [Ps 69; 74; 77-78].

3567 *Stefani, Piero* Formò la luce e creò le tenebre: a proposito di due benedizioni ebraiche. Servitium 31/1 (1997) 55-59 [Ps 136,7; Isa 45,7].

3568 ᴱ**Gryson, Roger** Esaias. Fasc. 5. Collab. *Auwers, Jean Marie; Baise, Ignace.* Vetus Latina 12/2. FrB 1995, Herder. 3-451-00124-1. ᴿJThS 48 (1997) 154-156 *(Elliott, J.K.)* [Isa 46,13-50,3];

3569 Esaias. Fasc. 6. Collab. *Auwers, Jean Marie; Baise, Ignace.* Vetus Latina 12/2. FrB 1996, Herder. 3-451-00124-6. ᴿJThS 48 (1997) 154-156 *(Elliott, J.K.)* [Isa 46,13-50,3].

3570 *Kruger, Paul A.* The slave status of the virgin daughter Babylon in Isaiah 47:2: a perspective from anthropology. JNSL 23/1 (1997) 143-151 [Isa 47,1-3].

3571 *Freedman, David Noel* 'Mistress forever': a note on Isaiah 47:7. Divine Commitment 2. 1997 <1970>, ⇒124. 241-248.

3572 *Odobašić, Božo* Radost povratka na Sion: Iz 49,14-26 [Die Freude der Rückkehr nach Zion]. ᶠTOMICA C.; Zsfg. 126. 1997; ⇒96. 108-127. **Croatian.**

3573 *Brenner, Athalya* Identifying the speaker-in-the-text and the reader's location in prophetic texts: the case of Isaiah 50. A feminist companion. 1997, ⇒180. ᴱBrenner, A., 136-150.

E8.5 *Isaiae 53ss, Carmina Servi YHWH:* **Servant Songs**

3574 *Blenkinsopp, Joseph* The servant and the servants in Isaiah and the formation of the book. Writing and reading... Isaiah. VT.S 70/2: 1997, ⇒181. ᴱBroyles, Craig C., 155-175.

3575 **Ekblad, Eugène Robert** An exegetical and theological study of the Septuagint translation of Isaiah's Servant poems. Diss. Montpellier 1997; ᴰ*Bourguet, D.*: 339 pp. [RTL 29,577].

3576 *Werlitz, Jürgen* Vom Knecht der Lieder zum Knecht des Buches: ein Versuch über die Ergänzungen zu den Gottesknechtstexten des Deuterojesajabuches. ZAW 109 (1997) 30-43 [Isa 42,5-9; 49,7-12; 50,10-11].

3577 *Van der Kooij, Arie* "The servant of the Lord": a particular group of Jews in Egypt according to the Old Greek of Isaiah: some com-

ments on LXX Isa 49,1-6 and related passages. BEThL 132: 1997,
⇒12. ᶠBEUKEN W., 383-396.

3578 *Abma, Richtsje* Travelling from Babylon to Zion: location and its function in Isaiah 49-55. JSOT 74 (1997) 3-28.

3579 *Stratton, Beverly J.* Engaging metaphors: suffering with Zion and the servant in Isaiah 52-53. Theological interpretation. 1997, ⇒244. ᴱFowl, E., 219-237.

3580 *Costen, James H.* Doing the right thing: Isaiah 53:1-12, Luke 23:13-25. JITC 24 (1996-1997) 207-213 [ZID 23,406].

3581 *Henning-Hess, Heike* Bemerkungen zum *ASCHAM*-Begriff in Jes 53,10. ZAW 109 (1997) 618-626.

3582 ᴱ**Janowski, Bernd; Stuhlmacher, Peter** Der leidende Gottesknecht. FAT 14: 1996, ⇒12,3432. ᴿZKTh 119 (1997) 225-226 *(Hasitschka, Martin)*.

3583 *Clines, David J. A.* Selections from I, he, we, they: a literary approach to Isaiah 53. Theological interpretation. 1997, ⇒244. ᴱFowl, E., 210-218.

3584 *Song, Jae-Jun* Die heilsuniversalistische Sendung Israels: exegetische und theologische Untersuchungen von Jes 55,1-5. Diss. Salzburg 1997; ᴰ*Reiterer, F.; Bodendorfer-Langer, G.*, 270 pp. [RTL 29,580].

3585 *Höffken, Peter* Zur Symmetrie in Jesaja lv, ein Gespräch mit M.C.A. KORPEL. VT 47 (1997) 249-252.

## E8.6 [Trito-]Isaias 56-66

3586 **Dafni, Nikoleta** Isaiah 56-66: prophecy or apocalypse?: the nature of the eschatological beliefs of Isaiah 56-66 and the investigation of the problem of its unity within the rest of the Isaianic corpus. Diss. London 1997; ᴰ*Knibb, M.* [RTL 29,577].

3587 **Lau, Wolfgang** Schriftgelehrte Prophetie in Jes 56-66: eine Untersuchung zu den literarischen Bezügen in den letzten elf Kapiteln des Jesajabuches. BZAW 225: 1994, ⇒10,3481... 12,3449. ᴿJBL 116 (1997) 127-129 *(Nogalski, James D.)*.

3588 *Michel, Diethelm* Zur Eigenart Tritojesajas. Studien zur Überlieferungsgeschichte. TB 93: 1997 <1966>, 181-197.

3589 *Minette de Tillesse, Caetano* Trito-Isaías. RBB 14/1-3 (1997) 135-139.

3590 *Oswalt, John N.* Righteousness in Isaiah: a study of the function of chapters 55-66 in the present structure of the book. Writing and reading... Isaiah. VT.S 70/2: 1997, ⇒181. ᴱBroyles, C., 177-191.

3591 *Polan, Gregory J.* Still more signs of unity in the book of Isaiah: the significance of Third Isaiah. SBL.SPS 36 (1997) 224-233.

3592 **Schramm, Brooks** The opponents of Third Isaiah: reconstructing the cultic history of the restoration. Diss. Chicago 1993; ᴰ*Levenson, J.*: JSOT.S 193: 1995, ⇒11/1,2298; 12,3450. ᴿBiOr 54 (1997) 174-176 *(Höffken, Peter)*; JAOS 117 (1997) 605-606 *(Hurowitz, Victor A.)*.

3593 **Smith, Paul A.** Rhetoric and redaction in Trito-Isaiah. VT.S 62: 1995, ⇒11/1,2299; 12,3451. ᴿJThS 48 (1997) 559-561 *(Clements, R.E.)*; CBQ 59 (1997) 359-360 *(Polan, Gregory J.)*.

3594 *Steck, Odil Hannes* Autor und/oder Redaktor in Jesaja 56-66. Writing and reading... Isaiah. VT.S 70/2: 1997, ⇒181. EBroyles, Craig C., 219-259.

3595 **Van Wieringen, Archibald L.H.M.** Computerized analysis of parallel texts between Isaiah 56-66 and Isaiah 40-66. 1993, ⇒9,3624. RBiOr 54 (1997) 447-450 *(Verheij, Arian).*

3596 *Gosse, Bernard* Isaïe 56-59, le livre d'Isaïe et la mémoire du prophète Isaïe. Henoch 19/3 (1997) 267-281 [Isa 8,16-9,6].

3597 *Van Winkle, D.W.* Isaiah LVI 1-8. SBL.SPS 36 (1997) 234-252;

3598 The meaning of *yad wašem* in Isaiah lvi 5. VT 47 (1997) 378-385;

3599 An inclusive authoritative text in exclusive communities. Writing and reading... Isaiah. VT.S 70/2: 1997, ⇒181. EBroyles, Craig C., 423-440 [Isa 56,6].

3600 *Schottroff, Willy* "Unrechtmäßige Fesseln auftun, Jochstricke lösen" Jesaja 58,1-2, ein Textbeispiel zum Thema 'Bibel und Ökonomie'. Bibl.Interp. 5 (1997) 263-278.

3601 *Witaszek, Gabriel* Bez sprawiedliwości społecznej nie ma zbawienia (Iz 58,1-13; 59) [Sine iustitia sociali non est salus (Is 58,1-13; 59)]. RBL 50 (1997) 105-113. **P.**

3602 *Hurowitz, Victor Avigdor* A forgotten meaning of *nepeš* in Isaiah lviii 10. VT 47 (1997) 43-52.

3603 *Levi, Abramo* Il tema della luce nell'Antico Testamento: commento spirituale al cap. 58 di Isaia. Servitium 31/1 (1997) 44-53.

3604 *Kruger, H.A.J.* Who comes: Yahweh or Nahar?: a few remarks on the translation of Isaiah 59:19c-d and the theological meaning of the passage. OTEs 10 (1997) 84-91; 268-278.

3605 *Moor, Johannes C. de* Structure and redaction in Isaiah 60,1-63,6. BEThL 132: 1997, ⇒12. FBEUKEN W., 325-346.

3606 *Croatto, José Severino* Wie ist die Befreiung anzukündigen?: hermeneutischer Kommentar zu Jes 61,1-3. 1997, ⇒29. FGERSTENBERGER E.S., 148-165.

3607 *Collins, John J.* A herald of good tidings: Isaiah 61:1-3 and its actualization in the Dead Sea Scrolls. 1997, ⇒77. FSANDERS J., 225-240.

3608 *Ravasi, Gianfranco* La veste, le nozze, i germogli: lettura simbolico-teologica di *Isaia* 61,10-11. Som., sum. 60. VivH 8 (1997) 47-60.

3609 *Sweeney, Marvin A.* Prophetic exegesis in Isaiah 65-66. Writing and reading... Isaiah. VT.S 70/2: 1997, ⇒181. EBroyles, Craig C., 455-474.

3610 *Steck, Odil Hannes* Der neue Himmel und die neue Erde: Beobachtungen zur Rezeption von Gen 1-3 in Jes 65,16b-25. BEThL 132: 1997, ⇒12. FBEUKEN W., 349-365.

3611 *Croatto, J. Severino* El origen isaiano de las bienaventuranzas de Lucas: estudio exegético de Isaías 65:11-16. RevBib 59/1 (1997) 1-16 [Lk 6,20-22].

E8.7 **Jeremias**

3612 EBogaert, Pierre-Maurice Le livre de Jérémie: le prophète et son milieu: les oracles et leur transmission. BEThL 54: Lv ²1997

<1981>, Peeters 448 pp. Journées bibliques de Louvain (1980). FB1.800. 90-6831-941-8.

3613 *Bogaert, Pierre-Maurice* De Baruch à Jérémie: les deux rédactions conservées du livre Jérémie. Le livre de Jérémie. ⇒3612. 168-173, 430-432;

3614 Introduction. Le livre de Jérémie. ⇒3612. 13-18.

3615 *Brooke, George J.* The book of Jeremiah and its reception in the Qumran scrolls. The book of Jeremiah. BEThL 128: 1997, ⇒186. ᴱCurtis, A., 183-205.

ᴱ**Curtis, A.H.W.** The book of Jeremiah ⇒186.

3616 **Fischer, Georg** Il libro di Geremia. 1995, ⇒11/1,2307. ᴿSal. 59 (1997) 557-558 *(Buzzetti, Carlo)*;

3617 El libro de Jeremías. 1996, ⇒12,3453. ᴿIter 8/2 (1997) 155-156 *(Frades, Eduardo)*.

3618 *Fischer, Georg* Zum Text des Jeremiabuches. Sum. 328. Bib. 78 (1997) 305-328.

3619 **Jones, Douglas Rawlinson** Jeremiah. NCBC: 1992, ⇒8,3764... 10,3495. ᴿVJTR 61 (1997) 133-134 *(Meagher, P.M.)*.

3620 **King, Philip J.** Jeremiah: an archaeological companion. 1993, ⇒9,3643... 11/1,2315. ᴿJNES 56 (1997) 67-69 *(Smith, Mark S.)*.

3621 **Lundbom, Jack R.** Jeremiah: a study in ancient Hebrew rhetoric. WL ²1997, Eisenbrauns xliii; 212 pp. 1-57506-016-7.

3622 **McKane, William** Jeremiah 2: XXVI-LII. ICC: 1996, ⇒12,3455. ᴿThLZ 122 (1997) 1001-1005 *(Liwak, Rüdiger)*.

3623 **Mello, A.** Geremia: commento esegetico-spirituale. Magnano 1997, Qiqajon 100 pp. L.12.000 [Asp. 45,427s—Casale, C.M.].

3624 ᴱ**Rabin, C.; Talmon, S.; Tov, E.** The book of Jeremiah. The Hebrew University Bible Project. J 1997, Magnes xlv; 303 pp. 965-223-933-X.

3625 **Stipp, Hermann-Josef** Das masoretische und alexandrinische Sondergut des Jeremiabuches. OBO 136: 1994, ⇒10,3516... 12,3473. ᴿThRv 93 (1997) 127-129 *(Fischer, Georg)*; ThZ 153 (1997) 373-374 *(Huwyler, Beat)*.

3626 *Stipp, Hermann-Josef* Linguistic peculiarities of the Masoretic edition of the book of Jeremiah: an updated index. JNSL 23/2 (1997) 181-202.

3627 *Tov, Emanuel* Some aspects of the textual and literary history of the book of Jeremiah. Le livre de Jérémie. ⇒3612. 145-167, 430.

3628 **Werner, Wolfgang** Das Buch Jeremia, 1: Kapitel 1-25. Neuer Stuttgarter Kommentar, AT 19: Stu 1997, Katholisches Bibelwerk 220 pp. DM44. 3-460-07191-5.

3629 *Berlyn, P.J.* Baruch Ben-Neriah: the man who was not a prophet. JBQ 25 (1997) 143-149.

3630 *Cazelles, Henri* La vie de Jérémie dans son contexte national et international. Le livre de Jérémie. ⇒3612. 21-39, 418-422.

3631 **Dubbink, J.** Waar is de Heer?: dynamiek en actualiteit van het woord van JHWH bij Jeremia. Diss. Amsterdam; ᴰ*Deurloo, K.A.*: Gorinchem 1997, Narratio 268 pp. *f*25. 90-5263-903-5 [ITBT 5/7,34].

3632 *Fuchs, Gisela* Die Klage des Propheten: Beobachtungen zu den Konfessionen Jeremias im Vergleich mit den Klagen Hiobs (Erster Teil). BZ 41 (1997) 212-228.

3633 *Gilbert, Maurice* Jérémie en conflit avec les sages?. Le livre de Jérémie. ⇒3612. 105-118, 427-428.
3634 *Goldman, Yohanan* Juda et son roi au milieu des nations: la derniè-re rédaction du livre de Jérémie. The book of Jeremiah. BEThL 128: 1997, ⇒186. ᴱCurtis, A., 151-182.
3635 *Gosse, Bernard* Les écrits de Jérémie, la réalisation du malheur voulu par Yahvé, et le pardon du péché dans le livre de Jérémie. EstB 55 (1997) 53-72.
3636 **Habel, Norman C.** The God of Jeremiah. 1996, ⇒12,3463. ᴿACR 74/1 (1997) 123 *(Webb, Freda)*.
3637 *Herrmann, Siegfried* Jeremia—der Prophet und die Verfasser des Buches Jeremia. Le livre de Jérémie. ⇒3612. 197-214, 433.
3638 **Hill, John Edward** Friend or foe?: the question of Babylon in the book of Jeremiah, Massoretic Text. Diss. Melbourne College of Divinity 1997-8; ᴰ*Campbell, Antony F.* [Sum. Pacifica 11,245].
3639 *Holladay, William L.* A coherent chronology of Jeremiah's early career. Le livre de Jérémie. ⇒3612. 58-73, 425-426.
3640 *Homerski, Józef* Powrót do Ojca: refleksje egzegetyczno-teogogiczne nad niektórymi wyroczniami Księgi Jeremiasza [Return to Father: exegetical and theological reflexions on some oracles from Jeremiah]. 1997, ⇒52. ᶠLACH J., 175-185. **P.**
3641 *Lust, Johan* "Gathering and return" in Jeremiah and Ezekiel. Le livre de Jérémie. ⇒3612. 119-142, 428-430.
3642 **Martini, Carlo Maria** A prophetic voice in the city: meditations on the prophet Jeremiah. ᵀ*Theisen, Vera Castelli*: ColMn 1997, Liturgical viii; 152 pp. $12. 0-8146-2412-X [ThD 45,180—Heiser, W. Charles].
3643 **McConville, J. Gordon** Judgment and promise: an interpretation of the book of Jeremiah. 1993, ⇒9,3666... 12,3466. ᴿSBET 15/1 (1997) 79-80 *(Herbert, Edward D.)*.
3644 *McLean, Paul D.* The Greek translation of *jhwdh* in the book of Jeremiah. BIOSCS 30 (1997) 45-80.
3645 **Orlandini, Guerrino** Il ramo di mandorlo in fiore: dalle immagini simboliche del profeta Geremia all'esperienza del mistero cristiano. Sussidi biblici 55: Reggio Emilia 1997, San Lorenzo (4) ii, 74 pp. 88-8071-066-4.
3646 *Scharbert, Josef* Jeremia und die Reform des Joschija. Le livre de Jérémie. ⇒3612. 40-57, 422-424.
3647 *Seidel, Bodo* Freunde und Feinde Jeremias unter den Beamten Judas der spätvorexilischen Zeit. BZ 41 (1997) 28-53.
3648 *Stipp, Hermann-Josef* Eschatologisches Schema im Alexandrini-schen Jeremiabuch?: Strukturprobleme eines komplexen Propheten-buchs. JNSL 23/1 (1997) 153-179.
3649 *Taylor, James* Jeremiah: the challenge of the prophet. Evangel 15/3 (1997) 66-69.
3650 *Tomes, Roger* The reception of Jeremiah in rabbinic literature and in the Targum. The book of Jeremiah. BEThL 128: 1997, ⇒186. ᴱCurtis, A., 233-253.
3651 *Vermeylen, Jacques* Essai de Redaktionsgeschichte des "Confes-sions de Jérémie";
3652 *Weippert, Helga* Der Beitrag ausserbiblischer Prophetentexte zum Verständnis der Prosareden des Jeremiabuches. Le livre de Jérémie. ⇒3612. 239-270, 435-436/83-104, 426-427.

3653 *Renaud, Bernard* Jér 1: structure et théologie de la rédaction. Le livre de Jérémie. ⇒3612. 177-196.

3654 *Gitay, Yehoshua* The projection of the prophet: a rhetorical presentation of the prophet Jeremiah (according to Jer 1:1-19). Prophecy and prophets. 1997, ⇒199. ᴱGitay, Yehoshua, 41-55.

3655 *Taylor, James* Jeremiah: the call to ministry, 1. Evangel 15/2 (1997) 34-37 [Jer 1].

3656 *Macchi, Jean-Daniel* Les doublets dans le livre de Jérémie. The book of Jeremiah. BEThL 128: 1997, ⇒186. ᴱCurtis, A., 119-150 [Jer 2; 32; 17,19-27; 33,01-13].

3657 *Soggin, J. Alberto* The ark of the covenant, Jeremiah 3,16. Le livre de Jérémie. ⇒3612. 215-221.

3658 *Jenni, Ernst* Jer 3,17 'nach Jerusalem': ein Aramaismus. Studien zur Sprachwelt. 1997 <1988>, ⇒138. 135-140.

3659 *Olson, Daniel C.* Jeremiah 4.5-31 and apocalyptic myth. JSOT 73 (1997) 81-107.

3660 *Hayes, Katherine M.* Jeremiah iv 23: tōhû without bōhû. VT 47 (1997) 247-249.

3661 *Curtis, Adrian H.W.* "Terror on every side!". The book of Jeremiah. BEThL 128: 1997, ⇒186. ᴱCurtis, A., 111-118 [Ps 31,14; Jer 6,25; 20,3; 20,10; 46,15; 49,29; Lam 2,22].

3662 **Biddle, Mark E.** Polyphony and symphony in prophetic literature: rereading Jeremiah 7-20. 1996, ⇒12,3483. ᴿCBQ 59 (1997) 530-531 *(McConville, J.G.)*.

3663 *Klimek, Piotr* Objawienie boga w Jr 9,22-23 [God's revelation by Jer 9,22-23]. Sum. 156. WST 10 (1997) 151-156. P.

3664 *Bogaert, Pierre-Maurice* Les mecanismes redactionnels en Jér 10,1-16 (LXX et TM) et la signification des suppléments;

3665 *Brekelmans, Christian* Jeremiah 18,1-12 and its redaction;

3666 *Hubmann, Franz D.* Jer 18,18-23 im Zusammenhang der Konfessionen. Le livre de Jérémie. ⇒3612. 222-238, 433-434/343-350/271-296, 436-439.

3667 *Costen, James H.* A new agenda for the nineties: Jeremiah 23:25-40. JITC 24 (1996-1997) 175-182 [ZID 23,406].

3668 *Kessler, Martin* Jeremiah 25,1-29: text and context: a synchronic study. ZAW 109 (1997) 44-70.

3669 *Lemaire, André* Jérémie xxv 10b et la stèle araméenne de Bukân. VT 47 (1997) 543-545.

3670 *Applegate, John* Jeremiah and the seventy years in the Hebrew Bible. The book of Jeremiah. BEThL 128: 1997, ⇒186. ᴱCurtis, A., 91-110 [2 Chr 35,25; 26,11-23; Ezra 1,1-11; Jer 25,11-12; 29,10; Dan 9; Zech 1,1-17].

3671 *Hoffman, Yair* Eschatology in the book of Jeremiah. Eschatology in the bible. JSOT.S 243: 1997, ⇒222. ᴱReventlow, Henning Graf, 75-97 [Jer 25,15-33; 23,5-6; 33,15-17; 35,5-7; 31,8-9].

3672 **Stipp, Hermann Josef** Jeremia im Parteienstreit: Studien zur Textentwicklung von Jer 26,36-43 und 45. BBB 82: 1992, ⇒8,3809; 9,3693. ᴿThRv 93 (1997) 127-129 *(Fischer, Georg)*.

3673 *Renkema, J.* A note on Jeremiah xxviii 5. VT 47 (1997) 253-255.

3674 **Fischer, Georg** Das Trostbüchlein: Text, Komposition und Theologie von Jer 30-31. SBB 26: 1993, ⇒9,3698; 10,3537. ᴿBZ 41 (1997) 297-300 *(Willmes, Bernd)*.

3675 *Lohfink, Norbert* Der junge Jeremia als Propagandist und Poet: zum Grundstock von Jer 30-31. Le livre de Jérémie. ⇒3612. 351-368, 439-445.

3676 **Schmid, Konrad** Buchgestalten des Jeremiabuches: Untersuchungen zur Redaktions- und Rezeptionsgeschichte von Jer 30-33 im Kontext des Buches. ᴰ*Steck, O.H.*: WMANT 72: 1996, ⇒12,3495. ᴿZAW 109 (1997) 468-469 *(Wanke, G.)*.

3677 *Gołębiewski, Marian* 'Nowy człowiek' według Jeremiasza i Ezechiela ['New man' according to Jeremiah and Ezekiel]. 1997, ⇒52. ꜰŁACH J., 129-137. **P**.

3678 *Bovati, Pietro* La nuova alleanza: Dio cambia il cuore umano. La biblia per la famiglia 7. 1997, ⇒1456. ᴱRavasi, G., 268-272 [Jer 31,31-34].

3679 **Marafioti, Domenico** Sant' Agostino e la nuova alleanza: l'interpretazione agostiniana di Geremia 31,31-34 nell'ambito dell'esegesi patristica. Aloisiana 26: 1995, ⇒11/1,2371; 12,3497. ᴿOrph. 18 (1997) 642-644 *(Cutino, Michele)*.

3680 *Marafioti, Domenico* Storia della salvezza e testamento nuovo: l'esegesi di Ger 31,31-34 in TEODORETO di Ciro e LEONE Magno. 1997, ⇒30. ꜰGIORDANO M., 205-216.

3681 *Bogaert, Pierre-Maurice* Loi(s) et alliance nouvelle dans les deux formes conservées du livre de Jérémie (Jr 31,31-37 TM; 38,31-37 LXX). La loi. LeDiv 168: 1997, ⇒195. ᴱFocant, C., 81-92.

3682 *Ego, Beate* "In meinem Herzen berge ich dein Wort": zur Rezeption von Jer 31,33 in der Torafrömmigkeit der Psalmen. JBTh 12 (1997) 277-289.

3683 *Applegate, John* "Peace, peace, when there is no peace" [Jer 32,1-5; 34,1-7];

3684 *Piovanelli, Pierluigi* JrB 33,14-26, ou la continuité des institutions à l'époque maccabéenne. The book of Jeremiah. BEThL 128: 1997, ⇒186. ᴱCurtis, A., 51-90/255-276.

3685 *Chavel, Simeon* 'Let my people go!': emancipation, revelation, and scribal activity in Jeremiah 34.8-14. JSOT 76 (1997) 71-95 [Lev 25,39; Dt 15,12; Neh 5,1-13].

3686 *Wijesinghe, S.L.G.* Tracing the shorter version behind the short text (LXX): a new approach to the redaction of Jeremiah 34,8-22. Muséon 110 (1997) 293-328.

3687 *Knights, Chris H.* The history of the Rechabites—an initial commentary. JSJ 28 (1997) 413-436 [Jer 35].

3688 *Migsch, Herbert* Die vorbildlichen Rechabiter: zur Redestruktur von Jeremia xxxv. VT 47 (1997) 316-328.

3689 *Knights, Chris H.* A century of research into the story/apocalypse of Zosimus and/or the history of the Rechabites. JSPE 15 (1997) 53-66 [Jer 35].

3690 *Römer, Thomas* La conversion du prophète Jérémie à la théologie deutéronomiste. The book of Jeremiah. BEThL 128: 1997, ⇒186. ᴱCurtis, A., 27-50 [2 Kgs 22-23; Jer 36].

3691 **Boyle, Brian** Fire in the city: a synchronic (narrative critical) and diachronic reading of Jeremiah 37:1-38:28a. Diss. Pont. Univ. Gregoriana 1997; ᴰ*Conroy, Charles*: extr. 4356, R 1997, 139 pp.

3692 *Bedriñán, Claudio* El 'retorno' a Egipto (Jr 42): studio de teología bíblica. Soleriana 22/1 (1997) 153-164.

3693 *Sharp, Carolyn J.* "Take another scroll and write": a study of the LXX and the MT of Jeremiah's oracles against Egypt and Babylon. VT 47 (1997) 487-516 [Jer 44; 50; 51].

3694 **Huwyler, Beat** Jeremia und die Völker: Untersuchungen zu den Völkersprüchen in Jeremia 46-49. FAT 20: Tü 1997, Mohr x; 433 pp. DM138. 3-16-146774-4.

3695 *Jong, C. de* Deux oracles contre les nations, reflets de la politique étrangère de Joaqim. Le livre de Jérémie. ⇒3612. 369-379 [Jer 46,3-12].

### E8.8 Lamentationes, *Threni;* Baruch

3696 *Brunet, Gilbert* Jérémie et les Qinot de son adversaire. Le livre de Jérémie. ⇒3612. 74-79.

3697 *Dennison, James T.* The lament and the lamenter: Lamentations 3:1-23. Kerux 12/3 (1997) 30-34.

3698 **Dobbs-Allsopp, F.W.** Weep, O daughter of Zion: a study of the city-lament genre in the Hebrew bible. BibOr 44: 1993, ⇒9,3719... 11/1,2385. RBZ 41 (1997) 312 *(Becker, Joachim).*

3699 *Dobbs-Allsopp, F.W.* Tragedy, tradition, and theology in the book of Lamentations. JSOT 74 (1997) 29-60.

3700 **Droin, Jean-Marc** Le livre des Lamentations. 1995, ⇒11/1,2386. RETR 72 (1997) 131-132 *(Balestier-Stengel, Guy).*

**Fischer, James A.** Cantico...Lamentazioni ⇒2395.

3701 *Linafelt, Tod* Margins of lamentation, or, the unbearable whiteness of reading. Reading bibles. 1997, ⇒172. EBeal, Timothy K., 219-231.

3702 *Linafelt, Tod* Surviving Lamentations. A feminist companion. 1997, ⇒180. EBrenner, A., 344-357.

3703 *Minette de Tillesse, Caetano* Lamentações. RBB 14/1-3 (1997) 65-69.

3704 **Feuerstein, Rüdiger** Das Buch Baruch: Studien zur Textgestalt und Auslegungsgeschichte. Diss. Eichstätt; DDiedrich, F.: EHS.T 614: Fra 1997, Lang 542 pp. 3-631-32359-X.

3705 *Wright, J. Edward* The social setting of the Syriac Apocalypse of Baruch. JSPE 16 (1997) 81-96.

3706 **Herzer, Jens** Die Paralipomena Jeremiae. TSAJ 43: 1994, ⇒10,3558b. RSal. 59/1 (1997) 158 *(Vicent, R.);* JSJ 28/1 (1997) 119-123 *(Flusser, David);* RTL 28 (1997) 519-522 *(Haelewyck, Jean-Claude).*

3707 *Kaestli, Jean-Daniel* L'influence du livre de Jérémie dans les Paralipomènes de Jérémie. The book of Jeremiah. BEThL 128: 1997, ⇒186. ECurtis, A., 217-231.

### E8.9 Ezekiel: *textus, commentarii; themata, versiculi*

3708 *(a)* **André, Georges** Ezechiele: un profeta del millennio. Valenza, AL 1996, "Il Messaggero Cristiano" 65 pp.; *(b)* **Asurmendi, Jesús-Naria** O profeta Ezequiel. Cadernos Bíblicos 59: Lisboa 1997, Difusora Bíblica 60 pp. [Bib(L) 7/7,188—Negreiros, Fernando de].

3709  **Block, Daniel I.** The book of Ezekiel: chapters 1-24. GR 1997, Eerdmans xxi; 887 pp. £33/$48. 0-8028-2534-4 [NThAR 1998,98].

3710  **Clements, Ronald Ernest** Ezekiel. Westminster Bible Companion. 1996, ⇒12,3533. RHBT 19/1 (1997) 84-85 *(Allen, Leslie C.)*; CBQ 59 (1997) 729-730 *(Strong, John T.)*.

3711  *Freedman, David Noel* The book of Ezekiel. Divine Commitment 1. 1997 <1954>, ⇒124. 8-30.

3712  **Greenberg, Moshe** Ezekiel 21-37: a new translation with introduction and commentary. AncB 22A: NY 1997, Doubleday 394-760 pp. $40. 0-385-18200-7.

3713  *Minette de Tillesse, Caetano* Ezequiel. RBB 14/1-3 (1997) 15-31.

3714  **Pohlmann, Karl-Friedrich** Das Buch des Propheten Hesekiel 1-19. ATD 22/1, 1996, ⇒12,3539. REstAg 32 (1997) 546-547 *(Mielgo, C.)*; JETh 11 (1997) 182-184 *(Renz, Thomas)*.

3715  ERibera Florit, Josep Targum Jonatán de los profetas posteriores en tradición babilónica: Ezequiel. TECC 62: M 1997, Instituto de Filología del CSIC 250 pp. 84-00-07698-2.

3716  *Angelini, Giuseppe* Meditazioni su Ezechiele. RCI 78 (1997) 300-309, 436-447, 661-674.

3717  **Berrigan, Daniel J.** Ezekiel: vision in the dust. Ill. *Lewis-Borbely, T.*: Maryknoll, NY 1997, Orbis xxi; 137 pp. $16. 1-57075-135-8.

3718  **Boggio, Giovanni** 'Lectio divina' del profeta Ezechiele. Leggere le Scritture 4: Padova 1997, Messaggero 252 pp. Bibl. L22.000. 88-250-0690-X [CiVi 52,510].

3719  *Chrostowski, Waldemar* Ezechiel jako świadek asyryjskiej diaspory Izraelitów [Ezekiel as a witness of the Assyrian diaspora of the Israelites]. 1997, ⇒52. FŁACH J., 81-94. **P.**

3720  *Davidson, Richard M.* The chiastic literary structure of the book of Ezekiel. 1997, ⇒83. FSHEA W., 71-93.

3721  *Lust, Johan* The vocabulary of LXX Ezekiel and its dependence upon the pentateuch. BEThL 133: 1997, ⇒17. FBREKELMANS C., 529-546.

3722  *Malamat, Abraham* New Mari documents and the prophecy of Ezekiel. 1997, ⇒34. MGREENBERG M., 71*-76* **H.**

3723  **McIver, Robert K.** Ezekiel: through crisis to glory. Abundant Life Bible Amplifier. Oshawa, Canada 1997, Pacific 285 pp. 0-8163-1377-6/8-4. Diss. [RB 105,157].

3724  **Mein, A.R.** Ezekiel and the ethics of exile. Diss. Oxf 1997 [RTL 29,579].

3725  *Sedlmeier, Franz* Gott erschüttert Gottvertrauen: das Ringen mit dem babylonischen Exil im Ezechielbuch. Prisma 9/2 (1997) 13-9.

3726  **Stevenson, Kalinda Rose** Vision of transformation: the territorial rhetoric of Ezekiel 40-48. SBL.DS 154: 1996, ⇒12,3585. REThL 73 (1997) 161-162 *(Lust, J.)*.

3727  *Tarlin, Jan William* Utopia and pornography in Ezekiel: violence, hope, and the shattered male subject. Reading bibles. 1997, ⇒172. EBeal, Timothy K., 175-183.

3728  *Whitman, Andrew* Ezekiel's 'leadership training seminar': Ezekiel 11-14. Evangel 15/3 (1997) 69-73.

3729 **Bodendorfer, Gerhard** Das Drama des Bundes: Ezechiel 16 in rabbinischer Perspektive. Herder's Biblical Studies 11: FrB 1997, Herder (6) 392 pp. 3-451-26236-3.

3730 *Lust, Johan* And I shall hang him on a lofty mountain: Ezek 17:22-24 and Messianism in the Septuagint. IX Congress IOSCS. SCSt 45: 1997, ⇒340. ᴱTaylor, Bernard A., 231-250.

3731 *Rumianek, Ryszard* Problem odpowiedzialności według Ez 18,2 [The problem of responsibility according to Ezek 18,2]. 1997, ⇒52. ᶠLACH J., 359-366. **P.**

3732 *Lust, Johan* Ezekiel salutes Isaiah: Ezekiel 20,32-44. BEThL 132: 1997, ⇒12. ᶠBEUKEN W., 367-382.

3733 *Ruiz, Jean-Pierre* Exile, history, and hope: a Hispanic reading of Ezekiel 20. BiTod 35 (1997) 106-113 [Mk 12,18-27].

3734 *Harland, P.J.* What kind of 'violence' in Ezekiel 22?. ET 108 (1997) 111-114.

3735 *Arthur, Joseph* O rei de Tiro em Ezequiel 28:12-19: seria ele Satanás. Vox Scripturae 7/1 (1997) 3-24 [ZID 23,415].

3736 *Porter, J.R.* Ezekiel xxx 16—a suggestion. VT 47 (1997) 128.

3737 *Homerski, Józef* Dobry pasterz: refleksje egzegetyczno-teologiczne nad tekstem Ez 34,1-31 [Good Shepherd: exegetical and theological reflections on Ez 34,1-31]. Sum. 129. WST 10 (1997) 123-129.

3738 *Talmon, Shemaryahu* Fragments of an Ezekiel scroll from Masada 1043-2220 (Ezekiel 35:11-38:14). 1997, ⇒34. ᴹGREENBERG M., 53*-69*. **H.**

3739 **Giuliano, Luca** L'acqua di purificazione e il dono dello spirito in Ezechiele 36,24-28. Diss. Pont. Univ. Urbaniana; ᴰ*Testa, Emmanuele*: Extract. Genuae 1997, 85 pp.

3740 *Costen, James H.* How can these bones live?: Ezekiel 37. JITC 24 (1996-97) 51-65 [ZID 23,406].

3741 *Gosse, B.* La réhabilitation des prophètes d'Israël en Ezéchiel 38:17-23. OTEs 10 (1997) 226-235 [Ezek 13].

3742 **Schmitt, John W.; Laney, J. Carl** Messiah's coming temple: Ezekiel's prophetic vision of the future temple. GR 1997, Kregel 191 pp. $11. 0-8254-3727-X. ᴿCBTJ 13 (1997) 70-73 *(McLain, Charles E.)* [Ezek 40-48].

3743 **Tuell, Steven Shaun** The law of the temple in Ezekiel 40-48. HSM 49: 1992, ⇒8,3893... 12,3584. ᴿJSSt 44 (1997) 389-390 *(Curtis, Adrian H.W.)*.

E9.1 **Apocalyptica VT**

3744 *Capelli, Piero* Periodizzazioni del tempo: la soluzione apocalittica. RStB 9/1 (1997) 193-214.

3745 *Collins, John J.* Apocalyptic eschatology as the transcendence of death <1974>;

3746 Genre, ideology and social movements in Jewish apocalypticism <1991>;

3747 Jewish apocalyptic against its Hellenistic Near Eastern environment <1975>;

3748 The origin of evil in apocalyptic literature and the Dead Sea scrolls <1995>;

3749 The place of apocalypticism in the religion of Israel <1987>;

3750 The sage in the apocalyptic and pseudepigraphic literature
<1990>. Seers. JSJ.S 54: 1997, ⇒119. 75-97/25-38/59-74/287-
299/39-57/339-350.
3751 **Collins, John Joseph** Apocalypticism in the Dead Sea Scrolls. The
Literature of the Dead Sea Scrolls: L 1997, Routledge xv; 187 pp.
£37.50/£12. 0-415-14636-4/7-2.
3752 *Hartmann, Lars* The functions of some so-called apocalyptic time-
tables <1976>;
3753 *Hartmann, Lars* Survey of the problem of apocalyptic genre
<1983>. Text-centered NT studies. WUNT 102: 1997, ⇒132.
107-124/89-105.
3754 **Jacobsen, David S.** As seeing the invisible: the cosmic scope of
apocalyptic preaching. Diss. Vanderbilt 1997; DButtrick, David
[RTL 29,585].
3755 *Jasper, David* Theology and postmodernity: poetry, apocalypse and
the future of God. SvTK 73/3 (1997) 97-103.
3756 **Johnson, Robert Van** The development of *sheol/hades* in the Jewish apocalypstic writings. Diss. Wycliffe, Toronto 1997;
DLongenecker, Richard [SR 26,528].
3757 **LaRondelle, Hans K.** How to understand end-time prophecies of
the bible: the biblical-contextual approach. Sarasota, FL 1997,
First Impressions x; 501 pp. 0-9659202-0-8 [NThAR 2000,62].
3758 *Marconcini, Benito* Ancora sull'"apocalittica": una luce da non
spegnere. RivBib 45 (1997) 179-182.
3759 **Moraleda Molero, Domingo** Influjo apocaliptico en los origenes y
comprensión de la vida religiosa. Diss. Salamanca 1997 [RTL
29,579].
3760 *Rohner, Manuel* "Die Prophezeiung des Nfr.tj": eine Vorübung zur
Struktur des Apokalyptischen. ThZ 53 (1997) 304-321.
3761 *Sacchi, Paolo* L'"attesa" come essenza dell'apocalittica?. RivBib
45 (1997) 71-78.
3762 **Schlomit, Adam** Zur Neubewertung der Apokalyptik: nach der
Veröffentlichung der Henochfragmente aus Qumran.     [n.p.]
1997, [n.p.] 52 pp.
3763 *Schwager, Raymund* Apokalyptik: über die Verbindlichkeit der
biblischen Bilder vom Ende der Geschichte. SaThZ 1 (1997) 2-14.
3764 *Vermeylen, Jacques* L'émergence et les racines de l'Apocalyptique.
Rés. 321. RThPh 129 (1997) 321-340.
3765 *Young, Ginger; Vintinner, David* That ol'time religion: American
folk artists depict apocalyptic texts. BiRe 13/5 (1997) 36-44.

E9.2 **Daniel:** *textus, commentarii; themata, versiculi*

3766 *Asurmendi, Jesús* El libro de Daniel en la investigación reciente.
EstB 55 (1997) 509-540.
3767 **Di Lella, Alexander** Daniel: a book for troubling times. Spiritual
Commentaries: Hyde Park, NY 1997, New City 232 pp. $12. 1-
56548-087-2 [ThD 44,88].
3768 **Meadowcroft, T.J.** Aramaic Daniel and Greek Daniel: a literary
comparison. JSOT.S 198: 1995, ⇒11/1,2475. RThLZ 122 (1997)
543-544 *(Koch, Klaus)*; BS 154 (1997) 501-502 *(Taylor, R.A.)*.
3769 **Miller, Stephen R.** Daniel. NAC 18: 1994, ⇒10,3614... 12,3607.
RAUSS 35 (1997) 134-136 *(Willis, Lloyd)*.

3770 *Minette de Tillesse, Caetano* Daniel. RBB 14/1-3 (1997) 194-203.
3771 **Stefanovic, Zdravko** The Aramaic of Daniel in the light of Old Aramaic. 1992, ⇒8,3934... 10,3630. ᴿBiOr 54 (1997) 746-754 *(Folmer, M.L.)*.
3772 **Van der Woude, A.S.** The book of Daniel in the light of new findings. BEThL 106: 1993, ⇒9,420... 11/1,2472. AfO 44-45 (1997-98) 438-439 *(Zaborski, Andrzej)*; EThL 73 (1997) 428-430 *(Schoors, A.)*.

3773 *Baldwin, Dalton D.* Free will and conditionality in Daniel. 1997, ⇒83. ᶠSʜᴇᴀ W., 163-172.
3774 *Bolognesi, Pietro* Religione e cultura: Daniele, un esempio biblico. Studi di Teologia 9/1 (1997) 89-96.
3775 *Collins, John J.* The meaning of 'the end' in the book of Daniel <1990>;
3776 Nebuchadnezzar and the kingdom of God <1990>. Seers. JSJ.S 54: 1997, ⇒119. 157-165/131-137.
3777 *Day, John* Resurrection imagery from Baal to the book of Daniel. Congress volume 1995. VT.S 66: 1997, ⇒323. ᴱEmerton, J.A., 125-133.
3778 *Flint, Peter W.* The Daniel tradition at Qumran. Eschatology, messianism. SDSSRL 1: 1997, ⇒276. ᴱEvans, Craig A., 41-60.
3779 *Gane, Roy* Genre awareness and interpretation of the book of Daniel. 1997, ⇒83. ᶠSʜᴇᴀ W., 137-148.
3780 *Jobes, Karen* Karen Jobes responds to Tim McLay. BIOSCS 30 (1997) 32-35.
3781 **Koch, Klaus** Europa, Rom und der Kaiser vor dem Hintergrund von zwei Jahrtausenden Rezeption des Buches Daniel. Berichte aus den Sitzungen der Joachim Jungius-Gesellschaft der Wissenschaften Hamburg 15: Gö 1997, Vandenhoeck & R 171 pp. DM49. 3-525-86291-1 [ThLZ 123,848—Haag, Ernst].
3782 *Koch, Klaus* Spätisraelitisch-jüdische und urchristliche Danielrezeption vor und nach der Zerstörung des zweiten Tempels. OBO 153: 1997, ⇒91. ᶠSᴛᴇᴄᴋ O., 93-123.
3783 *Leatherman, Donn W.* Apparent indicators of textual discontinuity in the book of Daniel. 1997, ⇒83. ᶠSʜᴇᴀ W., 149-161.
3784 *Millar, Fergus* Hellenistic history in a Near Eastern perspective: the book of Daniel. Hellenistic constructs. 1997, ⇒271. ᴱCartledge, P., 89-104.
3785 *Mitchell, T.C.* Achaemenid history and the book of Daniel. 1997, ⇒58. ᴹLᴜᴋᴏɴɪɴ V., 68-78.
3786 **Olyan, Saul M.** A thousand thousand served him: exegesis and the naming of angels in ancient Judaism. TSAJ 36: 1993, ⇒9,2205... 12,1696. ᴿJSSt 42 (1997) 154-159 *(Morray-Jones, C.R.A.)*.
3787 **Reaburn, Mary Ann** Jᴇʀᴏᴍᴇ's use of the psalms in his commentary on Daniel. Diss. Melbourne College of Divinity 1997-98; ᴰO'Hagan, Angelo [Sum. Pacifica 11,246].
3788 *Stefanovic, Zdravko* The presence of the *three and a fraction*: a literary figure in the book of Daniel. 1997, ⇒83. ᶠSʜᴇᴀ W., 199-203.
3789 **Steussy, M.J.** Gardens in Babylon: narrative and faith in the Greek legends of Daniel. SBL.DS 141: 1993, ⇒9,3819; 10,3639. ᴿJSSt 44 (1997) 396-397 *(Davies, Philip)*.

3790  *Vallejo Bozal, Javier* Contribution à l'étude de la transmission des cycles bibliques du haut moyen âge: les enluminures du livre de Daniel dans la Bible mozarabe de 960. Sum. 159. CCMéd 40 (1997) 159-174.

3791  *Venter, P.M.* Daniel and Enoch: two different reactions. HTS 53 (1997) 68-91.

3792  *Marconcini, Benito* Il tempo nella successione dei regni secondo Daniele (cc. 2-7). PSV 36 (1997) 95-107.

3793  *Lawson, Jack N.* 'The God who reveals secrets': the Mesopotamian background to Daniel 2.47. JSOT 74 (1997) 61-76.

3794  **Miegge, Mario** Il sogno del re di Babilonia: profezia e storia da Thomas MUENTZER a Isaac NEWTON. 1995, ⇒11/1,2476; 12,3626. RFilTeo 11 (1997) 419-423 *(Sorrentino, Sergio)* [Dan 2].

3795  *Dulaey, Martine* Les trois Hébreux dans la fournaise (Dn 3) dans l'interprétation symbolique de l'église ancienne. RevSR 71 (1997) 33-59.

3796  *Albertz, Rainer* Bekehrung von oben als "messianisches Programm": die Sonderüberlieferung der Septuaginta in Dan 4-6. Theologische Probleme. 1997, ⇒223. EReventlow, H. Graf, 46-62.

3797  *Waterhouse, Douglas S.* Why was Darius the Mede expunged from history?. 1997, ⇒83. FSHEA W., 173-189 [Dan 5,30-31].

3798  *Venter, P.M.* 'n Verkenning van postmodernisme en 'n ekskurs op Daniël 7-12. HTS 53 (1997) 580-598.

3799  *Fletcher-Louis, Crispin H. T.* The high priest as divine mediator in the Hebrew Bible: Dan 7:13 as a test case. SBL.SPS 36 (1997) 161-193.

3800  *Gulley, Norman R.* Why the Danielic little horn is not Antiochus IV Epiphanes. 1997, ⇒83. FSHEA W., 191-197 [Dan 7,21-22].

3801  *Collins, John J.* Stirring up the Great Sea: the religio-historical background of Daniel 7. Seers. JSJ.S 54: 1997 <1993>, ⇒119. 139-155.

3802  *Stuckenbruck, Loren T.* The throne-theophany of the book of Giants: some new light on the background of Daniel 7. The scrolls and the scriptures. JSPE.S 26: 1997, ⇒299. EPorter, S., 211-220.

3803  *Le Saux, Madeleine* Gabriel, l'ange de la parole du Seigneur: une lecture du livre de Daniel 9,20-25. DosB 70 (1997) 22-23.

3804  *Grabbe, Lester L.* The seventy-weeks prophecy (Daniel 9:24-27) in early Jewish interpretation. 1997, ⇒77. FSANDERS J., 595-611.

3805  *Ray, Paul J.* The *Abomination of Desolation* in Daniel 9:27 and related texts: theology of retributive judgment. 1997, ⇒83. FSHEA W., 205-213.

3806  *Blum, Erhard* Der "Schiqquz Schonem" und die Jehud-Drachme BMC Palestine S.181, Nr.29. BN 90 (1997) 13-27 [Dan 9,27; 1 Macc 1,44-51].

3807  **Rigger, Hansjörg** Siebzig Siebener: die 'Jahrwochenprophetie' in Dan 9. Diss. Trier. TThSt 57: Trier 1997, Paulinus ix; 344 pp. DM68 [CBQ 61,348s—Redditt, Paul L.].

3808  *Rowland, Christopher* A man clothed in linen: Daniel 10:5-9 and Jewish angelology. NT Backgrounds. 1997 <1985>, ⇒F1.1. EEvans, Craig A., 33-45.

3809  *Thompson, Steven* Those who are wise: the *maskilim* in Daniel and the New Testament. 1997, ⇒83. FSHEA W., 215-220 [Dan 11,33-35; 12,3; 12,10].

3810 *Van der Woude, Adam S.* Prophetic prediction, political prognosti-
cation, and firm belief: reflections on Daniel 11:40-12:3. 1997,
⇒77. ᶠSᴀɴᴅᴇʀs J. 63-73.

3811 **Stele, Artur A.** Resurrection in Daniel 12 and its contribution to
the theology of the book of Daniel. Diss. 1996, ⇒12,3633 [Abstr.
AUSS 35 (1997) 246].

3812 **Wysny, Andreas** Die Erzählungen von Bel und dem Drachen: Untersuchungen zu Dan 14. SBB 33: 1996, ⇒12,3646. ᴿRTL 28
(1997) 388-390 *(Bogaert, Pierre-Maurice)*; ThLZ 122 (1997) 801-
802 *(Haag, Ernst)*.

### E9.3 *Prophetae Minores,* Dōdekaprophetōn...Hosea, Joel

3813 *Ben Zvi, Ehud* A Deuteronomistic redaction in/among "The
twelve"?: a contribution from the standpoint of the books of
Micah, Zephaniah and Obadiah. SBL.SPS 36 (1997) 433-459.

3814 **Birch, Bruce C.** Hosea, Joel, and Amos. Westminster bible companion: LVL 1997, Westminster viii; 262 pp. $19. 0-664-25271-0.

3815 **Brown, William P.** Obadiah through Malachi. Westminster bible
companion: LVL 1996 Westminster xii; 209 pp. 0-664-25520-5.

3816 *Conrad, Edgar W.* The end of prophecy and the appearance of an-
gels/messengers in the book of the Twelve. JSOT 73 (1997) 65-79.

3817 *Dogniez, Cécile* Le Dieu des armées dans le Dodekapropheton:
quelques remarques sur une initiative de traduction. IX Congress
IOSCS. SCSt 45: 1997, ⇒340. ᴱTaylor, Bernard A., 19-36.

3818 **Gordon, Robert P.** Studies in the Targum to the Twelve Prophets:
from Nahum to Malachi. VT.S 51: 1994, ⇒10,3651... 12,3650.
ᴿJQR 88 (1997) 102-103 *(Schenker, Adrian)*.

3819 **Jeremias, Jörg** Hosea und Amos: Studien zu den Anfängen des
Dodekapropheton. FAT 13: 1996, ⇒12,3669. ᴿRExp 94/1 (1997)
137 *(Nogalski, James D.)*.

3820 **Jones, Barry Alan** The formation of the book of the Twelve.
SBL.DS 149: 1995, 11/1,2498; 12,3653. ᴿJSSt 44 (1997) 390-392
*(Gelston, A.)*; HebStud 38 (1997) 141-143 *(Ellis, Robert R.)*; JBL
118 (1999) 542-543 *(Simkins, Ronald A.)*.

3821 ᴱ**McComiskey, Thomas Edward** The Minor Prophets: an exegetical and expository commentary. 1992-3, 2 vols, ⇒8,3972...
11/1,2502. ᴿHebStud 38 (1997) 143-146 *(Oswalt, John N.)*.

3822 *Minette de Tillesse, Caetano* Joes-Abdias-Naum-Habacuc. RBB
14/1-3 (1997) 144-148.

3823 *Müller-Abels, Susanne* HIᴇʀᴏɴʏᴍᴜs, Prologe zu den Kommen-
taren zum Zwölfprophetenbuch: Exegese und Rhetorik. StPatr 33:
1997, ⇒351. ᴱLivingstone, Elizabeth A., 345-351.

3824 *Pearson, Brook W.R.* The book of the Twelve, Aqiba's messianic
interpretations, and the refuge caves of the second Jewish war. The
scrolls and the scriptures. JSPE.S 26: 1997, ⇒229. ᴱPorter,
Stanley E., 221-239.

3825 *Redditt, Paul L.* The production and reading of the book of the
Twelve. SBL.SPS 36 (1997) 394-419.

3826 *Rendtorff, Rolf* How to read the book of the Twelve as a theological unity. SBL.SPS 36 (1997) 420-432.

3827  **Van der Woude, A.S.** Amos—Obadja—Jona: een praktische bijbelverklaring. Tekst en Toelichting: Kampen 1997, Kok 158 pp.
ƒ35. 90-242-9182-8 [Str. 65,664—Beentjes, Panc].
3828  **Wilcock, Michael** Six minor prophets: understanding the signs of
the times. Crossway Bible Guide: Leicester 1997, Crossway 151
pp. 1-85684-141-3.
3829  **Yerushalmi, Shmuel** Me'am Lo'ez: the book of Trei-Asar (2): the
Twelve Prophets: Micah, Nahum, Habakkuk, Zephanya, Haggai,
Zechariah, Malachi. ᵀᴱ*Faier, Zvi*: J 1997, Moznaim xii; 548 pp.
Adapted by Zvi Faier.

3830  *De Menezes, Rui* Gone with the whirlwind!: Hoshea's critique of
the monarchy. 1997, ⇒89. ᶠSᴏᴀʀᴇs-Pʀᴀʙʜᴜ G., 219-238.
3831  **Eidevall, Göran** Grapes in the desert: metaphors, models, and themes in Hosea 4-14. CB.OT 43: 1996, ⇒3691. ᴿThLZ 122 (1997)
539-540 *(Neef, Heinz-Dieter)*; SEÅ 62 (1997) 153-165 *(Laato,
Antti)*.
3832  *Freedman, David Noel* Problems of textual criticism in the book of
Hosea. Divine Commitment 1. 1997 < 1979 >, ⇒124. 314-329.
3833  **Garrett, Duane A.** Hosea, Joel. NAC 19 A: Nv 1997, Broadman
& H 426 pp. Bibl. 0-8054-0119-9.
3834  **Guenther, Allen R.** Hosea, Amos. Believers Church Bible Commentary. Scottdale, PA 1997, Herald 430 pp. $20/CAN$28.50. 0-
8361-9072-6.
3835  **Holt, Else Kragelund** Prophesying the past: the use of Israel's history in the book of Hosea. JSOT.S 194: 1995, ⇒11/1,2513;
12,3667. ᴿCBQ 59 (1997) 122-124 *(Nash, Kathleen S.)*.
3836  **Landy, Francis** Hosea. 1995, ⇒11/1,2507. ᴿCBQ 59 (1997) 127-
128 *(Dearman, J. Andrew)*.
3837  **Macintosh, Andrew Alexander** A critical and exegetical commentary on Hosea. ICC: E 1997, Clark xcix; 600 pp. £40. 0-567-
08545-7. ᴿRBBras 14 (1997) 334-335.
3838  *Michel, Diethelm* Zum Geschichtsverständnis Hoseas. Studien zur
Überlieferungsgeschichte. TB 93: 1997 < 1996 >. 219-228.
3839  **Morris, Gerald** Prophecy, poetry and Hosea. JSOT.S 219: 1996,
⇒12,3671. ᴿCBQ 59 (1997) 744 *(Jones, Barry A.)*.
3840  **Nwaoru, Emmanuel** The imagery in the prophecy of Hosea: a literary and exegetical survey of Hosea's metaphors and similes. Diss.
Mü 1997; ᴰ*Görg, M.* [RTL 29,579].
3841  **Ortlund, Raymond C.** Whoredom: God's unfaithful wife in biblical theology. New Studies in Biblical Theology 2: GR 1997, Eerdmans 200 pp. $18. 0-8028-4285-2 [ThD 44,376—Heiser, W.
Charles].
3842  **Seifert, Brigitte** Metaphorisches Reden von Gott im Hoseabuch.
FRLANT 166: 1996, ⇒12,3675. ᴿThLZ 122 (1997) 663-664
*(Balz-Cochois, Helgard)*; Bib. 78 (1997) 412-415 *(Eidevall,
Göran)*; CBQ 59 (1997) 555-567 *(Dempsey, Carol J.)*.
3843  **Simian-Yofre, Horacio** El desierto de los dioses: teología e historia en el libro de Oseas. 1993, ⇒9,3854... 11/1,2518. ᴿPerTeol 29
(1997) 256-257 *(Vitório, Jaldemir)*.
3844  **Šporčić, Ivan** Das untreue Volk: zum Sprachfeld der Untreue bei
Hosea. Diss. ᴰ*Conroy, Charles* 1995, ⇒11/1,2520. ᴿBoSm 67/1
(1997) 104-107 *(Rebić, Adalbert)*.

3845 **Sherwood, Yvonne** The prostitute and the prophet: Hosea's marriage in literary-theoretical perspective. JSOT.S 212: 1996, ⇒12,3683. RCBQ 59 (1997) 557-558 *(Zulick, Margaret D.)* [Hos 1-3].

3846 *Silva Retamales, Santiago* Oseas 1-3: interpretación y teología. TyV 38 (1997) 347-370.

3847 *Gosse, Bernard* Osée 1,1-2,3, les enfants d'Osée et d'Isaïe et la rédaction d'ensemble du livre d'Isaïe. SEL 14 (1997) 65-68.

3848 *Dass, Maria; Ambrose, Devadass* The divorce (?) formula in Hos 2:4a. ITS 34/1-3 (1997) 56-88.

3849 *Moenikes, Ansgar* The rejection of cult and politics by Hosea. Henoch 19/1 (1997) 3-15 [Hos 3,1-4; 10,1-4].

3850 **Vicuna, Luis** Énoncé prophétique et traditions historiques selon Osée, chapitres 8-11. Diss. Strasbourg 1997; DHeintz, J.-G., 552 pp. [RTL 29,580].

3851 *Breytenbach, A.P.* Die herfsfees en die koningsrite by Bet-El as interteks van Amos 7:10-8:14 en Hosea 9:1-9. HTS 53 (1997) 513-528.

3852 **Oestreich, Bernhard** Metaphors and similes for Yahweh in Hosea 14:2-9 (1-9): a study of Hoseanic pictorial language. Diss. Andrews 1997; DYounker, R.W.: 377 pp. [RTL 29,579].

3853 **Crenshaw, James L.** Joel. AncB 24C: 1995, ⇒11/1,2548; 12,3698. RBS 154 (1997) 240-242 *(Taylor, Richard A.)*.

3854 **Garrett, Duane A.** Hosea, Joel. NAC 19 A: Nv 1997, Broadman & H 426 pp. Bibl. 0-8054-0119-9.

3855 **Simkins, Ronald** Yahweh's activity in history and nature in the book of Joel. ANETS 10: 1991, ⇒7,3411... 12,2554. RJNES 56 (1997) 156-157 *(Handy, Lowell K.)*.

3856 *Treier, Daniel J.* The fulfillment of Joel 2:28-32: a multiple-lens approach. JETS 40 (1997) 13-26.

3857 *Crenshaw, James L.* Freeing the imagination: the conclusion to the book of Joel. Prophecy and prophets. 1997, ⇒199. EGitay, Yehoshua, 129-147 [Joel 4,17-21].

### E9.4 Amos

3858 **Bovati, Pietro; Meynet, Roland** Le livre du prophète Amos. 1994, ⇒10,3690; 12,3702. REstB 55 (1997) 118-119 *(Arambarri, J.)*.

    **Guenther, Allen R.** Hosea, Amos ⇒3834.

3859 **Jeremias, Jörg** Der Prophet Amos. ATD 24/2: 1995, ⇒11/1,2566; 12,3706. RCBQ 59 (1997) 543-544 *(Craghan, John F.)*; JBL 116 (1997) 548-550 *(Biddle, Mark E.)*.

3860 **Paul, Shalom M.** Amos. 1991, ⇒7,3425... 10,3697. RVJTR 61 (1997) 134-136 *(Meagher, P.M.)*.

3861 **Smith, Billy K.; Page, Frank S.** Amos, Obadiah, Jonah. NAC 19B: 1995, ⇒11/1,2503; 12,3660. RHebStud 38 (1997) 146-149 *(Ogden, Graham S.)*.

3862 **Thompson, Henry O.** The book of Amos: an annotated bibliography. ATLA.BS 42: Lanham 1997, Scarecrow xxvii; (2) 433 pp. $54. 0-8108-3274-7.

3863 **Bovati, Pietro; Meynet, Roland** La fin d'Israël: paroles d'Amos. LiBi 101: 1994, ⇒10,3691... 12,3708. ᴿEstB 55 (1997) 545-546 *(Asenjo, J.)*.

3864 *Fritz, Volkmar* Amosbuch, Amos-Schule und historischer Amos. Studien zur Literatur. 1997 <1989>, ⇒126. 109-124.

3865 *Levin, Christoph* Das Amosbuch der Anawim. ZThK 94 (1997) 407-436.

3866 *Manakatt, Mathew* Was Amos a shepherd?: an investigation into the profession of prophet Amos. BiBh 23 (1997) 228-244.

3867 *Noble, Paul R.* Amos' absolute "no". VT 47 (1997) 329-340.

3868 **Reimer, Haroldo** Richtet auf das Recht! Studien zur Botschaft des Amos. SBS 149: 1992, ⇒8,4015... 11/1,2592. ᴿBZ 41 (1997) 100-102 *(Gerstenberger, Erhard S.)*.

3869 *Simian-Yofre, Horacio* Canonicidad, sincronía e diacronía: a propósito de Amós. EfMex 15 (1997) 177-197.

3870 **Watts, John D.W.** Vision and prophecy in Amos. Macon ²1997, Mercer University Press xi; 144 pp. 0-86554-534-0.

3871 *Fritz, Volkmar* Die Fremdvölkersprüche des Amos. Studien zur Literatur. 1997 <1987>, ⇒126. 97-108 [Amos 1,3-2,16].

3872 *Cimosa, Mario* Da quale testo tradurre nelle lingue moderne l'Antico Testamento (TM o LXX?): alcuni esempi dal profeta Amos. Sal. 59 (1997) 443-462 [Amos 1,3.6.14-15; 2,7; 3,3-4.9-11; 4,1; 5,25].

3873 *Orel, Vladimir* Textological notes. ZAW 109 (1997) 408-413 [Ezek 13,17-18; Amos 2,6-7].

3874 *Crocetti, Giuseppe* 'Cercate me e vivrete' (Am 5,1-17). PSV 35 (1997) 61-75.

3875 *Loss, Nicolò Maria* Il "giorno di Jahweh": tema profetico inaugurato da Amos. BSRel 125: 1997, ⇒45. ᶠJAVIERRE ORTAS A., 27-44 [Amos 5,18-20].

3876 *Romero, C.G.* Amos 5:21-24: religion, politics, and the Latino experience. Journal of HispanicLatino Theology 4/4 (1997) 21-41 [ZID 23,273].

3877 *O'Kennedy, D.F.* 'It shall not be': divine forgiveness in the intercessory prayers of Amos (Am 7:1-6). OTEs 10 (1997) 92-108.

3878 *Heyns, Dalene* Space and time in Amos 7: reconsidering the third vision. OTEs 10 (1997) 27-38 [Amos 7,7-9].

3879 *Cooper, Alan* The meaning of Amos's third vision (Amos 7:7-9). 1997, ⇒34. ᴹGREENBERG M., 13-21.

3880 *Gilbert, Pierre* A new look at Amos's prophetic status (Amos 7:10-17). EeT(O) 28 (1997) 291-300.

3881 *Heyns, Dalene* Space and time in Amos 8: an ecological reading. OTEs 10 (1997) 236-251.

3882 *Terblanche, M.D.* 'Rosen und Lavendel nach Blut und Eisen': intertextuality in the book of Amos. OTEs 10 (1997) 312-321 [Amos 9,11-15].

E9.5 **Jonas:** *commentarii; themata; versiculi*

**Craghan, John** Ester...Giona ⇒2693.
3883 **Limburg, James** Jonah. 1993, ⇒9,3915... 12,3737. RJNES 56 (1997) 209-210 *(Long, Gary Alan)*.
3884 *Minette de Tillesse, Caetano* Na Diáspora: Jonas. RBB 14/1-3 (1997) 157-160.
**Nowell, Irene** I libri di Giona... ⇒2694.

3885 **Bolin, Thomas M.** Freedom beyond forgiveness: the book of Jonah re-examined. JSOT.S 236; Copenhagen International Seminar 3: Shf 1997, Academic 217 pp. £35/$50. 1-85075-642-2.
3886 **Chow, Simon** The sign of Jonah reconsidered: a study of its meaning in the gospel traditions. CB.NT 27: 1995, RThLZ 122 (1997) 32-34 *(Frenschkowski, Marco)*; CritRR 10 (1997) 171-173 *(Matson, Mark A.)* [Mt 12,39-41; Lk 11,29-32].
3887 **Corti, G.** Un profeta ribelle all'amore: leggere e pregare il libro di Giona. Mi 1997, Paoline 134 pp. L14.500 [PaVi 44/6,54—Rolla, Armando].
3888 *Dorsey, David A.* Literary architecture and meaning in the book of Jonah. 1997, ⇒83. FSHEA W., 57-69.
3889 **Facey, A.** Giona profeta riluttante, Dio misericordioso. Bo 1997, EDB 64 pp. L8.000 [RivBib 45,255].
3890 **Laffite, Jacques** Pardon, mode d'emploi: précédé de procès pour Jonas. Turnhout 1997, Brepols 239 pp. 2-503-83025-0 [RHPhR 77,251].
3891 **Lux, Rüdiger** Jona, Prophet zwischen 'Verweigerung' und 'Gehorsam': eine erzählanalytische Studie. FRLANT 162: 1994, ⇒10,3732... 12,3738. RZAW 109 (1997) 146 *(Pfeifer, H.)*.
3892 **Maillot, Alphonse** Jonas ou le sourire de Dieu. P 1997, Lethielleux 112 pp. 2-283-60170-3.
3893 *Nahmia, Yvette* FREUD and FROMM read the book of Jonah. DBM 16 (1997) 83-94. G.
3894 **Person, Raymond F. Jr.** In conversation with Jonah. JSOT.S 220: 1996, ⇒12,3756. RBib. 78 (1997) 415-420 *(Miller, Cynthia L.)*; CBQ 59 (1997) 748-749 *(Craig, Kenneth M.)*.
3895 **Poucouta, Paulin** La mission à tous vents: le livre de Jonas. Bible et Mission 5: Limete-Kinshasa 1997, L'Epiphanie 104 pp. [LV.F 53,362].
3896 *Prout, Elmer* God and Jonah's prayers. RestQ 39 (1997) 115-118.
3897 **Room, H.J.** Jona, profeet van God: bijbelstudie over het book Jona. Barneveld 1997, De Vuurbaak 68 pp. 90-6015-929-2 [NThAR 1997,291].
3898 *Schöpflin, Karin* Notschrei, Dank und Disput: Beten im Jonabuch. Bib. 78 (1997) 389-404.
3899 *Sevilla Jiménez, C.* La crisis de Jonás. Carthaginensia 13 (1997) 19-37.
3900 *Sherwood, Yvonne* Rocking the boat: Jonah and the new historicism. Bibl.Interp. 5 (1997) 364-402.
3901 **Trible, Phyllis** Rhetorical criticism: context, method, and the book of Jonah. 1994, ⇒10,2740... 12,3758. JR 77 (1997) 122-123 *(Sommer, Benjamin D.)*.

3902  *Wendland, Ernst R.* Five key aspects of style in Jonah and (possibly) how to translate them. TPBT 48 (1997) 308-328.
3903  *Wendland, Ernst R.* Recursion and variation in the "prophecy" of Jonah: on the rhetorical impact of stylistic technique in Hebrew narrative discourse, with special reference to irony and enigma. AUSS 35 (1997) 67-98; 189-209.

3904  **Opgen-Rhein, Hermann J.** Jonapsalm und Jonabuch: Sprachgestalt, Entstehungsgeschichte und Kontextbedeutung von Jona 2. SBB 38: Stu 1997, Katholisches Bibelwerk 252 pp. Bibl. 3-460-00381-2.

E9.6 *Micheas,* **Micah**

3905  **Carbone, Sandro Paolo; Rizzi, Giovanni** Il libro di Michea. 1996, ⇒12,3766. RIsidorianum 6 (1997) 270-271 *(Guillén Torralba, Juan).*
3906  **Cha, Jun-Hee** Micha und Jeremia. BBB 107: 1996, ⇒12,3767. RThLZ 122 (1997) 434-435 *(Kessler, Rainer);* CBQ 59 (1997) 339-340 *(Biddle, Mark E.).*
3907  **Lescow, Theodor** Worte und Wirkungen des Propheten Micha: ein kompositionsgeschichtlicher Kommentar. AzTh 84: Stu 1997, Calwer 304 pp. 3-7668-3510-6 [NThAR 1997,259] [Jer 8,8-9].
3908  **Zapff, Burkard M.** Redaktionsgeschichtliche Studien zum Michabuch im Kontext des Dodekapropheton. Diss.-Habil. FrB 1997; DRuppert, Lothar: BZAW 256: B 1997, De Gruyter xii; 331 pp. DM184. 3-11-015764-0.

3909  *Fritz, Volkmar* Das Wort gegen Samaria in Mi 1,2-7. Studien zur Literatur. 1997 <1974>, ⇒126. 125-140.
3910  **Wagenaar, Jan A.** Oordeel en heil: een onderzoek naar samenhang tussen de heils- en onheilsprofetieën in Micha 2-5 [Judgment and salvation: an investigation of the connection between the prophecies of salvation and doom in Micah 2-5]. 1995, ⇒11/1,2652. RBiOr 54 (1997) 450-452 *(Otto, Eckart).*
3911  *McKane, William* Micah 2:1-5: text and commentary. JSSt 42 (1997) 7-22.
3912  *Wessels, W.J.* Conflicting powers: reflections from the book of Micah. OTEs 10 (1997) 528-544 [Mic 2,1-13; 3].
3913  *Williamson, H.G.M.* Marginalia in Micah. VT 47 (1997) 360-372 [Mic 2,8; 4,7; 5,4; 6,14; 7,12].
3914  **Niccacci, Alviero** Un profeta tra oppressori e oppressi: analisi esegetica del capitolo 2. SBFA 27: 1989, ⇒5,2669... 8,4062. RCDios 210/1 (1997) 346-347 *(Gutiérrez, J.).*
3915  *Himbaza, Innocent* "Se couvriront-ils la moustache?" (Michée 3:7). BN 88 (1997) 27-30.
3916  *Wessels, W.J.* Wisdom in the gate: Micah takes the rostrum. OTEs 10 (1997) 125-135.
3917  *Lust, Johan* Mic 5,1-3 in Qumran and in the New Testament, and messianism in the Septuagint. The scriptures in the gospels. BEThL 131: 1997, ⇒234. ETuckett, Christopher M., 65-88.
3918  *Pola, Thomas* Micha 6,7a. BN 86 (1997) 57-59.

3919 *Crüsemann, Frank* '...nichts als...mitgehen mit Deinem Gott' (Mi 6,8): nachdenken über ungegangene Wege. WuD 24 (1997) 11-28.
3920 *Heil, Christoph* Die Rezeption von Micha 7,6 LXX in Q und Lukas. ZNW 88 (1997) 211-222 [Mt 10,35-36; Lk 12,52-53].

### E9.7 *Abdias, Sophonias...*Obadiah, Zephaniah, Nahum

3921 **Ben Zvi, Ehud** A historical-critical study of the book of Obadiah. BZAW 242: 1996. ᴿThLZ 122 (1997) 894-896 *(Wehrle, Josef)*; CritRR 10 (1997) 156-158 *(Watts, John D.W.)*.
3922 *Tanghe, Vincent* Die Trinker in Obadja 16. RB 104 (1997) 522-27.

3923 **Berlin, Adele** Zephaniah. AncB 25A: 1994, ⇒10,3758; 12,3787. ᴿCBQ 59 (1997) 108-110 *(Raabe, Paul R.)*.
3924 **Ryou, Daniel Hojoon** Zephaniah's oracles against the nations... 2:1-3:8. 1995, ⇒11/1,2668. ᴿJThS 48 (1997) 561-562 *(Mason, Rex)*; CBQ 59 (1997) 749-751 *(Haak, Robert D.)*; JBL 116 (1997) 735-738 *(Sweeney, Marvin A.)*; ThLZ 122 (1997) 1116-1117 *(Neef, Heinz-Dieter)*.
3925 ᴱ**Dietrich, Walter; Schwantes, Milton** Der Tag wird kommen... Zefanja. SBS 170: 1996, ⇒12,3789. ᴿThLZ 122 (1997) 1000-1001 *(Neef, Heinz-Dieter)*.
3926 **Spreafico, Ambrogio** Sofonia. 1991, ⇒9,3956; 10,3762. ᴿEstB 55 (1997) 270-272 *(Arambarri, J.)*.
3927 *Weimar, Peter* Zefanja—Aufbau und Struktur einer Prophetenschrift. UF 29 (1997) 723-774.

3928 *Ball, E.* Interpreting the Septuagint: Nahum 2.2 as a case-study. JSOT 75 (1997) 59-75.
3929 **Spronk, Klaas** Nahum. Historical Commentary on the OT: Kampen 1997, Kok P 153 pp. ƒ49. 90-242-6355-7 [ITBT 5/5,32].

### E9.8 *Habacuc,* Habakkuk

ᴱ**Connolly, Seán** Beda Venerabilis... super Canticum Habacuc ⇒2695.
3930 *Heard, Chris* Hearing the children's cries: commentary, deconstruction, ethics, and the book of Habakkuk. Semeia 77 (1997) 75-89.
3931 *Martyn, J. Louis* The textual contradiction between Habakkuk 2:4 and Leviticus 18:5. Theological issues. 1997, ⇒146.
3932 *Van Ruiten, J.T.A.G.M.* "His master's voice"?: the supposed influence of the book of Isaiah in the book of Habakkuk. BEThL 132: 1997, ⇒12. ᶠBᴇᴜᴋᴇɴ W., 397-411.

### E9.9 *Aggaeus,* Haggai—*Zacharias,* Zechariah—*Malachias,* Malachi

3933 *Minette de Tillesse, Caetano* Ageu-Zacarias-Malaquias. RBB 14/1-3 (1997) 100-116.
3934 **Redditt, Paul L.** Haggai, Zechariah and Malachi. NCeB. 1995, ⇒11/1,2688; 12,3825. ᴿHebStud 38 (1997) 149-152 *(Norton, Gerard J.)*.

3935  *Sykes, Seth* Time and space in Haggai-Zechariah 1-8: a Bakhtinian analysis of a prophetic chronicle. JSOT 76 (1997) 97-124 [Zech 1,1-8,23].
3936  **Tollington, Janet E.** Tradition and innovation in Haggai and Zechariah 1-8. JSOT.S 150: 1993, ⇒9,3979... 11/1,2691. ᴿThRv 93 (1997) 217-218 *(Reventlow, Henning Graf)*.

3937  *Cimosa, Mario* Observations on the Greek translation of the book of Zechariah. IX Congress IOSCS. SCSt 45: 1997, ⇒340. ᴱTaylor, Bernard A., 91-108.
3938  *Floyd, Michael H.* Cosmos and history in Zechariah's view of the restoration (Zechariah 1:7-6:15). ᶠKɴɪᴇʀɪᴍ R., 1997, ⇒48. 125-144.
3939  *Fournier-Bidoz, Alain* Des mains de Zorobabel aux yeux du Seigneur: pour une lecture unitaire de Zacharie iv 1-14. VT 47 (1997) 537-542.
3940  *Hoet, Hendrik* Dromen met Zacharia. ITBT 5/8 (1997) 10-11.
3941  *Kline, Meredith G.* The exaltation of Christ. Kerux 12/3 (1997) 3-29 [Zech 6,9-15].
3942  **Kunz, Andreas** Auch heute sage ich—eine Wiederholung verkünde ich dir: Untersuchung zur literarischen Kontinuität und Diskontinuität in Sach 9,1-10; 11-17; 10,3b-12 und zum sozio-kommunikativen Hintergrund der Textentstehung. Diss. Leipzig 1996-97; ᴰLux, R.: 347 pp. [ThLZ 122,764].
3943  *Minette de Tillesse, Caetano* Zacarias 9-14. RBB 14/1-3 (1997) 140-143.
3944  *Overstreet, R. Larry* Israel responds to grace: a study of Zechariah 12:10. CBTJ 13/1 (1997) 1-30.
3945  **Rose, Wolter H.** Zerubbabel and Zemah: messianic expectations in the early post-exilic period. Diss. Oxford 1997; ᴰWilliamson, H.G.M. [TynB 49,373ss] [Zech 3,8; 6,9-15].
3946  **Schmidt, Werner H.** Hoffnung auf einen armen König: Sach 9,9f. als letzte messianische Weissagung des Alten Testaments. BZNW 86: 1997, ⇒41. ᶠHoꜰɪᴜs O., 689-709.
3947  **Tigchelaar, Eibert J.C.** Prophets of old and the day of the end: Zechariah, the Book of Watchers and Apocalyptic. OTS 35: 1996, ⇒12,3835. ᴿCBQ 59 (1997) 757-758 *(Cook, Stephen L.)*.

3948  **Lescow, Theodor** Das Buch Maleachi... Exkurs über Jeremiah 8:8-9. AzTh 75: 1993, ⇒9,3996; 11/1,2714. ᴿThLZ 122 (1997) 134-135 *(Zobel, Konstantin)*.
3949  *Meinhold, Arndt* Gottesungewißheit: zum Verhältnis von Form und Inhalt in Mal 1,2-5. CV 39/2-3 (1997) 128-154.
3950  *Vianès, Laurence* L'épaule comme part des lévites: le Rouleau du Temple et Ml 2,3. RB 104 (1997) 512-521 [Gen 34; Dt 18,1].

# VIII. NT Exegesis generalis

## ꜰ1.1 New Testament Introduction

3951  ᴱ**Aguirre Monasterio, Rafael; Rodríguez Carmona, Antonio** La investigación de los evangelios sinópticos y Hechos de los Apóstoles en el siglo XX. 1996, ⇒12,3855. ᴿActBib 34 (1997) 44-45 *(Boada, J.)*.
3952  *Aguirre, Rafael* La persecución en el cristianismo primitivo. RLAT 13 (1997) 11-42.

3953 **Aubrun, Jean** Les oubliés de l'évangile. Foi vivante: P 1997, Cerf 155 pp. [EeV.D 110,40—Marchal, Claude].

3954 **Barr, David L.** New Testament story: an introduction. Belmont, CA [2]1995, Wadsworth 574 pp. $43. [R]RStR 23 (1997) 241-242 *(Darr, J.A.)*.

3955 **Bartolomé, Juan José** El evangelio y Jesús de Nazaret. 1995, ⇒11/2,2090; 12,3858. [R]EstB 55 (1997) 121-122 *(Arambarri, J.)*; ScrTh 29 (1997) 930-931 *(Balaguer, V.)*.

3956 **Beeching, Paul Q.** Awkward reverence: reading the New Testament today. NY 1997, Continuum vi; 246 pp. $25. 0-8264-1000-6 [BTB 27,120].

3957 [E]**Benetti, Santos** La bibbia tematica, 2: Nuovo Testamento. Padova 1996, Messagero 376 pp. [Ter. 48,886—Pasquetto, Virgilio].

3958 *Best, Ernest* Recent continental New Testament literature. ET 108 (1997) 269-271.

3959 **Borgen, Peder** Early christianity and Hellenistic Judaism. 1996, ⇒12,116. [R]AUSS 35 (1997) 253 *(Maier, Paul L.)*.

3960 **Brown, Peter** El primer milenio de la cristiandad europea. Barc 1997, Crítica 324 pp. [RF 237,551 (España, Antonio)].

3961 **Brown, Raymond Edward** An introduction to the New Testament. AncB Reference Library: NY 1997, Doubleday xlii; (4) 878 pp. £30. 0-385-24767-2. [R]EThL 73 (1997) 443-445 *(Neirynck, F.)*.

3962 **Bruce, Frederick F.** In the steps of our Lord. GR 1997, Kregel 64 pp. 0-8254-2335-X [NThAR 1998,100] [Mainly ill].

3963 **Bulai, Alois; Budau, Anton** Sfintele Evanghelii. Iasi 1997, Presa Buna 363 pp.

3964 **Carmichael, Joel** The unriddling of Christian origins: a secular account. 1995, ⇒11/2,2111. [R]JRH 21/2 (1997) 228-229 *(Lieu, Judith M.)*.

3965 **Cook, Terry L.** The mark of the new world order. New Kensington 1997, Whitaker xiii; 385 pp. 0-88368-466-7 [NThAR 1998,270].

3966 **Court, John M.** Reading the New Testament. NT Readings: L 1997, Routledge xiv; 170 pp. £35/£11. 0-415-10367-3/8-1. [R]Tablet (6 Sept. 1997) 1132 *(Harvey, A.E.)*.

3967 **Crowe, Jerome** From Jerusalem to Antioch: the gospel across cultures. ColMn 1997, Liturgical xx; 160 pp. $15. 0-8146-2432-4 [BiTod 35,323].

3968 **Davies, Stevan L.** New Testament fundamentals. [2]1994, ⇒10,3825. [R]TJT 13/1 (1997) 99-101 *(Vaage, Leif E.)*.

3969 **Delorme, J.** Il rischio della parola: leggere i vangeli. Paralleli: Mi 1994, Vita e Pensiero 260 pp. L28.000. 88-343-3974-6. [R]Div. 40/1 (1997) 96 *(Stramare, Tarcisio)*.

3970 **Derrett, J. Duncan M.** Some telltale words in the New Testament. Shipston-on-Stour 1997, Drinkwater 82 pp. 0-946643-48-2 [EstB 55,568].

3971 **Doran, Robert** Birth of a worldview: early christianity in its Jewish and pagan context. 1995, ⇒11/2,2240. [R]ChH 66 (1997) 312-313 *(Grant, Robert M.)*.

3972 **Duling, Dennis C.; Perrin, Norman** The New Testament. Fort Worth [3]1994, Harcourt B 512 pp. [R]RStR 23 (1997) 242 *(Darr, John A.)*.

3973 **Ehrman, Bart D.** The New Testament: a historical introduction to the early christian writings. NY 1997, OUP xxii; 437 pp. $34. 0-19-508481-0. [R]JBL 116 (1997) 738-740 *(Meier, John P.)*.

3974 *Estevez Lopez, Elisa* Pluralidad y unidad en los orígenes cristianos. Almogaren 20 (1997) 31-51.

3975 [E]**Evans, Craig A.; Porter, Stanley E.** New Testament backgrounds. BiSe 43: Shf 1997, Academic 335 pp. $20. 1-85075-796-8 [EThL 73,168].

3976  Fanin, L. La proposta spirituale del Nuovo Testamento: l'esperienza fondante del vivere cristiano. CinB 1997, San Paolo 128 pp. L16.000 [RdT 38,575].

3977  EFiloramo, Giovanni; Menozzi, Daniele Storia del cristianesimo. R 1997, Laterza 5 (4) vols.

3978  Fornberg, Tord The holy gospel. ITS 34/1-3 (1997) 110-123.

3979  Frenschkowski, Marco Die verborgene Epiphanie in Spätantike und frühem Christentum. Offenbarung und Epiphanie, 2. Diss. Mainz 1994. WUNT 2/80: Tü 1997, Mohr ix; 385 pp. 3-16-146456-7 [NThAR 1997,194].

3980  Fusco, Vittorio Le prime comunità cristiane: tradizioni e tendenze nel cristianesimo delle origini. La Bibbia nella storia 8: Bo 1997, EDB 305 pp. L38.000. 88-10-40263-4. RBeO 39/1 (1997) 57-58 (De Virgilio, Giuseppe); LASBF 47 (1997) 610-613 (Chrupcała, L.D.).

3981  Garrison, Roman The Graeco-Roman context of early christian literature. JSNT.S 137: Shf 1997, Academic 123 pp. £24.50/$35. 1-85075-646-5.

3982  Guillaume, J.-M. Jésus-Christ en son temps: dates, lieux, personnes dans le Nouveau Testament. Vivre la parole: P 1997, Médiaspaul 206 pp. FF95 [VieCon 70,338—Luciani, Didier].

3983  Herranz Marco, Mariano Huellas de arameo en los evangelios y en la catequesis cristiana primitiva. Studia Semitica Novi Testamenti 5: M 1997, Ciudad N 354 pp. 84-89651-32-9 [EstAg 33,385—Cineira, D.A.].

3984  Hilton, Allen The dumb speak: early christian illiteracy and pagan criticism. Diss. Yale 1997; DMeeks, W.A.: 1997 [RTL 29,585].

3985  Hooker, Morna D. Beginnings: keys that open the gospels. L 1997, SCM xiv; 98 pp. 1996 Diocese of British Columbia Hall Lectures. £8. 0-334-02710-1 [RRT 1998/1,90];

3986  Hoornaert, Eduardo El movimiento de Jésus. 1996, ⇒12,3880. REfMex 15 (1997) 400-401 (Serraima Cirici, Enrique).

3987  Horsley, Richard A.; Silberman, Neil Asher The message and the kingdom: how Jesus and Paul ignited a revolution and transformed the ancient world. NY 1997, Grosset xi; 290 pp. 0-399-14194-4.

3988  Hyldahl, Niels The history of early Christianity. ARGU 3: Fra 1997, Lang x; 317 pp. £32. 3-631-30404-8.

3989  Kelly, Joseph F. The world of the early christians. Message of the Fathers of the Church 1: ColMn 1997, Liturgical ix; 231 pp. Bibl. $30/$23. 0-8146-5341-3/13-8. RJEarlyC 5 (1997) 619-621 (Finn, T.M.).

3990  Ketzel, James A. Panta: the philosophical basis of the New Testament. Lanham, Md 1997, University Press of America 395 pp. 0-7618-0582-6 [NThAR 1997,261].

3991  Lea, Thomas D. The New Testament: its background and message. 1996, ⇒12,3888. RCritRR 10 (1997) 188-189 (Orr, Mary).

3992  Lüdemann, Gerd Die Ketzer: die andere Seite des frühen Christentums. Studienausgabe. 1996, ⇒12,3891. RActBib 34 (1997) 49-50 (Fàbrega, Valentí); JAC 40 (1997) 225-229 (Löhr, Winrich A.).

3993  Mack, Burton L. Who wrote the New Testament?. 1995, ⇒11/2,2159. RBS 154 (1997) 205-221 (Ingolfsland, Dennis); CritRR 10 (1997) 190-194 (Duling, Dennis C.);

3994  Wie schreven het Nieuwe Testament werkelijk?: feiten, mythen en motieven. Deventer 1997, Ankh-Hermes [ITBT 6/8,27s—Mellink, Osger].

3995  Maggioni, Bruno, (al.), Annunciare il vangelo. Sussidi biblici 54: Reggio Emilia 1997, San Lorenzo x; 108 pp. 88-8071-065-6.

3996 Malina, Bruce J. The social world of Jesus and the gospels. 1996, ⇒12,3893. RRRT 4/2 (1997) 30-32 *(Need, Stephen W.)*.

3997 *Martian, Sorin* Lire les évangiles—proposition d'un exercice. Rez. 59. SUBB 42/1 (1997) 59-65.

3998 Martini, Carlo Maria Se retrouver soi-même: à la recherche de soi à travers les évangiles. P 1997, Brépols 238 pp. FF110 [EeV 107,99].

3999 Mestre i Godes, Jesús Els primers cristians: del divendres sant (any 30) al concili de Nicea (any 325). Libres a l'Abast 300: Barc 1997, Edicions 62 401 pp. [AHlg 7,483s—Blasi, F.].

4000 EMoo, Douglas The gospel and contemporary perspectives. Biblical Forum 2: GR 1997, Kregel 202 pp. $12. 0-8254-3349-5 [ThD 44,157].

4001 Müller, Peter 'Verstehst du auch, was du liest?': Lesen und Verstehen im Neuen Testament. Da:Wiss 1994, x; 241 pp. DM68. 3-534-12384-0. RNT 39 (1997) 197-199 *(Stenschke, Christoph)*.

4002 *Pearson, Birger A.* The emergence of the christian religion. The emergence. 1997, ⇒154. 7-22.

4003 *Pienaar, Henk* Sondaars in die tyd van Jesus. HTS 53 (1997) 751-772 [ZID 24,127].

4004 Ponizy, Bogdan Korzenie przeslania biblijnego Nowego Testamentu. Gniezno 1997, Gaudentinum 205 pp. 83-85654-67-4. P.

4005 Popkes, Wiard Paränese und Neues Testament. SBS 168: 1996, ⇒12,3900. RThLZ 122 (1997) 918-920 *(Horn, Friedrich W.)*.

4006 Pregeant, Russell Engaging the New Testament. 1995, ⇒11/2,2186. RRStR 23 (1997) 240-241 *(Darr, John A.)*; CritRR 10 (1997) 210-212 *(Sheeley, Steven)*.

4007 Ravasi, Gianfranco La buona novella: le storie, le idee, i personaggi del Nuovo Testamento. 1996, ⇒12,3903. RVP 80 (1997) 386-388 *(Senna, Paolo)*.

4008 Reddish, Mitchell G. An introduction to the gospels. Nv 1997, Abingdon 254 pp. $20. 0-687-00448-9 [BiTod 35,326].

4009 Riches, John El mundo de Jesús: el judaísmo del siglo I, en crisis. 1996, ⇒12,3905. RIsidorianum 6 (1997) 269-270 *(Camacho, Fernando)*.

4010 Riley, Gregory John One Jesus, many Christs: how Jesus inspired not one true christianity, but many: the truth about christian origins. SF 1997, HarperSanFrancisco (8) 228 pp. $22. 0-06-066799-0.

4011 Ruck-Schröder, Adelheid ONOMA: eine exegetisch-theologische Untersuchung zur Bedeutung der Namensaussagen im Neuen Testament. Diss. Berlin 1997-98; DOsten-Sacken, P. von der [RTL 29,588].

4012 Sánchez Mielgo, Gerardo Introducción a los escritos del Nuevo Testamento. Textos, Biblia 3: M 1997, Instituto Superior de Ciencias Catequéticas 'San Pío X' 463 pp. [EsVe 27,393-395].

4013 Saramagu, José Το καρά Ιησούν Εςαγγέλιον [The gospel according to Jesus]. Athens 1997, Kastaniote [DBM 18,132—Agourides, S.] G.

4014 Scott, J. Julius Customs and controversies: intertestamental Jewish backgrounds of the New Testament. 1995, ⇒11/2,2203. RCritRR 10 (1997) 217-219 *(Fonrobert, Charlotte)*.

4015 Sicre Diaz, José Luis La búsqueda. El cuadrante: introducción a los evangelios, 1. Estella ²1997, Verbo Divino 301 pp. 84-8169-118-6;

4016 La apuesta: el mundo de Jesús. El cuadrante, 2. Estella 1997, Verbo Divino 326 pp. 84-8169-154-2 [ActBib 34,207—González Faus, José I.].

4017 Söding, Thomas Blick zurück nach vorn: Bilder lebendiger Gemeinden im Neuen Testament. FrB 1997, Herder 220 pp. DM29.80. 3-451-26467-6 [OrdKor 38,512].

4018   **Stark, Rodney** The rise of christianity: a sociologist reconsiders history.
       1996, ⇒12,3918. [R]JEarlyC 5 (1997) 306-308 *(Leyerle, Blake)*; TS 58
       (1997) 354-356 *(Greeley, Dolores Lee)*; Sociology of Religion 58/2 (1997)
       191-195 *(Bryant, Joseph M.)*; RRelRes 39/1 (1997) 86-88 *(Braun, Willi)*;
       CHR 83 (1997) 739-741 *(Benko, Stephen)*; ChH 66 (1997) 779-780 *(Volz,
       Carl A.)*; CBQ 59 (1997) 593-595 *(Malina, Bruce J.)*.
4019   **Strecker, Georg** History of New Testament literature. [T]*Katter, Calvin;
       Mollenhauer, Hans-Joachim*: Harrisburg 1997, Trinity xiv; 238 pp. $24.
       1-563-38203-2.
4020   **Trocmé, Étienne** The childhood of christianity. L 1997, SCM xiv; 146
       pp. £13. 0-334-02709-8 [RRT 1998/1,92].
4021   [TE]**Van der Horst, Pieter Willem** Bronnen voor de studie van de wereld
       van het vroege christendom: joodse en pagane teksten uit de periode van
       Alexander de Grote tot keizer Constantijn. Kampen 1997, Kok 2 vols;
       268; 272 pp. Deel 1: Joodse bronnen; Deel 2: Pagane bronnen. *f*45+*f*45.
       90-242-7962-3/3-1. [R]EThL 73 (1997) 194-196 *(Verheyden, J.)*.
4022   **Wright, N.T.** The New Testament and the people of God. 1992,
       ⇒8,4209... 11/2,3427. [R]SJTh 50/1 (1997) 125-127 *(Marsh, Clive)*.

F1.2  *Origo Evangeliorum,* **the origin of the Gospels**

4023   **Burridge, Richard A.** Four gospels, one Jesus?: a symbolic reading.
       1994, ⇒10,3889; 12,3930. [R]VJTR 61 (1997) 210-211 *(Meagher, P.M.)*.
4024   **Frickenschmidt, Dirk** Evangelium als Biographie: die vier Evangelien im
       Rahmen antiker Erzählkunst. TANZ 22: Tü 1997, Francke xv; 549 pp.
       DM158. 3-7720-1873-4.
4025   **Gallo, Italo** Studi sulla biografia greca. Storie e testi 7: N 1997, D'Auria
       217 pp. 88-7092-129-8.
4026   **Morton, Andrew Queen** The gathering of the gospels: from papyrus to
       printout. Mellen Biblical Press 53: Lewiston 1997, Mellen vii; 143 pp.
       $70. 0-7734-2427-X. [R]CritRR 10 (1997) 196-198 *(Vinson, Richard)*.
4027   *Pastor Ramos, Federico* La historia de la redacción de los evangelios
       sinópticos. ResB 13 (1997) 23-30.
4028   **Schulz, Hans-Joachim** Die apostolische Herkunft der Evangelien. QD
       145: 1994, ⇒10,3906... 12,3935 [[[3]1997, 405 pp. DM68]. [R]ThPh 72
       (1997) 264-265 *(Beutler, J.)*.
4029   **Schulz, Hans-Joachim** L'origine apostolica dei vangeli. Pref. *Schnacken-
       burg, Rudolf;* Post. *Thiede, Carsten Peter.* La filocalia 4: Mi 1997, Gri-
       baudi 444 pp. L48.000. 88-7152-427-6 [Iter. 5/8,258].
4030   **Thiede, Carsten Peter; D'Ancona, Matthew** Testimone oculare di Gesù:
       la nuova sconvolgente prova sull'origine del vangelo. 1996, ⇒12,3937.
       [R]Cultura & Libri.S 112 (1997) 59-66 *(De Ritis, Luisa)*.
4031   **Vardy, Peter; Mills, Mary** The puzzle of the gospels. Armonk, N.Y.
       1997, Sharpe xi; 239 pp. 0-7656-0165-6.
4032   **Wills, Lawrence Mitchell** The quest of the historical gospel: Mark, John
       and the origins of the gospel genre. L 1997, Routledge vii; 285 pp. Bibl.
       £45. 0-415-15093-0.

F1.3  **Historicitas,** *chronologia* **Evangeliorum**

4033   *Ausín, Santiago; Chapa, Juan* Alcuni studi recenti sulla storicità dei van-
       geli. [T]*Musella, Marialetizia*: Cultura & Libri.S 112 (1997) 52-58.

4034 *Baillet, Maurice* I manoscritti della grotta 7 di Qumran e il Nuovo Testamento. Ridatare i vangeli? 1997 <1972>, ⇒4038. 71-82.

4035 *Baum, Armin Daniel* Die Publikationsdaten der Evangelien in den ältesten Quellen: zu IRENAEUS, Adversus Haereses 3.1.1. JETh 11 (1997) 77-92.

4036 **Blomberg, Craig L.** Jesus and the gospels: an introduction and survey. Nv 1997, Broadman & H 384 pp. $25. 0-85111-770-8.

4037 *Boismard, Marie-Émile* Riguardo a 7Q5 e Mc 6,52-53. Ridatare i vangeli? 1997 <1995>, ⇒4038. 163-167.

4038 ᴱ**Dalla Vecchia, Flavio** Ridatare i vangeli?. Giornale di teologia 247: Brescia 1997, Queriniana 218 pp. L28.000. 88-399-0747-5 [RdT 38,142].

4039 *Focant, Camille* Un frammento del secondo vangelo a Qumran: 7Q5=Mc 6,52-53?. Ridatare i vangeli? 1997 <1985>, ⇒4038. 83-95.

4040 *Grelot, Pierre* Note sulle proposte del prof. Carsten Peter THIEDE. Ridatare i vangeli? 1997 <1995>, ⇒4038. 175-178;

4041 Su un manoscritto del vangelo di Matteo. Ridatare i vangeli? 1997 <1995>, ⇒4038. 169-173.

4042 **Guillén Armendáriz, Fernando** Anuncio del evangelio e historicidad de los evangelios: retrospectiva y análisis crítico de los números 7 y 19 de la Dei Verbum. Theses ad Lauream 356: R 1997, Pont. Athenaeum Antonianum 175 pp. (Pars Diss.).

4043 **Harrison, Brian W.** The teaching of Pope Paul VI on scred scripture: with special reference to the historicity of the gospels. Diss. Pont. Athenaeum Sanctae Crucis; ᴰ*Tábet, Michael Angelus*: R 1997, 483 pp.

4044 **Heckel, Theo** Vom Evangelium des Markus zum viergestaltigen Evangelium. Diss.-Habil. Erlangen 1997-98; ᴰ*Roloff, J.* [RTL 29,585].

4045 *Kirchschläger, Walter* Frühdatierung der Evangelien?. BiLi 70 (1997) 36-38.

4046 *O'Callaghan, José* Papiri neotestamentari nella grotta 7 di Qumran?. Ridatare i vangeli? 1997 <1972>, ⇒4038. 11-23.

4047 *Penna, Romano* Kerygma e storia alle origini del cristianesimo: nuove considerazioni su di un annoso problema. AnScR 2 (1997) 239-256.

4048 *Puech, Émile* I frammenti greci della grotta 7 e il Nuovo Testamento?: 7Q4 e 7Q5, e il papiro Magdalen greco 17=$P^{64}$. Ridatare i vangeli? 1997 <1995>, ⇒4038. 127-147;

4049 Osservazioni sui frammenti greci del manoscritto 7Q4=1 Enoc 103 e 105. Ridatare i vangeli? 1997 <1996>, ⇒4038. 149-161.

4050 *Rosenbaum, Hans-Udo* Cave 7Q5!: contro il rinnovato tentativo di identificare 7Q5 di Qumran come frammento del più antico manoscritto dei vangeli. Ridatare i vangeli? 1997 <1987>, ⇒4038. 97-126.

4051 *Segalla, Giuseppe* Il dibattito sui manoscritti più antichi di Marco (?) e Matteo. Ridatare i vangeli? 1997, ⇒4038. 179-205.

4052 *Thiede, Carsten Peter* 7Q—frammenti di papiri neotestamentari della settima grotta di Qumran?. Ridatare i vangeli? 1997 <1984>, ⇒4038. 25-51;

4053 Il papiro Magdalen greco 17 (Gregory-Aland $P^{64}$): una rivalutazione. Ridatare i vangeli? 1997 <1995>, ⇒4038. 53-69.

4054 *Wischmeyer, Wolfgang* Zu den neuen Frühdatierungen von Carsten Peter THIEDE. ZAC 1 (1997) 280-290.

F1.4 *Jesus historicus*—The human Jesus

4055  **Aers, David; Staley, Lynn** The powers of the holy: religion, politics, and gender in late medieval English culture. 1996, ⇒12,3939. RTS 58 (1997) 542-544 *(Cole, Penny J.)*.

4056  **Angelini, Giuseppe** Lettera viva: i vangeli e la presenza di Gesù. Sestante 10: Mi 1997, Vita e Pensiero 200 pp. 88-343-3966-5 [NThAR 1999,4].

4057  *Arendse, Roger A.* Shifting boundaries in historical Jesus research?: some critical reflections on paradigms and images of Jesus in current North American scholarship. Scriptura 63 (1997) 435-449.

4058  *Arnal, William E.* Major episodes in the biography of Jesus: an assessment of the historicity of the narrative tradition. TJT 13 (1997) 201-226;

4059  Making and re-making the Jesus-sign: contemporary markings on the body of Christ. Whose historical Jesus?. SCJud 7: 1997, ⇒170. EArnal, W.E., 308-319.

4060  *Aune, David E.* Jesus and Cynics in first-century Palestine: some critical considerations. Hillel and Jesus. 1997, ⇒321. ECharlesworth, J.H., 176-192.

4061  *Autané, Maurice* Jésus selon les apocryphes: un personnage étrange. DosB 69 (1997) 25-26.

4062  *Bammel, Ernst* Jesus der Zauberer. Judaica et Paulina. WUNT 91: 1997, ⇒109. 3-14.

4063  **Barnett, Paul William** Jesus and the logic of history. New Studies in Biblical Theology: GR 1997, Eerdmans 182 pp. Bibl. $18. 0-8028-4410-3.

4064  **Bartley, Peter** The gospel Jesus: fact or fiction?. 1996, ⇒12,3946. RMillSt 40 (1997) 158-160 *(Rogers, Patrick)*.

4065  **Baudet, Gilbert** De traditie voorbij: een theologisch essay over 'vergeten' woorden van Jezus. Zoetermeer 1997, Meinema 172 pp. 90-211-3643-0 [NThAR 1997,226].

4066  *Bauer, Johannes B.* Unverbürgte Jesusworte < 1981 >;

4067  Vidisti fratrem, vidist dominum tuum (Agraphon 144 Resch und 126 Resch) < 1989 >. Studien zu Bibeltext. 1997, ⇒111. 3-36/37-44.

4068  **Becker, Jürgen** Jesus von Nazareth. 1996, ⇒12,3948. RBZ 41/1 (1997) 126-12128 *(Dormeyer, Detlev)*; LM 36/9 (1997) 43 *(Lindemann, Walter)*; Orien. 61/18 (1997) 193-196 *(Kügler, Joachim)*; CBQ 59 (1997) 568-569 *(McKnight, Scot)*.

4069  **Berger, Klaus** Wie was Jezus werkelijk?. 1996, ⇒12,3951. RITBT 5/1 (1997) 32-33 *(Wilhelm, Han)*.

4070  *Blázquez, Ricardo* El cristianismo es Jesucristo. 1997, ⇒76. MRuiz de la Pena J., 193-205.

4071  *Bloomquist, L. Gregory* Methodological considerations in the determination of the social context of Cynic rhetorical practice: implications for our present studies of the Jesus traditions. The rhetorical analysis. JSNT.S 146: 1997, ⇒336. EPorter, Stanley E., 200-231.

4072  *Bloomquist, L. Gregory* The rhetoric of the historical Jesus. Whose historical Jesus?. SCJud 7: 1997, ⇒170. EArnal, W.E., 98-117.

4073  *Bock, Darrell L.* Key Jewish texts on blasphemy and exaltation and the Jewish examination of Jesus. SBL.SPS 36 (1997) 115-160.

4074  *Boismard, Marie-Émile* Jésus, un homme de Nazareth. 1996, ⇒12,4796. RThLZ 122 (1997) 257-258 *(Rebell, Walter)*.

4075  **Borg, Marcus J.** Jesus in contemporary scholarship. 1994, ⇒10,3929; 11/2,2095. RCBQ 58 (1996) (1997) 150-152 *(Mercer, Calvin)*;

4076 Meeting Jesus again for the first time: the historical Jesus & the heart of contemporary faith. NY [12]1997, Harper & Row ix; 150 pp. 0-06-060916-8/7-6.

4077 *Boring, M. Eugene* The "third quest" and the apostolic faith. Gospel interpretation. 1997, ⇒210. [E]Kingsbury, J.D., 237-252.

4078 *Boshoff, Piet B.* The proclaimer became the proclaimed: Walter Schmithals's point of view. The JHiC 4/1 (1997) 89-119.

4079 *Braun, Willi* Socio-rhetorical interests: context. Whose historical Jesus?. SCJud 7: 1997, ⇒170. [E]Arnal, W.E., 92-97.

4080 *Camacho Acosta, Fernando* Jesús, el dinero y la riqueza. Sum. 393. Isidorianum 6 (1997) 393-415.

4081 **Casciaro, José María** Gesù di Nazaret: biografia terrena del Figlio di Dio. Mi 1997, Ares 568 pp. L45.000. 88-8155-146-2 [Itin(M) 7,264s— Zoccali, Vincenzo].

4082 *Casey, P.M.* In which language did Jesus teach?. ET 108 (1997) 326-328.

4083 *Cernuda, Antonio Vicent* El Testimonio Flaviano, alarde de solapada ironía. EstB 55 (1997) 355-385, 497-508.

4084 *Charlesworth, J.H.* Hillel and Jesus: retrospective and prospective reflections;

4085 Hillel and Jesus: why comparisons are important. Hillel and Jesus. 1997, ⇒321. [E]Charlesworth, James H., 460-462/3-30.

4086 *Chilton, Bruce* E.P. Sanders and the question of Jesus and purity. Jesus in context. AGAJ 39: 1997, ⇒183. 221-230;

4087 **Chilton, Bruce D.** Pure kingdom: Jesus' vision of God: studying the historical Jesus. [R]CritRR 10 (1997) 168-170 *(Blomberg, Craig L.)*.

4088 [E]**Chilton, Bruce; Evans, Craig A.** Studying the historical Jesus. 1994, ⇒10,239b; 12,3959. [R]SR 26 (1997) 232-233 *(Richardson, Peter)*.

4089 *Chilton, Bruce; Evans, Craig A.* Jesus in context: an introduction. Jesus in context. AGAJ 39: 1997, ⇒183. 1-24.

4090 **Click, E. Dale** Have you met Jesus?: eight studies on the life and times of Jesus. Lima, OH 1997, CSS 74 pp. 0-7880-1016-6 [NThAR 1998,270].

4091 *Cole, Juan R.* Behold the man: Bahaullah on the life of Jesus. JAAR 65 (1997) 47-71.

4092 Comisión episcopal de catequesis, biblia y ere. ¿JQuién dices que soy yo?: la persona y el mensaje de Jesús. Collab. *Pastore, Corrado; Wyssenbach, Jean-Pierre*. Caracas 1997, Paulinas 91 pp.

4093 **Crossan, Dominic** Der historische Jesus. [2]1995 <1994>, ⇒11/2,2119; 12,3962. [R]Orien. 61 (1997) 192-193 *(Kügler, Joachim)*.

4094 *Crossan, John Dominic* Itinerants and householders in the earliest Jesus movement. Whose historical Jesus?. SCJud 7: 1997, ⇒170. [E]Arnal, W.E., 7-24.

4095 **Crossan, John Dominic** Was Jesus wirklich lehrte: die authentischen Worte des historischen Jesus. [T]Hahlbrock, Peter: Mü 1997, Beck 220 pp. DM34. 3-406-41918-6. [R]EK (1997) 552 *(Rohrbach, Heiko)*.

4096 **Depoortere, Christian** Qui es-tu Jésus?. Namur 1997, Racine-Fidélité 168 pp. FB496 [EeV 107,470].

4097 *Dietzfelbinger, Christian* Reinheit: Neues Testament. TRE 28. 1997, ⇒420. 487-493.

4098 *Donaldson, Terence L.* Jesus and the Dead Sea scrolls: context. Whose historical Jesus?. SCJud 7: 1997, ⇒170. [E]Arnal, W.E., 188-189.

4099 **Drane, John** Jesús. Estella 1996, Verbo Divino 207 pp. Bibl. 84-7151-398-6.

4100   *Dunn, J.D.G.* Jesus and factionalism in early Judaism: how serious was the factionalism of late second temple Judaism?. Hillel and Jesus. 1997, ⇒321. ᴱCharlesworth, James H., 156-175.

4101   *Ellis, E. Earle* The historical Jesus and the gospels. 1997, ⇒92. ꟳSᴛᴜʜʟᴍᴀᴄʜᴇʀ P., 94-106.

4102   **Evans, C. Stephen** The historical Christ and the Jesus of faith. 1996, ⇒12,3979. ᴿJThS 48 (1997) 363-365 *(Page, Ruth)*; ThTo 54 (1997) 418, 420 *(Cook, Michael L.)*.

4103   *Evans, C.A.* Reconstructing Jesus' teaching: problems and possibilities. Hillel and Jesus. 1997, ⇒321. ᴱCharlesworth, James H., 397-426.

4104   **Evans, Craig A.** Jesus and his contemporaries: comparative studies. AGJU 25: 1995, ⇒11/2,2132. ᴿCBQ 59 (1997) 412-413 *(Black, C.C.)*;

4105   Life of Jesus research: an annotated bibliography. NTTS 24: 1996, ⇒12,3981. ᴿEThL 73 (1997) 169-171 *(Neirynck, F.)*; SEÅ 62 (1997) 169-170 *(Ekenberg, Anders)*.

4106   *Evans, Craig A.* Aspects of exile and restoration in the proclamation of Jesus and the gospels. Exile. JSJ.S 56: 1997, ⇒227. ᴱScott, James M., 299-328;

4107   Early rabbinic sources and Jesus research. Jesus in context. AGAJ 39: 1997 <1995>, ⇒183. 27-57;

4108   Jesus and the Dead Sea scrolls from Qumran cave 4. Eschatology, messianism. SDSSRL 1: 1997, ⇒276. ᴱEvans, Craig A., 91-100;

4109   The life of Jesus. Handbook. NTTS 25: 1997, ⇒971. ᴱPorter, Stanley E., 427-475;

4110   The "Real Jesus" in debate. BBR 7 (1997) 225-226;

4111   Reconstructing Jesus' teaching: problems and possibilities;

4112   'Who touched me?': Jesus and the ritually impure. Jesus in context. AGAJ 39: 1997, ⇒183. 145-176/353-376.

4113   *Feldmeier, Reinhard* Jesus—ein Radikaler?: Tempelreinigung, Zinsgroschenfrage und Liebesgebot. ᴿRKZ 138 (1997) 418-422.

4114   **Fernández-Carvajal, F.** Vida de Jésus (de acuerdo con los relatos evangélicos). M 1997, Palabra 720 pp. Ptas4.200. 84-8239-000-7 [Espíritu 46,242s—Forment, Eudaldo].

4115   *Fiensy, D.A.* Jesus' socioeconomic background. Hillel and Jesus. 1997, ⇒321. ᴱCharlesworth, James H., 225-255.

4116   *Fiorenza, Elisabeth Schüssler* Jesus and the politics of interpretation. HThR 90 (1997) 343-358.

4117   ᴱFlowers, F.A. III Leo Nikolaevich Tolstoi: the gospel in brief. ᵀHapgood, Isabel Florence: Lincoln, NE 1997, University of Nebraska Press 215 pp. 0-8032-9432-8.

4118   *Flusser, D.* Hillel and Jesus: two ways of self-awareness. Hillel and Jesus. 1997, ⇒321. ᴱCharlesworth, James H., 71-107.

4119   **Focant, Camille,** *(al.)*, Le Jésus de l'histoire. Connaître la Bible 4/5: Bru 1997, Lumen Vitae 111 pp. FB350. 2-87324-095-4 [RTL 29,248—Dermience, Alice].

4120   *Freyne, Seán* Galilean questions to Cʀossᴀɴ's Mediterranean Jesus. Whose historical Jesus?. SCJud 7: 1997, ⇒170. ᴱArnal, W.E., 63-91;

4121   La investigación acerca del Jesús histórico: reflexiones teológicas. Conc(D) 33/1,32-46; Conc(F) 269,49-64; Conc(I) 33/1,60-79; Conc(E) 269 (1997) 57-73;

4122   Archaeology and the historical Jesus. Archaeology and biblical interpretation. 1997, ⇒268. ᴱBartlett, John R., 117-144.

4123   **Funk, Robert Walter** Honest to Jesus: Jesus for a new millennium. 1996, ⇒12,3986. ᴿTS 58 (1997) 348-350 *(Brown, Schuyler)*; ThTo 54 (1997)

262, 264, 266 *(Kay, James F.)*; AsbTJ 52 (1997) 70-75 *(Stegner, William Richard)*.

4124 *Galvin, John P.* "I believe ... in Jesus Christ, his only son, our Lord": the earthly Jesus and the Christ of faith. Gospel interpretation. 1997, ⇒210. EKingsbury, J.D., 273-282.

4125 **García Blázquez, Manuel** Hipótesis sobre la personalidad de Jesús de Nazaret. Armilla 1997, Osuna 278 pp. 84-89717-96-6 [NThAR 1999,181].

4126 **Gnilka, Joachim** Jesus of Nazareth: message and history. Peabody 1997, Hendrickson xiii; 346 pp. $25. 1-56563-164-1 [BiTod 36,133—Senior, Donald].

4127 **Goldstein, Barbara** Jeschua ben Joseph: Leben, Umfeld und Predigt Jesu. Wü 1997, Königshausen & N 438 pp. 3-8260-1304-2 [NThAR 1998,100].

4128 *Goshen Gottstein, A.* Hillel and Jesus: are comparisons possible?. Hillel and Jesus. 1997, ⇒321. ECharlesworth, James H., 31-55.

4129 *Graham, Susan Lochrie; Moore, Stephen D.* The quest of the new historicist Jesus. Bibl.Interp. 5 (1997) 438-464.

4130 **Grenier, Brian** Jesús el maestro. M 1996, San Pablo. 84-285-1987-1. REE 72 (1997) 782-783 *(López Valdeón, F. Javier)*.

4131 *Guillet, Jacques* Comment Jésus a reçu sa mission. Tychique 125 (1997) 45-47 [Isa 61; John 8,29].

4132 **Guitton, Jean** Gesù. Leumann 1997 <1956>, Elle Di Ci 304 pp. L35.000 [Cultura & Libri.S 112,71 Scalabrin, Sandro].

4133 **Heiligenthal, Roman** Der verfälschte Jesus: eine Kritik moderner Jesusbilder. Da:Wiss. 1997, ix; 143 pp. DM19.90. 3-534-80206-3.

4134 *Hellwig, Monika K.* On rescuing the humanity of Jesus: implications for catholicism. 1997, ⇒88. FSLOYAN G., 40-48.

4135 **Henaut, Barry W.** Is "historical Jesus" a christological construct?. Whose historical Jesus?. SCJud 7: 1997, ⇒170. EArnal, W.E., 241-268.

4136 **Heyer, C.J. den** Jesus matters: 150 years of research. Valley Forge, PA 1997, Trinity xiv; 193 pp. $16. 1-56338-195-8 [ThD 44,365—Heiser, W. Charles].

4137 **Hooker, Morna Dorothy** The signs of a prophet: the prophetic actions of Jesus. L 1997, SCM x; 131 pp. Schaffer lectures, Yale, 1995; Bibl. £10/$14. 0-334-02702-0. RDSD 4 (1997) 360-362 *(Brooke, George J.)*.

4138 **Hoppe, Rudolf** Jesus: von der Krippe an den Galgen. 1996, ⇒12,3999. RLM 36/1 (1997) 40 *(Korsch, Dietrich)*; BiKi 52 (1997) 143-144 *(Krieger, Klaus-Stefan)*; BiLi 70 (1997) 240-242 *(Kühschelm, Roman)*.

4139 *Huffman, Douglas S.* The historical Jesus of ancient unbelief. JETS 40 (1997) 551-562.

4140 *Humphrey, Edith M.* Will the reader understand?: apocalypse as veil or vision in recent historical-Jesus studies. Whose historical Jesus?. SCJud 7: 1997, ⇒170. EArnal, W.E., 215-237.

4141 EHunwick, Andrew Paul Thiry, baron d'HOLBACH: histoire critique de Jésus Christ ou analyse raisonnée des évangiles. TLS 485: Genève 1997, Droz 710 pp. 2-600-00231-6 [ETR 73,308].

4142 *Hurtado, Larry W.* A taxonomy of recent historical-Jesus work. Whose historical Jesus?. SCJud 7: 1997, ⇒170. EArnal, W.E., 272-295.

4143 EJeanrond, Verner; Theobald, Christoph La redécouverte de Jésus: qui dites-vous que je suis?. P 1997, Beauchesne 167 pp. Conc(F) 269.

4144 **Johnson, Luke Timothy** The real Jesus. 1996, ⇒12,4003. RCTJ 32/1 (1997) 172-174 *(Holwerda, David E.)*; Horizons 24/1 (1997) 119-125

*(Reiser, William)*; CBQ 59 (1997) 159-161 *(McKnight, Scot)*; Thom. 61 (1997) 645-647 *(Martin, Francis)*; BBR 7 (1997): 227-232 *(Collins, Adela Yarbro)*; 233-248 *(Wink, Walter)*; 249-254 *(Johnson, Luke Timothy)*; JSNT 68 (1997) 101-120 *(Miller, Robert J.)*.

4145 **Jones, Laurie Beth** Jesus Christus, Manager: biblische Weisheiten für visionäres Management. W 1996, Signum 332 pp. ÖS350. 3-85436-202-1. ᴿZKTh 119 (1997) 484-486 *(Lies, Lothar)*.

4146 *Kereszty, Roch* El papel de la investigación sobre el 'Jesús de la historia' en el quehacer teológico: algunas precisiones metodológicas. Communio 19/2 (1997) 108-121; Com(US) 24,297-310.

4147 **Kieffer, R.** Jésus raconté: théologie et spiritualité des évangiles. LiBi 108: 1996, ⇒12,4007. ᴿNRTh 119 (1997) 262-263 *(Luciani, D.)*.

4148 *Klassen, William* The Mediterranean Jesus: context. Whose historical Jesus?. SCJud 7: 1997, ⇒170. ᴱArnal, W.E., 4-6.

4149 *Koester, Helmut* The sayings of Q and their image of Jesus. NT.S 89: 1997, ⇒7. ᶠBAARDA T., 137-154.

4150 *Körtner, Ulrich H.* Historischer Jesus—geschichtlicher Christus: zum Ansatz einer rezeptionsästhetischen Christologie. Lesen und Leben. 1997, ⇒205. 99-135.

4151 *Krieger, Klaus-Stefan* Die Zöllner: Jesu Umgang mit einem verachteten Beruf. BiKi 52 (1997) 124-130.

4152 *Kulisz, Józef; Baliszeuska, Aleksandra Mostowska* Jezus historii a Chrystus wiary [Jésus de l'histoire et le Christ de la foi]. Rés. 69. Bobolanum 8 (1997) 49-69.

4153 **Kümmel, Werner Georg** Vierzig Jahre Jesusforschung (1950-1990). ᴱ*Merklein, Helmut*: BBB 91: ²1994, ⇒10,3976. ᴿThRv 93 (1997) 289-291 *(Backhaus, Knut)*.

4154 *La Potterie, I. de* Jésus, témoin de la vérité et roi par la vérité. StMiss 46 (1997) 21-41.

4155 *La Rosa, Giuseppe* L'annuncio di Gesù evangelizzatore. Ambrosius 73/1 (1997) 73-82 [Lk 24,13-35].

4156 **Labbens, Jean** Le dessein temporel de Jésus. Religion et sciences humaines: P 1997, Harmattan 142 pp. 2-7384-5781-1 [Bulletin de l'Institut catholique de Lyon 117,79].

4157 **Laliberté, Madeleine** Jésus le Christ entre l'histoire et la foi: la vision de Paul TILLICH. Montréal 1997, Médiaspaul 324 pp. [Brot. 148,381s— Silva, I. Ribeiro da].

4158 *Langkammer, Hugolin* Il pellegrino Cristo e la sua sequela. Com(I) 153 (1997) 26-37; IKaZ 26,205-213.

4159 **Laurentin, René** Vie authentique de Jésus-Christ. 1996, ⇒12,4013. ᴿEeV 107 (1997) 85-86 *(Cothenet, E.)*;
4160 Vita autentica di Gesù Cristo. ᵀ*Basile, M.; Pref. Messori, Vittorio*: Mi 1997, Mondadori 518 pp. L28.000 [StPat 44,202—Segalla, Giuseppe].

4161 **Lee, Moonjang** The historical Jesus and *Mokmin* hermeneutics, with reference to the description of Jesus in *Minjung* theology in Korea. Diss. Edinburgh 1997, 246 pp. [RTL 29,575].

4162 *LeMarquand, Grant* The historical Jesus and African New Testament scholarship. Whose historical Jesus?. SCJud 7: 1997, ⇒170. ᴱArnal, W.E., 161-180.

4163 *Lichtenberger, H.* Jesus and the Dead Sea scrolls. Hillel and Jesus. 1997, ⇒321. ᴱCharlesworth, James H., 389-396.

4164 *Livi, Antonio* Storicità di Cristo e logica della fede. Cultura & Libri.S 112 (1997) 11-26.

4165 *Longenecker, Richard N.* A realized hope, a new commitment, and a de veloped proclamation: Paul and Jesus. The road from Damascus. 1997, ⇒330. ELongenecker, R.N., 18-42.

4166 *Mack, Burton L.* Q and a Cynic-like Jesus. Whose historical Jesus?. SCJud 7: 1997, ⇒170. EArnal, W.E., 25-36.

4167 *Malina, Bruce J.* Jesus as astral prophet. BTB 27 (1997) 83-98 [Mt 24,6-29; Mk 3,7-25; Lk 21,9-26; Rev 6,2-7,3.

4168 *Marsh, Clive* Quests of the historical Jesus in new historicist perspective. Bibl.Interp. 5 (1997) 403-437.

4169 *Marshall, John W.* The gospel of Thomas and the Cynic Jesus. Whose historical Jesus?. SCJud 7: 1997, ⇒170. EArnal, W.E., 37-60.

4170 *Martini, Carlo Maria* La risposta del vaso spezzato ossia 'tutto è Cristo per noi sacerdoti'. Ambrosius 73/2 (1997) 99-105.

4171 **McAteer, Michael R.; Steinhauser, Michael G.** The man in the scarlet robe: two thousand years of searching for Jesus. Etobicoke 1996, United Church 172 pp. [SR 26,139—Arnal, William].

4172 *McCready, Wayne O.* The historical Jesus and the Dead Sea scrolls. Whose historical Jesus?. SCJud 7: 1997, ⇒170. EArnal, W.E., 190-211.

4173 *McIntosh, Mark* In the pink: Jesus and his recent critics. RRT (1997/1) 73-76.

4174 *Meier, John P.* The circle of the twelve: did it exist during Jesus' public ministry?. JBL 116 (1997) 635-672;

4175 Dividing lines in Jesus research today: through dialectical negation to a positive sketch. Gospel interpretation. 1997, ⇒210. EKingsbury, J.D., 253-272;

4176 On retrojecting later questions from later texts: a reply to Richard BAUCKHAM. CBQ 59 (1997) 511-527.

4177 **Men', Aleksandr** Gesú maestro di Nazaret. EGuaita, Giovanni: 1996, ⇒12,4026. RStPav 44/2 (1997) 244-245 (Segalla, Giuseppe).

4178 **Messadié, Gerald** Ο 'Ανθρωπος που έγινε Θεός [The man who became God]. Nea Synora Athens 1995, Libane 730 pp. RDBM 16/1 (1997) 84-88 (Agourides, S.);

4179 L'homme qui devint Dieu 4: Jesús de Srinagar. Le livre de poche: P 1997, Laffont 533 pp. 2-253-14353-7 [NThAR 1998,271].

4180 *Meyers, Eric M.* Jesus and his Galilean context. Archaeology and the Galilee. SFSHJ 143: 1997, ⇒275. EEdwards, D.R., 57-66.

4181 *Mielgo, C.* El Jesús histórico y el *Jesus Seminar*. EstAg 32 (1997) 171-216.

4182 **Miller, John W.** Jesus at thirty: a psychological and historical portrait. Mp 1997, Fortress ix; 177 pp. $18. 0-8006-3107-2 [NThAR 1998,101].

4183 *Miller, Robert J.* Battling over the Jesus Seminar: why the ugly attacks?: scholars know some sayings are inauthentic. BiRe 13/2 (1997) 18-22, 47;

4184 Can the historical Jesus be made safe for orthodoxy: a critique of 'The Jesus Quest' by Ben WITHERINGTON III. JHiC 4/1 (1997) 120-137 [ZID 23,417];

4185 The gospel truth?: read the bible critically. BiRe 13/2 (1997) 25-26.

4186 **Morrice, William G.** Hidden sayings of Jesus: words attributed to Jesus outside the four gospels. L 1997, SPCK viii; 247 pp. $17. 0-281-04922-X.

4187 *Morrone, Fortunato* Gesù Maestro e Signore: annotazioni sulla pretesa cristiana. Vivarium 5 (1997) 39-59.

4188 *Moxnes, Halvor* The theological importance of the "Third Quest" for the historical Jesus. Whose historical Jesus?. SCJud 7: 1997, ⇒170. EArnal, W.E., 132-142.

4189   **Mugueta S., Mª Amparo** Jovenes con Cristo hacia el 2.000. Espirituali-
       dad Juvenil Salesiana 1: Caracas 1997, Equipo Nacional de Aso-
       ciacionismo Juvenil Salesiano 54 pp.

4190   [ET]**Negri, Antimo** G.W.F. HEGEL: la vita di Gesù. Economica Laterza
       37: Bari [3]1994 <1795>, Laterza 160 pp. L10.000. 88-420-4546-2. [R]Il
       Pensiero Politico 30/1 (1997) 86-89 *(Sciacca, Fabrizio)*.

4191   *Neufeld, Dietmar* Apocalypticism: context. Whose historical Jesus?.
       SCJud 7: 1997, ⇒170. [E]Arnal, W.E., 212-214.

4192   *O'Keeffe, Michael E.* Searching for the historical Jesus: examining the
       work of John Dominic CROSSAN and Marcus J. BORG. Horizons 24/2
       (1997) 175-192.

4193   **O'Neill, John** Who did Jesus think he was?. 1995, ⇒11/2,2174. [R]Theol.
       100 (1997) 57-58· *(Harvey, A.E.)*; Bib. 78 (1997) 122-124 *(Penna, Ro-
       mano)*; JThS 48 (1997) 579-581 *(Ziesler, John A.)*; CritRR 10 (1997) 202-
       204 *(Casey, P.M.)*.

4194   *Osiek, Carolyn* Jesus and cultural values: family life as an example. HTS
       53 (1997) 800-814.

4195   *Overman, J. Andrew* Jesus of Galilee and the historical peasant. Archaeo-
       logy and the Galilee. SFSHJ 143: 1997, ⇒275. [E]Edwards, D.R., 67-73.

4196   **Pastore, Corrado; Wyssenbach, Jean-Pierre** Jesús en los evangelios.
       Mes de la biblia 97: Caracas 1997, Comisión episcopal de catequesis,
       biblia y ere 40 pp.

4197   *Pearson, Birger A.* The gospel according to the "Jesus Seminar": on some
       recent trends in gospel research. The emergence. 1997, ⇒154. 23-57.

4198   *Pilch, John J.* Jesus, the holy man, and nature. BiTod 35 (1997) 114-119.

4199   **Piñero, Antonio** L'autre Jésus: vie de Jésus selon les évangiles apocry-
       phes. 1996, ⇒12,4043. [R]EeV 107 (1997) 87 *(Cothenet, E.)*.

4200   *Pixner, B.* Jesus and his community: between Essenes and Pharisees.
       Hillel and Jesus. 1997, ⇒321. [E]Charlesworth, James H., 193-224.

4201   *Porter, Stanley E.; Hayes, Michael A.; Tombs, David* Introduction. Ima-
       ges of Christ. 1997, ⇒256. 17-20.

4202   *Pozzoli, Luigi* La letteratura del '900 di fronte al personaggio Gesù.
       Ambrosius 73/1 (1997) 28-65.

4203   *Pridmore, John* The adolescence of Jesus and growing up in Christ.
       Way.S 90 (1997) 3-9.

4204   **Renan, Ernest** Vita di Gesù. R 1997, Newton 190 pp. L2.000 [Paramita
       17/1,47].

4205   *Richardson, Peter* Enduring concerns: desiderata for future historical-
       Jesus research. Whose historical Jesus?. SCJud 7: 1997, ⇒170. [E]Arnal,
       W.E., 296-307.

4206   *Riches, John K.* The social world of Jesus. Gospel interpretation. 1997,
       ⇒210. [E]Kingsbury, J.D., 283-294.

4207   *Riley, Gregory J.* Words and deeds: Jesus as teacher and Jesus as pattern
       of life. HThR 90 (1997) 427-436.

4208   *Robinson, James M.* Galilean upstarts: a sot's cynical disciples?. NT.S 89:
       1997, ⇒7. [F]BAARDA T., 223-249;

4209   The real Jesus of the sayings gospel Q. PSB 18 (1997) 135-151;

4210   Der wahre Jesus?: der historische Jesus im Spruchevangelium Q. PzB 6
       (1997) 1-14.

4211   *Saldarini, Anthony J.* Comparing the traditions: New Testament and rabbi-
       nic literature. BBR 7 (1997) 195-203.

4212   **Saucy, Mark** The kingdom of God in the teaching of Jesus in the 20th
       century. Dallas 1997, Word xl; 406 pp. $17. 0-8499-1329-2 [ThD
       45,187—Heiser, W. Charles].

4213  *Schaberg, Jane* A feminist experience of historical-Jesus scholarship. Whose historical Jesus?. SCJud 7: 1997, ⇒170. ᴱArnal, W.E., 146-160.

4214  *Schmeller, Thomas* Kollege Paulus: die Jesusüberlieferung und das Selbstverständnis des Völkerapostels. ZNW 88 (1997) 260-283.

4215  *Schmeller, Thomas* War Jesus Revolutionär?: neue Aspekte einer alten Frage. WiWei 60 (1997) 163-175.

4216  **Schnackenburg, Rudolf** El camino de Jesús. Estella 1997, Verbo Divino 124 pp. Ptas1.000 [Comunidades 26,64];

4217  The friend we have in Jesus. ᵀ*Christian, Mark A.*: LVL 1997, Westminster x; 80 pp. $12. 0-664-25731-3 [ThD 45,288—Heiser, W. Charles].

4218  *Schöni, Marc* The question of the "historical Jesus": a look from East and West. ThRev 18 (1997) 347-370.

4219  **Schürmann, H.** Jesus: Gestalt und Geheimnis. ᴱ*Scholtissek, K.*: 1994, ⇒10,224a. ᴿRSR 85/1 (1997) 157-158 *(Léon-Dufour, Xavier)*.

4220  **Schweizer, Eduard** Gesù Cristo: l'uomo di Nazareth e il Signore glorificato. Piccola Collana Moderna 69: 1992, ⇒8,4339; 9,4202. ᴿLaur. 38/1-2 (1997) 303-305 *(Martignani, Luigi)*;

4221  Jesus the parable of God: what do we really know about Jesus?. E 1997, Clark x; 120 pp. £10. 0-567-08585-6 [RRT 1998/1,87].

4222  *Scibona, Rocco* 7Q5, il frammento Magdalen (P$^{64+67}$) e il Gesù storico e il Cristo della fede. 1997, ⇒30. ᶠGɪᴏʀᴅᴀɴᴏ M., 121-156 [Mk 6,52-53].

4223  *Seeley, David* Jesus and the Cynics revisited. JBL 116 (1997) 704-712.

4224  *Segalla, Giuseppe* La 'terza ricerca' su Gesù: il ritorno al suo ambiente storico originario. RCI 78/3 (1997) 196-215.

4225  **Segundo, Juan Luis** A história perdida e recuperada de Jesus de Nazaré: dos sinóticos a Paulo. ᵀ*Furtado de Queiroz, Magda*: São Paulo 1997, Paulus 672 pp. 85-4-349-0742-0. REB 57 (1997) 985-987 *(Bingemer, Maria Clara Lucchetti)*.

4226  **Sesboüé, Bernard** Jésus-Christ à l'image des hommes: brève enquête sur les représentations de Jésus à travers l'histoire. P ²1997, Desclée de B 224 pp. [ScEs 50,382s—Dufort, Jean-Marc].

4227  **Shorto, Russell** Gospel truth: the new image of Jesus emerging from science and history and why it matters. NY 1997, Riverhead viii; 305 pp. $25. 1-57322-056-6 [ThD 44,383—Heiser, W. Charles].

4228  *Snodgrass, Klyne R.* Christology and the historical Jesus. BBR 7 (1997) 255-257.

4229  **Stanton, Graham** Gospel truth?: new light on Jesus and the gospels. 1995, ⇒11/2,2208; 12,4063. ᴿJSNT 67 (1997) 123-124 *(Gibson, Arthur)*;

4230  Dichter bij Jezus?: nieuw licht op de evangeliën. ᵀ*Dubbink, Joep*: Baarn 1997, Callenbach 224 pp. *f*40. 90-266-0636-2 [ITBT 6/1,34].

4231  Parole d'évangile?: un éclairage nouveau sur Jésus et les évangiles. ᵀ*Prignaud, Jean*: L'histoire à vif: P 1997, Cerf 252 pp. FF144. 2-204-05585-9. ᴿEeV 107 (1997) 266-267 & CEv 101 (1997) 61-62 *(Cothenet, Edouard)*; Qumran Chronicle 7/1-2 (1997) 125-126 *(Długosz, Mariusz)*; FV 96/5 (1997) 112-114 *(Trocmé, Étienne)*; RET 57 (1997) 497-499 *(Barrado Fernández, P.)*.

4232  *Stegner, William Richard* Some personal reflections on the Jesus seminar. AsbTJ 52 (1997) 71-80.

4233  *Strange, J.F.* The sayings of Jesus and archaeology. Hillel and Jesus. 1997, ⇒321. ᴱCharlesworth, James H., 291-305.

4234  **Tamayo-Acosta, Juan José** Imágenes de Jesús: condicionamientos sociales, culturales, religosos y de género. 1996, ⇒12,4067. ᴿSalTer 85 (1997) 349-350 *(Tamayo-Acosta, Juan J.)*; Seminarios 42/2 (1997) 260-261 *(Alquezar, Domingo)*.

4235  Tan, Kim Huat The Zion traditions and the aims of Jesus. Diss. MSSNTS 91: C 1997, CUP xiv; 276 pp. £37.50/$60. 0-521-58006-4 [ET 108 (1996-97) 342].

4236  Terribili, Muzio Se tu avessi pazientato... un inedito Gesù tra amici e nemici. Letteratura biblica 9: Mi 1997, Paoline 212 pp. L24.000. 88-315-1432-6 [RivBib 45,507].

4237  Theißen, Gerd; Merz, Annette Der historische Jesus: ein Lehrbuch. 1996, ⇒12,4068. RBZ 41 (1997) 267-269 (Dormeyer, Detlev).

4238  Theissen, Gerd; Winter, Dagmar Die Kriterienfrage in der Jesusforschung: vom Differenzkriterium zum Plausibilitätskriterium. NTOA 34: FrS 1997, Universitäsverlag 348 pp. FS98. 3-7278-1129-3 [NTS 44,625].

4239  Tilliette, Xavier La chasteté de Jésus. RCIC 19/1,28-32; Com(US) 24/1,51-56; Com(F) 22/1 (1997) 21-26.

4240  Tomson, Peter J. The core of Jesus' evangel: εὐαγγελίσασθαι πτωχοῖς (Isa 61). The scriptures in the gospels. BEThL 131: 1997, ⇒234. ETuckett, C.M., 647-658.

4241  Trujillo, L. Jésus el Hijo: un relato creyente. M 1997, Claretianas 410 pp. Pts2.250. 84-7966-137-2 [Proyecció 44,322].

4242  Tully, Mark Four faces: a journey in seach of Jesus the Divine, the Jew, the rebel, the sage. Introd. Moore, Thomas: Berkeley, Calif. 1997, Ulysses xiii; 237 pp. Bibl. 1-569-75090-4 [NThAR 1999,46].

4243  Vaage, Leif E. Recent concerns: the scholar as engagé. Whose historical Jesus?. SCJud 7: 1997, ⇒170. EArnal, W.E., 181-186.

4244  Valero, S. Memorias de María: memorias de Juan: la vida de Jesús contada por la madre y el discípulo. M 1997, Edibesa 251 pp. [Comunidades 26,158—González, M.].

4245  Van Aarde, Andries G. The continued importance of Jesus. HTS 53 (1997) 773-799.

4246  Van Oyen, Geert 'Jesus redt ... alle mensen opgelet': over de band tussen christologie en onderzoek naar Jezus. TTh 37 (1997) 331-342.

4247  Vergeer, Charles Het jong van de panter. Streven 64 (1997) 497-507.

4248  Vergeer, Charles Een nameloze Jezus de Nazarener. Nijmegen 1997, SUN 312 pp. ƒ39.50. 90-6168-498-6 [Streven 64,1051].

4249  Voorwinde, Stephen Jesus' tears: human or divine?. RTR 56/2 (1997) 68-81 [Lk 19,41; John 11,35].

4250  Walker-Ramisch, Sandra Academic engagement: context. Whose historical Jesus?. SCJud 7: 1997, ⇒170. EArnal, W.E., 143-145.

4251  Walter, Nikolaus 'Historischer Jesus' und Osterglaube: ein Diskussionsbeitrag zur Christologie. Praeparatio evangelica. WUNT 98: 1997 <1976>, ⇒167. 56-77.

4252  Webb, Robert L. Continuing historical-Jesus studies: context. Whose historical Jesus?. SCJud 7: 1997, ⇒170. EArnal, W.E., 269-271.

4253  EWilkins, Michael J.; Moreland, J.P. Jesus under fire: modern scholarship reinvents the historical Jesus. 1995, ⇒11/2,390; 12,4079. RCTJ 32/1 (1997) 174-175 (Holwerda, David E.).

4254  Witherington, Ben Buyer beware!: sensationalist claims sold here. BiRe 13/2 (1997) 23-25, 47.

4255  Wright, Nicholas Thomas Jesus and the victory of God. 1996, ⇒12,6939. RRRT (1997/2) 7-12; 12-14 (Bryan, David; Wright, N.T.); Theology 100 (1997) 295-297 (Harvey, A.E.); New Theology Review 10/4 (1997) 106-107 (Harrington, Daniel); StPat 44/3 (1997) 186-192 (Segalla, Giuseppe); NeoTest. 31 (1997) 416-417 (Yorke, Gosnell L.O.R.); HeyJ 38 (1997) 440-441 (Turner, Geoffrey); CritRR 10 (1997): 121-144 (Newman, Carey C.); 221-223 (Moser, Paul K.).

4256 **Zahrnt, Heinz** Jésus de Nazareth: une vie. [T]*Rey, F.; Guého, M.-T.*: 1996, ⇒12,4088. [R]Telema 23/3 (1997) 82-83 *(Delhez, Charles)*.

4257 **Zannoni, Arthur E.** Jesus of the gospels. Cincinnati 1996, St. Anthony Messenger ix; 205 pp. $13. 0-86716-241-4 [BiTod 38,64—Senior, D.].

### F1.5 *Jesus et Israel—*Jesus the Jew

4258 *Arnal, William E.* The Galilean Jewish Jesus: context. Whose historical Jesus?. SCJud 7: 1997, ⇒170. [E]Arnal, W.E., 61-62.

4259 *Bammel, Ernst* Eine übersehene Angabe zu den Toledoth Jeschu. Judaica et Paulina. WUNT 91: 1997 < 1989 >, ⇒109. 62-63.

4260 **Buzzard, Anthony F.** Our Father, who aren't in heaven: the forgotten christianity of Jesus, the Jew. Morrow 1995, Atlanta Bible College 277 pp. [R]EvQ 69/2 (1997) 163-164 *(Brower, K.E.)*.

4261 **Charlesworth, James H.** Jesus' jewishness. 1991, ⇒7,294... 12,4090. Horizons 24/1 (1997) 126-127 *(Loewe, William P.)*;

4262 Gesù nel giudaismo del suo tempo alla luce delle più recenti scoperte. 1994, ⇒10,4038; 12,4091. [R]FilTeo 11/1 (1997) 185-189 *(Gramaglia, Piero Angelo)*.

4263 *Chilton, Bruce* Jesus within Judaism. Jesus in context. AGAJ 39: 1997 < 1995 >, ⇒183. 179-201.

4264 **Flusser, David** Jesus. Collab. *Notley, R. Steven*: J [2]1997 < 1969 >, Magnes 297 pp. Bibl. 965-223-978-X;

4265 Jesus. Pref. *Cunz, M.*: Brescia 1997, Morcelliana 196 pp. L22.000. 88-372-1652-1 [Protest. 53,358—Soggin, J.A.].

4266 *Friedman, David B.* How Jesus observed the Torah in the gospels. ATA Journal 5/1 (1997) 81-94 [ZID 23,439].

4267 *Hegstad, Hans* Savior of the gentiles or Israel's messiah?. ThD 44/2 (1997) 111-116.

4268 *Kjaer-Hansen, Kai* Der dreieinige Gott und der Jude Jesus. Tod eines Messias. 1996, ⇒286. [E]Kjaer-Hansen, Kai, 146-151.

4269 *Lange, Nicholas de* Jesus Christ and Auschwitz. NBl 78 (1997) 308-316.

4270 **Lockhart, Douglas G.** Jesus, the heretic: freedom and bondage in a religious world. Shaftesbury 1997, Element x; 394 pp. 1-86204-001-X [NThAR 1998,101].

4271 **Manns, Frédéric** Jésus fils de David. 1994, ⇒10,4063. [R]LASBF 47 (1997) 605-607 *(Chrupcała, Lesław Daniel)*.

4272 *Manns, Frédéric* Una aproximación judía al Nuevo Testamento. TE 41 (1997) 335-349.

4273 **Meier, John P.** Mentor, message, and miracles. A marginal Jew: rethinking the historical Jesus, 2. 1994, ⇒10,4069; 12,4094. [R]BZ 41 (1997) 262-266 *(Schlosser, Jacques)*; JES 34/1 (1997) 139-140 *(Polish, Daniel)*; TrinJ 18 (1997) 99-102 *(Evans, Craig A.)*; AnnTh 11 (1997) 538-541 *(Estrada, Bernardo)*.

4274 *Moussé, Jean* Jésus le roi des juifs: l'éternité présente. Parole présente: P 1997, Cerf 191 pp. FF100 [EeV 107/22,174].

4275 **Neusner, Jacob** Disputa immaginaria tra un rabbino e Gesù: quale maestro seguire?. 1996, ⇒12,4098. [R]Vivarium 5 (1997) 253-261 *(Dilenge, Giovanni)*; RSEc 15 (1997) 133-135 *(Morandini, Simone)*;

4276 Ein Rabbi spricht mit Jesus: ein jüdisch-christlicher Dialog. [T]*Miedler, Karin; Heinemann, Enrico*: Mü 1997, Claudius 173 pp. DM25. 3-532-62208-4 [NThAR 1997,261] [Mk 14,3-9; 12,1-8].

4277  *Riches, John* Gesù l'ebreo: l'interazione con il giudaismo del suo tempo.
Conc(D) 33/1,47-55; Conc(F) 269,65-74; Conc(E) 269,75-85    Conc(I)
33/1 (1997) 80-91.

4278  ᵀᴱSalomon, H.P.; Sassoon, I.S.D. Uriel da Costa: examination of pharisaic traditions. 1993, ⇒9,4271; 11/2,7482. ᴿREJ 156 (1997) 407-410
*(Ayoun, Richard)*.

4279  *Sievers, Joseph* Gesù di Nazaret visto da scrittori ebrei del XX secolo.
Tertium Millennium 1/5 (1997) 48-53;

4280  Gesù, gli esseni e la reincarnazione. Sum. 217. Religioni e Sette nel
mondo 3/2 (1997) 37-49.

4281  *Stefani, Piero* Maria figlia di Sion e le radici ebraiche di Gesù: tracce per
una ricerca. Mar. 59/151 (1997) 17-30.

4282  **Vermes, Geza** La religión de Jesús el judío. 1996, ⇒12,4107. ᴿEE 72
(1997) 149-152 *(Piñero, Antonio)*.

4283  *Vermes, Geza* Reflections on Jesus the Jew, his world and his religion.
FolOr 33 (1997) 33-37.

4284  **Vidal, Marie** Un juif nommé Jésus. 1996, ⇒12,4108. ᴿEeV 107/4 (1997)
87-89 *(Monloubou, Louis)*; CEv 101 (1997) 62-63 *(Tassin, Claude)*;

4285  Un judío llamado Jesús. Bilbao 1997, Ega 285 pp. [Comunidades
26,37s—Sosa, Emilio R.].

4286  **Willems, Gerard F.** Jezus en de chassidim van zijn dagen. 1996,
⇒12,4109. ᴿColl. 27/3 (1997) 333-334 *(Tercic, Hans)*.

4287  *Wolf, Arnold Jacob* Jesus as an historical Jew. Jdm 46 (1997) 375-380.

4288  **Young, Brad H.** Jesus the Jewish theologian. 1995, ⇒11/2,2279;
12,4113. ᴿStPav 44/2 (1997) 245-246 *(Segalla, Giuseppe)*.

F1.6 *Jesus in Ecclesia*—The Church Jesus

4289  **Alunno, Luigi** La vita di Gesù Cristo—croce e martirio: meditazioni.
1996, ⇒12,4115. ᴿLa Sapienza della Croce 12/1 (1997) 79-80 *(Acciaretti,
Gino)*.

4290  *Arregui, Josune* Cómo animar una vida religiosa que sea hoy memoria de
Jesús. Confer 36/1 (1997) 103-122.

4291  **Bieritz, Karl-Heinrich** Grundwissen Theologie: Jesus Christus. Kaiser
Taschenbücher 148: Gü 1997 Kaiser 96 pp. 3-579-05148-2.

4292  *Blásquez, Ricardo* El cristianismo es Jesucristo. ᴹRuiz de la Peña, J.,
BSal.E 189: 1997, ⇒76. 193-205.

4293  **Bockmuehl, Markus N.A.** This Jesus: martyr, Lord, messiah. 1996,
⇒12,4117. Faith & Mission 15/1 (1997) 80-82 *(Köstenberger, A.J.)*.

4294  **Cabodevilla, José María** 365 nombres de Cristo. BAC 572: M 1997,
BAC 748 pp. 84-7914-279-0. ᴿMayéutica 23 (1997) 480-1 *(Eguiarte, E.)*.

4295  *Cagin, Michel* Voir Jésus. NV 72/1 (1997) 5-18 [ZID 23,197].

4296  **Chilton, Bruce** Jesus' prayer and Jesus' eucharist: his personal practice
of spirituality. Valley Forge 1997, Trinity viii; 103 pp. $9. 1-56338-204-0
[ThD 45,64—Heiser, W. Charles].

4297  **Colonna, C.** Gli splendori di Gesù: contemplazione e preghiera. R 1997,
ADP 134 pp. L15.000 [RivBib 45,383].

4298  *Cortina, Adela* La vida religiosa como memoria de Jesús: aportaciones de
una mujer laica desde la perspectiva ética. Confer 36/1 (1997) 137-150.

4299  **De Andrés, R.** Jesús siempre y más. M 1997, EDIBESA 525 pp. Ptas
1.900 [Comunidades 26,65].

4300  **Depoortere, K.** Wie is die Jezus?. 1996, ⇒12,4120. ᴿColl. 27 (1997)
325-326 *(Dessein, Jozef)*.

4301 **Dini, A.** Gesù nostro contemporaneo. Brescia 1997, Queriniana 166 pp. L18.000 [RdT 38,285].

4302 *Elenga, Yvon Christian* Jésus-Christ et les récits mythiques. Hekima Review 17 (1997) 19-25.

4303 **Espeja, Jesús** Creer en Jesucristo. M 1997, BAC 170 pp. [Mayéutica 23,500—Gómez, Vladimir].

4304 *García Paredes, José Cristo Rey* 'Memoria Jesu': un tiempo nuevo para la vida religiosa. Confer 36/1 (1997) 65-101.

4305 **Grelot, Pierre** Jésus de Nazareth, Christ et Seigneur: une lecture de l'évangile, 1. LeDiv 167: P 1997, Cerf 473 pp. FF220. 2-204-05493-3. RLV(B) 46/2 (1997) 93-94 *(Genuyt, F.)*; EeV 107 (1997) 265-266 *(Cothenet, Édouard)*.

4306 *Grey, Mary* Gesù, *guru* dell'invidualismo o cuore della comunità: discepolato cristiano e chiesa profetica. Conc(E) 269,159-169; Conc(I) 33/1 (1997) 167-178.

4307 **Joannes Paulus II, papa** Gesù di Nazaret: centro dell'universo e del tempo. CasM 1997, Piemme 238 pp. 88-384-2645-7.

4308 **Léonard, A.-M.** Jezus Christus, de mens van alle tijden: tien ontmoetingen in het vooruitzicht van het jaar 2000. Averbode 1997, Altiora 135 pp. 90-317-1283-3 [Coll. 27,335].

4309 **Lentzen-Deis, Fritzleo** Jesus in exegetical reflections and community experience. E*Mulloor, Augustine*: Evangelium et cultura 2: New Delhi 1997, Intercultural xvi; 168 pp. 81-85574-31-6 [NThAR 1999,251].

4310 **Maier, Johann** Gesù Cristo e il cristianesimo nella tradizione giudaica antica. StBi 106: 1994, ⇒11/2,7208. RFilTeo 11/1 (1997) 189-191 *(Gramaglia, Pier Angelo)*.

4311 *Okure, Teresa* Word of God—word of life: an African perspective. VSVD 38/3 (1997) 243-265.

4312 **Pemán, José M.ª** Los testigos de Jesús. M 1997, Edibesa 174 pp. [Comunidades 26,157—González, M.].

4313 **Recinos, Harold J.** Who comes in the name of the Lord?: Jesus at the margins. Nv 1997, Abingdon 158 pp. $15. 0-687-01002-0 [RRT 1998/2,91].

4314 *Rezza, Dario* Gesù Cristo, il testimone. PalCl 76/1-2 (1997) 43-58.

4315 **Sachot, Maurice** L'invention du Christ: genèse d'une religion. Le champ médiologique: P 1997, Jacob 251 pp. FF130. 2-7381-0534-3 [JSJ 29,347—Tromp, J.].

4316 *Susin, Luiz Carlo* Jesus na encruzilhada: reflexões sobre Jesus, desde a 'Vita Consecrata' até o pluralismo religioso contemporâneo. Convergência 32/1 (1997) 20-32.

4317 *Wanamaker, Charles A.* Jesus the ancestor: reading the story of Jesus from an African christian perspective. Scriptura 62 (1997) 281-298 [ZID 24,133].

4318 *Westerholm, Stephen* The Christ of faith: context. Whose historical Jesus?. SCJud 7: 1997, ⇒170. EArnal, W.E., 238-240.

4319 *Xeres, Saverio* Gesù mostra la via: il tempo di Quaresima. RCI 78/1 (1997) 69-77.

F1.7 *Jesus 'anormalis':* to atheists, psychoanalysts, romance...

4320 **Al-Assiouty, Sarwat Anis** Révolutionnaires et contre-révolutionnaires parmi les disciples de Jésus et les compagnons de Muhammad. 1994, ⇒10,4125. ᴿEstB 55 (1997) 558-560 *(Ribera, J.)*.

4321 **al-Markaz al-malakî li-l-dirâsât al-dîniyya** ʿÎsâ wa-Maryam fî l-Qurʾân wa-l-tafâsîr [Jésus et Marie dans le Coran et les commentaires]. ʿAmmân 1996, Dâr al-shurûq li-l-nashr wa-l-tawzîʿ 584 pp. [IslChr 25,284—Borrmans, Maurice].

4322 *Alkier, Stefan* Wunder Punkt Jesusfilm. PTh 86 (1997) 167-182.

4323 **Altizer, Thomas J.J.** The contemporary Jesus. Albany 1997, State Univ. of New York Press xxvii; 225 pp. $20. 0-7914-3376-5 [ThD 44,351—Heiser, W. Charles].

4324 **Andrés, Rafael de** Jesús sempre y más: 1.000 opiniones sobre Cristo. M 1997, Edibesa 552 pp. ᴿRF 182 (1997) 437-438 *(Abad, J.)*.

4325 *Anonby, John* Images of Christ in East African literature: the novels of Ngugi wa Thiong'o. Images of Christ. 1997, ⇒256. ᴱPorter, S.E., 239-258.

4326 **Baugh, Lloyd** Imaging the divine: Jesus and Christ figures in films. Kansas City 1997, Sheed & W x; 337 pp. $25. 1-55612-863-0 [ThD 45,61—Heiser, W. Charles].

4327 *Baulot, Alberto; Viganò, Dario* Dal tradimento alla traduzione: le figure di Gesù nel cinema. Ambrosius 73/1 (1997) 66-72.

4328 *Beaude, Pierre-Marie* Le Jésus de RENAN lu par un exégète. La Bible en littérature. 1997, ⇒315. ᴱBeaude, Pierre-Marie, 245-258.

4329 *Bergoza Martinez, R.* Jesús y la religión: claves para un diálogo y discernimiento teológico según H. de LUBAC. Burg. 38 (1997) 395-414.

4330 **Borrmans, Maurice** Jésus et les musulmans d'aujourd'hui. CJJC 69: 1996, ⇒12,4131. ᴿIslChr 23 (1997) 266-267 *(Lagarde, M.)*.

4331 *Campani, Giorgio* Il problema di Gesù Cristo nella società secolare. Presbyteri 31 (1997) 369-374.

4332 **Castelli, Ferdinando** Volti de Gesù nella letteratura moderna. 1987-1995, ⇒7,3716... 11/2,1820. ᴿCivCatt 148 II (1997) 562-572 *(Spadaro, Antonio)*.

4333 *DuToit, Cornel W.* The fictional transfiguration of Jesus: images of Jesus in literature. HTS 53 (1997) 815-839.

4334 ᴱ**Elliott, J.K.** The apocryphal Jesus. 1996, ⇒12,4136. ᴿCrossCur 47/1 (1997) 119-121 *(Fitzgerald, John T.)*; CritRR 10 (1997) 177-178 *(Penn, Michael)*.

4335 *Graham, David J.* Christ imagery in recent film: a saviour from celluloid?;

4336 *Graham, Susan Lochrie* The life of Jesus as comedy: plot structure in two contemporary historical Jesus portraits. Images of Christ. 1997, ⇒256. ᴱPorter, S.E., 305-314/73-94.

4337 *Guerra Gomez, M.* Jesucristo y las sectas religiosas, mágicas e ideológicas de nuestro tiempo. Burg. 38 (1997) 433-492.

4338 *Hahnen, Peter* 'Diese Show—das bin ich!': die Londoner Neuproduktion von *Jesus Christ Superstar* als Berührungspunkt zwischen Pop-/Rockmusik und Frömmigkeit. Orien. 61 (1997) 41-45.

4339 **Hamilton, William** A quest for the post-historical Jesus. 1994, ⇒11/2,1798; 12,891. ᴿTJT 13/1 (1997) 104-106 *(Husbands, M.)*.

4340 TIacovella, Angelo Il pettine e la brocca: detti arabi di Gesù. T 1997, Leone Verde 77 pp. [IslChr 24,270—Borrmans, Maurice].

4341 Jacomuzzi, Stefano Cominciò in Galilea: autobiografia di Gesù. CasM 1997, Piemme 230 pp. 88-384-2855-7 [NThAR 1999,45].

4342 Jaschke, Helmut Gesù—il guaritore: psicoterapia a partire dal Nuovo Testamento. Spiritualità 62: Brescia 1997, Queriniana 342 pp. Bibl. 88-399-1362-9.

4343 *Jiménez, José Demetrio* Cómo ven a Jesucristo los creyentes de otras religiones. RelCult 43 (1997) 751-765.

4344 Kaiser, Gerhard Christus im Spiegel der Dichtung: exemplarische Interpretationen vom Barock bis hin zur Gegenwart. FrB 1997, Herder 192 pp. DM29.80 [GuL 71,156—Steinmetz, Franz-Josef].

4345 Kindler, Helmut Leg mich wie ein Siegel auf dein Herz: ein Indizien-Roman über die kinderreiche 'Heilige Familie' in Nazareth. Mü 1997, Kindler 320 pp. DM45 [EK 1998/4,237s—Huizing, Klaas].

4346 *Kuschel, Karl-Josef* Espressione della cultura, protesta contro la cultura: il paradosso di Gesú nei film e nei romanzi del nostro tempo. Conc(F) 269,13-24; Conc(D) 33/1,4-13; Conc(E) 269,13-27; Conc(I) 33/1 (1997) 17-32.

4347 Mailer, Norman The gospel according to the Son. NY 1997, Random House (8) 242 pp. 0-679-45783-6.

4348 *McCarron, Kevin* 'The sudden look of some dead master': T.S. ELIOT and DANTE. Images of Christ. 1997, ⇒256. EPorter, S.E., 277-288.

4349 *Mette, Norbert* Ce Jésus si difficile à suivre: engager quelqu'un à devenir disciple, une entreprise difficile dans les conditions actuelles. Conc(F) 269 (1997) 25-34.

4350 Parazzoli, Ferruccio L'ago e il cammello: quarantatré storielle profane dal Nuovo Testamento. Mi 1996, Longanesi 171 pp. L25.000. RCivCatt 148 IV (1997) 622-624 *(Vanzan, P.)*.

4351 Parrinder, Geoffrey Jesus in the Qur'an. 1995, ⇒12,4141. RCTJ 32/1 (1997) 207-209 *(Madany, Bassam M.)*.

4352 Pelikan, Jaroslav Jan The illustrated Jesus through the centuries. NHv 1997, Yale Univ. Press 256 pp. $35. 0-300-07268-6 [ThD 45,85—Heiser, W. Charles].

4353 *Pell, Barbara* Images of Christ in Canadian literature: faith and fiction in the novels of CALLAGHAN, HOOD and MACLENNAN. Images of Christ. 1997, ⇒256. EPorter, S.E., 259-276.

4354 Phipps, William E. Muhammed and Jesus: a comparison of the prophets and their teachings. 1996, ⇒12,4142. Islam and Christian-Muslim Relations 8/1 (1997) 106-107 *(Forward, Martin)*; Studies in World Christianity 3/2 (1997) 243-244 *(Watt, W. Montgomery)*.

4355 *Pinsent, Pat* The image of Christ in the writings of two seventeenth-century English country parsons: George HERBERT and Thomas TRAHERNE;

4356 *Porter, Wendy J.* BACH, BEETHOVEN and STRAVINSKY masses: images of Christ in the credo. Images of Christ. 1997, ⇒256. EPorter, S.E., 227-238/375-398.

4357 *Pozzoli, Luigi* La letteratura del '900 de fronte al personaggio Gesù: l'accoglienza. Ambrosius 73/2 (1997) 173-191.

4358 Prigent, Pierre Jésus au cinéma. Entrée Libre 37: Genève 1997, Labor & F 89 pp. FS13. 2-8309-0806-6 [RHPhR 77,253].

4359 **Saramago, José** Das Evangelium nach Jesus Christus. ᵀ*Klotsch, Andreas*: Reinbek 1997, Rowohlt 511 pp. DM19.90 [LM 38/4,32—Zoske, Robert M.].

4360 **Sorel, Andrés** Jesús, llamado el Cristo. M 1997, Compañía Literaria 219 pp. 84-8213-051-X [EE 73,513s—Piñero, Antonio].

4361 *Soupa, Anne* Jésus à travers le septième art. DosB 69 (1997) 15-18.

4362 **Tatum, W. Barnes** Jesus at the movies: a guide to the first hundred years. Santa Rosa, CA 1997, Polebridge x; 245 pp. $18. 0-944344-67-4 [ThD 45,389—Heiser, W. Charles].

4363 *Thompson, John O.* Jesus as moving image: the question of movement. Images of Christ. 1997, ⇒256. ᴱPorter, S.E., 290-304.

4364 **Wessels, Anton** Images of Jesus: how Jesus is perceived and portrayed in non-European cultures. ᵀ*Vriend, John*: 1990, ⇒7,3748. ᴿThRev 18/1 (1997) 73-74 *(Worley, Robert)*.

F2.1 *Exegesis creativa*—innovative methods [⇒B5]

4365 ᴱ**Bernardelli, Andrea** The concept of intertextuality thirty years on: 1967-1997. Versus 77/78 (1997) 1-197.

4366 *Blanchard, Yves-Marie* Vers un nouveau paradigme exégétique. La théologie dans l'histoire. 1997, ⇒238. ᴱBousquet, F., 73-91 [EThL 74,166*].

4367 *Botha, J. Eugene* Style in the New Testament: the need for serious reconsideration. New Testament text. BiSe 44: 1997 <1991>, ⇒748. ᴱPorter, S.E., 114-129.

4368 **Egger, Wilhelm** Lecturas del Nuevo Testamento. 1990, ⇒8,4473. ᴿThX 47/2 (1997) 247-257 *(Novoa M., Carlos J.)*.

4369 **Egger, Wilhelm** How to read the New Testament: an introduction to linguistic and historical-critical methodology. 1996, ⇒12,4153. ᴿRevBib 59/3 (1997) 190-191 *(Levoratti, A.J.)*.

4370 *Goodacre, Mark* 'Drawing from the treasure both new and old': current trends in New Testament study. ScrB 27 (1997) 66-77.

4371 **Henderson, Ian H.** Jesus, rhetoric and law. 1996, ⇒12,4154. ᴿBZ 41 (1997) 270-272 *(Ebner, Martin)*; ThLZ 122 (1997) 568-569 *(Pöttner, Martin)*.

4372 **Kartveit, Magnar** Det Gamle Testamentet: analyse av tekstar i utval. Oslo 1997, Norske Samlaget 375 pp. 82-521-4474-6 [SJOT 12,152—Jeppesen, Knud].

4373 **Keßler, Hildrun** Bibliodrama und Leiblichkeit: leibhafte Textauslegung im theologischen und therapeutischen Diskurs. PTHe 20: 1996, ⇒12,4157. ᴿThLZ 122 (1997) 655-657 *(Bubenheimer, Ulrich)*; ZKTh 119 (1997) 488-489 *(Meyer, Hans Bernhard)*.

4374 *Kosch, Daniel; Fong, Maria Ko Ha* Wort Gottes—Quelle des Lebens: kontextuelle Bibelauslegungen. Collab. *Okure, Teresa*. BK 52 (1997) 53-79 [EThL 74,169*].

4375 *Mendonça, José Tolentino* Método pragmático de interpretação da bíblia. Did(L) 27/2 (1997) 137-145.

4376 **Onuki, Takashi** Sammelbericht als Kommunikation: Studien zur Erzählkunst der Evangelien. WMANT 73: Neuk 1997, Neuk xiii; 170 pp. 3-7887-1618-5.

4377 **Robbins, Vernon K.** The tapestry of early Christian discourse. 1996, ⇒12,4166. ᴿRRT 4/2 (1997) 35-37 *(Need, Stephen W.)*; ScEs 49 (1997) 377-378 *(Racine, Jean-François)*.

4378 <sup>E</sup>**Warns, Else Natalie; Fallner, Heinrich** Bibliodrama als Prozeß: Leitung und Beratung. Bielefeld 1994, Luther 262 pp. DM36. 3-7858-0364-8. <sup>R</sup>ThLZ 122 (1997) 655-657 *(Bubenheimer, Ulrich)*.

4379 **Wilson, Victor M.** Divine symmetries: the art of biblical rhetoric. Lanham 1997, University Press of America iii; 354 pp. $64.50/$37.50. 0-7618-0662-8/3-6.

## F2.2 *Unitas VT-NT et NT:* The Unity of OT-NT and NT

4380 <sup>E</sup>**Blanchetière, François; Herr, Moshé D.** Aux origines juives du christianisme. 1993, ⇒11/2,2229. <sup>R</sup>REJ 156 (1997) 196-199 *(Mimouni, Simon C.)*.

4381 *Childs, Brevard S.* Does the Old Testament witness to Jesus Christ?. 1997, ⇒92. <sup>F</sup>STUHLMACHER P., 57-64.

4382 *Dohmen, Christoph* Die Post eines anderen lesen ...?: christliches Verstehen der Bibel Israels. rhs 40 (1997) 93-103.

4383 *Freedman, David Noel* The unity of the bible. Divine Commitment 1. 1997, <1956>, ⇒124. 43-49.

4384 *Guillet, Jacques* The role of the bible in the birth of the church. The Bible in Greek christian antiquity. 1997 <c.1984>, ⇒177. <sup>ET</sup>Blowers, Paul M., 34-48.

4385 *Hagner, Donald A.* Balancing the old and the new: the law of Moses in Matthew and Paul. Interp. 51 (1997) 20-30.

4386 **Liebers, Reinhold** 'Wie geschrieben steht': Studien zu einer besonderen Art frühchristlichen Schriftbezuges. 1993, ⇒9,4383... 12,4180. <sup>R</sup>ThLZ 122 (1997) 36-39 *(Holtz, Traugott)*.

4387 *Lohfink, Norbert* Perikopenordnung "Patmos": Gedanken eines Alttestamentlers zu dem Leseordnungsentwurf von Hansjakob BECKER. BiLi 70 (1997) 218-232.

4388 *Michel, Diethelm* Annäherungen: Gedanken zum Problem der fundamentalen Bedeutung des Alten und der normativen Bedeutung des Neuen Testaments: Walter SCHMITHALS zum 70. Geburtstag. Studien zur Überlieferungsgeschichte. TB 93: 1997, ⇒149. 69-88.

4389 **Pesce, Mauro** Il cristianesimo e la sua radice ebraica. 1994, ⇒11/2,2262. <sup>R</sup>FilTeo 11/1 (1997) 207-208 *(Di Sante, Carmine)*; VetChr 34 (1997) 386-387 *(Aulisa, Immacolata)*.

4390 *Pickering, Stuart R.* Old Testament and New Testament. NTTRU 5 (1997) 41-58.

4391 *Porter, Stanley E.* The use of the Old Testament in the New Testament: a brief comment on method and terminology. Early christian interpretation. JSNT.S 148: 1997, ⇒191. <sup>E</sup>Evans, C., 79-96.

4392 *Smend, Rudolf* Beziehungen zwischen alttestamentlicher und neutestamentlicher Wissenschaft. Bibel, Theologie. 1997 <1995>, ⇒162. 46-58.

4393 *Soulen, R. Kendall* Karl BARTH and the future of the God of Israel. Pro Ecclesia 6/4 (1997) 413-428.

4394 *Stanley, Christopher* The social environment of 'free' biblical quotations in the New Testament;

4395 The rhetoric of quotations: an essay on method. Early christian interpretation. JSNT.S 148: 1997, ⇒191. <sup>E</sup>Evans, C., 18-27/44-58.

4396 *Tuckett, Christopher M.* Scripture and Q. The scriptures in the gospels. BEThL 131: 1997, ⇒234. <sup>E</sup>Tuckett, C.M., 3-26.

4397  *Werbick, Jürgen* Bibel Jesu und Evangelium Jesu Christi: systema-tisch-theologische Perspektiven. BiLi 70 (1997) 213-218.
4398  **Westermann, Claus** L'Ancien Testament et Jésus Christ. Foi Vi-vante—Bible: P 1997, Cerf 90 pp. [LV(L) 244,86s—Revellin, L.].
4399  **Wilson, Walter T.** The mysteries of righteousness: the literary composition and genre of the Sentences of Pseudo-Phocylides. TSAJ 40: 1994, ⇒10,3882... 11/2,2275. ᴿBZ 41 (1997) 151-153 *(Thomas, Johannes)*; JBL 116 (1997) 352-354 *(Holladay, Carl R.)*.
4400  *Zenger, Erich* "Gemäß der Schrift" (1Kor 15,3f): das Alte Testament und das christlich-jüdische Verhältnis. rhs 40 (1997) 74-83.

4401  **Aletti, Jean-Noël** Gesù Cristo: unità del Nuovo Testamento?. ᵀ*Valentino, Carlo*: Nuove vie dell'esegesi: R 1995, Borla 288 pp. L40.000. 88-263-1105-6. ᴿCivCatt 148 IV (1997) 515-516 *(Scaiola, D.)*.

F2.5 *Commentarii*—Commentaries on the whole NT

4402  ᵀ**Bateman, John J.** Paraphrases on Timothy, Titus, Philemon, Peter, Jude, James, John, Hebrews. Collected works of Erasmus 44. 1993, ⇒9,4395. ᴿSCJ 28/1 (1997) 354-355 *(Hoffmann, Manfred)*; Erasmus of Rotterdam Society Yearbook 17 (1997) 70-97 *(Vessey, Mark)*.
4403  **Cothenet, Édouard; Morgen, Michèle; Vanhoye, Albert** Les der-nières épîtres: Hébreux—Jacques—Pierre—Jean—Jude. Commen-taires: P 1997, Bayard 290 pp. FF120. 2-227-366-09-5.
4404  **Hübner, Hans** An Philemon: an die Kolosser: an die Epheser. HNT 12: Tü 1997, Mohr 277 pp. DM59. 3-16-146775-2 [OrdKor 38,512].
4405  ᴱ**Mills, Watson Early; Wilson, Richard Francis** Acts and Pauline writings. Mercer Commentary on the Bible 7: Macon, GA 1997, Mercer University Press lxxx; 291 pp. $19. 0-86554-512-X.
4406  ᴱ**Parr, John** Sowers & reapers: a companion to the four gospels and Acts. Nv 1997, Abingdon 459 pp. 0-687-07098-8.
4407  **Tuñi, Josep-Oriol; Alegre, Xavier** Scritti giovannei e lettere catto-liche. Introduzione allo studio della Bibbia 8: Brescia 1997, Paideia 312 pp. L47.000. 88-394-0545-3.

IX. Evangelia

F2.6 **Evangelia Synoptica;** *textus, synopses, commentarii*

4408  ᴱ**Gomis, Joaquim** Primera lectura del evangelio: Mateo, Marcos, Lucas, Juan. Emaús 23: Barc 1997, Centre de Pastoral Litúrgica 68 pp. Selección de textos y notas. 84-7467-406-9.
4409  **Kudasiewicz, Joseph** The synoptic gospels today. 1996, ⇒12,4195. ᴿHPR 97/8 (1997) 75-76 *(Reilly, Matthew V.)*.
4410  **Lasserre, Guy** Les synopses: élaboration et usage. SubBi 19: 1996, ⇒12,4196. ᴿNT 39 (1997) 192-193 *(Tuckett, Christopher)*; RivBib 45 (1997) 361-364 *(Poppi, Angelico)*.

4411 *Luke, K.* Vinegar and gall in Tatian's *Diatesseron*. BiBh 23/1 (1997) 45-59.
4412 **Price, Reynolds** Three gospels. 1996, ⇒12,4199. ᴿThTo 54/1 (1997) 92-94 *(Garrison, Joseph M. Jr.)*.
4413 *Schmithals, Walter* Vom Ursprung der synoptischen Tradition. ZThK 94 (1997) 288-316.
4414 *Van Zyl, H.C.* Objective display or textual engineering?: hermeneutical aspects in making and using a synopsis of the synoptic gospels. Neotest. 31 (1997) 361-388.

## F2.7 *Problema synopticum:* The Synoptic Problem

4415 *Aguirre Monasterio, Rafael* El enigma de los sinópticos. ResB 13 (1997) 5-13.
4416 **Allison, Dale C.** The Jesus tradition in Q. Harrisburg, Pennsylvania 1997, Trinity xii; 243 pp. Bibl. $27. 1-56338-207-5.
4417 *Arnal, William E.* Gendered couplets in Q and legal formulations: from rhetoric to social history. JBL 116 (1997) 75-94.
4418 **Arnal, William E.** The rhetoric of deracination in Q. Diss. Toronto 1997; ᴰ*Kloppenborg, John S.* [SR 26,527].
4419 **Baik, Woon Chul** La christologie de la source Q. Diss. 1996, ⇒12,4204. ᴿRICP 61 (1997) 348-350 *(Perrot, Charles)*.
4420 ᴱ**Borg, Marcus** Het verloren evangelie Q:; dichter bij de bron. Inleid. *Den Heyer, C.J.*: Zoetermeer 1997, Meinema 136 pp. ƒ25. 90-211-3678-3 [ITBT 6/3,31—Hoet, Hendrik].
4421 *Broadhead, Edwin K.* On the (mis)definition of Q. JSNT 68 (1997) 3-12.
4422 ᴱ**Carruth, Shawn; Garsky, Albrecht** The database of the International Q Project: Q 11:2b-4. 1996, ⇒12,4208. ᴿRStT 16/1 (1997) 91-93 *(Moore, Anne)*.
4423 **Catchpole, David R.** The quest for Q. 1993, ⇒9,4407... 11/2,240. ᴿSJTh 50 (1997) 507-508 *(Parker, D.C.)*.
4424 *De Santis, Andrea* La consegna di Dio: la tradizione fra visione sinottica e parola tramandata. StAns 124: 1997, ⇒57. ᶠLOEHRER M. — TRAGAN P., 185-207.
4425 **Fleddermann, Harry T.** Mark and Q: a study of the overlap texts. BEThL 122: 1995, ⇒11/1,2735; 12,4214. ᴿThLZ 122 (1997) 35-36 *(Schenk, Wolfgang)*.
4426 *Fuchs, Albert* Die Agreement-Redaktion von Mk 6,32-44 par Mt 14,13-21 par Lk 9,10b-17: ein vorläufiger Entwurf. SNTU.A 22 (1997) 181-203.
4427 **Head, Peter M.** Christology and the synoptic problem: an argument for Markan priority. MSSNTS 94: C 1997, CUP xviii; 337 pp. $60. 0-521-58488-4. ᴿFaith & Mission 15/1 (1997) 76-78 *(Köstenberger, Andreas J.)*.
4428 ᴱ**Heil, Christoph** Q 12:8-12: Confessing or denying, speaking against the Holy Spirit, hearings before synagogues. DQ: Lv 1997, Peeters xix; 812 pp. FB2.800. 90-6831-990-6 [EThL 74,433ss—Neirynck, F.].
4429 **Hoffmann, Paul** Tradition und Situation: Studien zur Jesusüberlieferung in der Logienquelle und den synoptischen Evangelien. NTA 28: 1995, ⇒11/1,2737; 12,4219. ᴿThLZ 122 (1997) 673-674 *(März, Claus-Peter)*.

4430  *Hoffmann, Paul* Betz and Q. ZNW 88 (1997) 197-210.
4431  <sup>E</sup>**Kloppenborg, John S.** Conflict and invention... studies on the sayings gospel Q. 1995, ⇒11/1,94; 12,4223. <sup>R</sup>TJT 13/1 (1997) 108-109 *(Sweder, Kristen M.)*.
4432  *McIver, Robert K.* Implications of new data pertaining to the problem of synoptic relationships. ABR 45 (1997) 20-39.
4433  *Moreland, Milton C.; Robinson, James M.* The international Q project: editorial board meetings 1-10 June, 16 November 1995, 16-23 August, 22 November 1996; work sessions 17 November 1995, 23 November 1996. JBL 116 (1997) 521-525.
4434  *Neirynck, F.* GOULDER and the minor agreements;
4435  Note on Q 4,1-2;
4436  Note on the argument(s) from order. EThL 73 (1997) 84-93/94-102/386-392.
4437  *Scholer, David M.* Q bibliography supplement VIII: 1997. SBL.SPS 36 (1997) 750-756.
4438  **Schröter, Jens** Erinnerung an Jesu Worte: Studien zur Rezeption der Logienüberlieferung in Markus, Q und Thomas. Diss.-Habil. Humboldt; <sup>D</sup>*Breytenbach, C.*: WMANT 76: Neuk 1997, Neuk xviii; 529 pp. DM148. 3-7887-1646-0.
4439  *Tuckett, Christopher M.* Q and the 'church': the role of the christian community within Judaism according to Q. 1997, ⇒93. <sup>F</sup>SWEET J., 65-77.
4440  *Tuckett, Christopher M.* The synoptic gospels and Acts. Handbook. NTTS 25: 1997, ⇒971. <sup>E</sup>Porter, S.E., 477-502.
4441  <sup>E</sup>**Uro, Risto** Symbols and strata: essays on the sayings gospel Q. SESJ 65: 1996, ⇒12,208. <sup>R</sup>EThL 73 (1997) 177-79 *(Neirynck, F.)*.
4442  *Van Oyen, Geert* The doublets in 19th-century gospel study. Sum. 306. EThL 73 (1997) 277-306.
4443  *Wilson, B.E.* The Two Notebook hypothesis: an explanation of seven synoptic patterns. ET 108 (1997) 265-268.

### F2.8 *Synoptica:* **themata**

4444  **Andreoli, Dante** Il 'velum scissum' nei sinottici: espressione, realtà e significato. Diss. Pont. Univ. Gregoriana 1997; <sup>D</sup>*Rasco, Emilio*: 297 pp. extr. 4463 [RTL 29,582].
4445  **Barton, Stephen C.** Discipleship and family ties in Mark and Matthew. MSSNTS 80: 1994, ⇒10,4736... 12,4247. <sup>R</sup>Bibl.Interp. 5/2 (1997) 212-214 *(Moxnes, Halvor)*.
4446  *Braun, Willi* Argumentation and the problem of authority: synoptic rhetoric of pronouncement in cultural context. The rhetorical analysis. JSNT.S 146: 1997, ⇒336. <sup>E</sup>Porter, Stanley E., 185-199.
4447  <sup>E</sup>**Carruth, Shawn** Q 12:49-59: children against parents—judging the time—settling out of court. DQ: Lv 1997, Peeters xvii; 434 pp. BEF1.800. 90-6831-931-0. <sup>R</sup>EThL 73 (1997) 458-9 *(Neirynck, F.)*.
4448  *Dewey, Joanna* Women in the synoptic gospels: seen but not heard?. BTB 27 (1997) 53-60.
4449  **Ennulat, A.** Die "Minor Agreements". WUNT 2/62: 1993, ⇒10,4253...12,4250. <sup>R</sup>TJT 13 (1997) 101-03 *(Kloppenborg, J.S.)*.

4450 **Inch, Morris A.** Exhortations of Jesus according to Matthew and up from the depths: Mark as tragedy. Lanham 1997, University Pr. of America 176 pp. Bibl. 0-7618-0696-2/7-0 [NThAR 1998,101].

4451 *Kasiłowski, Piotr* Przykazanie miłości boga i miłości bliźniego tradycji synoptycznej [The commandment of love in the synoptic tradition]. Sum. 150. WST 10 (1997) 141-150.

4452 **Kelber, Werner H.** The oral and written gospel: the hermeneutics of speaking and writing in the synoptic tradition: Mark, Paul, and Q. Foreword *Ong, Walter J.*: Voices in Performance and Text: Bloomington, IND [2]1997 <1983>, Indiana University Press xxxi; 254 pp. Bibl. $35/$18. 0-253-33230-3/21097-6. [R]BBR 7 (1997) 91-106 *(Hurtado, L.W.)*.

4453 *Liedenberg, Jacobus* The language of the Kingdom and Jesus: parable, aphorism and metaphor in the sayings material common to the synoptic tradition and the gospel of Thomas. Diss. B 1997-98; [D]*Breytenbach, C.* [RTL 29,586].

4454 **Marconcini, Benito** I vangeli sinottici: formazione, redazione, teologia. Universo teologia 55: CinB 1997, San Paolo 264 pp. L30.000. 88-215-3551-7.

4455 **Roh, Taeseong** Die *familia dei* in den synoptischen Evangelien: eine redaktions- und sozialgeschichtliche Untersuchung zu einem urchristlichen Bildfeld. Diss. Heidelberg 1997; [D]*Theissen, G.* [RTL 29,587].

4456 **Theissen, Gerd** Colorido local y contexto histórico en los evangelios: una contribución a la historia de la tradición sinóptica. Biblioteca de estudios bíblicos 195: S 1997, Sígueme 348 pp. [SalTer 87,437].

4457 **Tuckett, Christopher M.** Q and the history of early christianity: studies on Q. 1996, ⇒12,4260. [R]JThS 48 (1997) 191-194 *(Catchpole, David)*; EThL 73 (1997) 173-177 *(Neirynck, F.)*; OLZ 92 (1997) 702-705 *(Bull, Klaus-M.)*.

4458 **Vaage, Leif E.** Galilean upstarts: Jesus' first followers according to Q. 1994, ⇒10,4266... 12,4261. [R]TJT 13/1 (1997) 121-123 *(Arnal, William E.)*.

4459 *Weiss, Herold* The sabbath in the synoptic gospels. NT Backgrounds. 1997 <1990>, ⇒3975. [E]Evans, Craig A., 109-123.

## F3.1 Matthaei evangelium: *textus, commentarii*

4460 **Baarlink, Heinrich** Matteüs: een praktische bijbelverklaring [1-12], 1. Tekst en toelichting: Kampen 1997, Kok 226 pp. 90-242-7900-3 [NThAR 1997,291].

4461 [E]**Bauer, David R.; Powell, Mark Allan** Treasures new and old: recent contributions to Matthean studies. 1996, ⇒12,4265. [R]CBQ 59 (1997) 600-602 *(Doran, Robert)*; AsbTJ 52 (1997) 97-99 *(Brewer, B. Keith)*; ABR 45 (1997) 78-81 *(Watson, Nigel M.)*.

4462 **Buchanan, George Wesley** The gospel of Matthew. 1996, ⇒12,4267. [R]CritRR 10 (1997) 163-165 *(Carter, Warren)*.

4463 **Calloud, Jean; Genuyt, François** L'évangile de Matthieu, 2: lecture sémiotique des chapitres 11 à 20. La Tourette 1997, Centre Thomas More iv; 118 pp. FF70. 2-905600-15-2.

4464 *Davies, Margaret* Reading the book 8: the gospel according to Matthew. ET 108 (1997) 227-230.

4465 **Davies, W.D.; Allison, Dale C.** The gospel according to Saint Matthew III: XIX-XXVIII. ICC: E 1997, Clark 790 pp. £40. 0-567-08518-X [⇒4,4439...9,4446]. ᴿEThL 73 (1997) 448-450 *(Neirynck, F.)*; RBBras 14 (1997) 388-391.

4466 **Fallon, Michael B.** The gospel according to Matthew: an introductory commentary. Kensington, NSW Australia 1997, Chevalier 395 pp. 0-86940-232-3.

4467 **Frankemölle, Hubert** Matthäus Kommentar, 2. Dü 1997, Patmos 560 pp. 3-491-77026-2.

4468 **Grasso, Santi** Il vangelo di Matteo. CBi: 1995, ⇒11/1,2815. ᴿEstB 55 (1997) 550-552 *(Díaz Rodelas, J.M.)*; EstJos 51 (1997) 254-255 *(Llamas, Román)*; CivCatt 148 II (1997) 312-313 *(Scaiola, D.)*.

4469 **Gundry, Robert H.** Matthew: a commentary on his handbook for a mixed church under persecution. ²1994, ⇒10,4279; 11/1,2817. ᴿVJTR 61 (1997) 280-282 *(Meagher, P.M.)*.

4470 **Hagner, Donald A.** Matthew 14-28. WBC 33B: 1995, ⇒11/1,2819; 12,4272. ᴿJBL 116 (1997) 363-366 *(Allison, D.C.)*.

4471 **Hare, Douglas R.A.** Matthew. 1993, ⇒9,4452; 10,4281. ᴿBiBh 23/1 (1997) 61-62 *(Uppukunnel, M.)*.

4472 **Keener, Craig S.** Matthew. The IVP NT Commentary 1: Downers Grove, IL 1997, InterVarsity 444 pp. Bibl. 0-8308-1801-4.

4473 **Kiraz, George Anton** Comparative edition of the Syriac gospels, 1: Matthew. NTTS 21/1: 1996, ⇒12,4276. ᴿNT 39 (1997) 405-414 *(Barda, T.)*.

4474 **Krämer, Michael** Die Entstehungsgeschichte der synoptischen Evangelien: das Matthäusevangelium. Deutsche Hochschulschriften 1127: Egelsbach 1997, Hänse-Hohenhausen xiv; 156 pp. 3-8267-1127-0.

4475 **Long, Thomas G.** Matthew. Westminster Bible companion. LVL 1997, Westminster xii; 331 pp. Bibl. 0-664-25257-5.

4476 **Luz, Ulrich** Das Evangelium nach Matthäus: 3. Teilband: Mt 18-25. Evangelisch-katholischer Kommentar zum NT 1/3: Z 1997, Benziger xii; 561 pp. 3-545-23129-1.

4477 *Marin, Marcello* ILARIO de Poitiers e GEROLAMO. Motivi letterari. 1997, ⇒331. ᴱMoreschini, C., 137-157.

4478 **Matteüs: evangelie.** Den Bosch 1997, Katholieke Bijbelstichting 120 pp. ƒ14. 90-6173-675-7 [Str. 65,285].

4479 **Mello, Alberto** Evangelo secondo Matteo. 1995, ⇒11/1,2829. ᴿCivCatt 148 IV (1997) 200-202 *(Scaiola, D.)*.

4480 *Rayan, Samuel* With us—with whom?—is God?: good news of God's presence and solidarity with the oppressed. 1997, ⇒89. ᶠSOARES-PRABHU G., 37-83.

4481 **Riehl, Christian** Matthaeus & Markus. Bibel 2000, 15. Stu 1997, Katholisches Bibelwerk 176 pp. DM68. 3-460-02015-6 [OrdKor 39,255].

4482 *Selander, Sven-Åke* Birger GERHARDSSONS tryckta bidrag till de exegetiska studiet av Matteusevangeliet 1957-1996. ᶠGERHARDSSON B., Religio 48: 1997, ⇒28. 109-114 [RB 105,298—Langlamet, F.].

4483 **Senior, Donald P.** The gospel of Matthew. Interpreting Biblical Texts: Nv 1997, Abingdon 205 pp. $24. 0-687-00848-4.

4484 *Shedinger, Robert F.* The textual relationship between P45 and Shem-Tob's Hebrew Matthew. NTS 43 (1997) 58-71.

4485 **Swanson, Reuben J.** Matthew: NT Greek manuscripts, 1. 1995, ⇒11/1,2835. ᴿJBL 116 (1997) 159-160 *(Ehrman, Bart D.)*.

4486 **Thiede, Carsten Peter; Ancona, Matthew d'** Der Jesus-Papyrus [P64+67]. 1996, ⇒12,4287. ᴿZKTh 119 (1997) 220-222 *(Oberforcher, Robert)*;

4487 The Jesus papyrus. L 1997, Phoenix 258 pp. AUS$17. 1-85799-9584 [ACR 74,382].

4488 ᴱ**Zanchettin, Leo** Matthew: a devotional commentary. Ijamsville, Maryland 1997, The Word Among Us 306 pp. 0-8091-3775-5.

F3.2 **Themata** *de Matthaeo*

4489 *Adam, A.K.M.* Reading Matthew as cultural criticism. SBL.SPS 36 (1997) 253-272.

4490 *Bartnicki, Roman* Autorstwo ewangelii wedlug św. Mateusza w świetle świadectwa starożytnego Kościola i współczesnych dyskusji [Autorenschaft des Matthäusevangeliums im Lichte der Aussagen der Autoren der antiken Kirche und der modernen Exegeten]. Zsfg. 50. WST 10 (1997) 37-50.

4491 *Bauer, David R.* The major characters of Matthew's story: their function and significance. Gospel interpretation. 1997, ⇒210. ᴱKingsbury, J.D., 27-37.

4492 *Bossman, David M.* Christians and Jews read the gospel of Matthew today. BTB 27 (1997) 42-52.

4493 **Boyer, Mark G.** Day by ordinary day with Matthew. NY 1997, Alba xxii; 328 pp. $18 [BiTod 36,263—Senior, Donald].

4494 *Bravo Gallardo, Carlos* Matthew: good news for the persecuted poor. Subversive scriptures. 1997, ⇒263. ᴱVaage, L., 173-192.

4495 **Byrskog, Samuel** Jesus the only teacher: didactic authority and transmission in ancient Israel: ancient Judaism and the Matthean community. CB.NT 24: 1994, ⇒10,4301... 12,4298. ᴿJThS 48 (1997) 180-182 *(Hunter, Alastair G.)*; ThLZ 122 (1997) 1017-1019 *(Walter, Nikolaus)*.

4496 *Carter, Warren* Community definition and Matthew's gospel. SBL.SPS 36 (1997) 637-663.

4497 **Castaño Fonseca, Adolfo M.** Δικαιοσύνη en Mateo: una interpretación teológica a partir de 3,15 y 21,32. Diss. Pont. Univ. Gregoriana 1996; ᴰRasco, E.: TGr.Teologia 27: R 1997, Ed. Pont. Univ. Gregoriana 344 pp. L35.000. 88-7652-763-X.

4498 *Cuvillier, Élian* Justes et petits chez Matthieu: l'interprétation du lecteur à la croisée des chemins. ETR 72 (1997) 345-364.

4499 *Cuvillier, Élian* Particularisme et universalisme chez Matthieu: quelques hypothèses à l'épreuve du texte. Bib. 78 (1997) 481-502.

4500 ᴱ*Darling Young, Robin* Selections from John CHRYSOSTOM's homilies on Matthew. Theological interpretation. 1997, ⇒244. ᴱFowl, S., 239-247.

4501 *De Stefano, Francesco; Sferco, Luigi* Metafora e narrazione nel linguaggio religioso. BeO 39 (1997) 235-252.

4502 **Deutsch, Celia M.** Lady Wisdom, Jesus, and the sages... Matthew's gospel. 1996, ⇒12,4303. ᴿCBQ 59 (1997) 573-574 *(Carter, Warren)*.

4503 *Duling, Dennis C.* "Egalitarian" ideology, leadership, and factional conflict within the Matthean group. BTB 27 (1997) 124-137.

4504  *Eckstein, Hans-Joachim* Die Weisung Jesu Christi und die Tora des Mose nach dem Matthäusevangelium. BZNW 86: 1997, ⇒41. [F]HOFIUS O., 379-403.

4505  **Facey, A.** Matteo il narratore di Gesù. Bo 1997, EDB 58 pp. L8.000 [[RivBib 45,505].

4506  *Fornberg, Tord* Matteus och hans läsare: några exempel från tolkningshistorien. 1997, ⇒28. [F]GERHARDSSON B., 25-39.

4507  *Fuller, Christopher C.* Not to abolish the text, but displace it: the repositioning of the authorial audience in PASOLINI's *Il Vangelo secondo Matteo*. SBL.SPS 36 (1997) 1-19.

4508  **Fusco, Vittorio** La casa sulla roccia: temi spirituali di Matteo. Magnano (Vercelli) 1994, Qiqajon 136 pp. ⇒10,4309; 11/1,2854. [R]Asp. 44/1 (1997) 126-127 *(Rolla, Armando)*.

4509  *Geiger, Georg* Falsche Zitate bei Matthäus und Lukas. The scriptures in the gospels. BEThL 131: 1997, ⇒234. [E]Tuckett, C.M., 479-486.

4510  **Gench, Frances Taylor** Wisdom in the christology of Matthew. Lanham, Md 1997, University Press of America xi; 229 pp. Diss. Union Theol. Sem. in Virginia 1988. $57/$32.50. 0-7618-0743-8/4-6 [NThAR 1998,100].

4511  **Gendron, Philippe** Peur et foi dans l'évangile de Matthieu: l'acte de croire aujourd'hui. Parole d'actualité 6: Montréal 1997, Médiaspaul 80 pp. [SR 27,119—Mathieu, Yvan].

[F]**Gerhardsson, Birger** Matteus och hans läsare ⇒28.

4512  *Good, Deirdre* Moral dualism and virtues in Matthew's gospel. 1997, [F]SCROGGS R., ⇒82. 101-123.

4513  *Goulder, Michael* Matthew's vision for the church. 1997, ⇒93. [F]SWEET J., 19-32.

4514  **Grasso, Santi** Gesù e i suoi fratelli. RivBib.S 29: 1994, ⇒9,4481 ... 12,4313. [R]BeO 39 (1997) 123-124 *(De Virgilio, Giuseppe)*.

4515  *Kampen, John* 'Righteousness' in Matthew and the legal texts from Qumran. StTDJ 23: 1997, ⇒8. [F]BAUMGARTEN J., 461-487.

4516  **Kealy, Seán P.** Matthew's gospel and the history of biblical interpretation. Mellen Biblical Press 55a-55b: Lewiston, NY 1997, Mellen 2 vols; xi; 969 pp. $110. 0-7734-2431-8/3-4. [R]PIBA 20 (1997) 95-99 *(McNamara, Martin)*.

4517  **Kingsbury, Jack Dean** Matthew: structure, christology, kingdom. 1975, ⇒57,3592...60,5854. [R]DBM 16/1 (1997) 78-81 *(Agourides, S.)*.

4518  *Kingsbury, Jack Dean* The plot of Matthew's story. Gospel interpretation. 1997, ⇒210. [E]Kingsbury, J.D., 16-26.

4519  **Kvalbein, Hans** 'La hans blod komme over oss og våre barn!': var Matteusevangeliet jødefiendtlig?. 1997, ⇒28. [F]GERHARDSSON B., 55-69 [Mt 27,25].

4520  *LaGrand, James* The earliest christian mission to "all nations" in the light of Matthew's gospel. 1995, ⇒11/1,2870. [R]JBL 116 (1997) 742-744 *(Allison, Dale C.)*.

4521  *Le Saux, Madeleine* Jésus selon Matthieu: le maître unique. DosB 69 (1997) 3-5.

4522  **Luz, Ulrich** The theology of the gospel of Matthew. [T]Robinson, J. *Bradford*: 1995, ⇒11/1,2874; 12,4323. [R]EvQ 69 (1997) 276-281 *(Nolland, John)*; Interp. 51 (1997) 297-298 *(Carroll, John T.)*.

4523  *Maggioni, Bruno* Gesù nel vangelo di Matteo. Som. 339. RCI 78 (1997) 339-350.

4524 *Marguerat, Daniel* "Pas un iota ne passera de la loi ..." (Mt 5,18): la loi dans l'évangile de Matthieu. La loi. LeDiv 168: 1997, ⇒195. [E]Focant, C., 140-174.

4525 **Overman, J. Andrew** O evangelho de Mateus e o judaísmo formativo: o mundo social da comunidade de Mateus. [T]*Camargo Bartalotti, Cecília*: Bíblica Loyola 20: São Paulo 1997, Loyola 172 pp. 85-15-01442-4 [PerTeol 29,282].

4526 *Perez Herrero, F.* Identidad y misión de Jesús según san Mateo. Burg. 38/2 (1997) 321-346.

4527 *Powell, Mark Allen* Toward a narrative-critical understanding of Matthew. Gospel interpretation. 1997, ⇒210. [E]Kingsbury, J.D., 9-15.

4528 **Scheuermann, Georg** Gemeinde im Umbruch: eine sozialgeschichtliche Studie zum Matthäusevangelium. FzB 77: 1996, ⇒12,4339. [R]ThLZ 122 (1997) 336-337 *(Wrege, Hans-Theo)*.

4529 *Segalla, Giuseppe* L'etica matteana fra comandamenti di Dio (Legge e Profeti) e comandamenti del Signore (Il Vangelo). Teol(Br) 22 (1997) 111-162.

4530 *Senior, Donald* The lure of the formula quotations: re-assessing Matthew's use of the Old Testament with the passion narrative as test case. The scriptures in the gospels. BEThL 131: 1997, ⇒234. [E]Tuckett, C.M., 89-115.

4531 **Senior, Donald P.** What are they saying about Matthew?. [2]1996, ⇒12,4342. [R]ScrTh 29/1 (1997) 289-290 *(Heras, G.)*.

4532 *Smith, Christopher R.* Literary evidences of a fivefold structure in the gospel of Matthew. NTS 43 (1997) 540-551.

4533 *Snodgrass, Klyne R.* Matthew's understanding of the law. Gospel interpretation. 1997, ⇒210. [E]Kingsbury, J.D., 38-48.

4534 *Stanton, Graham N.* The communities of Matthew. Gospel interpretation. 1997, ⇒210. [E]Kingsbury, J.D., 49-62.

4535 **Stock, Augustine** The method and message of Matthew. 1994, ⇒10,4340; 11/2,2893. [R]Gr. 78 (1997) 156-57 *(Marconi, Gilberto)*.

4536 *Syreeni, Kari* Petrus och den ende läraren i Matteusevangeliet. 1997, ⇒28. [F]GERHARDSSON B., 71-84.

4537 **Van Aarde, Andries** God-with-us: the dominant perspective in Matthew's story and other essays. 1994, ⇒10,4296. [R]JBL 115 (1996) (1997) 143-145 *(Dean, Margaret E.)*.

4538 *Van Aarde, Andries G.* The First Testament in the gospel of Matthew. HTS 53 (1997) 126-145.

4539 *Vitório, Jaldemir* Destinatários do *kerygma* evangélico na perspectiva de Mateus. REB 57 (1997) 344-365.

4540 *Wainwright, Elaine* Rachel weeping for her children: intertextuality and the biblical testaments—a feminist approach. A feminist companion. 1997, ⇒180. [E]Brenner, Athalya, 452-469.

4541 *Walter, Nikolaus* Zum Kirchenverständnis des Matthäus. Praeparatio evangelica. WUNT 98: 1997 <1981>, ⇒167. 118-143.

4542 *Weren, Wim* Quotations from Isaiah and Matthew's christology (Mt 1,23 and 4,15-16). BEThL 132: 1997, ⇒12. [F]BEUKEN W., 447-465 [Isa 7,14; 8,23-9,1].

4543 **Yang, Yong-Eui** Jesus and the Sabbath in Matthew's gospel. JSNT.S 139: Shf 1997, Academic 352 pp. £47.50. 1-85075-654-6.

F3.3 *Mt 1s (Lc 1s ⇒F7.5) Infantia Jesu*—Infancy Gospels

4544 *Autané, Michel* Les annonces de naissance. DosB 70 (1997) 7-9.
4545 ᵀBastiaensen, A.A.R. Kerstmis en Epifanie: teksten uit de vroege kerk over de geboorte van Christus. Christelijke bronnen 12: Kampen 1997, Kok 106 pp. ƒ22.50. 90-242-9313-8 [Str. 65,857—Beentjes, Panc].
4546 ᴱBenyik, György Biblikus Konferencia (1996: Szeged): Gyermekségtörténet és mariológia [Storia d'infanzia e mariologia]. Szeged 1997, JATEPress 271 pp.
4547 Blanquet, Josep M. La Sagrada Familia, icono de la Trinidad. Barc 1996, Hijos de la Sagrada Familia 743 pp. ᴿDiv. 40/1 (1997) 97-98 *(Stramare, Tarcisio)*.
4548 ᴱBreen, Aidan A I L E R A N I interpretatio mystica et moralis progenitorum Domini Jesu Christi. 1995, ⇒11/1,2909. ᴿJThS 48 (1997) 720-721 *(Yarnold, E.J.)*; Latomus 56 (1997) 903-904 *(Meyers, J.)*.
4549 Brown, Raymond Edward Der kommende Christus: eine Auslegung der Evangelien im Advent. Wü 1997, Echter 85 pp. 3-429-01942-7.
4550 Centini, Massimo La vera storia dei re magi: dall'Oriente alla ricerca del Re Bambino. CasM 1997, Piemme 272 pp. Bibl. 88-384-2968-5.
4551 Deiss, Lucien Joseph, Marie, Jésus. Spiritualité contemporaine: P 1997, Saint Paul 200 pp. FF89 [EeV 107,47].
4552 *Farkasfalvy, Dénes* Jézus gyermeksége az evangéliumokban és a mariológia [Infancy narrative and mariology]. Gyermekségtörténet. 1997, ⇒316. ᴱBenyik, G., Sum—Zsfg—Rias—167-172. **Hungarian**.
4553 *Gianazza, Pier Giorgio* Natale a Betlemme: tra memoria evangelica e attese di pace. Asp. 44 (1997) 401-412.
4554 Un'infanzia disconosciuta: circoncisione, riscatto e purificazione nella famiglia di Gesù. Studi Fatti Ricerche 79 (1997) 7-10.
4555 Lüdemann, Gerd Jungfrauengeburt?: die wirkliche Geschichte von Maria und ihrem Sohn Jesus. Stu 1997, Radius-Verl. 148 pp. 3-87173-129-3.
4556 *Mans, M.J.* The early Latin Church Fathers on Herod and the infanticide. HTS 53 (1997) 92-102.
4557 *Merklein, Helmut* Die Kindheitsgeschichten der Evangelien;
4558 *Mimouni, Simon C.* Debatten über die Anfänge Jesu. . Welt und Umwelt der Bibel 6 (1997) 20-23, 25-28/29-30.
4559 *Orchard, Bernard* The betrothal and marriage of Mary to Joseph: a biblical meditation [Zaręczyny i związek małżeński Naryi z Józefem: medytacja biblijna]. Streszczenie 248. WST 10 (1997) 241-248.
4560 *Perrot, Charles* Die Bedeutung Betlehems bei Matthäus und Lukas. Welt und Umwelt der Bibel 6 (1997) 24.
4561 *Petrozzi, Maria Teresa* The nativity grotto. Holy Land 17 (1997) 171-175.
4562 *Rodger, Lynlea* The infancy stories of Matthew and Luke: an examination of the child as a theological metaphor. HBT 19/1 (1997) 58-81.

4563 **Roll, Susan** Toward the origins of Christmas. Liturgia Condenda 5: Kampen 1995, Kok 296 pp. reprint. f65/£25.50. 90-390-0531-1. RJThS 48 (1997) 233-234 *(Bradshaw, Paul)*.

4564 **Sanchez-Silva, José-María** La adolescencia de Jesús nunca contada. M 1997, Planeta 188 pp. [Mayéutica 24,298—Alonso, Gonzalo].

4565 **Schaberg, Jane D.** The illegitimacy of Jesus: a feminist theological interpretation of the infancy narratives. BiSe 28: 1995, ⇒11/1,2929. RETR 72 (1997) 302-303 *(Cuvillier, Élian)*.

4566 **Stramare, Tarcisio** Gesù lo chiamò Padre: rassegna storico-dottrinale su san Giuseppe. Città del Vaticano 1997, Libreria Editrice Vaticana 216 pp. 88-209-2269-X.

4567 *Stricher, Joseph* L'ange du Seigneur;
4568 Les anges de Noël;
4569 L'armée céleste;
4570 La nativité mystique de Sandro BOTTICELLI. DosB 70 (1997) 13-14/3-6/11-12/15-18.

4571 *Hooker, Morna D.* A prophetic key: Matthew 1-2. Beginnings. 1997, ⇒136. 23-43.

4572 *Moitel, Pierre* Matthieu 1-2: Jésus fils d'Israël. CEv 98 (1997) 47-52.

4573 **Besançon, M.** 'L'affaire' de David et Bethsabée et la généalogie du Christ. Saint-Maur 1997, Parole et Silence 341 pp. [NRTh 120,628s—Ska, J.L.] [Mt 1,1-16; Lk 3,23-38].

4574 *Nolland, John* The four (five) women and other annotations in Matthew's genealogy. NTS 43 (1997) 527-539 [Mt 1,1-17].

4575 *Weren, Wim J.C.* The five women in Matthew's genealogy. CBQ 59 (1997) 288-305 [Mt 1,1-17].

4576 *Birdsall, J. Neville* Genealogies of Jesus in the works of HIPPOLYTUS: a possible pointer in the questions of authorship. StPatr 31: 1997, ⇒351. ELivingstone, E.A., 243-251 [Mt 1,1-17].

4577 *Forte, Bruno* Encarnação: estudo bíblico sobre Mt 1,1-17. TDuque, João: Theologica 32/2 (1997) 323-329.

4578 *Jakubinyi, György* Az úr Jézus nemzetségtáblája Máténál (1,2-17) [The genealogy of Jesus in Matthew]. Gyermekségtörténet. 1997, EBenyik, G. Sum., Zsfg., Rias., 195-197. **Hungarian**.

4579 *Nolland, John* Jechoniah and his brothers (Matthew 1:11). BBR 7 (1997) 169-177.

4580 *Derrett, John Duncan M.* Shared themes: the virgin birth (Matthew 1:18-2:12). JHiC 4/2 (1997) 57-67.

4581 **Zannini, Paolo** I 'Kontakia' di ROMANO il Melode sull'Annunciazione: contenuti e fonti. R 1997, 74 pp. Diss. excerpt Pont. Institutum Orientale [Mt 1,18-25; Lk 1,26-38].

4582 *Da Spinetoli, Ortensio* A 'szentlélek műve általi fogantatás' (vö. Mt 1,18 és 20; Lk 1,35) [The role of the Holy Spirit in the conception of Jesus]. TTuray, Alfréd: Gyermekségtörténet. 1997, EBenyik, G. Sum., Zsfg., Rias., 9-37. **Hungarian**.

4583 *Bauer, Johannes B.* 'Josef gedachte Maria heimlich zu verlassen' (Mt 1,19; ASCIs 11,3). Studien zu Bibeltext. 1997 <1992>, ⇒111. 205-208.

4584 *Verburg, Winfried* Gehen, Sehen, Handeln: Mahnung wider die nur vermittelte Wahrnehmung: zur Magier-Perikope Mt 2,1-12. KatBl 122 (1997) 420-425.

4585  **Trexler, Richard C.** The journey of the Magi: meanings in history of a christian story. Princeton 1997, Princeton University Press 277 pp. £28. 0-691-01126-5 [Theol. 101,219s—Pickstone, Charles] [Mt 2,1-12].

4586  *Kügler, Joachim* Gold, Weihrauch und Myrrhe: eine Notiz zu Mt 2,11. BN 87 (1997) 24-33.

4587  *Orsatti, Mauro* Mt 1-2 alla luce di Es 2: un delicato rapporto tra storia e teologia. PaVi 42/1 (1997) 39-44.

4588  *Van Reisen, Hans* Op zoek nar een koningskind: AUGUSTINUS' verkondiging op epifanie, 2. ITBT 5/7 (1997) 9-12 [Mt 2].

F3.4  *Mt 3...Baptismus Jesus*, **Beginnings of the Public Life**

4589  *Bammel, Ernst* Johannes der Täufer in den Toledoth Jeschu. Judaica et Paulina. WUNT 91: 1997, ⇒109. 15-22.

4590  *Brown, Colin* What was John the Baptist doing?. BBR 7 (1997) 37-49.

4591  *Chilton, Bruce* John the purifier. Jesus in context. AGAJ 39: 1997 < 1994 >, ⇒183. 203-220.

4592  *Ernst, Josef* Johannes der Täufer und Jesus von Nazareth in historischer Sicht. NTS 43 (1997) 161-183.

4593  **Fichtner, Rudolf** Taufe und Versuchung Jesu in den Evangeliorum libri quattuor des Bibeldichters JUVENCUS (1, 346-408). 1994, ⇒10,4386. RGn. 69 (1997) 556-558 *(Roberts, Michael)*.

4594  *Goodall, Lawrence D.* None greater born of a woman: the theological figure of John the Baptist. Com(US) 24 (1997) 550-562.

4595  *Hevia Alvarez, José María* Juan Bautista y la 'liminalidad' en la iniciación cristiana. StOv 25 (1997) 25-52.

4596  **Kazmierski, Carl R.** John the Baptist: prophet and evangelist. 1996, ⇒12,4402. REeT(O) 28/1 (1997) 116-118 *(Dumais, Marcel)*; CBQ 59 (1997) 584-585 *(Newman, Carey C.)*.

4597  *Lupieri, Edmondo* Halakah qumranica e halakah battistica di Giovanni: due mondi a confronto. RStB 9/2 (1997) 69-98.

4598  *Martensen, Hans J.* Das Geheimnis der vierzig Tage: war Jesus ein Qumran-Dissident?: frohe Botschaft—verschlüsselte Botschaft?. LM 36/1 (1997) 27-29.

4599  *Smith, Daniel A.* IRENAEUS and the baptism of Jesus. TS 58 (1997) 618-642.

4600  **Tatum, Barnes W.** John the Baptist and Jesus: a report of the Jesus Seminar. 1994, ⇒10,4391. RTJT 13/1 (1997) 117-118 *(Bloomquist, L. Gregory)*; RB 104 (1997) 285-287 *(Prendergast, Terrence)*.

4601  **Taylor, Joan E.** The Immerser: John the Baptist within Second Temple Judaism. Studying the Historical Jesus: GR 1997, Eerdmans xvi; 360 pp. $30. 0-8028-4236-4.

4602  *Schwarz, Günther* "Wie eine Taube"? (Markus 1,10 par. Matthäus 3,16; Lukas 3,21.22; Johannes 1,32). BN 89 (1997) 27-29.

4603  *Callaghan, Denise Marie* The temptations of Jesus. Spiritual Life 43/4 (1997) 230-235 [Mt 4,1-11].

4604  *Hasitschka, Martin* Die Verwendung der Schrift in Mt 4,1-11. The scriptures in the gospels. BEThL 131: 1997, ⇒234. ETuckett, C.M., 487-490.

4605 *Batut, Jean-Pierre* Chasteté et 'refus de prendre': Jésus devant la tentation originaire. Rés. 5. Com(F) 22/1 (1997) 27-35 [Mt 4,1-11].

4606 *Pokorný, Petr* The temptation stories and their intention. Bibelauslegung. WUNT 100: 1997 <1974>, ⇒970. ᴱPokorný, Petr, 275-287 [Mt 4,1-11; Mk 1,12-13; Lk 4,1-13].

4607 *Stegner, William Richard* The use of scripture in two narratives of early Jewish christianity (Matthew 4.1-11; Mark 9.2-8). Early christian interpretation. JSNT.S 148: 1997, ⇒191. ᴱEvans, C., 98-120.

4608 *Bagni, Arcangelo* Figlio di dio, eppure provato! (Mt 4,1-11). PaVi 42/1 (1997) 59-62.

4609 *Söding, Thomas* Der Gehorsam des Gottessohnes: zur Christologie der matthäischen Versuchungserzählung (4,1-11). BZNW 86: 1997, ⇒41. ᶠHoꜰɪᴜs O., 711-750.

4610 *Callaghan, Denise Marie* The temptations of Jesus. Spiritual Life 43/4 (1997) 230-235 [Mt 4,1-11].

4611 **Gibson, Jeffrey B.** The temptations of Jesus in early Christianity. JSNT.S 112: 1995, ⇒11/1,2963; 12,4414. ᴿEvQ 69 (1997) 267-273 *(Nolland, John)*; CBQ 59 (1997) 379-381 *(Wainwright, Elaine)* [Mt 4,1-11; Mk 1,9-13; 8,1-13].

4612 *Calambrogio, Leone* La rinascita: Mt 4,12-17. Laós 4/1 (1997) 35-41.

4613 *Carter, Warren* Narrative/literary approaches to Matthean theology: the 'reign of the heavens' as an example (Mt. 4.17-5.12). JSNT 67 (1997) 3-27;

4614 Matthew 4:18-22 and Matthean discipleship: an audience-oriented perspective. CBQ 59 (1997) 58-75.

## F3.5 Mt 5...Sermon on the Mount [...plain, Lk 6,17]

4615 *Alegre, Xavier* La moral del sermón de la montaña de Mateo. RLAT 14 (1997) 243-264.

4616 *Bexell, Göran* Kommentar till Mogens Mᴜᴇʟʟᴇʀ om bergspredikans etik. 1997, ⇒28. ᶠGᴇʀʜᴀʀᴅssoɴ B., 99-108.

4617 *Blount, Brian K.* Righteousness from the inside: the transformative spirituality of the Sermon on the Mount;

4618 *Burrows, Mark S.* Selections from Martin Lᴜᴛʜᴇʀ's sermons on the Sermon on the Mount. Theological interpretation. 1997, ⇒244. ᴱFowl, S., 262-284/248-261.

4619 **Dumais, Marcel** Le sermon sur la montagne: état de la recherche: interprétation. 1995, ⇒11/1,2972; 12,4421. ᴿGr. 78 (1997) 157-158 *(Marconi, Gilberto)*; EeT(O) 28 (1997) 372-375 *(Gourgues, Michel)*; CBQ 59 (1997) 768-769 *(Edwards, Richard A.)*; SR 26 (1997) 361-362 *(Fraikin, Daniel)*.

4620 *Enermalm, Agneta* The Sermon on the Mount as foundational text: more than catechism. 1997, ⇒82. ᶠScʀoGGs R., 81-98.

4621 *Lischer, Richard* The Sermon on the Mount as radical pastoral care. Theological interpretation. 1997, ⇒244. ᴱFowl, S., 294-306.

4622 **Loader, William R.G.** Jesus' attitude towards the law: a study of the gospels. WUNT 2/97: Tü 1997, Mohr x; 563 pp. Bibl. DM128. 3-16-146517-2.

4623  *Müller, Mogens* Loven og hjertet: Bjergprœdikenen som pagt-steologi. 1997, ⇒28. <sup>F</sup>GERHARDSSON B., 41-54.

4624  *Pathrapankal, Joseph* The ethics of the Sermon on the Mount: its relevance for and challenge to our times. Jeevadhara 27 (1997) 389-407.

4625  *Sisson, Russell B.* Voices of authority in the Sermon on the Mount. SBL.SPS 36 (1997) 551-566.

4626  *Stock, Klemens* Die Bergpredigt als Programm für das Reich Gottes. StMiss 46 (1997) 1-20.

4627  **Strecker, Georg** The Sermon on the Mount. 1988, ⇒4,4571... 6,4772. <sup>R</sup>DBM 16/1 (1997) 74-78 *(Agourides, S.)*.

4628  *Viviano, Benedict T.* The Sermon on the Mount in recent study. Bib. 78 (1997) 255-265.

4629  **Worth, Roland H.** The Sermon on the Mount: its Old Testament roots. NY 1997, Paulist iv; (4) 285 pp. Bibl. $23. 0-8091-3746-1.

4630  *Robinson, Phil J.* The church in the public sphere: some perspectives from Matthew 5:13-16. Sum. 274. Missionalia 25/3 (1997) 274-284.

4631  *Wetzlaugk, Sigrun* Ermutigung zur Mitarbeit am Reich Gottes: sozialgeschichtliche Bibelauslegung zu Matthäus 5,13-16. JK 58 (1997) 359-361.

4632  *Lejeune, Charles* Les paroles du sel et de la lumière (Mt 5,13-16) et la portée missionnaire du Sermon sur la Montagne. Analecta Bruxellensia 2 (1997) 33-50.

4633  *Souček, Josef B.* Salz der Erde und Licht der Welt: zur Exegese von Matth. 5,13-16. Bibelauslegung. WUNT 100: 1997 <1963>, ⇒970. <sup>E</sup>Pokorný, Petr, 289-299.

4634  *Hainz, Josef* Salzloses Christentum?. 1997, ⇒46. <sup>F</sup>KAMPHAUS F., 107-123 [ThRv 94,625] [Mt 5,13].

4635  *Minear, Paul S.* The salt of the earth. Interp. 51 (1997) 31-41 [Mt 5,13].

4636  *Carotta, Alberto* 'Vedano le vostre opere buone e glorifichino il Padre' (Mt 5,16). Presbyteri 31/2 (1997) 133-137.

4637  *Byrskog, Samuel* Matthew 5:17-18 in the argumentation of the context. RB 104 (1997) 557-571.

4638  *Schellong, Dieter* Christus fidus interpres legis: zur Auslegung von Mt 5,17-20. BZNW 86: 1997, ⇒41. <sup>F</sup>HOFIUS O., 659-687.

4639  *Czyż, Stanisław* Zakaz przysięgania czy nakaz prawdomównosci? (Mt 5,33-37) [Interdiction of oaths or order to speak the truth? (Matt 5.33-37)]. 1997, ⇒52. <sup>F</sup>ŁACH J., 103-110. P.

4640  *Millet, Marc* 'Tends aussi l'autre joue' (Mt 5,38-42): parole prophétique du royaume de Dieu. Cahiers de l'Atelier 471 (1997) 97-101.

4641  *Brennecke, Hanns Christof* 'Niemand kann zwei Herren dienen': Bemerkungen zur Auslegung von Mt 6,24/Lk 16,13 in der Alten Kirche. ZNW 88 (1997) 157-169.

4642  *Carter, Warren* 'Solomon in all his glory': intertextuality and Matthew 6.29. JSNT 65 (1997) 3-25 [Mt 6,25-34].

4643  *Alexander, Philip S.* Jesus and the golden rule. Hillel and Jesus. 1997, ⇒321. <sup>E</sup>Charlesworth, James H., 363-388 [Mt 7,12].

4644  *Heil, John Paul* Parable of the wise and foolish builders in Matthew 7:24-27. Matthew's parables: audience-oriented perspectives

[E*Carter, Warren; Heil, John Paul.* CBQ.MS 30: Wsh 1997, Cath. Biblical Assoc. of America ix; 255 pp. $10. 0-915170-29-9]. 23-35.

### F3.6 Mt 5,3-11 (Lc 6,20-22) Beatitudines

4645 **Aparicio Rodríguez, A.** Las bienaventuranzas evangélicas en la vida consagrada. M 1997, Claretianas 340 pp. [EstAg 33,441— Domínguez, B.].

4646 *Bély, Marie-Etiennette; Gonneaud, Didier* La quête du bonheur et le don des béatitudes;

4647 *Biot, Christian* Béatitudes et service pastoral;

4648 *Chareire, Isabelle* Les béatitudes, espace de la vie théologale. LV(L) 47/3 (1997) 7-17/75-81/85-92.

4649 **Drewermann, Eugen** Dal discorso della montagna: le beatitudini e il Padre nostro. Meditazioni 133: Brescia 1997, Queriniana 158 pp. 88-399-1533-8.

4650 *Genuyt, François* Les béatitudes selon saint Matthieu (5,3-12);

4651 *Gira, Dennis* Béatitudes chrétiennes et bouddhisme 'occidental'. LV(L) 47/3 (1997) 21-30/67-73.

4652 **Gourgues, Michel** Foi, bonheur et sens de la vie: relire aujourd'hui les Béatitudes. 1995, ⇒11/1,3015. REeT(O) 28/1 (1997) 115-116 *(Dumais, Marcel).*

4653 TGuillamin, Jean-Yves; Parent, Gabrielle; Hamman, Adalbert Gauthier GREGORIUS Nyssenus: orationes VIII de beatitudinibus: les béatitudes. CPF 10: P ²1997, Migne 125 pp. FF95. 2-908587-30-0.

4654 *Kessler, Colette* Exégèse juive des béatitudes matthéennes. LV(L) 47/3 (1997) 51-61.

4655 **Lustiger, Jean-Marie** Soyez heureux: entretiens sur le bonheur et les béatitudes. P 1997, Nil 141 pp. FF85. 2-84111-083-4 [RTL 29,128].

4656 **Madre, Philippe** Beati i misericordiosi. 1996, ⇒12,4455. RAnime e Corpi 192 (1997) 586-587 *(Casera, Antonio).*

4657 *Nieuviarts, Jacques* Jésus, l'homme des béatitudes. LV(L) 47/3 (1997) 33-46.

4658 **Rouet, Albert** Le Christ des béatitudes, le maître de la joie. Spiritualité contemporaine: P 1997, Saint-Paul 211 pp. FF92 [EeV 107,47].

4659 *Russotto, Mario* Il vangelo delle beatitudini. Som. 921. Presenza Pastorale 67 (1997) 921-931.

4660 *Berrouard, Marie-François* 'Heureux les pauvres de cœur: le royaume des cieux est à eux' [Mt 5,3];

4661 *Jossua, Jean-Pierre* Heureux ceux qui pleurent, ils seront consolés [Mt 5,4];

4662 *Durand, Alain* Bienheureux ceux qui ont faim et soif de justice [Mt 5,6];

4663 *Sagne, Jean-Claude* 'Heureux les cœurs purs, ils verront Dieu' [Mt 5,8];

4664 *Hillairet, Martin* 'Heureux les artisans de paix ils seront appelés fils de Dieu [Mt 5,9]. LV(L) 47/3 (1997) 31-32/83-84/63-66/19-20/47-49.

4665  *Ai Yang, Seung* Jesus' saying on divorce: a Korean perspective. BiTod 35 (1997) 49-54.
4666  *Bartnicki, Roman* Nauka Jezusa o malzenstwie [Jesus' teaching about marriage]. 1997, ⇒52. FLACH J., 41-54 [Mt 5,32]. **P.**
4667  *Warden, Duane* The words of Jesus on divorce. RestQ 39/3 (1997) 141-153.
4668  **Wenham, Gordon J.; Heth, William E.** Jesus and divorce. Biblical and theological classics library: L ²1997, Paternoster 324 pp. 0-85364-768-2.


F3.7  *Mt 6,9-13 (Lc 11,2-4)* **Oratio Jesu,** Pater Noster, **Lord's Prayer**

4669  TE**Argárate, Pablo** MAXIMUS el Confesor: tratados espirituales: diálogo ascético, cenutrias sobre la caridad, interpetación del Padrenuestro: introducción, tradución y notas. Biblioteca de Patrística 37: M 1997, Ciudad Nueva 248 pp. 84-89651-23-X [Ang. 75,273s—Degórski, Bazyli].
4670  *Caro C, Cristián* 'Padre nuestro'. Revista Católica 97/4 (1997) 281-285.
4671  E**Cibotto, Gian Antonio; Merlo, Bernardino** Il Padre nostro ieri e oggi. Vicenza 1996, Pozza xii; 116 pp. L18.000. RCivCatt 148 III (1997) 93-94 *(Marucci, C.).*
4672  *Dube Shomanah, Musa W.* Praying the Lord's prayer in a global economic era. ER 49 (1997) 439-456.
4673  *Espinel Marcos, José Luis* El 'Padre Nuestro'. CTom 124 (1997) 205-220.
4674  **Evans, C.F.** The Lord's Prayer. L ²1997, SCM viii; 104 pp. £7. 0-334-02715-2 [RRT 1998/1,86].
4675  **Froidure, Michel** Prier avec les mots du Notre Père. Connaître la bible 2: Bru 1997, Lumen Vitae 64 pp. FB220. 2-87324-087-3 [RTL 29,125].
4676  T**Gaia, Pio** NICOLO Cusano: predica sul Padre nostro. T 1995, SEI. L16.000. RCivCatt 148 II (1997) 203-204 *(Forlizzi, G.).*
4677  *Gese, Hartmut* Bemerkungen zum Vaterunser unter dem Gesichtspunkt alttestamentlicher Gebetsformen. BZNW 86: 1997, ⇒41. FHOFIUS O., 405-437.
4678  *Haacker, Klaus* Stammt das Vater-Unser also doch von Jesus?: eine Antwort an Ulrich MELL. ThBeitr 28 (1997) 291-295.
4679  *Heither, Theresia* Das Vaterunser [Auslegung von Origenes]. EuA 73 (1997) 438-450.
4680  *Jamourlian, Serop* Il commento al 'Padre Nostro' di Elišē VARDAPET. Bazmavep 155 (1997) 207-268.
4681  *Jenni, Ernst* Kausativ und Funktionsverbgefüge: sprachliche Bemerkungen zur Bitte: 'Führe uns nicht in Versuchung'. Studien zur Sprachwelt. 1997 <1992>, ⇒138. EHuwyler, Beat, 162-173 [[Mt 6,13].
4682  **La Potterie, Ignace de** Modlitwa Jezusa: Mesjasza—Slugi Bozego—Syna Bozego [Het Gebed van Jezus]. T*Piotrowska, Barbara*: Mysl Teologiczna 6: Kraków 1996, WAM 138 pp. Bibl. 83-7097-158-X. **P.**
4683  *Lössl, Josef* Mt 6:13 in AUGUSTINE's later works. StPatr 33: 1997, ⇒351. ELivingstone, E.A., 167-171.

4684  *Mell, Ulrich* Das Vater-Unser als Gebet der Synagoge: eine Antwort an Klaus HAACKER. ThBeitr 28 (1997) 283-290.
4685  *Okorie, A.M.* The Lord's Prayer. Scriptura 60 (1997) 81-86 [ZID 23,278].
4686  *Philonenko, Marc* De la "Priére de Jésus" au "Notre Père" (Abba; targonum du Psaume 89,27; 4Q369,1,2,1-12; Luc 11,2). RHPhR 77 (1997) 133-140.
4687  *Pingleton, Jared P.* Why we don't forgive: a biblical and object relations theoretical model for understanding failures in the forgiveness process. Sum. 403. Psychology & Theology 25 (1997) 403-413.
4688  **Poveda, P.** Jesús, maestro de oración. [E]*González, Mª Encarnación:* M 1997, BAC xxiii; 268 pp. Estudio preliminar y edición crítica. Ptas2.400 [Proyección 45,78].
4689  *Russell, James R.* Scythian and Avesta in an Armenian vernacular paternoster and a Zok paternoster. Muséon 110/1-2 (1997) 91-114.
4690  **Staniloaë, Dumitru** Oración de Jesús y experiencia del Espíritu Santo. M 1997, Narcea 124 pp. 84-277-1211-1.
4691  [T]**Tolve-Vincenza, Umberto Antonio** S. Francesco Antonio FASANI: commento al 'Padre Nostro' (Expositio brevis). Lucera 1997, 'Padre Maestro' ix; 213 pp. [MF 99,406s—Costa, Francesco].

4692  *Menken, Maarten J.J.* The source of the quotation from Isaiah 53:4 in Matthew 8:17. NT 39 (1997) 313-327.
4693  *Arasakumar, R.* Insecurity vs. faith: meaning and purpose of Mt 8:18-27. Sum. 243. VJTR 61 (1997) 243-258.

F4.1 *Mt 9-12; Miracula Jesu*—The Gospel miracles

4694  **Berger, Klaus** Darf man an Wunder glauben?. 1996, ⇒12,4487. [R]BiLi 70 (1997) 237-238 *(Weiser, Alfons)*;
4695  Mag je in wonderen geloven?. Kampen 1997, Kok 176 pp. *f*30 [GThT 98,137].
4696  **Blum, Hans-Joachim** Biblische Wunder—heute: eine Anfrage an die Religionspädagogik. SBTB 23: Stu 1997, Kath. Bibelwerk 256 pp. DM26.80 [BiLi 71,275—Koller, Franz].
4697  *Brennecke, Hanns Christof* Heilen und Heilung in der Alten Kirche. BZNW 89: 1997, ⇒33. [F]GRAESSER E., 23-45.
4698  *Cotter, Wendy J.* Cosmology and the Jesus miracles. Whose historical Jesus?. SCJud 7: 1997, ⇒170. [E]Arnal, W.E., 118-131.
4699  **Davies, Stevan L.** Jesus the healer: possession, trance, and the origins of christianity. 1995, ⇒11/1,3056; 12,4490. [R]BTB 27 (1997) 71-72 *(Pilch, John J.)*; TJT 13 (1997) 269-270 *(Muir, Stephen C.)*.
4700  **De Grandis, R.** Il dono dei miracoli: testimonianze vissute della potenza di Dio. [T]*Marzo, S.*: Spiritualità carismatica: Mi 1994, Ancora 168 pp. L18.000. 88-7610-474-7. Anime e Corpi 189 (1997) 127-127 *(Casera, Antonio)*.
4701  [E]**Geivett, R. Douglas; Habermas, Gary R.** In defense of miracles: a comprehensive case for God's action in history. DG 1997, InterVarsity 330 pp. $18. 0-8308-1528-7 [ThD 45,371—Heiser, W. Charles].
4702  *Gräfrath, Bernd* Wissenschaftstheorie und Ästhetik der Wunder?. ThPh 72 (1997) 257-263.

4703  *Grosso, Michael* Miracles: illusions, natural events, or divine interventions?. JRPR 20/1 (1997) 2ff [ThD Index February 1997,7].

4704  **Kahl, Werner** New Testament miracle stories in their religious-
historical setting. FRLANT 163: 1994, ⇒10,4466; 12,4496. RJBL
115 (1996) 540-542 *(Just, Felix).*

4705  **Kollmann, Bernd** Jesus und die Christen als Wundertäter: Studien
zu Magie, Medizin und Schmanismus in Antike und Christentum.
FRLANT 170: 1996, ⇒12,4498. RBZ 41 (1997) 130-132 *(Trunk,
Dieter)*; OrdKor 38 (1997) 496-497 *(Giesen, Heinz)*; JThS 48
(1997) 594-596 *(Nielsen, H.K.).*

4706  *Lambert, Jean* Les miracles et la brèche. CBFV 36 (1997) 125-42.

4707  **Leone, Salvino** La medicina di fronte ai miracoli. Bo 1997, Dehoniane 223 pp. L28.000 [Asp. 45,436ss—Scognamiglio, Edoardo].

4708  *Overall, Christine* Miracles and God: a reply to Robert A.H.
LARMER. Canadian Philosophical Review 36 (1997) 741-752.

4709  *Paulsen, Henning* Die Wunderüberlieferung in der *Vita Apollonii*
des PHILOSTRATOS. Zur Literatur. WUNT 99: 1997, ⇒153.
220-234.

4710  *Percy, Martyn* The gospel miracles and modern healing movements. Theol. 100 (1997) 8-17.

4711  **Radoani, S.; Gagliardi, G.** Vattene, o Satana!: l'esorcismo: rito,
psichiatria e ministero. Bo 1997, EDB 255 pp. L27.000 [RivBib
45,256].

4712  *Reiser, Marius* Die Wunder Jesu—eine Peinlichkeit?. EuA 73
(1997) 425-437.

4713  **Trunk, Dieter** Der messianische Heiler: eine ... Studie zu den
Exorzismen im Matthäusevangelium. 1994, ⇒10,4487; 11/1,3069.
RRivBib 45 (1997) 233-238 *(Grasso, Santi).*

4714  *Trunk, Dieter* Jesus, der Exorzist. ThPQ 145 (1997) 3-13.

4715  **Twelftree, Graham H.** Jesus the exorcist. WUNT 2/54: 1993,
⇒10,4647... 12,4506. RJRH 21/1 (1997) 110-112 *(Harding,
Mark)*; TJT 13/1 (1997) 120-121 *(Cotter, Wendy)*; EvQ 69 (1997)
69-72 *(Blackburn, Barry L.).*

4716  **Park, Eung Chun** The mission discourse in Matthew's interpretation. WUNT 2/81: 1995, ⇒11/1,3072. RCritRR 10 (1997) 204-206
*(LaGrand, James)* [Mt 9,35-11,1].

4717  **Vledder, Evert-Jan** Conflict in the miracle stories: a socio-
exegetical study of Matthew 8 and 9. JSNT.S 152: Shf 1997, Academic 276 pp. £47.50. 1-85075-699-6.

4718  *Ellis, Pamela* 'Courage, my daughter'. Month 30 (1997) 199-203
[Mt 9,20-22; Mk 5,25-34].

4719  *Lichtenberger, Hermann* "Bittet den Herrn der Ernte, daß er Arbeiter in seine Ernte sende" (Mt 9,38/Lk 10,2). 1997, ⇒92.
FSTUHLMACHER P., 269-278.

4720  *O'Mara, V.M.* Late Middle English sermons on the apostles: a survey. Summarium 147. EL 111/2 (1997) 147-163 [Mt 10,2-4].

4721  **Lamont, Stewart** The life of Saint Andrew: apostle, saint and
enigma. L 1997, Hodder & S x; 102 pp. 0-340-67857-7 [Mt 10,2].

4722  **Bedouelle, Guy** Thomas l'Apôtre. Regards: Montrouge 1997,
Nouvelle Cité 152 pp. [Mt 10,3].

4723  **Lubega Muzindusi, Michael** The mission, persecution and consolation of Jesus' disciples: an exegetical-theological study of Mt
10,16-33. R 1997, Pont. Univ. Urbaniana 118 pp. Diss. Extract.

4724 *Bammel, Ernst* Weichet von Ort zu Ort (Matthäus 10,23). Judaica et Paulina. WUNT 91: 1997 < 1961 >, ⇒109. 140-153.

4725 *Derrett, J. Duncan M.* Light on sparrows and hairs (Mt 10,29-31). EstB 55 (1997) 341-353.

4726 *Walter, Nikolaus* 'Nicht Frieden, sondern das Schwert'?: Mt 10,34 (Lk 12,51) im Kontext der Verkündigung Jesu. Praeparatio evangelica. WUNT 98: 1997 < 1982 >, ⇒167. 169-186.

4727 **Lohmeyer, Monika** Der Apostelbegriff im Neuen Testament: eine Untersuchung auf dem Hintergrund der synoptischen Aussendungsreden. Diss. ᴰ*Broer, I.*: SBB 29: 1995, ⇒11/1,3082; 12,4510. ᴿThLZ 122 (1997) 447-449 *(Kraus, Wolfgang)* [Mt 10].

4728 **Roesler, Johannes** Erzählte Reden: die literarische Funktion der Missionsreden. Diss. Bonn 1997; ᴰ*Guttgemanns, E.*: 267 pp. [RTL 29,587] [Mt 10].

4729 *Kvalbein, Hans* Die Wunder der Endzeit: Beobachtungen zu 4Q521 und Matth 11,5p. ZNW 88 (1997) 111-125.

4730 *Marcato, Giorgio* Il logion 'giovanneo' di Mt 11,25-30: tradizione matteana e giovannea a confronto. Som. 3. Ang. 74 (1997) 3-29 [Lk 10,21-24; John 6,37-46].

4731 *Birdsall, J. Neville* The Marcosians' text of Jesus' cry of jubilation (Matt 11:26 // Luke 10:21) in Iʀᴇɴᴀᴇᴜs Adv. Haer. I.20.2. NT.S 89: 1997, ⇒7. ꜰBᴀᴀʀᴅᴀ T., 1-6.

4732 *De Virgilio, Giuseppe* La valenza teologica dell'espressione: "πραΰς εἰμι καὶ ταπεινὸς τῇ καρδίᾳ" (Mt 11,29). RivBib 45 (1997) 409-428.

4733 **Laansma, Jon** I will give you rest: the rest motif in the New Testament with special reference to Mt 11 and Heb 3-4. Diss. Aberdeen 1996; ᴰ*Marshall, I.H.*: WUNT 2/98: Tü 1997, Mohr xv; 459 pp. DM128. 3-16-146639-X.

4734 *Lybaek, Lena* Matthew's use of Hosea 6,6 in the context of the sabbath controversies. The scriptures in the gospels. BEThL 131: 1997, ⇒234. ᴱTuckett, C.M., 491-499 [Mt 12,1-14].

4735 ᴱ**Fizzotti, Eugenio** La sfida di Beelzebul: complessità psichica o possessione diabolica?. 1995, ⇒11/1,3091. ᴿAnime e Corpi 192 (1997) 577-578 *(Casera, Antonio)* [Mt 12,24-32].

### F4.3 Mt 13... *Parabolae Jesu*—The Parables

4736 **Bohiguez, R.** Nostro hoy en 31 párabolas de Jesús. M 1997, San Pablo 120 pp. Ptas1.000 [Comunidades 26,63].

4737 *Carter, Warren* An audience-oriented approach to Matthew's parables. Matthew's parables. 1997, ⇒4738. 1-22.

4738 **Carter, Warren; Heil, John Paul** Matthew's parables: audience-oriented perspectives. CBQ.MS 30: Wsh 1997, Cath. Biblical Assoc. of America ix; 255 pp. $10. 0-915170-29-9.

4739 *Clark, David J.* Parable openings. PPBT 48 (1997) 410-418.

4740 *Delville, Jean-Pierre* Jᴀɴsᴇɴɪᴜs de Gand (1510-1576) et l'exégèse des paraboles. RHE 92 (1997) 38-69.

4741 **Donahue, John R.** El evangelio como parábola. Bilbao 1997, Mensajero 303 pp. [RF 237,217—Vallarino, Jesús M.ª].

4742 **Fonck, Leopold** The parables of Christ: an exegetical and practical explanation. ᵀ*Leahy, E.*; ᴱ*O'Neill, George*: Fort Collins 1997

<1918>, Roman Catholic Books 829 pp. repr. $36. 0-912141-47-6 [ThD 45,69—Heiser, W. Charles].

4743 **Ford, Richard Q.** The parables of Jesus: recovering the art of listening. Mp 1997, Fortress viii; 183 pp. Bibl. $18. 0-8006-2938-8 [NThAR 1998,270].

4744 *García-Viana, F.* Las parábolas de Jesús: un proceso de transformación de la persona. SalTer 85 (1997) 295-305.
    **Green, B.G.** Like a tree planted: an exploration of the Psalms and parables ⇒2826.

4745 **Hedrick, Charles W.** Parables as poetic fiction: the creative voice of Jesus. 1994, ⇒10,4510; 12,4528. ᴿRevBib 59/1 (1997) 56-61 *(Levoratti, A.J.)*; TJT 13/2 (1997) 278-279 *(Batten, Alicia)*.

4746 **Huggett, Joyce** Praying the parables: a spiritual journey through the stories of Jesus. DG 1997, InterVarsity 120 pp. 0-8308-1355-1.

4747 **Jones, Ivor Harold** The Matthean parables: a literary and historical commentary. NT.S 80: 1995, ⇒11/1,3105. ᴿJThS 48 (1997) 182-187 *(Nolland, J.L.)*.

4748 *Jones, Peter R.* Preaching on the parable genre. RExp 94 (1997) 231-245.

4749 **Kähler, Christoph** Jesu Gleichnisse als Poesie und Therapie. WUNT 2/78: 1995, ⇒11/1,3106; 12,4530. ᴿThG 40 (1997) 153-154 *(Giesen, Heinz)*; CV 39/2-3 (1997) 278-282 *(Mrázek, Jiří)*; ThZ 153 (1997) 376-378 *(Raguse, Hartmut)*.

4750 **Keating, Thomas** El reino de Dios es como...: reflexiones sobre las parábolas y los dichos de Jesús. Bilbao 1997, Desclée de B 134 pp. 84-330-1214-2.

4751 ᵀ**Kooyman, Arie C.** Als een koning van vlees en bloed: rabbijnse parabels in midrasjiem. Baarn 1997, Ten Have 219 pp. Vertaald en toegelicht. *f*40. 90-259-4731-X [ITBT 6/3,32s—Monshouwer, Dirk].

4752 **Kunduru, Joji** Samhita: the parables of Christ. Secunderabad 1997, Andhra Jesuit Publications xv; 216 pp. Rs20. **Telugu.**

4753 **Maillot, A.** Le parabole di Gesù. CinB 1997, San Paolo 222 pp. L24.000 [RdT 38,286].

4754 *Matić, Marko* Kristološki kontekst isusova govora u prispodobama [Der christologische Kontext in den Gleichnissen]. 1997, ⇒96. ᶠTomⅰca C., Zsfg. 342. 320-342.

4755 *May, David M.* "Drawn from nature or common life": social and cultural reading strategies for the parables. RExp 94 (1997) 199-214.

4756 **Meurer, Herrmann-Josef** Die Gleichnisse Jesu als Metaphern: Paul RⅰcoeuⱤs Hermeneutik der Gleichniserzählung Jesu im Horizont des Symbols "Gottesherrschaft/Reich Gottes". Diss. Münster 1995-96; ᴰ*Vorgrimler, H.*: BBB 111: Bodenheim 1997, Philo 783 pp. DM178. 3-8257-0054-2 [NTS 44,624].

4757 *Oldenhage, Tania* Parables for our time?: post-holocaust interpretations of the parables of Jesus. Semeia 77 (1997) 227-241.

4758 *Ramaroson, Léonard* Paraboles évangéliques et autres textes néotestamentaires: "à double ou à triple pointe". ScEs 49 (1997) 175-180.

4759 **Ramos, Felipe Fernández** El reino en parábolas. 1996, ⇒12,4536. ᴿSalm. 44 (1997) 103-105 *(Pikaza, Xabier)*; TeCa 63 (1997) 139-140 *(Navarro, María)*.

4760 **Sáenz, Alfredo** Las parábolas del evangelio según los Padres de la Iglesia: la figura señorial de Cristo. BA 1997, Gladius 434 pp. [OCP 65,498s–Špidlik, T.].

4761 *Schmithals, Walter* The parabolic teachings in the synoptic gospels. JHiC 4/2 (1997) 3-32.

4762 *Shillington, V. George* Engaging with the parables. Jesus and his parables. 1997, ⇒230. EShillington, V.G., 1-20.

4763 **Sider, John W.** Interpretar las parábolas: guía hermenéutica de su significcado. Dabar 9: M 1997, San Pablo 317 pp. Ptas1.800. 84-285-1934-X [Qüestions de Vida Cristiana 187,193].

4764 **Trela, Janusz** Przypowiesci Jezusa: a starotestamentalne i rabinakkie meszalim. Katolicki Uniwersytet Lubelski. Wydzial Teologii: Lublin 1997, Katolickiego Uniwersytetu Lubelskiego 322 pp. Bibl. 83-228-0573-X. **P**.

4765 *Valavanolickal, Kuriakose* The use of the gospel parables in Ephrem. Ephrem's Theological Journal 1/1-2 (1997) 17-26.

4766 **Wright, Stephen** The voice of Jesus in six parables and their interpreters: a study in insight, influence and intention. Diss. Durham 1997; DDunn, J.D.G. 233 pp. [RTL 29,589].

4767 *Carter, Warren* The parables in Matthew 13:1-52 as embedded narratives;

4768 *Heil, John Paul* Narrative progression of the parables discourse in Matthew 13:1-52. Matthew's parables. CBQ.MS 30: 1997, ⇒4738. 36-63/64-95.

4769 *Agua, Agustín del* Eclesiología como discurso narrado: Mt 13,2-52: teoría y prática del análisis de discursos narrados en los evangelios. EE 72 (1997) 217-269.

4770 *Kerr, A.J.* Matthew 13:25: sowing *zizania* among another's wheat: realistic or artificial. JThS 48 (1997) 108-109.

4771 *Schwarz, Günther* "Verbarg es in drei Sea Mehl"? (Matthäus 13,33 / Lukas 13,20.21). BN 86 (1997) 60-62.

4772 *Rota Scalabrini, Patrizio* Scoperto un tesoro di grande valore... Vocazioni 14/1 (1997) 10-16 [Mt 13,44].

4773 EVidal, **Daniel** La perle évangélique. Atopia: Grenoble 1997, Millon 729 pp. Trad. franç. (1602). Édition établie et précédé de 'Le coup terrible du néant'. FF250. 2-84137-039-9 [RTL 29,132] [Mt 13,46].

4774 *Hagner, Donald A.* Nytt från den skriftlärdes förråd (Matt 13:52). 1997, ⇒28. FGERHARDSSON B., 11-24.

4775 *Tàrrech, Armand Puig i* Le récit de Mt 13. StAns 124: 1997, ⇒57. FLOEHRER M. — TRAGAN P., 267-286.

4776 *Seidel, Johannes* Entfaltete Dynamik: Himmelreichsgleichnisse in Mt 13. Entschluss 52/11 (1997) 4-5.

4777 *Czerny, Michael* 'Lecz i szczenięta...' (Mk 7,24-30, Mt 15,21-28): słowo o sprawiedliwości Królestwa w oczekiwaniu na jubileusz ['Even the puppies...' (Mk 7:24-30, Mt 15:21-28): justice of the Kingdom in advent of the jubilee]. TSzlufik-Szczęsna, Ela: Życie Duchowe 9/4 (1997) 99-114. **P**.

4778 *Guardiola-Sáenz, Leticia A.* Borderless women and borderless texts: a cultural reading of Matthew 15:21-28. Semeia 78 (1997) 69-81.

4779 *Gemünden, Petra von* La Cananéenne (Mt. 15.21-28). Sources 23/1 (1997) 28-32.

4780    *Mussies, Gerard* Jesus and 'Sidon' in Matthew 15/Mark 7. Sum. 278. Bijdr. 58 (1997) 264-278.

F4.5 Mt 16... *Primatus promissus*—The promise to Peter

4781    **Butler, Scott; Dahlgren, Norman; Hess, David** Jesus, Peter and the keys: a scriptural handbook on the papacy. Santa Barbara 1996, Queenship xxiii; 431 pp. $15. 1-882972-54-6 [ThD 44,257— Heiser, W. Charles].

4782    *Chilton, Bruce* Shebna, Eliakim, and the promise to Peter. Jesus in context. AGAJ 39: 1997, ⇒183. ᴱChilton, B., 319-337 [Isa 22,22].

4783    **Dschulnigg, Peter** Petrus im Neuen Testament. 1996, ⇒12,4557. ᴿThLZ 122 (1997) 906-907 *(Fornberg, Tord)*; ThGl 87 (1997) 658-659 *(Ernst, Josef)*.

4784    *Gnilka, Joachim* Der Petrusdienst—Grundlegung im Neuen Testament und Ausprägung in der frühen Kirche. Papstamt und Ökumene: zum Petrusdienst an der Einheit aller Getauften. ᴱHünermann, Peter Regensburg 1997, Pustet. 3-7917-1565-8. 9-24.

4785    *González Faus, José Ignacio* Algunos libros últimos sobre el ministerio de Pedro, 1. ActBib 34 (1997) 5-21.

4786    **Grappe, Christian** Images de Pierre aux deux premiers siècles. EHPR 75: 1995, 349 pp. FF150. 2-13-047054-8. ᴿVetChr 34 (1997) 175-176 *(Schirone, Salvatore)*; RB 104 (1997) 458-459 *(Taylor, Justin)*; CritRR 10 (1997) 178-179 *(Casurella, Anthony)*.

4787    *Häring, Bernhard* Meine Hoffnung für die Zukunft des Petrusdienstes. ThG 40 (1997) 254-261.

4788    *Karavidopoulos, John* Peter in the NT church. ThD 44 (1997) 149-154.

4789    **Lima, João Tavares de** 'Tu serás chamado ΚΗΦΑΣ': estudo exegético sobre Pedro no quarto evangelho. AnBib 265: 1994, ⇒10,5212. ᴿEstB 55 (1997) 279-281 *(López Fernández, E.)*; CivCatt 148 I (1997) 521-522 *(Scaiola, D.)*.

4790    **Minnerath, Roland** De Jérusalem à Rome: Pierre et l'unité de l'Église apostolique. ThH 101: 1994, ⇒10,4546; 12,4562. ᴿRSR 71 (1997) 521-523 *(Meslin, Michel)*.

4791    *Pannenberg, Wolfhart* Riflessioni evangeliche sul servizio petrino del vescovo di Roma. AnScR 2 (1997) 109-119.

4792    *Saint-Roch, Patrick* La tombe de Pierre. MoBi 103 (1997) 26-29.

4793    **Schatz, Klaus** Papal primacy. 1996, ⇒12,4566. ᴿTS 58 (1997) 565-566 *(Granfield, Patrick)*;

4794    El primado del Papa: su historia desde los orígenes a nuestros días. Santander 1996, Sal Terrae 253 pp. 84-293-1202-1. ᴿEE 72 (1997) 753-754 *(Sanz de Diego, Rafael M.ª)*;

4795    Il primato del papa: la sua storia dalle origini ai nostri giorni. Brescia 1996, Queriniana 260 pp. L40.000. ᴿCivCatt 148 III (1997) 336-337 *(Mazzolini, S.)*.

4796    **Wehr, Lothar** Petrus und Paulus—Kontrahenten und Partner. NTA 30: 1996, ⇒12,4567. ᴿBZ 41 (1997) 284-285 *(Dschulnigg, Peter)*.

4797    *Brock, Sebastian P.* The gates/bars of sheol revisited. NT.S 89: 1997, ⇒7. ᶠBAARDA T., 7-24 [Ps 106; Isa 45; Mt 16,8].

4798 *Law, David R.* Matthew's enigmatic reference to Jeremiah in Mt 16,14. The book of Jeremiah. BEThL 128: 1997, ⇒186. ᴱCurtis, A.H.W., 277-302.

4799 **Moses, A.D.A.** Matthew's transfiguration story and Jewish-Christian controversy. JSNT.S 122: Shf 1996, Academic 294 pp. £45/$65. 1-85075-576-0. ᴿCBQ 59 (1997) 585-587 *(Powell, Mark Allan)*; JBL 116 (1997) 560-562 *(Gundry, Robert H.)* [Mt 17,1-8].

4800 *Deutsch, Celia M.* The transfiguration: vision and social setting in Matthew's gospel (Matthew 17:1-9). 1997, ⇒82. ᶠSᴄʀᴏɢɢs R., 124-137.

4801 *Rouiller, Grégoire* La transfiguration comme 'icône biblique' dans *Vita consecrata*. Som. VieCon 69 (1997) 352-363 [Mt 17,1-9].

4802 *Soljačić, Ivo* Preobraženje Kristovo u očima fizikalnog kemičara [The transfiguration of Jesus Christ as seen by a physical chemist]. Sum. 160. Obnovljeni Život 52/2 (1997) 151-160. [Mt 17,1-9; Mk 9,2-9] **Croatian.**

4803 *Milner, Christine* The role of the prophet Elijah in the transfiguration mosaics at Sinai and Classe. ByF 24 (1997) 207-217 [Mt 17,1-13].

4804 *Chilton, Bruce* A coin of three realms (Matthew 17:24-27). Jesus in context. AGAJ 39: 1997 <1990>, ⇒183. ᴱChilton, B., 319-337.

4805 **Tellan, Sergio** La correzione fraterna nella chiesa di Matteo Mt 18,15-20. Diss. Pont. Univ. Gregoriana 1997; ᴰ*Rasco, Emilio*: Verona 94 pp. excerpt.

4806 *Heil, John Paul* Parable of the unforgiving forgiven servant in Matthew 18:21-35. Matthew's parables. CBQ.MS 30: 1997, ⇒4738. ᴱCarter, W., 96-123.

4807 *Larsen, Iver* Seventy-seven times or seventy times seven times. PPBT 48 (1997) 442-445 [Mt 18,22].

4808 *Bernabé Ubieta, Carmen* Lectura de un texto bíblico: Mateo 19,1-12. ResB 13 (1997) 61-65.

F4.8 **Mt 20...**_Regnum eschatologicum_—**Kingdom eschatology**

4809 *Cebulj, Christian* Wenn den Armen der Himmel gehört: zur Reich Gottes-Predigt Jesu im Neuen Testament. Entschluss 52/11 (1997) 14-17.

4810 **Durrwell, François Xavier** El mas allá: miradas cristianas. Verdad e Imagen minor 9: S 1997, Sígueme 144 pp. [EfMex 16,246—Ramírez Ayala, Manuel].

4811 *Erniakulathil, John* Kingdom of God in the teaching of Jesus. BiBh 23 (1997) 90-101.

4812 **Fuellenbach, John** The kingdom of God: the message of Jesus today. 1995, ⇒11/1,3160; 12,4587. ᴿPacifica 10/1 (1997) 105-107 *(Loader, William)*; New Theology Review 10/3 (1997) 120-121 *(Haight, Roger)*.

4813 *Hemelsoet, Ben; Touwen, Klaas* Parabels van het Koninkrijk. BTIT 5/1 (1997) 26-28.

4814 **Kloppenburg, Boaventura** [sic] Basiléia: o reino de Deus. São Paulo, 1997, Loyola 134 pp. 85-15-01565-X [PerTeol 29,282].

4815 *Lienhard, Fritz* Le royaume et la croix. FV 96/1 (1997) 7-19.

4816 **Reiser, Marius** Jesus and judgment: the eschatological proclamation in its Jewish context. [T]*Maloney, Linda M.*:        Mp 1997, Fortress x; 398 pp. Bibl. 0-8006-2623-0.
4817 *Roloff, Jürgen* Das Reich des Menschensohnes: ein Beitrag zur Eschatologie des Matthäus. BZNW 89: 1997, ⇒33. [F]GRAESSER E., 275-292.
4818 *Rordorf, Bernard* ¿Como hablar del juicio final?. [T]*Sala, Márius*: SelTeol 36 (1997) 319-326.
4819 *Scholtissek, Klaus* "Alles ist bereit, kommt zur Hochzeit!" (Mt 22,4): Heilszeit und Lebenszeit in der urchristlichen Jesusüberlieferung. BiLi 70 (1997) 169-176.
4820 *Wengst, Klaus* Aspects of the last judgement in the gospel according to Matthew. Eschatology in the bible. JSOT.S 243: 1997, ⇒222. [E]Reventlow, H. Graf, 233-245.

4821 *Shillington, V. George* Saving life and keeping sabbath (Matthew 20:1b-15): the parable of the labourers in the vineyard. Jesus and his parables. 1997, ⇒230. [E]Shillington, V.G., 87-101.
4822 *Carter, Warren* Parable of the householder in Matthew 20:1-16. Matthew's parables. CBQ.MS 30: 1997, ⇒4738. [E]Carter, W., 124-146.
4823 *Gnadt, Martina S.* Anwerbung zur Solidarität: sozialgeschichtliche Bibelauslegung zu Matthäus 20,1-16. JK 58 (1997) 32-35.
4824 *Pak, Chang Hyong* Die Arbeiter im Weinberg (Mt 20,1-16). BiKi 52 (1997) 136-137.
4825 *Reid, Barbara E.* Puzzling passages: Matt 20,12. BiTod 35 (1997) 247-248.
4826 *Autané, Maurice* L'entrée de Jésus à Jérusalem. DosB 67 (1997) 22-23 [Mt 21,1-11; Mk 11,1-10; Lk 19,28-40; John 12,12-19].
4827 *Weren, Wim* Jesus' entry into Jerusalem: Matthew 21,1-17 in the light of the Hebrew Bible and the Septuagint. The scriptures in the gospels. BEThL 131: 1997, ⇒234. [E]Tuckett, C.M., 117-141.
4828 *Bell, Theo* Der Mensch als Esel Christi [Humanity as donkey of Christ—M. Luther]. Adapted by *Rossol, Heinz D.*: Luther Digest 5 (1997) 2-4 [Mt 21,5].
4829 *Carter, Warren* The parables in Matthew 21:28-22:14. Matthew's parables. CBQ.MS 30: 1997, ⇒4738. [E]Carter, W., 147-176.
4830 *Evans, Craig A.* Are the wicked tenant farmers 'peasants'?: Jesus' parable and lease agreements in antiquity. Jesus in context. AGAJ 39: 1997 <1996>, ⇒183. [E]Chilton, B., 231-250 [Mt 21,33-46].
4831 *Genuyt, François* Matthieu 21. SémBib 85 (1997) 47-62.
4832 *Theobald, Michael* "Gebt dem Kaiser, was des Kaisers ist ...!" (Mt 22,15-22). Diak. 28 (1997) 140-142.
4833 *Genuyt, François* Matthieu 22. SémBib 86 (1997) 49-59.
4834 *Müller, Stefanie* Weh euch, ihr Heuchler!: zur Herkunft und Bedeutung der pharisäischen Bewegung im Judentum (Mt 23,1-39). Antijudaismus im NT. KT 149: 1997, ⇒κ8. [E]Henze, Dagmar, 138-150.
4835 **Del Verme, Marcello** Giudaismo e Nuovo Testamento: il caso delle decime. SGCA 1: 1989, ⇒5,4687*... 10,4574. [R]JSJ 28 (1997) 359-361 *(Malina, Bruce J.)* [Mt, 23,23].
4836 *Maccoby, Hyam* The law about liquids: a rejoinder. JSNT 67 (1997) 115-122 [Mt 23,25-26].

4837 *Weinfeld, Moshe* The Jewish roots of Matthew's vitriol. BiRe 13/5 (1997) 31 [Mt 23].

4838 *Saldarini, Anthony J.* Understanding Matthew's vitriol. BiRe 13/2 (1997) 32-39, 45 [Mt 23].

4839 **Dlungwana, Mlungisi Pius** Jesus' parousia in the context ofthe crucifixion: an exegetical analysis of Matt. 24:1-26:2 using some elements of the semiotic. Diss. Ottawa 1997; <sup>D</sup>*Laberge, L.*: 257 pp. [RTL 29,584].

4840 <sup>F</sup>THOMA, **Clemens** Tempelkult und Tempelzerstörung (70 n.Chr.). <sup>E</sup>**Lauer, Simon**: JudChr 15: 1995, ⇒11/1,33; 12,93. <sup>R</sup>JSSt 44 (1997) 380-382 *(Grabbe, Lester L.)* [Mt 24,2].

4841 *Heil, John Paul* Final parables in the eschatological discourse in Matthew 24-25. Matthew's parables. CBQ.MS 30: 1997, ⇒4738. <sup>E</sup>Carter, W., 177-209.

4842 *Lindemann, Andreas* Die Endzeitrede in Didache 16 und die Jesus-Apokalypse in Matthäus 24-25. NT.S 89: 1997, ⇒7. <sup>F</sup>BAARDA T., 155-174.

4843 *Wohlgemut, Joel R.* Entrusted money (Matthew 25:14-28): the parable of the talents/pounds. Jesus and his parables. 1997, ⇒230. <sup>E</sup>Shillington, V.G., 103-120.

4844 *Pizivin, Daniel* 'J'étais étranger et vous m'avez accueilli' (Mt 25,31-46): de l'usage d'un texte biblique en période de crise. Cahiers de l'Atelier 475 (1997) 58-65.

4845 *Niemand, Christoph* Matthäus 25,31-46 universal oder exklusiv?: Rekonstruktion der ursprünglichen Textintention im Spannungsfeld moderner Wertaxiome. StAns 124: 1997, ⇒57. <sup>F</sup>LOEHRER M. — TRAGAN P., 287-326.

4846 *Derrett, J. Duncan M.* Unfair to goats (Mt 25:32-33). ET 108 (1997) 177-178.

4847 *Mattam, Joseph* Judgement on the present economic order: Matthew twenty five. BiBh 23 (1997) 174-182.

F5.1 *Redemptio*, Mt 26, *Ultima coena;* **The Eucharist** [⇒H7.4]

4848 **Alonso Schökel, Luis** L'eucarestia: meditazioni bibliche. Bibbia e Preghiera 29: R 1997, ADP 121 pp. L15.000. 88-7357-169-7.

4849 *Bach, Jeff* The agape in the Brethren tradition. The Lord's supper. 1997, ⇒260. <sup>E</sup>Stoffer, D.R., 161-168.

4850 *Barile, Riccardo* Rendere grazie, chiedere grazie. RPLi 200 (1997) 23-31.

4851 *Bartnicki, Roman* Eucharystia w bożym planie zbawienia [De Eucharistia in oeconomia salutis] I-II. RBL 50 (1997) 2-16, 119-127. **P.**

4852 **Béraudy, Roger** Sacrifice et eucharistie: la dimension anthropologique du sacrifice dans la célébration de l'eucharistie. Théologies: P 1997, Cerf 134 pp. FF130. 2-204-05626-X [RTL 29,122].

4853 *Berzonsky, Vladimir* Observations from the Orthodox perspective. The Lord's supper. 1997, ⇒260. <sup>E</sup>Stoffer, D.R., 281-284.

4854 *Boendermaker, J.P.* Brood breken: de handeling der apostelen. ITBT 5/1 (1997) 4-6.

4855 *Boughton, Lynne C.* "Being shed for you / many": time-sense and consequences in the synoptic cup citations. TynB 48 (1997) 249-270.

4856 *Brackney, William H.* A Baptist response. The Lord's supper. 1997, ⇒260. ᴱStoffer, D.R., 278-280.

4857 *Brackney, William H.* Sacrament, ordinance, or both?: Baptist understandings of the Lord's supper. The Lord's supper. 1997, ⇒260. ᴱStoffer, D.R., 231-240.

4858 *Carmichael, Deborah Bleicher* David Dᴀᴜʙᴇ on the eucharist and the passover seder. NT Backgrounds. 1997, <1991>, ⇒3975. ᴱEvans, C.A., 89-108.

4859 ᴱ**Casanellas, Pere; Gendra, Jordi** Ritual de l'Hagadà de Pasqua: la celebración del sopar pasqual jueu. Collab. *Ricart, Ignasi; Marín, Joan Ramon;* Afterword *Benarroch, Carlos*: Paràbola 9: Barc 1997, Claret 105 pp. Ptas1.450. 84-8297-131-X [ActBib 35,170—Tuñí, J.O.].

4860 *Castellano, Jesús* La relación entre Eucaristía y libertad. Phase 37 (1997) 43-52.

4861 *Chilton, Bruce* Ideological diets in a feast of meanings. Jesus in context. AGAJ 39: 1997 <1994>, ⇒183. ᴱChilton, B., 59-89.

4862 *Clouse, Robert G.* Eschatology and the Lord's supper: hope for the triumph of God's reign. The Lord's supper. 1997, ⇒260. ᴱStoffer, D.R., 129-139.

4863 *Cummings, Owen F.* The reformers and eucharistic ecclesiology. OiC 33/1 (1997) 47-54.

4864 *Durnbaugh, Donald F.* Believers church perspectives on the Lord's supper. The Lord's supper. 1997, ⇒260. ᴱStoffer, D.R., 63-78.

4865 **Espinel Marcos, J.L.** La eucaristía del Nuevo Testamento. S 1997, San Esteban 300 pp. [Comunidades 26,33ss—Vázquez, Xaime].

4866 *Estep, William R.* Contrasting views of the Lord's supper in the Reformation of the sixteenth century;

4867 *Ewert, David* The Lord's supper in the Mennonite Brethren Church;

4868 *Ewert, David, (al.),* Report of the findings committee. The Lord's supper. 1997, ⇒260. ᴱStoffer, D.R., 46-62/263-265/285-288.

4869 *Falsini, Rinaldo* Rendere grazie tra memoria e attesa. RPLi 200 (1997) 13-22.

4870 *Ferguson, Everett* The Lord's supper in church history: the early church through the medieval period;

4871 *Finger, Reta Halteman* "Mary, please pass the bread": social implications of the Lord's supper in the early church;

4872 *Finger, Thomas* Proposed theses for a believers church theology of the Lord's supper. The Lord's supper. 1997, ⇒260. ᴱStoffer, D.R., 21-45/250-255/256-260.

4873 *Forde, Gerhard O.* The Lord's supper as the testament of Jesus. Word & World 17/1 (1997) 5ff [ThD Index February 1997, 15].

4874 *Frack, Kevin C.* A Moravian perspective on holy communion;

4875 *George, Timothy* Reflections on the conference. The Lord's supper. 1997, ⇒260. ᴱStoffer, D.R., 225-230/266-270.

4876 *Gesteria, Manuel* Jesucristo, hijo de Dios y salvador. Confer 36/2 (1997) 231-245.

4877 *Ghiberti, Giuseppe* La cène 'pascale' de Jésus. SIDIC 30/1 (1997) 7-11.

4878 *Gros, Jeffrey* The Lord's supper in ecumenical dialogue. The Lord's supper. 1997, ⇒260. ᴱStoffer, D.R., 271-277.

4879 *Hellwig, Monika K.* The eucharist and world hunger. Word & World 17/1 (1997) 61ff [ThD Index February 1997, 15].

4880 *Henderson, J. Frank* Jésus et le séder. SIDIC 30/1 (1997) 14-16.

4881 *Jeschke, Marlin* Making the Lord's supper meaningful;

4882 *Jones, T. Canby* A Quaker interpretation of the Lord's supper. The Lord's supper. 1997, ⇒260. EStoffer, D.R., 140-153/200-206.

4883 *Knutsen, Mary M.* What is a Lutheran theology of the Lord's supper?: a response to the three essays. Word & World 17/1 (1997) 28ff [ThD Index February 1997, 15].

4884 **Kreider, Eleanor** Communion shapes character. Scottdale, PA 1997, Herald 303 pp. $20/CAN$28.50. 0-8361-9064-5.

4885 *Lamberts, J.* Hoe fungeert de Bijbel in de eucharistie?. Emmaüs 28/2 (1997) 55-60.

4886 *Langkammer, Hugolin* Eucharystia jako ofiara i jako uczta [Eucharist as sacrifice and banquet]. 1997, ⇒52. FŁACH J., 211-217. **P.**

4887 **Long, Edward LeRoy** To liberate and redeem: moral reflections on the biblical narrative. Cleveland, Ohio 1997, Pilgrim xiii; 263 pp. Bibl. $19. 0-8298-1176-1 [NThAR 1998,98].

4888 *Manicardi, Luciano* 'In perenne rendimento di grazie': dall'eucaristia alla vita. RPLi 200 (1997) 41-55.

4889 **McAdoo, H.R.; Stevenson, Kenneth** The mystery of the Eucharist in the Anglican tradition. 1995, ⇒11/1,3193. ER 49/1 (1997) 114-118 *(Carroll, Thomas K.)*.

4890 *McCray, Thomas L.* The Lord's supper: the perspective of the African Methodist Episcopal Church. The Lord's supper. 1997, ⇒260. EStoffer, D.R., 219-224.

4891 **McNeil, Brian** The Master is here: biblical reflections on eucharistic adoration. Dublin 1997, Veritas 95 pp. [Milltown Studies 42,176ss—Moloney, Raymond].

4892 *Meyer, Ben F.* Recondite hermeneutics and the Last Supper rite. 1997, ⇒92. FSTUHLMACHER P., 296-309 [John 6; 1 Cor 11].

4893 *Mills, John* The Lord's supper as viewed and practiced by the Christian Churches, Churches of Christ, and the Disciples of Christ. The Lord's supper. 1997, ⇒260. EStoffer, D.R., 193-199.

4894 **Moloney, Francis J.** A body broken for a broken people: eucharist in the New Testament. Blackburn 21997 <1990>, HarperCollinsReligious xv; 212 pp. $15/AUS$17. 1-86371-698-X [ACR 74,382].

4895 *Mosso, Domenico* La preghiera eucaristica, azione dell'assemblea. RPLi 200 (1997) 32-40.

4896 *Murphy, G. Ronald* The night before he suffered. Spiritual Life 43/3 (1997) 131-144.

4897 *Mutta, Ruggero dalla* Gesù, unico salvatore: 1. l'eucologia del tempo di quaresima e della settimana santa. RPLi 200 (1997) 65-71;

4898 2. l'eucologia del triduo pasquale e del tempo di Pasqua. RPLi 201 (1997) 49-56.

4899 **O'Loughlin, Frank** The eucharist: doing what Jesus said. Homebush 1997, St. Paul 147 pp. AUS$15. 1-8755-7089-6 [Pacifica 11,94ss—Hamilton, Andrew].

4900 *Pasinelli, Nadia* Lodare, benedire e rendere grazie. RPLi 200 (1997) 5-12.

4901 *Pigna, Arnaldo* Gesù, nostra salvezza. RVS 51/2 (1997) 195-200.

4902  *Pothier, René; Aubin, Catherine* La fraction du pain et sa significa-
      tion. MD 209 (1997) 61-78.
4903  **Power, David N.** Il mistero eucaristico: infondere nuova vita alla
      tradizione. BTCon 93: Brescia 1997, Queriniana 462 pp. L70.000.
      RStPat 44/3 (1997) 181-184 *(Tura, Ermanno Roberto)*.
4904  *Prasannabhai, Fr.* Jesus the *arati* personified: the eucharist as our
      *mahâ-ârati.* Sum. 192. VJTR 61/3 (1997) 192-199.
4905  **Rempel, John D.** The Lord's Supper in Anabaptism: a study in the
      christology of Balthasar HUBMAIER, Pilgram MARPECK, and
      Dirk PHILIPS. SAMH 33: 1993, ⇒10,4613. RJThS 48 (1997) 314-
      316 *(Spinks, Bryan D.).*
4906  *Rempel, John D.* Toward an Anabaptist theology of the Lord's sup-
      per. The Lord's supper. 1997, ⇒260. EStoffer, D.R., 243-249.
4907  *Rosato, Philip J.* The eucharist and the kingdom of God. StMiss 46
      (1997) 149-169.
4908  *Scholtissek, Klaus* Das Herrenmahl im Spiegel der neueren exegeti-
      schen Forschung. BiLi 70 (1997) 39-44.
4909  *Sierra López, Juan Manuel* La participación eucarística: a proposito
      del volumen de Francisco Caro de Hojeda *Modo de ordenar el
      memento en el sacrosanto sacrificio de la misa* publicado en Sevilla
      en 1613. Sum. 211. Isidorianum 6 (1997) 211-226.
4910  *Snyder Howard A.* The Lord's supper in the Free Methodist tradi-
      tion;
4911  *Stoffer, Dale R.* Brethren heritage of the Lord's supper: introduc-
      tion;
4912  Brethren heritage of the Lord's supper: Eucharist;
4913  *Strege, Merle D.* Ecclesiology and the Lord's supper: the memorial
      meal of a peaceable commumity. The Lord's supper. 1997, ⇒260.
      EStoffer, D.R., 212-218/157-160/185-192/117-128.
4914  *Strohl, Jane E.* The Lord's supper in light of the piety of medieval
      women: a Lutheran view. Word & World 17/1 (1997) 21ff [ThD
      Index February 1997, 15].
4915  *Throntveit, Mark A.* The Lord's supper as new testament, not new
      passover. LuthQ 11/3 (1997) 271-289.
4916  *Van Bemmelen, Peter M.* Seventh-day Adventists and the Lord's
      supper. The Lord's supper. 1997, ⇒260. EStoffer, D.R., 207-211.
4917  *Wahle, Hedwig* Une lecture midrachique des récits de la dernière
      céne de Jésus. SIDIC 30/1 (1997) 17-20.
4918  *Witherington, Ben* "Making a meal of it": the Lord's supper in its
      first-century social setting. The Lord's supper. 1997, ⇒260.
      EStoffer, D.R., 81-113.

4919  **Thiede, Carsten Peter; Ancona, Matthew d'** Eyewitness to Jesus:
      amazing new manuscript evidence about the origin of the gospels.
      1996, ⇒12,4647. RIBSt 19/1 (1997) 32-45 *(MacAdam, Henry
      Innes)*; HPR 97/7 (1997) 78-79 *(Zabielski, Gregory)* [Mt 26,6-7].
4920  **Thiede, Carsten Peter** Il papiro Magdalen: la comunità di Qumran
      e le origini del vangelo. TBianchi, Francesco: CasM 1997, Piemme
      236 pp. Bibl. 88-384-2835-2 [Mt 26].
4921  **Thiede, Carsten Peter; D'Ancona, Matthew** Testimonio de Jesús.
      TBoune, C.; Elías, P.: La línea del horizonte: Barc 1997, Planeta
      262 pp. 84-08-01932-5 [ActBib 34,210—Boada, J.] [Mt 26].

### F5.3  Mt 26,30...// *Passio Christi;* Passion narrative

4922  *Alegre, Xavier* Los responsables de la muerte de Jesús. RLAT 14 (1997) 139-172.

4923  *Autané, Maurice* Les psaumes dans la Passion. DosB 68 (1997) 22-24.

4924  *Bammel, Ernst* Judas in der jüdischen Überlieferung. Judaica et Paulina. WUNT 91: 1997, ⇒109. 23-33.

4925  *Battaglia, Vincenzo* La passione di Cristo nei commenti al Cantico dei Cantici, 2. La Sapienza della Croce 12/3 (1997) 217-228.

4926  *Blanco Pacheco, Severiano* Judíos e romanos en el proceso de Jésus. Stauros 27 (1997) 7-16.

4927  **Brown, Raymond E.** The death of the Messiah. 1994, ⇒10,4634... 12,4657. RAtK 128/2 (1997) 304-305 *(Sławiński, Henryk)*; Bib 78 (1997) 124-128 *(Busse, Ulrich)*; Horizons 24/2 (1997) 297-298 *(Sloyan, Gerard S.)*; RBBras 14 (1997) 396-398; JBL 115 (1996) 351-353 *(Carroll, John T.)*.

4928  *Brown, Raymond E.* The Babylonian Talmud on the execution of Jesus. NTS 43 (1997) 158-159.

4929  *Buioni, Maurizio* Passione di Cristo, passione del mondo: un'interpretazione della Passione per una prassi di liberazione. La Sapienza della Croce 12/3 (1997) 247-259.

4930  *Coda, Piero* 'Sei tu sei figlio di Dio, scendi dalla croce': la prassi di pace come dono ed esperienza del Crocifisso. Nuova Umanità 19/5 (1997) 591-605.

4931  **Cohn, Chaim** Der Prozeß und Tod Jesu aus jüdischer Sicht. Fra 1997, Jüdischer Verlag 518 pp. DM58. 3-633-54141-1 [EK (1998/4),235s—Osten-Sacken, Peter von der].

4932  *Daccache, Salim* Texte arabe inédit de l'évêque Ğirmānus Farḥāt: *Soixante méditations sur la passion et la résurrection de Jésus.* Rés. Al-Machriq 71/1 (1997) 57-82.

4933  **Egger, Peter** "Crucifixus sub Pontio Pilato": das "Crimen" Jesu von Nazareth im Spannungsfeld römischer und jüdischer Verwaltungs- und Rechtsstrukturen. Diss. München 1995-96; DGnilka, J.: NTA 32: Mü 1997, Aschendorff viii; 243 pp. DM75. 3-402-04780-2.

4934  **Fischer, Kurt von** Die Passion: Musik zwischen Kunst und Kirche. Kassel 1997, Bärenreiter 145 pp. DM48. 3-7618-2011-9 [EK (1998/4),238—Mörchen, Roland].

4935  **Garsky, Albrecht** Jesus vor dem Hohen Rat: eine redaktionsgeschichtliche Untersuchung. Diss. Würzburg 1997; DMüller [BZ 42,319].

4936  **Gooch, Paul W.** Reflections on Jesus and Socrates: word and silence. NHv 1997, Yale University Press xii; 308 pp. £21. 0-300-06695-3 [Theol. 101,210—Macquarrie, John].

4937  *Haacker, Klaus* Zur Sinngebung des Todes Jesu. ThBeitr 28 (1997) 24-33.

4938  **Hermosilla Molina, Antonio** La pasión de Cristo vista por un médico. Sevilla 1997 Guadalquivir 279 pp. 84-8093-026-8 [Isidorianum 7,299ss—Calero, Antonio Mª].

4939  *Jinkins, Michael; Reid, Steven Breck* God's forsakenness: the cry of dereliction as an utterance within the Trinity. HBT 19/1 (1997) 33-57.

4940   **Kim, Chang-Sun** Das Leiden Jesu: exegetische Studien zu indirek-
       ten Leidensankündigungen Jesu und ihrem Verhältnis zu seiner
       Basileia-Verkündigung. Diss. Tübingen 1997-98; <sup>D</sup>*Jeremias, G.*
       233 pp. [RTL 29,585].

4941   **Klassen, William** Judas: betrayer or friend of Jesus?. 1996,
       ⇒12,4675. <sup>R</sup>RRT (1997/1) 36-38 *(Cane, Anthony)*; CBQ 59 (1997)
       771-772 *(Fleddermann, Harry T.)*; Theol. 100/3 (1997) 114-115
       *(France, R.T.)*; AThR 79 (1997) 266-267 *(Sowers, Sidney G.)*; NT
       39 (1997) 196-197 *(Oxford, Jim)*; SR 26 (1997) 367-368
       *(McCready, Wayne O.)*.

4942   **Krafft, Olivier** Les 3 procès de Jésus. P 1997, Godefroy de Bouil-
       lon 140 pp. 2-84191-037-7 [NThAR 1997,292].

4943   *Küppers, Karl Heinz* Datum und Wochentag des Todes Jesu, der
       14. und 15. Nisan. Theologisches 27 (1997) 4-7.

4944   **Légasse, Simon** La passion dans les quatre évangiles. Le procès de
       Jésus, 2. 1995, ⇒11/1,3231; 12,4679. <sup>R</sup>EstB 55 (1997) 553-554
       *(Alegre, X.)*;

4945   The trial of Jesus. L 1997, SCM viii; 184 pp. £15. 0-334-02679-2
       [ET 108 (1996-97) 343].

4946   **Maggioni, Bruno** I raconti evangelici della passione. 1994,
       ⇒10,4639; 11/1,3233. <sup>R</sup>La Sapienza della Croce 12/1 (1997) 56-59
       *(Diez, Luis)*;

4947   Los relatos de la Pasión en los cuatro evangelios. <sup>T</sup>*García, Pablo*:
       Nueva Alianza 145: S 1997, Sígueme 308 pp. 84-301-1333-9 [Ef-
       Mex 16,229—Cárdenas Pallares, José].

4948   **Marcus, Joel** Jesus and the Holocaust: reflections on suffering and
       hope. NY 1997, Doubleday 144 pp. $15 [ThTo 55/1,98—Linafelt,
       Tod].

4949   **Messori, Vittorio** Gelitten unter Pontius Pilatus?: eine Untersu-
       chung über das Leiden und Sterben Jesu. Köln 1997, Adamas 445
       pp. 3-925746-72-2.

4950   **Noll, Mark A.** Adding cross to crown: the political significance of
       Christ's passion. 1996, ⇒12,4693. <sup>R</sup>BS 154 (1997) 490-491 *(Spen-
       cer, Stephen R.)* .

4951   *Pardo, Carmen* Jesús en medio de la tormenta. Confer 36/2 (1997)
       281-288.

4952   **Pemán, José M.**<sup>a</sup> La pasión según Pemán. M 1997, Edibesa 147
       pp. [Comunidades 26,157—González, M.].

4953   **Pinckaers, Servais Th.** Un grand chant d'amour, la Passion selon
       saint Matthieu. Saint-Maur 1997, Parole et silence 156 pp. [Sedes
       Sapientiae 16/1,69ss—Bazelaire, Thomas-M. de].

4954   **Rivkin, Ellis** What crucified Jesus?: messianism, pharisaism, and
       the development of christianity. Foreword *Fisher, Eugene J.* NY
       1997 <1984>, UAHC Press viii; 181 pp. 0-8074-0630-9.

4955   **Ross, Ellen M.** The grief of God: images of the suffering Jesus in
       late medieval England. NY 1997, OUP xiii; 200 pp. $50. 0-19-
       510451-X.

4956   **Senior, Donald** The Passion of Jesus Christ. Union City 1997,
       Passionist 96 pp. $11 [BiTod 36,267—Senior, Donald].

4957   **Sloyan, Gerard S.** The crucifixion of Jesus: history, myth, faith.
       1995, ⇒11/1,3244; 12,4705. <sup>R</sup>CBQ 59 (1997) 172-173 *(Olsthoorn,
       Martin F.)*.

4958 **Spiegel, Yorick; Kutter, Peter** Kreuzwege: theologische und psychoanalytische Zugänge zur Passion Jesu. Stu 1997, Kohlhammer 248 pp. 13 ill. DM39.80 [EuA 73/5,406].

4959 *Stillman, Martha K.* Footprints of oral transmission in the canonical passion narratives. EThL 73 (1997) 393-400.

4960 *Tardieu, Michel* Le procès de Jésus vu par les manichéens. Sum. rés. 9. Apocrypha 8 (1997) 9-23.

4961 **Treanor, Oliver** This is my beloved Son: aspects of the Passion. L 1997, Darton, L & T 232 pp. £10 [Furrow 49,591—O'Donnell, Christopher].

4962 *Zeller, Dieter* Die Rede von Tod und Auferstehung Jesu im hellenistischen Kontext. BiKi 52 (1997) 19-24.

4963 *Derrett, J.D.* "I adjure thee" (Matthew 26,63). DR 115 (1997) 225-234.

4964 *Graham, Susan Lochrie* A strange salvation: intertextual allusion in Mt 27,39-43. The scriptures in the gospels. BEThL 131: 1997, ⇒234. ETuckett, C.M., 501-511.

4965 *Viviano, Benedict T.* A psychology of faith: Matt 27:54 in the light of Exod 14:30-31. RB 104 (1997) 368-372.

4966 *LaCocque, André* The great cry of Jesus in Matthew 27:50. 1997, ⇒82. FSCROGGS R., 138-164.

4967 *Cheney, Emily* The mother of the sons of Zebedee (Matthew 27.56). JSNT 68 (1997) 13-21.

## F5.6 **Mt 28//: Resurrectio**

4968 **Balthasar, Hans Urs von** Leben aus dem Tod: Betrachtungen zum Ostermysterium. Kriterien 97: FrB 1997, Johannes 88 pp. DM18. 3-8411-343-X [OrdKor 39,255].

4969 **Barker, Maragaret** The risen Lord. 1996, ⇒12,4725. RDoLi 47/3 (1997) 183-185 *(McCarthy, Carmel)*.

4970 *Boismard, Marie-Émile* Faut-il encore parler de "résurrection"?. 1995, ⇒11/1,3261. RATG 60 (1997) 377-379 *(Pozo, C.)*.

4971 *Boissieu, Béatrice de* La résurrection chez PANNENBERG. RICP 61 (1997) 193-210.

4972 *Brambilla, Franco Giulio* L'incontro con il Signore risorto: sul cammino, in fuga da Gerusalemme. RCI 78 (1997) 246-256, 326-338.

4973 **Brown, Raymond E.** Begegnung mit dem Auferstandenen: ein Begleiter durch die Osterevangelien. TLauble, Michael: Wü 1997, Echter 109 pp. 3-429-01892-7 [NThAR 1997,194].

4974 ED'Costa, Gavin Resurrection reconsidered. 1996, ⇒12,4731. RTheol. 100 (1997) 48 *(Wells, Samuel)*; HeyJ 38 (1997) 192-193 *(Alison, James)*.

4975 EDavis, Stephen T.; Kendall, Daniel: O'Collins, Gerald The resurrection: an interdisciplinary symposium on the resurrection of Jesus. Oxf 1997, OUP 400 pp. £30. 0-19-815091-1. RTablet (23 August 1997) 1072 *(Kerr, Fergus)*; Theology 798 (1997) 455-457 *(Barton, Stephen C.)*.

4976 **Deneken, M.** La foi pascale: rendre compte de la résurrection de Jésus aujourd'hui. Théologies: P 1997, Cerf 675 pp. FF195. 2-204-05764-9 [ETR 73,307].

4977   *Eisenbaum, Pamela M.* A speech act of faith: the early proclamation of the resurrection of Jesus. 1997, ⇒82. ᶠScROGGS R., 24-45.

4978   *Ellul, Yves* L'au-delà dans la religion chrétienne, une lecture protestante. BLE.S 4 (1997) 101-106.

4979   **Essen, Georg** Historische Vernunft und Auferweckung Jesu: Theologie und Historik im Streit um den Begriff geschichtlicher Wirklichkeit. TSTP 9: 1995, ⇒11/1,3269; 12,4732. ᴿETR 72 (1997) 465-466 *(Rakotoharintsifa, Andrianjatovo)*.

4980   **Federici, Tommaso** Resuscitò Cristo!: commento alle letture bibliche della divina liturgia bizantina. Quaderni di Oriente Cristiano 8: 1996, ⇒12,4733. ᴿRiCi 14/2 (1997) 194-197 *(Rosati, Cristina)*.

4981   *Ferraris, Maurizio* Cristo è veramente risorto?: l'estetica come filosofia prima. REst 37/4 (1997) 169-177.

4982   *Gubler, Marie-Louise* Auferweckt als Erstling der Entschlafenen. BiKi 52 (1997) 2-7.

4983   *Haik, Georges* L'au-delà dans la religion juive. BLE.S 4 (1997) 107-117.

4984   *Kallenberg, Arie* The resurrection in the early Carmelite liturgy. Carmelus 44/1 (1997) 5-20.

4985   *Kraus, Wolfgang* Volles Grab—leerer Glaube?: zum Streit um die Auferstehung Jesu. RKZ 138 (1997) 516-523.

4986   *Leipoldt, Johannes* The resurrection stories. JHiC 4/1 (1997) <1948> 138-149 [ZID 23,417].

4987   **Lüdemann, Gerd; Özen, A.** De opstanding van Jezus: een historische benadering. 1996, ⇒12,4745. ᴿColl. 27/2 (1997) 221-222 *(Van Soom, Willy)*.

4988   **McKenzie, Leon** Pagan resurrection myths and the resurrection of Jesus: a christian perspective. Southern Academic Editions: Charlottesville 1997, Bookwrights xvi; 180 pp. $22. 1-880404-13-3 [CBQ 60,196].

4989   *Müller, Karlheinz* Das Weltbild der jüdischen Apokalyptik und die Rede von Jesu Auferstehung. BiKi 52 (1997) 8-18.

4990   **Osborne, Kenan B.** The resurrection of Jesus: new considerations for its theological interpretation. Mahwah, NJ 1997, Paulist 194 pp. $15. 0-8091-3703-8 [HPR 98/10,71ss—Reilly, Matthew V.].

4991   *Osiek, Carolyn* The women at the tomb: what are they doing there?. HTS 53 (1997) 103-118.

4992   **Oyer, Linda** Interpreting the new in light of the old: comparative study of post-resurrection commissioning stories of Matthew and John. Diss. Institut catholique de Paris 1997; ᴰ*Cothenet, E.*: 490 pp. [RICP 65,257ss].

4993   *Pelser, G.M.* Rudolf BULTMANN oor die opstanding van Jesus. HTS 53 (1997) 455-475 [ZID 24,126].

4994   *Reichardt, Michael* Psychologische Erklärung der Ostererscheinungen?. BiKi 52 (1997) 28-33.

4995   **Riley, Gregory John** Resurrection reconsidered: Thomas and John in controversy. 1995, ⇒11/1,3296; 12,4752. ᴿJBL 116 (1997) 147-148 *(Davies, Stevan)*.

4996   **Russell, Jeffrey Burton** A history of heaven: the singing silence. Princeton, NJ 1997, Princeton Univ. Press xv; 220 pp. 0-691-01161-3.

4997   *Szabó, Ferenc* La résurrection et la transfiguration du cosmos. FolTh 8 (1997) 113-135.

4998 *Valsania, Maurizio* Trasformazioni fenomeniche dell'Eterno: critica all'unicità e al primato della resurrezione di Cristo nel panteismo britannico del secolo XVIII. REst 37/4 (1997) 179-189.

4999 **Veilleur, Jean-Marie** Flos florum: pour une date commune de la fête de Pâques conforme aux données astronomiques. P 1997, de Paris 35 pp. FF48/EUR7.32. 2-85162-007-X.

5000 *Walter, Nikolaus* Eine vormatthäische Schilderung der Auferstehung Jesu. Praeparatio evangelica. WUNT 98: 1997 <1973>, ⇒167. 12-27.

5001 **Wiebe, Phillip H.** Visions of Jesus: direct encounters from the New Testament to today. NY 1997, OUP viii; 278 pp. $30. 0-19-509750-5 [ThD 45,194—Heiser, W. Charles].

5002 *Williams, Trevor* The trouble with the resurrection. JSOT.S 153: 1997, ⇒4. FASHTON J., 219-235.

5003 *Byrskog, Samuel* Slutet gott, allting gott: Matteus 28:16-20 i narrativt perspektiv. 1997, ⇒28. FGERHARDSSON B., 85-98.

5004 **Nissen, Johannes** Ordet tog bolig iblandt os. 1997, Anis 200 pp. DK195. ΙΧΘΥΣ 24/2 (1997) 87-88 *(Christensen, Søren T.)* [Mt 28,19-20].

## F6.1 Evangelium Marci—*Textus, commentarii*

5005 *Álvarez Márquez, Carmen* Un manuscritto de BEDA, propiedad de Coluccio Saluti. Ms. 56-1-26 de la Biblioteca Capitular y Colombina de Sevilla. BHR 59 (1997) 613-620.

5006 *Bombeck, Stefan hallo* und *kona* im altäthiopischen Markusevangelium. BN 87 (1997) 5-12.

5007 ECahill, Michael Expositio evangelii secundum Marcum. CChr.SL 82: Turnhout 1997, Brepols 154*; 127 pp. 2-503-00821-6 [RBen 108,390s—Bogaert, P.-M.].

5008 ECilia, Lucio Marco e il suo vangelo. CinB 1997, San Paolo 156 pp. Atti del convegno internazionale di studi "il vangelo di Marco" Venezia, 30-31 maggio 1995. L28.000. 88-215-3436-7.

5009 **Fallon, Michael B.** The gospel according to Saint Mark: an introductory commentary. Kensington, NSW Australia 1997, Chevalier 293 pp. 0-86940-240-4.

5010 **Flanagan, Patrick J.** The gospel of Mark made easy. NY 1997, Paulist ix; 188 pp. Bibl. $20. 0-8091-3728-3.

5011 **Frinking, Bernard** La parole est tout près de toi: apprendre l'évangile pour apprendre à le vivre. 1996, ⇒12,4771. REeV 98 (1997) 64-65 *(Quesnel, M.)*.

5012 **Garland, David E.** Mark. NIV. application commentary. GR 1996, Zondervan 653 pp. Bibl. 0-310-49350-1.

5013 *Ghiberti, Giuseppe* Marco a Qumrân: esegesi e fede. Marco e il suo vangelo. 1997, ⇒5008. ECilia, Lucio, 141-149.

5014 **Gundry, Robert H.** Mark: a commentary on his apology for the cross. 1993, ⇒8,5144... 12,4772. REvQ 69/1 (1997) 72-74 *(Edwards, Ruth B.)*; SJTh 50/1 (1997) 118-120 *(Best, Ernest)*.

5015 **Hare, Douglas R.A.** Mark. 1996, ⇒12,4773. RABR 45 (1997) 81-82 *(Watson, Nigel M.)*.

5016 **Hooker, Morna D.** The Gospel according to Saint Mark. 1991, ⇒7,4268... 11/1,3314. RBTB 27 (1997) 72 *(McVann, Mark)*.

5017   **Kiraz, George Anton** Mark. Comparative edition of the Syriac gospels, 2. NTTS 21/2: 1996, ⇒12,4777. ᴿNT 39 (1997) 405-414 *(Baarda, T.)*.

5018   **Lafrenière, Bernard** Traduction interlinéaire de l'évangile selon saint Marc. Montréal 1996, Fides 224 pp. SR 26 (1997) 362-364 *(Bonneau, Guy)*.

5019   **Lamarche, Paul** Évangile de Marc: commentaire. EtB 33: 1996, ⇒12,4778. ᴿEThL 73 (1997) 179-180 *(Neirynck, F.)*; ETR 72 (1997) 611-612 *(Cuvillier, Élian)*.

5020   **Légasse, Simon** L'évangile de Marc. LeDiv.Commentaires 5: P 1997, Cerf 1047 pp.; 2 vols. FF500. 2-204-05588-3 [ETR 73,309].

5021   Marcus: evangelie. Den Bosch 1997, Katholieke Bijbelstichting 80 pp. *f*12.50. 90-6173-676-5 [Str. 65,285].

5022   **Mateos, Juan; Camacho Acosta, Fernando** Mc 1,1-6,6. Il vangelo di Marco: analisi linguistica e commento. Assisi 1997, Cittadella 559 pp. ᴿTer. 48 (1997) 883-886 *(Pasquetto, Virgilio)*.

5023   **Peter, Roger** Il vangelo: istruzioni per l'uso: con il testo integrale del vangelo secondo Marco. Bibbia e spiritualità: Mi 1997, Paoline 159 pp. 88-315-1316-8.

5024   **Riehl, Christian** Matthaeus & Markus. Bibel 2000, 15: Stu 1997, Katholisches Bibelwerk 176 pp. DM68. 3-460-02015-6 [OrdKor 39,255].

5025   **Standaert, Benoît** L'évangile selon Marc: commentaire. LiBi 61/2: P 1997, Cerf 207 pp. FF120. 2-204-05577-8 [EeV 107,63].

5026   *Thiede, Carsten Peter* San Marco e san Matteo: frammento di Qumrân 7Q5 e frammento dei Oxford P64: nuovi risultati della nostra ricerca sul papiro più antico. Marco e il suo vangelo. 1997, ⇒5008. ᴱCilia, Lucio, 124-140.

5027   ᵀTorró, Joaquín Pascual HIE RONYMUS: comentario al evangelio de San Marcos. ᴱGuerrero Martínez, Fernando: Biblioteca de Patrística 5: M 1995, Ciudad Nueva 133 pp. 84-86987-85-7.

5028   **Van Iersel, Bas** Marcus uitgelegd aan andere lezers. Baarn 1997, Gooi en Sticht 468 pp. *f*85. 90-317-1287-6 [Str. 65,665—Beentjes, Panc].

## F6.2 *Evangelium Marci*, Themata

5029   **Aichele, George** Jesus framed: biblical limits. 1996, ⇒12,4792. ᴿJThS 48 (1997) 582-584 *(Moore, Stephen D.)*; NeoTest. 31 (1997) 414-415 *(Van Eck, Ernest)*.

5030   *Aichele, George* Rewriting Superman. The monstrous. 1997, ⇒169. ᴱAichele, G., 75-101.

5031   ᴱ**Anderson, Janice Capel; Moore, Stephen D.** Mark and method. ⇒8,336; 9,4918. ᴿVJTR 61/9 (1997) 644-645 *(Meagher, P.M.)*.

5032   *Autané, Maurice* Le vrai secret de Jésus selon Marc. DosB 69 (1997) 6-8.

5033   **Beck, Robert R.** Nonviolent story: narrative conflict in the gospel of Mark. 1996, ⇒12,4794. ᴿAThR 79/2 (1997) 264-265 *(Good, Deirdre)*.

5034   *Biguzzi, Giancarlo* Marco, il tempio e la vera adorazione. Marco e il suo vangelo. 1997, ⇒5008. ᴱCilia, Lucio, 57-65.

5035  **Black, C. Clifton** Mark: images of an apostolic interpreter. 1994,
⇒10,4738... 12,4795. [R]TJT 13/1 (1997) 96-97 *(Kozar, Joseph V.)*.

5036  *Black, C.C.* The evangelist Mark: some reflections out of season.
Theol. 100 (1997) 35-42.

5037  **Bolt, Peter** 'Do you not care that we are perishing?': Jesus' defeat
of death and Mark's early readers. Diss. London 1997; [D]*Stanton,
G.* [RTL 29,583].

5038  **Bonneau, Guy** Le prophète Marc: fonctions communautaires et
stratégies rédactionelles du second évangile. Diss. Montréal 1995;
[D]*Myre, André* [SR 26,527].

5039  *Borrell, Agustí* Jesús i el mar en l'evangeli de Marc. La Bíblia i el
Mediterrani. 1997, ⇒385. [E]Borrell, d'Agustí, 263-279.

5040  *Botha, Pieter J.J.* Mark's story of Jesus and the search for virtue.
The rhetorical analysis. JSNT.S 146: 1997, ⇒336. [E]Porter, S.E.,
156-184.

5041  **Boyer, Mark G.** Day by ordinary day with Mark. NY 1997, Alba
xx; 204 pp. $13 [BiTod 36,263—Senior, Donald].

5042  *Breytenbach, Cilliers* Das Markusevangelium, Psalm 110,1 und
118,22f: Folgetext und Prätext. The scriptures in the gospels.
BEThL 131: 1997, ⇒234. [E]Tuckett, C.M., 197-222.

5043  *Campos, Dilmo Franco de* Quem é Jesus. RCB 21 (1997) 133-138.

5044  *Collins, Adela Yarbro* The appropriation of the Psalms of individual lament by Mark. The scriptures in the gospels. BEThL 131:
1997, ⇒234. [E]Tuckett, C.M., 223-241 [Ps 69].

5045  *Davies, Stevan L.; Johnson, Kevin* Mark's use of the Gospel of
Thomas, 2. Neotest. 31 (1997) 233-261.

5046  *Delorme, J.* Évangile et récit: la narration evangélique en Marc.
NTS 43 (1997) 367-384.

5047  **Dwyer, Timothy** The motif of wonder in the gospel of Mark.
JSNT.S 128: 1996, ⇒12,4804. [R]CBQ 59 (1997) 575-576
*(Thompson, Mary R.)*.

5048  [E]**Elliott, J.K.** The language and style of the gospel of Mark: an
edition of Ch.H. TURNER's "Notes on Marcan usage" together
with other comparable studies [*Kilpatrick, G.; Turner, N.*]. NT.S
71: 1993 <1928>, ⇒9,4936... 11/1,3351. [R]Augustinus 42 (1997)
408-409 *(Eguiarte, Enrique)*.

5049  *Elliott, J.K.* Mark and the teaching of Jesus: an examination of
λόγος and εὐαγγέλιον. NT.S 89: 1997, ⇒7. [F]BAARDA T., 37-45.

5050  **Feagin, Glyndle M.** Irony and the kingdom in Mark: a literary-
critical study. Mellen 56: Lewiston, NY 1997 Mellen iii; 264 pp.
Bibl. 0-7734-2435-0.

5051  **Fink, Renate Maria** Die Botschaft des heilenden Handelns Jesu:
Untersuchung der dreizehn exemplarischen Berichte von Jesu hei-
lendem Handeln im Markusevangelium. Diss. Innsbruck 1996/97;
[D]*Hasitschka, Martin* 226 pp. [BZ 42,316].

5052  *Focant, Camille* Le rapport à la loi dans l'évangile de Marc. La
loi. LeDiv 168: 1997, ⇒195. [E]Focant, Camille, 175-205.

5053  **Francis, Leslie J.** Personality type and scripture: exploring Mark's
gospel. Oxf 1997, Mowbray vi; 154 pp. £10. 0-304-70087-8.

5054  **Geysels, Luc** De weg van de dienaar: lezen in het Marcusevange-
lie. Lv 1997, Davidsfonds 279 pp. 90-6152-976-X [EThL
74,301*].

5055  **Harrington, Wilfrid J.** Mark: realistic theologian: the Jesus of
Mark. 1996, ⇒12,4812. [R]DoLi 47/1 (1997) 60-61 *(Mangan, C.)*.

5056  *Hartmann, Lars* Das Markusevangelium, 'für die lectio sollemnis im Gottesdienst abgefaßt'?. Text-centered NT studies. WUNT 102: 1997 <1996>, ⇒132. 25-51.

5057  *Heil, John Paul* The narrative strategy and pragmatics of the temple theme in Mark. CBQ 59 (1997) 76-100.

5058  *Hooker, Morna D.* Mark's vision for the church. 1997, ⇒93. FSweet J., 33-43.

5059  **Humphrey, Hugh M.** 'He is risen!': a new reading of Mark's gospel. 1992, ⇒8,5790; 10,4725. REstB 55 (1997) 552-553 *(Asenjo, J.).*

5060  *Iriarte, José Luiz* Perspectivas cristológicas de Marcos. RCB 21 (1997) 117-123.

5061  **Juel, Donald H.** A master of surprise: Mark interpreted. 1994, ⇒10,4768; 12,4818. RCBQ 59 (1997) 161-162 *(Rhoads, David).*

5062  **Kapkin, David** Marcos: historia humana del Hijo de Dios. Escuela Bíblica: Medellín 1997, Centro Carismático Minuto de Dios vii; 720 pp. Bibl.

5063  *Kato, Zenji* Das Reich Gottes, verkündigt durch den als Gottessohn bevollmächtigten Jesus: ein Entwurf der Interpretation des Markus-Evangeliums, 1. Kwansei-Gakuin-Daigaku 2 (1997) 1-18.

5064  *Kingsbury, Jack Dean* The significance of the cross within Mark's story. Gospel interpretation. 1997, ⇒210. EKingsbury, J., 95-105.

5065  **Kinukawa, Hisako** Women and Jesus in Mark: a Japanese feminist perspective. 1994, ⇒10,8738... 12,4819. RHBT 19/1 (1997) 89 *(Thurston, Bonnie).*

5066  **Kmiecik, Ulrich** Der Menschensohn im Markusevangelium. Diss. Bonn 1995; FzB 81: Wü 1997, Echter 335 pp. DM48. 3-429-01861-7 [NThAR 1997,292].

5067  *Magnante, Antonio* Missionary theology in the gospel of Mark. Omnis Terra 31 (1997) 78-85.

5068  **Marshall, Christopher D.** Faith as a theme in Mark's narrative. MSSNTS 94: 1995, ⇒5,4920... 12,4828. RAThR 79/1 (1997) 71-73 *(Graham, Holt).*

5069  *Martins Terra, João Evangelista* Cristo no evangelho de Marcos;

5070  O segredo messiânico;

5071  Questionário: evangelho de Marcos;

5072  *Matos Félix, Paulo de* Títulos de Jesus no evangelho de Marcos. RCB 21 (1997) 3-18/9-24/25-64/110-116.

5073  **Meadors, Edward P.** Jesus the messianic herald of salvation. WUNT 2/72: 1995, ⇒9,4958... 12,4831 [Peabody 1997, Hendrickson $20. 1-56563-268-0—BiTod 35,325]. REvQ 69 (1997) 161-162 *(France, Dick)*; TJT 13 (1997) 283-284 *(Kloppenborg, John S.).*

5074  **Monari, L.** Messagio del vangelo di Marco. Bo ²1997, EDB 192 pp. L18.000 [RivBib 45,256].

5075  *Monshouwer, Dirk* Marcus literair. ITBT 5/2 (1997) 25-26 [Jer 13,12; John 2,1-11].

5076  **Müller, Peter** 'Wer ist dieser?': Jesus im Markusevangelium. BThSt 27: 1995, ⇒11/1,3382; 12,4834. RZThK 119 (1997) 234-235 *(Huber, Konrad).*

5077  *Nascimento, Ademar L.* Perspectivas cristológicas de Marcos. RCB 21 (1997) 124-132.

5078  *Navarro, Mercedes* ¿Quién eres?: ¿quién soy?: siete encuentros con Jesús según el evangelio de Marcos. SalTer 85 (1997) 307-322.

5079 *O'Callaghan, José* Il vangelo di Marco e Qumran. Marco e il suo vangelo. 1997, ⇒5008. [E]Cilia, Lucio, 117-123.

5080 **Painter, John** Mark's gospel: worlds in conflict. NT Readings: L 1997, Routledge xvii; 245 pp. £40/£14. 0-415-11364-4/5-2 [NTS 43,622].

5081 **Perry, John Michael** Exploring the messianic secret in Mark's gospel. Kansas City 1997, Sheed & W xii; 173 pp. 1-55612-924-6.

5082 **Phillips, Vicki C.** Women's speech and silence in the gospel of Mark. Diss. Vanderbilt 1997; [D]*Patte, Daniel* [RTL 29,587].

5083 *Pokorný, Petr* 'Anfang des Evangeliums': zum Problem des Anfangs und des Schlusses des Markusevangeliums < 1977 >

5084 Die Bedeutung des Markusevangeliums für die Entstehung der christlichen Bibel < 1995 >. Bibelauslegung. WUNT 100: 1997, ⇒970. 237-253/255-273.

5085 *Powell, Mark Allen* Toward a narrative-critical understanding of Mark;

5086 *Rhoads, David* Losing life for others in the face of death: Mark's standards of judgment. Gospel interpretation. 1997, ⇒210. [E]Kingsbury, J.D., 65-70/83-94.

5087 **Robbins, Vernon K.** New boundaries in old territories: form and social rhetoric in Mark. 1994, ⇒10,4789. [R]TJT 13/1 (1997) 116-117 (*LeMarquand, Grant*).

5088 *Rodrigues dos Santos, Gilvan* Retalhos da cristologia de Marcos. RCB 21 (1997) 101-109.

5089 *Rohrbaugh, Richard L.* The social location of the Markan audience. Gospel interpretation. 1997, ⇒210. [E]Kingsbury, J.D., 106-122.

5090 **Rolin, Patrice** Les controverses dans l'évangile de Marc. Diss. Montpellier-Paris 1997; [D]*Vouga, M.* 383 pp. [RTL 29,587].

5091 *Santos, Narry F.* The paradox of authority and servanthood in the gospel of Mark. BS 154 (1997) 452-460.

5092 **Scholtissek, Klaus** Die Vollmacht Jesu: traditions- und redaktionsgeschichtliche Analysen zu einem Leitmotiv markinischer Christologie. NTA 25: 1992, ⇒8,5179... 11/1,3397. [R]BiKi 52/1 (1997) 49-50 (*Backhaus, Knut*); ThRv 93/5 (1997) 389-390 (*Fendler, Folkert*).

5093 *Schreiber, Johannes* Die Sonne im Markusevangelium: Hinweise zur Eschatologie und Schöpfungslehre des Markus. BZNW 89: 1997, ⇒33. [F]GRAESSER E., 355-374.

5094 *Silva Ramos, Jadson da* Uma leitura de política da história de Jesus em Marcos. RCB 21 (1997) 139-146.

5095 *Stock, Klemens* I discepoli nel vangelo di san Marco. Marco e il suo vangelo. 1997, ⇒5008. [E]Cilia, Lucio, 17-32.

5096 *Stowasser, Martin* Gottes Herrschaft: Überlegungen zur narrativen Soteriologie des Markusevangeliums. StAns 124: 1997, ⇒57. [F]LOEHRER M. — TRAGAN P., 327-364.

5097 *Swartley, Willard M.* The role of women in Mark's gospel: a narrative analysis. BTB 27 (1997) 16-22 [Mk 5,24-34; 7,24-30; 12,41-44; 14,3-9].

5098 *Tolbert, Mary Ann* How the gospel of Mark builds character. Gospel interpretation. 1997, ⇒210. [E]Kingsbury, J.D., 71-82.

5099 **Trombatore, Stefano** In compagnia degli ultimi: lettura del vangelo di Marco. R 1997, Città N 143 pp. 88-311-3621-6.

5100  **Van Eck, Ernest** Galilee and Jerusalem in Mark's story of Jesus: a narratological and social scientific reading. HTS.S 7: 1995, ⇒11/1,3348. ᴿJThS 48 (1997) 187-188 *(Carleton Paget, James)*; ThLZ 122 (1997) 802-804 *(Reinmuth, Eckart)*.

5101  **Van Oyen, Geert** De studie van de Marcusredactie in de twintigste eeuw. SNTA 18: 1993, ⇒9,4963... 11/1,3384. ThRv 93 (1997) 393-394 *(Suhl, Alfred)*.

5102  *Vignolo, Roberto* Cercare Gesù: tema e forma del vangelo di Marco. Marco e il suo vangelo. 1997, ⇒5008. ᴱCilia, Lucio, 77-114.

5103  *Vignolo, Roberto* 'Tutti ti cercano!' (Mc 1,37): cercare Gesù come tema e forma del vangelo di Marco. PSV 35 (1997) 89-125.

5104  *Vouga, François* Mündliche Tradition, soziale Kontrolle und Literatur als theologischer Protest: die Wahrheit des Evangeliums nach Paulus und Markus. Logos. TANZ 20: 1997, ⇒229. ᴱSellin, G., 195-209.

5105  *Walter, Nikolaus* Das Markus-Evangelium und Rom: das kanonische Markus-Evangelium als überarbeitete Fassung des ursprünglichen Textes. Praeparatio evangelica. WUNT 98: 1997 <1978>, ⇒167. 78-94.

5106  **Watts, Rikki E.** Isaiah's new exodus and Mark. WUNT 2/88: Tü 1997, Mohr xvi; 479 pp. Bibl. DM128. 3-16-146222-X.

5107  *Woodroof, Tim* The church as boat in Mark: building a seaworthy church. RestQ 39/4 (1997) 231-249.

5108  *Xavier, Aldo* O caminho do seguimento de Jesus. RCB 21 (1997) 94-100.

5109  **Zager, Werner** Gottesherrschaft und Endgericht in der Verkündigung Jesu: eine Untersuchung zur markinischen Jesusüberlieferung einschliesslich der Q-Parallelen. BZNW 82: 1996, ⇒12,4859. ᴿThLZ 122 (1997) 571-573 *(Oehler, Markus)*.

### F6.3 Evangelii Marci versiculi

5110  *Hooker, Morna D.* A dramatic key: Mark 1.1-13. Beginnings. 1997, ⇒136. 1-22.

5111  *Moitel, Pierre* Marc 1,1-15: commencement de la bonne nouvelle de Jésus Christ. CEv 98 (1997) 54-60.

5112  *Dormeyer, Detlev* Mk 1,1-15 als Prolog des ersten idealbiographischen Evangeliums von Jesus Christus. Bibl.Interp. 5 (1997) 181-211.

5113  *Rius-Camps, Josep* Les variants de la recensió occidental de l'*evangeli de Marc* (I) (Mc 1,1-15). RCatT 22 (1997) 163-177.

5114  *Biguzzi, Giancarlo* I tempi e i luoghi in Mc 1,1-39. PSV 36 (1997) 111-126.

5115  *Cárdenas Pallares, José* ¿Quién es Jesús?: primeros intentos por aclarar el enigma (Mc 1,9-10). EfMex 15 (1997) 247-263.

5116  *Sieg, Franciszek* 'Króleswo Boże przybliżyło się' (Mk 1,15) ['The kingdom of God is near' (Mark 1:15b)]. Sum. 318. WST 10 (1997) 309-318. P.

5117  *Rius-Camps, Josep* Les variants de la recensió occidental de l'*evangeli de Marc* (II) (Mc 1,16-28). RCatT 22 (1997) 409-419.

5118  *Granger Cook, John* In defence of ambiguity: is there a hidden demon in Mark 1.29-31?. NTS 43 (1997) 184-208.

FRAVANELLI V.,   Entrarono a Cafarnao: lettura interdisciplinare di Mc 1 ⇒74.

5119  **Klauck, Hans-Josef** Vorspiel im Himmel?: Erzähltechnik und Theologie im Markusprolog. BThSt 32: Neuk 1997, Neuk 128 pp. Bibl. DM38. 3-7887-1643-6.

5120  **Czajkowski, Michal** Galilejskie spory Jezusa: struktura kerygmatyczna Mk. 2,1-3,6. Wsz 1997, Wydawnictwa Akademii Teologii Katolickiej 203 pp. 83-7072-073-0. **P.**

5121  *Graziani, Domenico* Mc 2,18-20: la gioia incompiuta dell'incontro nell'attesta / II. ⇒12,4872. Vivarium 5 (1997) 17-37.

5122  *Schenk, Wolfgang* Die rhetorische Funktion der Fastenwarnung Mk 2,20. NT.S 89: 1997, ⇒7. FBAARDA T., 251-276.

5123  *Kanjirakompil, Cherian* New wine into fresh wineskins: an exegetical study on Mk 2:21-22. BiBh 23 (1997) 245-255.

5124  *Müller, Stefanie* Ist der Sabbat für den Menschen geschaffen?: zum jüdischen Sabbatverständnis (Mk 2,23-28). Antijudaismus im NT. KT 149: 1997, ⇒K8. EHenze, Dagmar, 114-125.

5125  *Gamba, Giuseppe Giov.* Struttura redazionale e tematica dottrinale di Marco 3,20-35. BSRel 125: 1997, ⇒45. FJAVIERRE ORTAS A., 69-99.

5126  *Ayers, James* Mark 3:20-35. Interp. 51 (1997) 178-182.

5127  *Fusco, Vittorio* Vangelo e parabola (Mc 4,1-34). Marco e il suo vangelo. 1997, ⇒5008. ECilia, Lucio, 33-45.

5128  *Peters, Donald* Vulnerable promise from the land (Mark 4:3b-8): the parable of the sower/soils. Jesus and his parables. 1997, ⇒230. EShillington, V.G., 69-84.

5129  *Focant, Camille* La recontextualisation d'Is 6,9-10 en Mc 4,10-12, ou un exemple de non-citation. The scriptures in the gospels. BEThL 131: 1997, ⇒234. ETuckett, C.M., 143-175.

5130  *Bauer, Johannes B.* Et adicietur vobis credentibus Mk 4,24f. Studien zu Bibeltext. 1997 < 1980 >, ⇒111. 209-214.

5131  *Kittel, Gisela* "Wer ist der?" Markus 4,35-41 und der mehrfache Sinn der Schrift. BZNW 86: 1997, ⇒41. FHOFIUS O., 519-542.

5132  *Cilia, Lucio* 'Perché avete paura?': la paura del discepolo nel racconto della tempesta sedata (Mc 4,35-41). Marco e il suo vangelo. 1997, ⇒5008. ECilia, Lucio, 46-56.

5133  *Ulrichs, Karl Friedrich* "... und viele miteinander waren bei ihm": ein textkritischer und formgeschichtlicher Vorschlag zu Mk 4,36b. ZNW 88 (1997) 187-196.

5134  *Marcus, Joel* Blanks and gaps in the Markan parable of the sower. Bibl.Interp. 5 (1997) 247-262 [Mk 4].

5135  *Müller, Peter* Wie werdet ihr alle Gleichnisse verstehen?: die Gleichnisse vom Säen, Wachsen und Fruchtbringen in Markus 4. Lesen und Leben. 1997, ⇒205. 53-97.

5136  *Juel, Donald H.* Plundering Satan's house: Mark 5:1-20. Word and World 17/3 (1997) 278-281 [ZID 23,415].

5137  **Oppel, Dagmar** Heilsam erzählen—erzählend heilen: die Heilung der Blutflüssigen und die Erweckung der Jairustochter in Mk 5,21-43 als Beispiel markinischer Erzählfertigkeit. BBB 102: 1995. ⇒9,5010; 11/1,3454. RThRv 93 (1997) 19-20 *(Scholtissek, Klaus)*.

5138  *Fonrobert, Charlotte* The woman with a blood-flow (Mark 5.24-34) revisited: menstrual laws and Jewish culture in christian feminist hermeneutics. Early christian interpretation. JSNT.S 148: 1997, ⇒191. EEvans, C.A., 121-140.

5139  *Loba-Mkole, Jean-Claude* Une femme qui sait se libérer (Mc 5,25-34). Revue africaine des sciences de la mission  7 (1997) 29-41 [ThIK 21/1,27].

5140  *Janssen, Claudia* Verachtet und ausgegrenzt?: Menstruation und jüdisches Frauenleben (Mk 5,25-34).      Antijudaismus im NT. KT 149: 1997, ⇒κ8. ᴱHenze, Dagmar, 98-106.

5141  *Bauer, Johannes B.* Das "Regelwort" Mk 6,4par und EvThom 31. BZ 41 (1997) 95-98.

5142  *Delorme, Jean* La tête de Jean Baptiste ou la parole pervertie: lecture d'un récit (Marc 6, 14-29). La bible en littérature. 1997, ⇒315. ᴱBeaude, Pierre-Marie, 293-311.

5143  *Zink-Sawyer, Beverly* Mark 6:30-34. Interp. 51 (1997) 288-291.

5144  *Borrell, Agustí* Gesù pastore e maestro in Mc 6,34. StAns 124: 1997, ⇒57. ꟳLOEHRER M. — TRAGAN P., 365-375.

5145  *Martins Terra, João Evangelista* Papiro 7Q5 de Qumran e a nova datação dos evangelhos sinóticos. RCB 21 (1997) 65-93.

5146  *Scibona, Rocco* Un frammento di Marco a Qumran?: ipotesi sulla comunità cristiana di Gerico. Asp. 44 (1997) 385-400 [Mk 6,52-53].

5147  *O'Callaghan, José* Il vangelo di Marco e Qumrán. Marco e il suo vangelo. 1997, ⇒5008. ᴱCilia, Lucio, 117-123 [Mk 6,52-53].

5148  *Carrón, Julián; González Núñez, Jacinto* Il testo del papiro 7Q5 e l'originale aramaico di Mc 6,53    Marco e il suo vangelo. 1997, ⇒5008. ᴱCilia, Lucio, 150-156.

5149  *Nardoni, Enrique* Lo puro y lo impuro en Marcos 7:1-23: la respuesta del lector. RevBib 59/3 (1997) 135-154.

5150  *Chilton, Bruce* A generative exegesis of Mark 7:1-23. Jesus in context. AGAJ 39: 1997, ⇒183. ᴱChilton, B., 297-317.

5151  *Pokorný, Petr* From a puppy to the child: some problems of contemporary biblical exegesis demonstrated from Mark 7.24-30/Matt 15.21-8. Bibelauslegung. WUNT 100: 1997 <1995>, ⇒970. 69-85.

5152  *Roure, Damia* The narrative of the Syro-Phoenician woman as metaphorical discourse (Mark 7,24-30). StAns 124: 1997, ⇒57. ꟳLOEHRER M. — TRAGAN P., 377-396.

5153  *Camacho Acosta, Fernando* La sirofenicia de Mc 7,26, figura representativa de la élite dirigente pagana. La Bíblia i el Mediterrani. 1997, ⇒385. ᴱBorrell, d'Agustí, 123-130.

5154  *Zani, Lorenzo* 'Effatà, cioè: apriti!' (Mc 7,31-37). Presbyteri 31 (1997) 304-310, 379-384.

5155  *Marcus, Joel* Scripture and tradition in Mark 7. The scriptures in the gospels. BEThL 131: 1997, ⇒234. ᴱTuckett, C.M., 177-195.

5156  **García Pérez, Prudencio** Mc 8,22b-26: el itinerario de los discípulos hacia la fe. Diss. Pont. Univ. S. Thomae 1997; ᴰDe Santis, Luca M. xi; 234 pp. excerpt.

5157  *Kasiłowski, Piotr* Zapowiedź śmierci Jezusa a postawy uczniów w Mk 8,27-10,52 [L'annonce de la mort de Jésus et les attitudes des disciples (Mc 8,27-10,52)]. Rés. 124. Bobolanum 8 (1997) 111-125.

5158  *Jonge, Henk Jan de* The sayings on confessing and denying Jesus in Q 12:8-9 and Mark 8:38. NT.S 89: 1997, ⇒7. ꟳBAARDA T., 105-121.

5159 *Vidović, Marinko* Isusovo preobraženje (Mk 9,2-9) [Jesus' transfiguration (Mk 9,2-9)]. Sum. 150. Obnovljeni Život 52/2 (1997) 111-150. **Croatian.**

5160 *Bagni, Arcangelo* 'Ascoltatelo' (Mc 9,2-10). PaVi 42/2 (1997) 52-55.

5161 *Bammel, Ernst* Markus 10,11f und das jüdische Eherecht. Judaica et Paulina. WUNT 91: 1997 <1991>, ⇒109. 171-177.

5162 *Mangatt, George* Jesus and children (Mk 10:13-16). BiBh 23/1 (1997) 14-26.

5163 *Guenzi, Pier Davide* Anche la fede ha problemi di qualità. Vocazioni 14/1 (1997) 17-23 [Mk 10,17-22].

5164 **Leal Salazar, Gabriel** El seguimiento de Jesús según la tradición del rico: estudio redaccional y diacrónico de Mc 10,17-31. EMISJ 31: 1996, ⇒12,4921. [R]LASBF 47 (1997) 586-588 *(Bissoli, Giovanni)*.

5165 *Pavanello, Massimo* Gesù fissatolo lo amò (Mc 10,20): un difficile dialogo tra i giovani e Cristo. Ambrosius 73/1 (1997) 83-88.

5166 *Bosowski, Andrzej* Hipotetyczna pierwsza katecheza Jezusa o dobrach materialnych ze szczególnym uwzględnieniem logionu Mk 10,24 [The first hypothetical catechesis of Jesus about material goods and the logion Mk 10.24]. 1997, ⇒52. [F]LACH J., 55-75. **P.**

5167 *Gundry, Robert H.* Mark 10:29: order in the list. CBQ 59 (1997) 465-475.

5168 *Eltrop, Bettina* Dienen ist ein Männerproblem: sozialgeschichtliche Bibelauslegung zu Markus 10,35-45. JK 58 (1997) 93-95.

5169 *Collins, Adela Yarbro* The signification of Mark 10:45 among gentile christians. HThR 90 (1997) 371-382.

5170 *Charlesworth, J.H.* The Son of David: Solomon and Jesus (Mark 10.47). NT and Hellenistic Judaism. 1997, ⇒318. [E]Borgen, P., 72-87.

5171 *Krause, Deborah* The one who comes unbinding the blessing of Judah: Mark 11.1-10 as a midrash on Genesis 49.11, Zechariah 9.9, and Psalm 118.25-26. Early christian interpretation. JSNT.S 148: 1997, ⇒191. [E]Evans, C.A., 141-153.

5172 *Böttrich, Christfried* Jesus und der Feigenbaum: Mk 11:12-14,20-25 in der Diskussion. NT 39 (1997) 328-359.

5173 *Evans, Craig A.* From "House of Prayer" to "Cave of Robbers": Jesus' prophetic criticism of the temple establishment. 1997, ⇒77. [F]SANDERS J., 417-442 [Isa 56,1-7; Jer 7,11-15; Mk 11,15-18].

5174 *Betz, Hans Dieter* Jesus and the purity of the temple (Mark 11:15-18): a comparative religion approach. JBL 116 (1997) 455-472.

5175 *Bauer, Johannes B.* Christus sidereus: die Tempelaustreibung, HIERONYMUS und das Nazaräerevangelium. Studien zu Bibeltext. 1997 <1989>, ⇒111. 226-241 [Mk 11,15-18; John 2,13-22].

5176 *Evans, Craig A.* Jesus' action in the temple: cleansing or portent of destruction?. Jesus in context. AGAJ 39: 1997 <1989>, ⇒183. [E]Chilton, B., 395-439 [Mk 11,15-18].

5177 *Casey, P. M.* Culture and historicity: the cleansing of the temple. CBQ 59 (1997) 306-332 [Mk 11,15-18].

5178 **Mell, Ulrich** Die "anderen" Winzer... Mk 11,27-12,34. WUNT 2/77: 1994, ⇒10,4850...12,4932. [R]JBL 116 (1997) 744-746 *(Marcus, Joel)*.

5179 *Van Veldhuizen, Piet* De boom en de berg in Marcus 11. ITBT 5/1 (1997) 15-17.

5180 *Bammel, Ernst* Das Gleichnis von den bösen Winzern (Mk 12,1-9) und das jüdische Erbrecht. Judaica et Paulina. WUNT 91: 1997 <1959>, ⇒109. 178-184.

5181 *Schottroff, Luise* Sind die Juden schuld am Tod Jesu?: das Kreuz Christi (Mk 12,1-12). Antijudaismus im NT. KT 149: 1997, ⇒к8. EHenze, Dagmar, 70-78.

5182 *Robinson, Bernard P.* 'They are as angels in heaven': Jesus' alleged riposte to the Sadducees (Mark 12:18-27; par. Mt 22:23-33, Lk 20:27-40). NBl 78 (1997) 530-537.

5183 *Koet, Bart J.* Mk 12,28-34: Übereinstimmung im Kern der Sache. The scriptures in the gospels. BEThL 131: 1997, ⇒234. ETuckett, C.M., 513-523.

5184 *Norfleet, Agnes W.* Mark 12:28-34. Interp. 51 (1997) 403-406.

5185 *Schwarz, Günther* "Die Häuser der Witwen verzehren"? (Markus 12,40 / Lk 20,47). BN 88 (1997) 45-46.

5186 *Beutler, Johannes* Die Gabe der armen Witwe: Mk 12,41-44. FKAMPHAUS F., 1997, ⇒46. 125-136 [ThRv 94,625].

5187 *Smith, Geoffrey* A closer look at the widow's offering: Mark 12:41-44. JETS 40 (1997) 27-36.

5188 *Jensen, Darcy D.* The widow's mite. Word and World 17/3 (1997) 282-288 [Mk 12,42] [ZID 23,415].

5189 *Verheyden, Joseph* Describing the parousia: the cosmic phenomena in Mk 13,24-25. The scriptures in the gospels. BEThL 131: 1997, ⇒234. ETuckett, C.M., 525-550.

5190 *Lamb, Regene* Endgericht oder Verheißung?: Eschatologie/Apokalyptik zur Zeit des Zweiten Tempels (Mk 13,28-33). Antijudaismus im NT. KT 149: 1997, ⇒к8. EHenze, Dagmar, 158-163.

5191 *Taylor, N.H.* Interpretation of scripture as an indicator of socio-historical context: the case of eschatological discourses of Mark and Q. The scriptures in the gospels. BEThL 131: 1997, ⇒234. ETuckett, C.M., 459-467 [Mk 13; Lk 17,22-37].

5192 *Standaert, Benoît* Il discorso in Mc 13. PSV 36 (1997) 127-138.

5193 *Zuurmond, Rochus* Profetische exegese. ITBT 5/1 (1997) 8-11 [Mk 13].

5194 *Adams, Edward* Historical crisis and cosmic crisis in Mark 13 and Lucan's "civil war". TynB 48 (1997) 329-344.

F6.8 Passio secundum Marcum, 14,1... [⇒5.3]

5195 **Hanhart, Karel** The open tomb, a new approach: Mark's Passover haggada (72 C.E.). 1995, ⇒11/1,3551. RCBQ 59 (1997) 156-158 *(Pilch, John J.)*.

5196 *Maggioni, Bruno* Passione e croce nel vangelo di Marco. Marco e il suo vangelo. 1997, ⇒5008. ECilia, Lucio, 66-76.

5197 **Wilkinson, Nicole** Making life make sense: ritual and meaning in Mark's Passion. Diss. Vanderbilt 1997; DPatte, Daniel [RTL 29,588].

5198 **Willert, Niels** Den korsfæstede konge kristologi og discipelbillede i Markus-eveangeliets passionsfortelling [The crucified king: christology and discipleship theme in Mark's Passion Narrative]. Diss. Aarhus 1997; 574 pp. [RTL 29,588].

5199 **Broadhead, Edwin K.** Prophet, son, messiah: narrative form and function in Mark 14-16. JSNT.S 97: 1994, ⇒10,4861; 11/1,3523. RCBQ 58 (1996) 152-153 *(Olsthoorn, Martin)*.

5200 *Wagner, Guy* L'onction de Béthanie: essai sur la genèse du récit de Marc 14/3-9 et sa reprise par Matthieu, Luc et Jean. ETR 72 (1997) 437-446.

5201 *McLain, Charles E.* Did Christ defend the status quo?: an examination of Mark 14:7. CBTJ 13/1 (1997) 31-56.

5202 *Casey, Maurice* The date of the passover sacrifices and Mark 14:12. TynB 48 (1997) 245-247.

5203 *Luke, K.* "This is my flesh" (Mark 14:22 and par.). ITS 34/1-3 (1997) 150-167.

5204 *Jonge, Marinus de* Mark 14:25 among Jesus' words about the kingdom of God. NT.S 89: 1997, ⇒7. FBAARDA T., 123-135.

5205 *Ghidelli, Carlo* 'Questo e il mio sangue, il sangue dell'alleanza' (Mc 14,29). PaVi 42/5 (1997) 34-40.

5206 *Derrett, J.D.* The prayer in Gethsemane (Mark 14:35-36). JHiC 4/1 (1997) 78-88.

5207 *Baarda, T.* 'Abba, Vader'. KeTh 48/1 (1997) 3-8 [Mk 14,35-36; Rom 8,15; Gal 4,6].

5208 *Jackson, Howard M.* Why the youth shed his cloak and fled naked: the meaning and purpose of Mark 14:51-52. JBL 116 (1997) 273-289.

5209 *Chilton, Bruce* The trial of Jesus reconsidered. Jesus in context. AGAJ 39: 1997 <1995>, ⇒183. EChilton, B., 481-500 [Mk 14,53-72].

5210 *Paulsen, Henning* Mk 16,1-8. Zur Literatur. WUNT 99: 1997 <1980>, ⇒153. 75-112.

5211 *Collins, Adela Yarbro* Apotheosis and resurrection. NT and Hellenistic Judaism. 1997 <1992>, ⇒318. EBorgen, P., 88-100 [Mk 16,1-8].

5212 *Dannemann, Irene* Aufstehen gegen die Entmutigung: sozialgeschichtliche Bibelauslegung zu Markus 16,1-8. JK 58 (1997) 157-160.

5213 *Perroni, Marinella* L'annuncio pasquale alle/delle donne (Mc 16,1-8): alle origini della tradizione kerygmatica. StAns 124: 1997, ⇒57. FLOEHRER M. — TRAGAN P., 397-436.

5214 **Danove, Paul L.** The end of Mark: a methodological study. 1993, ⇒9,5058; 11/1,3549. RAugustinus 42 (1997) 409-410 *(Éguiarte, Enrique)* [Mk 16].

# X. Opus Lucanum

## F7.1 *Opus Lucanum*—Luke-Acts

5215 **Allen, Oscar Wesley, Jr.** The death of Herod: the narrative and theological function of retribution in Luke-Acts. Diss. Emory, 1996; DJohnson, Luke Timothy: SBL.DS 158: Atlanta 1997, Scholars xi; 222 pp. $30. 0-7885-0359-6.

5216  **Arlandson, James Malcolm** Women, class, and society in early christianity: models from Luke-Acts. Peabody 1997, Hendrickson xvi; 238 pp. $25. 1-565-63181-1 [RRT 1998/1,44—Need, S.W.].

5217  *Ashworth, John* Hospitality in Luke-Acts. BiTod 35 (1997) 300-04.

5218  **Bergholz, Thomas** Der Aufbau des lukanischen Doppelwerkes. 1995, ⇒11/1,2554; 12,4988. ᴿThLZ 122 (1997) 31-32 *(Klein, Hans)*.

5219  **Böhm, Martina** Samarien und die Samaritai bei Lukas: eine Studie zum religionshistorischen und traditionsgeschichtlichen Hintergrund der lukanischen Samarientexte und zu deren topographischer Verhaftung. Diss. Leipzig 1997; ᴰ*Kähler, C.* 250 pp. [RTL 29,583].

5220  *Bovon, François* La loi dans l'oeuvre de Luc. La loi. LeDiv 168: 1997, ⇒195. ᴱFocant, C., 206-225.

5221  **Brawley, Robert Lawson** Text to text pours forth speech: voices of Scripture in Luke-Acts. 1995, ⇒11/1,3563. ᴿCBQ 59 (1997) 571-572 *(Gowler, David B.)*.

5222  *Brent, Allen* Luke-Acts and the imperial cult in Asia Minor. JThS 48 (1997) 411-438.

5223  **Cunningham, Scott** 'Through many tribulations': the theology of persecution in Luke-Acts. Diss. Dallas Theol. Sem. 1993; ᴰ*Bock, D.L.*: JSNT.S 142: Shf 1997, Academic 376 pp. $45. 1-85075-661-9.

5224  **Denova, Rebecca I.** The things accomplished among us: prophetic tradition in the structural pattern of Luke-Acts. JSNT.S 141: Shf 1997, Academic 260 pp. £40/$66. 1-85087-656-2.

5225  *Dickerson, Patrick L.* The new character narrative in Luke-Acts and the synoptic problem. JBL 116 (1997) 291-312.

5226  **Fletcher-Louis, Crispin H.T.** Luke-Acts: angels, christology and soteriology. WUNT 2/94: Tü 1997, Mohr xv; 357 pp. DM118. 3-16-146764-7.

5227  *Gilbert, Gary* The disappearance of the gentiles: God-fearers and the image of the Jews in Luke-Acts. 1997, ⇒82. ᶠSᴄʀᴏɢɢs R., 172-184.

5228  *González Echegaray, Joaquín* Las ciudades palestinas del siglo I: trasfondo cultural y su significado en la obra lucana. La Bíblia i el Mediterrani. 1997, ⇒385. ᴱBorrell, d'Agustí, 305-314.

5229  *Grilli, Massimo* Il tema dell''oggi' nell'opera lucana. PSV 36 (1997) 139-151.

5230  **Held, Heinz J.** Den Reichen wird das Evangelium gepredigt: die sozialen Zumutungen des Glaubens im Lukasevangelium und in der Apostelgeschichte. Neuk 1997, Neuk 88 pp. DM19.80. 3-7887-1641-X.

5231  **Kato, Takashi** La pensée sociale de Luc-Actes. EHPhR 76: P 1997, Presses Universitaires de France xii; 377 pp. FF198. 2-13-0478-514 [RHPhR 77,251].

5232  *Kudasiewicz, Józef* 'Gdy Duch Święty zstąpi na was, otrzymacie Jegto moc i będziecie moimi świadkami...' (Dz 1,8; Łk 24,48n): studium z teologii świętego Łukasza [...When the Holy Spirit has come upon you, you shall receive power and you shall be my witnesses...' (Acts 1.8; Luke 24.48f): a study on the theology of Saint Luke]. 1997, ⇒52. ᶠLᴀᴄʜ J., 187-209. **P.**

5233  *Kunnatholy, Abraham* The Lucan Jesus: the Indian missionary model. Sum. 335. VJTR 61 (1997) 335-347.

5234 *Kurz, William S.* The open-ended nature of Luke and Acts as inviting canonical actualisation. Neotest. 31 (1997) 289-308.

5235 **Lane, Thomas Joseph** Luke and the gentile mission: gospel anticipates Acts. EHS.T 571: 1996, ⇒12,5006. RMilltown Studies 39 (1997) 147-150 *(Byrne, Patrick)*.

5236 **Löning, Karl** Israels Hoffnung und Gottes Geheimnisse. Das Geschichtswerk des Lukas, 1. UB 455: Stu 1997, Kohlhammer 261 pp. DM34. 3-17-013121-4.

5237 *Löning, Karl* Neuschöpfung und religiöse Kultur: zur Begründung christlicher Identität im Geschichtswerk des Lukas. Religion und Gesellschaft. AOAT 248: 1997, ⇒235. EAlbertz, Rainer, 203-215.

5238 **Marconi, Gilberto** Lo Spirito di Dio nella vita interiore: l'opera di Luca vangelo dello Spirito. Quaderni di Camaldoli, Meditazioni 6: Bo 1997, EDB 142 pp. L16.000. 88-10-41111-0 [RivBib 45,383].

5239 *Marguerat, Daniel* Le premier historien du christianisme (Luc-Actes). CBFV 36 (1997) 19-34.

5240 *Marshall, I. Howard* Reading the book 7: Luke-Acts. ET 108 (1997) 196-200.

5241 **Penney, John Michael** The missionary emphasis of Lukan pneumatology. JPentec.S 12: Shf 1997, Academic 143 pp. £15. 1-85075-800-X [EvQ 69,369].

5242 *Perez Herrero, Francisco* La obra de San Lucas y su mensaje para el cristiano de hoy. Burgense 38/1 (1997) 11-31.

5243 *Pokorný, Petr* '...bis an das Ende der Erde': ein Beitrag zum Thema Sammlung Israels und christliche Mission bei Lukas. Bibelauslegung. WUNT 100: 1997 <1995>, ⇒970. 315-325.

5244 **Price, Robert M.** The widow traditions in Luke-Acts: a feminist-critical scrutiny. SBL.DS 155: Atlanta, GA 1997, Scholars xli; 281 pp. $30. 0-7785-0224-7 [ET 108,378].

5245 **Ravens, David** Luke and the restoration of Israel. JSNT.S 119: 1995, ⇒11/1,3588. RCBQ 59 (1997) 171-172 *(Darr, John A.)*; JBL 116 (1997) 366-368 *(Paffenroth, Kim)*.

5246 **Reinhardt, Wolfgang** Das Wachstum des Gottesvolkes... im lukanischen Doppelwerk. 1995, ⇒11/1,3589; 12,5013. RThLZ 122 (1997) 261-263 *(Klein, Hans)*; CritRR 10 (1997) 213-215 *(Stenschke, Christoph W.)*.

5247 **Reinmuth, Eckart** Pseudo-PHILO und Lukas. WUNT 2/74: 1994, ⇒10,4907... 12,5014. RCBQ 59 (1997) 396-398 *(Adler, William)*; JBL 115 (1996) 145-147 *(Murphy, Frederick J.)*.

5248 **Roth, S. John** The blind, the lame, and the poor: character types in Luke-Acts. JSNT.S 144: Shf 1997, Academic 253 pp. Diss. Vanderbilt 1994. £37.50/$62. 1-85075-667-8.

5249 *Speckman, McGlory T.* Beggars and gospel in Luke-Acts: preliminary observations on an emerging model in the light of recent developmental theories. Neotest. 31 (1997) 309-337.

5250 **Strauss, Mark L.** The Davidic messiah in Luke-Acts. Diss. DTurner, M.: JSNT.S 110: 1995, ⇒11/1,3595; 12,5022. RThLZ 122 (1997) 149-151 *(Bendemann, Reinhard von)*; JThS 48 (1997) 188-189 *(Franklin, Eric)*; EvQ 69/1 (1997) 80-81 *(Clark, Andrew C.)*; JBL 116 (1997) 370-372 *(Juel, Donald)* [Lk 4,16-30; Acts 2,14-41; 13,16-41].

5251 **Stricher, Joseph** La parité hommes-femmes dans l'oeuvre de Luc. 1996, ⇒12,5024. RCahiers de l'Atelier 471 (1997) 103-104 *(Guillermain, Chantal)*.

5252 *Stronstad, Roger* The prophethood of all believers: a study in Luke's charismatic theology. JPentec.S 11: 1997, ⇒63. ᶠMENZIES W., 60-77.

5253 *Sweetland, Dennis M.* Luke-Acts: an overview. BiTod 35 (1997) 332-339.

5254 **Turner, Max** Power from on high: the spirit in Israel's restoration and witness in Luke-Acts. JPentec.S 9: 1996, ⇒12,5026. ᴿBib. 78 (1997) 428-432 *(Pervo, Richard I.)*.

5255 *Wagner, J. Ross* Psalm 118 in Luke-Acts: tracing a narrative thread. Early christian interpretation. JSNT.S 148: 1997, ⇒191. ᴱEvans, C.A., 154-178.

5256 **Watt, Jonathan M.** Code-switching in Luke and Acts. Berkeley Insights in Linguistics and Semiotics 31: NY 1997, Lang 307 pp. $54. 0-8204-3695-X [BiTr 49,349ss—Noss, Philip A].

5257 **Zwiep, Arie W.** The ascension of the Messiah in Lukan christology. Diss. Durham, 1996: ᴰ*Dunn, J.D.*: NT.S 87: Lei 1997, Brill xiii; 291 pp. *f*176. 90-04-10897-1.

### ꜰ7.3 Evangelium Lucae—*Textus, commentarii*

5258 **Bock, Darrell L.** Luke. 1994-96, ⇒10,4921... 12,5030. ᴿJETh 11 (1997) 206-208 *(Baum, Armin Daniel)*; BS 154/1 (1997) 109-111 *(Harris, W. Hall)*;

5259 Luke. NIV application commentary: GR 1996, Zondervan 640 pp. Bibl. 0-310-49330-7.

5260 **Boismard, Marie-Émile** En quête du Proto-Luc. EtB 37: P 1997, Gabalda 364 pp. FF320. 2-85021-100-1. ᴿEThL 73 (1997) 453-455 *(Neirynck, F.)*.

5261 **Bovon, François** El evangelio según san Lucas (Lc 1-9). ᵀ*Ortiz García, A.*: 1995, ⇒11/1,3604; 12,5031. ᴿEfMex 15/1 (1997) 114-116 *(Lugo Rodríguez, Raul H.)*;

5262 L'évangile selon saint Luc (9,51-14,35). 1996, ⇒12,5032. ᴿRThPh 129 (1997) 106-107 *(Brandt, Pierre-Yves)*; Bib. 78 (1997) 425-428 *(Talbert, Charles H.)*; ETR 72 (1997) 612-613 *(Cuvillier, Élian)*; EeV 107 (1997) 449-450 *(Cothenet, Édouard)*.

5263 *Brodie, Thomas L.* Intertextuality and its use in tracing Q and Proto-Luke. The scriptures in the gospels. BEThL 131: 1997, ⇒234. ᴱTuckett, C.M., 469-477.

5264 **Corsato, Celestino** La *Expositio euangelii secundum Lucam* di sant'AMBROGIO. SEAug 43: 1993, ⇒9,5117... 11/1,3606. ᴿREAug 43/1 (1997) 217-219 *(Savon, Hervé)*; CrSt 18/2 (1997) 445-447 *(Gori, Franco)*; Div. 40/3 (1997) 99 *(Noce, C.)*.

5265 **Ernst, Josef** Das Evangelium nach Lukas. 1993, ⇒10,4925. ᴿThPh 72 (1997) 575-576 *(Beutler, J.)*; ThRv 93 (1997) 214 *(Radl, Walter)*; CDios 209 (1996) 761-762 *(Gutiérrez, J.)*.

5266 **Fallon, Michael B.** The gospel according to Saint Luke: an introductory commentary. Kensington, NSW Australia 1997. Chevalier 375 pp. 0-86940-248-X.

5267 **Gargano, I.** Lectio divina su il vangelo di Luca, 2. Bo 1997, EDB 154 pp. L23.000 [RivBib 45,256].

5268 *Graumann, Thomas* Die theologische Grundlage der Auslegung in der *Expositio evangelii secundum Lucam* des AMBROSIUS von Mailand. StPatr 30: 1997, ⇒351. ᴱLivingstone, E.A., 19-27.

5269 **Green, Joel B.** The gospel of Luke. NICNT: GR 1997, Eerdmans xcii; 928 pp. $50. 0-8028-2315-7 [ETR 73,308].

5270 E*Hirunuma, Toshio* Praxis: (769) Luc. 10.17;

5271 (771) Luc. 10.19. Studia Textus Novi Testamenti 333 (1997) 2754-5/2761-2.

5272 **Just, Arthur A.** Luke 9:51 - 24:53. Concordia Commentary: Saint Louis 1997, Concordia xxxi; 419 - 1067 pp. 0-570-04254-2 [NThAR 1999,5].

5273 **Katholisches Bibelwerk,** Lukas entdecken: Lese- und Arbeitsbuch zum Lukasevangelium. Bibel im Jahr: Stu 1997, 142 pp. 3-460-19983-3f.

5274 **Kiraz, George Anton** Luke. Comparative edition of the Syriac gospels, 3. NTTS 21/3: 1996, ⇒12,5037. RNT 39 (1997) 405-414 *(Baarda, T.)*.

5275 **Lieu, Judith M.** The gospel of Luke. Epworth Commentaries: Peterborough 1997, Epworth xxi; 212 pp. Bibl. £10. 0-7162-0516-5.

5276 **Lucas: evangelie.** Den Bosch 1997, Katholieke Bijbelstichting 136 pp. *f*15.75. 90-6173-677-3 [Str. 65,285].

5277 (*a*) **Mosconi, Luis** Evangelho de Jesus Cristo segundo Lucas: para cristãos e cristãs rumo ao novo milênio. São Paulo 1997, Loyola 134 pp. 85-15-01626-5 [PerTeol 29,438]; (*b*) **Prod'hom, S.** L'evangelo di Luca. Valenza 1997, "Il Messaggero Cristiano" (4) 302 pp.

5278 **Rius-Camps, Josep** O evangelho de Lucas: o êxodo do homem livre. 1995, ⇒11/1,3615. RPerTeol 29 (1997) 277-278 & REB 227 (1997) 736-737 *(Libanio, João Batista)*.

F7.4 *Lucae themata*—Luke's Gospel, topics

5279 *Adkin, Neil* Jerome on AMBROSE: the preface to the translation of ORIGEN's homilies on Luke. RBen 107 (1997) 5-14.

5280 *Beavis, Mary Ann* "Expecting nothing in return": Luke's picture of the marginalized. Gospel interpretation. 1997, ⇒210. EKingsbury, J.D., 142-154.

5281 **Bieberstein, Sabine** Gebrochene Konzepte: der Weg der galiläischen Frauen und die Vorstellungen von Nachfolge und Besitzverzicht im Lukasevangelium. Diss. FrS 1997/98; D*Venetz, H.-J.* [BZ 42,316].

5282 **Bonney, Gillian** AMBROSII et BEDAE exegesis Lucana quae mulierum coetum spectat. Thesis ad Doctoratum 373; D*Dal Covolo, Enrico*: R 1997, Pont. Univ. Salesiana 140 pp. excerpt.

5283 **Böhlemann, Peter** Jesus und der Täufer: Schlüssel zur Theologie und Ethik des Lukas. Diss. Bethel, 1993; D*Lindemann, A.*: MSSNTS 99: C 1997, CUP xiii; 379 pp. £45. 0-521-59421-9.

5284 *Bovon, François* Réception apocryphe de l'"Evangile de Luc' et lecture orthodoxe des actes apocryphes des apôtres. Sum. rés. 137. Apocrypha 8 (1997) 137-146.

5285 **Boyer, Mark G.** Day by ordinary day with Luke. NY 1997, Alba xxii; 330 pp. $18 [BiTod 36,263—Senior, Donald].

5286 **Buckwalter, H. Douglas** The character and purpose of Luke's christology. MSSNTS 89: 1996, ⇒12,5409. RCritRR 10 (1997) 165-168 *(Chance, J. Bradley)*.

5287 *Cárdenas Pallares, José* The kingdom of God or the kingdom of money. Subversive scriptures. 1997, ⇒263. EVaage, L., 60-74.

5288  Cenci, Anna Maria La parola di Dio nel vangelo di Luca. Pref.
      Galbiati, Enrico: CasM 1997, Piemme 302 pp. 88-384-2895-6.
5289  Del Agua, Agustín La hermenéutica del "relato" lucano. La Bíblia i
      el Mediterrani. 1997, ⇒385. EBorrell, d'Agustí, 235-253.
5290  Diefenbach, Manfred Die Komposition des Lukas-Evangeliums
      unter Berücksichtigung antiker Rhetorikelemente. FTS 43: 1993,
      ⇒9,5136... 12,5053. ROrdKor 38/1 (1997) 107-108 (Fobes, R.).
5291  Doble, Peter The paradox of salvation: Luke's theology of the
      cross. MSSNTS 87: 1996, ⇒12,5054. RNT 39 (1997) 289-291
      (Muir, Steven); JThS 48 (1997) 586-587 (Beck, Brian E.); Cross-
      Cur 47 (1997-8) 553-554 (Mowery, Robert L.).
5292  García Pérez, José M. San Lucas: evangelio y tradición: sustrato
      arameo en Lc 1,39; 8,26-39; 21,36; 22,28-30; 23,39-43. 1995,
      ⇒11/1,3625; 12,5056. ActBib 34 (1997) 26-28 (Fàbrega, Valentí);
      EstTr 31/1-2 (1997) 189-190 (Pikaza, Xabier); EstB 55 (1997)
      548-550 (Ribera, J.).
5293  Gillman, John Poverty, riches, and the challenge of discipleship.
      BiTod 35 (1997) 356-362.
5294  Gourgues, Michel Les paraboles de Luc: d'amont en aval. Scien-
      ces bibliques: Montréal: Médiaspaul 269 pp. CAN$29. 2-89420-
      361-6 [RTL 28,292].
5295  Graves, Mike Preaching Lukan parables: a socio-rhetorical
      approach. SWJT 40/1 (1997) 17-32.
5296  Hemelsoet, Ben; Touwen, Klaas     Handelingen: Lucas ten
      tweeden male: parabels van het Koninkrijk. Zoetermeer 1997,
      Boekencentrum 144 pp. ƒ28.50. 90-239-0462-1.
5297  Hermant, Dominique Un procédé d'écriture de Luc: le transfert.
      RB 104 (1997) 528-556 [Lk 4,16-37; 5,10-11; 8,19-20; 22,25-27;
      3,19-20].
5298  Jackson, Paul N. Allegiance to Jesus from the transfiguration to his
      death in Luke's gospel. SWJT 40/1 (1997) 48-62.
5299  Karris, Robert J. Women and discipleship in Luke. BiTod 35
      (1997) 351-355.
5300  Kimball, Charles A. Jesus' exposition of the Old Testament in
      Luke's gospel. JSNT.S 94: 1994, ⇒10,4945; 11/1,3630. REvQ 69
      (1997) 160-161 (Bock, Darrell L.).
5301  Kingsbury, Jack Dean The plot of Luke's story of Jesus. Gospel
      interpretation. 1997, ⇒210. EKingsbury, J.D., 155-165.
5302  Klein, Günter Eschatologie und Schöpfung bei Lukas: eine kosmi-
      sche Liturgie im dritten Evangelium. BZNW 89: 1997, ⇒33.
      FGRAESSER E.. 145-154.
5303  Krüger, René Gott oder Mammon: das Lukasevangelium und die
      Ökonomie. Luzern 1997, Exodus 91 pp. DM24.80. 3-905577-19-
      4. RBiKi 52 (1997) 141-142 (Helsper, Michael).
5304  Kügler, Joachim Pharao und Christus?: religionsgeschichtliche
      Untersuchung zur Frage einer Verbindung zwischen altägyptischer
      Königstheologie und neutestamentlicher: Christologie im Lukase-
      vangelium. Diss.-Habil. Bonn 1996-97; BBB 113: Bodenheim
      1997, Philo 360 pp. 3-8257-0072-0 [Acts 13,32-33].
5305  Laconi, Mauro Cercare Dio in Luca: le parabole nel terzo vangelo.
      PSV 35 (1997) 127-138.
5306  TLienhard, Joseph ORIGEN: homilies on Luke. FaCh 94: 1996,
      ⇒12,5060. RJEarlyC 5 (1997) 452-453 (Pang-White, Ann A.).

5307 **Marconi, Gilberto** La comunicazione visiva nel vangelo di Luca: per cogliere il mistero con la vista. Fede e comunicazione 3: Mi 1997, Paoline 116 pp. 88-315-1461-X [[NThAR 1999,182].

5308 *Martini, Carlo Maria* El itinerario del discípulo: a la luz del evangelio de Lucas. Santander 1997, Sal Terrae 224 pp. [Comunidades 24,138].

5309 **Mazzocchi, L.; Forzani, J.** Il vangelo secondo Luca e lo Zen. Pref. *Maggioni, B.*: Bo 1997, EDB 346 pp. L39.000. 88-10-80797-9 [RivBib 45,506].

5310 *Moxnes, Halvor* The social context of Luke's community. Gospel interpretation. 1997, ⇒210. ᴱKingsbury, J.D., 166-177.

5311 **Paffenroth, Kim** The story of Jesus according to L. JSNT.S 147: Shf 1997, Academic 200 pp. £35/$58. 0-85075-675-9.

5312 *Peretto, Elio* ORIGENE: l'esegesi biblica nelle omelie XV, XVI, XVII sul vangelo di Luca. 1997 <1977>, ⇒155. Saggi, 115-130.

5313 *Phiri, Isabel A.* Women in the gospel of Luke: an African woman's perspective. Journal of Constructive Theology 3/1 (1997) 35-48 [ZID 24,128].

5314 *Powell, Mark Allan* Toward a narrative-critical understanding of Luke. Gospel interpretation. 1997, ⇒210. ᴱKingsbury, J.D., 125-131.

5315 **Prieur, Alexander** Die Verkündigung der Gottesherrschaft: exegetische Studien zum lukanischen Verständnis von βασιλεια του θεου. WUNT 2/89: 1996, ⇒12,5067. ᴿLASBF 47 (1997) 588-592 *(Chrupcała, Lesław Daniel)*.

5316 **Ramis, F.** Lucas, evangelista de la ternura de Dios: diez catequesis. Estella 1997, Verbo Divino 208 pp. Ptas1.300.

5317 **Rohr, Richard** The good news according to Luke. NY 1997, Crossroad 192 pp. $20. 0-8245-1490-4 [BiTod 35,327].

5318 *Seccombe, David* Luke's vision for the church. 1997, ⇒93. ᶠSWEET J., 45-63.

5319 **Seland, Torrey** Establishment violence in PHILO and Luke. 1995, ⇒11/1,3649; 12,5072. ᴿJAOS 117/1 (1997) 154-155 *(Feldman, Louis H.)*; TJT 13 (1997) 289-290 *(Gowler, David B.)*; JBL 116 (1997) 368-370 *(Sterling, Gregory E.)* [Acts 6,8-7,60; 21,15-36; 23,12-15].

5320 *Stagg, Frank* Luke's theological use of parables. RExp 94 (1997) 215-229.

5321 *Stein, Robert H.* Interpreting the parables of Luke. SWJT 40/1 (1997) 6-16.

5322 *Steyn, Gert J.* Luke's use of μιμησις?: re-opening the debate. The scriptures in the gospels. BEThL 131: 1997, ⇒234. ᴱTuckett, C.M., 551-557.

5323 *Stricher, Joseph* Comme il faisait route vers Jérusalem: Jérusalem dans l'évangile de Luc;

5324 Jésus selon Luc: le Seigneur qui visite son peuple;

5325 Nouvelles fiches bibliques sur l'évangile de Luc. DosB 67 (1997) 19-21/9-11/28-30.

5326 *Tannehill, Robert C.* "Cornelius" and "Tabitha" encounter Luke's Jesus. Gospel interpretation. 1997, ⇒210. ᴱKingsbury, J.D., 132-141.

5327 **Terrinoni, Ubaldo** Il vangelo dell'incontro: riflessioni su Luca. Lettura pastorale della bibbia: bibbia e spiritualità 1: Bo 1997, EDB 240 pp. Bibl. 88-10-20147-7 [NThAR 2000,5].

5328 **Thayse, André** Luc: l'évangile revisité. Bru 1997, Racine 251 pp. 2-87386-123-1 [RTL 29,131].

5329 <sup>E</sup>**Tuckett, C.M.** Luke's literary achievement: collected essays. JSNT.S 116: 1995, ⇒11/1,3599. <sup>R</sup>EvQ 69 (1997) 78-80 *(Marshall, I.H.)*; JThS 48 (1997) 588-589 *(Nolland, J.L.)*.

5330 *Van Cangh, Jean M.* Women in the gospel of Luke. DBM 16/2 (1997) 31-60. **G.**

5331 *Van Zyl, Sanrie; Van Aarde, Andries G.* Die Lukaanse Jesusbeeld: in dialoog met Wilhelm Bousset se "Kyrios Christos". HTS 53 (1997) 185-208.

5332 *Vanhoye, Albert* L'anno giubilare nel vangelo di Luca. Tertium Millennium 1 (1997) 22-25.

5333 *Wolter, Michael* Israels Zukunft und die Parusieverzögerung bei Lukas. BZNW 89: 1997, ⇒33. <sup>F</sup>Graesser E., 405-426.

F7.5 *Infantia, cantica*—Magnificat, Benedictus: Luc. 1-3

5334 **Boismard, Marie-Émile** L'évangile de l'enfance (Luc 1-2) selon le Proto-Luc. EtB 35: P 1997, Gabalda 278 pp. FF200. 2-85021-097-8. <sup>R</sup>RB 104 (1997) 602-607 *(Taylor, Justin)*; EThL 73 (1997) 450-452 *(Neirynck, F.)*.

5335 **Martini, Carlo Maria** Por los senderso de la visitación. Estella 1997, Verbo Divino 136 pp. Ptas1.200 [Comunidades 26,64].

5336 *Masini, Mario* Tre icone della fede: Zaccaria Elisabetta Maria. Sum. 706. Theotokos 5 (1997) 691-706.

5337 **Pigeaud, Olivier** Syméon et l'enfant: lendemains de Noël au seuil de l'évangile. Poliez-le-Grand 1997, Moulin 84 pp. FF56 [ETR 73,310].

5338 *Plevnik, Joseph* As imádság szerepe Lukács gyermekségtörténeté-ben [The role of prayers in Luke's infancy narratives] <sup>T</sup>*Thorday, Attila*;

5339 *Schmatovich, János* Ószövetségi gyökerek szent Lukács gyermekség-evangéliumában [The roots of Luke's infancy narrative based on the Old Testament];

5340 *Serra, Aristide* Máriának, Jézus anyjának alakja a Lukács-evangélium gyermekségtörténetének néhány szakasza alapján [Die Gestalt Mariä, der Mutter Jesu im Hinblick auf einige Texte der Kindheitsgeschichte]. <sup>T</sup>*Kiss, Imre*;

5341 *Vojnović, Tadej* Néhány gondolat máté és Lukács gyermekség-evangéliumának történetiségéről és hitelességéről [Historicity and midrash in Luke's infancy narrative]. <sup>T</sup>*Harmath, Károly*. Gyer-mekségtörténet. 1997, ⇒316. <sup>E</sup>Benyik, G. Sum., Zsfg., Rias., 83-92/101-113/51-81/237-242. **Hungarian.**

5342 **Radl, Walter** Der Ursprung Jesu: traditionsgeschichtliche Untersu-chungen zu Lukas 1-2. 1996, ⇒12,5081. <sup>R</sup>BZ 41 (1997) 132-134 *(Müller, Christoph G.)*; ThLZ 122 (1997) 145-147 *(Klein, Hans)*; CV 39/1 (1997) 60-94 *(Kaut, Thomas)*.

5343 *Hooker, Morna D.* A spiritual key: Luke 1-2. Beginnings. 1997, ⇒136. 43-63.

5344 *Bogaert, Pierre-Maurice* Luc et les écritures dans l'évangile de l'enfance à la lumière des "Antiquités Bibliques": histoire sainte et livres saints. The scriptures in the gospels. BEThL 131: 1997, ⇒234. ᴱTuckett, C.M., 243-270.

5345 *Pokorný, Petr* Lukas 1,1-4 als Prolog zum lukanischen Doppelwerk [Łk 1,1-4 jako prolog do podwójnego dziela św. Łukasza]. Streszczenie 276. WST 10 (1997) 271-276.

5346 *Ryan, Judith M.* Luke's infancy narrative. BiTod 35 (1997) 340-344 [Lk 1,5-2,52].

5347 *Sulyok, Elemér* Örvendj, isten kegyeltje (Lk 1,26-38) [The annunciation of the birth of John the Baptist and of Jesus]. Gyermekségtörténet. 1997, ⇒316. ᴱBenyik, G. Sum., Zsfg., Rias., 93-100. **Hungarian**.

5348 *Maggioni, Corrado* L'annunciazione: cardine della storia umana. Consacrazione e Servizio 46/3 (1997) 45-54 [Lk 1,26-38].

5349 *Sheridan, J. Mark* 'Steersman of the mind': the Virgin Mary as ideal nun (an interpretation of Luke 1:29 by Rufus of Shotep). StPatr 30. 1997, ⇒351. ᴱLivingstone, E.A., 265-269.

5350 *Kilgallen, John J.* The conception of Jesus (Luke 1,35). Sum. 246. Bib. 78 (1997) 225-246.

5351 *Gambero, Luigi* Antiche riletture patristiche di Lc 1,39-45. Sum. 52. Theotokos 5/1 (1997) 25-52;

5352 *Maggioni, Bruno* La madre del mio Signore: esegesi di Lc 1,39-45. Sum. 23. 11-24;

5353 *Ko Ha Fong, Maria* Lectio divina su Lc 1,39-45. Sum. 195. 177-195;

5354 *Occhipinti, Vilma* Visitazione. Sum. 119. 113-119;

5355 *Nicola, Giulia Paola di* Maria ed Elisabetta. Sum. 134. 121-135;

5356 *Guglielmoni, Luigi* Catechesi sulla visitazione. Sum. 175. 137-175;

5357 *Castelli, Ferdinando* Poeti e narratori dinanzi alla Visitazione. Sum. 212. 197-212;

5358 *Sebastiani, Lilia* Una rilettura in chiave di solidarietà. Sum. 111. 83-111;

5359 *Sorci, Pietro* La visitazione nella liturgia. Sum. 81. 53-81;

5360 *Soranzo, Micaela* Iconografia della Visitazione. Sum. 241. Theotokos 5/1 (1997) 213-241.

5361 *Bianchi, Enzo* Lectio divina. Sum. 615. Theotokos 5/1 (1997) 599-615 [Lk 1,46-55].

5362 *Valentini, Alberto* Approcci esegetici a Lc 1,46b-55. Sum. 422. Theotokos 5/1 (1997) 403-422.

5363 *Fabiny, Tibor* A Magnificat narratív-kritikai és hatástörténeti megközelítése [A narrative-critical and effect-history approach to the Magnificat]. Gyermekségtörténet. 1997, ⇒316. ᴱBenyik, G. Sum., Zsfg., Rias., 147-166. **Hungarian**.

5364 *Farina, Marcella* Un umanesimo oltre le false dialettiche. Sum. 500. Theotokos 5 (1997) 487-500

5365 *Gaál, Endre* A Magnificat. Gyermekségtörténet. 1997, ⇒316. ᴱBenyik, G. Sum., Zsfg., Rias., 173-178. **Hungarian**.

5366 *Gallo, Luis A.* Il Magnificat nel documento di Puebla: un caso emblematico di contestualizzazione dell'annuncio evangelico. Sum. 563. Theotokos 5 (1997) 551-563 [Lk 1,46-55];

5367 *Gharib, Georges* Il Magnificat nella lliturgia orientale specie bizantina. Sum. 485. 463-485;

5368 *Gila, Angelo* Riletture patristiche. Sum. 460. 423-461 [Lk 1,46-55];

5369 *Golasmici, Marilena* Griglie interpretative di Lc 1,46-55. Sum. 690. 675-690;

5370 *Visentin, Maria Cecilia* Il Magnificat in musica. Sum. 642. Theotokos 5 (1997) 617-642.

5371 *Klauck, Hans-Josef* Gottesfürchtige im Magnificat?. NTS 43 (1997) 134-139.

5372 *Klein, Hans* Das Magnifikat als jüdisches Frauengebet. KuD 43 (1997) 258-267.

5373 *Masciarelli, Michele G.* 'Grammatica' di catechesi: considerazioni teologiche e spunti pastorali. Sum. 597;

5374 *Valentini, Alberto* Il problema dell'attribuzione del Magnificat in musica. Sum. 674;

5375 *Bertalot, Renzo* Il Magnificat di LUTE RO. Sum. 549. Theotokos 5 (1997) 565-597/643-674/539-549.

5376 **Terrien, Samuel** The Magnificat. 1995, ⇒11/1,3669. RMar. 59 (1997) 324-326 *(Zannini, Paolo M.).*

5377 *Palumbieri, Sabino* L'irruzione di Dio nella storia. Sum. 538. Theotokos 5 (1997) 501-538 [Lk 1,46-55].

5378 *Buth, Randall* Hebrew poetic tenses and the Magnificat. New Testament text. BiSe 44: 1997 <1984>, ⇒748. EPorter, S.E., 240-255.

5379 *Valentini, Alberto* Il senso degli aoristi in Lc 1,51-53. Sum. 729. Theotokos 5 (1997) 725-729.

5380 *Dornisch, Loretta* A woman reads the gospel of Luke: introduction and Luke 1: the infancy narratives. BR 42 (1997) 7-22.

5381 *Peretto, Elio* Zaccaria Elisabetta Giovanni visti dal primo lettore di Luca (cap. I). 1997 <1978>, ⇒155. Saggi. 157-177.

5382 *Krieger, Klaus-Stefan* Die Historizität des Census des Quirinius. BN 87 (1997) 17-23 [Lk 2,1-3].

5383 *Mussies, Gerard* Lucas 2:1-6 in enig recent onderzoek. NedThT 51 (1997) 89-103.

5384 **Prazer, José Raimundo** Lucas "Nasceu vos hoje um Salvador": o título sotér em Lc 2,1-20. Diss. Pontificia Univ. a S. Thoma, R 1997; DDe Santis, Luca: 96 pp. Bibl. Rxtr.

5385 *Winandy, Jacques* Le signe de la mangeoire et des langes. NTS 43 (1997) 140-146 [Lk 2,1-20];

5386 Le recensement dit de Quirinius (Lc 2,2) une interpolation?. RB 104 (1997) 373-377.

5387 *Bolyki, János* Nunc dimittis: Simeon története—Lk 2,25-35 ['Nunc dimittis...' and the story of Simeon (Lk 2,25-35)]. Gyermekségtörténet. 1997, ⇒316. EBenyik, G., Sum., Zsfg., Rias., 127-132. **Hungarian.**

5388 **Simón Muñoz, Alfonso** El Mesías y la hija de Sion: teología de la redención en Lc 2,29-35. 1994, ⇒10,4983... 12,5100. RJBL 115 (1996) 545-546 *(Brown, Raymond E.).*

5389 *Bauckham, Richard* Anna of the tribe of Asher (Luke 2:36-38). RB 104 (1997) 161-191.

5390 *Peretto, Elio* La lettura origeniana di Lc 2,41-52. 1997 <1975>, ⇒155. Saggi, 59-76.

5391 *Van der Horst, Pieter W.* Notes on the Aramaic background of Luke 2.41-52. New Testament text. BiSe 44: 1997 <1980>, ⇒748. EPorter, S.E., 235-239.

5392 *Madigan, Kevin* Did Jesus "progress in wisdom"?: THOMAS Aquinas on Luke 2:52 in ancient and high-medieval context. Tr. 52 (1997) 179-200.
5393 **Hendrickx, Herman** Ministry in Galilee (Luke 3:1-6:49). The third gospel for the third world, 2A. Quezon City, Philippines 1997 <1996> ⇒12,5101, Claretian viii; 376 pp. 971-501-748-7 [EThL 74,306*].

### F7.6 Evangelium Lucae 4,1...

5394 *Kirk, Alan* Some compositional conventions of Hellenistic wisdom texts and the juxtaposition of 4:1-13; 6:20b-49; and 7:1-10 in Q. JBL 116 (1997) 235-257.
5395 *Thévenot, Xavier* Conflit de conditions filiales: les tentations de Jésus. VS 722 (1997) 7-15 [Lk 4,1-13].
5396 *Mattam, Zacharias* The temptations of Christ: Lk 4:1-13 (a kerygmatic, patristic and theological interpretation). BiBh 23 (1997) 102-120.
5397 *Boismard, Marie-Emile* La deuxième tentation du Christ d'après Lc 4,5-8. StAns 124: 1997, ⇒57. FLOEHRER M. — TRAGAN P., 455-464.
5398 *Schubert, Judith* Jesus as prophet. BiTod 35 (1997) 345-350 [Lk 4,16-30].
5399 **Prior, Michael** Jesus the liberator (Luke 4:16-30). 1995, ⇒11/1,3698; 12,5104. RCBQ 59 (1997) 169-171 *(Harrington, Wilfrid J.)*.
5400 *Pereira, Francis* Jesus and the good news of the kingdom to the poor (Lk 4:18f., 43). 1997, ⇒89. FSOARES-PRABHU G., 178-205.
5401 *Peretto, Elio* Evangelizare pauperibus (Lc 4,18; 7,22-23) nella lettura patristica dei secoli II-III. 1997 <1977>, ⇒155. Saggi. 131-156.
5402 *Rius-Camps, Josep* Dos versiones divergentes de la llamada de los primeros discípulos (Lc 5,1-11) según D⁰⁵ (d) y P⁷⁵-B⁰³ (vg). StAns 124: 1997, ⇒57. FLOEHRER M. — TRAGAN P., 437-453.
5403 *Bagni, Arcangelo* 'Sii sanato!' (Lc 5,12-16). PaVi 42/4 (1997) 48-52.
5404 *Neirynck, Frans* Q 6,20b-21; 7,22 and Isaiah 61. The scriptures in the gospels. BEThL 131: 1997, ⇒234. ETuckett, C.M., 27-64.
5405 **Moscoso Pacheco, Arturo** Ay de los ricos!... la imprecación unida al macarismo, fundamentada en el paralelismo antitético, una forma de imprecación desarrolado. Diss. Belo Horizonte 1997; DKonings, Johan [Lk 6].
5406 *Gafner, Philippe* Le cercueil et la rosée—le mot σορος en Luc 7.14. BN 87 (1997) 13-16.
5407 *Borse, Udo* Der lukanische Verzicht auf Betanien. SNTU.A 22 (1997) 5-24 [Lk 7,36-50].
5408 *Foster, Ruth A.; Shiell, William D.* The parable of the sower and the seed in Luke 8:1-10: Jesus' parable of parables. RExp 94 (1997) 259-267.
5409 **Nayak, Vijay Kumar** Exousía and kingdom of God: a study of the missionary discourse in Lk 9:1-6. Diss. Pont. Univ. Urbaniana, R 1997, Extr. xii; 71 pp.

5410   *Kariamadam, Paul* Transfiguration and Jesus' ascended glory (an explanation of Lk. 9:28-36). BiBh 23/1 (1997) 1-13.

F7.7  *Iter hierosolymitanum—Lc 9,51...—*Jerusalem journey

5411   *Denaux, Adelbert* Old Testament models for the Lukan travel narrative: a critical survey. The scriptures in the gospels. BEThL 131: 1997, ⇒234. ᴱTuckett, C.M., 271-305.
5412   *Parsons, Mikeal C.* Landmarks along the way: the function of the "L" parables in the Lukan travel narrative. SWJT 40/1 (1997) 33-47.
5413   *Székely, János* Structure and purpose of the Lucan travel account. FolTh 8 (1997) 61-112.
5414   **Székely, János** Structure and theology of the Lucan itinerarium. Diss. Universitas Catholica a Petro Pázmány; Budapest 1997 [FolTh 8,232].

5415   *Evans, Craig A.* 'Do this and you will live': targumic coherence in Luke 10:25-28. Jesus in context. AGAJ 39: 1997, ⇒183. ᴱChilton, B., 377-393.
5416   *Graves, Mike* Luke 10:25-37: the moral of the "good Samaritan" story?. RExp 94 (1997) 269-275.
5417   *Noël, Filip* The double commandment of love in Lk 10,27: a deuteronomistic pillar or Lukan redaction of Mk 12,29-33;
5418   *Verhoef, Eduard* (Eternal) life and following the commandments: Lev 18,5 and Luke 10,28. The scriptures in the gospels. BEThL 131: 1997, ⇒234. ᴱTuckett, C.M., 559-570/571-577.
5419   *McDonald, J. Ian H.* Alien grace (Luke 10:30-36): the parable of the good Samaritan. Jesus and his parables. 1997, ᴱShillington, V.G., 35-51.
5420   **Constable, Giles** Three studies in medieval religious and social thought: the interpretation of Mary and Martha. 1995, ⇒11/1,3728; 12,5125. ᴿCCMéd 40 (1997) 184-185 *(Cazelles, Brigitte)*; ChH 66 (1997) 567-568 *(Borgehammar, Stephan)* [Lk 10,38-42].
5421   *Devillers, Luc* Marthe et Marie: en quête de l'unique nécessaire. Vie Spirituelle 77 (1997) 617-621 [Lk 10,38-42].
5422   *Kudasiewicz, Józef* Dom Marty i Marii małym kościołem (Łk 10,38-42) [Das Haus von Martha und Maria als kleine Kirche (Ecclesiola) (Lk 10,38-42)]. Zsfg. 178. WST 10 (1997) 169-178.
5423   *Rebera, Ranjini* Polarity or partnership?: retelling the story of Martha and Mary from Asian women's perspective. Semeia 78 (1997) 93-107 [Lk 10,38-42].
5424   **Fornari-Carbonell, Isabel M.** La escucha del huésped (Lc 10,38-42). EMISJ 30: 1995, ⇒11/1,3726; 12,5124. ᴿCBQ 59 (1997) 378-379 *(Reid, Barbara E.)*.
5425   *North, J. Lionel* ὀλίγων δέ ἐστιν χρεία ἢ ἑνὸς (Luke 10.42): text, subtext and context. JSNT 66 (1997) 3-13.

5426   *Snodgrass, Klyne* Anaideia and the friend at midnight (Luke 11:8). JBL 116 (1997) 505-513.
5427   *Hengel, Martin* Der Finger und die Herrschaft Gottes in Lk 11,20. La main de Dieu. WUNT 94: 1997, ⇒328. ᴱKieffer, R., 87-106.

5428  *Van der Horst, Pieter W.* "The finger of God": miscellaneous notes
      on Luke 11:20 and its Umwelt. NT.S 89: 1997, ⇒7. FBAARDA
      T., 89-103.

5429  **Cholakis, Arthur** Luke's first eschatological discourse: form,
      function and contextual integration of Luke 12:1-13:9. Diss. Ford-
      ham 1997; DGiblin, C. [RTL 29,583].

5430  *Stacy, R.W.* Luke 12:13-21: the parable of the rich fool. RExp 94
      (1997) 285-292.

5431  *Crüsemann, Marlene* Der Habgier nicht ausgeliefert: sozialge-
      schichtliche Bibelauslegung zu Lukas 12,15-21. JK 58 (1997) 506-
      509.

5432  *Beavis, Mary Ann* The foolish landowner (Luke 12:16b-20): the
      parable of the rich fool. Jesus and his parables. 1997, ⇒230.
      EShillington, V.G., 55-68.

5433  **Harmansa, H.-Konrad** Die Zeit der Entscheidung: Lk 13,1-9 als
      Beispiel für das lukanische Verständnis der Gerichtspredigt Jesu an
      Israel. EThSt 69: 1995, ⇒11/1,3735. RCBQ 59 (1997) 582-583
      *(Rogers, Patrick)*; JBL 116 (1997) 748-749 *(Reed, Jonathan)*.

5434  *Hedrick, Charles W.* Prolegomena to reading parables: Luke 13:6-9
      as a test case. RExp 94 (1997) 179-197.

5435  *May, David M.* The straightened woman (Luke 13:10-17): Paradise
      lost and regained. PRSt 24/3 (1997) 245-258.

5436  **York, John O.** The last shall be first; the rhetoric of reversal in
      Luke. JSNT.S 46: 1991, ⇒7,4550... 9,5237. RAsp. 44/1 (1997)
      114-116 *(Pitta, Antonio)* [Lk 13,6-9].

5437  *Rasco, Emilio* Jesús y los "Buenos Modales" en un banquete, Lc
      14,1-24: narración y sociología, cristología y eclesiología. StAns
      124: 1997, ⇒57. FLOEHRER M. — TRAGAN P., 465-490.

5438  *Wendland, Ernst R.* 'Blessed is the man who will eat at the feast in
      the kingdom of God' (Lk 14:15): internal and external intertextual
      influence on the interpretation of Christ's parable of the Great Ban-
      quet. Neotest. 31 (1997) 159-194.

5439  *Swartley, Willard M.* Unexpected banquet people (Luke 14:16-24):
      the parable of the great feast. Jesus and his parables. 1997, ⇒230.
      EShillington, V.G., 177-190.

5440  *Van Staden, Piet* Transformerende riglyne vir die kerk uit Lukas
      14: mense is belangriker as reëls en grense. HTS 53 (1997) 650-
      669.

5441  **Braun, Willi** Feasting and social rhetoric in Luke 14. MSSNTS
      85: 1995, ⇒11/1,3741; 12,5134. RTJT 13/1 (1997) 97-98 *(Gowler,
      David B.)*; CBQ 59 (1997) 149-150 *(O'Toole, Robert F.)*.

5442  *Lampe-Densky, Sigrid* Suchen, was verloren ging: sozialgeschicht-
      liche Bibelauslegung zu Lukas 15,1-7. JK 58 (1997) 288-291,

5443  *Pokorný, Petr* Lukas 15,11-32 und die lukanische Soteriologie.
      Bibelauslegung. WUNT 100: 1997 <1989>, ⇒970. 301-314.

5444  *Keillor, Garrison* Prodigal son. Word and World 17 (1997) 289-
      294 [ZID 23,415].

5445  *Rohrbaugh, Richard L.* A dysfunctional family and its neighbours
      (Luke 15:11b-32): the parable of the prodigal son. Jesus and his
      parables. 1997, ⇒230. EShillington, V.G., 141-164.

5446  **Mesquita Galvão, Antônio** O Pai misericordioso. Petrópolis 1997,
      Vozes 54 pp. [REB 57,488] [Lk 15,11-32].

5447  *Sahi, Iyoti* Reflections on the image of the prodigal son. ITS 34/1-3 (1997) 168-184 [Lk 15,11-32].

5448  **Berder, Michel; Foerster, Jean-Luc-Marie,** *(al.)*, La parabole du fils prodigue (Lc 15,11-32). CEv.S 101: P 1997, Cerf 99 pp. FF50. 0222-9706.

5449  *Batten, Alicia* Dishonour, gender and the parable of the prodigal son. TJT 13 (1997) 187-200 [Lk 15,11-32].

5450  *Bagni, Arcangelo* Un padre incompreso (Lc 15,11-32). PaVi 42/3 (1997) 47-51.

5451  *Kilgallen, John J.* Luke 15 and 16: a connection. Bib. 78 (1997) 369-376.

5452  *Chance, J.B.* Luke 15: seeking the outsiders. RExp 94 (1997) 249-257.

5453  *Trudinger, Paul* Exposing the depth of oppression (Luke 16:1b-8a): the parable of the unjust steward. Jesus and his parables. 1997, ⇒230. ᴱShillington, V.G., 121-137.

5454  *Lee, Martin* The wasteful steward. NBl 78 (1997) 520-528 [Lk 16,1-13].

5455  *Schröter, Jens* Erwägungen zum Gesetzesverständnis in Q anhand von Q 16,16-18. The scriptures in the gospels. BEThL 131: 1997, ⇒234. ᴱTuckett, C.M., 441-458.

5456  *Rigato, Maria-Luisa* "Mosè e i profeti" in chiave cristiana: un pronunciamento e un midrash (Lc 16,16-18 + 19-31). RivBib 45 (1997) 143-177.

5457  **Hanska, Jussi** 'And the rich man also died; and he was buried in hell': the social ethos in mendicant sermons. Bibliotheca Historica 28: Helsinki 1997, Suomen Historiallinen Seura 196 pp. [Spec. 74,762s—Wiethaus, Ulrike] [Lk 16,19-31].

5458  *Knight, George W.* Luke 16:19-31: the rich man and Lazarus. RExp 94 (1997) 277-283.

5459  **Wailes, Stephen L.** The Rich Man and Lazarus on the Reformation stage: a contribution to the social history of German drama. Selinsgrove 1997, Susquehanna University Press 359 pp. $48.50. ᴿSCJ 28 (1997) 1444-1446 *(Bell, Dean Phillip)* [Lk 16,19-31].

5460  *Bock, Darrell L.* The parable of the rich man and Lazarus and the ethics of Jesus. SWJT 40/1 (1997) 63-72 [Lk 16,19-31].

5461  *Kreisel-Liebermann, Hanna* Solidarisch sein kann nur, wer eigenes Leid nicht vergißt: sozialgeschichtliche Bibelauslegung zu Lukas 17,11-19. JK 58 (1997) 434-437.

5462  *Patte, Daniel* Whither critical New Testament studies for a new day?: some reflections on Luke 17:11-19. 1997, ⇒82. ᶠSᴄʀᴏɢɢs R., 277-293.

5463  *Morgen, Michèle* Lc 17,20-37 et Lc 21,8-11.20-24: arrière-fond scripturaire. The scriptures in the gospels. BEThL 131: 1997, ⇒234. ᴱTuckett, C.M., 307-326.

5464  *Hartmann, Lars* Reading Luke 17:20-37. Text-centered NT studies. WUNT 102: 1997 <1992>, ⇒132. 53-67.

5465  *Chrupcała, Lesław* 'Il regno di Dio non verrà μετὰ παρατηρήσεως' (Lc 17,20b). Sum. 39. Anton. 72 (1997) 39-52.

5466  *Bovon, François* Apocalyptic traditions in the Lukan special material: reading Luke 18:1-8. HThR 90 (1997) 383-391.

5467 *Paulsen, Henning* Die Witwe und der Richter (Lk 18,1-8). Zur Literatur. WUNT 99: 1997 <1984>, ⇒153. 113-138.
5468 *Stemm, Sönke von* Der betende Sünder vor Gott: Lk 18,9-14: zur Rezeption von Psalm 51(50),19. The scriptures in the gospels. BEThL 131: 1997, ⇒234. ETuckett, C.M., 579-589.
5469 *Joji, Kunduru* From brokenness to wholeness: the Jesus' way: hermeneutical study of Lk 18:9-14. Sum. 469. VJTR 61 (1997) 469-479.
5470 *Farris, Michael* A tale of two taxations (Luke 18:10-14b): the parable of the Pharisee and the toll collector. Jesus and his parables. 1997, ⇒230. EShillington, V.G., 23-33.
5471 *Guy, Laurie* The interplay of the present and future in the kingdom of God (Luke 19:11-44). TynB 48 (1997) 119-137.
5472 *Reid, Barbara* Puzzling passages: Luke 19:26. BiTod 35 (1997) 363-364.
5473 **Kinman, Brent** Jesus' entry into Jerusalem. AGJU 28: 1995, ⇒11/1,3767. RJThS 48 (1997) 584-586 *(Catchpole, David)*; JBL 116 (1997) 746-747 *(Tyson, Joseph B.)* [Lk 19,28-48].
5474 *Kariamadam, Paul* 'Peace in heaven...' (Lk 19:38b)—an explanation. BiBh 23 (1997) 256-268.
5475 *Hughes, Kent* Sovereign in his temple: the SBJT sermon; Luke 19:45-48. Southern Baptist Convention 1/3 (1997) 68-73.
5476 *O'Neill, J.C.* The shocking prospect of killing the Messiah (Luke 20:9-19): the parable of the wicked tenants. Jesus and his parables. 1997, ⇒230. EShillington, V.G., 165-176.

F7.8 **Passio—***Lc 22...*

5477 *Bottini, G. Claudio* Is 52,13-53,12 nel racconto della Passione di Lc 22-23. Sum. 451. LASBF 47 (1997) 57-78.
5478 *Brawley, Robert L.* Scripture resisting the carnivalesque in the Lucan passion. The scriptures in the gospels. BEThL 131: 1997, ⇒234. ETuckett, C.M., 591-595.
5479 *Coleridge, Mark* "You are witnesses" (Luke 24:48): who sees what in Luke. ABR 45 (1997) 1-19.
5480 **Prete, Benedetto** La passione e la morte di Gesù nel racconto di Luca, 1: ... l'arresto. StBi 112: 1996, ⇒12,5164. RPaVi 42/6 (1997) 57-58 *(Rolla, Armando)*;
5481 2: la passione e la morte. StBi 115: Brescia 1997, Paideia 198 pp. L32.000. 88-394-0546-1 [RTL 29,129].

5482 *Evans, Craig A.* The twelve thrones of Israel: scripture and politics in Luke 22:24-30. Jesus in context. AGAJ 39: 1997 <1993>, ⇒183. EChilton, B., 455-479.
5483 **Nelson, Peter K.** Leadership and discipleship: a study of Luke 22:24-30. SBL.DS 138: 1994, ⇒10,5042; 12,5165. RRB 104 (1997) 120-123 *(Prendergast, Terrence)*.
5484 *Kruger, H.A.J.* A sword over his head or in his hand? (Luke 22,35-38). The scriptures in the gospels. BEThL 131: 1997, ⇒234. ETuckett, C.M., 597-604.
5485 **Tremolada, Pierantonio** "E fu annoverato fra iniqui": prospettive di lettura della Passione secondo Luca alla luce di Lc 22,37 (Is

53,12d). Diss. Pont. Inst. Biblicum 1996, <sup>D</sup>*Vanhoye, Albert*:
AnBib 137: R 1997, Ed. Pont. Istit. Biblico 288 pp. L36.000. 88-
7653-137-8.

5486 *Smit Sibinga, J.* The making of Luke 23:26-56: an analysis of the
composition technique in Luke's crucifixion narrative. RB 104
(1997) 378-404.

5487 *Delobel, Joel* Luke 23:34a: a perpetual text-critical crux?. NT.S
89: 1997, ⇒7. <sup>F</sup>BAARDA T., 25-36.

5488 *Carras, George P.* A pentateuchal echo in Jesus' prayer on the
cross: intertextuality between Numbers 15,22-31 and Luke 23,34a.
The scriptures in the gospels. BEThL 131: 1997, ⇒234. <sup>E</sup>Tuckett,
C.M., 605-616.

5489 *Terrinoni, Ubaldo* Il buon ladrone: la salvezza passa attraverso la
croce, Lc. 23,40-43. RVS 51/2 (1997) 201-221.

5490 *Grández, Rufino María* Crítica textual de Lc 23,45a: καὶ ἐσκοτίσθη
ὁ ἥλιος. ScrVict 44 (1997) 5-20.

5491 **San Silvester, Tung Kiem** Experience of the risen lord in Luke
24:13-35. Diss. extract Pont. Univ. Urbaniana; R 1997, x; 95 pp.
Bibl.

5492 *Ochs, Robert* Die Emmaus-Erzählung: Beispielerzählung für das
pastorale Handlungsmodell der Begleitung. KatBl 122 (1997) 107-
109.

5493 *Moore, Thomas S.* The Lucan great commission and the Isaianic
Servant. BS 154 (1997) 47-60 [Lk 24,46-49].

5494 *Wind, Renate* Der Gott, der bei uns ist, ist der Gott, der uns verlä-
ßt: sozialgeschichtliche Bibelauslegung zu Lukas 24,50-53. JK
58/4, Beih. (1997) 224-227.

5495 *Moitel, Pierre* Luc 24: 'il est ressuscité selon les Ecritures'. CEv
98 (1997) 15-21.

5496 *Carroll, Conard* Hermes, the fantastic and the burning heart. The
monstrous. 1997, ⇒169. <sup>E</sup>Aichele, G., 148-167 [Lk 24; Acts 14].

5497 *Biemer, Günter* Sonntag—der Auferstehungstag der Woche (zu Lk
24,35ff). Diak. 28 (1997) 281-283.

F8.1 *Actus Apostolorum*, Acts—*text, commentary, topics*

5498 **Barrett, Charles Kingsley** Acts I-XIV. ICC: 1994, ⇒12,5177.
<sup>R</sup>RBBras 14 (1997) 408-409.

5499 <sup>E</sup>**Bateman, John J.** In Acta apostolorum paraphrasis [Paraphrase
on the Acts of the Apostles]. <sup>T</sup>*Sider, Robert D.*: Collected works of
Erasmus 50: 1995, ⇒11/1,3783; 12,5178. <sup>R</sup>SR 26 (1997) 120-122
*(Starnes, Colin)*.

5500 <sup>E</sup>**Bauckham, Richard** The book of Acts in its Palestinian setting.
1995, ⇒11/1,3748; 12,5179. <sup>R</sup>CBQ 59 (1997) 404-406 *(McLaren,
James S.)*; TJT 13 (1997) 265-267 *(Oakman, Douglas E.)*.

5501 **Boice, James Montgomery** Acts: an expositional commentary. GR
1997, Baker 454 pp. $30. 0-8010-1137-X.

5502 **Boismard, Marie-Émile; Lamouille, A.** Les Actes des deux Apôtres. EtB 12-14: 1990, 3 vols. ⇒6,5466... 8,5476. <sup>R</sup>RivBib 45
(1997) 368-371 *(Fabris, Rinaldo)*.

5503 *Bondi, Richard A.* Become such as I am: St. Paul in the Acts of the
Apostles. BTB 27 (1997) 164-177.

5504 **Bossuyt, Philippe; Radermakers, Jean** Lettura pastorale degli Atti degli Apostoli. Lettura Pastorale della Bibbia 25: Bo 1997, EDB 720 pp. L82.000. 88-10-20589-8.

5505 **Brüning, Gerhard** Apostelgeschichte: ihr werdet meine Zeugen sein. Roter Faden: Wu 1997, Brockhaus 143 pp. 3-417-25082-X.

5506 *Caballero Cuesta, José M.ª* La oración en la iglesia primitiva: estudio sobre el libro de los Hechos de los Apósteles (1). Burgense 38/1 (1997) 33-65.

5507 *Cancik, Hubert* The history of culture, religion, and institutions in ancient historiography: philological observations concerning Luke's history. JBL 116 (1997) 673-695.

5508 *Dunn, James D.G.* κύριος in Acts. BZNW 86: 1997, ⇒41. FHoFIUS O., 363-378.

5509 **Gaukroger, Stephen** Acts. Crossway Bible Guide: Leicester 1997, Crossway 201 pp. 1-85684-163-4.

5510 *Geer, Thomas C.* The presence and significance of Lukanisms in the 'western' text of Acts. New Testament text. BiSe 44: 1997 <1990>, EPorter, S.E., 34-51.

5511 EGill, **David W.J.; Gempf, Conrad** The book of Acts in its Graeco-Roman setting. 1994, ⇒10,5064... 12,5191. REvQ 69 (1997) 283-284 *(Walton, Steve)*.

5512 **González, Justo L.** Tres meses en la escuela del Espíritu: estudios sobre Hechos. Nv 1997, Abingdon vii; 168 pp. 0-687-02568-0.

5513 E*Hirunuma, Toshio* Notes on Acts: (22) Act. 1.21. Studia Textus Novi Testamenti 332 (1997) 2755-2756.

5514 **Jervell, Jacob Stephan** The theology of the Acts of the Apostles. 1996, ⇒12,5193. RAThR 79 (1997) 437-438 *(Carroll, John T.)*.

5515 **Johnson, Dennis E.** The message of Acts in the history of redemption. Phillipsburg 1997, P&R xiv; 248 pp. Bibl.; 0-87552-235-1 [NThAR 1998,270].

5516 **Johnson, Luke Timothy** The Acts of the Apostles. Sacra Pagina 5: 1992, ⇒8,5483... 11/1,3801. RVJTR 61 (1997) 841-843 *(Raj, M.I.)*.

5517 **Kee, Howard Clark** To every nation under heaven: the Acts of the Apostles. The New Testament in context: Harrisburg, Pennsylvania 1997, Trinity vi; 361 pp. Bibl. $24. 1-56338-221-0.

5518 **Kettenbach, Günter** Das Logbuch des Lukas: das antike Schiff in Fahrt und vor Anker. EHS.T 276: Fra ²1997, Lang 244 pp. 3-631-31238-5 [NThAR 1997,261].

5519 **Kjær-Hansen, Kai** Studieudgave af Apostlenes Gerninger. 1997, Det Danske Bibelselskab 223 pp. DK225. RΙΧΘΥΣ 24/2 (1997) 85-87 *(Nyborg, Poul-Arne)*.

5520 **Larkin, William J.** Acts. 1995, ⇒11/1,3804. RBib. 78 (1997) 128-130 *(Talbert, Charles H.)*.

5521 **Levinskaya, Irina** The book of Acts in its diaspora setting. 1996, ⇒12,5197. RJJS 48 (1997) 369-371 *(Noy, David)*.

5522 Lukas: Handelingen van de apostelen. Den Bosch 1997, Katholieke Bijbelstichting 128 pp. ƒ14. 90-6173-679-X/90-6597-198-X [Str. 65,285].

5523 *Marguerat, Daniel* Actes de Paul et Actes canoniques: un phénomène de relecture. Apocrypha 8 (1997) 207-224.

5524 *Marzotto, Damiano* Figure di donne negli Atti degli Apostoli: contributi per un'antropologia cristiana. Anthropotes 13 (1997) 457-480.

5525  **Matthews, Shelley** High-standing women and mission and conversion: a rhetorical-historical analysis of the *Antiquities* and Acts. Diss. Harvard 1997 [HThR 90,441].

5526  **Monari, Luciano** Sulla via di Gesù: la vita nello Spirito a partire dagli Atti degli Apostoli. Pres. *Ruini, Card. Camillo*: Reggio Emilia 1997, San Lorenzo 173 pp. 88-8071-070-2.

5527  **Nodet, Etienne; Taylor, Justin** Essai sur les origines du christianisme: une secte éclatée. Initiations: P 1997, Cerf 429 pp. 2-204-05819-X [RSR 86,437ss—Guillet, Jacques].

5528  *Osburn, Carroll D.* The search for the original text of Acts—the international project on the text of Acts. New Testament text. BiSe 44: 1997 <1991>, EPorter, S.E., 17-33.

5529  *Overman, J. Andrew* The God-fearers: some neglected features. NT backgrounds. 1997 <1988>, ⇒3975. EEvans, C.A., 253-262.

5530  *Panimolle, Salvatore A.* L'elezione divina negli Atti degli apostoli. DSBP 15 (1997) 98-126.

5531  *Pathrapankal, Joseph* The church in the Acts of the Apostles: a challenge for our times. ITS 34/1-3 (1997) 202-223.

5532  *Pichler, Josef* Dimensionen des Zeugenbegriffs in der Apostelgeschichte. 1997, ⇒106. FWOSCHITZ K., 394-403.

5533  *Rasco, Emilio* Le tappe fondamentali della ricerca sugli Atti degli Apostoli. Res. 32. Gr. 78 (1997) 5-32.

5534  *Read-Heimerdinger, Jenny* The 'long' and the 'short' texts of Acts: a closer look at the quantity and types of variation. Res. 261. RCatT 22 (1997) 245-261.

5535  **Reimer, Ivoni Richter** Women in the Acts of the Apostles. TMaloney, Linda M.: 1995, ⇒11/1,3816. RCBQ 59 (1997) 590-592 *(Reid, Barbara E.)*.

5536  *Richard, Pablo* El movimiento de Jesús después de su resurrección y antes de la iglesia: claves hermenéuticas para interpretar los Hechos de los apóstoles, 1. RLAT 13 (1996) 257-280; 2-4. RLAT 14 (1997) 61-82, 193-218, 285-307.

5537  *Seaford, Richard* Thunder, lightning and earthquake in the *Bacchae* and the Acts of the Apostles. What is a god?. ELloyd, A.B., 1997, ⇒M5.1. 139-151 [Acts 9,3-7; 16,26].

5538  **Spencer, F. Scott** Acts. Readings, a new biblical commentary: Shf 1997, Academic 266 pp. £40/£12.50. 1-85075-673-2/817-4.

5539  **Steyn, G.J.** Septuagint quotations in the context of the Petrine and Pauline speeches in the Acta Apostolorum. 1995, ⇒11/1,3823; 12,5212. RJThS 48 (1997) 194-196 *(Barrett, C.K.)*; CrSt 18 (1997) 659-662 *(Passoni Dell'Acqua, Anna)*.

5540  *Stricher, Joseph* Le nouveau visage du Ressuscité: les Actes des Apôtres. DosB 69 (1997) 19-21.

5541  **Talbert, Charles H.** Reading Acts: a literary and theological commentary on the Acts of the Apostles. Reading the NT: NY 1997, Crossroad 269 pp. $30. 0-8245-1669-9 [ThD 45,92—Heiser, W.].

5542  **Tavardon, Paul** Le texte alexandrin et le texte occidental des Actes des Apôtres: doublets et variantes de structure. Préf. *Boismard, Marie-Émile* CRB 37: P 1997, Gabalda iii; 201 pp. FF210. 2-85021-098-6 [RTL 29,131].

5543  **Taylor, Justin** Commentaire historique (Act. 18,23-28,31). Les Actes des deux apôtres, 6. EtB 30: 1996, ⇒12,5215. RRivBib 45 (1997) 373-374 *(Fabris, Rinaldo)*; RB 104 (1997) 412-416 *(Mora, Vincent)*.

5544 *Trevijano Etcheverría, Ramón* El contrapunto Lucano (Hch 9,26-30; 11,27-30; 12,25 y 15,1-35) a Gal 1,18-20 y 2,1-10. Salm. 44 (1997) 295-339.

5545 **Vouga, François** Les premiers pas du christianisme: les écrits, les acteurs, les débats. MoBi 35: Genève 1997, Labor et F 264 pp. FF140. 2-8309-0871-6 [ETR 73,311].

5546 *Walter, Nikolaus* Hellenistische Diaspora-Juden an der Wiege des Urchristentums. NT and Hellenistic Judaism. 1997, ⇒318. EBorgen, P., 37-58.

5547 **Weiß, Wolfgang** "Zeichen und Wunder": eine Studie zu der Sprachtradition und ihrer Verwendung im Neuen Testament. WMANT 67: 1995, ⇒11/1,3829. RThPQ 145/2 (1997) 173-175 *(Schreiber, Stefan)*.

5548 EWinter, Bruce W.; Clarke, Andrew D. The book of Acts in its ancient literary setting. 1993, ⇒9,5310... 12,5221. REvangel 15/2 (1997) 60-61 *(Bill, Howard C.)*; EvQ 69 (1997) 281-282 *(Walton, Steve)*.

## F8.3 *Ecclesia primaeva Actuum:* Die Urgemeinde

5549 *Dujarier, Michel* L'hospitalité chez les premiers chrétiens. Mission de l'Église 114 (1997) 9-17.

5550 **Goulder, Michael** St. Paul versus St. Peter: a tale of two missions. 1994, ⇒10,5108a; 12,5229. RCTJ 32/1 (1997) 164-168 *(DeBoer, Willis P.)*.

5551 **Manns, Frédéric** L'Israël de Dieu: essais sur le christianisme primitif. ASBF 42: 1996, ⇒12,5230. RAnton. 72 (1997) 698-699 *(Nobile, Marco)*.

5552 **Trocmé, Étienne** L'enfance du christianisme. P 1997, Noêsis 218 pp. FF130. 2-911606-09-4. RETR 72 (1997) 610-611 *(Cuvillier, Élian)*; BLE 98 (1997) 397-398 *(Debergé, P.)*.

5553 *Walter, Nikolaus* Apostelgeschichte 6,1 und die Anfänge der Urgemeinde in Jerusalem. Praeparatio evangelica. WUNT 98: 1997 <1983>, ⇒167. 187-211.

## F8.5 **Ascensio, Pentecostes; ministerium Petri**—*Act 1...*

5554 *González Faus, José Ignacio* Algunos libros últimos sobre el ministerio de Pedro. RLAT 14 (1997) 17-39, 111-137.

5555 **Matson, David L.** Household conversion narratives in Acts: pattern and interpretation. JSNT.S 123: 1996, ⇒12,5238. REvQ 69 (1997) 349-351 *(Marshall, I. Howard)*; CritRR 10 (1997) 194-196 *(Brawley, Robert L.)*.

5556 *Paulsen, Henning* Das Kerygma Petri und die urchristliche Apologetik. Zur Literatur. WUNT 99: 1997 <1977>, 173-209.

5557 *Moore, Thomas S.* "To the end of the earth": the geographical and ethnic universalism of Acts 1:8 in light of Isaianic influence on Luke. JETS 40 (1997) 389-399.

5558 *Heimerdinger, Jenny* La tradition targumique et le Codex de Bèze: Actes 1:15-26. La Bíblia i el Mediterrani. 1997, ⇒385. EBorrell, d'Agustí, 171-180.

5559  *Schieffer, Elisabeth* "Wieso kann sie jeder von uns in seiner Mut-
      tersprache hören?" (Apg 2,8): eine biblische Besinnung zu Pfing-
      sten. LS 48 (1997) 105-107.
5560  *Van der Horst, Pieter W.* Hellenistic parallels to the Acts of the
      Apostles (2.1-47). NT backgrounds. 1997 <1985>, ⇒3975.
      ᴱEvans, C.A., 207-219.
5561  *Grillo, José G.* O discurso de Pedro em Pentecostes: estudo do gê-
      nero literário em Atos 2:14-40. Vox Scripturae 7/1 (1997) 37-52
      [ZID 23,415].
5562  *Rasmussen, Keld Hvolbol* L'écriture de Luc et le discours de Pierre
      en Ac 2. SémBib 86 (1997) 39-47.
5563  *Schreiber, Stefan* Der Glaube in der Wunderdeutung von Apg 3,16.
      SNTU.A 22 (1997) 25-46.
5564  *Van der Horst, Pieter W.* Hellenistic parallels to Acts (chapters 3
      and 4). NT backgrounds. 1997 <1989>, ⇒3975. ᴱEvans, C.A.,
      220-229.
5565  *Havelaar, Henriette* Hellenistic parallels to Acts 5.1-11 and the
      problem of conflicting interpretations. JSNT 67 (1997) 63-82.
5566  *Barbi, A.* 'Bisogna obbedire a Dio piuttosto che agli uomini (*At*
      5,29)' nel contesto della persecuzione gerosolimitana.
      L'obbedienza. 1997, ⇒216. ᴱMarrocu, G., 93-113.
5567  *Lyons, William John* The words of Gamaliel (Acts 5.38-39) and the
      irony of indeterminacy. JSNT 68 (1997) 23-49.
5568  *Bodinger, Martin* Les "Hébreux" et les "Hellénistes" dans le livre
      des Actes des Apôtres. Henoch 19/1 (1997) 39-58.
5569  *Reinmuth, Eckart* Beobachtungen zur Rezeption der Genesis bei
      Pseudo-Pʜɪʟᴏ (LAB 1-8) und Lukas (Apg 7.2-17). NTS 43
      (1997) 552-569.
5570  *Donaldson, T.L.* Moses typology and the sectarian nature of early
      christian anti-Judaism: a study in Acts 7. NT backgrounds. 1997
      <1981>, ⇒3975. ᴱEvans, C.A., 230-252.
5571  *Brehm, H. Alan* Vindicating the rejected one: Stephen's speech as a
      critique of the Jewish leaders. Early christian interpretation.
      JSNT.S 148: 1997, ⇒191. ᴱEvans, C.A., 266-299 [Acts 7].
5572  *Dickerson, Patrick L.* The sources of the account of the mission to
      Samaria in Acts 8:5-25. NT 39 (1997) 210-234.
5573  **Heintz, Florent** Simon "le Magicien": Actes 8, 5-25 et l'accusation
      de magie contre les prophètes thaumaturges dans l'antiquité. CRB
      39: P 1997, Gabalda (6) 179 pp. Bibl. FF225. 2-85021-104-4.
5574  **Stachow, Mary Ann** 'Do you understand what you are reading?'
      (Acts 8:30): a historical-critical reexamination of the pericope of
      Philip and the Ethiopian (Acts 8:26-40). Diss. Catholic Univ. of
      America 1997; ᴰFitzmyer, J.A., Microfilm: Ann Arbor [RTL
      29,588].
5575  *Sánchez de Toca, Melchor* Πορεύου κατὰ μεσημβρίαν (Hch 8,26).
      EstB 55 (1997) 107-115.
5576  *Clerget, Joël* La lumière du nom ou le parcours subjectif dans un
      corps social: Actes 9,1-19. SémBib 86 (1997) 31-38.
5577  *Barber, John L.* The paradoxical courage of Ananias. RfR 56
      (1997) 571-577 [Acts 9,10-16].
5578  *Dougherty, Charles T.* Did Paul fall off a horse?: a deceptively
      simple question reveals differences in bible interpretation. BiRe
      13/4 (1997) 42-44 [Acts 9].

5579   Kurz, William S. Effects of variant narrators in Acts 10-11. NTS
       43 (1997) 570-586.

F8.7 Act 13...Itinera Pauli; Paul's Journeys

5580   Jewett, Robert Mapping the route of Paul's "second missionary
       journey" from Dorylaeum to Troas. TynB 48 (1997) 1-22.
5581   Rapske, Brian The book of Acts and Paul in Roman custody.
       1994, ⇒10,5191; 12,5275. RCBQ 59 (1997) 783-785 (Kazmierski,
       Carl R.).
5582   Schreiber, Stefan Paulus als Wundertäter: redaktionsgeschichtliche
       Untersuchungen zur Apostelgeschichte und den authentischen Pau-
       lusbriefen. BZNW 79: 1996, ⇒12,5278. RJThS 48 (1997) 596-598
       (Nielsen, H.K.).
5583   Taşlialan, Mehmet Pisidian Antioch: 'the journeys of St. Paul to
       Antioch'. Göltaş Cultural Series 2: Ankara 1997, 82 pp. [CoTh
       69/4,195—Chrostowski, Waldemar].
5584   Toni, Roberto 'E accoglieva tutti...': l'itinerario di Paolo. Horeb
       18/3 (1997) 34-42 [1 Kgs 17].

5585   Lin, Bonaventura Wundertaten und Mission: dramatische Episo-
       den in Apg 13-14. Diss. Würzburg 1997/98; DKlauck [BZ
       42,319].
5586   Kilgallen, John J. Acts 13:4-12: the role of the Magos. EstB 55
       (1997) 223-237.
5587   Pichler, Josef Paulusrezeption in der Apostelgeschichte: Untersu-
       chungen zur Rede im pisidischen Antiochien. Diss. Graz, 1995,
       DZeilinger, F.: IThS 50: Innsbruck 1997, Tyrolia 404 pp. 3-7022-
       2096-8 [Acts 13,16-52].
5588   Bechard, Dean Paul among the rustics: a study of Luke's socio-
       geographical universalism in Acts 13:48-14:20. Diss. Yale 1997;
       DMeeks, W.A. [RTL 29,583].
5589   Fournier, Marianne The episode at Lystra: a rhetorical and se-
       miotic analysis of Acts 14:7-20a. Diss. DDumais, Marcel:
       AmUSt.TR 197: NY 1997, Lang xvi; 265 pp. $47. 0-8204-3384-5
       [EeT(O) 29,152].
5590   Barnes, Colin Paul and Johanan ben Zakkai. ET 108 (1997) 366-
       367 [Acts 14].
5591   Rolin, Patrice Pierre, Paul, Jacques à Jérusalem. CBFV 36 (1997)
       99-114 [Acts 15,1-21; Gal 2,1-10].
5592   Peretto, Elio Pietro e Paolo e l'anno 49 nella complessa situazione
       palestinese. 1997 <1967>, ⇒155. Saggi. 13-24 [Acts 15,1-29;
       Gal 2,11-21].
5593   Ádna, Jostein Die Heilige Schrift als Zeuge der Heidenmission: die
       Rezeption von Amos 9,11-12 in Apg 15,16-18. 1997, ⇒92.
       FSTUHLMACHER P., 1-23.
5594   Rius-Camps, Josep La compareixença de Pau davant l'Areòpag
       d'Atenes: primer contacte del cristianisme amb la filosofia grega.
       La Bíblia i el Mediterrani. 1997, ⇒385. EBorrell, d'Agustí, 203-
       223 [Acts 15,41-16,10; 17,16-34].
5595   Wehnert, Jürgen Die Reinheit des "christlichen Gottesvolkes" aus
       Juden und Heiden: Studien zum historischen und theologischen

Hintergrund des sogenannten Aposteldekrets. FRLANT 173: Gö 1997 Vandenhoeck & R 311 pp. Diss. Gö 1995. DM124. 3-525-53856-1 [Acts 15; 21,15-26; Gal 2,1-14].

5596  Scott, J. Julius The church's progress to the council of Jerusalem according to the book of Acts. BBR 7 (1997) 205-224 [Acts 15].

5597  Pokorný, Petr 'Ihr Männer von Athen!': Apg 17,16-34 und die Role der theologischen Fakultät im Rahmen der Universitätswissenschaften. Bibelauslegung. WUNT 100: 1997, ⇒970. 87-95.

5598  Isizoh, Denis Chukwudi The resurrected Jesus preached in Athens: the Areopagus speech (Acts 17,16-34): an inquiry into the reasons for the Greek reaction to the speech and a reading of the text from the African traditional religious perspective. Diss. Pont Univ. Gregoriana 1996; DGrech, Prosper: Lagos—R 1997, Ceedee xvi; 244 pp. 88-900030-1-4.

5599  Barbi, Augusto Le genti cercano Dio 'come a tentoni': Paolo ad Athene (At 17,16-34). PSV 35 (1997) 161-175.

5600  Külling, Heinz Geoffenbartes Geheimnis: eine Auslegung von Apostelgeschichte 17,16-34. AThANT 79: 1993, ⇒9,5387. RNT 39 (1997) 96-99 (Stenschke, Christoph).

5601  Croy, N. Clayton Hellenistic philosophies and the preaching of the resurrection (Acts 17:18, 32). NT 39 (1997) 21-39.

5602  Díaz Rodelas, Juan Miguel Hechos 17,22-34: un paradigma de inculturación de la fe?. La Bíblia i el Mediterrani. 1997, ⇒385. EBorrell, d'Agustí, 131-144.

5603  Horn, Friedrich W. Paulus, das Nasiräat und die Nasiräer. NT 39 (1997) 117-137 [Acts 18,18-22; 21,15-27].

5604  Doughty, Darrell J. Luke's story of Paul in Corinth: fictional history in Acts 18. JHiC 4/1 (1997) 3-54.

5605  Sampathkumar, P.A. Aquila and Priscilla: a family at the service of the word. ITS 34/1-3 (1997) 185-201 [Acts 18].

5606  Selinger, Reinhard Die Demetriosunruhen (Apg. 19,23-40): eine Fallstudie aus rechtshistorischer Perspektive. ZNW 88 (1997) 242-259.

5607  Hemer, Colin The name of Felix again < 1987 >;

5608  Bruce, F.F. The full name of the procurator Felix < 1978 >. New Testament text. BiSe 44: 1997, EPorter, S.E., 259-262/256-258 [Acts 23,24-26].

5609  Chrupcała, Lesław D. Il disegno di Dio e l'annuncio del regno alla luce di At 28,17-31. Sum. 452. LASBF 47 (1997) 79-96.

5610  Winandy, Jacques La finale des Actes: histoire ou théologie. EThL 73 (1997) 103-106 [Acts 28,30-31].

# XI. Johannes

## G1.1  Corpus johanneum: John and his community

5611  Charlesworth, James H. The beloved disciple. 1995, ⇒11/1,3938. RCThMi 24 (1997) 286-287 (Hoops, Merlin H.); ThTo 54/1 (1997) 116-120 (Stanton, Graham N.).

5612  Cothenet, Édouard Les communautés johanniques. EeV 107 (1997) 433-440.

5613  *Doglio, Claudio* Gesù, la dimora di Dio. PaVi 42/6 (1997) 35-41.

5614  **Hill, Robert Allan** An examination and critique of the understanding of the relationship between apocalypticism and gnosticism in Johannine studies. Lewiston, NY 1997, Mellen (8) iii; 258 pp. Bibl. 0-7734-2282-X.

5615  *Kaltenbrunner, Gerd-Klaus* Johannes auf der Insel Patmos: der vierte Evangelist als der Gottesmutter Sohn: mit der Übersetzung eines Briefes des Heiligen Dionysius. Theologisches 27 (1997) 497-504.

5616  *Létourneau, Pierre* Traditions johanniques dans *Le Dialogue du Sauveur* (NH III, 5). Muséon 110/1-2 (1997) 33-61.

5617  *Niederwimmer, Kurt* Zur Eschatologie im Corpus Johanneum. NT 39 (1997) 105-116.

5618  *Painter, John* The Johannine literature. Handbook. NTTS 25: 1997, EPorter, S.E., 555-590.

5619  *Pasquetto, Virgilio* Il lessico antropologico del vangelo e delle lettere di Giovanni. Ter. 48 (1997) 185-232.

5620  **Rathnakara Sadananda, Daniel** The Johannine exegesis of God: an exploration into the Johannine understanding of God. Diss. Bethel 1997; DLindermann, A. [RTL 29,587].

5621  **Rinke, Johannes** Kerygma und Autopsie: der christologische Disput als Spiegel johanneischer Gemeindegeschichte. Herder's Biblical Studies 12: FrB 1997, Herder xi; 346 pp. 3-451-26349-1.

5622  **Rossé, Gérard** La spiritualità di comunione negli scritti giovannei. 1996, ⇒12,4641. RRdT 38 (1997) 851-852 *(Casalegno, Alberto)*.

5623  *Sánchez Navarro, Luis A.* Acerca de ὁράω en Jn. EstB 55 (1997) 263-266.

5624  **Santos, Pedro Paulo Alves dos** Do Espírito da Verdade ao Espírito da Profecia: o Espírito Santo em contacto direto com a vida eclesial no ambito do movimento joanino. Diss. Pont. Univ. Gregoriana 1997; DVanni, Ugo: 489 pp. extr. 4385 [RTL 29,582].

5625  *Segalla, Giuseppe* Qumran e la letteratura giovannea (vangelo e lettere): il dualismo antitetico di luce-tenebra. RStB 9/2 (1997) 117-153.

5626  *Smalley, Stephen S.* The Johannine community and the letters of John. 1997, ⇒93. FSweet J., 95-104.

5627  *Tragan, Pius Ramon* La luce negli scritti giovannei: percorso di un simbolo biblico. Servitium 31/1 (1997) 33-43.

5628  **Tuñi, Josep Oriol; Alegre, Xavier** Escritos joánicos y cartas católicas. 1995 [²1997], ⇒11/1,3955; 12,5326. REstB 55 (1997) 277-278 *(García-Moreno, A.)*.

5629  *Tuñí, Josep Oriol* La escuela joánica: evangelio, cartas y Apocalipsis. ResB 13 (1997) 31-39.

5630  **Vidal, Senén** Los escritos originales de la comunidad del discípulo 'amigo' de Jesús: el evangelio y las cartas de Juan. Biblioteca de Estudios Bíblicos 93: S 1997, Sígueme 653 pp. Pts4.500. 84-301-1321-5. REstAg 32/2 (1997) 338-339 *(Cineira, D.A.)*; EstTrin 31 (1997) 439-440 *(Pikaza, X.)*; ActBib 34 (1997) 192-199 *(Tuñi, Josep O.)*.

5631  *Wahlde, Urban C. von* Community in conflict: the history and social context of the Johannine community. Gospel interpretation. 1997, ⇒210. EKingsbury, J.D., 222-233.

5632  *Zumstein, Jean* Zur Geschichte des johanneischen Christentums. ThLZ 122 (1997) 417-428.

G1.2 **Evangelium Johannis:** *textus, commentarii*

5633 **Barclay, Ian** John's gospel. Crossway Bible Guides: Leicester 1997, Crossway 222 pp. 1-85684-165-0.

5634 **Blanchard, Yves-Marie** Des signes pour croire?: une lecture de l'évangile de Jean. LiBi 106: 1995, ⇒11/1,3960; 12,5332. ᴿRB 104 (1997) 407-412 *(Devillers, Luc)*.

5635 ᴱ**Elliott, W.J.; Parker, David C.** The gospel according to St. John, 1: the papyri. The New Testament in Greek, 1. NTTS 20: 1995, ⇒11/1,3965. ᴿNT 39 (1997) 90-92 *(Rodgers, Peter R.)*; ThLZ 122 (1997) 1120-1122 *(Wachtel, Klaus)*.

5636 ᴱ**Feld, Helmut** In evangelium secundum Johannem commentarius. Pars prior. Ioannis Calvini opera exegetica 16/1. Genève 1997, Droz xlix; 361 pp. 2-600-00192-1. ᴿThLZ 122 (1997) 930-931 *(Rogge, Joachim)*.

5637 **García Moreno, Antonio** El evangelio según San Juan: introducción y exegesis. 1996, ⇒12,5337. ᴿScrTh 29/1 (1997) 286-287 *(Ausín, S.)*.

5638 *Gorman, Michael* The oldest epitome of AUGUSTINE's Tractatus in Euangelium Ioannis and commentaries on the gospel of John in the early Middle Ages. REAug 43 (1997) 63-103.

5639 **Grua, Antonella** Comparazioni tra le citazioni del vangelo secondo Giovanni, presenti nelle opere di LUCIFERO di Cagliari, nel codice a di Vercelli e nella 'Vulgata'. Introd. *Capellino, Mario*. Vercelli 1997, 47 pp. [Nouarien 26,268s—Gavinelli, Simona].

5640 **Guillerand, Augustin** San Giovanni: una lettura spirituale del quarto vangelo. CinB 1995, San Paolo 446 pp. L40.000. ᴿCivCatt 148 III (1997) 330-332 *(Scaiola, D.)*.

5641 **Hofrichter, Peter Leander** Modell und Vorlage der Synoptiker: das vorredaktionelle 'Johannesevangelium'. Theologische Texte und Studien 6: Hildesheim 1997, Olms 205 pp. DM48. 3-487-10371-0 [NThAR 1997,292].

5642 *Johannes: evangelie*, Den Bosch 1997, Katholieke Bijbelstichting 104 pp. ƒ13.50. 90-6173-678-1 [Str. 65,285].

5643 **Keil, Günther** Das Johannesevangelium: ein philosophischer und theologischer Kommentar. Gö 1997, Vandenhoeck & R 254 pp. 3-525-53642-9.

5644 **Kiraz, George Anton** John. Comparative edition of the Syriac gospels. NTTS 21/4: 1996, ⇒12,5340. ᴿNT 39 (1997) 405-414 *(Baarda, T.)*.

5645 **Konings, Johan** João. A Bíblia Passo a Passo: São Paulo 1997, Loyola 88 pp. 85-15-01657-5 [PerTeol 29,437].

5646 **Léon-Dufour, Xavier** Les adieux du Seigneur (chapitres 13-17). Lecture de l'évangile selon Jean, 3. Parole de Dieu 31: 1993, ⇒9,5435...11/1,3970. ᴿThPh 72 (1997) 265-267 *(Sievernich, M.)*.

5647 ᵀ**Leone, Luigi** CIRILLO di Alessandria: commento al vangelo di Giovanni. CTePa 111-113: 1994, ⇒10,5231. ᴿAsp. 44/1 (1997) 116-117 *(Fatica, Luigi)*.

5648 **Moloney, Francis J.** Signs and shadows: reading John 5-12. 1996, ⇒12,5346. New Theology Review 10/4 (1997) 120-121 *(Karris, Robert J.)*; AThR 79 (1997) 596-597 *(Wahlde, Urban C. von )*.

5649 **Morris, Leon** The gospel according to John. NICNT: [2]1995, ⇒11/1,3973; 12,5347. [R]Cart. 13 (1997) 222-223 *(Sanz Valdivieso, R.)* AUSS 35 (1997) 293-294 *(Coutsoumpos, Panayotis)*.

5650 [T]**Paul, Rudolf** Johannes (Apostolus): 'S Johannes-Evangeliom. D' Bibel für Schwoba. Stu 1997, Silberburg 127 pp. Ens Schwäbische übers. 3-87407-247-9.

5651 [T]**Rettig, John W.** AUGUSTINE: tractates on the gospel of John 112-24: tractates on the first epistle of John. FC 92: 1995, ⇒11/1,3977; 12,5350. [R]JEarlyC 5/1 (1997) 131-132 *(Teske, Roland J.)*.

5652 **Ridderbos, Herman N.** The gospel according to John: a theological commentary. [T]*Vriend, John*: GR 1997, Eerdmans xiv; 721 pp. $42. 0-8028-0453-5. [R]WThJ 59 (1997) 334-335 *(Silva, Moisés)*.

5653 **Schwank, Benedikt** Evangelium nach Johannes. 1996, ⇒12,5351. [R]TThZ 106 (1997) 155-156 *(Reiser, M.)*.

5654 [T]**Segalla, Giuseppe** Vangelo secondo Giovanni: traduzione strutturata. Sussidi biblici 56: Reggio Emilia 1997, San Lorenzo 130 pp. 88-8071-068-0.

5655 **Van Houwelingen, P.H.R.** Johannes: het evangelie van het woord. CNT(K): Kampen 1997, Kok 478 pp. *f*79. 90-242-6098-1 [ITBT 6/4,32—Bekker, Ype].

5656 **Witherington III, Ben** John's wisdom: a commentary on the fourth gospel. 1996, ⇒12,5354. [R]CBQ 59 (1997) 790-792 *(Sweetland, Dennis M.)*; CritRR 10 (1997) 219-221 *(Michaels, J. Ramsey)*.

5657 **Zevini, Giorgio** Evangelio según San Juan. 1995, ⇒11/1,3985. [R]CDios 210/1 (1997) 356-357 *(Gutiérrez, J.)*.

### G1.3 Introductio *in Evangelium Johannis*

5658 [E]**Ashton, John** The interpretation of John. E [2]1997, Clark xiv; 330 pp. £15. 0-567-08546-5 [RRT 1998/1,86].

5659 *Ashton, John* Introduction: the problem of John. The interpretation of John. 1997, ⇒5658. 7-25.

5660 *Cothenet, Édouard* Autour du iv[e] évangile. EeV 107 (1997) 440-442.

5661 **Edwards, Ruth B.** Reading the book, 4: the gospel according to John. ET 108 (1997) 101-105.

5662 **Farmer, Craig S.** The gospel of John in the sixteenth century: the Johannine exegesis of Wolfgang MUSCULUS. Oxford Studies in Historical Theology: NY 1997, OUP xiv; 250 pp. $50. 0-19-509903-6 [ChH 67,149ss—Wengert, Timothy J.].

5663 **García-Moreno, Antonio** Introducción al mistero: evangelio de San Juan. Pamplona 1997, Eunate 398 pp. 84-7768-073-6 [RTL 29,125].

5664 *Gebauer, Roland* Sehen und Glauben: zur literarisch-theologischen Zielsetzung des Johannesevangeliums. ThFPr 23/2 (1997) 39-57.

5665 **Hengel, Martin** Die johanneische Frage. Collab. *J. Frey*. WUNT 2/67: 1993, ⇒9,5477... 12,5362. [R]Bijdr. 58 (1997) 457-458 *(Bieringer, Reimund)*.

5666 **Mannucci, Valerio** Giovanni, il vangelo narrante. 1993, ⇒9,5486 ... 12,5366. [R]Hum(B) 52 (1997) 667-668 *(Dalla Vecchia, Flavio)*.

5667 *Motyer, Steve* Method in fourth gospel studies: a way out of the impasse?. JSNT 66 (1997) 27-44.
5668 [E]**Padovese, Luigi** Atti del V Simposio di Efeso su S. Giovanni Apostolo. 1995, ⇒11/2,520; 12,262. [R]RivBib 45 (1997) 103-108 *(Marcheselli, Maurizio)*.
5669 **Schenke, Ludger** Das Buch Johannes: Roman des vierten Evangeliums. Dü 1997, Patmos 320 pp. 3-491-77017-3 [NThAR 1997,195].
5670 *Wenham, David* The enigma of the fourth gospel: another look. JSNT.S 153: 1997, ⇒4. [F]AsHTON J., 102-128 [=TynB 48 (1997) 149-178].

G1.4 *Themata de evangelio Johannis*—John Gospel, topics

5671 **Anderson, Paul N.** The christology of the fourth gospel... John 6. 1996, ⇒12,5375. [R]Cart. 13 (1997) 223-224 *(Sanz Validivieso, R.)*.
5672 *Augenstein, Jörg* "Euer Gesetz"—ein Pronomen und die johanneische Haltung zum Gesetz. ZNW 88 (1997) 311-313.
5673 *Balfour, Glenn M.* Is John's gospel anti-Semitic?. Diss. abstract. TynB 48 (1997) 369-372.
5674 **Ball, David Mark** 'I Am' in John's gospel: literary function, background and theological implications. JSNT.S 124: 1996, ⇒12,5376. [R]CBQ 59 (1997) 566-567 *(Koester, Craig R.)*; JBL 116 (1997) 749-751 *(Wahlde, Urban C. von)*.
5675 *Barreto, Juan* Señales y discernimiento en el evangelio de Juan. RLAT 14 (1997) 41-59.
5676 *Bauckham, Richard* Qumran and the fourth gospel: is there a connection?. The scrolls and the scriptures. JSPE.S 26: 1997, ⇒299. [E]Porter, S.E., 267-279.
5677 **Beck, David R.** The discipleship paradigm: readers and anonymous characters in the fourth gospel. Bibl.Interp. 27: Lei 1997, Brill vii; 173 pp. Bibl. ƒ105/$65.75. 90-04-10700-2.
5678 **Bekker, Ype** Zoon van God, messias, mensenzoon: de structuur van het evangelie naar Johannes [Fils de Dieu, Messie, Fils de l'homme: structure de l'évangile selon Jean]. Diss. Amsterdam; [D]*Zuurmond, R.*: Kampen 1997, Kok 192 pp. 90-242-6128-7. [R]ITBT 6/1 (1997) 32-33 *(Monshouwer, Dirk)*.
5679 **Benedetti, Ugolino** Il vangelo secondo Giovanni alla fine dell'epoca moderna: fede cristiana come interpretazione del senso. 1994, ⇒10,5268; 12,5379. [R]RivBib 45 (1997) 238-240 *(Cilia, Lucio)*.
5680 *Benoît, Frère* Deux dialogues philosophiques dans l'évangile de saint Jean. Aletheia 11 (1997) 89-105 [ŽID 23,307].
5681 **Berger, Klaus** Im Anfang war Johannes: Datierung und Theologie des Evangeliums. Stu 1997, Quell 312 pp. DM38. 3-7918-1435-4 [BZ 42,271—Reim, Günter].
5682 *Beutler, Johannes* Die Stunde Jesu im Johannesevangelium. BiKi 52 (1997) 25-27.
5683 *Busse, Ulrich* Die Tempelmetaphorik als ein Beispiel von implizitem Rekurs auf die biblische Tradition im Johannesevangelium. The scriptures in the gospels. BEThL 131: 1997, ⇒234. [E]Tuckett, C.M., 395-428.
5684 *Cardellino, Lodovico* Testimoni che Gesù è il Cristo (Gv 20,31) affinché tutti credano δι' αὐτοῦ (Gv 1,7). RivBib 45 (1997) 79-85.

5685 **Caron, Gérald** Qui sont les 'juifs' de l'évangile de Jean?. RFTP 35: Quebec 1997, Bellarmin 316 pp. $30. 2-89007-830-2 [RivBib 45,383].

5686 **Casey, Maurice** Is John's Gospel true?. 1996, ⇒12,5390. ET 109 (1997-98) 242-243 *(Edwards, Ruth)*.

5687 *Collins, Raymond F.* From John to the beloved disciple: an essay on Johannine characters;

5688 *Culpepper, R. Alan* The plot of John's story of Jesus. Gospel interpretation. 1997, ⇒210. ᴱKingsbury, J.D., 200-211/188-199.

5689 **Danna, Elizabeth** Which side of the line?: a study of the characterisation of non-Jewish characters in the gospel of John. Dissertation Durham 1997; ᴰBarton, S. [RTL 29,583].

5690 *Devillers, Luc* Les trois témoins: une structure pour le quatrième évangile. RB 104 (1997) 40-87.

5691 *Dietzfelbinger, Christian* Sühnetod im Johannesevangelium?. 1997, ⇒92. ᶠSᴛᴜʜʟᴍᴀᴄʜᴇʀ P., 65-76.

5692 *Draper, J. A.* Temple, tabernacle and mystical experience in John. Neotest. 31 (1997) 263-288.

5693 *Dunderberg, Ismo* John and Thomas in conflict?. Nag Hammadi... · after fifty years. 1997, ⇒341. ᴱTurner, J.D., 361-380.

5694 **DuToit, David S.** Theios anthropos: zur Verwendung von theios anthropos und sinnverwandten Ausdrücken in der Literatur der Kaiserzeit. WUNT 2/91: Tü 1997, Mohr xviii; 457 pp. Diss. Humboldt 1996. DM128. 3-16-146631-4.

5695 **Ensor, P.W.** Jesus and his 'works': the Johannine sayings in historical perspective. WUNT 2/85: 1996, ⇒12,5403. ᴿThG 40 (1997) 233-235 *(Giesen, Heinz)*; JThS 48 (1997) 589-591 *(Grayston, Kenneth)*; ThQ 177 (1997) 312-313 *(Theobald, Michael)*; JETh 11 (1997) 203-205 *(Baum, Armin Daniel)*.

5696 *Fabris, Rinaldo* Caratteristiche dell'antropologia nel quarto vangelo. Som., sum. 139. VivH 8 (1997) 111-139.

5697 *Farfán Navarro, Enrique* Agua viviente. 1997, ⇒76. ᴹRᴜɪᴢ ᴅᴇ ʟᴀ Pᴇɴᴀ J., 85-96.

5698 **Ferraro, Giuseppe** Lo Spirito Santo nel quarto vangelo. OCA 246: 1995, ⇒11/1,4040; 12,5407. ᴿGr. 78 (1997) 203-204;

5699 Lo spirito e l'"ora" di Cristo: l'esegesi di san Tᴏᴍᴍᴀsᴏ d'Aquino sul quarto vangelo. 1996, ⇒12,5409. ᴿTer. 48 (1997) 888-889 *(Pasquetto, Virgilio)*;

5700 Il Paraclito, Cristo, il Padre nel quarto vangelo. 1996, ⇒12,5408. ᴿRdT 38 (1997) 573-574, 717-718 *(Casalegno, Alberto)*; Ter. 48 (1997) 882-883 *(Moriconi, Bruno)*; Mar. 59 (1997) 348-349 *(Pasquetto, Virgilio)*; CivCatt 148 III (1997) 303-304 *(Scaiola, D.)*.

5701 **Ford, J. Massyngbaerde** Redeemer—friend and mother: salvation in antiquity and in the gospel of John. Mp 1997, Fortress 336 pp. £20. 0-8006-2778-4 [Theol. 101,217—Edwards, Ruth B.].

5702 **Frey, Jörg** Die johanneische Eschatologie I: ihre Probleme im Spiegel der Forschung seit Rᴇɪᴍᴀʀᴜs. Diss. Tübingen 1996; ᴰHengel, M.: WUNT 2/96: Tü 1997, Mohr xx; 551 pp. DM188. 3-16-146716-7 [OrdKor 38,512];

5703 II: Zeitverständnis und Eschatologie in den johanneischen Texten. Diss.-Habil. Tübingen 1997-98; ᴰHengel, M. [RTL 29,584].

5704 **García Moreno, Antonio** El cuarto evangelio: aspectos teológicos. 1996, ⇒12,5411. ᴿRF 181 (1997) 327-328 *(Vallarino, Jesús Marí-*

*a)*; Cart. 13 (1997) 224-226 *(Álvarez Barredo, M.)*; Gr. 78 (1997) 775-776 *(Ferraro, Giuseppe)*; CDios 210 (1997) 916-917 *(Gutiérrez, J.)*; ATG 60 (1997) 383-384 *(Contreras Molina, Francisco)*.

5705 García-Moreno, Antonio El agua y el espíritu: aspectos joánicos. La Bíblia i el Mediterrani. La Bíblia i el Mediterrani. 1997, ⇒385. EBorrell, d'Agustí, 281-295.

5706 *Grassi, Joseph A.* Women's leadership roles in John's gospel. BiTod 35 (1997) 312-317.

5707 **Grelot, Pierre** Les juifs dans l'évangile selon Jean: enquête historique et réflexion théologique. CRB 34: 1995, ⇒11/1,4044; 12,5415. RGr. 78 (1997) 158-159 *(Ferraro, Giuseppe)*; NRTh 119 (1997) 117-118 *(Simoens, Y.)*; RB 104 (1997) 288-298 *(Devillers, Luc)*; RICP 62 (1997) 287-288 *(Blanchard, Yves-Marie)*; JBL 116 (1997) 564-566 *(Just, Felix)*.

5708 **Hammes, Axel** Der Ruf ins Leben: eine theologisch-hermeneutische Untersuchung zur Eschatologie des Johannesvangeliums mit einem Ausblick auf ihre Wirkungsgeschichte. Diss. Bonn 1996; DMerklein, H.: BBB 112: Bodenheim 1997, Philo 353 pp. DM98. 3-8257-0060-7.

5709 **Hergenröder, Clemens** Wir schauten seine Herrlichkeit: das johanneische Sprechen vom Sehen im Horizont von Selbsterschliessung Jesu und Antwort des Menschen. FzB 80: 1996, ⇒12,5419. RBoSm 67/1 (1997) 101-104 *(Dugandžić, Ivan)*; ThGl 87/3 (1997) 456-457 *(Ernst, Josef)*.

5710 **Hofius, Ottfried Friedrich; Kammler, Hans-Christian** Johannesstudien. WUNT 2/88: 1996, ⇒12,5420. RDBM 16/1 (1997) 69-74 *(Karakolis, Chr.)*; NT 39 (1997) 394-396 *(Menken, Maarten J.J.)*.

5711 **Howard-Brook, Wes** John's Gospel & the renewal of the Church. Maryknoll, N.Y. 1997, Orbis xi; 179 pp. 1-57075-114-5.

5712 **Jensen, Alexander S.** The struggle for language: John's gospel as a witness to the development of the early christian language of faith. Diss. Durham 1997; DBarton, S.C. 232 pp. [RTL 29,575].

5713 **Jerumanis, Pascal-Marie** Réaliser la communion avec Dieu: croire, vivre et demeurer dans l'évangile selon Saint Jean. 1996, ⇒12,5423. RBLE 98/1 (1997) 80-81 *(Légasse, S.)*; LV(L) 235 (1997) 86 *(Lemonon, J.-P.)*.

5714 **Jones, Larry Paul** The symbol of water in the gospel of John. Diss. 1995, DSegovia, Fernando F.: JSNT.S 145: Shf 1997, Academic 267 pp. £40/$66. 0-85075-668-6.

5715 (a) **Karakole, Chrestou K.** 'E Theologiké semasía tôn thaumaton stò katà Ioánnen Evangélio. Thessalonike 1997, Ekdoseis Pournara 614 pp. Bibl. G; (b) *Kieffer, René* La main du père et du fils dans le quatrième évangile. La main de Dieu. WUNT 94: 1997, ⇒328. EKieffer, R., 107-116 [John 3,35; 10,27-29; 13,03].

5716 **Kieschke, Hans G.** Rekonstruktion des Evangeliums nach St. Johannes. 1995, ⇒11/1,4057. RThLZ 122 (1997) 329-331 *(Bull, Klaus-M.)*.

5717 **Korting, Georg** Die esoterische Struktur des Johannesevangeliums, 1-2. BU 25: 1994, ⇒10,5265... 12,5364. RRevBib 59 (1997) 248-9 *(Martín, José Pablo)*; JBL 115 (1996) 361-363 *(Painter, John)*.

5718 **Kraus, Wolfgang** Johannes und das Alte Testament: Überlegungen zum Umgang mit der Schrift im Johannesevangelium im Horizont Biblischer Theologie. ZNW 88 (1997) 1-23.

5719 *Kügler, Joachim* Der andere König: religionsgeschichtliche Anmerkungen zum Jesusbild des Johannesevangeliums. ZNW 88 (1997) 223-241.

5720 *La Potterie, Ignace de* Jésus, témoin de la vérité et roi par la vérité. The kingdom of God and the mission. StMiss 46 (1997) 21-41;

5721 Santificazione e missione secondo san Giovanni. 30 giorni 4 (1997) 76-77 [AcBib 10/3,268].

5722 **Leclerc, Eloi** Le maître du désir. P 1997, DDB 236 pp. [Telema 23/4,91].

5723 **Lee, Dorothy A.** The symbolic narratives of the fourth gospel. JSNT.S 95: 1994, ⇒10,5277. RHeyJ 38 (1997) 67-68 *(Turney, G.)*.

5724 **Maccini, Robert Gordon** Her testimony is true: women as witnesses according to John. JSNT.S 125: 1996, ⇒12,5437. RCBQ 59 (1997) 776-777 *(Mangan, Céline)*.

5725 *MacGrath, James F.* Uncontrived Messiah or passover plot?: a study of a Johannine apologetic motif. IBSt 19 (1997) 2-16.

5726 *Manns, Frédéric* El evangelio de Juan a la luz del judaísmo. TE 41 (1997) 351-365;

5727 La sagesse nourricière dans l'Évangile de Jean. BeO 39/4 (1997) 207-234;

5728 La Galilée dans le quatrième évangile. Sum. 351. Anton. 72 (1997) 351-364.

5729 *Martyn, J. Louis* John and Paul on the subject of gospel and scripture. Theological issues. 1997 <1992>, ⇒146. 209-230.

5730 *McGrath, James F.* Going up and coming down in Johannine legitimation. Neotest. 31 (1997) 107-118.

5731 **Menichelli, Ernesto** I simboli biblici nel vangelo di Giovanni. Mi 1995, Àncora 166 pp. L18.000. RCivCatt 148 I (1997) 619-620 *(Scaiola, D.)*.

5732 **Menken, Maarten J.J.** Old Testament quotations in the fourth gospel. 1996, ⇒12,5445. RJThS 48 (1997) 591-594 *(North, W.S.)*.

5733 *Menken, Maarten J.J.* The use of the Septuagint in three quotations in John: Jn 10,34; 12,38; 19,24. The scriptures in the gospels. BEThL 131: 1997, ⇒234. ETuckett, C.M., 367-393.

5734 *Moldovan, Ioan* Învăţătorul Isus—potrivit evangheliei după sfântul Ioan [Le maitre Jésus, d'après l'évangile de saint Jean]. Rés. 31. SUBB 42/1 (1997) 31-43.

5735 **Motyer, Stephen** Your father the devil?: a new approach to John and 'the Jews'. Carlisle 1997, Paternoster 260 pp. [RTR 57,156—Salier, Bill].

5736 *Muñoz León, Domingo* Jesucristo, don del padre a la humanidad: perspectiva del cuarto evangelio. ScrTh 29 (1997) 493-510.

5737 *Müller, Peter* "Was ich geschrieben habe, das habe ich geschrieben": Beobachtungen am Johannesevangelium zum Verhältnis von Mündlichkeit und Schriftlichkeit. Logos. TANZ 20: 1997, ⇒229. ESellin, G., 153-173.

5738 *Ndombi, Jean-Roger* Le langage des lieux dans l'évangile de Jean. Hekima Review 17 (1997) 53-65.

5739 *Neufeld, Dietmar* "And when that one comes": aspects of Johannine messianism. Eschatology, messianism. SDSSRL 1: 1997, ⇒276. EEvans, C.A., 120-140.

5740 *O'Day, Gail R.* Toward a narrative-critical study of John. Gospel interpretation. 1997, ⇒210. EKingsbury, J.D., 181-187.

5741  *O'Neill, J. C.* A vision for the church: John's gospel. 1997, ⇒93.
FSWEET J., 79-93.

5742  **Obermann, Andreas** Die christologische Erfüllung der Schrift im
Johannesevangelium. WUNT 2/83: 1996, ⇒12,5453. ROrdKor 38
(1997) 236-237 *(Giesen, Heinz)*; CritRR 10 (1997) 200-202
*(Köstenberger, Andreas J.)*.

5743  *Panimolle, Salvatore A.* La escatologia dell'evangelista Giovanni.
DSBP 16 (1997) 154-171.

5744  *Penna, Romano* Lessico di rivelazione e cristologia nel quarto vangelo. Som., sum. 167. VivH 8 (1997) 141-168.

5745  *Peretto, Elio* La voce 'donna' segno di continuità dinamica tra
Giovanni 2,3-4; 19,26-27 e Apocalisse 12,1-6: prospettive eccle-
siali. 1997 <1991>, ⇒155. Saggi. 607-635.

5746  **Petersen, Norman R.** The gospel of John and the sociology of
light. 1993, ⇒9,5532... 12,5457. RJBL 116 (1997) 562-564
*(Fortna, Robert T.)*.

5747  **Plumer, Eric** The absence of exorcisms in the fourth gospel. Sum.
368. Bib. 78 (1997) 350-368.

5748  *Pokorný, Petr* Der irdische Jesus im Johannesevangelium.
Bibelauslegung. WUNT 100: 1997 <1984>, ⇒970. 327-339.

5749  **Reilly, John** Praying John. Strathfield 1997, St Paul's 248 pp.
AUS$18 [ACR 74,382].

5750  *Reinhartz, Adele* A nice Jewish girl reads the gospel of John. Semeia 77 (1997) 177-193.

5751  *Rowland, Christopher* Ιωαννης συνκοινωνος. JSNT.S 153: 1997,
⇒4. FASHTON J., 236-246.

5752  **Schvartz, Alain** Le visage du Père dans l'évangile de Jean. Tychique 17 (1997) 29-34.

5753  *Segovia, Fernando F.* The significance of social location in reading
John's story. Gospel interpretation. 1997, ⇒210. EKingsbury,
J.D., 212-221.

5754  **Sevrin, Jean-Marie** Jésus et le sabbat dans le quatrième évangile.
La loi. LeDiv 168: 1997, ⇒195. EFocant, C., 226-242.

5755  **Simoens, Yves** Selon Jean, 1: une traduction; 2-3: une interprétation. Collection 17: Bru 1997, Éd. de l'Institut d'Études Théologiques 3 vols. 2-930067-29-2. RVieCon 69/5 (1997) 331-332 *(Luciani, Didier)*; LV(L) 235 (1997) 87-88 *(Lemonon, J.-P.)*.

5756  FSMITH D.M., Exploring the gospel of John. ECulpepper, R.
Alan; Black, C. Clifton 1996, ⇒12,82. RBiKi 52 (1997) 94-96
*(Weidemann, Hans-Ulrich)*; BTB 27 (1997) 117-118 *(Craghan,
John F.)*; Faith & Mission 14/2 (1997) 91-92 *(Beck, David R.)*.

5757  **Smith, D. Moody** The theology of the gospel of John. 1995,
⇒11/1,4098; 12,5479. REvQ 69/1 (1997) 74-75 *(Edwards, Ruth
B.)*; Kerux 12/3 (1997) 49-50 *(Dennison, James T.)*.

5758  **Smith, T.C.** Reading the signs. Macon 1997, Smyth & H 144 pp.
$13. 1-57312-156-3 [NTS 44,625].

5759  *Snyder, Graydon F.* The social context of the ironic dialogues in
the gospel of John. 1997, ⇒82. FSCROGGS R., 3-23.

5760  **Soupa, Anne** Jésus selon Jean: le Verbe s'est fait chair. DosB 69
(1997) 12-14.

5761  **Staley, Jeffrey L.** Reading with a passion: rhetoric, autobiography, and the American West in the gospel of John. 1995,
⇒11/1,4100. RRExp 94/1 (1997) 141-143 *(Lewis, Gladys S.)*; CBQ
59/2 (1997) 400-402 *(Burton-Christie, Douglas)*.

5762 **Tovey, Derek** Narrative art and act in the fourth gospel. JSNT.S 151: Shf 1997, Academic 296 pp. £45. 1-85075-687-2.

5763 **Van 't Riet, Peter** Het evangelie uit het leerhuis van Lazarus: een speurtocht naar de joodse herkomst van het vierde evanglie. 1996, ⇒12,5485. ^RKeTh 48/2 (1997) 163-164 *(Monshouwer. D.)*.

5764 *Van der Merwe, Dirk G.* Towards a theological understanding of Johannine discipleship. Neotest. 31 (1997) 339-359.

5765 *Van der Watt, Jan G.* Liefde in die familie van God: 'n beskrywende uiteensetting van familiale liefdesverhoudinge in die Johannesevangelie. HTS 53 (1997) 557-569.

5766 **Van Tilborg, Sjef** Reading John in Ephesus. NT.S 83: 1996, ⇒12,5488. ^RThLZ 122 (1997) 570-571 *(Frey, Jörg)*.

5767 *Vignolo, Roberto* 'Io sono' nel vangelo di Giovanni. PaVi 42/2 (1997) 38-41.

5768 *Walter, Nikolaus* Glaube und irdischer Jesus im Johannesevangelium. Praeparatio evangelica. WUNT 98: 1997 <1982>, ⇒167. 144-150.

5769 *Widdicombe, Peter* Knowing God: ORIGEN and the example of the beloved disciple. StPatr 31: 1997, ⇒351. ^ELivingstone, E., 554-8.

5770 *Zevini, Giorgio* Cercare Dio in Gesù nel vangelo di Giovanni. PSV 35 (1997) 139-160;

5771 L''ora' di Gesù nel vangelo di Giovanni. PSV 36 (1997) 153-169.

5772 *Zumstein, Jean* Das Johannesevangelium: eine Strategie des Glaubens. ThBeitr 28 (1997) 350-363.

### G1.5 Johannis Prologus 1,1...

5773 *Coloe, Mary* The structure of the Johannine prologue and Genesis 1. ABR 45 (1997) 40-55.

5774 *Guidetti, Vittoria Luisa* I Bektashi e il prologo del vangelo di Giovanni. Studi sull'Oriente Cristiano 1 (1997) 75-78.

5775 **Harris, Elizabeth** Prologue and gospel: the theology of the fourth evangelist. JSNT.S 107: 1994, ⇒10,5339... 12,5500. ^RStPat 44/1 (1997) 183-184 *(Segalla, Giuseppe)*.

5776 *Hooker, Morna D.* A glorious key: John 1.1-18. Beginnings. 1997, ⇒136. 64-83.

5777 *Jasper, Alison* Communicating: the word of God. JSNT 67 (1997) 29-44.

5778 *Khoo Kay-keng* Logos, Tao and wisdom. ChFe 40/2 (1997) 149-173.

5779 *Kurz, William S.* Intertextual permutations of the Genesis word in the Johannine prologue. Early christian interpretation. JSNT.S 148: 1997, ⇒191. ^EEvans, C.A., 179-190.

5780 **La Potterie, Ignace de** La concepción virginal de Jesús según San Juan: el texto del Prólogo. Lima 1997, VE 63 pp. 9972-600-26-2.

5781 *MacGrath, James F.* Prologue as legitimation: christological controversy and the interpretation of John 1:1-18. IBSt 19 (1997) 98-120.

5782 *Munitiz, Joseph A.* Nikephoros BLEMMYDES on John: a Byzantine scholar's reactions to John's prologue. JSNT.S 153: 1997, ^FASHTON J., 247-253.

5783   **Paczkowski, Mieczyslaw C.** Esegesi, teologia e mistica: il prologo di Giovanni nelle opere di S. BASILIO Magno. ASBF 39: 1995, ⇒11/1,4122. RCBQ 59 (1997) 390-391 *(Madigan, Kevin)*.

5784   *Pasquier, Anne* Interpretation of the prologue to John's Gospel in some gnostic and patristic writings: a common tradition. Nag Hammadi... after fifty years. 1997, ⇒341. ETurner, J.D., 484-495.

5785   **Pazzini, Domenico** Il prologo di Giovanni in CIRILLO di Alessandria. StBi 116: Brescia 1997, Paideia 218 pp. L33.000. 88-394-0548-8 [RivBib 45,506].

5786   *Salier, Bill* What's in a world?: Κόσμος in the Prologue of John's gospel. RTR 56 (1997) 105-117.

5787   *Segalla, Giuseppe* Il prologo di Giovanni (1,1-18) nell'orizzonte culturale dei suoi primi lettori. Teol(Br) 22 (1997) 14-47.

5788   *Swetnam, James* John's prologue: a suggested interpretation. Melita Theologica 48 (1997) 75-91.

5789   *Zevini, Giorgio* Il prologo nel vangelo di Giovanni: struttura e teologia. BSRel 125: 1997, ⇒45. FJAVIERRE ORTAS A., 101-126.

5790   *Edwards, Ruth B.* χάριν ἀντὶ χάριτος (John 1.16): grace and the law in the Johannine Prologue. NT backgrounds. 1997 <1988>, ⇒3975. EEvans, C.A., 190-202.

5791   *Lataire, Bianca* The son on the father's lap: the meaning of εἰς τὸν κόλπον in John 1:18. SNTU.A 22 (1997) 125-138.

5792   *Kügler, Joachim* Der Sohn im Schoß des Vaters: eine motivgeschichtliche Notiz zu Joh 1,18. BN 89 (1997) 76-87.

5793   *Peretto, Elio* Il logion giovanneo 'agnello di Dio, che toglie il peccato del mondo' (Gv 1,29). 1997 <1982>, ⇒155. Saggi, 285-319.

5794   **Francis, John** The vision of discipleship according to John 1,35-51. Diss. extract Pont. Univ. Urbaniana; R 1997, xiv; 120 pp.

5795   *Hill, C.E.* The identity of John's Nathanael. JSNT 67 (1997) 45-61 [John 1,45-51].

5796   *Lawless, George* The wedding at Cana: AUGUSTINE on the gospel according to John tractates 8 and 9. AugSt 28/2 (1997) 35-80.

5797   *Hübner, Ulrich* Das Weinwunder von Kana auf einer byzantinischen Bleibulle. ZDPV 113 (1997) 133-139.

5798   *Cidrac, Charles de* Pour qui ce vin?: Jn 2.1-11. SémBib 85 (1997) 63-71.

5799   *Guinot, Jean-Noël* Les lectures patristiques grecques (IIIe-Ve s.) du miracle de Cana (*Jn* 2,1-11): constantes et développements christologiques. StPatr 30: 1997, ⇒351. ELivingstone, E.A., 28-41.

5800   *Monshouwer, Dirk* De wijn van de gramschap. ITBT 5/1 (1997) 6-7 [Jer 13,12].

5801   **Prakash, Kujur Jai** The sign at Cana and its influence in the life of faith (Jn 2:1-12). Diss. extract Pont. Univ. Urbaniana; DFederici, Tommaso: R 1997, 64 pp.

5802   *Schwank, Benedikt* 'Sechs steinerne Wasserkrüge' (Joh 2,6). EuA 73 (1997) 314-316.

5803   *Bauer, Johannes B.* 'Literarische' Namen und 'literarische' Bräuche (zu Joh 2,10 und 18,39). Studien zu Bibeltext. 1997 <1982>, ⇒111. 215-225.

5804 *Trudinger, Paul* The cleansing of the temple: St. John's indepen-
dent, subtle reflections. ET 108 (1997) 329-330.
5805 *Chilton, Bruce* The whip of ropes ([ὡς] φραγέλλιον ἐκ σχοινίων)
in John 2:15. Jesus in context. AGAJ 39: 1997 <1991>, ⇒183.
ᴱChilton, B., 441-454.

### G1.6 Jn 3ss... Nicodemus, Samaritana

5806 **Chevalley, Bernard** Nicodème [roman]. Écritures: P 1997,
L'Harmattan 207 pp. 2-7384-6067-4 [ETR 74,139—Lienhard, F.].
5807 *Pryor, John W.* John the Baptist and Jesus: tradition and text in
John 3.25. JSNT 66 (1997) 15-26.

5808 **Link, Andrea Hildegard** Was redest du mit ihr?:... Joh 4,1-42.
1992, ⇒8,5794...10,5365. ᴿRHPhR 77 (1997) 218-219 *(Grob,
Fr.)*.
5809 *Kim, Jean K.* A Korean feminist reading of John 4:1-42. Semeia 78
(1997) 109-119.
5810 **Tosello, Vincenzo** La dimensione simbolica di Gv 4,5-42: studio
ermeneutico interdisciplinare. Diss. excerpt Pont. Athenaeum S.
Anselmi. Thesis ad Lauream 238: R 1997, 121 pp.
5811 *Camprodon, Jaume* A la vora del pou (Jn 4,6). Qüestions de Vida
Cristiana 187 (1997) 12-19.
5812 *Farfán Navarro, Enrique* Agua viviente. ᴹRuiz de la Pena J.,
BSal.E 189: 1997, ⇒76. 85-96 [RB 105,299—Langlamet, F.]
[John 4,14].
5813 **Kalonga, Joachim Kabatuswile.** L'adoration du Père en esprit et
vérité selon Jn 4,23-24: de l'architecture du sens au contenu
dogmatico-spirituel. Diss. 1995, 11/1,4168. ᴿTer. 48 (1997) 889-
891 *(Pasquetto, Virgilio)*.
5814 ᴱ**Bori, Pier Cesare** In spirito e verità: letture di Giovanni 4,23-24.
1996, ⇒12,5539. ᴿRdT 38 (1997) 572-573 *(Casalegno, Alberto)*;
LASBF 47 (1997) 619-623 *(Paczkowski, Mieczysław Celestyn)*.
5815 *Mean, A.H.* The βασιλικός in John 4.46-53. NT backgrounds.
1997 <1985>, ⇒3975. ᴱEvans, C.A., 203-206.

5816 ᴱ**Boismard, Marie-Émile; Lamouille, A.** Jean 5,1-47. Un évangile pré-johannique, 3/1-2. EtB 28-29: 1996, ⇒12,5545. ᴿThLZ
122 (1997) 563 *(Wiefel, Wolfgang)*; RB 104 (1997) 451-452
*(Taylor, Justin)*; RivBib 45 (1997) 487-488 *(Segalla, Giuseppe)*;
POC 46 (1996) 481-483 *(Ternant, P.)*.
5817 *Huie-Jolly, Mary R.* Like father, like son, absolute case, mythic
authority: constructing ideology in John 5:17-23. SBL.SPS 36
(1997) 567-595.
5818 *Huie-Jolly, Mary R.* Threats answered by enthronement: death/re-
surrection and the divine warrior myth in John 5.17-29, Psalm 2
and Daniel 7. Early christian interpretation. JSNT.S 148: 1997,
⇒191. ᴱEvans, C.A., 191-217.

G1.7  **Panis Vitae**—*Jn 6...*

5819  <sup>E</sup>**Culpepper, R. Alan** Critical readings of John 6. Bibl.Interp. 22:
Lei 1997, Brill xiv; 289 pp. *f*155. 90-04-10579-4.

5820  *Philippe, Marie D.* Commentaire de l'évangile de saint Jean: la
multiplication des pains. Aletheia 11 (1997) 153-165 [ZID 23,307]
[John 6,1-14].

5821  *Hemelsoet, Ben* De wonderbare spijziging volgens Johannes. ITBT
5/7 (1997) 24-26 [John 6,1-15].

5822  *O'Day, Gail R.* John 6:15-21: Jesus walking on water as narrative
embodiment of Johannine christology. Critical readings of John 6.
1997, ⇒5819. 149-159.

5823  **Madden, Patrick J.** Jesus' walking on the sea: an investigation of
the origin of the narrative account. BZNW 81: B 1997, De Gruyter
x; 156 pp. DM108. 3-11-015247-9 [Mt 14,22-33; Mk 6,45-52;
John 6,16-21; 21,1-14].

5824  *Swancutt, Diana M.* Hungers assuaged by the bread from heaven:
'eating Jesus' as Isaian call to belief: the confluence of Isaiah 55
and Psalm 78(77) in John 6.22-71. Early christian interpretation.
JSNT.S 148: 1997, ⇒191. <sup>E</sup>Evans, C.A., 218-251.

5825  *Kysar, Robert* The dismantling of decisional faith: a reading of
John 6:25-71. Critical readings of John 6. 1997, ⇒5819. 161-181.

5826  *Menken, Maarten J.J.* John 6:51c-58: eucharist or christology?.
Critical readings of John 6. 1997, ⇒5819. 183-204.

5827  *Fernández, Aurelio* Eucaristia y resurrección: comentario patrístico
a Jn 6,54. <sup>M</sup>RUIZ DE LA PENA J., BSal.E 189: 1997, ⇒76. 521-
542.

5828  *Schenke, Ludger* The Johannine schism and the "Twelve" (John
6:60-71). Critical readings of John 6. 1997, ⇒5819. 205-219.

5829  *Meye Thompson, Marianne* Thinking about God: wisdom and theology in John 6. Critical readings of John 6. 1997, ⇒5819. 221-246.

5830  *Moitel, Pierre* Jean 6: 'c'est moi le pain de la vie'. CEv 8 (1997)
23-26, 43-45.

5831  *Moloney, Francis J.* The function of prolepsis in the interpretation
of John 6. Critical readings of John 6. 1997, ⇒5819. 129-148.

5832  *Mosetto, Francesco* Il vero pane disceso dal cielo. PaVi 42/4
(1997) 35-41.

5833  *Painter, John* Jesus and the quest for eternal life. Critical readings
of John 6. 1997, ⇒5819. 61-94.

5834  *Culpepper, R. Alan* John 6: current research in retrospect. Critical
readings of John 6. 1997, ⇒5819. 247-257.

5835  *Philippe, Marie D.* Commentaire de l'évangile de saint Jean: le discours sur le pain de vie (1). Aletheia 12 (1997) 121-126 [ZID
24,119].

5836  **Caba, José** Pan de vida: teología eucarística del IV Evangelio:
estudio exegético de Jn 6. BAC 531: 1993, ⇒9,5582... 12,5557.
<sup>R</sup>Laur. 38/1-2 (1997) 300-301 *(Martignani, Luigi)*.

5837  *Borgen, Peder* John 6: tradition, interpretation and composition.
Critical readings of John 6. 1997, ⇒5819. 95-114.

5838  *Beutler, Johannes* The structure of John 6. Critical readings of
John 6. 1997, ⇒5819. 115-127.

5839  *Theobald, Michael* Schriftzitate im "Lebensbrot"-Dialog Jesu (Joh
6): ein Paradigma für den Schriftgebrauch des vierten Evangelisten.

The scriptures in the gospels. BEThL 131: 1997, ⇒234. ETuckett, C.M., 327-366.

5840 *Anderson, Paul N.* The Sitz im Leben of the Johannine bread of life discourse and its evolving context. Critical readings of John 6. 1997, ⇒5819. 1-59.

5841 **Camarero Maria, Lorenzo** Revelaciones solemnes de Jesús: derás cristológico en Jn 7-8 (fiesta de las tendas). Diss. Madrid 1993; DMuñoz Léon, D.: Monografías 4: M 1997, Claretianas 482 pp. PTA4.327. 84-7966-140-2 [EThL 74,316*].

5842 *Cory, Catherine* Wisdom's rescue: a new reading of the tabernacles discourse (John 7:1-8:59). JBL 116 (1997) 95-116.

5843 *Ketterer, Eliane* 'Si quelqu'un a soif...'. Sum., som. 117. Cahiers Ratisbonne 2 (1997) 103-117 [John 7,37-39].

5844 *Da Silva, Anthony* 'Neither do I condemn you': a psychological study of the gospel story of the woman taken in adultery. 1997, ⇒89. MSOARES-PRABHU G., 84-101 [John 7,53-8,11].

5845 *Petersen, William L.* Οὐδὲ ἐγώ σε (κατα)κρίνω: John 8:11, the Protevangelium Iacobi, and the history of the Pericope Adulterae. NT.S 89: 1997, ⇒7. FBAARDA T., 191-221.

5846 *Wehn, Beate* Jesus, der erste neue Mann?: Jesus in Begegnungen mit Frauen (Joh 7,53-8,11). Antijudaismus im NT. KT 149: 1997, ⇒K8. EHenze, D., 126-137.

5847 *Grillo, Margherita* Non voglio più volerti bene. TS(I) (luglio-agosto 1997) 11-14 [John 8,2-11].

5848 *Mandonico, Franco* La verità vi farà liberi (Gv 8,3). Presbyteri 31 (1997) 213-217.

5849 *Taulero, Giovanni [Tauler, Johann]* Io sono la luce del mondo. Servitium 31/1 (1997) 74-79 [John 8,12].

5850 **Babra Blanco, Antonio** 'La verdad os hará libres' (Jn 8,32) en la doctrina social, la prensa y el apostolado, según el cardenal HERRERA Oria (1886-1968). Diss. Pont. Univ. Gregoriana 1997, extr. 4366; DJoblin, J. 463 pp. [RTL 29,582].

5851 *Bondi, Richard A.* John 8:39-47: children of Abraham or the devil?. JES 34 (1997) 473-498.

5852 **Rein, Matthias** Die Heilung des Blindgeborenen (Joh 9). WUNT 2/73: 1995, ⇒11/1,4204; 12,5569. RBZ 41 (1997) 137-140 *(Schwankl, Otto)*; ThLZ 122 (1997) 333-335 *(Dettwiler, Andreas)*; CBQ 59 (1997) 395-396 *(Swetnam, James)*.

5853 *Lawless, George* Listening to AUGUSTINE: tractate 44 on John 9. AugSt 28/1 (1997) 51-66.

5854 **Kowalski, Beate** Die Hirtenrede (Joh 10,1-18) im Kontext des Johannesevangeliums. SBB 31: 1996, ⇒12,5572. RBZ 41 (1997) 140-2 *(Scholtissek, Klaus)*; ThLZ 122 (1997) 1026-8 *(Taeger, J.-W.)*.

5855 *Deeley, Mary Katharine* Ezekiel's shepherd and John's Jesus: a case study in the appropriation of biblical texts. Early christian interpretation. JSNT.S 148: 1997, ⇒191. EEvans, C.A., 252-264 [Ezek 34; John 10].

5856 *Thompson, Philip E.* John 10:11-18. Interp. 51 (1997) 182-186.

5857 **Cachia, Nicholas** 'I am the good shepherd; the good shepherd lays down his life for the sheep' (John 10,11): the image of the good

shepherd as a source for the spirituality of the ministerial priesthood. Diss. Pont. Univ. Gregoriana 1995, <sup>D</sup>*Martinez, Ernest R.*:
TGr.Spirituality 4: R 1997, Ed. PUG 392 pp. L39.000/$28. 88-
7652-736-2.

5858 *Santos, José C. dos* Da funcionalidade redactorial de Joao 10,40-
11,54: para uma leitura do episódio da ressuscitaçao de Lázaro como causa da morte de Jesus no 4. evangelho. Itin. 43 (1997) 23-70.

5859 *Mendes dos Santos, José Carlos* Da funcionalidade redactorial de
João 10,40-11,54\*: para uma leitura do episódio da ressuscitação
de Lázaro como causa da morte de Jesus no 4.º evangelho. Itin.
43/1 (1997) 23-70.

5860 *Rodríguez-Ruiz, Miguel* Significado cristológico y soteriológico de
Jn 11,25-27. EstB 55 (1997) 199-222.

5861 *Katz, Paul* Wieso gerade nach Efrajim?: (Erwägungen zu Jh
11,54). ZNW 88 (1997) 130-134.

5862 *Cunningham, Mary B.* ANDREAS of Crete's homilies on Lazarus
and Palm Sunday: the preacher and his audience. StPatr 30: 1997,
⇒351. <sup>E</sup>Livingstone, E.A., 22-41.

5863 *Metzing, Erich* Textkritische Beobachtungen zu ἐκβληθήσεται ἔξω
in Joh. 12,31. ZNW 88 (1997) 126-129.

### G1.8  Jn 13... Sermo sacerdotalis et Passio

5864 **Boer, Martinus C. de** Johannine perspectives on the death of
Jesus. 1996, ⇒12,5583. <sup>R</sup>BZ 41 (1997) 135-137 *(Van der Watt,
Jan)*; JThS 48 (1997) 189-190 *(Smalley, Stephen S.)*; JBL 116
(1997) 372-374 *(Carroll, John T.)*.

5865 **Derrett, J. Duncan M.** The victim—the Johannine passion narrative re-examined. 1993, ⇒8,5849... 12,5586. <sup>R</sup>CDios 210/1 (1997)
357-358 *(Gutiérrez, J.)*.

5866 **Dietzfelbinger, Christian** Der Abschied des Kommenden: eine
Auslegung der johanneischen Abschiedsreden. WUNT 2/95: Tü
1997, Mohr xvi; 369 pp. DM84. 3-16-146687-X [OrdKor 38,511].

5867 **Joulin, Marc** La passion selon saint Jean. P 1997, Desclée de B
224 pp. FF130. 2-220-03948-X [BCLF 583,1119].

5868 **Léon-Dufour, Xavier** L'heure de la glorification. Lecture de
l'évangile selon Jean, 4. 1996, ⇒12,5591. <sup>R</sup>EeV 107 (1997) 83-85
*(Cothenet, Émile)*; Angelicum 74 (1997) 283-285 *(Jurič, Stipe)*;
ThLZ 122 (1997) 445-447 *(Wiefel, Wolfgang)*; ATG 60 (1997)
388-389 *(Contreras Molina, Francisco)*.

5869 *Müller, Ulrich B.* Zur Eigentümlichkeit des Johannesevangeliums:
das Problem des Todes Jesu. ZNW 88 (1997) 24-55.

**Oyer, L.** Interpreting the new in light of the old... commissioning stories of Matthew and John ⇒4992.

5870 **Neugebauer, Johannes** Die eschatologischen Aussagen in den johanneischen Abschiedsreden: eine Untersuchung zu Johannes 13-
17. BWANT 140: 1995, ⇒11/1,4234. <sup>R</sup>ThLZ 122 (1997) 449-454
*(Thyen, Hartwig)*.

5871 **Winter, Martin** Das Vermächtnis Jesu und die Abschiedsworte der
Väter: gattungsgeschichtliche Untersuchung der Vermächtnisrede

im Blick auf Joh. 13-17. FRLANT 161: 1994, ⇒10,5410...
12,5593. RNT 39 (1997) 94-96 *(Stenschke, Christoph)*; ThRv 93
(1997) 223-225 *(Scholtissek, Klaus)*.

5872 **Tolmie, D.F.** Jesus' farewell to the disciples: John 13:1-17:26 in
narratological perspective. 1995, ⇒11/1,4235. RCBQ 59 (1997)
177-79 *(Carter, Warren)*; CDios 210 (1997) 918-9 *(Gutiérrez, J.)*.

5873 *Gangemi, Attilio* La lavanda dei piedi: il coinvologimento dei discepoli nell'esodo di Gesù mediante l'amore. Synaxis 15/1 (1997) 7-
87 [John 13,1-5].

5874 *Simonetti, Manlio* ORIGENE e la lavanda dei piedi. Orpheus 18/1
(1997) 66-79 [John 13,2-11].

5875 *Shae, Gam Seng* Why feet, hands and head?. PPBT 48 (1997) 221-
228 [John 13,9].

5876 *Cerbelaud, Dominique* 'Et trempant la bouchée...' (Jn 13:26): une
curieuse exégèse des Pères syriens. Muséon 110/1-2 (1997) 33-80
[John 13,26].

5877 **Dettwiler, Andreas** Die Gegenwart des Erhöhten... Abschiedsreden (Joh 13,31-16,33). FRLANT 169: 1995, ⇒11/1,4240;
12,5600. ROrdKor 38 (1997) 237-238 *(Giesen, Heinz)*.

5878 **Hoegen-Rohls, Christina** Der nachösterliche Johannes: die Abschiedsreden als hermeneutischer Schlüssel zum vierten Evangelium. WUNT 2/84: 1996, ⇒12,5588. RThLZ 122 (1997) 443-445
*(Beutler, Johannes)*; ThQ 177 (1997) 314 *(Theobald, Michael)*.

5879 **Thomas, John C.** Footwashing in John 13 and the Johannine community. JSNT.S 61: 1991, ⇒7,4943... 12,5602. RAUSS 35 (1997)
301-303 *(Jolliffe, Ronald L.)*.

5880 *Thomas, John Christopher* Footwashing within the context of the
Lord's supper. The Lord's supper. 1997, ⇒260. EStoffer, Dale R.,
169-184 [John 13].

5881 **Matabaro, Chubaka Pierre** La paix de Jésus: étude exégétique de
Jn 14,27. Diss. Studium Biblicum Franciscanum 1997; DManns, F.
ix; 250 pp. pars. publ.: Thesis ad Doctoratum 352: J 1997, Pont.
Athenaeum Antonianum xi; 63 pp. [LASBF 47,641-646].

5882 **Haldimann, Konrad** Rekonstruktion und Entfaltung: exegetische
Untersuchungen zu Joh 15 und 16. Diss. Zürich 1997; DWeder,
H.: 350 pp. [RTL 29,585].

5883 *Moloney, Francis J.* To make God known: a reading of John 17:1-
26. Sal. 59 (1997) 463-489.

5884 **Wierbse, Warren W.** The prayer of Jesus. Leicester 1997, Crossway 153 pp. £5. 1-85684-167-7 [Evangel 17,26] [John 17].

5885 **Heil, John Paul** Blood and water: the death and resurrection of
Jesus in John 18-21. CBQMS 27: 1995, ⇒11/1,4257; 12,5615.
RLASBF 47 (1997) 593-595 *(Chrupcała, Lesław Daniel)*.

5886 *Van Belle, Gilbert* L'accomplissement de la parole de Jésus: la parenthèse de Jn 18,9. The scriptures in the gospels. BEThL 131:
1997, ⇒234. ETuckett, C.M., 617-627.

5887 **Diebold-Scheuermann, Carola** Jesus vor Pilatus... (Joh 18,28-
19,16a). SBB 32: 1996, ⇒12,5616. RThLZ 122 (1997) 904-906
*(Vogler, Werner)*.

5888 *Svensson, Jan* Johannespåsken och Qumrankalendern. SEÅ 62
(1997) 87-110 [John 18-19].

5889 *Culpepper, R. Alan* The theology of the Johannine passion narrative: John 19:16b-30. Neotest. 31 (1997) 21-37.

5890 *Mędala, Stanisław* Historia i teologia w Janowym opisie śmierci
Jezusa (J 19,16b-42) [History and theology in the Johannine
description of the death of Jesus (John 19,16b-42)]. 1997, ⇒52.
ᶠŁACH J., 233-271. **P.**
5891 *Jetter, Hartmut* Das Wort vom Kreuz: (Joh 19,17-18). ThBeitr 28
(1997) 1-7.
5892 *Zumstein, Jean* Johannes 19,25-27. ZThK 94 (1997) 131-154.
5893 *Simoens, Yves* La mort de Jésus selon Jn 19,28-30. NRTh 119
(1997) 3-19.
5894 *Kraus, Wolfgang* Die Vollendung der Schrift nach Joh 19,28:
Überlegungen zum Umgang mit der Schrift im Johannesevangelium. The scriptures in the gospels. BEThL 131: 1997, ⇒234.
ᴱTuckett, C.M., 629-636.
5895 **Bender, Jorge Alberto** La muerte de Jesús como cumplimiento de
su mision terrena: Jn 19,30 en comentarios de Padres, de Maestros
medievales y de exegetas contemporáneos: hiptesis de confronta-
ción. Fac. Theol. Diss. ad Doctoratum 345: R 1997, Pontificium
Athenaeum Antonianum 120 pp. Pars Diss.

5896 *Moitel, Pierre* Jean 20-21: 'nous avons vu le Seigneur'. CEv 98
(1997) 7-13.
5897 *Schlumberger, Sophie* Un récit qui fait histoire: Jean 20,1-18.
CBFV 36 (1997) 85-98.
5898 *Scholtissek, Klaus* "Mitten unter euch steht er, den ihr nicht kennt"
(Joh 1,26): die Messias-Regel des Täufers als johanneische
Sinnlinie-aufgezeigt am Beispiel der relecture der Jüngerberufungen
in der Begegnung zwischen Maria von Magdala und Jesus. MThZ
48 (1997) 103-121 [John 20,1-18].
5899 *Hansen, Steven E.* Forgiving and retaining sin: a study of the text
and context of John 20:23. HBT 19/1 (1997) 24-32.
5900 **Bonney, William** Why did the risen Jesus appear to Thomas?: an
analysis of John 20:24-29 in the context of a synchronic reading of
the gospel. Diss. Fordham 1997; ᴰGiblin, C. [RTL 29,583].
5901 *De Conick, April D.* "Blessed are those who have not seen" (Jn
20:29): Johannine dramatization of an early christian discourse.
Nag Hammadi... after fifty years. 1997, ⇒341. ᴱTurner, J.D.,
381-398.

5902 *Derret, J. Duncan M.* Ἄρτος and the comma (Jn 21:9). FgNT 10
(1997) 117-128.
5903 *Oladipo, Caleb O.* John 21:15-17. Interp. 51 (1997) 65-66.
5904 *Béré, Paul* Pourquoi Pierre est-il peiné?: une lecture exégétique et
théologique de Jean 21,15-19. Hekima Review 17 (1997) 66-80.
5905 *Cardellino, Lodovico* Chi rifiuta la parola di Dio non comprende-
rebbe neppure se fossero scritte tutte le conversioni (Gv 21,25).
RivBib 45 (1997) 429-437.
5906 *Hartmann, Lars* An attempts at a text-centred exegesis of John 21.
Text-centered NT studies. WUNT 102: 1997 <1984>, ⇒132. 70-
87.

## G2.1 Epistulae Johannis

5907 *Morgen, Michèle* Les épîtres de Jean. Les dernières épîtres. 1997, ⇒4403. 189-265.

5908 **Rensberger, David** 1 John, 2 John, 3 John. Abingdon NT Commentaries: Nv 1997, Abingdon 174 pp. $20. 0-687-05722-1 [BiTod 36,136—Senior, Donald].

5909 **Strecker, Georg** The Johannine letters: a commentary on 1, 2, and 3 John. TMaloney, Linda M.: Hermeneia: 1996, ⇒12,5643. RTS 58 (1997) 352-354 *(Brown, Raymond E.)*; JThS 48 (1997) 615-620 *(Grayston, Kenneth)*.

5910 *Watson, Duane F.* Rhetorical criticism of Hebrews and the Catholic Epistles since 1978. CurResB 5 (1997) 175-207.

5911 *Załeski, Jan* Główne myśli teologiczne w Listach św. Jana [Haupttheologische Gedanken in den Johannesbriefen]. Zsfg. 434. WST 10 (1997) 427-434. **P.**

5912 **Dalbesio, Anselmo** "Quello che abbiamo udito e veduto": l'esperienza cristiana nella prima lettera di Giovanni. RivBib.S 22: 1990, ⇒6,5912...12,5645. RRivBib 45 (1997) 243-47 *(Marcheselli, M.)*.

5913 TLuis, **Pío de** San AGUSTIN: homilías sobre la primera carta de San Juan. Valladolid 1997, Estudio Agustiniano 524 pp. Ptas2.300 [EstAg 33,453].

5914 *Reno, R.R.* Theological exegesis of the first letter of John for Easter. Pro Ecclesia 6/1 (1997) 43-54.

   TRettig, **J.W.** AUGUSTINE: Tractates... on the first epistle of John ⇒5651.

5915 *Shim, Ezra S.* The Holy Spirit in 1 John in the light of structural analysis. Chongshin Review 2/2 (1997) 109-126 [ZID 23,439].

5916 *Wallraff, Martin* Das Zeugnis des Kirchenhistorikers Sokrates zur Textkritik von 1 Joh 4,3. ZNW 88 (1997) 145-148.

5917 **Fuller, Robert** Naming the Antichrist: the history of an American obsession. 1995, ⇒11/2,k582. RChH 66 (1997) 880-881 *(Albanese, Catherine L.)*.

5918 **Guadalajara Medina, José** Las profecías del Anticristo en la Edad Media. 1996, ⇒12,5659. RIsidorianum 6 (1997) 287-288 *(Martín Riego, Manuel)*.

5919 **Heid, Stefan** Chiliasmus und Antichrist-Mythos. 1993, ⇒9,5674... 12,5660. RJEarlyC 5/1 (1997) 124-125 *(Wilken, Robert L.)* [1 John 2,18].

5920 **Lietaert Peerbolte, Lambertus J.** The antecedents of antichrist: a traditio-historical study of the earliest christian views on eschatological opponents. JStJudS 49: 1996, ⇒12,5661. RBZ 41 (1997) 285-287 *(Klauck, Hans-Josef)*; JSJ 28 (1997) 338-342 *(Frankfurter, David)*; CritRR 10 (1997) 206-208 *(Royalty, Robert M.)*.

5921 **Lorein, Geert Wouter** Het thema van de antichrist in de intertestamentaire periode. Groningen 1997, Diss. Rijksuniversiteit 562 pp. BEF1.050.

5922 *Whitman, Andrew* 3 John: helping or hindering with the spread of the gospel?. Evangel 15/2 (1997) 37-42.

G2.3  *Apocalypsis Johannis*—Revelation: text, introduction

5923  **Aune, David Edward** Revelation, 1: 1-5. WBC 52A: Dallas 1997, Word ccxi; 374 pp. $33. 0-8499-0251-7. RFaith & Mission 14/2 (1997) 88-90 *(Patterson, Paige)*.

5924  **Backus, Iréna** Les sept visions et la fin des temps: les commentaires genevois de l'Apocalypse entre 1539 et 1584. CRThPh 19: Lausanne 1997, RThPh 82 pp. FS18 [ETR 73,305].

5925  **Bandera, Armando** El Apocalipsis: Patmos? Roma?. Barc 1997, Esin 260 pp. 84-88017-38-3 [NThAR 2000,3].

5926  **Burr, David** OLIVI's peaceable kingdom: a reading of the Apocalypse Commentary. 1993, ⇒9,5682; 12,5666. RHeyJ 38 (1997) 339-340 *(Hamilton, Alastair)*.

5927  **Corsani, Bruno** L'Apocalisse e l'apocalittica del Nuovo Testamento. La Bibbia nella storia 14: Bo 1997, EDB 171 pp. L24.000. 88-10-40264-2.

5928  *Court, John M.* Reading the book 6: the book of Revelation. ET 108 (1997) 164-167.

5929  TEDulaey, **Martine** VICTORIN de Poetovio: sur l'Apocalypse: (suivi de) fragment chronologique (et de) la construction du monde. SC 423: P 1997, Cerf 246 pp. Edition bilingue latin-français; introduction, text critique, commentaire et index. FF154. 2-204-05738-X [BCLF 585-6,1735].

5930  *Elliott, J.K.* The distinctiveness of the Greek manuscripts of the book of Revelation. JThS 48 (1997) 116-124.

5931  **Fiorenza, Elisabeth Schüssler** Apocalisse: visione di un mondo giusto. TDe Santis, *Luca*: 1994, ⇒10,5483. RRivBib 45 (1997) 374-378 *(Biguzzi, Giancarlo)*;

5932  Apocalipsis: visión de un mundo justo. Agora 3: Estella (Navarra) 1997, Verbo Divino 216 pp. 84-8169-155-0.

5933  **Garrow, Alan John Philip** Revelation. NT Readings: L 1997, Routledge xi; 140 pp. £35/£13. 0-415-14640-2/1-0 [NTS 43,621].

5934  **Giblet, Jean** L'Apocalypse: une lecture commentée. Préf. *La Potterie, Ignace de*: Présences 15: Namur 1997, Culture et Vérité 240 pp. FB840. 2-87299-059-3 [RTL 29,93s—Ponthot, J.].

5935  **Giesen, Heinz** Die Offenbarung des Johannes. RNT: Regensburg 1997, Pustet 562 pp. DM98. 3-7917-1520-8.

5936  ETGonzález Echegaray, **Joaquin**, *(al.)*, Obras completas de BEATO de Liébana. 1995, ⇒11/1,4324; 12,5669. RAHIg 6 (1997) 535-536 *(Viciano, A.)*.

5937  **González, Catherine Gunsalus & Justo L.** Revelation. Westminster Bible Companion: LVL 1997, Westminster x; 149 pp. $16. 0-664-25587-6 [BiTod 35,324].

5938  **González, Justo L.** Tres meses en la escuela de Patmos: estudios sobre el Apocalipsis. Nv 1997, Abingdon vii; 168 pp. 0-687-03328-4.

5939  *Gryson, Roger* Les commentaires patristiques latins de l'Apocalypse. RTL 28 (1997) 305-337, 484-502;

5940  Fragments inédits du commentaire de TYCONIUS sur l'Apocalypse. RBen 107 (1997) 189-226.

5941  **Hélou, Clémence** L'Apocalypse de Jésus-Christ. P 1997, Cariscript 311 pp. Bibl. 2-87601-2553.

    *Leonardi, Lino* Volgarizzare la Bibbia nell'Italia medievale... (con appunti sull'*Apocalisse*) ⇒1344.

5942 *Lichtenberger, Hermann* Überlegungen zum Verständnis der Johannes-Apokalypse. BZNW 86: 1997, ⇒41. ᶠHoᖴɪᵁs O., 603-618.

5943 *Mackay, Thomas W.* Sources and style in Bᴇᴅᴇ's commentary on the Apocalypse. StPatr 30: 1997, ⇒351. ᴱLivingstone, E., 54-60.

5944 *Maier, Gerhard* Das Verständnis der Johannesoffenbarung in der Kirchengeschichte. KuD 43/2 (1997) 151-163.

5945 ᴱ**Mamiani, M.** Nᴇᴡᴛᴏɴ: Trattato sull'Apocalisse. 1994 <1733>, ⇒11/1,4329; 12,5675. ᴿAIHS 47 (1997) 419-420 *(Hutton, Sarah).*

5946 **McIlraith, Donal A.** Everyone's Apocalypse: a reflection guide. Suva, Fiji 1997, A Pacific Regional Seminary Publication ix; 124 pp. Bibl. 982-342-001-7.

5947 **Michaels, J. Ramsey** Revelation. IVP NT Commentary: DG 1997, InterVarsity 265 pp. Bibl. 0-8308-1820-0.

5948 *Morton, A.Q.* Revelation. IBSt 19 (1997) 81-91.

5949 *(a) Nardi, Carlo* L'ermeneutica di Aɴᴅʀᴇᴀ e Aʀᴇᴛᴀ di Cesarea: il triplice senso biblico nei loro *Commenti all'Apocalisse.* Som. 195. VivH 8 (1997) 169-196; *(b)* **Negri, Samuele** Rivelazione di Gesù Cristo: commento all'Apocalisse. Rimini 1997, Movimento Biblico Giovanile 366 pp. Bibl.

5950 *Nevius, Richard C.* Papyri witnesses to the text of the nomina sacra in the Apocalypse. 21. Papyrologenkongress, 2. 1997, ⇒367. ᴱKramer, Bärbel, 750-755.

5951 **Prévost, Jean-Pierre** Apocalisse. Fame e Sete della Parola 25: CinB 1997, San Paolo 192 pp. L23.000. 88-215-3455-3 [RdT 38,576].

5952 **Richard, Pablo** Apocalypse. 1995, ⇒11/1,4332. ᴿCritRR 10 (1997) 215-217 *(Rowland, Christopher).*

5953 **Schwarz, Hans** O mistério das sete estrelas: uma interpretação do Apocalipse de João. ᵀ*Trein, Hans Alfred*: São Leopoldo 1997, Sinodal 124 pp. 85-233-0438-X [PerTeol 29,284].

5954 ᵀ**Tagliapietra, Andrea** Gɪᴏᴀᴄᴄʜɪɴᴏ da Fiore sull'Apocalisse: testo originale a fronte. 1994, ⇒11/1,4338. ᴿTeol. 34/1 (1997) 126-128 *(Hubeñák, Florencio).*

5955 **Wall, Robert W.** Revelation. NIBC 18: 1991, ⇒7,5022... 12,5683. ᴿEvQ 69 (1997) 351-352 *(Maile, J.E.).*

## G2.4 *Apocalypsis,* Revelation, topics

5956 *Abir, Peter A.* More than blood-witness. ITS 34 (1997) 233-261.

5957 *Arens K., Eduardo* La composicion del Apocalipsis. RevBib 60 (1997) 13-30.

5958 *Barr, David L.* Towards an ethical reading of the Apocalypse: reflections on John's use of power, violence, and misogyny. SBL.SPS 36 (1997) 358-373.

5959 *Barr, George K.* The structure of revelation. IBSt 19 (1997) 121-132.

5960 **Bauckham, Richard** La teologia dell'Apocalisse. 1994 <1993>, ⇒9,5703...12,5690. ᴿRivBib 45 (1997) 488-492 *(Biguzzi, G.).*

5961 *Beale, G.K.* The hearing formula and the visions of John in Revelation. 1997, ⇒93. ᶠSᴡᴇᴇᴛ J., 167-180.

5962 *Beale, G.K.* Solecisms in the Apocalypse as signals for the presence of Old Testament allusions: a selective analysis of Revelation 1-22. Early christian interpretation. JSNT.S 148: 1997, ⇒191. [E]Evans, C.A., 421-446.

5963 **Bedriñán, Claudio** La dimensión socio-politica del mensaje teológico del Apocalipsis. TGr.T 11: 1996, ⇒12,5692. [R]StPav 44 (1997) 239-241 *(Segalla, Giuseppe)*.

5964 *Biguzzi, B.* 'Sii fedele fino alla morte' *(Ap 2,10)*. L'obbedienza. 1997, ⇒216. [E]Marrocu, G., 183-203.

5965 **Biguzzi, Giancarlo** I settenari nella struttura dell'Apocalisse. SRivBib 31: 1996, ⇒12,5694. [R]Bib. 78 (1997) 294-297 *(Prigent, Pierre)*; StPav 44/2 (1997) 242-243 *(Segalla, Giuseppe)*; LASBF 47 (1997) 595-599 *(Chrupcała, Lesław Daniel)*; PaVi 42/6 (1997) 56-7 *(Doglio, Claudio)*; RdT 38 (1997) 847-8 *(Cuadrado, J.T.)*.

5966 *Boxall, Ian* 'For Paul' or 'for Cephas'?: the book of Revelation and early Asian christianity. JSOT.S 153: 1997, ⇒4. [F]ASHTON J., 198-218.

5967 **Burdon, Christopher** The Apocalypse in England: revelation unravelling, 1700-1834. L 1997, MacMillan xiv; 251 pp. £42.50 [Theol. 101,220—Newport, Kenneth].

5968 **Carrell, Peter R.** Jesus and the angels. Diss. Durham; [D]*Dunn, James D.G.*: MSSNTS 95: NY 1997, CUP xxii; 270 pp. $55. 0-521-59011-6 [BiTod 36,133—Senior, Donald].

5969 *Caza, Lorraine* ¿De qué esperanza nos habla el libro del Apocalipsis?. [T]*García Fernández, Fernando*: Anámnesis 7/1 (1997) 19-29.

5970 **Chevalier, Jacques M.** A postmodern revelation: signs of astrology and the Apocalypse. Toronto 1997, University of Toronto Press xiii; 415 pp. $60/$23 [JR 79,122s—Malina, Bruce J.].

5971 **Christe, Yves** L'Apocalypse de Jean: sens et développements de ses visions synthétiques. BCAr 15: 1996, ⇒12,5704. [R]RHEF 83 (1997) 501-503 *(Paul, Jacques)*.

5972 *Cothenet, Édouard* Liturgie céleste et liturgie de l'église d'après l'Apocalypse. EeV 107 (1997) 529-535.

5973 **Cothenet, Édouard** Il messagio dell'Apocalisse. Leumann 1997, Elle Di Ci 168 pp. L15.000 [RivBib 45,255].

5974 *Cothenet, Édouard* La venue ou les venues du Christ dans l'Apocalypse. EeV 107 (1997) 481-486.

5975 *DeVilliers, Pieter G.* Oracles and prophecies in the Graeco-Roman world and the book of Revelation in the New Testament. Acta Patristica et Byzantina 8 (1997) 79-96.

5976 *Doglio, Claudio* 'Il tempo è vicino' (Apocalisse). PSV 36 (1997) 239-254.

5977 **Donegani, Isabelle** "A cause de la parole de Dieu et du témoignage de Jésus...": le témoignage comme parole de sens et d'espérance dans l'Apocalypse de Jean: son enracinement extra-biblique et biblique: sa force comme parole de sens. Diss. FrS 1995; [D]*Rouiller, G.*: EtB 36: P 1997, Gabalda xi; 578 pp. FF350. 2-85021-099-4 [RTL 29,124].

5978 **Finamore, S.F.** God, order and chaos: a history of the interpretation of Revelation's plague sequences (6.1-17; 8.1-9.2; 11.15-19; 15.1, 15.7-16.21) and an assessment of the value of René GIRARD's thought for the understanding of these visions. Diss. Oxford 1997 [RTL 29,578].

5979 **Gentry, Kenneth L., Jr.** Before Jerusalem fell: dating the book of Revelation: an exegetical and historical argument for a pre-A.D. 70 composition. SF 1997, Christian University Press xi; 409 pp. Bibl. 1-57309-154-5.

5980 **Gilbertson, Michael** 'See, I am making all things new': God and human history in the book of Revelation and in twentieth-century theology, with particular reference to Wolfhart PANNENBERG and Jürgen MOLTMANN. Diss. Durham 1997; ᴰ*Barton, S.* 299 pp. [RTL 29,575].

5981 *Goranson, Stephen* Essene polemic in the Apocalypse of John. StTDJ 23: 1997, ⇒8. ᶠBAUMGARTEN J., 453-460.

5982 **Grubb, Nancy** Revelations: art of the Apocalypse. NY 1997, Abbeville 144 pp. 0-7892-0398-7 [NThAR 1999,254].

5983 *Hahn, Ferdinand* Die Schöpfungsthematik in der Johannesoffenbarung. BZNW 89: 1997, ⇒33. ᶠGRAESSER E., 85-93.

5984 **Hangyas, Laszlo I.** The use and abuse of authority: an investigation of the exousia passages in Revelation. Diss. Andrews 1997; ᴰ*Paulien, Jon* [Abstr. AUSS 35,245].

5985 *Haoornaert, Eduardo* Cristãos de terceira geração (100-130). Petrópolis 1997, Vozes 144 pp. [REB 57,1009].

5986 *Holtz, Traugott* Literatur zur Johannesapokalypse 1980-1996. ThR 62 (1997) 368-413.

5987 **Keller, Catherine** Apocalypse now and then: a feminist approach to the end of the world. 1996, ⇒12,5715. ᴿThTo 54 (1997) 243-246 *(Peters, Ted)*; CritRR 10 (1997) 296-298 *(Pippin, Tina)*.

5988 *Kollbrunner, Fritz* Zur missions- und religionstheologischen Bedeutung der Johannesoffenbarung. NZM 53 (1997) 284.

5989 *Lee, Judith* Sacred horror: faith and fantasy in the Revelation to John. The monstrous. 1997, ⇒169. ᴱAichele, G., 220-239.

5990 **MacKenzie, Robert K.** The author of the Apocalypse: a review of the prevailing hypothesis of Jewish-Christian authorship. Mellen Biblical Pr. 51: Lewiston 1997, Mellen v; 201 pp. 0-7734-2423-7.

5991 **Malina, Bruce J.** On the genre and message of Revelation. 1995, ⇒11/1,4386; 12,5721. ᴿETR 72 (1997) 308-309 *(Campbell, Gordon)*; JSNT 65 (1997) 126 *(Pearson, Brook W.R.)*; CBQ 59 (1997) 165-167 *(Morton, Russell)*; TJT 13 (1997) 281-282 *(Janzen, Anna)*; JBL 116 (1997) 763-765 *(deSilva, David A.)*.

5992 **Marshall, John W.** Parables of the war: reading the Apocalypse within Judaism and during the Juaean war. Diss. Princeton, Univ. 1997 [RTL 29,586].

5993 **Mazzeo, Michele** La sequela di Cristo nel libro dell'Apocalisse. Cammini dello Spirito, Spiritualità 4: Mi 1997, Paoline 315 pp. 88-315-1372-9.

5994 *Mondati, Franco* La struttura generale dell'Apocalisse. RivBib 45 (1997) 289-327.

5995 **Moyise, Steve** The OT in the book of Revelation. JSNT.S 115: 1995, ⇒11/1,4393; 12,5728. ᴿCBQ 59 (1997) 167-168 *(Thomas, Carolyn)*.

5996 **Pezzoli-Olgiati, Daria** Täuschung und Klarheit: zur Wechselwirkung zwischen Vision und Geschichte in der Johannesoffenbarung. FRLANT 175: Gö 1997, Vandenhoeck & R 272 pp. DM58. 3-525-53858-8.

5997 *Philippe, Marie D.* Réflexion théologique sur la révélation du sacerdoce du Christ dans l'Apocalypse. Aletheia 11 (1997) 19-34 [ZID 23,307].

5998 **Pippin, Tina** Death and desire: the rhetoric of gender in the Apocalypse of John. 1992, ⇒9,5733... 11/1,4404. ᴿABR 45 (1997) 90-92 *(Ince, Gwen)*.

5999 *Poythress, Vern S.* Counterfeiting in the book of Revelation as a perspective on non-Christian culture. JETS 40 (1997) 411-418.

6000 **Raguer Suner, Hilari** Llegir avui l'Apocalipsi. El Gra de Blat 128: Barc 1997, Publicacions de l'Abadia de Montserrat 169 pp. 84-7826-892-8.

6001 *Rand, Jan A. du* "Your kingdom come 'on earth as it is in heaven'": the theological motif of the Apocalypse of John. Neotest. 31 (1997) 59-75.

6002 **Rehmann, Luzia Sutter** Geh, frage die Gebärerin!: feministisch-befreiungstheologische Untersuchungen zum Gebärmotiv in der Apokalyptik. Diss. Kassel. Gü 1995 Gü'er 264 pp. DM68. ᴿActBib 34 (1997) 66-67 *(Boada, J.)*; JBL 116 (1997) 575-576 *(Pippin, Tina)*; CritRR 10 (1997) 298-299 *(Schuengel-Straumann, Helen)*.

6003 **Reichelt, Hansgünter** Angelus interpres—Texte in der Johannes-Apokalypse. EHS.T 507: 1994, ⇒10,5521; 12,5741. ᴿNeoTest. 31 (1997) 228-231 *(Villiers, J.L. de)*.

6004 **Richard, Pablo** Apocalipsis: reconstrucción de la esperanza. 1995, ⇒11/1,4413. ᴿEfMex 15 (1997) 133-5 *(Cepeda Salazar, A.)*;

6005 Apocalipse: reconstrução da esperança. 1996, ⇒12,5742. ᴿFranciscanum 39/1 (1997) 109-111 *(Noratto Gutiérrez, José Alfredo)*.

6006 **Riley, William** The spiritual adventure of the Apocalypse. 1996, ⇒12,5743. ᴿDoLi 47 (1997) 443-444 *(Greehy, J.J.)*.

6007 *Roosimaa, Peeter* Die Bezeugung von Gerichtsvorstellungen in der Offenbarung des Johannes. Engel und Dämonen. FARG 29: 1997, ⇒343. ᴱAhn, G., 151-160.

6008 *Roure, Damià* L'Apocalipsi de Joan com a discurs sobre l'home. Qüestions de Vida Cristiana 188 (1997) 70-77.

6009 *Rowland, Christopher* The lamb and the beast, the sheep and the goats: 'the mystery of salvation' in Revelation. 1997, ⇒93. ᶠSᴡᴇᴇᴛ J., 181-191.

6010 *Royalty, Robert M.* The rhetoric of Revelation. SBL.SPS 36 (1997) 596-617.

6011 **Simojoki, Anssi** Apocalypse interpreted: the types of interpretation of the book of Revelation in Finland 1944-1995, from the Second World War to the Post-Cold War world. Diss. Åbo 1996; ᴰ*Cleve, F.*: Åbo 1997, Åbo Akademi University Press 220 pp. 952-9616-78-3 [EThL 74,339*].

6012 **Söllner, Peter** Jerusalem, die hochgebaute Stadt: eschatologisches und himmlisches Jerusalem im Frühjudentum und im frühen Christentum. Diss. Heidelberg 1997; ᴰ*Berger, K.* [RTL 29,582].

6013 **Spatafora, Andrea** From the 'temple of God' to God as the temple: a biblical theological study of the temple in the book of Revelation. Diss. Pont. Univ. Gregoriana; ᴰ*Vanni, Ugo*: TGr.T 27: R 1997, PUG 340 pp. L35.000. 88-7652-761-3.

6014 **Stuckenbruck, Loren T.** Angel veneration and christology... Apocalypse of John. WUNT 2/70: 1995, ⇒11/1,4422; 12,5755. ᴿJAC 40 (1997) 217-218 *(Böcher, Otto)*.

6015 *Trummer, Peter* Offenbarung in Bildern—die Bilder der Offenbarung. 1997, ⇒106. <sup>F</sup>Woschitz K., 384-393.
6016 *Vassiliadis, Petros* Apocalypse and liturgy. SVTQ 41/2-3 (1997) 95-112.
6017 *Vetrali, Tecle* Gli eletti nell'Apocalisse. DSBP 15 (1997) 157-173;
6018 L'escatologia dell'Apocalisse. DSBP 16 (1997) 172-194.
6019 *Walter, Nikolaus* Die Botschaft des Sehers Johannes zwischen apokalyptischer Tradition und urchristlichem Osterglauben: Thesen zur theologischen Interpretation der Johannesoffenbarung. Praeparatio evangelica. WUNT 98: 1997 <1990>, ⇒167. 303-310.
6020 *Wright, Rosemary Muir* The great whore in the illustrated Apocalypse cycles. Sum. 191. Journal of Medieval History 23/3 (1997) 191-210.

## G2.5 *Apocalypsis,* Revelation 1,1...

6021 **Jędrzejewski, Sylwester** U korzeni zła: Rdz 1-11 w interpretacij apokaliptyki żydowskiej. Lublin 1997, KUL 192 pp. 83-228-0485-7 [NThAR 1998,99].
6022 *Hartmann, Lars* Form and message: a preliminary discussion of 'partial texts' in Revelation 1-3 and 22:6ff. Text-centered NT studies. WUNT 102: 1997 <1980>, ⇒132. 125-149.
6023 **Synnes, Martin** Sju profetiske budskap til menighetene: en gjennomgåelse av sendebrevene i Johannes' Åpenbaring. 1996, ⇒12,5762. IXΘΥΣ 24/2 (1997) 95-96 *(Adamsen, Georg S.).*
6024 **Poucouta, Paulin** Lettres aux églises d'Afrique: Apocalypse 1-3. P 1997, Karthala 288 pp. FF160 [EeV 107,175].
6025 **McDonough, Sean** The One Who is and Who was and Who is to come: Revelation 1:4 in its Hellenistic and early Jewish setting. Diss. St. Andrew's 1997; <sup>D</sup>*Bauckham, R.* 227 pp. [RTL 29,586].
6026 *Pikaza, Xabier* El fundamentalismo apocalíptico. BiFe 23 (1997) 211-243 [Rev 2-3].
6027 **Bach, Daniel** Je viens à toi: sept lettres aux églises dans l'épreuve: Apocalypse 2-3. Poliez-le-Grand 1994, Moulin 89 pp. <sup>R</sup>EstB 55 (1997) 557-558 *(Asenjo, J.).*
6028 *Bordreuil, Pierre* Qui étaients les nicolaïtes de l'*Apocalypse de Jean*?. Sum. 105. Sem. 47 (1997) 105-109 [Rev 2,6; 2,15].
6029 *Coutsoumpos, Panayotis* The social implication of idolatry in Revelation 2:14: Christ or Caesar?. BTB 27 (1997) 23-27 [Acts 15,20.29; 1 Cor 10,19-22; 8,1-13].
6030 *Duff, Paul B.* 'I will give to each of you as your works deserve': witchcraft accusations and the fiery-eyed Son of God in Rev 2.18-23. NTS 43 (1997) 116-133.
6031 (*a*) **Contreras Molina, Francisco** Estoy a la puerta y llamo (Ap 3,20): estudio temático. Biblioteca de Estudios Bíblicos 84: 1995, ⇒11/1,4443; 12,576. <sup>R</sup>EfMex 15/1 (1997) 118-119 *(Ramírez Ayala, Manuel);* PerTeol 29 (1997) 249-250 *(Konings, Johan);* EstB 55 (1997) 421-422 *(Muñoz León, D.);* (*b*) **Müller, Ekkehardt** Microstructural analysis of Revelation 4-11. Andrews University Seminary, Doctoral Dissertation 21: Berrien Springs, Michigan 1996, Andrews University Press ix; 788 pp. Bibl. 1-883925-11-8.
6032 *Giesen, Heinz* Im Dienst der Weltherrschaft Gottes und des Lammes: die vier apokalyptischen Reiter (Offb 6,1-8). SNTU.A 22 (1997) 92-124.

6033  *Laiti, Giuseppe* Gli inni dell'Apocalisse nella liturgia delle ore/2: il giudizio che ci salva (Ap 11,17-18. 12,10-12). Presbyteri 31 (1997) 68-72.

6034  *Wong, Daniel K.K.* The two witnesses in Revelation 11. BS 154 (1997) 344-354.

6035  **Ulland, Harald** Die Vision als Radikalisierung der Wirklichkeit in der Apokalypse des Johannes: das Verhältnis der sieben Sendschreiben zu Apokalypse 12-13. Diss. Bethel 1995; DVouga, *Fr.*: TANZ 21: Tü 1997, Francke ix; 369 pp. 3-7720-1872-6.

6036  *Wink, Walter* La bestia apocalíptica: la cultura de la violencia. Conc(I) 33,992-1002; Conc(GB) 1997/5,71-77; Conc(F) 273,97-104; (D33,647-653); Conc(E) 273 (1997) 915-923 [Rev 12-13].

6037  *Dochhorn, Jan* Und die Erde tat ihren Mund auf: ein Exodusmotiv in Apc 12,16. ZNW 88 (1997) 140-142.

6038  *Valentini, Alberto* Il "grande segno" di Apocalisse 12: una Chiesa ad immagine della Madre di Gesù. Mar. 59/151 (1997) 31-63.

6039  **Busch, Peter** Der gefallene Drache: Mythenexegese am Beispiel von Apokalypse 12. TANZ 19: 1996, ⇒12,5772. RThLZ 122 (1997) 1119-1120 *(Pezzoli-Olgiati, Daria)*.

6040  **Farkaš, Pavol** La "donna" di Apocalisse 12: storia, bilancio, nuove prospettive. Diss. Pont. Univ. Gregoriana; DVanni, *Ugo*: TGr.T 25: R 1997, 274 pp. L28.000. 88-7652-758-3. RRSEc 15 (1997) 599-600 *(Mirri, Luciana)*.

6041  *Newport, Kenneth G.C.* Revelation 13 and the papal antichrist in eighteenth-century England: a study in New Testament *eis*egesis. BJRL 79/1 (1997) 143-160.

6042  *Olson, Daniel C.* "Those who have not defiled themselves with women": Revelation 14:4 and the book of Enoch. CBQ 59 (1997) 492-510.

6043  **Jürgens, Burkhard** Zweierlei Anfang: kommunikative Konstruktionen heidenchristlicher Identität in Gal 2 und Apg 15. Diss. Münster 1997/98; DLöning [BZ 42,317].

6044  *Míguez, Néstor O.* La apocalíptica y la economia: lectura de textos apocalípticos desde la experiencia de la exclusión económica. RevBib 59/1 (1997) 17-31 [Rev 17-18].

6045  **Rissi, Mathias** Die Hure Babylon und die Verführung der Heiligen. BWANT 136: 1995, ⇒11/1,4464; 12,5779. RThRv 93 (1997) 124-127 *(Giesen, Heinz)* [Rev 17].

6046  *Mattingly, Gerald L.* The Palmyrene luxury trade and Revelation 18:12-13: a neglected analogue. Aram 7 (1995) 217-231.

6047  *Ramírez Fernández, Dagoberto* The judgment of God on the multinationals: Revelation 18. Subversive scriptures. 1997, ⇒263. EVaage, L., 75-100.

6048  *Laiti, Giuseppe* Gli inni dell'Apocalisse nella liturgia delle ore: l'umanità salvata canta la gioia dell'amore di Di (Ap 19,1b-2a.5.6b-7a), 4. Presbyteri 31 (1997) 226-230.

6049  **Ruiz, Jean-Pierre** The politics of praise: a reading of Revelation 19:1-10. SBL.SPS 36 (1997) 374-393.

6050  *Pikaza Ibarrondo, X.* Triunfo de Cristo, reino de Dios: relectura de Ap 19,11-20,15. RET 57 (1997) 211-240.

6051  *Morandi, Giacomo* Il signore dei signori: teologia della passione in Apocalisse 19,11-16, 2. La Sapienza della Croce 12/1 (1997) 5-14;

6052 Porta scrito sul mantello e sul femore: Re dei re e Signore dei signori, 3. La Sapienza della Croce 12/3 (1997) 203-215 [Rev 19,11-16].

## G2.7 **Millenniarismus,** *Apc 20...*

6053 **Bachicha, Martin R.** The kingdom of the bride: a book on the last days. Lafayette, LA 1997, Prescott 239 pp. $10 [BS 156,494—Witmer, J.A.].

6054 **Delumeau, Jean** Mille ans de bonheur. Une histoire du paradis, 2. ⇒11/1,4468; 12,5782. Collationes 27/1 (1997) 100-101 *(Vanden Berghe, Eric)*; RHEF 83/1 (1997) 234-235 *(Venard, Marc)*; RTL 28 (1997) 270 *(Gilmont, J.-Fr.)*.

6055 *Delumeau, Jean* Une traversée du millénarisme occidental. BLE.S 4 (1997) 143-152.

6056 **Fuster, Sebastián** Milenarismos: el cristianismo en la encrucijada del año 2000. M 1997, Edibesa 244 pp. [TE 42,125].

6057 *Kolarić, Juraj* Hilijazam u kršćanskoj tradiciji [Il millenaresimo nella tradizione cristiana]. 1997, ⇒96. <sup>F</sup>Tomica C.; Rias. 272. 249-272. **Croatian.**

6058 Multiple Jérusalem: Jérusalem terrestre, Jérusalem céleste. Dédale 3-4. 1996, ⇒12,5786. <sup>R</sup>Esprit 228 (1997) 198-200 *(Grandguillaume, Gilbert)*.

6059 <sup>E</sup>**Nardi, Carlo** Il millenarismo: testi dei secoli I-II. 1995, ⇒11/1, 4474; 12,5787. <sup>R</sup>CivCatt 148 IV (1997) 94-95 *(Cremascoli, G.)*.

6060 **O'Leary, Stephen D.** Arguing the Apocalypse: a theory of millennial rhetoric. 1994, ⇒10,5562...: 12,5788. <sup>R</sup>AUSS 35 (1997) 294-296 *(Strand, Kenneth A.)*.

6061 **Ralph, Margaret N.** The bible and the end of the world. Mahwah 1997, Paulist vii; 166 pp. $12 [BiTod 36,266—Senior, Donald].

6062 <sup>E</sup>**Robbins, Thomas; Palmer, Susan J.** Millennium, messiahs, and mayhem: contemporary apocalyptic movements. NY 1997, Routledge ix; 334 pp. 0-415-91649-6.

6063 *(a)* **Stackhouse, Reginald** The end of the world?: a new look at an old belief. Mahwah 1997, Paulist viii; 136 pp. Bibl. $12. 0-8091-3727-5; *(b)* <sup>E</sup>**Strozier, Charles B.; Flynn, Michael** The year 2000: essays on the end. NY 1997, University Press ix; 343 pp. 0-8147-8031-8.

6064 *Pikaza Ibarrondo, Xabier* Santa ciudad, nueva Jerusalén: relectura de Ap 21,1-22,5. 1997, ⇒76. <sup>M</sup>Ruiz de la Pena J., 497-519.

6065 *Heide, Gale Z.* What is new about the new heaven and the new earth?: a theology of creation from Revelation 21 and 2 Peter 3. JETS 40 (1997) 37-56.

6066 *Goranson, Stephen* The text of Revelation 22.14. NTS 43 (1997) 154-157.

6067 *Philonenko, Marc* 'Dehors les chiens' (Apocalypse 22.16 et 4QMMT B 58-62). NTS 43 (1997) 445-450.

## XII. Paulus

### G3.1 Pauli biographia

6068  **Anderson, R. Dean** Ancient rhetorical theory and Paul. 1996, ⇒12,5797. [R]NT 39 (1997) 291-294 *(Van Halsema, Johan D.F.)*.

6069  *Arnold, J.P.* The relationship of Paul to Jesus. Hillel and Jesus. 1997, ⇒321. [E]Charlesworth, J.H., 256-288.

6070  **Bartolomé, Juan José** Pablo de Tarso: una introduccíon a la vida y a la obra de un apóstol de Cristo. Claves Cristianas 7: M 1997, Ed. CCS 390 pp. 84-7043-989-8.

6071  *Boespflug, François* Von Jerusalem nach Damaskus: ein Bekehrungsweg. Welt und Umwelt der Bibel 3 (1997) 47-49.

6072  **Bornkamm, Günther** Paulo: vida e obra. 1992, [R]RBBras 14 (1997) 413-415.

6073  **Buscemi, Alfio Marcello** Paolo: vita, opera e messaggio. ASBF 43: 1996, ⇒12,5804. [R]Ang. 74 (1997) 457-458 *(Jurič, Stipe)*.

6074  *Busto Saíz, José R.* Momentos cruciales en la vida de Pablo. SalTer 85 (1997) 363-375.

6075  *De Lorenzi, Lorenzo* Paolo e 'la pienezza del tempo'. PSV 36 (1997) 171-197.

6076  *Degórski, Bazyli* Un nuovo indizio per la datazione della *Vita S. Pauli* di GIROLAMO?. StPatr 33: 1997, ⇒351. [E]Livingstone, E., 302-310.

6077  *Förster, Niclas* Sprach Paulus einen kilikischen Koine-Dialekt?: ein bisher übersehener Aspekt in der Biographie des Paulus. ZNW 88 (1997) 316-321.

6078  **Gnilka, Joachim** Paulus von Tarsus: Zeuge und Apostel. 1996, ⇒12,5807. [R]ThGl 87 (1997) 454-455 *(Ernst, Josef)*; OrdKor 38 (1997) 497-498 *(Giesen, Heinz)*; JETh 11 (1997) 220-224 *(Schnabel, Eckhard)*; RBL 50 (1997) 311-313 *(Pindel, Roman)*.

6079  **Haacker, Klaus** Paulus: der Werdegang eines Apostels. SBS 171: Stu 1997, Katholisches Bibelwerk 140 pp. Bibl. DM39.80. 3-460-04711-9.

6080  **Hengel, Martin; Schwemer, Anna Maria** Paul between Damascus and Antioch. [T]*Bowden, John*: L 1997, SCM xiv; 530 pp. £20. 0-334-02661-X. [R]ET 109 (1997-98) 118 *(Barclay, John)*.

6081  **Holzner, Joseph** Paul de Tarse. Préf. *Laubier, Patrick de*: P 1997, Téqui 592 pp. FF180. 2-7403-0500-1 [BCLF 598-599,1563].

6082  **Hubaut, Michel** Sulle orme di San Paolo: guida storica e spirituale. Guida alla Bibbia 16: CinB 1997, San Paolo 312 pp. L32.000. 88-215-3180-5 [RdT 38,186].

6083  **Lohse, Eduard** Paulus: eine Biographie. 1996, ⇒12,5810. [R]LM 36/10 (1997) 44 *(Lindemann, Walter)*; JETh 11 (1997) 220-224 *(Schnabel, Eckhard)*.

6084  **Murphy-O'Connor, Jerome** Paul: a critical life. 1996, ⇒12,5811. [R]RB 104 (1997) 592-598 *(Richardson, Peter)*; TS 58 (1997) 724-726 *(Byrne, Brendan)*.

6085  **Pitta, Antonio** Paolo, la vita, le lettere, il suo vangelo. La bibbia nelle nostre mani 1: CinB 1997, S. Paolo 64 pp. L7.000. 88-215-3497-9 [RdT 38,576].

6086  **Riesner, Rainer** Die Frühzeit des Apostels Paulus. WUNT 2/71: 1994, ⇒10,5588... 12,5814. [R]Gn. 69 (1997) 235-239 *(Botermann, Helga)*; TJT 13/1 (1997) 115-116 *(Donaldson, Terence L.)*; JBL 115 (1996) 153-155 *(Scott, James M.)*.

6087  **Sánchez Bosch, Jordi** Nacido a tiempo: una vida de Pablo, el apóstol. 1994, ⇒10,5589... 12,5815. [R]AnVal 23 (1997) 464-466 *(Díaz Rodelas, Juan Miguel)*;

6088  Nascido a tempo: vida de Paulo, o apóstolo. São Paulo, 1997, AM 355 pp. 85-276-0430-2.

6089  **Sanders, E.P.** San Paolo. Genova 1997, Melangolo 143 pp. [R]Henoch 19 (1997) 381-383 *(Gianotto, Claudio)*.

6090  [E]**Schlosser, Jacques** Paul de Tarse: congrès de l'ACFEB 1995. LeDiv 165: 1996, ⇒12,273. [R]EeV 107 (1997) 447-449 *(Cothenet, Édouard)*.

6091  **Schonfield, Hugh Joseph** Proclaiming the Messiah: the life and letters of Paul of Tarsus, envoy to the nations. L 1997, Open Gate 245 pp. Bibl. 1-871871-328.

6092  **Tajra, Harry W.** The martyrdom of St Paul. WUNT 2/67: 1994, ⇒11/1,4499; 12,5820. [R]JBL 116 (1997) 751-753 *(Bauman, R.A.)*.

6093  **Wansink, Craig S.** Chained in Christ: the experience and rhetoric of Paul's imprisonments. JSNT.S 130: 1996, ⇒12,5822. [R]JBL 116 (1997) 571-573 *(Hawthorne, Gerald F.)*.

6094  **Wenham, David** Paul: follower of Jesus or founder of christianity?. 1995, ⇒11/1,4500; 12,5823. [R]StPat 44/1 (1997) 184-186 *(Segalla, Giuseppe)*; EvQ 69 (1997) 164-166 *(Proctor, John)*; EThL 73 (1997) 181-182 *(Neirynck, F.)*; CBQ 59 (1997) 180-181 *(Hensell, Eugene)*; AUSS 35 (1997) 305-306 *(Badenas, Roberto)* [1 Cor 9; 1 Thess 4-5].

6095  **Wilson, A.N.** Paul, the mind of the apostle. L 1997, Sinclair-Stevenson xiii; 274 pp. £18. 1-85619-542-2. [R]Tablet (15 March 1997) 364 *(Wansbrough, Henry)*.

## G3.2  Corpus paulinum; *generalia, technica epistularis*

6096  [E]**Aland, Barbara; Juckel, Andreas** 2. Korintherbrief, Galaterbrief, Epheserbrief, Philipperbrief und Kolosserbrief. Das Neue Testament in syrischer Überlieferung II: die Paulinischen Briefe, 2. ANTT 23: 1995, ⇒11/1,4501. [R]NT 39 (1997) 88-89 *(Elliott, J.K.)*; JBL 116 (1997) 161-164 *(Petersen, William L.)*.

6097  *Aletti, Jean-Noël* Bulletin d'exégèse du Nouveau Testament: bulletin paulinien. RSR 85 (1997) 85-112.

6098  *Arzt, Peter* Analyse der Paulusbriefe auf dem Hintergrund dokumentarischer Papyri. 21. Papyrologenkongress, 1. 1997, ⇒367. [E]Kramer, B., 31-36.

6099  **Ballarini, L.** Paolo e il dialogo Chiesa-Israele: proposta di un cammino esegetico. CSB 31: Bo 1997, EDB 112 pp. L17.000. 88-10-40732-6 [RivBib 45,255].

6100  [T]**Barbaglio, Giuseppe** Lettere, 1: Lettere autentiche; 2: Lettere della scuola di Paolo. Classici della BUR 1190-1191: Mi 1997, Biblioteca Universale Rizzoli 2 vols; 435+233 pp. 88-17-17190-5/1-3.

6101  **Baumert, Norbert** Woman and man in Paul. [T]*Madigan, Patrick; Maloney, Linda M.*: 1996, ⇒12,5828. [R]ScrB 27 (1997) 86-89 *(Mills, Mary E.)*.

6102  **Betz, Hans Dieter** Paulinische Studien. Gesammelte Aufsätze, 3. 1994, ⇒10,160; 12,5829. [R]Protest. 52/1 (1997) 78-80 *(Redalié, Yann)*; SEÅ 62 (1997) 190-191 *(Fornberg, Tord)*.

6103  *Given, Mark D.* True rhetoric: ambiguity, cunning, and deception in Pauline discourse. SBL.SPS 36 (1997) 526-550.

6104  *Hartmann, Lars* On reading others' letters. Text-centered NT studies. WUNT 102: 1997 <1986>, ⇒132. 167-177.

6105  **Heckel, Ulrich** Schwachheit und Gnade: Trost im Leiden bei Paulus und in der Seelsorgepraxis heute. Stu 1997, Quell 274 pp. 3-7918-3450-9 [NThAR 1997,194].

6106  *Holland, Glenn* Paul's use of irony as a rhetorical technique. The rhetorical analysis. JSNT.S 146: 1997, ⇒336. [E]Porter, S., 234-48. [E]**Horsley, Richard A.** Paul and empire ⇒204.

6107  **Hübner, Hans** Corpus Paulinum. Vetus Testamentum in Novo, 2. Gö 1997, Vandenhoeck & R xxiv; 663 pp. DM188. 3-525-50108-0. [R]BZ 41 (1997) 255-256 *(Klauck, Hans-Josef)*; OTEs 10 (1997) 555-557 [Afrikaans] *(du Toit, A.B.)*.

6108  **Jasinski, Andrzej Sebastian** Dzieje Apostolskie Listy sw. Pawla [Introduction to the letters of St Paul]. Wprowadzenie w mysl i wezwanie ksiag Biblijnych 9: Wsz 1997, Akademia Teologii Katolickiej 608 pp. 83-7072-085-4. **P**.

6109  **Lambrecht, Jan** Pauline studies. Collected essays. BEThL 115: 1994, ⇒10,195...12,5841. [R]EThL 73 (1997) 182-83 *(Focant, C.)*.

6110  *Le Saux, Madeleine* Le Seigneur Jésus selon Paul. DosB 69 (1997) 22-24.

6111  **Lim, Timothy H.** Holy Scripture in the Qumran commentaries and Pauline letters. Diss. Oxford 1991. Oxf 1997, Clarendon xiii; 221 pp. £40. 0-19-826206-X [NThAR 1998,98].

6112  *Lim, Timothy H.* Midrash pesher in the Pauline letters. The scrolls and the scriptures. JSPE.S 26: 1997, ⇒299. [E]Porter, S., 280-292.

6113  *Makhloufi, Mustapha; Penicaud, Anne* Notes sur le genre épistolaire. SémBib 88 (1997) 56-64.

6114  **Meißner, Stefan** Die Heimholung des Ketzers: Studien zur jüdischen Auseinandersetzung mit Paulus. WUNT 2/87: 1996, ⇒12,5844. [R]FrRu 4 (1997) 295-296 *(Reichrath, Hans L.)*.

6115  **Moreschini, C.; Norelli, E.** Da Paolo all'età costantiniana. Storia della letteratura cristiana antica greca e latina, 1. 1995, ⇒11/1,4522. [R]RdT 38 (1997) 257-261 *(Cattaneo, Enrico)*; CivCatt 148 III (1997) 546-547 *(Cremascoli, G.)*.

6116  **Murphy-O'Connor, Jerome** Paul et l'art épistolaire. 1994, ⇒12,5845. [R]RHPhR 77/2 (1997) 221-222 *(Grappe, Ch.)*.

6117  *Nikopulos, Basileios E.* "Debt" and "debtor": basic ideas of contractual law in the letters of the apostle Paul. DBM 16/2 (1997) 95-120. **G**.

6118  **Noormann, Rolf** IRENAEUS als Paulus Interpret. WUNT 2/66: 1994, ⇒10,5721; 12,10880. [R]RSR 85 (1997) 629-630 *(Sesboüé, Bernard)*.

6119  [E]**Padovese, Luigi** Atti del II Simposio di Tarso su S. Paolo Apostolo. 1994, ⇒10,328. [R]Laur. 38/1-2 (1997) 302-303 *(Martignani, Luigi)*;

6120 Atti del IV Simposio di Tarso su S. Paolo Apostolo. 1996, ⇒12,263. ᴿGr. 78 (1997) 558-559 *(Ferraro, Giuseppe)*; Letteratura Liturgica 84/4-5 (1997) 652-653 *(Troía, Pasquale)*.

6121 *Perrone, Lorenzo* Questioni paoline nell'epistolario di GEROLAMO. Motivi letterari. 1997, ⇒331. ᴱMoreschini, C., 81-103.

6122 *Porter, Stanley E.* Ancient rhetorical analysis and discourse analysis of the Pauline corpus. The rhetorical analysis. JSNT.S 146: 1997, ⇒336. ᴱPorter, S.E., 249-274;

6123 Exegesis of the Pauline letters, including the Deutero-Pauline letters. Handbook. NTTS 25: 1997, ⇒971. ᴱPorter, S.E., 503-553.

6124 *Price, Robert M.* The evolution of the Pauline canon. HTS 53 (1997) 36-67 [ZID 23,443].

6125 *Puigdollers Noblom, Rodolf* La primera collecció de cartes paulines: les cartes autèntiques. La Bíblia i el Mediterrani. 1997, ⇒385. ᴱBorrell, d'Agustí, 329-350.

6126 **Reynier, Chantal; Trimaille, Michel** Éphésiens, Philippiens, Colossiens, 1-2 Thessaloniciens, 1-2 Timothée, Tite, Philémon. Les épîtres de Paul, 3. Commentaires: P 1997, Bayard 393 pp. FF140. 2-227-36607-9 [RTL 29,129].

6127 *Sánchez Bosch, Jordi* Escritos paulinos y postpaulinos. ResB 13 (1997) 41-50.

6128 **Schmid, Ulrich** MARCION und sein apostolos: Rekonstruktion... der marcionitischen Paulusbriefausgabe. ANTT 25: 1995, ⇒11/1,4536; 12,5857. ᴿNT 39 (1997) 396-405 *(Güting, E.)*.

6129 *Smith, Abraham* "There's more in the text than that": William Wells BROWN's *Clotel*, slave ideology and Pauline hermeneutics. SBL.SPS 36 (1997) 618-636.

6130 **Tatum, Gregory** Putting Galatians in its place: the sequence of Paul's undisputed letters. Diss. Duke 1997; ᴰ*Sanders, E.P.* [RTL 29,588].

6131 **Thomson, Ian H.** Chiasmus in the Pauline letters. JSNT.S 111: 1995, ⇒11/1,4539; 12,5860 [sic].

6132 *Weima, Jeffrey A.D.* What does ARISTOTLE have to do with Paul?: an evaluation of rhetorical criticism. CTJ 32 (1997) 458-468.

6133 **Winninge, Mikael** Sinners and the righteous: a comparative study of the Psalms of Solomon and Paul's letters. CB.NT 26: 1995, ⇒11/1,4547; 12,5867. ᴿETR 72 (1997) 305-306 *(Cuvillier, Élian)*; NRTh 119 (1997) 271-272 *(Ska, J.-L.)*; JBL 116 (1997) 566-567 *(Trafton, Joseph L.)*.

## G3.3 Pauli theologia

6134 *Agurides, Sabbas C.* The influence of Pauline theological thought on European civilization. DBM 16/2 (1997) 5-15. G.

6135 **Bammel, Ernst** Paul and Judaism. Judaica et Paulina. WUNT 91: 1997 <1963>, ⇒109. 327-333.

6136 **Barrett, Charles K.** La teologia di San Paolo: introduzione al pensiero dell'apostolo. 1996, ⇒12,5873. ᴿStPav 44/2 (1997) 238-239 *(Segalla, Giuseppe)*.

6137 *Bartolomé, Juan J.* 'Soy lo que soy por la gracia': apóstol por gracia: apóstol de la gracia. SalTer 85 (1997) 377-389.

6138  **Boers, Hendrikus** The justification of the gentiles: Paul's letters to the Galatians and Romans. 1994, ⇒10,11608*; 11/2,a232. RJBL 115 (1996) 368-370 *(Cosgrove, Charles H.)*.

6139  *Burchard, Christoph* Glaubensgerechtigkeit als Weisung der Tora bei Paulus. BZNW 86: 1997, ⇒41. FHoFIUS O., 341-362.

6140  *Byrne, Brendan* Christ's pre-existence in Pauline soteriology. TS 58 (1997) 308-330.

6141  **Cooper, John Charles** The "spiritual presence" in the theology of Paul TILLICH: TILLICH's use of St. Paul. Macon, GA 1997, Mercer University Press ix; 263 pp. Bibl. 0-86554-535-9.

6142  *Davies, W.D.* Paul and the new exodus. 1997, ⇒77. FSANDERS J., 443-463.

6143  **Díaz-Rodelas, Juan Miguel** Pablo y la ley: la novedad de Rom 7,7-8,4 en el conjunto de la reflexión paulina sobre la ley. 1994, ⇒10,5803... 12,6094. RCart. 13 (1997) 226-227 *(Cueca Molina, J.F.)*; CBQ 59 (1997) 374-375 *(Gillman, John)*.

6144  **Dunn, James D.G.** Paul and justification by faith. The road from Damascus. 1997, ⇒330. ELongenecker, R.N., 85-101;

6145  In quest of Paul's theology: retrospect and prospect. Pauline theology, 4. 1997, ⇒6157. EJohnson, E.E., 95-115.

6146  **Fee, Gordon D.** God's empowering presence: the Holy Spirit in the letters of Paul. 1994, ⇒10,7529; 12,5880. RTJT 13/1 (1997) 103-104 *(LeMarquand, Grant)*; NeoTest. 31 (1997) 225-226 *(Gräbe, P.J.)*; SR 26 (1997) 119-120 *(Hurtado, Larry W.)*; JBL 116 (1997) 150-152 *(Lull, David J.)*.

6147  *Georgi, Dieter* God turned upside down. Paul and empire. 1997, ⇒204. EHorsley, R.A., 148-157.

6148  **Giglioli, Alberto** L'uomo o il creato?: Κρίσις in S. Paolo. Bo 1994, EDB 139 pp. L15.000. 88-10-40724-5. RHum(B) 52 (1997) 307 *(Montagnini, Felice)*.

6149  *Gignac, Alain* Comment élaborer une "théologie paulinienne" aujourd'hui? (2ème partie: essai d'application). ScEs 49 (1997) 25-38.

6150  **Goveas, Stany** 'Of the heart, by the Spirit': an exegetical-theological study of the Pauline idea of spiritual circumcision. Diss. Pont. Univ. Gregoriana 1997; DSwetnam, James: 1997, 375 pp. [RTL 29,584].

6151  *Hafemann, Scott J.* The spirit of the new covenant, the law, and the temple of God's presence: five theses on Qumran self-understanding and the contours of Paul's thought. 1997, ⇒92. FSTUHLMACHER P., 172-189.

6152  *Haubeck, Wilfrid* Rechtfertigung und Sühne bei Paulus. JETh 11 (1997) 93-104.

6153  *Hay, David M.* Pauline theology after Paul. Pauline theology, 4. 1997, ⇒6157. EJohnson, E.E., 181-195.

6154  *Hengel, Martin* Präexistenz bei Paulus?;

6155  *Herms, Eilert* Äußere und innere Klarheit des Wortes Gottes bei Paulus, LUTHER und SCHLEIERMACHER. BZNW 86: 1997, ⇒41. FHoFIUS O., 479-518/3-72.

6156  **Hotze, Gerhard** Paradoxien bei Paulus: Untersuchungen zu einer elementaren Denkform in seiner Theologie. Diss. Münster 1995; DKertelge, K.: NTA 33: Müns 1997, Aschendorff xiii; 380 pp. DM98. 3-402-04781-0 [EThL 74,322*].

6157 EJohnson, E. Elizabeth; Hay, David M. Looking back, pressing on. Pauline theology, 4. SBL Symposium 4: Atlanta 1997, Scholars 222 pp. $25. 0-7885-0306-5.

6158 *Kim, Seyoon* God reconciled his enemy to himself: the origin of Paul's concept of reconciliation. The road from Damascus. 1997, ⇒330. ELongenecker, R.N., 102-124.

6159 *Klinghardt, Matthias* Sünde und Gericht von Christen bei Paulus. ZNW 88 (1997) 56-80.

6160 **Kraus, Wolfgang** Das Volk Gottes... Ekklesiologie bei Paulus. WUNT 2/85: 1996, ⇒12,5893. ROrdKor 38 (1997) 239-240 *(Giesen, Heinz)*; Bib. 78 (1997) 286-290 *(Pastor-Ramos, Federico)*; ScrTh 29 (1997) 932-933 *(Villar, J.R.)*; JETh 11 (1997) 210-213 *(Schnabel, Eckhard)*; ATG 60 (1997) 390-391 *(Rodríguez Carmona, A.)*.

6161 *Kraus, Wolfgang* "Volk Gottes" als Verheißungsbegriff bei Paulus. KuI 12/2 (1997) 134-147.

6162 **Küng, Hans** Great christian thinkers. 1994, ⇒10,14021; 14974. RTJT 13/1 (1997) 146-147 *(Donovan, Daniel)*.

6163 *Lang, Friedrich* Das Verständnis der Taufe bei Paulus. 1997, ⇒92. FSTUHLMACHER P., 255-268.

6164 *Lindemann, Andreas* 'Nehmet einander an': paulinisches Kirchenverständnis und die Zukunft des Christentums. WuD 24 (1997) 29-50.

6165 *Lohse, Eduard* Theologie der Rechtfertigung im kritischen Disput: zu einigen neuen Perspektiven in der Interpretation der Theologie des Apostels Paulus. GGA 249/1-2 (1997) 66-81.

6166 *Longenecker, Bruce W.* Contours of covenant theology in the postconversion Paul;

6167 *Marshall, I. Howard* A new understanding of the present and the future: Paul and eschatology. The road from Damascus. 1997, ⇒330. ELongenecker, R.N., 125-146/43-61.

6168 *Martyn, J. Louis* The daily life of the church in the war between the spirit and the flesh;

6169 Leo BAECK's reading of Paul < 1990 >. Theological issues. 1997, ⇒146. 251-266/47-69.

6170 **Matand Bulembat, Jean-Bosco** Noyau et enjeux de l'eschatologie paulinienne: de l'apocalyptique juive et de l'eschatologie hellénistique dans quelques argumentations de l'apôtre Paul: études rhétorico-exégétique de 1 Co 15,35-58; 2 Co 5,1-10 et Rm 8,18-30. Diss. Pont. Inst. Biblicum 1995; DAletti, Jean-Noël: BZNW 84: B 1997, De Gruyter xx; 328 pp. DM188. 3-11-015387-4.

6171 **McLean, Bradley Hudson** The cursed Christ: Mediterranean expulsion rituals and Pauline soteriology. JSNT.S 126: 1996, ⇒12,5899. RCBQ 59 (1997) 780-782 *(Gormley, Joan F.)*.

6172 *Meagher, P.M.* Jesus Christ in God's plan, interreligious dialogue, theology of religions and Paul of Tarsus. VJTR 61 (1997) 742-755.

6173 **Minguet Mico, José** El Espíritu Santo según San Pablo. Valencia 1997, Edicep 158 pp. [AnVal 24,253].

6174 **Penna, Romano** Paul the apostle: a theological and exegetical study. TWahl, Thomas P.: 1996, ⇒12,5904. RCBQ 59 (1997) 610-611 *(Turro, James C.)*.

6175 *Pitta, Antonio* Aspetti kerygmatici e implicazioni morali nella cristologia paolina. ThViat(P) 2 (1997) 235-256.

6176   **Plevnik, Joseph** Paul and the parousia: an exegetical and theologi-
       cal investigation. Peabody, Mass. 1997, Hendrickson xli; 351 pp.
       $30. 1-56563-180-3 [NThAR 1997,195].
6177   *Porter, Stanley E.* Images of Christ in Paul's letters. Images of
       Christ. 1997, ⇒256. ᴱPorter, S.E., 95-112.
6178   *Price, Robert M.* The evolution of the Pauline canon. HTS 53
       (1997) 36-67.
6179   *Riesner, Rainer* Paulus und die Jesus-Überlieferung. 1997, ⇒92.
       ᶠSᴛᴜʜʟᴍᴀᴄʜᴇʀ P., 347-365.
6180   *Roetzel, Calvin J.* No "Race of Israel" in Paul. 1997, ⇒82.
       ᶠSᴄʀᴏɢɢs R., 230-244.
6181   *Schrage, Wolfgang* Der gekreuzigte und auferweckte Herr: zur
       theologia crucis und theologia resurrectionis bei Paulus. ZThK 94
       (1997) 25-38;
6182   Das messianische Zwischenreich bei Paulus. BZNW 89: 1997,⇒33.
       ᶠGʀᴀᴇssᴇʀ E., 343-354.
6183   *Souček, Josef B.* Israel und die Kirche im Denken des Apostel Pau-
       lus. Bibelauslegung. WUNT 100: 1997 <1971>, ⇒970.
       ᴱPokorný, P., 171-182.
6184   *Söding, Thomas* Heilige Schriften für Israel und die Kirche: die
       Sicht des "Alten Testaments" bei Paulus ⇒6185, 222-247.
6185   **Söding, Thomas** Das Wort vom Kreuz: Studien zur paulinischen
       Theologie. WUNT 93: Tü 1997, Mohr viii; 408 pp. DM158. 3-16-
       146618-7.
6186   **Tarocchi,    Stefano**   Il   Dio   longanime:   la   longanimità
       nell'epistolario   paolino.   RivBib.S   28:   1993,   ⇒9,5860...
       11/1,4591. ᴿRivBib 45 (1997) 241-243 *(Pitta, Antonio)*.
6187   *Wehnert, Jürgen* Die Teilhabe der Christen an der Herrschaft mit
       Christus—eine eschatologische Erwartung des frühen Christentums.
       ZNW 88 (1997) 81-96 [Mark 12,1-12].
6188   *Weiss, Herold* The sabbath in the Pauline corpus. StPhilo 9 (1997)
       287-315.
6189   **Westerholm, Stephen** Preface to the study of Paul. GR 1997,
       Eerdmans 128 pp. £9/$13. 0-8028-4285-5. ᴿScrB 27 (1997) 90-91
       *(Campbell, W.S.)*.
6190   *Winger, Michael* Freedom and the apostle: Paul and the paradoxes
       of necessity and choice. 1997, ⇒82. ᶠSᴄʀᴏɢɢs R., 217-229.
6191   *Wright, N. T.* Good news for a pagan world. BiRe 13/3 (1997) 23,
       54.
6192   **Young, Brad H.** Paul the Jewish theologian: a pharisee among
       christians. Peabody 1997, Hendrickson xx; 164 pp. $13. 1-56563-
       248-6 [ThD 45,295—Heiser, W. Charles].
6193   *Young, Norman H.* Reconciliation in Pʜɪʟᴏ, Jᴏsᴇᴘʜᴜs, and
       Paul. 1997, ⇒83. ᶠSʜᴇᴀ W., 233-244.


       ɢ3.4 *Pauli stylus et modus operandi*—Paul's image

6194   **Cirignano, Giulio; Montuschi, Ferdinando** La personalità di Pao-
       lo. CSB 27: 1996, ⇒12,5927. ᴿAng. 74 (1997) 455-457 *(De San-
       tis, Luca)*.
6195   **Elliott, Neil** Liberating Paul: the justice of God and the politics of
       the Apostle. BiSe 27: 1995, ⇒11/1,4600; 12,5932. ᴿBibl.Interp. 5
       (1997) 285-287 *(Horrell, David)*.

6196   **Glad, Clarence E.** Paul and Philodemus: adaptability in Epicurean and early Christian psychagogy. NT.S 81: Lei 1995, Brill xiv; 414 pp. $117.25. 90-04-10067-9. [R]ThLZ 122 (1997) 142-144 *(Zeller, Dieter)*; JBL 116 (1997) 376-377 *(Attridge, Harold W.)*.

6197   **Heininger, Bernhard** Paulus als Visionär: eine religionsgeschichtliche Studie. 1996, ⇒12,5935. [R]BZ 41 (1997) 272-274 *(Zeilinger, Franz)*.

6198   *Langenhorst, Georg* Paulus—Mann der bleibenden Widersprüche: Spurensuche in der modernen Literatur. EuA 73 (1997) 119-137.

6199   **Malina, Bruce J.** Portraits of Paul. 1996, ⇒12,5940. [R]TS 58 (1997) 532-3 *(Soards, Marion L.)*; CBQ 59 (1997) 777-778 *(Pervo, Richard I.)*; RThPh 129 (1997) 161-172 *(Brandt, Pierre-Yves)*.

6200   **Martini, Carlo Maria** Saint Paul face à lui-même. [T]*Lemoine, J.O.*: Maranatha 3: P 1997, Médiaspaul 158 pp. FF69. [EeV 107,46].

6201   *Meyendorf, Rudolf* Der Apostel auf der Couch: Paulus, mit den Augen eines Psychiaters betrachtet. Zeitschrift für Theologie und Gemeinde 2 (1997) 9-22.

6202   [E]**Swüste, Gerard** De handelingen van Paulus: portret van een bevlogen gelovige. 1996, ⇒12,5945. [R]ITBT 5/1 (1997) 33 *(Schelling, Piet)*.

6203   *Turek, Waldemar* La figura di Paolo nelle 'lettere' di A M B R O G I O. Ricerche Teologiche 8/2 (1997) 385-399.

6204   **Walton, Stephen John** Paul in Acts and Epistles: the Miletus speech and 1 Thessalonians as a test case. Diss. Sheffield 1997; [D]*Lincoln, Andrew T.; Alexander, L.C.A.* [TynB 48,377-380].

6205   **Wright, Nicholas T.** What Saint Paul really said: was Paul of Tarsus the real founder of christianity?. GR 1997, Eerdmans 192 pp. Bibl. $14. 0-8028-4445-6 [NThAR 1998,101].

### G3.5 Apostolus Gentium [⇒G4.6, Israel et Lex/ Jews & Law]

6206   *Aguirre, Rafael* ¿Cómo evangelizaba Paolo?: estrategias del anuncio evangélico. SalTer 85 (1997) 407-420.

6207   **Alvarez Cineira, David** Die Religionspolitk des Kaisers Claudius und die paulinische Mission. Diss. Würzburg 1997/98; [D]*Klauck* [BZ 42,319].

6208   **Badiou, A.** Saint-Paul: la fondation de l'universalisme. Les essais du collège international de philosophie: P 1997, PUF 119 pp. FF90. 2-13-048847-1 [ETR 73,305].

6209   **Becker, J.** Paolo l'apostolo dei popoli. BiBi(B) 20: 1996, ⇒12,5951. [R]Gr. 78 (1997) 776-777;

6210   Paul: l'apôtre des nations. 1995, ⇒11/1,4612; 12,5952. [R]RHR 214 (1997) 368-370 *(Mehat, André)*.

6211   **Beckheuer, Burkhard** Paulus und Jerusalem: Kollekte und Mission im theologischen Denken des Heidenapostels. Diss. Göttingen 1996/97; EHS.T 611: Fra 1997, Lang 287 pp. 3-631-32093-0 [NThAR 1999,4].

6212   **Boyarin, Daniel** A radical Jew: Paul and the politics of identity. 1994, ⇒10,5677... 12,5954. [R]JQR 87 (1997) 389-390 *(Gaston, Lloyd)*; KuL 12 (1997) 185-188 *(Stegemann, Wolfgang)*.

6213 **Donaldson, Terence L.** Paul and the gentiles: remapping the apostle's convictional world. Mp 1997, Fortress xviii; 409 pp. Bibl. $34. 0-8006-2993-0 [NTS 44,623].

6214 *Donaldson, Terence L.* Israelite, convert, apostle to the gentiles: the origin of Paul's gentile mission. The road from Damascus. 1997, ⇒330. ELongenecker, R.N., 62-84.

6215 EDunn, **James D.G.** Paul and the Mosaic law. WUNT 89: 1996, ⇒12,176. RThG 40 (1997) 231-233 *(Giesen, Heinz)*; ETR 72 (1997) 615-616 *(Cuvillier, Élian)*.

6216 **Ellis, E. Earle** Pauline theology: ministry and society. Lanham, Md. 1997 <1989>, University Press of America xv; 182 pp. $27.50. 0-7618-0612-1 [CTJ 33,563—DeBoer, Willis P].

6217 **Fabris, Rinaldo** Paolo: l'apostolo delle genti. Donne e uomini nella storia 6: Mi 1997, Paoline 623 pp. L40.000. 88-315-1468-7.

6218 *Gnilka, Joachim* La mission d'après Paul [Misja według Pawła apostoła]. Streszczenie 108. WST 10 (1997) 99-108.

6219 *Hofius, Otfried* Paulus—Missionar und Theologe. 1997, ⇒92. FSTUHLMACHER P., 224-237.

6220 *Legrand, Lucien* Inculturation and hermeneutics: the example of St Paul. IMR 19/1 (1997) 5-17.

6221 *Martyn, J. Louis* A tale of two churches. Theological issues. 1997, ⇒146. 25-36.

6222 **O'Brien, P.T.** Gospel and mission in the writings of Paul. 1995, ⇒11/1,4622. REvQ 69/3 (1997) 284-285 *(Oakes, Peter)*.

6223 *Richard, Pablo* Fundamento cristológico de la práctica apostólica de Pablo. MisEx(M) 161 (1997) 433-441.

6224 *Scott, James M.* Paul's "Imago Mundi" and scripture. 1997, ⇒92. FSTUHLMACHER P., 366-381 [Gen 10].

6225 *Starnitzke, Dierk* 'Griechen und Barbaren...bin ich verpflichtet' (Röm 1,14): die Selbstdefinition der Gesellschaft und die Individualität und Universalität der paulinischen Botschaft. WuD 24 (1997) 187-207.

G3.6 *Pauli fundamentum* philosophicum [G4.3] *et* morale

6226 **Finsterbusch, Karin** Die Thora als Lebensweisung für Heidenchristen. StUNT 20: 1996, ⇒12,5964. RThLZ 122 (1997) 669-670 *(Reinmuth, Eckart)*.

6227 **Graakjær Hjort, Birgitte** En analyse af etikkens fundering hos Paulus med inddragelse af spørgsmålet om dens aktuelle relevans, belyst ud fra Emil BRUNNER [An analysis of the foundation of ethics in Paul together with a discussion of its relevance today as seen from the standpoint of Emil Brunner]. Diss. Aarhus 1997 [StTh 51,80].

6228 *MacDonald, J. Ian* The crucible of Pauline ethics: a cross-cultural approach to ethics-in-the-making. Studies in World Christianity 3/1 (1997) 1-21.

6229 **Matlock, R. Barry** Unveiling the apocalyptic Paul: Paul's interpreters and the rhetoric of criticism. JSNT.S 127: 1996, ⇒12,5969. RJThS 48 (1997) 611-613 *(Watson, Francis)*; CBQ 59 (1997) 778-780 *(Boisclair, Regina A.)*.

6230  **O'Toole, Robert F.** Chi è cristiano?: saggio sull'etica paolina.
      1995, ⇒11/1,4641; 12,5970. ᴿPaVi 42/2 (1997) 61-62 *(Fumagalli,
      Aristide)*.
6231  ᴱ**Rosner, Brian S.** Understanding Paul's ethics: twentieth century
      approaches. 1995, ⇒11/1,110; 12,5972. ᴿPacifica 10/1 (1997) 97-
      99 *(Harding, Mark)*.
6232  **Söding, Thomas** Das Liebesgebot bei Paulus. NTA 26: 1995,
      ⇒10,5705; 12,5973. ᴿJThS 48 (1997) 199-202 *(Furnish, Victor
      Paul)*; ThRv 93 (1997) 390-393 *(Schrage, Wolfgang)*.
6233  *Willert, Niels* The catalogues of hardships in the Pauline correspon-
      dence: background and function. NT and Hellenistic Judaism.
      1997, ⇒318. ᴱBorgen, P., 217-243.


## G3.7 *Pauli* communitates *et* spiritualitas

6234  *Aasgaard, Reidar* Brotherhood in PLUTARCH and Paul: its role
      and character. Constructing... families. 1997, ⇒295. ᴱMoxnes, H.,
      166-182.
6235  **Ascough, Richard Stephen** Voluntary associations and community
      formation: Paul's Macedonian christian communities in context.
      Diss. Toronto, St. Michael 1997; ᴰ*Kloppenborg, J.S.* 604 pp.
      [RTL 29,582].
6236  **Bentoglio, Gabriele** Apertura e disponibilità: l'accoglienza
      nell'epistolario paolino. TGr.T 2: 1995, ⇒12,4657. ᴿRdT 38
      (1997) 845-846 *(Penna, Romano)*; CivCatt 148 IV (1997) 92-94
      *(Scaiola, D.)*.
6237  *Chester, Andrew* The Pauline communities. 1997, ⇒93. ᶠSweet
      J., 105-120.
6238  *Corley, Bruce* Interpreting Paul's conversion—then and now. The
      road from Damascus. 1997, ⇒330. ᴱLongenecker, R.N., 1-17.
6239  *Debergé, Pierre* Vocation et exercise de l'autorité: l'exemple de
      Paul. UnChr 126 (1997) 2-5.
6240  *Fee, Gordon D.* Paul's conversion as key to his understanding of
      the spirit. The road from Damascus. 1997, ⇒330. ᴱLongenecker,
      R.N., 166-183.
6241  *Fiorenza, Elisabeth Schüssler* The praxis of coequal discipleship.
      Paul and empire. 1997, ⇒204. ᴱHorsley, R.A., 224-241.
6242  **Gebauer, Roland** Paulus als Seelsorger: ein exegetischer Beitrag
      zur praktischen Theologie. Diss.-Habil. Erlangen, Nürnberg
      1995/96; ᴰ*Merk, O.*: CThM.BW 18: Stu 1997, Calwer x; 389 pp.
      3-7668-3512-2.
6243  **Gianantoni, Luigi** La paternità apostolica di Paolo: il kerygma,
      l'evangelizzatore, la comunità. 1993, ⇒9,5906. ᴿRivBib 45 (1997)
      101-103 *(Penna, Romano)*.
6244  *González-Carvajal Santabárbara, Luis* La libertad de los hijos de
      Dios. SalTer 85 (1997) 391-405.
6245  *Jankowski, Augustyn* Proces doczesnego upodabniania się wiernych
      do Chrystusa według świętego Pawła [The temporal process of
      achieving resemblance to Christ by the faithful according to St.
      Paul]. Sum. 140. WST 10 (1997) 131-140. **P.**
6246  *Krentz, Edgar* Paul: all things to all people—flexible and welcom-
      ing. CThMi 24 (1997) 238-244.

6247 *Martyn, J. Louis* A formula for communal discord!. Theological issues. 1997, ⇒146. 267-278 [Rom 7; Gal 5,17].

6248 **Meeks, Wayne A.** Urchristentum und Stadtkultur: die soziale Welt der paulinischen Gemeinden. ᵀ*Denzel, Sieglinde; Naumann, Susanne*: Gü 1993, Gü'er 454 pp. Nachwort *Gerd Theissen*. DM148. 3-579-01824-8. ᴿThRv 93 (1997) 123-124 *(Bickmann, Jutta)*.

6249 *Merklein, Helmut* Im Spannungsfeld von Protologie und Eschatologie: zur kurzen Geschichte der aktiven Beteiligung von Frauen in paulinischen Gemeinden. BZNW 89: 1997, ⇒33. ᶠGRAESSER E., 231-259.

6250 **Peterson, Eugene H.** Praying with Paul. SF 1995, HarperSanFrancisco 383 pp. $10 [BiTod 37,398—Senior, Donald].

6251 **Pinckaers, S.** La vita spirituale del cristiano secondo San Paolo e San TOMMASO d'Aquino. 1996, ⇒12,5995. ᴿAnnTh 11 (1997) 250-253 *(Bosch, Vicente)*.

6252 *Scott, James M.* Throne-chariot mysticism in Qumran and in Paul. Eschatology, messianism. SDSSRL 1: 1997, ⇒276. ᴱEvans, C.A., 101-119.

6253 *Venetz, Hermann-Josef* Jesus und Paulus: bibeltheologische Elemente eines "Kirchenspiegels". Pfarrei in der Postmoderne?. 1997, ⇒259. ᴱSchifferle, A., 117-128.

6254 *Walter, Nikolaus* Christusglaube und heidnische Religiosität in paulinischen Gemeinden. Praeparatio evangelica. WUNT 98: 1997 <1979>, ⇒167. 95-117.

6255 *Wolter, Michael* Ethos und Identität in paulinischen Gemeinden. NTS 43 (1997) 430-444.

### G3.8 *Pauli receptio,* history of research

*Aletti, J.-N.* Bulletin d'exégèse du NT: bulletin paulinien ⇒6097.

6256 *Bovon, François* Notes and observations after "Paul after Paul". HThR 90 (1997) 105-108.

6257 **Fabris, Rinaldo** La tradizione paolina. 1995, ⇒11/1,4681; 12,6003. ᴿAnton. 72 (1997) 317-319 *(Buscemi, Marcello A.)*.

6258 *Furnish, Victor Paul* Where is "the truth" in Paul's gospel?: a response to Paul W. MEYER;

6259 *Kraftchick, Steven J.* An asymptotic response to DUNN's retrospective and proposals;

6260 *Meyer, Paul W.* Pauline theology: a proposal for a pause in its pursuit. Pauline theology, 4. 1997, ⇒6157. ᴱJohnson, E.E., 161-177/116-139/140-160.

### G3.9 *Themata particularia de Paulo,* details

6261 **Bash, Anthony** Ambassadors for Christ: an exploration of ambassadorial language in the New Testament. Diss. C 1995: WUNT 2/92: Tü 1997, Mohr xvii; 322 pp. DM98. 3-16-146718-3.

6262 *Bernabé, Carmen* Pablo y las mujeres. SalTer 85 (1997) 421-437.

6263 **Brown, Peter** Die Keuschheit der Engel: sexuelle Entsagung, Askese und Körperlichkeit am Anfang des Christentums. ᵀ*Pfeiffer, Martin* 1991, ⇒9,8418; 10,8226. ᴿThRv 93 (1997) 137-138 *(Lutterbach, Hubertus)*.

6264 *Gundry-Volf, Judith M.* Paul on women and gender: a comparison with early Jewish views. The road from Damascus. 1997, ⇒330. ELongenecker, R.N., 184-212.

6265 **Mills, Kevin** Justifying language: Paul and contemporary literary theory. 1995, ⇒11/1,4698. RAThR 79 (1997) 288-9 *(Jones, J.N.)*.

6266 *Obrycki, Kazimierz* Apokryficzna korespondencja między Seneką i świętym Pawłem [De scriptis apocryphis quae Lucii Annaei Senecae epistulae ad Sanctum Paulum missae et ab eo acceptae ferebantur]. Summarium 240. WST 10 (1997) 219-240. **P**.

6267 *Pérez Gordo, Angel* La cruz interpretada por S.Pablo (II): las fiestas de Israel tipo de las nuevas realidades. Stauros 27 (1997) 17-43 [⇒11/1,4701].

6268 **Pedersen, Sigfred** Pauls som brevskriver. Frederiksberg 1997, A-nis 373 pp. DAK325. RΙΧΘΥΣ 24/3 (1997) 136-143 *(Legarth, Peter V.)*.

6269 *Ramelli, Ilaria* L'epistolario apocrifo Seneca—san Paolo: alcune osservazioni. VetChr 34 (1997) 299-310.

6270 **Rolland, Philippe** James and Paul in dialogue. Kephas 1/1: P 1997, de Paris 33 pp.

6271 *Sànchez Bosch, Jordi* Pau l'apòstol i el mar. La Bíblia i el Mediterrani. 1997, ⇒385. EBorrell, d'Agustí, 365-374.

6272 **Saß, Gerhard** Leben aus den Verheißungen. FRLANT 164: 1995, ⇒11/1,4703; 12,6020. RJETh 11 (1997) 213-216 *(Schnabel, Eckhard)*.

6273 **Winter, Bruce W.** PHILO and Paul among the sophists. Diss. Macquarie 1988; DJudge, E.A., MSSNTS 96: C 1997, CUP xvi; 289 pp. £35. 0-521-59108-2.

## G4.1 **Ad Romanos** *Textus, commentarii*

6274 EBammel, Caroline P. Hammond Der Römerbriefkommentar des ORIGENES: kritische Ausgabe der Übersetzung RUFINS: Buch 4-6. FrB 1997, Herder 545 pp. 3-451-21945-X [Mayéutica 24,250— Eguiarte, Enrique].

6275 **Barth, Karl** De brief aan de Romeinen kort verklaard. TSpijkerboer, A.A.: Kampen 1997, Kok 168 pp. ƒ39.90 [GThT 97/3,144].

6276 **Bénétreau, Samuel** L'épître de Paul aux Romans, 2. Commentaire Évangélique de la Bible 19: Vaux-sur-Seine 1997, Edifac 280 pp. 2-904407-23-5 [NThAR 1999,4] [⇒12,6026].

6277 (*a*) **Bosio, Enrico** Epistole di S. Paolo ai Romani; I-II Corinzi. Commentario esegetico-pratico del Nuovo Testamento: T 1997, Claudiana pag. varia. 88-7016-093-9; (*b*) **Bruce, Frederick Fyvie** La Lettera di Paolo ai Romani: introduzione e commentario. Commentari al Nuovo Testamento: Roma 1997, GBU 364 pp. Bibl.

6278 **Byrne, Brendan** Romans. Sacra Pagina 6: 1996, ⇒12,6031. RBib. 78 (1997) 284-286 *(Lambrecht, Jan)*; TS 58 (1997) 534-535 *(Heil, John P.)*.

6279 EDíaz García, Gonzalo Fray LUIS de León: in epistolam ad Romanos expositio. 1993, ⇒10,5733. REstB 55 (1997) 415-417 *(Urbán, A.)*.

6280 **Fitzmyer, Joseph A.** Romans. AncB 33: 1993, ⇒9,5945... 12,6033. REstB 55 (1997) 417-418 *(Alegre, X.)*.

6281 EFrede, Hermann Josef; Stanjek, Herbert SEDULII SCOTTI collectaneum in apostolum I: in epistolam ad Romanos. AGLB 31:

1996, ⇒12,6034. RREAug 43 (1997) 401-403 *(Dolbeau, François)*.

6282 **Grayston, Kenneth** The Epistle to the Romans. Epworth Commentaries: Peterborough 1997, Epworth Press xiv; 130 pp. 0-7162-
0511-4.

6283 TE**Heither, Theresia** ORIGENES: commentarii in epistulam ad
Romanos, liber quintus, liber sextus. FC 2/3: 1993, ⇒12,6037.
RThPQ 145/1 (1997) 100 *(Kertsch, Manfred)*.

6284 **Johnson, Luke Timothy** Reading Romans: a literary and theological commentary. Reading the New Testament: NY 1997, Crossroad
xii; 224 pp. $13. 0-8245-1624-9.

6285 **Moo, Douglas J.** The epistle to the Romans. NIC: 1996,
⇒12,6043. RRRT (1997/3) 56-59 *(Campbell, W.S.)*; Bib. 78
(1997) 432-435 *(Lambrecht, Jan)*; RBBras 14 (1997) 419-421.

6286 **Morgan, Robert** Romans. NT Guides: Shf 1995, Academic 164
pp. £6/$10. 1-85075-739-9. RScrB 27 (1997) 39-40 *(Robinson,
Bernard P.)*.

6287 **Mounce, Robert H.** Romans. NAC 27: 1995, ⇒11/1,4718. RBS
154/1 (1997) 120-121 *(Constable, Thomas L.)*; EvQ 69/1 (1997)
85-86 *(Grogan, Geoffrey W.)*.

6288 **Murray, John** The epistle to the Romans. GR 1997 <1959-
1965>, Eerdmans 736 pp. $30. 0-8028-4341-7 [NTS 44,624].

6289 **Peterson, Erik** Der Brief an die Römer. E*Nichtweiss, Barbara;*
Collab. *Hahn, Ferdinand.* Aus dem Nachlass. Ausgewählte Schriften 6. Wü 1997, Echter xxxiii; 382 pp. DM98. 3-429-01887-0.

6290 **Rao, Ontimetta Madhusudhana** Paul and Romans. Delhi 1997,
I.S.P.C.K. 72 pp. 81-7214-387-7 [NThAR 1999,254].

6291 **Schlatter, Adolf** Romans: the righteousness of God. T*Schatzmann,
S.S.*: 1995 <1935>, ⇒11/1,4724. REThL 73 (1997) 184-185
*(Verheyden, J.)*.

G4.2 *Ad Romanos: themata*, topics

6292 *Achtemeier, Paul J.* Unsearchable judgments and inscrutable ways:
reflections on the discussion of Romans. Pauline theology, 4.
1997, ⇒6157. EJohnson, E.E., 3-21.

6293 **Aletti, Jean-Noël** La lettera ai Romani e la giustizia di Dio. Nuove
vie dell'esegesi: R 1997, Borla 301 pp. L40.000. 88-263-1193-5.

6294 *Branick, Vincent* Romans: an overview. BiTod 35 (1997) 72-76.

6295 E**Cipriani, Settimio** La lettera ai Romani ieri e oggi. 1995,
⇒11/1,74; 12,6055. REstB 55 (1997) 125-126 *(Pastor-Ramos, F.)*;
RdT 38 (1997) 562-564 *(Pitta, Antonio)*; Orph. 18 (1997) 573-578
*(Isetta, Sandra)*.

6296 **Cosgrove, Charles H.** Elusive Israel: the puzzle of election in
Romans. LVL 1997, Westminster xiii; 134 pp. $20. 0-664-25696-
1 [BTB 27,120].

6297 *Davidsen, Ole* The structural typology of Adam and Christ: some
modal-semiotic comments on the basic narrative of the letter to the
Romans. NT and Hellenistic Judaism. 1997, ⇒318. EBorgen, P.,
244-262.

6298 *DuToit, Andries B.* The ecclesiastical situation of the first generation Roman christians. HTS 53 (1997) 498-512 [ZID 24,126] [Col
1,13-20].

6299 **Garlington, Don B.** Faith, obedience and perseverance: aspects of Paul's letter to the Romans. 1994, ⇒10,5749; 12,6057. ᴿEvQ 69/1 (1997) 82-84 *(Gundry-Volf, Judith M.)*; TrinJ 18 (1997) 254-258 *(Karlberg, Mark W.)*.

6300 *Gemünden, Pétra von* Image de Dieu—Image de l'être humain dans l'Épître aux Romains. RHPhR 77 (1997) 31-49.

6301 *Grenholm, Cristina* The process of the interpretation of Romans. SBL.SPS 36 (1997) 306-336.

6302 ᴱ**Hay, David M.; Johnson, E. Elizabeth** Romans. Pauline theology, 3. 1995, ⇒11/1,4737. ᴿJThS 48 (1997) 598-599 *(Grayston, Kenneth)*; CBQ 59 (1997) 608-609 *(Byrne, Brendan)*.

6303 *Hofius, Otfried* Der Psalter als Zeuge des Evangeliums: die Verwendung der Septuaginta-Psalmen in den ersten beiden Hauptteilen des Römerbriefes. Theologische Probleme. 1997, ⇒223. ᴱReventlow, H. Graf, 72-90.

6304 *Holtz, Traugott* Die historischen und theologischen Bedingungen des Römerbriefes. 1997, ⇒92. ᶠSᴛᴜʜʟᴍᴀᴄʜᴇʀ P., 238-254.

6305 *Jewett, Robert* Honor and shame in the argument of Romans. 1997, ⇒82. ᶠSᴄʀᴏɢɢs R., 258-273.

6306 *Jolivet, Ira J.* An argument from the letter and intent of the law as the primary argumentative strategy in Romans. The rhetorical analysis. JSNT.S 146: 1997, ⇒336. ᴱPorter, S.E., 309-335.

6307 *Keck, Leander E.* Searchable judgments and scrutable ways: a response to Paul J. Aᴄʜᴛᴇᴍᴇɪᴇʀ. Pauline theology, 4. 1997, ⇒6157. ᴱJohnson, E.E., 22-32.

6308 *Lippi, Adolfo* La rinascita della *teologia crucis* nel secolo ventesimo: il *Römerbrief* di Karl Bᴀʀᴛʜ. La Sapienza della Croce 12/1 (1997) 21-46.

6309 *Longenecker, Richard N.* Prolegomena to Paul's use of scripture in Romans. BBR 7 (1997) 145-168.

6310 **Nanos, Mark D.** The mystery of Romans. 1996, ⇒12,6062. ᴿJSJ 28 (1997) 345-347 *(Tomson, Peter J.)*; JThS 48 (1997) 599-602 *(Dunn, James D.G.)*; TJT 13 (1997) 284-286 *(Campbell, Douglas A.)*; CBQ 59 (1997) 587-589 *(Elliott, Neil)*.

6311 *Penna, Romano* I pagani e la ricerca di Dio (nella lettera ai Romani). PSV 35 (1997) 177-191.

6312 *Rafiński, Grzegorz* Rozum jako źródło wartości moralnej czynu ludzkiego w Liście św. Pawła do Rzymian [Reason as the source of the moral value of human acts in Romans]. 1997, ⇒52. ᶠŁᴀᴄʜ J., 335-357. P.

6313 *Wright, N.T.* The two faces of faithfulness. BiRe 13/5 (1997) 16, 47.

## G4.3 *Naturalis cognitio Dei*, Rom 1-4

6314 **Moores, John D.** Wrestling with rationality in Paul: Romans 1-8 in a new perspective. MSSNTS 82: 1995, 11/1,4748; 12,6068. ᴿCBQ 59 (1997) 782-783 *(Porter, Stanley E.)*.

6315 *Byrskog, Samuel* Epistolography, rhetoric, and letter prescript: Romans 1.1-7 as a test case. JSNT 65 (1997) 27-46.

6316 *Bonneau, Normand* The gospel: God's power for salvation. BiTod 35 (1997) 77-82 [Rom 1,16-3,31].

6317  *Lohse, Eduard* "Die Juden zuerst und ebenso die Griechen".
      BZNW 89: 1997, ⇒33. ᶠGRAESSER E., 201-212 [Rom 1,16].
6318  *Walter, Nikolaus* Gottes Zorn und das 'Harren der Kreatur': zur
      Korrespondenz zwischen Römer 1,18-32 und 8,19-22. Praeparatio
      evangelica. WUNT 98: 1997 <1989>, ⇒167. 293-302.
6319  *Ward, Roy Bowen* Why unnatural?: the tradition behind Romans
      1:26-27. HThR 90 (1997) 263-284.
6320  *Adams, Edward* Abraham's faith and gentile disobedience: textual
      links between Romans 1 and 4. JSNT 65 (1997) 47-66 [Rom 1; 4].
6321  *Finamore, Steve* The gospel and the wrath of God in Romans 1.
      JSOT.S 153: 1997, ⇒4. ᶠASHTON J., 137-154.

6322  *Bell, Richard H.* Extra ecclesiam nulla salus?: is there a salvation
      other than through faith in Christ according to Romans 2.12-16?.
      1997, ⇒92. ᶠSTUHLMACHER P., 31-43.
6323  *Gryziec, Piotr R.* 'Z uczynków prawa nikt nie może dostąpić uspra-
      wiedliwienia' (Rz 3,20) ['Ex operibus legis non iustificabitur
      omnis caro' (Rom 3,20)]. RBL 50 (1997) 16-21. **P.**
6324  *Penna, Romano* Le 'opere della legge' in s. Paolo e 4QMMT.
      RStB 9/2 (1997) 155-176 [Rom 3,20].
6325  **Neubrand, Maria** Abraham—Vater von Juden und Nichtjuden: ei-
      ne exegetische Studie zu Röm 4. FzB 85: Wü 1997, Echter xiii;
      329 pp. DM48. 3-429-01978-8 [ThLZ 124,745—Klumbies, P.G.].
6326  *Brawley, Robert L.* Multivocality in Romans 4. SBL.SPS 36 (1997)
      285-305.


                    G4.4 *Redemptio cosmica:* **Rom 5-8**

6327  *Sánchez Ramiro, Demetrio* Pecado original y bautismo en el co-
      mentario de LUTERO a Romanos. ᴹRUIZ DE LA PENA J.,
      BSal.E 189: 1997, ⇒76. 245-261 [RB 105,299—Langlamet, F.].
6328  *Testa, Michael* NEWMAN on the doctrine of original sin. NBl 78
      (1997) 230-236.

6329  *Aletti, Jean-Noël* The rhetoric of Romans 5-8. The rhetorical analy-
      sis. JSNT.S 146: 1997, ⇒336. ᴱPorter, S.E., 294-308.
6330  *McDonald, Patricia M.* United in Christ. BiTod 35 (1997) 83-87
      [Rom 5,1-11].
6331  *Aletti, Jean-Noël* Romains 5,12-21: logique, sens et fonction. Sum.
      32. Bib. 78 (1997) 3-32.
6332  *Manicardi, E.* L'antitesi tra Adamo e Gesù nelle lettere paoline.
      L'obbedienza. 1997, ⇒216. ᴱMarrocu, G., 129-156 [Rom 5,12-21;
      1 Cor 15,21-22; 15,44-49].
6333  **Reid, Marty L.** Augustinian and Pauline rhetoric in Romans five.
      1996, ⇒12,6085. ᴿRHE 92 (1997) 528-531 *(Savon, Hervé)*; JBL
      116 (1997) 755-757 *(Watson, Duane F.).*

6334  *Eckstein, Hans J.* Auferstehung und gegenwärtiges Leben nach
      Röm 6,1-11: präsentische Eschatologie bei Paulus?. ThBeitr 28
      (1997) 8-23.
6335  *Arens, Edmund* Participación y testimonio: ¿qué significa hoy la
      muerte y la vida en Jesucristo?. Conc(E) 269 (1997) 147-157;
      (F133-141); (P133-142); (I33/1,156-166) [Rom 6; 8].

6336 *Tanghe, Vincent* Die Vorlage in Römer 6. EThL 73 (1997) 411-414.

6337 *Hellholm, David* Die argumentative Funktion von Römer 7.1-6. NTS 43 (1997) 385-411.

6338 *Schottroff, Luise* Selbstgerechtigkeit vor Gott oder Gnade?: zum Verständnis von Sünde im Neuen Testament (Röm 7,14-25). Antijudaismus im NT. KT 149: 1997, ⇒κ8. EHenze, D., 151-157.

6339 *Martin, Thomas F.* AUGUSTINE on Romans 7:24-25a. StPatr 33: 1997, ⇒351. ELivingstone, E., 178-182.

6340 *Lichtenberger, Hermann* Der Beginn der Auslegungsgeschichte von Römer 7: Röm 7,25b. ZNW 88 (1997) 284-295.

6341 **Huggins, Ronald Vincent** Romans 7 and the 'ordo salutis' in the nineteenth-century American revivalist tradition. Diss. Wycliffe, Toronto 1997; DLincoln, Andrew [SR 26,528].

6342 (a) *Keidel, Anne Gordon* BASIL of Caesarea's use of Romans 7 as a reflection of inner struggle. StPatr 32: 1997, ⇒351. ELivingstone, E., 136-140; (b) **Middendorf, Michael Paul** The "I" in the storm: a study of Romans 7. St. Louis, Mo. 1997, Concordia Acad. Press 303 pp. 0-570-04261-5.

6343 *Moreno García, Abdón* La tradición targúmica en Rom 8,5-8. La Bíblia i el Mediterrani. 1997, ⇒385. EBorrell, d'Agustí, 181-194.

6344 *Stefani, Piero* I gemiti dello Spirito: Romani 8,14-27. Sum. 300. RSEc 15 (1997) 291-300.

6345 **Chang, Hae-Kyung** Die Knechtschaft und Befreiung der Schöpfung: eine exegetische Untersuchung zu Röm 8,19-22. Diss. Tübingen 1997-98; DHofius, O. vi; 399 pp. [RTL 29,583].

6346 **Hahne, Harry A.** The corruption and redemption of creation: an exegetical study of Romans 8:19-23 in the light of Jewish apocalypticism. Diss. Wycliffe, Toronto 1997; DLongenecker, Richard [SR 26,527].

6347 **Ndiaye, Benjamin** Jésus 'premier-né d'une multitude de frères': étude de Rm. 8,28-30. Diss. Institut Catholique de Paris 1996; DQuesnel, Michel 266 pp. RRICP 61 (1997) 343-47 (Quesnel, M.).

G4.6 *Israel et Lex;* **The Law and the Jews,** *Rom 9-11*

6348 *Bammel, Ernst* Rückkehr zum Judentum. Judaica et Paulina. WUNT 91: 1997 <1987>, ⇒109. 47-56.

6349 *Beauchamp, Paul* Saint Paul et l'Ancien Testament: loi et foi. La loi. LeDiv 168: 1997, ⇒195. EFocant, C., 110-139.

6350 **Bell, Richard H.** Provoked to jealousy: the origin and purpose of the jealousy motif in Romans 9-11. WUNT 2/63: 1994, ⇒10,5801; 11/1,4800. RIBSt 19 (1997) 92-93 (McCullough, J.C.); CBQ 59 (1997) 145-147 (Spencer, F. Scott).

6351 *Elliott, Neil* Figure and ground in the interpretation of Romans 9-11. Theological interpretation. 1997, ⇒244. EFowl, S.E., 371-389.

6352 EFritsch-Oppermann, Sybille Juden und Christen—Juden und Deutsche: zur Auslegungs- und Wirkungsgeschichte von Röm 9-11. Loccumer Protokolle 93,60: Rehburg-Loccum 1997, Evangelische Akademie Loccum, Protokolstelle 192 pp. Dokumentation einer Tagung der Evangelischen Akadmie Loccum vom 1. bis 3. November 1993. 3-8172-6093-8 [NThAR 1997,292].

6353 **Gignac, Alain** La théologie paulinienne de l'élection en Rm 9-11 et son apport au dialogue entre juifs et chrétiens: analyse structurelle et intertextuelle. Diss. Montréal 1997; <sup>D</sup>*Mainville, O.* [RTL 29,584].

6354   <sup>E</sup>*Gorday, Peter* Selections from AUGUSTINE's Propositions from the epistle to the Romans and To Simplician—on various questions. Theological interpretation. 1997, ⇒244. <sup>E</sup>Fowl, S.E., 307-319.

6355   *Haacker, Klaus* Die Geschichtstheologie von Röm 9-11 im Lichte philonischer Schriftauslegung. NTS 43 (1997) 209-222.

6356   *Johnson, Elizabeth E.* Divine initiative and human response. Theological interpretation. 1997, ⇒244. <sup>E</sup>Fowl, S.E., 356-370.

6357   *Kraus, Wolfgang* Paulinische Perspektiven zum Thema "bleibende Erwählung Israels". Christen und Juden. 1997, ⇒212. <sup>E</sup>Kraus, W., 143-170.

6358   **Kruse, Colin G.** Paul, the law and justification. 1996, ⇒12,6112. <sup>R</sup>Pacifica 10/1 (1997) 95-97 *(Byrne, Brendan).*

6359   *La Potterie, Ignacio de* L'Israele di Dio. TS(I) (gen-feb 1997) 16-17, 55-56.

6360   *Peretto, Elio* Ebrei e cristiani a confronto nella lettura di Rom 9-11 di BRUNO, il certosino. 1997, ⇒155. Saggi, 701-716.

6361   *Remaud, Michel* 'Leur voix a retenti par toute la terre...': allusions à quelques traditions juives dans Romains 9-11. Sum., som. 102. Cahiers Ratisbonne 2 (1997) 78-102.

6362   <sup>E</sup>*Rogers, Eugene F.* Selections from THOMAS Aquinas's Commentary on Romans. Theological interpretation. 1997, ⇒244. <sup>E</sup>Fowl, S.E., 320-337.

6363   *Ryan, Judith M.* God's fidelity to Israel and mercy to all. BiTod 35 (1997) 89-93.

6364   **Sänger, Dieter** Die Verkündigung des Gekreuzigten und Israel. WUNT 2/75: 1994, ⇒10,5810; 12,6116. <sup>R</sup>JBL 116 (1997) 374-375 *(Räisänen, Heikki).*

6365   *Westerholm, Stephen* Law and the early christians. JDH 22 (1997) 396-417;

6366   Sinai as viewed from Damascus: Paul's reevaluation of the Mosaic law. The road from Damascus. 1997, ⇒330. <sup>E</sup>Longenecker, R.N., 147-165.

6367   *Wolter, Michael* Recht/Rechtswesen im Neuen Testament. TRE 28. 1997, ⇒420. 209-213.

6368   *Baldanza, Giuseppe* L'unione tra giudei e gentili: la metafora sponsale in Rom 9,23-26. Sal. 59 (1997) 237-248.

6369   *Lang, Friedrich* Erwägungen zu Gesetz und Verheißung in Römer 10,4-13. BZNW 86: 1997, ⇒41. <sup>F</sup>HOFIUS O., 579-602.

6370   *Meyer, Paul W.* Romans 10:4 and the "end" of the law. Theological interpretation. 1997, ⇒244. <sup>E</sup>Fowl, S.E., 338-355.

6371   *Bekken, Per Jarle* Paul's use of Deut 30,12-14 in Jewish context: some observations. NT and Hellenistic Judaism. 1997, ⇒318. <sup>E</sup>Borgen, P., 183-203 [Rom 10].

6372   *Havemann, J.C.T.* Cultivated olive-wild olive: the olive tree metaphor in Romans 11:16-24. Neotest. 31 (1997) 87-106.

6373   *Maartens, Pieter J.* A critical dialogue of structure and reader in Romans 11:16-24. HTS 53 (1997) 1030-1051.

6374   *Kim, Seyoon* The "mystery" of Rom 11.25-6 once more. NTS 43 (1997) 412-429.

6375  *Seewann, Maria I.* "Verstockung", "Verhärtung" oder "Nicht-Erkennen"?: Überlegungen zu Röm 11,25. KuI 12/2 (1997) 161-172.
6376  *Sievers, Joseph* "God's gifts and call are irrevocable": the interpretation of Rom 11:29 and its uses. SBL.SPS 36 (1997) 337-357;
6377  A history of the interpretation of Romans 11:29. ASEs 14 (1997) 381-442.
6378  *Mindling, Joseph A.* Thoughts on Romans 11. BiTod 35 (1997) 95-99.

## G4.8  Rom 12...

6379  *Thompson, Michael B.* Romans 12.1-2 and Paul's vision for worship. 1997, ⇒93. ᶠSwᴇᴇᴛ J., 121-132.
6380  *Gubler, Marie-Louise* Gegen den Strom schwimmen ...: zu Röm 12,1-3 und Mt 16,21-26. Diak. 28 (1997) 350-352.
6381  *Beré, Paul* Rom. 12,2-3: exhortation au renouvellement intérieur (essai d'exégèse). Hekima Review 18 (1997) 82-96.
6382  *Elliott, Neil* Romans 13:1-7 in the context of imperial propaganda. Paul and empire. 1997, ⇒204. ᴱHorsley, R.A., 184-204.
6383  *Coleman, Thomas M.* Binding obligations in Romans 13:7: a semantic field and social context. TynB 48 (1997) 307-327.
6384  *Elliot, John H.*, (*al.*), Forum: subject to whose authority?. Neotest. 31 (1997) 195-222 [Rom 13].
6385  **Botha, Jan** Subject to whose authority?: multiple readings of Romans 13. 1994, ⇒10,5831; 11/1,4823. ᴿBibl.Interp. 5 (1997) 214-216 (*Moxnes, Halvor*).
6386  *Bammel, Ernst* Romans 13. Judaica et Paulina. WUNT 91: 1997 <²1985>, ⇒109. 286-304.
6387  *Wagner, J. Ross* The Christ, servant of Jew and gentile: a fresh approach to Romans 15:8-9. JBL 116 (1997) 473-485.

### G5.1  Epistulae ad Corinthios I, *textus, commentarii*

6388  ᵀ**Barbaglio, Giuseppe** La prima lettera ai Corinzi. Scritti delle origini cristiane 7: 1995, ⇒11/1,4829; 12,6142. ᴿJThS 48 (1997) 602-604 (*Hickling, C.J.A.*).
6389  ᴱ**Bieringer, Reimund** The Corinthian correspondence. BEThL 125: 1996, ⇒12,6143. ᴿRB 104 (1997) 433-434 (*Langlamet, F.*); CBQ 59 (1997) 793-795 (*Harrill, J. Albert*).
6390  **Blazen, Ivan T.** The gospel on the street: Paul's first letter to the Corinthians. Nampa, Idaho 1997, Pacific 127 pp. 0-8163-1411-X [NThAR 2000,123].
       **Bosio, Enrico** Epistole di S. Paolo... I-II Corinzi ⇒6277.
6391  ᴱᵀ**Donnelly, John Patrick** Philip Mᴇʟᴀɴᴄʜᴛᴏɴ: annotations on First Corinthians. 1995, ⇒11/1,4831. ᴿSCJ 28 (1997) 603-604 (*Eppley, Dan*).
6392  ᴱ**Frede, Hermann Josef; Stanjek, Herbert** Sᴇᴅᴜʟɪɪ Scotti collectaneum in apostolum II: in epistolas ad Corinthios usque ad Hebraeos. Collectanea in omnes beati Pauli epistulas. AGLB 32: FrB 1997, Herder 512 pp. DM300. 3-451-21952-2. ᴿREAug 43 (1997) 401-403 (*Dolbeau, François*).

6393   **Frör, Hans** Jullie Korintiërs!: de briefwisseling van de gemeente in Korinthe met Paulus. 1996, ⇒12,6148. ᴿITBT 5/1 (1997) 18-19 *(Roukema, Riemer)*.

6394   **Hannah, Darrel D.** The text of I Corinthians in the writings of ORIGEN. SBL.The NT in the Greek Fathers 4: Atlanta, GA 1997 Scholars xi; 308 pp. $45. 0-7885-0338-3 [NTS 43,621].

6395   **Haykin, Michael A.G.** The Spirit of God: the exegesis of 1 and 2 Corinthians in the pneumatomachian controversy of the fourth century. SVigChr 27: 1994, ⇒10,5855; 12,6149. ᴿChH 66/1 (1997) 83-84 *(Balás, David L.)*.

6396   **Hays, Richard B.** First Corinthians. Interpretation: LVL 1997, Knox xiv; 299 pp. $24. 0-8042-3144-3 [NThAR 1998,100].

6397   **Hodge, Charles** 1 and 2 Corinthians. The Crossway Classic Commentaries. 1995, ⇒11/1,4834. SBET 15/1 (1997) 81-82 *(Boyd, A.C.)*.

6398   **Hollander, H.W.** 1 Korintiërs. 1996, ⇒12,6150. ᴿITBT 5 (1997) 18-19 *(Roukema, Riemer)*.

6399   **Kremer, Jacob** Der erste Brief an die Korinther. RNT: Regensburg 1997, Pustet 428 pp. DM78. 3-7917-1519-4.

6400   **Lambrecht, Jan** 1 Korintiërs. Belichting van het bijbelboek: 's-Hertogenbosch 1997, Katholieke Bijbelstichting 96 pp. 90-6173-951-9.

6401   **Murphy-O'Connor, Jerome** 1 Corinthians. People's Bible Commentary: Oxf 1997, Bible Reading Fellowship 195 pp. £8. 0-7459-3280-0 [RB 104,476].

6402   **Reiling, J.** Die eerste brief van Paulus aan de Korintiërs. De prediking van het Nieuwe Testament: Baarn 1997, Callenbach 320 pp. ƒ79. 90-266-0348-7 [CBQ 60,197].

6403   **Witherington III, Ben** Conflict and community in Corinth: a socio-rhetorical commentary on 1 and 2 Corinthians. 1995, ⇒11/1,4839; 12,6155. ᴿAUSS 35 (1997) 156-158 *(DeSilva, D.A.)*.


G5.2   *1 & 1-2 ad Corinthios—themata*, topics

6404   *Bammel, Ernst* Rechtsfindung in Korinth. Judaica et Paulina. WUNT 91: 1997, ⇒109. 279-285 [=EThL 73 (1997) 107-113].

6405   *Bowe, Barbara E.* Paul and First Corinthians. BiTod 35 (1997) 268-274.

6406   *Carter, Timothy L.* 'Big men' in Corinth. JSNT 66 (1997) 45-71.

6407   *Chow, John K.* Christians in an ever-changing world: lessons from I Clement and I Corinthians. Listening 32/1 (1997) 39-47;

6408   Patronage in Roman Corinth. Paul and empire. 1997, ⇒204. ᴱHorsley, R.A., 104-125.

6409   *Collins, Raymond F.* Preaching the gospel according to Paul;

6410   *Harrill, J. Albert* Slavery and society at Corinth. BiTod 35 (1997) 280-285/287-293.

6411   *Horsley, Richard A.* 1 Corinthians: a case study of Paul's assembly as an alternative society. Paul and empire. 1997, ⇒204. ᴱHorsley, R.A., 242-252.

6412   *Hughes, Frank W.* Rhetorical criticism and the Corinthian correspondence. The rhetorical analysis. JSNT.S 146: 1997, ⇒336. ᴱPorter, S.E., 336-350.

6413 **Hunt, Allen Rhea** The inspired body: Paul, the Corinthians, and divine inspiration. 1996, ⇒12,6168. RCritRR 10 (1997) 185-187 *(Gillespie, Thomas W.)*.

6414 *Hyldahl, Niels* Paul and Hellenistic Judaism in Corinth. NT and Hellenistic Judaism. 1997, ⇒318. EBorgen, P., 204-216.

6415 **Lanci, John R.** A new temple for Corinth: rhetorical and archaeological approaches to Pauline imagery. Studies in Biblical Literature 1: NY 1997, Lang xi; 155 pp. Bibl. £25. 0-8204-3676-3.

6416 **Martin, Dale B.** The Corinthian body. 1995, ⇒11/1,4849; 12,6174. RMoTh 13 (1997) 269-271 *(Ward, Graham)*; CBQ 59 (1997) 384-386 *(Scroggs, Robin)*.

6417 *Mauser, Ulrich* Trinitarische Sprachformen in den Korintherbriefen des Paulus. 1997, ⇒92. FSTUHLMACHER P., 288-295.

6418 *Mickiewicz, Franciszek* Świątynia duchowa jako motywacja napomnień moralnych w listach św. Pawła do Koryntian [Spiritual temple as the motivation of moral admonitions in the epistles to the Corinthians]. 1997, ⇒52. FŁACH J., 273-285. **P.** [1 Cor 3,16-17; 6,19-20; 2 Cor 6,16-18].

6419 **Pickett, Raymond** The cross in Corinth: the social significance of the death of Jesus. Diss. Sheffield; DLincoln, A.: JSNT.S 143: Shf 1997, Academic 230 pp. £40/$66. 1-85075-663-5 [EThL 74,327*].

6420 *Pytel, Jam Kanty* Słudzy Ewangelii w Pierwszym Liście do Koryntian [Servants of the gospel in 1 Corinthians]. 1997, ⇒52. FŁACH J., 325-333. **P.**

6421 **Quast, Kevin** Reading the Corinthian correspondence. 1994, ⇒10,5863; 12,6176. RTJT 13/1 (1997) 113-114 *(Campbell, Douglas A.)*.

6422 *Rakotoharintsifa, Andrianjatovo* Historiographie et lecture sociohistorique de 1 Corinthiens. CBFV 36 (1997) 115-123;

6423 Jérémie en action à Corinthe: citations et allusions jérémiennes dans 1 Corinthiens. The book of Jeremiah. BEThL 128: 1997, ⇒186. ECurtis, A.H.W., 207-216.

6424 *Sanders, Jack T.* Paul between Jews and gentiles in Corinth. JSNT 65 (1997) 67-83.

6425 **Song, Bong-Mo** The Pauline concept of 'weakness' in 1 Corinthians and its usage within the context of Paul's resolution of the opposition betweeen the strong and the weak in 1 Cor 8:7-13. Diss. Catholic Univ. of America 1997; DCollins, R.F.; Microfilm: Ann Arbor [RTL 29,588].

6426 *Tomlin, Graham* Christians and Epicureans in 1 Corinthians. JSNT 68 (1997) 51-72.

6427 **Welborn, Laurence L.** Politics and rhetoric in the Corinthian epistles. Macon, Ga. 1997, Mercer viii; 238 pp. $30. 0-86554-463-8 [NThAR 1998,101].

6428 *Wenham, David* Whatever went wrong in Corinth?. ET 108 (1997) 137-141.

### G5.3 1 Cor 1-7: *sapientia crucis... abusus matrimonii*

6429 *Elliott, Neil* The anti-imperial message of the cross. Paul and empire. 1997, ⇒204. EHorsley, R.A., 167-183.

6430 *Helewa, Giovanni* Sotto la croce con Paolo apostolo. RVS 51/1 (1997) 7-18.

6431 *Kreitzer, Larry J.* The scandal of the cross: crucifixion imagery and Bram STOKER's Dracula. The monstrous. 1997, ⇒169. EAichele, G., 181-219.

6432 *Martin, Dale B.* Paul without passion: on Paul's rejection of desire in sex and marriage. Constructing... families. 1997, ⇒295. EMoxnes, H., 201-215.

6433 **Rotzetter, Anton** Im Kreuz ist Leben. 1996, ⇒12,6186. RGuL 70/6 (1997) 477 *(Steinmetz, Franz-Josef)*.

6434 **Brown, Alexandra R.** The cross and human transformation. 1995, ⇒11/1,4864. RCBQ 59 (1997) 150-2 *(Jaquette, J.L.)* [1 Cor 1-2].

6435 *Vadakkedom, Jose* The Corinthian community: a divided church?: a study based on I Corinthians 1-4. BiBh 23/1 (1997) 27-44.

6436 **Yamsat, Pandang** Partners not rivals, 1: a study of 1 Corinthians 1-6. Jos 1997, TCNN 218 pp. 978-2949-03-5 [[NThAR 1999,182].

6437 **Pöttner, Martin** Realität als Kommunikation: Ansätze zur Beschreibung der Grammatik des paulinischen Sprechens in 1 Kor 1,4-4,21 im Blick auf literarische Problematik und Situationsbezug des 1. Korintherbriefs. Diss. Marburg 1995; DHarnisch, W.: Theologie 2: Müns 1995, LIT iv; 370; xxi pp. 3-8258-2687-2 [ThLZ 125,518ss—Schenk, Wolfgang].

6438 *Brown, Alexandra R.* The cross and moral discernment, 1. DoLi 47 (1997) 196-203 [1 Cor 1,17-18].

6439 *Merklein, Helmut* Das paulinische Paradox des Kreuzes. TThZ 106 (1997) 81-98 [1 Cor 1,18-25].

6440 **Bullmore, Michael A.** St. Paul's theology of rhetorical style... 1 Cor 2.1-5. 1995, ⇒11/1,4873. RJBL 116 (1997) 568-570 *(Litfin, Duane)*.

6441 *Selby, Gary S.* Paul, the seer: the rhetorical persona in 1 Corinthians 2.1-16. The rhetorical analysis. JSNT.S 146: 1997, ⇒336. EPorter, S.E., 351-373.

6442 **Rosner, Brian S.** Paul, scripture and ethics: a study of 1 Corinthians 5-7. AZGATU 22: 1994, ⇒10,5881... 12,6198. RBibl.Interp. 5 (1997) 221-223 *(Horrell, David)*; EvQ 69/1 (1997) 86-88 *(Thiselton, Anthony C.)*.

6443 *Jacobs, Lambert D.* Establishing a new value system in Corinth: 1 Corinthians 5-6 as persuasive argument. The rhetorical analysis. JSNT.S 146: 1997, ⇒336. EPorter, S.E., 374-387.

6444 **Pascuzzi, Maria** Ethics, ecclesiology and Church discipline: a rhetorical analysis of 1 Corinthians 5. Diss. Pont. Univ. Gregoriana; DSwetnam, James: TGr.T 32: R 1997, Ed. Pont. Univ. Gregoriana 234 pp. L24.000. 88-7652-767-2.

6445 *Kuhn, Heinz-Wolfgang* A legal issue in 1 Corinthians 5 and in Qumran. StTDJ 23: 1997, ⇒8. FBAUMGARTEN J., 489-499.

6446 *Kinman, Brent* "Appoint the despised as judges!" (1 Corinthians 6:4). TynB 48 (1997) 345-354.

6447 *Derrett, J. Duncan M.* Right and wrong sticking (1 Cor 6,18)?. EstB 55 (1997) 89-106.

6448 *Winter, Bruce W.* 1 Corinthians 7:6-7: a caveat and a framework for "the sayings" in 7:8-24. TynB 48 (1997) 57-65.

6449 *Warzeszak, Józef* Próba jurydycznego naświetlenia 1 Kor 7,14.16 [Prova di spiegazione giuridica del 1 Cor 7,14.16)]. Rias. 412. WST 10 (1997) 407-412.

6450 *Bauer, Johannes B.* Was las TERTULLIAN 1 Kor 7,39?. Studien zu Bibeltext. 1997 <1986>, ⇒111. 249-254.

6451 **Gordon, J.** Dorcas Sister or wife?: 1 Corinthians 7 and cultural anthropology. JSNT.S 149: Shf 1997, Academic 248 pp. Bibl. £32.50. 1-85075-685-6.

6452 *Osiek, Carolyn* First Corinthians 7 and family questions. BiTod 35 (1997) 275-279.

6453 **Deming, Will** Paul on marriage and celibacy: the Hellenistic background of 1 Corinthians 7. MSSNTS 83: 1995, ⇒11/1,4893; 12,6209. ᴿEstB 55 (1997) 282-283 *(Pastor-Ramos, F.)*; JThS 48 (1997) 604-06 *(Horrell, David G.)*; JBL 116 (1997) 155-156 *(Yarbrough, O. Larry)*; JR 77 (1997) 289-290 *(Fitzgerald, John T.)*.

6454 *Mateo-Seco, Lucas F.* La exégesis de San AGUSTIN en 1 Cor 13,12 y 1 Jn 3,2. RevAg 38 (1997) 529-559.

## G5.4 *Idolothyta... Eucharistia:* 1 Cor 8-11

6455 *Dalmais, Irénée-Henri* Biblical themes in Greek eucharistic anaphoras. The Bible in Greek christian antiquity. 1997 <c.1984>, ⇒177. ᴱᵀBlowers, Paul M., 329-341.

6456 **Heil, Christoph** Die Ablehnung der Speisegebote durch Paulus. BBB 96: 1994, ⇒10,5896; 11/1,4894. ᴿEstB 55 (1997) 554-556 *(Rodríguez-Ruiz, M.)*; CBQ 58 (1996) 753-754 *(Muller, Earl C.)*; CritRR 9 (1996) 227-229 *(Schreiner, Thomas R.)*.

6457 **Klinghardt, Matthias** Gemeinschaftsmahl und Mahlgemeinschaft: Soziologie und Liturgie frühchristlicher Mahlfeiern. TANZ 13: Tü 1996, Francke xi; 633 pp. 3-7720-1879-3. ᴿThR 62 (1997) 342-344 *(Lohse, Eduard)*.

6458 *Passakos, Demetrius C.* Eucharist in First Corinthians: a sociological study. RB 104 (1997) 192-210.

6459 *Smit, Joop F. M.* The rhetorical disposition of First Corinthians 8:7-9:27. CBQ 59 (1997) 476-491.

6460 *Lemonon, Jean-Pierre* Liberté chrétienne et respect du frère: la communion ecclésiale: à propos de 1Co 8,1-11,1. UnChr 125 (1997) 4-7.

6461 *Horrell, David* Theological principle or christological praxis?: Pauline ethics in 1 Corinthians 8.1-11.1. JSNT 67 (1997) 83-114.

6462 *Smit, Joop* Paulus 'over de afgodsoffers': de kerk tussen joden en grieken (1 Kor. 8,1-11,1). TTh 37 (1997) 228-242.

6463 *Lambrecht, Jan* El universalismo de 1 Cor 8,1-11,1. RevBib 59/3 (1997) 155-163.

6464 *Hofius, Otfried* "Einer ist Gott—Einer ist Herr": Erwägungen zu Struktur und Aussage des Bekenntnisses 1.Kor 8,6. BZNW 89: 1997, ⇒33. ᶠGRAESSER E., 95-108.

6465 **Yeo, Khiok-khing** Rhetorical interaction in 1 Corinthians 8 and 10. 1995, ⇒11/1,4897. TJT 13/1 (1997) 124-125 *(LeMarquand, Grant)*; ETR 72 (1997) 466-467 *(Rakotoharintsifa, Andrianjatovo)*.

6466  *Lohse, Eduard* "Kümmert sich Gott etwa um die Ochsen?": zu 1Kor 9,9. ZNW 88 (1997) 314-315.
6467  *Horrell, David G.* 'The Lord commanded ... but I have not used ...': exegetical and hermeneutical reflections on 1 Cor 9.14-15. NTS 43 (1997) 587-603.
6468  *Papathomas, Amphilochios* Das agonistische Motiv 1 Kor 9.24ff im Spiegel zeitgenössischer dokumentarischer Quellen. NTS 43 (1997) 223-241.
6469  *Schwankl, Otto* "Lauft so, daß ihr gewinnt": zur Wettkampfmetaphorik in 1 Kor 9. BZ 41 (1997) 174-191.
6470  **Palma, Paul Victor Hugo** 1 Co. 9: Paulus, apostolus liber: teología de la libertad cristiana y del apostolado. Diss. Pont. Univ. Gregoriana 1997; 396 pp. [RTL 29,587].

6471  *Aitken, Bradshaw Ellen* Τα δρωμενα και τα λεγομενα: Jesus' words in First Corinthians. HThR 90 (1997) 359-370 [1 Cor 10-11].
6472  *Sandelin, Karl-Gustav* Does Paul argue against sacramentalism and over-confidence in 1 Cor 10.1-14?. NT and Hellenistic Judaism. 1997, ⇒318. ᴱBorgen, P., 165-182.
6473  *Smit, J.* "Do not be idolaters": Paul's rhetoric in First Corinthians 10:1-22. NT 39 (1997) 40-53.
6474  *Smit, Joop F.M.* The function of First Corinthians 10,23-30: a rhetorical anticipation. Bib. 78 (1997) 377-388.

6475  **Blattenberger, David E.** Rethinking 1 Corinthians 11:2-16 through archaeological and moral-rhetorical analysis. SBEC 36: Lewiston, NY 1997, Mellen xiii; 96 pp. Bibl. 0-7734-8562-7.
6476  *Holmyard, Harold R.* Does 1 Corinthians 11:2-16 refer to women praying and prophesying in the church?. BS 154 (1997) 461-472.
6477  *Pastor Ramos, Federico* La cabeza "cubierta" en 1 Cor 11,2-16. La Bíblia i el Mediterrani. 1997, ⇒385. ᴱBorrell, d'Agustí, 311-328.
6478  *Gundry-Volf, Judith M.* Gender and creation in 1 Corinthians 11:2-16: a study in Paul's theological method. 1997, ⇒92. ᶠSᴛᴜʜʟᴍᴀᴄʜᴇʀ P., 151-171.
6479  *Larsen, Iver* 1 Corinthians 11.10 revisited. TPBT 48 (1997) 345-350.
6480  *Paulsen, Henning* Schisma und Häresie: Untersuchungen zu 1 Kor 11,18.19. Zur Literatur. WUNT 99: 1997 <1982>, ⇒153. 43-74.
6481  *Vives, Josep* 'Cal que hi hagi heretyies' (1C 11,19). Qüestiones de Vida Cristiana 185 (1997) 71-84.
6482  *Neugebauer, Fritz* Wege zum Herrenmahl. 1997, ⇒92. ᶠSᴛᴜʜʟᴍᴀᴄʜᴇʀ P., 325-336 [1 Cor 11].

### G5.5  1 Cor 12s... Glossolalia, charismata

6483  *Fee, Gordon D.* Toward a Pauline theology of glossolalia. JPentec.S 11: 1997, ⇒63. ᶠMᴇɴᴢɪᴇs W., 24-37.
6484  *Filoramo, Giovanni* Pour une histoire comparée du prophétisme chrétien: réflexions méthodologiques entre histoire des religions et histoire religieuse. Le comparatisme. 1997, ⇒346. ᴱBoespflug, F., 73-87.

6485 **Forbes, Christopher** Prophecy and inspired speech in early christianity and its Hellenistic environment. WUNT 2/75: 1995, ⇒11/2, 2072. ᴿLetteratura Liturgica 84 (1997) 596-597 *(Vicent, Rafael)*; CBQ 59 (1997) 580-581 *(Pelser, Gert M.M.)*.

6486 *Garhammer, Erich* Die vielen Gaben und der eine Geist. LS 48 (1997) 129-132.

6487 *Georgi, Dieter* Who Is the true prophet?. Paul and empire. 1997, ⇒204. ᴱHorsley, R.A., 36-46.

6488 **Gillespie, Thomas W.** The first theologians: a study in early christian prophecy. 1994, ⇒10,5918; 11/1,4916. ᴿJBL 115 (1996) 538-540 *(Boring, M. Eugene)*; CBQ 58 (1996) 747-749 *(McGinn, Sheila Elizabeth)*.

6489 *Goede, Juan Bek de* Pablo y el modelo carismatico de la iglesia en Corinto: ¿exito o fracaso?. RevBib 59 (1997) 193-222.

6490 **Grudem, Wayne A.** Die Gabe der Prophetie im Neuen Testament und heute. Nürnberg 1994, Immanuel 336 pp. Vorwort von *Mike Bickle*. DM29.80. ᴿJETh 11 (1997) 232-233 *(Schmidt, Norbert)*.

6491 **Howard, Roland** Charisma: when christian fundamentalism goes wrong. L 1997, Mowbray 150 pp. £10. 0-264-67409-X [RRT 1998/1,90].

6492 *Menzies, Robert P.* Spirit-baptism and spiritual gifts. JPentec.S 11: 1997, ⇒63. ᶠMᴇɴᴢɪᴇs W., 48-59.

6493 *Murphy, David J.* Prophecy as charism. 1997, ⇒70. ᶠMᴜʀᴘʜʏ R., Master, 317-334.

6494 *Penney, John* The testing of New Testament prophecy. JPentec 10 (1997) 35-84 [ZID 23,360].

6495 *Trocmé, Etienne* Le prophétisme chez les premiers chrétiens. Oracles. 1997, ⇒374. ᴱHeintz, J.-G., 259-270.

6496 **Zaleski, Philip; Kaufman, Paul** Gifts of the spirit: living the wisdom of the great religious traditions. SF 1997, HarperSanFrancisco xiii; 271 pp. 0-06-069701-6.

6497 **Omara, Robert** Spiritual gifts in the church: a study of 1 Cor 12:1-11. Diss. extract Pont. Univ. Urbaniana 1997; ᴰ*Federici, Tommaso* xiii; 139 pp.

6498 *Roberts, P.* Seers or overseers?. ET 108 (1997) 301-305 [1 Cor 12,28].

6499 *Hartmann, Lars* 1 Cor 14:1-25: argument and some problems. Text-centered NT studies. WUNT 102: 1997, ⇒132. 211-233.

6500 *Msafiri, Aidan G.* Diversity in 1 Corinthians 14:12-14, as a challenge towards church unity: an African perspective. African Christian Studies 13/1 (1997) 28-41.

6501 *Hasitschka, Martin* "Die Frauen in den Gemeinden sollen schweigen": 1 Kor 14,33b-36—Anweisung des Paulus zur rechten Ordnung im Gottesdienst. SNTU.A 22 (1997) 47-56.

6502 *Niccum, Curt* The voice of the manuscripts on the silence of women: the external evidence for 1 Cor 14.34-5. NTS 43 (1997) 242-255.

6503 *Eriksson, Anders* "Tig, tungomålstalerskor!": Paulus förbud för kvinnorna att tala i 1 Kor 14:34. SEÅ 62 (1997) 123-150.

6504 *Zerhusen, Bob* The problem tongues in 1 Cor 14: a reexamination. BTB 27 (1997) 139-152.

6505  *Mateo-Seco, Lucas F.* 1 Cor 13,12 in Gregory of Nyssa's
theological thinking. StPatr 32: 1997, ⇒351. ᴱLivingstone, E.,
153-162.

G5.6 **Resurrectio;** *1 Cor 15...* [ꜰ5.6]

6506  **Bynum, Caroline Walker** The resurrection of the body in western
christianity. LHR 15: 1995, ⇒11/1,4940; 12,6251. ᴿMAe 66/1
(1997) 122-123 *(Hirsh, John C.)*.
6507  *Raffin, Pierre* La risurrezione dei corpi fondamento dell'identità
cristiana. Sum. 219. Religioni e Sette nel mondo 3/2 (1997) 128-
153.
6508  **Thomas, Pascal** Réincarnation, résurrection. 1995, ⇒11/1,4953.
ᴿTelema 23/3 (1997) 84-86 *(Delhez, Charles)*.

6509  *Smit Sibinga, Joost* 1 Cor. 15:8/9 and other divisions in 1 Cor.
15:1-11. NT 39 (1997) 54-59.
6510  *Bammel, Ernst* Herkunft und Funktion der Traditionselemente in
1.Kor. 15,1-11. Judaica et Paulina. WUNT 91: 1997 <1959>,
⇒109. 260-278.
6511  **Lucas, Roger** The time of the reign of Christ in 1st Corinthians
15:20-28 in light of early christian session theology. Diss.
Andrews 1997; ᴰYounker, R.W. 358 pp. [RTL 29,586].
6512  *White, Joel R.* "Baptized on account of the dead": the meaning of 1
Corinthians 15:29 in its context. JBL 116 (1997) 487-499.
6513  *Załęski, Jan* Chrzest za zmarłych (1 Kor 15,29) [Baptism on behalf
of the dead (1 Cor 15,29)]. 1997, ⇒52. ꜰŁach J., 455-460. **P.**
6514  **Teani, Maurizio** Corporeità e risurrezione: l'interpretazione di 1
Corinti 15,35-49 nel Novecento. Aloi. 24: 1994, ⇒10,5947...
12,6262. ᴿEstB 55 (1997) 418-421 *(Urbán, A.)*; Hum(B) 52 (1997)
665-666 *(Montagnini, Felice)*; CivCatt 148 I (1997) 305-306
*(Scaiola, D.)*.
6515  **Peterson, Jeffrey** The image of man from heaven: christological
exegesis in 1 Corinthians 15:45-49. Diss. Yale; ᴰFraade, S.D.
[RTL 29,587].
6516  *Lindemann, Andreas* Die Auferstehung der Toten: Adam und Christus nach 1.Kor 15. BZNW 89: 1997, ⇒33. ꜰGraesser E., 155-
167.
6517  **Verburg, Winfried** Endzeit und Entschlafene... Analyse von 1
Kor 15. 1996, ⇒12,6269. ᴿBZ 41 (1997) 145-147 *(Dautzenberg,
Gerhard)*.
6518  *Panimolle, Salvatore* 'Maràn athá' = Signore, vieni!. DSBP 16
(1997) 7-19 [1 Cor 16,22].

G5.9 **Secunda epistula ad Corinthios**

6519  **Barnett, Paul William** The second epistle to the Corinthians. New
International Commentary on the NT: GR 1997, Eerdmans xxx;
662 pp. £30/$45. 0-8028-2300-9.
6520  ᴱ**Feld, Helmut** Commentarii in Secundum Pauli epistolam ad Corinthios. Ioannis Calvini Opera exegetica 15. 1994, ⇒10,5952...

12,6273. <sup>R</sup>Zwing. 24 (1997) 162-164 *(Saxer, Ernst)*; ChH 66 (1997) 808-809 *(Ocker, Christopher)*.

6521 <sup>E</sup>**Mills, Watson E.** 2 Corinthians. Bibliographies for biblical research. Lewiston, NY 1997, Mellen xiv; 139 pp. 0-7734-2442-3 [NThAR 1998,335].

6522 **Zeilinger, Franz** Krieg und Frieden in Korinth: Kommentar zum 2. Korintherbrief des Apostels Paulus, 2: die Apologie. W 1997, Böhlau 487 pp. 3-205-98746-2 [⇒8,6454; 9,6149].

6523 **Bosenius, Bärbel** Die Abwesenheit des Apostels als theologisches Programm: der zweite Korintherbrief als Beispiel für die Brieflichkeit der paulinischen Theologie. TANZ 11: 1994, ⇒10,5955; 11/1,4963. <sup>R</sup>JBL 115 (1996) 560-562 *(Scott, James M.)*.

6524 **Harvey, Anthony Ernest** Renewal through suffering: a study of 2 Corinthians. 1996, ⇒12,6279. <sup>R</sup>CritRR 10 (1997) 180-181 *(Tatum, Gregory)*.

6525 *Hotze, Gerhard* Schatz in tönernen Gefäßen—der zweite Korintherbrief. BiLi 70 (1997) 47-52, 147-152, 204-208, 305-309.

6526 *Quesnel, Michel* Circonstances de composition de la seconde épitre aux Corinthiens. NTS 43 (1997) 256-267.

6527 **Savage, Timothy B.** Power through weakness: Paul's understanding of the Christian ministry in 2 Corinthians. MSSNTS 86: 1996, ⇒12,6281. <sup>R</sup>EvQ 69 (1997) 166-169 *(Clarke, Andrew D.)*; JThS 48 (1997) 606-611 *(Hickling, C.J.A.)*; CBQ 59 (1997) 592-593 *(Hensell, Eugene)*; JBL 116 (1997) 570-571 *(Gillespie, Thomas)*.

6528 **Wünsch, Hans-Michael** Der paulinische Brief 2Kor 1-9 als kommunikative Handlung. 1996, ⇒12,6283. <sup>R</sup>BZ 41 (1997) 274-276 *(Dautzenberg, Gerhard)*.

6529 **Cyran, Włodzimierz** Kultyczny wymiar posługi apostolskiej według 2 Kor 1-7 [La dimension cultuelle du ministère apostolique selon 2 Co 1-7]. Diss. Lublin 1997; <sup>D</sup>*Langkammer, H.* xxxi; 366 pp. [RTL 29,583].

6530 **Brendle, Albert** Im Prozeß der Konfliktüberwindung... 2 Kor 1,1-2,13; 7,4-16. EHS.T 533: 1995, ⇒11/1,4964. <sup>R</sup>BZ 41 (1997) 147-149 *(Dautzenberg, Gerhard)*; ThLZ 122 (1997) 140-2 *(Sellin, G.)*.

6531 *Scholla, Robert W.* Into the image of God: Pauline eschatology and the transformation of believers. Rés. 54. Gr. 78 (1997) 33-54 [2 Cor 2,14-3,18].

6532 **Gruber, M. Margarete (Brigitte)** 'DOXA' in der Apologie des Paulus: Struktur, Gedankengang und Theologie von 2 Kor 2,14-6,13. Diss. St. Georgen 1997; <sup>D</sup>*Baumert, N.* 525 pp. [BZ 42,316].

6533 *Gleason, Randall C.* Paul's covenantal contrasts in 2 Corinthians 3:1-11. BS 154 (1997) 61-79.

6534 *Bammel, Ernst* Paulus, der Moses des Neuen Bundes. Judaica et Paulina. WUNT 91: 1997 <1983>, ⇒109. 205-214 [2 Cor 3].

6535 **Hafemann, Scott J.** Paul, Moses, and the history of Israel... 2 Corinthians 3. WUNT 2/81: 1995, ⇒11/1,4979; 12,6294. <sup>R</sup>JThS 48 (1997) 196-199 *(Hickling, C.J.A.)*; EvQ 69/1 (1997) 88-90 *(Thrall, Margaret E.)*; CBQ 59 (1997) 381-382 *(Branick, Vincent P.)*; TJT 13 (1997) 275-276 *(Donaldson, Terence L.)*; WThJ 59 (1997) 123-125 *(Silva, Moisés)* [1 Cor 3,7-18].

6536 *Pitta, Antonio* Forza e debolezza del proprio minstero (2Cor 4,1-12). 1997, <sup>F</sup>GIORDANO M., ⇒30. 103-119.

6537  *Helewa, Giovanni* 'Predichiamo Cristo Gesù Signore'. RVS 51 (1997) 319-333 [2 Cor 4,5].
6538  *Hanhart, Karel* Hope in the face of death: preserving the original text of 2 Cor 5:3. Neotest. 31 (1997) 77-86.
6539  *Kim, Seyoon* 2 Cor. 5:11-21 and the origin of Paul's concept of "reconciliation". NT 39 (1997) 360-384.
6540  *Souček, Josef B.* Wir kennen Christus nicht mehr nach dem Fleisch. Bibelauslegung. WUNT 100: 1997 <1959>, ⇒970. ᴱPokorný, P., 183-197 [2 Cor 5,16].
6541  *Martyn, J. Louis* Epistemology at the turn of the ages. Theological issues. 1997 <1967>, ⇒146. 89-110 [2 Cor 5,16-17].
6542  *Kertelge, Karl* "Neue Schöpfung": Grund und Maßstab apostolischen Handelns (2.Kor 5,17). BZNW 89: 1997, ⇒33. ᶠGRAESSER E., 139-144.
6543  *Köstenberger, Andreas J.* 'We plead on Christ's behalf: "be reconciled to God"'. TPBT 48 (1997) 328-331 [2 Cor 5,20].
6544  *Härle, Wilfried* Christus factus est peccatum metaphorice: zur Heilsbedeutung des Kreuzestodes Jesu Christi [Christ was made sin metaphorically: on the salvific meaning of the death of Jesus Christ on the cross];
6545  *Ebeling, Gerhard* Christus... factus est peccatum metaphorice. Adapted by *Posset, Franz*: Luther Digest 5 (1997) 17-20/9-12 [2 Cor 5,21].
6546  *Peterson, Brian K.* 2 Corinthians 6:1-13. Interp. 51 (1997) 409-415.
6547  **Wodka, Andrzej** Una teologia biblica del dare nel contexto della colletta paolina (2 Cor 8-9). Diss. Pont. Univ. Gregoriana 1997; ᴰ*O'Toole, R.F.* 452 pp. [RTL 29,588].
6548  **Angstenberger, Pius** Der reiche und der arme Christus: die Rezeptionsgeschichte von 2 Kor 8,9 zwischen dem zweiten und dem sechsten Jahrhundert. Hereditas 12: Bonn 1997, Borengässer lvii; 373 pp. DM74. 3-923946-31-7 [ThGl 87,678].
6549  *Hartmann, Lars* A sketch of the argument of 2 Cor 10-13. Text-centered NT studies. WUNT 102: 1997, ⇒132. ᴱHellholm, D., 235-252.
6550  **DiCicco, Mario M.** Paul's use of ethos, pathos and logos in 2 Corinthians 10-13. 1995, ⇒11/1,4988. ᴿCBQ 59 (1997) 375-376 *(Neyrey, Jerome H.)*.
6551  *Böttrich, Christfried* 2Kor 11,1 als Programmwort der "Narrenrede". ZNW 88 (1997) 135-139.
6552  *Andrews, Scott B.* Enslaving, devouring, exploiting, self-exalting, and striking: 2 Cor 11:19-20 and the tyranny of Paul's opponents. SBL.SPS 36 (1997) 460-490.
6553  *Lambrecht, Jan* Strength in weakness: a reply to Scott B. ANDREW's exegesis of 2 Cor 11.23b-33. NTS 43 (1997) 285-290.
6554  *Jegher-Bucher, Verena* 'The thorn in the flesh' / 'Der Pfahl im Fleisch': considerations about 2 Corinthians 12.7-10 in connection with 12.1-13. The rhetorical analysis. JSNT.S 146: 1997, ⇒336. ᴱPorter, S.E., 388-397.
6555  **Nicdao, Victor S.** Power in times of weakness according to 2 Corinthians 12,1-10: an exegetical investigation of the relationship between δύναμις and ἀσθένεια. Diss. Leuven 1997; ᴰ*Bieringer, R.* 3 vols; lxxxiv; 854 pp. [RTL 29,586].

6556  *Brown, Perry C.* What is the meaning of 'examine yourselves' in 2 Corinthians 13:5?. BS 154 (1997) 175-188.

## G6.1  Ad Galatas

6557  <sup>T</sup>**Childress, Kathy** John CALVIN's sermons on Galatians. Carlisle 1997, Banner of Truth xii; 671 pp. £22/$47. 0-85151-699-8. <sup>R</sup>SCJ 28 (1997) 840-842 *(Payton, James R.)*.

6558  *Eshbaugh, Howard* Textual variants and theology: a study of the Galatians text of Papyrus 46. New Testament text. BiSe 44: 1997 <1979>, ⇒748. <sup>E</sup>Porter, S.E., 81-91.

6559  **Hagen, Kenneth** LUTHER's approach to Scripture as seen in his "Commentaries" on Galatians 1519-1538. 1993, ⇒8,6502... 12,6328. <sup>R</sup>KHÅ 97 (1997) 212-213 *(Fagerberg, Holsten)*.

6560  **Hume, C.R.** Reading through Galatians. L 1997, SCM viii; 104 pp. £7. 0-334-02705-5 [RRT (1998/1) 90].

6561  **Martyn, J. Louis** Galatians: a new translation with introduction and commentary. AncB 33a: NY 1997, Doubleday 614 pp. $40. 0-385-08838-8 [ETR 73,615—Cuvillier, Élian].

6562  **Morris, Leon** Galatians: Paul's charter of christian freedom. 1996, ⇒12,6332. <sup>R</sup>SBET 15/1 (1997) 82-83 *(Wilson, Alistair)*.

6563  **Ramsay, William Mitchell** Historical commentary on Galatians. <sup>E</sup>*Wilson, Mark* GR 1997, Kregel 366 pp. $14. 0-8254-3638-9 [ThD 45,87—Heiser, W. Charles].

6564  <sup>T</sup>**Ring, T.G.** AUGUSTINUS: die Auslegung des Briefes an die Galater—die angefangene Auslegung des Briefes an di Römer—über dreiundachtzig verschiedene Fragen: Fragen 66-68. Augustinus: Schriften über die Gnade, Schriften gegen die Pelagianer, 2. Wü 1997, Augustinus 456 pp.

6565  **Saretto, D.L.** Chiamata divina e risposta umana: uno studio esegetico-teologico della lettera ai Galati. Diss. Navarra 1995 [Laur. 40,538—Gonzalez, Manuel].

6566  **Vanhoye, Albert** La lettera ai Galati: seconda parte. R <sup>3</sup>1997, Ed. Pont. Ist. Biblico 226 pp.

6567  **Wachtel, Klaus; Witte, Klaus** Die paulinischen Briefe, Teil 2. ANTT 22: 1994, ⇒10,5995; 11/1,5007. ThRv 93 (1997) 23-24 *(Elliott, J.K.)*.

6568  **Williams, Sam K.** Galatians. Abingdon NT Commentaries: Nv 1997, Abingdon 176 pp. Bibl. $20. 0-687-05707-8.

6569  *Dunn, James D.G.* 4QMMT and Galatians. NTS 43 (1997) 147-153.

6570  **Elliott, Susan Margaret** The rhetorical strategy of Pauls letter to the Galatians in its Anatolian cultic context: circumcision and the castration of the Galli of the mother of the gods. Diss. Loyola, Chicago, 1997 xx; 738 pp. microfiche [NThAR 2000,124].

6571  *Geerlings, Wilhelm* Das Verständnis von Gesetz im Galaterbrief-kommentar des AMBROSIASTER. BZNW 85: 1997, ⇒105. <sup>F</sup>WICKERT U., 101-113.

6572  *Hansen, G. Walter* Paul's conversion and his ethic of freedom in Galatians. The road from Damascus. 1997, ⇒330. <sup>E</sup>Longenecker, R.N., 213-237.

6573	**Holmstrand, Jonas** Markers and meaning in Paul: an analysis of 1 Thessalonians, Philippians and Galatians. Diss. Uppsala, 1996; <sup>D</sup>*Kieffer, R.*: CB.NT 28: Sto 1997, Almqvist & W 244 pp. 91-22-01761-5 [EThL 74,333*].

6574	*Keesmaat, Sylvia C.* Paul and his story: Exodus and tradition in Galatians. Early christian interpretation. JSNT.S 148: 1997, ⇒191. <sup>E</sup>Evans, C.A., 300-333.

6575	*Lémonon, Jean-Pierre* Dans l'épître aux Galates Paul considère-t-il la loi mosaïque comme bonne?. La loi. LeDiv 168: 1997, ⇒195. <sup>E</sup>Focant, C., 243-270.

6576	*Martyn, J. Louis* Apocalyptic antinomies <1985>;
6577	Christ and the elements of the cosmos <1995>;
6578	Galatians, an anti-Judaic document?;
6579	A law-observant mission to gentiles <1985>;
6580	Romans as one of the earliest interpretations of Galatians <1988>. Theological issues. 1997, ⇒146. 111-123/125-140/77-84/7-24/37-45.

6581	*Plumer, Eric* The influence of MARIUS Victorinus on AUGUSTINE's commentary on Galatians. StPatr 33: 1997, ⇒351. <sup>E</sup>Livingstone, E., 221-228.

6582	**Russell, Walter Bo** The flesh/spirit conflict in Galatians. Lanham 1997, University Press of America xi; 290 pp. Bibl. $36.50. 0-7618-0797-7.

6583	**Scott, James M.** Paul and the nations. WUNT 2/84: 1995, ⇒11/1, 5026; 12,6345. <sup>R</sup>NT 39 (1997) 294-297 *(Schnabel, Eckhard J.)*; FrRu 4 (1997) 298-9 *(Oberforcher, Robert)*; CBQ 59 (1997) 398-9 *(Matera, Frank J.)*; JBL 116 (1997) 753-755 *(Meadors, Edward)*.

6584	*Walter, Nikolaus* Paulus und die Gegner des Christusevangeliums in Galatien. Praeparatio evangelica. WUNT 98: 1997 <1986>, ⇒167. 273-280.

6585	*Zager, Werner* Albert SCHWEITZERs Interpretation des Galaterbriefs: ein Impuls für die heutige Paulus- und Actaforschung. BZNW 89: 1997, ⇒33. <sup>F</sup>GRAESSER E., 427-448.

6586	*Hagen, Kenneth* It is all in the et cetera: LUTHER and the elliptical reference. Adapted by *Skocir, Joan*: Luther Digest 5 (1997) 13-16 [Gal 1,9-10].

6587	*Dunn, James D.G.* Paul's conversion—a light to twentieth century disputes. 1997, ⇒92. <sup>F</sup>STUHLMACHER P., 77-93 [Gal 1,13-16].

6588	*Bammel, Ernst* Galater 1,23. Judaica et Paulina. WUNT 91: 1997 <1968>, ⇒109. 222-226.

6589	*Schmithals, Walter* Probleme des "Apostelkonzils" (Gal 2,1-10). HTS 53 (1997) 6-35.

6590	**Wechsler, Andreas** Geschichtsbild und Apostelstreit: eine forschungsgeschichtliche und exegetische Studie über den antiochenischen Zwischenfall (Gal 2,11-14). BZNW 62: 1991, ⇒7,5549... 11/2,6030. <sup>R</sup>BBras 14 (1997) 425-428.

6591	**Amadi-Azuogu, Chinedu Adolphus** Paul and the law in... Galatians... 2,14-6,2. BBB 104: 1996, ⇒12,6355. <sup>R</sup>ThLZ 122 (1997) 1117-1118 *(Betz, Hand Dieter)*.

6592	**Eckstein, Hans-Joachim** Verheissung und Gesetz... Galater 2,15-4,7. WUNT 2/86: 1996, ⇒12,6356. <sup>R</sup>ThG 40 (1997) 235-237 *(Giesen, Heinz)*.

6593 *Martyn, J. Louis* God's way of making right what is wrong. Theological issues. 1997 <1993>, ⇒146. 141-156 [Gal 2,16].

6594 *Walker, William O.* Translation and interpretation of ἐὰς μὴ in Galatians 2:16. JBL 116 (1997) 515-520.

6595 **Jürgens, Burkhard** Zweierlei Anfang: kommunikative Konstruktionen heidenchristlicher Identität in Gal 2 und Apg 15. Diss. Münster 1997/98; ᴰ*Löning* [BZ 42,317].

6596 *Thatcher, Tom* The plot of Gal 3:1-18. JETS 40 (1997) 401-410.

6597 *Garlington, Don* Role reversal and Paul's use of scripture in Galatians 3.10-13. JSNT 65 (1997) 85-121 [Lev 18,5; Dt 21,23; 27,26; Hab 2,4].

6598 *Bonneau, Normand* The logic of Paul's argument on the curse of the law in Galatians 3:10-14. NT 39 (1997) 60-80.

6599 *Gundry-Volf, Judith M.* Christ and gender: a study of difference and equality in Gal 3,28. BZNW 86: 1997, ⇒41. ᶠHOFIUS O., 439-477.

6600 *Röhser, Günter* Mann und Frau in Christus: eine Verhältnisbestimmung von Gal 3,28 und 1 Kor 11,2-16. SNTU.A 22 (1997) 57-78.

6601 *Hafemann, Scott J.* Paul and the exile of Israel in Galatians 3-4. Exile. JSJ.S 56: 1997, ⇒227. ᴱScott, J.M., 329-371.

6602 *Navarro Puerto, Mercedes* Nacido de mujer (Gal 4,4): perspectiva antropologica. Sum. som. 337. EphMar 47 (1997) 327-337.

6603 *Cserháti, Sándor* 'Asszonytól született' (Máriának, Jézus anyjának szerepe Pál teológiájában Gal 4,4 szerint) ['Geboren aus einer Frau, dem Gesetz unterstellt' (Gal 4:4)]. Gyermekségtörténet. 1997, ⇒316. ᴱBenyik, G. Sum., Zsfg., Rias. 141-45. **Hungarian.**

6604 *Esler, Philip F.* Family imagery and Christian identity in Gal 5:13 to 6:10. Constructing... families. 1997, ⇒295. ᴱMoxnes, H., 121-149.

6605 *Martyn, J. Louis* A formula for communal discord as a clue to the nature of pastoral guidance. 1997, ⇒82. ᶠSCROGGS R., 203-216 [Gal 5,17].

6606 **Costa, Giuseppe** Gal 5,19-23: le opere della carne e il frutto dello Spirito: una rilettura biblico-teologica dell'agire cristiano. Diss. Pont. Univ. Gregoriana 1997; ᴰ*Grech, P.* 358 pp. extr. 4362 [RTL 29,583].

6607 *Lambrecht, Jan* Paul's coherent admonition in Galatians 6,1-6: mutual help and individual attentiveness. Sum. 56. Bib. 78 (1997) 33-56.

6608 *Fenz, Augustinus Kurt* "Das Gesetz Christi" (Gal 6,2): zur Rechtsposition in der theologia spiritualis biblica. Iustitia in caritate: Festgabe für Ernst Rößler zum 25jährigen Dienstjubiläum als Offizial der Diözese Rottenburg-Stuttgart. ᴱ**Puza, Richard; Weiß, Andreas:** Adnotationes in ius canonicum 3: Fra 1997, Lang. 3-631-31004-8. 31-58.

6609 *Luis, Pío de* Ga 6,2 en la obra agustiniana. EstAg 32 (1997) 217-266.

6610 *Saldhana, Assisi* Gal 6:16: the 'Israel of God': christianity's ultimate break with Judaism?. ITS 34/1-3 (1997) 224-232.

6611 *Martyn, J. Louis* The Abrahamic covenant, Christ, and the church. Theological issues. 1997 <1993>, ⇒146. 161-175 [Gal 3,6-4,7; 4,21-5,1].

6612   *Hartmann, Lars* Gal 3:15-4,11 as part of a theological argument on a practical issue. Text-centered NT studies. WUNT 102: 1997 <1993>, ⇒132. 179-194.

6613   *Bammel, Ernst* Gottes διαθηκη (Gal. III.15-17.) und das jüdische Rechtsdenken. Judaica et Paulina. WUNT 91: 1997 <1960>, ⇒109. 313-319.

6614   *Paulsen, Henning* Einheit und Freiheit der Söhne Gottes—Gal 3,26-29. Zur Literatur. WUNT 99: 1997 <1980>, ⇒153. 21-42.

6615   *Borgen, Peder* Some Hebrew and pagan features in PHILO's and Paul's interpretation of Hagar and Ishmael. NT and Hellenistic Judaism. 1997, ⇒318. EBorgen, P., 151-164 [Gal 4,21-5,1].

6616   *Martyn, J. Louis* The covenants of Hagar and Sarah: two covenants and two gentile missions <1990> [Gen 16-21; Gal 4,21-5,1];

6617   The crucial event in the history of the law <1996> [Gal 5,13-6,10]. Theological issues. 1997, 191-208/235-249.

### G6.2  Ad Ephesios

6618   TAdams, **Michael** The Navarre Bible St. Paul's Captivity Epistles: in the Revised Standard Version and New Vulgate. The Navarre Bible. Dublin 1996, Four Courts 207 pp. Commentary by the Faculty of Theology of the University of Navarre. 1-85182-079-5.

6619   **Best, Ernest** Essays on Ephesians. E 1997, Clark xv; 221 pp. £20. 0-567-08566-X [RTL 29,122].

6620   **Hahn, Eberhard** Der Brief des Paulus an die Epheser. WStB: 1996, ⇒12,6380. RJETh 11 (1997) 208-210 *(Dumm, Manfred)*.

6621   **Kreitzer, Larry Joseph** The epistle to the Ephesians. Epworth Commentaries. Peterborough 1997, Epworth 215 pp. £10. 0-7162-0515-7.

6622   **Perkins, Pheme** Ephesians. Abingdon NT Commentaries: Nv 1997, Abingdon 160 pp. Bibl. $20. 0-687-05699-3.

6623   **Reynier, Chantal; Trimaille, Michel** Éphésiens, Philippiens, Colossiens, 1-2 Thessaloniciens, 1-2 Timothée, Tite, Philémon. Les épîtres de Paul, 3. Commentaires: P 1997, Bayard 393 pp. FF140 2-227-36607-9 [RTL 29,129].

6624   *Baldanza, Giuseppe* L'ecclesiologia sponsale della lettera agli Efesini e la sua interpretazione in alcuni riti matrimoniali di lingua siriaca. Summarium 209. EL 111/3 (1997) 209-241.

6625   *Best, E.* Who used whom?: the relationship of Ephesians and Colossians. NTS 43 (1997) 72-96.

6626   **Cooper, Stephen Andrew** Metaphysics and morals in Marius VICTORINUS' commentary on the letter to the Ephesians. AmUSt.P 155. 1995, ⇒11/1,5066. RJThS 48 (1997) 268-270 *(Rist, J.M.)*; JEH 48 (1997) 521-522 *(McGuckin, John)*.

6627   **Gese, Michael** Das Vermächtnis des Apostels: die Rezeption der paulinischen Theologie im Epheserbrief. WUNT 2/99: Tü 1997, Mohr xii; 321 pp. Bibl. 3-16-146844-9.

6628   **Hinkle, Mary** Proclaiming peace: the use of scripture in Ephesians. Diss. Duke 1997; DHays, R. [RTL 29,585].

6629   *Mouton, Elna* The transformative potential of Ephesians in a situation of transition. Semeia 78 (1997) 121-143.

6630 *Olson, Ronald* 'Thinking and practicing reconciliation': the Ephesians texts for Pentecost. Word and World 17/3 (1997) 8-14, 322-328 [ZID 23,416].

6631 *Porter, Stanley E.; Clarke, Kent D.* Canonical-critical perspective and the relationship of Colossians and Ephesians. Sum. 86. Bib. 78 (1997) 57-86.

6632 **Strelan, Rick** Paul, Artemis, and the Jews in Ephesus. BZNW 80: 1996, ⇒12,6408. ᴿBZ 41 (1997) 278-281 *(Roloff, Jürgen)*; RHPhR 77 (1997) 226-227 *(Grappe, Ch.)*.

6633 *Jennings, Eric* Peragence. ET 108 (1997) 368-369 [Eph 1,6].

6634 *Korting, Georg* Das Partizip in Eph 1,23. ThGl 87 (1997) 260-265.

6635 *MacCoy, Timothy A.* The gospel truth: the SBJT sermon: Ephesians 2:1-10. Southern Baptist Convention 1/1 (1997) 70-78.

6636 *Konings, Johan* Welches sind die Werke, die nicht erkösen?. 1997, ⇒29. ᶠGERSTENBERGER S., 401-404 [Eph 2,8-9].

6637 *Olávarri Goicoechea, Emilio* La escatología en Ef. 2,47. StOv 25 (1997) 53-68.

6638 *Hollon, Vicky; Hollon, Leslie* Ephesians 3:14-21—Hebrews 12:1-2: for the joy set before us. RExp 94 (1997) 583-588.

6639 *Ballenger, Isam E.* Ephesians 4:1-16. Interp. 51 (1997) 292-295.

6640 *Holladay, James F.* Ephesians 4:30: do not grieve the spirit. RExp 94 (1997) 81-87.

6641 *Zovkić, Mato* Svjetlost u gospodinu (Ef 5,8-14) [Light in the Lord (Eph 5,8-14)]. 1997, ⇒96. ᶠTOMICA C.; Sum. 202. 181-203. **Croatian**.

6642 *Montagnini, Felice* Riscattare il tempo (Ep 5,16). PSV 36 (1997) 199-208.

6643 *Volonté, Ernesto W.* Generare-educare: un inscindibile binomio nel contesto sponsale di Ef 5,21-33. Sum., rés., Zsfs., som. 218s. RTLu 2/2 (1997) 205-219.

6644 **Fleckenstein, Karl-Heinz** Ordnet euch einander unter... Eph. 5,21-33. 1994, ⇒10,6089; 11/1,5081. ᴿThGl 87 (1997) 452-454 *(Backhaus, Knut)*.

6645 *Lindner, Helgo* "Ihr Frauen! ...—ihr Männer, ..." (Epheser 5). ThBeitr 28 (1997) 249-253.

6646 *Smillie, Gene R.* Ephesians 6:19-20: a mystery for the sake of which the apostle is an ambassador in chains. TrinJ 18 (1997) 199-222.

## G6.3 Ad Philippenses

6647 **Fee, Gordon D.** Paul's letter to the Philippians. NIC.NT 1995, ⇒11/1,5089; 12,6425. ᴿRB 104 (1997) 143-145 *(Murphy-O'Connor, J.)*; Interp. 51 (1997) 302-304 *(Kaylor, R. David)*; CBQ 59 (1997) 577-578 *(deSilva, David A.)*; AUSS 35 (1997) 262-263 *(Coutsoumpos, Panayotis)*; SR 26 (1997) 234-235 *(Westerholm, Stephen)*; ABR 45 (1997) 86-87 *(Watson, Nigel M.)*.

6648 **Ferguson, Sinclair B.** Let's study Philippians. Carlisle, Pa. 1997, Banner of Truth xvii; 136 pp. $10 [CTJ 34,259—Greenway, R.S.].

6649 **Harrington, Daniel J.** Paul's prison letters: spiritual commentaries on Paul's letters to Philemon, the Philippians, and the Colossians. Spiritual Commentaries: Hyde Park, NY 1997, New City 136 pp. $12. 1-56548-087-2 [ThD 44,88].

**Holmstrand, J.** Markers... in Paul... Philippians ⇒6573.

6650 **Pilhofer, Peter** Die erste christliche Gemeinde Europas. WUNT 2/87: 1995, ⇒11/1,5106; 12,6427. RThLZ 122 (1997) 331-333 *(Müller, Ulrich B.)*; JThS 48 (1997) 621-627 *(Bockmuehl, Markus)*; RB 104 (1997) 452-454 *(Murphy-O'Connor, J.)*; CBQ 59 (1997) 589-590 *(Thompson, Leonard L.)*; JBL 116 (1997) 757-758 *(Reumann, John)*.

**Reynier, C.; Trimaille, M.** Éphésiens, Philippiens... ⇒6623.

6651 **Abrahamsen, Valerie Ann** Women and worship at Philippi. 1995, ⇒11/1,5092. RJBL 116 (1997) 557-558 *(Snyder, Graydon F.)*.

6652 **Bloomquist, L. Gregory** The function of suffering in Philippians. JSNT.S 78: 1993, ⇒9,6273... 11/1,5095. RThLZ 122 (1997) 665-667 *(Walter, Nikolaus)*.

6653 **Peterlin, Davorin** Paul's letter to the Philippians in the light of disunity in the Church. NT.S 79: 1995, ⇒11/1,5104. RCBQ 59 (1997) 391-393 *(McDonald, Patricia M.)*; Fil.Neotest. 10 (1997) 162-164 *(Black, David Alan)*.

6654 **Reed, Jeffrey T.** A discourse analysis of Philippians: method and rhetoric in the debate over literary integrity. JSNT.S 136: Shf 1997. Academic 525 pp. £55. 1-85075-638-4 [NTS 43,622].

6655 *Watson, Duane F.* The integration of epistolary and rhetorical analysis of Philippians. The rhetorical analysis. JSNT.S 146: 1997, ⇒336. EPorter, S.E., 398-426.

6656 **Williams, Demetrius Kelvin** Enemies of the cross of Christ: a rhetorical analysis of the 'theology of the cross' in conflict in Paul's Philippian correspondence. Diss. Harvard 1997 [HThR 90,443].

6657 *Oakes, Peter* Jason and Penelope hear Philippians 1.1-11. JSOT.S 153: 1997, ⇒4. FASHTON J., 155-164.

6658 *Landmesser, Christof* Der paulinische Imperativ als christologisches Performativ: eine begründete These zur Einheit von Glaube und Leben im Anschluß an Phil 1,27-2,18. BZNW 86: 1997, ⇒41. FHOFIUS O., 543-577.

6659 **Martin, Ralph P.** A hymn of Christ: Philippians 2:5-11 in recent interpretation & in the setting of early christian worship. DG 1997, InterVarsity lxxvi; 372 pp. $30. 0-8308-1894-4 [ThD 45,377— Heiser, W. Charles].

6660 **Brucker, Ralph** "Christushymnen" oder "epideiktische Passagen"?: Studien zum Stilwechsel im Neuen Testament und seiner Umwelt. Diss. Hamburg 1996; DPaulsen, H.: FRLANT 176: Gö 1997, Vandenhoeck & R viii; 400 pp. DM160. 3-525-53859-6 [Phil 2,6-11].

6661 *Testa, Emmanuele* Un inno prepaolino della catechesi primitiva (Fil 2,6-11). Sum. 453. LASBF 47 (1997) 97-116.

6662 *Maggioni, B.* Obbediente fino alla morte di croce. L'obbedienza. 1997, ⇒216. EMarrocu, G., 115-127 [Phil 2,6-11].

6663   **Capizzi, Nunzio** L'uso di Fil 2,6-11 nella cristologia contempora-
       nea. Diss. Pont. Univ. Gregoriana; [D]*O'Collins, Gerald*: TGr.T 21:
       R 1997, Ed. Pont. Univ. Greg. 528 pp. L52.000. 88-7652-749-4.
6664   **Bockmuehl, Markus** 'The form of God' (Phil. 2:6): variations on
       a theme of Jewish mysticism. JThS 48 (1997) 1-23.

6665   *Weidmann, Frederick W.* An (un)accomplished model: Paul and the
       rhetorical strategy of Philippians 3:3-17. 1997, ⇒82. [F]Sᴄʀᴏɢɢs
       R., 245-257.
6666   **Koperski, Veronica** The knowledge of Christ Jesus my Lord: the
       high christology of Philippians 3:7-11. 1996, ⇒12,6169. [R]BZ 41
       (1997) 276-278 *(Vollenweider, Samuel)*; CBQ 59 (1997) 772-774
       *(Soards, Marion L.)*.
6667   *Moiser, Jeremy* The meaning of *koilia* in Philippians 3:19. ET 108
       (1997) 365-366.
6668   **Peterman, Gerald W.** Paul's gift from Philippi: conventions of
       gift-exchange and christian giving. Diss. King's College 1992.
       SBL.MS 92: C 1997, CUP xi; 246 pp. £35/$55. 0-521-57220-7
       [Phil 4,10-20].

## G6.4  Ad Colossenses

6669   **Aletti, Jean-Noël** Saint Paul: epître aux Colossiens. Ebib 20:
       1993, ⇒9,6299... 12,6447. [R]CoTh 67 (1997) 240-5 *(Zalęski, Jan)*.
6670   **Barclay, John M.G.** Colossians and Philemon. Shf 1997, Aca-
       demic 132 pp. £7. 1-85075-818-2 [RRT (1998/1) 88].
6671   *Best, E.* Who used whom?: the relationship of Ephesians and Co-
       lossians. NTS 43 (1997) 72-96.
6672   **Dunn, James D.G.** The epistles to the Colossians and to Phile-
       mon. NIGTC: 1996, ⇒12,6450. [R]JThS 48 (1997) 202-205 *(Moule,
       C.F.D.)*; JSNT 66 (1997) 122-124 *(Pearson, Brook W.R.)*; ThLZ
       122 (1997) 907-909 *(Schweizer, Eduard)*; CBQ 59 (1997) 574-575
       *(Montague, George T.)*; JBL 116 (1997) 759-760 *(Donelson, Lewis
       R.)*.
       **Harrington, D.J.** Paul's letters to... Colossians ⇒6649.
6673   *Hartmann, Lars* Doing things with the words of Colossians. Text-
       centered NT studies. WUNT 102: 1997, ⇒132. 195-209.
6674   **Legarth, Peter V.** Kolossenserbrevet og Brevet til Filemon. Credo
       Kommentaren: 1995, Credo 255 pp. DK225. ΙΧΘΥΣ 24/2 (1997)
       92-94 *(Adamsen, Georg S.)*.
6675   **Martin, Troy W.** By philosophy and empty deceit: Colossians as
       response to a Cynic critique. JSNT.S 118: 1996, ⇒12,6452. [R]CBQ
       59 (1997) 386-387 *(Crawford, Barry S.)*.
       *Porter, S.E.* Canonical-critical perspective and the relationship of
       Colossians and Ephesians ⇒6631.
       **Reynier, C.** Éphésiens... Colossiens ⇒6623.
6676   *Van Broekhoven, Harold* The social profiles in the Colossian de-
       bate. JSNT 66 (1997) 73-90.
6677   **Wilson, Walter T.** The hope of glory: education in the epistle to
       the Colossians. NT.S 88: Lei 1997, Brill xiv; 297 pp. ƒ170/$100.
       90-04-10937-4 [RB 105,318].

6678  *Roberts, J.H.* Die belydenisuitspraak Kolossense 1:13-20: eenheid, struktuur en funksie. HTS 53 (1997) 476-497 [ZID 24,126].
6679  *Schottroff, Luise* Ist allein in Christus Heil?: das Bekenntnis zu Christus und die Erlösung (Kol 1,15-20). Antijudaismus im NT. KT 149: 1997, ⇒κ8. ᴱHenze, D., 79-89.
6680  *Bammel, Ernst* Col. 1.15-20. Judaica et Paulina. WUNT 91: 1997 <1961>, ⇒109. 305-312.
6681  *Peretto, Elio* L'inno cristologico di Col 1,15-20 dagli gnostici ad IRENEO. 1997 <1975>, ⇒155. Saggi. 43-57.
6682  *Campbell, Douglas A.* The Scythian perspective in Col. 3:11: a response to Troy MARTIN. NT 39 (1997) 81-84.
6683  *Hartmann, Lars* Some unorthodox thoughts on the 'household-code form'. Text-centered NT studies. WUNT 102: 1997 <1988>, ⇒132. 179-194 [Col 3,18-4,1].

### G6.5  Ad Philemonem

**Barclay, J.** Colossians and Philemon ⇒6670.
6684  **Bradley, Keith R.** Slavery and society at Rome. Key Themes in Ancient History: C 1997, CUP xiv; 202 pp. Bibl. 0-521-37887-7.
6685  **Callahan, Allen Dwight** Embassy of Onesimus: the letter of Paul to Philemon. The NT in context: Valley Forge, PA 1997, Trinity xiv; 96 pp. Bibl. $11. 1-56338-147-8.
   **Dunn, J.** The epistles to the Colossians and to Philemon ⇒6672.
   **Harrington, D.** Paul's prison letters: Philemon... ⇒6649.
   **Legarth, P.** Kolossenserbrevet og Brevet til Filemon ⇒6674.
6686  *Nordling, John G. Onesimus fugitivus*: a defense of the runaway slave hypothesis in Philemon. NT Backgrounds. 1997 <1991>, ⇒3975. ᴱEvans, C.A., 263-283.
   **Reynier, C.** Éphésiens... Philémon ⇒6623.
6687  *Wilson, Andrew* The pragmatics of politeness and Pauline epistolography: a case study of the letter to Philemon. NT Backgrounds. 1997 <1992>, ⇒3975. ᴱEvans, C.A., 284-295.

### G6.6  Ad Thessalonicenses

6688  ᵀAdams, Michael The Navarre Bible: St. Paul's Epistles to the Thessalonians and the Pastoral Epistles. The Navarre Bible: Dublin 1996, Four Courts 183 pp. 1-85182-077-9.
6689  *Allen, Pauline* John CHRYSOSTOM's homilies on I and II Thessalonians: the preacher and his audience. StPatr 31: 1997, ⇒351. ᴱLivingstone, E., 3-21.
6690  *Crook, Zeba Antonin* Paul's riposte and praise of the Thessalonians. BTB 27 (1997) 153-163.
6691  **Ironside, Henry A.** 1 & 2 Thessalonians. Ironside Commentaries: Neptune, NJ ²1997, Loizeaux 89 pp. 0-87213-414-8 [NThAR 1998,270].
6692  **Orsatti, Mauro** 1-2 Tessalonicesi. LoB.NT 10: 1996, ⇒12,6462. ᴿPaVi 42/2 (1997) 62-63 *(Rolla, Armando)*.
   **Reynier, C.** Éphésiens... 1-2 Thessaloniciens ⇒6623.

6693 *Verhoef, Eduard* The relation between 1 Thessalonians and 2 Thessalonians and the inauthenticity of 2 Thessalonians. HTS 53 (1997) 163-171.

6694 *Alkier, Stefan* Der 1. Thessalonicherbrief als kulturelles Gedächtnis. Logos. TANZ 20: 1997, ⇒229. ᴱSellin, G., 175-194.
6695 *Bammel, Ernst* Judenverfolgung und Naherwartung: zur Eschatologie des Ersten Thessalonicherbriefs. Judaica et Paulina. WUNT 91: 1997, <1959>, ⇒109. 237-259.
6696 *Bwanali, Peter N.* We believe that Jesus died and rose again: a reply to Paul. Rés. 97. Hekima Review 18 (1997) 97-104.
6697 *Donfried, Karl P.* The imperial cults of Thessalonica and political conflict in 1 Thessalonians. Paul and empire. 1997, ⇒204. ᴱHorsley, R.A., 215-223.
6698 *Fatum, Lone* Brotherhood in Christ: a gender hermeneutical reading of 1 Thessalonians. Constructing... families. 1997, ⇒295. ᴱMoxnes, H., 183-197.
     **Holmstrand, J.** Markers... in Paul... 1 Thessalonians ⇒6573.
6699 *Hoppe, Rudolf* Der erste Thessalonicherbrief und die antike Rhetorik: eine Problemskizze. BZ 41 (1997) 229-237.
6700 *Koester, Helmut* Imperial ideology and Paul's eschatology in I Thessalonians. Paul and empire. 1997, ⇒204. ᴱHorsley, R.A., 158-166.

6701 *Weima, Jeffrey A.D.* An apology for the apologetic function of 1 Thessalonians 2.1-12. JSNT 68 (1997) 73-99.
6702 *Légasse, Simon* Paul et les Juifs d'après 1 Thessaloniciens 2,13-16. RB 104 (1997) 572-591.
6703 *Pearson, Birger A.* 1 Thessalonians 2:13-16: a deutero-Pauline interpolation. The emergence. 1997, ⇒154. 58-74.
6704 **Schlueter, Carol J.** Filling up the measure: polemical hyperbole in 1 Thessalonians 2.14-16. JSNT.S 98: 1994, ⇒10,6166... 12,6476. ᴿABR 45 (1997) 87-88 *(Byrne, Brendan).*
6705 *Bammel, Ernst* Preparation for the perils of the last days: 1 Thessalonians 3:3. Judaica et Paulina. WUNT 91: 1997 <1981>, ⇒109. 227-236.
6706 *Légasse, Simon* Vas suum possidere (1Th 4,4). FgNT 10 (1997) 105-115.
6707 *Elgvin, Torleif* 'To master his own vessel': 1 Thess 4.4 in light of new Qumran evidence. NTS 43 (1997) 604-619.
6708 *Merk, Otto* 1. Thessalonicher 4,13-18 im Lichte des gegenwärtigen Forschungsstandes. BZNW 89: 1997, ⇒33. ᶠGRAESSER E., 213-230.
6709 *Barbaglio, Giuseppe* Analisi formale di 1 Ts 4-5. StAns 124: 1997, ⇒57. ᶠLOEHRER M. — TRAGAN P., 491-504.

6710 *Hartmann, Lars* The eschatology of 2 Thessalonians as included in a communication. Text-centered NT studies. WUNT 102: 1997 <1990>, ⇒132. 283-300.

6711 *Peerbolte, L.J. Lietaert* The κατέχον/κατέχων of 2 Thess. 2:6-7. NT 39 (1997) 138-150.
6712 *Powell, Charles E.* The identity of the 'restrainer' in 2 Thessalonians 2:6-7. BS 154 (1997) 320-332.

## G7.0 Epistulae pastorales

<sup>T</sup>Adams, Michael The Navarre Bible... Pastoral Epistles ⇒6684.

6713 **Arichea, Daniel C.; Hatton, Howard A.** A handbook on Paul's letters to Timothy and to Titus. 1995, 11/1,5180. <sup>R</sup>AUSS 35 (1997) 103-104 *(Coutsoumpos, P.)*.

6714 *Bird, Anthony E.* The authorship of the Pastoral Epistles—quantifying literary style. RTR 56 (1997) 118-137.

6715 **Cothenet, Edouard** As Cartas Pastorais. Cadernos Bíblicos 57: Lisboa 1997, Difusora Bíblica 60 pp. [Bib(L) 7/7,188—Negreiros, Fernando de].

6716 **Hutson, Christopher** My true child: the rhetoric of youth in the Pastoral Epistles. Diss. Yale 1997; <sup>D</sup>*Malherbe, A.* [RTL 29,585].

6717 **Merkel, Helmut** Le lettere pastorali. NT 2/9,1: Brescia 1997, Paideia 150 pp. Bibl. L27.000. 88-394-0554-2.

6718 **Miller, James D.** The Pastoral Letters as composite documents. MSSNTS 93: C 1997, CUP x; 214 pp. Bibl. $35. 0-521-560489-9.

6719 *Pietersen, Lloyd* Despicable deviants: labelling theory and the polemic of the Pastorals. Sum. 343. Sociology of Religion 58/4 (1997) 343-352.

6720 **Ravasi, Gianfranco** Lettere a Timoteo e a Tito. Conversazioni bibliche: Bo 1997, EDB 135 pp. Ciclo di conferenze tenute al Centro culturale S. Fedele di Milano. L18.000. 88-10-70959-4.

6721 *Söding, Thomas* Mysterium fidei: zur Auseinandersetzung mit der "Gnosis" in den Pastoralbriefen. IKaZ 26 (1997) 502-524.

6722 **Stott, John R.W.** Guard the truth: the message of 1 Timothy & Titus. The Bible Speaks Today: DG 1997, InterVarsity 232 pp. Bibl. 0-8308-1992-4.

6723 **Wagener, Ulrike** Die Ordnung des "Hauses Gottes": der Ort von Frauen in der Ekklesiologie und Ethik der Pastoralbriefe. WUNT 2/65: 1994, ⇒10,6188... 12,6499. <sup>R</sup>ActBib 34 (1997) 50-51 *(Fàbrega, Valentí)* [1 Tim 2,9-3,1; 5,3-16].

## G7.2 1-2 ad Timotheum

6724 *DeVilliers, Pieter G.* The vice of conceit in 1 Timothy: a study in the ethics of the New Testament within its Graeco-Roman context. Acta Patristica et Byzantina 7 (1996) 37-67.

6725 **Martini, Carlo Maria** Camino de Timoteo. M 1997, PPC 192 pp. Ptas1.575 [Comunidades 26,64].

6726 **Synnes, Martin** Vakthold om den skjønne skatt: innføring i pastoralbrevene og kommentar til første Timoteusbrev. Oslo 1996, Luther 284 pp. NOK248. <sup>R</sup>TTK 68 (1997) 308-309 *(Legarth, P.V.)*.

6727 <sup>E</sup>**Köstenberger, Andreas J.,** *(al.),* Women in the church: a fresh analysis of 1 Timothy 2:9-15. 1995, ⇒12,6505. <sup>R</sup>BS 154 (1997) 122-123 *(Pyne, Robert A.)*; AUSS 35 (1997) 272-274 *(Vyhmeister, Nancy J.)*.

6728 *Köstenberger, Andreas J.* Ascertaining women's God-ordained roles: an interpretation of 1 Timothy 2:15. BBR 7 (1997) 107-144.

6729 *Porter, Stanley E.* What does it mean to be 'saved by childbirth' (1 Timothy 2.15)?. New Testament text. BiSe 44: 1997 <1993>, ⇒748. [E]Porter, S.E., 160-175.

6730 *Campbell, Barth* Rhetorical design in 1 Timothy 4. BS 154 (1997) 189-204.

6731 *Aageson, James W.* 2 Timothy and its theology: in search of a theological pattern. SBL.SPS 36 (1997) 692-714.

6732 *Donelson, Lewis R.* Studying Paul: 2 Timothy as remembrance;

6733 *Fee, Gordon D.* Toward a theology of 2 Timothy—rom a Pauline perspective. SBL.SPS 36 (1997) 715-731/732-749.

6734 **Martin, Seán Charles** Pauli testamentum: 2 Timothy and the last words of Moses. Diss. Pont. Univ. Gregoriana 1994; [D]*Vanni, Ugo*: TGr.T 18: R 1997, Ed. Pont. Univ. Gregoriana 308 pp. L32.000. 88-7652-739-7.

6735 *Hutson, Christopher R.* Was Timothy timid?: on the rhetoric of fearlessness (1 Corinthians 16:10-11) and cowardice (2 Timothy 1:7). BR 42 (1997) 58-73.

6736 *Bammel, Ernst* Semper aut aliquotiens. Judaica et Paulina. WUNT 91: 1997, ⇒109. 334-336 [Rom 12,11; 2 Tim 4,2].

## G7.3 Ad Titum

6737 *Classen, C. Joachim* A rhetorical reading of the epistle to Titus. The rhetorical analysis. JSNT.S 146: 1997, ⇒336. [E]Porter, S.E., 427-444.

6738 **Oberlinner, Lorenz** Kommentar zum Titusbrief. Die Pastoralbriefe, 3. HThK 11/2-3: 1996, ⇒12,6512. [R]BZ 41 (1997) 281-282 *(Weiser, Alfons)*.

**Reynier, C.** Éphésiens... Tite ⇒6623.

## G8 Epistula ad Hebraeos

6739 **Gräßer, Erich** An die Hebräer, 3. Teilband: Hebr 10,19-13,25. Evangelisch-katholischer Kommentar zum Neuen Testament 17/3: Z 1997, Benziger x; 428 pp. 3-545-23130-5.

6740 **Hume, C.R.** Reading through Hebrews. L 1997, SCM 136 pp. £7. 0-334-02689-X [ET 108,383].

6741 **Long, Thomas G.** Hebrews. Interpretation Commentaries: LVL 1997, Westminster xii; 153 pp. $21. 0-8042-3133-8 [BiTod 35,324].

6742 [E]**Parker, T.H.L.** Ioannis CALVINI: opera exegetica: commentarius in epistolam ad Hebraeos. 1996, ⇒12,6520. [R]SCJ 28 (1997) 552-554 *(Holder, R. Ward)*.

6743 **Pfitzner, Victor** Hebrews. Abingdon NT Commentaries: Nv 1997, Abingdon 218 pp. $21. 0-687-05724-8 [BiTod 36,136—Senior, Donald].

6744 **Strobel, August** La lettera agli Ebrei. Nuovo Testamento 2/9,2. Brescia 1997, Paideia 270 pp. Bibl. L49.000. 88-394-0556-9.

6745 **Trotter, Andrew H.** Interpreting the epistle to the Hebrews. GNTE 6: GR 1997, Baker 222 pp. 0-8010-2095-6.

6746  Vanhoye, Albert L'épître aux Hébreux. Les dernières épîtres.
      ᴱCothenet, É., (al.), 1997, ⇒4403. 8-108.

6747  Barr, George K. The structure of Hebrews and of 1st and 2nd
      Peter. IBSt 19 (1997) 17-31.
6748  Beauchamp, Paul Quelle typologie dans l'épître aux Hébreux?.
      Sum., som. 32. Cahiers Ratisbonne 2 (1997) 10-32.
6749  Bockmuehl, Markus The church in Hebrews. 1997, ⇒93. ᶠSᴡᴇᴇᴛ
      J., 133-151.
6750  deSilva, David Arthur Despising shame: the social function of the
      rhetoric of honor and dishonor in the epistle to the Hebrews.
      SBL.DS 152: 1995, ⇒11/1,5225. ᴿEThL 73 (1997) 185-187 (Ver-
      heyden, J.); ThLZ 122 (1997) 667-669 (Weiß, Hans-Friedrich);
      BiOr 54 (1997) 484-486 (Hollander, Harm W.); JBL 116 (1997)
      378-379 (Malina, Bruce J.).
6751  Garuti, Paolo Alle origini dell'omiletica cristiana: la lettera agli
      Ebrei. ASBF 38: 1995, ⇒11/1,5228. ᴿGr. 78 (1997) 159-160
      (Marconi, Gilberto); EstB 55 (1997) 141-142 (Huarte, J.); Bib. 78
      (1997) 290-293 (Attridge, Harold W.); CDios 210 (1997) 643-645
      (Gutiérrez, J.); JBL 116 (1997) 573-575 (Pesce, Mauro); CivCatt
      148 III (1997) 202-203 (Scaiola, D.).
6752  Gianotto, Claudio Qumran e la lettera agli Ebrei. RStB 9/2 (1997)
      211-230.
6753  Gieschen, Charles A. The different functions of a similar Melchize-
      dek tradition in 2 Enoch and the epistle to the Hebrews. Early
      christian interpretation. JSNT.S 148: 1997, ⇒191. ᴱEvans, C.A.,
      364-379.
6754  Gonnet, Dominique L'utilisation christologique de l'épître aux
      Hébreux dans les Orationes contra Arianos d'Aᴛʜᴀɴᴀsᴇ
      d'Alexandrie. StPatr 32: 1997, ⇒351. ᴱLivingstone, E., 19-24.
6755  Guthrie, George H. The structure of Hebrews. NT.S 72: 1994,
      ⇒10,6222... 12,6531. ᴿAUSS 35 (1997) 274-276 (Kent, Matthew).
6756  Guthrie, George H. New Testament exegesis of Hebrews and the
      Catholic Epistles. Handbook. NTTS 25: 1997, ⇒971. ᴱPorter,
      S.E., 591-606.
6757  Isaacs, Marie E. Priesthood and the epistle to the Hebrews. HeyJ
      38 (1997) 51-62.
6758  Jones, Darryl L. The sermon as "art" of resistance: a comparative
      analysis of the rhetorics of the African-American slave preacher
      and the preacher to the Hebrews. Semeia 79 (1997) 11-26.
6759  Leschert, Dale F. Hermeneutical foundations of Hebrews.
      NABPR.DS 10: 1994, ⇒10,6228. ᴿThLZ 122 (1997) 259-261
      (Löhr, Hermut); CBQ 59 (1997) 774-775 (Kurz, William S.).
6760  Löhr, Hermut Anthropologie und Eschatologie im Hebräerbrief:
      Bemerkungen zum theologischen Interesse einer frühchristlichen
      Schrift. BZNW 89: 1997, ⇒33. ᶠGʀᴀᴇssᴇʀ E., 169-199.
6761  Manzi, Franco Melchisedek e l'angelologia nell'epistola agli Ebrei
      e a Qumran. Diss. Pont. Institutum Biblicum 1996; ᴰVanhoye,
      Albert: AnBib 136: R 1997, Ed. PIB xvii; 433 pp. L52.000. 88-
      7653-136-X. ᴿET 111 (1997) 299-300 (Ward, Anthony).
6762  Punt, Jeremy Hebrews, thought-patterns and context: aspects of the
      background of Hebrews. Neotest. 31 (1997) 119-158.
6763  Schenck, Kenneth Keeping his appointment: creation and enthrone-
      ment in Hebrews. JSNT 66 (1997) 91-117.

6764  *Schmithals, Walter* Der Hebräerbrief als Paulusbrief: Beobachtungen zur Kanonbildung. BZNW 85: 1997, ⇒105. [F]WICKERT U., 319-337.

6765  *Schmithals, Walter* Über Empfänger und Anlaß des Hebräerbriefes;

6766  *Schröer, Henning* Die Exegese des Hebräerbriefs als Herausforderung für die Praktische Theologie. BZNW 89: 1997, ⇒33. [F]GRAESSER E., 321-342/375-385.

6767  **Tauf, Konrad Ludwig** Anleitung zum Schriftverstĕndnis?: die heiligen Schriften nach dem Hebräerbrief. Diss. Leipzig 1997; [D]*Vogler, W.* 163 pp. [RTL 29,588].

6768  **Vanhoye, Albert** La cristología sacerdotal de la Carta a los Hebreos: curso ofrecido a los Señores Obispos de la Conferencia Episcopal Argentina. BA 1997, Conferencia Episcopal Argentina 207 pp. 950-9325-97-X.

6769  *Vanhoye, Albert* La loi dans l'épître aux Hébreux. La loi. LeDiv 168: 1997, ⇒195. [E]Focant, C., 271-298.

6770  *Walter, Nikolaus* Christologie und irdischer Jesus im Hebräerbrief. Praeparatio evangelica. WUNT 98: 1997 <1982>, ⇒167. 151-68.

6771  *Watson, Duane F.* Rhetorical criticism of Hebrews and the Catholic Epistles since 1978. CurResB 5 (1997) 175-207.

6772  **Wider, David** Theozentrik und Bekenntnis: Untersuchungen zur Theologie des Reden Gottes im Hebräerbrief. Diss. Bern; [D]*Hasler, V.*: BZNW 87: B 1997, De Gruyter ix; 230 pp. DM158. 3-11-015554-0.

6773  *Ruager, Soren* Die Hermeneutik des Hebräerbriefes (Hebr 1,1+2a). TVGMS 424: 1997, ⇒59. [F]MAIER G., 205-217.

6774  **Ha, Hong Pal** Heb 1:2-3, the threefold characterization of the person of Christ as prerequisite for the fulfillment of a complete atonement. Diss. Sahmyook 1995. Korean Sahmyook University monographs: doctoral dissertation 4: Seoul 1996, Institute for Theological Research xii; 314 pp.

6775  *Heininger, Bernhard* Sündenreinigung (Hebr 1,3): christologische Anmerkungen zum Exordium des Hebräerbriefs. BZ 41 (1997) 54-68.

6776  **Bateman, Herbert W.** Early Jewish hermeneutics and Hebrews 1:5-13: the impact of early Jewish exegesis on the interpretation of a significant New Testament passage. AmUSt TR 193: NY 1997, Lang xiv; 438 pp. Bibl. £38. 0-8204-3324-1.

6777  *Enns, Peter* The interpretation of Psalm 95 in Hebrews 3.1-4.13. Early christian interpretation. JSNT.S 148: 1997, ⇒191. [E]Evans, C.A., 352-363.

6778  *Theobald, Michael* Vom Text zum "lebendigen Wort" (Hebr 4,12): Beobachtungen zur Schrifthermeneutik des Hebräerbriefs. BZNW 86: 1997, ⇒41. [F]HOFIUS O., 751-790.

6779  *Muddiman, John* Wrestling with Hebrews: a note on τετραχηλισμένα at Hebrews 4.13. JSOT.S 153: 1997, ⇒4. [F]ASHTON J., 165-173.

6780  *Bentué, Antoni* Probado en todo como nosotros, excepto en el pecado (Heb 4,15). Sum. 156. RCatT 22 (1997) 139-156.

6781  *Kuthirakkattel, Scaria* Christ, the self-emptying high priest: meaning and function of Heb 5:1-10. 1997, ⇒89. [F]SOARES-PRABHU G., 102-177.

6782 *Lee, John A.L.* Hebrews 5:14 and ἕξις: a history of misunderstanding. NT 39 (1997) 151-176.
6783 *Reding, Franklin S.* Hebrews 9:11-14. Interp. 51 (1997) 67-70.
6784 **Rose, Christian** Die Wolke der Zeugen: eine exegetisch-traditionsgeschichtliche Untersuchung zu Hebräer 10,32-12,3. WUNT 2/60: 1994, ⇒10,6253; 12,6553. RRHPhR 77 (1997) 231 *(Grappe, Ch.).*
6785 *Baker, Kimberly F.* Hebrews 11—the promise of faith. RExp 94 (1997) 439-445.
6786 *Eisenbaum, Pamela* Heroes and history in Hebrews 11. Early christian interpretation. JSNT.S 148: 1997, ⇒191. EEvans, C.A., 380-396.
6787 **Eisenbaum, Pamela Michelle** The Jewish heroes of christian history: Hebrews 11 in literary context. SBL.DS 156: Atlanta, GA 1997, Scholars xii; 250 pp. $40. 0-7885-0246-8.
6788 **Modersohn, Ernst** Durch den Glauben: Gedanken zu Hebräer 11. TELOS 1366: Lahr 1997, VLM 192 pp. 3-88002-620-3 [NThAR 1998,302].
6789 *Gisana, Rosario* Cristo, Signore del tempo in Eb 13,8. PSV 36 (1997) 209-222.
6790 *Isaacs, Marie E.* Hebrews 13.9-16 revisited. NTS 43 (1997) 268-284.

### G9.1  1 Petri

6791 EAmphoux, **Christian-Bernard; Bouhot, Jean-Paul** La lecture liturgique des épîtres catholiques dans l'Église ancienne. 1996, ⇒12,6559. RMD 209 (1997) 138-139 *(Dalmais, I.H.);* JThS 48 (1997) 682-683 *(Spinks, Bryan D.).*
6792 *Lugo Rodríguez, Raúl Humberto* 'Wait for the day of God's coming and do what you can to hasten it...' (2 Pet 3:12): the non-Pauline letters as resistance literature. Subversive scriptures. 1997, ⇒263. EVaage, L., 193-206 [1 Peter 2,13-17].
6793 *Marconi, G.* 'Sia fatta la tua volontà' (*Mt* 26,41): il discepolo tra legge della carne e obbedienza alla fede: obbedienza e moralità nelle lettere cattoliche. L'obbedienza. 1997, ⇒216. EMarrocu, G., 157-181 [Jas 3; 1 Pet 2,11-3,7].
     **Tuñi, Josep Oriol; Alegre, Xavier** Escritos joánicos y cartas católicas. Estella ²1997, Verbo Divino 392 pp. 84-7151-909-7 ⇒5628.
6794 **Wachtel, Klaus** Der byzantinische Text der Katholischen Briefe. ANTT 24: 1995, ⇒11/1,5273; 12,6574. RCBQ 59 (1997) 789-790 *(Cody, Aelred).*

6795 **Achtemeier, Paul J.** 1 Peter. Hermeneia: 1996, ⇒12,6577. RTS 58 (1997) 535-537 *(Neyrey, Jerome H.).*
6796 **Beck, Johann Tobias** Petrusbriefe. 1995, ⇒11/1,5261. RJETh 11 (1997) 205-206 *(Stenschke, Christoph).*
6797 **Casurella, Anthony** Bibliography of literature on First Peter. NTTS 23: 1996, ⇒12,6581. RNT 39 (1997) 297-98 *(Elliott, J.K.).*
6798 *Cothenet, Édouard* Les épîtres de Pierre. Les dernières épîtres. 1997, ⇒4403. 143-187.

6799 **Davids, Peter H.** The first epistle of Peter. 1990, ⇒6,6729... 8,6772. RVJTR 61 (1997) 212-213 *(Meagher, P.M.)*.

*Barr, G.* The structure of Hebrews and of 1st and 2nd Peter ⇒6747.

6800 **Bosetti, Elena** Il Pastore: Cristo e la chiesa nella prima lettera di Pietro. RivBib.S 21: 1990, ⇒6,6727... 9,6440. REstB 55 (1997) 129-131 *(Rodríguez Ruiz, M.)*.

6801 *Bosetti, Elena* Tempo e attesa nella prima lettera di Pietro. PSV 36 (1997) 223-237.

6802 **Elliott, John H.** Un hogar para los que no tienen patria ni hogar: estudio crítico social de la carta primera de Pedro y de su situación y estrategia. 1995, ⇒11/1,5275. REfMex 15 (1997) 283-285 *(Zesati Estrada, Carlos)*.

6803 *Johnson, Ronald W.* Acts 6:2-4,7—1 Peter: recovery of passion in missiological concern. RExp 94 (1997) 599-603.

6804 **Metzner, Rainer** Die Rezeption des Matthäusevangeliums im 1. Petrusbrief. WUNT 2/74: 1995, ⇒11/1,5279; 12,6588. RCBQ 59 (1997) 387-389 *(Davids, Peter H.)*.

6805 *Schweizer, Eduard* Neue Botschaft alter Traditionen: der erste Petrusbrief. StAns 124: 1997, ⇒57. FLOEHRER M. — TRAGAN P., 505-524.

6806 *Segalla, Giuseppe* Salvación cristologica universal en Filipenses y 1 Pe. RevBib 59/3 (1997) 165-180.

6807 *Souček, Josef B.* Das Gegenüber von Gemeinde und Welt nach dem ersten Petrusbrief. Bibelauslegung. WUNT 100: 1997 <1960>, ⇒970. EPokorný, P., 199-209.

6808 *Stewart-Sykes, A.* The function of 'Peter' in I Peter. ScrB 27 (1997) 8-21.

6809 **Thurén, Lauri Toumas** Argument and theology in 1 Peter: the origins of Christian paraenesis. JSNT.S 114: 1995, ⇒11/1,5286. RCBQ 59 (1997) 597-598 *(Elliott, John H.)*.

6810 **Waldmann, Helmut** Der Königsweg der Apostel in Edessa, Indien und Rom. Tübinger Gesellschaft, Wissenschaftliche Reihe 5: Tü ²1997, Verlag der Tübinger Gesellschaft xxxvi; 236 pp. Bibl. 3-928096-11-7.

6811 **Tite, Philip L.** Compositional transitions in 1 Peter: an analysis of the letter-opening. SF 1997, International Scholars Publications (6) viii; (2) 147 pp. Bibl. 1-57309-148-0 [1 Pet 1,1-14].

6812 *Horrell, David* Whose faith(fulness) is it in 1 Peter 1:5?. JThS 48 (1997) 110-115.

6813 *Evang, Martin* "Jedes menschliche Geschöpf" und "treuer Schöpfer": Schöpfungstheologische Aspekte in 1.Petr 2,13; 4,19. BZNW 89: 1997, ⇒33. FGRAESSER E., 53-67.

6814 *Schlosser, Jacques* "Aimez la fraternité" (1 P 2,17): à propos de l'ecclésiologie de la première lettre de Pierre. StAns 124: 1997, ⇒57. FLOEHRER M. — TRAGAN P., 525-545.

6815 *Bauer, Johannes B.* Aut maleficus aut alieni speculator (1 Petr 4,15). Studien zu Bibeltext. 1997 <1978>, ⇒111. 255-264.

6816 **Sakkos, S.N.** Καθηγητοῦ Πανεπιστημίου Θεσσαλονίκης, ἡ Βαβυλὼν τοῦ ᾿αποστόλου Πέτρου (Α´ Πε 5,13), ᾿η Βαβυλὼν τῆς Αἰγύπτου. Thessalonica 1993, 117 pp. RΘΕΟΛΟΓΙΑ 68 (1997) 611-614 *(Simotas, Pan.)*. G.

G9.2 **2 Petri**

6817 **Barra, Domenico** La seconda epistola di Pietro. Commentari biblici: Palermo 1997, Gesù vive 80 pp. [SdT 11,109s—Mattioli, A.].
6818 *Paulsen, Henning* Kanon und Geschichte: Bemerkungen zum Zweiten Petrusbrief. Zur Literatur. WUNT 99: 1997 <1983>, ⇒153. 154-161.
6819 *Pearson, Birger A.* The Apocalypse of Peter (NHC VII,3) and canonical 2 Peter. The emergence. 1997, ⇒154. 88-98.
6820 **Speyr, Adrienne von** L'avènement du Seigneur: commentaire de la seconde épitre de saint Pierre. ᵀ*David, Isabelle*: Bru 1997, Culture et Vérité 128 pp. BEF520. 2-87299-055-0 [Coll. 27,336].

6821 **Charles, J. Daryl** Virtue amidst vice: the catalog of virtues in 2 Peter 1. JSNT.S 150: Shf 1997, Academic 194 pp. Bibl. 1-85075-686-4.
6822 *Pearson, Birger A.* A reminiscence of classical myth at 2 Peter 2:4. The emergence. 1997, ⇒154. 75-87.

G9.4 **Epistula Jacobi**...data on both apostles James

6823 ᴱ**Aland, B.**, (*al.*), Die katholischen Briefe: 1, Text: 1) Der Jakobusbrief; 2) Begleitende Materialien. Novum Testamentum graecum, 4: editio maior critica. Stu 1997, Deutsche Bibelgesellschaft 102 + 39 pp. Institut für neutestamentliche Textforschung; 2 Fasc. DM27. 3-438-05600-3. ᴿEThL 73 (1997) 441-443 *(Neirynck, F.)*.
6824 **Bernheim, Pierre-Antoine** Jacques, frère de Jésus. 1996, ⇒12,6613. ᴿCEv 101 (1997) 64-65 *(Quesnel, Michel)*; BLE 98 (1997) 394-396 *(Debergé, P.)*;
6825 James, brother of Jesus. ᵀ*Bowden, John*: L 1997, SCM viii; 324 pp. £15. 0-334-02695-4.
6826 *Cothenet, Édouard* L'épître de Jacques. Les dernières épîtres. 1997, ⇒4403. 109-141.
6827 **Eisenman, Robert** James the brother of Jesus: recovering the true history of early christianity. L 1997, Faber xxxvi; 1074 pp. £25. 0-571-17573-2 [DSD 5,95ss—Brent, Allen].
6828 **Johnson, Luke Timothy** The letter of James: a new translation with introduction and commentary. AncB 37A: 1995, ⇒11/1,5303 ... 12,6608. ᴿTS 58 (1997) 350-352 *(Giblin, Charles Homer)*.
6829 ᵀ**Karsten, Matthias** BEDAs Kommentar zum Jakobusbrief: Einführung, Übersetzung, Kurzkommentar. Diss. Paderborn 1997/98; ᴰ*Frankemölle* [BZ 42,318].
6830 **Kopp, Herbert** Authentic living: bringing belief and lifestyle together: studies in James. Luminaire Studies: Winnipeg 1996, Kindred xv; 127 pp. 0-921788-33-9 [NThAR 2000,4].
6831 **Loh, I-Jin; Hatton, Howard A.** The letter of James. UBS Handbook: NY 1997, UBS 225 pp. [Sal. 61,621s—Buzzetti, Carlo].
6832 **Nystrom, David, P.** James. NIV application commentary: GR 1997, Zondervan 338 pp. Bibl. 0-310-49360-9.
6833 **Painter, John** Just James. Columbia 1997, University of South Carolina Press xiv; 326 pp. $35. 1-5703-174-6 [BiTod 36,266—Senior, Donald].

6834  **Palmer, Earl F.** The book that James wrote. GR 1997, Eerdmans xiv; 90 pp. $10. 0-8028-0136-6.

6835  **Peters, Hans-Jürgen** Der Brief des Jakobus erklärt. WStB: Wu 1997, Brockhaus 213 pp. Bibl. 3-417-25024-2.

6836  **Richardson, Kurt A.** James. NAC 36: Nv 1997, Broadman & H 272 pp. $28. 0-8054-0136-9 [NThAR 1999,5].

6837  *Townsend, Michael J.* Reading the book 5: the epistle of James. ET 108 (1997) 134-137.

6838  **Vries, E.** de Jakobus: een praktische bijbelverklaring. 1996, ⇒12,6610. ITBT 5/5 (1997) 32-33 *(Veen, Wilken)*.

6839  **Wall, Robert W.** Community of the wise: the letter of James. The NT Testament in Context: Valley Forge, PA 1997, Trinity xi; 354 pp. Bibl. $24. 1-56338-145-5.

6840  **Baker, William R.** Personal speech-ethics in the epistle of James. WUNT 2/68: 1995, ⇒11/1,5306; 12,6612. REvQ 69/1 (1997) 90-91 *(Warrington, Keith)*; ThG 40/2 (1997) 152-153 *(Giesen, Heinz)*.

6841  *Hartin, Patrick J.* The poor in the epistle of James and the gospel of Thomas. HTS 53 (1997) 146-162.

6842  *Hogan, Maurice* The law in the epistle of James. SNTU.A 22 (1997) 79-91.

6843  **Klein, Martin** "Ein vollkommenes Werk": Vollkommenheit, Gesetz und Gericht als theologische Themen des Jakobusbriefes. BWANT 139: 1995, ⇒11/1,5313; 12,6620. RBiLi 70/1 (1997) 77-78 *(Kühschelm, Roman)*.

6844  **Konradt, Matthias** Christliche Existenz nach dem Jakobusbrief: eine Studie zu seiner soteriologischen und ethischen Konzeption. Diss. Heidelberg 1996-1997; DBurchard, Ch. [ThLZ 122,763].

6845  **Ludwig, Martina** Wort als Gesetz. EHS.T 502: 1994, ⇒10,6290*. RJBL 115 (1996) 372-375 *(Jackson-McCabe, Matt)*.

6846  *März, Claus-Peter* Von der 'evangelischen Art' der 'strohernen Epistel'. 1997, ⇒98. FULLRICH L., 44-62.

6847  *Neudorfer, Heinz-Werner* Ist Sachkritik nötig?: Anmerkungen zu einem Thema der biblischen Hermeneutik am Beispiel des Jakobusbriefs. KuD 43 (1997) 279-302.

6848  *Neudorfer, Heinz-Werner* "Nur der Glaubende ist gehorsam, und nur der Gehorsame glaubt": Anmerkungen zum Thema "Sachkritik an der Bibel" am Beispiel des Jakobusbriefs. TVGMS 424: 1997, ⇒59. FMAIER G., 219-235.

6849  **Penner, Todd C.** The epistle of James and eschatology. JSNT.S 121: 1996, ⇒12,6622. RJThS 48 (1997) 613-615 *(Martin, Ralph P.)*; CritRR 10 (1997) 209-210 *(Davids, Peter H.)*.

6850  *Popkes, Wiard* The composition of James and intertextuality: an exercise in methodology. StTh 51/2 (1997) 91-112.

6851  *Souček, Josef B.* Zu den Problemen des Jakobusbriefes. Bibelauslegung. WUNT 100: 1997 <1958>, ⇒970. EPokorný, P., 211-219.

6852  *Tollefson, Kenneth D.* The epistle of James as dialectical discourse. BTB 27 (1997) 62-69.

6853  **Tsuji, Manabu** Glaube zwischen Vollkommenheit und Verweltlichung: eine Untersuchung zur literarischen Gestalt und zur inhaltlichen Kohärenz des Jakobusbriefes. Diss. Bern. WUNT 2/93: Tü 1997, Mohr xi; 244 pp. DM118. 3-16-146620-9.

6854  *Llewelyn, S.R.* The prescript of James [Jas 1,1];
6855  *Verseput, Donald J.* James 1:17 and the Jewish morning prayers. NT 39 (1997) 385-393/177-191.
6856  *Wall, Robert W.* "The perfect law of liberty" (James 1:25). 1997, ⇒77. ᶠSANDERS J., 475-497.
6857  *Verseput, Donald J.* Reworking the puzzle of faith and deeds in James 2.14-26. NTS 43 (1997) 97-115.
6858  *Limberis, Vasiliki* The provenance of the Caliphate church: James 2.17-26 and Galatians 3 reconsidered. Early christian interpretation. JSNT.S 148: 1997, ⇒191. ᴱEvans, C.A., 397-420.
6859  *Dannemann, Irene* Kämpferisch geduldig sein: sozialgeschichtliche. Bibelauslegung zu Jakobus 5,7 und 8. JK 58 (1997) 630-632.

### G9.6  Epistula Judae

6860  *Cothenet, Édouard* L'épître de Jude. Les dernières épîtres. 1997, ⇒4403. 267-276.
6861  *Joubert, Stephan J.* "Die einde is hier!": tekstuele strategie en historiese verstaan in die Judasbrief. HTS 53 (1997) 543-556.
6862  *Thurén, Lauri* Hey Jude!: asking for the original situation and message of a catholic epistle. NTS 43 (1997) 451-465.

## XIII.  Theologia Biblica

### H1.1  Biblical Theology [OT] God

6863  **Alonso Schökel, Luis** Dios: cien máximas bíblicas. Enseñamos a orar 8: Bilbao 1997, Mensajero 119 pp. 84-271-2123-7.
6864  **Armstrong, Karen** Storia di Dio: 4000 anni di religioni monoteiste. Venezia 1995, Marsilio 492 pp. L58.000. ᴿRdT 38 (1997) 139-140 *(Rizzi, Armido)*;
6865  Histoire de Dieu: d'Abraham à nos jours. ᵀ*Médina, Jean-Baptiste*: P 1997, Seuil 516 pp. [SR 27,123—Mager, Robert].
6866  *Auld, Graeme* Does God speak [Hebrew]?: a response to Professor McKANE. ET 108 (1997) 177.
6867  **Baldick, Julian** Black God: the Afroasiatic roots of the Jewish, Christian and Muslim religions. L 1997, Tauris viii; (2) 197 pp. 1-86064-123-7.
6868  **Baudler, Georg** El Jahwe Abba: wie die Bibel Gott versteht. 1996, ⇒12,6636. ᴿThLZ 122 (1997) 324-325 *(Särkiö, Pekka)*.
6869  *Berger-Holzknecht, Ruth* Gottesbilder in der Bibel. HlD 51 (1997) 72-74.
6870  *Brenner, Athalya* The Hebrew God and his female complements. Reading bibles. 1997 <1992>, ⇒172. ᴱBeal, T.K., 56-71.
6871  **Briend, Jacques** Dios en la Escritura. ᵀ*Montes, M.*: Biblioteca Manual Desclée 9: Bilbao 1995, Desclée de B 141 pp. ᴿEfMex 15 (1997) 116-117 *(Zesati Estrada, Carlos)*; RF 181 (1997) 319-320 *(Tamayo-Acosta, Juan José)*.
6872  *Eid, Volker* Gott—der Herr der Geschichte?. BiKi 52 (1997) 191-192.

6873 *Feldmeier, Reinhard* Nicht Übermacht noch Impotenz: zum bibli- schen Ursprung des Allmachtsbekenntnisses. Der Allmächtige. 1997, ⇒1563. 13-42.

6874 **Friedman, Richard Elliott** The disappearance of God. 1995, ⇒11/2,2774; 12,6639. RJR 77 (1997) 311-313 *(Kaminsky, Joel S.)*.

6875 *Gibson, Arthur* God's semantic logic: some functions in the Dead Sea scrolls and the bible. The scrolls and the scriptures. JSPE.S 26 1997, ⇒299. EPorter, S.E., 68-106.

6876 **Goodman, Lenn E.** God of Abraham. 1996, ⇒12,6641. RRelSt 33 (1997) 354-356 *(Sagi, Avi)*; Teol. 34 (1997) 545-546 *(Burrell, David B.)*; CrossCur 47 (1997-8) 564-566 *(Flage, Daniel E.)*.

6877 *Hendel, Ronald S.* Aniconism and anthropomorphism in ancient Israel. The image. 1997, ⇒2073. EVan der Toorn, K., 205-228.

6878 *Henry, Carl F.* The living God of the bible. Southern Baptist Con- vention 1/1 (1997) 16-31.

6879 *Hoaas, Geir* Passion and compassion of God in the Old Testament: a theological survey of Hos 11,8-9; Jer 31,20, and Isa 63,9 + 15. SJOT 11 (1997) 138-159.

6880 **Jeremias, Jörg** Die Reue Gottes: Aspekte alttestamentlicher Got- tesvorstellung. BThSt 31: Neuk ²1997, Neuk 160 pp. 3-7887- 1625-8.

6881 **Klement, Herbert H.** Gott und die Götter im Alten Testament. JETh 11 (1997) 7-41.

6882 **Miles, Jack** Dios: una biografía. 1996, ⇒12,6653. RRelCult 43/1 (1997) 195-203 *(Jiménez, José Demetrio)*.

6883 **Monsabré, H.; Bottero, J.; Moingt, J.** La plus belle histoire de Dieu: qui est le Dieu de la Bible?. P 1997, Seuil 180 pp. RTelema 23/4 (1997) 82-83 *(Delhez, Charles)*.

6884 **Neufeld, Thomas R. Yoder** 'Put on the armour of God': the di- vine warrior from Isaiah to Ephesians. JSNT.S 140: Shf 1997, Academic 182 pp. £30/$45. 1-85075-655-4 [Wisd 5; Isa 59; Eph 6; 1 Thess 5].

6885 **Neusner, Jacob; Chilton, Bruce D.** God in the world. Christianity and Judaism, the formative categories. Harrisburg 1997, Trinity xvi; 175 pp. $17. 1-56338-202-4 [ThD 45,379—Heiser, W. Charles].

6886 **Peels, H.G.L.** De omkeer van God in het Oude Testament. Apel- doornse Studies 34: Apeldoorn 1997, Theologische Universiteit 54 pp. [ZAW 111,309—Kinet, D.]. *f*17.50.

6887 *Puhvel, Jaan* Gods versus demons: all in the family. Engel und Dä- monen. FARG 29: 1997, ⇒343. EAhn, G., 145-150.

6888 *Rauhaus, Alfred* Gottes Bild. RKZ 138 (1997) 291-295.

6889 *Ritter, Werner H.* "Gott, der Allmächtige" im religionspädagogi- schen Kontext: zur Problematik einer Glaubensaussage. Der Allmä- chtige. 1997, ⇒1563. 97-151.

6890 **Satinover, Jeffrey** Cracking the bible code: the real story of the scientific search for the existence of God. NY 1997, Morrow xvii; 346 pp. bibl. 0-688-15463-8 [NThAR 1998,99].

6891 *Schenker, Adrian* Le monothéisme Israélite: un dieu qui transcende le monde et les dieux. Bib. 78 (1997) 436-448.

6892 *Schoberth, Wolfgang* Gottes Allmacht und das Leiden. Der All- mächtige. 1997, ⇒1563. 43-67.

6893 *Schreiner, Josef* Zur Personwirklichkeit Gottes im Alten Testa- ment. FSCHREINER J., 1997 <1996>, ⇒80. 30-46.

6894 *Schwemer, Anna Maria* Gottes Hand und die Propheten: zum Wandel der Metapher "Hand Gottes" in frühjüdischer Zeit. La main de Dieu. WUNT 94: 1997, ⇒328. [E]Kieffer, R., 65-85.

6895 *Shiffren, Mara* Biblical hypostases and the concept of God. SBL.SPS 36 (1997) 194-223.

6896 **Soulen, R. Kendall** The God of Israel and christian theology. 1996, ⇒12,6660. [R]ThTo 54/1 (1997) 86-88 *(Schramm, Brooks)*; EE 72 (1997) 376-378 *(Uríbarri, G.)*; CThMi 24/4 (1997) 365 *(Giere, Samuel D.)*; TJT 13 (1997) 345-347 *(Verbin, Nehama)*; AThR 79 (1997) 627-8, 630 *(Malcolm, Lois)*.

6897 *Westermann, Claus* Gottes Handeln und Gottes Reden im Alten Testament. 1997, ⇒48. [F]KNIERIM R., 389-403.

H1.4 *Femininum in Deo*—God as father and mother

6898 *Baarda, T.* "Abba, Vader". KeTh 48/1 (1997) 3-8.

6899 *Caro C., Cristián* 'Padre nuestro'. La Revista Católica 97/2 (1997) 103-108, 116-121.

6900 **Grelot, Pierre** Dieu, le Père de Jésus Christ. CJJC 60: 1994, ⇒10,7407... 12,6671. [R]EstB 55 (1997) 120-121 *(Ibarzábal, S.)*.

6901 **Juung, Wonyong** The divine Father concept in the Old Testament. Diss. Silang Theol. Seminary 1996. Sahmyook University Monographs 5: Seoul 1997, Inst. for Theol. Reseach Sahmyook University ix; 168 pp. [NThAR 1999,252].

6902 *Lys, Daniel* La figure du Père dans l'Ancien Testament. Tychique 127 (1997) 23-28.

6903 **Speyr, Adrienne von** The countenance of the Father. [T]*Kipp, David*: SF 1997, Ignatius 131 pp. $10. 0-89870-620-3 [ThD 45,92—Heiser, W. Charles].

6904 *Stansell, Gary* Mothers and sons in ancient Israel. 1997, ⇒29. [F]GERSTENBERGER E.S., 269-290.

6905 **Widdicombe, Peter** The fatherhood of God from ORIGEN to ATHANASIUS. 1994, ⇒11/2,2866; 12,6678. [R]TJT 13/1 (1997) 133-135 *(Egan, John P.)*.

H1.7 **Revelatio**

6906 *Anderson, Bernhard W.* Israel and revelation. BiRe 13/5 (1997) 17, 46-47.

6907 [E]**Avis, Paul** Divine revelation. GR 1997, Eerdmans viii; 215 pp. 0-8028-4219-4.

6908 **Bruns, Peter** Das Offenbarungsverständnis THEODORS von Mopsuestia im Zwölfprophetenkommentar. StPatr 32: 1997, ⇒351. [E]Livingstone, E.A., 272-277.

6909 Comisión mixta de diálogo entre la Iglesia Católica y el Consejo Metodista Mundial. La palabra de vida: declaración sobre la revelación y la fe (1995). [T]*Herrera García, Rosa María*: DiEc 32 (1997) 317-364 [Eng. orig. 'The word of life: a statement on revelation and faith' (1995) [PCPUC: Information Service 92 (1996-III)].

6910 *Escribano-Alberca, Ignacio* GREGORS von Nyssa *in Cant.*: einige Beobachtungen zur mystischen Konstruktion biblischer Offenbarung. StPatr 32: 1997, ⇒351. [E]Livingstone, E.A., 108-120.

6911 **Fackre, Gabriel** The doctrine of revelation: a narrative interpretation. Edinburgh Studies in Constructive Theology: GR 1997, Eerdmans x; 230 pp. £40. 0-8028-4336-0.
6912 **Knoch, Wendelin** Gott sucht den Menschen: Offenbarung, Schrift, Tradition. AMATECA 4: Paderborn 1997, Bonifatius 317 pp. DM68. 3-87088-911-X [EuA 75,70].
6913 *Moses, Stéphane* Rivelazione e linguaggio secondo le fonti bibliche. Studi Fatti Ricerche 78 (1997) 4-7.
6914 *Ravasi, Gianfranco* 'In principio...': la concezione biblica del tempo. PSV 36 (1997) 13-23.
6915 **Solov'ëv, Vladimir Sergeevic** La sofia: l'eterna sapienza mediatrice tra Dio e il mondo. Introd. *Nina Kauchtschischwili*. Opere, i giorni: i protagonisti della cultura 18: CinB 1997, San Paolo 137 pp. 88-215-3258-5.
6916 **Tillich, Paul** Religione e rivelazione: l'essere di Dio. Teologia sistematica, 1. 1996, ⇒12,6689. StPat 44/1 (1997) 259-260 *(Sartori, Luigi)*.
6917 **Via, Dan Otto** The revelation of God and/as human reception: in the New Testament. Valley Forge 1997, Trinity ix; 245 pp. Bibl. $20. 1-563-38198-2 [NThAR 1998,271].

### H1.8 Theologia fundamentalis

6918 *Caviglia, Giovanni* Presenza e assenza del miracolo nell'odierna teologia fondamentale. BSRel 125: 1997, ⇒45. [F]JAVIERRE ORTAS A., 397-434.
6919 [E]**Latourelle, René; Fisichella, Rino** Dictionary of fundamental theology. 1995, ⇒12,6692. [R]AUSS 35 (1997) 286-288 *(Hasel, Frank M.)*.
6920 *Lemonon, Jean-Pierre* L'enfer, écriture et dogme. LV(L) 46/3 (1997) 19-25.
6921 **Waldenfels, Hans** Einführung in die Theologie der Offenbarung. Die Theologie. 1996, ⇒12,6696. [R]ThGl 87 (1997) 460-461 *(Schlochtern, Josef Meyer zu)*.

### H2.1 Anthropologia theologica—VT & NT

6922 *Alonso Schökel, Luis* Il credente di fronte al mistero del dolore. Sulla soglia del tempio: credenti e non credenti a dialogo. [E]**Liberti, V.**: Mi 1997, San Paolo 67-82, 102-108.
6923 **Alonso Schökel, Luis** Símbolos matrimoniales en la biblia. Estella 1997 Verbo Divino 284 pp. 84-8169-182-8.
6924 [E]**Aune, David E.; McCarthy, John** The whole and divided self. NY 1997, Crossroad viii; 251 pp. $30. 0-8245-1668-0 [ThD 45,194—Heiser, W. Charles].
6925 *Balch, David L.* Political friendship in the historian DIONYSIUS of Halicarnassus, *Roman Antiquities*. Greco-Roman perspectives. 1997, ⇒6942. [E]Fitzgerald, J.T., 123-144.
6926 *Barclay, John M.G.* The family as the bearer of religion in Judaism and early christianity. Constructing... families. 1997, ⇒295. [E]Moxnes, H., 66-80.

6927] *Barreau, Hervé* La réflexion humaine devant la souffrance: les figures de Job, Bouddha et Jésus. Sedes Sapientiae 61 (1997) 42-60.
6928] *Barton, Stephen C.* The relativisation of family ties in the Jewish
and Graeco-Roman traditions. Constructing... families. 1997,
⇒295. EMoxnes, H., 81-100.
6929] *Blenkinsopp, Joseph* Life expectancy in ancient Palestine. SJOT 11
(1997) 44-55.
6930] *Bons, Eberhard* Der Umgang mit Leiden, Sterben und Trauer: ein
Überblick über Zeugnisse aus der Bibel und ihrer Umwelt. ZME
43 (1997) 301-314.
6931] *Brüning, Christian* 'Die Freude Jahwes—eure Stärke'. EuA 73
(1997) 254-287 [Neh 8,10].
6932] *Calduch-Benages, Nuria* L'affettività alla luce della parola di Dio.
Consacrazione e Servizio 46/4 (1997) 49-55.
6933] *Camus, Jean* La bible et l'étranger: donner ou recevoir?. Mission
de l'Église 114 (1997) 3-8.
6934] **Costacurta, Bruna** La vita minacciata: il tema della paura nella
Bibbia Ebraica. AnBib 119: R ²1997 <1988>, Ed. Pont. Ist.
Biblico 360 pp. L54.000. 88-7653-119-X. RCivCatt 148 IV (1997)
619-620 *(Prato, G.L.).*
6935] *Deist, Ferdinand* Boundaries and humour: a case study from the
ancient Near East. Scriptura 63 (1997) 415-424.
6936] **Destro, Adriana; Pesce, Mauro** Antropologia delle origini cristiane. Quadrante 78: R ²1997 <1995>, Laterza xv; 243 pp.
L25.000.
6937] *Eilberg-Schwartz, Howard* The problem of the body for the people
of the book. Reading bibles. 1997 <1991>, ⇒172. EBeal, T.K.,
34-55.
6938] **Ercoleo, Marisa; Vecchio, Sebastiano** Filosofia e scritture. Palermo 1997, Vito Fazio 223 pp. [FilTeo 13,411ss—Acerra, Maria
Grazia].
6939] *Evans, Katherine G.* Friendship in Greek documentary papyri and
inscriptions: a survey. Greco-Roman perspectives. 1997, ⇒6942.
EFitzgerald, J.T., 181-202.
6940] *Fiore, Benjamin* The theory and practice of friendship in CICERO.
Greco-Roman perspectives. 1997, ⇒6942. EFitzgerald, J., 59-76.
6941] *Fischer, Irmtraud* Mütter und Kinder im Alten Testament. Welt
und Umwelt der Bibel 6 (1997) 4-9.
6942] EFitzgerald, John T. Greco-Roman perspectives on friendship.
SBL Resources for Biblical Study 34: Atlanta, Georgia 1997,
Scholars xiii; 330 pp. $45. 0-7885-0272-7.
6943] *Fitzgerald, John T.* Friendship in the Greek world prior to
ARISTOTLE;
6944] Introduction.     Greco-Roman     perspectives.     1997,     ⇒6942.
EFitzgerald, J.T., 13-34/1-11.
6945] EGagey, Henri-Jérôme Le bonheur: deuxième cycle de théologie
biblique et systématique. Sciences théologiques et religieuses 5: P
1996, Beauchesne 241 pp. 2-7010-1336-4 [EE 72,594—Quinzá
Lleó, Xavier].
6946] *García Trapiello, Jesús* Juicio bíblico sobre el miedo humano.
Rias. 57. Ang. 74 (1997) 31-58 [Mt 11,25-30; Lk 10,21-24; John
6,37-46].

6947 **Gelabert, M.** Jesucristo, revelación del misterio del hombre: ensayo de antropología teológica. S 1997, San Esteban 266 pp. <sup>R</sup>TE 41/2 (1997) 311-313 *(Botella, Vicente)*.

6948 *Gemünden, Petra von* La femme passionnelle et l'homme rationnel?: un chapitre de psychologie historique. Sum. 480. Bib. 78 (1997) 457-480.

6949 **Gilhus, Ingvild Saelid** Laughing gods, weeping virgins: laughter in the history of religion. L 1997, Routledge vii; 173 pp. 0-415-16197-5.

6950 **Gioia, Francesco** Il libro della gioia: per una teologia biblica dei sentimenti. CasM 1997, Piemme 230 pp. [Lat. 63,340—Marinelli, Francesco].

6951 *Guijarro, Santiago* The family in first-century Galilee. Constructing ... families. 1997, ⇒295. <sup>E</sup>Moxnes, H., 42-65.

6952 *Halder, Alois* Aufbruch in die Fremde wie Abraham: das Denken des Anderen nach Emmanuel LEVINAS. Das Prisma 9/1 (1997) 14-18.

6953 *Hartnagel, Henri* Mes brebis entendent ma voix. Tychique 125 (1997) 3-6.

6954 **Hidal, Sten** Nästan till en Gud: människobild och människosyn i Gamla testamentet. Sto 1996, Verbum 207 pp. <sup>R</sup>TTK 68 (1997) 149-152 *(Stordalen, Terje)*.

6955 *Hill, Brennan R.* Hebrew biblical anthropology and modern environmental concerns. 1997, ⇒70. <sup>F</sup>MURPHY R., Master, 253-275.

6956 *Hobbs, T. Raymond* Reflections on honor, shame, and covenant relations. JBL 116 (1997) 501-503.

6957 *Hock, Ronald F.* An extraordinary friend in CHARITON's Callirhoe: the importance of friendship in the Greek romances. Greco-Roman perspectives. 1997, ⇒6942. <sup>E</sup>Fitzgerald, J.T., 145-162.

6958 *Huizing, Klaas* Das Gesicht der Schrift: Grundzüge einer bibelliterarischen Anthropologie. Lesen und Leben. 1997, ⇒205. 13-51.

6959 *Kriechbaum, Friedel* Behinderte Theologie?. 1997, ⇒29. <sup>F</sup>GERSTENBERGER E.S., 405-416.

6960 *Krüger, Thomas* Das menschliche Herz und die Weisung Gottes: Elemente einer Diskussion über Möglichkeiten und Grenzen der Tora-Rezeption im Alten Testament. OBO 153: 1997, ⇒91. <sup>F</sup>STECK O., 65-92 [Qoh 8,06; 7,29; Sir 37,13-14; Jer 31,33; Ezek 36,26-27].

6961 *Lassen, Eva Marie* The Roman family: ideal and metaphor. Constructing ... families. 1997, ⇒295. <sup>E</sup>Moxnes, H., 103-120.

6962 **Magnante, A.** Why suffering?: the mystery of suffering in the bible. <sup>T</sup>*Antolin, J.*: Nairobi 1997, Paulines 143 pp. [EstAg 32,564].

6963 *Malina, Bruce J.* Mediterranean cultural anthropology and the New Testament. La Bíblia i el Mediterrani. 1997, ⇒385. <sup>E</sup>Borrell, d'Agustí, 151-178.

6964 *Mannucci, Valerio* 'Ecco l'uomo': appunti per una 'antropologia biblica'. Som., sum. 21. VivH 8 (1997) 7-21.

6965 <sup>E</sup>**McCarthy, John** The whole and divided self: the bible and theological anthropology. NY 1997, Crossroad 251 pp. $30. 0-8245-1668-0 [NTS 44,624].

6966 **McDermott, John M.** La sofferenza umana nella Bibbia. 1990, ⇒7,1302... 9,1297. <sup>R</sup>Anime e Corpi 192 (1997) 583-585 *(Casera, Antonio)*.

6967 ᴱ**Milano, Lucio** Drinking in ancient societies. 1994, ⇒10,480...
    12,10627. ᴿBSOAS 60/1 (1997) 125-126 *(George, A.R.)*; BiOr 54
    (1997) 62-65 *(Limet, Henri)*; JNES 56 (1997) 233-234 *(Biggs,
    Robert D.)*.

6968 *Mitchell, Alan C.* "Greet the friends by name": New Testament
    evidence for the Greco-Roman topos on friendship. Greco-Roman
    perspectives. 1997, ⇒6942. ᴱFitzgerald, J.T., 225-262.

6969 *Moxnes, Halvor* Introduction;

6970 What is family?: problems in constructing early Christian families.
    Constructing... families. 1997, ⇒295. ᴱMoxnes, H., 1-9/13-41.

6971 *Nikić, Mijo* Savršena ljubav izgoni strah: psihološko-teološko raz-.
    mišljanje o strahu [Fear is driven out by perfect love
    (psychological-theological reflection about fear)]. 1997, ⇒96.
    ᶠTomica C.; Sum. 223. 214-224. **Croatian.**

6972 *O'Neil, Edward N.* Plutarch on friendship. Greco-Roman
    perspectives. 1997, ⇒6942. ᴱFitzgerald, J.T., 105-122.

6973 **Osiek, Carolyn; Balch, David** Families in the New Testament
    world: households and house churches. LVL 1997, Westminster x;
    301 pp. $25. 0-664-25546-9 [BTB 27,120].

6974 **Overholt, Thomas W.** Cultural anthropology and the Old Testa-
    ment. Guides to Biblical Scholarship, OT: Mp 1996, Fortress ix;
    116 pp. $13. 0-8006-2889-6. ᴿCBQ 59 (1997) 747-748 *(Matthews,
    Victor H.)*.

6975 *Peretto, Elio* Ricerche sul concetto di 'riparazione' nella letteratura
    biblica e patristica e ipotesi d'attualizzazione. 1997 <1990>,
    ⇒155. Saggi. 547-575.

6976 *Pervo, Richard I.* With Lucian: who needs friends?: friendship in
    the *Toxaris*. Greco-Roman perspectives. 1997, ⇒6942. ᴱFitzgerald,
    J.T., 163-180.

6977 **Pikaza, Xabier** Antropología bíblica. Biblioteca de Estudios Bíbli-
    cos 80: 1993, ⇒9,7255... 11/2,2985. ᴿEfMex 15/1 (1997) 105-108
    *(Castillo Solano, Ezequiel)*.

6978 **Poudrier, Roger** L'umorismo nella bibbia. Mi 1996, San Paolo
    [Anime e corpi 37,336—Casera, A.].

6979 *Pryor, John W.* Jesus and family—a test case. ABR 45 (1997) 56-
    69.

6980 *Sandnes, Karl Olav* Equality within patriarchal structures: some
    New Testament perspectives on the Christian fellowship as a
    brother- or sisterhood and a family. Constructing... families. 1997,
    ⇒295. ᴱMoxnes, H., 150-165.

6981 *Satlow, Michael L.* Jewish constructions of nakedness in late anti-
    quity. JBL 116 (1997) 429-454.

6982 *Schlageter, Johannes* Die Auseinandersetzung zwischen griechi-
    schem und biblischem Menschenbild im franziskanischen Freiheits-
    verständnis des Petrus Johannes Olivi OFM. WiWei 60 (1997)
    65-86.

6983 *Schroeder, Frederic M.* Friendship in Aristotle and some peri-
    patetic philosophers. Greco-Roman perspectives. 1997, ⇒6942.
    ᴱFitzgerald, J.T., 35-57.

6984 *Seifert, Elke* Frauen und Brunnen: Gedanken zu einem literarischen
    Motiv. 1997, ⇒29. ᶠGerstenberger E.S., 291-295 [Gen 21;
    27; Exod 2; Judg 13-14; 1 Sam 1-2; 1 Kgs 1-2].

6985) *Sterling, Gregory E.* The bond of humanity: friendship in PHILO of Alexandria. Greco-Roman perspectives. 1997, ⇒6942. EFitzgerald, J.T., 203-223.

6986) **Stienstra, Nelly** YHWH is the husband of his people. 1993, ⇒9,9760; 11/2,8721. RBZ 41 (1997) 311-312 *(Becker, Joachim).*

6987) **Strijp, Ruud** Cultural anthropology of the Middle East: a bibliography, 2: 1988-1992. HO 1: The Near and Middle East 27: L 1997, Brill xx; 259 pp. 90-04-10745-2.

6988) *Szesnat, Holger* Human sexuality, history, and culture: the essentialist/social constructionist controversy and the methodological problem of studying 'sexuality' in the New Testament and its world. Scriptura 62 (1997) 336-361 [ZID 24,133].

6989) *Tarocchi, Stefano* 'Fino a quando...': (Mc 9,19; Ap 6,10): dinamiche d'attesa e di compimento come riprova della longanimità. Som., sum. 108. VivH 8 (1997) 91-109 [Mk 9,19; Rev 6,10].

6990) *Thom, Johan C.* "Harmonious equality": the topos of friendship in Neopythagorean writings. Greco-Roman perspectives. 1997, ⇒6942. EFitzgerald, J.T., 77-103.

6991) **Vidovic, Franjo** Homo patiens: Leid und Leibewältigung im biblischen Schrifttum und seinem antiken Umfeld. Diss. Graz 1997; DWoschitz, K.M.; Larcher, G. 240 pp. [RTL 29,580].

6992) EVolker, Gäckle; Rieger, Joachim Der Mensch in Gottes Heilsgeschehen: eine biblische Anthropologie für die Gemeinde. Lehre und Leben 7: Neuhausen-Stuttgart 1996 Hänssler 224 pp. DM20. 3-7751-2477-2. RJETh 11 (1997) 219-220 *(Stenschke, Christoph).*

6993) *Vorster, J.N.* The body as strategy of power in religious discourse. Neotest. 31 (1997) 389-411.

6994) EWilkins, J.; Harvey, D.; Dobson, M. Food in antiquity. 1995, ⇒11/2,710. RCIR 47/1 (1997) 145-146 *(Dalby, Andrew)*; REA 99 (1997) 567-568 *(Amouretti, Marie-Claire).*

6995) *Winter, S.C.* Why is christianity anti-body?: or is it?. 1997, ⇒82. FSCROGGS R., 46-57.

6996) **Wolff, Hans Walter** Antropologia del Antiguo Testamento. Biblioteca de Estudios Biblicos 99: S 21997, Sígueme 341 pp. 84-301-0618-9.

## H2.8 Œcologia VT & NT— saecularitas

6997) *Becquet, Gilles* 'Aimer cette terre'. Sève 585 (1997) 57-62.

6998) **Boersema, Jan J.** Thora en Stoa over mens en natuur: een bijdage aan het milieudebat over duurzaamheid en kwaliteit [Ce que la Thora et la stoa disent de l'homme et de la nature: une contribution au débat écologique sur la durabilité et la qualité]. Diss. Groningen 1997; DVan der Woude, A.S.; Schoot, A.J.M.: Baarn 1997, Callenbach 319 pp. 90-266-0901-9 [RTL 29,581].

6999) **Clatworthy, Jonathan** Good God: green theology and the value of creation. Charlbury 1997, Spendlove Centre vi; 234 pp. £13. 1-897766-37-8 [RRT 1998/1,89].

7000) **Edwards, Denis** Jesus the wisdom of God: an ecological theology. 1995, ⇒11/2,3031. RCBQ 59 (1997) 152-153 *(Bergant, Dianne).*

7001) ELorenzani, Massimo La natura e l'ambiente nella Bibbia. 1996, ⇒12,189. RMedicina e Morale 47/1 (1997) 209-211 *(Fisso, Maria Beatrice).*

7002  *Martens, Elmer A.* Yahweh's compassion and ecotheology. 1997,
      ⇒48. ᶠKnierim R., 234-248.
7003  **Murray, Robert** The cosmic covenant: biblical themes of justice,
      peace and the integrity of creation. HeyM 7: 1992, ⇒8,7266...
      12,6727. ᴿSJTh 50/1 (1997) 123-124 *(Harvey, Graham).*
7004  *Neuhaus, Richard J.* Christ and creation's longing. First Things 78
      (1997) 20-25.
7005  *Poucouta, Paulin* Jésus et l'argent. Spiritus 38/146 (1997) 53-61.
7006  **Primavesi, Anne** Del Apocalipsis al Génesis: ecología, feminismo,
      cristianismo. ᵀ*Martínez Riu, Antonio*: 1995, ⇒12,6732. ᴿEeT(O)
      28/1 (1997) 316-319 *(Arana, María José).*
7007  *Tucker, Gene M.* Rain on a land where no one lives: the Hebrew
      Bible on the environment. JBL 116 (1997) 3-17.
7008  **Winkler, Ulrich** Vom Wert der Welt: das Verständnis der Dinge in
      der Bibel und bei Bonaventura: ein Beitrag zu einer ökologi-
      schen Schöpfungstheologie. Salzburger theologische Studien 5:
      Innsbruck 1997, Tyrolia 512 pp. Bibl. SCH680. 3-7022-2076-3.

## h3.1 *Foedus*—The Covenant; the Chosen People; Providence

7009  *Barclay, John M.G.* Universalism and particularism: twin compo-
      nents of both Judaism and early christianity. 1997, ⇒93. ᶠSweet
      J., 207-224.
7010  *Briglia, Sergio* 'Acuerdate, Señor, de tu alianza': la memoria y el
      jubileo. RevBib 60 (1997) 31-51.
7011  **Christiansen, Ellen Juhl** The covenant in Judaism and Paul.
      AGJU 27: 1995, ⇒11/2,3120. ᴿThLZ 122 (1997) 328-329 *(Räisä-
      nen, Heikki)*; SJOT 11 (1997) 305-306 *(Jeppesen, Knud).*
7012  *Fabris, Rinaldo* L'elezione-vocazione-predestinazione dell'umanità
      nell'epistolario del Nuovo Testamento;
7013  L'elezione-vocazione-predestinazione dell'umanità nei quattro van-
      geli. DSBP 15 (1997) 127-156/67-97.
7014  **Faley, Roland James** Bonding with God: a reflective study of
      biblical covenant. NY 1997, Paulist iii; 151 pp. 0-8091-3706-2.
7015  *Fenske, Wolfgang* Das Ringen des Volkes um die Stellung der Völ-
      ker. SJOT 11 (1997) 181-199.
7016  **Iori, R.** Due testamenti una alleanza: l'alleanza nell'antico e nel
      nuovo testamento: il cammino di una storia che continua. Pubblica-
      zioni dell'Istituto Superiore di Scienze Religiose 1: Sassari 1997,
      Istituto Superiore di Scienze Religiose 190 pp. Bibl. L35.000.
7017  *La Potterie, Ignace de* Jesus the bridegroom and Mary the bride in
      the mystery of the covenant. The theology of the alliance of the
      two hearts. R 1997, Two Hearts Media Organization.     Testo
      inglese e versione italiana. 11-64 [AcBIB 10/3,267].
7018  **Novak, David** The election of Israel. 1995, ⇒11/2,3145; 12,6749.
      ᴿAJS Review 22/1 (1997) 129-132 *(Arkush, Allan).*
7019  *Pickering, Stuart R.* Issues of newness and covenant in the Old and
      New Testaments. NTTRU 5 (1997) 21-38.
7020  *Ratzinger, Cardinal Joseph* Nouvelle alliance: la théologie de
      l'alliance dans le Nouveau Testament. Com(F) 22/5 (1997) 93-112.
7021  *Rodríguez Ruiz, Miguel* ¿Sigue en vigor la alianza con el pueblo
      juío?: respuesta del Nuevo Testamento. EstB 55 (1997) 393-403.

7022 **Röhser, Günther** Prädestination und Verstockung: Untersuchungen zur frühjüdischen, paulinischen und johanneischen Theologie. TANZ 14: 1994, ⇒10,7286... 12,6755. ᴿThLZ 122 (1997) 147-149 *(Frey, Jörg)*.

7023 **Simian-Yofre, Horacio** La "chiesa" dell'Antico Testamento: costituzione, crisi e speranza della comunità credente dell'Antico Testamento. Teologia Viva 27: Bo 1997, EDB 175 pp. L22.000. 88-10-40933-7.

7024 *Spieckermann, Hermann* Rechtfertigung: Altes Testament. TRE 28. 1997, ⇒420. 282-286.

7025 **Vogel, Manuel** Das Heil des Bundes: Bundestheologie im Frühjudentum und im frühen Christentum. TANZ 18: 1996, ⇒12,6759. ᴿBZ 41 (1997) 149-151 *(Backhaus, Knut)*.

### H3.5 *Liturgia, spiritualitas VT—OT prayer*

7026 **Alonso Schökel, Luis** Apostolato ed esercizi spirituali. Bibbia e Preghiera 28: R 1997, ADP 140 pp. L15.000. 88-7357-168-9 [RdT 38,287].

7027 **Balentine, Samuel E.** Prayer in the Hebrew Bible. 1993, ⇒9,7414 ... 11/2,3163. ᴿHebStud 38 (1997) 106-108 *(Schrieber, Paul L.)*; CritRR 10 (1997) 155-156 *(Harrelson, Walter)*.

7028 *Barrado Fernández, Pedro* Biblia y oración. TeCa 64 (1997) 31-55.

7029 **Bermejo, Luis M.** Alone with God alone: a biblical 30-day retreat. Anand, Gujarat 1997, Gujarat Sahitya Prakash xii; 272 pp. Rs95/$12; Rs86/$10 [IMR 19/3-4,218].

7030 **Bianchi, Enzo** Gott im Wort: die geistliche Schriftlesung. Eichstätt 1997, Franz-Sales 104 pp. DM21.80. 3-7721-0198-4 [OrdKor 38,511].

7031 *Brunon, Mgr.* La parole de Dieu source de vie spirituelle. EeV 107 (1997) 313-320.

7032 ᴱ**De Zan, Renato** Dove rinasce la parola. Bibbia e liturgia, 3. Padova 1993, EMP 288 pp. L30.000. 88-250-0214-9. ᴿLetteratura Liturgica 84 (1997) 567-569 *(Troía, Pasquale)*.

7033 *Figueiredo Frias, Agostinho* La 'lectio Scripturae' nella tradizione agostiniana portoghese. Santo 37/1-2 (1997) 9-25.

7034 ᴱ**Franz, Ansgar** Streit am Tisch des Wortes?: zur Deutung und Bedeutung des Alten Testaments und seiner Verwendung in der Liturgie. PiLi 8: St. Ottilien 1997, EOS 927 pp. 3-88096-288-X [NThAR 1998,301].

7035 *Gargano, Guido Innocenzo* Dalla parola scritta alla parola viva: la 'lectio divina'. Presenza Pastorale 67 (1997) 817-825.

7036 Un giorno, una parola: letture bibliche quotidiane per il 1998. Introd. **Ricca, Paolo**: T 1997, Claudiana 288 pp. Federazione delle chiese evangeliche in Italia. L12.000.

7037 ᴱ**Kiley, Mark** Prayer from Alexander to Constantine: a critical anthology. L 1997, Routledge xx; 332 pp. $23. 0-415-13235-5.

7038 *Kirchschläger, Walter* Feuer: biblisches Motiv und liturgisches Zeichen. HID 51 (1997) 145-157.

7039 *Larini, Riccardo* Dall'esperienza orante di Israele alla preghiera comune dei cristiani. Itinerari di Preghiera 67 (1997) 495-506.

7040  *Lohfink, Norbert* Altes Testament und Liturgie: unsere Schwierig-
keiten und unsere Chancen. LJ 47 (1997) 3-22.

7041  *Lorenzin, Tiziano* La 'lectio Scripturae' di ANTONIO per una at-
tualizzazione. Rias., sum. 104. Santo 37/1-2 (1997) 89-104.

7042  *Maldonado Arenas, Luis* Oración bíblica—oración litúrgica. RET
57 (1997) 163-188 [Ps 115].

7043  *Marie Jérôme, (Frère)* L'adoration dans la bible. Aletheia 12
(1997) 11-31 [ZID 24,119].

7044  **Masini, Mario** La 'lectio divina': teologia, spiritualità, metodo.
1996, ⇒12,6773. ᴿAng. 74/1 (1997) 129-131 *(Rossi, Margherita
Maria)*.

7045  *Monloubou, Louis* La Bible et la prière des hommes. EeV 107
(1997) 321-328.

7046  **Nolan, Albert** Espiritualidad bíblica: espiritualidad de la justicia y
el amor. Biblia y Vida: México 1993, Dabar 63 pp. ᴿThX 47
(1997) 365-367 *(Arango, José Roberto)*.

7047  *Nowack, Petrus* 'Excitate nos scriptura' (RB PR 8): das Hören auf
die heilige Schrift und die Antwort im Gebet: eine bleibende
exemplarische Dimension der benediktinischen Liturgie. Neunter
Internationaler Regula-Benedicti-Kongreß. RBS 19: St. Ottilien
1997, Eos. 3-88096-293-6. 79-98.

7048  *Nübold, Elmar* Das Alte Testament in der gegenwärtigen Perikopenordnung. LJ 47 (1997) 174-189.

7049  *Odasso, Giovanni* Dalla 'lectio Scripturae' di FRANCESCO alla
lectio Scripturae' di ANTONIO. Sum. 52. Santo 37/1-2 (1997) 27-
52.

7050  *Pompei, Alfonso M.* Dalla 'lectio Scripturae' di ANTONIO alla lectio Scripturae' di BONAVENTURA e della prima Scuola francescana. Sum. 87. Santo 37/1-2 (1997) 53-87.

7051  **Ravasi, Gianfranco** Il Dio vicino: la preghiera biblica tra storia e
fede. Saggi: Mi 1997, Mondadori 266 pp. 88-04-43399-X [NThAR
1999,2].

7052  **Rossier, François** L'intercession entre les hommes dans la Bible
hébraïque. OBO 152: 1996, ⇒12,6782. ᴿEThL 73 (1997) 149-150
*(Lust, J.)*.

7053  *Rouwhorst, G.* Jewish liturgical traditions in early Syriac Christianity. VigChr 51 (1997) 72-93.

7054  *Schaalman, Herman E.* Judaic spirituality. ChiSt 36/1 (1997) 39-
46.

7055  **Schlegel, Helmut** Ich bin das Feuer und du bist der Wind: biblische Meditationen zum Werden und Wachsen des inneren Menschen. Wü 1997, Echter 116 pp. DM19.80. 3-429-01934-6 [Ord-
Kor 39,360—Heinemann, Franz Karl].

7056  *Schreiner, Josef* Biblische Spiritualität: Worte zur Einkehr. 1997
<1996>, ⇒80. ᶠSCHREINER J., 277-322 [Dt 6,4-7; 2 Kgs 5,14-
17; Jer 1; John 20,21; 1 Tim 6,13-16].

7057  *Silva, Santiago* Conocer, comprender y orar con la biblia, 1. La
Revista Católica 97/1 (1997) 19-27.

7058  **Wargnies, Ph.** Connaître et prier l'Ancien Testament. Namur
1997, Fidélité 120 pp. FB280 [NRTh 120,286].

7059  **Warnier, Philippe; Valentino, Carlo** Pregare con la Bibbia: 215
preghiere bibliche. Itinerari Biblici: R 1997, Borla 298 pp. 30.000.
88-263-1184-6.

7060  **West, Fritz** Scripture and memory: the ecumenical hermeneutic of the three-year lectionaries. Pueblo Book: ColMn 1997, Liturgical xii; 228 pp. $25. 0-8146-6157-2 [BTB 27,120].

### H3.7  *Theologia moralis VT*—OT moral theology

7061  *Alvarez Verdes, Lorenzo* Ética bíblica y hermenéutica: una reflexión desde la post-modernidad. Sum., res. 342. StMor 35 (1997) 313-343.

7062  *Bexell, Göran* Theological interpretation of biblical texts on moral issues. StTh 51/1 (1997) 3-14.

7063  *Botha, S.W.J.* The social-ethical contribution of the reflective proverbs to a meaningful life in the farming community of ancient Israel. OTEs 10 (1997) 198-212.

7064  **Börschlein, Wolfgang** Häsäd: der Erweis von Solidarität—als eine ethische Grundhaltung im Alten Testament: ein Beispiel für ein Modell in christlicher Ethik heute?. Diss. Eichstätt 1997; D*Diedrich, F.* 508 pp. [RTL 29,576].

7065  **Bovati, Pietro** Ristabilire la giustizia: procedure, vocabolario, orientamenti. AnBib 110: R 1997 <1986>, Ed. PIB 448 pp. L54.000. 88-7653-110-6. RCivCatt 148 II (1997) 616-617 *(Scaiola, D.)*.

7066  E**Brawley, Robert Lawson** Biblical ethics and homosexuality: listening to scripture. 1996, ⇒12,6794. RCBQ 59 (1997) 795-796 *(Willis, Wendell)*.

7067  **Bretzke, James T.** Bibliography on scripture and christian ethics. SRS 39: Lewiston 1997, Mellen 364 pp. $100. 0-7734-8460-4 [ThD 45,358—Heiser, W. Charles].

7068  *Christensen, Kurt* Bibelsk etik over for bioetikkens problemer. IXΘΥΣ 24/3 (1997) 102-112.

7069  *Dietrich, Walter; Link, Christian* Die dunklen Seiten Gottes: Willkür und Gewalt. Neuk ²1997, Neuk 238 pp. [FrRu 4,299s—Oberforcher, Robert].

7070  *Doyle, Áilín* The bible and homosexuality. DoLi 47/4 (1997) 233-239 [1 Cor 1,17-18].

7071  *Fabry, Heinz-Josef* Deuteronomium 15: Gedanken zur Geschwister-Ethik im Alten Testament. ZAR 3 (1997) 92-111 [Exod 23; Lev 25; Dt 15].

7072  *Fleckenstein, Wolfgang* "Einen Fremden sollst du nicht ausnützen oder ausbeuten" (Ex 22,20): alttestamentliche Orientierungshilfen zu einem immer wieder aktuellen Thema. MThZ 48 (1997) 1-8.

7073  *Freund, Richard A.* Individual vs. collective responsibility: from the ancient Near East and the bible to the Greco-Roman world. SJOT 11 (1997) 279-304.

7074  *Kaiser, Walter C. Jr.* Approches récentes en éthique de l'Ancien Testament. T*Gallopin, Marc*: Hokhma 64 (1997) 31-43.

7075  **Kaminsky, Joel S.** Corporate responsibility in the Hebrew Bible. JSOT.S 196: 1995, ⇒11/2,3240. RBib. 78 (1997) 100-103 *(Clements, Ronald E.)*; JBL 116 (1997) 331-332 *(Schoors, Antoon)*.

7076  *Kaminsky, Joel S.* The sins of the fathers: a theological investigation of the biblical tension between corporate and individualized retribution. Jdm 46 (1997) 319-332.

7077 *Knierim, Rolf P.* On two cases of the biblical hermeneutic of justice. 1997, ⇒29. <sup>F</sup>GERSTENBERGER E.S., 238-255.

7078 *Meves, Christa* Schamgefühl III: biblische Gründung. Theologisches 27 (1997) 73-79.

7079 *Míguez, Néstor O.* Compartir o acumular: una aproximación bíblica. RevBib 59 (1997) 223-237.

7080 *Milgrom, Jacob* The blood taboo. BiRe 13/4 (1997) 21, 46.

7081 *Mouton, Elna* The (trans)formative potential of the bible as resource for christian ethos and ethics. Scriptura 62 (1997) 245-257 [ZID 24,133].

7082 **Nardoni, Enrique** Los que buscan la justicia: un estudio de la justicia en el mundo bíblico. Estudios Bíblicos 14: Estella 1997, Verbo Divino 337 pp. 84-8169-201-8.

7083 *Niehr, Herbert* The constitutive principles for establishing justice and order in Northwest Semitic societies with special reference to ancient Israel and Judah. ZAR 3 (1997) 112-130.

7084 *Noguez A., Armando* La fundamentación bíblica de la ética teológica. Voces 10 (1997) 19-43.

7085 **Otto, Eckart** Theologische Ethik des Alten Testaments. 1994, ⇒10,7238... 12,6814. <sup>R</sup>EstB 55 (1997) 267-268 *(Mielgo, C.)*; OTEs 10 (1997) 561-562 *(van Tonder, C.A.P.)*.

7086 *Otto, Eckart* Programme der sozialen Gerechtigkeit: die neuassyrische *(an-)duraru*-Institution sozialen Ausgleichs und das deuteronomische Erlaßjahr in Dtn 15. ZAR 3 (1997) 26-63.

7087 *Patte, Daniel* When ethical questions transform critical biblical studies. Semeia 77 (1997) 271-284.

7088 *Phillips, A.C.J.* Old Testament and moral tradition. ET 108 (1997) 231-232.

7089 *Pinckaers, Servais* La parole de Dieu et la morale. Revue d'Éthique et de Théologie Morale—Supplément 200 (1997) 21-38.

7090 *Punt, Jeremy* Biblical studies in South Africa?: the case for moral values. Scriptura 60 (1997) 1-13 [ZID 23,278].

7091 <sup>E</sup>**Rogerson, John W.** The Bible in ethics. JSOT.S 207: 1995, ⇒11/2,529. <sup>R</sup>CBQ 59 (1997) 613-615 *(Janzen, Waldemar)*.

7092 *Roux, Cornelia* Biblical values and multi-religious education in the primary school: problems and proposals. Scriptura 60 (1997) 63-69 [ZID 23,278].

7093 *Świerczek, Edmund* Zamysły serca, czyli skłonność dobra i zła w nauczaniu biblijnym [De inclinatione ad bonum et malum in doctrina biblica]. RBL 50 (1997) 22-28. **P**.

7094 <sup>E</sup>**Seow, Choon-Leong** Homosexuality and christian community. 1996, ⇒12,6820. <sup>R</sup>Interp. 51/2 (1997) 197-199 *(Busey, Robert S.)*.

7095 **Sheriffs, Deryck** The friendship of the Lord: an Old Testament spirituality. 1996, ⇒12,6821. <sup>R</sup>JETh 11 (1997) 199-201 *(Bluedorn, Wolfgang)*.

7096 *Spieckermann, Hermann* Konzeption und Vorgeschichte des Stellvertretungsgedankens im Alten Testament. Congress volume 1995. VT.S 66: 1997, ⇒323. <sup>E</sup>Emerton, J.A., 281-295 [Isa 53].

7097 *Stone, Ken* Biblical interpretation as a technology of the self: gay men and the ethics of reading. Semeia 77 (1997) 139-155.

7098 **Vasey, Michael** Strangers and friends: a new exploration of homosexuality and the bible. L 1995, Hodder & S xii; 276 pp. £10. <sup>R</sup>Theol. 100 (1997) 63-64 *(Coleman, P.E.)*.

7099 *Wenham, G.J.* The gap between law and ethics in the bible. JJS 48 (1997) 17-29.

7100 *Witczyk, Henryk* Powrót do Boga wspólnoty: zadośćuczynienie za grzechy według Deutero-Izajasza i księgi Psalmów [Reditus ad Deum et communitatem: de satisfactione pro peccatis in Dt-Is et Ps]. RBL 50 (1997) 86-104. **P.**

7101 *Wojciechowski, Michał* Jedność etyki Starego i Nowego Testamentu [Unity of the Old and New Testament ethic]. 1997, ⇒52. ᶠLACH J., 443-454. **P.**

7102 **Wright, Christopher J.H.** Walking in the ways of the Lord: the ethical authority of the Old Testament. 1995, ⇒11/2,3268. ᴿNRTh 119 (1997) 113-114 *(Ska, J.L.)*; ThLZ 122 (1997) 28-30 *(Otto, Eckart)*.

7103 *Zerafa, P.* La retribuzione nella bibbia. Rias. 145. Ang. 74 (1997) 145-170.

### H3.8 *Bellum et pax VT-NT*—War and peace in the whole Bible

7104 **Boyd, Gregory A.** God at war: the bible and spiritual conflict. DG 1997, InterVarsity 414 pp. $18. 0-8308-1885-5.

7105 **Colvin, John** Lions of Judah. L 1997, Quartet 309 pp. 0-7043-7108-1 [NThAR 1999,2].

7106 **Dalla Vecchia, Flavio** L'arte della guerra nella bibbia. CasM 1997, Piemme 210 pp. L38.000. 88-384-2794-1 [Itinerari di Preghiera 67,570].

7107 ᴱ**Dierkens, Alain** Le penseur, la violence, la religion. Problèmes d'histoire des religions 7: Bru 1996, Éd. de l'Université de Bruxelles 160 pp. 2-8004-1155-4.

7108 *Fewell, Danna Nolan* Imagination, method, and murder: un/framing the face of post-exilic Israel. Reading bibles. 1997, ⇒172. ᴱBeal, T.K., 132-152.

7109 *Häring, Hermann* Ploegscharen omgesmeed tot zwaarden (Joël 4,10): de wortels van het geweld in de religie. TTh 37 (1997) 265-290.

7110 **Herzog, Chaim; Gichon, Mordechai** Battles of the Bible. L ²1997, Greenhill 320 pp. 1-85367-266-1.
  **Johnson, J.** The Holy War idea in Western and Islamic traditions ⇒2341.

7111 *Manjaly, Thomas* Reconciliation—peace: biblical reflections. IMR 19/1 (1997) 82-92.
  **Partner, P.** God of battles: holy wars of christianity and Islam ⇒2346

7112 **Schwartz, Regina M.** The curse of Cain: the violent legacy of monotheism. Ch 1997, University of Chicago Press xv; 211 pp. 0-226-74199-0. ᴿFirst Things 78 (1997) 48, 50-52 *(Alison, James)*.

7113 **Williams, James G.** The bible, violence and the sacred: liberation from the myth of sanctioned violence. 1996, ⇒12,6845. ᴿJRHe 36 (1997) 297 *(Liechty, Daniel)*.

### H4.1 Messianismus

7114  *Amir, Yehoshua* Messianism and Zionism. Eschatology in the bible. JSOT.S 243: 1997, ⇒222. ᴱReventlow, H. Graf, 13-30.

7115  *Andersen, Ole* Qumran: die Messiasgestalten. Tod eines Messias. 1996, ⇒286. ᴱKjær-Hansen, K., 46-54.

7116  *Ausín, Santiago* El mesías, don salvífico. ScrTh 29 (1997) 447-472.

7117  ᴱ**Bailão, Marcos Paulo; Borges de Sousa, Ágabo** Messias e messianismo. Estudos Bíblicos 52: Petrópolis 1997, Vozes 102 pp. [NThAR 1997,224].

7118  *Bammel, Ernst* "Verzehrt haben die Israeliten ...". Judaica et Paulina. WUNT 91: 1997, ⇒109. 125-132.

7119  *Becker, Michael* 4Q521 und die Gesalbten. RdQ 18 (1997) 73-96.

7120  *Bornkamm, Günther* Das überlebensgroße Ich: der messianische Typos der alttestamentlichen *Confessio*. Schuld. 1997, ⇒236. ᴱAssmann, J., 102-117.

7121  *Buchholz, René* Erlösung und Destruktion: zur Didaktik des Messianischen bei Gershom Sᴄʜᴏʟᴇᴍ. LebZeug 52 (1997) 183-211.

7122  *Calise, Carol* Die Chabad-Bewegung und ihr Messias. Tod eines Messias. 1996, ⇒286. ᴱKjær-Hansen, K., 102-110.

7123  **Cohn-Sherbok, Dan** The Jewish Messiah. E 1997, Clark xx; 211 pp. Bibl. $25. 0-567-08586-4.

7124  *Collins, John J.* The background of the "Son of God" text. BBR 7 (1997) 51-61 [2 Sam 7; Ps 2; Lk 1,32.35].

7125  **Delgado, Mariano** Die Metamorphosen des Messianismus in den iberischen Kulturen. NZM.S 34: 1994, ⇒11/2,3322. ᴿZMR 81/3 (1997) 244-245 *(Schiffers, Norbert)*.

7126  *Erder, Yoram* The negation of the exile in the messianic doctrine of the Karaite mourners of Zion. HUCA 68 (1997) 109-140.

7127  *Evans, Craig A.* Mishna and Messiah 'in context': some comments on Jacob Nᴇᴜsɴᴇʀ's proposals. Jesus in context. AGAJ 39: 1997 <1993>, ⇒183. 109-143.

7128  *Fruchtenbaum, Arnold* Jüdische Einwände gegen Jesus;

7129  *Glasser, Arthur F.* Judenchristentum im ersten Jahrhundert;

7130  *Goldberg, Louis* Der messianische Gedanke im Judentum. Tod eines Messias. 1996, ⇒286. ᴱKjær-Hansen, K., 132-140/83-91/92-101.

7131  *Hathaway, Jane* The grand vizier and the false messiah: the Sabbatai Sᴇᴠɪ controversy and the Ottoman reform in Egypt. JAOS 117 (1997) 665-671.

7132  *Hendren, Noam* Der Messias Gottes im Tanach, im Alten Testament. Tod eines Messias. 1996, ⇒286. ᴱKjær-Hansen, K., 35-45.

7133  *Hess, Richard S.* The image of the messiah in the Old Testament. Images of Christ. 1997, ⇒256. ᴱPorter, S.E., 22-33.

7134  **Kaiser, Walter C.** The messiah in the Old Testament. 1995, ⇒11/2,3327. BS 154 (1997) 497-498 *(Howard, James M.; Allen, Ronald B.)*.

7135  *Kimelman, Reuven* The Messiah of the Amidah: a study in comparative messianism. JBL 116 (1997) 313-320.

7136  *Kjaer-Hansen, Kai* Gelobt sei der König Messias. Tod eines Messias. 1996, ⇒286. ᴱKjær-Hansen, K., 11-21.

7137 **Levinson, Nathan P.** Il messia nel pensiero ebraico. Pref. *Prato, Gian L.* R 1997, Città Nuova 187 pp. L28.000. 88-311-3501-5 [RdT 38,720].

7138 *Lust, Jan* Septuagint and messianism, with a special emphasis on the pentateuch. Theologische Probleme. 1997, ⇒223. [E]Reventlow, H. Graf, 26-45.

7139 **Marks, Richard G.** The image of Bar Kokhba in traditional Jewish literature. 1993, ⇒10,11355; 11/2,9807. [R]Bibl.Interp. 5/1 (1997) 106-107 *(Davila, James R.).*

7140 *Meyer, Robert* Die eschatologische Wende des politischen Messianismus im Ägypten der Spätzeit: historisch-kritische Bemerkungen zu einer spätägyptischen Prophetie. Saec. 48 (1997) 177-212.

7141 **Oegema, Gerbern S.** Der Gesalbte. 1994, ⇒10,7371... 12,6871. [R]DSD 4 (1997) 364-367 *(Brooke, George J.).*

7142 *Oppenheimer, Aharon* Leadership and messianism in the time of the mishnah. Eschatology in the bible. JSOT.S 243: 1997, ⇒222. [E]Reventlow, H. Graf, 152-168.

7143 *Perlman, Susan* Was die Presse über Rabbi SCHNEERSON geschrieben hat. Tod eines Messias. 1996, ⇒286. [E]Kjær-Hansen, K., 22-34.

7144 *Pinho, Arnaldo de* Messianismos e expectativas de Cristo, hoje. Theologica 32/1 (1997) 49-58.

7145 *Pritz, Ray* Über die Berechnung der Zeit, in der der Messias erscheint. Tod eines Messias. 1996, ⇒286. [E]Kjær-Hansen, K., 121-131.

7146 *Puech, Émile* Messianisme, eschatologie et résurrection dans les manuscrits de la Mer Morte. RdQ 18 (1997) 255-298.

7147 **Ravasi, Gianfranco** L'attesa del Salvatore nell'Antico Testamento. Conversazioni bibliche: Bo 1997, EDB 111 pp. Ciclo di conferenze tenute al Centro culturale S. Fedele di Milano. L18.000. 88-10-70961-6.

7148 **Rose, Wolter H.** Zerubbabel and Zemah: messianic expectations in the early post-exilic period. Diss. Oxford 1997; [D]Williamson, H.G.M. [TynB 49,373ss] [Zech 3,8; 6,9-15].

7149 **Rowland, Christopher** Christian origins. 1985, ⇒2,3148... 11/2,3344. [R]VJTR 61 (1997) 421-422 *(Meagher, P.M.).*

7150 *Rubin, Barry A.* Der Messias—der Erstling von denen, die auferstehen. Tod eines Messias. 1996, ⇒286. [E]Kjær-Hansen, K., 75-82.

7151 *Sadan, Tsvi* Neues Interesse an messianischen Texten. Tod eines Messias. 1996, ⇒286. [E]Kjær-Hansen, K., 111-120.

7152 **Schwartz, Dov** Messianism in medieval Jewish thought. Ramat Gan 1997, Bar-Ilan Univ. Press 292 pp. [AJSR 24,384ss—Berger, David]. H.

7153 *Sedaca, David* Die Wiedergeburt des messianischen Judentums. Tod eines Messias. 1996, ⇒286. [E]Kjær-Hansen, K., 152-161.

7154 *Seim, Jürgen* Jesus der Messias: Christologie im jüdisch-christlichen Gespräch. RKZ 138 (1997) 505-513.

7155 *Skjott, Bodil F.* Messiasgläubige in Israel und ihr Messias;

7156 *Telchin, Stan* Mein Weg zum Messias. Tod eines Messias. 1996, ⇒286. [E]Kjær-Hansen, K., 162-171/182-190.

7157 *Wimmer, Joseph E.* Isaiah's messianism. BiTod 35 (1997) 216-221.

7158 **Zimmermann, Johannes** Messianische Vorstellungen in den Schriftfunden von Qumran. Diss. Tübingen 1997; [D]Hengel, M. [RTL 29,589].

H4.3 *Eschatologia VT*—OT hope of future life

7159 EBremer, J.M., (al.), Hidden futures: death and immortality in ancient Egypt, Anatolia, the classical, biblical and Arabic-Islamic world. 1994, ⇒11/2,552; 12,6879. RBiOr 54 (1997) 311-315 *(Tobin, Vincent Arieh)*.

7160 *Cimosa, Mario* Il giorno del Signore e l'escatologia nell'Antico Testamento. DSBP 16 (1997) 20-61.

7161 ECoward, Harold Life after death in world religions. Faith meets faith: Maryknoll, NY 1997, Orbis vii; 131 pp. $15. 1-57075-119-6 [ThD 44,369—Heiser, W. Charles].

7162 Lane, Dermot A. Keeping hope alive: stirrings in christian theology. 1996, ⇒12,6882. RDoLi 47/1 (1997) 28-34 *(Mills, John Orme)*.

7163 *Michel, Diethelm* Ich aber bin immer bei dir: von der Unsterblichkeit der Gottesbeziehung. Studien zur Überlieferungsgeschichte. TB 93: 1997 <1987>, ⇒149. 155-179 [Ps 73; 142; Isa 26,19; 2 Macc 7,13].

7164 *Rebić, Adalbert* Nada u Starome Zavjetu [Die Hoffnung im Alten Testament]. 1997, ⇒96. FTomic C. Zsfg. 78. 71-78. **Croatian.**
EReventlow, H. Eschatology in the Bible ⇒222.

7165 Tornos, Andrés Esperança e o além na Bíblia. TOrth, Lúcia M.E. O Mundo da Bíblia: Petrópolis 1995, Vozes 158 pp. TPerTeol 29 (1997) 112-115 & REB 57 (1997) 987-990 *(Libânio, J.B.)*.

7166 *Uffenheimer, Benjamin* From prophetic to apocalyptic eschatology;
7167 *Weinfeld, Moshe* Expectations of the divine kingdom in biblical and postbiblical literature. Eschatology in the bible. JSOT.S 243: 1997, ⇒222. EReventlow, H. Graf, 200-217/218-232.

H4.5 *Theologia totius VT*—General Old Testament theology

7168 *Brettler, Marc Zvi* Biblical history and Jewish biblical theology. JR 77 (1997) 563-583.

7169 *Brooke, George J.* The Qumran Scrolls and Old Testament theology. 1997, ⇒48. FKnierim R., 59-75.

7170 Brueggemann, Walter Theology of the Old Testament: testimony, dispute, advocacy. Mp 1997, Fortress 777 pp. Bibl. $48. 0-8006-3087-4 [BiTod 36,128—Bergant, Dianne].

7171 *Dinter, Paul E.* The once and future text. 1997, ⇒77. FSanders J., 375-392.

7172 Gunneweg, Antonius H.J. Biblische Theologie des Alten Testaments. 1993, ⇒9,7650*... 12,6885. RJBL 115 (1996) 327-329 *(Diamond, A.R. Pete)*.

7173 *Holman, Jan* La théologie de l'Ancien Testament de Gerhard von RAD: d'où vient un tel succès?. SémBib 87 (1997) 31-47.

7174 *Hossfeld, Frank-Lothar* Schwerpunkte der Theologie. Lebendige Welt. 1997, ⇒565. EZenger, E., 152-175.

7175 JBTh 10 (1995). RBiKi 52/3 (1997) 144-146 *(Stendebach, Franz Josef)*.

7176 *Kalimi, Isaac* History of Israelite religion or Old Testament theology?: Jewish interest in biblical theology. SJOT 11 (1997) 100-123.

7177 **Knierim, Rolf** The task of Old Testament theology. 1995, ⇒11/2,3381; 12,6891. ᴿNRTh 119 (1997) 110-112 *(Ska, J.L.)*; ThLZ 122 (1997) 132-134 *(Reventlow, Henning Graf)*; ScrB 27 (1997) 33-35 *(Mills, Mary E.)*; Anton. 72/1 (1997) 133-135 *(Nobile, Marco)*; RStT 16/1 (1997) 101-103 *(Lee, Bernon)*; JThS 48 (1997) 567-568 *(Clements, R.E.)*.

7178 *Knierim, Rolf P.* On the task of Old Testament theology. JSOT.S 240: 1997, ⇒20. ᶠCoᴀᴛs G., 153-166.

7179 *Lemcio, Eugene E.* Kerygmatic centrality and unity in the First Testament?. 1997, ⇒77. ᶠSᴀɴᴅᴇʀs J., 357-373.

7180 **Lohfink, Norbert** Studien zur biblischen Theologie. SBAB 16: 1993, ⇒9,212; 11/2,3383. ᴿJThS 48 (1997) 139-141 *(Schaper, Joachim)*; FZPhTh 44/1-2 (1997) 195-196 *(Schenker, Adrian)*; EstB 55 (1997) 406-407 *(González García, F.)*.

7181 **Martens, Elmer A.** Old Testament Theology. IBR Bibliographies 13: GR 1997, Baker 139 pp. $12. 0-8010-2146-4 BoL (1998) 6— Grabbe, Lester L.].

7182 **Michel, Diethelm** Einheit in der Vielheit des Alten Testaments. Studien zur Überlieferungsgeschichte. TB 93: 1997 <1993>, ⇒149. 53-68.

7183 ᴱ**Ollenburger, B.C.**, *(al.)*, The flowering of Old Testament theology. 1992, ⇒8,363; 11/2,3388. ᴿThRev 18 (1997) 75-76 *(Derksen, John)*.

7184 *Pannenberg, Wolfhart* Problems in a theology of (only) the Old Testament. 1997, ⇒48. ᶠKɴɪᴇʀɪᴍ R., 275-280.

7185 **Preuss, Horst Dietrich** Old Testament theology, 1. ᵀ*Perdue, Leo G.*: 1995, ⇒11/2,3390. ᴿJThS 48 (1997) 141-143 *(Davidson, R.)*; TS 58 (1997) 150-153 *(Wimmer, Joseph F.)*;

7186 Old Testament theology, 2. ᵀ*Perdue, Leo G.*: 1996, ⇒12,6894. ᴿTheology 100 (1997) 293 *(Coggins, Richard)*; HebStud 38 (1997) 103-105 *(Gillingham, Susan)*.

7187 *Rendtorff, Rolf* Approaches to Old Testament theology. 1997, ⇒48. ᶠKɴɪᴇʀɪᴍ R., 13-26.

7188 *Rofé, Alexander* The historical significance of secondary readings. 1997, ⇒77. ᶠSᴀɴᴅᴇʀs J., 393-402.

7189 **Schmidt, Werner H.** Psalmen und Weisheit: theologische Anthropologie und Jeremia: Theologie des Alten Testaments. Vielfalt und Einheit alttestamentlichen Glaubens, 2. 1995. ᴿThLZ 122 (1997) 229-230 *(Wagner, Siegfried)*.

7190 **Schmitt, Armin** Wende des Lebens: Untersuchungen zu einem Situations-Motiv der Bibel. BZAW 237: 1996, ⇒12,6899. ᴿVT 47 (1997) 400-402 *(Schunck, K.-D.)*; ThLZ 122 (1997) 661-663 *(Hermann, Wolfram)*; RSR 85 (1997) 433-434 *(Gibert, Pierre)*.

7191 **Schroven, Brigitte** Theologie des Alten Testaments zwischen Anpassung und Widerspruch. 1996, ⇒12,6901. ᴿThR 62 (1997) 461-462 *(Smend, Rudolf)*.

7192 *Sweeney, Marvin A.* Tanak versus Old Testament: concerning the foundation for a Jewish theology of the bible. 1997, ⇒48. ᶠKɴɪᴇʀɪᴍ R., 353-372.

7193 **Van Leeuwen, J.H.** En Ik zal uw God zijn: wegwijzer in het Oude Testament. Schrift en Liturgie 20: Bonheiden 1995, Abdij Bethlehem 159 pp. FB410/f25. 90-71837-50-5. ᴿBijdr. 58 (1997) 455 *(Schrama, Martijn)*.

7194  **Vasholz, Robert I.** Pillars of the kingdom: five features of the kingdom of God progressively revealed in the Old Testament. Lanham 1997, University Press of America ix; 238 pp. 0-7618-0918-X.

7195  ᴱ**Zuck, Roy B.** A biblical theology of the Old Testament. Chicago 1997, Moody 446 pp. 0-8042-0738-2 [NThAR 2000,62].

### н5.1  *Deus—NT—God* [as Father н1.4]

7196  *Bernabé Ubieta, Carmen* Del dios desconocido al Dios universal: la ciudad, los extranjeros y los inicios del cristianismo. La Bíblia i el Mediterrani. 1997, ⇒385. ᴱBorrell, d'Agustí, 279-289.

7197  *Cummings, Brian* Justifying God in Tᴜɴᴅᴀʟᴇ's English. Reformation 2 (1997) 143-171.

7198  **Duquesne, Jacques** Le Dieu de Jésus. P 1997, Grasset 237 pp. FF98. 2-246-44911-1. ᴿTelema 23/4 (1997) 80-82 *(Delhez, Charles).*

7199  *Gunton, Colin E.* The God of Jesus Christ. ThTo 54 (1997) 325-334.

7200  **Placher, William C.** Narratives of a vulnerable God: Christ, theology, scripture. 1994, ⇒10,7036... 12,6694. ᴿThom. 61/2 (1997) 328-331 *(Martin, Francis).*

7201  **Schlosser, Jacques** El Dios de Jesús: estudio exegético. 1995, ⇒11/2,3418; 12,6907. ᴿRF 181 (1997) 322-323 *(Tamayo-Acosta, Juan José).*

7202  **Viau, Marcel** Le Dieu du Verbe. Théologies: P 1997, Cerf 256 pp. 2-204-05875-0.

### н5.2  **Christologia ipsius NT**

7203  *Amaladoss, Michael* Cristología y misión. ᵀ*Alarcia, Juan José*: MisEx(M) 161 (1997) 451-460.

7204  *Barrett, Charles Kingsley* Christocentricity at Antioch. BZNW 86: 1997, ⇒41. ꜰHoꜰɪᴜs O., 323-339.

7205  *Binz, Stephen J.* 1997: a year for biblical renewal. BiTod 35 (1997) 45-48.

7206  **Brown, Raymond Edward** Introduzione alla cristologia del Nuovo Testamento. BiBi(B) 19: 1995, ⇒11/2,3433. ᴿStPat 44/1 (1997) 188-191 *(De Marchi, Sergio)*;

7207  *Jesús en el Nou Testament: introducció a la cristologia bíblica.* ᵀ*Serra, Joan Manuel*: Paràbola 8: Barc 1997, Claret 253 pp. Ptas2.350. 84-8297-098-4. ᴿRCatT 22 (1997) 221-223 *(Serra i Oller, Joan Manuel).* () () () () () () () ()

7208  *Bueno de la Fuente, Eloy* Dimensión misionera de la cristología. MisEx(M) 161 (1997) 442-450.

7209  *Combes, Isobel H.* Nursing mother, ancient shepherd, athletic coach?: some images of Christ in the early church. Images of Christ. 1997, ⇒256. ᴱPorter, S.E., 113-125.

7210  **Cook, Michael L.** Christology as narrative quest. ColMn 1997, Liturgical 219 pp. $22. 0-8146-5854-7 [ThD 44,357—Heiser, W.].

7211  **Cullmann, Oscar** Cristología del Nuevo Testamento. ᵀ*Gattinoni, Carlos T.; Pikaza, Xabier*: Biblioteca de estudios bíblicos 63: S

1997, Sígueme 456 pp. Ptas3.300. 84-301-1315-0 [ActBib 71,24—Boada, J.].

7212 **Davis, Carl J.** The name and way of the Lord... NT christology. JSNT.S 129: 1996, ⇒12,6915. ᴿCBQ 59 (1997) 766-768 *(Ascough, Richard S.)*; CritRR 10 (1997) 146-148 *(Fisk, Bruce N.)*.

7213 *Evans, Craig A.* Images of Christ in the canonical and apocryphal gospels. Images of Christ. 1997, ⇒256. ᴱPorter, S.E., 34-72.

7214 *Ferrer Mayer, Víctor* Imágenes de Jesucristo en los evangelios: Jesucristo salvador y evangelizador. RTLi 31 (1997) 255-286.

7215 *Fisichella, Rino* El rostro de Cristo. Communio 19/2 (1997) 84-92.

7216 **Fitzmyer, J.A.** Catecismo cristológico, respuesta del Nuevo Testamento. Nueva Alianza 146: S 1997, Sígueme 173 pp. [RevAg 40,381s—Rodríguez, Vicente].

7217 *Gronchi, Maurizio* 'Per Cristo nostro Signore': il mediatore e il sacerdote. RPLi 201 (1997) 10-17.

7218 *Gubler, Marie-Louise* Der du die Zeit in Händen hast... StAns 124: 1997, ⇒57. ᶠLOEHRER M. — TRAGAN P., 127-155.

7219 **Gunton, Colin E.** Yesterday and today: a study of continuities in christology. L 1997, SPCK viii; 248 pp. £13. 0-281-05083-X [RRT 1998/1,90].

7220 **Hengel, Martin** Studies in early christology. 1995, ⇒11/2,268(!); 12,127. ᴿCart. 13 (1997) 219-220 *(Sanz Valdivieso, R.)*; SEÁ 62 (1997) 173-175 *(Hartman, Lars)*.

7221 *Herman, Zvonimir Izidor* Inkulturacija ranokrscanske kerigme. BoSm 67 (1997) 43-55. **Croatian.**

7222 *Hoffmeier, James K.* Son of God: from Pharaoh to Israel's kings to Jesus. BiRe 13/3 (1997) 44-49, 54.

7223 **Iammarrone, Giovanni** Gesù di Nazaret messia del regno e figlio di Dio: lineamenti di cristologia. 1996, ⇒12,6921. ᴿCivCatt 148 II (1997) 198-200 *(Ferraro, G.)*.

7224 *Lacey, D.R. de* Jesus as mediator. NT Backgrounds. 1997 <1987>, ⇒3975. ᴱEvans, C.A., 169-189.

7225 ᴱ**Laufen, Rudolf** Gottes ewiger Sohn: die Präexistenz Christi. Pd 1997, Schöningh 301 pp. 3-506-75118-2.

7226 **Maloney, George A.** L'incredibile misericordia: Gesù rivela l'amore del Padre. R 1992, Città Nuova. ᴿAnime e Corpi 192 (1997) 585-586 *(Casera, Antonio)*.

7227 **Manns, Frédéric** Mais pour vous, qui suis-je?: éléments de christologie. Vivre la Parole: P 1997, Médiaspaul 206 pp. F120 [EeV 107/10 (1997) 79].

7228 *Marchesi, Giovanni* Il volto di Gesù nel Nuovo Testamento. CivCatt 148 IV (1997) 553-566.

7229 *Martin, Frère* Le Christ come prêtre selon saint Paul et saint Jean. Aletheia 11 (1997) 75-88 [ZID 23,307].

7230 *Nouailhat, René* La genèse du christianisme: de Jérusalem à Chalcédoine. Histoire des Religions: P 1997, Cerf 334 pp. 2-204-05684-7.

7231 **O'Collins, Gerald** Christology. 1995, ⇒11/2,3545; 12,6929. ᴿAThR 79/1 (1997) 73-75 *(Hefling, Charles)*; CBQ 59 (1997) 168-169 *(Montague, George T.)*; BBR 7 (1997) 255-258 *(Snodgrass, Klyne R.)*; EE 72 (1997) 551-552 *(Gesteira, Manuel)*;

7232 Cristologia: uno studio biblico, storico e sistematico su Gesù Cristo. BTCon 90: Brescia 1997, Queriniana 333 pp. L50.000 [RdT 38,143].

7233  *O'Collins, Gerald* Images of Jesus: reappropriating titular christology. Sum. 303. Bellarmine Lecture, Saint Louis University 1997.
ThD 44 (1997) 303-318.

7234  [E]**Ohlig, Karl-Heinz** Christologie, 1: des origines à l'antiquité tardive. 1996, ⇒12,6931. [R]Telema 23/1-2 (1997) 87-92 *(Ntima,
Kanza)*.

7235  **Pastore, Corrado; Wyssenbach, Jean-Pierre** Cristo en el Nuevo
Testamento. Caracas 1997, Iter 32 pp.

7236  **Penna, Romano** I ritratti originali di Gesù il Cristo. 1996,
⇒12,6932. [R]PaVi 42/3 (1997) 59-60 *(Migliasso, Secondo)*; StPat
44/3 (1997) 203-204 *(Segalla, Giuseppe)*.

7237  *Pilgaard, Aage* The Hellenistic *theios aner*—a model for early christian christology?. NT and Hellenistic Judaism. 1997, ⇒318.
[E]Borgen, P., 101-122.

7238  *Pokorný, Petr* Christologie et baptême à l'époque du christianisme
primitif. Bibelauslegung. WUNT 100: 1997 <1981>, ⇒970. 223-
235.

7239  **Ravasi, Gianfranco** La manifestazione di Gesù Cristo nel Nuovo
Testamento. Conversazioni bibliche: Bo 1997, EDB 148 pp. Ciclo
di conferenze tenute al Centro culturale S. Fedele di Milano.
L19.000. 88-10-70962-4.

7240  **Riley, Gregory John** One Jesus, many Christs: how Jesus inspired
not one true christianity, but many: the truth about christian origins. SF 1997, Harper San Francisco (8) 228 pp. $22. 0-06-
066799-0.

7241  **Schlatter, Adolf von** The history of the Christ: the foundation for
New Testament theology. [T]*Köstenberger, Andreas J.*: GR 1997,
Baker 426 pp. 0-8010-2089-1.

7242  **Schnackenburg, Rudolf** Die Person Jesu Christi im Spiegel der
vier Evangelien. 1993, ⇒9,7600... 12,6935. [R]CoTh 67/2 (1997)
232-239 *(Załęski, Jan)*;

7243  Jesus in the gospels: a biblical christology. 1995, ⇒11/2,3447.
[R]VJTR 61 (1997) 564-565 *(Meagher, P.M.)*; JBL 116 (1997) 559-
560 *(Stanton, Graham)*; CBQ 58 (1996) 773-4 *(Matera, Frank J.)*.

7244  *Scriba, Albrecht* Religionsgeschichte des Urchristentums. TRE 28.
1997, ⇒420. 604-618.

7245  **Sesboüé, Bernard** Cristologia fondamentale. Theologica: CasM
1997, Piemme 207 pp. 88-384-2787-9.

7246  *Van Wyk, D.J.* Die oorspronge van die belydenis 'Jesus is God' in
die vroegste Christendom: 'n odersoek na metodes en kriteria. HTS
53 (1997) 722-750 [ZID 24,127].

7247  *Walker, William O. Kyrios* and *epistates* as translations of
rabbi/rabbouni. JHiC 4/1 (1997) 56-77.

7248  *Walter, Nikolaus* Geschichte und Mythos in der urchristlichen Prä-
existenzchristologie. Praeparatio evangelica. WUNT 98: 1997
<1988>, ⇒167. 281-292 [Phil 2,6-11; Col 1,15-20].

7249  *Wiederkehr, Dietrich* Parallelen mit Querverbindungen: Wechsel-
wirkungen zwischen Christologie und Eschatologie. StAns 124:
1997, ⇒57. [F]LOEHRER M. — TRAGAN P., 111-126.

7250  *Wilckens, Ulrich* Monotheïsmus und Christologie. JBTh 12 (1997)
87-97.

## H5.3 *Christologia praemoderna*—**Patristic to Reformation**

7251 **Benericetti, Ruggero** Il Cristo nei sermoni di S. Pier CRISOLO-GO. StRav 6: 1995, ⇒12,6941. RChH 66/2 (1997) 316-318 *(Hester, David Paul)*.

7252 *Biffi, Card.* Giacomo L'unico salvatore nella riflessione di sant' AMBROGIO. Ambrosius 73/2 (1997) 106-122.

7253 *Bonato, Antonio* La figura di Cristo in sant'AMBROGIO. Sum. 289. Teol(M) 22 (1997) 244-290.

7254 **Boulnois, Marie-Odile** Le paradoxe trinitaire chez CYRILLE d'Alexandrie: herméneutique, analyses philosophiques et argumentation théologique. EAug, Antiquité 143: 1994, ⇒10,7559; 12,7059. RJThS 48 (1997) 287-290 *(Wickham, L.R.)*.

7255 TCongourdeau, M.-H. MAXIME le Confesseur: l'agonie du Christ. CPF 64: 1996, ⇒12,6942. RETR 72 (1997) 474-475 *(Pérès, Jacques-Noël)*; RHPhR 77 (1997) 350-352 *(Larchet, J.-C.)*.

7256 *Downey, Deane E.D.* Images of Christ in corpus Christi medieval mystery play cycles. Images of Christ. 1997, ⇒256. EPorter, S.E., 206-226.

7257 *Feiss, Hugh Bernard* The christology of Gerhard GROTE's *Getijdenboek*. ABenR 48/2 (1997) 161-185.

7258 *Foley, Desmond* The christology of AMBROSIASTER, I-II. MillSt 39-40 (1997) 27-47, 31-52.

7259 **Grillmeier, Alois** Jesus der Christus im Glauben der Kirche 2/4: die Kirche von Alexandrien mit Nubien und Äthiopien nach 451. 1990, ⇒6,7463*. RThPQ 145/1 (1997) 78-79 *(Schulte, Raphael)*;

7260 Cristo en la tradición cristiana: desde el tiempo apostólico hasta el Concilio de Calcedonia (451). TOlasagasti Gaztelumendi, M.: Velm 143: S 1997, Sígueme 930 pp. 84-301-1327-4 [EstAg 33,402—Sala, R.].

7261 Fragmente zur Christologie: Studien zum altkirchlichen Christusbild. EHainthaler, Theresia: FrB 1997, Herder 484 pp. DM98. 3-451-26411-0 [OrdKor 38,512].

7262 Christ in christian tradition 2/2: the church of Constantinople in the sixth century. 1995, ⇒11/2,3464; 12,6945. RJThS 48 (1997) 290-294 *(Louth, Andrew)*;

7263 Christ in Christian tradition 2/4: the church of Alexandria with Nubia and Ethiopia after 451. TDean, O.C.: 1996, ⇒12,6946. RJThS 48 (1997) 290-294 *(Louth, Andrew)*; SVTQ 41/1 (1997) 81-84 *(Bouteneff, Peter)*;

7264 Le Christ dans la tradition chrétienne 2/4: l'église d'Alexandrie, la Nubie et l'Ethiopie après 451. CFi 192: 1996, ⇒12,6947. RLe Monde Copte 27-28 (1997) 236-242 *(Cannuyer, Christian)*.

7265 *Hallman, Joseph M.* The seed of fire: divine suffering in the christology of CYRIL of Alexandria and NESTORIUS of Constantinople. JEarlyC 5 (1997) 369-391.

7266 *Henne, Philippe* Pour JUSTIN, Jésus est-il un autre Dieu?. RSPhTh 81 (1997) 57-68.

7267 **Iammarrone, Giovanni** La cristologia francescana: impulsi per il presente. Studi Francescani 1: Padova 1997, Messagero 368 pp. L30.000. 88-250-0557-1. RSanto 37/1 (1997) 200-202 *(Santolin, Federico)*; CFr 67 (1997) 592-596 *(Armellada, Bernardino de)*.

7268 *Kannengiesser, Charles* The bible in the Arian crisis. The Bible in Greek christian antiquity. 1997 <c.1984>, ⇒177. ETBlowers, P.M., 217-228.

7269 **Martínez Fraseda, Francisco** La gracia y la ciencia de Jesucristo: historia de la cuestión en ALEJANDRO de Hales, ODON Rigaldo, Summa Halensis y BUENAVENTURA. Publicaciones Instituto Teológico Franciscano, Ser. Mayor 23: Murcia 1997, Espigas 340 pp. RRCatT 22 (1997) 220-221 *(Castanyé, Josep).*

7270 **Meunier, Bernard** Le Christ de CYRILLE d'Alexandrie: l'humanité, le salut et la question monophysite. Diss. École pratique 1993; ThH 104: P 1997, Beauchesne 304 pp. FF270 [Vie Spirituelle 724,591—Dalmais, I.-H.].

7271 *Moingt, Joseph* La cristología de la iglesia primitiva: el precio de una mediación cultural. Conc(E) 269 (1997) 87-95 (P77-85); (F269,75-83); (I33/1,92-102).

7272 *Paciorek, Antoni* Tajemnica Chrystusa w egzegezie św. CYRYLA z Aleksandrii [Mystery of Christ in the exegesis of St. Cyril of Alexandria]. 1997, ⇒52. FŁACH J., 287-302. P.

7273 **Pons, Guillermo** Jesucristo en los Padres de la iglesia. Textos Patristicos: M 1997, Ciudad Nueva 251 pp. Ptas2.400. 84-89651-20-5. RRelCult 43 (1997) 961-967 *(Langa, Pedro).*

7274 **Rey Escapa, Jaime** La libertad de Cristo según el beato Juan DUNS ESCOTO. 1996, ⇒12,6956. RCFr 67/1-2 (1997) 314-315 *(Armellada, Bernardino de).*

7275 *Thümmel, Hans Georg* Logos und Hypostasis;
7276 *Wirsching, Johannes* Menschwerdung: von der wahren Gestalt des Göttlichen. BZNW 85: 1997, ⇒105. FWICKERT U., 347-398/399-441.

### H5.4 *(Commentationes de) Christologia* **moderna**

7277 *Amato, Angelo* La riscoperta di Cristo salvatore ed evangelizzatore. Orientamenti Pastorali 45/1 (1997) 30-35.

7278 EAscione, A.; **Giustiniani, P.** Il Cristo: nuovo criterio in filosofia e teologia?. N 1995, D'Auria 258 pp. Postfazio Andrea Milano. RFilTeo 11 (1997) 413-414 *(Festa, Francesco S.).*

7279 *Barreda, Jesús-Ángel* Jesús, el Santo de Dios, revelador y evangelizador. Studium 37/2 (1997) 205-234.

7280 **Barth, Ulrich** Die Christologie Emanuel HIRSCHS. 1992, ⇒9,7639*. RZKG 108/1 (1997) 117-119 *(Korsch, Dietrich).*

7281 *Brambilla, Franco Giulio* Dire Gesù oggi. Ambrosius 73/1 (1997) 3-27.

7282 **Brennan, John P.** Christ, the one sent. ColMn 1997, Liturgical 191 pp. $16. 0-8146-2445-6 [ThD 45,163—Heiser, W. Charles].

7283 *Brüske, Martin* Christologie und Schriftauslegung: Anmerkungen zu GUARDINIS "Der Herr" anläßlich seines Erscheinens vor 60 Jahren. IKaZ 26 (1997) 155-162.

7284 **Bueno, Eloy** Los rostros de Cristo. M 1997, BAC 154 pp. [StLeg 39,325s—Trobajo, Antonio].

7285 *Butler, Sara* Contemporary christology: getting one's bearings. ChiSt 36/2 (1997) 159-171.

7286 *Carruth, Shawn* Christ as wisdom: imagination for a renewed world. BiTod 35 (1997) 153-157.

7287 *Casciaro, José María* La autodonación de Dios en Cristo. ScrTh 29 (1997) 473-492.

7288 *Castro C., Javier Alonso* El absoluto moral en la reflexión cristológica de Jon SOBRINO. ThX 47/1 (1997) 55-64.

7289 *Chapman, G. Clarke* JUNG and christology. Sum. 414. Psychology & Theology 25 (1997) 414-426.

7290 **Claussen, Johann Hinrich** Die Jesus-Deutung von Ernst TROELTSCH im Kontext der liberalen Theologie. BHTh 99: Tü 1997, Mohr xi; 324 pp. DM148. 3-16-146744-2 [JThS 51,389ss— Chapman, Mark D.].

7291 Commissione theologica internazionale. Cristo, verbo del Padre. 1996, ⇒12,6973. ᴿOrientamenti Pastorali 45/1 (1997) 30-35 *(Amato, Angelo)*.

7292 *Cote, Richard G.* Cristología e imaginación pascual. Conc(E) 269 (1997) 109-118 (F97-105); (P99-108); (I33/1,117-128).

7293 *Coutinho, Jorge O* 'processo de Cristo' nos últimos sécolos. Theologica 32/1 (1997) 35-48.

7294 **Cowdell, Scott** Is Jesus unique?: a study of recent christology. 1996, ⇒12,6974. ᴿRRT (1997/1) 96-97 *(Jones, Gareth)*.

7295 **D'hert, Ignace** Een spoor voor ons getrokken: de Jezustrilogie van Edward SCHILLEBEECKX. Baarn 1997, Nelissen 95 pp. ƒ19.50. 90-244-1540-3 [Bijdr. 58,357].

7296 **Danz, Christian** Die philosophische Christologie F.W.J. SCHELLINGS. 1996, ⇒12,6976. ᴿArPh 60/1 (1997) 155-58 *(Tilliette, X.)*.

7297 **Dupuis, Jacques** Who do you say I am?: introduction to christology. 1993, ⇒10,7478; 11/2,3504. ᴿTJT 13/1 (1997) 145-146 *(Raab, Joseph Quinn)*.

7298 *Fédou, Michel* La teología de las religiones: a los diez años de A-sís. ᵀ*De Balle, Teodoro*: SelTeol 36 (1997) 349-354.

7299 **Ferraro, B.** Cristologia em tempos de ídolos e sacrifícios. São Paulo 1993, Paulinas 112 pp. 85-05-01477-4. ᴿPerTeol 29 (1997) 124-126 *(Motta A. de Lacerda, Rosa Emília)*.

7300 **Fraijó, M.** El cristianismo: una aproximación. M 1997, Trotta 132 pp. Ptas1.500 [Proyección 45,73].

7301 **Frosini, G.** Chi dite che io sia?: una cristologia per tutti. Bo 1997, EDB 188 pp. L22.000 [RivBib 45,255].

7302 **Gabus, Jean-Paul** La nouveauté de Jésus Christ, témoin de Dieu pour le monde. 1996, ⇒12,6984. ᴿRHPhR 77/1 (1997) 92-93 *(Siegwalt, G.)*.

7303 *Gisel, Pierre* Los límites de la cristología o la tentación de absolutizar. Conc(E) 269 (1997) 97-108 (P86-98); (I33/1,103-116); (F269,85-96).

7304 *Gispert-Sauch, G.* Notes for an Indian christology. VJTR 61 (1997) 757-764.

7305 **Hackmann, Geraldo Luiz Borges** Jesus Cristo nosso redentor: iniciação à cristologia como soteriologia. Teologia: Porto Alegre 1997, EDIPUCRS 216 pp. [Theologica 32/1,185].

7306 **Honoré, Jean** La pensée christologique de NEWMAN. CJJC 68: 1996, ⇒12,6993. ᴿRThom 97 (1997) 610-611 *(Bavaud, Georges)*.

7307 **Hünermann, Peter** Cristología. ᵀ*Gancho, C.; Villanueva, M.*: Barc 1997, Herder 496 pp. Pts4.300. 84-254-1955-7 [Proyección 44,335].

7308   **Johnson, Elizabeth; Rakoczy, Susan** Who do you say that I am?: introducing contemporary christology. Pietermaritzburg 1997, Cluster 92 pp. [NZM 54,238—Peter, Anton].

7309   **Kay, James F.** Christus praesens: a reconsideration of Rudolf BULTMANN's christology. 1994, ⇒11/2,3525; 12,7000. RJThS 48 (1997) 342-344 *(Jones, Gareth)*.

7310   **Knitter, Paul** The uniqueness of Jesus: a dialogue with Paul KNITTER. ESwidler, Leonard; Mojzes, Paul: Maryknoll 1997, Orbis 189 pp. £13. [Theol. 101,208s—Race, Alan];

7311   Jesus and the other names: christian mission and global responsibility. 1996, ⇒12,7002. RDoLi 47 (1997) 509-510 *(May, John D'Arcy)*; Horizons 24/2 (1997): 267-274 *(Haight, Roger)*; 275-277 *(Ruether, Rosemary Radford)*; 277-280 *(Clooney, Francis X.)*; 280-283 *(Keller, Catherine)*; 283-285 *(Baum, Gregory)*; 283-296 *(Knitter, Paul F.)*.

7312   **Kuschel, Karl-Josef** Born before all time: the dispute over Christ's origin. 1992, ⇒8,7532... 12,6925. RTJT 13/1 (1997) 147-149 *(Donovan, Daniel)*;

7313   Generato prima di tutti i secoli?: la controversia sull'origine di Cristo. ⇒12,7004. RStPat 44/3 (1997) 176-181 *(De Marchi, Sergio)*; CivCatt 148 III (1997) 338-341 *(Ferraro, G.)*.

7314   *Lippi, Adolfo* Gesù di Nazareth, figlio di Davide, figlio di Dio: semplici riflessioni sulla cristologia. Sum. 323. La Sapienza della Croce 12/4 (1997) 323-338.

7315   **Marchesi, Giovanni** La cristologia trinitaria di Hans Urs VON BALTHASAR: Gesù Cristo pienezza della revelazione e della salvezza. BTCon 94: Queriniana 1997, Brescia 666 pp. L80.000. 88-399-0394-1. RFKTh 13 (1997) 316-317 *(Lochbrunner, Manfred)*.

7316   *Marie Jérôme, Frère* Un problème fondamental de christologie: la foi déforme-t-elle la réalité de Jésus?. Aletheia 11 (1997) 141-152 [ZID 23,307].

7317   *McDermott, John M.* Jesus: parable or sacrament of God?: an ecumenical discussion on analogy and freedom with E. SCHWEIZER, K. BARTH, and R. BULTMANN. Rés. 499. Gr. 78 (1997) 477-499.

7318   **Menacherry, Cheriyan** Christ: the mystery in history: a critical study on the christology of Raymond PANIKKAR. THEION 5: 1996, ⇒12,7013. RVSVD 38/1-2 (1997) 205-208 *(Mantovani, Ennio)*; ThLZ 122/10 (1997) 953-954 *(Pöhlmann, Horst Georg)*.

7319   **Moingt, Joseph** El hombre que venía de Dios. 1995, ⇒11/2,3536. RAtualidade Teológica 1/1 (1997) 100-102 *(Lucchetti Bingemer, Maria Clara)*.

7320   **Moltmann, Jürgen** Jésus, le messie de Dieu. CFi 171: 1993, ⇒9,7683; 11/2,3539. RScEs 49/2 (1997) 246-247 *(Petit, Jean-Claude)*;

7321   Cristo para nosotros hoy. M 1997, Trotta 123 pp. [ThX 48,362ss—Gutiérrez Jaramillo, Mario].

7322   **Murphy, Francesca Aran** Christ the form of beauty. 1995, ⇒11/2,3542. RNBl 78 (1997) 250-252 *(Loughlin, Gerard)*; Teol. 34/1 (1997) 412-414 *(Wood, Ralph C.)*.

7323   *Müller, Gerhard Ludwig* Confesar a Jesucristo como único mediador de la salvación en el contexto de una cultura pluralista. Communio 19/2 (1997) 93-107.

7324 **Neuenschwander, Ulrich** Christologie—verantwortet vor den Fragen der Moderne: mit Beiträgen zu Person und Werk Albert SCHWEITZERS. [E]*Zagen, Werner*: Albert Schweitzer Studien 5: Bern 1997, Haupt 343 pp. DM33. 3-258-05593-9 [RHPhR 78,97— Kaempf, B.].

7325 **Nicolosi, Carmelo** Gesù Cristo unico salvatore del mondo ieri, oggi e sempre: catechesi cristologica. Città del Vaticano 1997, LEV 280 pp. [R]SapDom. 50 (1997) 345-6 *(Sorrentino, Domenico)*.

7326 **Ntima, Kanza** Non: je ne mourrai pas, je vivrai: méditation sur le cheminement christologique en Afrique. Kinshasa 1996, Loyola 190 pp. [R]Telema 23/1-2 (1997) 79 *(Ciervide, Joaquin)*.

7327 *Nyamiti, Charles* Cristologías africanas actuales. [T]*Dávila, Ricardo*: MisEx(M) 161 (1997) 475-498.

7328 *O'Collins, Gerald* Images of Jesus and modern theology. Images of Christ. 1997, ⇒256. [E]Porter, S.E., 128-143.

7329 [E]**Ohlig, Karl-Heinz** Christologie, 2: du moyen âge à l'époque contemporaine. 1996, ⇒12,7018. [R]Telema 23/1-2 (1997) 87-92 *(Ntima, Kanza)*.

7330 **Pagazzi, Giovanni Cesare** La singolarità di Gesù come criterio di unità e differenza nella chiesa. Diss. Romana 16: R 1997, Pontificio Seminario Lombardo x; 222 pp. L32.000. 88-399-0394-1 [Sal. 59,599].

7331 *Parappally, Jacob* One Jesus—many christologies. VJTR 61 (1997) 708-718.

7332 **Pavlidou, E.** Cristologia e pneumatologia tra Occidente cattolico e Oriente ortodosso neo-greco: per una lettura integrata di W. KASPER e J. ZIZIOULAS in prospettiva ecumenica. Contributi teologici: R 1997, Dehoniane 191 pp. Bibl. 88-396-0692-0. [R]RSEc 15 (1997) 264-266 *(Morandini, Simone)*.

7333 **Pavlou, Teleosphora** Saggio di cristologia neo-ortodossa. R 1995, Ed. Pont. Univ. Gregoriana xvi; 250 pp. L40.000/EUR20,65. 88-7652-684-6. [R]OCP 63/1 (1997) 266-267 *(Farrugia, E.G.)*.

7334 **Peelman, Achiel** Christ is a native American. 1995, ⇒12,7023. [R]Pro Dialogo 95/2 (1997) 264-265 *(Fitzgerald, Michael L.)*; CrossCur 47 (1997) 415-417 *(Treat, James)*.

7335 *Perera, Rienzie* The task of rewriting christology. VFTW 20/1 (1997) 27-55 [ZID 23,414].

7336 *Pieris, Aloysius* Jesucristo: la palabra que entienden los asiáticos. [T]*Alarcia, Juan José*: MisEx(M) 161 (1997) 461-474.

7337 **Pikaza, X.** Éste es el hombre: manual de cristología. S 1997, Secretariado Trinitario 508 pp. [SalTer 87,440].

7338 *Porter, Stanley E.; Hayes, Michael A.; Tombs, David* Introduction. Images of Christ. 1997, ⇒256. [E]Porter, S.E., 17-20.

7339 *Renwart, Léon* Que dit-on de Jésus?: chronique de christologie. NRTh 119 (1997) 573-585.

7340 **Richard, Lucien** Christ, the self-emptying of God. Mahwah 1997, Paulist iii; 236 pp. 0-8091-3668-6 [ThD 44,380—Heiser, W.C.].

7341 *Ross, Kenneth R.* Current christological trends in northern Malawi. JRA 27/2 (1997) 160-176.

7342 **Ruíz Arenas, Octavio** Jesus, epifania do amor do Pai. [T]*Moreira, Orlando Soares*: Textos Básicos para Seminários Latino-Americanos 3: São Paulo 1995, Loyola 431 pp. [R]REB 57 (1997) 477-478 *(Alves de Melo, Antônio)*.

7343  **Sanna, Ignazio** Teologia come esperienza di Dio: la prospettiva cristologica di Karl RAHNER. BTCon 97: Brescia 1997, Queriniana 352 pp. Bibl. 88-399-0397-6.

7344  *Sarmiento, Pedro M.* Perfiles de la cristología existencial e imágenes de Jesucristo para la postmodernidad. Sum. 220. REphMar 47/3 (1997) 199-220.

7345  **Scharlemann, Robert P.** The reason of following: christology and the ecstatic, 1. 1991, ⇒8,7560... 10,7517. RRStR 23/1 (1997) 32-34 *(Grigg, Richard).*

7346  **Schillebeeckx, E.** Le Christ sacrement de la rencontre de Dieu. FoiViv Formation 133: P 1997, Cerf 262 pp.

7347  **Schleiermacher, Friedrich D.E.** La festa di Natale: un dialogo [*Schelling, Friedrich W.J.; Barth, Karl*]. 1994 <1806>, ⇒12,7027. RStudium 93/1 (1997) 143-144 *(Miccoli, Paolo).*

7348  *Sesboüé, Bernard* Bulletin de théologie dogmatique: christologie. RSR 85 (1997) 113-126.

7349  **Sesboüé, Bernard** Pédagogie du Christ: éléments de christologie fondamentale. 1994, ⇒11/2,3558; 12,7028. ScrTh 29/1 (1997) 320-321 *(Mateo-Seco, L.F.);* EE 72 (1997) 416-17 *(Gesteira, M.).*

7350  *Silva Lima, José da* 'Quem dizem as pessoas que Eu sou?' (Mc 8,27-30; Mt 16,13-20; Lk 9,18-20). Theologica 32/1 (1997) 15-33.

7351  *Sobrino, Jon* 'Jésus y pobres': lo meta-paradigmático de las cristologías africanas actuales. TDávila, Ricardo: MisEx(M) 161 (1997) 499-511.

7352  **Stock, Alex** Namen. Poetische Dogmatik: Christologie, 1. 1995, ⇒11/2,3560. RLM 36/3 (1997) 40 *(Fritsch-Opermann, Sybille).*

7353  **Strahm, D.** Vom Rand in die Mitte: Christologie aus der Sicht von Frauen in Asien, Afrika und Lateinamerika. Luzern 1997, 447 pp. DM64. 3-905577-11-9. RThG 40/3 (1997) 225-226 *(Fuchs, Gotthard).*

7354  *Sugirtharajah, R.S.* The Magi from Bengal and their Jesus: Indian construals of Christ during colonial-times. Images of Christ. 1997, ⇒256. EPorter, S.E., 144-158.

7355  **Thangaraj, M. Thomas** The crucified guru: an experiment in cross-cultural christology. 1994, ⇒11/2,3563. RER 49 (1997) 386-387 *(Lipner, Julius);* Japan Mission Journal 51/2 (1997) 136-137 & Gr. 78 (1997) 781-783 & New Theology Review 10/4 (1997) 115-117 & IMR 19/3-4 (1997) 223-225 *(Kroeger, James H.).*

7356  *Thomas, Frère* La simplicité du Verbe dans l'humanité de Jésus. Aletheia 11 (1997) 107-121 [ZID 23,307].

7357  **Thompson, William H.** The struggle for theology's soul: contesting scripture in christology. 1996, ⇒12,7031. RWorship 71/1 (1997) 88-90 *(Loewe, William P.);* Thomist 61/1 (1997) 133-137 *(Kereszty, Roch);* ThTo 54 (1997) 432, 434-5 *(Hays, Richard B.);* TJT 13 (1997) 349-350 *(Donovan, Daniel).*

7358  **Tilliette, Xavier** El Cristo de la filosofía. 1994, ⇒12,7032. RAnVal 23 (1997) 466-470 *(Ruiz Aldaz, Juan Ignacio);*

7359  Il Cristo della filosofia: prolegomeni a una cristologia filosofica. Brescia 1997, Morcelliana 320 pp. L35.000 [Cultura & Libri.S 112,71—Scalabrin, Sandro].

7360  *Tombs, David* Liberating christology: images of Christ in the work of Aloysius PIERIS. Images of Christ. 1997, ⇒256. EPorter, S.E., 173-188.

7361 **Van den Toren, Benno** Kwame BEDIAKO's christology in its African evangelical context. Exchange 26 (1997) 218-232.

7362 **Wainwright, Geoffrey** For our salvation: two approaches to the work of Christ. GR 1997, Eerdmans xi; 186 pp. $18. 0-8028-0846-8 [ThD 45,94—Heiser, W. Charles].

7363 ᴱ**Zuck, Roy B.** Vital christology issues: examining contemporary and classic concerns. Vital Issues 10: GR 1997, Kregel 192 pp. $13. 0-8254-4096-3 [ThD 44,387—Heiser, W. Charles].

## H5.5 *Spiritus Sanctus; penumatologia*—The Holy Spirit

7364 *Anthonysomy, S.J.* Models of Spirit activity in the New Testament in the context of Neo-Pentecostalism today. ITS 34/1-3 (1997) 138-149;

7365 Biblical and theological perspectives of Neo-Pentecostalism, 2. Sum. 161. VJTR 61/3 (1997) 161-169.

7366 *Block, Daniel Isaac* Empowered by the Spirit of God: the Holy Spirit in the histographic writings of the Old Testament. Southern Baptist Convention 1/1 (1997) 42-61.

7367 **Canipe, John Cliff** The Holy Spirit and power in evangelism as demonstrated in selected Pauline texts in 1 Thessalonians and 1 Corinthians. Diss. Southwestern Baptist Theological Seminary 1997; 198 pp. [NThAR 2000,34].

7368 *Dassmann, Ernst* Die Früchte des Heiligen Geistes in der frühchristlichen Katechese. LS 48 (1997) 86-89.

7369 **Fagaras, Sabin** Lo spirito santo, la risurrezione e il tempo della storia. R 1997, 88 pp. Sum. Diss. Pont. Univ. Urbaniana.

7370 ᵀ**Faustus Reiensis** Lo Spirito Santo: de Spiritu santo. CTePa 136: R 1997, Città Nuova 128 pp. Introduzione, traduzione e note. 88-311-3136-2.

7371 *Ferraro, Giuseppe* Vedere il regno e nascere da acqua e da spirito. StMiss 46 (1997) 43-64.

7372 *Fuente, Alfonso de la* Del Espíritu Santo antes del Nuevo Testamento: Biblia Hebrea y literatura targúmica. RET 57 (1997) 191-209.

7373 *González, Carlos I.* El espíritu del Señor en el Antiguo Testamento;

7374 El Espiritu del Señor en el Nuevo Testamento. RTLi 31 (1997) 5-24/307-328.

7375 **González, Carlos Ignacio** El Espíritu del Señor que da la vida: teología del Espíritu santo. Perú 1997, Conferencia Episcopal Peruana 294 pp. [Revista Católica 1998,167—Arias R., Maximino].

7376 ᵀ**Granado, Carmelo** DIDIMO el Ciego: tratado sobre el Espíritu Santo. Biblioteca de Patrística: M 1997, Ciudad Nueva 202 pp. [EfMex 16,245s—Villanueva, Jesús Guízar].

7377 *Heinz, Hanspeter* Der Geist weht, wo er will, er läßt sich nicht festhalten. LS 48 (1997) 89-94.

7378 **Holl, Adolf** The left hand of God: a biography of the Holy Spirit. ᵀ*Cullen, John*: NY 1997, Doubleday xiii; 352 pp. 0-385-49284-7.

7379 *Kaiser, Walter C.* The Holy Spirit in the Old Testament. JPentec.S 11: 1997; ⇒63. ᶠMENZIES W., 38-47.

7380  **Keener, Craig S.** The Spirit in the Gospels and Acts: divine purity and power. Peabody 1997, Hendrickson xxxi; 282 pp. $25. 1-56563-169-2.
7381  **Lison, Jacques** L'Esprit répandu: la pneumatologie de GREGOIRE Palamas. 1994, ⇒11/2,3584. RJThS 48 (1997) 308-310 *(Louth, Andrew)*.
7382  **Minguet Mico, José** El Espíritu Santo según San Pablo. Valencia 1997, Edicep 158 pp. [AnVal 24,253].
7383  **Moltmann, Jürgen** Die Quelle des Lebens: der Heilige Geist und die Theologie des Lebens. Kaiser Taschenbücher 150: Gü 1997, Kaiser 141 pp. Bibl. 3-579-05150-4;
7384  The source of life: the Holy Spirit and the theology of life. L 1997, SCM x; 148 pp. 0-334-02698-0.
7385  **Monari, Luciano** Sulla via di Gesù: la vita nello Spirito a partire dagli Atti degli Apostoli. Pres. *Ruini, Card. Camillo*: Reggio Emilia 1997, San Lorenzo 173 pp. 88-8071-070-2.
7386  **Pastore, Corrado; Wyssenbach, Jean-Pierre** Señor y dador de vida: la presencia y la acción del Espíritu Santo. Caracas 1997, Comisión episcopal de catequesis, biblia, ere. 112 pp.; Manual para agentes de pastoral. 980-207-488-8.
7387  *Pemsel-Maier, Sabine* Der heilige Geist—das Weibliche an Gott. LS 48 (1997) 95-99.
7388  *Pesch, Otto Hermann* Ich glaube an Gott, den heiligen Geist. LS 48 (1997) 74-80.
7389  *Piva, Pompeo* Lo Spirito e la libertà del cristiano. Sum. 311. RSEc 15 (1997) 301-311.
7390  **Poudrier, Roger** Souffle de vie: l'Esprit Saint dans la bible. P 1997, Médiaspaul 127 pp. 2-89420-090-0.
7391  **Schweizer, Eduard** El Espíritu Santo. S 1997, Sígueme 168 pp. Ptas1.200 [Comunidades 26,65].
7392  **Turner, Max** The Holy Spirit and spiritual gifts: then and now. 1996, ⇒12,7054. RJETh 11 (1997) 258-261 *(Kaiser, Bernhard)*.
7393  *Venetz, Hermann-Josef* Der Geist stiftet Kirche. LS 48 (1997) 80-85.
7394  *Viviana, Marco de* Lo spirito di Dio: dimensione collettiva nella pneumatologia di Michael WELKER. Nuova Umanità 19/2 (1997) 329-349.

H5.6 *Spiritus et Filius;* 'Spirit-Christology'

7395  *Bertalot, Renzo* Unità e diversità nello Spirito. Sum. 357. RSEc 15 (1997) 351-357.
7396  **Bordoni, Marcello** La cristologia nell'orizzonte dello Spirito. BTCon 82: 1995, ⇒12,7055. RStPat 44/1 (1997) 258-259 *(Sartori, Luigi)*; ActBib 34 (1997) 22-23 *(Vives, Josep)*; AnnTh 11 (1997) 245-8 *(Ducay, Antonio)*; CivCatt 148 I (1997) 90-91 *(Ferraro, G.)*.
7397  Comité para el jubileo del año 2000. El Espíritu del Señor. M 1997, BAC 188 pp. [StLeg 39,313s—Trobajo, Antonio].
7398  *Dal Ferro, Giuseppe* Il regno, i confini della chiesa e i confini dello Spirito. Sum. 420. RSEc 15 (1997) 409-420.
7399  **Del Colle, Ralph** Christ and the Spirit: spirit-christology in trinitarian perspective. 1994, ⇒9,7753... 11/2,3597. RJThS 48 (1997)

359-363 *(Gaine, Simon Francis)*; JR 77 (1997) 159-160 *(Gaither, Linda L.)*.

7400 **Dunn, James D.G.** Jesus and the Spirit. GR 1997, Eerdmans xii; 515 pp. reprint; $30. 0-8028-4291-7 [NTS 44,623].

7401 **Durrwell, François-Xavier** Jésus fils de Dieu dans l'Esprit Saint. Préf. *Doré, Joseph*: CJJC 71: P 1997, Desclée 140 pp. ᴿStMor 35 (1997) 511-514 *(Mimeault, Jules)*.

7402 **González, Carlos Ignacio** El espíritu del Señor que santifica: meditaciones bíblicas para el jubileo de la encarnación. Perú 1997, Conferencia Episcopal Peruana 190 pp. [Revista Católica 1998,167—Arias R., Maximino].

7403 **Pixley, Jorge V.** Vida no Espírito: o projeto messiânico de Jesus depois da ressurreição. ᵀ*Clasen, Jaime A.*: Petrópolis 1997, Vozes 282 pp. 85-326-1793-0 [PerTeol 29,284].

7404 *Varó, Francisco* Jesucristo y el don del espíritu. ScrTh 29 (1997) 511-539.

### H5.7 *Ssma Trinitas*—The Holy Trinity

7405 **Beck, Horst W.** Biblische Universalität und Wissenschaft: interdisziplinäre Theologie im Horizont trinitarischer Schöpfungslehre. Weilheim-Bierbronnen ²1994, Siewerth lviii; 730 pp. DM60. ᴿJETh 11 (1997) 225-226 *(Schwarz, Hans)*.

7406 *Fuller, Reginald H.* The *Vestigia Trinitatis* in the Old Testament. 1997, ⇒77. ᶠSᴀɴᴅᴇʀs J., 499-508.

7407 *Juel, Donald H.* The Trinity and the New Testament. ThTo 54 (1997) 312-324.

7408 *Middleton, Kathleen; Poorthuis, Marcel* Joodse kritiek op de christelijke triniteitsidee: de theologische vruchtbaarheid van het verschil. TTh 37 (1997) 343-367.

7409 *Muller, Earl C.* The trinity and the kingdom. StMiss 46 (1997) 91-117.

7410 **Reid, Duncan** Energies of the Spirit: trinitarian models in eastern Orthodox and western Theology. Academy 96: Atlanta, GA 1997, AAR xiv; 149 pp. Bibl. 0-7885-0345-6.

### H5.8 *Regnum messianicum, Filius hominis*— Messianic kingdom, Son of Man

7411 *Afzal, Cameron* The communal icon: complex cultural schemas, elements of the social imagination (Matthew 10:32//Luke 12:8 and Revelation 3:5, a case study). 1997, ⇒82. ᶠSᴄʀᴏɢɢs R., 58-80.

7412 ᴱ**Benyik, György** Szegedi Biblikus Konferencia: A messiási kérdés [Conferenza biblica di Szeged: la questione messianica]. Szeged 1995, szept. 4-7. Szeged 1997, JATEPress 132 pp. **Hungarian.**

7413 *Bianchi, Enzo* Il regno di Dio: dono e responsabilità. Som. 933. Presenza Pastorale 67 (1997) 933-942.

7414 *deHaven-Smith, Lance* How Jesus planned to overthrow the Roman Empire. RStT 16/1 (1997) 48-59.

7415 *Kieffer, René* Reinado de Dios: justificación y salvación. Conc(E) 269 (1997) 135-146 (F121-131); (P121-132); (I133/1,143-155).

7416  *Kjaer-Hansen, Kai* Der kommende Messias und die Wiederkunft Jesu. Tod eines Messias. 1996, ⇒286. ᴱKjær-Hansen, K., 191-95.
7417  *Levinson, Pnina Navè* Das Reich Gottes im jüdischen Glauben. Entschluss 52/11 (1997) 18, 23-24.
7418  **Mateos, Juan; Camacho, Fernando** El hijo del hombre: hacia la plenitud humana. En los orígines del cristianismo 9: 1995, ⇒11/2,3662. ᴿEstB 55 (1997) 414-415 *(Gesteira, M.)*.
7419  *Nebe, Gottfried* The Son of man and the angels: reflections on the formation of christology in the context of eschatology. Eschatology in the bible. JSOT.S 243: 1997, ⇒222. ᴱReventlow, H., 111-131.
7420  *Riggans, Walter* Was für eine Person ist Jesus?. Tod eines Messias. 1996, ⇒286. ᴱKjær-Hansen, K., 141-145.
7421  **Schenk, Wolfgang** Das biographische Ich-Idiom 'Menschensohn' in den frühen Jesus-Biographien: der Ausdruck, seine Codes und seine Rezeptionen in ihren Kontexten. FRLANT 177: Gö 1997, Vandenhoeck & R 264 pp. Bibl. 3-525-53860-X.
7422  **Schrupp, Ernst** Israel und der Messias: Versöhnung durch Jesus Christus in endzeitlicher Perspecktive. Wu 1997, Brockhaus 219 pp. DM17. 3-417-24147-2.
7423  *Taylor, Joan E.* Ho huios tou anthrōpou, 'The Son of Man': some remarks on an androcentric convention of translation. Response by *Paul Ellingworth* 109-113. TPBT 48 (1997) 101-109.
7424  *Toll, Christopher* The meaning of the Aramaic expression "son of man": an addition to J.-C. Loba Mᴋᴏʟᴇ's "synthèse d'opinions philologiques". JNSL 23/1 (1997) 225-226.
7425  *Zaretsky, Tuvya* Jesus, Israels Messias—ein Messias für Israel. Tod eines Messias. 1996, ⇒286. ᴱKjær-Hansen, K., 172-181.

H6.1  *Creatio, sabbatum NT;* **The Creation** [⇒E1.6]

7426  *Alves, Manuel Isidro* Cristo princípio e fim. As origens da vida. 1997, ⇒344. 231-250.
7427  **Burrell, David B.** Freedom and creation in three traditions. 1994, ⇒11/2,2815. ᴿRelSt 33/1 (1997) 121-125 *(Schwöbel, Christoph)*.
7428  ᴱ**Delver, J.A.**, *(al.)*, Van zondag naar sabbat: een dagboek bij de Schrift in het perspectief van kerk en Israël. Zoetermeer 1997, Boekencentrum 221 pp. *f*25. 90-239-1657-3 [ITBT 6/3,34—Stroes, Herman].
7429  *Farrelly, Brian J.* La creación como encuentro del ser y de la nada en la teología del maestro Eᴄᴋʜᴀʀᴛ de Hochheim O.P. (1260-1327). Sapientia 52 (1997) 33-39.
7430  **Mildenberger, Friedrich** Biblische Dogmatik: eine biblische Theologie in dogmatischer Perspektive. 1991-1993. ⇒7,9042... 12,7084. ᴿKeTh 48/3 (1997) 263-265 *(Knijff, H.W. de)*.
7431  **Noemi Callejas, Juan** El mundo: creación y promesa de Dios. 1996, ⇒12,7086. ᴿRevista Católica 97/1 (1997) 81 *(Arteaga Manieu, Andrés)*.
7432  *Philippe, Marie-Dominique* Saint Tʜᴏᴍᴀs et le mystère de la création: une réponse aux interrogations de l'homme d'aujourdhui. Sapientia 52 (1997) 145-158.
7433  *Pinnock, Clark H.* The role of the Spirit in creation. AsbTJ 52/1 (1997) 47-54.

7434 *Quacquarelli, Antonio* Dal settimo all'ottavo giorno: dal sabato all'origine del nuovo mondo: la domenica. VetChr 34 (1997) 203-210.

7435 *Rhoads, David* Reading the New Testament in the environmental age. CThMi 24 (1997) 259-266.

7436 *Watts, David* Creation in the New Testament. Evangel 15/3 (1997) 80-85.

## H6.3 *Fides, veritas in NT*—Faith and truth

7437 **Aguirre, Rafael** Raíces bíblicas de la fe cristiana. M 1997, PPC 207 pp. 84-288-1407-4. RSalTer 85 (1997) 699-700 *(Aguirre, R.)*.

7438 *Becquet, Gilles* La 'vérité'. Sève 584 (1997) 45-48.

7439 **Brossier, François** Relatos bíblicos y comunicación de la fe. Estella (Navarra) 1997, Verbo Divino 161 pp. 84-7151-531-8.

7440 *Dumais, Marcel* Le salut en dehors de la foi en Jésus-Christ?: observations sur trois passages des Actes des Apôtres. EeT(O) 28/2 (1997) 161-190.

7441 **Farrelly, M. John** Faith in God through Jesus Christ. Foundational Theology 2: ColMn 1997, Liturgical 350 pp. $30 [BTB 27,120].

7442 **Ferdinand, Kenneth S.** Reflections on outlines of bible faith doctrines. Delhi 1996, ISPCK xii; 188 pp. 81-7214-300-0f [NThAR 2000,1].

7443 *Hainthaler, Theresia* La foi au Christ dans l'église éthiopienne: une synthèse des éléments judéo-chrétiens et helléno-chrétiens. RevSR 71 (1997) 329-337.

7444 *Hamm, Dennis* Preaching biblical justice to nurture the faith that does it. Studies in the Spirituality of Jesuits 29/1 (1997) 1-33.

7445 **Kriegbaum, Bernhard** "Konfessionalisierung" des Glaubens im Frühchristentum. Entschluss 52/7-8 (1997) 40-43.

7446 **Landmesser, Christof** Wahrheit als Grundbegriff neutestamentlicher Wissenschaft. Diss. Münster 1997; DHofius, O. xi; 548 pp. [ThLZ 124,244].

7447 **Levy, David M.** Guarding the gospel of grace: contending for the faith in the face of compromise (Galatians and Jude). Bellmawr, NJ 1997, Friends of Israel Gospel Ministry 206 pp. 0-915540-26-6 [NThAR 2000,34].

7448 *Melchiore, Virgilio* L'*eros* nella spiritualità cristiana: esperienza umana e fede biblica. Som. 351. RCI 78 (1997) 351-362.

7449 **Rossi De Gasperis, Francesco** Cominciando da Gerusalemme (Lc 24, 47): la sorgente della fede e dell'esistenza cristiana. Pref. *Martini, Carlo Maria Card.*: CasM 1997, Piemme 588 pp. 88-384-2845-X.

7450 **Taylor, Brian C.** Setting the gospel free: experiential faith and contemplative practice. L 1997, SCM 156 pp. 0-334-02678-4.

7451 *Vanhetloo, Warren* Dealing with doubt. CBTJ 13 (1997) 57-78.

7452 *Vanhoye, Albert* Per crescere nella fede. Il Messaggio del Cuore di Gesù 20 (1997) 21-26 [AcBib 10/3,270].

7453 **Wallis, Ian G.** The faith of Jesus Christ in early christian traditions. MSSNTS 84: 1995, ⇒11/2,2218; 12,7096. RJBL 116 (1997) 141-143 *(Winger, Michael)*.

H6.6　*Peccatum NT*—Sin, evil [E1.9]

7454　*Abel, Olivier* Mal, responsabilité, pardon. RHPhR 77 (1997) 309-329.
7455　**Arnold, Clinton E.** Three crucial questions about spiritual warfare. GR 1997, Baker 224 pp. $12 [TrinJ 20,247ss—Larkin, W.J.]
7456　*Hanson, K.C.* Sin, purification, and group process. 1997, ⇒48. ᶠKNIERIM R., 167-191 [Lev 4-5; Jer 7; 26; Acts 2].
7457　*Häring, Hermann* 'Ni él ni sus padres pecaron...': el castigo, la culpa y la exclusión. Conc(I) 33 (1997) 944-957; (GB/5,35-44); (F237,53-63); (E273,871-883).

H7.0　**Soteriologia NT**

7458　ᴱ**Ancona, Giovanni** La giustificazione. Padova 1997, Messagero 383 pp. Atti del VII Corso di Aggiornamento per docenti di Teologia Dogmatica, Roma, 2-4 gennaio 1997. ᴿMF 97 (1997) 755-758 *(Iammarrone, Giovanni).*
7459　*Beilner, Wolfgang* Versöhnung oder Widerstand. Diakonia 28/1 (1997) 65-68.
7460　**Borges Hackmann, Geraldo Luiz** Jesus Cristo, nosso redentor (iniciaçã à cristologia como soteriologia). Teologia 7: Porto Alegre 1997, Pontifícia Universidade Católica do Rio Grande do Sul (EDIPUCRS) 213 pp. [REB 57,495].
7461　*Brinkman, Martien E.* De rechtvaardiging als centraal paradigma van heil? perspectieven vanuit een gemeenschappelijke verklaring protestanten en katholieken. TTh 37 (1997) 149-165.
7462　*Carson, Donald A.* Reflections on salvation and justification in the New Testament. JETS 40 (1997) 581-608.
7463　*De Virgilio, Giuseppe* Salvezza universale in Cristo: aspetti della riflessione neotestamentaria per il dialogo interreligioso. RdT 38 (1997) 313-345.
7464　*Estrada-Barbier, Bernardo; Grafinger, Christine Maria* La fede e le opere a confronto con il giudaismo. Città del Vaticano 1997, LEV 63-72 pp. [Estratto da 'La giustificazione in Cristo', J.M. Galvan (ed.)].
7465　*Fishbane, Michael* Justification through living—Martin BUBER's third alternative. BJSt 313: 1997, ⇒85. ᶠSILBERMAN L., 219-230.
7466　ᴱ**Frankemölle, Hubert** Sünde und Erlösung im Neuen Testament. QD 161: 1996, ⇒12,181. ᴿOrdKor 38 (1997) 235-236 *(Giesen, Heinz)*; ThLZ 122 (1997) 670-673 *(Bendemann, Reinhard von).*
7467　**Goorden, C.** De heilsbetekenis van Christus' leven en dood: een actualiserende interpretatie. Antwerpen 1997, Eigen Beheer 83 pp. BEF150. 90-8033785-1-8 [Coll. 27,335].
7468　**Gorringe, Timothy** God's just vengeance: crime, violence and the rhetoric of salvation. Cambridge Studies in Ideology and Religion 9: C 1996, CUP xiv; 280 pp. 0-521-55762-3. ᴿTheol. 100 (1997) 49 *(Page, Ruth).*
7469　**Heyer, Cornelius J. den** Verzoening: bijbelse notities bij een omstreden thema. Kampen 1997, Kok 144 pp. ƒ27.50. 90-242-7789-2 [NThAR 1997,257].

7470 *Hutton, Rodney R.* Innocent or holy?: justification and sanctification in Old Testament theology. Word and World 17/3 (1997) 312-321 [ZID 23,416].

7471 *Kertelge, Karl* Rechtfertigung: Neues Testament. TRE 28. 1997, ⇒420. 286-307.

7472 **Letham, Robert** The work of Christ. 1993, ⇒10,7720*. ᴿRTR 56 (1997) 149-150 *(Milne, Douglas J.W.)*.

7473 *Marto, António* Jesus Cristo, salvador do homem. Theologica 32/1 (1997) 59-74.

7474 *Martyn, J. Louis* Paul's understanding of the textual contradiction between Habakkuk 2:4 and Leviticus 18:5. 1997, ⇒77 [⇒3931]. ᶠSANDERS J., 465-473.

7475 *Meves, Christa* Seelische Gesundheit und biblisches Heil. Theologisches 27 (1997) 191-194, 245-250.

7476 *Phillips, Peter* SCHILLEBEECKX's soteriological agnosticism. NBl 78 (1997) 76-84.

7477 *Pinnock, Clark H.* The role of the Spirit in redemption. AsbTJ 52/1 (1997) 55-62.

7478 *Van Beek, Franz Josef* Kingdom of God and salvation (a note on rearranging the great tradition). StMiss 46 (1997) 195-210.

H7.2 *Crux, sacrificium;* **The Cross; the nature of sacrifice** [⇒E3.4]

7479 **Anselmi, M.** La spiritualità della passione alla luce di S. PAOLO della Croce: la ricerca di Stanislas BRETON. Teramo 1997, Staurós 173 pp. L20.000 [RVS 52,210].

7480 *Asnaghi, Adolfo* Croce... epifania di verità e di bellezza: nella tradizione ortodossa russa. Servitium 112 (1997) 18-25.

7481 **Barth, Gerhard** Il significato della morte di Gesù Cristo: l'interpretazione del NT. PBT 38: 1995, ⇒11/2,3919. ᴿStPat 44/1 (1997) 263-264 *(Sartori, Luigi)*; Ho Theológos 15/2 (1997) 345-347 *(Iovino, Paolo)*; Lat. 63 (1997) 328-329 *(Ancona, Giovanni)*.

7482 *Baudler, Georg* Jesus—der vollkommene Sündenbock?: zu René GIRARDS Revision seines Opferbegriffs. LebZeug 52 (1997) 212-223.

7483 **Baudler, Georg** Das Kreuz: Geschichte und Bedeutung. Patmos 1997, Dü 375 pp. DM90. 3-491-77013-0 [ThG 41/1,67ss—Häring, Bernhard].

7484 ᴱBeckwith, **Roger T.; Selman, Martin J.** Sacrifice in the Bible. 1995, ⇒11/2,483. ᴿRRT (1997/1) 93-95 *(Norton, Gerard J.)*.

7485 *Bruni, Giancarlo* La croce, epifania di verità e di bellezza: introduzione al quaderno. Servitium 112 (1997) 5-7.

7486 *Clancy, Finbarr G.* The cross in AUGUSTINE's *Tractatus in Iohannem*. StPatr 33: 1997, ⇒351. ᴱLivingstone, E.A., 55-62.

7487 *D'Este, Raffaella* L'icona della crocifissione;

7488 *Derungs, Ursicin Gion Gieli* La croce come paradosso estetico. Servitium 112 (1997) 34-46/9-12.

7489 **Deselaers, Manfred** 'Mein Gott, warum hast du mich verlassen...?': Kreuzwegmeditationen in Auschwitz. Aachen 1995, Einhard 64 pp. ᴿFrRu 4/1 (1997) 51 *(Mechtenberg, Theo)*.

7490 ᵀᴱDrijvers, **Han Jan Willem** The finding of the true cross: the Judas Kyriakos legend in Syriac. CSCO 565; CSCO.Sub 93: Lv 1997, Peeters 99 pp. Bibl. 90-6831-891-8.

7491  *Ducay Real, Antonio* La croce: nuovo patto, autocomunicazione trinitaria e gesto supremo di salvezza: riflessioni sulla causalità salvifica della croce. AnnTh 11 (1997) 459-477.

7492  *Edallo, Edoardo* La croce e l'architettura. Servitium 112 (1997) 47-52.

7493  *Elgvin, Torleif* Der Messias, der am Holz verflucht wurde. Tod eines Messias. 1996, ⇒286. ᴱKjær-Hansen, K., 55-62.

7494  ᴱ**Knubben, Jürgen** Via crucis: das Kreuz in der Kunst der Gegenwart. Rottweil 1997, Dominikaner-Forum des Dominikanermuseums 130 pp. DM48. 3-9805461-2-8 [ETR 74,133s—Cottin, J.].

7495  *Koester, Helmut* Rediscovering the message of Lent. BiRe 13/1 (1997) 16, 46.

7496  **Kretzenbacher, Leopold** Bild-Gedanken der spätmittelalterlichen Hl. Blut-Mystik und ihr Fortleben in mittel- und südosteuropäischer Volksüberlieferung. Bayerische Akad. der Wissenschaften, Phil.-Hist. Kl. Abh. 114: Mü 1997, Bayerische Akad. der Wissenschaften 117 pp. 3-7696-0109-2.

7497  *Langenhorst, Georg* Die Absurdität von Kreuz, Kreuzigung und Gekreuzigtem: auf den Spuren der Gegenwartsliteratur. Ren. 53/1 (1997) 39-51.

7498  *Nadler, Sam* Der Messias, der für unsere Sünden gestorben ist. Tod eines Messias. 1996, ⇒286. ᴱKjær-Hansen, K., 63-74.

7499  *Pokorný, Petr* Antigone und Jesus (Opfer und Hoffnung). Bibelauslegung. WUNT 100: 1997 <1996>, ⇒970. 133-146.

7500  *Preus, Robert* The theology of the cross. Adapted *Maschke, Timothy H.*: Luther Digest 5 (1997) 121-131.

7501  *Puech, Émile* Notes sur 11Q19 LXIV 6-13 et 4Q524 14,2-4: à propos de la crucifixion dans le Rouleau du Temple et dans Judaïsme ancien. RdQ 18 (1997) 109-124.

7502  *Remondi, Giordano* La celebrazione del venerdì santo. Servitium 112 (1997) 27-33.

7503  ᴱ**Schenker, Adrian** Studien zu Opfer und Kult im AT. 1992, ⇒8,491; 11/2,3957. ᴿBZ 41 (1997) 102-103 *(Grünwaldt, Klaus)*.

7504  *Schmidt, Thomas* Jesus' triumphal march to crucifixion: the sacred way as Roman procession. BiRe 13/1 (1997) 30-37.

7505  **Screech, Michael Andrew** Laughter at the foot of the Cross. Harmondsworth, Middlesex 1997, Penguin xxiii; 328 pp. 0-713-99012-0.

7506  *Stefani, Piero* Morire per amore del Dio unico. Servitium 112 (1997) 13-17 [Dt 6,4].

7507  *Trabucco, Giovanni* La croce come verità e bellezza in Simone WEIL. Servitium 112 (1997) 72-85.

7508  **Wierbse, Warren W.** The cross of Jesus: what his words from Calvary mean for us. Leicester 1997, Crossway 134 pp. £4. 1-85684-168-5 [Evangel 17,26].

7509  **Ziehr, Wilhelm** Das Kreuz: Symbol, Gestalt, Bedeutung. Stu 1997, Belser 240 pp. 388 pl. 3-7630-2343-7 [ETR 74,134s—Cottin, Jérôme].

### H7.4 *Sacramenta, gratia*

7510  *Baudry, Gérard-Henry* Le baptême: mise au tombeau avec le Christ. EeV 107 (1997) 121-127.

7511 **Bentué, Antonio** La experiencia bíblica: gracia y ética. M 1997, PPC 181 pp. [Mayéutica 24,249—Martínez, Carlos Jesús].

7512 **Booth, Robert R.** Children of the promise: the biblical case for infant baptism. Darlington, UK 1995, Evangelical 206 pp. $10. 0-87552-167-5. RCTJ 32/1 (1997) 176-177 *(Van Dyk, Wilbert M.)*.

7513 *Caillot, Joseph* Baptême et déploiement de l'existence chrétienne. MD 209 (1997) 9-22.

7514 *Ferrua, Valerio* "Nudus nudum Christum sequi": sulla nudità battesimale. BSRel 125: 1997, ⇒45. FJAVIERRE ORTAS A., 205-216.

7515 *Figura, Michael* Christus und die Kirche—das große Geheimnis (Eph 5,32): zur Sakramentalität der christlichen Ehe. IKaZ 26 (1997) 33-43.

7516 **Geissler, Rex** Born of water: what the bible really says about baptism. Long Beach, CA 1997, Great Commission Illustrated 172 pp. 0-9653469-0-0 [NThAR 2000,124].

7517 **Hartman, Lars O.** 'Into the name of the Lord Jesus': baptism in the early church. Studies of the NT and its world: E 1997, Clark x; 214 pp. Bibl. £20. 0-567-08589-9.

7518 **Magrassi, M.** Gesù e il malato: il sacramento che porta salvezza. 1996, ⇒12,7165. RAnime e Corpi 189 (1997) 123-124 *(Casera, Antonio)*.

7519 *Malfèr, Benno* Die Lehre vom Sakrament der Ehe vom Konzil von Trient bis zum II. Vatikanischen Konzil: eine Überlieferungsgeschichte?. StAns 124: 1997, ⇒57. FLOEHRER M. — TRAGAN P., 749-758.

7520 **McPartlan, Paul** Sacrament of salvation: an introduction to eucharistic ecclesiology. 1995, ⇒12,7167. RMonth 30 (1997) 76-77 *(Barreiro, Alvaro)*.

7521 *Pozo Abejón, Gerardo del* El matrimonio en el horizonte de la nueva alianza. RCIC 19/1 (1997) 4-12.

7522 **Rocchetta, C.** I sacramenti della fede: saggio di teologia biblica dei sacramenti: 1 Sacramentaria biblica fondamentale; 2 Sacramentaria biblica speciale. Bo ⁷1997, EDB 2 vols; 294 + 392 pp. L35.000 + 48.000 [RdT 39,948].

7523 *Santorski, Andrzej* Małżeństwo jako znak łaski nadprzyrodzonej w świetle Nowego Testamentu [Die Ehe als Zeichen der Gnade im Licht der neutestamentlichen Texte]. Zsfg.303. WST 10 (1997) 293-303. P.

7524 **Stevick, Daniel B.** By water and the word: the scriptures of Baptism. NY 1997, Church 313 pp. $21. 0-8986-9296-2 [Worship 73,78ss—McKenna, John H.].

7525 **Vanstone, W.H.** Fare well in Christ. L 1997, Darton, L & T 147 pp. £9 [Theology 797,364].

7526 **Vogel, Arthur A.** Radical christianity and the flesh of Jesus: the roots of eucharistic living. 1995, ⇒11/2,4028. RAThR 79 (1997) 464-465 *(Slocum, Robert B.)*.

7527 *Volz, Carl A.* Holy Communion in the Lutheran confessions. Word & World 17/1 (1997) 10ff [ThD Index February 1997,15].

## H7.6 Ecclesiologia, theologia missionis, laici—The Church

7528 **Alonso Schökel, Luis** Como mi padre me envió, yo os envio: a-postolado y ejercicios espirituales. El Pozo de Siquem 81: Sdr

1997, Sal Terrae 158 pp. 84-293-1215-3 [ActBib 34,243— O'Callaghan, J.].

7529 *Amaladoss, Michael* Images of Christ and orientations in mission: a historical overview. VJTR 61 (1997) 732-741.

7530 *Bauckham, Richard* James, 1 Peter, Jude and 2 Peter. 1997, ⇒93. FSWEET J., 153-166.

7531 *Becker, Jürgen* Endzeitliche Völkermission und antiochenische Christologie. BZNW 89: 1997, ⇒33. FGRAESSER E., 1-21.

7532 **EBergamelli, F.** Laici e laicità nei primi secoli della chiesa. Letture cristiane del primo millennio 21: Mi 1995, Paoline 435 pp. L48.000. 88-315-1125-4. RStPat 44/1 (1997) 222-223 *(Corsato, Celestino)*.

7533 **Beyerhaus, Peter** Die Bibel in der Mission. 1996, ⇒12,7180. RJETh 11 (1997) 352-354 *(Padberg, Lutz E. von)*.

7534 *Binz, Stephen J.* Parish bible study: foundation for evangelization. BiTod 35 (1997) 249-254.

7535 **Bonanate, U.** Il difficile universalismo di Bibbia e Corano. T 1997, Bollati Boringhieri 181 pp. [Henoch 19,249—Soggin, J.A.].

7536 *Buetubela, Balembo* Aux sources de l'église-famille de Dieu: la fraternité en Jésus Christ, premier-né (Rm 8,29). Telema 23/1/2 (1997) 69-75.

7537 *Callahan, James* The bible says: evangelical and postliberal biblicism. ThTo 53 (1997) 449-463.

7538 **ECarro, Daniel; Wilson, Richard F.** Contemporary gospel accents: doing theology in Africa, Asia, Southeast Asia, and Latin America. Baptist World Alliance. Macon, GA 1997, Mercer xv; 142 pp. 0-86554-505-7.

7539 *Castillo, José María* Jesús, el pueblo y la teología I-II. RLAT 14 (1997) 111-138, 279-324.

7540 *Chica Arellano, Fernando* Jesús evangelizador: nosotros evangelizadores con Él. RelCult 43 (1997) 511-539.

7541 *Dhavamony, Mariasusai* The kingdom of God and religious pluralism. StMiss 46 (1997) 227-249.

7542 *Ebner-Golder, Roswitha* Hommes et femmes: que dit l'Esprit dans l'Écriture et aux églises aujourd'hui à propos de leur ministère?. UnChr 126 (1997) 10-15.

7543 **Evans, G.R.** The reception of the faith: reinterpreting the gospel for today. L 1997, SPCK x; 230 pp. £16. 0-281-05092-9 [RRT 1998/1,89].

7544 *Fackre, Gabriel* The church of the center. Interp. 51 (1997) 130-142.

7545 **Ferguson, Everett** The church of Christ: a biblical ecclesiology for today. 1996, ⇒12,7185. RFaith & Mission 14/2 (1997) 98-100 *(Hammett, John S.)*.

7546 *Flemming, Dean* Biblical theological foundations for a response to religious pluralism. AsbTJ 52 (1997) 43-61.

7547 *Gil i Ribas, Josep* D'una llar evangelitzada a una llar evangelitzadora (i II). Sum. 347. RCatT 22 (1997) 307-347.

7548 *Grech, Prospero* La chiesa, sacramento di unità di tutto il genere humano. Som., sum. 45. VivH 8 (1997) 33-45.

7549 *Henn, William* The church and the kingdom of God. StMiss 46 (1997) 119-147.

7550 *Horbury, William* Septuagintal and New Testament conceptions of the church. 1997, ⇒93. FSWEET J., 1-17.

7551 **Houlden, James L.** The public face of the gospel: New Testament ideas of the church. L 1997, SCM viii; 103 pp. £8. 0-334-02666-0. ᴿTheology 797 (1997) 384 *(Muddiman, John)*.

7552 **Kee, Howard Clark** Who are the people of God?: early christian models of community. 1995, ⇒11/2,4093; 12,7196. ᴿCBQ 58 (1996) 156-157 *(Harrington, Daniel J.)*.

7553 *Kirchschläger, Walter* Bleibendes und Veränderbares in der Kirche: ein biblischer Beitrag zur Systemanalyse. Pfarrei. 1997, ⇒259. ᴱSchifferle, A., 129-139;

7554 Kirche als Nachfolgegemeinschaft Jesu Christi: Dynamik im Kontext als Grundmerkmal für das Leben von Kirche. Diak. 28 (1997) 394-398.

7555 **Klaiber, Walter** Call and response: biblical foundations of a theology of evangelism. ᵀ*Perry-Trauthig, Howard; Dwyer, James A.*: Nv 1997, Abingdon 272 pp. $20. 0-687-04602-5 [RRT 1998/2,91].

7556 *Klein, Ralph W.* Israel/today's believers and the nations: three test cases. CThMi 24 (1997) 232-237 [Gen 34; Neh 9; Jonah 3-4].

7557 **Küng, Hans** El cristianismo: esencia e historia. Estructuras y Procesos: Religión: M 1997, Trotta 905 pp.

7558 *Legrand, Lucien* Good news of the kingdom or good news of Jesus Christ?. StMiss 46 (1997) 211-225.

7559 *Morley, Jean-Paul* Un divorce entre attentes populaires et discours religieux: des fraternités de la Mission Populaire Évangélique dans les années 40. RHPhR 77 (1997) 81-85.

7560 **Nobile, Marco** Ecclesiologia biblica. CSB 30: 1996, ⇒12,7207. ᴿPaVi 42/5 (1997) 58-60 *(Manzi, Franco)*.

7561 *Padberg, Lutz E. v.* Bibel und Mission im Spiegel der Briefe des BONIFATIUS;

7562 *Riesner, Rainer* Wenn sich pneumatische Exegese beim Geist widerspricht. TVGMS 424: 1997, ⇒59. ᶠMAIER G., 333-344/113-132.

7563 *Ritter, Adolf Martin* Ulrich WICKERT, Wolfhart PANNENBERG und das Problem der "Hellenisierung des Christentums". BZNW 85: 1997, ⇒105. ᶠWICKERT U., 303-318.

7564 **Roloff, Jürgen** Die Kirche im Neuen Testament. GNT 10: 1993, ⇒9,8174... 12,7210. ᴿEE 72 (1997) 378-379 *(Madrigal, S.)*.

7565 *Roure, Damia* La producció del Nou Testament en el marc de la missió cristiana mediterrània. La Bíblia i el Mediterrani. 1997, ⇒385. ᴱBorrell, d'Agustí, 181-190.

7566 *Sänger, Dieter* Kultisches Amt und priesterliche Gemeinde: neutestamentliche Erwägungen zum Priestertum aller Gläubigen. BZNW 86: 1997, ⇒41. ᶠHOFIUS O., 619-657.

7567 *Seibold, Jorge R.* La sagrada escritura en la primera evangelización americana: el sermonario del Padre Valdivia y el teatro bíblico indiano. Strom. 53 (1997) 251-276.

7568 ᴱ**Shenk, Wilbert R.** The transfiguration of mission: biblical, theological and historical foundations. Missionary Studies 12: 1993, ⇒10,396. ᴿIRM 86 (1997) 342 *(Matthey, Jacques)*.

7569 **Sieben, Hermann Josef** Vom Apostelkonzil zum Ersten Vatikanum: Studien zur Geschichte der Konzilsidee. KonGe.U: 1996, ⇒12,7214. ᴿSapienza 50/2 (1997) 241-243 *(Miele, Michele)*.

7570  ᴱStenico, Tommaso Il concilio Vaticano II: carisma e profezia.
      Città del Vaticano 1997, Ed. Vaticana 484 pp. Colloquio con S.E.
      card. Francis Arinze et al. 88-209-2325-4.
7571  Sugden, Chris Seeking the Asian face of Jesus: the practice and
      theology of christian social witness in Indonesia and India 1974-
      1996. Oxf 1997, Regnum xix; 496 pp. 1-870345-26-6.
7572  Van Engen, John Christening the Romans. Tr. 52 (1997) 1-45.
7573  Venetz, Hermann-Josef Jesus und Paulus: bibeltheologische Ele-
      mente eines "Kirchenspiegels". Pfarrei. 1997, ⇒259. ᴱSchifferle,
      A., 117-128.
7574  Vernet, Joan M. L'universalisme bíblic fet realitat a Cesarea. La
      Bíblia i el Mediterrani. 1997, ⇒385. ᴱBorrell, d'Agustí, 395-415.
7575  Walker, Andrew Telling the story: gospel, mission and culture.
      1996, ⇒12,7221. ᴿTheol. 100 (1997) 52-53 (Pickstone, Charles).
7576  Wengst, Klaus Das Volk und die Völker nach dem Neuen Testa-
      ment. 1997, ⇒25. ᶠFRIEDLANDER A., 259-266.

### н7.7  Œcumenismus—The ecumenical movement

7577  Amaladoss, Michael A. À la rencontre des cultures: comment con-
      juguer unité et pluralité dans les Églises?. Questions ouvertes: P
      1997, L'Atelier 172 pp. 2-7082-3291-6.
7578  Freedman, David Noel Modern scripture research and ecumenism.
      Divine Commitment 1. 1997 <1963>, ⇒124. 161-167.
7579  Greeley, Andrew M.; Neusner, Jacob Common ground: a priest
      and a rabbi read Scripture together. 1996, ⇒12,7227. ᴿAThR 79
      (1997) 438-439 (Portaro, Sam).
7580  Henn, William One faith: biblical and patristic contributions to-
      ward understanding unity in faith. 1995, ⇒11/2,3740; 12,7229.
      ᴿJEarlyC 5 (1997) 309-310 (Turcescu, Lucian).
7581  Lanne, Emmanuel Tradition et communion des églises: recueil
      d'études. BEThL 129: Lv 1997, Peeters xxv; 704 pp. 90-6831-
      892-6.
7582  Mesters, Frei Carlos De Santa Maria para São Luís: reflexões em
      torno do uso da bíblia no IX Intereclesial. REB 57 (1997) 825-842.
7583  Pittner, Bertram Wolfgang TRILLING (1925-1993)—exegetische
      Beiträge zum ökumenischen Gespräch. 1997, ⇒98. ᶠULLRICH L.,
      63-72.
7584  Urban, Hans Jörg Die Überlieferung des "Patrimonium fidei" und
      die Ökumene. StAns 124: 1997, ⇒57. ᶠLOEHRER M. —
      TRAGAN P., 81-95.

### н7.8  Amt—Ministerium ecclesiasticum

7585  Bartlett, David Ministry in the New Testament. 1993, ⇒9,8412;
      11/2,4333. New Theology Review 10/3 (1997) 101-102 (McDo-
      nald, Patricia M.).
7586  Becquet, Gilles Ministères et Nouveau Testament. Sève 586 (1997)
      57-61.
7587  Blandenier, Jacques Le Nouveau Testament et les structures ecclé-
      siales d'autorité: quels sont les 'modeles' néotestamentaires de
      structure ecclésiales?. Ḥokhma 66 (1997) 28-48.

7588 **Campenhausen, Hans von** Ecclesiastical authority and spiritual power in the church of the first three centuries. Peabody 1997 <1969>, Hendrickson vii; 308 pp. 1-56562-272-279 [LouvSt 23,377s—Verheyden, Joseph].

7589 ᴱ**Cattaneo, Enrico** I ministeri nella Chiesa antica: testi patristici dei primi tre secoli. Letture cristiane del primo millennio 25: T 1997, Paoline 828 pp. L78.000. 88-315-1370-2. ᴿThViat(P) 2 (1997) 259-260 *(Telesca, Luigi)*.

7590 **Dassmann, Ernst** Ämter und Dienste in den frühchristlichen Gemeinden. 1994, ⇒11/2,4351; 12,7237. ᴿBLE 98/1 (1997) 81-82 *(Denis, Y.)*; WiWei 60/1 (1997) 154-156 *(Bey, Horst von der)*; ThQ 177 (1997) 231-232 *(König, Hildegard)*; VM 39/1 (1997) 239-240 *(Olivar, A.)*.

7591 *Eckert, Jost* Die Befähigung zu "Dienern des Neuen Bundes" (2 Kor 3,6): neutestamentliche Perspektiven zum Amt in der Kirche. TThZ 106 (1997) 60-78.

7592 *Eggen, Wiel* The gender of the crucified. Sum. 267. VSVD 38 (1997) 267-287.

7593 *Ego, Beate* Priester/Priestum: Judentum. TRE 27. 1997, ⇒419. 391-396.

7594 **Eisen, Ute E.** Amtsträgerinnen im frühen Christentum. FKDG 61: 1996, ⇒12,7240. ᴿThLZ 122 (1997) 457-459 *(Dörfler-Dierken, Angelika)*.

7595 **Forestell, J. Terence** As ministers of Christ: the christological dimension of ministry in the NT. 1991, ⇒7,8128... 10,8075. ᴿEeT(O) 28/1 (1997) 119-120 *(Bonneau, Normand)*.

7596 *Geist, Heinz* El sacerdocio según la revelación: novedad del sacerdocio cristiano. EstTrin 31 (1997) 275-294.

7597 *Gonsalves, Francis* Shepherds after my own heart. VJTR 61 (1997) 775-783.

7598 **Haag, Herbert** Worauf es ankommt: wollte Jesus eine Zwei-Stände-Kirche?. FrB 1997, Herder 123 pp. 3-451-26049-2.

7599 **Heid, Stefan** Zölibat in der frühen Kirche: die Anfänge einer Enthaltsamkeitspflicht für Kleriker in Ost und West. Pd 1997, Schöningh 339 pp. DM39.80. ᴿGuL 70 (1997) 471-472 *(Baur, Franz Josef)*.

7600 **Hermans, Theo** Oʀɪɢᴇɴᴇ: théologie sacrificielle du sacerdoce des chrétiens. ThH 102: 1996, ⇒12,7248. ᴿJThS 48 (1997) 244-246 *(Edwards, M.J.)*; MD 209 (1997) 130-132 *(Laporte, Jean)*; StPat 44/3 (1997) 211-212 *(Corsato, Celestino)*.

7601 **Kaufman, Peter Ivan** Church, book, and bishop: conflict and authority in early Latin christianity. 1996, ⇒12,7251. ᴿAThR 79 (1997) 440-441 *(Lyman, J. Rebecca)*.

7602 *Maffei, Giuseppe* L'apporto di A.M. Jᴀᴠɪᴇʀʀᴇ al dialogo con O. Cᴜʟʟᴍᴀɴɴ sulla successione. BSRel 125: 1997, ⇒45. ᶠJᴀᴠɪᴇʀʀᴇ Oʀᴛᴀs A., 505-533.

7603 *Mappes, David* The discipline of a sinning elder;
7604 The 'elder' in the Old and New Testaments;
7605 The 'laying on of hands' of elders;
7606 The New Testament elder, overseer, and pastor. BS 154 (1997) 333-343/80-92/473-479/162-174.

7607 *Marucci, Corrado* Storia e valore del diaconato femminile nella chiesa antica. RdT 38 (1997) 771-795.

7608  *McLain, Charles E.* Standing between God and culture: 'heedership' or leadership?. CBTJ 13/2 (1997) 13-36.
7609  **Nelson, Richard D.** Raising up a faithful priest: community and priesthood in biblical theology. 1993, ⇒9,8498... 12,7256. ᴿThLZ 122 (1997) 1005-1007 *(Reventlow, Henning Graf)*.
7610  *Neymeyr, Ulrich* Presbyteroi bei CLEMENS von Alexandrien. St-Patr 31: 1997, ⇒351. ᴱLivingstone, E.A., 493-496.
7611  *Odasso, Giovanni* La formazione biblica in relazione al ministero presbiterale. Seminarium 37 (1997) 56-79.
7612  *Reventlow, Henning Graf* Priester/Priestum: Altes Testament. TRE 27. 1997, ⇒419. 383-391.
7613  **Rolland, P.** La succession apostolique dans le Nouveau Testament. P 1997, Éd. de Paris 123 pp. FF124. 2-85162-010-X [ETR 73,310].
7614  *Roloff, Jürgen* Church leadership according to the NT. ThD 44 (1997) 139-147.
7615  *Sänger, Dieter* Priester/Priestum: Neues Testament. TRE 27. 1997, ⇒419. 396-401.
7616  *Schöllgen, Georg* Der Abfassungszweck der frühchristlichen Kirchenordnungen: Anmerkungen zu den Thesen Bruno STEIMERS. JAC 40 (1997) 55-77.
7617  *Schwarz, Roland* Verbieten Bibeltexte die Frauenordination?. Diak. 28 (1997) 167-173.
7618  *Servais, Jacques* Il regno di Dio e la vita consacrata. StMiss 46 (1997) 171-194.
7619  **Ysebaert, Joseph** Die Amtsterminologie im Neuen Testament und in der alten Kirche. 1994, ⇒10,8139... 12,7275. ᴿRB 104 (1997) 459-460 *(Taylor, Justin)*.
7620  *Zardoni, Serafino* La storia del diaconato permanente. Seminarium 37 (1997) 733-751.

H8.0 **Oratio,** *spiritualitas personalis*

7621  **Alphonso Liguori** Pratica di amar Gesù Cristo. ᴱ*Desideri, F.* 1996, ⇒12,7276. Asp. 44/1 (1997) 128-129 *(Langella, Alfonso)*.
7622  ᴱ**Barbaglio, Giuseppe** Espiritualidad del Nuevo Testamento. Nueva Alianza 129: 1994, ⇒11/2,4422. ᴿCDios 210/1 (1997) 349-350 *(Gutiérrez, J.)*.
7623  **Barrado, Pedro** La oración del barro. M 1997, Narcea 166 pp. ᴿEphMar 47/3 (1997) 311-312 *(Navarro Puerto, Mercedes)*.
7624  *Blowers, Paul* The bible and spiritual doctrine: some controversies within the early eastern christian ascetic tradition. The Bible in Greek christian antiquity. 1997 <c.1984>, ⇒177. ᴱᵀBlowers, P.M., 229-255.
7625  **Brown, Raymond Edward** Leggere i vangeli con la chiesa: da Natale a Pasqua. Meditazioni 132: Brescia 1997, Queriniana 132 pp. 88-399-1532-X.
7626  *Bruni, Giancarlo* Corro verso ció che mi sta davanti: risalita alle sorgenti neotestamentarie dell'ascesi. Servitium 31 (1997) 476-489.
7627  *Charles, Francois-Dominique* Le pelerinage a Jerusalem. VS 77 (1997) 664-666.

7628    **Creedon, Joseph D.** Lenten light: daily scripture meditations and prayers. Mystic 1997, Twenty-Third 48 pp. [BiTod 36,129—Bergant, Dianne].

7629    **Cullmann, Oscar** Prayer in the NT. 1995, ⇒11/2,4430. [R]NT 39 (1997) 92-4 *(Moessner, David P.)*; Interp. 51 (1997) 80-1 *(Sowers, Sidney)*; CBQ 59 (1997) 765-766 & CritRR 10 (1997) 173-175 *(Kiley, Mark)*;

7630    La preghiera nel NT. PBT 39: 1995, ⇒11/2,4432; 12,7282. [R]Ho Theológos 15 (1997) 347-349 *(Iovino, Paolo)*;

7631    La prière dans le NT. 1995, ⇒11/2,4431; 12,7283. [R]FV 96/1 (1997) 68-69 *(Flichy, Odile)*; RThPh 129 (1997) 298-299 *(Cochand, Nicolas)*;

7632    Das Gebet im Neuen Testament: zugleich Versuch einer vom Neuen Testament aus zu erteilenden Antwort auf heutige Fragen. Tü [2]1997, Mohr xi; 196 pp. 3-16-146685-3.

7633    **Fenske, Wolfgang** "Und wenn ihr betet..." (Mt. 6,5): Gebete in der zwischenmenschlichen Kommunikation der Antike als Ausdruck der Frömmigkeit. Diss. München 1994; [D]*Kuhn, H.-W.*: StUNT 21: Gö 1997, Vandenhoeck & R 348 pp. DM128. 3-525-53373-X [NThAR 1997,132].

7634    **Finn, Thomas M.** From death to rebirth: ritual and conversion in antiquity. NY 1997, Paulist vi; 286 pp. $20. 0-8091-3689-9.

7635    **García Rubio, S.** A solas con el evangelio. San Lorenzo del Escurial 1997, Escurialenses 151 pp. [EstAg 32,596—Fernández, A.].

7636    [E]**Giraudo, Cesare** Liturgia e spiritualità nell'Oriente cristiano: in dialogo con Miguel ARRANZ. Rdt Library 3: CinB 1997, San Paolo 319 pp. 88-215-3630-0.

7637    *Gonnet, Dominique* Jésus et la demande. Vie Chrétienne 425 (1997) 1-4.

7638    **Hamman, Adalbert Gautier** La preghiera nella Chiesa antica. TC 6: 1994, ⇒11/2,4447; 12,7286. [R]AHIg 6 (1997) 516-519 *(Pasquato, O.)*.

7639    *Janeras, Sebastià* El Trisagi, una professió de fe biblicolitúrgica al llarg de la Mediterrània. La Bíblia i el Mediterrani. 1997, ⇒385. [E]Borrell, d'Agustí, 297-310.

7640    *Juel, Donald* The strange silence of the bible. Interp. 51 (1997) 5-19.

7641    **Kern, Kathleen** We are the pharisees. 1995, 11/2,4452. [R]AUSS 35 (1997) 130-132 *(Maynard-Reid, Pedrito U.)*.

7642    **Lopez Melus, Francisco Maria** Desierto: una experiencia de gracia. 1994, ⇒9,8586... 11/2,4457. [R]EstB 55 (1997) 426-427 *(Munoz Leon, D.)*.

7643    **Martini, Carlo Maria** El seguimiento de Cristo. Sdr 1997, Sal Terrae 93 pp. [RF 237,556];

7644    Alla fine del millennio lasciateci sognare. CasM 1997, Piemme 240 pp. 88-384-2957-X.

7645    **McGinn, B.** Storia della mistica cristiana in Occidente, 1: le origini (I-V secolo). Genova 1997, Marietti. [Firmana 19-20,321ss—Petruzzi, Paolo].

7646    **Miller, Patrick D.** They cried to the Lord: the form and theology of biblical prayer. 1994, ⇒10,8179; 11/2,4470. [R]JBL 116 (1997) 732-733 *(Bellinger, W.H.)*; CBQ 58 (1996) 323-324 *(McCann, J. Clinton)*.

7647  **Monaca, Eliana** Cantico. Mi 1997, Mondadori 158 pp. L12.000.
RAMi 22 (1997) 484-488 *(Vannini, Marco)*.
7648  *Osuna, Javier* La persona de Jesús en los Ejercicios de San
IGNACIO. Confer 36/2 (1997) 272-280.
7649  [E]**Ryan, Gregory** The burning heart: reading the New Testament
with John Main. 1996, ⇒12,7297. [R]ScrB 27 (1997) 89-90 *(Mills,
Mary E.)*.
7650  **Schürmann, Heinz** Ein Jahr der Jesusbegegnung: die Evangelien
der liturgischen Leseordnung für Werktage ins Gebet genommen:
ein Werkbuch für geistliche Schriftlesung und inneres Gebet.
[E]*Christian, Paul*: Pd 1997, Bonifatius 400 pp. DM39.80. 3-87088-
979-9.
7651  *Ségalen, Jean-Marie* Prier avec Jésus... Tychique 127 (1997) 51-
55.
7652  *Silva, Santiago* Conocer, comprender y orar con la Biblia, 2. La
Revista Católica 97/2 (1997) 109-115.
7653  *Spittler, Russell P.* What to read in New Testament spirituality and
beyond: a bibliographic essay. JPentec.S 11: 1997, ⇒63.
[F]MENZIES W., 151-172.
7654  [E]**Terrin, A.N.** Scriptura crescit cum orante: bibbia e liturgia, 2.
1994, ⇒12,6783. [R]Ben. 44 (1997) 451-452 *(Lapponi, Massimo)*.
7655  **Vanhoye, Albert** Vivere nella nuova alleanza: meditazioni bibliche. 1995, ⇒11/2,4493. [R]CivCatt 148 III (1997) 547-548
*(Scaiola, D.)*;
7656  Per progredire nell'amore. Seoul 1997, Living with Scripture 318
pp. [AcBib 10/4,395]. **K.**
7657  *Vanni, Ugo* La preghiera e il regno. StMiss 46 (1997) 65-90.
7658  *Viviano, B.T.* Hillel and Jesus on prayer. Hillel and Jesus. 1997,
⇒321. [E]Charlesworth, J.H., 427-457.
7659  **Zink, Jörg** Cento giorni con Gesù. T 1997, Claudiana 224 pp.
L29.000. 88-7016-64-8 [Protest. 53,358—Bottazzi, Roberto].

H8.1 *Spiritualitas publica:* **Liturgia, vita communitatis, Sancti**

7660  *Abir, Peter Antonysamy* More than blood-witness. ITS 34/1-3
(1997) 233-261 [Rev 16,6].
7661  *Bacq, Philippe* Comunidad y misión según Jesús. Confer 36/2
(1997) 219-230.
7662  **Barnes, Elizabeth B.** The story of discipleship: Christ, humanity,
and church in narrative perspective. 1995, ⇒11/2,4037; 12,7177.
[R]RExp 94 (1997) 314-315 *(Stassen, Glen)*.
7663  *Bermejo, Enrique* El influjo de la liturgia de Jerusalén en las demás
liturgias. TE 41 (1997) 393-409.
7664  *Borrell, Agustí* 'La paraula de Jesús és mateix': TERESA de Lisieux i la bíblia. Qüestiones de Vida Cristiana 185 (1997) 9-22.
7665  **Brown, Peter** The body and society: men, women and sexual re-
nuncation in early christianity. 1988, ⇒4,9307... 11/2,4543. [R]Gn.
69 (1997) 657-665 *(Habermehl, Peter)*.
7666  *Burton-Christie, Douglas* Oral culture, biblical interpretation, and
spirituality in early christian monasticism. The Bible in Greek
christian antiquity. 1997 <c.1984>, ⇒177. [ET]Blowers, P.M.,
415-440.

7667 *Cavagnoli, Gianni* Il mistero di Cristo: oggetto della celebrazione. RPLi 201 (1997) 3-9.

7668 Comité del Gran Jubileo Comisión Litúrgica. Encontrar a Jesucristo en la liturgia. Phase 37 (1997) 7-20.

7669 *Cothenet, Édouard* Liturgie et évangélisation dans le Nouveau Testament. EeV 107 (1997) 97-104.

7670 *Dahlgrün, Corinna* Ethik statt Eschaton?: Überlegungen zur Reduktion der Worte von Apokalypse und Jüngstem Gericht in den Perikopenrevisionen. PTh 86 (1997) 429-437.

7671 *Dal Covolo, Enrico* La donna vergine di Cristo nelle comunità dei primi tre secoli. BSRel 125: 1997, ⇒45. FJAVIERRE ORTAS A., 217-225.

7672 *Davis, Stephen M.* Toward a theology of worship. CBTJ 13/2 (1997) 52-68.

7673 *De Zan, Renato* Il cultuale e l'economico nella bibbia. RivLi 84 (1997) 209-219;

7674 La teologia liturgico-biblica della gloria nel tempo di Pasqua. StAns 124: 1997, ⇒57. FLOEHRER M. — TRAGAN P., 759-778.

7675 *Della Mutta, Ruggero* Gesù, unico salvatore: l'eucologia del tempo ordinario, 3. RPLi 35/3 (1997) 65-70.

7676 *Diefenbach, Manfred* "Berufen als Heilige": eine Klärung des Heiligenbegriffes tut not. IKaZ 26 (1997) 249-257.

7677 *Dugandžić, Ivan* Učitelju, Gdje stanuješ? (Iv 1,38): pojam učenika i nasljedovanja u novom zavjetu [Meister, wo wohnst Du?]. 1997, ⇒96. FTOMICA C., Zsfg. 318. 303-319. **Croatian**.

7678 *Durken, Daniel* The bible and the Benedictines. BiTod 35 (1997) 236-240.

7679 *Falsini, Rinaldo* I modi della presenza di Cristo nella liturgia: un invito alla riflessione. RPLi 201 (1997) 18-24.

7680 *Fortin-Melkevik, Anne* L'identità del cristiano al seguito di Gesù Cristo. TCrespi, Pietro: Conc(I) 33/1 (1997) 129-142.

7681 *García Mateo, R.* San IGNACIO de Loyola y San Pablo. Zsfg. 544. Gr. 78 (1997) 523-544.

7682 **Lang, Bernhard** Sacred games: a history of christian worship. NHv 1997, Yale University Press xiii; 527 pp. $40 [CHR 84,702s—Baldovin, John F.].

7683 *Luchetti, María Clara* La alteridad crística. Confer 36/2 (1997) 261-271.

7684 *Madera Vargas, Ignacio* Identidad de la vida religiosa desde el seguimiento de Jesucristo. Confer 36/2 (1997) 189-197.

7685 *Martínez González, Emilio J.* El rostro de Cristo en TERESA de Lisieux. Confer 36/2 (1997) 297-320.

7686 *Martini, Carlo Maria* Experiencia de itinerario vocacional y *lectio divina*. Seminarios 43 (1997) 489-496.

7687 *Masseroni, Enrico* Lascio tutto... eccomi!. Consacrazione e Servizio 46/4 (1997) 9-16.

7688 **Menestrina, Giovanni** Bibbia, liturgia e letteratura cristiana antica. Brescia 1997, Morcelliana 199 pp. L30.000. 88-372-1634-3.

7689 **Mesters, Carlos** Seguir a Jesús en los evangelios. Tu Palabra es Vida 5: México 1997, Dabar 286 pp. [EfMex 16,260—Cabello Ramos, Rubén].

7690 *Nichols, Bridget* The bible in the liturgy: a hermeneutical discussion of faith and language. StLi 27 (1997) 200-216.

7691 *Novoa, Laurentino* Vida consagrada y misterio de la cruz. Confer 36/2 (1997) 247-258.
7692 *Paulsen, Henning* Werdet Vorübergehende... Zur Literatur. WUNT 99: 1997, ⇒153. 1-17.
7693 *Petras, David M.* The gospel lectionary of the Byzantine church. SVTQ 41/2-3 (1997) 113-140.
7694 *Pfeifer, Michaela* Wie evangelisch sind die evangelischen Räte?: der Stachel der historisch-kritischen Exegese im Fleisch der modernen Ordenstheologie. StAns 124: 1997, ⇒57. FLOEHRER M. — TRAGAN P., 697-727.
7695 *Pina, Abilio* Tomar en serio a Jesucristo. Confer 36/2 (1997) 289-293.
7696 *Renoux, Charles* The reading of the bible in the ancient liturgy of Jerusalem. The Bible in Greek christian antiquity. 1997 <c.1984>, ⇒177. ETBlowers, P.M., 389-414.
7697 **Ribeiro, Cláudio de Oliveira,** (*al.*), Communidades e massa a partir da Bíblia. Estudos bíblicos 55: Petrópolis 1997, Vozes 121 pp. [NThAR 1998,98].
7698 ERichter, Klemens; Kranemann, Benedikt Christologie der Liturgie: der Gottesdienst der Kirche—Christusbekenntnis und Sinaibund. QD 159: 1995, ⇒11/2,634; 12,7317. RMD 210 (1997) 157-165 *(Prétot, Patrick)*.
7699 *Rodríguez Quiroga, Silvia* Estudiar... también es amar. CuMon 32 (1997) 177-194, 308-327.
7700 *Rordorf, Willy* The bible in the teaching and the liturgy of early christian communities. The Bible in Greek christian antiquity. 1997 <c.1984>, ⇒177. ETBlowers, P.M., 69-102.
7701 *Russell, John* Saint THERESE of Lisieux and scripture. 1997, ⇒70. FMURPHY R., Master, 335-351.
7702 *Saxer, Victor* The influence of the bible in early christian martyrology. The Bible in Greek christian antiquity. 1997 <c.1984>, ⇒177. ETBlowers, P.M., 342-374.
7703 *Sullivan, Lisa M.* "I responded, 'I will not ...'": christianity as catalyst for resistance in the Passio Perpetuae et Felicitatis. Semeia 79 (1997) 63-74.
7704 *Susin, Luis Carlos* Jesús en la encrucijada. Confer 36/2 (1997) 199-217.
7705 *Taft, Robert F.* Quaestiones disputatae: the Skeuophylakion of Hagia Sophia and the entrances of the liturgy revisited. OrChr 81 (1997) 1-35.
7706 **Ton, Josef** Suffering, martyrdom, and rewards in heaven. Lanham 1997, University Press of America xviii; 516 pp. $68/$48.50. 0-7618-0832-9/66-7 [NTS 44,625].
7707 *Uríbarri, Gabino* La conformación plena con Cristo: peculiaridad de la vida religiosa. Confer 36/2 (1997) 169-187.
7708 **Uríbarri, Gabino** 'Reavivar el don de Dios' (2 Tim 1,6): una propuesta de promoción vocacional. Sdr 1997, Sal Terrae 239 pp. RMCom 55 (1997) 560 *(Aleixandre, Dolores)*.
7709 *Vandenbroeck, Paul* Racines bibliques pour une compréhension chrétienne de la sainteté. SIDIC 30/3 (1997) 11-14.
7710 *Vanhoye, Albert* Vita consacrata sanitaria: fondamenti biblici. Dizionario di teologia pastorale sanitaria. ECinà, G.: T 1997, Camillane. 1388-1393 [AcBib 10/4,395].

7711 *Verhelst, Stéphane* Pesiqta de-Rav Kahana, chapitre 1, et la liturgie chrétienne. Sum. 453. LASBF 47 (1997) 129-138.
7712 *Vilanova, Evangelista* Teología y mística: a propósito del Maestro ECKHART. StAns 124: 1997, ⇒57. <sup>F</sup>LOEHRER M. — TRAGAN P., 729-748.

## H8.2 Theologia moralis NT

7713 *Beilner, Wolfgang* Versöhnung oder Widerstand. Diak. 28 (1997) 65-68.
7714 **Bilkes, Laurens W.** Theological ethics and holy scripture in the works of James M. GUSTAFSON, R. Paul RAMSEY, and Allen D. VERHEY. Diss. Apeldoorn 1997; <sup>D</sup>*Velema, W.H.*: Heerenveen 1997, Groen 274 pp. *f*50 [GThT 98,187s—Lange, F. de].
7715 **Bretzke, James T.** Bibliography on scripture and christian ethics. SRS 39: Lewiston 1997, Mellen 364 pp. $100. 0-7734-8460-4 [ThD 45,358—Heiser, W. Charles].
7716 *Bultmann Lemke, Antje* Albert SCHWEITZERs Ethik und die Menschenrechte: "Ethik ist bis ins Unendliche erweiterte Verantwortung". BZNW 89: 1997, ⇒33. <sup>F</sup>GRAESSER E., 47-51.
7717 **Carter, Philippa** The servant-ethic in the New Testament. AmUSt.TR 196: NY 1997, Lang xi; 155 pp. Bibl. $36. 0-8204-3393-4.
7718 **Desjardins, Michel R.** Peace, violence and the New Testament. BiSe 46: Shf 1997, Academic 131 pp. 1-85075-799-2.
7719 **Dziuba, Andrzej F.** Orędzie moralne Jezusa Chrystusa [Messaggio morale di Gesù Cristo]. 1996, ⇒12,7329. <sup>R</sup>Ter.48/1 (1997) 435-436 *(Praśkiewicz, Szczepan T.)*; CoTh 67/3 (1997) 218-220 *(Góralczyk, Pawel)*. P.
7720 **Faul, Fabien** Morale biblique et système théologique: la recherche des moralistes francophones entre 1945 et le Concile Vatican II. Diss. Pont. Univ. Gregoriana; <sup>D</sup>*Demmer, Klaus*: Metz 1997, 76 pp. excerpt.
7721 *Gustafson, James M.* The use of scripture in christian ethics. StTh 51/1 (1997) 15-29.
7722 *Haas, Guenther* Exegetical issues in the use of the bible to justify the acceptance of homosexual practice. CScR 26 (1997) 386-412.
7723 *Hagner, Donald A.* Ethics and the sermon on the mount. StTh 51/1 (1997) 44-59.
7724 **Hays, Richard B.** The moral vision of the NT. 1996, ⇒12,7334. <sup>R</sup>TS 58 (1997) 537-539 *(Matera, Frank J.)*; First Things 78 (1997) 61-64 *(Meilaender, Gilbert)*.
7725 *Jefford, Clayton N.* Household codes and conflict in the early church. StPatr 31: 1997, ⇒351. <sup>E</sup>Livingstone, E.A., 121-127.
7726 **Jones, David C.** Biblical christian ethics. GR 1994, Baker. $13 [WThJ 61,300—Krabbendam, Henry].
7727 *Kollmann, Bernd* Jesu Verbot des Richtens und die Gemeindediszi-plin. ZNW 88 (1997) 170-186 [Mt 7,1-2; Lk 6,37-38].
7728 *Kosch, Daniel* Das Gesetz der Freiheit: zum Toraverständnis von Jesus und Matthäus. PzB 6 (1997) 47-71.
7729 *Kügler, Hermann* Die Nachtseite des Christentums?: ein Beispiel zur "dunklen" Seite der Sexualität und Erotik im frühen Christen-tum. Entschluss 52/6 (1997) 25-29.

7730  *Kvalbein, Hans* The kingdom of God in the ethics of Jesus. StTh 51/1 (1997) 60-84.

7731  *LaHurd, Carol Schersten* The 'other' in biblical perspective. CThMi 24 (1997) 411-424.

7732  *Martin, Troy* The christian's obligation not to forgive. ET 108 (1997) 360-362.

7733  **Martini, Carlo Maria** Das Evangelium als Lebensnorm. [T]*Kohlhaas, Radbert*: Trier 1997, Paulinus 135 pp. 3-7902-0097-2.

7734  **Matera, Frank J.** New Testament ethics. 1996, ⇒12,7341. [R]TS 58 (1997) 723-724 *(Topel, John)*.

7735  **Meeks, Wayne A.** The origins of Christian morality: the first two centuries. 1993, ⇒9,8809...12,7343. [R]Bibl.Interp. 5/1 (1997) 107-09 *(Muddiman, John)*; NeoTest. 31 (1997) 223-4 *(Tite, Philip L.)*;

7736  As origens da moralidade cristã: os dois primeiros séculos. [T]*Fiorotti, Adaury*: Bíblia e Sociologia: São Paulo 1997, Paulus 255 pp. 85-349-0592-0 [PerTeol 30,322].

7737  *Mouton, Elna* The (trans)formative potential of the bible as resource for christian ethos and ethics. Scriptura 62 (1997) 245-257.

7738  *Nissen, Johannes* The distinctive character of the New Testament love command in relation to Hellenistic Judaism: historical and hermeneutical reflections. NT and Hellenistic Judaism. 1997, ⇒318. [E]Borgen, P., 123-150 [Mk 12,28-34].

7739  *Öhler, Markus* Homosexualität und neutestamentliche Ethik. PzB 6 (1997) 133-147.

7740  *Paretsky, Albert* The two ways and *dipsychia* in early christian literature: an interesting dead end in moral discourse. Rés. 334. Ang. 74 (1997) 305-334.

7741  *Pearson, Birger A.* Philanthropy in the Greco-Roman world and in early christianity. The emergence. 1997, ⇒154. 186-213.

7742  *Peschke, Karl-Heinz* Apologie pour la monogamie: l'évangile et les critères de l'ethique sexuelle. Rés. 6. Com(F) 22/1 (1997) 37-54 (IKaZ 26,16-32).

7743  *Phillips, Gary A.; Fewell, Danna Nolan* Ethics, bible, reading as if. Semeia 77 (1997) 1-21.

7744  *Rodriguez, Edmundo* Jesus, power, and the ONE. RfR 56/1 (1997) 87-94.

7745  *Rousselle, Aline* Die antike Familie und das Christentum. Welt und Umwelt der Bibel 6 (1997) 32-36.

7746  *(a) Saldarini, Anthony J.* Taking law seriously. BiRe 13/2 (1997) 17, 44; *(b)* [E]**Sauter, Gerhard** "Versöhnung" als Thema der Theologie. Collab. *Assel, Heinrich.* TB 92: Mü 1997, Kaiser 270 pp. Bibl. 3-579-02009-9.

7747  **Schenk-Ziegler, Alois** Correctio fraterna im Neuen Testament: die 'brüderliche Zurechtweisung' in biblischen, frühjüdischen und hellenistischen Schriften. Diss. Tübingen; [D]*Theobald, M.*: FzB 84: Wü 1997, Echter 492 pp. DM56. 3-429-01979-6.

7748  **Schmitz, Philipp** Fortschritt ohne Grenzen?: christliche Ethik und technische Allmacht. QD 164: FrB 1997, Herder 256 pp. Bibl. 3-451-02164-1.

7749  **Siker, Jeffrey S.** Scripture and ethics: twentieth-century portraits. NY 1997, OUP (10) 294 pp. $17. 0-19-510104-9. [R]ET 109 (1997-98) 1-3 *(Rodd, C.S.)*.

7750  *Stowasser, Martin* Homosexualität und Bibel: exegetische und hermeneutische Überlegungen zu einem schwierigen Thema. NTS 43 (1997) 503-526.

7751 *Turner, P.D.* Biblical texts relevant to homosexual orientation and practice: notes on philology and interpretation. CScR 26 (1997) 435-445.

7752 *Van Leeuwen, Mary Stewart* To ask a better question: the heterosexuality-homosexuality debate revisited. Interp. 51 (1997) 143-158.

7753 *Waele, Daniël H. de* De herkomst van de nieuwtestamentische "huistafels": een korte geschiedenis van het onderzoek. Analecta Bruxellensia 2 (1997) 163-179.

7754 *Welch, Sharon D.* Biblical interpretation in christian feminist ethics. StTh 51/1 (1997) 30-43.

7755 **Wheeler, Sondra Ely** Wealth as peril and obligation: the New Testament on possessions. 1995, ⇒11/2,4719; 12,7361. [R]RStT 16/1 (1997) 114-115 *(Wilkinson, Bruce W.)*.

7756 *Williams, Rowan D.* Interiority and epiphany: a reading in New Testament ethics. MoTh 13/1 (1997) 29-51.

7757 *Winter, Martin* Die Bedeutung des Lohngedankens bei Jesus und Paulus. WuD 24 (1997) 169-185.

7758 *Wölfel, Eberhard* Ethik im Kontext eines evolutionären Weltbildes. BZNW 89: 1997, ⇒33. [F]GRAESSER E., 387-403.

7759 *Zehetbauer, Markus Barmherzigkeit* als Lehnübersetzung: die Etymologie des Begriffes im Hebräischen, Griechischen, Lateinischen und Deutschen—eine kleine Theologiegeschichte. BN 90 (1997) 67-83.

H8.4 *NT ipsum de reformatione sociali*—**Political action in Scripture**

7760 *Manenschijn, Gerrit* 'Jesus is the Christ': the political theology of Leviathan. [T]*Vriend, John*: Sum. 35. JRE 25/1 (1997) 35-64.

7761 **O'Donovan, Oliver** The desire of the nations: rediscovering the roots of political theology. 1996, ⇒12,7368. [R]JThS 48 (1997) 756-758 *(Forrester, Duncan B.)*.

H8.5 **Theologia liberationis latino-americana**

7762 [E]**Fornet-Betancourt, Raúl** Befreiungstheologie: kritischer Rückblick und Perspektiven für die Zukunft. Mainz 1997, Grünewald 3 vols. [R]Jahrbuch für kontextuelle Theologie 5 (1997) 176-191 *(Bey, Horst von der)*.

7763 *Gerstenberger, Erhard S.* Der befreiende Gott: zum Standort lateinamerikanischer Theologie. 1997, ⇒48. [F]KNIERIM R., 145-166.

7764 *Giroud, Nicole* Presencia de la redención en la teología de la liberación. Anámnesis 7/1 (1997) 55-82.

7765 *Maier, Martin* Teología de la liberación en Latinoamérica. RF 236 (1997) 281-296;

7766 Theologie der Befreiung in Lateinamerika. StZ 215 (1997) 723-35.

7767 *Mesters, Carlos* The liberation reading of the bible in the base ecclesial communities in Brazil. 1997, ⇒70. [F]MURPHY R., Master, 301-315.

7768 **Schürger, Wolfgang** Theologie auf dem Weg der Befreiung: Geschichte und Methode des Zentrums für Bibelstudien in Brasilien.

Diss. Erlangen 1994. EMMÖ: Erlangen 1995, Ev.-Luth. Mission 280 pp. ᴿThLZ 122 (1997) 130-131 *(Frieling, Reinhard)*.

7769 *Silvestre, Giuseppe* La lettura popolare della bibbia speranza di liberazione per l'Africa e l'America Latina e cammino per l'ecumenismo. Vivarium 5 (1997) 397-415.

7770 **Sobrino, Jon** Jesus the liberator. 1993, ⇒10,8550... 12,7386. ᴿTJT 13/1 (1997) 156-157 *(Whelan, Gerard K.)*.

7771 ᴱᵀ**Vaage, Leif E.** Subversive scriptures: revolutionary readings of the christian bible in Latin America. Valley Forge 1997, Trinity x; 213 pp. $19. 1-56338-200-8.

7772 *Vanzan, Piersandro* La teologia della liberazione in America Latina e nel primo mondo. 1997, ⇒30. ᶠGɪᴏʀᴅᴀɴᴏ, 759-778.

## ʜ8.6 *Theologiae emergentes*—Theologies of emergent groups

7773 *Beyerhaus, Peter* Die Bibel im Werden einheimischer Kirchen. TVGMS 424: 1997, ⇒59. ᶠMᴀɪᴇʀ G., 345-356.

7774 ᴱ**Jiménez, Luz** A palavra se fez Índia. RIBLA 26: Petrópolis 1997, Vozes 152 pp. [REB 57,1008].

7775 *Ma, Wonsuk* The spirit of God upon leaders of Israelite society and Igorot tribal churches. JPentec.S 11: 1997, ⇒63. ᶠMᴇɴᴢɪᴇs W., 291-316.

7776 ᴱ**Mukonyora, Isabel,** *(al.),* 'Rewriting' the bible. 1993, ⇒9,9186; 10,8621. ᴿTPBT 48 (1997) 150-152 *(Mojola, Aloo O.)*.

7777 *Naber, Gerhard* 'Die Bibel mit den Augen eines Palästineners lesen...': eine Annäherung an die palästinesische Befreiungstheologie. RKZ 138/9 (1997) 390-394 [ZID 23,448].

7778 *Rakotsoane, Francis C.L.* Jesus Christ as the leader of the ancestors. Challenge 39 (1997) 20-21 [ThIK 18/2,20].

7779 **Sherman, Amy L.** The soul of development: biblical christianity and economic transformation in Guatemala. NY 1997, OUP xviii; 214 pp. $45. 0-19-510671-7 [JR 79,187s—Brusco, Elizabeth E.].

## ʜ8.7 *Mariologia*—The mother of Jesus in the NT

7780 **Bartha, Tibor** Maria, Jézus anyija [Mary, mother of Jesus]. Gyermeksegtortenet. 1997, ⇒316. ᴱBenyik, G., Sum., Zsfg., Rias., 115-120. **Hungarian.**

7781 **Bartosik, Grzegorz M.** Z niej nrodzit sic Jezus: szkice z mariologii biblijnej [Da lei è nato Gesù: saggio di mariologia biblica]. 1996, ⇒12,7396. ᴿMF 97/1-2 (1997) 346-349 *(Siwak, Waclaw)*.

7782 *Benyik, György* Mária az apokrif irodalomban. Gyermeksegtortenet. 1997, ⇒316. ᴱBenyik, G., Sum., Zsfg., Rias., 121-126. **Hungarian.**
ᴱ**Benyik, G.** Biblikus Konferencia (1996: Szeged): Gyermeksegtortenet es mariologia ⇒316.

7783 *Bolewski, Jacek* Godzina laski: Maryja droga zycia duchowego [The hour of grace: Mary as the way to a spiritual life]. Sum. 3. Zycie Duchowe 9/4 (1997) 29-48. **P.**

7784 *Bridcut, William J.* Did Mary remain a virgin?. ChM 111/1 (1997) 48-52 [ZID 23/6,191].

7785 $^E$**Buono, Anthony** Dictionary of Mary. New Jersey 1997, Catholic Book 552 pp. [Miles Immaculatae 35,536s—Calkins, Arthur B.].

7786 *Canal, Jose Maria* Maria, reina de misericordia y nueva Ester: historia de estos títulos. StLeg 38 (1997) 119-155.

7787 *Carroll, Eamon R.* With Mary his mother: a theologian reflects on recent scripture studies. 1997, ⇒70. $^F$MURPHY R., Master, 219-234.

7788 **Colzani, G.** Maria: mistero di grazia e di fede. 1996, ⇒12,7408. $^R$Theotokos 5 (1997) 738-741 *(De Fiores, Stefano)*.

7789 **Cunneen, Sally** In search of Mary: the woman and the symbol. 1996, ⇒12,7410. $^R$CrossCur 47 (1997-8) 574-5 *(Moynihan, R.B.)*.

7790 $^E$**De Fiores, Stefano; Meo, Salvatore** Dicionario de mariologia. $^T$*Cunha, Alvaro A.*, *(al.)*: Sao Paulo 1995, Paulus xxiii; 1381 pp. $^R$REB 57 (1997) 459-463 *(Taborda, Francisco)*.

7791 Dombes, Groupe des. Marie dans le dessein de Dieu et la communion des saints, 1: dans l'histoire et l'écriture. P 1997, Bayard 100 pp. F55. $^R$ScEs 50 (1998) 389-390 *(Lison, Jacques)*.

7792 *Falgueras Salinas, Ignacio* Sedes sapientiae. Burg. 38 (1997) 493-525.

7793 **Garcia de Paredes, Jose Cristo Rey** Mariologia. 1995, ⇒11/2,5123; 12,7417. $^R$Theotokos 5 (1997) 349-351 *(De Fiores, Stefano)*; RdT 38 (1997) 570-572 *(De Fiores, Stefano)*;

7794 Santa Maria del 2000. M 1997, BAC 124 pp. Pts750 [Proyeccion 44,319].

7795 **Gaventa, Beverly R.** Mary: glimpses of the mother of Jesus. Studies on personalities of the New Testament: 1995, ⇒11/2,5124; 12,7418. $^R$CBQ 59 (1997) 153-154 *(Cahill, Michael)*.

7796 *Gaventa, Beverly R.* "All generations will call me blessed": Mary in biblical and ecumenical perspective. PSB 18 (1997) 250-261.

7797 *Grisez, Germain* Mary, mother of Jesus: sketch of a theology. NBl 78 (1997) 418-423.

7798 *Hallet, Carlos* María de Nazareth y TERESA de Lisieux. La Revista Catolica 97/2 (1997) 125-134.

7799 *Heine, Susanne* Glauben mit Leib und Seele: Maria—Jesu Mutter als Mutter Gottes in evangelischer Sicht. LM 36/11 (1997) 3-6.

7800 **Hock, Ronald F.** The life of Mary. Berkeley 1997, Ulysses 104 pp. $16 [BiTod 36,134—Senior, Donald] [Judg 11].

7801 *Imrenyi, Tibor* Vladjmir LOSSKY: Panagia. Gyermeksegtortenet. 1997, ⇒316. $^E$Benyik, G., Sum., Zsfg., Rias., 187-194. **Hungarian**.

7802 $^E$**Kießig, M.** Maria, la madre di nostro Signore: un contributo della chiesa evangelico-luterana tedesca. 1996, ⇒12,7426. $^R$Theotokos 5 (1997) 358-363 *(Cereti, Giovanni)*.

7803 *Lenkeyne Semsey, Klara* Jezus, Maria megvaltoja [Jesus as redeemer of Mary]. Gyermeksegtortenet. 1997, ⇒316. $^E$Benyik, G., Sum., Zsfg., Rias., 199-210. **Hungarian**.

7804 *Lucci, Laila* La figlia di Sion sullo sfondo delle culture extrabibliche. RivBib 45 (1997) 257-287.

7805 **McKenna, Megan** Die verkannte Frau: Maria von Nazaret neu entdeckt. $^T$*Schellenberger, Bernardin*: FrB 1997, Herder 173 pp. DM30. 3-45126034-4. $^R$ThGl 87 (1997) 675-676 *(Beinert, Wolfgang)*.

7806 **Mimouni, Simon Claude** Dormition et assomption de Marie: histoire des traditions anciennes. ThH 98: 1995, ⇒11/2,5142;

12,7432. <sup>R</sup>RB 104 (1997) 310-311 *(Taylor, Justin)*; EThL 73 (1997) 463-466 *(Verheyden, J.)*; Mar. 59 (1997) 329-335 *(Stiernon, Daniel)*.

7807 *Mirri, Luciana* La verginità nel mistero di Maria in San GIROLAMO. StPatr 33: 1997, ⇒351. <sup>E</sup>Livingstone, E.A., 325-344.

7808 *Murad, Afonso* O que queremos dizer quando proclamamos 'Maria, mae de Deus'. <sup>R</sup>PerTeol 29/1 (1997) 53-73.

7809 *Myszor, Wincenty* Maryja w wypowiedziach chrzescijanskich gnostykow [Maria, Mutter Jesu in einigen Aussagen der christlichen Gnostikern]. Zsfg. 217. WST 10 (1997) 211-217. **P**.

7810 *Nowell, Irene* Mary, seat of wisdom. BiTod 35 (1997) 158-163.

7811 **Nunez, Jose Miguel** Nacido de mujer: María, la madre de Jesus. M 1997, CCS 126 pp. [Mayeutica 23,509—Shonibare, Joseph].

7812 *Okland, Jorunn* "Den historiske Maria" og Dea Creatrix. NTT 98 (1997) 205-220.

7813 **Ossanna, Tullio Faustino** Il vangelo racconta Maria. Borgonuovo di Pontecchio Marconi 1997, Immacolata 100 pp. L12.000 [CiVi 52,414].

7814 **Pelikan, J.** María a traves de los siglos: su presencia en veinte siglos de cultura. M 1997, PPC 233 pp. [EstAg 33,397—Sierra de la Calle, B.];

7815 Mary through the centuries: her place in the history of culture. 1996, ⇒12,7437. <sup>R</sup>Carmelus 44/1 (1997) 210-211 *(Carroll, Eamon Richard)*; CrossCur 47 (1997-8) 572-574 *(O'Toole, James M.)*; Mar. 59 (1997) 337-338 *(Brennan, Walter)*.

7816 **Ponce Cuellar, Miguel** Maria, madre del redentor y madre de la Iglesia. Manual de Mariologia. 1995 (²1996), ⇒12,7441. <sup>R</sup>AnVal 23 (1997) 229-230 *(Girones, Gonzalo)*; RTLi 31/2 (1997) 215-216 *(Gonzalez, Carlos Ignacio)*; EE 72 (1997) 412-413 *(Martinez Sierra, A.)*; San Juan de la Cruz 13/1 (1997) 208-209 *(Bengoechea, Ismael)*; Augustinus 42 (1997) 198-199 *(Gomez, Enrique)*; Phase 37 (1997) 528-529 *(Aldazabal, J.)*; AnnTh 11 (1997) 548-549 *(Riestra, Jose Antonio)*; Cart. 13 (1997) 463 *(Hernandez Valenzuela, J.)*.

7817 *Ribeiro, Abilio Pina* Maria, mulher consagrada para a missao. Igreja e Missão 49/1 (1997) 83-96.

7818 **Rossi De Gasperis, Francesco** Maria di Nazaret: icona di Israele e della Chiesa. Spiritualita biblica: Magnano 1997, Qiqajon 142 pp. 88-85227-94-5.

7819 **Schreiner, Klaus** Maria, virgen, madre, reina. 1996, ⇒12,7444. <sup>R</sup>Cart. 13 (1997) 465 *(Chavero Blanco, F.)*; RTLi 31 (1997) 350-351 *(Gonzalez, Carlos Ignacio)*.

7820 **Serra, Aristide M.** Miryam figlia di Sion: la donna di Nazaret e il femminile a partire dal giudaismo antico. Maria di Nazaret 3: Mi 1997, Paoline 238 pp.

7821 *Siebel, Wigand* Hat Maria den Satan besiegt?: zur Frage nach der Schlangenkopfzertreterin. Theologisches 27 (1997) 121-128, 185-190 [Gen 3.15].

7822 *Speyr, Adrienne von* Il Golgotha. Com(I) 154-155 (1997) 64-70.

7823 **Stock, Klemens** Maria, la madre del Signore, nel Nuovo Testamento. Bibbia e preghiera 30: R 1997, ADP 144 pp. L15.000. 88-7357-170-0.

7824  **Tavard, George Henry** The thousand faces of the Virgin Mary. 1996, ⇒12,7448. RDoLi 47/3 (1997) 189-191 *(Flanagan, Donal)*; Tablet (17 May 1997) 636 *(Beattie, Tina)*; TS 58 (1997) 177-178 *(Johnson, Elizabeth A.)*.

7825  La vergine madre nella chiesa delle origini: itinerari mariani dei due millenni. 1996, ⇒12,7449. RTheotokos 5 (1997) 749-752 *(Bottino, Adriana)*.

### H8.8 *Feminae NT*—Women in the NT and church history

7826  TEAmonville Alegría, Nicole d' El amor de Magdalena: l'amour de Madeleine: sermón anónimo francés del siglo XVII, descubierto por Rainer Maria Rilke en la tienda de un anticuario parisino. 1996, ⇒12,7453. RIsidorianum 6 (1997) 589-595 *(Ordóñez García, José)*; RTLi 31 (1997) 351-353 *(Varela Gómez, Milagros)*.

7827  **Arjava, Antti** Women and law in late antiquity. 1996, ⇒12,7454. RJThS 48 (1997) 642-643 *(Barnes, T.D.)*.

7828  **Barry, Catherine** Des femmes parmi les apôtres: 2000 ans d'histoire occultée. Grandes Conférences: Saint-Laurent 1997, Fides 56 pp. [LTP 54,215].

7829  **Boer, Esther A. de** Mary Magdalene: beyond the myth. L 1997, SCM xiv; 147 pp. £13/$15. 1-56338-212-1 [BiTod 36,133—Senior, Donald].

7830  **Bonanate, Mariapia** Il vangelo secondo una donna: ieri e oggi. Letteratura biblica 7: 1996, ⇒12,7457. RHum(B) 52 (1997) 674-675 *(Grassino, Liliana Bestagno)*.

7831  EBoucherat, Jean-Luc Charles de SAINT-PAUL: tableau de la Magdeleine en l'état de parfaite amante de Jésus, 1628. Atopia Grenoble 1997, Million 138 pp. FF50. 2-84137-062-3 [RHPR 79,415—Chevallier, M.]

7832  **Burke, Christine** Through a woman's eyes: encounters with Jesus. Blackburn 1997, HarperCollinsReligious 130 pp. AUS$17. 1-86371-721-8 [ACR 75,250].

7833  **Coon, Lynda L.** Sacred fictions: holy women and hagiography in late antiquity. The Middle Ages. Philadelphia 1997, University of Pennsylvania Press xxiii; 228 pp. Bibl. 0-8122-3371-9.

7834  *Eggen, William* Mary Magdalene's touch in a family church. NBl 78 (1997) 429-438.

7835  **Grelot, Pierre** La condition de la femme d'après le Nouveau Testament. 1995, ⇒11/2,5199; 12,7464. REstB 55/1 (1997) 131-133 *(Pastor-Ramos, F.)*;

7836  La donna nel Nuovo Testamento. 1996, ⇒12,7463. RAnnTh 11 (1997) 531-535 *(Tábet, Miguel Ángel)*.

7837  **Haldas, Georges** Marie de Magdala. Regards Montrouge 1997, Nouvelle Cité 124 pp.

7838  **Luter, Boyd; McReynolds, Kathy** Women as Christ's disciples. GR 1997, Baker 200 pp. Bibl. 0-8010-5711-6.

7839  **MacDonald, Margaret Y.** Early christian women and pagan opinion: the power of hysterical women. 1996, ⇒12,7474. RAThR 79 (1997) 602-603 *(Krahmer, Shawn Madison)*.

7840  **Marjanen, Atti** The woman Jesus loved: Mary Magdalene in the Nag Hammadi library and related documents. NHS 40: 1996,

⇒12,7475. RThLZ 122 (1997) 462-463 *(Schenke-Robinson, Gesine)*; JThS 48 (1997) 639-642 *(Wilson, R. McL.)*.

7841 **Melzer-Keller, Helga** Jesus und die Frauen: eine Verhältnisbestimmung nach der synoptischen Überlieferung. Diss. Würzburg 1996-97; D*Müller, K.*: Herders Biblische Studien 14: FrB 1997, Herder xix; 487 pp. DM98. 3-451-26410-2.

7842 **Mohri, Erika** Maria Magdalena: Frauenbilder in Evangelientexten des 1. bis 3. Jahrhunderts. Diss. Marburg 1997; D*Bienert, W.* [RTL 29,586].

7843 *Osiek, Carolyn* The women at the tomb: what are they doing there?. HTS 53 (1997) 103-118.

7844 *Peters, Diane E.* The life of Martha of Bethany by Pseudo-MARCILIA. TS 58 (1997) 441-460.

7845 **Pinto-Mathieu, Élisabeth** Marie-Madeleine dans la littérature du Moyen Age. Diss. Sorbonne 1992; D*Zink, Michel*: P 1997, Beauchesne xiv; 306 pp. FF240. 2-7010-1356-9.

7846 **Quaglia, Rocco** Gli incontri de Gesù: le donne 'minori'. Moncalvo (At) 1997, Sharòn [Anime e Corpi 36,526].

7847 **Queré, France** Las mujeres del evangelio. Bilbao 1997, Mensajero 240 pp. [RF 237,334].

7848 **Saunders, Ross** Outrageous women, outrageous God: women in the first two generations of christianity. 1996, ⇒12,883. RPacifica 10 (1997) 258-260 *(Lee, Dorothy A.)*.

7849 **Sawyer, Deborah F.** Women and religion in the first christian centuries. 1996, ⇒12,884. RStudies in World Christianity 3/2 (1997) 258-259 *(Wright, D.F.)*; AThR 79 (1997) 603-604 *(Krahmer, Shawn Madison)*.

7850 *Setzer, Claudia* Excellent women: female witness to the resurrection. JBL 116 (1997) 259-272.

7851 *Stegemann, Wolfgang* Women in the Jesus movement in social-scientific perspective. Listening 32/1 (1997) 8-21.

7852 **Tepedino, Ana Maria** Las discípulas de Jesús. M 1994, Narcea 192 pp. REfMex 15/1 (1997) 135-136 *(Cepeda Salazar, Antonino)*.

7853 **Thompson, Mary R.** Mary of Magdala, apostle and leader: an amazing re-discovery of a woman in the early church. 1995, ⇒11/2,5252. RScrTh 29/1 (1997) 287-289 *(Heras, G.)*.

7854 **Watson, Elizabeth G.** Wisdom's daughters: stories of women around Jesus. Cleveland, OH 1997, Pilgrim xvii; 167 pp. Bibl. $13. 0-8298-1221-0.

7855 *Zalleski, Jan* Czy kobiety powinny milczeć w Kościele? (1 Kor 14,34-35). CoTh 67/4 (1997) 5-20. **P**.

H8.9 *Theologia feminae*—Feminist theology

7856 *Asher-Greve, Julia M.* Feminist research and ancient Mesopotamia: problems and prospects. A feminist companion. 1997, ⇒180. EBrenner, A., 218-237.

7857 **Bail, Ulrich** Gegen das Schweigen klagen: eine intertextuelle Studie zu Ps 6, Ps 55 und 2 Sam 13,1-22. Diss. Bochum 1997; D*Ebach, J.*.

7858 *Beach, Eleanor Ferris* Transforming goddess iconography in Hebrew narrative. Women and goddess traditions. 1997, ⇒249. EKing, K., 239-263.

**Bird, P.** Missing persons... women and gender in ancient Israel ⇒114.

7859 Bird, Phyllis A.; Sakenfeld, Katharine Doob; Ringe, Sharon H. Introduction. Semeia 78 (1997) 1-9.

7860 Boer, Esther de Feministische exegese. PrakTh 24 (1997) 434-445.

7861 **Brenner, Athalya** The intercourse of knowledge: on gendering desire and 'sexuality' in the Hebrew Bible. Bibl.Interp. 26: Lei 1997, Brill ix; 190 pp. ƒ116. 90-04-10155-1.

7862 Brenner, Athalya Introduction. A feminist companion. 1997, ⇒180. ᴱBrenner, A., 17-28.

7863 Cama-Calderón, Ahida; Bachmann, Mercedes García About "the other" and "the this". Semeia 78 (1997) 161-165.

7864 Camp, Claudia V. Feminist theological hermeneutics: canon and christian identity. Theological interpretation. 1997, ⇒244. ᴱFowl, S.E., 53-69.

7865 Caron, Gérald Des femmes aussi faisaient route avec Lui: perspectives féministes sur la bible. Sciences Bibliques: Études/Instruments 1: Montréal 1995, Médiaspaul 230 pp. ᴿCBQ 59 (1997) 186-7 (Mangan, Céline); RThPh 129 (1997) 391-2 (Graesslé, I.).

7866 **Cheney, Emily** She can read: feminist reading strategies for biblical narrative. 1996, ⇒12,7500. ᴿMissionalia 25 (1997) 470-471 (de Wet Strauss, J.J.).

7867 Clark Wire, Antoinette A North American perspective. Semeia 78 (1997) 145-149.

7868 Dube, Musa W. Toward a post-colonial feminist interpretation of the bible. Semeia 78 (1997) 11-26.

7869 ᴱFiorenza, Elisabeth Schüssler A feminist commentary. Searching the Scriptures, 2: 1994, ⇒10,1166... 12,1228. ᴿTJT 13 (1997) 288-289 (Badley, Jo-Ann); JBL 116 (1997) 359-361 (Scholer, David M.).

7870 **Fiorenza, Elisabeth Schüssler** As origens cristãs a partir da mulher: uma nova hermenêutica. São Paulo 1992, Paulinas 400 pp. ᴿRBBras 14 (1997) 369-370;

7871 Jesus, Miriam's child, Sophia's prophet: critical issues in feminist christology. 1994, ⇒11/2,5351; 12,7506. ᴿJBL 115 (1996) 345-347 (Ruether, Rosemary Radford); CBQ 58 (1996) 344-346 (Rosenblatt, Marie-Eloise);

7872 Bread not stone: the challenge of feminist biblical interpretations. 1995 <1984>, ⇒1,8622... 11/2,5353. ᴿRStT 16/1 (1997) 93-95 (Moore, Anne);

7873 Gesù figlio di Miriam, profeta di Sophía: questioni critiche di cristologia femminista. 1996, ⇒12,7508. ᴿRSEc 15 (1997) 597-599 (Morandini, Simone);

7874 Jezus: kind van Mirjam, profeet van Sophia: kritische bijdragen tot de feministische christologie. Kampen 1997, Kok 279 pp. ƒ49. 90-242-6046-9 [ITBT 6/4,32—Vander Stichele, Caroline];

7875 Jesus—Miriams Kind, Sophias Prophet: kritische Anfragen feministischer Christologie. ᵀGraffam-Minkus, Melanie; Mayer-Schärtel, Bärbel: Gü 1997, Gü'er 302 pp. DM68. 3-579-01838-8 [BZ 42,284—Melzer-Keller, Helga].

7876 Fischer, Irmtraud Das Alte Testament—ein Buch für Frauen?. Lebendige Welt. 1997, ⇒565. ᴱZenger, E., 176-183.

7877  *Fontaine, Carole R.* The abusive bible: on the use of feminist method in pastoral contexts. A feminist companion. 1997, ⇒180. ᴱBrenner, A., 84-113.

7878  *Grenholm, Cristina* Gesù in una prospettiva femminista: incarnazione ed esperienza della gravidanza. Conc(I) 33/1 (1997) 47-59—Conc(D) 33/1,23-31; Conc(F) 269,35-45; Conc(E) 269,43-54.

7879  *Grey, Mary* 'Ne pleurez pas sur moi, mais sur vous et sur vos enfants': la religion et la fin de la violence envers les femmes. Conc(F) 272 (1997) 91-99 (D33,503-510);

7880  Who do you say that I am?: images of Christ in feminist liberation theology. Images of Christ. 1997, ⇒256. ᴱPorter, S.E., 189-203.

7881  **Groothuis, Rebecca Merrill** Good news for women: a biblical picture of gender equality. GR 1997, Baker 272 pp. 0-8010-5720-5.

7882  **Hopkins, Julie M.** Towards a feminist christology: Jesus of Nazareth, European women and the christological crisis. 1995, ⇒11/2,5310. ᴿThLZ 122 (1997) 600-602 *(Link-Wieczorek, Ulrike)*; TJT 13 (1997) 322-323 *(Gordon, Dorcas)*; EThL 73 (1997) 491-493 *(Brito, E.)*;

7883  Verso una cristologia femministica. GdT 243: 1996, ⇒12,7516. ᴿStPat 44/1 (1997) 257-258 *(Segalla, Giuseppe)*.

7884  *Jordon, Sherry* Women as proclaimers and interpreters of the word. CThMi 24 (1997) 33-43.

7885  *Kellenbach, Katharina von* Overcoming the teaching of contempt. A feminist companion. 1997, ⇒180. ᴱBrenner, A., 190-202.
      ᴱ**King, K.** Women and goddess traditions ⇒249.

7886  ᴱ**Lautman, Françoise** Ni Ève ni Marie: luttes et incertitudes des héritières de la bible. Histoire et société 36: Genève 1997, Labor et F 352 pp. [RThPh 130,462—Graesslé, Isabelle.

7887  ᴱ**Loades, Ann** Teología feminista. Bilbao 1997, Desclée de B 404 pp. 84-330-1201-0. ᴿEE 72 (1997) 729-733 *(Pastor-Ramos, Federico)*.

7888  *Masenya, Madipoane* Redefining ourselves: a bosadi (womanhood) approach. OTEs 10 (1997) 439-448.

7889  *McKay, Heather A.* On the future of feminist biblical criticism. A feminist companion. 1997, ⇒180. ᴱBrenner, A., 61-83.

7890  *Melanchthon, Monica J.* The Indian voice. Semeia 78 (1997) 151-160.

7891  *Meyers, Carol* Recovering objects, re-visioning subjects: archaeology and feminist biblical study;

7892  *Milne, Pamela J.* Toward feminist companionship: the future of feminist biblical studies and feminism. A feminist companion. 1997, ⇒180. ᴱBrenner, A., 270-284/39-60.

7893  *Müller, Stefanie* Frauen in der Sprache sichtbar machen. Antijudaismus im NT. 1997, ⇒κ8. KT 149: ᴱHenze, D., 53-55.

7894  ᴱ**Newsom, Carol A.** Da Genesi a Neemia. La Biblia delle donne, 1. 1996, ⇒12,1232. ᴿStPat 44/1 (1997) 269-270 *(Sartori, Luigi)*.

7895  *Njoroge, Nyambura* "Woman, why are you weeping?". ER 49 (1997) 427-438.

7896  **Noller, Annette** Feministische Hermeneutik: Wege einer neuen Schriftauslegung. Neuk 1995, Neuk xii; 272 pp. DM58. 3-7887-1520-0. ᴿBiLi 70/1 (1997) 82-83 *(Silber, Ursula)*.

7897  *Osiek, Carolyn* The feminist and the bible: hermeneutical alternatives. HTS 53 (1997) 956-968.

7898 *Ostriker, Alicia Suskin* A triple hermeneutic: scripture and revisionist women's poetry. A feminist companion. 1997, ⇒180. EBrenner, A., 164-189.

7899 *Perroni, Marinella* L'interpretazione biblica femminista tra ricerca sinottica ed ermeneutica politica. RivBib 45 (1997) 439-468.

7900 *Porcile, María Teresa* Cristología en femenino. Sum. 198. EphMar 47/3 (1997) 183-198.

7901 **Primavesi, Anne** Do Apocalipse ao Gênesis: ecologia, feminismo e cristianismo. TCosta, Alberto: 1996, ⇒12,7531. RAtualidade Teológica 1/1 (1997) 85-96 *(Corrêa Pinto, Maria Conceição)*.

7902 *Reid, Barbara E.* Choosing the better part. BR 42 (1997) 23-31.

7903 *Reinhartz, Adele* Feminist criticism and biblical studies on the verge of the twenty-first century;

7904 *Ringe, Sharon H.* An approach to a critical, feminist, theological reading of the bible [Phil 2,5-11]. A feminist companion. 1997, ⇒180. EBrenner, A., 30-38/156-163.

7905 ERussell, **Letty M.** Interpretación feminista de la biblia. Bilbao 1995, Desclée de B 184 pp. 84-330-1124-95. REE 72 (1997) 729-733 *(Pastor-Ramos, Federico)*.

7906 **Rutledge, David** Reading marginally: feminism, deconstruction and the Bible. 1996, ⇒12,7535. RJBL 116 (1997) 527-528 *(Jobling, David)*.

7907 *Schearing, Linda S.* A wealth of women: looking behind, within, and beyond Solomon's story. The age of Solomon. 1997, ⇒282. EHandy, L.K., 428-456.

7908 **Schottroff, Luise** Lydia's impatient sisters. TRumscheidt, Martin; Rumscheidt, Barbara: 1995. ⇒11/2,5240; 12,7483. RHeyJ 38 (1997) 208-210 *(King, Nicholas)*; ChH 66 (1997) 303-304 *(Clark, Elizabeth)*; Missionalia 25 (1997) 240-241 *(Landman, Christina)*; JBL 116 (1997) 554-555 *(Matthews, Shelly)*; SR 26 (1997) 368-370 *(Carter, Philippa)*.

7909 **Schottroff, Luise; Schroer, Silvia; Wacker, Marie-Theres** Feministische Exegese. 1995, ⇒11/2,1766; 12,7538. RBiKi 52 (1997) 93-94 *(Schüngel-Straumann, Helen)*.

7910 *Seim, Turid Karlsen* Searching for the silver coin: a response to Loretta Dornisch and Barbara Reid. BR 42 (1997) 32-42.

7911 *Sibeko, Malika; Haddad, Beverly* Reading the bible "with" women in poor and marginalized communities in South Africa. Semeia 78 (1997) 83-92 [Mt 5,21-6,1].

7912 **Souzenelle, Annick de** Le féminin de l'être: pour en finir avec la côte d'Adam. P 1997, Albin M 340 pp. [INTAMS.R 5,216ss—Pelletier, Anne-Marie] [Isa 7,1-17; 29,1-8].

7913 *Stratton, Beverly J.* Here we stand: Lutheran and feminist issues in biblical interpretation. CThMi 24 (1997) 23-32.

7914 **Taube, Roselies; Tietz-Buck, Claudia; Klinge, Christiane** Frauen und Jesus Christus: die Bedeutung von Christologie im Leben protestantischer Frauen. Stu 1995, Kohlhammer 205 pp. DM 34.80. 3-17-013232-6. RThLZ 122 (1997) 595-597 *(Eckholt, M.)*.

7915 *Teubal, Savina J.* The rise and fall of female reproductive control as seen through images of women. Women and goddess traditions. 1997, ⇒249. EKing, K., 281-309.

7916 *Troy, Lana* Engendering creation in ancient Egypt: still and flowing waters. A feminist companion. 1997, ⇒180. EBrenner, A., 238-268.

7917 *Troyer, Kristin de* Septuagint and gender studies: the very beginning of a promising liaison. A feminist companion. 1997, ⇒180. ᴱBrenner, A., 326-343.

## H9.0 Eschatologia NT, *spes,* hope

7918 *Austad, Torleiv* The biblical vision of hope in today's world. European Journal of Theology 6/1 (1997) 21-29.
7919 **Balabanski, Vicky** Eschatology in the making: Mark, Matthew and the Didache. Diss. Melbourne 1993, ᴰ*Moloney, F.*: MSSNTS 97: C 1997, CUP xvii; 241 pp. £35. 0-521-59147-6 [Mt 24; 25; Mk 13].
7920 *Balz, Horst* Early Christian faith as "hope against hope". Eschatology in the bible. JSOT.S 243: 1997, ⇒222. ᴱReventlow, H., 31-48.
7921 *Bayer, Oswald* Wann endlich hat das Böse ein Ende?. 1997, ⇒92. ꟳStᴜʜʟᴍᴀᴄʜᴇʀ P., 24-30.
7922 **Beck, Norman A.** Anti-Roman cryptograms in the New Testament: symbolic messages of hope and liberation. Westminster College Library of Biblical Symbolism 1: NY 1997, Lang 191 pp. $30. 0-8204-2771-3 [NTHÄR 1997,226].
7923 **Berger, Klaus** Ist mit dem Tod alles aus?. Stu 1997, Quell 227 pp. 3-7918-1953-4.
7924 *Collins, John J.* The christian appropriation of the apocalyptic tradition. Seers. JSJ.S 54: 1997, ⇒119. 115-127.
7925 **Cuvillier, Élian** L'Apocalypse, c'était demain: protestations de l'espérance au cœur du Nouveau Testament. Poliez-le-Grand ²1996, Moulin 90 pp. FF56 [VS 153,768].
7926 *Dunn, James D.G.* He will come again. Interp. 51 (1997) 42-56 [1 Cor 16,22].
7927 *Elior, Rachel* Not all is in the hands of heaven: eschatology and kabbalah. Eschatology in the bible. JSOT.S 243: 1997, ⇒222. ᴱReventlow, H., 49-61.
7928 **Erlemann, Kurt** Naherwartung und Parusieverzögerung im NT. TANZ 17: 1995, ⇒11/2,5426; 12,7552. ᴿJBL 116 (1997) 136-138 *(Carroll, John T.)*.
7929 *Evans, Craig A.; Flint, Peter W.* Introduction. Eschatology, messianism. SDSSRL 1: 1997, ⇒276. ᴱEvans, C.A., 1-9.
7930 *Fabris, Rinaldo* La escatologia del Nuovo Testamento. DSBP 16 (1997) 84-153.
7931 *Frey, Christofer* Eschatology and ethics: their relation in recent continental protestantism. Eschatology in the bible. JSOT.S 243: 1997, ⇒222. ᴱReventlow, H., 62-74.
7932 *Garcia-Viana, Luis F.* La escatologia reinterpretada: una mirada a la segunda y tercera generacion cristiana. Almogaren 21 (1997) 35-51.
7933 *González Blanco, Antonino* La apocalíptica, fenómeno mediterráneo. La Bíblia i el Mediterrani. 1997, ⇒385. ᴱBorrell, d'Agustí, 205-225.
7934 *Hendel, Ronald S.* Knocking on heaven's gate. BiRe 13/4 (1997) 20.

7935 **Holman, Charles L.** Till Jesus comes: origins of christian apocalyptic expectation. Peabody 1996, Hendrickson xli; 181 pp. 0-943575-74-5. [R]RevBib 59/3 (1997) 191-192 *(Levoratti, A.J.)*.

7936 [E]**Jonge, H.J. de; Ruyter, B.W.J. de** Totdat hij komt: een discussie over de wederkomst van Jezus Christus. 1995, ⇒11/1,91. [R]Bijdr. 58 (1997) 348-350 *(Schreurs, Nico)*.

7937 *Lafont, Ghislain* En attendant Jésus: simples pensées sur l'eschatologie. StAns 124: 1997, ⇒57. [F]LOEHRER M. — TRAGAN P., 97-110.

7938 *Légasse, Simon* Les Juifs, au temps de Jésus, croyaient-ils à l'immortalité de l'âme?: pour introduire à la doctrine du Nouveau Testament sur les fins dernières. Sum. 121. BLE 98 (1997) 103-121.

7939 *Link, Christian* Points of departure for a christian eschatology. Eschatology in the bible. JSOT.S 243: 1997, ⇒222. [E]Reventlow, H., 98-110.

7940 **Marquardt, Friedrich-Wilhelm** Was dürfen wir hoffen, wenn wir hoffen dürften?: eine Eschatologie, 3. Gü 1996, Gü'er 564 pp. DM148. 3-579-01946-5. [R]LM 36/4 (1997) 45 *(Schmidt, Joachim)*; TTh 36 (1996) 429-430 *(Logister, W.)*; FrRu 4 (1997) 292-293 [3 vols] *(Trutwin, Werner)*.

7941 *Monloubou, Louis* 'Les coeurs purs verront Dieu': le culte et l'eschatologie. EeV 107 (1997) 487-490.

7942 *Niebuhr, Karl-Wilhelm* Die Werke des eschatologischen Freudenboten (4Q521 und die Jesusüberlieferung). The scriptures in the gospels. BEThL 131: 1997, ⇒234. [E]Tuckett, C.M., 637-646.

7943 **Oegema, Gerbern S.** Zwischen Hoffnung und Gericht: Untersuchungen zur Rezeption der Apokalyptik im frühen Christentum und Judentum. Diss.-Habil. Tübingen 1996-97; [D]*Lichtenberger, H.* [ThLZ 122,764].

7944 *Pöhlmann, Wolfgang* Bestimmte Zukunft: die Einheit von 'Eschaton' und 'Eschata' in neutestamentlicher Sicht. 1997, ⇒92. [F]STUHLMACHER P., 337-346.

**Reventlow, H.** Eschatology in the Bible ⇒222.

7945 *Rozman, Francè* Prišel bo na oblakih neba [Er wird auf den Wolken des Himmels kommen]. 1997, ⇒96. [F]TOMIC C., Zsfg. 213. 204-213. **Croatian.**

7946 **Ruiz de la Peña, Juan L.** La pascua de la creación: escatología. Sapientia Fidei 11: M 1996, BAC 298 pp. 84-7914-261-8. [R]ATG 60 (1997) 437 *(Olivares, E.)*.

7947 **Souletie, Jean-Louis** La croix de Dieu: eschatologie et histoire dans la perspective christologique de Jürgen MOLTMANN. P 1997, Cerf 409 pp. [ED 51/2-3,364s—Muya, J. Ilunga].

7948 **Steiger, Johann Anselm** Bibel-Sprache und Jüngster Tag bei Johann Peter HEBEL. APTh 25: 1994, ⇒12,7572. [R]ThR 62 (1997) 241-242 *(Kühlmann, Wilhelm)*.

7949 *Vugdelija, Marijan* Uskrznuće i nada (1 Pt 1,3-5.21) [Risurrezione e speranza]. 1997, ⇒96. [F]TOMIC C., Zsfg. 180. 145-180. **Croatian.**

7950 *Walter, Nikolaus* Die Botschaft vom Jüngsten Gericht im Neuen Testament < 1991 >;

7951 'Hellenistische Eschatologie' im Neuen Testament < 1985 >;

7952 'Hellenistische Eschatologie' im Frühjudentum—ein Beitrag zur 'Biblischen Theologie'? < 1985 >;

7953   Zur theologischen Relevanz apokalyptischer Aussagen <1975>.
       Praeparatio evangelica. WUNT 98: 1997, ⇒167. 311-340/152-
       272/234-251/28-55.

## H9.5 *Theologia totius [VT-] NT*—General [OT-] NT theology

7954   **Adam, A.K.M.** Making sense of New Testament theology: 'mod-
       ern' problems and prospects. 1995, ⇒11/2,5640. [R]Interp. 51
       (1997) 204, 206 *(Morgan, Robert)*; CBQ 59 (1997) 367-368
       *(Seeley, David)*; ThTo 54 (1997) 404, 406 *(Fowl, Stephen)*.
7955   **Balla, Peter** Challenges to New Testament theology: an attempt to
       justify the enterprise. WUNT 2/95: Tü 1997, Mohr xv; 279 pp.
       Bibl. DM98. 3-16-146752-3.
7956   *Bammel, Ernst* Die Anfänge der Kirchengeschichte im Spiegel der
       jüdischen Quellen. Judaica et Paulina. WUNT 91: 1997 <1988>,
       ⇒109. 34-46.
7957   *Bellia, Giuseppe* Teologia biblica: riflessione e proposte. Ho
       Theológos 15 (1997) 355-378.
7958   *Brueggemann, Walter* Biblical theology appropriately postmodern.
       BTB 27 (1997) 4-9.
7959   **Caird, G.B.** New Testament theology. [E]*Hurst, L.D.*, 1994,
       ⇒10,8923... 12,7579. [R]Pro Ecclesia 6 (1997) 502-503 *(Rhoads,
       David)*; TJT 13 (1997) 267-268 *(Lincoln, Andrew T.)*; SJTh 50
       (1997) 511-515 *(Towner, Philip)*; JBL 115 (1996) 134-136 *(Mi-
       near, Paul S.)*.
7960   **Carroll, Robert P.** Wolf in the sheepfold: the bible as problematic
       for theology. L [2]1997, SCM xv; 159 pp. 0-334-02677-6.
7961   **Childs, Brevard S.** Biblical theology of the Old and New Testa-
       ments. 1993, ⇒8,9322...12,7581. [R]SJTh 50 (1997) 391-3 *(Provan,
       Iain)*;
7962   Die Theologie der einen Bibel, 1: Grundstrukturen. [T]*Oeming, Ch.
       & M.*: 1994, ⇒11/2,5648; 12,7582. [R]ZKTh 119 (1997) 92-93 *(O-
       berforcher, Robert)*; ThLZ 122 (1997) 647-648 *(Barth, Gerhard)*;
7963   2: Hauptthemen. 1996, ⇒12,7583. [R]ThLZ 122 (1997) 648-651
       *(Barth, Gerhard)*; JETh 11 (1997) 186-187 *(Dreytza, Manfred)*.
7964   **Conzelmann, Hans** Grundriss der Theologie des Neuen Testa-
       ments. [E]*Lindemann, Andreas*: UTB 1446: Tü [6]1997, Mohr xx; 433
       pp. 3-16-146811-2.
7965   **Espeja, Jesús** El evangelio en un cambio de época. 1996,
       ⇒12,7585. [R]SalTer 85/1 (1997) 81-82 *(Lago, Luis)*.
7966   **Fuller, Daniel P.** The unity of the bible. 1992, ⇒8,4502; 12,4177.
       [R]AUSS 35 (1997) 118-120 *(Norman, Bruce)*.
7967   **Gnilka, Joachim** Theologie des Neuen Testaments. 1994, CoTh
       67/2 (1997) 245-255 *(Zelęski, Jan)*; RBBras 14 (1997) 361-362.
7968   **Hübner, Hans** Biblische Theologie des Neuen Testaments. 1990-
       1995, 3 vols. ⇒9,9650... 11/2,5661s. [R]JThS 48 (1997) 627-630
       *(Morgan, Robert)*; [I-II:] NeoTest. 31 (1997) 417-421 *(Loubser,
       J.A.)*;
7969   Hebräerbrief, Evangelien und Offenbarung Epilegomena. Biblische
       Theologie des Neuen Testaments, 3. 1995, ⇒11/1,5230; 12,6519.
       [R]LM 36/4 (1997) 46 *(Lohse, Eduard)*;

7970 Teologia biblica del Nuovo Testamento, 1: prolegomeni. Commentario teologico del NT.S 5: Brescia 1997, Paideia 323 pp. L51.000. 88-394-0542-9.

7971 **Ingraffia, Brian D.** Postmodern theory and biblical theology: vanquishing God's shadow. 1995, ⇒11/2,5663; 12,7592. RRT (1997/2) 69-70 *(Moberly, Walter)*.

7972 *Knierim, Rolf P.* On biblical theology. 1997, ⇒77. FSANDERS J., 117-128.

7973 **Ladd, George Eldon** A theology of the New Testament. E*Hagner, Donald Alfred*: GR ²1997, Eerdmans xiv; 764 pp. 0-8028-0680-5.

7974 E**Léon-Dufour, X.** 25 noms propres pour entrer dans la bible: extraits du Vocabulaire de théologie biblique. P 1997, Cerf 128 pp. FF60. 2-204-05701-0 [ETR 73,309];

7975 35 mots pour entrer dans la Bible: extraits du Vocabulaire de théologie biblique. P 1997, Cerf 366 pp. FF140. 2-204-05700-2 [ETR 73,309].

7976 *Long, Burke O.* Letting rival gods be rivals: biblical theology in a postmodern age. 1997, ⇒48. FKNIERIM R., 222-233.

7977 *Luz, Ulrich* Ein Traum auf dem Weg zu einer Biblischen Theologie der ganzen Bibel: ein Brief an Peter STUHLMACHER. 1997, ⇒92. FSTUHLMACHER P., 279-287.

7978 *Murphy, Roland E.* Reflections on a critical biblical theology. 1997, ⇒48. FKNIERIM R., 265-274.

7979 *Müller, Mogens* Neutestamentliche Theologie als Biblische Theologie: einige grundsätzliche Überlegungen. NTS 43 (1997) 475-490.

7980 *Paulsen, Henning* Prolegomena zur Geschichte der frühchristlichen Theologie;

7981 Synkretismus im Urchristentum und im Neuen Testament <1990>;

7982 Von der Unbestimmtheit des Anfangs: zur Entstehung von Theologie im Urchristentum <1991>. Zur Literatur. WUNT 99: 1997, ⇒153. 237-283/301-309/284-300.

7983 *Pedersen, Sigfred* Biblische Theologie: eine Frage nach dem Gottesverständnis. JBTh 12 (1997) 67-85.

7984 **Penchansky, David** The politics of biblical theology: a postmodern reading. SABH 10: 1995, ⇒11/2,5679; 12,7605. RCBQ 59 (1997) 133-135 *(Biddle, Mark E.)*.

E**Pokorný, P.** Bibelauslegung als Theologie ⇒970.

7985 *Pokorný, Petr* Probleme biblischer Theologie. Bibelauslegung. WUNT 100: 1997 <1981>, ⇒970. 109-119.

7986 **Schmithals, Walter** The theology of the first christians. TDean, O.C. Jr.: LVL 1997, Westminster xii; 396 pp. Bibl. $29. 0-664-25615-5.

7987 **Strecker, Georg** Theologie des Neuen Testaments. E*Horn, Friedrich Wilhelm*: 1996, ⇒12,7608. RThLZ 122 (1997) 676-678 *(Schweizer, Eduard)*; NT 39 (1997) 200-02 *(Stenschke, Christoph)*; CBQ 59 (1997) 174-176 *(Mowery, Robert L.)*; JBL 116 (1997) 740-742 *(Boers, Hendrikus)*.

7988 **Stuhlmacher, Peter** Biblische Theologie des Neuen Testaments, 1: Grundlegung: von Jesus zu Paulus. Gö ²1997, Vandenhoeck & R xii; 419 pp. 3-525-53595-3.

7989 *Thiselton, Anthony C.* Biblical theology and hermeneutics. Modern Theologians. 1997, ⇒243. EFord, D., 520-537.

7990  *Vos, J.S.* De theologie van het Nieuwe Testament: een overzicht over recent verschenen werken, 2. GThT 97/1 (1997) 15-27.

7991  *Vouga, François* Derselbe ungleiche Gott: zum Problem einer biblischen Theologie des Neuen Testaments. WuD 24 (1997) 159-168.

7992  **Warzecha, Julian** Idźcie i wy: z zagadnień biblijnej teologii apostolstwa, "Apostolicum". 1996, ⇒12,7614. ᴿCoTh 67/3 (1997) 228-230 *(Weron, Eugeniusz).* **P.**

7993  **Watson, Francis** Text and truth: redefining biblical theology. E 1997, Clark viii; 344 pp. £25. 0-567-08556-2.

7994  **Weiser, Alfons** Die Theologie der Evangelien. Theologie des Neuen Testaments, 2. KStTh 8: 1993, ⇒10,8953; 11/2,5692. ᴿBiKi 52/1 (1997) 46 *(Porsch, Felix).*

7995  *Wiles, Virginia* On transforming New Testament theology: (re)-claiming subjectivity. 1997, ⇒82. ᶠScʀᴏɢɢs R., 311-335.

## XIV. Philologia biblica

### J1.1 Hebraica *grammatica*

7996  *Althann, Robert* Approaches to prepositions in Northwest Semitic studies <1994>;

7997  Does Biblical Hebrew know a third person singular suffix in *-y*?: a reconsideration of the evidence;

7998  On verbal forms: the case of *\*taqtul*. Studies in NWS. BibOr 45: 1997, ⇒108. 5-24/61-78/25-59.

7999  **Auvray, Paul** Bibelhebräisch zum Selbststudium: Kurzgrammatik, erläuterte Texte, Vocabular. UTB.WG: 1996, ⇒12,7616. ᴿZKTh 119 (1997) 104-105 *(Oesch, Josef M.).*

8000  *Bartelmus, Rüdiger* Prima la lingua, poi le parole: David Kɪᴍᴄʜɪ und die Frage der hebräischen Tempora: sprachwissenschaftliche und exegetische Überlegungen zu IISam 14,5b und 15,34a, ausgehend von der Behandlung beider Stellen in Kimchi's Kommentar zu den Vorderen Propheten. ThZ 53 (1997) 7-16.

8001  *Behrens, Achim* "Grammatik statt Ekstase!": das Phänomen der syntaktischen Wiederaufnahme am Beispiel von Am 7,1-8,2. Studien zur hebräischen Grammatik. OBO 156: 1997, ⇒310. ᴱWagner, A., 1-9.

8002  *Ben-David, Israel* עתיד הקצר ומלרע, עתיד הקצר ועתיד הקצר ומלרע, עתיד השלם כהיותם במקרא [Simple imperfect, *waw*-consecutive, and other a-pocopate verb forms in the Bible];

8003  *Blau, Joshua* בעיות בתורת ההגה והצורות של עברית המקרא [Issues in biblical phonetics and morphology]. Sum. II. Leš. 60/3-4 (1997) 191-276/181-189. **H.**

8004  **Bolozky, Shmuel** 501 Hebrew verbs: fully conjugated in all the tenses... 1996, ⇒12,7625. ᴿHebStud 38 (1997) 89-91 *(Glinert, Lewis),*

8005  **Bombeck, Stefan** Das althebräische Verbalsystem aus aramäischer Sicht: Masoretischer Text, Targume und Peschitta. EHS.T 591: Fra 1997, Lang 251 pp. FS64. 3-631-30674-1.
      *Buth, R.* Hebrew poetic tenses and the Magnificat ⇒5378.

8006 **Casanellas i Bassols, Pere** Transliteració i transcripció de l'hebreu: eines, propostes, qüestions pendents. Butlletí de l'Associació Bíblica de Catalunya 58: n.p. 1997, Associació Bíblica de Catalunya 72 pp.

8007 *Chabane, Jacob S.* Teaching Biblical Hebrew to non-theological students. NAOTS 2 (1997) 8-9.

8008 **Dawson, David Allan** Text-linguistics and Biblical Hebrew. JSOT.S 177: 1994, ⇒10,8963. ᴿCBQ 58 (1996) 111-115 *(Dobbs-Allsopp, F.W.)*.

8009 **Deiana, G.; Spreafico, A.** Guida allo studio dell'ebraico biblico. 1991, ⇒6,9156... 9,9676. ᴿAnnTh 11 (1997) 527-528 *(Tábet, Miguel Ángel)*;

8010 Guía para el estudio del hebreo bíblico. M 1995, Sociedad Bíblica 225 pp. ᴿAnnTh 11 (1997) 527-528 *(Tábet, Miguel Ángel)*.

8011 *Diem, Werner* Suffixkonjugation und Subjektspronomina. ZDMG 147 (1997) 10-76.

8012 ᵀᴱ**Dotan, Aron** The dawn of Hebrew linguistics: the book of Elegance of the language of the Hebrews by SAADIA Gaon. Sources for the Study of Jewish Culture 3: J 1997, World Union of Jewish Studies 2 vols. Introduction and critical edition. 965-90148-2-1.

8013 *Ehrensvärd, Martin* Once again: the problem of dating Biblical Hebrew. SJOT 11 (1997) 29-40.

8014 *Fischler, Bracha* להר"ם and its related expressions. Sum. vii. Leš. 60/1-2 (1997) 33-51. H. [Qoh 1,10].

8015 *Freedman, David Noel* Archaic forms in early Hebrew poetry <1960>;

8016 *Freedman, David Noel* Some observations on Early Hebrew <1972>. Divine Commitment, 2. 1997, ⇒124. 5-12/61-69.

8017 *García-Jalón de la Lama, Santiago* El origen de la puntuación vocálica en las gramáticas hebreas europeas del siglo XVI. La Bíblia i el Mediterrani. 1997, ⇒385. ᴱBorrell, d'Agustí, 29-38.

8018 *Groß, Walter* Ein verdrängter bibelhebräischer Satztyp: Sätze mit zwei oder mehr unterschiedlichen Konstituenten vor dem Verbum finitum. JNSL 23/1 (1997) 15-41.

8019 **Hadas-Lebel, Mireille** Histoire de la langue hébraique, des origines à l'époque de la mishna. REJ.Collection 21: Lv ⁴1995, Peeters 199 pp. FB900. ᴿJSSt 44 (1997) 369-377 *(Elwolde, J.F.)*; CBQ 59 (1997) 734 *(Greenspahn, Frederick E.)*.

8020 **Hatav, Galia** The semantics of aspect and modality: evidence from English and Biblical Hebrew. Diss. Tel Aviv. Studies in Language Companion Ser. 34: Amst 1997, John Benjamins x; 224 pp. Bibl. 90-272-3037-4.

8021 **Häusl, Maria** Bedecken, Verdecken, Verstecken: Studien zur Valenz althebräischer Verben. ATSAT 59: St. Ottilien 1997, EOS 126 pp. 3-88096-559-5.

8022 *Jenni, Ernst* Philologische und linguistische Probleme bei den hebräischen Präpositionen;

8023 *zāqēn*: Bemerkungen zum Unterschied von Nominalsatz und Verbalsatz <1977>;

8024 Zur Funktion der reflexiv-passiven Stammformen im Biblisch-Hebräischen <1973>. Studien zur Sprachwelt. 1997, ⇒138. 174-188/61-71/51-60.

8025   *Joosten, Jan* The indicative system of the Biblical Hebrew verb and its literary exploitation. Narrative syntax. 1997, ⇒342. <sup>E</sup>Van Wolde, E., 51-71.

8026   **Joüon, Paul** A grammar of Biblical Hebrew. <sup>ET</sup>*Muraoka, Takamitsu:* 1991, ⇒7,9063...10,8974. <sup>R</sup>JNES 56 (1997) 144-7 *(Pardee, Dennis)*.

8027   *Kedar-Kopfstein, Benjamin; Lichtenberger, Hermann; Müller, Hans-Peter* Bibliographische Dokumentation: lexikalisches und grammatisches Material. ZAH 10 (1997) 99-114, 207-224.

8028   *Khan, Geoffrey* ʾAbū al-Faraj Hārūn and the early Karaite grammatical tradition. JJS 48 (1997) 314-334.

8029   *Kogut, Simcha* הַמִּקְרָה בֵּין טְעָמִים לְפַרְשָׁנוּת: בְּחִינָה [קוּגוּת, שִׂמְחָה] לְפַרְשָׁנוּתטְעָמִים פַּרְשָׁנוּת הַלְּשׁוֹנִית וְעִנְיָינִית שֶׁל זִיקוּת וּמַחְלוֹקוֹת בֵּין הַמְּסוֹרָתִית [Correlations between biblical accentuation and traditional Jewish exegesis]. 1994, ⇒10,8978; 11/2,5727. <sup>R</sup>HebSt 38 (1997) 188-191 *(Revell, E.J.)*. **H**.

8030   *Kroeze, Jan H.* Alternatives for the accusative in Biblical Hebrew. Studien zur hebräischen Grammatik. OBO 156: 1997, ⇒310. <sup>E</sup>Wagner, Andreas, 11-25;

8031   Semantic relations in construct phrases of Biblical Hebrew: a functional approach. ZAH 10 (1997) 27-41.

8032   *Lehmann, Reinhard G.* Überlegungen zur Analyse und Leistung sogenannter Zusammengesetzter Nominalsätze. Studien zur hebräischen Grammatik. OBO 156: 1997, ⇒310. <sup>E</sup>Wagner, A., 27-43.

8033   **Malone, Joseph L.** Tiberian Hebrew phonology. 1993, ⇒10,8983; 11/2,5729. MEAH.H 46 (1997) 169-178 *(Torres, Antonio)*.

8034   *Michel, Andreas* Gespaltene Koordinaten in biblisch-hebräischen Verbalsätzen: am Beispiel von Ex 34,27/Ps 11,5/Neh 10,36-37. Studien zur hebräischen Grammatik. OBO 156: 1997, ⇒310. <sup>E</sup>Wagner, Andreas, 45-71.

8035   **Michel, Andreas** Theologie aus der Periphrie: die gespaltene Koordination im Biblischen Hebräisch. Diss. Tübingen 1996; <sup>D</sup>*Gross, W.*: BZAW 257: B 1997, De Gruyter xi; 420 pp. DM218. 3-11-015689-X.

8036   *Michel, Diethelm* hæsæd wæʾæmæt. Studien zur hebräischen Grammatik. OBO 156: 1997, ⇒310. <sup>E</sup>Wagner, A., 73-82.

8037   **Miller, Cynthia Lynn** The representation of speech in Biblical Hebrew narrative: a linguistic analysis. HSM 55: 1996, ⇒12,7655. <sup>R</sup>Bib. 78 (1997) 421-424 *(Groß, Walter)*; JNSL 23/2 (1997) 245-247 *(Van der Merwe, C.H.J.)*; HebStud 38 (1997) 97-100 *(Waard, Jan de)*.

8038   *Muraoka, T.* Ancient Hebrew semantics database. ZAH 10 (1997) 98.

8039   <sup>E</sup>**Muraoka, Takamitsu** Studies in ancient Hebrew semantics. Abr-n.S 4: 1995, ⇒11/2,516; 12,7657. <sup>R</sup>JThS 48 (1997) 144-147 *(Williamson, H.G.M.)*.

8040   *Muraoka, Takamitsu* The alleged final function of the Biblical Hebrew syntagm (waw + a volitive verb form);

8041   Workshop: notes on the use of Hebrew tenses in Exodus 19-24. Narrative syntax. 1997, ⇒342. <sup>E</sup>Van Wolde, E., 229-241/242-249.

8042   *Müller, Hans-Peter* Zu einigen ungewöhnlichen Partikelfunktionen. Studien zur hebräischen Grammatik. OBO 156: 1997, ⇒310. <sup>E</sup>Wagner, A., 101-113.

8043 *Niccacci, Alviero* Basic facts and theory of the Biblical Hebrew verb system in prose;

8044 Workshop: narrative syntax of Exodus 19-24. Narrative syntax. 1997, ⇒342. <sup>E</sup>Van Wolde, E., 167-202/203-228.

8045 *Peckham, Brian* Tense and mood in Biblical Hebrew. ZAH 10 (1997) 139-168.

8046 *Qimron, E.* The contribution of the Judaean Desert scrolls to the study of ancient Hebrew. Qad. 30 (1997) 82-85. **H**.

8047 **Rechenmacher, Hans** Personennamen als theologische Aussagen: die syntaktischen und semantischen Strukturen der satzhaften theophoren Personenennamen in der hebräischen Bibel. ATSAT 50: St. Ottilien 1997, EOS viii; 125 pp. 3-88096-550-1 [EThL 74,185*].

8048 <sup>F</sup>RUBINSTEIN E. Studies in Hebrew language. <sup>E</sup>*Dotan, Aron; Tal, Abraham*: 1995, ⇒11/2,161. <sup>R</sup>JSSt 44 (1997) 426-428 *(Fassberg, Steven E.)*. **H**.

8049 **Sáens-Badillos, Angel** A history of the Hebrew language. 1993, ⇒10,8990... 12,7663. <sup>R</sup>ETR 72 (1997) 463-464 *(Margain, Jean)*.

8050 **Sarfatti, Gad B.** In the language of my people: essays on Hebrew. Studies in language 1: J 1997, Academy of the Hebrew Language (10) 339 pp. 965-481-009-3. **H**.

8051 *Sasson, Victor* Some observations on the use and original purpose of the waw consecutive in Old Aramaic and Biblical Hebrew. VT 47 (1997) 111-127.

8052 *Schüle, Andreas* Zur Bedeutung der Formel וַיְהִי im Übergang zum mittelhebräischen Tempussystem;

8053 *Schwiderski, Dirk* "Wer ist dein Knecht?: ein Hund!": zu Aufmerksamkeitserregern und Überleitungsformeln in hebräischen Briefen. Studien zur hebräischen Grammatik. OBO 156: 1997, ⇒310. <sup>E</sup>Wagner, A., 115-126/127-141.

8054 *Sciumbata, Maria Patrizia* Un progetto europeo di un database sulla semantica dell'ebraico antico (SAHD): gli studi preliminari. Henoch 19/2 (1997) 237-242.

8055 **Seidl, Theodor** Untersuchungen zur Valenz althebräischer Verben: 3. THR - "rein sein". ATSAT 57: St. Ottilien 1997, EOS vii; 307 pp. 3-88096-557-9.

8056 **Shlonsky, Ur** Clause structure and word order in Hebrew and Arabic: an essay in comparative Semitic syntax. Oxford Studies in comparative syntax. NY 1997, OUP xi; 289 pp. Bibl. 0-19-510866-3.

8057 **Shulman, Ahouva** The use of modal verb forms in Biblical Hebrew prose. Diss. Toronto 1996; <sup>D</sup>*Revell, E.J.* [SR 26,527].

8058 *Stolz, Fritz* Determinationsprobleme und Eigennamen. ThZ 53 (1997) 142-151.

8059 *Talstra, Eep* A hierarchy of clauses in Biblical Hebrew narrative. Narrative syntax. 1997, ⇒342. <sup>E</sup>Van Wolde, E., 85-118;

8060 Tense, mood, aspect and clause connections in Biblical Hebrew: a textual approach. JNSL 23/2 (1997) 81-103 [Josh 23];

8061 Workshop: clause types, textual hierarchy, translation in Exodus 19, 20 and 24. Narrative syntax. 1997, ⇒342. <sup>E</sup>Van Wolde, E., 119-132.

8062 *Testen, David* Morphological observations on the stems of the Semitic 'nota accusativi'. Sum. 215. AfO 44-45 (1997) 215-221.

8063    **Tschirschnitz, Alfred; Wojciechowska, Kalina** Gramatyka języka hebrajskiego w zarysie. Wsz 1996, ChAT vii; 331 pp. [CoTh 69/4,189—Dreja, Antoni]. P.

8064    *Tsumura, David Toshio* Vowel sandhi in Biblical Hebrew. ZAW 109 (1997) 575-588.

8065    *Van der Merwe, C.H.J.* "Reference time" in some biblical temporal constructions. Sum. 524. Bib. 78 (1997) 503-524;

8066    A critical analysis of narrative syntactic approaches, with special attention to their relationship to discourse analysis;

8067    An overview of Hebrew narrative syntax. Narrative syntax. 1997, ⇒342. EVan Wolde, E. 133-156/1-20;

8068    Reconsidering Biblical Hebrew temporal expressions. ZAH 10 (1997) 42-62.

8069    *Van Wolde, Ellen* Linguistic motivation and biblical exegesis. Narrative syntax. 1997, ⇒342. EVan Wolde, E., 21-50.

8070    *Verheij, Arian J.C.* Early?: late?: a reply to F.H. CRYER. SJOT 11 (1997) 41-43.

8071    **Volgger, David** Notizen zur Phonologie des Bibelhebräischen. ATSAT 36: 1992, ⇒9,9707... 12,7669. RJNES 56 (1997) 71-73 *(Goerwitz, Richard L.)*.

8072    *Wagner, Andreas* Der Lobaufruf im israelitischen Hymnus als indirekter Sprechakt. Studien zur hebräischen Grammatik. OBO 156: 1997, ⇒310. EWagner, A., 143-154.

8073    **Wagner, Andreas** Sprechakte und Sprechaktanalyse im Alten Testament: Untersuchungen im biblischen Hebräisch an der Nahtstelle zwischen Handlungsebene und Grammatik. BZAW 253: B 1997, De Gruyter xiii; 360 pp. Bibl. DM188. 3-11-015549-4.

8074    *Willi, Thomas* Basel und die Kontroverse um die Veritas Hebraica *[Buxtorf, Johannes]*. ThZ 53 (1997) 165-176.

8075    **Young, Ian** Diversity in pre-exilic Hebrew. FAT 5: 1993, ⇒9,9708... 11/2,5748. RSyr. 74 (1997) 243 *(Margain, Jean)*; LASBF 47 (1997) 577-586 *(Niccacci, Alviero)*; JBL 116 (1997) 730-732 *(White, Marsha)*.

8076    *Young, Ian* Evidence of diversity in pre-exilic Judahite Hebrew. Sum. 7. HebStud 38 (1997) 7-20.

8077    *Zewi, Tamar* Subjects preceded by the preposition ʾet in Biblical Hebrew. Studien zur hebräischen Grammatik. OBO 156: 1997, ⇒310. EWagner, A., 171-183.

### J1.2 Lexica et inscriptiones hebraicae; later Hebrew

8078    **Alonso Schökel, Luis** Dicionário bíblico hebraico-português. São Paulo 1997, Paulinus 798 pp. [RBBras 15,438].

8079    *Baasten, Martin F. J.* Nominal clauses containing a personal pronoun in Qumran Hebrew. The Hebrew of the DSS. StTDJ 26: 1997, EMuraoka, T., 1-16.

8080    **Beit-Arieh, Malachi; Sirat, Colette; Glatzer, Mordechai** Codices hebraicis litteris exarati quo tempore scripti fuerint exhibentes, 1: jusqu'à 1020. Monumenta Palaeographica Medii Aevi, hebraica 1: Turnhout 1997, Brepols 135 pp. 2-503-99015-0 [BiOr 57,172ss—Schenker, Adrian].

8081  *Bij de Vaate, Alice J.; Van Henten, Jan Willem* Jewish or non-Jewish?: some remarks on the identification of Jewish inscriptions from Asia Minor. BiOr 53 (1996) 16-28.

8082  *Blau, Joshua* The structure of biblical and Dead Sea Scrolls Hebrew in light of Arabic diglossia and Middle Arabic. Sum. v. Leš. 60/1-2 (1997) 21-32. **H.**

8083  *Bordreuil, Pierre; Israel, Felice; Pardee, Dennis* Deux ostraca paléo-hébreux de la collection Sh. Moussaïeff. Sum. 49. Sem. 46 (1996) 49-76.

8084  **Ceccherelli, Ignazio Marino** Origine e significato dei nomi di persona. BeO.S 6: Bornato in Franciacorta (Brescia) 1996, Sardini 211 pp. Bibl. 88-7506-166-1.

8085  [E]**Clines, David J.A.** א. The dictionary of classical Hebrew, 1. 1993, ⇒9,9718... 12,7680. [R]BZ 41 (1997) 110-112 *(Maier, Johann)*; Bibl.Interp. 5/1 (1997) 110-111 *(Horbury, William)*; VT 47 (1997) 390-393 *(Khan, Geoffrey)*; EvQ 69 (1997) 345-347 *(Satterthwaite, P.E.)*;

8086  The dictionary of classical Hebrew, 2-3. 1995-1996, ⇒12,7681-2. [R]VT 47 (1997) 390-393 *(Khan, Geoffrey)*.

8087  *Derby, Josiah* From Yerushalem to Yerushlayim. JBQ 25/4 (1997) 241-245.

8088  *Deutsch, Robert; Heltzer, Michael* ʿAbday on eleventh-century B.C.E. arrowheads. IEJ 47 (1997) 111-112.

8089  [E]**Doniach, N.S.; Kahane, A.** The Oxford English-Hebrew dictionary. 1996, ⇒12,7687. [R]JSSt 44 (1997) 429-430 *(Shivtiel, Avihai)*; BSOAS 60 (1997) 557-559 *(Ullendorff, Edward)*.

8090  *Ego, Beate, (al.),* Dokumentation neuer Texte. ZAH 10 (1997) 115-122; 225-236.

8091  *Elwolde, John* Developments in Hebrew vocabulary between Bible and Mishnah. The Hebrew of the DSS. StTDJ 26: 1997, [E]Muraoka, T., 17-55.

8092  *Emerton, J.A.* Comparative semitic philology and Hebrew lexicography. Congress volume 1995. VT.S 66: 1997, ⇒323. [E]Emerton, J.A., 1-24.

8093  **Fohrer, Georg** Dizionario ebraico e aramaico dell'Antico Testamento. 1996, ⇒12,7691. [R]PaVi 42/3 (1997) 58-59 *(Balzaretti, Claudio)*; CivCatt 148 I (1997) 620-622 *(Prato, G.L.)*.

8094  *Fox, Michael V.* Words for folly. ZAH 10 (1997) 4-15.

8095  *Freedman, David Noel* The Massoretic Text and the Qumran scrolls: a study in orthography <1962>;

8096  The orthography of the Arad ostraca <1969>. Divine Commitment, 2. 1997, ⇒124. 13-28/39-43.

8097  *Gitin, S.; Dotan, T.; Naveh, J.* A royal dedication inscription from Tel Miqneh/Ekron [=IEJ 47 (1997) 1-16]. Qad. 30/1 (1997) 38-43.

8098  **Glazerson, Matityahu** Building blocks of the soul: studies on the letters and words of the Hebrew language. Northvale, NJ 1997 Jason Aronson ix; 362 pp. 1-56821-932-6.

8099  *Hackett, Jo Ann, (al.),* Defusing pseudo-scholarship: the Siloam inscription ain't Hasmonean. BArR 23/2 (1997) 41-50, 68.

8100  *Jenni, Ernst* Verba gesticulationis im Hebräischen <1991>. Studien zur Sprachwelt. 1997, ⇒138. 150-161.

8101 **Kaltner, John** The use of Arabic in Biblical Hebrew lexicography. CBQMS 28: 1996, ⇒12,7847. ᴿCBQ 59 (1997) 736-738 *(Zahniser, A.H. Mathias)*; LASBF 47 (1997) 627-630 *(Chiesa, Bruno)*.

8102 ᴱ**Koehler, Ludwig; Baumgartner, Walter** ᵀᴱ*Richardson, Mervyn E.J.* The Hebrew and Aramaic lexicon of the Old Testament, 1.: 1994, ⇒10,9012... 12,7698. ᴿJThS 48 (1997) 143-144 *(Gordon, Robert P.)*;

8103 2.: 1995, ⇒12,7699. ᴿBS 154 (1997) 496-497 *(Chisholm, Robert B.)*.

8104 *Lemaire, André* Paleography's verdict: they're fakes! [*Shapira, Moses W.*]. BArR 23/3 (1997) 36-39.

8105 *Mashiah, Rachel* Parallel realizations of dichotomy patterns in biblical accentution. Sum. v. Leš. 60/1-2 (1997) 11-19. H.

8106 *McCarter, P. Kyle Jr.* Why all the fuss? [*Shapira, Moses W.*]. BArR 23/3 (1997) 40.

8107 *Mishor, Mordechay* El destino, la recompensa... y la morfosintaxis [Destiny, recompense... and morphosyntax]. Sum. res. 3. MEAH.H 46 (1997) 3-10.

8108 *Mittmann, Siegfried* Sakraler Wein und die Flüssigmaße Hin und Log. AOAT 247: 1997, ⇒75. ᶠRОELLIG W., 269-280.

8109 *Morag, Shelomo* Lo studio delle tradizioni linguistiche delle comunità ebraiche della Diaspora. Henoch 19/1 (1997) 69-79.

8110 *Muraoka, Takamitsu* Verb complementation in Qumran Hebrew. The Hebrew of the DSS. StTDJ 26: 1997, ᴱMuraoka, T., 92-149.

8111 *Na'aman, Nadav* Transcribing the theophoric element in North Israelite names. Discusssion with *Zadok, R.*: Nouvelles Assyriologiques Brèves et Utilitaires 1 (1997) 19-20.

8112 *Nebe, G. Wilhelm* Die hebräische Sprache der Naḥal Ḥever Dokumente 5/6Ḥev 44-46. The Hebrew of the DSS. StTDJ 26: 1997, ᴱMuraoka, T., 150-157.

8113 **Noy, David** Jewish inscriptions of western Europe, 2: the city of Rome. 1995, ᴿJSSt 44 (1997) 417-419 *(Trebilco, Paul)*.

8114 *Noy, David* Writing in tongues: the use of Greek, Latin and Hebrew in Jewish inscriptions from Roman Italy. JJS 48 (1997) 300-311.

8115 *Orel, V.; Stolbova, O.* On addenda et corrigenda to the Hamito-Semitic etymological dictionary. ZDMG 147 (1997) 212-217.

8116 **Ortiz Valdivieso, Pedro** Léxico hebreo-español y arameo-español. M 1997, Sociedad Bíblica 216 pp. Pres. *Victor Morla Asensio*. 84-80830-49-2 [NThAR 1999,180].

8117 *Pavoncello, Nello* Epigrafi ebraiche del vecchio cimitero di Senigallia. Henoch 19/2 (1997) 203-213.

8118 **Pérez Fernández, Miguel** An introductory grammar of Rabbinic Hebrew. ᵀ*Elwolde, John*: Lei 1997, Brill xxii; 327 pp. Bibl. 90-04-10890-4.

8119 ᴱ**Perani, Mauro; Campanini, Saverio** I frammenti ebraici di Bologna: Archivio di Stato e collezioni minori. Inventario dei manoscritti delle Biblioteche d'Italia 108: F 1997, Olschki 168 pp. 200 tables [RivBib 46,229—Fumagalli, Pier Francesco];

8120 I frammenti ebraici di Modena. Archivio storico comunale. Inventario dei manoscritti delle Biblioteche d'Italia 110: F 1997, Olschki 84 pp. 100 tables [RivBib 46,229—Fumagalli, Pier Francesco].

8121 *Qimron, E.* A new approach to the use of forms of the imperfect without personal endings. The Hebrew of the DSS. StTDJ 26: 1997, <sup>E</sup>Muraoka, T., 174-181.

8122 **Reif, Stefan C.** Hebrew manuscripts at Cambridge University Library: a description and introduction. UCOP 52: NY 1997, CUP xx; 626 pp. 32 pl. $125. 0-521-58339-X [ThD 44,379—Heiser, W. Charles].

8123 *Reiner, Fred* Tracking the SHAPIRA case: a biblical scandal revisited. BArR 23/3 (1997) 32-41, 66-67.

8124 **Renz, Johannes** Die althebräischen Inschriften, I-II. 1995, ⇒11/2,5774; 12,7710. <sup>R</sup>BiOr 54 (1997) 161-166 *(Lemaire, A.)*; OLZ 92 (1997) 342-352 *(Lehmann, Reinhard G.)*; WO 28 (1997) 216-220 *(Pardee, Dennis)*;

8125 Schrift und Schreibertradition. ADPV 23: Wsb 1997, Harrassowitz x; 111 pp. DM48. 3-447-03923-X [BiOr 55,486—Lemaire, A.].

8126 **Reymond, Philippe** Dizionario di ebraico e aramaico biblici. 1995, ⇒11/2,5775. <sup>R</sup>PaVi 42/2 (1997) 58-59 *(Balzaretti, Claudio)*; Synaxis 15/1 (1997) 364-368 *(Minissale, Antonino)*.

8127 *Särkiö, Pekka* Hilferuf zu Jahwe aus dem Versteck: eine neue Deutung der Inschrift *yšr mḥr* aus Ḥirbet Bet Ley. ZDPV 113 (1997) 39-60.

8128 *Sérandour, A.* Remarques complémentaires sur la contribution ordonnée par le roi ʾŠyhw pour le temple de YHWH. Sum. 77. Sem. 46 (1996) 77-80.

8129 *Shanks, Hershel* Three shekels for the Lord: ancient inscription records gift to Solomon's temple. BArR 23/6 (1997) 28-32.

8130 *Solomon, Avi* The prohibition against Ṭevul Yom and defilement of the daily whole offering in the Jerusalem temple in CD 11:21-12:1: a new understanding. DSD 4 (1997) 1-20.

8131 *Talmon, Shemaryahu* A Masada fragment of Samaritan origin. IEJ 47 (1997) 220-232.

8132 **Targarona Borrás, Judit** Diccionario hebreo-español. 1995, ⇒12,7718. <sup>R</sup>Sef. 57/1 (1997) 213-215 *(Girón, L.-F.)*.

8133 <sup>E</sup>**Weinberg, Werner** Essays on Hebrew. SFSHJ 46: 1993, ⇒11/2, 5746; 12,7670. <sup>R</sup>JSSt 42 (1997) 139-141 *(Glinert, Lewis H.)*.

8134 **Yahalom, Joseph** Palestinian vocalised Piyyut manuscripts in the Cambridge Genizah collections. Cambridge Genizah 7: C 1997, CUP vii; 87 pp. 0-521-58399-3.

8135 *Zehnder, Markus* Zentrale Aspekte der Semantik der hebräischen Weg-Lexeme. Studien zur hebräischen Grammatik. OBO 156: 1997, ⇒310. <sup>E</sup>Wagner, A., 155-170.

## J1.3 **Voces** *ordine alphabetico consonantium* **hebraicarum**

### *Akkadian*

8136 *baqaru*: Dombradi, Eva baqaru: ein Fall von lexikalischem Transfer infolge von Plurilingualismus?: Probleme der lexikalischen Interferenz in Sprachkontaktsituationen. WO 28 (1997) 31-57.

8137 *inūma*: Zewi, Tamar On similar syntactical roles of *inūma* in El Amarna and הנה, והנה and הן in Biblical Hebrew. JANES 25 (1997) 71-86.

8138   *naparšudu; nābutu*: Jenni, Ernst 'Fliehen' im akkadischen und im hebräischen Sprachgebrauch <1978>. Studien zur Sprachwelt. 1997, ⇒138. 72-81.

### Aramaic

8139   חמן Fritz, Volkmar Die Bedeutung von *hammān* im Hebräischen von *hmn*ʾ in den palmyrenischen Inschriften. Studien zur Literatur. 1997 <1981>, ⇒126. 285-296.
8140   מטר Lund, Jerome A. The noun *maṭṭar* 'prison': a possible ghost word in the lexicon of middle western Aramaic. Or. 66 (1997) 71-77.

### Hebrew

8141   אבד Jenni, Ernst Faktitiv und Kausativ von אבד 'zugrunde gehen' <1967>. Studien zur Sprachwelt. 1997, ⇒138. 11-24.
8142   iŝ Voigt, Rainer Die Wurzel iŝ (*iΘ) im Hebräischen sowie im Frühnord- und Altsüdarabischen. ZAH 10 (1997) 169-176.
8143   אבה ;מוט ;יאל Jenni, Ernst 'Wollen' und 'nicht wollen' im Hebräischen. Studien zur Sprachwelt <1971>. 1997, ⇒138. 36-42.
8144   אהב Deist, Ferdinand E. 'To love God and your neighbour'—a sociolinguistic perspective. OTEs 10 (1997) 7-17.
8145   בוא Jenni, Ernst 'Kommen' im theologischen Sprachgebrauch des Alten Testaments <1970>. Studien zur Sprachwelt. 1997, ⇒138. 25-35.
8146   בחר Cimosa, Mario L'elezione divina nell'Antico Testamento. DSBP 15 (1997) 16-50.
8147   במה Emerton, J.A. The biblical high place in the light of recent study. PEQ 129 (1997) 116-132 [Isa 53,9].
8148   גבירה Ackerman, Susan The queen mother and the cult in the ancient Near East. Women and goddess traditions. 1997, ⇒249. ᴱKing, K., 179-209.
8149   גער Klopfenstein, Martin Wenn der Schöpfer die Chaosmächte "anherrscht" (gʿr) und so das Leben schützt: zu einem wenig beachteten Aspekt des Zorns Gottes im Alten Testament. ThZ 53 (1997) 33-43 [Isa 51,20; 54,9].
8150   גת Michaux-Colombot, Danièle La *gat* de Gédéon, pressoir ou fief?. UF 29 (1997) 579-598.
8151   גר Sedlmeier, Franz "Fremdlinge sind wir, wie alle unsere Väter" (1 Chr 29,15): "Fremdsein" im Alten Testament. Prisma 9/1 (1997) 6-13.

        הן ;הנה ;והנה ⇒8137.
8152   זנה Bird, Phyllis A. 'To play the harlot': an inquiry into an Old Testament metaphor. Missing persons. 1997 <1989>, ⇒114. 219-236.
8153   זרע Regt, Lénart J. de Multiple meaning and semantic domains in some Biblical Hebrew lexicographical projects: the description of *zeraʿ*. ZAH 10 (1997) 63-75.
8154   (a) חדל Jenni, Ernst Lexikalisch-semantische Strukturunterschiede: hebräisch *ḥdl*—deutsch 'aufhören / unterlassen' <1994>. Studien

zur Sprachwelt. 1997, ⇒138. 196-205. (b) חליפה *Müller, Hans-Peter* Zur Semantik von *ḥªlîpā* (Ijob 10,17; 14,14 u.ö.). ZAH 10 (1997) 123-133.

חמן *Fritz, V.* Die Bedeutung von *hammān* ⇒8139.

8155 חֶסֶד **Börschlein, Wolfgang** Häsäd: der Erweis von Solidarität—als eine ethische Grundhaltung im Alten Testament: ein Beispiel für ein Modell in christlicher Ethik heute?. Diss. Eichstätt 1997; ᴰ*Diedrich, F.* 508 pp. [RTL 29,576].

8156 חרש *Barrado, Pedro* El silencio en el Antiguo Testamento: aproximación a un símbolo ambiguo. EstB 55 (1997) 5-27.

8157 ידע *Vervenne, Marc* The phraseology of "knowing YHWH" in the Hebrew Bible: a preliminary study of its syntax and function. BEThL 132: 1997, ⇒12. ᶠBᴇᴜᴋᴇɴ W., 467-492.

8158 יתרון *Bardski, Krzysztof* Yitrôn (יתרון) nelle traduzioni dell'Ecclesiaste di Gɪʀᴏʟᴀᴍᴏ [Yitrôn (יתרון) w Hierronimowych tłī ḥḥlḥniach księgi Eklezjastesa (Streszczenie)]. WST 10 (1997) 31-36.

8159 כוש *Holter, Knut* Should Old Testament 'Cush' be rendered 'Africa'?. TPBT 48 (1997) 331-336.

8160 כי; ל; מ *Althann, Robert* Misunderstood vocative particles. Studies in NWS. BibOr 45: 1997, ⇒108. 93-119.

8161 כפר *Soloff, Rav A.* Yom Kippur: cover up or plea for probation?. JBQ 25/2 (1997) 86-89.

8162 למד *Braulik, Georg* Das Deuteronomium und die Gedächtniskultur Israels: redaktionsgeschichtliche Beobachtungen zur Verwendung von *lmd*. Studien zu Dt. SBAB 24: 1997 <1993>, ⇒117. 119-46.

8163 למד *Engelen, Jan C.M.* Leren למד. ITBT 5/1 (1997) 29-30.

8164 למה; מדוע *Michel, Diethelm* "Warum" und "wozu"?: eine bisher übersehene Eigentümlichkeit des Hebräischen und ihre Konsequenzen für das alttestamentliche Geschichtsverständnis. Studien zur Überlieferungsgeschichte. TB 93: 1997 <1988>, ⇒149. 13-34.

8165 מבקר *Marcheselli-Casale, Cesare* Tracce del *mebaqqêr* di Qumran nell'*epískopos* del NT?: per uno 'status quaestionis'. RStB 9/2 (1997) 177-210.

8166 מן *Jenni, Ernst* Die Präposition *min* in zeitlicher Verwendung bei Deuterojesaja. Studien zur Sprachwelt. 1997 <1980>, ⇒138. 91-105.

8167 מִשְׁפָּט; צְדָקָה *Weinfeld, Moshe* Social justice in ancient Israel and in the ancient Near East. 1995, ⇒11/2,3266; 12,6827. ᴿVT 47 (1997) 571-572 *(Emerton, John A.E.)*; CBQ 59 (1997) 141-142 *(Gossai, Hemchand)*; JBL 116 (1997) 722-725 *(Smith-Christopher, Daniel L.)*; CThMi 24 (1997) 533-534 *(Hutton, Rodney R.)*.

נוס; ברח *Jenni, Ernst* 'Fliehen' im akkadischen und im hebräischen Sprachgebrauch ⇒8138.

8168 נחה *Loretz, Oswald* Ugaritisch *nhw* und hebräisch *nhh* II im Kontext der Legende vom syrisch-ephraimitischen Krieg. UF 29 (1997) 511-528 [2 Kgs 16,5-9; Isa 7,1-17].

8169 נחם *Freedman, David Noel* When God repents. Divine Commitment 1. 1997 <1989>, ⇒124. 409-446.

8170 (a) נקם *Peels, Hendrik G.L.* The vengeance of God: the meaning of the root NQM. OTS 31: 1995, ⇒11/2,5845; 12,7752. ᴿJBL 115 (1996) 517-518 *(Vogels, Walter)*. (b) סוד **Neef, Heinz-Dieter** Gottes himmlischer Thronrat: Hintergrund und Bedeutung von *sôd JHWH* im AT. AzTh 79: 1994, ⇒10,9046; 12,7753. ᴿJBL 116 (1997) 117-119 *(Pardee, Dennis)*.

8171  ספר *Hurvitz, Avi* On the borderline between biblical criticism and Hebrew linguistics: the emergence of the term *spr-mšh*. 1997, ⇒34. ᴹGʀᴇᴇɴʙᴇʀɢ M., 37*-43*. **H.**

8172  עבד *Freedman, David Noel* The slave of Yahweh. Divine Commitment 1. 1997 <1959>, ⇒124. Divine Commitment 1. 53-71.

8173  עבד *Eaton, Margaret* The intractable servant of the Septuagint: translating ʿ*ebed*. TPBT 48 (1997) 114-122.

8174  עלם *Niehr, Herbert* Zur Semantik von nordwestsemitisch ʿ*lm* als "Unterwelt" und "Grab". AOAT 247: 1997, ⇒75. ꜰRᴏᴇʟʟɪɢ W., 295-305.

8175  עתה *Jenni, Ernst* Zur Verwendung von ʿ*ttā* 'jetzt' im Alten Testament. Studien zur Sprachwelt. 1997 <1972>, ⇒138. 43-50.

8176  פחז *Hoop, Raymond de* The meaning of *pḥz* in classical Hebrew. ZAH 10 (1997) 16-26.

8177  פסח *Büchner, Dirk* פסח: pass over or protect?. BN 86 (1997) 14-17 [Exod 12,13].

8178  פ *Althann, Robert* A review of the evidence for *p*, 'and' in Biblical Hebrew. Studies in NWS. BibOr 45: 1997, ⇒108. 79-92 [Cant 3,10].

8179  קהת *Schorch, Stefan* Die hebräische Wurzel *QHT*. ZAH 10 (1997) 76-84.

8180  קנא *Gross, Carl D.* 'Jealous' in the Old Testament: the Hebrew *qanaʾ* and related words. PPBT 48 (1997) 228-235, 418-432.

8181  קנא *Péter-Contesse, René* Dieu est-il jaloux?. Cahiers de Traduction Biblique 28 (1997) 11-17.

8182  רע; ירא *Myhill, John* Problems in lexical semantics in the Old Testament: *raʿ* and *yrʾ*. Translating sensitive texts. 1997, ⇒231. ᴱSimms, K., 207-230.

8183  רפא **Brown, Michael L.** Israel's divine healer. 1995, ⇒11/2,c419; 12,10633. SdT 9 (1997) 111-112 *(Piccolo, Giuseppe)*.

8184  רוח *Luzzatto, Amos* Ruach: il pensiero ebraico. RSEc 15 (1997) 281-289.

8185  (a) שבת *Willi-Plein, Ina* Anmerkungen zu Wortform und Semantik des Sabbat. ZAH 10 (1997) 201-206.

        (b) שלום *Stendebach, Franz Josef* Shalom im alten Orient und in Ägypten. 1997, ⇒46. ꜰKᴀᴍᴘʜᴀᴜs F., 59-74.

8186  שלום *Talmon, Shemaryahu* The signification of *šlwm* and its semantic field in the Hebrew Bible. 1997, ⇒77. ꜰSᴀɴᴅᴇʀs J., 75-115.

8187  שלום *Jenni, Ernst* 'Gehe hin in Frieden (*lšlwm/bšlwm*). Studien zur Sprachwelt. 1997 <1988>, ⇒138. 125-134.

8188  שמים *Nam, Daegeuk* The biblical meanings of heaven;

8189  תמיד *Núñez, Samuel* The usage and meaning of the Hebrew word תמיד in the Old Testament. 1997, ⇒83. ꜰSʜᴇᴀ W., 291-300/95-102.


## Syriac

8190  *šlḥ: Joosten, Jan* 'Le Père envoie le Fils': la provenance occidentale d'une locution syriaque. Som., sum. 299. RHR 214 (1997) 299-309.

*Ugaritic*

*nḥw*: *Loretz, Oswald* Ugaritisch *nḥw* und hebräisch *nḥh* II ⇒8167.

### J1.5 *Phoenicia, ugaritica*—Northwest Semitic [⇒т5.4]

**Althann, Robert** Studies in Northwest Semitic ⇒108.

8191 *Amadasi Guzzo, Maria* L'accompli à la 3e personne du féminin singulier et le pronom suffixe à l'accusatif de la 3e personne du singulier: note de grammaire phénicienne. AOAT 247: 1997, ⇒75. FROELLIG W., 1-9.

8192 *Arnaud, Daniel* L'édition ougaritaine de la série astrologique 'Éclipses du dieu-Soleil'. Sum. 7. Sem. 45 (1996) 7-18.

8193 *Aufrecht, Walter E.* Urbanization and Northwest Semitic inscriptions of the late Bronze and Iron Ages. Urbanism. JSOT.S 244: 1997, ⇒265. EAufrecht, W.E., 116-129.

8194 *Bordreuil, P.; Briquel-Chatonnet, F.; Gubel, E.* Inédits épigraphiques des fouilles anciennes et récentes a Tell Kazel. Sum. 37. Sem. 45 (1996) 37-47.

8195 *Bron, F.* Sur quelques stèles puniques. Sum. 65. Sem. 45 (1996) 65-71.

8196 EBrooke, George J. Ugarit and the Bible. UBL 11: 1994, ⇒10,308; 12,10290. RJAOS 117 (1997) 375-378 *(Pardee, Dennis)*.

8197 *Cochavi-Rainey, Zipora* מבחר דימויים, תיאותים ומטבעות לשון במכתבי אל־עמארנה והשוואתם למקרא [Selected similes, descriptions, and figures of speech from the El-Amarna Letters and their biblical parallels]. Sum. I. Leš. 60/3-4 (1997) 165-179. **H.**

8198 **Cunchillos, Jesús-Luis; Vita, Juan-Pablo** Concordancia de palabras ugaríticas. BDFSN 1/2: 1995, ⇒11/2,5889.R OLZ 92 (1997) 465-467 *(Tropper, Josef)*; OLoP 28 (1997) 249-250 *(Schoors, A.)*.

8199 **Cunchillos, Jesús-Luis; Zamora, José-Ángel** Gramática fenicia elemental. BDFSN 2/1: M 1997, Consjeo Superior de Investigaciones Científicas xv; 170 pp. 84-00-07702-4 [NThAR 1999,250].

8200 *Cunchillos-Ilarri, Jesus L.* Des outils pour le développement de l'herméneumatique sémitique nord-occidentale. Congress volume 1995. VT.S 66: 1997, ⇒323. EEmerton, J.A., 97-124.

8201 **Dietrich, Manfried; Loretz, Oswald** Analytic Ugaritic bibliography 1972-1988. AOAT 20/6: 1996, ⇒12,7778. ROLZ 92 (1997) 460-462 *(Tropper, Josef)*;

8202 Word-List of *The cuneiform alphabetic texts from Ugarit.* ALASP 12: 1996, ⇒12,7779. RArOr 65/1 (1997) 132-133 *(Segert, Stanislav)*; OLZ 92 (1997) 464-465 *(Tropper, Josef)*.

8203 **Dietrich, Manfried; Loretz, Oswald; Sanmartín, Joaquín** The cuneiform alphabetic texts from Ugarit. ALASP 8: ⇒11/2,5891; 12,7780. RJSSt 42 (1997) 132-137 *(Pardee, Dennis)*; JAOS 117 (1997) 714-715 *(Parker, Simon B.)*.

8204 *Ferjaoui, Ahmed* Une épitaphe néopunique d'une grande prêtresse de Cérès provenant de ʿAyin Zakkar (Tunisie). Sum. 25. Sem. 46 (1996) 25-35.

8205 *Freedman, David Noel* The pronominal suffixes of the third person singular in Phoenician <1951>;

8206 A second Mesha inscription <1964>. Divine Commitment 2. 1997, ⇒124. 1-4/29-30.

8207 **Hoftijzer, Jean; Jongeling, K.** Dictionary of the North-West Semitic inscriptions: Part I ' - L: Part II M - T. 1995, ⇒11/2,5895; 12,7791. ᴿArOr 65 (1997) 312-314 *(Segert, Stanislav)*.

8208 **Lindenberger, James M.** Ancient Aramaic and Hebrew letters. 1994, ⇒11/2,5954...12,7792. ᴿJAOS 117 (1997) 370-371 *(Porten, Bezalel)*.

8209 **Olmo Lete, Gregorio del; Sanmartín, Joaquín** Diccionario de la lengua ugarítica 1: (↑ >i/u)-l. AulOr.S 7: 1996, ⇒12,7794. ᴿOLZ 92/4-5 (1997) 456-460 *(Tropper, Josef)*.

8210 *Pardee, D.* Quelques remarques relatives à l'étude des textes hippiatriques en langue ougaritique. Sum. 19. Sem. 45 (1996) 19-26.

8211 **Pettinato, Giovanni** Testi amministrativi di Ebla: archivio L. 2752. 1996, ⇒12,10337. ᴿBiOr 54 (1997) 397-399 *(Pomponio, Francesco)*.

8212 *Sasson, Victor* The inscription of Achish, governor of Eqron, and Philistine dialect, cult and culture. UF 29 (1997) 627-639.

8213 **Sivan, Daniel** A grammar of the Ugaritic language. HO 1/28: Lei 1997, Brill xxi; 327 pp. £71/$96.25. 90-04-10614-6. ᴿAfO 44-45 (1997-98) 429-438 *(Tropper, Josef)*.

8214 *Sivan, Daniel* Two notes on Ugaritic. Sum. ix. Leš. 60/1-2 (1997) 67-71 [*bhtm*] [Qoh 1,10]. **H.**

8215 *Southern, Mark* Where have all the nasals gone?: nC > CC in North Semitic. JSSt 42 (1997) 263-282.

8216 *Sznycer, Maurice* A propos de l'inscription punique de Carthage *CIS* I 4483. Sum. 17. Sem. 46 (1996) 17-24.

8217 *Testen, David* The Phoenician direct-object marker in the inscription of Yhwmlk. UF 29 (1997) 655-660.

8218 **Tropper, Josef** Die Inschriften von Zincirli. 1993, ⇒9,9833... 12,7804. BiOr 54 (1997) 464-468 *(Muraoka, T.)*.

8219 *Tropper, Josef* Bedeutende Neuerscheinungen der Ugaritistik. OLZ 92 (1997) 455-467.

8220 *Vattioni, Francesco* Gli ordinali nel Fenicio-Punico. SEL 13 (1996) 75-77.

8221 *Vita, J.P.* Bemerkungen zum ugaritischen Dual. OLoP 28 (1997) 33-41.

8222 **Zemánek, Petr** Ugaritischer Wortformenindex. Lexicographia Orientalis 4: Hamburg 1995, Buske xii; 294 pp. ᴿOLZ 92 (1997) 462-464 *(Tropper, Josef)*.

## ᴊ1.6 Aramaica

8223 *Ayad, Boulos Ayad* From the archive of Ananiah son of Azariah: a Jew from Elephantine. JNES 56 (1997) 37-50.

8224 *Bertolino, Roberto* Une stèle inédite de Hatra. Sum. 143. Sem. 46 (1997) 143-146.

8225 *Bordreuil, Pierre; Briquel-Chatonnet, Françoise* Aramaic documents from Til Barsib. Abr-n. 34 (1996-97) 100-107.

8226 *Briquel-Chatonnet, Françoise; Nehmé, Laïla* Graffitti nabatéens d'Al-Muwayh et de Bi'r al-Ḥammāmāt (Égypte). Sum. 81. Sem. 47 (1997) 81-88.

8227 *Colombo, V.* Nabataeans and Palmyreans: an analysis of the Tell el-Shuqafiyye inscriptions. Aram 7 (1995) 183-187.

8228 ECotton-Paltiel, Hannah M.; Yardeni, Ada Aramaic, Hebrew and Greek documentary texts from Naḥal Hever and other sites: with an appendix containing alleged Qumran Texts (The Seiyal collection II). DJD 27: Oxf 1997, Clarendon xxvii; 383 pp. Bibl. £95. 0-19-826394-3.

8229 Dalman, Gustav H. Aramäisch-Neuhebräisches Handwörterbuch zu Targum, Talmud und Midrasch, mit Lexikon der Abbreviaturen von G.H. Händler und einem Verzeichnis der Mischna-Abschnitte. Hildesheim ³1997, Olms ix; 457; 120 pp. Nachdr. 3-487-01602-8.

8230 Díez Merino, Luis El arameo, lengua mediterránea y española. La Bíblia i el Mediterrani. 1997, ⇒385. EBorrell, d'Agustí, 3-27.

8231 Dijkstra, Meindert The other side of darkness: once more smr in the Deir ʿAlla inscription. ZAW 109 (1997) 272-274.

8232 Emerton, J.A. Further comments on the use of tenses in the Aramaic inscription from Tel Dan. VT 47 (1997) 429-440.

8233 EEphʿal, Israel; Naveh, Joseph Aramaic ostraca of the fourth century BC from Idumaea. 1996, ⇒12,7813. RIEJ 48 (1997) 283-286 (Sokoloff, Michael); WO 28 (1997) 220-222 (Röllig, Wolfgang).

8234 Fales, Frederick Mario An Aramaic tablet from Tell Shioukh Fawqani, Syria. Sum. 81. Sem. 46 (1997) 81-121.

8235 Fitzmyer, Joseph A. The Aramaic inscriptions of Sefire. BibOr 19/A: ²1995, ⇒11/2,5934; 12,7816. ROr. 66 (1997) 204-205 (Lemaire, André).

8236 Grosby, Steven ʾrm klh and the worship of Hadad: a nation of Aram?. Aram 7 (1995) 337-352.

8237 EHealey, John F. The Nabataean tomb inscriptions of Madaʾin Salih. JSSt.S 1: 1993, ⇒11/2,5941. RSyr. 74 (1997) 244-245 (Briquel-Chatonnet, Françoise); AfO 44-45 (1997-98) 446-450 (Sima, Alexander).

8238 Healey, John F.; Schmitt-Korte, Karl; Wenning, Robert Scripta Nabataea und Sela Aretas: epigraphische Zeugnisse und Münzwesen der Nabatäer. Petra antike Felsstadt. 1997, ⇒311. EWeber, T., 99-104.

Herranz Marco, M. Huellas de arameo en los evangelios ⇒3983.

8239 Hillers, Delbert R. Notes on Palmyrene Aramaic texts. Aram 7 (1995) 73-88.

8240 Hillers, Delbert R.; Cussini, Eleonora Palmyrene Aramaic texts. 1996, ⇒12,7819. RBiOr 54 (1997) 468-471 (Lipiński, E.).

8241 Huehnergard, John What is Aramaic?. Aram 7 (1995) 261-282.

8242 Klingbeil, Gerald A. A semantic analysis of Aramaic ostraca of Syria-Palestine during the Persian period. AUSS 35 (1997) 33-46.

8243 Knauf, Ernst Axel Eine nabatäische Inschrift von der oberen Wasserleitung am Theaterberg (Gebel el-Madbaḥ), Petra. ZDPV 113 (1997) 68-69.

8244 Koehler, Ludwig; Baumgartner Walter Aramäisches Lexikon. Hebräisches und aramäisches Lexikon zum Alten Testament, 5. ³1995. ⇒11/2,5765. RWZKM 87 (1997) 301-303 (Segert, Stanislav); FolOr 33 (1997) 237-239 (Dombrowski, Bruno W.W.).

8245 Kottsieper, Ingo Anmerkungen zu Pap. Amherst 63 Teil II-V. UF 29 (1997) 385-434.

8246 Lemaire, André Contrat de prêt d'orge sur tablette araméenne (VIIe s. av. J.-C.). Sum. 47. Sem. 47 (1997) 47-51.

8247 **Lemaire, André** Nouvelles inscriptions araméennes d'Idumée au Musée d'Israël. Transeuphr.S 3: 1996, ⇒12,7824. RIEJ 48 (1997) 290-3 *(Eph'al, Israel)*; WO 28 (1997) 220-222 *(Röllig, Wolfgang)*.

8248 *Lozachmeur, Hélène; Lemaire, André* Nouveaux ostraca araméens d'Idumée (collection Sh. Moussaïeff). Sum. 123. Sem. 46 (1996) 123-142.

8249 *Makujina, John* On the possible old Persian origin of the Aramaic טעם שׂים, "to issue a decree". HUCA 68 (1997) 1-9.

8250 **Martínez Borobio, Emiliano** Gramática del arameo antiguo. 1996, ⇒12,7826. RSef. 57/1 (1997) 205-208 *(Sanmartín, J.)*.

8251 EMuraoka, **Takamitsu** Studies in Qumran Aramaic. Abr-n.S 3: 1992, ⇒8,9586... 12,7828. RAfO 44-45 (1997-98) 439-441 *(Zaborski, Andrzej)*.

8252 *Nehmé, Laila* La géographie des inscriptions de Pétra (Jordanie). Des Sumériens. 1997, ⇒377. ESérandour, A., 125-143.

8253 *Oelsner, Joachim* Neu/spätbabylonische und aramäische Kaufverträge. AOAT 247: 1997, ⇒75. FROELLIG W., 307-314.

8254 *Ribera Florit, Josep* L'arameu com a signe d'identitat semiticooccidental enfront de la cultura grecoromana. La Bíblia i el Mediterrani. 1997, ⇒385. EBorrell, d'Agustí, 67-75.

8255 **Ribera-Florit, Josep** Manual de gramática aramea: arameo clásico (oficial). Textos Docentes 13: Barc 1994, Univ. de Barcelona 83 pp. RSef. 57/1 (1997) 212-213 *(Ferrer, J.)*.

8256 **Rodrigues Pereira, Alphons S.** Studies in Aramaic poetry (c. 100 B.C.E. - c. 600 C.E.). SSN 34: Assen 1997, Van Gorcum viii; 456 pp. $58/f120. 90-232-3261-5 [BiOr 55,497—Lipiński, E.].

8257 *Stolper, Matthew W.* A paper chase after the Aramaic on TCL 13 193. JAOS 116 (1997) 517-521.

8258 *Teixidor, Javier* Nouvelles inscriptions palmyréniennes. Sum. 65. Sem. 47 (1997) 65-71.

8259 *Tropper, Josef* Lexikographische Untersuchungen zum Biblisch-Aramäischen. JNSL 23/2 (1997) 105-128.

## л1.7 Syriaca

8260 *Balzaretti, Claudio* Ancient treatises on Syriac homonyms. OrChr 81 (1997) 73-81.

8261 *Bombeck, Stefan* Das syrische Partizip von ḥwh aktiv. BN 88 (1997) 59-74.

8262 **Briquel-Chatonnet, Françoise** Manuscrits syriaques de la Bibliothèque nationale de France (nos 356-435, entrés depuis 1911), de la bibliothèque Méjanes d'Aix-en-Provence, de la bibliothèque municipale de Lyon et de la Bibliothèque nationale et universitaire de Strasbourg: catalogue. P 1997, Bibliothèque nationale de France 261 pp. 2-7177-2019-07.

8263 **Brock, Sebastian Paul** Syriac Studies: a classified bibliography (1960-1990). Kaslik 1996, Parole de l'Orient 308 pp.

8264 **Muraoka, Takamitsu** Classical Syriac: a basic grammar with a chrestomathy. PLO 19: Wsb 1997, Harrassowitz xxv; 147; 1-88 pp. Select bibliography compiled by S.P. Brock. 3-447-03890-X.

8265 *Voigt, Rainer* Das Vokalsystem des Syrischen nach BARHEBRAEUS. OrChr 81 (1997) 36-72.

J1.8 **Akkadica** (sumerica)

8266 *Beaulieu, Paul-Alain* Akkadische Lexikographie: CAD S2 und S3. Or. 66 (1997) 157-180.

8267 *Cathcart, Kevin J.* The age of decipherment: the Old Testament and the ancient Near East in the nineteenth century. Congress volume 1995. VT.S 66: 1997, ⇒323. ᴱEmerton, J.A., 81-95.

8268 **De Odorico, Marco** The use of numbers and quantifications in the Assyrian royal inscriptions. 1995, ⇒11/2,6004; 12,7843. ᴿOLZ 92 (1997) 512-516 *(Friberg, Jöran)*; WO 28 (1997) 199-201 *(Soden, Wolfram von)*.

8269 ᵀ**Durand, Jean-Marie** Les documents épistolaires du palais de Mari. LAPO 16: P 1997, Cerf 654 pp. Bibl. FF185. 2-204-05685-5.

8270 **Frahm, Eckart** Einleitung in die Sanherib-Inschriften. AfO 26: W 1997, Institut für Orientalistik der Universität Wien viii; 304 pp. ÖS890. 3-900345-04-X. ᴿUF 28 (1996) 787-790 *(Loretz, O.)*.

8271 **Frayne, Douglas** Royal inscriptions of Mesopotamia, early periods 4: Old Babylonian period (2003-1595 BC). 1990, ⇒6,e438; 10,12574. ᴿZA 87/1 (1997) 122-141 *(Krebernik, M.)*;

8272 3/2: Ur III period (2112-2004 BC). Toronto 1997, University of Toronto Press xliv; 489 pp. Bibl. 0-8020-4198-1.

8273 *Galter, H.D.* Assyrische Königsinschriften des 2. Jts. v. Chr.: die Entwicklung einer Textgattung. Assyrien im Wandel. 1997, ⇒379. ᴱWaetzoldt, H., 53-59.

8274 *Gensler, Orin D.* Mari Akkadian is "to, for" and preposition-hopping in the light of comparative Semitic syntax. Or. 66 (1997) 129-156.

8275 *Gianto, Agustinus* Script and word order in EA 162: a case study of Egyptian Akkadian. Or. 66 (1997) 426-433.

8276 **Hayes, John L.** Sumerian. Languages of the world, Materials 68: Newcastle 1997, Lincom-Europa 41 pp. Bibl. 3-929075-39-3.

8277 *Horowitz, Wayne* The Amarna Age inscribed clay cylinder from Beth-Shean. BA 60/2 (1997) 97-100.

8278 *Huehnergard, John* Akkadian grammar. Or. 66 (1997) 434-444.

8279 **Huehnergard, John** A grammar of Akkadian. HSM 45: Atlanta, GA 1997, Scholars xl; 647 pp. $25. 0-7885-0318-9. ᴿRA 91 (1997) 93-95 *(Charpin, D.)*.

8280 **Hurowitz, Victor (Avigdor)** Divine service and its rewards: ideology and poetics in the Hinke Kudurru. Beer-Sheva 10: Beer-Sheva 1997, Ben-Gurion University of the Negev Press viii; 106 pp. 0334-2255. ᴿRA 91 (1997) 89-90 *(Lion, B.)*.

8281 *Jeyes, U.* Assurbanipal's *barûtu*;

8282 *Kienast, B.* Altakkadische und assyrische Königsinschriften. Assyrien im Wandel. 1997, ⇒379. ᴱWaetzoldt, H., 61-65/67-69.

8283 **Kienast, Burkhart; Volk, Konrad** Die sumerischen und akkadischen Briefe des III. Jahrtausends aus der Zeit vor der III. Dynastie von Ur. 1995, ⇒11/2,6025. ᴿBiOr 54 (1997) 720-727 *(Zólyomi, Gábor)*.

8284 *Lipiński, E.* The personal names Handî, Harranay and Kurillay in Neo-Assyrian sources. Assyrien im Wandel. 1997, ⇒379. ᴱWaetzoldt, H., 89-93.

8285 *Maul, Stefan M.* Küchensumerisch oder hohe Kunst der Exegese?: Überlegungen zur Bewertung akkadischer Interlinearübersetzungen von Emesal-Texten. AOAT 247: 1997, ⇒75. FROELLIG W., 253-267.

8286 ᵀMichalowski, Piotr Letters from early Mesopotamia. 1993, ⇒9,9900. ᴿJAOS 117 (1997) 707-712 (Neumann, Hans).

8287 Miller, Douglas B.; Shipp, R. Mark An Akkadian handbook: paradigms, helps, glossary, logograms, and sign lists. WL 1996, Eisenbrauns vi; 163 pp. $15. 0-931464-86-2. ᴿAfO 44-45 (1997-98) 428 (Hunger, H.).

8288 Negri Scafa, P. Die "assyrischen" Schreiber des Königtums Arraphe;

8289 Neumann, H. Assur in altakkadischer Zeit: die Texte. Assyrien im Wandel. 1997, ⇒379. ᴱWaetzoldt, H., 123-132/133-138.

8290 Parpola, Simo The man without a scribe and the question of literacy in the Assyrian empire. AOAT 247: 1997, ⇒75. FROELLIG W., 315-324.

8291 Pedersén, O. Use of writing among the Assyrians;

8292 Penglase, Ch. Mesopotamian influence on the Homeric hymn to Demeter in Assyrian times. Assyrien im Wandel. 1997, ⇒379. ᴱWaetzoldt, H., 139-152/153-158.

8293 Pettinato, Giovanni L'uomo cominciò a scrivere: iscrizioni cuneiformi della Collezione Michail. Mi 1997, Electa 215 pp. 88-435-6343-2.

8294 Postgate, J.N. Middle-Assyrian to Neo-Assyrian: the nature of the shift;

8295 Renger, J. Aspekte von Kontinuität und Diskontinuität in den assyrischen Königsinschriften. Assyrien im Wandel. 1997, ⇒379. ᴱWaetzoldt, H., 159-168/169-175.

8296 Rollinger, Robert Zur Bezeichnung von "Griechen" in Keilschrifttexten. RA 91 (1997) 167-172.

8297 Römer, W.H.Ph. Sumerische Emesallieder. BiOr 54 (1997) 604-619.

8298 Seminara, Stefano Note di lessicografia emarita. Sum. 24. RSO 71 (1997) 15-24.

8299 ᴱSjöberg, Åke W. The Sumerian dictionary of the University of Pennsylvania 1: A: part I; part II. 1992-1994, ⇒11/2,6042. ᴿAfO 44-45 (1997-98) 277-288 (Maaijer, Remco; Jagersma, Bram);

8300 A: part II. Ph 1994, Univ. of Pennsylvania. $60. 0-924171-35-9. ᴿJAOS 117 (1997) 736-741 (Bauer, Josef).

8301 Soden, W. von Einige Bemerkungen zur Übernahme babylonischer Literaturwerke im neuassyrischen Großreich. Assyrien im Wandel. 1997, ⇒379. ᴱWaetzoldt, H., 177-180.

8302 Soden, Wolfram von Grundriss der akkadischen Grammatik. ᴱMayer, Werner R.: AnOr 33: ³1995. ⇒11/2,6044. ᴿBiOr 54 (1997) 399-402 (Kouwenberg, N.J.C.); AfO 44-45 (1997-98) 310-314 (Streck, Michael P.).

8303 Tadmor, Hayim The inscriptions of Tiglath-pileser III, king of Assyria. 1994, ⇒10,11149; 12,9286. ᴿBSOAS 60 (1997) 124-125 (George, A.R.); RB 104 (1997) 299-305 (Steymans, H.U.); AfO 44-45 (1997-98) 399-404 (Frahm, Eckart); IEJ 47 (1997) 104-110 (Oded, Bustanay).

8304 Talon, Philippe Old Babylonian texts from Chagar Bazar. Akkadica. Suppl. 10: Bru 1997, FAGD (6) 157 pp. Hand copies by Hamido Hammade; Bibl. 90-9010838-6.

8305 *Tsukimoto, Akio* From Lullû to Ebla: an Old Babylonian document concerning a shipment of horses. AOAT 247: 1997, ⇒75. FRoellig W., 407-412.

8306 **Visicato, Giuseppe** Indices of early dynastic administrative tablets of Suruppak. IUO.S 6/A: N 1997, Istituto Orientale di Napoli x; 136 pp.

8307 EVogelzang, E.; Vanstiphout, H.L.J. Mesopotamian poetic language: Sumerian and Akkadian. Cuneiform Monographs 6: Groningen 1996, STYX xviii; 236 pp. Proceedings of the Groningen Group for the study of Mesopotamian literature 2. ƒ125. 90-72371-84-4. ROLZ 92 (1997) 685-689 *(Reynolds, Frances)*.

8308 **Volk, Konrad** A Sumerian reader. Collab. *Votto, Silvano; Ganter, Annette*: StP.SM 18: R 1997, Ed. Pont. Istituto Biblico xviii; 113 pp. L26.000. 88-7653-610-8.

8309 *Westenholz, Joan Goodnick* Studying poetic language. Or. 66 (1997) 181-195.

8310 *Wilhelm, Gernot* Der mittelassyrische Brief eines Verwalters an seinen Herrn. AOAT 247: 1997, ⇒75. FRoellig W., 431-434.

8311 **Wiseman, Donald John; Black, J.A.** Literary texts from the temple of Nabû. Cuneiform Texts from Nimrud 4: L 1996, British School of Archaeology in Iraq x; 62 pp. 157 pl. 0-903472-15-5. RRA 91 (1997) 188-190 *(Charpin, D.)*.

### J2.7 Arabica

8312 *Bron, François* Quatre inscriptions sabéennes provenant d'un temple de Dhu-Samawi. Syr. 74/1 (1997) 73-80.

8313 *Knauf, Ernest Axel* Supplementa Ismaelitica 17: אין לה ולד Gen 11,30; 18: "Ross und Wagen warf er ins Meer" [Ex 15,21]. BN 86 (1997) 49-50, 50-51.

8314 EKratchkovsky, Ignace Histoire de Yahya ibn Saʾid d'Antioche. TMicheau, Françoise; Troupeau, Gérard: PO 47/4; PO 212: Turnhout 1997, Brepols 373-559 pp.

8315 **Sharon, Moshe** Corpus Inscriptionum Arabicarum Palaestinae (CIAP): A, vol. 1. HO 1/30: Lei 1997, Brill. Bibl. 90-04-11006-2.

8316 *Tropper, Josef* Subvarianten und Funktionen der sabäischen Präfixkonjugation. Or. 66 (1997) 34-57.

8317 *Viladrich, Mercé* La llengua àrab en el context del Mediterrani: algunes qüestions de terminologia teològica en relació amb la doctrina del *taḥrif*. La Bíblia i el Mediterrani. 1997, ⇒385. EBorrell, d'Agustí, 101-110.

### J3.0 Aegyptia

8318 **Depauw, Mark** A companion to Demotic studies. Papyrologica Bruxellensia 28: Bru 1997, Fondation Égyptologique Reine Élisabeth 198 pp. FB800.

8319 *Depuydt, Leo* Four thousand years of evolution: on a law of historical change in ancient Egypt. JNES 56 (1997) 21-35.

8320 EFischer-Elfert, Hans-Werner Lesefunde im literarischen Steinbruch von Deir-el-Medineh. Kleine ägyptische Texte 12: Wsb 1997, Harrassowitz xv; 192 pp. DM78. 3-447-03905-1.

8321  <sup>T</sup>**Foster, John L.** Hymns, prayers, and songs: an anthology of ancient Egyptian lyric poetry. SBL.WAW 8: 1995, ⇒11/2,6127. <sup>R</sup>CBQ 59 (1997) 538-540 *(Higginbotham, Carolyn R.)*.

8322  *Görg, Manfred* Didaktik der Entzifferung Georg EBERS und die Einführung in die Hieroglyphenkunde. BN 87 (1997) 56-68.

8323  **Grandet, Pierre; Mathieu, Bernard** Cours d'égyptien hiéroglyphique. P 1997, Khéops xxii; 845 pp. Nouvelle édition revue et augmentée. 2-9504368-2-X.

8324  **Hoch, James E.** Semitic words in Egyptian texts of the New Kingdom and third intermediate period. 1994, ⇒10,9205; 12,7868. <sup>R</sup>WZKM 87 (1997) 277-288 *(Vittmann, Güunter)*.

8325  *Jansen-Winkeln, Karl* Hervorgehobenes Objekt und königliche Widmungsformel. Or. 66 (1997) 15-33.

8326  **Jürgens, Peter** Grundlinien einer Überlieferungsgeschichte der altägyptischen Sargtexte. 1995, ⇒11/2,6150. <sup>R</sup>BiOr 54 (1997) 643-646 *(DuQuesne, Terence)*.

8327  <sup>T</sup>**Kitchen, K.A.** Translations: Ramesses II: royal inscriptions. Series A. Oxf 1996, Blackwell xxviii; 618 pp. £125/$150. <sup>R</sup>Or. 66 (1997) 449-451 *(Jansen-Winkeln, Karl)*.

8328  **Koenig, Yvan** Les ostraca hiératiques inédits de la Bibliothèque nationale et universitaire de Strasbourg. DFIFAO 33: Le Caire 1997, Institut Français d'Archéologie Orientale du Caire. (8) 23 pp. 135 pl. 2-7247-0210-7.

8329  *Meeks, Dimitri* Les emprunts égyptiens aux langues sémitiques durant le Nouvel Empire et la troisième période intermédiaire: les aléas du comparatisme. BiOr 54 (1997) 32-61.

8330  *Morenz, Ludwig D.* Ein hathorisches Kultlied und ein königlicher Archetyp des Alten Reiches-Sinuhe B 270f. und eine Stele der späten XI. Dynastie (Louvre C 15). WO 28 (1997) 7-17;

8331  Zu zwei Beispielen von Soldaten- und Räubersprache in Altägypten. BN 88 (1997) 39-44.

8332  **Murnane, William J.** Texts from the Amarna period in Egypt. SBLWAW 5: Atlanta 1996, Scholars xviii; 289 pp. $50/$35. 1-55-540-965-2/6-0. <sup>R</sup>CBQ 59 (1997) 132-133 *(Morschauser, Scott N.)*.

8333  <sup>T</sup>**Parkinson, Richard B.** The tale of Sinuhe and other Egyptian poems 1940-1640 BC. Oxf 1997, Clarendon ix; 317 pp. 0-19-814963-8 [ClR 48,508—Montserrat, Dominic].

8334  *Quack, Joachim Friedrich* Die Klage über die Zerstörung Ägyptens: Versuch einer Neudeutung der "Admonitions" im Vergleich zu den altorientalischen Städteklagen. AOAT 247: 1997, ⇒75. <sup>F</sup>ROELLIG W., 345-354.

8335  *Rendsburg, Gary A.* Semitic words in Egyptian texts. JAOS 116 (1996) 508-511.

8336  **Shirun-Grumach, Irene** Offenbarung, Orakel und Königsnovelle. 1993, ⇒9,11990. <sup>R</sup>CEg 72 (1997) 273-276 *(Mathieu, Bernard)*.

8337  **Wilson, Penelope** A Ptolemaic lexikon: a lexicographical study of the texts in the temple of Edfu. OLA 78: Lv 1997, Peeters xliii; 1300 pp. Bibl. 90-6831-933-7.

8338  **Zauzich, Karl-Theodor** Papyri von der Insel Elephantine. 1993, ⇒11/2,6198. <sup>R</sup>Enchoria 24 (1997/8) 194-205 *(Smith, Mark)*.

### J4.0 Anatolica

8339  <sup>E</sup>**Gomi, Tohru; Yildiz, Fatma** Die Umma-Texte aus den archäologischen Museen zu Istanbul (Nr. 2301-3000): Istanbul Arkeoloji

Müzelerinde Bulunan Umma Metinleri (Nr. 2301-3000). Bethesda, MD 1997, CDL 338 pp. 1-883053-33-1.

8340 *Haas, Volkert; Wegner, Ilse* Literarische und grammatikalische Betrachtungen zu einer hurritischen Dichtung. OLZ 92 (1997) 437-455.

8341 *Polvani, Anna Maria* La cometa e gli annali di Mursili II. SEL 14 (1997) 17-28.

8342 **Puhvel, Jaan** Hittite etymological dictionary, 3: words beginning with H. 1991, ⇒9,10057. RBiOr 54 (1997) 727-734 *(Van den Hout, Theo)*.

8343 **Salvini, Mirjo** The Ḫabiru Prism of King Tunip-Teššup of Tikunani. Documenta Asiana 3: R 1996, Istituti Editoriali e Poligrafici Internazionali 128 pp. ill. L120.000/L80.000. 88-8147-094-2. ROLZ 92 (1997) 689-692 *(Freydank, Helmut)*; AulOr 14 (1996) 292-295 *(Márques Rowe, I.)*; WO 28 (1997) 197-199 *(Röllig, Wolfgang)*.

## J4.8 Armena

8344 *Terian, Abraham* Surpassing the biblical worthies: an early motif in Armenian religious literature. Saint Nersess theological review 1 (1996) 117-144;

8345 Biblical interpretation in the epic poetry of GRIGOR Magistros. Saint Nersess theological review 2/1 (1997) 77-93.

8346 *Thomson, Robert W.* Sebeos and the bible. Saint Nersess theological review 2/1 (1997) 65-76.

## J5.1 Graeca *grammatica*

8347 EAdrados, Francisco R. Diccionario griego-español, 5: δαίνυμι - διώνυχος. M 1997, Consejo Superior de Investigaciones Científicas xlv; 865-1135 pp. Ptas9.615 [CÉg. 73,377—Nachtergael, G.].

8348 EBanfi, Emanuele Atti del secondo incontro internazionale di linguistica greca. Labirinti 27: Trento 1997, Dipartimento di scienze filologiche e storiche 570 pp. 88-86135-62-9.

8349 **Blass, Friedrich Wilhelm; Debrunner, Albert** Grammatica del greco del Nuovo Testamento. ERehkopf, Friedrich. Introduzione allo studio della Bibbia, Supplementi 2: Brescia 1997, Paideia 709 pp. Nuova edizione. 88-394-0541-0.

8350 EBrixhe, Claude La concurrence. La koiné grecque antique. Études anciennes: Nancy 1996, Association pour la diffusion de la recherche sur l'antiquité 212 pp. FF180. 2-9509726-2-4 [ClR 49,460ss—Horrocks, Geoffrey].

8351 **Buzzetti, Carlo** Nuovi studenti del Nuovo Testamento greco?: proposte e strumenti per un 'corso-base'. 1995, ⇒12,7894. RProtest. 52 (1997) 192-194 & Seminarium 37 (1997) 83-88 *(Provera, Laura)*; Lat. 63 (1997) 320-321 *(Cardellini, Innocenzo)*.

8352 **Chadwick, John** Lexicographica graeca: contributions to Greek lexicography. Oxf 1996, Clarendon vi; 343 pp. $85 [AJP 120,636—Crane, Gregory R.].

8353  **Cooper, Guy L.; Krüger, Karl Wilhelm** Attic Greek prose syntax. After K.W. Krüger. Ann Arbor, MI 1997, University of Michigan Press 2 vols; 1875 pp. £95. 0-472-10843-3/4-1.

8354  **Dover, Kenneth** The evolution of Greek prose style. Oxf 1997, OUP xxii; 198 pp. Bibl. 0-19-814028-2.

8355  **Easley, Kendell H.** User-friendly Greek: a common sense approach to the Greek New Testament. 1994, ⇒11/2,6285. ᴿAUSS 35 (1997) 259-261 *(Jolliffe, Ronald L.)*.

8356  **Fink, Gerhard** Die griechische Sprache: eine Einführung und eine kurze Grammatik des Griechischen. Da:Wiss ³1997, 384 pp.

8357  *Goodacre, Mark S.* "Wenham": an appreciation of the elements of New Testament Greek. EvQ 69/1 (1997) 3-6.

8358  **Haubeck, Wilfrid; Siebenthal, Heinrich von** Neuer sprachlicher Schlüssel zum griechischen Neuen Testament I: Matthäus bis Apostelgeschichte. TVG-Lehrbücher: Giessen 1997, Brunnen xxxvi; 896 pp. 3-7655-9391-5 [NThAR 1998,100].

8359  *Hirunuma, Toshio* NT diction (120) οὐκ ἔνι non est. Studia Textus Novi Testamenti 333 (1997) 2762-2768.

8360  **Horrocks, Geoffrey C.** Greek: a history of the language and its speakers. Longman Linguistics Library: L 1997, Longman xxi; 393 pp. Bibl. 0-582-03191-5.

8361  *Horsley, G.H.R.; Lee, John A.L.* A lexicon of the New Testament with documentary parallels: some interim entries, 1. FgNT 10 (1997) 55-84.

8362  **Kassühlke, Rudolf** Kleines Wörterbuch zum Neuen Testament: griechisch-deutsch. Stu 1997, Dt. Bibelges. 211 pp. 3-438-05127-3.

8363  **McKay, Kenneth L.** A new syntax of the verb in New Testament Greek: an aspectual approach. 1994, ⇒11/2,6297; 12,7907. ᴿEvQ 69 (1997) 67-68 *(Morrice, W.G.)*.

8364  **Melbourne, Bertram L.** Alpha through omega: a user friendly guide to New Testament Greek. Lanham 1997, University Press of America xiv; 168 pp. 0-7618-0457-9.

8365  **Moulton, James H.; Milligan, George** Vocabulary of the Greek New Testament. Peabody 1997 <1930>, Hendrickson xxxi; 736 pp. $40 [BiTod 36,265—Senior, Donald].

8366  **Muraoka, Takamitsu** A Greek-English lexicon of the Septuagint: Twelve Prophets. 1993, ⇒9,10120... 11/2,6307. ᴿNT 39 (1997) 101-102 *(Elliott, J.K.)*.

8367  *Mussies, Gerard* Double vocatives. NT.S 89: 1997, ⇒7. ᶠBAARDA T., 175-189.

8368  ᴱ**Nesselrath, Heinz-Günther** Einleitung in die griechische Philologie. Collab. *Ameling, Walter.* Einleitung in die Altertumswissenschaft: Stu 1997, Teubner xvi; 773 pp. 3-519-07435-4.

8369  *New, David S.* The injunctive future and existential injunctions in the New Testament. NT text. BiSe 44: 1997 <1991>, ⇒748. ᴱPorter, S.E., 130-144.

8370  **Ortiz Valdivieso, Pedro** Concordancia manual y diccionario griego-español del Nuevo Testamento. M 1997, Sociedad Bíblica 411 pp. 84-80830-50-6 [NThAR 1999,182].

8371  *Porter, Stanley E.* The Greek language of the New Testament. Handbook. NTTS 25: 1997, ⇒971. ᴱPorter, S.E., 99-130.

8372 *Rodríguez Somolinos, J.; Berenguer Sánchez, J.A.* Lexicographie grecque et papyrologie: le *Diccionario Griego-Español*. 21. Papyrologenkongress, 2. 1997, ⇒367. ᴱKramer, B., 858-866.

8373 ᶠRuɪᴊɢʜ C.J., New approaches to Greek particles: proceedings of the Colloquium held in Amsterdam, January 4-6, 1996 to honour... ᴱ*Rijksbaron, Albert*. Amsterdam Studies in Classical Philology 7: Amst 1997, Gieben v; (2) 285 pp. 90-5063-097-9.

8374 **Sollamo, Raija** Repetition of the possessive pronouns in the Septuagint. 1995, ⇒11/2,2600; 12,1082. ᴿHebSt 38 (1997) 185-188 *(Hiebert, Robert J.V.)*.

8375 **Spicq, Ceslas** Note di lessicografia neotestamentaria, 2. ᴱ*Viero, Franco Luigi*. Supplementi al Grande Lessico del Nuovo Testamento 4: 1994, ⇒10,9319; 12,7918. ᴿSal. 59/1 (1997) 161-62.

8376 **Summers, Ray; Sawyer, Thomas** Essentials of New Testament Greek. 1995, ⇒11/2,6327. ᴿRevBib 59 (1997) 243-244 *(Ricciardi, Alberto)*.

8377 **Swetnam, James** Il greco del NT 1: morfologia. 1995, ⇒11/2, 6329; 12,7921. ᴿAng. 74 (1997) 604-605 *(De Santis, Luca)*.

8378 **Waanders, Frederik M.J.** Studies in local case relations in Mycenaean Greek. Amst 1997, Gieben vii; 134 pp. Bibl. 90-5063-107-X.

8379 **Wallace, Daniel B.** Greek grammar beyond the basics: an exegetical syntax of the New Testament. GR 1996, Zondervan xxxii; 797 pp. ᴿBS 154/1 (1997) 118-120 *(Coover-Cox, Dorian)*.

8380 **West, M.L.** The east face of Helicon: west Asiatic elements in Greek poetry and myth. Oxf 1997, Clarendon xx; 662 pp. [ZAR 5,357—Kaiser, Otto].

8381 **Wong, Simon S.M.** A classification of semantic case-relations in the Pauline epistles. Studies in Biblical Greek 9: NY 1997, Lang xviii; 316 pp. Bibl. 0-8204-3680-1.

8382 **Woodard, Roger D.** Greek writing from Knossos to Homer: a linguistic interpretation of the origin of the Greek alphabet and the continuity of ancient Greek literacy. NY 1997, OUP xiv; 287 pp. Bibl. 0-19-510520-6.

8383 **Woods, Michael** Conditionals. ᴱ*Wiggins, David;* comment. *Edgington, Dorothy*. Oxf 1997, Clarendon vii; (2) 152 pp. Bibl. 0-19-875126-5.

8384 **Young, Richard A.** Intermediate NT Greek. 1994, ⇒10,9331. ᴿAUSS 35 (1997) 309-310 *(Jolliffe, Ronald L.)*.

8385 **Zerwick, Maximilian** El griego del Nuevo Testamento. Instrumentos para el estudio de la Biblia: Estella 1997, Verbo Divino 229 pp. 84-8169-168-2. ᴿCDios 210 (1997) 641-643 *(Gutiérrez, J.)*.

## J5.2 **Voces** *ordine alphabetico consonantium* **graecarum**

8386 'αγάπη *Boers, Hendrikus* 'Αγάπη and χάρις in Paul's thought. CBQ 59 (1997) 693-713;

8387 *Kottackal, Joseph* The merit of christian love. BiBh 23 (1997) 269-280.

8388 ἁγιωσύνη *Raurell, Frederic* Il binomio 'santità' (ἁγιωσύνη) e 'gloria' (δόχα) di Dio nei LXX. Sum. 244. RCatT 22 (1997) 231-244.

8389  αἰών *Bracchi, Remo* 'Saeculum': analisi semantica di un termine di uso biblico e liturgico. Summarium 3; sum., som. 27. EL 111/1 (1997) 3-27.

8390  ῞αλας *Sebastian, V.* Salt—disciples of Jesus. BiBh 23 (1997) 121-126.

8391  'αποσυνάγωγοσ *Boshoff, Piet B.* Die 'aposunagogos' se invloed op die geskrifte van die Nuwe Testament volgens Walter SCHMITHALS. HTS 53 (1997) 599-608 [ZID 24,127].

8392  ἀρραβών *Hirunuma, Toshio* NT diction (119) ἀρραβών pledge. Studia Textus Novi Testamenti 332 (1997) 2757-2760.

8393  Βοανηργές *Buth, Randall* Mark 3.17 BONEREGEM and popular etymology. New Testament text. BiSe 44: 1997 <1981>, ⇒748. ᴱPorter, S.E., 263-266.

8394  διαθήκη *Giversen, Søren* The covenant—theirs or ours? [Introduction]. NT and Hellenistic Judaism. 1997, ⇒318. ᴱBorgen, P., 14-18.

δόχα ⇒8388.

8395  δοῦλος; *Wright, Benjamin G.* δοῦλος and παῖς as translations of ʿbd: lexical equivalences and conceptual transformations. IX Congress IOSCS. SCSt 45: 1997, ⇒340. ᴱTaylor, B.A., 263-277.

8396  εἰκών *Steenburg, Dave* The case against the synonymity of *Morphē* and *Eikōn*. New Testament text. BiSe 44: 1997 <1988>, ⇒748. ᴱPorter, S.E., 191-200.

8397  ἐπιούσιος *Hemer, Colin* ἐπιούσιος. New Testament text. BiSe 44: 1997 <1984>, ⇒748. ᴱPorter, S.E., 222-234 [Acts 16,11].

8398  ἐπίτροπος *Cotton, Hannah M.* The guardian (ἐπίτροπος) of a woman in the documents from the Judaean Desert. ZPE 113 (1997) 267-273.

8399  καιρός *Eynikel, Erik; Hauspie, Katrin* The use of καιρος and χρονος in the Septuagint. EThL 73 (1997) 369-385;

8400  *Dôle, R.* Le concept de Kairos dans la théologie de Paul TILLICH et dans le Nouveau Testament grec. RHPhR 77 (1997) 302-307.

8401  καρδιογνώστης *Bauer, Johannes B.* Καρδιογνώστης, ein unbeachteter Aspekt (Apg 1,24; 15,8). Studien zu Bibeltext. 1997 <1988>, ⇒111. 242-248.

8402  λαικός *Bergamelli, Ferdinando* "Laico" nella prima lettera di Clemente Romano (1 Clem 40,5): osservazioni e rilievi in margine alla storia del termine *laikós*. BSRel 125: 1997, ⇒45. ᶠJAVIERRE ORTAS A., 127-141.

μορφή ⇒8396.

8403  νόμος **Winger, Michael** By what law?: the meaning of *nomos* in the letters of Paul. SBL.DS 128: 1992, ⇒9,6032; 10,5817. ᴿABR 45 (1997) 89 *(Kruse, Colin G.)*;

8404  *Bammel, Ernst* Νόμος Χριστοῦ. Judaica et Paulina. WUNT 91: 1997 <1964>, ⇒109. 320-326 [1 Cor 9,20; Gal 6,2].

8405  οἰκία *Brandt, Pierre-Yves; Lukinovich, Alessandra* Οἶκος et οἰκία chez Marc comparé à Matthieu et Luc. Sum. 533. Bib. 78 (1997) 525-533.

οἶκος ⇒8405.

8406  παιδαγωγός *Hanson, A.T.* The origin of Paul's use of παιδαγωγός for the law. New Testament text. BiSe 44: 1997 <1988>, ⇒748. ᴱPorter, S.E., 201-206.

παῖς ⇒8395.

8407 παράκλητος Grayston, Kenneth The meaning of Parakletos. New Testament text. BiSe 44: 1997 <1981>, ⇒748. EPorter, S.E., 207-221.

8408 πειρασμός Ekenberg, Anders "Utsätt oss inte för prövning". SEÅ 62 (1997) 111-122.

8409 πίστις Campbell, Douglas A. False presuppositions in the πίστις Χριστοῦ debate: a response to Brian DODD. JBL 116 (1997) 713-719 [Rom 1,17];

8410 Achtemeier, Paul J. Apropos the faith of/in Christ: a response to HAYS and DUNN;

8411 Dunn, James D.G. Once more πίστις Χριστοῦ;

8412 Hays, Richard B. πίστις and Pauline christology: what is at stake? Pauline theology 4. 1997, ⇒6157. EJohnson, E.E., 82-92/61-81/35-60;

8413 Lindsay, Dennis R. The roots and development of the πίστ-word group as faith terminology. New Testament text. BiSe 44: 1997 <1993>, ⇒748. EPorter, S.E., 176-190.

8414 πώρωσις Seewann, Maria-Irma Semantische Untersuchung zu πώρωσις, veranlasst durch Röm 11,25. FgNT 10 (1997) 139-156.

8415 συνείδησις Borghi, Ernesto La notion de conscience dans le Nouveau Testament: une proposition de lecture. FgNT 10 (1997) 85-98.

8416 φιλέω Graham Brock, Ann The significance of φιλέω and φίλος of Jesus' sayings in the early christian communities. HThR 90 (1997) 393-409.
φίλος ⇒8416.
χάρις ⇒8386.
χρόνος ⇒8399.

## J5.4 Papyri et incriptiones graecae—Greek epigraphy

8417 Arzt, Peter Ägyptische Papyri und das Neue Testament: zur Frage der Vergleichbarkeit von Texten. PzB 6 (1997) 21-29.
EBakker, Egbert J. Grammar as interpretation ⇒266.

8418 Blomkvist, Vemund An early Christian inscription?. ZNW 88 (1997) 143-144.

8419 Boffo, Laura Iscrizioni greche e latine per lo studio della bibbia. 1994, ⇒10,9379. RAt. 85 (1997) 647-651 (Pucci Ben Zeev, M.).

8420 Bohak, Gideon Good Jews, bad Jews, and non-Jews in Greek papyri and inscriptions;

8421 Capasso, Mario Il corpus dei papiri storici greci e latini;

8422 Cotton, Hannah M. Deeds of gift and the law of succession in the documents from the Judaean Desert. 21. Papyrologenkongress, 1. 1997, ⇒367. EKramer, B., 105-112/155-157/179-186.

8423 Daris, Sergio Papiri documentari greci del fondo Palau-Ribes (Palau Rib.). 1995, ⇒11/2,6442. RRivBib 45 (1997) 227-228 (Passioni Dell'Acqua, Anna); EstB 55 (1997) 562-565 (Urbán, A.).

8424 De Martino, Manuel Dottrina e poesia in una iscrizione greca metrica dell'Egitto paleocristiano. RivAC 73 (1997) 413-423.

8425 De Meyer, Luc Vers l'invention de la rhétorique: une perspective ethno-logique sur la communication en Grèce ancienne. Préf. Ladrière, Jean: BCILL 91: Lv 1997, Peeters 314 pp. 90-6831-942-6.

8426 ᴱEdwards, Mark J.; Swain, Simon Portraits: biographical representation in the Greek and Latin literature of the Roman Empire. Oxf 1997, Clarendon xi; 267 pp. Bibl. £40. 0-19-814937-9.

8427 *Epp, Eldon Jay* The New Testament papyri at Oxyrhynchus in their social and intellectual context. NT.S 89: 1997, ⇒7. ᶠBAARDA T., 47-68.

8428 *Ernst, Michael* "... verkaufte alles, was er besass, und kaufte die Perle" (Mt 13,46): der ἔμπορος im Neuen Testament und in dokumentarischen Papyri. PzB 6 (1997) 31-46.

8429 *Feissel, Denis* The bible in Greek inscriptions. The bible in Greek christian antiquity. 1997 <c.1984>, ⇒177. ᴱᵀBlowers, P.M., 289-298.

8430 *Fitzgerald, John T.* The catalogue in ancient Greek literature. Rhetorical analysis. JSNT.S 146: 1997, ⇒336. ᴱPorter, S.E., 275-293.

8431 ᴱGamillscheg, Ernst Repertorium der griechischen Kopisten 800-1600: Handschriften aus Bibliotheken Roms mit dem Vatikan. Collab. *Harlfinger, Dieter; Eleuteri, Paolo*: Veröffentlichungen der Kommission für Byzantinistik 3A-C: W 1997, Verl. der Österr. Akademie der Wissenschaften 3 vols; 344 pl. Bibl. 3-7001-2632-8.

8432 ᴱHandley, E.W., (al.), The Oxyrhynchus papyri: 64. PEES.GR 84: L 1997, Egypt Exploration Soc. for the Brit. Acad. xii; 209 pp. 19 pl. 0-85698-129-X.

8433 *Harrauer, Hermann* Wie finden Papyri den Weg nach Wien—und haben sie uns etwas zu sagen?. PzB 6 (1997) 15-19.

8434 *Horbury, William* A proselyte's 'ἐις θεός' inscription near Caesarea. PEQ 129 (1997) 133-137.

8435 Hughes, George Robert; Jasnow, Richard Oriental Institute Hawara papyri: Demotic and Greek texts from an Egyptian family archive in the Fayum (fourth to third century B.C.). Collab. *Keenan, James G.*: UCOIP 113: Ch 1997, The Oriental Institute of the University of Chicago xxviii; 101 pp. Bibl. 1-885923-02-3.

8436 Irigoin, Jean Tradition et critique des textes grecs. Histoire: P 1997, Les Belles Lettres viii; 304 pp. FF155. 2-251-44116-6.

8437 *Kaimio, Maarit; Koenen, Ludwig* Reports on decipherment of Petra papyri. ADAJ 41 (1997) 459-462.

8438 ᴱKambitsis, Sophie Papyrus Graux III: P. Graux 30. HEMGR 23: Genève 1997, Droz (8) 105 pp. 2-600-00213-8.

8439 Kayser, François Reueil des inscriptions grecques et latines (non funéraires) d'Alexandrie impériale 1er - 3e s. apr. J.-C. 1994, ⇒10,9400. ᴿBiOr 54 (1997) 691-695 *(Lajtar, Adam)*.

8440 *Lajtar, Adam* Greek funerary inscriptions from Old Dongola: general note. OrChr 81 (1997) 107-126.

8441 ᴱLaks, André; Most, Glenn W. Studies on the Derveni Papyrus. Oxf 1997, Clarendon viii; 204 pp. Bibl. 0-19-815032-6.

8442 LiDonnici, Lynn R. The Epidaurian miracle inscriptions: text, translation and commentary. SBL.TT 36: 1995, ⇒11/2,6466. ᴿCBQ 59 (1997) 164-165 *(Harrill, J. Albert)*.

8443 ᴱLilla, Salvatore Codices Vaticani Graeci, codices 2644-2663. Bibliothecae Apostolicae Vaticanae Codices Manvscripti recensiti: Città del Vaticano 1996, Bibliotheca Vaticana 189 pp.

8444 ᴱLlewelyn, S.R. A review of Greek inscriptions and papyri published in 1982-83. New documents illustrating early christianity, 7. 1994, ⇒10,9401. ᴿTJT 13/1 (1997) 110-111 *(Kloppenborg, John S.)*; JThS 48 (1997) 217-219 *(Winter, Bruce W.)*;

8445 A review... 1984-85. New documents...8. GR 1997, Eerdmans 198 pp. $35. 0-8028-4518-5.

8446 ᴱᵀ**Manning, Joseph Gilbert** The Hauswaldt papyri: a third century B.C. family dossier from Edfu. Demotische Studien 12: Sommerhausen 1997, Zauzich ix; 213 pp. Transcription, commentary. 3-924151-05-9.

8447 The Oxyrhynchus papyri, 65. PEES.GR 85: L 1997, Egypt Exploration Soc. for the Brit. Acad. 0-85698-130-3 [⇒8432]

8448 *Pokorný, Petr* Griechische Sprichwörter im Neuen Testament. Bibelauslegung. WUNT 100: 1997 <1994>, ⇒970. 147-154.

8449 *Porat, Pinhas* A fragmentary Greek inscription from Tel Jezreel. TelAv 24 (1997) 167-168.

8450 *Porter, Stanley E.* The Greek papyri of the Judaean desert and the world of the Roman east. The scrolls and the scriptures. JSPE.S 26: 1997, ⇒299. ᴱPorter, S.E., 293-316.

8451 *Rochette, Bruno* Bilinguisme, traductions et histoire des textes dans l'Orient grec (Iᵉʳ-IVᵉ siècle après J.-C.). RHT 27 (1997) 1-28.

8452 **Rupprecht, Hans-Albert** Sammelbuch griechischer Urkunden aus Ägypten 20. [Nr. 14069-15202]. Collab. *Hengstl, Joachim:* Wsb 1997, Harrassowitz xv; 724 pp. DM398 [CÉg 73,180s—Nachtergael, G.].

8453 **Sartre, Maurice** Inscriptions de la Jordanie: Pétra et la Nabatène méridionale. IGLS 21: 1993, ⇒9,10237. ᴿGn. 69 (1997) 239-243 *(Negev, Avraham)*.

8454 *Sartre, Maurice* Bornes du territoire ou marques de propriété?. Syr. 74/1 (1997) 139-140.

8455 **Small, Jocelyn Penny** Wax tablets of the mind: cognitive studies of memory and literacy in classical antiquity. L 1997, Routledge xviii; 377 pp. Bibl. 0-415-14983-5.

8456 *Thiede, Carsten Peter; Masuch, Georg* Neue mikroskopische Verfahren zum Lesen und zur Schadensbestimmung von Papyrushandschriften. 21. Papyrologenkongress, 2. 1997, ⇒367. ᴱKramer, B., 1102-1112.

8457 *Uthemann, Karl-Heinz* Erster Bericht über griechische Editionen, Handschriften und Hilfsmittel. ZAC 1 (1997) 17-41.

8458 *Verhelst, Stéphane* L'Isopséphie "réduite" à ʿAin Fattir et l'Hérodion (église-nord): une hypothèse vérifiée. RB 104 (1997) 223-236.

8459 **Woodhead, Geoffrey** Agora 16: the decrees. Princeton 1997, American School of Classical Studies at Athens xvii; 527 pp. 31 pl. $100. 0-87661-216-8 [AJA 103,710s—Osborne, Michael J.].

8460 ᴱ**Worp, Klaas Anthony; Rijksbaron, Albert** Isocrates: the Kellis Isocrates codex (P. Kell. III Gr. 95). Introd. ch. *Sharpe III, J.L.*: Oxbow Monograph 88: Oxf 1997, Oxbow 292 pp. Bibl. 1-900188-43-0.


### J6.0 Iranica

8461 *Lecoq, Pierre* L'empire perse et le grand roi: les peuples de l'empire dans les inscriptions. MoBi 106 (1997) 29-30.

8462 **Lecoq, Pierre** Les inscriptions de la Perse achéménide. L'aube des peuples: P 1997, Gallimard 327 pp. 2-07-073090-5.

8463   *Lecoq, Pierre* Le rocher de Bisotun. MoBi 106 (1997) 26-28.

### J6.5 Latina

8464   **Berry, Paul** The christian inscription at Pompeii. 1995, ⇒11/2,c056. [R]CBQ 59 (1997) 570-571 *(Osiek, Carolyn)*.
8465   [E]**Berschin, Walter** Miscellanea Bibliothecae Apostolicae Vaticanae V: Palatina-Studien: 13 Arbeiten zu Codices Vaticani Palatini latini und anderen Handschriften aus der alten Heidelberger Sammlung. StT 365: Città del Vaticano 1997, Biblioteca Apostolica Vaticana 380 pp. Bibl. 88-210-0685-9.
8465*  *Bracchi, Remo* 'Saeculum': analisi semantica di un termine di uso biblico e liturgico. EL 111/1 (1997) 3-27.
8466   [E]**Dominik, William J.** Roman eloquence: rhetoric in society and literature. L 1997, Routledge xii; 268 pp. [SCI 17,238—Winterbottom, Michael].
8467   [E]**Harrington, Karl Pomeroy** Medieval Latin. Rev. by *Pucci, Joseph Michael;* introd. *Elliott, Alison Goddard*: Ch [2]1997, University of Chicago Press xxii; 679 pp. 0-226-31712-9.
8468   [E]**Herzog, Reinhart; Schmidt, P.L.** Die Literatur des Umbruchs: von der römischen zur christlichen Literatur. Handbuch der lateinischen Literatur der Antike, 4. Mü 1997, Beck xxxii; 651 pp. DM238. 3-406-39020-X [JRS 89,246s—Powell, J.G.F.].
8469   *Leclercq, H.* Le 'passage' des noms propres latins dans le grec du Nouveau Testament: une comparaison avec des textes contemporains. EtCl 65/4 (1997) 289-308.
8470   [E]**Marucchi, Adriana** I codici latini datati della Biblioteca apostolica vaticana, I: nei fondi archivio S. Pietro, Barberini, Boncompagni, Borghese, Borgia,; Capponi, Chigi, Ferrajoli, Ottoboni, testo/tavole. Collab. *Albinia C. de la Mare*: Città del Vaticano 1997, Biblioteca Apostolica Vaticana 2 vols. 142 pl. 88-210-0632-8.
8471   **Porebski, Stanislaw Andrzej** Paleografia Lacinska: podrecznik dla studentów. Wsz 1997, Wydawnictwo Akademii Teologii Katolikkiej 87 pp. 83-7072-091-9.

### J8 Language, writing and the Bible

8472   **Aichele, George** Sign, text, scripture: semiotics and the bible. Interventions 1: Shf 1997, Academic 163 pp. £10. 1-85075-691-0.
8473   **Bradford, Richard** Stylistics. The new critical idiom: L 1997, Routledge xii; 215 pp. Bibl. 0-415-09769-X.
8474   [E]**Brugnatelli, Vermondo** Sem Cam Iafet. 1994, ⇒11/2,715. [R]JAOS 117 (1997) 374-375 *(Kaye, Alan S.)*.
8475   **Chierchia, Gennaro** Semantica. Le strutture del linguaggio: Bo 1997, Il Mulino 478 pp. fig. 88-15-05790-0.
8476   **Chomsky, Noam** Probleme sprachlichen Wissens. [T]*Schiffmann, M.*: 1996, ⇒12,7986. [R]ThLZ 122 (1997) 326-327 *(Schenk, Wolfgang)*;
8477   Language and problems of knowledge. The Managua Lectures. Current studies in linguistics 16: CM 1997, MIT Press x; 205 pp. 0-262-53070-8.

8478 **Clark, Herbert H.** Using language. C 1997, CUP xi; 432 pp. Bibl. 0-521-56745-9.

8479 **Cooke, Maeve** Language and reason: a study of HABERMAS's Pragmatics. CM 1997, MIT Pr. xv; 207 pp. Bibl. 0-262-53145-3.

8480 [E]**Costermans, Jean; Fayol, Michel** Processing interclausal relationships: studies in the production and comprehension of text. Mahwah 1997, Erlbaum x; 290 pp. 0-8058-1847-2.

8481 **Crystal, David** A dictionary of linguistics and phonetics. The Language Library: Oxf [4]1997, Blackwell xvi; 426 pp. 0-631-20097-5.

8482 *Dard, Pierre* Langues naturelles, informatique et sciences cognitives. SémBib 85 (1997) 35-45.

8483 *Diakonoff, Igor M.* Some reflections on the Afrasian linguistic macrofamily. JNES 55 (1996) 293-294.

8484 **Fabb, Nigel** Linguistics and literature: language in the verbal arts of the world. Blackwell Textbooks in Linguistics 12: L 1997, Blackwell xvi; 297 pp. Bibl. 0-631-19243-3.

8485 *Geninasca, Jacques* Stylistique et sémiosis. SémBib 85 (1997) 3-7.

8486 *Hayajneh, Hani; Tropper, Josef* Die Genese des altsüdarabischen Alphabets. UF 29 (1997) 183-198.

8487 *Jabłoński, Przemysław ; Van der Lans, Jan; Hermans, Chris* Children's interpretation of biblical narratives: a proposal for a research design. ARPs 22 (1997) 28-47.

8488 **Jackson, Howard** Words and their meaning. Learning about language. L 1996, Longman viii; 279 pp. Bibl. 0-582-29154-2.

8489 [E]**Joy, Morny** Paul RICOEUR and narrative: context and contestation. Calgary, Alberta 1997, University of Calgary Press 1; 232 pp. 1-895176-90-5.

8490 [E]**Kaye, Alan S.; Daniels, Peter T.** Phonologies of Asia and Africa (including the Caucasus). WL 1997, Eisenbrauns 2 vols. Technical Advisor *Peter T. Daniels*. 1-57506-019-1.

8491 [E]**Keefe, Rosanna; Smith, Peter** Vagueness: a reader. CM 1997, MIT Press vii (2) 352 pp. Bibl. 0-262-61145-7.

8492 **Lipinski, Edouard** Semitic languages: outline of a comparative grammar. OLA 80: Lv 1997, Peeters 754 pp. Bibl. 90-6831-939-6.

8493 **Palmer, Frank Robert** Semantics. C [2]1997, CUP viii; 221 pp. 0-521-28376-0.

8494 [E]**Porter, Stanley E.** Handbook of classical rhetoric in the Hellenistic period 330 B.C.- A.D. 400. Lei 1997, Brill xv; 901 pp. *f*430. 90-04-09965-4.

8495 **Raurell, Frederic** 'I Déu digué...': la paraula feta història. 1995, ⇒11/2,1129; 12,468. [R]CBQ 59 (1997) 135-136 *(Bernas, Casimir)*.

8496 *Reimer, Marga* "Competing" semantic theories. Noûs 31 (1997) 457-477.

8497 *Ruijgh, C.J.* La date de la création de l'alphabet grec et celle de l'épopée homérique. BiOr 54 (1997) 533-603.

8498 *Sadoulet, Pierre* Jacques GENINASCA: un modèle dynamique de sémiotique littéraire (I-III). SémBib 86-88 (1997) 3-29/3-29/27-55.

8499 *Sanmartín, Joaquín* El contexto lingüístico del Levante Mediterráneo Antiguo (III-II milenios). La Bíblia i el Mediterrani. 1997, ⇒385. [E]Borrell, d'Agustí, 77-85.

8500 *Seelenfreund, Morton H.; Schneider, Stanley* Leah's eyes. JBQ 25/1 (1997) 18-22 [Gen 29,17].

8501 *Spero, Shubert* And the writing was the writing of God. JBQ 25/1 (1997) 3-11.

8502   **Stiver, Dan R.** The philosophy of religious language: sign, symbol and story. Oxf 1997, Blackwell xiii; 258 pp. Bibl. 1-55786-582-5.
8503   **Trask, Robert Lawrence** Historical linguistics. L 1997, Arnold xvii; 430 pp. Bibl. 0-340-60758-0.
8504   **Van Bekkum, Wout Jac.**, *(al.)*, The emergence of semantics in four linguistic traditions: Hebrew, Sanskrit, Greek, Arabic. Amsterdam studies in the theory and history of linguistic science, 3: Studies in the history of the language sciences 82: Amst 1997, Benjamins ix; 322 pp. 90-272-4568-1.
8505   *Van de Mieroop, Marc* Why did they write on clay?. Klio 79 (1997) 7-18.
8506   **Van Heusden, Barend** Why literature?: an inquiry into the nature of literary semiosis. Probleme der Semiotik 18: Tü 1997, Stauffenburg viii; 278 pp. DM68. 3-86057-094-3.
8507   **Yardeni, Ada** The book of Hebrew script. J 1997, Carta 364 pp. 290 ill.; 53 script charts; $60 [BArR 24/5,64—Vaughn, A.G.].

# XV. Postbiblica

## κ1.1  Pseudepigrapha [=catholicis 'Apocrypha'] *VT generalia*

8508   Apocrypha and Pseudepigrapha, Jewish-Hellenistic literature, Dead Sea scrolls [bibliography]. QS 67 (1997) 414-417.
8509   [T]**Azar, Éphrem** Les Odes de Salomon. 1996, ⇒12,8048. [R]RB 104 (1997) 309-310 *(Taylor, Justin)*; EE 72 (1997) 375-376 *(Raczkiclovicz, Mavek)*.
8510   *Bammel, Ernst* Das Buch Nimrod. Judaica et Paulina. WUNT 91: 1997 <1992>, ⇒109. 157-160.
8511   *Charlesworth, James H.* Pseudepigraphen des Alten Testaments. TRE 27. 1997, ⇒419. 639-645.
8512   *Collins, John J.* The kingdom of God in the Apocrypha and Pseudepigrapha. Seers. JSJ.S 54: 1997 <1987>, ⇒119. 99-114.
8513   **Ehrmann, Michael** Klagephänomene in zwischentestamentlicher Literatur. Diss. Berlin 1994, [D]*Welten, P.*: BEAT 41: Fra 1997, Lang 354 pp. 3-631-31015-3.
8514   **Franzmann, Majella** The Odes of Solomon. NTOA 20: 1991, ⇒9,10457... 12,8049. [R]BiOr 54 (1997) 486-490 *(Harrak, Amir)*.
8515   *Hartmann, Lars* 'Teste Sibylla': construction and message in the fourth book of the Sibylline oracles. Text-centered NT studies. WUNT 102: 1997 <1987>, ⇒132. 151-164.
8516   *Infante, Renzo* Michele nella letteratura apocrifa del giudaismo del secondo tempio. VetChr 34 (1997) 211-229.
8517   *Jonge, M. de* The so-called Pseudepigrapha of the Old Testament and early christianity. NT and Hellenistic Judaism. 1997, ⇒318. [E]Borgen, P., 59-71.
8518   *Keefer, Kyle* A postscript to the book: authenticating the Pseudepigrapha. Reading bibles. 1997, ⇒172. [E]Beal, T.K., 232-241.
8519   **Mengozzi, Alessandro** Trattato di Sem e altri testi astrologici. TVOA 7; Letteratura della Siria cristiana 1: Brescia 1997, Paideia 106 pp. Bibl. L20.000. 88-394-0552-6.

8520 *Minette de Tillesse, Caetano* Pseudepígrafes. RBB 14/1-3 (1997) 214-237.
8521 *Norelli, Enrico* D'où viennent les Apocryphes?: panorama d'une littérature méconnue. BCPE 49/2-3 (1997) 3-16.
8522 *Petit, Madeleine* Génération et transformation de thèmes appartenant aux 'Vitae prophetarum'. Sum. rés. 273. Apocrypha 8 (1997) 273-286.
8523 *Pokorný, Petr* Pseudepigraphie: Altes und Neues Testament. TRE 27. 1997, ⇒419. 645-655.
8524 *Sacchi, Paolo* L'escatologia negli scritti giudaici apocrifi fra IV sec. a.C. e I sec. d.C. DSBP 16 (1997) 62-83.
8525 **Satran, David** Biblical prophets in Byzantine Palestine: reassessing the Lives of the Prophets. SVTP 11: 1995, ⇒11/2,6745. <sup>R</sup>JSJ 28/1 (1997) 119-123 *(Flusser, David)*; RB 104 (1997) 598-601 *(Verhelst, Stéphane)*.
8526 <sup>TE</sup>**Schwemer, Anna Maria** Studien zu den frühjüdischen Prophetenlegenden: *Vitae prophetarum*. TSAJ 49-50: 1995-1996, ⇒12,8036. <sup>R</sup>FrRu 4/4 (1997) 297-298 *(Rapp, Hans A.)*;
8527 Die Viten der kleinen Propheten und der Propheten aus den Geschichtsbüchern. Studien zu den frühjüdischen Prophetenlegenden: *Vitae prophetarum*, 2. TSAJ 50: 1996, ⇒12,8036. <sup>R</sup>ThG 40/3 (1997) 229-231 *(Giesen, Heinz)*; RTL 28/2 (1997) 244-246 *(Bogaert, Pierre-Maurice)*; RHPhR 77/2 (1997) 240-241 *(Grappe, Ch.)*;
8528 Vitae prophetarum: jüdische Schriften aus hellenistisch-römischer Zeit 1/7. Gü 1997, Kaiser 539-658 pp. 3-579-03918-0.
8529 *Scott, James M.* Geographic aspects of Noachic materials in the scrolls at Qumran. The scrolls and the scriptures. JSPE.S 26: 1997, ⇒299. <sup>E</sup>Porter, S.E., 368-381.
8530 *Stemberger, Günter* Pseudepigraphie: Judentum. TRE 27, ⇒419. 1997, 656-659.
8531 <sup>E</sup>**Troiani, Lucio** Letteratura giudaica di lingua greca. Apocrifi dell'Antico Testamento 5. Biblica, testi e studi 5: Brescia 1997, Paideia 254 pp. L50.000. 88-394-0547-X [RTL 29,130].
8532 *Walter, Nikolaus* Kann man als Jude auch Grieche sein?: Erwägungen zur jüdisch-hellenistischen Pseudepigraphie. Praeparatio evangelica. WUNT 98: 1997 <1994>, ⇒167. 370-382.

## κ1.2 Henoch

8533 **Adam, Schlomit** Zur Neubewertung der Apokalyptik nach der Veröffentlichung der Henochfragmente aus Qumran. n.p. <sup>2</sup>1997 Adam, Schlomit 52 pp.
8534 **Böttrich, Christfried** "Die Vögel des Himmels haben ihn begraben": Überlieferungen zu Abels Bestattung. SIJD 3: 1995, ⇒11/2,6752. <sup>R</sup>JSJ 28/1 (1997) 92-94 *(Van der Woude, A.S.)*.
8535 *Böttrich, Christfried* Astrologie in der Henochtradition. ZAW 109 (1997) 222-245.
8536 **Chialà, Sabino** Libro delle parabole di Enoc: testo e commento. StBi 117: Brescia 1997, Paideia 374 pp. L50.000. 88-394-0555-0. <sup>R</sup>Henoch 19 (1997) 380-381 *(Ubigli, Liliana Rosso)*.

8537  **Davidson, M.J.** Angels at Qumran: a comparative study of 1 Enoch 1-36, 72-108 and sectarian writings from Qumran. JSPE.S 11: 1992, ᴿJSPE 16 (1997) 123-124 *(Brooke, George J.)*.

8538  *Ego, Beate* Trauer und Erlösung: zum Motiv der Hand Gottes in 3Hen §§ 68-70. La main de Dieu. WUNT 94: 1997, ⇒328. ᴱKieffer, R., 171-188.

8539  *Muro, Ernest A.* The Greek fragments of Enoch from Qumran cave 7 (7Q4, 7Q8 & 7Q12 = 7QEn gr = Enoch 103:3-4, 7-8). RdQ 18 (1997) 307-312.

8540  *Pomykala, Kenneth E.* A scripture profile of the book of the Watchers. Bibl.Interp. 28: 1997, ⇒77. ᶠSᴀɴᴅᴇʀs J., 263-284.

8541  *Puech, Émile* Sept fragments grecs de la lettre d'Hénoch (1 Hén 100, 103 et 105) dans la grotte 7 de Qumrân (=7QHéngr). RdQ 18 (1997) 313-323.

8542  **VanderKam, James C.** Enoch: a man for all generations. 1996, ⇒12,8045. ᴿHebSt 38 (1997) 182-184 *(Hollander, Harm W.)*; CritRR 10 (1997) 153-154 *(Collins, John J.)*.

## κ1.3 Testamenta

8543  ᵀᴱColafemmina, C. Il Testamento di Abramo. CTePa 118: R 1995, Città Nuova 112 pp. L12.000. 88-311-3118-4. ᴿHum(B) 52 (1997) 1002-1004 *(Pieri, Silvia)*.

8544  *Konradt, Matthias* Menschen- und Bruderliebe?: Beobachtungen zum Liebesgebot in den Testamenten der Zwölf Patriarchen. ZNW 88 (1997) 296-310.

8545  **Kugler, Robert A.** From patriarch to priest: the Levi-Priestly tradition from Aramaic Levi to Testament of Levi. 1996, ⇒12,8047. ᴿJSJ 28/1 (1997) 115-117 *(Jonge, M. de)*.

8546  *O'Neill, J.C.* The Lamb of God in the *Testaments of the Twelve Patriarchs*. NT Backgrounds. 1997 <1979>, ⇒3975. ᴱEvans, C.A., 46-66.

8547  *Tromp, Johannes* Two references to a Levi document in an epistle of Ammonas. NT 39 (1997) 235-247.

## κ1.6 Jubilaea, Adam, Asenet, Ezekiel

8548  *Albani, Matthias* Zur Rekonstruktion eines verdrängten Konzepts: der 364-Tage Kalender in der gegenwärtigen Forschung. Studies in... Jubilees. TSAJ 65: 1997, ⇒8549. ᴱAlbani, M., 79-125.

8549  ᴱ**Albani, Matthias; Frey, Jörg; Lange, Armin** Studies in the book of Jubilees. TSAJ 65: Tü 1997, Mohr viii; 344 pp. DM228. 3-16-146793-0.

8550  *Böttrich, Christfried* Gottesprädikationen im Jubiläenbuch;

8551  *Brooke, George A.* Exegetical strategies in Jubilees 1-2: new light from 4QJubilees[a];

8552  *Doering, Lutz* The concept of the Sabbath in the book of Jubilees;

8553  *Ego, Beate* Heilige Zeit—heiliger Raum—heiliger Mensch: Beobachtungen zur Struktur der Gesetzesbegründung in der Schöpfungs- und Paradiesgeschichte des Jubiläenbuches;

8554  *Eiss, Werner* Das Wochenfest im Jübiläenbuch und im antiken Judentum;

8555 *Frey, Jörg* Zum Weltbild im Jubiläenbuch;
8556 *Gleßmer, Uwe* Explizite Aussagen über kalendarische Konflikte im Jubiläenbuch: Jub 6,22-32.33-38. Studies in... Jubilees. TSAJ 65: 1997, ⇒8549. EAlbani, M., 221-241/39-57/179-205/207-219/165-178/261-292/127-164.
8557 *Halpern-Amaru, Betsy* Exile and return in Jubilees. Exile. JSJ.S 56: 1997, ⇒227. EScott, J.M., 127-144.
8558 *Lange, Armin* Divinatorische Träume und Apokalyptik im Jubiläenbuch;
8559 *Martínez, Florentino García* The heavenly tablets in the book of Jubilees;
8560 *Scott, James M.* The division of the earth in Jubilees 8:11-9:15 and early Christian chronography;
8561 *Van Ruiten, Jacques T.A.G.M.* The interpretation of Genesis 6:1-12 in Jubilees 5:1-19;
8562 *VanderKam, James C.* The origins and purposes of the book of Jubilees. Studies in... Jubilees. TSAJ 65: 1997, ⇒8549. EAlbani, M., 25-38/243-260/295-323/59-75/3-24.
8563 *Wacholder, Ben Zion* Jubilees as the super canon: torah-admonition versus torah-commandment. StTDJ 23: 1997, ⇒8. FBAUMGARTEN J., 195-211.
8564 *Werman, Cana* Jubilees 30: building a paradigm for the ban on intermarriage. HThR 90 (1997) 1-22.

8565 *Glickler Chazon, Esther* The creation and fall of Adam in the Dead Sea scrolls. The book of Genesis. 1997, ⇒196. EFrishman, J., 13-24 [Gen 2-3; Sir 17,1-10].
8566 **Jonge, Marinus de; Tromp, Johannes** *The Life of Adam and Eve* and related literature. Guides to Apocrypha & Pseudepigrapha: Shf 1997, Academic 104 pp. 1-85075-764-X.
8567 *Stone, Michael E.* Adam, Eve and the incarnation. Saint Nersess theological review 2/2 (1997) 167-179.
8568 *Tromp, Johannes* Literary and exegetical issues in the story of Adam's death and burial (GLAE 31-42). The book of Genesis. 1997, ⇒196. EFrishman, J., 25-41.

8569 **Chesnutt, Randall D.** From death to life: conversion in Joseph and Aseneth. JSPE.S 16: Shf 1995, Academic 308 pp. £37.50. 1-85075-516-7. RBibl.Interp. 5 (1997) 281-283 *(Longenecker, B.W.)*.
8570 **Humphrey, Edith McEwan** The ladies and the cities: transformation and apocalyptic identity in Joseph and Aseneth... JSPE.S 17: 1995, ⇒11/2,6798. RJThS 48 (1997) 219-221 *(Lieu, Judith M.)*; CBQ 59 (1997) 158-159 *(Osiek, Carolyn)*; TJT 13 (1997) 279-281 *(Harland, Philip A.)*.

8571 *Hilhorst, A.* Das Lebensende des Ezechiel. AnBoll 115 (1997) 249-251.
8572 **Mueller, James R.** The five fragments of the *Apocryphon of Ezekiel*: a critical study. JSPE.S 5: 1994, ⇒10,9608; 12,8063. RJBL 115 (1996) (1997) 532-534 *(Cook, Stephen L.)*.

## κ1.7 Apocalypses, ascensiones

8573 *Bauckham, Richard* The Apocalypses in the new Pseudepigrapha. NT Backgrounds. 1997 <1986>, ⇒3975. EEvans, C.A., 67-88.

8574  <sup>E</sup>Bettiolo, Paolo, (al.), Ascensio Isaiae: textus. CChr.SA 7: 1995,
⇒11/2,6810. <sup>R</sup>Henoch 19/1 (1997) 122-123 (Lusini, Gianfrancesco); EThL 73 (1997) 459-463 (Verheyden, J.).

8575  Dangl, Oskar Vom Traum zum Trauma: apokalyptische Literatur im aktuellen Kontext. PzB 6 (1997) 123-132.

8576  Harlow, Daniel C. The Greek Apocalypse of Baruch (3 Baruch) in Hellenistic Judaism and early christianity. SVTP 12: 1996, ⇒12,8066. <sup>R</sup>ThLZ 122 (1997) 1105-1106 (Kaestli, Jean-Daniel).

8577  Lucchesi, Enzo Une (Pseudo-)Apocalypse d'Athanase en copte [Apocalypse of Paul]. Sum. 243. AnBoll 115 (1997) 241-248.

8578  Maier, Harry O. Staging the gaze: early Christian apocalypses and narrative self-representation. HThR 90 (1997) 131-154.

8579  Norelli, Enrico L'Ascensione di Isaia. 1994. <sup>R</sup>Henoch 19/1 (1997) 122-126 (Lusini, Gianfrancesco).

8580  Norelli, Enrico Pertinence théologique et canonicité: les premières apocalypses chrétiennes. Sum. rés. 147. Apocrypha 8 (1997) 147-164.

8581  <sup>E</sup>Schneemelcher, Wilhelm Apostolische Apokalypsen und Verwandtes. Neutestamentliche Apokryphen in deutscher Übersetzung, 2. Tü <sup>6</sup>1997, Mohr viii; 703 pp. DM148. 3-16-146756-6 [EuA 73,406].

8582  <sup>E</sup>Silverstein, Theodore; Hilhorst, Anthony Apocalypse of Paul: a new critical edition of three long Latin versions. Cahiers d'orientalisme 21: Genève 1997, Cramer 213 pp. 54 pl. FS120.

8583  VanderKam, James C. Exile in Jewish apocalyptic literature. Exile. JSJ.S 56: 1997, ⇒227. <sup>E</sup>Scott, J.M., 89-109.

### к2.1 Philo judaeus alexandrinus

8584  Begg, Christopher T. The ceremonies at Gilgal/Ebal according to PSEUDO-PHILO. Supplementary note by J. Verheyden 83. EThL 73 (1997) 72-83.

8585  Birnbaum, Ellen The place of Judaism in Philo's thought: Israel, Jews, and proselytes. BJSt 290: 1996, ⇒12,8074. <sup>R</sup>JJS 48 (1997) 366-367 (Reinhartz, Adele).

8586  Borgen, Peder Philo of Alexandria: an exegete for his time. NT.S 86: Lei 1997, Brill x; 332 pp. ƒ180/$106. 90-04-10388-0 [JJS 49,350ss—Mendelson, Alan].

8587  Borgen, Peder Philo of Alexandria: reviewing and rewriting biblical material. StPhilo 9 (1997) 37-53.

8588  Borgen, Peder Johan; Fuglseth, Kare; Skarsten, Ronald The Philo index: a complete Greek word index to the writings of Philo of Alexandria lemmatised & computer-generated. UniTrel Studieserie 25: Dragvoll (Norway)] 1997, University of Trondheim ix; 340 pp. 82-7546-026-3.

8589  Cohen, Naomi Earliest evidence of the Haftarah cycle for the sabbaths between בתמוז ז"י and סוכות in Philo. JJS 48 (1997) 225-249.

8590  Cohen, Naomi G. Philo Judaeus: his universe of discourse. BEAT 24: 1995, ⇒11/2,6818. <sup>R</sup>Cart. 13 (1997) 446-447 (Sanz Valdivieso, R.).

Cohen, N. The names of the separate books of the pentateuch in Philo's writings ⇒1495.

8591 *De Francesco, Sergio* Filone maestro di esegesi nelle 'Quaestiones': interpretare domandando e coordinando. Ricerche Teologiche 8/2 (1997) 253-269.
8592 **Decharneux, Baudouin** L'ange, le devin et le prophète: chemins de la parole dans l'oeuvre de Philon d'Alexandrie. 1994, ⇒12,8081. RRevBib 59 (1997) 245-248 *(Martín, José Pablo)*.
8593 *DesCamp, Mary Therese* Why are these women here?: an examination of the sociological setting of Pseudo-Philo through comparative reading. JSPE 16 (1997) 53-80.
8594 *Dillon, John* The pleasures and perils of soul-gardening;
8595 *Hay, David M.* Putting extremism in context: the case of Philo, *De migrazione* 89-93. StPhilo 9 (1997) 190-197/126-142.
8596 **Jacobson, Howard** A commentary on Pseudo-Philo's *Liber antiquitatum biblicarum*. AGJU 31: 1996, ⇒12,8087. RThLZ 122 (1997) 552-555 *(Tilly, Michael)*; JJS 48 (1997) 363-366 *(Hayward, Robert)*; VigChr 51 (1997) 440-443 *(Runia, D.T.)*; Tarb. 66/1 (1997) 135-138 [H.] *(Flusser, David)*.
8597 *Jacobson, Howard* Thoughts on the *Chronicles of Jerahmeel*, Ps-Philo's *Liber antiquitatum biblicarum*, and their relationship. StPhilo 9 (1997) 239-263.
    *Kamesar, A.* The literary genres of the pentateuch... the testimony of Philo ⇒1498.
8598 *Lluch Baixauli, Miguel* El tratado de Fílon sobre el decálogo. ScrTh 29 (1997) 415-441.
8599 *Long, A.A.* Allegory in Philo and etymology in Stoicism: a plea for drawing distinctions. StPhilo 9 (1997) 198-210.
8600 *Mealand, David* The paradox of PHILO's views on wealth. NT Backgrounds. 1997 < 1985 >, ⇒3975. EEvans, C.A. 28-32.
8601 *Mendelson, Alan* Philo's dialectic of reward and punishment;
8602 *Milgrom, Jacob* Philo the biblical exegete. StPhilo 9 (1997) 104-125/79-83.
8603 **Nikiprowetzky, Valentin** Études philoniennes. 1996, ⇒12,8094. RVetChr 34 (1997) 173-174 *(Veronese, Maria)*; OrChrP 63 (1997) 367-368 *(Luisier, Ph.)*.
8604 *Passoni Dell'Acqua, Anna* Il testo biblico di Filone e i LXX. AnScR 2 (1997) 175-196.
8605 *Royse, James R.* Heraclitus B 118 in Philo of Alexandria;
8606 *Runia, David T.* A provisional bibliography 1995-97;
8607 The reward for goodness: Philo, *De Vita Contemplativa* 90;
8608 *Runia, David T.; Geljon, A.C.; Martín, J.P.* Philo of Alexandria: an annotated bibliography 1994. StPhilo 9 (1997) 211-216/356-366/3-18/332-355.
8609 *Schmidt, T. Ewald* Hostility to wealth in PHILO of Alexandria. NT Backgrounds. 1997 < 1983 >, ⇒3975. EEvans, C.A., 15-27.
8610 **Sly, Dorothy I.** Philo's Alexandria. 1996, ⇒12,8101. Ancient Philosophy 17 (1997) 489-490 *(Winston, David)*.
8611 *Sterling, Gregory E.* Prepositional metaphysics in Jewish wisdom speculation and early christian liturgical texts;
8612 *Terian, Abraham* Back to creation: the beginning of Philo's grand commentary. StPhilo 9 (1997) 219-238/19-36.
8613 *Thoma, Clemens* Philo von Alexandrien: Inspirator für Deutungen von Christentum und Judentum. Edith Stein Jahrbuch 3 (1997) 37-49.

8614    *Tobin, Thomas H.* Philo and the Sibyl: interpreting Philo's eschatology. StPhilo 9 (1997) 84-103.
8615    **Torallas Tovar, S.** Filón de Alejandría: sobre los sueños; sobre José. Biblioteca Clásica Gredos 235: M 1997, Gredos 286 pp. [CDios 211,658—Gutiérrez, J.].
8616    *Van den Hoek, Annewies* The "catechetical" school of early christian Alexandria and its Philonic heritage. HThR 90 (1997) 59-87.
8617    *Van der Horst, Pieter W.* Pseudo-Philo. TRE 27. 1997, ⇒419. 670-672.
8618    **Winter, Bruce W.** Philo and Paul among the sophists. Diss. Macquarie 1988, D*Judge, E.A.*: MSSNTS 96: C 1997, CUP xvi; 289 pp. £35. 0-521-59108-2.

## κ2.4 *Evangelia apocrypha*—Apocryphal gospels

8619    E**Izydorczyk, Zbigniew** The medieval 'Gospel of Nicodemus': text, intertexts, and contexts in Western Europe. MRTS 158: Tempe 1997, Arizona State University [BuBbgB 24,6].
8620    *Dooley, Ann* The *Gospel of Nicodemus* in Ireland. The medieval 'Gospel of Nicodemus' ⇒8619, 361-401 [BuBbgB 24,18].
8621    TE**Gounelle, Rémi** L'Évangile de Nicodème ou les Actes faits sous Ponce Pilate (recension latine A) suivi de la Lettre de Pilate à l'empereur Claude. Apocryphes, (L'Aelac) 9: Turnhout 1997, Brepols 271 pp. Introduction et notes par *Rémi Gounelle* et *Zbigniew Izydorczyk*, traduction par *Rémi Gounelle*, à partir d'un texte mis au point par *Zbigniew Izydorczyk*. Bibl. BF800. 2-503-50581-3.
8622    *Gounelle, Rémi* La divinité du Christ est-elle une question centrale dans le procès de Jésus rapporté par les 'Acta Pilati'?. Sum. rés. 121. Apocrypha 8 (1997) 121-136.
8623    *Gounelle, Rémi* VOLTAIRE, traducteur et commentateur de l'évangile de Nicodème. REAug 43 (1997) 173-200.
8624    *Gounelle, Rémi; Izydorczyk, Zbigniew* Thematic bibliography of the *Acts of Pilate*. The medieval 'Gospel of Nicodemus'. 1997, ⇒8619. 419-519 [BuBbgB 24,19].
8625    *Hoffmann, Werner J.* The *Gospel of Nicodemus* in Dutch and Low German literatures of the Middle Ages. The medieval 'Gospel of Nicodemus'. 1997, ⇒8619. 337-360 [BuBbgB 24,18];
8626    The *Gospel of Nicodemus* in High German literature of the Middle Ages. The medieval 'Gospel of Nicodemus'. 1997, ⇒8619. 287-336 [BuBbgB 24,18].
8627    *Ianucci, Amilcare A.* The *Gospel of Nicodemus* in Medieval Italian literature: a preliminary assessment. The medieval 'Gospel of Nicodemus'. 1997, ⇒8619. 165-205 [BuBbgB 24,18].
8628    *Izquierdo, Josep* The *Gospel of Nicodemus* in medieval Catalan and Occitan literatures. The medieval 'Gospel of Nicodemus'. 1997, ⇒8619. 133-164 [BuBbgB 24,18].
8629    *Izydorczyk, Zbigniew* The *Evangelium Nicodemi* in the Latin Middle Ages. The medieval 'Gospel of Nicodemus'. 1997, ⇒8619. 43-101 [BuBbgB 24,18].
8630    *Izydorczyk, Zbigniew* Introduction. The medieval 'Gospel of Nicodemus'. 1997, ⇒8619. 1-19 [BuBbgB 24,18].
8631    *Izydorczyk, Zbigniew; Dubois, Jean-Daniel* Nicodemus's gospel before and beyond the medieval West;

8632 *Klausner, David N.* The *Gospel of Nicodemus* in the literature of medieval Wales. The medieval 'Gospel of Nicodemus'. 1997, ⇒8619. 21-41/403-418 [BuBbgB 24,18].

8633 [E]**Mahan, W.D.** Gesta Pilati: The Acts of Pilate: and ancient records recorded by contemporaries of Jesus Christ regarding the facts concerning his birth, death, resurrection. [T]*Dr. McIntosh; Dr. Twyman*: Kirkwood, MO 1997, Impact Christian Books viii; 215 pp. 089-228-127-8.

8634 *Marx, C.W.* The *Gospel of Nicodemus* in Old English and Middle English;

8635 *O'Gorman, Richard* The *Gospel of Nicodemus* in the vernacular literature of medieval France;

8636 *Wolf, Kirsten* The influence of the *Evangelium Nicodemi* on Norse literature. The medieval 'Gospel of Nicodemus'. 1997, ⇒8619. 207-259/103-131/261-286 [BuBbgB 24,18].

8637 **Baldock, John** The alternative gospel: the hidden teaching of Jesus. Shaftesbury 1997, Element xx; 232 pp. 1-86204-165-2 [NThAR 2000,34].

8638 **Bernabé Pons, L.F.** El evangelio de San Bernabé: un evangelio islámico español. Alicante 1995, Universidad 260 pp. [R]ATG 60 (1997) 472-473 *(Sotomayor, Manuel)*.

8639 *Bertrand, Daniel A.* Fragments évangéliques. Ecrits Apocryphes Chrétiens, 1. 1997, ⇒8641 [BuBbgB 24,16].

8640 [T]*Beyers, Rita* Livre de la nativité de Marie. Ecrits Apocryphes Chrétiens, 1. 1997, ⇒8641. 141-161 [BuBbgB 24,17].

8641 [E]**Bovon, François; Geoltrain, Pierre** Ecrits apocryphes chrétiens, 1. Collab. *Voicu, Server J.*: Bibliothèque de la Pléiade 442: P 1997, Gallimard 1782 pp. FF450. 2-07-011387-6 [Etudes (avril 1998) 551].

8642 *Cartlidge, David R.* The christian Apocrypha: preserved in art. BiRe 13/3 (1997) 24-31, 56.

8643 *Di Berardino, Angelo* The christian Apocrypha and their significance. History of Theology, 1. 1997, ⇒241. [E]Di Berardino, A., 225-250.

8644 [T]*Frey, Albert* Protévangile de Jacques. Ecrits Apocryphes Chrétiens, 1. 1997, ⇒8641. 71-104 [BuBbgB 24,17].

8645 *Geerard, Maurits* Der gute Schächer: ein neues unediertes Apokryphon [Pseudo-Matthew interpolation]. 1997, ⇒101. [F]Voordeckers E., 85-89.

8646 [T]*Genequand, Charles* Vie de Jésus en arabe. Ecrits Apocryphes Chrétiens, 1. 1997, ⇒8641. 205-238 [BuBbgB 24,18].

8647 [T]*Gijsel, Jan* Évangile de l'enfance du Pseudo-Matthieu. Ecrits Apocryphes Chrétiens, 1. 1997, ⇒8641. 105-140 [BuBbgB 24,17].

8648 [E]**Gijsel, Jan Baptist Matthijs; Beyers, Rita** Libri de nativitate Mariae: Pseudo Matthaei evangelium; Libellus de nativitate sanctae Mariae. CChr.SA 9-10: Turnhout 1997, Brepols xvi; 520; 456 pp. Textus et commentarius cura Jan Gijsel [Ps-Matt.]; Rita Beyers [Libellus]. 2-50341-102-9.

8649 [E]**González Núñez, J.** El Protoevangelio de Santiago. Introd. gen. J. González Núñez; introd., notas, trad.: del texto griego: *C. Isart Hernández*; del texto siríaco: *P. González Cadado*. M 1997, Ciudad Nueva 224 pp. 84-89651-24-8. [R]EphMar 47 (1997) 452-

453 *(Largo Domínguez, Pablo)*; Salm. 44 (1997) 459-460 *(Trevi-jano, Ramón)*.

8650 T*Junod, Eric* Évangile de Pierre. Ecrits Apocryphes Chrétiens, 1. 1997, ⇒8641. 239-254 [BuBbgB 24,16].

8651 T*Kaestli, Jean-Daniel* Évangile secret de Marc. Ecrits Apocryphes Chrétiens, 1. 1997, ⇒8641. 55-69 [BuBbgB 24,16].

8652 *Kaestli, Jean-Daniel* Le *Protévangile de Jacques* en latin: état de la question et perspectives nouvelles. Sum. RHT 26 (1996) 41-102;

8653 Questions de Barthélemy. Ecrits Apocryphes Chrétiens, 1. 1997, ⇒8641. 255-295 [BuBbgB 24,19].

8654 *Kaestli, Jean-Daniel; Cherix, Pierre* Livre de la résurrection de Jésus-Christ par l'apôtre Barthélemy. Ecrits Apocryphes Chrétiens, 1. 1997, ⇒8641. 297-356 [BuBbgB 24,19].

8655 *Karavidopoulos, Jean* 'Hapax legomena' et autres mots rares dans l''Évangile apocryphe de Pierre'. Sum. rés. 225. Apocrypha 8 (1997) 225-230.

8656 ET*Leloup, Jean-Yves* L'évangile de Marie Myriam de Magdala: évangile copte du IIIᵉ siècle. Spiritualités Vivantes: P 1997, Albin M 225 pp. F89. [EeV 107,331].

8657 *Lucchesi, E.* Un évangile apocryphe imaginaire. OLoP 28 (1997) 167-178;

8658 Feuillets Coptes non identifiés du prétendu Évangile de Barthélemy. VigChr 51 (1997) 273-275.

8659 **Moraldi, Luigi** I vangeli sconosciuti del Natale. CasM 1997, Piemme 191 pp. 88-384-2973-1.

8660 *Morard, Françoise* Un évangile écrit par une femme?: l'évangile de Marie. BCPE 49/2-3 (1997) 27-34.

8661 *Outtier, Bernard* Paralytique et ressuscité (Cant 85 et 62): vie des apocryphes en arménien. Apocrypha 8 (1997) 111-119.

8662 *Pagels, Elaine* Ritual in the Gospel of Philip. Nag Hammadi... after fifty years. 1997, ⇒341. ETurner, J.D., 280-291.

8663 *Pérès, Jacques-Noel* L'Épître des apôtres et l'Anaphore des a-pôtres: quelques convergences. Apocrypha 8 (1997) 89-96.

8664 *Peretto, Elio* Criteri d'impiego di alcune citazioni bibliche nel 'Protovangelo di Giacomo'. 1997 <1970>, ⇒155. Saggi, 25-42.

8665 **Piñero, Antonio** Der geheime Jesus: sein Leben nach den apokryphen Evangelien. Dü 1997, Patmos 187 pp. 3-491-77022-X.

8666 *Pokorný, Petr* Das theologische Problem der neutestamentlichen Pseudepigraphie. Bibelauslegung. WUNT 100: 1997 <1984>, ⇒970. 121-131.

8667 *Porter, Stanley E.* The Greek apocryphal gospels papyri: the need for a critical edition. 21. Papyrologenkongress, 2. 1997, ⇒367. EKramer, B., 795-803.

8668 **Prieur, Jean-Marc** Apocryphes chrétiens: un regard inattendu sur le christianisme ancien. 1995, ⇒11/2,6875. REstB 55 (1997) 560-562 *(Urbán, A.)*.

8669 *Slomp, Jan* The 'gospel of Barnabas' in recent research. Sum. 81; rés. 109. IslChr 23 (1997) 81-109.

8670 *Starowieyski, Marek* Apokryfy jako utwory apologetyczne [Aspetto apologetico degli apocrifi] [Protoevangelo di Giacomo; Atti di Pilato]; Rias. 365. WST 10 (1997) 357-365;

8671 Quelques remarques sur la méthode apocryphe. StPatr 30, 1997, ⇒351. ELivingstone, E.A., 102-113.

8672 *Stillman, Martha K.* The gospel of Peter: a case for oral-only dependency?. EThL 73 (1997) 114-120.
8673 *Thomassen, Einar* How Valentinian is the gospel of Philip?. Nag Hammadi... after fifty years. 1997, ⇒341. ETurner, J.D., 251-279.
8674 **Turner, Martha Lee** The gospel according to Philip. NHMS 38: 1996, ⇒12,8123. RJThS 48 (1997) 636-639 *(Wilson, R. McL.)*.
8675 *Turner, Martha Lee* On the coherence of the gospel according to Philip. Nag Hammadi... after fifty years. 1997, ⇒341. ETurner, J.D., 223-250.

## κ2.7 *Alia apocrypha NT—*Apocryphal Acts of apostles

8676 *Albrile, Ezio* La libagione d'immortalità: note sul *martirio di santo Stefano*. Sal. 59 (1997) 601-620.
8677 *Amsler, Frédéric* Remarques sur la réception liturgique et folklorique des 'Actes de Philippe' (APH VIII-XV et 'Martyre'). Sum. rés. 251. Apocrypha 8 (1997) 251-264.
8678 *Artés Hernández, José Antonio* Gnosis y Acta Apostolorum apocrypha: "Hechos de Pablo y Tecla" y "Martirio de Pedro". EstB 55 (1997) 387-392.
8679 *Aymer, Margaret P.* Hailstorms and fireballs: redaction, world creation, and resistance in the Acts of Paul and Thecla. Semeia 79 (1997) 45-61.
8680 *Bottecchia Dehò, M. Elisabetta* Nota in margine alla Grande Dossologia delle Costituzioni Apostoliche. OCP 63 (1997) 163-170.
8681 T*Boud'Hors, Anne* Éloge de Jean-Baptiste. Ecrits Apocryphes Chrétiens, 1. 1997, ⇒8641. 1553-1578 [BuBbgB 24,24].
8682 T*Bouvier, Bertrand; Bovon, François* Actes de Philippe. Ecrits Apocryphes Chrétiens, 1. 1997, ⇒8641. 1179-1320 [BuBbgB 24,21].
8683 E**Bremmer, Jan M.** The apocryphal Acts of John. 1995, ⇒11/2,6886. RNT 39 (1997) 99-101 & JThS 48 (1997) 227-228 *(Elliott, J.K.)*; ThLZ 122 (1997) 258-259 *(Wehnert, Jürgen)*; CBQ 59 (1997) 184-185 *(Pervo, Richard I.)*.
8684 *Calzolari, Valentina* Réécriture des textes apocryphes en arménien: l'exemple de la légende de l'apostolat de Thaddée en Arménie. Som. rés. 97. Apocrypha 8 (1997) 97-110;
8685 Les textes apocryphes chrétiens en langue arménienne: un aperçu. BCPE 49/2-3 (1997) 17-25.
8686 T*Cambe, Michel* Prédication de Pierre. Ecrits Apocryphes Chrétiens, 1. 1997, ⇒8641. 3-22 [BuBbgB 24,20].
8687 *Cowe, S.P.* Text critical investigation of the Armenian version of Third Corinthians. Saint Nersess theological review 2/1 (1997) 39-51.
8688 T*Desreumaux, Alain* Doctrine de l'apôtre Addaï. Ecrits Apocryphes Chrétiens, 1. 1997, ⇒8641. 1471-1525 [BuBbgB 24,22].
8689 *Desreumaux, Alain* Abgar, le roi converti à nouveau: les chrétiens d'Edesse selon la 'Doctrine d'Addai'. De la conversion. EAttias, Jean-Christophe. Patr.RL: P 1997, Cerf. 217-227 [BuBbgB 24,1, 22];
8690 Remarques sur le rôle des Apocryphes dans la théologie des églises syriaques: l'exemple de 'Testimonia' christologiques inédits. Sum. rés. 165. Apocrypha 8 (1997) 165-177.

8691 *Dubois, Jean-Daniel* La version copte des Actes de Pilate. Apocrypha 8 (1997) 81-88.

8692 *González Luis, José* En torno a la correspondencia de Séneca y Pablo. La Bíblia i el Mediterrani. 1997, ⇒385. ᴱBorrell, d'Agustí, 161-169.

8693 **González Núñez, J.** La leyenda del Rey Abgar y Jesús. 1995, ⇒11/2,5990. ᴿATG 60 (1997) 404-406 *(Pozo, C.)*.

8694 *Hanig, Roman* Simon Magus in den Petrusakten und die Theodotianer. StPatr 31, 1997, ⇒351. ᴱLivingstone, E.A., 112-120.

8695 *Hoffman, R. Joseph* Confluence in early christian and gnostic literature: the *Descensus Christi ad inferos (Acts of Pilate* 17-27). NT Backgrounds. 1997 <1981>, ⇒3975. ᴱEvans, C.A., 296-311.

8696 *Hovhanessian, Vahan* Third Corinthians: its relationship to the apocryphal Acts of Paul. Saint Nersess theological review 2/1 (1997) 53-64.

8697 **Hvalvik, Reidar** The struggle for scripture and covenant: the purpose of the epistle of Barnabas and Jewish-Christian competition in the second century. WUNT 2/82: 1996, ⇒12,10844. ᴿNT 39 (1997) 302-304 *(Barnard, L.W.)*.

8698 **Jones, F. Stanley** An ancient Jewish christian source on the history of christianity: Pseudo-Clementine *Recognitions* 1.27-71. SBL.TT 27: CA 2: 1995, ⇒12,10833. ᴿEThL 73 (1997) 188-191 *(Verheyden. J.)*; JSSt 44 (1997) 420-421 *(Bauckham, Richard)*; Muséon 110 (1997) 468-471 *(Haelewyck, J.-C.)*; RHR 214 (1997) 370-371 *(Le Boulluec, Alain)*.

8699 ᵀ*Junod, Eric; Kaestli, Jean-Daniel* Actes de Jean. Ecrits Apocryphes Chrétiens, 1. 1997, ⇒8641. 973-1037 [BuBbgB 24,20].

8700 ᵀ*Kappler, Claude-Claire; Kappler, René* Apocalypse de Paul. Ecrits Apocryphes Chrétiens, 1. 1997, ⇒8641. 775-826 [BuBbgB 24,23].

8701 ᵀ*Kappler, René* Correspondance de Paul et Sénèque. Ecrits Apocryphes Chrétiens. 1. 1997, ⇒8641. 1579-94 [BuBbgB 24,22].

8702 *Karakoles, Chrestos K.* "Συνερχομενοι επι το αυτο..." (Letter of Barnabas 4,10b): edificatory or eucharistic the church-assembly in the Letter of Barnabas?. DBM 16/2 (1997) 61-82. G.

8703 *King, Karen L.* Approaching the variants of the Apocryphon of John. Nag Hammadi... after fifty years. 1997, ⇒341. ᴱTurner, J.D., 105-137.

8704 *Marguerat, Daniel* 'Actes de Paul' et 'Actes' canoniques: un phénomène de relecture. Súm. rés. 207. Apocrypha 8 (1997) 207-224.

8705 *Marrassini, Paulo; Bauckham, Richard J.* Apocalypse de Pierre;

8706 ᵀ*Mimouni, Simon Claude* Dormition de Marie du Pseudo-Jean. Ecrits Apocryphes Chrétiens, 1. 1997, ⇒8641. 745-774/163-188 [BuBbgB 24,23].

8707 *Molinari, Andrea Lorenzo* The Acts of Peter and the twelve apostles: a reconsideration of the source question. Nag Hammadi... after fifty years. 1997, ⇒341. ᴱTurner, J.D., 461-483.

8708 ᵀ*Morard, Françoise* Légende de Simon et Théonoé. Ecrits Apocryphes Chrétiens, 1. 1997, ⇒8641. 1527-1551 [BuBbgB 24,22].

8709 *Outtier, Bernard* Paralytique et ressuscité (CANT 85 et 62): vie des apocryphes en arménien. Sum. rés. 111. Apocrypha 8 (1997) 111-119.

8710 *Pearson, Birger A.* Ancient Alexandria in the Acts of Mark. SBL.SPS 36 (1997) 273-284.

8711 *Pérès, Jacques-Noël* L'"Epître des apôtres et l'"Anaphore des a-pôtres': quelques convergences. Sum. rés. 81. Apocrypha 8 (1997) 89-96.

8712 [T]*Pérès, Jacques-Noël* Epître des apôtres. Ecrits Apocryphes Chrétiens, 1. 1997, ⇒8641. 357-392 [BuBbgB 24,22].

8713 *Plümacher, Eckhard* Der Θεος αρηθονος von *Acta Iohannis* 55 und sein historischer Kontext. BZNW 85: 1997, ⇒105. [F]WICKERT U., 249-301.

8714 [T]*Poupon, Gérard* Actes de Pierre. Ecrits Apocryphes Chrétiens, 1. 1997, ⇒8641. 1039-1114 [BuBbgB 24,20].

8715 [T]*Prieur, Jean-Marc* Actes d'André. Ecrits Apocryphes Chrétiens, 1. 1997, ⇒8641. 875-972 [BuBbgB 24,21].

8716 *Rodman, Rosamond C.* Who's on third?: reading Acts of Andrew as a rhetoric of resistance. Semeia 79 (1997) 27-43.

8717 *Siegert, Folker* Analyses rhétoriques et stylistiques portant sur les 'Actes de Jean' et les 'Actes de Thomas'. Sum. rés. 231. Apocrypha 8 (1997) 231-250.

8718 *Starowieyski, Marek* Scena 'Quo vadis?' (*Acta Petri, Martyrium* 6) [L'épisode 'Quo vadis?' (*Acta Petri, Martyrium* 6)] [*Sienkiewicz, Henryk*]. Rés. 390. Vox Patrum 17 (1997) 381-390. P.

8719 *Stewart-Sykes, A.* The Asian context of the new prophecy and of *Epistula Apostolorum*. VigChr 51 (1997) 416-438.

8720 *Tchkhikvadzé, Nestan* Une traduction géorgienne d'un original perdu: l'histoire de l'apocryphe de l'église de Lydda (Cant 77). Sum. rés. 179. Apocrypha 8 (1997) 179-191.

8721 *Vorster, Johannes N.* Construction of culture through the construction of person: the Acts of Thecla as an example. Rhetorical analysis. JSNT.S 146: 1997, ⇒336. [E]Porter, S.E., 445-473.

8722 *Waldstein, Michael* The primal triad in the Apocryphon of John;

8723 *Williams, Michael A.* Response to the papers of Karen KING, Frederik WISSE, Michael WALDSTEIN and Sergio LA PORTA;

8724 *Wisse, Frederik* After the synopsis: prospects and problems in establishing a critical text of the Apocryphon of John and defining its historical location. Nag Hammadi... after fifty years. 1997, ⇒341. [E]Turner, J.D., 154-187/208-220/138-153.

8725 *Zervos, George T.* An early non-canonical annunciation story. SBL.SPS 36 (1997) 664-691.

κ3.1 **Qumran**—*generalia*

8726 Apocrypha and Pseudepigrapha, Jewish-Hellenistic literature, Dead Sea scrolls [bibliography]. QS 67 (1997) 414-417.

8727 *Bartlett, John R.* The archaeology of Qumran. Archaeology and biblical interpretation. 1997, ⇒268. [E]Bartlett, J.R., 67-94.

8728 [E]**Brooke, George J.** New Qumran texts and studies. StTDJ 15: 1994, ⇒10,307; 12,8162. [R]JThS 48 (1997) 161-163 (*Gordon, Robert P.*);

8729 Introduction and catalogue: the Allegro Qumran collection: supplement to the Dead Sea Scrolls on microfiche. Collab. *Bond, Helen K.*: 1996, ⇒12,8163. [R]RdQ 18/1 (1997) 149-153 (*García Martínez, Florentino*).

8730 *Broshi, M.* Radiocarbon dating the Judaean Desert scrolls and its implications. Qad. 30 (1997) 71-73.

8731 *Broshi, Magen; Eshel, Hanan, (al.)*, La vie quotidienne [à Qumrân]. MoBi 107 (1997) 16-33.

8732 **Campbell, Jonathan** Deciphering the Dead Sea scrolls. 1996, ⇒12,8164. ᴿJJS 48/2 (1997) 360-361 *(Brooke, George J.)*.

8733 **Cansdale, Lena** Qumran and the Essenes: a re-evaluation of the evidence. TSAJ 60: Tü 1997, Mohr xii; 230 pp. DM168. 3-16-146719-1.

8734 *Caquot, André, (al.)*, Les manuscrits. MoBi 107 (1997) 33-49.

8735 *Cryer, Frederick H.* The Qumran conveyance: a reply to F.M. CROSS and E. ESHEL. SJOT 11 (1997) 232-240.

8736 *Daoust, Joseph* Le point sur les manuscrits de la Mer Morte. EeV 107 (1997) 454-456.

8737 **Davies, Philip R.** Sects and scrolls: essays on Qumran and related topics. SFSHJ 134: 1996, ⇒12,122. ᴿDSD 4/1 (1997) 120-124 *(Hempel, Charlotte)*.

8738 *Demsky, Aaron* Qumran epigraphy and mishnaic geography: the identification of ḤṬLʾ with Ḥaṭṭulim (Menaḥoth 8:6). DSD 4 (1997) 157-161.

8739 *Dombrowski, Bruno W.W.* Qumranologica IV, V. FolOr 33 (1997) 197-208, 209-222.

8740 *Doudna, Greg* Radiocarbon dating and the scrolls: report on Israel CARMI's talk at the Jerusalem conference. Qumran Chronicle 7/1-2 (1997) 11-13.

8741 *Elgvin, Torleif* Nyere bidrag til Qumranforskningen. TTK 68/1 (1997) 49-66.

8742 *Eshel, H.; Broshi, M.* The archaeological remains on the marl terrace around Qumran. Qad. 30 (1997) 129-133. **H.**

8743 ᴱFabry, Heinz-Josef; Lange, Armin; Lichtenberger, Hermann Qumranstudien. 1996, ⇒12,307. ᴿWZKM 87 (1997) 299-301 *(Maier, Johann)*; CBQ 59 (1997) 413-15 *(VanderKam, James C.)*.

8744 **Fitzmyer, Joseph A.** 101 perguntas sobre os manuscritos do Mar Morto. São Paulo 1997, Loyola 192 pp. 85-15-01530-7 [PerTeol 29,282].

8745 ᴱFlint, Peter W.; Vanderkam, James C. The Dead Sea scrolls after fifty years: a comprehensive assessment, 1. Lei 1996, Brill xxii; 544 pp. 15 pl. [CV 41,173ss—Segert, Stanislav].

8746 *García Martínez, Florentino* Qumran: le ultime scoperte e lo stato delle pubblicazioni. RStB 9/2 (1997) 11-47.

8747 ᴱarcía Martínez, Florentino The Dead Sea scrolls translated. 1994, ⇒10,9661...12,8177. ᴿRSR 85 (1997) 448-449 *(Gibert, P.)*.

8748 *García Martínez, Florentino* Les grandes batailles de Qumrân. MoBi 107 (1997) 4-10.

8749 **García Martínez, Florentino; Parry, Donald W.** A bibliography of the finds in the Desert of Judah 1970-1995. StTDJ 19: 1996, ⇒12,8181. ᴿJSJ 28/1 (1997) 111-112 *(Lange, Armin)*; Henoch 19/1 (1997) 118-119 *(Martone, Corrado)*.

8750 ᴱGarcía Martínez, Florentino; Tigchelaar, Eibert J.C. IQI-4Q273. The Dead Sea scrolls: study edition, 1. Lei 1997, Brill. ƒ186/$109.50. 90-04-10813-0.

8751 **García Martínez, Florentino; Trebolle Barrera, Julio** The people of the Dead Sea scrolls. 1995, ⇒11/2,7103; 12,8349. ᴿBArR 23/2 (1997) 62-63 *(Cook, Edward)*;

8752 Os homens de Qumran. ᵀGonçalves Pereira, Fernando. 1996, ⇒12,8182. ᴿREB 57 (1997) 482-484 *(Silva, Valinor da)*;

8753 Gli uomini di Qumran. StBi 113: 1996, ⇒12,8183. ᴿAnton. 72 (1997) 498-500 *(Nobile, Marco)*; RSLR 33 (1997) 409-411 *(Martone, Corrado)*.

8754 **García Martínez, Florentino; Van der Woude, A.S.** Die rollen van de Dode Zee, 2. Kampen 1995, Kok P. ᴿStr. 64/1 (1997) 86-87 *(Beentjes, Panc)*.

8755 **Gillièron, Bernard** De Qumrân à l'évangile: les manuscrits de la Mer Morte et les origines chrétiennes. Poliez-le-Grand 1997, Du Moulin 97 pp. FF58 [EstB 55,568].

8756 **Golb, Norman** Who wrote the Dead Sea scrolls?. 1995, ⇒11/2,6935; 12,8185. ᴿDSD 4/1 (1997) 124-128 *(Grabbe, Lester L.)*.

8757 *Grabbe, Lester L.* The current state of the Dead Sea scrolls: are there more answers than questions?. The scrolls and the scriptures. JSPE.S 26: 1997, ⇒299. ᴱPorter, S.E., 54-67.

8758 **Hanson, Kenneth** Qumran: the untold story. Tulsa, OK 1997, Council Oak Books 223 pp. Bibl. 1-57178-030-0.

8759 *Harrington, Daniel J.* Ten reasons why the Qumran wisdom texts are important. DSD 4 (1997) 245-254.

8760 *Hempel, Charlotte* Qumran communities: beyond the fringes of second temple society. The scrolls and the scriptures. JSPE.S 26: 1997, ⇒299. ᴱPorter, S.E., 43-53.

8761 *Kapera, Zdisław J.* Interpretacje archeologiczne osiedla Qumrań - kiego: zwięzły przegląd hipotez w pięćdziesięciolecie odkryć nad Morzem Martwym [De interpretationibus archaeologicis Qumran: repertorium hypothesum in 50 annos post inventionem]. RBL 50 (1997) 237-250. P.;

8762 Current bibliography on the Dead Sea Scrolls 1997: I-II. Qumran Chronicle 7 (1997) 127-144, 263-287;

8763 Józef Tadeusz MILIK: the scrollery's fastest man with a fragment. FolOr 33 (1997) 5-20.

8764 **Lange, Armin** Weisheit und Prädestination... in den Textfunden von Qumran. StTDJ 18: 1995, ⇒11/2,7107. ᴿThLZ 122 (1997) 252-254 *(Bergmeier, Roland)*; DSD 4/1 (1997) 129-132 *(Tigchelaar, Eibert J.C.)*.

8765 *Lange, Armin; Lichtenberger, Hermann* Qumran. TRE 28. 1997, ⇒420. 45-79.

8766 ᴱ**Laperrousaz, Ernest-Marie** Qoumrân et les manuscrits de la Mer Morte: un cinquantenaire. P 1997, Cerf 458 pp. FF220. 2-204-05549-2. ᴿOrChrP 63 (1997) 565-566 *(Lavenant, R.)*; Qumran Chronicle 7/1-2 (1997) 123-124 *(Długosz, Mariusz)*; EstTrin 31 (1997) 442-3 *(Vázquez Allegue, Xaime)*.

8767 *Magness, J.* The archaeology of Qumran. Qad. 30 (1997) 119-124. **H.**;

8768 The archaeology of Qumran at the Jerusalem Dead Sea Scrolls Congress, 1997. Qumran Chronicle 7/1-2 (1997) 1-10.

8769 **Maier, Johann** Die Qumran-Essener: die Texte vom Toten Meer. ⇒12,8196. ᴿFrRu 4/1 (1997) 57-59 *(Rapp, Hans A.)*; OrdKor 38 (1997) 372-373 *(Giesen, Heinz)*.

8770 *Maier, Johann* Der "Neue Bund im Land Damaskus" und die Qumran-Schriftrollen. WUB 3 (1997) 44-46.

8771 *Martone, C.* Molteplicità di calendari e identità di gruppo a Qumran. RStB 9/1 (1997) 119-138.

8772  *Nebe, Wilhelm* 4Q559 "Biblical chronology". ZAH 10 (1997) 85-88.

8773  **Nitzan, Bilhan** Qumran prayer and religious poetry. StTDJ 12: 1994. <sup>R</sup>BiOr 54 (1997) 475-476 *(VanderKam, James C.)*; JQR 88 (1997) 104-107 *(Schuller, Eileen)*.

8774  *Ortkemper, Franz-Josef* 50 Jahre Qumran. BiKi 52 (1997) 37-40.

8775  <sup>E</sup>**Parry, Donald W.; Ricks, Stephen D.** Current research and technological developments on the Dead Sea scrolls. StTDJ 20: 1996, ⇒12,293. <sup>R</sup>VT 47 (1997) 563-565 *(Emerton, John A.E.)*; DSD 4 (1997) 226-229 *(VanderKam, James C.)*; TTK 68 (1997) 305-306 *(Aschim, Anders)*.

8776  *Porter, Stanley E.; Evans, Craig A.* From Qumran to Roehampton: fifty years of research and reflection on the scrolls. The scrolls and the scriptures. JSPE.S 26: 1997, ⇒299. <sup>E</sup>Porter, S.E., 15-21.

8777  *Puech, Émile, (al.),* Les grandes questions. MoBi 107 (1997) 50-73.

8778  *Rainbow, Paul A.* The last Oniad and the teacher of righteousness. JJS 48 (1997) 30-52.

8779  <sup>E</sup>**Reed, Stephen A.** The Dead Sea scrolls catalogue. SBLRBS 32: 1994, ⇒10,9673... 12,8204. <sup>R</sup>CBQ 59 (1997) 136-138 *(Flint, Peter W.)*.

8780  *Reich, R. Miqwaʿot* (ritual baths) at Qumran. Qad. 30 (1997) 125-128. **H**.

8781  *Rochman, Bonnie* It takes a lickin' and keeps on tickin': studial from Qumran identified. BArR 23/4 (1997) 20.

8782  **Rohrhirsch, Ferdinand** Wissenschaftstheorie und Qumran. NTOA 32: 1996, ⇒12,8206. <sup>R</sup>ZKTh 119 (1997) 455-457 *(Oberforcher, Robert)*.

8783  **Roitman, Adolfo** A day at Qumran: the Dead Sea sect and its scrolls. J 1997 [Jud. 54/1-2,117s—Krupp, Michael].

8784  **Schiffman, Lawrence H.** Reclaiming the Dead Sea scrolls. 1994, ⇒10,9676... 12,8208. <sup>R</sup>AJS Review 22/1 (1997) 77-93 *(Bernstein, Moshe J.)*;

8785  *Schiffman, Lawrence H.* Non-Jews in the Dead Sea scrolls. Bibl.Interp. 28: 1997, ⇒77. <sup>F</sup>SANDERS J., 153-171.

8786  *Schuller, Eileen* The Dead Sea scrolls at fifty years. BiTod 35 (1997) 365-371.

8787  <sup>E</sup>**Shanks, Hershel** L'aventure des manuscrits de la mer Morte. 1996, ⇒12,8211. <sup>R</sup>ETR 72 (1997) 135-136 *(Cuvillier, Élian)*.

8788  *Shanks, Hershel* Golden anniversary of the scrolls. BArR 23/6 (1997) 62-65.

8789  *Shapiro, Shahar* Concerning the identity of Qumran. Qumran Chronicle 7 (1997) 91-116, 215-223.

8790  *Shiloh, Dina* Fierce protest over bones threatens to halt archaeology in Israel. BArR 23/6 (1997) 54-55, 76-77.

8791  *Tov, Emanuel* A status report on the publication of the Judaean Desert scrolls. Qad. 30 (1997) 66-70. **H**.

8792  <sup>E</sup>**Ulrich, Eugene; VanderKam, James** The community of the renewed covenant. CJAn 10: 1994, ⇒11/2,538; 12,8221. <sup>R</sup>JThS 48 (1997) 163-170 *(Davies, Philip R.)*; VT 47 (1997) 567-569 *(Emerton, John A.E.)*; RdQ 18 (1997) 156-160 *(Steudel, Annette)*.

8793  **VanderKam, James C.** The Dead Sea scrolls today. 1994, ⇒10,9683... 12,8224. <sup>R</sup>FolOr 33 (1997) 235-237 *(McGrath, James F.)*; JBL 115 (1996) 132-134 *(Matthews, Victor H.)*.

8794 **Vaux, Roland de** Die Ausgrabungen von Qumran und Ein Feschka 1A: die Grabungstagebücher. <sup>TE</sup>*Rohrhirsch, Ferdinand; Hofmeir, Bettina.* 1996, ⇒12,8226. <sup>R</sup>Qumran Chronicle 7 (1997) 225-234 *(Leonard, Robert D.).*

8795 <sup>T</sup>**Vermes, Geza** The complete Dead Sea scrolls in English. Harmondsworth 1997, Allen Lane xix; 648 pp. Bibl. £25/$50. 0-713-99131-3.

8796 <sup>E</sup>**Wacholder, Ben Zion; Abegg, Martin G.; Bowley, James** Concordance of fascicles 1-3: a preliminary edition of the unpublished Dead Sea Scrolls: the Hebrew and Aramaic texts from cave four. 1996, ⇒12,8228. <sup>R</sup>DSD 4/2 (1997) 229-241 *(Elwolde, J.F.).*

8797 <sup>T</sup>**Wise, Michael Owen**, *(al.),* The Dead Sea scrolls: a new translation. 1996, ⇒12,8230. <sup>R</sup>ABR 45 (1997) 92-93 *(O'Sullivan, M.M.K.);* RBBras 14 (1997) 443-444.

8798 <sup>E</sup>**Wise, Michael Owen** *(al.),* Methods of investigation of the Dead Sea Scrolls and the Khirbet Qumran site. 1994, ⇒11/2,540; 12,8229. <sup>R</sup>DSD 4/2 (1997) 241-243 *(Tov, Emanuel).*

## κ3.4 *Qumran,* libri biblici et parabiblici

8799 <sup>E</sup>**Attridge, H.** Qumran Cave 4, VIII: parabiblical texts, 1. DJD 13: 1994, ⇒10,9687... 12,8233. <sup>R</sup>DSD 4 (1997) 102-112 *(Bernstein, Moshe J.);* JSSt 44 (1997) 401-402 *(Davila, James R.);* CBQ 59 (1997) 333-335 *(Endres, John C.).*

8800 **Berger, Klaus** I salmi di Qumran. 1995, ⇒11/2,6976. <sup>R</sup>EstTr 31/1-2 (1997) 192-193 *(Pikaza, Xabier);*

8801 Salmos de Qumrán. 1996, ⇒12,8235. <sup>R</sup>Revista de Teología 33 (1997) 61-62 *(Castiglioni, Mario).*

8802 <sup>E</sup>**Broshi, Magen,** *(al.),* Qumran Cave 4, XIV: parabiblical texts, 2. DJD 19: 1995, ⇒11/2,6969. <sup>R</sup>JThS 48 (1997) 574-575 *(Lim, Timothy H.);* JJS 48 (1997) 130-145 *(Morgenstern, Matthew).*

8803 *Cross, Frank Moore; Parry, Donald W.* A preliminary edition of a fragment of 4QSam<sup>b</sup> (4Q52). BASOR 306 (1997) 63-74.

8804 <sup>E</sup>**Elgvin, Torleif** Qumran Cave 4, XV: sapiential texts, 1. Collab. *Fitzmyer, Joseph A.; Milik, Jozef T.; Strugnell, John.* DJD 20: Oxf 1997, Clarendon x; 247 pp. £60. 0-19-826938-2. <sup>R</sup>DSD 4 (1997) 357-360 *(Harrington, Daniel J.).*

8805 *Eshel, Esther* Hermeneutical approaches to Genesis in the Dead Sea scrolls. The book of Genesis. 1997, ⇒196. <sup>E</sup>Frishman, J., 1-12. *Eshel, H. & E.* 4Q448, Psalm 154 and 4QpIsa<sup>a</sup>. H. ⇒2989.

8806 *Flint, Peter W.* The "11QPs<sup>a</sup>-Psalter" in the Dead Sea Scrolls, including the preliminary edition of 4QPs<sup>e</sup>. Bibl.Interp. 28: 1997, ⇒77. <sup>F</sup>SANDERS J., 173-196;

8807 The Isaiah scrolls from the Judean Desert. Writing and reading... Isaiah. VT.S 70/2: 1997, ⇒181. <sup>E</sup>Broyles, C.C., 481-489.

8808 *Flint, Peter W.; Alvarez, Andrea E.* The oldest of all the psalms scrolls: the text and translation of 4QPs<sup>a</sup>. The scrolls and the scriptures. JSPE.S 26: 1997, ⇒299. <sup>E</sup>Porter, S.E., 142-169.

8809 *Freedman, David Noel* The 'House of Absalom' in the Habakkuk scroll <1949>;

8810 The Old Testament at Qumran <1968>. Divine Commitment 1. 1997, ⇒124. 1-2/233-240;

8811 Orthography (of the Paleo-Hebrew Leviticus scroll). Divine Commitment 2. 1997 <1985>, ⇒124. 123-170;

8812 The Prayer of Nabonidus. Divine Commitment 1. 1997 <1957>, ⇒124. 50-52;

8813 The use of aleph as a vowel letter in the Genesis Apocryphon. Divine Commitment 2. 1997 <1967>, ⇒124. 31-38.

8814 [E]García Martínez, Florentino Testi di Qumran. [T]Martone, Corrado: Studi e Testi 4: 1996, ⇒12,8252. [R]PaVi 42/2 (1997) 57-58 (Segalla, Giuseppe); Lat. 63 (1997) 135-144 (Penna, Romano).

8815 Garnet, Paul Cave 4MS parallels to 1QS 5.1-7: towards a Serek text history. JSPE 15 (1997) 67-78.

8816 Herbert, Edward D. 4QSam[a] and its relationship to the LXX: an exploration in stemmatological analysis. IX Congress IOSCS. SCSt 45: 1997, ⇒340. [E]Taylor, B.A., 37-55.

8817 Herbert, Edward D. Reconstructing biblical Dead Sea scrolls: a new method applied to the reconstruction of 4QSam[a]. StTDJ 22: Lei 1997, Brill xv; 293 pp. Diss. Cambridge. ƒ325/$191.50. 90-04-10684-7 [NThAR 1998,100].

8818 Hess, Richard S. The Dead Sea scrolls and higher criticism of the Hebrew Bible: the case of 4QJudg[a] [Judg 6,2-13; 1 Kgs 7,19-8,19];

8819 Jarick, John The bible's 'festival scrolls' among the Dead Sea scrolls. The scrolls and the scriptures. JSPE.S 26: 1997, ⇒299. [E]Porter, S.E., 122-128/170-182.

8820 Lim, Timothy H. Holy Scripture in the Qumran commentaries and Pauline letters. Oxf 1997, Clarendon xiii; 221 pp. Diss. Oxford 1991. £40. 0-19-826206-X [NThAR 1998,98].

8821 Martone, Corrado I LXX e le attestazioni testuali ebraiche di Qumran. AnScR 2 (1997) 159-174;

8822 Un inno di Qumran dedicato a "re Gionata" (4Q448). Henoch 19/2 (1997) 131-141 [Ps 154].

8823 Nickelsburg, George W.E. 4Q551: a vorlage to Susanna or a text related to Judges 19?. JJS 48 (1997) 349-351.

8824 Owen, Elizabeth 4QDeut[n]: a pre-samaritan text?. DSD 4 (1997) 162-178.

8825 Pfann, Stephen J. 4Q249 Midrash sefer Moshe. StTDJ 23: 1997, ⇒8. [F]Baumgarten J., 11-18.

8826 Raurell, Frederic Isaïas-LXX i Isaïas-Qumran. RCatT 22 (1997) 395-407.

8827 Rogers, Jeffrey S. Scripture is a scripturalists do: scripture as a human activity in the Qumran scrolls. Early christian interpretation. JSNT.S 148: 1997, ⇒191. [E]Evans, C.A., 28-43.

8828 Schuller, Eileen M.; DiTomasso, Lorenzo A bibliography of the Hodayot, 1948-1996. DSD 4 (1997) 55-101.

8829 [ET]Stuckenbruck, Loren T. The book of Giants from Qumran: text, translation, and commentary [1Q23-24]. TSAJ 63: Tü 1997, Mohr xvi; 289 pp. Bibl. DM198. 3-16-146270-5.

8830 Tov, Emanuel The biblical scrolls from the Judaean Desert. Qad. 30 (1997) 73-81 H.

8831 Tronina, Antoni '...aż do przyjścia proroka i mesjaszy Aarona i Izraela' (1QS 9,11) ['...until the prophet comes, and the messiahs of Aaron and Israel']. 1997, ⇒52. [F]Łach J., 401-408. P.

8832 [T]Tyloch, Witold Rękopisy z Qumran nad Morzem Martwym [Manuscripts from Qumran at the Dead Sea]. Wsz 1997, Kaiążka i

Wiedza 8\*; 392 pp. Zł30. 83-05-12908-X. RQumran Chronicle 7 (1997) 235-252 *(Kapera, Zdzisław)*.

8833 EUlrich, Eugene Qumran Cave 4 IX: Deuteronomy, Joshua, Judges, Kings. DJD 12: 1995, ⇒11/2,6967. RJJS 48/1 (1997) 149-150 *(Herbert, Edward D.)*; JThS 48 (1997) 568-574 *(Brooke, George J.)*; CBQ 59 (1997) 759-760 *(Fitzmyer, Joseph A.)*.

8834 *Ulrich, Eugene* An index to the contents of the Isaiah manuscripts from the Judean desert. Writing and reading... Isaiah. VT.S 70/2: 1997, ⇒181. EBroyles, C.C., 477-480.

8835 EUlrich, Eugene Charles Qumran Cave 4, X: the Prophets. DJD 15: Oxf 1997, Clarendon xv; 327 pp. £80. 0-19-826937-4.

8836 EUlrich, Eugene; Cross, Frank Moore Qumran Cave 4 VII: Genesis to Numbers. DJD 12: 1994, ⇒11/2,6966a; 12,8278. RCBQ 59 (1997) 558-560 *(Falk, Daniel K.)*.

8837 Wise, Michael; Abegg, Martin; Cook, Edward Die Schriftrollen von Qumran: Übersetzung und Kommentar mit bisher unveröffentlichen Texten. ELäpple, Alfred: Augsburg 1997, Pattloch 544 pp. [Jud. 54,105ss—Krupp, Michael].

8838 *Xeravits, Géza* Notes sur le 11QPsa<sup>Creat</sup> 7-9. RdQ 18 (1997) 145-148 [Ps 135,7; Jer 10,12-13].

8839 Zdun, Pawel Pieśni ofiary szabatoweij z Qumran i Masady [Songs of the sabbath sacrifice from Qumran and Masada]. 1996, ⇒12,8281. RQumran Chronicle 7 (1997) 253-255 *(Kapera, Zdzisław J.)*. P.

## κ3.5 *Qumran—varii rotuli et fragmenta*

8840 *Abegg, Martin G.* Who ascended to heaven?: 4Q491, 4Q427, and the teacher of righteousness. Eschatology, messianism. SDSSRL 1: 1997, ⇒276. EEvans, C.A., 61-73.

8841 *Avemarie, Friedrich* "Tohorat ha-Rabbim" and "Mashqeh ha-Rabbim": Jacob LICHT reconsidered. StTDJ 23: 1997, ⇒8. FBAUMGARTEN J., 215-229.

8842 EBaumgarten, Joseph Qumran Cave 4 XIII: the Damascus Document (4Q266-273). DJD 18: 1996, ⇒12,8283. RRT (1997/2) 93-95 *(Hempel, Charlotte)*.

8843 *Baumgarten, Joseph M.* Some notes on 4Q408. RdQ 18 (1997) 143-144.

8844 *Beckwith, Roger T.* The Temple scroll and its calendar: their character and purpose. RdQ 18 (1997) 3-19.

8845 *Brin, Gershon* Studies in 4Q424 1-2. RdQ 18 (1997) 21-42;

8846 Wisdom issues in Qumran: the types and status of the figures in 4Q424 and the phrases of rationale in the document. DSD 4 (1997) 297-311.

8847 *Brooke, George J.* The explicit presentation of scripture in 4QMMT. StTDJ 23: 1997, ⇒8. FBAUMGARTEN J., 67-88.

8848 *Broshi, Magen; Eshel, Esther* The Greek king is Antiochus IV (4QHistorical Text=4Q248). JJS 48 (1997) 120-129.

8849 *Callaway, Phillip R.* A second look at Ostracon no. 1 from Khirbet Qumrân. Qumran Chronicle 7/3-4 (1997) 145-170.

8850 *Caquot, André* Les cantiques qoumrâniens de l'holocauste du sabbat. RHPhR 77 (1997) 1-29.

8851  ᴱCharlesworth, J.H. Pseudepigraphic and non-Masoretic psalms
      and prayers. The Dead Sea Scrolls 4a. Tü 1997, Mohr xxiii; 296
      pp. DM168. 3-16-146649-7 [JSOT 78,122];
8852  Damascus Document, War Scroll, and related documents. The
      Dead Sea Scrolls: Hebrew, Aramaic, and Greek texts with English
      translations, 2. 1994, ⇒12,8286. ᴿDSD 4/1 (1997) 116-120 *(Falk,
      Daniel)*; JThS 48 (1997) 576-579 *(Brooke, George J.)*.
8853  **Chyutin, Michael** The new Jerusalem scroll from Qumran: a
      comprehensive reconstruction. JSPE.S 25: Shf 1997, Academic
      167  pp.  £32.50/$53.50.  1-85075-683-X  [RdQ  18,453ss—
      Tigchelaar, Eibert].
8854  *Cross, F.M.; Eshel, E.* A new ostracon from Qumran. Qad. 30
      (1997) 134-136. **H.**;
8855  Ostraca from Khirbet Qumrân. IEJ 47 (1997) 17-28. **H.**
8856  *Derrett, J. Duncan M.* The reprobate's peace: 4QDᵃ (4Q266) (18 V
      14-16). StTDJ 23: 1997, ⇒8. ᶠBᴀᴜᴍɢᴀʀᴛᴇɴ J., 245-249.
8857  *Dombrowski, Bruno W.W.* On the context of 1QS VIII 1f. Qumran
      Chronicle 7/3-4 (1997) 175-191;
8858  Fragmente und Verwandte des *Manual of Discipline* aus Höhle 4.
      Qumran Chronicle 7/1-2 (1997) 15-49.
8859  *Dunn, James D.G.* 'Son of God' as 'son of man' in the Dead Sea
      scrolls?: a response to John Cᴏʟʟɪɴs on 4Q246. The scrolls and
      the scriptures. JSPE.S 26: 1997, ⇒299. ᴱPorter, S.E., 198-210.
8860  *Fabry, Heinz-Josef* Der Begriff "Tora" in der Tempelrolle. RdQ 18
      (1997) 63-72.
8861  *Golb, Norman* Qadmoniot and the 'yahad' claim. Qumran Chron-
      icle 7/3-4 (1997) 171-173.
8862  *Grabbe, Lester L.* 4QMMT and second temple Jewish society.
      StTDJ 23: 1997, ⇒8. ᶠBᴀᴜᴍɢᴀʀᴛᴇɴ J., 89-108.
8863  *Gramaglia, Pier Angelo* 1QS, XI, 21-22: osservazioni lessicali.
      Henoch 19/2 (1997) 143-147.
8864  *Harrington, Hannah K.* Holiness in the laws of 4QMMT. StTDJ
      23: 1997, ⇒8. ᶠBᴀᴜᴍɢᴀʀᴛᴇɴ J., 109-128.
8865  *Hempel, Charlotte* The text of 4QDa (4Q266) 2 ii 3. RdQ 18
      (1997) 299-301.
8866  *Ibba, Giovanni* Alcune considerazioni sul tempo escatologico di
      1QM I. Henoch 19/3 (1997) 283-294;
8867  Gli angeli del "Rotolo della guerra" (1QM). Henoch 19/2 (1997)
      149-159;
8868  Il patto nel *Rotolo della Guerra* e negli *Inni*. Nuova Umanità 19/2
      (1997) 271-299.
8869  *Lemaire, André* Un fragment araméen inédit de Qumrân. RdQ 18
      (1997) 331-333.
8870  *Main, Emmanuelle* הערה עלם מגילה 448 ממערה 4 של קומראן [A
      note on 4Q448]. Sum. VI. Tarb. 67/1 (1997) 103-119.
8871  *Martone, Corrado* A proposito di un passo di 4Q visioni di
      ʿAmram in alcune interpretazioni recenti. RSLR 33 (1997) 615-
      621.
8872  **Metso, Sarianna** The textual development of the Qumran Commu-
      nity Rule. StTDJ 21: Lei 1997, Brill xi; 173 pp. $84.50. 90-04-
      10683-9.
8873  *Metso, Sarianna* The textual traditions of the Qumran Community
      Rule. StTDJ 23: 1997, ⇒8. ᶠBᴀᴜᴍɢᴀʀᴛᴇɴ J., 141-147.

8874 *Minette de Tillesse, Caetano* Qumrân. RBB 14/1-3 (1997) 238-260.
8875 *Nebe, G. Wilhelm* Qumranica II: zu unveröffentlichten Handschriften aus Höhle 4 von Qumran [4QUnid; 4Q334]. ZAH 10 (1997) 134-138.
8876 *Nitzan, Bilhah* The laws of reproof in 4QBerakhot (4Q286-290) in light of their parallels in the Damascus covenant and other texts from Qumran. StTDJ 23: 1997, ⇒8. <sup>F</sup>BAUMGARTEN J., 149-165.
8877 *Parry, Donald W.* Notes on divine name avoidance in scriptural units of the legal texts of Qumran. StTDJ 23: 1997, ⇒8. <sup>F</sup>BAUMGARTEN J., 149-165/437-449.
8878 *Pérez Fernández, Miguel* 4QMMT: redactional study. RdQ 18 (1997) 191-205.
8879 *Puech, Émile* Fragments du plus ancien exemplaire du Rouleau du temple (4Q524). StTDJ 23: 1997, ⇒8. <sup>F</sup>BAUMGARTEN J., 19-64.
8880 *Puech, Émile* Quelques résultats d'un nouvel examen du Rouleau de Cuivre (3Q15). RdQ 18 (1997) 163-190.
8881 <sup>E</sup>**Qimron, Elisha** The Temple Scroll: a critical edition with extensive reconstructions. 1996, ⇒12,8306. <sup>R</sup>Or. 66/1 (1997) 125 *(Gianto, Agustinus)*; OLZ 92 (1997) 78-79 *(Pfeifer, Gerhard)*; BiOr 54 (1997) 472-475 *(Brooke, George J.)*.
8882 *Roo, Jacqueline C.R. de* Is 4Q525 a Qumran sectarian document?. The scrolls and the scriptures. JSPE.S 26: 1997, ⇒299. <sup>E</sup>Porter, S.E., 338-367.
8883 *Schiffman, L.H.* The Temple Scroll after thirty years. Qad. 30 (1997) 101-104 **H.**;
8884 Some laws pertaining to animals in Temple Scroll column 52. StTDJ 23: 1997, ⇒8. <sup>F</sup>BAUMGARTEN J., 167-178.
8885 *Schmidt, Francis* Astrologie juive ancienne: essai d'interprétation de 4QCryptique (4Q186). RdQ 18 (1997) 125-141.
8886 *Sharp, Carolyn J.* Phinehan zeal and rhetorical strategy in 4QMMT. RdQ 18 (1997) 207-222.
8887 *Stone, Michael E.; Greenfield, Jonas C.* The fifth and sixth manuscripts of *Aramaic Levi Document* from Qumran (4QLevi<sup>e</sup> and 4QLevi<sup>f</sup> aram). Muséon 110 (1997) 271-291.
8888 *Stuckenbruck, Loren T.* The sequencing of fragments belonging to the Qumran book of Giants: an inquiry into the structure and purpose of an early Jewish composition. JSPE 16 (1997) 3-24.
8889 **Swanson, Dwight D.** The Temple Scroll and the Bible: the methodology of 11QT. StTDJ 14: 1995, ⇒11/2,7046. <sup>R</sup>CBQ 59 (1997) 140-141 *(Schuller, Eileen)*.
8890 *Tigchelaar, Eibert J.C.* 4Q499 48 + 47 (par 4Q369 1 II): a forgotten identification;
8891 Some more small 11Q1 fragments. RdQ 18 (1997) 303-306/325-330.
8892 *VanderKam, James C.* The calendar, 4Q327, and 4Q394. StTDJ 23: 1997, ⇒8. <sup>F</sup>BAUMGARTEN J., 179-194.
8893 *Wise, M.O.* To know the times and the seasons: a study of the Aramaic chronograph 4Q559. JSPE 15 (1997) 3-51.
8894 *Wolters, Al* The shekinah in the copper scroll: a new reading of 3Q15 12.10. The scrolls and the scriptures. JSPE.S 26: 1997, ⇒299. <sup>E</sup>Porter, S.E., 382-391.
8895 *Yardeni, Ada* A draft of a deed on an ostracon from Khirbet Qumrân. IEJ 47 (1997) 233-237.

к3.6 **Qumran et Novum Testamentum**

8896 [E]**Charlesworth, James Hamilton** Gesù e la comunità di Qumran. CasM 1997, Piemme 382 pp. Bibl.
8897 **Gillieron, B.** De Qumran à l'évangile: les manuscripts de la mer Morte et les origines chrétiennes. Pouliez-le-Grand 1997, Du Moulin 97 pp. [StPat 45,526—Segalla, Giuseppe].
8898 *Norelli, Enrico* Risonanze qumraniche nella letteratura cristiana tra I e II secolo: questioni di methodo ed esempi;
8899 *Penna, Romano Introduzione*: Qumran e le origini cristiane. RStB 9/2 (1997) 265-294/5-10.
8900 **Pilgaard, Aage** Dødehavsskrifterne og det Ny Testamente. Frederiksberg 1997, Anis 123 pp. [SJOT 11,313].
8901 *Sacchi, Paolo* Qumran e Gesù. RStB 9/2 (1997) 99-115.
8902 **Stegemann, Hartmut** Los esenios, Qumrán, Juan Bautista y Jesús. 1996, ⇒12,8332. [R]EfMex 15 (1997) 418-419 *(Zesati Estrada, Carlos)*;
8903 Gli Esseni, Qumran, Giovanni Battista e Gesù: una monografia. 1996, ⇒12,8333. [R]CivCatt 148 III (1997) 306-309 *(Prato, G.L.)*.

к3.8 **Historia et doctrinae Qumran**

8904 *Abegg, Martin G.* Exile and the Dead Sea scrolls. Exile. JSJ.S 56: 1997, ⇒227. [E]Scott, J.M., 111-125.
8905 *Alexander, Philip S.* 'Wrestling against wickedness in high places': magic in the worldview of the Qumran community. The scrolls and the scriptures. JSPE.S 26: 1997, ⇒299. [E]Porter, S.E., 318-337.
8906 *Baumgarten, A.I.* The Zadokite priests at Qumran: a reconsideration. DSD 4 (1997) 137-156.
8907 *Baumgarten, J.* The religious law of the Qumran community. Qad. 30 (1997) 97-100. **H.**
8908 *Betz, Otto* Sühne in Qumran. 1997, ⇒92. [F]STUHLMACHER P., 44-56.
8909 *Brin, Gerson* Divorce at Qumran. StTDJ 23: 1997, ⇒8. [F]BAUMGARTEN J., 231-244.
8910 *Collins, John J.* The expectation of the end in the Dead Sea scrolls. Eschatology, messianism. SDSSRL 1: 1997, ⇒276. [E]Evans, C.A., 74-90;
8911 The origin of the Qumran community: a review of the evidence <1989>;
8912 Prophecy and fulfillment in the Qumran scrolls <1987>;
8913 Was the Dead Sea sect an apocalyptic movement? <1990>;
8914 Wisdom, apocalypticism and the Dead Sea scrolls <1996>. Seers. JSJ.S 54: 1997, ⇒119. 239-260/301-314/261-285/369-383.
8915 *Doering, Lutz* New aspects of Qumran sabbath law from cave 4 fragments. StTDJ 23: 1997, ⇒8. [F]BAUMGARTEN J., 251-274.
8916 **Dombrowski, Bruno W.W.** Major texts mainly of Qumran Cave 1, CD and 4QMMT. 1994, ⇒11/2,7098. [R]CBQ 59 (1997) 116-117 *(Duhaime, Jean)*.
8917 *Eshel, Esther* 4Q414 fragment 2: purification of a corpse-contaminated person. StTDJ 23: 1997, ⇒8. [F]BAUMGARTEN J., 3-10.

8918 *Eshel, H.* The history of the Qumran community and historical details in the Dead Sea scrolls. Qad. 30 (1997) 86-93. **H.**

8919 **Falk, Daniel K.** Daily, sabbath and festival prayers in the Dead Sea scrolls. StTDJ 27: Lei 1997, Brill x; 302 pp. 90-04-10817-3.

8920 **Fisdel, Steven A.** The Dead Sea scrolls: understanding their spiritual message. Northvale, NJ 1997, Jason Aronson viii; 354 pp. Bibl. 1-56821-973-3.

8921 *Frey, Jörg* Different patterns of dualistic thought in the Qumran library: reflections on their background and history;

8922 *Hempel, Charlotte* The penal code reconsidered;

8923 *Jastram, Nathan* Hierarchy at Qumran. StTDJ 23: 1997, ⇒8. FBAUMGARTEN J., 275-335/337-348/349-376.

8924 EKampen, John; Bernstein, Moshe J. Reading 4QMMT: new perspectives on Qumran law and history. 1996, ⇒12,8353. RJSJ 28 (1997) 331-333 *(Tigchelaar, Eibert)*.

8925 *Kugler, Robert A.* Halakic interpretive strategies at Qumran: a case study. StTDJ 23: 1997, ⇒8. FBAUMGARTEN J., 131-140.

8926 *Lange, Armin* Physiognomie oder Gotteslob?: 4Q301 3. DSD 4 (1997) 282-296.

8927 *Magris, Aldo* Qumran e lo gnosticismo. RStB 9/2 (1997) 231-264.

8928 *McCarron, Kevin* History and hermeneutics: the Dead Sea scrolls. The scrolls and the scriptures. JSPE.S 26: 1997, ⇒299. EPorter, S.E., 107-120.

8929 *Mickiewicz, Franciszek* Koncepcje świątyni w tekstach wspólnoty z Qumran [De figuris templi in scriptis e Qumran]. RBL 50 (1997) 250-266. **P.**

8930 *Nitzan, Bilhah* Eschatological motives in Qumran literature: the messianic concept. Eschatology in the bible. JSOT.S 243: 1997, ⇒222. EReventlow, H., 132-151.

8931 **Paul, André** Les manuscrits de la mer Morte: la voix des Esséniens retrouvés. P 1997, Bayard 334 pp. FF138. 2-227-350-14-8. RQumran Chronicle 7 (1997) 260-262 *(Długosz, Mariusz)*.

8932 *Sacchi, Paolo* A new step towards a deeper knowledge of the Jewish second temple thought. Henoch 19/3 (1997) 367-372.

8933 *Schmidt, F.* Astrologie et prédestination à Qoumrân. Qad. 30 (1997) 115-118 **H.**

8934 *Shemesh, Aharon* "The holy angels are in their council": the exclusion of deformed persons from holy places in Qumranic and rabbinic literature. DSD 4 (1997) 179-206.

8935 **Sheres, Ita**, *(al.)*, The truth about the virgin: sex and ritual in the Dead Sea scrolls. 1995, ⇒11/2,7124. RCritRR 10 (1997) 152-153 *(Fuchs, Esther)*.

8936 *Talmon, S.* The calendar of the Qumran sect. Qad. 30 (1997) 105-114 **H.**

8937 *Tantlevskij, Igor R.* Elements of mysticism in the Dead Sea scrolls (thanksgiving hymns, War Scroll, text of two columns) and their parallels and possible sources. Qumran Chronicle 7/3-4 (1997) 193-213.

8938 *Tiller, Patrick A.* The "eternal planting" in the Dead Sea scrolls. DSD 4 (1997) 312-335.

8939 *Van Uchelen, N.A.* Halakhah at Qumran?. RdQ 18 (1997) 243-253.

8940 *VanderKam, James C.* Mantic wisdom in the Dead Sea scrolls. DSD 4 (1997) 336-353.

## κ4.1 Sectae iam extra Qumran notae: Esseni, Zelotae

8941 **Bergmeier, Roland** Die Essenerberichte des... JOSEPHUS. 1993, ⇒9,10651... 12,8369. ᴿBZ 41 (1997) 118-119 *(Maier, Johann)*.

8942 *Bergmeier, Roland* Die Leute aus Essa. ZDPV 113 (1997) 75-87.

8943 *Boccaccini, Gabriele* E se l'essenismo fosse il movimento eno-chiano?: una nuova ipotesi circa il rapporto tra Qumran e gli esseni. RStB 9/2 (1997) 49-67.

8944 **Bordeaux Székely, Edmond** The teachings of the Essenes from Enoch to the Dead Sea scrolls. Saffron Walden 1997, Daniel 93 pp. 0-85207-141-8.

8945 *Flusser, D.* The sect of the Essenes and its beliefs. Qad. 30 (1997) 94-96 **H**.

8946 *Genot-Bismuth, J.* Zoroastrisme et culture judéenne scribe sous influence perse: archéologie de l'essénisme à la lumière de l'étude comparée du Psaume 119 et du Yasna 45. TEuph 13 (1997) 107-121.

8947 **Hengel, Martin** The Zealots. 1989 <1976>, ⇒5,a59... 9,10652. ᴿVJTR 61 (1997) 416-418 *(Meagher, P.M.)*;

8948 Gli zeloti: ricerche sul movimento di liberazione giudaico dai tempi di Erode I al 70 d.C. 1996, ⇒12,8374. ᴿPaVi 42/6 (1997) 54-55 *(Balzaretti, Claudio)*.

8949 *Lange, Armin* The Essene position on magic and divination. StTDJ 23: 1997, ⇒8. ᶠBAUMGARTEN J., 377-435.

8950 *Pixner, Bargil* Jerusalem's Essene gateway: where the community lived in Jesus' time. BArR 23/3 (1997) 22-31, 64-66.

8951 **Puech, Émile** La croyance des esséniens en la vie future: immortalité, résurrection, vie éternelle?. 1993, ⇒9,7555... 12,6883. ᴿBZ 41 (1997) 308-311 *(Maier, Johann)*.

8952 *Rochman, Bonnie* The missing link?: rare tombs could provide evidence of Jerusalem Essenes. BArR 23/4 (1997) 20-21.

8953 *Schremer, Adiel* The name of the Boethusians: a reconsideration of suggested explanations and another one. JJS 48 (1997) 290-299.

8954 **Stemberger, Günter** Jewish contemporaries of Jesus: Pharisees, Sadducees, Essenes. 1995, ⇒11/2,7141; 12,8377. ᴿJJS 48 (1997) 372-373 *(Pearce, Sarah)*; CBQ 59 (1997) 787-788 *(Oakman, Douglas E.)*.

## κ4.3 Samaritani

8955 *Jamgotchian, A.S.* On the history of Samaritan studies in Russia. Sum. 149. VDI 221 (1997) 145-149 **R**.

8956 **Macchi, J.-D.** Les Samaritains: histoire d'une légende: Israel et la province de Samarie. 1994, ⇒11/2,7152. ᴿCDios 210 (1997) 636-637 *(Gutiérrez, J.)*.

8957 **Pummer, Reinhard** Samaritan marriage contracts and deeds of divorce, 1-2. Wsb 1993-1997, Harrassowitz 2 vols. Bibl. DM218 + 268. 3-447-03316-9.

8958 *Tournay, Raymond Jacques* Polémique antisamaritaine et le feu du Tofet. RB 104 (1997) 354-367 [Judg 5,14; 12,15; Sir 50,26; Isa 66,24.

8959 **Zangenberg, Jürgen** ΣΑΜΑPΕΙΑ: Antike Quellen zur Geschichte und Kultur der Samaritaner in deutscher Übersetzung. 1994, ⇒10,9764; 11/2,7153. [R]JBL 115 (1996) 567-569 *(Pummer, Reinhard)*.

8960 *Zevit, Ziony* The Gerizim-Samarian community in and between texts and times: an experimental study. 1997, ⇒77. [F]SANDERS J., 547-572.

## к4.5 *Sadoqitae, Qaraitae*—Cairo Genizah; Zadokites, Karaites

8961 The Cairo Genizah: one hundred years of discovery and research. Bulletin of the Israeli Academic Center in Cairo 21: J 1997, The Israel Academy of Sciences and Humanities 48 pp.

8962 **Campbell, Jonathan G.** The use of scripture in the Damascus Document 1-8, 19-20. BZAW 228: 1995, ⇒11/2,7155. [R]ZKTh 119 (1997) 103-4 *(Oesch, Josef M.)*; DSD 4 (1997) 112-6 *(Brooke, George J.)*; CBQ 58 (1996) 503-504 *(VanderKam, James C.)*.

8963 *Erder, Yoram* The observance of the commandments in the diaspora on the eve of the redemption in the doctrine of the Karaite mourners of Zion. Henoch 19/2 (1997) 175-202 [Dt 12,20].

8964 *Philonenko, Marc; Marx, Alfred* Quatre "chants" pseudo-davidiques trouvés dans la Gueniza du Caire et d'origine esséno-qoumrânienne. RHPhR 77 (1997) 385-406.

8965 **Schur, Nathan** The Karaite encyclopedia. BEAT 38: Fra 1995, Lang 295 pp. £33. 3-631-47742-2. [R]Jud. 53/3 (1997) 183-184 *(Schreiner, Stefan)*.

8966 *Veltri, Giuseppe* Letteratura etico-sapienziale del primo medioevo: alcuni frammenti dalla Geniza del Cairo. Henoch 19/3 (1997) 349-366.

## к5 Judaismus prior vel totus

8967 *Anderlini, Giampaolo* Il cammino della tradizione. Sette e Religioni 7/1 (1997) 20-47.

8968 *Atkinson, Kenneth* On further defining the first-century CE synagogue: fact or fiction?. NTS 43 (1997) 491-502.

8969 **Avemarie, Friedrich** Tora und Leben: Untersuchungen zur Heilsbedeutung der Tora in der frühen rabbinischen Literatur. TSAJ 55: 1996, ⇒12,8398. [R]ThLZ 122 (1997) 1010-11 *(Bergmeier, Roland)*.

8970 *Bammel, Ernst* Was ist Wissenschaft des Judentums?. Judaica et Paulina. WUNT 91: 1997, ⇒109. 187-202.

8971 *Barth, Lewis M.* The ban and the "Golden Plate": interpretation in Pirqe d'Rabbi ELIEZER 38. Bibl.Interp. 28: 1997, ⇒77. [F]SANDERS J., 625-640.

8972 **Baumgarten, Albert I.** The flourishing of Jewish sects in the Maccabean era: an interpretation. JSJ.S 55: Lei 1997, Brill xiii; 240 pp. Bibl. ƒ143/$84. 90-04-10751-7.

8973 **Bel Bravo, María Antonia** Sefarad: los judíos de España. M 1997, Sílex 430 pp. [HispSac 50,362—Andrés-Gallego, José].

8974 *Benoualid, Anne* Les bénédictions dans la tradition juive. Tychique 127 (1997) 13-18.

8975 **Berquist, Jon L.** Judaism in Persia's shadow: a historical and sociological approach. 1995, ⇒11/2,7172. ᴿBTB 27 (1997) 28 *(Burns, John Barclay)*; CBQ 59 (1997) 529-530 *(Cody, Aelred)*; JR 77 (1997) 656-658 *(Smith-Christopher, Daniel L.)*.

8976 *Boccaccini, Gabriele* Tra predeterminismo e responsabilità umana: riflessioni sul concetto di elezione nel giudaismo medio. DSBP 15 (1997) 51-66.

8977 **Cagiati, Annie** Settanta domande sull'ebraismo: un popolo e la sua storia. Padova 1997, Messagero 267 pp. L25.000. Amicizia Ebraico-Cristiana 32 (1997) 156-158 *(Salzano, Teresa)*.

8978 ᴱCohen, Shaye J.D. The Jewish family in antiquity. BJSt 289: 1993, ⇒11/2,495. ᴿJAOS 117 (1997) 364-365 *(Gilner, David J.)*.

8979 *Cohen, Shaye J.D.* Were pharisees and rabbis the leaders of communal prayer and torah study in antiquity?: the evidence of the New Testament, Joseph us, and the church fathers. BJSt 313: 1997, ⇒85. ᶠSɪʟʙᴇʀᴍᴀɴ L., 99-114.

8980 *Collins, John J.* A symbol of otherness: circumcision and salvation in the first century. Seers. JSJ.S 54: 1997 <1985>, ⇒119. 211-235.

8981 *Davies, Philip R.* Qumran and the quest for the historical Judaism. The scrolls and the scriptures. JSPE.S 26: 1997, ⇒299. ᴱPorter, S.E., 24-42.

8982 **Deines, Roland** Die Pharisäer im Spiegel christlicher und jüdischer Forschung seit Wᴇʟʟʜᴀᴜsᴇɴ und Gʀᴀᴇᴛᴢ. Diss. Tübingen, ᴰHengel, M.: WUNT 101: Tü 1997, Mohr xviii; 642 pp. 3-16-146808-2.

8983 *Feldman, Louis H.* Reflections on Jews in Graeco-Roman literature. JSPE 16 (1997) 39-52.

8984 ᴱFeldman, Louis H.; Reinhold, Meyer Jewish life and thought among Greeks and Romans: primary readings. 1996, ⇒12,8416. ᴿBZ 41 (1997) 256-257 *(Klauck, Hans-Josef)*; CBQ 59 (1997) 769-771 *(Neusner, Jacob)*.

8985 *Fenton, Paul B.* Le symbolisme du rite de la circumambulation dans le judaïsme et dans l'islam: une étude comparative. Le comparatisme. 1997, ⇒346. ᴱBoespflug, F., 197-218.

8986 **Fine, Steven** This holy place: on the sanctity of the synagogue during the Greco-Roman period. CJAn 11: Notre Dame, IN 1997, University of Notre Dame Press ix; 280 pp. Bibl. $35. 0-268-04205-5.

8987 **Fröhlich, Ida** 'Time and times and half a time': historical consciousness in the Jewish literature of the Persian and Hellenistic eras. JSJ.S 19: 1996, ⇒12,8417. ᴿCBQ 59 (1997) 732-733 *(Endres, John C.)*.

Goldberg, A. Mystik und Theologie des rabbinischen Judentums ⇒128.

8988 **Goldenberg, Robert** The ʟations that know thee not: ancient Jewish attitudes towards other religions. BiSe 52: Shf 1997, Academic xi; 215 pp. £13/$20 [CBQ 61,540s—Patton, Corrine].

8989 *Goldenberg, Robert* Reinheit: Judentum. TRE 28. 1997, ⇒420. 483-487.

8990 **Gordis, Daniel** God was not in the fire: the search for a spiritual Judaism. NY 1996, Simon & S 254 pp. Bibl. 0-684-82526-0.

8991 **Grabbe, Lester L.** An introduction to first century Judaism. 1996, ⇒12,8422. JJS 48 (1997) 371-372 *(Pearce, Sarah)*.

8992 EGreen, William Scott Approaches to ancient Judaism. BJSt 10; SFSHJ 1: Missoula 1997, Scholars viii; 222 pp. 0-7885-0330-8 [NThAR 1997,260].

8993 *Hoffman, Joel E.* Jewish education in biblical times: Joshua to 933 B.C.E. JBQ 25/2 (1997) 114-119.

8994 *Honigman, Sylvie* PHILON, Flavius JOSRPHE, et la citoyenneté alexandrine: vers une utopie politique. JJS 48 (1997) 62-90.

8995 Hruby, Kurt Aufsätze zum nachbiblischen Judentum und zum jüdischen Erbe der frühen Kirche. EOsten-Sacken, Peter von der: ANTZ 5: 1996, ⇒12,8428. RSIDIC 30/2 (1997) 32 *(Wahle, H.)*.

8996 Ilan, Tal Mine and yours are hers: retrieving women's history from rabbinic literature. AGJU 41: Lei 1997, Brill xiii; 346 pp. 90-04-10860-2.

8997 *Jacobs, Louis* Sainteté selon la tradition juive. SIDIC 30/3 (1997) 2-5.

8998 Jaffee, Martin S. Early Judaism. Upper Saddle River, NJ 1997, Prentice H xi; 259 pp. 0-13-519323-0 [NThAR 1997,159].

8999 *Jaffee, Martin S.* A rabbinic ontology of the written and spoken word: on discipleship, transformative knowledge, and the living texts of oral Torah. JAAR 65 (1997) 525-549.

9000 Joannes, Fernando L'Ebraismo. Le grandi religioni del mondo. Mi 1997, Rizzoli 95 pp. Bibl. 88-17-14624-2.

9001 *Kaplan, Edward K.* Sous le regard de Dieu: vénération, morale, et sainteté juive. SIDIC 30/3 (1997) 15-19.

9002 *Krochmalnik, Daniel* Die Schrift und ihre Auslegung in der jüdischen Tradition. rhs 40 (1997) 84-92.

9003 Levine, Lee I. The pre-70 C.E. Judean synagogue: its origins and character reexamined. 1997, ⇒34. MGREENBERG M., 143*-162* H.

9004 *Levinson, Nathan Peter* Die Exegese der Heiligen Schrift Israels im Lichte der rabbinischen Interpretation. 1997, ⇒25. FFRIEDLANDER A., 113-117.

9005 Levison, John R. The Spirit in first-century Judaism. AGJU 29: Lei 1997, Brill xiv; 302 pp. ƒ158/$93. 90-04-10739-8 [JSJ 30,104ss—Piñero, Antonio].

9006 Mélèze-Modrzejewski, Joseph Les juifs d'Égypte, de Ramsès II à Hadrien. P 1997, Presses Universitaires de France vii; 374 pp. Bibl. 2-13-048753-X.

9007 Mendels, Doron The rise and fall of Jewish nationalism. GR ²1997 <1992>, Eerdmans xiv; 450 pp. $35. 0-8028-4329-8 [NTS 44,624].

9008 Momigliano, Arnaldo Essays on ancient and modern Judaism. EBerti, Silvia: 1994, ⇒10,207f; 12,8447. RZion 62 (1997) 423-428 [H.] *(Schwartz, Daniel R.)*.

9009 ENeusner, Jacob Judaism in late antiquity I-II. HO 16-17: 1995, ⇒11/2,376; 12,8450. RLatomus 56 (1997) 893-895 *(Lipiński, E.)*.

9010 *Neusner, Jacob* Exile and return as the history of Judaism. Exile. JSJ.S 56: 1997, ⇒227. EScott, J.M., 221-237;

9011 German scholarship on rabbinic Judaism: the Goldberg-Schäfer school. Archaeology and the Galilee. SFSHJ 143: 1997, ⇒275. EEdwards, D., 75-81.

9012 Nodet, Étienne A search for the origins of Judaism: from Joshua to the Mishnah. TCrowley, Ed.: JSOT.S 248: Shf 1997, Academic

423 pp. £45/$65. 1-85075-445-4. RCritRR 10 (1997) 160-162 *(Pomykala, Kenneth E.)*.

9013 Perani, Mauro La "Genizah italiana": caratteri generali e rapporto su quindici anni di scoperte. RivBib 45 (1997) 31-70.

9014 Perani, Mauro L'interpretazione della bibbia presso i rabbi: aspetti dell'ermeneutica rabbinica. RivBib 45 (1997) 329-346.

9015 **Porton, Gary G.** The stranger within your gates: converts and conversion in rabbinic literature. 1994, ⇒10,9812; 11/2,7228. RCBQ 59 (1997) 393-395 *(Cohen, Shaye J.D.)*; JQR 88 (1997) 99-101 *(Rubenstein, Jeffrey L.)*.

9016 Puig i Tàrrech, Armand La diàspora mediterrània. La Bíblia i el Mediterrani. 1997, ⇒385. EBorrell, d'Agustí, 103-150.

9017 Rash, Yehoshua Attitudes juives à l'égard de non-juifs: références bibliques, talmudiques et actuelles. RSR 85 (1997) 177-197.

9018 Safrai, C. Sayings and legends in the Hillel tradition;

9019 The sayings of Hillel: their transmission and reinterpretation. Hillel and Jesus. 1997, ⇒321. ECharlesworth, J.H., 306-320/321-334.

9020 Safrai, Shmuel & Chana All are invited to read. Sum. vii. Tarbiz 66 (1997) 395-401 **H**.

9021 **Saperstein, Marc** 'Your voice like a ram's horn': themes and texts in traditional Jewish teaching. Kiev Library: Cincinnati 1996, Hebrew Union College Press xix; 522 pp. $50 [HR 38,414—Sommer, B.D.].

9022 **Schach, Stephen R.** The structure of the Siddur. Northvale, NJ 1997, Jason Aronson xvi; 287 pp. 1-56821-974-1.

9023 **Schäfer, Peter** Judeophobia: attitudes towards the Jews in the ancient world. CM 1997, Harvard University Press ix; 306 pp. $35. 0-674-48777-X [JEarlyC 5,316].

9024 Schoeman, S. Early Hebrew education and its significance for present-day educational theory and practice. HTS 53 (1997) 407-427.

9025 Scott, James M. Exile and the self-understanding of diaspora Jews in the Greco-Roman period. Exile. JSJ.S 56: 1997, ⇒227. EScott, J.M., 173-218.

9026 **Setzer, Claudia** Jewish responses to early christians: history and polemics, 30-150 C.E. 1994, ⇒11/2,7236. RJQR 87 (1997) 383-385 *(Efroymson, David P.)*; AJSR 22 (1997) 248-249 *(Schuller, Eileen)*; JBL 115 (1996) 165-167 *(Sanders, Jack T.)*; CBQ 58 (1996) 361-362 *(McLaren, James S.)*.

9027 Shemesh, Aharon The origins of the laws of separatism: Qumran literature and Rabbinic halacha. RdQ 18 (1997) 223-241.

9028 ESierra, Sergio J. La lettura ebraica delle Scritture. La Bibbia nella Storia 18: 1995. ⇒11/2,388; 12,205. RNRTh 119 (1997) 106-107 *(Ska, J.L.)*; SIDIC 30/1 (1997) 27-28 *(Serra, Aristide)*; Anton. 72 (1997) 697-698 *(Nobile, Marco)*; VetChr 34 (1997) 385-386 *(Aulisa, Immacolata)*.

9029 Sievers, J. Who were the Pharisees?. Hillel and Jesus. 1997, ⇒321. ECharlesworth, J.H., 137-155.

9030 **Slingerland, H. Dixon** Claudian policymaking and the early imperial repression of Judaism at Rome. SFSHJ 160: Atlanta 1997, Scholars. $70 [RHPhR 78,337s—Blanchetière, F.].

9031 **Stefani, Piero** Introduzione all'ebraismo. Introduzioni e trattati 6: Brescia 1995, Queriniana 392 pp. L42.000. 88-399-2156-7. RRdT 38 (1997) 554-555 *(Neudecker, Reinhard)*.

9032 *Stemberger, Günter* Vollkommener Text in vollkommener Sprache: zum rabbinischen Schriftverständnis. JBTh 12 (1997) 53-65.
9033 **Stern, Sacha** Jewish identity in early rabbinic writings. 1994, ⇒10,9821. RJQR 87 (1997) 391-395 *(Goldenberg, Robert)*.
9034 **Tilly, Michael** So lebten Jesu Zeitgenossen: Alltag und Frömmigkeit im antiken Judentum. Bibelkompaß: Mainz 1997, Matthias-Grünewald 144 pp. 3-7867-2030-4.
9035 *Tomson, Peter J.* Het nut van de rabbijnse literatuur voor de studie van het Nieuwe Testament. Analecta Bruxellensia 2 (1997) 180-96.
9036 *Trebilco, Paul R.* Jewish backgrounds. Handbook. NTTS 25: 1997, ⇒971. EPorter, S.E., 359-388.
9037 **Vetter, Dieter** Die Wurzel des Ölbaums: das Judentum. Kleine Bibliothek der Religionen 5: 1996, ⇒12,8478. RBiLi 70 (1997) 244-245 *(Bodendorfer, Gerhard)*.
9038 *Weinberg, Zwi* Judentum und Eros. Entschluss 52/6 (1997) 13-15.
9039 *Weinfeld, M.* Hillel and the misunderstanding of Judaism in modern scholarship. Hillel and Jesus. 1997, ⇒321. ECharlesworth, J.H., 56-70.
9040 *Weitzman, Steven* Revisiting myth and ritual in early Judaism. DSD 4 (1997) 21-54.
9041 EWerblowsky, R.J. Zwi; Wigoder, Geoffrey The Oxford dictionary of the Jewish religion. Oxf 1997, OUP xviii; 764 pp. £80. 0-19-508605-8. RJJS 48 (1997) 352-353 *(Frank, Daniel)*.
9042 **Wise, Michael Owen** Thunder in Gemini and other essays on the history, language and literature of second temple Palestine. JSPE.S 15: 1994, ⇒10,231; 12,8483. RCoTh 67/2 (1997) 228-231 *(Chrostowski, Waldemar)*.
9043 *Zeplowitz, Irwin A.* Jewish law. JDH 22 (1997) 379-395.

## κ6.0 Mišna, tosepta; Tannaim

9044 *Cohen, Shaye J. D.* Are there tannaitic parallels to the gospels? [*Smith, Morton*]. JAOS 116 (1997) 85-89.
9045 TCortès, Enric; Martinez, Teresa Pisqa. Sifre Deuteronomio: comentario tannaítico al libro del Deuteronomio, 2. Barc 1997, Facultat de Teologia de Catalunya 161-357 pp. Bibl. 84-86065-47-X.
9046 **Houtman, Alberdina** Mishnah and tosefta: a synoptic comparison of the tractates Berakhot and Shebiit. TSAJ 59: 1996, ⇒12,8487. RFJB 24 (1997) 157-162 *(Stemberger, Günter)*.
9047 *Houtman, Alberdina* The job, the craft and the tools: using a synopsis for research on the relationship(s) between the mishnah and the tosefta. JJS 48 (1997) 91-104.
9048 **Lapin, Hayim** Early rabbinic civil law and the social history of Roman Galilee... mishnah tractate Baba' Mesi'a'. BJSt 307: 1996, ⇒12,8491. RZion 62 (1997) 289-297 [H.] *(Ze'ev, Safrai)*.
9049 *Lightstone, Jack N.* Whence the rabbis?: from coherent description to fragmented reconstructions. Sum. 275. SR 26 (1997) 275-295.
9050 **Mayer, Günter** Die Tosefta: Seder I: Zeraim. 1,2: Terumot - Orla. RT I/1,2: Stu 1997, Kohlhammer vi; 190 pp. Bibl. 3-17-015112-6.
9051 **Moore, George Foot** Judaism in the first centuries of the christian era: the age of tannaim. Peabody, MA 1997 <1927-1930>, Hendrickson xii; 552; viii; 485; ix; 206 pp. 3 vol. in 2. $60. 1-56563-286-9 [ThD 45,282—Heiser, W. Charles].

9052  *Neudecker, Reinhard* Meister und Jünger im rabbinischen Judentum. Dialog der Religionen 7 (1997) 42-53 [AcBiB 10/3,265].
9053  **Neusner, Jacob** Il giudaismo nella testimonianza della mishnah. 1995, ⇒11/2,7264. ᴿRivBib 45 (1997) 108-111 *(Stemberger. Günther)*; PaVi 42/2 (1997) 59-60 *(Pesce, Mauro)*;
9054  Religion and law. 1996, ⇒12,8494. ᴿAcOr 58 (1997) 202-204 *(Groth, Bente)*.
9055  *Pérez Fernández, Miguel* Tres parábolas de allende los mares (medinat ha-yam) en los maestros tannaítas. La Bíblia i el Mediterrani. 1997, ⇒385. ᴱBorrell, d'Agustí, 327-343.
9056  **Schlüter, Margarete** Auf welche Weise wurde die Mishna geschrieben?: das Antwortschreiben des Rav Sherira Gᴀᴏɴ. 1993, ⇒10,9837; 11/2,7270. ᴿZion 62 (1997) 193-196 **[H.]** *(Brody, Robert)*.
9057  ᴱᵀStern, **Chaim** Pirke Avot: divre hakhamim [Pirké Avot: wisdom of the Jewish sages]. Hoboken 1997, KTAV x; 270 pp. $18. 0-88125-595-5 [ThD 45,82—Heiser, W. Charles].
9058  **Toperoff, Shlomo Pesach** Avot: a comprehensive commentary on the ethics of the fathers. Northvale, NJ 1997, Aronson 440 pp. $40. 0-7657-5970-5 [ThD 45,191—Heiser, W. Charles].
9059  ᴱValle, **C. del** La misná. S ²1997 <1981>, Sígueme 1.525 pp. Ptas8.000. 84-301-1342-8 [Proyección 45,75].
9060  *Vana, Liliane* Les relation sociales entre Juifs et païens à l'époque de la mishna: la question du banquet privé (mšwh gwjjm). RevSR 71 (1997) 147-170.

## κ6.5  Talmud; midraš

9061  *Aaron, David H.* Shedding light on God's body in rabbinic midrashim: reflections on the theory of a luminous Adam. HThR 90 (1997) 299-314.
9062  *Bardski, Krzystof* Grzech Adama i Ewy w midraszowej tradycji Rabbi Eʟᴇᴀᴢᴀʀᴀ [Sin of Adam and Eve in the midrashic tradition of Rabbi Eliezer]. 1997, ⇒52. ᶠLᴀᴄʜ J., 31-40 **P**.
9063  ᵀBecker, **H.J.** Der Jerusalemer Talmud: sieben ausgewählte Kapitel. 1995, ⇒11/2,7276. ᴿNRTh 119 (1997) 112-113 *(Ska, J.L.)*.
9064  ᵀBörner-Klein, **Dagmar** Der Midrasch Sifre zu Numeri. Tannaitische Midraschim, 3. Rabbinische Texte, 2. Reihe 3: Stu 1997, Kohlhammer xiv; (2) 796 pp. DM440. 3-17-013634-8. ᴿMEAH.H 46 (1997) 163-165 (Pérez Fernández, Miguel).
9065  **Boyarin, Daniel** Intertextuality and the reading of midrash. 1994, ⇒7,9988... 11/2,7278. ᴿHebSt 38 (1997) 191-193 *(Elman, Yaakov)*.
9066  *Boyarin, Daniel* Torah study and the making of Jewish gender. A feminist companion. 1997, ⇒180. ᴱBrenner, A., 515-546.
9067  *Dorff, Elliot N.* Hammer on the rock: ongoing Jewish exegesis. Bibl.Interp. 28: 1997, ⇒77. ᶠSᴀɴᴅᴇʀs J., 511-530.
9068  **Fisch, Menachem** Rational rabbis: science and talmudic culture. Jewish Literature and Culture: Bloomington, IND 1997, Indiana University Press xxii; 263 pp. 0-253-33316-4.
9069  *Fishbane, Michael* "Orally write therefore aurally right": an essay on midrash. Bibl.Interp. 28: 1997, ⇒77. ᶠSᴀɴᴅᴇʀs J., 531-546 [=Logos und Buchstabe, ed. Sellin, G., ⇒229, 91-102];

9070 Rabbinic mythmaking and tradition: the great dragon drama in b. Baba Batra 74b-75a. 1997, ⇒34. MGREENBERG M., 273-283.
9071 EFriedman, Shamma Talmud Arukh: BT Bava Mezi'a VI: vol. 1: text; vol. 2: commentary: critical edition with comprehensive commentary. NY 1996, Jewish Theological Seminary of America 438 + 422 pp. 0-87334-066-3 [JSSt 44,316s—Jacobs, Louis].
9072 EGinzberg, Louis La création du monde, Adam, les dix générations, Noé. TSed-Rajna, Gabrielle: Les légendes des juifs, 1. Patrimoines, Judaïsme: P 1997, Cerf; Institut Alain-de-Rothschild 332 pp. FF185. 2-204-05310-4 [BCLF 584,1417].
9073 Goldin, Judah A law and its interpretation. 1997, ⇒34. MGREENBERG M., 285-289 [Num 15,37-41].
9074 Hauptman, Judith Rabbinic interpretation of scripture. A feminist companion. 1997, ⇒180. EBrenner, A., 472-486 [Ex 22,15-16; Dt 22,28-29].
9075 Hayes, Christine Elizabeth Between the Babylonian and Palestinian talmuds: accounting for halakhic difference in selected sugyot from Tractate Avodah Zarah. NY 1997, OUP xvii; 270 pp. Bibl. £42.50. 0-19-509884-6.
9076 Hezser, Catherine The social structure of the rabbinic movement in Roman Palestine. TSAJ 66: Tü 1997, Mohr ix; 557 pp. DM228. 3-16-146797-3 [JJS 49,362ss—Schwartz, Joshua].
9077 Hyman, Naomi Mara Biblical women in the midrash: a sourcebook. Northvale, NJ 1997, Aronson xlii; 194 pp. Bibl. 0-7657-6030-4.
9078 Jacobs, Irving The midrashic process: tradition and interpretation in rabbinic Judaism. 1995, ⇒11/2,7292; 12,8513. RSal. 59/1 (1997) 158-159 (Vicent, R.).
TKooyman, A. Als een koning... rabbijnse parabels in midrasjiem ⇒4751.
9079 Levinas, Emmanuel Cuatro lecturas talmùdicas. 1996, ⇒12,8524. REstFil 46 (1997) 552-553 (Luis Carballada, Ricardo de).
9080 Midrashic and Halakhic literature, Jewish law [bibliography]. QS 67 (1997) 422-440.
9081 Milikowsky, Chaim Notions of exile, subjugation and return in rabbinic literature. Exile. JSJ.S 56: 1997, ⇒227. EScott, J., 265-296.
9082 Naeh, Shlomo Freedom and celibacy: a talmudic variation on tales of temptation and fall in Genesis and its Syrian background. The book of Genesis. 1997, ⇒196. EFrishman, J., 73-89.
9083 Neusner, Jacob Scripture and midrash in Judaism. JudUm 47-49: 1994-1995, ⇒11/2,7308; 12,8532. RThLZ 122 (1997) 557-559 (Oegema, Gerbern S.);
9084 Tractate Berakhot, Enlandisement- Tractates...: introduction: faith, thanksgiving. Between Israel and God, 1. The Halakhah of the Oral Torah; SFSHJ 159: Atlanta, GA 1997, Scholars;
9085 The components of the rabbinic documents: from the whole to the parts. South Florida academic commentary 80, 86, 87, 100, 101: Atlanta, GA 1997, Scholars 5 vols. v.3, Ruth Rabbah; v.7, Sifré to Deuteronomy II,5-10; Part III: a topical and methodical outline; v.9, Genesis Rabbah IV,4: Genesis Rabbah Chapters 76-100; v.11, Pesiqta deRab Kahana I: a topical and methodical outline. 0-7885-.
9086 Neusner, Jacob German scholarship on rabbinic Judaism: the GOLDBERG-SCHAEFER school. Archaeology and the Galilee. SFSHJ 143: 1997, ⇒275. EEdwards, D.R., 75-81.

9087 **Neusner, Jacob** Jerusalem and Athens: the congruity of talmudic and classical philosophy. JSJ.S 52: Lei 1997, Brill xvi; 166 pp. $87.50. 90-04-10698-7.

9088 *Peskowitz, Miriam* Rabbis, feminists and patriarchy's ordinariness. A feminist companion. 1997, ⇒180. ᴱBrenner, A., 487-514.

9089 *Porton, Gary G.* The idea of exile in early rabbinic midrash. Exile. JSJ.S 56: 1997, ⇒227. ᴱScott, J.M., 249-264.

9090 **Quarles, Charles L.** Midrash criticism: introduction and appraisal. Lanham 1997, University Press of America 176 pp. $49/$27.50. 0-7618-0924-4/5-2 [NTS 44,625].

9091 *Ragacs, Ursula* The forged midrashim of Raymond MARTINI—reconsidered. Henoch 19/1 (1997) 59-68.

9092 *Rovner, Jay* Pseudepigraphic invention and diachronic stratification in the stammaitic component of the Bavli: the case of Sukka 28. HUCA 68 (1997) 11-62.

9093 *Rubin, Nissan; Kosman, Admiel* The clothing of the primordial Adam as a symbol of apocalyptic time in the midrashic sources. HThR 90 (1997) 155-174.

9094 ᴱ**Schäfer, Peter; Becker, Hans-Jürgen** Ordnung Neziqin, Seder Toharot: Nidda. Synopse zum Talmud Yerushalmi, 4. TSAJ 47: 1995, ⇒11/2,7316; 12,8550. ᴿSal. 59 (1997) 356-357 *(Vicent, R.)*.

9095 *Schwartz, D.R.* Hillel and scripture: from authority to exegesis. Hillel and Jesus. 1997, ⇒321. ᴱCharlesworth, J.H., 335-362.

9096 *Shinan, Avigdor* "Moses had written about many deeds ... and David came and explained them" (Exodus Rabbah 15:22). 1997, ⇒34. ᴹGREENBERG M., 235*-244* H. [Gn 1; Ps 104].

9097 **Steinsaltz, Adin** Le talmud, 1: guide et lexiques. ᵀ*Gugenheim, Jean-Jacques; Grunewald, Jacquot.* P 1995 Ramsay 290 pp. FF290. 2-84114-104-7. ᴿBCLF 587-589 (1997) 2060-2062.

9098 **Stemberger, Günter** Introduzione al Talmud e al Midrash. 1995, ⇒11/2,7319; 12,8555. ᴿStPat 44/1 (1997) 194-198 *(Leonardi, Giovanni)*.

9099 *Tomson, Peter J.* Het nut van de rabbijnse literatuur voor de studie van het Nieuwe Testament. Analecta Bruxellensia 2 (1997) 180-196 [ZID 24,344].

9100 ᵀ**Townsend, John T.** Exodus and Leviticus. Midrash Tanhuma. Hoboken, NJ 1997, Ktav v; 394 pp. (S. Buber recension). $79.50. 0-88125-379-0 [RB 105,159].

9101 *Van der Heide, Albert* Midrash and exegesis. The book of Genesis. 1997, ⇒196. ᴱFrishman, J., 43-56.

9102 *Visotzky, Burton L.* The priest's daughter and the thief in the orchard: the soul of Midrash Leviticus Rabbah. 1997, ⇒82. ᶠScROGGS R., 165-171.

9103 *Viterbi, Benedetto Carucci* 'Cercate il signore dove si fa trovare': il *midrash* come ricerca di Dio. PSV 35 (1997) 77-86.

9104 *Wehn, Beate* Halacha—Diskussion/Streitgespräch. Antijudaismus im NT. KT 149: 1997, ⇒9221. ᴱHenze, D., 39-41.

## κ7.1 Judaismus mediaevalis, *generalia*

9105 *Ahrend, Moshe* L'adaptation des commentaires du *midrash* par RASHI et ses disciples à leur exégèse biblique. Som., sum. 275. REJ 156 (1997) 275-288.

9106 *Beeri, Tova* Early stages in the Babylonian Piyyut: Hayim al-Baradani and his poetic heritage. HUCA 68 (1997) 1*-33* **H**.

9107 *Emanuel, Simcha* The "European Genizah" and its contribution to Jewish studies. Henoch 19/3 (1997) 313-340.

9108 *Gamoran, Hillel* Mortgages in Geonic times in light of the law against usury. HUCA 68 (1997) 97-108.

9109 *Henkin, Judah H.* P'shat: an innovative method in torah commentary. JBQ 25/4 (1997) 234-240.

9110 **Hood, John Y.B.** Aquinas and the Jews. 1995, ⇒11/2,7334b. RJR 77 (1997) 133-134 *(Burrell, David)*.

9111 *Lecker, Michael; Thabit, Zayd B.* "A Jew with two sidelocks": Judaism and literacy in pre-Islamic Medina (Yathib). JNES 56 (1997) 259-273.

9112 <sup>E</sup>**Linder, Amnon** The Jews in the legal sources of the early Middle Ages. Detroit, MICH 1997, Wayne State University Press 717 pp. 0-8143-2403-7.

9113 **Saenz-Badillos, Ángel; Targarona Borras, Judit** Los judíos de Sefarad ante la Biblia. 1996, ⇒12,8580. MEAH.H 46 (1997) 180-181 *(Ferre, Lola)*.

9114 *Signer, Michael A.* Do Jews read the "letter"?: reflections on the sign ('wt) in medieval Jewish biblical exegesis. Bibl.Interp. 28: 1997, ⇒77. <sup>F</sup>Sanders J., 613-624.

9115 *Simon, Uriel* Peshat exegesis of biblical historiography: historicism, dogmatism, and medievalism. 1997, ⇒34. <sup>M</sup>Greenberg M., 171*-203* **H**.

9116 **Simonsohn, Shlomo** The Jews in Sicily, 1: 383-1300. Studia post-biblica 48/3; A Documentary History of the Jews in Italy 12: Lei 1997, Brill lxxxii; 598 pp. 90-04-10977-3.

9117 <sup>E</sup>**Ulmer, Rivka** Pesiqta Rabbati: a synoptic edition of Pesiqta Rabbati based upon all extant manuscripts and the editio princeps. SFSHJ 155: Atlanta, GA 1997, Scholars liv; 617 pp. $120. 0-7885-0362-6.

9118 **Veltri, Giuseppe** Magie und Halakha: Ansätze zu einem empirischen Wissenschaftsbegriff im spätantiken und frühmittelalterlichen Judentum. TSAJ 62: Tü 1997, Mohr xiii; 370 pp. DM178. 3-16-146671-3 [RB 105,317].

## к7.3 Magistri Judaismi mediaevalis

9119 *Charlap, Luba* Ibn Ezra's method in explaining unusual words in the bible. HUCA 68 (1997) 51*-61* **H**.

9120 *Lazarus-Yafeh, Hlava* Was Maimonides influenced by Al-Ghazzali?. 1997, ⇒34. <sup>M</sup>Greenberg M., 163*-169* **H**.

9121 <sup>ET</sup>**Niclós, José-Vicente** Šem Ṭob Ibn Šaprut, 'La piedra de toque' *(Eben bohan)*: una obra de controversia judeo-cristiana. BHBib 16: M 1997, Consejo Superior de Investigaciones Científicas iv; 474 pp. Introd... al libro I. 84-00-07664-8 [RB 105,315].

9122 *Nolan, Simon* Moses Maimonides and the eternity of the world debate. MillSt 40 (1997) 73-86.

9123 <sup>T</sup>**Rosner, Fred** Moses Maimonides' treatise on resurrection. Northvale, NJ 1997, Jason Aronson xv; 126 pp. Bibl. 0-7657-5954-3.

9124   *Sáenz-Bedillos, Ángel* Hermeneutik, Messianismus und Eschatologie bei MAIMONIDES. ᵀ*Romor, Renate M.; Sánchez de Murillo, José*: Edith Stein Jahrbuch 3 (1997) 74-85.
9125   *Woolf, Jeffrey R.* MAIMONIDES revised: the case of the Sefer Miṣwot Gadol. HThR 90 (1997) 175-203.


κ7.4  *Qabbalâ, Zohar, Merkabā*—Jewish mysticism

9126   **Besserman, Perle** The Shambhala guide to kabbalah and Jewish mysticism. Ill. *Besserman, Zoë Trigère*: Boston 1997, Shambhala xiii; (2) 160 pp. 1-57062-215-9.
9127   **Chasin, Esther Gordon** Mitzvot as spiritual practices: a Jewish guidebook for the soul. Northvale, NJ 1997, Jason Aronson xxi; 145 pp. 0-7657-5961-6.
9128   Der Chassidismus. 1996, ⇒12,8593. ᴿFrRu 4/1 (1997) 49-50 *(Bothe, Bernd)*.
9129   ᴱ**Dan, Joseph** The christian kabbalah: Jewish mystical books & their christian interpreters. CM 1997, Harvard College Library 231 pp. Symposium together with the catalogue of an exhibition at the Houghton Library, Harvard University 12 March - 26 April 1996. 0-914630-19-9.
9130   **De Léon-Jones, Karen Silvia** Giordano BRUNO and the kabbalah: prophets, magicians, and rabbis. Yale studies in hermeneutics: NHv 1997, Yale University Press ix; 273 pp. Bibl. $37.50. 0-300-06807-7.
9131   **Drosnin, Michael** O código da Bíblia. Lisboa 1997, Gradiva [Did(L) 28,219s—*Dos Santos Vaz, Armindo*] [⇒1135; 2091].
9132   **Fishbane, Michael** The kiss of God: spiritual and mystical death in Judaism. 1994, ⇒11/2,7431. ᴿHR 37 (1997) 172-174 *(Mendes-Flohr, Paul)*.
9133   *Gerhardsson, Birger* Hugo ODEBERG and his vision "Christ and scripture". 1997, ⇒92. ᶠSTUHLMACHER P., 112-125.
9134   *Goldberg, Arnold Pereq Re'uyot Yehezqe'el*: eine formanalytische Untersuchung. Mystik. TSAJ 61: 1997, ⇒128. 93-147.
9135   **Green, Arthur** Keter: the crown of God in early Jewish mysticism. Princeton, NJ 1997, Princeton University Press xv; 226 pp. Bibl. 0-691-04372-8.
9136   **Kamenetz, Rodger** Stalking Elijah: adventures with today's Jewish mystical masters. SF 1997, Harper SF xi; 370 pp. 0-06-064231-9.
9137   **Kuyt, Annelies** The 'descent' to the chariot... the Yeridah in Hekhalot literature. TSAJ 45: 1995, ⇒11/2,7443; 12,8599. ᴿSal. 59 (1997) 350-351 *(Vicent, R.)*.
9138   **Maier, Johann** La cabbala: introduzione. Testi classici spiegazione: Bo 1997, EDB 512 pp. L59.000. 88-10-40796-2 [RivBib 45,506].
9139   *Matt, Daniel C.* Varieties of mystical nothingness: Jewish, christian and Buddhist. StPhilo 9 (1997) 316-331.
9140   *Muñoz León, Domingo* La mística judía. BiFe 23 (1997) 324-341.
9141   Mysticism, kabbalah and hasidism [bibliography]. QS 67 (1997) 452-464.
9142   *Niclós, Josep-Vicent* Misticismo y filosofía judía en la edad media: una cita de 'los capítulos de Rabbí Eliezer' en MAIMONIDES y en Shem Tob Ibn ŠAPRUT. Sum. 74. RCatT 22 (1997) 57-74.

9143 **Umbach, Rolf** Vom Flug der Fische: die Bibel kabbalistisch gelesen. Neuk 1995, Christliche 304 pp. DM36. 3-7673-7504-4. RThLZ 122 (1997) 27-28 *(Beyse, Karl-Martin)*.

### κ7.5 Judaismus saec. 14-18

9144 *Bodian, Miriam* Biblical Hebrews and the rhetoric of republicanism: seventeenth-century Portuguese Jews on the Jewish community. AJSR 22 (1997) 199-221.
9145 **Stow, Kenneth** The Jews in Rome, 2: 1551-1557. Studia postbiblica 48; A Documentary History of the Jews in Italy 12: Lei 1997, Brill 413-951 pp. 90-04-10806-8.

### κ7.7 Hasidismus et Judaismus saeculi XIX

9146 *Bartolini, Elena* Narrazione e salvezza nelle storie chassidiche. Sette e Religioni 7/1 (1997) 48-56.
9147 **Bechtholdt, Hans-Joachim** Die jüdische Bibelkritik im 19. Jahrhundert. 1995, ⇒11/2,k288b; 12,11021. RThLZ 122 (1997) 123-124 *(Feist, Udo)*.
9148 **Gurary, Natan (Guraryeh)** Chasidism: its development, theology, and practice. Northvale, NJ 1997, Jason Aronson ix; 192 pp. 0-7657-5960-8.
9149 Judah ben Samuel Hεε-Hαsιd: Sefer Chasidim: the book of the pious. Northvale, NJ 1997, Jason Aronson xxxvi; 409 pp. 1-56821-920-2.
        Mysticism... Hasidism [bibliography] ⇒9141.
9150 **Nadler, Allan** The faith of the mithnagdim: rabbinic responses to hasidic rapture. Johns Hopkins Jewish Studies: Baltimore, MD 1997, Johns Hopkins xi; (2) 254 pp. Bibl. 0-8018-5560-8.
9151 **Rapoport-Albert, Ada** Hasidism reappraised. 1996, ⇒12,8624. RJJS 48/1 (1997) 175-178 *(Krassen, Miles)*.

### κ7.8 Judaismus contemporaneus

9152 *Aleksejeva, Tatjana* Zur Geschichte der Juden in Kurland und Semgallen. Jud. 53 (1997) 215-227.
9153 *Ben Chorin, Schalom* Die Bedeutung der hebräischen Bibel für das Judentum. Edith Stein Jahrbuch 3 (1997) 30-36.
9154 **Ben-Chorin, Schalom** La fede ebraica: lineamenti di una teologia dell'ebraismo sulla base del credo di Maimonide. ELoewy, Margherita: Opuscula 76: Genova 1997, Il melangolo 293 pp. 88-7018-325-4.
9155 *Bensimon, Doris* Die Juden Nordafrikas in Frankreich: dreissig Jahre später. Jud. 53 (1997) 135-142.
9156 *Comeau, Geneviève* Le Judaïsme dans le monde moderne: l'exemple du Conservative Judaism. RSR 85 (1997) 199-224.
9157 *Danow, David K.* Epiphany and apocalypse in holocaust writing: Aharon Appelfeld. RL 29/2 (1997) 61-74.
9158 *Domhardt, Yvonne* Auswahlbibliographie von Werken mit juedisch-judaistischer Thematik, die im Jahre 1996 in Schweizer

Verlagen erschienen sind bzw. durch Inhalt oder Verfasser/in die Schweiz betreffen, sowie bei der Redaktion eingegangene Beiträge von Mitgliedern der SGJF/SSEJ. Bulletin der Schweizerischen Gesellschaft für Judaistische Forschung 6 (1997) 51-59.

9159  *Dribins, Leo* Juden in der ersten lettischen Republik;
9160  *Erlanger, Simon* Zionismus heute. Jud. 53 (1997) 242-252/34-45.
9161  *Fackenheim, Emil L.* Zwei Briefe aus Jerusalem. 1997, ⇒25. ᶠFRIEDLANDER A., 55-59.
9162  *Feigmanis, Aleksandrs* Zur Geschichte der Juden in Livland;
9163  *Ferrero, Shaul Dominique* Der Zionismus und die Schweiz: Eidgenössische Behörden und zionistische Aktivitäten: ein wenig herzliches Verhältsnis. Jud. 53 (1997) 228-241/15-33.
9164  *Greenberg, Gershon* Der Holocaust und die Juden Amerikas: die Konzepte der Misrahi während des Zweiten Weltkrieges. 1997, ⇒25. ᶠFRIEDLANDER A., 61-80.
9165  *Hayoun, Maurice-Ruben* Einige Beobachtungen über die aktuelle Entwicklung des französischen Judentums. Jud. 53 (1997) 164-167.
9166  **Hayoun, Maurice-Ruben** La liturgia ebraica. ᵀ*Vogelmann, Vanna Lucattini*: Schulim Vogelmann 66: F 1997, La Giuntina 145 pp. Pref. *Joseph Levi*. Bibl. 88-8057-052-8.
9167  *Henrix, Hans Hermann* Morgendämmerung—die Stunde von Zweifel und Hoffnung: Erwägungen eines Christen zu Heil und Erlösung. 1997, ⇒25. ᶠFRIEDLANDER A., 81-92.
9168  *Janner, Sara* Friedrich HEMAN und die Anfänge des Zionismus in Basel: "Oh, wenn ich Missionar sein könnte, möchte ich Missionar des Zionismus sein";
9169  *Kaufmann, Uri* Bibliographie zur Geschichte der Juden in Frankreich nach 1945;
9170  Auswahlbibliographie zur Geschichte der zionistischen Bewegung 1897-1948. Jud. 53 (1997) 84-96/168-169/122-126.
9171  **Krabbe, Dieter** Freuet euch mit Jerusalem: jüdisches Leben, Denken und Gedenken: eine Einführung. Mü 1995, Claudius 286 pp. ᴿFrRu 4/1 (1997) 53-56 *(Rapp, Gertrud)*.
9172  *Lange, Dierk* Das hebräische Erbe der Yoruba, I. ZDMG 147 (1997) 77-136.
9173  *Lawee, Eric* The path to felicity: teachings and tensions in Even SHETIYYAH of Abraham Ben Judah, disciple of Hasdai CRESCAS. MS 59 (1997) 183-223.
9174  *Leitane, Iveta* Bibliographie zur Geschichte der Juden in Lettland;
9175  *Leitane, Iveta* Jakob GORDIN: die jüdische Moderne?: zum 50. Todesjahr eines jüdischen Philosophen aus Daugavpils. Jud. 53 (1997) 268-269/253-267.
9176  *Levinson, Pnina Navè* Altes und Neues in der Liturgie von Jüdinnen. Entschluss 52/9-10 (1997) 13-15;
9177  Gedanken zur jüdischen Kontinuität. 1997, ⇒25. ᶠFRIEDLANDER A., 119-126.
9178  ᴱ**Magonet, Jonathan** Seder hat-tefillôt: das jüdische Gebetbuch, 1: Gebete für Schabbat, Wochentage und Pilgerfeste; 2: Gebete für die Hohen Feiertage. Gü 1997, Gü 623+736 pp. 3-579-02216-4.
9179  *Magonet, Jonathan* Einige theologische Überlegungen zur Hebräischen Bibel. 1997, ⇒25. ᶠFRIEDLANDER A., 127-139.
9180  *Marten-Finnis, Susanne* Der Bund: wie weit darf Anpassung gehen?: ein pressegeschichtlicher Abriss 1897-1906;

9181 *Minczeles, Henri* 1897: Die Entstehung des jüdischen Sozialismus: der Bund. Jud. 53 (1997) 57-83/46-56.
9182 *Mosès, Stéphane* Franz ROSENZWEIGS Einstellungen zum Zionismus. Jud. 53 (1997) 8-14.
9183 *Nahon, Gérard* Jüdische Studien in Frankreich 1976-1996. Jud. 53 (1997) 143-163.
9184 ᴱ**Neusner, Jacob** Faith renewed: the Judaic affirmation beyond the holocaust. Judaism transcends catastrophe: God, torah, and Israel beyond the holocaust, 1. Macon, GA 1997, Mercer University Press x; 196 pp. 0-86554-460-3 [JSOT 75,127].
9185 **Newman, Louis E.** Covenantal responsibility in a modern context: recent work in Jewish ethics. Sum. 185. JRE 25/1 (1997) 185-210.
9186 *Petitdemange, Guy* LEVINAS phénoménologie et Judaïsme. RSR 85 (1997) 225-247.
9187 **Roth, Sol** The Jewish idea of culture. Hoboken 1997, KTAV xviii; 174 pp. $23. 0-88125-543-2 [ThD 45,89—Heiser, W. Charles].
9188 *Schreiner, Stefan* "Das Studium der Schrift ist die grösste Mizwa": Anmerkungen zum Beitrag des Wilner GAON zur Bibelwissenschaft. Jud. 53 (1997) 204-214.
9189 *Seim, Jürgen* Klage und Antwort: ein poetischer Gesprächsversuch zwischen Paul CELAN und Johannes BOBROWSKI. 1997, ⇒25. ᶠFRIEDLANDER A., 199-209.
9190 *Steindler Moscati, Gabriella* Gli scrittori ebrei d'origine irachena e la loro fortuna in Israele. Henoch 19/3 (1997) 373-377.
9191 **Wachs, Sharona R.** American Jewish liturgies: a bibliography of American Jewish liturgy from the establishment of the press in the colonies through 1925. Introd. *Goldman, Karla; Friedland, Eric L.*: BJud 14: Cincinnati 1997, Hebrew Union College ix; 221 pp. 0-87820-912-3.
9192 *Wohlmuth, Josef* Jüdische Hermeneutik. JBTh 12 (1997) 193-220.

### к8 *Philosemitismus*—Judeo-Christian relations

9193 *Angelini, Giuseppe* Cristiani ed ebrei equivoci di un difficile "dialogo". Teol(Br) 22 (1997) 199-206.
9194 Arbeitsgemeinschaft christlicher Kirchen Nürnberg: zur Erneuerung des Verhältnisses von Christen und Juden. Eine Handreichung der Theologischen Kommission der AcK Nürnberg an alle, die zu predigen oder im Raum der Kirche zu reden haben. FrRu 4/1 (1997) 25-30.
9195 *Bammel, Ernst* GREGOR der Große und die Juden < 1991 >;
9196 Heidentum und Judentum in Rom nach einer christlichen Darstellung des fünften Jahrhunderts < 1994 >;
9197 Die Zeugen des Christentums < 1990 >. Judaica et Paulina. WUNT 91: 1997, ⇒109. 87-95/77-86/96-106.
9198 *Blanchetiere, François* Comment le même est-il devenu l'autre?: ou comment Juifs et Nazaréens se sont-ils séparés?. RevSR 71 (1997) 9-32.
9199 **Boccara, Elia** Il peso della memoria: una lettura ebraica del Nuovo Testamento. 1994, ⇒10,4031… 12,4174. ᴿAmicizia Ebraico-Cristiana 32 (1997) 146-148 *(Martini, Luciano)*.

9200  *Boshoff, Piet B.* Die "aposunagogos" se invloed op die geskrifte van die Nuwe Testament volgens Walter Schmithals. HTS 53 (1997) 599-608.

9201  *Carleton Paget, James* Anti-Judaism and early christian identity. ZAC 1 (1997) 195-225.

9202  *Cerbelaud, Dominique* Thèmes de la polémique chrétienne contre le Judaïsme au IIe siècle. RSPhTh 81 (1997) 193-218.

9203  **Chilton, Bruce; Neusner, Jacob** Judaism in the NT. 1996, ⇒12,3867. ᴿJRH 21 (1997) 348-349 *(Lieu, Judith)*; CBQ 59 (1997) 764-765 *(McLaren, James S.)*;

9204  Trading places: the intersecting histories of Judaism and christianity. Trading places sourcebook. Cleveland 1997, Pilgrim ix; 293 pp. $17. 0-8298-1154-0 [ThD 44,356—Heiser, W. Charles].

9205  **Cohn-Sherbok, Dan** The crucified Jew: twenty centuries of christian anti-Semitism. GR 1997, Eerdmans 258 pp. $18. 0-8028-4311-5. ᴿScrB 27/2 (1997) 78-79 *(Cheetham, David)*.

9206  *Collins, John J.* Jewish monotheism and christian theology. Aspects of monotheism. 1997, ⇒339. ᴱShanks, H., 81-105.

9207  Comité épiscopal français pour les relations avec le judaisme: lire l'Ancien Testament: contribution à une lecture catholique de l'Ancien Testament pour permettre le dialogue entre juifs et chrétiens. Documents des Églises: P 1997, Cerf 44 pp. FF29. 2-204-05898-X [ETR 73,306].

9208  *Czajkowski, Michal* Judaizm w optyce nowotestamentowej [NT view of Judaism]. 1997, ⇒52. ᶠŁACH J., 95-101 P.

9209  Early christianity in connection with Judaism [bibliography]. QS 67 (1997) 417-422.

9210  *Ehrlich, Ernst Ludwig* Leonhard Ragaz und das Judentum. 1997, ⇒25. ᶠFriedlander A., 47-53.

9211  *Felle, Antonio Enrico* Echi della polemica antigiudaica nella documentazione epigrafica cristiana occidentale: un primo approccio. Sum. 5. ASEs 14/1 (1997) 207-219.

9212  *Foschepoth, Josef* Christen und Juden nach dem Holocaust. FrRu 4/1 (1997) 32-40.

9213  *Freedman, David Noel* Reader response: an essay on Jewish christianity. Divine Commitment 1. 1997 <1969>, ⇒124. 241-248.

9214  *Friedmann, Friedrich Georg* Als Jude in Deutschland. IKaZ 26 (1997) 182-192.

9215  *Fry, Helen* The Russian Orthodox Church and Judaism. ET 108 (1997) 367-368.

9216  *Gargano, Guido-Innocenzo* Le relazioni ebraico-cristiane come fondamento e motivazione dell'ecumenismo. Amicizia Ebraico-Cristiana 32 (1997) 99-103.

9217  ᴱ**Gargano, Innocenzo** Jerushalaim: 'i nostri piedi stanno alle tue porte, Gerusalemme'. Koinonia 4: Verucchio 1997, Pazzini 136 pp. Atti del XVII Colloquio ebraico cristiano di Camaldoli (27 nov-1 dic 1996). 88-85124-50-X.

9218  **Goldmann, Manuel** 'Die große ökumenische Frage...': zur Strukturverschiedenheit christlicher und jüdischer Tradition und ihrer Relevanz für die Begegnung der Kirche mit Israel. Neuk 1997, Neuk xii; 455 pp. [FrRu 4,297s—Mayer, Reinhold].

9219  **Harvey, Graham** The true Israel: uses of the names Jew, Hebrew and Israel in ancient Jewish and early Christian literature. AGJU 35: 1996, ⇒12,8659. ᴿJThS 48 (1997) 620-1 *(Brewer, D. Instone)*.

9220 *Heither, Theresia* Juden und Christen: Anregungen des ORIGENES zum Dialog. ThQ 177 (1997) 15-25.

9221 ᴱHenze, Dagmar, (*al.*), Antijudaismus im Neuen Testament?: Grundlagen für die Arbeit mit biblischen Texten. KT 149: Gü 1997, Kaiser 175 pp. DM24.80. 3-579-05149-0 [NThAR 1997,291].

9222 *Hirschberg, Peter* Probleme und Chancen bei der Rezeption des Themas Judentum in den Gemeinden. Christen und Juden. 1997, ⇒212. ᴱKraus, W., 95-106.

9223 *Kampling, Rainer* Antijudaismus von Anfang an?: zur Diskussion um den neutestamentlichen Ursprung des christlichen Antijudaismus. rhs 40 (1997) 110-120.

9224 **Keith, Graham** Hated without cause: a survey of anti-semitism. Foreword *Goldsmith, Martin*: Carlisle 1997, Paternoster xii; 301 pp. 0-85364-783-6 [RTL 29,127].

9225 *Kelley, Shawn* Aesthetic fascism: HEIDEGGER, anti-semitism, and the quest for Christian origins. Semeia 77 (1997) 195-225.

9226 *Kirn, Hans-Martin* Antijudaismus und spätmittelalterliche Bußfrömmigkeit: die Predigten des Franziskaners BERNHARDIN von Busti (um 1450-1513). ZKG 108 (1997) 147-175.

9227 *Klappert, Bertold* Der Midrasch aus Theresienstadt und das Testament Leo BAECKs: einige Erwägungen zu DIESES VOLK: jüdische Existenz. 1997, ⇒25. ᶠFRIEDLANDER A., 93-104.

9228 *Körtner, Ulrich* Il guideocristianesismo. Conc(I) 33/3 (1997) 78-87 (D33,333-339).

ᴱKraus, W. Christen und Juden ⇒212.

9229 *Kraus, Wolfgang* Christologie ohne Antijudaismus?: ein Überblick über die Diskussion. Christen und Juden. 1997, ⇒212. ᴱKraus, W., 21-48.

9230 **Krauss, Samuel** The Jewish-Christian controversy from the earliest times to 1789, 1: History. ᴱHorbury, William: TSAJ 56: 1996, ⇒12,8668. ᴿJJS 48/1 (1997) 163-165 (*Lasker, Daniel J.*).

9231 *Kula, Marcin* Z ostrożnym optymizmem. CoTh 67/2 (1997) 9-26 P.

9232 *Küng, Hans* Erfahrungen mit dem Judentum. 1997, ⇒25. ᶠFRIEDLANDER A., 105-111.

9233 *Lanne, Emmanuel* Notes sur la situation d'Israël par rapport aux schismes dans l'église chrétienne < 1954 >;

9234 Le schisme en Israël < 1953 >. Tradition. BEThL 129: 1997, ⇒142. 667-683/659-666.

9235 **Logister, Wiel** Een dramatische breuk: de plaats van Israël in de eerste eeuwen van het christendom. Verkenning en Bezinning 12: Kampen 1997, Kok 91 pp. *f*20. ᴿITBT 5/5 (1997) 21-23 *(Brouwer, Rinse Reeling)*.

9236 ᴱMarguerat, Daniel Le déchirement: Juifs et chrétiens au premier siècle. MoBi 32: 1996, ⇒12,192. ᴿNRTh 119 (1997) 260-261 *(Luciani, D.)*; RHPhR 77 (1997) 243 *(Prigent, P.)*; REJ 156 (1997) 199-204 *(Mimouni, Simon C.)*.

9237 **Martin, Vincent** A house divided: the parting of the ways between synagogue and church. 1995, ⇒11/2,7680. FrRu 4 (1997) 293-295 *(Zimmermann, Heidy)*.

9238 **Mayer, Reinhold** Zeit ist's: zur Erneuerung des Christseins durch Israel-Erfahrung. 1996, ⇒12,8683. ᴿFrRu 4/1 (1997) 59-61 *(Mußner, Franz)*.

9239 *Metz, Johann Baptist* Athen versus Jerusalem?: was das Christentum dem europäischen Geist schuldig geblieben ist. 1997, ⇒25. F FRIEDLANDER A., 149-152.

9240 *Mildenberger, Friedrich* Das Gesetz als Voraussetzung des Evangeliums: dogmatische und ethische Folgen eines lutherischen Theologumenons. Christen und Juden. 1997, ⇒212. E Kraus, W., 49-66.

9241 *Mimouni, Simon C.* La "Birkat Ha-Minim": une prière juive contre les Judéo-Chrétiens (1). RevSR 71 (1997) 275-298.

9242 *Mopsik, Charles* Nouvelles approches du Judaïsme et vieilles controverses. ASSR 100 (1997) 32-45.

9243 *Moritzen, Niels-Peter* Die Judenmission als Problem im Verhältnis zwischen Christen und Juden. Christen und Juden. 1997, ⇒212. E Kraus, W., 89-93.

9244 *Mosis, Rudolf* Nachbemerkungen: zum Beitrag von Erich ZENGER: eine neue "Einleitung in das Alte Testament", vor der man warnen muß? [⇒9296];

9245 Eine neue "Einleitung in das Alte Testament" und das christlich-jüdische Gespräch. TThZ 106 (1997) 316-319/232-240.

9246 **Much, Theodor** Judentum, wie es wirklich ist: die bedeutendsten Prinzipien und Traditionen: die verschiedenen Strömungen: die häufigsten Antijudaismen. W 1997, Kremayr & S 191 pp. 3-218-00635-X.

9247 *Müller, Stefanie* Die Darstellung religiöser Strömungen in den Evangelien;

9248 Erklärungen zu nichtbiblischen Quellen. Antijudaismus im NT. KT 149: 1997, ⇒9221. E Henze, D., 50-52/167-175.

9249 *Neuhaus, David M.* L'idéologie judéo-chrétienne et le dialogue Juifs-Chrétiens. RSR 85 (1997) 249-276.

9250 **Neusner, Jacob; Chilton, Bruce** The intellectual foundations of christian and Jewish discourse; the philosophy of religious argument. L 1997, Routledge xvi; 184 pp. £14. 0-415-15399-9 [RRT 1998/1,91].

9251 **Nicholls, William** Christian antisemitism: a history of hate. 1993, ⇒9,11055. R SR 26 (1997) 506-508 *(Davies, Alan)*.

9252 **O'Hare, Padraic** The enduring covenant: the education of christians and the end of antisemitism. Valley Forge, PA 1997, Trinity xi; 195 pp. $17. 1-563-38186-9.

9253 *Otranto, Giorgio* La polemica antigiudaica da BARNABA a GIUSTINO. Sum. 3. ASEs 14/1 (1997) 55-82.

9254 *Pawlikowski, John T.* Christian-Jewish bonding and the liturgy of Holy Week. New Theology Review 10/1 (1997) 100-106.

9255 *Pesce, Mauro* Antigiudaismo nel Nuovo Testamento e nella sua utilizzazione: riflessioni metodologiche. Sum. 3. ASEs 14/1 (1997) 11-38.

9256 *Pilch, John J.* Are there Jews and christians in the bible?. HTS 53 (1997) 119-125 [ZID 23,443].

9257 E **Poulain, Gaston; Dujardin, Jean** Lire l'Ancien Testament: réflexion du comité episcopal pour les relations avec le judaïsme. DC 94 (1997) 626-635.

9258 **Ragacs, Ursula** "Mit Zaum und Zügel muss man ihr Ungestüm bändigen": Ps 32,9: ein Beitrag zur christlichen Hebraistik und antijüdischen Polemik im Mittelalter. JudUm 65: Fra 1997, Lang 202 pp. 3-631-31916-9.

9259 *Raguse, Hartmut* Im Gespräch: christlicher Judenhass: Identitätsbildung auf Kosten der "Anderen". Jud. 53 (1997) 170-182.

9260 *Ratzinger, Kard. Joseph* Der Dialog der Religionen und das jüdisch-christliche Verhältnis. IKaZ 26 (1997) 419-429.

9261 *Rendtorff, Rolf* Ist Christologie ein Thema zwischen Christen und Juden?. 1997, ⇒25. [F]FRIEDLANDER A., 165-177.

9262 *Roloff, Jürgen* Die Predigt über Texte der Passionsgeschichte und der Antijudaismus;

9263 Ein weiterer Schritt auf einem schwierigen Weg: die Studie "Christen und Juden II" der EKD. Christen und Juden. 1997, ⇒212. [E]Kraus, W., 107-118/7-20.

*Saldhana, A.* Gal 6:16: the "Israel of God" ⇒6610.

9264 *Sauter, Gerhard* Rechenschaft über die Hoffnung im Vertrauen auf Gottes Treue: zur Selbstprüfung der Kirche im Blick auf Israel. BZNW 89: 1997, ⇒33. [F]GRAESSER E., 293-320.

9265 *Schäfer, Peter* Die Manetho-Fragmente bei JOSEPHUS und die Anfänge des antiken 'Antisemitismus'. Collecting fragments. 1997, ⇒294. [E]Most, G., 186-206.

**Schäfer, P.** Judeophobia: attitudes towards the Jews in the ancient world ⇒9023.

9266 *Schindler Alexander M.* Die Beziehungen zwischen Katholiken und Juden aus der amerikanischen Perspektive. 1997, ⇒25. [F]FRIEDLANDER A., 179-184.

9267 *Schottroff, Luise* Zur historischen Einordnung der neutestamentlichen Texte. Antijudaismus im NT. KT 149: 1997, ⇒9221. [E]Henze, D., 20-25.

9268 **Schreckenberg, Heinz** Die christlichen Adversus-Judaeos-Texte. 1991-1995, 3 vols. ⇒10,10145; 11/2,7718. [R]ZKTh 119 (1997) 107-108 *(Oberforcher, Robert)*; ThR 62 (1997) 117-119 *(Ohst, Martin)*;

9269 Die christlichen Adversus-Judaeos-Texte... (13.-20. Jh.). EHS.T 497: 1994, ⇒10,10145. [R]Sal. 59/1 (1997) 154-155 *(Vicent, R.)*; JSSt 44 (1997) 422-423 *(Efroymson, David P.)* [⇒9271];

9270 Die Juden in der Kunst Europas. 1996, ⇒12,8701. [R]BiLi 70 (1997) 245-246 *(Schubert, Kurt)*;

9271 Die christlichen Adversus-Judaeos-Texte... (13.-20. Jh.). EHS.T 335: Fra [3]1997, Lang 739 pp. Bibliographische Nachträge. 3-631-31665-8. [R]JQR 88 (1997) 82-84 *(Limor, Ora)* [⇒9269];

9272 The Jews in christian art: an illustrated history. NY 1997, Continuum 400 pp. $120. 0-8264-0936-9 [ThD 44,86].

9273 *Schwöbel, Christoph* Gemeinsamkeiten entdecken—Spannungen aushalten: Bermerkungen zu einer theologischen Hermeneutik des christlich-jüdischen Dialogs. KuI 12/2 (1997) 173-177.

9274 *Seidel, Esther* Leo BAECK und die liberale jüdische Theologie. 1997, ⇒25. [F]FRIEDLANDER A., 185-198.

9275 *Setzer, Claudia* Jews, Jewish christians, and Judaizers in north Africa. 1997, ⇒82. [F]SCROGGS R., 185-200.

9276 **Simon, Marcel** Verus Israel: a study of the relations between christians and Jews in the Roman empire (135-425). Littman Library of Jewish Civilization: Oxf 1996, OUP xviii; 533 pp. 1-874774-27-7.

9277 *Simon, Marcel* The bible in the earliest controversies between Jews and christians. The Bible in Greek christian antiquity. 1997 <c.1984>, ⇒177. [ET]Blowers, P.M., 49-68.

9278 *Sölle, Dorothee* Gott war sehr klein in jener Zeit;
9279 *Stegemann, Ekkehard W.* Vom christlichen Umgang mit jüdischen heiligen Schriften;
9280 Das Verhältnis von Kirche und Israel als christliches Identitätsproblem;
9281 *Stöhr, Martin* "Die Freiheit wird überall sprechen können und ihre Sprache wird biblisch sein". 1997, ⇒25. FFRIEDLANDER A., 211-216/217-227/229-238/239-249.
9282 *Tábet, Miguel Ángel* El diálogo judeo-cristiano en las obras de diálogo y polémica de los escritores cristianos prenicenos de las diversas áreas del Mediterráneo. La Bíblia i el Mediterrani. 1997, ⇒385. EBorrell, d'Agustí, 375-393.
9283 **Taylor, Miriam S.** Anti-Judaism and early christian identity. StPB 46: 1995, ⇒11/2,7732; 12,8706. RJThS 48 (1997) 643-649 *(Kinzig, Wolfram)*; ChH 66 (1997) 304-305 *(Kaminsky, Joel S.)*; JQR 87 (1997) 380-382 *(Efroymson, David P.)*; SR 26 (1997) 235-236 *(Davies, Alan).*
9284 **Tomson, Peter J.** Als dit uit de hemel is... Jezus en de schrijvers van het Niuwe Testament in hun verhouding tot het jodendom. Zoetermeer 1997, Boekencentrum 414 pp. FB900/*f*45. 90-239-0621-7 [Streven 64,853].
9285 *Trott zu Solz, Heinrich von* Der Wüstenwanderer im Land der Morgenröte. 1997, ⇒25. FFRIEDLANDER A., 251-258.
9286 *Ulrich, Hans G.* Israels bleibende Erwählung und die christliche Gemeinde: systematisch-theologische Perspektiven;
9287 Ein Wort—und zwei Sprachen?: Überlegungen zur Praxis der Begegnung von Juden und Christen. Christen und Juden. 1997, ⇒212. EKraus, W., 171-191/67-88.
9288 *Vian, Giovanni M.* Le versioni greche della Scrittura nella polemica tra giudei e cristiani. ASEs 14 (1997) 39-54.
9289 **Voltaire** Juifs. Il manifesto dell'antisemitismo moderno a cura del padre della tolleranza. Volti e anime 2: Mi 1997, Gallone xlv; 81 pp. Commento di *Elena Loewenthal;* nota al testo di *Ulisse Jacomuzzi*. 88-8217-013-6.
9290 **Wahle, Hedwig** Juifs et chrétiens en dialogue: vivre d'un héritage commun. Trajectoires 5: Bru 1997, Lumen Vitae 208 pp. Préf. *Albert Guigui:* RSR 26 (1997) 518-519 *(Brodeur, Patrice).*
9291 **Wander, Bernd** Trennungsprozesse zwischen Frühem Christentum und Judentum im 1. Jahrhundert n.Chr. TANZ 16: 1994, ⇒11/2,7747; 12,8712. RRHPhR 77 (1997) 244-245 *(Grappe, Ch.)*; FolOr 33 (1997) 224-227 *(Zangenberg, Jürgen).*
9292 **Wilson, Stephen G.** Related strangers: Jews and christians 70-170 CE. 1995, ⇒11/2,7752; 12,8714. RJThS 48 (1997) 214-216 *(Horbury, William)*; JEarlyC 5/1 (1997) 135-137 *(Horner, Timothy J.)*; JSJ 28 (1997) 362-363 *(Hogeterp, Albert)*; JJS 48 (1997) 373-374 *(Pearce, Sarah)*; ChH 66 (1997) 778-779 *(King, Noel Q.)*; CBQ 59 (1997) 598-599 *(Saldarini, Anthony J.)*; JBL 116 (1997) 555-557 *(Sanders, Jack T.).*
9293 **Yavetz, Zvi** Judenfeindschaft in der Antike: die Münchener Vorträge. Beck'sche Reihe 1222: Mü 1997, Beck 117 pp. DM17.80. 3-406-42022-2.
9294 *Zenger, Erich* Gemeinsame Bibel für Juden und Christen. Lebendige Welt. 1997, ⇒565. EZenger, E., 184-191;

9295 Judentum und Christentum—ein schwieriges Verhältnis. Das Evangelium. 1997, ⇒255. EMüller, H.-P., 47-61;
9296 Eine neue "Einleitung in das Alte Testament", vor der man warnen muß?. TThZ 106 (1997) 309-315 [⇒9244].

## XVI. Religiones parabiblicae

### M1.1 Gnosticismus classicus

9297 *Aland, Barbara* Die frühe Gnosis zwischen platonischem und christlichem Glauben: Kosmosfrömmigkeit versus Erlösungstheologie;
9298 *Alt, Karin* Glaube, Wahrheit, Liebe, Hoffnung bei PORPHYRIOS. BZNW 85: 1997, ⇒105. FWICKERT U., 1-24/25-43.
9299 *Aranda Pérez, Gonzalo* Corrientes gnósticas en el mundo mediterráneo. La Bíblia i el Mediterrani. 1997, ⇒385. EBorrell, d'Agustí, 227-246.
9300 **Casadio, Giovanni** Vie gnostiche all'immortalità. Letteratura cristiana antica: Brescia 1997, Morcelliana 109 pp. L20.000. 88-372-1648-3.
9301 *Figura, Michael* Erneute Herausforderungen der Kirche durch Gnosis und Gnostizismus. IKaZ 26 (1997) 543-550.
9302 **Förster, Niclas** Marcus Magus: Kult, Lehre und Gemeindeleben einer valentinianischen Gnostikergruppe: Sammlung der Quellen und Kommentar. Diss. Göttingen 1997, DLüdemann, G., 385 pp. [RTL 29,584].
9303 EGaeta, **Giancarlo** Valentino Tolomeo—Eracleone Teodoto: la passione di Sophia: ermeneutica gnostica dei Valentiniani. Genova 1997, Marietti 166 pp. [FilTeo 31,195s—Tugnoli, Claudio].
9304 *Gilhus, Ingvild Sælid* Family structures in gnostic religion. Constructing... families. 1997, ⇒295. EMoxnes, H., 235-249.
9305 *Gros, Miquel S.* Les tres oracions finals de l'*Exposició Valentiniana* (NH XI, 2). Sum. 55. RCatT 22 (1997) 47-55.
9306 *Hengel, Martin* Die Ursprünge der Gnosis und das Urchristentum. 1997, ⇒92. FSTUHLMACHER P., 190-223.
9307 *Hodges, Horace Jeffery* Gnostic liberation from astrological determinism: Hipparchan "Trepidation" and the breaking of fate. VigChr 51 (1997) 359-373.
9308 **Holladay, Carl R.** Orphica. Fragments from Hellenistic Jewish authors, 4. Atlanta 1997, Scholars x; 301 pp. $50. 0-7885-0743-7 [NTS 44,624].
9309 **Jonas, Hans** Von der Mythologie zur mystischen Philosophie. Gnosis und spätantiker Geist, 2/1.2. FRLANT 159: 1993, ⇒11/2,7777. RThLZ 122 (1997) 237-239 *(Schenke, Hans-Martin)*.
9310 *Le Boulluec, Alain* The bible in use among the marginally orthodox in the second and third centuries. The Bible in Greek christian antiquity. 1997 <c.1984>, ⇒177. ETBlowers, P.M., 197-216.
9311 *Logan, Alastair H.B.* The mystery of the five seals: Gnostic initiation reconsidered. VigChr 51 (1997) 188-206.
9312 **Löhr, Gebhard** Verherrlichung Gottes durch Philosophie: der hermetische Traktat II im Rahmen der antiken Philosophie- und Reli-

gionsgeschichte. WUNT 2/97: Tüb 1997, Mohr xi; 402 pp. 3-16-146616-0.

9313 **Lüdemann, Gerd; Janßen, Martina** Unterdrückte Gebete: gnostische Spiritualität im frühen Christentum. Stu 1997, Radius 128 pp. 3-87173-118-8.

9314 **Magris, Aldo** La logica del pensiero gnostico. Scienze delle religioni: Brescia 1997, Morcelliana 523 pp. Bibl. 88-372-1651-3.

9315 *Markschies, Christoph* Nochmals: Valentinus und die Gnostikoi: Beobachtungen zu IRENAEUS, Haer. I 30,15 und TERTULLIAN, Val. 4,2. VigChr 51 (1997) 179-187;

9316 Valentinian gnosticism: toward the anatomy of a school. Nag Hammadi... after fifty years. 1997, ⇒341. ᴱTurner, J.D., 401-438.

9317 *McGinn, Sheila E.* The 'Montanist' oracles and prophetic theology. StPatr 31. 1997, ⇒351. ᴱLivingstone, E.A., 128-135.

9318 *McGowan, Andrew* Valentinus poeta: Notes on θερος. VigChr 51 (1997) 158-178.

9319 *Pearson, Birger A.* EUSEBIUS and Gnosticism;

9320 Old Testament interpretation in gnostic literature;

9321 The problem of "Jewish Gnostic" literature. The emergence. 1997, ⇒154. 147-168/99-121/122-146.

9322 *Pokorný, Petr* Der Ursprung der Gnosis. Bibelauslegung. WUNT 100: 1997 <1967>, ⇒970. 155-167.

9323 *Rousselle, Aline* A propos d'articulations logiques dans les discours gnostiques. Apocrypha 8 (1997) 25-44.

9324 *Schmitz, Kenneth L.* Gnostizismus im Denken der deutschen Aufklärung. IKaZ 26 (1997) 525-542.

9325 *Scholer, David M.* Bibliographia Gnostica: Supplementum XXIV. NT 39 (1997) 248-285.

9326 *Scholten, Clemens* Probleme der Gnosisforschung: alte Fragen—neue Zugänge. IKaZ 26 (1997) 481-501.

9327 ᴱ**Segal, Robert A.** The allure of gnosticism: the gnostic experience and contemporary culture. 1995, ⇒11/2,447. ᴿJR 77 (1997) 673-674 *(Gallagher, Eugene V.)*.

9328 *Shoemaker, Stephen J.* Gnosis and paideia: education and heresy in late ancient Egypt. StPatr 31. 1997, ⇒351. ᴱLivingstone, E.A., 535-539.

9329 *Sudbrack, Josef* Gnosis, Gnostizismus in der Moderne. IKaZ 26 (1997) 551-562.

9330 *Trevett, Christine* Eschatological timetabling and the Montanist prophet MAXIMILLA. StPatr 31. 1997, ⇒351. ᴱLivingstone, E.A., 218-224.

### M1.5 Mani, *dualismus;* Mandaei

9331 *Albrile, Ezio* ALESSANDRO di Licopoli e il manecheismo: ontologia e soteriologia in un mito gnostico. Ter. 48 (1997) 737-759.

9332 *BeDuhn, Jason; Harrison, Geoffrey* The Tebessa codex: a Manichaean treatise on biblical exegesis and church order. Emerging from darkness. NHMS 43: 1997, ⇒9343. ᴱMirecki, P., 33-87.

9333 *Buckley, Jorunn J.* Professional fatigue: 'Hibil's lament' in the Mandaean *Book of John.* Muséon 110 (1997) 367-381.

9334 ᴱ**Cirillo, Luigi; Van Tongerloo, Alois** Atti del terzo congresso internationale di studi 'Manicheismo e Oriente cristiano Antico'.

Manichaean Studies 3: Turnhout 1997, Brepols 460 pp. Arcavacate di Rende, Amantea, 31.8-5.9 1993. 2-503-50602-X [OLZ 94,511ss—Taillieu, Dieter].

9335 *Clark, Larry* The Turkic Manichaean literature. Emerging from darkness. NHMS 43: 1997, ⇒9343. ᴱMirecki, P., 89-141.

9336 *Frankfurter, David* Apocalypses real and alleged in the Mani Codex. Sum. 60. Numen 44 (1997) 60-73.

9337 *Funk, Wolf-Peter* The reconstruction of the Manichaean Kephalaia;
9338 *Gardner, Iain* The Manichaean community at Kellis: a progress report;

9339 *Gulácsi, Zsuzsanna* Identifying the corpus of Manichaean art among the Turfan remains. Emerging from darkness. NHMS 43: 1997, ⇒9343. ᴱMirecki, P., 143-159/161-175/177-215.

9340 **Lieu, Samuel N.C.** Manichaeism in Mesopotamia and the Roman east. 1994, ⇒10,10190; 12,8764. ᴿJThS 48/1 (1997) 256-258 *(Lyman, J.R.)*.

9341 **Mayer, Gabriele** Und das Leben ist siegreich: ein Kommentar zu den Kapiteln 18-33 des Johannesbuches der Mandäer: der Traktat über Johannes den Täufer. Diss. Heidelberg 1996-97, ᴰBerger, K. [ThLZ 122,763].

9342 **Mikkelsen, Gunner B.** Bibliographia Manichaica: a comprehensive bibliography of Manichaeism through 1996. Fontium Manichaeorum Subsidia 1: Turnhout 1997, Brepols xlvi; 314 pp. EUR74. 2-503-50653-4 [VigChr 53,442s—Schipper, H.G.].

9343 ᴱ**Mirecki, Paul Allan; BeDuhn, Jason** Emerging from darkness: studies in the recovery of Manichaean sources. NHMS 43: Lei 1997, Brill x; 294 pp. 90-04-10760-6.

9344 *Mirecki, Paul; BeDuhn, Jason* Emerging from darkness: Manichaean studies at the end of the 20th century ⇒9343. vii-x.

9345 *Mirecki, Paul; Gardner, Iain; Alcock, Anthony* Magical spell, Manichaean letter ⇒9343. 1-32.

9346 **Polotsky, Hans-Jacob** Il manicheismo. 1996, ⇒12,8766. ᴿRSO 71 (1997) 275-277 *(Contini, Riccardo)*.

9347 *Reeves, John C.* Manichaean citations from the Prose Refutations of Ephrem ⇒9343. 217-288.

9348 *Schenke, Hans-Martin* Marginal notes on Manichaeism from an outsider ⇒9343. 289-294.

9349 **Sundermann, Werner** Der Sermon von der Seele: eine Lehrschrift des östlichen Manichäismus. Berliner Turfantexte 19: Turnhout 1997, Brepols 189 pp. Edition der parthischen und soghdischen Version mit einem Anhang von *Peter Zieme*: die türkischen Fragmente des "Sermons von der Seele". Bibl. 2-503-50635-6.

9350 **Villey, André** Psaumes des errant: écrits manichéens de Fayyūm. Sources Gnostiques et Manichéennes 4: 1994, ⇒10,10198... 12,8781. ᴿJThS 48 (1997) 251-255 *(Lieu, S.N.C.)*; BiOr 54 (1997) 490-491 *(Helderman, J.)*.

9351 **Wurst, Gregor** Die Bêma-Psalmen. 1996, ⇒12,8782. ᴿEnchoria 24 (1997/8) 186-193 *(Schenke, Hans-Martin)*.

## м2.1 Nag Hammadi, *generalia*

9352 **Cherix, Pierre** Concordance des textes de Nag Hammadi: le Codex VI. 1993, ⇒9,11168. ᴿJEarlyC 5 (1997) 120-121 *(Yamauchi, Edwin M.)*; OLZ 92 (1997) 661-673 *(Schenke, Hans-Martin)*;

9353 Concordance des textes de Nag Hammadi: le codex I. 1995, ⇒11/2,7838. ᴿOLZ 92 (1997) 661-673 *(Schenke, Hans-Martin)*.

9354 *Emmel, Stephen* Religious tradition, textual transmission, and the Nag Hammadi codices. Nag Hammadi... after fifty years. 1997, ⇒341. ᴱTurner, J.D., 34-43.

9355 *Filoramo, Giovanni* L'antigiudaismo nei testi gnostici di Nag Hammadi. Sum. 4. ASEs 14/1 (1997) 83-100.

9356 **Flory, Wayne S.** The gnostic concept of authority and the Nag Hammadi documents. 1995, ⇒11/2,7840. ᴿCBQ 59 (1997) 376-378 *(Timble, Janet).*

9357 **Khosroyev, Alexander** Die Bibliothek von Nag Hammadi. 1995, ⇒11/2,7841; 12,8785. ᴿJAC 40 (1997) 239-241 *(Schenke, Hans-Martin).*

9358 *Luttikhuizen, Gerard P.* The thought pattern of gnostic mythologizers and their use of biblical traditions. Nag Hammadi... after fifty years. 1997, ⇒341. ᴱTurner, J.D., 89-101.

9359 ᵀ**Lüdemann, Gerd; Janßen, Martina** Bibel der Häretiker: die gnostischen Schriften aus Nag Hammadi. Stu 1997, Radius. DM96. 3-87173-128-5 [ThLZ 124,138ss—Bethge, Hans-Gebhard].

9360 *McGuire, Anne; Rudisill, Kristen* Bibliography. Nag Hammadi... after fifty years. 1997, ⇒341. ᴱTurner, J.D., 499-531.

9361 *Painchaud, Louis; Janz, Timothy* La "Génération sans roi" et la réécriture polémique de quelques textes de Nag Hammadi. Apocrypha 8 (1997) 45-69;

9362 The "kingless generation" and the polemical rewriting of certain Nag Hammadi texts. Nag Hammadi... after fifty years. 1997, ⇒341. ᴱTurner, J.D., 439-460.

9363 ᴱ**Pearson, Birger A.** Nag Hammadi Codex VII. NHMS 30: 1996, ⇒12,8786. ᴿThLZ 122 (1997) 785-787 *(Lattke, Michael)*; JThS 48 (1997) 633-636 *(Wilson, R.McL.).*

9364 *Peretto, Elio* Maria: nome e ruolo nei codici della biblioteca gnostica di Nag Hammadi. 1997 <1989>, ⇒155. Saggi. 435-455.

9365 ᴱ**Piñero, Antonio; Montserrat Torrents, J.; García Bazán, F.** Textos gnósticos: Biblioteca de Nag-Hammadi I: tratados filosóficos y cosmológicos. Paradigmas 14: M 1997, Trotta 483 pp. 84-8164-138-3 [CDios 211—Gutiérrez, J.].

9366 *Piñero, Antonio; Montserrat, Josep* Sincretismo helénico-judío en los textos gnóstico-coptos: a propósito de la edición española de los escritos de Nag Hammadi. La Bíblia i el Mediterrani. 1997, ⇒385. ᴱBorrell, d'Agustí, 195-201.

9367 *Richter, Siegfried* Exegetisch-literarkritische Untersuchungen von Herakleidespsalmen des koptisch-manichäischen Psalmenbuches. 1994, ⇒10,10193... 12,8788. ᴿOLZ 92 (1997) 321-325 *(Plisch, Uwe-Karsten).*

9368 *Robinson, James M.* Nag Hammadi: the first fifty years;

9369 *Schenke, Hans-Martin* The work of the Berliner Arbeitskreis: past, present, and future;

9370 *Yamauchi, Edwin M.* The issue of pre-christian gnosticism reviewed in the light of the Nag Hammadi texts. Nag Hammadi... after fifty years. 1997, ⇒341. ᴱTurner, J.D., 3-33/62-71/72-88.

ᴍ2.2 *Evangelium etc. Thomae*—The Gospel of Thomas

9371 *Asgeirsson, Jon Ma.* Arguments and audience(s) in the gospel of Thomas, 1. SBL.SPS 36 (1997) 47-85.

9372 *Baarda, Tjitze* "Vader-Zoon-Heilige Geest": Logion 44 van "Thomas". NedThT 51 (1997) 13-30.

9373 *Bernard, Philippe* Un passage perdu des Acta Thomae latins conservé dans une anaphore mérovingienne. RBen 107 (1997) 24-39.

9374 *Callahan, Allen* "No rhyme or reason": the hidden logia of the gospel of Thomas. HThR 90 (1997) 411-426.

9375 *Cameron, Ron* Myth and history in the gospel of Thomas. Sum. rés. 193. Apocrypha 8 (1997) 193-205.

9376 **DeConick, April D.** Seek to see Him: ascent & vision mysticism in the gospel of Thomas. SVigChr 33: 1996, ⇒12,8792. ᴿJEarlyC 5 (1997) 583-584 *(Bingham, D. Jeffrey)*; ThLZ 122 (1997) 456-457 *(Fieger, Michael)*.

9377 L'évangile de Thomas. Mazamet 1997, Babel 78 pp. FF65. 2-909264-40-8 [ETR 73,307].

*Hartin, P.* The poor in... the gospel of Thomas ⇒6841.

9378 *Helderman, Jan* Die Herrenworte über das Brautgemach im Thomasevangelium und im Dialog des Erlösers. NT.S 89: 1997, ⇒7. ᶠBAARDA T.,69-88.

9379 **Hock, Ronald F.** The infancy gospels of James and Thomas. Scholars Bible 2: Santa Rosa, CA 1996, Polebridge 168 pp. $18. 0-944344-47-X. ᴿNT 39 (1997) 299-300 *(Elliott, J.K.)*.

9380 *Johnson, Steven R.* The gospel of Thomas 76:3 and canonical parallels: three segments in the tradition history of the saying. Nag Hammadi... after fifty years. 1997, ⇒341. ᴱTurner, J.D., 308-326 [Mt 6,19-20; Lk 12,33; Jn 6,27].

9381 ᵀOlgiati, Gaspard L'évangile selon Thomas: paroles de Jésus. Écrits apocryphes chrétiens: P 1997, Babel 78 pp. FF65. 2-909264-40-8 [BCLF 602,2260].

9382 *Peretto, Elio* Loghia del Signore e vangelo di Tommaso. 1997 <1976>, ⇒155. Saggi, 77-113.

9383 *Poirier, Paul-Hubert* The writings ascribed to Thomas and the Thomas tradition. Nag Hammadi... after fifty years. 1997, ⇒341. ᴱTurner, J.D., 295-307.

9384 ᵀ*Poirier, Paul-Hubert; Tissot, Yves* Actes de Thomas. Ecrits apocryphes chrétiens, 1. 1997, ⇒8641. ᴱBovon, F., 1321-1470 [BuBbgB 24,21].

9385 *Robbins, Vernon K.* Rhetorical composition and sources in the gospel of Thomas. SBL.SPS 36 (1997) 86-114.

9386 *Sellew, Philip* Death, the body, and the world in the gospel of Thomas. StPatr 31. 1997, ⇒351. ᴱLivingstone, E.A., 530-534;

9387 The gospel of Thomas: prospects for future research. Nag Hammadi... after fifty years. 1997, ⇒341. ᴱTurner, J.D., 327-346.

9388 *Sevrin, Jean-Marie* L'interprétation de l'évangile selon Thomas, entre tradition et rédaction. Nag Hammadi... after fifty years. 1997, ⇒341. ᴱTurner, J.D., 347-360.

*Siegert, Folker* Analyses rhétoriques... Actes de Thomas ⇒8717.

9389 **Trevijano Etchevarria, Ramón** Estudios sobre el evangelio de Tomás. Fuentes Patrísticas—Estudios 2: M 1997, Ciudad Nueva 452 pp. 84-89651-27-2. Salm. 44 (1997) 407-412 *(Aranda Pérez, Gonzalo)*.

9390 *Trevijano Etcheverría, Ramón* La antropología del evangelio de Tomás. 1997, ⇒76. ᶠRUIZ DE LA PENA J., 209-229.

9391 *Tubach, Jürgen* Der Apostel Thomas in China: die Herkunft einer Tradition. ZKG 108 (1997) 58-74.

9392   *Uro, Risto* Asceticism and anti-familial language in the gospel of Thomas. Constructing... families. 1997, ⇒295. ᴱMoxnes, H., 216-234.

9393   **Valantasis, Richard** The gospel of Thomas. New Testament Readings: L 1997, Routledge xvii; 221 pp. £13. 0-415-11621-X.

9394   *Van Eck, Ernest* Die Tomasevangelie: inleidende opmerkings. HTS 53 (1997) 623-649.

9395   ᵀ*Voicu, Sever J.* Histoire de l'enfance de Jésus. Ecrits apocryphes chrétiens, 1. 1997, ⇒8641. ᴱBovon, F., 189-204 [BuBbgB 24,17].

## M2.3  *Singula scripta*—Various titles [K3.4]

9396   **Barry, Catherine** La sagesse de Jésus-Christ (BG,3; NH III,4). 1993, ⇒11/2,7876b. ᴿJNES 56 (1997) 122-123 *(Wilfong, T.G.)*.

9397   ᴱᵀ**Bethge, Hans-Gebhard** Der Brief des Petrus an Philippus: ein neutestamentliches Apokryphhon aus dem Fund von Nag Hammadi. TU 141: B 1997, Akademie xxii; 248 pp. Diss. Humboldt 1985. DM220. 3-05-002494-1 [ThIK 18/2,132].

9398   *Buckley, Jorunn J.; Good, Deirdre J.* Sacramental language and verbs of generating, creating, and begetting in the *Gospel of Philip*. JEarlyC 5/1 (1997) 1-19.

9399   **Charron, Régine** Concordance des textes de Nag Hammadi: (*a*) le Codex VII. 1992, ⇒8,a849... 12,8783. ᴿOLZ 92 (1997) 661-673 *(Schenke, Hans-Martin)*;

9400   (*b*) le Codex III. 1995, ⇒11/2,7836. ᴿOLZ 92 (1997) 661-673 *(Schenke, Hans-Martin)*.

9401   *Filoramo, Giovanni* L'antigiudaismo nei testi gnostici di Nag Hammadi. ASEs 14 (1997) 83-100.

9402   *Kasser, Rodolphe* L'Eksêgêsis etbe tpsukhê (NH II,6): histoire de l'âme puis exégèse parénétique de ce mythe gnostique. Apocrypha 8 (1997) 71-80.

9403   *La Porta, Sergio* Sophia-Mêtêr: reconstructing a gnostic myth. Nag Hammadi... after fifty years. 1997, ⇒341. ᴱTurner, J.D., 188-207.

9404   *Montserrat-Torrents, J.* The social and cultural setting of the Coptic gnostic library. StPatr 31. 1997, ⇒351. ᴱLivingstone, E.A., 464-481.

9405   *Pearson, Birger A.* The CGL edition of Nag Hammadi codex VII. Nag Hammadi...after 50 years. 1997, ⇒341. ᴱTurner, J.D., 44-61.

9406   **Piñero, A; Monserrat Torrents, J.; García Bazán, F.** Tratados filosóficos cosmológicos. Textos gnósticos. Biblioteca de Nag Hammadi 1: M 1997, Trotta 483 pp. [Proyección 44,163].

9407   ᵀᴱ**Plisch, Uwe-Karsten** Die Auslegung der Erkenntnis. TU 142: 1996, ⇒12,8798. ᴿThLZ 122 (1997) 788-789 *(Rudolph, Kurt)*; OLZ 92 (1997) 538-541 *(Bethge, Hans-Gebhard)*.

9408   ᴱᵀ**Schenke, Hans-Martin** Das Philippus-Evangelium (Nag-Hammadi-Codex II,3). TU 143: B 1997, Akademie xxv; 571 pp. 3-05-003199-9.

9409   ᴱ**Waldstein, Michael; Wisse, Frederik** The Apocryphon of John. NHMS 33: 1995, ⇒11/2,7865; 12,8800. ᴿCBQ 59 (1997) 179-180 *(Wilfong, Terry)*; ThLZ 122 (1997) 1099-1100 *(Strutwolf, Holger)*.

## M3.5 Religiones mundi cum christianismo comparatae

EBoespflug, F. Le comparatisme en histoire des religions ⇒346.

9410 Bonanate, Ugo Il Dio degli altri: il difficile universalismo di Bibbia e Corano. Nuova cultura 56: T 1997, Bollati Boringhieri 181 pp. L40.000. 88-339-1015-6.

9411 Chlackalackal, Saju The word in the world: a study on the use of the scriptures of world religions in christian worship. Bangalore 1995, Vidya Vanam xvii; 110 pp. Rs60/$9. Tanima 5 (1997) 67-68 *(Mundadan, Mathias A.)*.

9412 Dupuis, Jacques Vers une théologie chrétienne du pluralisme religieux. T*Parachini, Olindo*: CFi 200: P 1997, Cerf 655 pp. FF290. 2-204-05759-2 [RB 105,475];

9413 Toward a christian theology of religious pluralism. Maryknoll, NY 1997, Orbis xiv; 433 pp. Bibl. 1-57075-125-0.

9414 *Favaro, Gaetano* Sunyata buddhista e kenosi cristologica: confronto dialogico tra il pensiero di Masao ABE e la teologia di Hans Urs von BALTHASAR. RTLu 2/1 (1997) 119-138.

9415 Ganeri, Anita Unter dem weiten Regenbogen: biblische Geschichten und Mythen aus den Religionen der Welt. Stu 1997, Katholisches Bibelwerk 96 pp. [Diak. 29,354—Bee-Schroedter, Heike].

9416 Gauchet, Marcel The disenchantment of the world: a political history of religion. T*Burge, Oscar*. Foreword *Taylor, Charles*: New French thought: Princeton, NJ 1997, Princeton University Press xv; 228 pp. Bibl. 0-691-04406-6.

9417 *Geffré, Claude* Le comparatisme en théologie des religions;

9418 *Gira, Dennis* Comparaisons trompeuses et points de rencontre entre bouddhisme et christianisme. Le comparatisme. 1997, ⇒346. EBoespflug, F., 415-431/405-414.

9419 Hanh, Thich Nhat Living Buddha, living Christ. Putnam 1995, NY 208 pp. $20. 1-57322-018-3. RBudCS 17 (1997) 250-255 *(Aitken, Robert)*;

9420 Bouddha vivant, Christ vivant. 1996, ⇒12,8808. RPro Dialogo 95/2 (1997) 272-273 *(Give, Bernard de)*.

9421 *Kwok, Pui L.* Discovering the bible in the non-biblical world: the journey continues. JAAT 2/1 (1997) 64-77.

9422 *Lambert, Jean* Le comparatisme dumézilien est-il transposable dans le domaine sémitique?. Le comparatisme. 1997, ⇒346. EBoespflug, F., 109-121;

9423 L'originalité du christianisme dans le système des monothéismes. BCPE 49/4 (1997) 5-28.

9424 Leong, Kenneth S. The Zen teachings of Jesus. 1995, ⇒11/2,9141. RBudCS 17 (1997) 246-250 *(Ingwersen, Sonya Anne)*.

9425 Magliola, Robert R. On deconstructing life-worlds: Buddhism, Christianity, culture. AAR, Cultural Criticism 3: Atlanta, GA 1997, AAR xxiii; 202 pp. 0-7885-0296-4.

9426 *Mitescu, Adriana* The pattern of the religious disputes: Judaism, Christianity and Islam from Spain to Caucasus. Ter. 48 (1997) 313-372.

9427 EMüller, Hans Peter Das Evangelium und die Weltreligionen: theologische und philosophische Herausforderungen. Stu 1997, Kohlhammer 120 pp. 3-17-014983-0.

9428 ENeusner, Jacob God. Pilgrim library of world religions 1: Cleveland 1997, Pilgrim xxxvii; 132 pp. $15. 0-8298-1177-X [ThD 45,172—Heiser, W. Charles].

9429 Newbigin, Lesslie L'evangelo in una società pluralistica. EGirardet, Maria Sbaffi: PBT 37: 1995. RGr. 78 (1997) 173-174 (Wolanin, Adam).

9430 Oguibénine, Boris Un thème indo-européen dans le Rgveda et dans un jataka bouddhique. Le comparatisme. 1997, ⇒346. EBoespflug, F., 259-277.

9431 Smith, Wilfred Cantwell What is scripture?: a comparative approach. 1993, ⇒9,11418... 12,8810. RCBQ 58 (1996) 136-138 (Smith-Christopher, Daniel L.).

9432 Sonô Fazion, G., (al.), Dharma e vangelo: due progetti di salvezza a confronto. 1996, ⇒12,8811. RPro Dialogo 95/2 (1997) 265-267 (Fitzgerald, Michael L.).

9433 Spineto, Natale Le comparatisme de Mircea ELIADE;

9434 Stroumsa, Guy G. Comparatisme et philologie: Richard SIMON et la naissance de l'orientalisme. Le comparatisme. 1997, ⇒346. EBoespflug, F., 93-108/47-62.

9435 Werblowsky, R.J. Zvi Magie, Mystik, Messianismus: vergleichende Studien zur Religionsgeschichte des Judentums und des Christentums. Hildesheim 1997, Olms 272 pp. DM68 [GuL 71,153—Sudbrack, Josef].

### m3.6  Sectae—Cults

9436 Abraham, William J. Confessing Christ: a quest for renewal in contemporary christianity. Interp. 51 (1997) 117-129.

9437 Aurenche, Christian Tokombéré au pays des grands prêtres: religions africaines et évangile peuvent-ils inventer l'avenir?. P 1996, L'Atelier 141 pp. RSources 23 (1997) 140-143 (Fontaine, Michel).

9438 Boring, M. Eugene Disciples and the bible: a history of Disciples biblical interpretation in North America. St. Louis 1997, Chalice 502 pp. [HR 37,475—Baird, William].

9439 Heyrman, Christine Leigh Southern Cross: the beginnings of the Bible Belt. NY 1997, Knopf xi; 336 pp. Faith & Mission 15/1 (1997) 92-93 (Harper, Keith).

9440 Jacobsen, Douglas Re-forming a sloppy center by and with grace. Interp. 51 (1997) 159-174.

9441 McElveen, Floyd The Mormon illusion: what the bible says about the Latter-Day Saints. GR ²1997, Kregel 223 pp. [Faith & Mission 14,125].

9442 Tilley, Maureen A. The bible in christian north Africa: the Donatist world. Diss. DClark, Elizabeth: Mp 1997, Fortress viii; 232 pp. Bibl. $32. 0-8006-2880-2.

### m3.8  Mythologia

9443 EBillington, Sandra; Green, Miranda The concept of the goddess. 1996, ⇒12,213. Antiquity 71 (1997) 246, 248 (Bailey, Douglas W.).

9444 Bottéro, Jean; Herrenschmidt, Clarisse; Vernant, Jean-Pierre L'Orient ancien et nous: l'écriture, la raison, les dieux. 1996, ⇒12,8830. RBiOr 54 (1997) 619-622 *(Koch, Heidemarie)*.

9445 Kubiak, Zygmunt Mitologia Greków i Rzymian. Wsz 1997, Świat Książki 575 pp. [CoTh 69/4,203—Warzecha, Julian].

9446 EOlmo Lete, Gregorio del Semitas occidentales. 1995. ⇒11/2,474. REstB 55 (1997) 428-429 *(Ibarzábal, S.)*.

9447 *Williams, Michael A.* Negative theologies and demiurgical myths in late antiquity. SBL.SPS 36 (1997) 20-46.

## M4.0 Religio romana; Mithraismus

9448 Arnaldi, Adelina Ricerche storico-epigrafiche sul culto di 'Neptunus' nell'Italia romana. Studi Pubblicati dall'Istituto Italiano per la Storia Antica 64: R 1997, Istituto Italiano per la Storia Antica viii; 295 pp. Bibl.

9449 ECancik, Hubert; Rüpke, Jörg Römische Reichsreligion und Provinzialreligion. Tü 1997, Mohr x; 318 pp. DM138. 3-16-146760-4.

9450 Clerc, Jean-Benoit Homines magici: étude sur la sorcellerie et la magie dans la société romaine imperiale. EHS.G 673: Fra 1995, Lang 355 pp. FF280/EUR42.69. 3-906754-05-7. RHZ 264/3 (1997) 172-174 *(Kakridi, Christina)*.

9451 De Filippis Cappai, Chiara Imago mortis: l'uomo romano e la morte. Studi latini 26: N 1997, Loffredo 181 pp. Bibl. 88-8096-547-6.

9452 Fless, Friederike Opferdiener und Kultmusiker auf stadtrömischen Reliefs. Mainz 1995, Von Zabern. RMes. 32 (1997) 393-396 *(Conti, M.C.)*; AJA 101 (1997) 612-613 *(Rose, C. Brian)*; Numen 44/1 (1997) 95-96 *(Rüpke, Jörg)*.

9453 *Gordon, Richard* The veil of power. Paul and empire. 1997, ⇒204. EHorsley, R.A., 126-137.

9454 Graf, Fritz Gottesnähe und Schadenzauber: die Magie in der griechisch-römischen Antike. Mü 1996, Beck 273 pp. [HR 39,203—Betz, Hans Dieter].

9455 Klauck, Hans-Josef Stadt- und Hausreligion, Mysterienkulte, Volksglaube. 1995, ⇒11/2,8396; 12,8845. RTThZ 106 (1997) 79-80 *(Reiser, M.)*; BZ 41 (1997) 253-255 *(Schenk, Wolfgang)*; ETR 72 (1997) 471-473 *(Siegert, Folker)*; EThL 73 (1997) 192-194 *(Verheyden, J.)*; JBL 116 (1997) 357-359 *(Betz, Hans Dieter)*.

9456 Mirón Pérez, María Dolores Mujeres, religión y poder: el culto imperial en el occidente mediterráneo. Feminae 14: Granada 1996, Universidad de Granada 376 pp. Diss. 84-338-2207-1 [Latomus 59,167s—Castillo, Carmen].

9457 Potter, David Prophets and emperors: human and divine authority from Augustus to Theodosius. 1994, ⇒11/2,a011. RInternational Journal of the Classical Tradition 4/1 (1997) 124-126 *(Liebeschuetz, Wolfgang)*.

9458 *Price, S.R.F.* Rituals and power. Paul and empire. 1997, ⇒204. EHorsley, R.A., 47-71.

9459 Ruggiero, Isabella I luoghi di culto. Vita e costumi dei Romani antichi 20: R 1997, Quasar 109 pp. Bibl. 88-7140-108-5.

9460  **Sauron, Gilles** Quis Deum?: l'expression plastique des idéologies politiques et religieuses à Rome à la fin de la république et au début du principat. BEFAR 285: 1994, ⇒10,10544. ᴿAJA 101 (1997) 185-7 *(Castriota, David)*; Latomus 56 (1997) 895-8 *(Perrin, Yves)*.

9461  **Schowalter, Daniel N.** The emperor and the gods. HDR 28: 1993, ⇒9,11677...11/2,8425. ᴿJEarlyC 5 (1997) 121-23 *(Calvert, K.R.)*.

9462  *Shaw, Brent D.* Ritual brotherhood in Roman and post-Roman societies. Tr. 52 (1997) 327-355.

9463  **Takács, Sarolta A.** Isis and Sarapis in the Roman world. 1995, ⇒11/2,8433; 12,8851. ᴿCBQ 59 (1997) 176-77 *(Wild, Robert A.)*.

9464  *Zanker, Paul* The power of images. Paul and empire. 1997, ⇒204. ᴱHorsley, R.A., 72-86.

9465  **Merkelbach, Reinhold** Mithras: ein persisch-römischer Mysterienkult. 1994, ⇒10,10568. ᴿBiOr 54 (1997) 738-739 *(Boeft, J. den)*.

м5.1 *Divinitates Graeciae*—Greek gods and goddesses

9466  ᴱ**Arslan, Ermanno A.; Tiradritti, Francesco** Iside: il mito, il mistero, la magia. Mi 1997, Electa 726 pp. Bibl. 88-435-5968-0.

9467  **Burkert, Walter** Homo necans: Interpretationen altgriechischer Opferriten und Mythen. RVV 32: B ²1997, De Gruyter xii; 378 pp. Bibl. 3-11-015099-9.

9468  **Calame, Claude** Mythe et histoire dans l'Antiquité grecque. 1996, ⇒12,8863. ᴿRHR 214 (1997) 481-485 *(Payen, Pascal)*.

9469  *Chaniotis, Angelos* Reinheit des Körpers—Reinheit des Sinnes in den griechischen Kultgesetzen;

9470  *Furley, William D.* Religiöse Schuld in attischen Gerichtsverfahren. Schuld. 1997, ⇒236. ᴱAssmann, J., 142-179/64-82.

9471  ᴱ**Hägg, Robin** Early Greek cult practice. 1988, ⇒5,792; 6,a841. ᴿGn. 69 (1997) 51-55 *(Thomas, Eberhard)*;

9472  Ancient Greek cult practice from the epigraphical evidence. 1994, ⇒11/2,8597. ᴿNumen 44 (1997) 346-347 *(Auffarth, Christoph)*.

9473  ᴱ**Hellström, Pontus; Alroth, Brita** Religion and power in the ancient Greek world. BOREAS 24: 1996, ⇒12,290. ᴿJHS 117 (1997) 222-3 *(Parker, Robert)*; AJA 101 (1997) 792-3 *(Aleshire, Sara B.)*.

9474  **Jesnick, Ilona Julia** The image of Orpheus in Roman mosaic: an exploration of the figure of Orpheus in Graeco-Roman art and culture with special reference to its expression in the medium of mosaic in late antiquity. BAR International 671: Oxf 1997, Archaeopress viii; 276 pp. Bibl. 0-86054-862-7.

9475  ᴱ**Lloyd, Alan B.** What is a god?: studies in the nature of Greek divinity. L 1997, Duckworth vii; 187 pp. 0-7156-2779-1.

9476  **Merkelbach, Reinhold** Isis regina—Zeus Sarapis: die griechisch-ägyptische Religion nach den Quellen dargestellt. 1995, ⇒11/2,8792; 12,9015. ᴿVigChr 51 (1997) 445-447 *(Boeft, J. den)*.

9477  **Motz, Lotte** The faces of the goddess. NY 1997, OUP vii; 280 pp. Bibl. 0-19-508967-7.

9478  **Pulleyn, Simon** Prayer in Greek religion. Oxford Classical Monographs: Oxf 1997, Clarendon xv; 245 pp. Bibl. $75. 0-19-815088-1.

9479  **Rakoczy, Thomas** Böser Blick, Macht des Auges und Neid der Götter: eine Untersuchung zur Kraft des Blickes in der griechischen

Literatur. Classica Monacensia 13: Tü 1996, Narr ix; 309 pp. [Gn. 71,719s—Fauth, Wolfgang].

9480 ESieveking, W. Plutarchus: de E apud Delphos: Pythici dialogi. Rev. *Gärtner, Hans*: BSGRT: Stu 1997, Teubner xi; 124 pp. 3-8154-1695-7.

9481 Thornton, Bruce S. Eros: the myth of ancient Greek sexuality. Boulder, CO 1997, Westview xvii; 282 pp. Bibl. 0-8133-3225-7.

9482 Van Straten, F.T. *Hierà kalá*: images of animal sacrifice in archaic and classical Greece. 1995, ⇒11/2,8508; 12,8885. RAt. 85 (1997) 639-643 *(De Maria, Sandro)*.

9483 TEVictor, Ulrich LUCIANUS Samosatensis: Alexandros oder der Lügenprophet. RGRW 132: Lei 1997, Brill viii; 180 pp. Bibl. 90-04-10792-4.

M5.2 *Philosophorum critica religionis*—Greek philosopher religion

9484 EBranham, Bracht; Goulet-Cazé, Marie-Odile The Cynics: the Cynic movement in antiquity and its legacy. Berkeley, CA 1997, University of California ix; 456 pp. 0-520-20449-2.

9485 *Brenk, Frederick* PLUTARCH, Judaism and christianity. Studies in PLATO and the Platonic tradition. EJoyal, M.: Aldershot 1997, Ashgat Essays presented to John Whittaker. 97-118 [AcBib 10,389].

9486 EKlauck, Hans-Josef PLUTARCHUS: moralphilosophische Schriften. Universal-Bibliothek 2976: Stu 1997, Reclam 256 pp. 3-15-002976-7.

9487 *Ludlam, Ivor* The God of Moses according to STRABO. 1997, Sum. vi. Tarbiz 66 (1997) 337-349 H.

M5.3 *Mysteria eleusinia; Hellenistica*—Mysteries; Hellenistic cults

9488 Alvar, J. Cristianismo primitivo y religiones mistéricas. Historia: M 1995, Cátedra 546 pp. RCDios 210 (1997) 637-9 *(Gutiérrez, J.)*.

9489 *Beatrice, Pier Franco* Hellénisme et christianisme aux premiers siecles de notre ère: parcours méthodologiques et bibliographiques. Kernos 10 (1997) 39-56;

9490 Das Orakel von Baalbek und die sogenannte Sibyllentheosophie. RQ 92 (1997) 177-189.

9491 Boardman, John The great god Pan: the survival of an image. Walter Neurath Memorial Lectures 29: L 1997, Thames & H 48 pp. 0-500-55030-1.

9492 *Bonnechère, Pierre* La πομπή sacrificielle des victimes humaines en Grèce ancienne. Sum. rés. 63. RREA 99/1-2 (1997) 63-89.

9493 *Brown, David; Linssen, Marc* BM 134701=1965-10-14,1 and the Hellenistic period eclipse ritual from Uruk. RA 91 (1997) 147-166.

9494 *Capelli, Piero* Le Menadi e le Sirene degli ebrei d'Egitto: nota a Oracula Sibyllina 5,55. Henoch 19/3 (1997) 341-348.

9495 Iacubovici-Boldisor, Constantin Die urchristlichen Mysterienkulte in Palästina, Kleinasien und Griechenland: quellenmässig wiedererkannt und rekonstruiert. Hochschulschriften 91: Müns 1997, Lit 304 pp. 3-8258-3213-9.

9496 **Klauck, Hans-Josef** Herrscher- und Kaiserkult, Philosophie, Gnosis. KStTh 9/2: 1996, ⇒12,8901. ᴿBZ 41 (1997) 253-255 *(Schenk, Wolfgang)*; TThZ 106 (1997) 79-80 *(Reiser, M.)*; ETR 72 (1997) 471-473 *(Siegert, Volker)*; EThL 73 (1997) 192-194 *(Verheyden, J.)*; ThPQ 145 (1997) 420-421 *(Niemand, Christoph)*.

9497 ᴱ**Marinatos, Nanno; Hägg, Robin** Greek sanctuaries. 1995, ⇒11/2,471. ᴿGn. 69 (1997) 578-580 *(Wirbelauer, Eckhard)*.

9498 **Pernot, Laurent** La rhétorique de l'éloge dans le monde gréco-romain. 1993, ⇒11/2,8579. ᴿOrpheus 18/1 (1997) 245-248 *(Greco, Giusy M.)*; Gn. 69 (1997) 307-310 *(Vallozza, Maddalena)*.

9499 **Pettazzoni, Raffaele** I misteri: saggio di una teoria storico-religiosa. Pres. *Sabbatucci, Darioby*: Biblioteca di Studi Religiosi 1: Cosenza 1997, Giordano 248 pp. Bibl. 88-86919-05-0.

9500 **Stroumsa, Guy G.** Hidden wisdom: esoteric traditions and the roots of christian mysticism. Lei 1996, Brill xxi; 195 pp. $71 [HR 38,389—McGinn, Bernard].

9501 ᵀᴱ**Vian, Francis** NONNOS de Panopolis: les dionysiaques: *(a)* tome V, chants XI-XIII. P 1995, Belles Lettres 280 pp. 2-251-00447-5. ᴿREA 99 (1997) 578-579 *(Cusset, Christophe)*;

9502 *(b)* Tome X, chants XXX-XXXII. P 1997, Belles Lettres 172 pp. 2-251-00457-2. REA 99 (1997) 579-580 *(Cusset, Christophe)*.

ᴍ6.0 **Religio canaanaea, syra; Religiones anatolicae**

9503 *Ackerman, Susan* The prayer of Nabonidus, Elijah on Mount Carmel, and the development of monotheism in Israel. BJSt 313: 1997, ⇒85. ᶠSɪʟʙᴇʀᴍᴀɴ L., 51-65 [1 Kgs 18; Dan 3,31-4,34].

9504 **Albertz, Rainer** A history of Israelite religion in the Old Testament period, 1: from the beginnings to the end of the monarchy. 1994, ⇒10,10690... 12,8926. ᴿBibl.Interp. 5 (1997) 279-281 *(Johnston, Philip)*; Interp. 51/1 (1997) 73-77 *(Lewis, Theodore J.)*; JAOS 117 (1997) 371-372 *(Smith, Mark S.)*;

9505 2: from the exile to the Maccabees. 1994, ⇒10,10690... 12,8927. Interp. 51 (1997) 73-77 *(Lewis, Theodore J.)*; CBQ 59 (1997) 103-105 *(Hoppe, Leslie J.)*;

9506 Religionsgeschichte Israels in alttestamentlicher Zeit, 2: vom Exil bis zu den Makkabäern. GAT 8: Gö ²1997 <1992>, Vandenhoeck & R vi; 376-726 pp. 3-525-51675-4.

9507 *Bammel, Ernst* 'αρχιερευς προψητευων. Judaica et Paulina. WUNT 91: 1997 <1954>, ⇒109. 133-139.

9508 *Becking, Bob* Assyrian evidence for iconic polytheism in ancient Israel?. The image. 1997, ⇒2073. ᴱVan der Toorn, K., 157-171.

9509 **Binger, Tilde** Asherah: goddesses in Ugarit, Israel and the Old Testament. JSOT.S 232; Copenhagen International Seminar 2: Shf 1997, Academic 190 pp. Bibl. £37.50/$62. 1-85075-637-6.

9510 *Bird, Phyllis A.* The end of the male cult prostitute: a literary-historical and sociological analysis of Hebrew *qadeš-qedešim*. Congress volume 1995. VT.S 66: 1997, ⇒323. ᴱEmerton, J.A., 37-80 [Dt 23,18; Job 36,14].

9511 *Bonnet, Corinne* Le culte d'Isis à Carthage: à propos de l'inscription funéraire punique CIS I, 6000 bis. AOAT 247: 1997, ⇒75. ᶠRoᴇʟʟɪɢ W., 43-56;

9512 De l'histoire des mentalités à l'histoire des religions: à propos de Leucothéa et de trois petits cochons. SEL 14 (1997) 91-104.

9513 *Braulik, Georg* Die Ablehnung der Göttin Aschera in Israel: war sie erst deuteronomistisch, diente sie der Unterdrückung der Frauen?. Studien zu Dt. SBAB 24: 1997 <1991>, ⇒117. 81-118 [Hos 4,18; 14,9].

9514 *Conti, Giovanni* Incantation de l'eau bénite et de l'encensoir et textes connexes. Mari 8 (1997) 253-272.

9515 **Cornelius, Izak** The iconography of the Canaanite gods Reshef and Ba'al. OBO 140: 1994, ⇒10,10699... 12,8931. [R]BArR 23/3 (1997) 46, 68-69 *(Hurowitz, Victor)*; OTEs 10 (1997) 345-348 *(Boshoff, W.S.)*.

9516 *Croatto, J. Severino* La crítica a los dioses en la Biblia: (a propósito de dos artículos de Revista Bíblica). RevBib 59/3 (1997) 181-9.

9517 *D'Agostino F.; Seminara, S.* Sulla continuità del mondo culturale della Siria settentrionale: la "Maš'artum" ad Ebla ed Emar. RA 91/1 (1997) 1-20.

9518 **Dearman, J. Andrew** Religion and culture in ancient Israel. 1992, ⇒8,b424...11,2,8655. [R]BZ 41 (1997) 105-107 *(Bohlen, Reinhold)*.

9519 *Demsky, Aaron* The name of the goddess of Ekron: a new reading. JANES 25 (1997) 1-5.

9520 *Dever, William G.* Folk religion in early Israel: did Yahweh have a consort?. Aspects of monotheism. 1997, ⇒339. [E]Shanks, H., 27-56.

9521 *Dietrich, Manfried* Die Parhedra im Pantheon von Emar: Miscellanea Emariana (I). UF 29 (1997) 115-122.

9522 *Dietrich, Manfried; Loretz, Oswald* Der Charakter der Göttin 'Anat 'nn und weitere Schreibfehler in KTU 1.96;

9523 Wohnorte Els nach Ugarit- und Bibeltexten: eine Studie zu ug. *ğr ll ‖ hr m'd* und he. *hr mw'd ‖ yrkty spwn* (KTU 1.2 I 20; Jes 14,13). UF 29 (1997) 151-160/123-149.

9524 *Dietrich, Manfried; Mayer, Walter* Das hurritische Pantheon von Ugarit. UF 29 (1997) 161-181.

9525 *Dijkstra, Meindert* Semitic worship at Serabit el-Khadim (Sinai). ZAH 10 (1997) 89-97.

9526 *Dirven, Lucinda* The author of De Dea Syria and his cultural heritage. Sum. 153. Numen 44 (1997) 153-179.

9527 **Doorly, William J.** The religion of Israel: a short history. NY 1997, Paulist vi; 206 pp. $17. 0-8091-3705-4 [BTB 27,120].

9528 [E]**Edelman, Diana Vikander** The triumph of Elohim. 1995, ⇒11/2,362; 12,8934. [R]VT 47 (1997) 393-400 *(Emerton, J.A.)*; BTB 27 (1997) 118 *(Burns, John Barclay)*.

9529 **Feldtkeller, Andreas** Im Reich der syrischen Göttin: eine religiös plurale Kultur als Umwelt des frühen Christentums. Studien zum Verstehen fremder Religionen 8: Gü 1994, Gü'er 333 pp. 3-579-01790-X. [R]ThLZ 122 (1997) 337-340 *(Markschies, Christoph)*.

9530 [E]**Fine, Steven** Sacred realm: the emergence of the synagogue in the ancient world. 1996, ⇒12,8937. [R]Worship 71/4 (1997) 376-380 *(Chiat, Marilyn J.)*.

9531 **Freedman, David Noel** History and eschatology: the nature of biblical religion and prophetic faith <1960>;

9532 KAUFMANN's *The religion of Israel* (review) <1962>;

9533 'Who is like thee among the gods?': the religion of early Israel <1987>;

9534  Yahweh of Samaria and his Asherah <1987>. Divine Commitment 1. 1997, ⇒124. 72-81/94-98/383-402/403-408.
9535  **Geller, Stephen A.** Sacred enigmas: literary religion in the Hebrew Bible. 1996. ᴿCritRR 10 (1997) 158-160 *(Wright, John W.)*.
9536  **Grätz, Sebastian** Der strafende Wettergott: Erwägungen zur Traditionsgeschichte des Abad-Fluchs im Alten Orient und im Alten Testament. Diss. Kiel 1997, ᴰ*Rüterswörden, U.*, 328 pp.
9537  *Guichard, Michaël* Présages fortuits à Mari (copies et ajouts à ARMT XXVI/1). Mari 8 (1997) 305-328;
9538  Zimrî-Lîm à Nagar. Mari 8 (1997) 329-337.
9539  *Gysens, Jacqueline Calzini* Dieux ancestraux et Baals syriens attestés à Rome. Orientalia Sacra. 1997, ⇒345. ᴱBellelli, G., 261-276.
9540  *Hadley, Judith M.* Chasing shadows?: the quest for the historical goddess. Congress volume 1995. VT.S 66: 1997, ⇒323. ᴱEmerton, J.A., 169-184 [Job 28];
9541  From goddess to literary construct: the transformation of Asherah into Ḥokmah. A feminist companion. 1997, ⇒180. ᴱBrenner, A., 360-399.
9542  ᴱ**Haider, Peter W.** Religionsgeschichte Syriens: von der Frühzeit bis zur Gegenwart. 1996, ⇒12,217. ᴿThLZ 122 (1997) 428-430 *(Hage, Wolfgang)*; StEL 14 (1997) 128-129 *(Niehr, Herbert)*.
9543  *Healey, John F.* Das Land ohne Wiederkehr: die Unterwelt im antiken Ugarit und im Alten Testament. ThQ 177 (1997) 94-104.
9544  *Husser, Jean-Marie* Shapash psychopompe et le pseudo hymne au soleil (KTU 1.6 vi 42-53). UF 29 (1997) 227-244.
9545  ᴱ**Janowski, Berndt** *(al.)*, Religionsgeschichtliche Beziehungen zwischen Kleinasien, Nordsyrien und dem Alten Testament. OBO 129: 1993, ⇒9,567; 10,10718. ᴿJAOS 117 (1997) 604-05 *(Singer, Itamar)*.
9546  *Jean-Marie, Marylou* À propos de certaines offrandes funéraires à Mari. Mari 8 (1997) 693-705.
9547  *Kaizer, T.* De Dea Syria et aliis diis deabusque: a study of the variety of appearances of God in Aramaic inscriptions and on sculptures from the Near East in the first three centuries AD, 1. OLoP 28 (1997) 147-166.
9548  *Kottsieper, Ingo* El—ferner oder naher Gott?: zur Bedeutung einer semitischen Gottheit in verschiedenen sozialen Kontexten im 1. Jtsd.v.Chr. Religion und Gesellschaft. AOAT 248: 1997, ⇒235. ᴱAlbertz, R., 25-74.
9549  *Levine, Baruch A.* The next phase in Jewish religion: the land of Israel as sacred space. 1997, ⇒34. ᴹGʀᴇᴇɴʙᴇʀɢ M., 245-257.
9550  *Masetti-Rouault, Maria Grazia* Adad ou Šamaš?: notes sur le culte local aux sources du Khabour, Xᵉ-IXᵉ siècles avant J.-C. Sum. 9. Sem. 47 (1997) 9-45.
9551  *Mayes, Andrew D.H.* Kuntilett ʿAjrud and the history of Israelite religion. Archaeology and biblical interpretation. 1997, ⇒268. ᴱBartlett, J.R., 51-66.
9552  *McCarter, P. Kyle* The religious reforms of Hezekiah and Josiah. Aspects of monotheism. 1997, ⇒339. ᴱShanks, H., 57-80.
9553  *Merlo, Paolo* Note critiche su alcune presunte iconografie della dea Ašera. SEL 14 (1997) 43-63.
9554  *Mettinger, Tryggve N.D.* Israelite aniconism: developments and origins. The image. 1997, ⇒2073. ᴱVan der Toorn, K., 173-204;

9555 The roots of aniconism: an Israelite phenomenon in comparative perspective. Congress volume 1995. VT.S 66: 1997, ⇒323. EEmerton, J.A., 219-233.

9556 *Müller, Hans-Peter* Sterbende auf auferstehende Vegetationsgötter?: eine Skizze. ThZ 53 (1997) 74-82;

9557 Unterweltsfahrt und Tod des Fruchtbarkeitsgottes. Religion und Gesellschaft. AOAT 248: 1997, ⇒235. EAlbertz, R., 1-13.

9558 **Niditch, Susan** Ancient Israelite religion. NY 1997, OUP 146 pp. $25. 0-19-509127-2 [ThD 44,375—Heiser, W. Charles].

9559 *Podella, Thomas* Nekromantie. ThQ 177 (1997) 121-133.

9560 **Pomponio, Francesco; Xella, Paolo** Les dieux d'Ebla: étude analytique des divinités éblaïtes à l'époque des archives royales du IIIe millénaire. AOAT 245: Müns 1997, Ugarit-Verlag 551 pp. DM116. 3-927120-46-4. RAfO 44-45 (1997) 276-277 *(Hirsch, H.)*.

9561 *Stolz, Fritz* Religionsgeschichte Israels. TRE 28. 1997, ⇒420. 585-603.

9562 **Theuer, Gabriele** Der Mondgott in den Religionen Syrien-Palästinas während der Spätbronze- und Eisenzeit unter besonderer Berücksichtigung von KTU 1.24. Diss. Tübingen 1997, DNiehr [BZ 42,318].

9563 **Tillich, P.** Bijbelse religie en de vraag naar het zijn. Comm., trans. *Schonewille, Fake; Woudenberg, Aad*: Paul Tillich Genootschap Nederland/België. Bolswaard 1997, Witte 76 pp. f15. 90-70365-84-7 [Coll. 28/1,112].

9564 **Trémouille, Marie-Claude** dHebat: une divinité syro-anatolienne. Eothen 7: F 1997, LoGisma 271 pp. [Mes. 33,377s—Jasink, A.].

9565 *Uehlinger, Christoph* Anthropomorphic cult statuary in Iron Age Palestine and the search for Yahweh's cult images. The image. 1997, ⇒2073. EVan der Toorn, K., 97-155.

9566 *Van der Toorn, Karel* Ein verborgenes Erbe: Totenkult im frühen Israel. ThQ 177 (1997) 105-120.

9567 **Weippert, Manfred** Jahwe und die anderen Götter: Studien zur Religionsgeschichte des antiken Israel in ihrem syrisch-palästinischen Kontext. FAT 18: Tü 1997, Mohr xiv; 281 pp. Bibl. DM228. 3-16-146592-X.

9568 *Wenning, Robert* Bemerkungen zur Gesellschaft und Religion der Nabatäer. Religion und Gesellschaft. AOAT 248: 1997, ⇒235. EAlbertz, R., 177-201.

9569 *Wenning, Robert; Merklein, Helmut* Die Götter in der Welt der Nabatäer. Petra antike Felsstadt. 1997, ⇒311. EWeber, T., 105-110.

9570 *Zayadine, Fawzi* Die Götter der Nabatäer. Petra und das Königreich. 1997, ⇒289. ELindner, M., 113-123.

9571 **Haas, Volkert** Geschichte der hethitischen Religion. HO 1/15: 1994, ⇒11/2,8621. RNumen 44/1 (1997) 74-90 *(Hutter, Manfred)*; BiOr 54 (1997) 411-416 *(Martino, Stefano de)*; WO 28 (1997) 209-214 *(Taracha, Piotr)*; JNES 56 (1997) 226-228 *(Hoffner, Harry A.)*; ZA 87 (1997) 281-286 *(Beckman, G.)*.
    **Trémouille, M.-C.** Hebat, une divinité syro-anatolienne ⇒9564.

## M6.5 Religio aegyptia

9572 **Abitz, Friedrich** Pharao als Gott in den Unterweltsbüchern des Neuen Reiches. OBO 146: 1995, ⇒11/2,8735. RDiscEg 37 (1997)

93-97 *(DuQuesne, Terence)*; BiOr 54 (1997) 646-648 *(Englund, Gertie)*.

9573 **Assmann, Jan** Egyptian solar religion in the New Kingdom. 1995, ⇒11/2,8736; 12,8991. JESHO 40 (1997) 299-300 *(Poo, Mu-chou)*.

9574 *Assmann, Jan* Eine liturgische Inszenierung des Totengerichts aus dem Mittleren Reich: altägyptische Vorstellungen von Schuld, Person und künftigem Leben. Schuld. 1997, ⇒236. ᴱAssmann, J., 27-63.

9575 *Baines, John* Temples as symbols, guarantors, and participants in Egyptian civilization. The temple in ancient Egypt. 1997, ⇒300. ᴱQuirke, S., 216-241.

9576 *Bauks, Michaela* Präfigurationen der hermopolitanischen Achtheit in den Sargtexten?. BN 88 (1997) 5-8.

9577 *Beinlich, Horst* Hieratische Fragmente des "Buches vom Fayum" und ein Nachtrag zu BF CARLSBERG. ZÄS 124/1 (1997) 1-22.

9578 **Bolshakov, Andrey O.** Man and his double in Egyptian ideology of the Old Kingdom. AAT 37: Wsb 1997, Harrassowitz 336 pp. 3-447-03892-6 [OLZ 93,619ss—Jánosi, Peter].

9579 **Bongioanni, Alessandro; Tosi, Mario** Spiritualità dell'Antico Egitto: i concetti di Akh, Ba e Ka. Homo Absconditus: Rimini 1997, Cerchio 193 pp. Pref. *Donadoni, Sergio*; Post. *Magris, Aldo*.

9580 *Bonnet, Charles; Valbelle, Dominique* The middle kingdom temple of Hathor at Serabit el-Khadim. The temple in ancient Egypt. 1997, ⇒300. ᴱQuirke, S., 82-89.

9581 **Bradshaw, Joseph** The night sky in Egyptian mythology. 85 Balfour Road, London N5 2HE 1997, privately printed 182 pp. 50 fig. £8. ᴿDiscEg 39 (1997) 139-141 *(Griffiths, J. Gwyn)*.

9582 *Bryan, Betsy M.* The statue program for the mortuary temple of Amenhotep III. The temple in ancient Egypt. 1997, ⇒300. ᴱQuirke, S., 57-81.

9583 ᵀᴱ**Burkard, Günter** Spätzeitliche Osiris-Liturgien im Corpus der Asasif-Papyri. AAT 31: Wsb 1995, Harrassowitz xi; 329 pp. Kommentar, formale und inhaltliche Analyse. 3-447-03715-6. ᴿBiOr 54 (1997) 346-349 *(Koemoth, Pierre P.)*; OLZ 92 (1997) 317-321 *(Jansen-Winkeln, Karl)*.

9584 *Cannuyer, Christian* Aton, nourrice dans le sein, succédané des maîtresses de la ménat. GöMisz 157 (1997) 11-14.

9585 ᵀᴱ**Cauville, Sylvie** Dendera: les chapelles osiriennes, 1: transcription et traduction, 2: commentaire, 3: index. Bibliothèque d'Etude 117-119: Cairo 1997, Institut français d'archéologie orientale 3 vols; 669 pp. [JARCE 36,170—Bianchi, Robert Steven].

9586 **Cauville, Sylvie** Le Zodiaque d'Osiris. Lv 1997, Peeters 81 pp. 90-6831-971-X.

9587 *Ciałowicz, Krzysztof M.* Le plus ancien témoignage de la tradition du heb-sed. FolOr 33 (1997) 39-48.

9588 *Cozi, Massimo* A propos des origines du culte atonien. GöMisz 156 (1997) 33-36.

9589 *Cruz-Uribe, Eugene* Atum, Shu, and the gods during the Amarna period. JSSEA 25 (1995) 15-22.

9590 **Depuydt, Leo** Civil calendar and lunar calendar in ancient Egypt. OLA 77: Lv 1997, Peeters xiv; 272 pp. FB2400. 90-6831-908-6.

9591 *Derchain, Philippe* La différence abolie: Dieu et Pharaon dans les scènes rituelles ptolémaïques. Selbstverständnis und Realität. ÄAT 36/1: 1997, ⇒394. <sup>E</sup>Gundlach, R., 225-232.

9592 **Dunand, Françoise; Zivie-Coche, Christiane** Dieux et hommes en Égypte 3000 av. J.-Chr.-395 apr. J.-C. 1991, ⇒8,b474. <sup>R</sup>CÉg 72 (1997) 67-70 *(Van Rinsveld, Bernard)*.

9593 *el-Aswad, el-Sayed* Archaic Egyptian cosmology. Anthr. 92 (1997) 69-81.

9594 *Favard-Meeks, Christine* The temple of Behbeit el-Hagara. The temple in ancient Egypt. 1997, ⇒300. <sup>E</sup>Quirke, S., 102-111.

9595 **Forman, Werner; Quirke, Stephen** Hieroglyphs and the afterlife in ancient Egypt. 1996, ⇒12,9000. <sup>R</sup>AJA 101 (1997) 406-407 *(Wilfong, Terry G.)*.

9596 Das Gericht des Osiris. WUB 5 (1997) 13.

9597 **Germer, Renate** Mummies: life after death in ancient Egypt. NY 1997, Prestel 141 pp. Bibl. 3-7913-1804-7.

9598 *Goedicke, Hans* Ancient Egyptian vision of eschatology. JSSEA 25 (1995) 38-45.

9599 *Görg, M.* Ptah in der Bibel. BN 86 (1997) 24-28.

9600 **Graindorge-Héreil, Catherine** Le dieu Sokar à Thèbes au Nouvel Empire. GOF.Ä 28/2: 1994, ⇒10,10755. <sup>R</sup>DiscEg 37 (1997) 99-109 *(Gimelli, Marilinda)*.

9601 **Haring, B.J.J.** Divine households: administrative and economic aspects of the New Kingdom memorial temples in western Thebes. Egyptologische Uitgaven 11: Lei 1997, Nederlands Historisch-Archaeologisch Instituut xxii; 485 pp. *f*110. 90-6258-212-5 [DiscEg 44,123ss—Warburton, David].

9602 **Herbin, François René** Le livre de parcourir l'éternité. OLA 58: 1994, ⇒10,12675; 12,10416. <sup>R</sup>BiOr 54 (1997) 652-658 *(Hoffmann, Friedhelm)*.

9603 <sup>T</sup>**Hornung, Erik** Die Unterweltsbücher der Ägypter. Z 1997, Artemis 528 pp. Eingeleitet, erläutert. Bibl. 3-7608-1061-6;

9604 Altägyptische Jenseitsbücher: ein einführender Überblick. Da 1997, Primus x; 181 pp. DM64. 3-89678-043-3.

9605 **Koch, Klaus** Geschichte der ägyptischen Religion. 1993, ⇒9,11967... 12,9010. <sup>R</sup>CBQ 58 (1996) 118-120 *(Jacobs, Paul F.)*.

9606 **Koemoth, Pierre** Osiris et les arbres. 1994, ⇒10,13405. <sup>R</sup>BiOr 54 (1997) 639-643 *(Pantalacci, L.)*.

9607 *Lacaze, Ginette* L'au-delà dans la religion égyptienne. BLE.S 4 (1997) 119-126.

9608 **Lapp, Günther** The Papyrus of Nu (BM EA 10477). Collab. *Schneider, T.*: Catalogue of Books of the Dead in the British Museum 1: L 1997, British Museum 93 pp. 0-7141-1902-4.

9609 *Leblanc, Christian* Quelques reflexions sur le programme iconographique et la fonction des temples de "millions d'années". The temple in ancient Egypt. 1997, ⇒300. <sup>E</sup>Quirke, S., 49-56.

9610 *Leprohon, R.J.* Gatekeepers of this and the other world. JSSEA 24 (1994) 77-91.

9611 **Lichtheim, Miriam** Moral values in ancient Egypt. OBO 155: Gö 1997, Vandenhoeck & R vii; 110 pp. FS38. 3-525-53791-3.

9612 **Meeks, Christine & Dimitri** La vie quotidienne des dieux égyptiens. P 1993, Hachette 364 pp. 16 pl. FF125. <sup>R</sup>CÉg 72 (1997) 292-294 *(Degardin, Jean-Claude)*.

9613    **Meeks, Dimitri; Favard-Meeks, Christine** Daily life of the Egyptian gods. $^T$*Goshgarian, G.M.*. Ithaca 1996, Cornell University Press vii (2) 249 pp. 22 pl. $45/$18. 0-8014-8248-8.

9614    **Munro, Irmtraut** Die Totenbuch-Handschriften der 18. Dynastie im Ägyptischen Museum Cairo. ÄA 54: 1994, 2 vols ⇒10,9219. $^R$OLZ 92 (1997) 313-317 *(Luft, Ulrich)*;

9615    Das Totenbuch des Jah-mes (pLouvre E. 11085) aus der frühen 18. Dynastie. Handschriften des Altägyptischen Totenbuches 1: Wsb 1995, Harrassowitz xiv; 21 pp.;

9616    Das Totenbuch-Papyrus des Hohenpriesters Pa-nedjem II (pLondon BM 10793/pCampbell). Handschriften des Altägyptischen Totenbuches 3: Wsb 1996, Harrassowitz xiv; 54 pp. Beitrag vom *Ursula Rößler-Köhler*: 33 pl. 33 Umschrift-Tafeln; DM168;

9617    Das Totenbuch des Nacht-Amun aus der Ramessidenzeit (pBerlin P. 3002). Handschriften des Altägyptischen Totenbuches 4: Wsb 1997, Harrassowitz xi; 41 pp. 29 pl. 36 Umschrift-Tafeln. DM158. 3-447-03951-5 [LASBF 48,566—Niccacci, Alviero].

9618    *Osing, Jürgen* Zur Dekoration der Säulen an Prozessionswegen des Amonre. MDAI.K 53 (1997) 227-232.

9619    *Pikaza, Xabier* El culto de Isis en el Oriente mediterráneo (Plutarco y Apuleyo). La Bíblia i el Mediterrani. 1997, ⇒385. $^E$Borrell, d'Agustí, 345-372.

9620    **Poo, Mu-Chou** Wine and wine offering in the religion of ancient Egypt. 1995, ⇒11/2,8799. $^R$RStT 16/1 (1997) 107-109 *(Smith, Richard C.)*.

9621    *Quaegebeur, Jan* Excavating the forgotten temple of Shenhur (Upper Egypt). The temple in ancient Egypt. 1997, ⇒300. $^E$Quirke, S., 159-167.

9622    **Quirke, Stephen** Ancient Egyptian religion. 1992, ⇒8,b501; 10,10773. CÉg 143 (1997) 65-67 *(Franco, Isabelle)*;

9623    Altägyptische Religion. 1996, ⇒12,9020. $^R$DiscEg 37 (1997) 111-117 *(Hermsen, Edmund)*.

9624    *Quirke, Stephen* Gods in the temple of the king: Anubis at Lahun. The temple in ancient Egypt. 1997, ⇒300. $^E$Quirke, S., 24-48.
        $^E$**Quirke, S.** The temple in ancient Egypt ⇒300.

9625    $^{TE}$**Rachet, Guy** Il libro dei morti degli antichi egizi: testo e raffigurazioni del papiro di Ani. CasM 1997, Piemme 251 pp. Bibl. 88-384-2887-5.

9626    *Redford, Donald B.* The monotheism of Akhenaten. Aspects of monotheism. 1997, ⇒339. $^E$Shanks, H., 11-26.

9627    **Roulin, Gilles** Le livre de la nuit. OBO 147/1-2: 1996, ⇒12,9022. $^R$ETR 72 (1997) 125-126 *(Smyth, Françoise)*; WO 28 (1997) 177-181 *(Quack, Joachim Friedrich)*.

9628    **Römer, Malte** Gottes- und Priesterherrschaft in Ägypten am Ende des Neuen Reiches. ÄAT 21: 1994, ⇒10,10774. $^R$BiOr 54 (1997) 633-635 *(Naguib, Saphinaz-Amal)*.

9629    *Satzinger, Helmut* Gott gibt dem König Leben: mit Anhängen über djˁnḫ und die Weihformel. ZÄS 124/2 (1997) 142-156.

9630    **Siliotti, Alberto** Egitto: templi, uomini e dei. Vercelli 1997, White Star 290 pp. Bibl. 88-8095-092-4.

9631    **Simonet, Jean-Luc** Le collège des dieux maîtres d'autel: nature et histoire d'une figure tardive de la religion égyptienne. Orientalia Monspeliensia 7: Montpellier 1994, Université Paul Valéry vi; 214 pp. ill. $^R$BiOr 54 (1997) 649-651 *(Derchain, Philippe)*.

9632 *Spieser, Cathie* L'eau et la régénération des morts d'après les représentations des tombes thébaines du Nouvel Empire. CÉg 72 (1997) 211-228.

9633 **Stricker, B.H.** Zijn en worden, I. Amst 1997, Faculteit der Godgeleerdheid van de Universiteit 88 pp. [DiscEg 41,81—DuQuesne, Terence].

9634 **Teeter, Emily** The presentation of Maat: ritual and legitimacy in Ancient Egypt. SAOC 57: Ch 1997, The Oriental Institute of the University of Chicago l; 142 pp. Bibl. 1-885923-05-8.

9635 *Traunecker, Claude* Lessons from the Upper Egyptian temple of el-Qalʾa. The temple in ancient Egypt. 1997, ⇒300. EQuirke, S., 168-178.

9636 *Wilkinson, Richard H.* The motif of the path of the sun in Ramesside royal tombs: an outline of recent research. JSSEA 25 (1995) 78-84.

9637 *Wilson, Penelope* Slaughtering the crocodile at Edfu and Dendera. The temple in ancient Egypt. 1997, ⇒300. EQuirke, S., 179-203.

9638 *Woodhouse, Susanne* The sun god, his four *bas* and the four winds in the sacred district at Saïs: the fragment of an obelisk (BM EA 1512). The temple in ancient Egypt. 1997, ⇒300. EQuirke, S., 132-151.

9639 **Zandee, J.** Der Amunhymnus des Papyrus I 334, verso. 1992, 3 vols. ⇒8,b518. RJAOS 117/1 (1997) 155-160 *(Allen, James P.)*.

9640 **Zivie-Coche, Christiane M.** Sphinx!: le Père la terreur. P 1997, Noêsis 146 (4) pp. Bibl. 2-911606-12-4.

## м7.0 Religio mesopotamica; Religio persiana

9641 *Beaulieu, Paul-Alain* The cult of An.Šár/Aššur in Babylonia after the fall of the Assyrian empire. State Archives of Assyria Bulletin 11 (1997) 55-73.

9642 *Berlejung, Angelika* Washing the mouth: the consecration of divine images in Mesopotamia. The image. 1997, ⇒2073. EVan der Toorn, K., 45-72.

9643 **Bongenaar, A.C.V.M.** The Neo-Babylonian Ebabbar temple at Sippar: its administration and its prosopography. Publications de l'Institut historique-archéologique néerlandais de Stamboul 80: Lei 1997, Nederlands Historisch-Archaeologisch Instituut te Istanbul xvi; 559 pp. Bibl. 90-6258-081-5.

9644 **Chiodi, Silvia Maria** Offerte "funebri" nella Lagas presargonica. Materiali per il vocabolario sumerico 5,1-2: R 1997, Univ. di Roma "La Sapienza", Dipart. di Studi Orientali 2 vols. Bibl.

9645 *Colbow, G.* Der Stiermensch als Opfertierträger: beeinflußte ein assyrisches Motiv die babylonische Glyptik der altbabylonischen Zeit?. Assyrien im Wandel. 1997, ⇒379. EWaetzoldt, H., 235-38.

9646 *Cornelius, Izak* The many faces of God: divine images and symbols in ancient Near Eastern religions. The image. 1997, ⇒2073. EVan der Toorn, K., 21-43.

9647 **Cunningham, Graham** 'Deliver me from evil': Mesopotamian incantations 2500-1500 BC. StP.SM 17: R 1997, Ed. Pont. Ist. Biblico 203 pp. L37.000. 88-7653-608-6.

9648 *Dalley, Stephanie* Statues of Marduk and the date of *Enūa eliš*. Altorientalische Forschungen 24/1 (1997) 163-171.

9649 *Dietrich, Manfried sukkallu*—der mesopotamische Götterbote: eine Studie zur "Angelologie" im Alten Orient. Engel und Dämonen. FARG 29: 1997, ⇒343. ᴱAhn, G., 49-74.

9650 **Dijkstra, Klaas** Life & loyalty: a study in the socio-religious culture of Syria and Mesopotamia in the Graeco-Roman period based on epigraphical evidence. 1995, ⇒11/2,8834. ᴿMes. 32 (1997) 367-368 *(Bertolino, R.)*; BiOr 54 (1997) 754-756 *(Lipiński, E.)*.

9651 *Durand, Jean-Marie* La divination par les oiseaux. Mari 8 (1997) 273-282.

9652 *Farber, W. Bit rimki-ein* assyrisches Ritual?. Assyrien im Wandel. 1997, ⇒379. ᴱWaetzoldt, H., 41-46.

9653 ᴱ**Finkel, I.L.; Geller, M.J.** Sumerian gods and their representations. Cuneiform Monographs 7: Groningen 1997, Styx ix; 249 pp. 90-5693-005-2 [[SEL 15,124s—Xella, Paolo].

9654 *Frame, Grant* The God Aššur in Babylonia. Assyria 1995. 1997, ⇒376. ᴱParpola, S., 55-64.

9655 *Freydank, H.* Mittelassyrische Opferlisten aus Assur. Assyrien im Wandel. 1997, ⇒379. ᴱWaetzoldt, H., 47-52.

9656 *George, A.R.* Studies in cultic topography and ideology. BiOr 53 (1996) 363-395;

9657 Marduk and the cult of the gods of Nippur at Babylon. Or. 66 (1997) 65-70.

9658 *Groneberg, Brigitte* Ein Ritual an Ištar. Mari 8 (1997) 291-303.

9659 **Groneberg, Brigitte R.M.** Lob der Ištar: Gebet und Ritual an die altbabylonische Venusgöttin: Tanatti Ištar. Cuneiform Monographs 8: Groningen 1997, STYX xix; 227 pp. 8 ill. ƒ150. 90-5693-006-0 [OLZ 93,453ss—Reynolds, Frances].

9660 *Heimpel, Wolfgang* The river ordeal in Hit. RA 90 (1996) 7-18.

9661 *Horowitz, Wayne; Wasserman, Nathan* Another Old Babylonian prayer to the gods of the night. JCS 48 (1996) 57-60.

9662 *Hurowitz, Victor Avigdor* Reading a votive inscription Simbar-Shipak and the ellilification of Marduk. RA 91/1 (1997) 39-45.

9663 **Hutter, Manfred** Religionen... 1: Babylonier, Syrer, Perser. 1996, ⇒12,9050. ᴿOLZ 92 (1997) 673-677 *(Thiel, Winfried)*.

9664 *Joannès, F.* Le monde occidental vu de Mésopotamie, de l'époque néo-babylonienne à l'époque hellénistique. TEuph 13 (1997) 141-153.

9665 **Jonker, Gerdien** The topography of remembrance: the dead, tradition and collective memory in Mesopotamia. SHR 68: 1995, ⇒11/2,8841; 12,9051. ᴿNumen 44/1 (1997) 91-94 *(Assmann, Jan)*.

9666 *Kessler, Karlheinz* Über "Löwenmenschen" und Türhüter in Uruk/Warka. AOAT 247: 1997, ⇒75. ᶠRoELLIG W., 153-161.

9667 *Lambert, W.G.* Processions to the Akitu house. RA 91/1 (1997) 49-80;

9668 Syncretism and religious controversy in Babylonia. Altorientalische Forschungen 24/1 (1997) 158-162.

9669 ᴱ**Lara Peinado, Federico** Himno al templo Eninnu: cilindros A y B de Gudea. Paradigmas 9: M 1996, Trotta 188 pp. Bibl. 84-8164-082-4.

9670 **Lawson, Jack N.** The concept of fate in ancient Mesopotamia of the first millennium: toward an understanding of *šimtu*. 1994, ⇒10,10798; 12,9053. ᴿOLZ 92 (1997) 56-61 *(Reynolds, Frances)*; WZKM 87 (1997) 289-292 *(Glassner, J.-J.)*; BiOr 54 (1997) 713-717 *(Böck, Barbara)*.

9671 *Leichty, Erle* Divination, magic, and astrology in the Assyrian royal court;
9672 *Livingstone, Alasdair* New dimensions in the study of Assyrian religion. Assyria 1995. 1997, ⇒376. ᴱParpola, S., 161-164/165-177.
9673 *Margueron, Jean-Claude* Palais de Mari: figurines et religion populaire. Mari 8 (1997) 731-753.
9674 *Mayer, Walter* Der Gott Assur und die Erben Assyriens. Religion und Gesellschaft. AOAT 248: 1997, ⇒235. ᴱAlbertz, R., 15-23.
9675 *Michel, Cécile* Une incantation paléo-assyrienne contre Lamaštum. Or. 66 (1997) 58-64.
9676 *Nunn, Astrid* Helden und Mischwesen in der altbabylonischen Glyptik. Zsfg. 222. ZA 87 (1997) 222-246.
9677 *Pomponio, Francesco* Cuori strappati e quisling Babilonesi. SEL 14 (1997) 69-89.
9678 *Pongratz-Leisten, Beate* The interplay of military strategy aned cultic practice in Assyrian politics. Assyria 1995. 1997, ⇒376. ᴱParpola, S., 245-252;
9679 Das "negative Sündenbekenntnis" des Königs anläßlich des babylonischen Neujahrsfestes und die *kidinnutu* von Babylon. Schuld. 1997, ⇒236. ᴱAssmann, J., 83-101.
9680 **Reiner, Erica** Astral magic in Babylonia. TAPhS 85/4: 1995, ⇒11/2,8847. ᴿAfO 44-45 (1997-98) 417-419 *(Veldhuis, Niek)*; BiOr 54 (1997) 710-713 *(Dalley, Stephanie)*.
9681 *Robbins, Ellen* Tabular sacrifice records and the cultic calendar of Neo-Babylonian Uruk. JCS 48 (1996) 61-87.
9682 *Rochberg, Francesca* Personifications and metaphors in Babylonian celestial omina. JAOS 116 (1996) 475-485.
9683 *Sallaberger, Walther* Nippur als religiöses Zentrum Mesopotamiens im historischen Wandel. Die orientalische Stadt. 1997, ⇒406. ᴱWilhelm, G., 147-168.
9684 *Scurlock, JoAnn* Ghosts in the ancient Near East: weak or powerful?. HUCA 68 (1997) 77-96.
9685 *Van der Toorn, Karel* The iconic book: analogies between the Babylonian cult of images and the veneration of the Torah. The image. 1997, ⇒2073. ᴱVan der Toorn, K., 229-248.
9686 **Westenholz, Joan M. Goodnick** Legends of the kings of Akkad: the texts. Mesopotamian Civilizations 7: WL 1997, Eisenbrauns. 0-931464-85-4.
9687 **Zgoll, Annette** Der Rechtsfall der En-hedu-Ana: im Lied nin-me-sara. AOAT 246: Müns 1997, Ugarit-Verlag xii; 632 pp. 3-927120-50-2.

9688 *Dombrowski, B.W.W.* Socio-religious implications of foreign impact on Palestine Jewry under Achaemenid rule. TEuph 13 (1997) 65-89.
9689 *Philonenko, Marc* Les 'oracles d'Hystaspe' et deux textes qoumrâniens *(Règle de la Communauté* 8, 12-14 et *4Q* 385, 3, 2-7). Sum. 111. Sem. 47 (1997) 111-115.

## M8 Islam; Religions of Africa and Asia

9690 **Adang, Camilla** Muslim writers on Judaism and the Hebrew Bible: from Ibn RABBAN to Ibn HAZM. IPTS 22: 1996, ⇒12,9074. ᴿJQR 87 (1997) 373-376 *(Brinner, William M.)*.
9691 **Gil, Moshe** A history of Palestine, 634-1099. C ²1997, CUP 968 pp. £90 [StIsl 87,159ss—Mouton, Jean-Michel].

9692 **Gimaret, Daniel** Dieu à l'image de l'homme: les anthropomorphismes de la *sunna* et leurs interprétations par les théologiens. Patrimoines, Islam: P 1997, Cerf 338 pp. FF250 [VS 153,768—Cousin, Hugues].

9693 Grupo de Investigación Islamo-Cristiano. Inerpelados por las escrituras: Biblia y Corán. Pliegos de Encuentro Islamo-Cristiano 20: M 1997, Darek Nyumba 97 pp. [Proyecció 44,320].

9694 *Knappert, J.* The Islamic literatures of Africa. OLoP 28 (1997) 193-221.

9695 **Moucarry, Chawkat Georges** Pardon, repentir, conversion: études de ces concepts en Islam et de leurs équivalents bibliques. Diss. E.P.H.E. Paris 1994, D*Gimaret, Daniel*: Villeneuve d'Asq 1997, Presses Universitaires du Septentrion 336 pp. [IslChr 24,254—Gabus, Jean-Paul].

9696 *Pinto, Desiderio* MUHAMMAD and Jesus. Sum. 460. VJTR 61 (1997) 460-468.

9697 *Raeder, Siegfried* Biblische Traditionen im Koran. JBTh 12 (1997) 309-331.

9698 **Räisänen, Heikki** MARCION, MUHAMMAD and the MAHATMA: exegetical perspectives on the encounter of cultures and faiths. L 1997, SCM xi; 239 pp. £15. 0-334-02693-8.

9699 **Renard, John** All the king's falcons: RUMI on prophets and revelation. 1994, ⇒10,10861. RJAOS 117/1 (1997) 183-185 *(Lewisohn, Leonard)*.

9700 **Riccardi, Andrea** Mediterraneo: cristianesimo e Islam tra coabitazione e conflitto. Frontiere 11: Mi 1997, Guerini 209 pp. 88-7802-820-7.

9701 *Rodinò, Nerina* Bibbia e Corano: due mondi a confronto. RdT 38 (1997) 821-827.

9702 *Sánchez Nogales, José Luis* Biblia y Coran: esas escrituras que se cuestionan. EE 72 (1997) 433-468.

9703 *Schirrmacher, Christine* La Bible et le Coran comparés. RRef 48/3 (1997) 25-30.

9704 **Sfar, Mondher** Le Coran, la Bible et l'Orient ancien. P 1997, Sfar 438 pp. FF129. 2-9511936-0-2 [BCLF 604,27].

9705 *Siddiqui, Mona* The image of Christ in Islam: scripture and sentiment. Images of Christ. 1997, ⇒256. E*Porter, S.E.*, 159-172.

9706 E*Wilson, Richard Francis; Carro, Daniel* Contemporary gospel accents: doing theology in Africa, Asia, Southeast Asia, and Latin America. Macon, GA 1997, Mercer University Press xv (2) 142 pp. Baptist World Alliance. 0-86554-505-7.

9707 **Young, R.F.; Jebanesan, S.** The bible trembled: the Hindu-Christian controversies of nineteenth-century Ceylon. Publications of the De Nobili Reseearch Library 22: W 1995, Sammlung de Nobili 204 pp. [RHR 216,496—Clémentin-Ojha, Catherine].

9708 **Young, R.F.; Somaratna, G.P.V.** Vain debates: the Buddhist-Christian controversies of nineteenth-century Ceylon. Publications of the De Nobili Research Library 23: W 1996, Sammlung de Nobili 236 pp. [RHR 216,496—Clémentin-Ojha, Catherine].

## XVII. Historia Medii Orientis Biblici

### Q1 *Syria prae-islamica, Canaan* Israel Veteris Testamenti

9709 **Ahlström, Gösta W.** The history of ancient Palestine. JSOT.S 146: 1993, ⇒9,12326... 12,9093. RSyr. 74 (1997) 223-224 *(Will, Ernest)*.

9710 **Andelković, Branislav** The relations between Early Bronze Age I Canaanites and Upper Egyptians. Centre for Archaeological Research 14: Belgrade 1995, Univ. of Belgrade Fac. of Philosophy 88 pp. Abbrev. M.A. thesis. 86-80269-17-4.

9711 *Arata Mantovani, Piera* L'archeologia siro-palestinese e la storia di Israele: rassegna di studi archeologici-IX. Henoch 19/1 (1997) 95-113.

9712 *Arnaud, Daniel* Mariage et remariage des femmes chez les Syriens du moyen-Euphrate, à l'âge du Bronze récent d'après deux nouveaux documents. Sum. 7. Sem. 46 (1996) 7-16.

9713 *Astour, Michael C.* Ḫaššu and Ḫasuwan: a contribution to North Syrian history and geography. UF 29 (1997) 1-66.

9714 **Barstad, Hans** The myth of the empty land: a study in the history and archaeology of Judah during the 'exilic' period. SO.S 28: 1996. ⇒12,9095. RSJOT 11 (1997) 311-312 *(Jeppesen, Knud)*; SEÅ 62 (1997) 165-167 *(Oredsson, Dag)*.

9715 **Becking, Bob** The fall of Samaria. 1992, ⇒8,2991... 11/2,9189. RIEJ 48 (1997) 145-147 *(Cogan, Mordechai)*.

9716 *Ben-Tor, Daphna* The relations between Egypt and Palestine in the Middle Kingdom as reflected by contemporary Canaanite scarabs. IEJ 47 (1997) 162-189.

9717 *Bonechi, Marco* Lexique et idéologie royale à l'époque proto-syrienne. Mari 8 (1997) 477-535.

9718 *Bonechi, Marco; Catagnoti, Amalia* Deux nouvelles lettres de Yaqqim-Addu, gouverneur de Saggarâtum. Mari 8 (1997) 777-780.

9719 *Bonneterre, Daniel* Surveiller, punir et se venger: la violence d'état à Mari. Mari 8 (1997) 537-561.

9720 *Borgonovo, Gianantonio* Significato numerico delle cronologie bibliche e rilevanza delle varianti testuali (TM—LXX—SAM). RStB 9/1 (1997) 139-170.

9721 *Bretschneider, Joachim; Jans, Greta* Palast und Verwaltung: Synchronismen im Ḫaburgebiet im 3. Jahrtausend v. Chr. UF 29 (1997) 67-93.

9722 **Bruce, Frederick Fyvie** Israel and the nations. EPayne, David F.: Carlisle ²1997, Paternoster xii; 258 pp. Bibl. 0-85364-762-3.

9723 **Canovesi, A.** Sui passi del Dio d'Israele: panorama di storia biblica. Mi 1997, Paoline 182 pp. L14.000 [RivBib 45,505].

9724 *Ceresko, Anthony R.* Potsherds and pioneers: recent research on the origins of Israel. ITS 34/1-3 (1997) 5-22.

9725 *Charpin, Dominique; Ziegler, Nele* Mekum, roi d'Apišal. Mari 8 (1997) 243-247.

9726 *Chavalas, Mark W.* Inland Syria and the East-of-Jordan region in the first millennium BCE before the Assyrian intrusions. The age of Solomon. 1997, ⇒282. EHandy, L.K., 167-178.

9727  <sup>E</sup>**Chavalas, Mark W.; Hayes, John L.** New horizons in the study
of ancient Syria. 1992, ⇒8,705*... 12,9109. 9,559. <sup>R</sup>JNES 56
(1997) 285-287 *(Joffe, Alexander H.)*.

9728  *Daoust, Joseph* Coup d'oeil sur les philistins. EeV 107 (1997) 452-
453.

9729  **Davies, Philip R.** In search of 'Ancient Israel'. JSOT.S 148: 1992,
⇒10,303b... 12,9112. <sup>R</sup>JNES 56 (1997) 148-149 *(Holloway, Steven W.)*.

9730  *Davies, Philip R.* 'Ancient Israel' and history: a response to Norman WHYBRAY. ET 108 (1997) 211-212.

9731  **DeBlois, L; Van der Spek, R.J.** An introduction to the ancient
world. <sup>T</sup>*Mellor, Susan*: NY 1997, Routledge xx; 321 pp. $26
[BTB 29,45—Eddinger, Terry W.].

9732  *Dever, William G.* Archaeology and the "age of Solomon": a case-
study in archaeology and historiography. The age of Solomon.
1997, ⇒282. <sup>E</sup>Handy, L.K., 217-251;

9733  Archaeology, urbanism, and the rise of the Israelite state. Urbanism. JSOT.S 244: 1997, ⇒265. <sup>E</sup>Aufrecht, W.E., 172-193;

9734  Philology, theology, and archaeology: what kind of history of
Israel do we want, and what is possible?. The archaeology of
Israel. JSOT.S 237: 1997, ⇒9790. <sup>E</sup>Silberman, N.A., 290-310.

9735  **Dietrich, Walter** Die frühe Königszeit in Israel: 10. Jahrhundert v.
Chr. Biblische Enzyklopädie 3: Stu 1997, Kohlhammer 312 pp.
Rudolf Smend zum 65. Geburtstag. DM44. 3-17-012332-7 [NT-
hAR 1998,98].

9736  **Dion, Paul Eugène** Les araméens à l'Âge du fer: histoire politique
et structures sociales. EtB 34: P 1997, Gabalda 473 pp. FF390. 2-
85021-096-X.

9737  **Drews, Robert** The end of the Bronze Age: changes in warfare and
the catastrophe ca. 1200 B.C. 1993, ⇒9,13755... 11/2,a925. <sup>R</sup>HZ
264 (1997) 425-426 *(Maier, Franz Georg)*; At. 85 (1997) 637-639
*(Benzi, Mario)*; JNES 56 (1997) 127-129 *(Cline, Eric H.)*.

9738  *Duarte Castillo, Raúl* Israel acuño su identidad en la epoca Persa.
EfMex 15 (1997) 165-176.

9739  <sup>E</sup>**Edelman, Diana Vikander** You shall not abhor an Edomite for
he is your brother: Edom and Seir in history and tradition. 1995,
⇒11/2,500; 12,10228. <sup>R</sup>CBQ 59 (1997) 189-90 *(Jacobs, Paul F.)*.

9740  *Ehrlich, Carl S.* "How the mighty are fallen": the Philistines in
their tenth century context. The age of Solomon. 1997, ⇒282.
<sup>E</sup>Handy, L.K., 179-201.

9741  *Eph<sup>c</sup>al, Israel* The Philistine entity and the origin of the name "Palestine". 1997 ⇒34. <sup>M</sup>GREENBERG M., 31*-35* **H.**

9742  *Finkelstein, Israel* Pots and people revisited: ethnic boundaries in
the Iron Age I. The archaeology of Israel. JSOT.S 237: 1997,
⇒9790. <sup>E</sup>Silberman, N.A., 216-237.

9743  *Fleming, Daniel E.* Counting time at Mari and in early second millennium Mesopotamia. Mari 8 (1997) 675-692.

9744  *Freedman, David Noel* 'Son of Man, can these bones live?': the
exile. Divine Commitment 1. 1997 <1975>, ⇒124. 251-266.

9745  *Galil, Gershon* The Canaanite city states in the fourteenth century
BCE. Sum. 189. Cathedra 84 (1997) 7-52 **H.**

9746  **Garbini, Giovanni** I filistei: gli antagonisti di Israele. Orizzonti
della storia: Mi 1997, Rusconi 288 pp. Bibl. L60.000. 88-18-
88046-2.

9747 **García Trapiello, Jesús** La autoridad política en la biblia: origen y desarollo en el Antiguo Testamento. BAC 579: M 1997, BAC xvii; 282 pp. Bibl. 84-7914-319-3.

9748 *Gatgounis, George J.* The role of the Philistines in the Hebrew Bible. Ter. 48 (1997) 373-385.

9749 *Gonçalves, Francolino J.* El "destierro" consideraciones históricas. EstB 55 (1997) 431-461.

[E]**Grabbe, L.** Can a 'History of Israel' be written? ⇒200.

9750 **Hadas-Lebel, Mireille** Le peuple hébreu: entre la bible et l'histoire. Découvertes Gallimard 313: P 1997, Gallimard 160 pp. 2-07-053356-5 [NThAR 1998,268].

9751 **Hallo, William W.** Origins: the ancient Near Eastern background of some modern Western institutions. 1996, ⇒12,9123. [R]Mes. 32 (1997) 341-4 *(Liverani, M.)*; ZAR 3 (1997) 250-58 *(Otto, Eckart)*.

9752 *Handy, Lowell K.* Phoenicians in the tenth century BCE: a sketch of an outline;

9753 Postlude and prospects. The age of Solomon. 1997, ⇒282. [E]Handy, L.K., 154-166/493-502.

9754 *Herr, Larry G.* The Iron Age II period: emerging nations. BA 60/3 (1997) 114-183.

9755 **Hess, Richard S.** Hurrians and other inhabitants of Late Bronze Age Palestine. Levant 29 (1997) 153-156.

9756 **Hostetter, Edwin C.** Nations mightier and more numerous: the biblical view of Palestine's pre-Israelite peoples. 1995, ⇒11/2,9217. [R]ThLZ 122 (1997) 131-132 *(Weippert, Helga)*.

9757 **Jullien, C. & F.** La bible en exil. 1995, ⇒12,9131. [R]RSR 85 (1997) 287-289 *(Gibert, Pierre)*.

9758 *Kallai, Zecharia* The twelve-tribe systems of Israel. VT 47 (1997) 53-90.

9759 *Kellenberger, Edgar* Die Besiedlung des zentralpalästinischen Berglands zur Eisen-I-Zeit. ThZ 53 (1997) 177-194.

9760 *Klengel, H.* Beute, Tribut und Abgaben: Aspekte assyrischer Syrienpolitik. Assyrien im Wandel. 1997 ⇒379. [E]Waetzoldt, H., 71-6.

9761 **Knoppers, Gary N.** The vanishing Solomon: the disappearance of the united monarchy from recent histories of ancient Israel. JBL 116 (1997) 19-44.

9762 **Kuhrt, Amélie** The ancient Near East c.3000-330 BC. 1995, 2 vols. ⇒11/2,9457. [R]BSOAS 60 (1997) 541 *(Reynolds, Frances)*; Or. 66 (1997) 103-104 *(Dandamayev, M.)*; AJA 101 (1997) 166-167 *(Potts, D.T.)*; ZA 87 (1997) 297-299 *(Yoffee, N.)*.

9763 *Lacambre, Denis* La bataille de Hirîtum. Mari 8 (1997) 431-454.

9764 *Lafont, Bertrand* Nouvelles lettres de Şidqum-Lanasi, vizir du royaume de Karkémish. Mari 8 (1997) 781-784.

9765 *Lemche, Niels Peter* Response to William G. DEVER, 'Revisionist Israel revisited'. CurResB 5 (1997) 9-14.

9766 *Levy, Thomas E.*, (al.), Egyptian-Canaanite interaction at Nahal Tillah, Israel (ca. 4500-3000 B.C.E.): an interim report on the 1994-1995 excavations. BASOR 307 (1997) 1-51.

9767 *Long, Burke O.* Historical imaginings, ideological gestures: W.F. ALBRIGHT and the 'reasoning faculties of man'. The archaeology of Israel. JSOT.S 237: 1997, ⇒9790. [E]Silberman, N.A., 82-94.

9768 [E]**Maier, Gerhard** Israel in Geschichte und Gegenwart. 1996, ⇒12,9139. [R]Cart. 13 (1997) 212-213 *(Marín Heredia, F.)*; JETh 11 (1997) 191-193 *(Gugler, Werner)*.

9769 **Maier, Johann** Entre los dos testamentos: historia y religión en la época del segundo templo. BEB 89: 1996, ⇒12,9140. ᴿCDios 210/1 (1997) 348-349 *(Gutiérrez, J.)*; EfMex 15 (1997) 404-406 *(Muñoz Tónix, Reyes)*.

9770 *Małecki, Zdzisław* Król perski Cyrus wielki i jego rola w historii Izraela. Saeculum Christianum 4/1 (1997) 189-197.

9771 *Marello, Pierre* Liqtum, reine du Burundum. Mari 8 (1997) 455-9.

9772 **Margalith, Othniel** The Sea Peoples in the Bible. 1994, ⇒10,12194. ᴿCBQ 59 (1997) 354-355 *(Matthews, Victor H.)*; JQR 88 (1997) 108-112 *(Stone, Bryan Jack)*.

9773 *Mazar, Amihai* Iron Age chronology: a reply to I. Fɪɴᴋᴇʟsᴛᴇɪɴ. Levant 29 (1997) 157-167.

9774 *Menezes, Rui de* Societies in transition: Israel and the tribes of North East India. ITS 34/1-3 (1997) 23-55.

9775 *Morenz, Ludwig D.* Kanaanäisches Lokalkolorit in der Sinuhe-Erzählung und die Vereinfachung des *Urtextes*. ZDPV 113 (1997) 1-18.

9776 *Muth, Richard F.* Economic influences on early Israel. JSOT 75 (1997) 77-92.

9777 *Naʾaman, Nadav* King Mesha and the foundation of the Moabite monarchy. IEJ 47 (1997) 83-92;

9778 The network of Canaanite Late Bronze kingdoms and the city of Ashdod. UF 29 (1997) 599-626.

9779 **Nosovskij, Gleb V.** Matematičeskaja chronologija biblejskich so-bytij. Kibernetika: Moskva 1997, Nauka 406 pp. 5-02-013532-1 [NThAR 1999,2] **R**.

9780 *Oredsson, Dag* Salomos, Omris och Jehus Jisreel. SEÅ 62 (1997) 13-26.

9781 *Prato, Gian Luigi* La cronologia archeologica: tra il tempo mitico e il tempo reale;

9782 Sintesi dei contributi e suggerimenti conclusivi;

9783 'Un tempo per nascere e un tempo per morire': cronologie norma-tive e razionalità della storia nell'antico Israele: introduzione al tema. RStB 9/1 (1997) 9-34/215-218/5-7.

9784 **Redford, Donald B.** Egypt, Canaan and Israel in ancient times. 1992, ⇒8,b836... 12,9154. ᴿProtest. 52/1 (1997) 72-73 *(Soggin, J.A.)*.

9785 *Redford, Donald B.* Observations on the sojourn of the *bene*-Israel. Exodus. 1997, ⇒325. ᴱFrerichs, E., 57-66.

9786 **Ricciotti, Giuseppe** Storia d'Israele. Pref. *Sacchi, Paolo*; Introd. *Erba, Achille*: Religione: T 1997 < 1932-33 >, Società Ed. Inter-nazionale lxxviii; 885 pp. 88-05-05536-0.

9787 **Sacchi, Paolo** Storia del secondo tempio: Israele tra il IV secolo a.C. ed il I d.C. 1994, ⇒11/2,9237; 12,9158. ᴿBib. 78 (1997) 548-564 *(Nodet, Étienne)*.

9788 *Shanks, Hershel* The biblical minimalists: expunging ancient Israel's past. BiRe 13/3 (1997) 32-39, 50-52;

9789 Face to face: biblical minimalists meet their challengers. BArR 23/4 (1997) 26-42, 66.

9790 ᴱ**Silberman, Neil Asher; Small, David B.** The archaeology of Israel: constructing the past, interpreting the present. JSOT.S 237: Shf 1997, Academic 350 pp. $65/£45. 0-85075-650-3.

9791 *Silberman, Neil Asher; Small, David B.* Introduction /to The ar-chaeology of Israel/. 17-31 ⇒9790.

9792 *Small, David B.* Group identification and ethnicity in the construction of the early state of Israel: from the outside looking in. 271-288 ⇒9790.

9793 **Snell, Daniel C.** Life in the ancient Near East, 3100-332 B.C.E. NHv 1997, Yale University Press 270 pp. £21. 0-300-06615-5 [ET 108,376].

9794 **Soggin, J.A.** Nueva historia de Israel: de los orígenes a Bar Kochbá. Bilbao 1997, Desclée de B 513 pp. Ptas3.600 [Proyección 45,75].

9795 *Strong, John T.* Tyre's isolationist policies in the early sixth century BCE: evidence from the prophets. VT 47 (1997) 207-219.

9796 **Sturm, Josef** La guerre de Ramsès II contre les hittites. [T]*Vandersleyen, Claude.* 1996, ⇒12,9165. [R]DiscEg 39 (1997) 143-144 *(Gurney, O.R.).*

9797 'Un tempo per nascere e un tempo per morire': cronologie normative e razionalità della storia nell'antico Israele. RStB 1: Bo 1997, EDB 218 pp. L43.000 [RivBib 45,255].

9798 **Thompson, Thomas L.** Early history of the Israelite people from the written and archaeological sources. 1994, ⇒8,b848...12,9166. [R]JNES 56 (1997) 65-67 *(Bloch-Smith, Elizabeth).*

9799 *Weippert, Manfred* Israélites, Araméens et Assyriens dans la Transjordanie septentrionale. ZDPV 113 (1997) 19-38.

9800 **Westermann, Claus** Une histoire d'Israël—mille ans et un jour. 1996, ⇒12,9170. [R]LV(L) 47/3 (1997) 107-109 *(Revellin, Louise).*

9801 **Whitelam, Keith W.** The invention of ancient Israel: the silencing of Palestinian history. 1996, ⇒12,9172. [R]JSSt 44 (1997) 283-300 *(Provan, Iain).*

9802 **Willi, Thomas** Juda—Jehud—Israel: Studien zum Selbstverständnis des Judentums in persischer Zeit. FAT 12: 1995. ⇒11/2,9263. [R]ThLZ 122 (1997) 248-249 *(Wallis, Gerhard)*; CBQ 59 (1997) 564-565 *(Mandell, Sara).*

9803 **Wudke, Kurt** Von der Sippe zum Staat: aus den Berichten des Alten Testaments zum Werden eines Volkes. Fra 1997, Haag & H 142 pp. 3-86137-614-8 [NThAR 1998,335].

## Q2 **Historiographia**—*theologia historiae*

9804 **Bakker, Nico** Geschiedenis in opspraak: over de legitimatie van het concept geschiedenis: een theologische verhandeling. 1996, ⇒12,9179. [R]ITBT 5/3 (1997) 24-27 *(Boer, Dick).*

9805 *Barstad, Hans M.* History and the Hebrew Bible;

9806 *Becking, Bob* Inscribed seals as evidence for biblical Israel?: Jeremiah 40.7-41.15 *par exemple*. Can a 'History of Israel' be written?. JSOT.S 245: 1997, ⇒200. [E]Grabbe, L., 37-64/65-83.

9807 *Bevir, Mark* Mind and method in the history of ideas. HTh 36 (1997) 167-189.

9808 *Carroll, Robert P.* Madonna of silences: Clio and the bible;

9809 *Davies, Philip R.* Whose history?: whose Israel?: whose bible?: biblical histories, ancient and modern. Can a 'History of Israel' be written?. JSOT.S 245: 1997, ⇒200. [E]Grabbe, L., 84-103/104-122.

9810 *Deist, Ferdinand E.* The Yehud Bible: a belated divine miracle?. JNSL 23/1 (1997) 117-142.

9811 **Demandt, Alexander** Antike Staatsformen. 1995, ⇒11/2,c613.
RFolOr 33 (1997) 223-224 *(Dombrowski, Bruno W.W.)*.

9812 *Dever, William G.* "On listening to the text—and the artifacts".
BJSt 313: 1997, ⇒85. FSILBERMAN L., 1-23.

9813 *Freedman, David Noel* The biblical idea of history. Divine Commitment 1. 1997 <1967>, ⇒124. 218-232.

9814 *Fritz, Volkmar* Weltalter und Lebenszeit: mythische Elemente in
der Geschichtsschreibung Israels und bei HESIOD. Studien zur Literatur. 1997 <1990>, 13-31.

9815 *Gafni, Isaiah M.* Between Babylonia and the land of Israel: ancient
history and the clash of ideologies in modern Jewish historiography. Sum. xxi. Zion 62 (1997) 213-242 **H.**

9816 *Gall, Lothar* Das Argument der Geschichte: Überlegungen zum
gegenwärtigen Standort der Geschichtswissenschaft. HZ 264 (1997)
1-20.

9817 *Gottwald, Norman K.* Triumphalist versus anti-triumphalist
versions of early Israel: a response to articles by LEMCHE and
DEVER in volume 4 (1996). CurResB 5 (1997) 15-42.

9818 *Grabbe, Lester L.* Are historians of ancient Palestine fellow creatures—or different animals;

9819 Reflections on the discussion. Can a 'History of Israel' be written?.
JSOT.S 245: 1997, ⇒200. EGrabbe, L., 19-36/188-196.

9820 **Grant, Michael** Greek and Roman historians: information and mis-
information. L 1997, Routledge xii; 172 pp. Bibl. 0-415-11770-4.

9821 *Guest, P. Deryn* The historical approach in crisis?: fact, fiction and
current debate in Old Testament study. ScrB 27 (1997) 42-54.

9822 *Hall, Robert G.* Ancient historical method and the training of an
orator. The rhetorical analysis. JSNT.S 146: 1997, ⇒336. EPorter,
S.E., 103-118.

9823 **Halpern, Baruch** The first historians: the Hebrew Bible and history. University Park, Pa. 1996, Pennsylvania State Univ. Press
xxxvi; 285 pp. 0-271-01615-9.

9824 *Halpern, Baruch* Text and artifact: two monologues?. The archaeology of Israel. JSOT.S 237: 1997 ⇒9790. ESilberman, N., 311-41.

9825 *Hengel, Martin* Problems of a history of earliest christianity. Sum.
144. Bib. 78 (1997) 131-144.

9826 *Heyns, Dalene* Considering aspects of history, knowledge and
world-view: is Old Testament history relevant for South Africa?.
OTEs 10 (1997) 387-400.

9827 *Hoffmeier, James K.* The evangelical contribution to understanding
the (early) history of ancient Israel in recent scholarship. BBR 7
(1997) 77-89.

9828 *Kallai, Zecharia* The patriarchal boundaries, Canaan and the land
of Israel: patterns and application in biblical historiography. IEJ 47
(1997) 69-82.

9829 *Lampe, Peter* Wissenssoziologische Annäherung an das Neue Testament. NTS 43 (1997) 347-366.

9830 *Le Morvan, Michael* The bible as history: reflections on the
approach of David ROHL. ScrB 27 (1997) 55-65.

9831 *Lemche, Niels Peter* Clio is also among the Muses!: Keith W.
WHITELAM and the history of Palestine: a review and commentary. Can a 'History of Israel' be written?. JSOT.S 245: 1997,
⇒200. EGrabbe, L., 123-155.

9832 **Marincola, John** Authority and tradition in ancient historiography. C 1997, CUP xvi; 361 pp. Bibl. 0-521-48019-1.

9833 *Michel, Diethelm* Geschichte und Zukunft im Alten Testament. Studien zur Überlieferungsgeschichte. TB 93: 1997 <1991>, ⇒149. 35-52.

9834 ᴱ**Millard, A.R.**, (*al.*), Faith, tradition, and historiography: OT historiography in its ancient Near Eastern context. 1994, ⇒10,326*... 12,9195. ᴿWThJ 59 (1997) 128-131 *(Enns, Peter).*

9835 **Mortley, Raoul** The idea of universal history from Hellenistic philosophy to early christian historiography. Lewiston 1996, Mellen 233 pp. [IJCT 5,292ss—Eckstein, Arthur M.].

9836 *Mutschler, F.-H.* Vergleichende Beobachtungen zur griechischrömischen und altchinesischen Geschichtsschreibung. Saec. 48 (1997) 213-253.

9837 *Neusner, Jacob* Paradigmatic versus historical thinking: the case of rabbinic Judaism. HTh 36 (1997) 353-377.

9838 *Niehr, Herbert* Some aspects of working with the textual sources. Can a 'History of Israel' be written?. JSOT.S 245: 1997, ⇒200. ᴱGrabbe, L., 156-165.

9839 *Römer, T.* Transformations et influences dans "l'historiographie" juive de la fin du VIIe s. av. notre ère jusqu'à l'époque perse. TEuph 13 (1997) 47-63;

9840 Transformations in deuteronomistic and biblical historiography. ZAW 109 (1997) 1-11 [2 Kgs 22; 23; 25,27-30].

9841 *Simian-Yofre, Horacio* Lenguaje bíblico e historia de frente al tercer milenio. Caminando hacia el tercer milenio. ᴱRivas, L.H.: BA 1997, San Pablo. 39-90.

9842 *Simonetti, Manlio* Tra innovazione e tradizione: la storiografia cristiana. VetChr 34 (1997) 51-65.

9843 **Smelik, Klaas D.** Converting the past: studies in ancient Israelite and Moabite historiography. OTS 28: 1992, ⇒8,110... 11/2,9342. ᴿBiOr 54 (1997) 442-443 *(Rogerson, J.W.).*

9844 *Thompson, Thomas L.* Defining history and ethnicity in the south Levant. Can a 'History of Israel' be written?. JSOT.S 245: 1997, ⇒200. ᴱGrabbe, L., 166-187.

9845 *Van de Mieroop, Marc* On writing a history of the ancient Near East. BiOr 54 (1997) 285-305.

9846 **Van der Veen, J.E.** The significant and the insignificant: five studies in Herodotus' view of history. Amsterdam Studies in Classical Philology 6: Amst 1996, Gieben (8) 146 pp. Bibl. 90-5063-296-3.

9847 **Vernus, Pascal** Essai sur la conscience de l'histoire dans l'Égypte pharaonique. BEHE.H 332: P 1995, Champion 187 pp. FF240 [CÉg 74,272—Vandersleyen, Claude].

9848 *Zuurmond, Rochus* De aanvaarding van het nieuwe. ITBT 5/7 (1997) 17-19.

### Q3 *Historia Ægypti*—Egypt

9849 **Alston, R.** Soldier and society in Roman Egypt: a social history. 1998 <1995>, ⇒11/2,c564. ᴿCÉg 72 (1997) 184-185 *(Martin, Alain).*

9850 **Assmann, Jan** Ägypten: eine Sinngeschichte. 1996, ⇒12,9204. RActBib 34 (1997) 270-271 *(Boada, J.)*.

9851 *Assmann, Jan* Ägypten als Argument: Rekonstruktion der Vergangenheit und Religionskritik im 17. und 18. Jahrhundert. HZ 264 (1997) 561-585;

9852 Religion im Zeitalter Ramses' II. WUB 5 (1997) 23-25.

9853 **Bagnall, Roger S.; Frier, Bruce W.** The demography of Roman Egypt. 1994, ⇒10,13788... 12,10774. RJAOS 117 (1997) 160-161 *(Wilfong, Terry G.)*; BiOr 54 (1997) 696-702 *(Jördens, Andrea)*.

9854 *Baines, John* Kingship before literature: the world of the king in the Old Kingdom. Selbstverständnis und Realität. ÄAT 36/1: 1997, ⇒394. EGundlach, R., 125-174.

9855 **Bard, Kathryn A.** From farmers to Pharaohs: mortuary evidence for the rise of complex society in Egypt. 1994, ⇒11/2,13565. RPEQ 129 (1997) 78-79 *(Filer, J.M.)*; AJA 101 (1997) 165-166 *(Richards, Janet E.)*.

9856 *Beckerath, J. von* Nochmals zu den Thronbesteigungsdaten Ramses' V. und VII. GöMisz 157 (1997) 7-10.

9857 **Beckerath, Jürgen von** Chronologie des ägyptischen Neuen Reiches. HÄB 39: 1994, ⇒10,11078; 12,9207. RBiOr 54 (1997) 78-82 *(Spalinger, Anthony)*;

9858 Chronologie des pharaonischen Ägypten: die Zeitbestimmung der ägyptischen Geschichte von der Vorzeit bis 332 v. Chr. MÄST 46: Mainz 1997, Von Zabern xix; 244 pp. DM98. 3-8053-2310-7.

9859 **Bowman, Alan K.** Egypt after the pharaohs: 332 BC-AD 642 from Alexander to the Arab conquest. ²1996, ⇒12,9208. RDiscEg 38 (1997) 135-137 *(La'da, Csaba A.)*.

9860 *Boyer, Frédéric* Israel und der Pharao;

9861 *Briend, Jacques* Der Pharao als politische Autorität. WUB 5 (1997) 26-28/31-33.

9862 ECamplani, Alberto L'Egitto cristiano: aspetti e problemi in età tardo-antica. SEAug. 56: R 1997, Institutum Patristicum Augustinianum 358 pp. L60.000. 88-7961-041-4. RAug. 37/1 (1997) 241-243 *(Grossi, Vittorino)*.

9863 **Clayton, Peter A.** Crónica de los faraones: todos los soberanos y dinastías del antiguo Egipto. TLopez-Guix, Juan Gabriel; Ferrer, Isabel: Barc 1996, Destino, 350 ill. 84-233-2604-7 [BAEO 35,393ss—Pardo Mata, Pilar].

9864 **Currid, John D.** Ancient Egypt and the Old Testament. Foreword Kitchen, Kenneth A.: GR 1997, Baker 269 pp. Bibl. $22. 0-8010-2137-5.

9865 *Daoust, Joseph* Akhénaton et Ramsès II. EeV 107 (1997) 143-144.

9866 *Darnell, John Coleman* The message of king Wahankh Antef II to Khety, ruler of Heracleopolis. ZÄS 124/2 (1997) 101-108.

9867 *Darnell, John Coleman & Deborah* New inscriptions of the late first intermediate period from the Theban western desert and the beginnings of the northern expansion of the eleventh dynasty. JNES 56 (1997) 241-258.

9868 *Dautzenberg, N.* Die Wahl des Königsnamens in der Hyksoszeit: das Entstehen einer eigenen Tradition, Bezüge zu den thebanischen Herrschern und Schlußfolgerungen für die Chronologie. GöMisz 159 (1997) 43-51.

9869 *Derchain, Philippe* La différence abolie: Dieu et Pharaon dans les scènes rituelles ptolémaïques. Selbstverständnis und Realität. ÄAT 36/1: 1997, ⇒394. <sup>E</sup>Gundlach, R., 225-232.

9870 *Doxey, Denise* Searching for ancient Egypt. BA 60/2 (1997) 107.

9871 <sup>E</sup>**Eide, T.** Fontes historiae Nubiorum, 1: from the eighth to the mid-fifth century B.C. 1994, ⇒10,11088... 12,9218.<sup>R</sup> Aeg. 77 (1997) 137-139 *(Piacentini, Patrizia)*.

9872 *El-Mosallamy, A.H.* The evolution of the position of the woman in ancient Egypt. 21. Papyrologenkongress, 1. 1997, ⇒367. <sup>E</sup>Kramer, B., 251-272.

9873 *Eyre, Christopher J.* Peasants and 'modern' leasing strategies in ancient Egypt. Sum. 367. JESHO 40/4 (1997) 367-390.

9874 *Fernández Sangrador, Jorge Juan* Origen de la comunidad cristiana de Alejandría. La Bíblia i el Mediterrani. 1997, ⇒385. <sup>E</sup>Borrell, d'Agustí, 291-303.

9875 **Feucht, Erika** Das Kind im Alten Ägypten: die Stellung des Kindes in Familie und Gesellschaft nach altägyptischen Texten und Darstellungen. Fra 1995, Campus 610 pp. 53 fig. DM98. <sup>R</sup>RdE 48 (1997) 292-296 *(Durisch, Nicole)*; JEA 83 (1997) 228-231 *(Janssen, Jac. J.)*;

9876 *Franke, Detlef* "Schöpfer, Schützer, Guter Hirte": zum Königsbild des Mittleren Reiches;

9877 *Gestermann, Louise* Sesostris III.—König und Nomarch. Selbstverständnis und Realität. ÄAT 36/1: 1997, ⇒394. <sup>E</sup>Gundlach, R., 175-209/37-47.

9878 **Görg, Manfred** Die Beziehungen zwischen dem alten Israel und Ägypten: von den Anfängen bis zum Exil. EdF 290: Da:Wiss 1997, vi; 190 pp. DM45. 3-534-08426-8.

9879 *Görg, Manfred* Ein Namenseintrag der Scheschonq-Liste von Karnak. BN 88 (1997) 16-18;

9880 Ramses II.—Pharao des Exodus?. WUB 5 (1997) 28-30.

9881 *Gundlach, Rolf* Die Legitimationen des ägyptischen Königs— Versuch einer Systematisierung;

9882 Zu Inhalt und Bedeutung der ägyptischen Königsideologie. Selbstverständnis und Realität. ÄAT 36/1: 1997, ⇒394. <sup>E</sup>Gundlach, R., 11-20/1-8.

9883 *Hollis, Susan Tower* Queens and goddesses in ancient Egypt. Women and goddess traditions. 1997, ⇒249. <sup>E</sup>King, K., 210-238.

9884 *Hölbl, Günther* Zur Legitimation der Ptolemäer als Pharaonen. Selbstverständnis und Realität. ÄAT 36/1: 1997, ⇒394. <sup>E</sup>Gundlach, R., 21-34.

9885 *Ignatjeva, Lilia* New data for early Egyptian chronology. DiscEg 37 (1997) 11-22.

9886 *Jansen-Winkeln, Karl* Die Hildesheimer Stele der Chereduanch. MDAI.K 53 (1997) 91-100;

9887 Ein Kaufmann aus Naukratis. ZÄS 124/2 (1997) 108-115.

9888 **Janssen, Rosalind M. & Jac J.** Getting old in ancient Egypt. 1996, ⇒12,9228. <sup>R</sup>DiscEg 39 (1997) 125-127 *(Dodson, Aidan)*.

9889 *Kitchen, Kenneth A.* Egypt and East Africa. The age of Solomon. 1997, ⇒282. <sup>E</sup>Handy, L.K., 106-125;

9890 Glanz und Geheimnis eines Pharaos. WUB 5 (1997) 8-10, 12-16.

9891 **Lacovara, Peter** The New Kingdom royal city. Studies in Egyptology: L 1997, Kegan P xiv; 202 pp. £85/$144.50. 0-7103-0544-3.

9892  *Leblanc, Christian* Die Bauten für die Ewigkeit der "Großen Sonne Ägyptens". WUB 5 (1997) 44-47.
9893  **Lewis, Naphtali** The compulsory public services of Roman Egypt. Papyrologica Florentina 28: F ²1997, Gonnelli 191 pp.
9894  **Luft, Ulrich** Die chronologische Fixierung des ägyptischen Mittleren Reiches nach dem Tempelarchiv von Illahun. 1992, ⇒9,12456; 10,11102. ᴿJNES 56 (1997) 119-121 *(Rose, Lynn E.)*.
9895  ᴱ**Lustig, Judith** Anthropology and egyptology: a developing dialogue. Monographs in Mediterranean Archaeology 8: Shf 1997, Academic 147 pp. £32.50/$53.50. 1-85075-676-7.
9896  **Luvino, Alfredo** Il dono del Nilo: introduzione alla civiltà dei faraoni. Pref. *Gabutti, Diego*: T 1997, Ananke 283 pp. Bibl. 88-86626-21-5.
9897  *Maderna-Sieben, Claudia* Der König als Kriegsherr und oberster Heerführer in den Eulogien der frühen Ramessidenzeit. Selbstverständnis und Realität. ÄAT 36/1: 1997, ⇒394. ᴱGundlach, R., 49-79.
9898  *Malek, Jaromir* La division de l'histoire d'Égypte et l'égyptologie moderne. BSFE 138 (1997) 6-17.
9899  **Mélèze Modrzejewski, Joseph** Les juifs d'Égypte de Ramsès II à Hadrien. P 1997, Presses Universitaires de France viii; 371 pp. FF98 [CÉg 73,187—Straus, Jean A.];
9900  The Jews of Egypt: from Rameses II to Emperor Hadrian. 1995, ⇒11/2,7212. VDI 222 (1997) 191-193 *(Fikhman, I.F.)*.
9901  **Montserrat, Dominic** Sex and society in Graeco-Roman Egypt. 1996, ⇒12,9237. ᴿAJA 101 (1997) 619-621 *(Meskell, Lynn)*; CÉg 72 (1997) 185-190 *(Bagnall, Roger S.)*.
9902  **Moreno Garcia, Juan Carlos** Études sur l'administration, le pouvoir et l'idéologie en Égypte, de l'Ancien au Moyen Empire. Aegyptiaca Leodiensia 4: Liège 1997, C.I.P.L. (6) iv; 174 pp.
9903  *Moreno García, Juan Carlos* Administration territoriale et organisation de l'espace en Egypte au troisième millénaire avant J.-C. (II): *swnw*. ZÄS 124/2 (1997) 116-130.
9904  ᴱ**O'Connor, David; Silverman, David P.** Ancient Egyptian kingship. 1995, ⇒11/2,9409. ᴿJEA 83 (1997) 227-8 *(Malek, Jaromir)*.
9905  ᴱ**Oren, Eliezer D.** The Hyksos: new historical and archaeological perspectives. University Museum Monographs 98: Ph 1997, University Museum, Univ. of Penn. xxvi; 434 pp. 188 fig. 23 pl. 16 tables; Seminar, Univ. Museum of Archaeology and Anthropology, Jan.-April 1992 [JARCE 36,169—Riggins, Thomas].
9906  *Pamminger, Peter* Contribution à la prosopographie militaire du Nouvel Empire. BiOr 54 (1997) 3-31.
9907  **Peden, A.J.** The reign of Ramesses IV. 1994, ⇒10,11107; 11/2,9411. ᴿBiOr 54 (1997) 631-633 *(Haring, Ben)*.
9908  *Putter, Thierry de* Ramsès II, géologue?: un commentaire de la stèle de Manshiyet es-Sadr, dite "de lan 8". ZÄS 124/2 (1997) 131-141.
9909  **Rice, Michael** Egypt's legacy: archetypes of western civilization 3000-30 BC. L 1997, Routledge xvi; 233 pp. £37.50. 0-415-15779-X.
9910  **Rohl, David** Pharaonen und Propheten: das AT auf dem Prüfstand. 1996, ⇒12,9242. ᴿJETh 11 (1997) 195-199 *(Fischer, Stefan)*.
9911  *Roth, Silke* Königin, Regentin oder weiblicher König?: zum Verhältnis von Königsideologie und "female sovereignty" in der Früh-

zeit. Selbstverständnis und Realität. ÄAT 36/1: 1997, ⇒394. EGundlach, R., 99-123.
9912  **Ryholt, K.S.B.** The political situation in Egypt during the Second Intermediate Period c. 1800-1550 B.C. Appendix *Bülow-Jacobsen, Adam*: Carsten Niebuhr Institute 20: K 1997, Carsten Niebuhr. 87-7289-421-0 [AcOr 60,207—Pierce, Richard Holton].
9913  *Schade-Busch, Mechthild* Bemerkungen zum Königsbild Thutmosis' III. in Nubien. Selbstverständnis und Realität. ÄAT 36/1: 1997, ⇒394. EGundlach, R., 211-223.
9914  **Schneider, Thomas** Lexikon der Pharaonen: die altägyptischen Könige von der Frühzeit bis zur Römerherrschaft. 1994, ⇒10,571*. ROr. 66/1 (1997) 123 *(Roccati, Alessandro)*.
9915  ESpencer, **Jeffrey** Aspects of early Egypt. 1996, ⇒12,243. RDiscEg 37 (1997) 85-88 *(Ciałowicz, Krzysztof M.)*; BiOr 54 (1997) 626-630 *(Trigger, Bruce G.)*.
9916  *Tefnin, Roland* Die Schlacht von Kadesch. WUB 5 (1997) 10-11.
9917  **Török, László** The kingdom of Kush: handbook of the Napatan-Meroitic civilization. HO 1/31: Lei 1997, Brill xvii; 591 pp. Bibl. 90-04-10448-8.
9918  **Trigger, Bruce G.** Early civilizations: ancient Egypt in context. 1993. RAJA 101/1 (1997) 164 *(Renfrew, Colin)*.
9919  **Vandersleyen, Claude** De la fin de l'Ancien Empire à la fin du Nouvel Empire. L'Égypte et la vallée du Nil, 2. 1995, ⇒11/2,9427; 12,9247. ROr. 66 (1997) 98-99 *(Berlev, Oleg D.)*; JARCE 34 (1997) 263-264 *(Delia, Robert D.)*.
9920  **Vernieux, Robert; Gondran, Michel** Amenophis IV et les pierres du soleil: Akhénaton retrouvé. P 1997, Arthaud 198 pp. 2-7003-1149-3.
9921  **Vernus, Pascal** Affaires et scandales sous les Ramsès. 1993, ⇒11/2,9429. RCÉg 72 (1997) 276-279 *(Kruchten, Jean-Marie)*.
9922  *Vernus, Pascal* Königliche Ideologie und gesellschaftliche Wirklichkeit. WUB 5 (1997) 17-22.
9923  **Warburton, David A.** State and economy in ancient Egypt: fiscal vocabulary of the New Kingdom. OBO 151: FrS 1997, University Press 379 pp. FS110. 3-7278-1080-7. RDiscEg 39 (1997) 149-151 *(Wilkinson, Toby A.H.)*.
9924  **Watterson, Barbara** The Egyptians. Oxf 1997, Blackwell 367 pp. 28 fig. 7 maps. 0-631-18272-1 [AJA 101,821].
9925  **Way, Thomas von der** Göttergericht und 'Heiliger Krieg' im alten Agypten. 1992, ⇒8,b977... 11/2,9432. RAfO 44-45 (1997-98) 522-523 *(Brein, G.)*;
9926  Untersuchungen zur Spätvor- und Frühgeschichte Unterägyptens. 1993, ⇒11/2,9431. RJNES 56 (1997) 294-298 *(Williams, Bruce)*.
9927  **Wilkinson, Toby A.H.** State formation in Egypt: chronology and society. 1996, ⇒12,9250. RAntiquity 71 (1997) 778-9 *(Snape, S.)*.
9928  *Zibelius-Chen, Karola* Theorie und Realität im Königtum der 25. Dynastie. Selbstverständnis und Realität. ÄAT 36/1: 1997, ⇒394. EGundlach, R., 81-95.
9929  *Zivie, Alain* Ramses II. WUB 5 (1997) 2-5;
9930  Von Hauptstadt zu Hauptstadt. WUB 5 (1997) 34-43.
9931  *Zonhoven, Louis* Was het oude Egypte een luikkerland?. Phoe. 43/2 (1997) 63-74.

Q4.0  **Historia Mesopotamiae**

9932  *Artzi, P.* The middle-Assyrian kingdom as precursor to the Assyrian empire. Assyrien im Wandel. 1997 ⇒379. ᴱWaetzoldt, H., 3-6.

9933  **Blois, Lukas de; Van der Spek, R.J.** An introduction to the ancient world. ᵀ*Mellor, Susan*: L 1997, Routledge xx; 321 pp. Bibl. 0-415-12773-4.

9934  **Brack-Bernsen, Lis** Zur Entstehung der babylonischen Mondtheorie: Beobachtung und theoretische Berechnung von Mondphasen. Boethius 40: Stu 1997, Steiner viii; 142 pp. Bibl. DM48. 3-515-07089-3.

9935  *Brinkmam, J.A.* Unfolding the drama of the Assyrian Empire. Assyria 1995. 1997, ⇒376. ᴱParpola, S., 1-16.

9936  *Cancik-Kirschbaum, Eva* Rechtfertigung von politischem Handeln in Assyrien im 13./12. Jh. v. Chr. AOAT 247: 1997, ⇒75. ᶠRoᴇʟʟɪɢ W., 69-77.

9937  *Charpin, Dominique; Durand, Jean-Marie* Asššur avant l'Assyrie. Mari 8 (1997) 367-391.

9938  *Cifola, Barbara* Ashurnasirpal II's 9th campaign: seizing the grain bowl of the Phoenician cities. Sum. 156. AfO 44-45 (1997) 156-8.

9939  ᴱ**Curtis, John** Later Mesopotamia and Iran: tribes and empires 1600-539 B.C.: proc. of a seminar in honour of **Lukonin, V.J.**: 1995, ⇒11/2,b371. ᴿBSOAS 60/1 (1997) 126-127 *(Cotterell, Peter)*; AfO 44-45 (1997-98) 478-481 *(Stiehler-Alegria, G.)*.

9940  *Donbaz, Veysel; Galter, Hannes D.* Assurnasirpal II. und die Subnatquelle. MDOG 129 (1997) 173-185.

9941  **Edzard, Dietz Otto** Gudea and his dynasty. The Royal Inscriptions of Mesopotamia, Early Periods 3/1: Toronto 1997, Univ. Toronto Press xvii; 233 pp. Bibl. $150. 0-8020-4187-6.

9942  *Eidem, J.; Højlund, F.* Assyria and Dilmun revisited. Assyrien im Wandel. 1997 ⇒379. ᴱWaetzoldt, H., 25-31.

9943  **Frayne, Douglas R.** The royal Inscriptions of Mesopotamia, early periods II: Sargonic and Gutian periods (2334-2113 BC). 1993, ⇒9,12587; 10,12583. ᴿRA 91 (1997) 91-93 *(Charpin, D.)*.

9944  *Freedman, David Noel* The Babylonian Chronicle. Divine Commitment 1. 1997 <1956>, ⇒124. 31-49.

9945  *George, A.R.* Assyria and the western world;

9946  *Gitin, Seymour* The Neo-Assyrian Empire and its western periphery: the Levant, with a focus on Philistine Ekron. Assyria 1995. 1997, ⇒376. ᴱParpola, S., 69-75/77-103.

9947  **Grayson, Albert Kirk** Assyrian rulers of the early first millennium BC II (858-745 BC). 1996, ⇒12,9226. ᴿAfO 44-45 (1997-98) 393-396 *(Schramm, Wolfgang)*.

9948  *Haerinck, E.* Babylonia under Achaemenid rule. 1997, ⇒58. ᴹLᴜᴋᴏɴɪɴ V., 26-34.

9949  *Holloway, Steven W.* Assyria and Babylonia in the tenth century BCE. The age of Solomon. 1997, ⇒282. ᴱHandy, L.K., 202-216.

9950  *Lanfranchi, G.B.* Consensus to empire: some aspects of Sargon II's foreign policy. Assyrien im Wandel. 1997 ⇒379. ᴱWaetzoldt, H., 81-87;

9951  Assyrische Kultur. Land der Bibel. 1997, ⇒9960. ᴱSeipel, W., 129-141.

9952 *Machinist, Peter* The fall of Assyria in comparative ancient perspective. Assyria 1995. 1997, ⇒376. ᴱParpola, S., 179-195.
9953 **Mayer, Walter** Politik und Kriegskunst der Assyrer. 1995, ⇒11/2,9466. ᴿAfO 44-45 (1997) 409-417 *(Fuchs, Andreas)*.
9954 *Pearce, Laurie E.* The number-syllabary texts. JAOS 116 (1996) 453-474.
9955 **Pingree, David** From astral omens to astrology: from Babylon to Bikaner. SOR 78: R 1997, Istituto Italiano per L'Africa e l'Oriente 125 pp.
9956 *Pongratz-Leisten, Beate* Genealogien als Kulturtechnik zur Begründung des Herrschaftsanspruchs in Assyrien und Babylonien. State Archives of Assyria Bulletin 11 (1997) 75-108;
9957 Toponyme als Ausdruck assyrischen Herrschaftsanspruchs. AOAT 247: 1997, ⇒75. ᶠRoɛʟʟɪɢ W., 325-343.
9958 **Sack, Ronald H.** Neriglissar—king of Babylon. AOAT 236: 1994, ⇒11/2,9475. ᴿOr. 66 (1997) 111-116 *(Zawadzki, Stefan)*.
9959 **Saggs, H.W.F.** Babylonians. 1995, ⇒11/2,9476. ᴿJAOS 117 (1997) 609-610 *(Chavalas, Mark W.)*.
9960 ᴱ**Seipel, Wilfried** Land der Bibel: Jerusalem und die Königsstädte des Alten Orients, Schätze aus dem Bible Lands Museum Jerusalem: Katalog; Textband. W 1997, Kunsthistorisches Museum 141: 239 pp. ill. 3-900325-76-6/5-8.
9961 *Sigrist, Marcel; Westenholz, Joan Goodnick* Das Neusumerische Reich: Geschichte, Kultur und Religion 39-49 ⇒9960.
9962 *Steele, J.M.; Stephenson, F.R.* Canon of solar and lunar eclipses for Babylon: 750 B.C. - A.D. 1. Sum. 195. AfO 44-45 (1997) 195-209.
9963 *Stronach, David* Notes on the fall of Niniveh;
9964 *Tadmor, Hayim* Propaganda, literature, historiography: cracking the code of the Assyrian royal inscriptions. Assyria 1995. 1997, ⇒376. ᴱParpola, S., 307-324/325-338.
9965 *Weisberg, David* Das Neubabylonische Reich 163-169 ⇒9960.
9966 *Zadok, R.* The ethnolinguistic composition of Assyria proper in the 9th-7th centuries BC. Assyrien im Wandel. 1997 ⇒379. ᴱWaetzoldt, H., 209-216;
9967 Historical and ethno-linguistic notes. UF 29 (1997) 797-814.

## Q4.5 *Historia Persiae*—Iran

9968 *Abadie, Philippe; Méroz, Christianne* La Perse et la Bible. MoBi 106 (1997) 70-75.
9969 *Amiet, Pierre* L'Iran avant les perses: la révélation du monde iranien. MoBi 106 (1997) 8-11.
9970 *Benoit, Agnès* Musée du Louvre: les salles iraniennes. MoBi 106 (1997) 12-16.
9971 **Briant, Pierre** Histoire de l'empire perse: de Cyrus à Alexandre. 1996, ⇒12,9291. ᴿBASOR 60 (1997) 347-349 *(Bivar, A.D.H.)*; CBFV 36 (1997) 159-161 *(Smyth, Françoise)*.
9972 *Briant, Pierre* Du Danube à l'Indus, l'histoire d'un empire. MoBi 106 (1997) 22-26.
9973 *Collins, John J.*, *(al.)*, L'héritage perse. MoBi 106 (1997) 76-85.

9974 **Koch, Heidemarie** Es kündet Dareios der König...: vom Leben im persischen Großreich. Kulturgeschichte der antiken Welt 55: Mainz 1996, Von Zabern 309 [32] pp. 3-8053-1934-7.

9975 [E]**Laperrousaz, Ernest-Marie; Lemaire, André** La Palestine à l'époque perse. 1994, ⇒10,252... 12,10014. [R]EstB 55 (1997) 547-548 *(Ribera, J.)*; Syr. 74 (1997) 242-243 *(Will, Ernest)*.

9976 *Lemaire, A.* Les Minéens et la Transeuphratène à l'époque perse: une première approche. TEuph 13 (1997) 123-139.

9977 *Menu, B.* Réglementation et modalités du prêt en Égypte à l'époque de la première domination perse. TEuph 13 (1997) 187-188.

9978 *Miroschedji, Pierre de* D'où venaient les perses?. MoBi 106 (1997) 17-21.

9979 [E]**Sancisi-Weerdenburg, H.; Kuhrt, A.; Root, M.** Cool Continuity and change: Proc. of the last Achaemenid history workshop, 1990. ⇒10,11156. [R]ClR 47/1 (1997) 104-105 *(Tsetskhladze, Gocha R.)*.

9980 *Walker, Christopher* Achaemenid chronology and the Babylonian sources. 1997, ⇒58. [M]LUKONIN V., 17-25.

9981 **Weber, Ursula; Wiesehöfer, Josef** Das Reich der Achaimeniden: eine Bibliographie. AMI.E 15: 1996, ⇒12,9300. [R]OLZ 92 (1997) 228-239 *(Kettenhofen, Erich)*; Mes. 32 (1997) 361-362 *(Invernizzi, A.)*; ZA 87 (1997) 291-292 *(Koch, H.)*.

9982 *Zawadzki, Stefan* Cyrus-Cambyses coregency. RA 90 (1996) 171-183.

### Q5 *Historia Anatoliae*—Asia Minor, Hittites [⇒T8.2]

9983 **Beckman, Gary** Hittite diplomatic texts. 1996, ⇒12,9302. [R]CBQ 59 (1997) 725-726 *(Younger, K. Lawson)*.

9984 *Czichon, Rainer M.* Studien zur Regionalgeschichte von Ḫḫī-tuša/Boğazköy 1996. MDOG 129 (1997) 89-102.

9985 **Dörtlük, Kayhan** Phaselis. Istanbul ²1996, Net Turistik Yayinlar 47 pp. 975-479-175-9.

> **Güterbock, H.** Perspectives on Hittite civilization ⇒131.
> **Hoffner, H.** The laws of the Hittites ⇒2108.

9986 *Polvani, Anna Maria* La cometa e gli annali di Mursili II. SEL 14 (1997) 17-28.

9987 *Sperlich, Waltraud; Schendzielorz, Ulrich* Zuflucht am schwarzen Berg: Karatepe—die letzte Bastion der Hethiter. Bild der Wissenschaft 25 (1997) 82-91.

9988 *Van der Hout, Theo P.J.* Twee tot driemaal daags eten en eetgewoontes bij de Hettieten. Phoe. 43/2 (1997) 75-92.

### Q6.1 Historia Graeciae classicae

9989 **Boegehold, Alan L.** The lawcourts at Athens. 1995, ⇒11/2,9540. [R]AJA 101 (1997) 797-798 *(Todd, S.C.)*.

9990 **Fitton, Lesley J.** The discovery of the Greek Bronze Age. 1996, ⇒12,9318. [R]AJA 101 (1997) 408-409 *(Thomas, Carol G.)*.

9991 Hellenische Mythologie/Vorgeschichte: die Hellenen und ihre Nachbarn von der Vorgeschichte bis zur klassischen Periode. Altenburg 1996, Verlag für Kultur und Wissenschaft 344 pp. Verein zur Förderung der Aufarbeitung der hellenischen Geschichte. 3-9804823-0-8. ᴿZDPV 113 (1997) 144-146 *(Vieweger, D.)*.

9992 ᴱ**Langdon, Susan** New light on a dark age: exploring the culture of Geometric Greece. Columbia 1997, Univ. of Missouri Press xii; 247 pp. 69 fig. $35. 0-8262-1099-6 [AJA 102,630s—Antonaccio, Carla M.].

9993 **Manville, Philip Brook** The origins of citizenship in ancient Athens. Princeton, NJ 1997, Princeton Univ. Press xiv; 265 pp. Bibl. 0-691-01593-7.

9994 *Martin, Jochen* Zwei alte Geschichten: vergleichende historisch-anthropologische Betrachtungen zu Griechenland und Rom. Saec. 48 (1997) 1-20.

9995 **Miller, Margaret Christina** Athens and Persia in the fifth century BC: a study in cultural receptivity. C 1997 University Press xiv; 331 pp. 0-521-49598-9.

9996 **Reden, Sitta von** Exchange in ancient Greece. 1995, ⇒12,9324. ᴿAJA 101 (1997) 175-176 *(Kroll, John H.)*.

9997 **Santosusso, Antonio** Soldiers, citizens, and the symbols of war: from classical Greece to republican Rome, 500-167 BC. Boulder 1997, Westview x; 277 pp. $22 [IHR 20,944ss—Hodgkinson, M.].

9998 *Schwinn, Thomas* Die Entstehung neuer Ordnungen im antiken Griechenland: eine struktur- und akteurtheoretische Analyse. KZSS 49 (1997) 391-409.

9999 *Yamauchi, Edwin M.* Greece and Babylon revisited. 1997, ⇒83. ᶠSʜᴇᴀ W., 127-135.

## Q6.5 Alexander, Seleucidae; historia Hellenismi

10000 **Barclay, John M.G.** Jews in the Mediterranean diaspora from Alexander to Trajan (323 BCE-117 CE). 1996, ⇒12,9326. ᴿTheol. 100 (1997) 56-57 *(Alexander, Loveday)*; RRT (1997/2) 55-57 *(Chaplin, Doug)*; JJS 48/1 (1997) 155-156 *(Gera, Dov)*; ThLZ 122 (1997) 546-549 *(Frenschkowski, Marco)*; JSSt 44 (1997) 412-417 *(Trebilco, Paul)*; RB 104 (1997) 448-450 *(Taylor, Justin)*.

10001 *Beaulieu, Paul-Alain; Rochberg, Francesca* The horoscope of Anu-Belšunu. JCS 48 (1996) 89-94.

10002 *Berlin, Andrea M.* Between large forces: Palestine in the Hellenistic period. BA 60/1 (1997) 2-51.

10003 *Berlin, Andrea M.* From monarchy to markets: the Phoenicians in Hellenistic Palestine. BASOR 306 (1997) 75-88.

10004 ᴱ**Bilde, Per,** *(al.)*, Aspects of Hellenistic kingship, 7. 1996, ⇒12,9327. ᴿMes. 32 (1997) 362-364 *(Invernizzi, A.)*;

10005 Conventional values of the Hellenistic Greeks. Studies in Hellenistic civilization 8: Aarhus 1997, Aarhus Univ. Press 327 pp. 87-7288-555-6.

10006 *Bloedow, Edmund F.; Loube, Heather M.* Alexander the Great "under fire" in Persepolis. Klio 79 (1997) 341-353.

10007 **Brown, John Pairman** Israel and Hellas. BZAW 231: 1995, ⇒11/2,9197; 12,9103. ᴿETR 72 (1997) 132 *(Römer, Thomas)*; OTEs 10 (1997) 550-553 *(Muntingh, L.M.)*; ᴿCBQ 59 (1997) 728-729 *(Hawk, L. Daniel)*.

10008 ᴱCartledge, P.; Garnsey, P.; Gruen, E. Hellenistic constructs: essays in culture, history and historiography  Hellenistic Culture and Society 26: Berkeley 1997: Univ. of California Press vii; 319 pp. £40/$50. 0-520-20676-2 [ClR 48,380ss—Davidson, James].

10009 *Collins, John J.* The Jewish transformation of Sibylline oracles;

10010 The Sybil and the potter: political propaganda in Ptolemaic Egypt <1994>. Seers. JSJ.S 54: 1997, ⇒119. 181-197/199-210.

10011 **Del Monte, Giuseppe F.** Testi dalla Babilonia ellenistica. Studi ellenistici 9: Pisa 1997, Istituti Editoriali e Poligrafici Internazionali xiv; 296 pp. Bibl. 88-8147-020-9.

10012 **Durand, Xavier** Des grecs en Palestine au IIIe siècle avant Jésus-Christ: le dossier syrien des archives de Zénon de Caunos. CRB 38: P 1997, Gabalda 304 pp. Bibl. FF280. 2-85021-101-X.

10013 *Ellens, J. Harold* The ancient library of Alexandria: the west's most important repository of learning. BiRe 13/1 (1997) 18-29, 46.

10014 ᴱ**Funck, Bernd** Hellenismus: Beiträge zur Erforschung von Akkulturation und politischer Ordnung in den Staaten des hellenistischen Zeitalters. Tü 1997, Mohr xvi; 798 pp. Akten des Internationalen Hellenismus-Kolloquium 9.-14. März 1994 in Berlin. DM298. 3-16-146526-1 [JSJ 28,366].

10015 *Gera, Dov; Horowitz, Wayne* Antiochus IV in life and death: evidence from the Babylonian astronomical diaries. JAOS 117 (1997) 240-252.

10016 **Grainger, John D.** A Seleukid prosopography and gazetteer. Mn.S 172: Lei 1997, Brill xxii; 828 pp. 90-04-10799-1.

10017 **Habicht, C.** Athens from Alexander to Antony. CM 1997, Harvard Univ. Press x; 406 pp. £26.50. 0-674-05111-4 [ClR 48,385s—Ogden, Daniel].

10018 **Hall, Jonathan M.** Ethnic identity in Greek antiquity. C 1997, CUP viii; 228 pp. Bibl. £35. 0-521-58017-X.

10019 **Hammond, N.G.L.** The genius of Alexander the Great. L 1997, Duckworth xiii; 220 pp. £35. 0-7156-2692-2 [ClR 48,378—Devine, A.M.].

10020 *Hartman, Lars* 'Guiding the knowing vessel of your heart': on bible usage and Jewish identity in Alexandrian Judaism. NT and Hellenistic Judaism. 1997, ⇒318. ᴱBorgen, P., 19-36.

10021 ᴱ**Hoepfner, Wolfram; Brands, Gunnar** Basileia: die Paläste der hellenistischen Könige. 1996, Symposium, Berlin 1992, ⇒12,314. ᴿMes. 32 (1997) 381-384 *(Invernizzi, A.)*.

10022 *Gera, Dov* Antiochus IV in life and death: evidence from the Babylonian astronomical diaries. JAOS 117 (1997) 240-252.

10023 **Inwood, B.; Gerson, L.P.** Hellenistic philosophy: introductory readings. Indianapolis ²1997, Hackett xxi; 441 pp. £10. 0-87220-378-6 [ClR 48,516—Ireland, Stanley].

10024 *Jasnow, Richard* The Greek Alexander romance and demotic Egyptian literature. JNES 56 (1997) 95-103.

10025 *Orth, Wolfgang* Hellenistische Monarchie und römischer Prinzipat. Klio 79 (1997) 354-361.

10026 *Roche, Marie-Jeanne* Remarques sur les Nabatéens en Méditerranée. Sum. 73. Sem. 45 (1997) 73-99.

10027 **Sachs, Abraham J.; Hunger, Hermann** Diaries from 164 B.C. to 61 B.C. Astronomical diaries and related texts from Babylonia, 3. DÖAW.PH 247: W 1996, Verlag ÖAW 517 pp. 166-297 pl. ᴿAfO 44-45 (1997-98) 167-175 *(Van der Spek, R.J.)*.

10028 *Sterling, Gregory E.* Hellenistic philosophy and the New Testament. Handbook. NTTS 25: 1997, ⇒971. EPorter, S.E., 313-358.

10029 **Stern, Menahem** Hasmonean Judaea in the Hellenistic world. E*Schwartz, Daniel R.*, J 1995, Shazar Center for Jewish History 298 pp. RAJS Review 22/1 (1997) 112-114 *(Goodblatt, David)* H.

10030 **Stoneman, R.** Alexander the Great. L 1997, Routledge xx; 101 pp. £7. 0-415-15050-7 [CIR 48,525s—Ogden, Daniel].

10031 ETritle, **Lawrence A.** The Greek world in the fourth century: from the fall of the Athenian empire to the successors of Alexander. L 1997, Routledge xvii; 296 pp. Bibl. 0-415-10582-X.

10032 *Troiani, Lucio* Cronologie apologetiche presso gli storici ellenisti. RStB 9/1 (1997) 171-182.

10033 *Tuplin, C.J.* Medism and its causes. TEuph 13 (1997) 155-185.

10034 **Voegelin, Eric** Hellenism, Rome, and early christianity. History of political ideas, 1. E*Moulakis, Athanasios*: Collected Works of Eric Voegelin 19: Columbia 1997, Univ. of Missouri Press 281 pp. $35 [JR 79,136ss—Heilke, Thomas].

10035 *Waldbaum, Jane C.* Greeks in the east or Greeks and the east?: problems in the definition and recognition of presence. BASOR 305 (1997) 1-17.

10036 *Walter, Nikolaus* Frühe Begegnungen zwischen jüdischem Glauben und hellenistischer Bildung in Alexandrien <1964>;

10037 Hellenistische Diaspora-Juden an der Wiege des Urchristentums <1995>. Praeparatio evangelica. WUNT 98: 1997, ⇒167. 1-11/383-404.

## Q7 Josephus Flavius

10038 *Bammel, Ernst* Von Josephus zu HEGESIPP <1993>;

10039 Der Zeuge des Judentums <1987>. Judaica et Paulina. WUNT 91: 1997, 64-76/109-114.

10040 *Barzanò, Alberto* L'uso delle cronologie in Giuseppe Flavio e la storia ebraica universalizzata. RStB 9/1 (1997) 183-191.

10041 *Begg, C.T.* Israel's treaty with Gibeon according to Josephus. OLoP 28 (1997) 123-145 [Josh 9,3-27];

10042 The Cisjordanian altar(s) and their associated rites according to Josephus. BZ 41 (1997) 192-211;

10043 Israel's battle with Amalek according to Josephus. JSQ 4 (1997) 201-216 [Ex 17,8-16];

10044 Israel's demand for a king according to Josephus. Muséon 110 (1997) 329-348;

10045 Jeremiah under King Zedekiah according to *Ant.* 10.102-130. Som., sum. 7. REJ 156 (1997) 7-42;

10046 Samuel's farewell discourse according to Josephus. SJOT 11 (1997) 56-77 [1 Sam 12];

10047 The Jeroboam-Ahijah encounter according to Josephus. Abr-n. 34 (1996-97) 1-17 [1 Kgs 11,26-40];

10048 David's second sparing of Saul according to Josephus. TynB 48 (1997) 93-117 [1 Sam 26];

10049 David's transfer of the ark according to Josephus. BBR 7 (1997) 11-35 [2 Sam 6; 1 Chr 13-16];

10050 The exploits of David's heroes according to Josephus. Sum. 454. LASBF 47 (1997) 139-169 [2 Sam 21,15-22; 23,8-37];
10051 Joash of Judah according to Josephus. JSOT.S 238: 1997, ⇒61. ᶠMcKenzie S., 301-320 [2 Kgs 12,1-22; 2 Chr 24,1-27];
10052 The massacre of the priests of Nob in Josephus and Pseudo-Philo. EstB 55 (1997) 171-198 [1 Sam 21-22];
10053 Samuel leader of Israel according to Josephus. Riass. 199. Anton. 72 (1997) 199-216 [1 Sam 7,2-17];
10054 The Transjordanian altar (Josh 22:10-34) according to Josephus (Ant.5.100-114) and Pseudo-Philo (LAB 22.1-8). AUSS 35 (1997) 5-19;
10055 The Ziklag interlude according to Josephus. Ter. 48 (1997) 713-736 [1 Sam 30].
10056 **Bergmeier, Roland** Die Essenerberichte des Flavius Josephus. 1993, ⇒9,10651. ᴿBZ 41 (1997) 118-119 *(Maier, Johann).*
10057 *Botha, Pieter J.J.* History, rhetoric and writings of Josephus. Neotest. 31 (1997) 1-20.
10058 *Feldman, Louis H.* The concept of exile in Josephus. Exile. JSJ.S 56: 1997, ⇒227. ᴱScott, J.M., 145-172;
10059 Josephus' view of Solomon. The age of Solomon. 1997, ⇒282. ᴱHandy, L., 348-374;
10060 Josephus' portrait of Isaiah. Writing and reading... Isaiah. VT.S 70/2: 1997, ⇒181. ᴱBroyles, C.C., 583-608;
10061 Josephus' portrait of Jehu. JSQ 4/1 (1997) 12-32 [2 Kgs 9,1-10,36];
10062 Josephus' portrait of Jethro. Bibl.Interp. 28: 1997, ⇒77. ᶠSanders J., 573-594;
10063 Josephus' portrait of Rehoboam. StPhilo 9 (1997) 264-286 [1 Kgs 12].
10064 ᴱ**Feldman, Louis H; Levinson, John R.** Josephus' *Contra Apionem.* AGJU 34: 1996, ⇒12,9384. ᴿEThL 73 (1997) 434-437 *(Verheyden, J.).*
10065 **Gerber, Christine** Ein Bild des Judentums für Nichtjuden von Flavius Josephus: Untersuchungen zu seiner Schrift *Contra Apionem.* Diss. München, 1996, ᴰ*Hahn, F.*: AGJU 40: Lei 1997, Brill xiv; 456 pp. Bibl. ƒ250. 90-04-10753-3.
10066 **Hadas-Lebel, Mireille** Flavio Josefo. 1994, ⇒10,11270; 11/2,9687. ᴿAnnTh 11 (1997) 529-531 *(Bermúdez, Catalina).*
10067 ᵀ**Harsberg, Erling** Flavius Josefus: den jødiske krig. K 1997, Museum Tusculanum 477 pp. Inledning og kommentarer. 87-7289-386-9 [NTT 98/3,181].
10068 **Krieger, Klaus-Stefan** Geschichtsschreibung als Apologetik bei Flavius Josephus. 1994, ⇒11/2,9694. ᴿJBL 116 (1997) 129-132 *(Mason, Steve).*
10069 *Mason, Steve* Will the real Josephus please stand up?. BArR 23/5 (1997) 58-65, 67-68.
10070 **Mayer-Schärtel, Bärbel** Das Frauenbild des Josephus: eine sozialgeschichtliche und kultanthropologische Untersuchung. 1995, ⇒11/2,9699. ᴿBZ 41 (1997) 257-261 *(Trautmann, Maria).*
10071 ᵀ**Nieto Ibáñez, Jesús M.ª** Flavio Josefo: la guerra de los judíos: libros I-III. Biblioteca Clásica Gredos 247: M 1997, Gredos 516 pp. Introd., notas. 84-249-1886-X [FgNT 11,139—Peláez, Jesús].

10072    *Pastor, Jack* Josephus and social strata: an analysis of social attitudes. Henoch 19/3 (1997) 295-312.

10073    *Spottorno, Victoria* The books of Chronicles in Josephus' *Jewish Antiquities*. IX Congress IOSCS. SCSt 45: 1997, ⇒340. ᴱTaylor, B.A., 381-390.

10074    ᴱ**Vara Donado, José** Josephus, Flavius: antigüedades judías: v.1, libros I-XI; v.2, libros XII-XX. Akal. Clásica 45-46: M 1997, Torrejón de Ardoz 2 vols. 84-4600-782-7.

10075    *Williams, David S.* Josephus or Nɪcoʟᴀᴜs on the pharisees?. Som., sum. 43. REJ 156 (1997) 43-58;

10076    Tʜᴀᴄᴋᴇʀᴀʏ's assistant hypothesis: a stylometric evaluation. JJS 48 (1997) 262-275.


## Q8.1  *Roma Pompeii et Caesaris*—Hyrcanus to Herod

10077    **Kunkel, Wolfgang; Wittmann, Roland** Die Magistratur. ᴱ*Glasterer, Hartmut; Meier, Christian.* Staatsordnung und Staatspraxis der römischen Republik, 2. HAW 10: Mü 1995, Beck xvii; 806 pp. DM278. 3-406-33827-5. ᴿHZ 264 (1997) 718-720 *(Libero, Loretana de)*.

10078    *Regev, Eyal* How did the Temple Mount fall to Pompey?. JJS 48 (1997) 276-289.

10079    **Richardson, Peter** Herod: king of the Jews and friend of the Romans. 1996, ⇒12,9411. ᴿTheology 798 (1997) 452-453 *(Freyne, Sean)*.


## Q8.4  Zeitalter Jesus Christ: *particular/general*

10080    *Aguirre, Rafael* Los estudios actuales sobre Galilea y la exégesis de los evangelios [Lk 7,24-26; 11,17; 9,57-58];

10081    *Alonso Schökel, Luis* El Mediterráneo y la biblia. La Bíblia i el Mediterrani. 1997, ⇒385. ᴱBorrell, d'Agustí, 249-262/3-10.

10082    *Evenari, Michael* Die Nabatäer im Negev. Petra und das Königreich. 1997, ⇒289. ᴱLindner, M., 162-182.

10083    **Galinsky, Karl** Augustan culture: an interpretive introduction. 1996, ⇒12,9413. ᴿAJA 101 (1997) 610-612 *(Kampen, Natalie B.)*.

10084    *Hirschfeld, Yizhar* Jewish rural settlement in Judaea in the early Roman period. Early Roman Empire. 1997, ⇒357. ᴱAlcock, S., 72-88.

10085    **Horsley, Richard A.** Galilee: history, politics, people. 1995, ⇒11/2,b077. ᴿTS 58/1 (1997) 155-156 *(Witherington III, Ben)*.

10086    *Khouri, Rami G.* "Meine geliebten Brüder und Schwestern": das nabatäische Königtum und die modernen arabischen Monarchien;

10087    *Knauf, Ernst Axel* "Der sein Volk liebt": Entwicklung des nabatäischen Handelsimperiums zwischen Stamm, Königtum und Klientel. Petra antike Felsstadt. 1997, ⇒311. ᴱWeber, T., 164-167/14-24.

10088    *Levine, L.I.* Archaeology and the religious ethos of pre-70 Palestine. Hillel and Jesus. 1997, ⇒321. ᴱCharlesworth, J.H., 110-120.

10089  *Lindner, Manfred* Die Geschichte der Nabatäer. Petra und das
       Königreich. 1997, ⇒289. <sup>E</sup>Lindner, M., 37-112.
10090  *Robinson, S.E.* Apocalypticism in the time of Hillel and Jesus.
       Hillel and Jesus. 1997, ⇒321. <sup>E</sup>Charlesworth, J.H., 121-136.
10091  *Saldarini, Anthony J.* Jewish responses to Greco-Roman culture,
       332 B.C.E. to 200 C.E. The Cambridge companion. 1997,
       ⇒429. <sup>E</sup>Kee, H.C., 288-440.
10092  **Schürer, Emil** Storia del popolo giudaico al tempo di Gesù Cri-
       sto (175 a.C.-135 d.C.), 3/1. <sup>E</sup>*Vermes, Geza, (al.)*: BSSTB 12:
       Brescia 1997, Paideia 901 pp. L170.000. 88-394-0549-6 [RB
       105,316].
10093  **Winkes, Rolf** Livia, Octavia, Iulia: Porträts und Darstellung.
       Archeologica Transatlantica 13: Providence 1995, Art and Ar-
       chaeology 238 pp. 292 fig. $61 [AJA 103,721s—Wood, Susan].

### Q8.7 *Roma et Oriens,* prima decennia post Christum

10094  *Álvarez, David* El edicto de CLAUDIO y la comunidad judía de
       Roma. La Bíblia i el Mediterrani. 1997, ⇒385. <sup>E</sup>Borrell,
       d'Agustí, 263-277.
10095  **Botermann, Helga** Das Judenedikt des Kaisers CLAUDIUS:
       römischer Staat und *Christiani* im 1. Jahrhundert. Hermes.E 71:
       1996, ⇒12,9421. <sup>R</sup>VigChr 51 (1997) 217 *(Teitler, H.C.)*; JETh
       11 (1997) 217-8 *(Baum, Armin Daniel)*; ThLZ 122 (1997) 1128-
       1131 *(Freudenberger, Rudolf)*; TThZ 106 (1997) 154-155 *(Rei-
       ser, M.)*.
10096  *Brunt, P.A.* Laus imperii. Paul and empire. 1997, ⇒204.
       <sup>E</sup>Horsley, R.A., 25-35.
10097  <sup>T</sup>**Callu, J.-P.** Introduction générale: vies d'Hadrien, Aelius, An-
       tonin. Histoire Auguste 1/1. 1992, ⇒10,11379. <sup>R</sup>Gn. 69 (1997)
       336-341 *(Szidat, Joachim)*.
10098  **Fell, Martin** Optimus princeps?: Anspruch und Wirklichkeit der
       imperialen Programmatik Kaiser Traians. 1991, ⇒11/2,9788.
       <sup>R</sup>Gn. 69 (1997) 81-84 *(Scardigli, Barbara)*.
10099  *Garnsey, Peter; Saller, Richard* Patronal power relations. Paul
       and empire. 1997, ⇒204. <sup>E</sup>Horsley, R.A., 96-103.
10100  *Gill, David W.J.* The Roman empire as a context for the New
       Testament. Handbook. NTTS 25: 1997, <sup>E</sup>Porter, S.E., 389-406.
10101  *Jones, Christopher P.* Egypt and Judaea under Vespasian. Hist.
       46 (1997) 249-253.
       **Mendels, D.** The rise and fall of Jewish nationalism ⇒9007.
10102  **Millar, Fergus** The Roman Near East 31 BC-AD 337. 1993,
       ⇒11/2,9914. <sup>R</sup>Gn. 69 (1997) 79-81 *(Pekáry, Thomas)*.
10103  **Shotter, David** Nero. Lancaster Pamphlets: L 1997, Routledge
       xvii; 101 pp. £7. 0-415-12931-1 [AnCl 67,494ss—Benoist, S.].
10104  **Southern, Pat** Domitian: tragic tyrant. L 1997, Routledge viii;
       164 pp. Bibl. £40. 0-415-16525-3.

### Q9.1 *Historia Romae generalis et* post-christiana

10105  <sup>E</sup>**Alcock, Susan E.** The early Roman Empire in the East. Oxbow
       Monograph 95: Oxf 1997, Oxbow x; 212 pp. £24. 1-900188-52-
       X.
10106  **Bowersock, G.W.** Martyrdom and Rome. 1995, ⇒11/2,9847;
       12,9430. <sup>R</sup>JR 77 (1997) 128-129 *(Trumbower, Jeffrey A.)*.

10107 **Carandini, Andrea** La nascita di Roma: dèi, lari, eroi e uomini all'alba di una civiltà. Biblioteca di cultura storica 219: T 1997, Einaudi xxx; 766 pp. Bibl. 88-06-14494-4.

10108 [E]**Clauss, Manfred** Die römischen Kaiser: 55 historische Portraits von Caesar bis Iustinian. Mü 1997, Beck 501 pp. [ZSSR.R 115,729s—Jakab, Éva].

10109 *Fernández-Ardanaz, Santiago* El papel del mundo neopúnico en la cristianización del Mediterráneo occidental y en la posición antiromana (siglos III-V). La Bíblia i el Mediterrani. 1997, ⇒385. [E]Borrell, d'Agustí, 145-153.

10110 **Goodman, Martin** The Roman world, 44 BC-AD 180. Collab. *Sherwood, Jane*: Routledge history of the ancient world: L 1997, Routledge xxiii; 380 pp. Bibl. £50/£17. 0-415-04969-5/70-9.

10111 **Grandazzi, Alexandre** The foundation of Rome: myth and history. [T]*Todd, Jane Marie*: Ithaca 1997, Cornell Univ. Press x; 236 pp. Bibl. 0-8014-3114-X.

10112 **Haensch, Rudolf** Capita provinciarum: Statthaltersitze und Provinzverwaltung in der römischen Kaiserzeit. Diss. Köln. Kölner Forschungen 7: Mainz 1997, Von Zabern 863 pp. [GGA 251,189—Wesch-Klein, Gabriele].

10113 **Hamman, A.-G.** A vita cotidiana dos primeiros cristãos (95-197). [T]*Lemos, Benôni*: Patrologia: São Paulo 1997, Paulus 248 pp. [REB 57,1020].

10114 [E]**Hawley, R; Levick, B.** Women in antiquity: new assessments. L 1995, Routledge 296 pp. $63. 0-415-11368-7. [R]CIR 47 (1997) 373-375 *(Gardner, Jane F.)*.

10115 I sabini: la vita, la morte, gli dèi. R 1997, Armando 142 pp. Bibl. Ministero per i Beni Culturali e Ambientali. 88-7144-782-4.

10116 [E]**Jones, P.; Sidwell, K.** The world of Rome: an introduction to Roman culture. C 1997, CUP xvii; 399 pp. £45/£16. 0-521-38421-4/600-4 [ClR 48,417ss—Barker, Peter].

10117 **Kienast, Dietmar** Römische Kaisertabelle: Grundzüge einer römischen Kaiserchronologie. Da:Wiss [2]1996, xxvii; 399 pp. DM78. [R]CÉg 72 (1997) 176-181 *(Kettenhofen, Erich)*.

10118 **König, Ingemar** Die Kaiserzeit. Der römische Staat, 2. Reclam Wissen 9615: Stu 1997, Reclam 550 pp. DM20. 3-15-009615-4 [AnCl 67,474—Desy, Philippe].

10119 **Lendon, J.E.** Empire of honour: the art of government in the Roman world. Oxf 1997, Clarendon xii; 320 pp. £40 [HZ 267,728s—Schulz, Raimund].

10120 **Lintott, Andrew** Imperium romanum: politics and administration. 1993, ⇒10,11413; 11/2,9909. [R]Gn. 69 (1997) 330-336 *(Galsterer, Hartmut)*.

10121 **Löhr, Winrich Alfred** Basilides und seine Schule. WUNT 2/83: 1996, ⇒12,9450. [R]JThS 48 (1997) 238-241 *(Edwards, M.J.)*.

10122 *Meinardus, Otto* Les débuts du christianisme alexandrin et les églises d'Alexandrie. Sum. 104. Le Monde Copte 27-28 (1997) 99-104.

10123 **Migliardi Zingale, Livia** I testamenti romani nei papiri e nelle tavolette d'Egitto: silloge di documenti dal I al IV secolo d.C. T [3]1997, Giappichelli 179 pp. 88-348-7047-6.

10124   **Orlin, Eric M.** Temples, religion and politics in the Roman Republic. Mn.S 164: Lei 1997, Brill ix; 227 pp. 90-04-10708-8.
10125   ᴱ**Rawson, Beryl; Weaver, Pau** The Roman family in Italy: status, sentiment, space. Humanities Research Centre. Oxford 1997, Clarendon xvi; 378 pp. Bibl. 0-19-815052-0.
10126   **Robert, Jean-Noël** De Rome à la Chine: sur les routes de la soie au temps des Césars. P ²1997, Belles Lettres 390 pp. Bibl. 2-251-44006-2.
10127   **Rutgers, L.V.** The Jews in late ancient Rome. 1995, ⇒11/2,a014. ᴿClR 47 (1997) 365-366 *(Goodman, M.D.)*; JAOS 117 (1997) 719-720 *(Price, Jonathan J.)*.
10128   **Schulz, Raimund** Herrschaft und Regierung: Roms Regiment in den Provinzen in der Zeit der Republik. Pd 1997, Schöningh 330 pp. 3-506-78207-X.
10129   *Straus, Jean A.* Les autorités responsables de l'ἀνάκρισις des esclaves dans l'Égypte romaine. CÉg 72 (1997) 332-340.
10130   *Sznycer, Maurice* Permanence de l'organisation administrative des territoires africains aux époques punique et romaine d'après les témoignages épigraphiques. Des Sumériens. 1997, ⇒377. ᴱSérandour, A., 111-123.
10131   **Thomas, Yan** 'Origine' et 'commune patrie': étude de droit public romain (89 av. J.-C. - 212 ap. J.C.). CEFR 221: R 1996, Ecole française xv; 221 pp. 2-7083-0358-4 [AnCl 68,562—Raepsaet-Charlier, Marie-Thérèse].

# XVIII. Archaeologia terrae biblicae

## T1.1 General biblical-area archaeologies

10132   **Bahn, Paul G.** The Cambridge illustrated history of archaeology. 1996, ⇒12,9466. ᴿAJA 101 (1997) 776-777 *(Silberman, Neil A.)*.
10133   ᴱ**Ben-Tor, Amnon** The archaeology of Ancient Israel. ᵀGreenberg, R.: 1992. ᴿJSSt 42 (1997) 141-143 *(Prag, Kay)*; JNES 56 (1997) 134-137 *(Hallote, Rachel)*.
10134   **Bouzek, Jan** Greece, Anatolia and Europe: cultural interrelations during the early Iron Age. Studies in Mediterranean Archaeology 122: Jonsered 1997, Åström 321 pp. 34 pl. 317 fig. Bibl. SEK750. 91-7081-168-7 [Antiquity 72,934—Sinclair, Anthony].
10135   ᴱ**Briese, C.**, *(al.)*, Interactions in the Iron Age. 1996, ⇒12,9469. ᴿMes. 32 (1997) 386-390 *(Conti, M.C.)*.
10136   **Dever, W.G.** Recent archaeological discoveries and biblical research. 1990, ⇒6,b908... 12,9472. ᴿPEQ 129 (1997) 166-167 *(Cobbing, Felicity J.)*.
10137   *Ehrlich, Ernst Ludwig* Das Land Israel. WUB 4 (1997) 48-50.
10138   **Finkelstein, Israel** Living on the fringe: the archaeology and history of the Negev, Sinai and neighbouring regions in the bronze and iron ages. Monographs in Mediterranean Archaeology 6: Shf 1995, Academic 197 pp. 40 fig. 8 plans; 13 maps. $60. 1-85075-555-8. ᴿAJA 101 (1997) 171-172 *(Bienkowski, Piotr)*; BiOr 54

(1997) 227-228 *(Van der Steen, Eveline J.)*; AUSS 35 (1997) 263-265 *(Hasel, Michael G.)*.

10139 **Forsberg, Stig** Near Eastern destruction datings as sources for Greek and Near Eastern Iron Age chronology. Boreas 19: 1995, ⇒11/2,a929. ᴿOLZ 92 (1997) 518-522 *(Novák, Mirko)*.

10140 **Frascati, Simona** La collezione epigrafica di Giovanni Battista De ROSSI presso il Pontificio Istituto di Archeologia Cristiana. SSAC 11: Città del Vaticano 1997, Pontificio Istituto di Archeologia Cristiana 243 pp. Bibl. 88-85991-19-X.

10141 *Freedman, David Noel* Archaeology and the future of biblical studies: the biblical languages. Divine Commitment 1. 1997 <1965>, ⇒124. 185-199.

10142 **Fritz, Volkmar** An introduction to biblical archaeology. JSOT.S 172: 1994 <1985>, ⇒11/2,a045. ᴿBiOr 54 (1997) 231-234 *(Holland, T.A.)*; AUSS 35 (1997) 266-267 *(Hasel, Michael G.)*.

10143 *Gądecki, Stanisław* Archeologia biblijna. 1994, ⇒10,11497. Saeculum Christianum 4/2 (1997) 243-245 *(Nowogórski, Przemysław)*.

10144 **González Echegaray, Joaquín** Arqueología y evangelios. 1994, ⇒10,11500. ᴿEstB 55 (1997) 273-275 *(Sánchez de Toca, M.)*.

10145 *Hossfeld, Frank-Lothar* Israel/Palästina—Gelobtes und Heiliges Land. WUB 4 (1997) 41-43.

10146 *Korfmann, Manfred* Hisarlik und das Troia Homers—ein Beispiel zur kontroversen Einschätzung der Möglichkeiten der Archäologie. AOAT 247: 1997, ⇒75. ᶠROELLIG W., 171-184.

10147 *Piccirillo, Michele* Sesenta años de actividad arqueológica en la tierra bíblica de Transjordania (en el monte Nebo donde murió Mosés). TE 41 (1997) 367-379.

10148 *Quesnel, Michel* Das Land, in dem Gott Mensch wurde. WUB 4 (1997) 44-47.

10149 **Rast, Walter E.** Through the ages of Palestinian archaeology: an introductory handbook. Ph 1997, Trinity xiii; 221 pp. 1-56338-055-2.

10150 *Sabbah, Michel* Heiliges Land, alltägliches Land. WUB 4 (1997) 51-52.

10151 ᴱ**Shanks, Hershel** Biblical archaeology: from the ground down. 1996, Video. ⇒12,9480. ᴿRExp 94/1 (1997) 139-140 *(Drinkard, Joel F. Jr.)*.

10152 *Shanks, Hershel* Leading archaeologist chastised for publishing artifacts in private collections: debate over antiquities market continues. BArR 23/6 (1997) 33.

10153 **Stefoff, Rebecca** Finding the lost cities: the golden age of archaeology. L 1997, British Museum 190 pp. 0-7141-2124-X.

10154 *Wenning, Robert* Von einer Bibelwissenschaft zu einer Landesarchäologie. WUB 4 (1997) 60-69.

10155 **Wimmer, Hans H.** Die Strukturforschung in der klassischen Archäologie. EHS 38/60: Bern 1997, Lang 276 pp. $48. 3-906756-31-9 [AJA 101,821].

10156 **Zwickel, W.** Die Welt des Alten und Neuen Testaments: ein Sach- und Arbeitsbuch. Stu 1997, Calwer 272 pp. DM38 [ZAW 111,323—Wegner, A.-C.].

## T1.2 Musea, organismi, exploratores

10157   **D'Amicone, Elvira** Nella valle del Nilo: Antico Egitto da toccare. T 1997, Celid 127 pp. Mostra a Moncalieri dal 24 sett. a 20 dic. 1997; Bibl. 88-7661-299-8.

10158   Dalla terra alle genti: la diffusione del cristianesimo nei primi secoli: guida alla mostra. Mi 1996, Electa 31 pp.

10159   Geheimnisvolle Königin Hatschepsut: ägyptische Kunst des 15. Jahrhunderts v. Chr. Wsz 1997, Nationalmuseum 181 pp. Bibl. 83-7100-107-X.

10160   [E]**Krauspe, Renate** Das Ägyptische Museum der Universität Leipzig. Photo. *Liepe, Jürgen*: Zaberns Bildbände zur Archäologie: Mainz 1997, Von Zabern 136 pp. DM58. 3-8053-2007-8.

10161   [E]**Morello, Giovanni** Pierre et Rome: vingt siècles d'élan créateur. Città del Vaticano 1997, Musei Vaticani 255 pp. Paris—Hotel de Ville 10.7-9.11 1997; Bibl. 88-374-1573-7.

10162   Museo Nazionale Romano: Palazzo Altemps. Guide Electa per la Soprintendenza archeologica di Roma. Mi 1997, Electa 67 pp. 88-435-6381-5.

10163   New antiquities: recent discoveries from archaeological excavations in Israel. J 1997, Israel Museum 32 pp. 965-278-212-2.

10164   **Nielsen, Anne Marie; Østergaard, Jan Stubbe** The eastern Mediterranean in the Hellenistic period: Ny Carlsberg Glyptotek. K 1997, Ny Carlsberg Glyptotek 159 pp. Contrib. *M. Moltesen; B. Lundgreen;* ill. 87-7452-218-3 [Mes. 33,396s—Invernizzi, A.].

10165   *Poulin, Joan; Briend, Jacques* Das Heilige Land in den Museen Jerusalems. WUB 4 (1997) 79-85.

10166   **Schmidt, Stefan** Katalog der ptolemäischen und kaiserzeitlichen Objekte aus Ägypten im Akademischen Kunstmuseum Bonn. Mü 1997, Biering & B 157 pp. Beitrag von *Barbara Borg;* 31 fig. 78 pl. [CÉg 73,191s—Nachtergael, Georges].

10167   [E]**Seipel, Wilfried** Land der Bibel: Schätze aus dem Israel Museum Jerusalem. W 1997, Kunsthistorisches Museum 150 pp. 3-900325-77-4.
        Land der Bibel: Schätze aus dem Bible Lands Museum Jerusalem ⇒9960;

10168   [E]**Ziegler, Christiane**, (*al.*), Musée du Louvre, Département des antiquités égyptiennes: les antiquités égyptiennes: guide du visiteur. P 1997, Réunion des Musées Nationaux 2 vols. 2-7118-.

10169   *Ziegler, Christiane; Barbotin, Christophe* Die Schätze des Louvre. WUB 5 (1997) 56-59.

## T1.3 *Methodi*—Science in archaeology

10170   **Bernbeck, Reinhard** Theorien in der Archäologie. Tü [2]1997 <1964>, Francke 404 pp. DM39.80. 3-7720-2254-5 [ThLZ 124,1203—Conrad, Diethelm].

10171   **Drennan, Robert D.** Statistics for archaeologists: a commonsense approach. 1996, ⇒12,9509. [R]AJA 101 (1997) 628-629 *(Lock, Gary)*.

10172 *Finkelstein, Israel* Method of field survey and data recording 11-24 ⟹10174.

10173 [E]**Finkelstein, Israel; Lederman, Zvi** Highlands of many cultures: the southern Samaria survey: the sites, I-II. Tel Aviv University, Nadler Institute of Archaeology MS 14: J 1997, Graphit xvi; 959 pp. 965-440-007-3.

10174 **Hodder, Ian**, *(al.)*, Interpreting archaeology: finding meaning in the past. L 1997, Routledge ix; 275 pp. Bibl. 0-415-15744-7.

10175 *Lehrer-Jacobson, Gusta* Fake!: the many facets of the forger's art. BArR 23/2 (1997) 36-38, 67.

10176 *Longstaff, Thomas R.W.; Hussey, Tristram C.* Palynology and cultural process: an exercise in the new archaeology. Archaeology and the Galilee. SFSHJ 143: 1997, ⟹275. [E]Edwards, D.R., 151-162.

## T1.4 *Exploratores*—Excavators, pioneers

10177 **Aström, Paul** 'Fantastic years on Cyprus': the Swedish Cyprus expedition. 1994, ⟹10,11548. [R]BiOr 54 (1997) 218-220 *(Al-Radi, Selma)*.

10178 ALBRIGHT, William Foxwell: **Long, Burke O.** Planting and reaping Albright: politics, ideology, and interpreting the bible. University Park, PA 1997, Pennsylvania State University Press x; 162 pp. $32.50. 0-271-01576-4. [R]BArR 23/4 (1997) 62-64 *(Hendel, Ronald S.)*.

10179 BURCKHARDT, Johann Ludwig; BANKES, William John: *Stucky, Rolf A.; Lewis, Norman, N.* Johann Ludwig Burckardt und William John Bankes: die ersten neuzeitlichen Europäer in Petra. Petra antike Felsstadt. 1997, ⟹311. [E]Weber, T., 5-13.

10180 CARTER, Howard: **James, T.G.H.** Howard Carter: the path to Tutankhamun. 1992, ⟹8,d546. [R]CÉg 143 (1997) 41-43 *(Mekhitarian, A.)*.

10181 LAWRENCE, Thomas E.: *Tabachnick, Stephen E.* Lawrence of Arabia as archaeologist. BArR 23/5 (1997) 40-47, 70-71.

10182 LLOYD, Seton H.F.: *Wright, G.R.H.* Lloyd, Seton—his work in Middle Eastern archaeology. BiOr 53 (1996) 317-324.

10183 PRITCHARD, James B.: *Muhly, James* James Bennett Pritchard. BArR 23/2 (1997) 12.

10184 TURVILLE-PETRE, Francis: *Bar-Yosef, Ofer; Callander, Jane* A forgotten archaeologist: the life of Francis Turville-Petre. PEQ 129 (1997) 2-18.

10185 WOOLEY, Leonard: *Luby, Edward M.* The Ur-archaeologist Leonard Woolley and the treasures of Mesopotamia. BArR 23/2 (1997) 60-61.

## T1.5 *Materiae primae*—metals, glass; stone

10186 *Gorin-Rosen, Yael* כלי זכוכית מקברים באשרת [Glass vessels from burial caves in Asherat]. Sum. 12*. ʿAtiqot 33 (1997) 61-67 **H**.

10187 **Lilyquist, C.; Brill, R.H.** Studies in Early Egyptian glass. 1993, ⟹9,13042...12,9530. [R]JNES 56 (1997) 298-301 *(Meyer, Carol)*.

10188  **Liritzis, Veronica McGeehan** The role and development of met-
allurgy in the Late Neolithic and Early Bronze Age of Greece.
SIMA-PB 122: 1996, ⇒12,9531. ᴿAJA 101 (1997) 771-772
*(Muhly, J.D.).*

10189  *Marchetti, N.; Nigro, L.* Observations on the distribution of the
technological and typological features of glass and vitreous materials in Assyria during the late Bronze Age: the case of Assur,
Nuzi, Tell Rimah and Tell Brak. Assyrien im Wandel. 1997,
⇒379. ᴱWaetzoldt, H., 299-313.

10190  *Mirau, Neil A.* The social context of early iron working in the
Levant. Urbanism JSOT.S 244: 1997, ⇒265. ᴱAufrecht, W.E.,
99-115.

10191  *Plantzos, Dimitris* Crystals and lenses in the Graeco-Roman
world. Sum. 451. ᴿAJA 101 (1997) 451-464.

10192  **Reiter, Karin** Die Metalle im Alten Orient: unter besonderer
Berücksichtigung altbabylonischer Quellen. AOAT 249: Müns
1997, Ugarit-Verlag xlvii; 471, 160* pp. Bibl. 3-927120-49-9.

10193  *Roman, Itzhak* Hazor: metallurgical study of Hazor copper in-
gots;

10194  *Shalev, Sariel* Hazor: metal objects from Hazor. Hazor V. 1997,
⇒269. ᴱBen-Tor, A., 387-389/348-352.

10195  **Stern, Marianne E.** Roman mold-blown glass: the first through
sixth centuries. Bretschneider 1995, R 388 pp. Num. pl., fig.
$100. 88-7062-916-3. ᴿAJA 101 (1997) 422-423 *(Whitehouse,
David)*; Ber. 42 (1995-96) 178-180 *(Abdallah, Joanna)*; RAr
(1997/2) 388-392 *(Foy, Danièle)*.


T1.7  **Technologia antiqua; Architectura**

10196  *Lamberg-Karlovsky, C.C.* Our past matters: materials and in-
dustries of the ancient Near East. JAOS 117 (1997) 87-102.

10197  **Miron, Eli** Axes and adzes from Canaan. 1992, ⇒9,13362;
12,11813. JNES 56 (1997) 132-133 *(Joffe, Alexander H.).*

10198  **Ainian, Alexander Mazarakis** From ruler's dwellings to
temples: architecture, religion and society in early Iron Age
Greece (1100-700 BC). Studies in Mediterranean Archaeology
121: Jonsered 1997, Åströms 424 pp. 6 maps, 11 tables, 512 fig.
91-7081-152-0 [BiOr 56,742—Crielaard, Jan Paul].

10199  **Anderson, James C.** Roman architecture and society. Baltimore
1997, Johns Hopkins Univ. Press xiii; 442 pp. 8 fig. 21 plans.
$40. 0-2018-5546-2 [AJA 103,570s—Gros, Pierre].

10200  **Balty, Jean Ch.** Curia ordinis: recherches d'architecture et
d'urbanisme antiques sur les curies provinciales du monde romain. 1991, ⇒11/2,a237; 12,9550. ᴿGn. 69 (1997) 636-645
*(Schalles, Hans-Joachim).*

10201  ᴱ**Castel, Corinne; al-Maqdissi, Michel; Villeneuve, François**
Les maisons dans la Syrie antique du IIIᵉ millénaire aux débuts de
l'Islam: pratiques et représentations de l'espace domestique.
BAHI 150: Beyrouth 1997, Institut Français d'Archéologie du
Proche-Orient iv; xvii; 332 pp. (franç.); xii pp. (arabe). Actes du
Colloque International, Damas 27-30 juin 1992; ill. 2-7053-0567-
X [RB 105,634].

10202  ᴱD'Andria, Francesco; Mannino, Katia Ricerche sulla casa in Magna Graecia e in Sicilia. 1996. ᴿREA 99 (1997) 590-592 *(Lamboley, Jean-Luc)*.

10203  *Deblauwe, F.* A test study of circulation and access patterns in Assyrian architecture. Assyrien im Wandel. 1997, ⇒379. ᴱWaetzoldt, H., 239-246.

10204  DeVries, LaMoine F. Cities of the biblical world. Peabody, MA 1997, Hendrickson xviii; 398 pp. $35. 1-56563-145-5 [BTB 27,120].

10205  *Dolce, R.* The city of Kar-Tukulti-Ninurta: cosmic characteristics and topographical aspects. Assyrien im Wandel. 1997, ⇒379. ᴱWaetzoldt, H., 251-258.

10206  *Drinkard, Joel F.* New volute capital discovered. BA 60/4 (1997) 249-250.

10207  *Hachlili, Rachel* Aspects of similarity and diversity in the architecture and art of ancient synagogues and churches in the land of Israel. ZDPV 113 (1997) 92-122.

10208  *Hauben, H.* An American architect in Iran and Afghanistan: the John B. McCooʟ correspondence (August-December 1937), 1: introduction and timetable. OLoP 28 (1997) 223-248.

10209  Hirschfeld, Yizhar The Palestinian dwelling in the Roman-Byzantine period. 1995, ⇒11/2,a257. RivBib 45 (1997) 247-248 *(Rolla, Armando)*.

10210  *Ji, Chang-Ho C.* A note on the Iron Age four-room house in Palestine. Or. 66 (1997) 387-413.

10211  Kiderlen, Moritz Megale oikia: Untersuchungen zur Entwicklung aufwendiger griechischer Stadthhausarchitektur: von der Früharchaik bis ins 3. Jh. v. Chr. I-II. Hürth 1995, Lange 2 vols; 270 pp. I: text; II: ill.: 58 fig.; 164 plans; 8 maps. DM138. 3-9804934-0-7. ᴿAJA 101 (1997) 602-603 *(Nevett, Lisa)*.

10212  Konecny, Andreas Hellenistische Turmgehöfte in Zentral- und Ostlykien. Wiener Forschungen zur Archäologie 2: W 1997, Phoibos 112 pp. 72 pl. 3-901232-08-7.

10213  *Liégey, Anne* Analyse de quelques briques crues et de leurs dégraissants. Mari 8 (1997) 189-193.

10214  Mainstone, Rowland J. Hagia Sophia: architecture, structure and liturgy of Jᴜsᴛɪɴɪᴀɴ's great church. L 1997, Thames and H 288 pp. 305 ill. 56 pl. Bibl. 0-500-27945-4.

10215  *Margueron, Jean-Claude* Notes d'archéologie et d'architecture orientales. Syr. 74/1 (1997) 15-32.

10216  *Miglus, P.A.* Eine assyrische Stadt im Wandel: Einblicke in die Wohnarchitektur von Assur. Assyrien im Wandel. 1997, ⇒379. ᴱWaetzoldt, H., 317-324.

10217  Negev, Avraham The architecture of Oboda: final report. Qedem 36: J 1997, Institute of Archaeology, Hebrew University xx; 214 pp. 27 fig. 294 phot. 5 pl. 0333-5844 [RB 105,315].

10218  Pringle, Denys Secular buildings in the Crusader Kingdom of Jerusalem: an archaeological gazetteer. C 1997, CUP xx; 159 pp. 113 pl. 62 fig. $70. 0-521-46010-7 [AJA 103,582s—Ivison, E.A.].

10219  Segal, Arthur Theatres in Roman Palestine and Provincia Arabia. Mn.S 140: 1995, ⇒11/2,a287. ᴿRAr (1997/2) 421-422 *(Dentzer-Feydy, Jacqueline)*;

10220   From function to monument: urban landscapes of Roman Pal-estine, Syria and Provincia Arabia. Oxf 1997, Oxbow viii; 184 pp. 207 fig. $38. 0-900188-13-9 [AJA 103,164s—Roller, Duane W.].

10221   *Tatischwili, I.* Zur É ḫalentu-Frage. Assyrien im Wandel. 1997, ⇒379. EWaetzoldt, H., 181-183.

10222   **Vandeput, Lutgarde** The architectural decoration in Roman Asia Minor: Sagalassos: a case study. Studies in Eastern Mediterra-nean Archaeology 1: Lv 1997, Brepols 353 pp. 2-503-50540-6.

10223   *Weiss, Zeev; Netzer, Ehud* Architectural development of Seppho-ris during the Roman and Byzantine periods. Archaeology and the Galilee. SFSHJ 143: 1997, ⇒275. EEdwards, D.R., 117-133.

10224   **White, Michael L.** The social origins of christian architecture: 1. building God's house in the Roman world: architectural adaption among pagans, Jews, and christians; 2. texts and monuments for the christian domus ecclesiae in its environment. HThS 42: CM 1997, Harvard Univ. Press xi; 211; xvi; 524 pp. 1-56338-180-X/1-8.

10225   **Whittaker, Helène** Mycenaean cult buildings: a study of their architecture and function in the context of the Aegean and the eastern Mediterranean. Monographs from the Norwegian Institute at Athens 1: Bergen 1997, The Norwegian Institute at Athens x; 338 pp. Bibl. 82-91626-03-0.

10226   **Youkana, Doni George** Tell Es-Sawwan: the architecture of the sixth millennium B.C. EDUBBA 5: L 1997, NABU 72 pp. 22 maps; 42 pl. 1-857750-05-6.

T1.9   *Supellex*—**Artifacts**; *Res militaris*—**military matters;** *Nautica*

10227   *Raban, Avner* Stop the charade: it's time to sell artifacts. BArR 23/3 (1997) 42-45.

10228   *Córdoba, J.* Die Schlacht am Ulaya-Fluß: ein Beispiel assyrischer Kriegführung während der letzten Jahre des Reiches. Assyrien im Wandel. 1997, ⇒379. EWaetzoldt, H., 7-18.

10229   *Eph'al, Israel* Ways and means to conquer a city, based on Assy-rian queries to the Sungod. Assyria 1995. 1997, ⇒376. EParpola, S., 49-53.

10230   *Kupper, Jean-Robert* Béliers et tours de siège. RA 91 (1997) 121-133.

10231   *Lafont, Sophie* Un "cas royal" à l'époque de Mari. RA 91 (1997) 109-119.

10232   **McNicoll, Anthony W.** Hellenistic fortifications from the Aegean to the Euphrates. Rev. *Milner, Nicholas P.*: Oxford Monographs on Classical Archaeology: Oxf 1997, Clarendon xxv; 230 pp. £65. 0-19-813228-X.

10233   *Pilch, John J.* Military occupation. BiTod 35 (1997) 305-310.

10234   **Vita, Juan-Pablo** El ejército de Ugarit. 1995, ⇒11/2,a349. RAfO 44-45 (1997-98) 369-376 *(Márquez Rowe, I.)*; OLoP 28 (1997) 251-252 *(Schoors, A.)*.

10235   **Göttlicher, Arvid** Die Schiffe im Alten Testament. B 1997, Mann 251 pp. Bibl. 3-7861-1958-9.

## T2.4 *Athletica*—Sport, games; *Musica,* dance

10236 **Decker, Wolfgang** Sport in der griechischen Antike: vom minoischen Wettkampf bis zu den Olympischen Spielen. Mü 1995, Beck 255 pp. Num. ill. DM58/48. 3-406-39669-0/-8-2. [R]HZ 264 (1997) 712-714 *(Schuller, Wolfgang)*;

10237 **Decker, Wolfgang; Herb, Michael** Bildatlas zum Sport im Alten Ägypten. 1994, 2 vols. ⇒9,13235. [R]ZDMG 87 (1997) 249-251 *(Hölzl, Regina).*

10238 **Fortuin, Rigobert W.** Der Sport im augusteischen Rom. 1996, ⇒12,9608. [R]HZ 265 (1997) 752-753 *(Weiler, Ingomar).*

10239 **Futrell, A.** Blood in the arena. Austin 1997, Univ. of Texas Press xii; 328 pp. 36 fig. 6 maps. $39.50. 0-292-72504-3 [JRS 89,236—Plass, Paul].

10240 *Bartolini, Elena* La danza come espressione di lode a Dio nell'ebraismo biblico. Sette e Religioni 7/1 (1997) 78-86.

10241 *Boroskaya, N.F.* Lyres from the royal tombs of Ur as monuments of Sumer culture of the early dynastic period. Sum. 13. Journal of Ancient History 223 (1997) 3-13 **R**.

10242 *Crocker, Richard L.* Mesopotamian tonal systems. Iraq 59 (1997) 189-202.

10243 *Dohmen, Christoph* Das Alte Testament in Oratorien und Opern. Lebendige Welt. 1997, ⇒565. [E]Zenger, E., 45-56.

10244 *Hahnen, Peter* Der leichte Gott: Kritik und Ertrag der kommerziellen Bibel-Musicals. ThG 40 (1997) 107-118.

10245 *Kilmer, Anne; Tinney, Steve* Old Babylonian music instruction texts. JCS 48 (1996) 49-56.

10246 *Ragazzi, Cesare* La musica: l'ebraismo come etica dell'ascolto. Sette e Religioni 7/1 (1997) 105-129.

10247 *Saulnier, Daniel* La résurrection de Lazare. EtGr 25 (1997) 7-11.

10248 *Theobald, Michael* Vita aeterna ohne Resurrectio mortuorum?: Franz SCHUBERT zum 31. Januar 1997. ThQ 177 (1997) 56-58.

10249 [E]*Troía, P.* La musica e la bibbia. 1992, ⇒8,455; 9,13301. Letteratura Liturgica 84 (1997) 691-694 *(Pappalardo, Emanuele).*

## T2.6 *Vestis,* clothing; *Ornamenta,* jewellry

10250 **Vogelsang-Eastwood, Gillian** Pharaonic Egyptian clothing. 1993, ⇒9,13325... 12,9627. [R]CEg 72 (1997) 77-78 *(Rassart-Debergh, M.).*

10251 *Bohak, Gideon* A note on the Chnoubis gem from Tel Dor. IEJ 47 (1997) 255-256.

10252 [E]*Calinescu, Adriana* Ancient jewelry and archaeology. 1996, ⇒12,224. [R]AJA 101 (1997) 808-809 *(Henig, Martin).*

10253 *Groot, A. de; Greenhut, Z.* A sceptre head from Moza. Qad. 30/1 (1997) 44-45 **H**.

10254 *Kotansky, Roy* The Chnoubis gem from Tel Dor. IEJ 47 (1997) 257-260.

10255 **Musche, Brigitte** Vorderasiatischer Schmuck von den Anfängen bis zur Zeit der Achaemeniden (ca. 10,000-330 v.Chr.). 1992,

⇒8,d896... 11/2,a488. ᴿJNES 56 (1997) 307-309 *(Wilson, Karen L.)*.

10256  *Rodríguez, Angel Manuel* Jewelry in the Old Testament: a description of its functions. 1997, ⇒83. ᶠSʜᴇᴀ W., 103-125.

### т2.8 Utensilia; *Pondera et mensurae*—Weights and measures

10257  *Hikade, Thomas* Ein außergewöhnliches Silexmesser aus Abydos. MDAI.K 53 (1997) 85-89.

10258  **Lilyquist, Christine** Egyptian stone vessels: Khian through Thutmosis IV. NY 1995, Metropolitan Museum of Art 123 pp. Appendix by *E.W. Castle;* 163 fig. $25. 0-87099-760-2. ᴿAJA 101 (1997) 780-781 *(Lacovara, Peter)*.

10259  **Müller-Karpe, Michael** Prähistorische Bronzefunde Abt. II. Metallgefäße in Iraq I/14. 1993, ⇒11/2,a511. ᴿBiOr 54 (1997) 763-765 *(Curtis, John)*.

10260  **Rosen, Steven A.** Lithics after the Stone Age: a handbook of stone tools from the Levant. L 1997, Walnut Creek 184 pp. £35/£20. 0-7619-9123-9/4-7 [RB 105,158].

10261  *Albani, M.; Glessmer, U.* Un instrument de mesures astronomiques à Qumrân. RB 104 (1997) 88-115.

10262  *Élayi, Josette; Planas Palau, Antonio* Poids inscrits de l'île d'Ibiza. Sum. 37. Sem. 46 (1996) 37-47.

10263  *Gradwohl, Roland* Drei Tage und der dritte Tag. VT 47 (1997) 373-378 [Ex 3,18].

10264  *Heyns, Dalene* Of plumb lines, gnomons and sundials: reviewing ancient Israel's measuring of space and time. OTEs 10 (1997) 252-267.

10265  *Kushinir-Stein, Alla* On the chronology of some inscribed lead weights from Palestine. ZDPV 113 (1997) 88-91.

10266  **Leitz, Christian** Altägyptische Sternuhren. OLA 62: 1995, ⇒11/2,a520. ᴿOr. 66 (1997) 99-102 *(Beckerath, Jürgen von)*.

### т3.0 Ars antiqua, *motiva, picturae* [icones т3.1 infra]

10267  *Albenda, P.* Assyrian wall reliefs: a study of compositional styles. Assyrien im Wandel. 1997, ⇒379. ᴱWaetzoldt, H., 223-26.

10268  **Arnold, Dorothea** Royal women of Amarna: images of beauty in ancient Egypt. NY 1997, The Metropolitan Museum of Art xxii; 169 pp. Bibl. $45. 0-8109-6504-6.

10269  *Bergman, Jan* Darstellungen und Vorstellungen von Götterhänden im Alten Ägypten. La main de Dieu. WUNT 94: 1997, ⇒328. ᴱKieffer, R., 1-18.

10270  **Bingöl, O.** Malerei und Mosaik der Antike in der Türkei. Mainz 1997, Von Zabern 148 pp. 32 pl; 96 fig. DM45. 3-8053-1880-4 [CIR 48,546—Ling, Roger].

10271  *Börker-Klähn, J.* Mauerkronenträgerinnen. Assyrien im Wandel. 1997, ⇒379. ᴱWaetzoldt, H., 227-234.

10272 **Cohen, Ada** The Alexander mosaic: stories of victory and defeat. Cambridge Studies in Classical Art and Iconography: C 1997, CUP 279 pp. Bibl. 0-521-56339-9.

10273 **Collon, Dominique** Ancient Near Eastern art. 1995, ⇒11/2,a527. <sup>R</sup>BiOr 54 (1997) 203-207 *(Muscarella, Oscar White)*; AJA 101 (1997) 167-169 *(Marchetti, Nicolò)*.

10274 *Ehrenberg, E.* An Old Assyrian precursor of the Neo-Assyrian royal image. Assyrien im Wandel. 1997, ⇒379. <sup>E</sup>Waetzoldt, H., 259-264.

10275 **Eschweiler, Peter** Bildzauber im alten Ägypten. OBO 137: 1994, ⇒12,9671. <sup>R</sup>WO 28 (1997) 185-188 *(Quack, Joachim Friedrich)*.

10276 *Görg, Manfred* Zur Rezeptionsgeschichte der Asiaten-Szene von Beni-Hassan. BN 88 (1997) 9-15.

10277 *Gubel, Eric* Cinq bulles inédites des archives tyriennes de l'époque achéménide. Sum. 53. Sem. 47 (1997) 53-64.

10278 **Hackländer, Nele** Der archaistische Dionysos: eine archäologische Untersuchung zur Bedeutung archaistischer Kunst in hellenistischer und römischer Zeit. 1996, ⇒12,9674. <sup>R</sup>AJA 101 (1997) 799-800 *(Fullerton, Mark D.)*.

10279 *Herrmann, G.* The Nimrud ivories 3: the Assyrian tradition. Assyrien im Wandel. 1997, ⇒379. <sup>E</sup>Waetzoldt, H., 285-290.

10280 **Hoff, Ralf von den** Philosophenporträts des Früh- und Hochhellenismus. 1994, ⇒11/2,a649. <sup>R</sup>AJA 101 (1997) 414-415 *(Smith, R.R.R.)*.

10281 *Hurowitz, Victor* Picturing imageless deities: iconography in the ancient Near East. BArR 23/3 (1997) 46-51, 68-69.

10282 *Kaper, Olaf E.* A painting of the gods of Dakhla in the temple of Ismant el-Kharab. The temple in ancient Egypt. 1997, ⇒300. <sup>E</sup>Quirke, S., 204-215.

10283 **Keel, Othmar; Uehlinger, Christoph** Altorientalische Miniaturkunst. Collab. *Gasser, Madeleine*: <sup>2</sup>1996, ⇒12,9681. <sup>R</sup>OLZ 92 (1997) 531-533 *(Stoof, Magdalena)*.

10284 **Kilmer, Martin F.** Greek erotica on Attic red-figure vases. 1993, ⇒9,13635; 10,12037. <sup>R</sup>AJA 101 (1997) 413-414 *(Sutton, Robert F.)*.

10285 **Koch, Nadia** De picturae initiis: die Anfänge der griechischen Malerei im 7. Jahrhundert v. Chr. 1996, ⇒12,9684. AJA 101 (1997) 814-815 *(Cook, R.M.)*.

10286 *Leblanc, Christian* Quelques reflexions sur le programme iconographique et la fonction des temples de "millions d'années". The temple in ancient Egypt. 1997, ⇒300. <sup>E</sup>Quirke, S., 49-56.

10287 *Margueron, Jean-Claude* Autour de la tête d'une statuette du temple de Ninni-zaza. Mari 8 (1997) 725-730.

10288 **Matheson, Susan B.** Polygnotos and vase painting in classical Athens. Madison 1995, Univ. of Wisconsin Press xvii; 537 pp. $60. 0-299-13870-4. <sup>R</sup>AJA 101 (1997) 412-413 *(Neils, Jenifer)*.

10289 *Metzger, Thérèse* Note sur l'hospitalité d'Abraham dans l'iconographie juive. Le comparatisme. 1997, ⇒346. <sup>E</sup>Boespflug, F., 345-359.

10290 *Minas, Martina* Die Dekorationstätigkeit von Ptolemaios VI: Philometor und Ptolemaios VIII. Euergetes II. an ägyptischen Tempeln (Teil 2). OLoP 28 (1997) 87-121 [⇒12,9691].

10291 *Mittmann, Siegfried* Das Symbol der Hand in der altorientalischen Ikonographie. La main de Dieu. WUNT 94: 1997, ⇒328. EKieffer, R., 19-47.

10292 *Morenz, Ludwig D.; Schorch, Stefan* Der Seraph in der Hebräischen Bibel und in Altägypten. Or. 66 (1997) 365-386 [Num 21,6; Isa 14,29; 6].

10293 *Norin, Stig* Die Hand Gottes im Alten Testament. La main de Dieu. WUNT 94: 1997, ⇒328. EKieffer, R., 49-63.

10294 *O'Bryhim, Shawn* The sphere-bearing anthropomorphic figurines of Amathus. BASOR 306 (1997) 39-45.

10295 **Preston, Percy** Metzler Lexikon antiker Bildmotive. Stu 1997, Metzler xiv; 249 pp. DM58. 3-476-01541-6 [AnCl 68,580—Massar, Natacha].

10296 *Ragazzi, Cesare* Le arti figurative [*Chagall, Marc*]. Sette e Religioni 7/1 (1997) 132-161.

10297 **Rose, Charles Brian** Dynastic commemoration and imperial portraiture in the Julio-Claudian period. Cambridge Studies in Classical Art and Iconography: C 1997, CUP 362 pp. 96 pl. $85. 0-521-45382-8 [AJA 101,821].

10298 **Rouveret, Agnès** Histoire et imaginaire de la peinture ancienne. 1989, ⇒6,d552... 8,d977. RGn. 69 (1997) 55-60 *(Scheibler, I.)*.

10299 **Scham, Sandra A.** Shiqmim's violin-shaped figurines and Ghassulian bone artifacts. BA 60/2 (1997) 108.

10300 **Spivey, N.** Greek art. L 1997, Phaidon 448 pp. 254 ill. £15. 0-714-83368-1 [Prudentia 30/1,68—Stevenson, Tom].

10301 **Stewart, Andrew** Art, desire, and the body in ancient Greece. C 1997, CUP xiv; 272 pp. 8 pl. 159 fig. £45. 0-521-45064-0 [AJA 102,438—Kampen, Natalie Boymel].

10302 **Teissier, B.** Egyptian iconography on Syro-Palestinian cylinder seals of the Middle Bronze Age. OBO.A 11: 1996, ⇒12,9701. RRSFen 25/1 (1997) 105-108 *(Matthiae, Gabriella Scandone)*; AcOr 58 (1997) 196-198 *(Groth, Bente)*; CÉg 72 (1997) 89-92 *(Ward, William M.)*.

10303 *Venit, Marjorie Susan* The tomb from Tigrane Pasha Street and the iconography of death in Roman Alexandria. Sum. 701. AJA 101 (1997) 701-729.

10304 **Walker, Susan; Bierbrier, Morris L.** Ancient faces: mummy portraits from Roman Egypt. Collab. *Roberts, Paul; Taylor, John*: L 1997, British Museum 224 pp. 135 col. fig. 79 fig. £19. 0-7141-1905-9/0989-4 [AJA 101,821];

10305 Fayum: misteriosi volti dall'Egitto. Collab. *Roberts, Paul; Taylor, John*: R 1997, Leonardo Arte 271 pp. Esposizione Palazzo Ruspoli, Roma 22 ottobre 1997 al 28 febbraio 1998. Bibl. 88-7813-913-0.

10306 *Winter, Irene J.* Art *in* empire: the royal image and the visual dimensions of Assyrian ideology. Assyria 1995. 1997, ⇒376. EParpola, S., 359-381.

10307 **Zanker, Paul** The mask of Socrates: the image of the intellectual in antiquity. 1995, ⇒11/2,8576. RAJA 101 (1997) 415-416 *(Pollitt, J.J.)*.

10308 *Ziffer, Irit* Die Kunst der Achämeniden. Land der Bibel. 1997, ⇒9960. ESeipel, W., 187-203.

## T3.1 *Theologia iconis*—ars postbiblica

10309 **Balicka-Witakowska, Ewa** La crucifixion sans crucifié dans l'art éthiopien: recherches sur la survie de l'iconographie chrétienne de l'antiquité tardive. Bibliotheca nubica et aethiopica 4: Wsz 1997, ZAS PAN xi; 188 pp. Bibl. 83-901809-4-4.

10310 *Barber, John* Images of Christ in the works of REMBRANDT. Images of Christ. 1997, ⇒256. ᴱPorter, S.E., 338-341.

10311 *Bauer, Anton* Biblische Botschaft in Bildern: Lebens-Atem. WUB 6 (1997) 12-19.

10312 *Beauchamp, Paul* Art funéraire et mémoire biblique. MoBi 103 (1997) 36-41.

10313 **Ben-Arieh, Yehoshua** Painting the Holy Land in the nineteenth century. J 1997, Yad Izhak Ben-Zvi 320 pp. Bibl. 965-217-135-2.

10314 **Berthoud, Émile** 2000 ans d'art chrétien. Chambray 1997, CLD 473 pp. 266 pl. FF270. 2-85443-335-1 [ETR 74,135s—Cottin, J.].

10315 *Bertolone, Vincenzo* Il volto dei volti, Cristo. Introduzione al primo Congresso Internazionale—una ricerca interdisciplinare, Istituto di ricerca sul santo Volto di Cristo—Pontificia Università Urbaniana 12 ott. 1997. PalCl 76/8-9 (1997) 615-636.

10316 *Bourguet, Pierre du* The first biblical scenes depicted in christian art. The bible in Greek christian antiquity. 1997 <c.1984>, ⇒177. ᴱᵀBlowers, P.M., 299-326.

10317 **Butzkamm, Aloys** Christliche Ikonographie: zum Verstehen mittelalterlicher Kunst. Pd 1997, Bonifatius. DM58. 3-87088-932-2. ᴿTheologisches 27 (1997) 477-478 *(Meyer zu Schlochtern, Josef)*.

10318 *Cannuyer, Christian* Osiris et Jésus, les bons pélicans. Le comparatisme. 1997, ⇒346. ᴱBoespflug, F., 223-238.

10319 *Contessa, Andreina* Arte e *midrash*: l'illustrazione biblica tra testo e interpretazione. Sum., rés. 63. Cahiers Ratisbonne 2 (1997) 33-77.

10320 *Dohmen, Christoph* Das Alte Testament in Bildprogrammen christlicher Kunst. Lebendige Welt. 1997, ⇒565. ᴱZenger, E., 22-33.

10321 *Dourado Fernandes, Jorge Aristides Campos* O Cristo che se vê: análise de formas iconográficas seleccionadas do dealbar do cristianismo. Theologica 32/1 (1997) 89-103.

10322 *Egender, Nikolaus* Die Dornbusch-Ikone. EuA 73 (1997) 388-393 [Ex 3,1-16].

10323 **Elsner, Jaś** Art and the Roman viewer: the transformation of art from the pagan world to christianity. 1995, ⇒12,9720. ᴿChH 66 (1997) 320-322 *(Norris, Frederick W.)*; JHS 117 (1997) 265-266 *(Pollitt, J.J.)*.

10324 **Engemann, Josef** Deutung und Bedeutung frühchristlicher Bildwerke. Da 1997, Primus 185 pp. 138 ill. 3-89678-041-7 [RQ 93,137ss—Heid, Stefan].

10325 *Eörsi, Anna* Haec scala significat ascensum virtutum: remarks on the iconography of Christ mounting the cross on a ladder. ACr 85 (1997) 151-166.

10326 **Finney, Paul Corby** The invisible God: the earliest christians on art. 1994, ⇒11/2,a574; 12,9723. ᴿJThS 48 (1997) 231-233

*(Murray, Mary Charles)*; JAC 40 (1997) 245-49 *(Rutgers, Leonard V.)*.

10327   *Fischer, Irmtraud* Alttestamentliche Gestalten als politische Programme in der europäischen Malerei und Plastik. Lebendige Welt. 1997, ⇒565. [E]Zenger, E., 34-44 [Gen 19,30-37].

10328   **Franchi De Bellis, Annalisa** I cippi prenestini. Pubbl. dell'Univ. di Urbino, linguistica...13: Urbino 1997, Univ. di Urbino 245 pp. Bibl. 88-392-0427-6.

10329   **Gharib, Georges** Le icone di Cristo: storia e culto. R 1993, Città Nuova 300 pp. L50.000. 88-311-7011-2. [R]Letteratura Liturgica 84 (1997) 603-605 *(Amato, Angelo)*.

10330   *Gnemmi, Dario* Appunti d'iconologia: in margine ad alcune ipotesi formulate circa la presunta 'concezione di sant'Anna', opera di TANZIOanzio da Varallo conservata nelle raccolte della Galleria Sabauda di Torino;

10331   Il *Cristo morto* di palazzo Silva in Domodossola: è possibile definirlo autografo di Daniele CRESPI (1598?-1630)?;

10332   'Deposizione di Cristo' di Giacomo CAVEDONI: una variante d'autore o l'archetipo per una serie di varianti?;

10333   La 'natività' del sacro Monte di Pietà di Novara. BSPNov 88 (1997) 123-126/107-121/679-688/663-678.

10334   *Grappe, Christian* Main de Dieu et mains des apôtres: réflexions à partir d'Actes 4,30 et 5,12. La main de Dieu. WUNT 94: 1997, ⇒328. [E]Kieffer, R., 117-134 [Acts 4,30; 5,12].

10335   [TE]**Griffith, Sidney Harrison** A treatise on the veneration of the holy icons written in Arabic by Theodore ABU QURRAH, Bishop of Harran. Eastern Christian Texts in Translation 1: Lv 1997, Peeters xxii; 99 pp. Bibl. 90-6831-928-0.

10336   **Grubb, Nancy** Christliche Kunst: vom 6.-20. Jahrhundert. [T]*Würmli, M.*: Stu 1997, Katholisches Bibelwerk 143 pp. 184 pl. DM39.80. 3-460-33082-1 [ETR 74,132—Cottin, Jérôme].

10337   *Gupta, Suman* Images of Christ in the paintings of Jamini ROY. Images of Christ. 1997, ⇒256. [E]Porter, S.E., 342-357.

10338   *Hadermann-Misguich, Lydie* L'exploitation d'une gravure maniériste du Jugement dernier dans le codex de Georges KLONTZAS à la Biblioteca Marciana (Gr. VII,22). 1997, ⇒101. [F]VOORDECKERS E., 91-100.

10339   *Hallak, Sami* La Vierge et l'Enfant dans l'art byzantin. Rés., Al-Machriq 71/1 (1997) 195-228.

10340   **Hecht, Christian** Katholische Bildertheologie im Zeitalter von Gegenreformation und Barock: Studien zu Traktaten von Johannes MOLANUS, Gabriele PALEOTTI und anderen Autoren. B 1997, Mann 506 pp. 3-7861-1930-9.

10341   *Jensen, Robin M.* The femininity of Christ in early christian iconography. StPatr 29. 1997, ⇒351. [E]Livingstone, E.A., 269-282.

10342   [E]**Knubben, Jürgen** Via crucis: das Kreuz in der Kunst der Gegenwart. Rottweil 1997, Dominikaner-Forum des Dominikanermuseums 130 pp. DM48. 3-980-5461-2-8 [ETR 74,133s—Cottin, J.].

10343   *Kogman-Appel, Matrin* The picture cycles of the Rylands haggadah and the so-called brother haggadah and their relation to the western tradition of Old Testament illustration. BJRL 79/2 (1997) 3-19.

10344  *Köpf, Ulrich* Produktive Christusfrömmigkeit. BZNW 86: 1997, ⇒41. [F]HOFIUS O., 823-874.

10345  **Langener, Lucia** Isis lactans—Maria lactans: Untersuchungen zur koptischen Ikonographie. 1996, ⇒12,9732. [R]ThLZ 122 (1997) 959-961 *(Müller, C. Detlef G.).*

10346  **Lazarev, Viktor Nikititch** Icones russes. 1996, ⇒12,9733. [R]Contacts 49 (1997) 275-276 *(Evdokimov, Michel).*

10347  *Lepage, Claude* Première iconographie chrétienne de Palestine: controverses anciennes et perpectives [sic] à la lumière des liturgies et monuments éthiopiens. CRAI 3 (1997) 739-782.

10348  **MacDonnell, Joseph F.** Gospel illustrations; a reproduction of the 153 images from Jerome NADAL's 1595 book 'Adnotationes et meditationes in evangelia'. Fairfield, CT 1997, MacDonnell, J.F. 153 pp. $20. 0-9657731-2-4 [ThD 45,178—Heiser, W. Charles].

10349  *Maraval, Pierre* Les mains de Dieu dans la création: quelques interpretations patristiques d'une image biblique. La main de Dieu. WUNT 94: 1997, ⇒328. [E]Kieffer, R., 157-169.

10350  *Marsh, Clive* Christ on the road to Belleville: christology through conversation with Georges ROUAULT (1871-1958). Images of Christ. 1997, ⇒256. [E]Porter, S.E., 358-374.

10351  **Mathews, Thomas F.** The clash of gods: a reinterpretation of early christian art. 1993, ⇒9,13453... 12,9736. International Journal of the Classical Tradition 4 (1997) 291-293 *(Finney, Paul C.).*

10352  **Milano. Museo Poldi Pezzoli** La tunica dell'Egitto cristiano: restauro e iconografia dei tessuti copti del Museo Poldi Pezzoli. [E]*Zanni, Annalisa*: Quaderni di studi e restauri del Museo Poldi Pezzoli 3: T 1997, Artema 65 pp. 88-8052-007-5.

10353  *Monfrin, Françoise* Quand les mosaïques nous racontent la bible. MoBi 103 (1997) 42-49.

10354  **Muller, Frank** Heinrich VOGTHERR l'Ancien: un artiste entre Renaissance et Réforme. Wolfenbütteler Forschungen 72: Wsb 1997, Harrassowitz 386 pp. 300 reprod. DM198. 3-447-03914-0 [ETR 74,130s—Cottin, Jérôme].

10355  *Murray, Mary Charles* The art of the early church: christian or pagan? Month 30 (1997) 388-391.

10356  *Muzj, Maria Giovanna* La cruz de Pentecostés. CuMon 32 (1997) 328-332.

10357  **Onasch, Konrad** Ikone: Kirche, Gesellschaft. 1996, ⇒12,9742. [R]OrdKor 38 (1997) 505 *(Weis, Jessica).*

10358  **Ott, Martin** Dialog der Bilder: die Begegnung von Evangelium und Kultur in afrikanischer Kunst. FThSt 157: FrB 1995, Herder xv; 505 pp. DM68. 3-451-23743-1. [R]JRA 27 (1997) 431-433 *(Schoffeleers, Matthew).*

10359  **Panofsky, Erwin** Hercules am Scheidewege: und andere antike Bildstoffe in der neueren Kunst. Nachwort *Wuttke, Dieter*: Studien der Bibliothek Warburg 18: B 1997 <1930>, Mann xx; 217; 96 pp. Rpr. 3-7861-1826-4.

10360  **Partridge, Loren** MICHELANGELO: the *Last Judgment*: a glorious restoration. Collab. *Mancinelli, Fabrizio; Colalucci, Gianluigi.* NY 1997, Abrams 208 pp. [SCJ 29,503ss—Shrimplin, V.].

10361   *Peers, Glenn* Holy man, supplicant, and donor: on representations of the miracle of the archangel Michael at Chonae. MS 59 (1997) 173-182.

10362   *Philonenko, Marc* Main gauche et main droite de Dieu. La main de Dieu. WUNT 94: 1997, ⇒328. ᴱKieffer, R., 135-140.

10363   **Prigent, Pierre** L'arte dei primi cristiani: l'eredità culturale e la nuova fede. La via dei simboli: R 1997, Arkeios 277 pp. Bibl. 88-86495-40-4.

10364   *Prigent, Pierre* La main de Dieu dans l'iconographie du paléochristianisme. La main de Dieu. WUNT 94: 1997, ⇒328. ᴱKieffer, R., 141-155.

10365   **Quenot, Michel** Ikona—okno ku wieczności. ᵀ*Paprocki, Henryk*: Białystok 1997, Orthdruk [CoTh 69,207ss—Mendyk, Elżbieta] **P.**

10366   **Rice, Louise** The altars and altarpieces of new St. Peter's: outfitting the basilica, 1621-1666. Monuments of Papal Rome: C 1997, CUP xvi; 478 pp. Bibl. 0-521-55470-5.

10367   **Riess, Jonathan B.** The renaissance Antichrist: Luca Sɪɢɴᴏ-ʀᴇʟʟɪ's Orvieto frescoes. 1995, ⇒11/2,a606. ᴿChH 66/2 (1997) 347-348 *(Gill, Meredith J.)*.

10368   **Rosier, Bart Alexander** The bible in print; Netherlandish bible illustration in the sixteenth century. ᵀ*Weterings, Chris F.*: Lei 1997, Foleor 2 vols; xv; 359; 216 pp. 529 pl. ƒ460. 90-75035-09-8 [NThAR 1997,257].

10369   **Ross, Ellen M.** The grief of God: images of the suffering Jesus in late medieval England. NY 1997, OUP xiii; 200 pp. $50. 0-19-510451-X.

10370   *Schmitt, Jean-Claude* Pour une histoire comparée des images religieuses. Le comparatisme. 1997, ⇒346. ᴱBoespflug, F., 361-377.

10371   **Schrenk, Sabine** Typos und Antitypos in der frühchristlichen Kunst. JAC.E 21: 1995, ⇒11/2,a611; 12,9748. ᴿRQ 92/1-2 (1997) 136-137 *(Heid, Stefan)*.

10372   *Semff, Michael* Ein wiedergewonnenes Hauptwerk mittelalterlicher Holzskulptur in Italien [Crucifix]. Kunst Chronik 50/2 (1997) 61-64.

10373   *Sessner, Horst* Le Christ de verre: Aʟᴀɪɴ et la sculpture funèbre. RICP 61 (1997) 235-245.

10374   *Sirgant, Pierre* L'abbaye de Moissac, une bible ouverte. Sum. 373. BLE 98 (1997) 363-373.

10375   *Spieser, Jean-Michel* Comparatisme et diachronie: à propos de l'histoire de l'iconographie dans le monde paléochrétien et byzantin. Le comparatisme. 1997, ⇒346. ᴱBoespflug, F., 383-399.

10376   **Steinberg, Leo** The sexuality of Christ in Renaissance art and in modern oblivion. Ch ²1997, Univ. of Chicago Press viii; 417 pp. $30. 0-226-77187-3 [ThD 44,89].

10377   **Thoumieu, Marc** Dictionnaire d'iconographie romane. Introduction à la nuit des temps 15: La Pierre-qui-Vire, Saint-Léger-Vauban 1997, Zodiaque 370 pp. 140 pl. dessins de frère *Noël Deney*. FF250. 2-7369-0225-4 [ETR 74,128—Cottin, Jérôme].

10378   *Tudor-Craig, Pamela* The iconography of Corpus Christi. Images of Christ. 1997, ⇒256. ᴱPorter, S.E., 315-337.

10379   **Van Moorsel, Paul**, *(al.)*, Les peintures du monastère de Saint-Antoine près de la Mer Rouge. Mémoires de l'Institut Français d'archéologie orientale 2 vols. 2-7247-0156-9/7-7.

10380 <sup>E</sup>Verdon, T. Arte e la Bibbia: immagine come esegesi biblica. 1992, ⇒8,456. <sup>R</sup>BeO 39/1 (1997) 58-61 *(De Virgilio, Giuseppe)*.

10381 *Wallace, William E.* Michelangelo's *Risen Christ.* Sum. 1251. SCJ 28/4 (1997) 1251-1280.

10382 **Yaniv, Bracha** The torah-case: its history and design. Ramat Gan 1997, Bar Ilan Univ. Press 267 pp. Bibl. 965-235-071-0.

10383 *Zenger, Erich* Das Alte Testament in der Kunst und Literatur des 20. Jahrhunderts. Lebendige Welt. 1997, ⇒565. <sup>E</sup>Zenger, E., 57-65.

## т3.2 Sculptura

10384 **Baumer, Lorenz E.** Vorbilder und Vorlagen: Studien zu klassischen Frauenstatuen und ihrer Verwendung für Reliefs und Statuetten des 5. und 4. Jahrhunderts vor Christus. Acta Bernensia 12: Bern 1997, Stämpfli 178 pp. 51 pl. FS128. 3-7272-0517-2 [AJA 102,634s—Lawton, Carol L.].

10385 **Berger, Ernst; Gisler-Huwiler, Madeleine** Der Parthenon in Basel: Dokumentation zum Fries I-II. Studien der Skulpturhalle Basel 3: 1996, ⇒12,9761. <sup>R</sup>AJA 101 (1997) 774-775 *(Jenkins, Ian)*.

10386 **Boardman, John** Greek sculpture: the late classical period and sculpture in colonies and overseas. L 1995, Thames and H 248 pp. 377 fig. $15. 0-500-20285-0. <sup>R</sup>AJA 101 (1997) 590-591 *(Hurwitt, Jeffrey M.)*.

10387 **Charbonneau-Lassay, Louis** Le pietre misteriose del Cristo. La via dei simboli: R 1997, Arkeios 179 pp. L36.000. 88-86495-38-2. <sup>R</sup>MF 97/1-2 (1997) 343-344 *(Gualdana, Claudia)*.

10388 *Desreumaux, Alain; Briquel-Chatonnet, Françoise* Deux bas-reliefs palmyréniens au musée de Gaziantep. Sum. 73. Sem. 47 (1997) 73-79.

10389 **Faulstich, Elisabeth Ida** Hellenistische Kultstatuen und ihre Vorbilder. EHS 38/70: Fra 1997, Lang 225 pp. 47 fig. DM68. 3-631-30668-7 [AnCl 68,605—Hermary, Antoine].

10390 *Geiger, Joseph* Die Olympiodorbüste aus Caesarea. ZDPV 113 (1997) 70-74.

10391 *Guralnick, E.* A preliminary study of the proportions of some Assyrian sculptured figures from Khorsabad. Assyrien im Wandel. 1997, ⇒379. <sup>E</sup>Waetzoldt, H., 265-270.

10392 *Hawass, Zahi* The discovery of a pair-statue near the pyramid of Menkaure at Giza. MDAI.K 53 (1997) 289-293.

10393 *Hübner, Ulrich; Weber, Thomas* Götterbüsten und Königsstatuen: nabatäische und römische Plastik im Spannungsfeld zwischen Konvention und Staatsraison. Petra antike Felsstadt. 1997, ⇒311. <sup>E</sup>Weber, T., 111-125.

10394 **Josephson, Jack A.** Egyptian royal sculpture of the Late Period 400-246 B.C. Mainz 1997, Von Zabern x; 54 pp. DM88. 3-8053-1987-8 [BiOr 55,123—Meulenaere, H.J.A. de].

10395 **Lehmann, Stefan** Mythologische Prachtreliefs. Studien zur Kunst der Antike und ihrem Nachleben 1: Bamberg 1996, Weiss 226 pp. 17 fig. 48 pl. [RAr 1999/2, 425—Turcan, Robert].

10396 <sup>E</sup>**Marcadé, Jean** Sculptures déliennes. 1996, ⇒12,231. <sup>R</sup>AJA 101 (1997) 815 *(Stieber, Mary C.)*.

10397  **Mattusch, Carol C.** Classical bronzes: the art and craft of Greek and Roman statuary. 1996, ⇒12,9772. ᴿAJA 101 (1997) 589-590 *(Hurwitt, Jeffrey M.)*;

10398  The fire of Hephaistos: large classical bronzes from North American collections. 1996, ⇒12,9773. ᴿAJA 101 (1997) 806-807 *(Dillon, Sheila)*.

10399  **Métraux, Guy P.R.** Sculptors and physicians in fifth-century Greece: a preliminary study. Montreal 1995, McGill xvi; 154 pp. 15 pl. 4 fig. $40. 0-7735-1231-4. ᴿAJA 101 (1997) 604-605 *(King, Helen)*.

10400  **Pasqua, Roberta Belli** Scultura di età romana in 'basalto'. Xenia Antiqua 2: R 1995, Bretschneider 163 pp. 89 pl. 42 fig. 88-7062-885-X. ᴿAJA 101 (1997) 613-614 *(Fullerton, Mark D.)*.

10401  *Pittman, H.* Unwinding the white obelisk. Assyrien im Wandel. 1997, ⇒379. ᴱWaetzoldt, H., 347-354.

10402  *Putter, Thierry de; Karlshausen, Christina; Van Rinsveld, Bernard* Un relief thébain d'Amenhotep Iᵉʳ au Musée du Cinquantenaire. CÉg 72 (1997) 203-210.

10403  **Schlögl, Hermann A.; Meves-Schlögl, Christa** Uschebti: Arbeiter im ägyptischen Totenreich. 1993, ⇒11/2,a673. ᴿJEA 83 (1997) 237-238 *(Taylor, John H.)*.

10404  **Sirgant, Pierre** Moissac Bible ouverte. Montauban 1996, 394 pp. Préf. de *Jean-Claude Fau*. ᴿBLE 98 (1997) 405-406 *(Passerat, G.)*.

10405  **Spivey, Nigel** Understanding Greek sculpture: ancient meanings, modern readings. 1996, ⇒12,9779. ᴿAJA 101 (1997) 587-589 *(Hurwitt, Jeffrey M.)*.

10406  **Ziegler, Christiane** Statues égyptiennes de l'Ancien Empire. P 1997, Réunion des Musées nationaux [CRAI 1999,960s—Leclant, Jean].


т3.3  *Glyptica;* **stamp and cylinder seals,** scarabs, amulets


10407  *Amiet, Pierre* Observations sur les sceaux de Haft Tépé (Kabnak). RA 90 (1996) 135-143;

10408  Quelques observations à propos des sceaux-cylindres de Tell Suleimeh (Hamrin). RA 91 (1997) 97-108.

10409  **Amorai-Stark, Shua** Wolfe family collection of Near Eastern prehistoric stamp seals. OBO.A 16: FrS 1997, Univ.-Verl. 185 pp. FS75. 3-7278-1136-6.

10410  *Aufrecht, Walter E.; Shury, Wendy D.* Three Iron Age seals: Moabite, Aramaic and Hebrew. IEJ 47 (1997) 57-68.

10411  **Avigad, Nahman** Corpus of West Semitic stamp seals. ᴱ*Sass, Benjamin*: J 1997, Israel Academy of Sciences and Humanities 640 pp. $90. 965-208-138-8. ᴿUF 29 (1997) 819-825 *(Heltzer, M.)*.

10412  *Boehmer, Rainer Michael* Einige ältere, in jüngeren Zeiten wiederbenutzte altorientalische Siegel. AOAT 247: 1997, ⇒75. ᶠRoellig W., 23-41.

10413  ᴱ**Collon, Dominique** 7000 years of seals. L 1997, British Museum 240 pp. 0-7141-1143-0.

10414  **Deutsch, Robert** Messages from the past: Hebrew bullae from the time of Isaiah through the destruction of the first temple. Old

Jaffa 1997, Archaeological Center 171 pp. Shlomo Moussaieff Collection and an up to date Corpus. 965-222-795-1 [BiOr 56,174s—Lemaire, A.].

10415 **Deutsch, Robert; Heltzer, Michael** Windows to the past. TA 1997, Archaeological Center 93 pp. 80 photos; 48 drawings. $48. 965-222-839-7 [BAR 24/4,58].

10416 *Dittmann, R.; Larsen, P.* Eine altassyrische Siegelabrollung aus Assur: Ausgrabungen der FU Berlin im Jahre 1989. Assyrien im Wandel. 1997, ⇒379. ᴱWaetzoldt, H., 247-250.

10417 *Farber, Walter* ištu api ilâmma ezezu ezzet: ein bedeutsames neues Lamaštu-Amulett;

10418 *Gamer-Wallert, Ingrid* Eine mesopotamisch-ägyptische Synthese. AOAT 247: 1997, ⇒75. ᶠRoᴇʟʟɪɢ W., 115-128/145-151.

10419 *Gualandi, Guido* Terqa: Rapport préliminaire (1987-1989): les sceaux et les impressions de sceaux (TQ 10-12): étude préliminaire. Mari 8 (1997) 149-157.

10420 *Güterbock, Hans G.* Observations on the Tarsus seal of Puduhepa, Queen of Hatti. JAOS 117 (1997) 143-144.

10421 ᴱ**Gyselen, Rika** Sceaux d'Orient et leur emploi. Res Orientales 10: Bures-sur-Yvette 1997, Groupe pour l'Étude de la Civilisation du Moyen-Orient 174 pp. 2-9508266-4-4 [Mes. 33,388-390—Bollati, A.].

10422 *Herbordt, S.* Neo-Assyrian royal and administrative seals and their use. Assyrien im Wandel. 1997, ⇒379. ᴱWaetzoldt, H., 279-283.

10423 **Herrmann, Christian** Ägyptische Amulette aus Palästina/Israel. OBO 138: 1994, ⇒10,11978... 12,9805. ᴿOLZ 92 (1997) 31-38 *(Hüttner, Michaela)*; WO 28 (1997) 189-191 *(Gamer-Wallert, Ingrid)*.

10424 *Horsley, G.H.R.* Reconstructing a biblical codex: the prehistory of MPER n.s. XVII.10 (P.*Vindob.* G 29 831). 21. Papyrologenkongress, 1. 1997, ⇒367. ᴱKramer, B., 473-481 [John 1,5-6].

10425 **Jakob-Rost, Liane** Die Stempelsiegel im Vorderasiatischen Museum. Beitrag *Gerlach, Iris*: Mainz 1997, Von Zabern 118 pp. DM35. 3-8053-2029-9 [WO 29,200—Röllig, Wolfgang].

10426 **Jaroš, Karl** Die ältesten Fragmente eines biblischen Textes: zu den Silberamuletten von Jerusalem. Kulturgeschichte der antiken Welt: Mainz 1997, Von Zabern 30 pp. Othmar Kehl zum 60. Geburtstag. 3-8053-2401-4 [NThAR 1998,300].

10427 **Keel, Othmar** Studien zu den Stempelsiegeln aus Palästina/Israel, 4. OBO 135: 1994, ⇒10,11981... 12,9807. ᴿWZKM 87 (1997) 292-294 *(Klengel-Brandt, Evelyn)*;

10428 Corpus der Stempelsiegel-Amulette aus Palästina/Israel, 1: von den Anfängen bis zur Perserzeit: (*a*) Einleitung. OBO.A 10: 1995, ⇒11/2,a706; 12,9808. ᴿThLZ 122 (1997) 239-240 *(Hartenstein, Friedhelm)*; OLZ 92 (1997) 199-206 *(Stoof, Magdalena)*; WZKM 87 (1997) 294-296 *(Klengel-Brandt, Evelyn)*; CBQ 59 (1997) 544-545 *(Aufrecht, Walter E.)*; JAOS 117 (1997) 673-679 *(Ward, William A.)*; JBL 116 (1997) 767-768 *(Chavalas, Mark W.)*; CÉg 72 (1997) 93-95 *(Clerc, Gisèle)*;

10429 (*b*) Katalog. OBO.A 13: Gö 1997, Vandenhoeck & R viii; 802 pp. DM269. 3-525-53894-4.

10430 ᴱ**Klengel-Brandt, Evelyn** Mit sieben Siegeln versehen: das Siegel in Wirtschaft und Kunst des Alten Orients. Collab. *Amiet,*

*Pierre*: Mainz 1997, Zabern 192 pp. Ein Handbuch. DM68. 3-8053-2032-9 [EuA 73,329].

10431   *Kühne, Hartmut* Stempel- oder Siegelringe des Tukulti-Ninurta I. AOAT 247: 1997, ⇒75. FRoELLIG W., 193-218.

10432   **Leith, M.J. Winn** Wadi Daliyeh I: the Wadi Daliyeh seal impressions. DJD 24: Oxf 1997, Clarendon xxii; 249 pp. 24 pl. £65. 0-19-826935-8 [ZAW 110,322—Lange, A.].

10433   *Lemaire, André* Sceau phénicien de la région de Karaman (Turquie). Epigraphica Anatolica 29 (1997) 123-125.

10434   *Lemaire, André; Sass, Benjamin* Sigillographie ouest-sémitique: nouvelles lectures. Sum. 27. Sem. 45 (1996) 27-35.

10435   *Margain, Jean; Lozachmeur, Hélène* Un anneau-sceau samaritain avec motif ornemental (collection Sh. Moussaïeff). Sum. 97. Sem. 47 (1997) 97-104.

10436   **Matthews, Donald M.** The early glyptic of Tell Brak: cylinder seals of third millennium Syria. OBO.A 15: FrS 1997, Universitätsverlag xiv; 313 pp. 59 ill. FS120. 3-7278-1104-8 [RB 104,475].

10437   *McCollough, C. Thomas; Glazier-McDonald, Beth* Magic and medicine in Byzantine Galilee: a bronze amulet from Sepphoris. Archaeology and the Galilee. SFSHJ 143: 1997, ⇒275. EEdwards, D.R., 143-149.

10438   *Naveh, Joseph* A Syriac amulet on leather. JSSt 42 (1997) 33-38.

10439   ESass, **Benjamin; Uehlinger, Christoph** Studies in the iconography of Northwest Semitic inscribed seals. OBO 125: 1993. Symposium, FrS, 1991. ⇒12,9827. RSyr. 74 (1997) 240-242 *(Mora, Clelia)*.

10440   **Sbonias, Kostas** Frühkretische Siegel: Ansätze für eine Interpretation der sozial-politischen Entwicklung auf Kreta während der Frühbronzezeit. BAR-Is 620: Oxf 1995, Tempus Reparatum vi; 198 pp. 60 fig. £35. 0-86054-801-5. RAJA 101 (1997) 597-598 *(Wiencke, Martha Heath)*.

10441   *Vieweger, Dieter* An Early Bronze Age handle with cylinder seal impression from Dayr Qiqub, Jordan. Levant 29 (1997) 147-152.

T3.4 **Mosaica**

10442   **Bingöl, O.** Malerei und Mosaik der Antike in der Türkei. Mainz 1997, Von Zabern 148 pp. 32 pl. 96 fig. DM45. 3-8053-1880-4 [ClR 48,546—Ling, Roger].

10443   **Jolly, Penny Howell** Made in God's image?: Eve and Adam in the Genesis mosaics at San Marco, Venice. California Studies in the History of Art, Discovery 4: Berkeley 1997, Univ. of California Press xv; 142 pp. 12 col. pl. 33 ill. $45 [Spec. 74,777s—Givens, Jean A.].

10444   **Lancha, Janine** Mosaïque et culture dans l'Occident romain (Ier-IVe s.). R 1997, Bretschneider 439 pp. 140 pl. $463. 88-7062-952-X [AJA 103,162s—Westgate, Ruth].

10445   **Magness, Jodi** Jerusalem ceramic chronology: circa 200-800 C.E. 1993, ⇒9,13643; 11/2,a767. RJNES 56 (1997) 133-134 *(Harrison, Timothy P.)*.

10446   **Osborne, J.; Claridge, A.** Other mosaics paintings, sarcophagi and small objects. Paper Museum of Cassiano dal Pozzo, A. Antiquities and Architecture, II, Early Christian and Medieval Antiquities. L 1997, Harvey Miller 2 vols; 304 + 315 pp. £150. 1-872501-67-2.

## T3.5 *Ceramica,* pottery

10447 **Abay, Eşref** Die Keramik der Frühbronzezeit in Anatolien mit 'syrischen Affinitäten'. Altertumskunde des Vorderen Orients 8: Müns 1997, Ugarit-Verlag xiv; 461 pp. DM228. 3-927-120-58-8. RUF 29 (1997) 817-819 *(Zwickel, Wolfgang).*

10448 **Adan-Bayewitz, D.** Common pottery in Roman Galilee: a study of local trade. 1993, ⇒9,13610... 12,9844. RPEQ 129 (1997) 162-163 *(Watson, Pamela).*

10449 **Berlin, Andrea; Slane, Kathleen Warner** Tel Anafa II.1: the Hellenistic and Roman pottery: the plain wares and the fine wares. Journal of Roman Archaeology Suppl. 10.II.1: Ann Arbor 1997, Journal of Roman Archaeology 418 pp. $89.50. 1-887829-98-9.

10450 **Campenon, Christine** La céramique attique à figures rouges autour de 400 avant J.-C. De l'archéologie à l'histoire. 1994, ⇒11/2,a757. RGn. 69 (1997) 85-87 *(Paul-Zinserling, Verena).*

10451 *Conrad, Diethelm* Zur Rekonstruktion phönikischer Figurinen vom Tel Akko. 1997, ⇒29. FGERSTENBERGER S., 333-349.

10452 *Di Paolo, Silvana* Sulla tipologia e l'origine degli unguentari *à canard* nella Siria-Palestina del Bronzo Tardo. Sum. 53. RSO 71 (1997) 25-53.

10453 **Garfinkel, Yosef** Human and animal figurines of Munhata (Israel). Cahiers des Missions archéologiques françaises en Israël 8: P 1995, Association Paléorient 150 pp. 41 fig. 9 tables. 22 pl. FF180. 2-902485-03-4. RSyr. 74 (1997) 225-226 *(Contenson, Henri de).*

10454 E**Hallager, Erik; Hallager, Birgitta P.** Late Minoan III pottery: chronology and terminology. Monographs of the Danish Institute at Athens 1: Aarhus University Press 1997, Aarhus 420 pp. 371 figs. $40. 87-7288-731-1 [AJA 102,435—Rutter, Jeremy B.].

10455 *Hausleiter, A.* Neuassyrische Keramik-Aspekte der Erforschung. Assyrien im Wandel. 1997, ⇒379. EWaetzoldt, H., 271-278.

10456 **Hayes, John W.** Handbook of Mediterranean Roman pottery. L 1997, British Museum Press 108 pp. 40 pl. 34 fig. £15. 0-7141-2216-5 [AnCl 67,574—Raepsaet, Georges].

10457 **Hendrix, Ralph E.,** (*al.*), Ancient pottery of Transjordan: an introduction utilizing published whole forms, late Neolithic through late Islamic. 1996, ⇒12,9865. RAUSS 35 (1997) 276-278 *(Bienkowski, Piotr).*

10458 **Herr, Larry G.; Trenchard, Warren C.** Published pottery of Palestine. 1996, ⇒12,9868. ROLZ 92 (1997) 677-678 *(Hübner, Ulrich).*

10459 **Hoffmann, Herbert** Sotades: symbols of immortality on Greek vases. Ill. *Lissarague, François*: Oxf 1997, OUP xviii; 206 pp. 108 ill. £70. 0-19-815061-X [Antiquity 72,967s—Spivey, Nigel].

10460 **Jenkins, Ian; Sloan, Kim** Vases and volcanoes: Sir William HAMILTON and his collection. 1996, ⇒12,9871. RAJA 101 (1997) 424-425 *(Gill, David W.J.).*

10461   *McAdam, Ellen* The figurines from the 1982-1985 seasons of excavations at Ain Ghazal. Levant 29 (1997) 115-145.

10462   **Moignard, E.** Corpus vasorum antiquorum, Great Britain, Fascicule 18: the Glasgow collections. Oxf 1997, OUP 54 pp. 60 pl. £55. 0-19-726168-X [ClR 48,430s—Stafford, Emma J.].

10463   *Parlasca, Ingemarie* Terrakotten, Trinkschalen und Goldschmuck: nabatäisches Kunsthandwerk—exquisite Massenware. Petra antike Felsstadt. 1997, ⇒311. ᴱWeber, T., 126-144.

10464   *Pfälzner, P.* Keramikproduktion und Provinzverwaltung im mittelassyrischen Reich. Assyrien im Wandel. 1997, ⇒379. ᴱWaetzoldt, H., 337-345.

10465   *Pic, Marielle* Le matériel de Tell Ashara-Terqa au musée du Louvre. Mari 8 (1997) 159-178.

10466   **Postgate, Carolyn; Oates, David; Oates, Joan** The excavations at Tell al Rimah: the pottery. Iraq archaeological reports 4: Warminster 1997, British School of Archaeology in Iraq 275 pp. Bibl. £48. 0-85668-700-6.

10467   ᴱ**Rasmussen, Tom; Spivey, Nigel Jonathan** Looking at Greek vases. C 1997, CUP xvii; 282 pp. Bibl. 0-521-37679-3.

10468   **Rotroff, Susan I.** Hellenistic pottery: Athenian and imported wheelmade tableware and related material. Princeton 1997, American School of Classical Studies at Athens xxxviii; 575 pp. 2 vols. $175. 0-87661-229-X [AnCl 68,610—Raepsaet, Georges].

10469   *Schmitt-Korte, Karl* Die bemalte nabatäische Keramik: Verbreitung, Typologie und Chronologie;

10470   Die Entwicklung des Granatapfel-Motivs in der nabatäischen Keramik. Petra und das Königreich. 1997, ⇒289. ᴱLindner, M., 205-227/228-232.

10471   ᴱ**Söldner, Magdalene** Corpus vasorum antiquorum, 3: Deutschland, 59. Akademisches Kunstmuseum 13: Mü 1990, Beck 119 pp. 42 ill. 64 pl. ᴿGn. 69 (1997) 87-89 (*Güntner, Gudrun*).

10472   *Stocks, Denys A.* Derivation of ancient Egyptian faience core and glaze materials. Antiquity 71 (1997) 179-182.

10473   *Tassignon, Isabelle* Terqa: rapport préliminaire (1987-1989): la poterie des campagnes de 1988 et 1989. Mari 8 (1997) 125-140.

10474   *Van der Steen, Eveline J.* Pots and potters in the central Jordan valley. ADAJ 41 (1997) 81-93.

10475   *Waldbaum, Jane C.; Magness, Jodi* The chronology of early Greek pottery: new evidence from seventh-century B.C. destruction levels in Israel. Sum. 23. AJA 101 (1997) 23-40.

10476   *Wolff, Samuel R.* 'Ironian' casseroles from Nizzana and Iskandil Burnu, Turkey. IEJ 47 (1997) 93-96.

10477   *Yannai, Eli* The possible origin of the tournette?: a group of ceramic bowls made in stone moulds from ʿEn Asawir. TelAv 24 (1997) 253-257.

10478   **Zimhoni, Orna** Studies in the Iron Age pottery of Israel: typological, archaeological and chronological aspects. Tel Aviv occasional publications 2: TA 1997, Tel Aviv Univ., Inst. of Archaeology 263 pp. 965-266-010-8.

T3.6 *Lampas*; **Cultica**

10479   **Loffreda, Stanislao** Lucerne bizantine in Terra Santa con iscrizioni in greco. 1989, ⇒5,d571... 8,e248. ᴿIEJ 48 (1997) 293-295 (*Gichon, Mordechai*).

10480 **Mackensen, Michael** Die spätantiken Sigillata und Lampentöpfereien von El Mahrine (Nordtunesien). 1993, ⇒10,12064. <sup>R</sup>IEJ 48 (1997) 147-150 *(Gichon, Mordechai)*.

10481 **Młynarczyk, Jolanta** Alexandrian and Alexandria-influenced mould-made lamps of the Hellenistic period. Oxf 1997, Archaeopress vii; 161 pp. 201 fig. 8 pl. £35 [CÉg 73,194s—Nachtergael, Georges].

10482 **Tezgor, Dominique Kassab; Sezer, Tahsin** Catalogue des lampes en terre cuite du Musée archéologique d'Istanbul I: époque protohistorique... hellénistique. Institut français d'études anatoliennes d'Istanbul, Varia Anatolica 6/1: P 1995, De Boccard 200 pp. 79 pl. 467 fig. FF300. 2-906053-38-4. <sup>R</sup>AJA 101 (1997) 625-626 *(Williams, Hector)*.

10483 *Al-Jadir, W.* Le dégagement de la Ziggurat à Sippar. Assyrien im Wandel. 1997, ⇒379. <sup>E</sup>Waetzoldt, H., 291-293.

10484 **Cooper, Frederick A.** The temple of Apollo Bassitas I: architecture; II: illustrations. 1996, ⇒12,9900. <sup>R</sup>AJA 101 (1997) 796-797 *(Coulton, J.J.)*.

10485 *Dentzer-Feydy, Jacqueline* Remarques sur les temples de Hebrân et de Sleim (Syrie du Sud) dessinés par W.J. BANKES (1786-1855). Syr. 74/1 (1997) 161-164.

10486 **Draeger, Olaf** Religionem significare: Studien zu römischen Altaren. MDAI.RE 33: 1994, ⇒11/2,a797; 12,9901. <sup>R</sup>Mes. 32 (1997) 390-393 *(Conti, M.C.)*.

10487 *Frenkel, R.* The sanctuary from the Persian period at Mount Mizpe Yamim. Qad. 30/1 (1997) 46-53 **H**.

10488 *Kurth, Dieter* The present state of research into Graeco-Roman temples. The temple in ancient Egypt. 1997, ⇒300. <sup>E</sup>Quirke, S., 152-158.

10489 *Levine, Lee I.* The revolutionary effects of archaeology on the study of Jewish history: the case of the ancient synagogue. The archaeology of Israel. JSOT.S 237: 1997, ⇒9790. <sup>E</sup>Silberman, N.A., 166-189.

10490 *Metzler, Dieter* "Abstandsbetonung": zur Entwicklung des Innenraumes griechischer Tempel in der Epoche der frühen Polis. Religion und Gesellschaft. AOAT 248: 1997, ⇒235. <sup>E</sup>Albertz, R., 155-175.

10491 **Pfeifer, Michael** Der Weihrauch: Geschichte, Bedeutung, Verwendung. Rg 1997, Pustet 221 pp. 3-7917-1566-6 [EL 112,414ss—Raffa, Vincenzo].

10492 *Roussin, Lucille A.* The Zodiac in synagogue decoration. Archaeology and the Galilee. SFSHJ 143: 1997, ⇒275. <sup>E</sup>Edwards, D.R., 83-96.

10493 **Siebenmorgen, Harald** Delphi: Orakel am Nabel der Welt. 1996, ⇒12,9907. <sup>R</sup>AJA 101 (1997) 794-795 *(Herzog, Horst)*.

10494 *Stadelmann, Rainer* The development of the pyramid temple in the fourth dynasty. The temple in ancient Egypt. 1997, ⇒300. <sup>E</sup>Quirke, S., 1-16.

10495 *Tarzi, Zemaryalaï* Préservation des sites de Hadda: monastères bouddhiques de Tape Shotor et de Tape Tope Kalân. Mari 8 (1997) 207-222.

10496 <sup>E</sup>**Urman, Dan; Flesher, Paul V.M.** Ancient synagogues: historical analysis and archaeological discovery. StPB 47/1: 1995,

⇒11/2,a812; 12,9909. ᴿQad. 30/1 (1997) 61 *(Patrich, J.)* JAOS 117 (1997) 367-368 *(Magness, Jodi)*.

### т3.8 Funeraria; *Sindon,* the Shroud

10497 *Abu Ghanime, Khaled* Les coutumes funéraires dans l'Épipaléolithique Jordanien. Syr. 74/1 (1997) 3-13.

10498 *Abu Uqsa, Ḥana* מערת קבורה מהתקופה הרומית ממזרח לגבעת יוסף [תל אל-סומיריה] [A burial cave from the Roman period east of Givʿat Yasaf]. Sum. 10*;

10499 *Aviam, Mordechai* מערת קבורה בכפר שעב [A rock-cut tomb at Shaʿab]. Sum. 14*;

10500 *Aviam, Mordechai; Gorin-Rosen, Yael* מערות קבורה בחורפיש [Three burial caves from the Roman period at Ḥurfeish]. Sum. 9*. ʿAtiqot 33 (1997) 39-46/79-80/25-37 H.

10501 **Baima Bollone, Pier Luigi** Sepoltura del messia e sudario di Oviedo. Religione: T 1997, Società Ed. Internazionale x; 237 pp. 88-05-05788-6.

10502 *Barbet, Alix; Gatier, Pierre-Louis; Lewis, Norman N.* Un tombeau peint inscrit de Sidon. Syr. 74/1 (1997) 141-160.

10503 *Bartoloni, P.* Un sarcofago antropoide filisteo da Neapolis (Oristanot-Sardegna). RSFen 25/1 (1997) 97-103.

10504 ᴱ**Bierbrier, Morris L.** Portraits and masks: burial customs in Roman Egypt. L 1997, British Museum viii; 131 pp. 48 pl. £40. 0-7141-1904-0.

10505 **Boehmer, Rainer Michael; Pedde, Friedhelm; Salje, Beate** Uruk: die Gräber. ADFGUW: Endberichte 10: 1996, ⇒12,9918. ᴿAJA 101 (1997) 170 *(Emberling, Geoff)*.

10506 **Branigan, Keith** Cemetery and society in the Aegean Bronze Age. Shf 1997, Academic 173 pp. 65 pl. fig. $21.50; £13. 1-8505-822-0 [Antiquity 72,934—Sinclair, Anthony].

10507 **Breuer, Christine** Reliefs und Epigramme griechischer Privatgrabmäler: Zeugnisse bürgerlichen Selbstverständnisses vom 4.-2. Jahrhundert v. Chr. Arbeiten zur Archäologie: Köln 1995, Böhlau 151 pp. 51 pl. DM148. 3-412-15893-3. ᴿAJA 101 (1997) 179-180 *(Day, Joseph W.)*.

10508 ᴱ**Broshi, M.** Burial caves of the Roman and Byzantine periods in western Galilee. 1997, 162; 19* pp. Eng. sum. ʿAtiqot 33.

10509 ᴱ**Campbell, Stuart; Green, Anthony** The archaeology of death in the ancient Near East. Oxbow Monograph 51: 1995, ⇒11/2,a822. ᴿAJA 101 (1997) 169-170 *(Emberling, Geoff)*; Mes. 32 (1997) 322-323 *(Fiorina, P.)*.

10510 **Corcoran, Lorelei H.** Portrait mummies from Roman Egypt. 1995, ⇒11/2,a826a. ᴿCÉg 72 (1997) 376-378 *(Montserrat, Dominic)*; AJA 101 (1997) 187-188 *(Borg, Barbara)*.

10511 *Di Giglio, Alberto* La sindone come 'monumento' storico. Cultura & Libri.S 112 (1997) 43-51.

10512 *Dietrich, Manfried; Mayer, Walter* Ein hurritisches Totenritual für ʿAmmištamru III (KTU 1.125). AOAT 247: 1997, ⇒75. ᶠROELLIG W., 79-89.

10513 **Eslava Glan, Juan** El fraude de la sábana santa y las reliquias de Cristo. M 1997, Planeta 352 pp. [Mayéutica 23,500—Acero, F. Javier].

10514 *Gnirs, Andrea Maria; Grothe, Elina; Guksch, Heike* Zweiter Vorbericht über die Aufnahme und Publikation von Gräbern der 18. Dynastie der thebanischen Beamtennekropole. MDAI.K 53 (1997) 57-83.

10515 *Gorin-Rosen, Yael* מערת קבורה בכפר יסיף [A burial cave at Kafr Yasif]. Sum. 13*. ʿAtiqot 33 (1997) 71-77 **H.**

10516 *Griesheimer, Marc* Cimetières et tombeaux des villages de la Syrie du Nord. Syr. 74/1 (1997) 165-211.

10517 *Hachlili, Rachel* A Jericho ossuary and a Jerusalem workshop. IEJ 47 (1997) 238-247.

10518 **Hodel-Hoenes, Sigrid** Vita e morte nell'Antico Egitto: le tombe private tebane del Nuovo Rego. Archeologia 3: CinB 1997, San Paolo 219 pp. [LASBF 48,568—Niccacci, Alviero].

10519 *Ji, Chango-ho C.* New dolmen field near Iraq al-Amir, Jordan. BA 60/4 (1997) 251-252.

10520 *Maeir, Aren M.* Tomb 1181: a multiple-interment burial cave of the transitional Middle Bronze Age IIA-B. Hazor V. 1997, ⇒269. ᴱBen-Tor, A., 295-340.

10521 **Marinelli, Emanuela** La sindone: un'immagine 'impossibile'. 1996, ⇒12,9961. ᴿPalCl 76/1-2 (1997) 153-155 *(Pedrini, Arnaldo)*; RdT 38 (1997) 567-568 *(Pfeiffer, Heinrich)*.

10522 *Marinelli, Emanuela* Flagelli e spine: S. Sindone, 1. TS(I) (mag.-giu. 1997) 15-20;

10523 Fu crocifisso sotto Pilato: S. Sindone, 2. TS(I) (lug.-ago. 1997) 15-19, 55-56.

10524 **Martin, Geoffrey Thorndike**, (al.), The tomb of Tia and Tia: a royal monument of the Ramesside period in the Menphite necropolis. ᵀ*Van Dijk, Jacobus*: The Egypt Exploration Fund, Memoir 58: L 1997, Egypt Exploration Society xxv; 113 pp. 175 pl. Bibl. 0-85698-121-4.

10525 *Mendecki, Norbert* Czy ossuraria z epigrafami rodziny Jezusa z Jerozolimy mogą być autentyczne? [De autenticitate ossuariorum sic dictae familiae Iesu in Ierusalem]. RBL 50 (1997) 150-151 **P.**

10526 **Mercky, Annette** Römische Grabreliefs und Sarkophage auf den Kykladen. EHS 38, Archäologie 55: Fra 1995, Lang. ᴿRivista di Archeologia 21 (1997) 148-150 *(Sperti, Luigi)*.

10527 **Metcalf, Peter; Huntington, Richard** Celebrations of death: the anthropology of mortuary ritual. CM ²1997, CUP xiii; 236 pp. Bibl. 0-521-42375-9.

10528 *Montserrat, Dominic; Meskell, Lynn* Mortuary archaeology and religious landscape at Graeco-Roman Deir el-Medina. Sum. 179. ᴿJEA 83 (1997) 179-197.

10529 *Mouton, Michel* Les tours funéraires d'Arabie, nefesh monumentales. Syr. 74/1 (1997) 81-98.

10530 *Peskowitz, Miriam* The gendering of burial and the burial of gender: notes from Roman-period archaeology. JSQ 4/2 (1997) 105-124.

10531 *Polz, Daniel* An architect's sketch from the Theban necropolis. MDAI.K 53 (1997) 233-240.

10532 *Porat, Lea* מערות קבורה ומחצבה בחורבת כנס — כרמיאל [Quarry and burial caves at Ḥ. Kenes (Karmiel)]. Sum. 15*. ʿAtiqot 33 (1997) 81-88 **H.**

10533 **Raffard de Brienne, D.** Dictionnaire du Linceul de Turin. P 1997, de Paris 103 pp. FF98 [EeV 107/5,39].

10534   *Riesner, Rainer* Archäologie und Politik: die Patriarchengräber in Hebron. BiKi 52 (1997) 91-92.

10535   *Scaltriti, Giacinto Arturo* Il mistero della sindone. PalCl 76 (1997) 731-743.

10536   *Shapiro, Anastasia* Petrographic analysis of Roman clay sarcophagi from northwestern Israel and Cyprus. ʿAtiqot 33 (1997) 1*-5*.

10537   **Siliato, Maria Grazia** Sindone: mistero dell'impronta di duemila anni fa. CasM 1997, Piemme 354 pp. Bibl. L32.000. 88-384-2965-0 [Presenza Pastorale 68,91].

10538   *Smithline, Howard* שלוש מערות קבורה מהתקופה הרומית באשרת [Three burial caves from the Roman period in Asherat]. Sum. 11*. ʿAtiqot 33 (1997) 47-60 H.

10539   *Stern, Edna J.; Gorin-Rosen, Yael* מערות קבורה ליד כברי [Burial caves near Kabri]. Afterword *Aviam, Mordechai*. Sum. 7*-8*; Appendix: The significance of the coin of Agrippa II from Cave 3 near Kabri (p. 23). ʿAtiqot 33 (1997) 1-22 H.

10540   *Torremans, René* Burial practices in neolithic Anatolia. Orient-Express 2 (1997) 53-43.

10541   **Van Walsem, René** The coffin of Djedmonthuiufankh in the National Museum of Antiquities at Leiden. Egyptologische uitgaven 10: Lei 1997, Nederlands Instituut voor het Nabije Oosten 2 vols, v.1, (Text) Technical and iconographic/iconological aspects; v.2, (Tables, graphs etc. illustrations) Technical and iconographic/iconological aspects. 90-6258-210-9.

10542   [F]VENTZKE, W.: Kāmid el-Lōz 16: 'Schatzhaus'-Studien. [E]**Hachmann, R.**, 1996, ⇒12,9941. [R]ZAW 109 (1997) 457-459 *(Kaiser, Otto)*.

10543   *Weeks, Kent R.* Die Geheimnisse des Grabes Nr. 5. WUB 5 (1997) 49-53.

10544   *Wenning, Robert* Bestattungen im königszeitlichen Juda. ThQ 177 (1997) 82-93.

10545   *Wissa, Myriam* Die Mumie Ramses' II. WUB 5 (1997) 6-7.

10546   *Zorn, Jeffrey* More on Mesopotamian burial practices in ancient Israel. IEJ 47 (1997) 214-219.


т3.9 *Numismatica,* coins

10547   *Alföldi, Maria R.; Perrone, Micaela* Fundmünzen der Antike I: reperti numismatici antichi a Roma: nuove prospettive e problematiche; II: un progretto per il recupero di oltre 32.000 monete del Medagliere Capitolino. Bollettino dei musei comunali di Roma 11 (1997) 132-138.

10548   *Arslan, Ermanno A.* Il deposito monetale della trincea XII nel cortile della sinagoga di Cafarnao. Sum. 455;

10549   *Callegher, Bruno* Un ripostiglio di monete d'oro bizantine dalla sinagoga di Cafarnao. Sum. 456. LASBF 47 (1997) 245-328/329-338.

10550   *Deutsch, R.; Heltzer, M.* Numismatic evidence from the Persian period from the Sharon plains (Pls. IV-V). TEuph 13 (1997) 17-20.

10551 **Forzoni, Angiolo** La moneta nella storia, 4: dai figli di Costantino a Giustiniano. R 1997, Istituto Poligrafico dello Stato, Libreria dello Stato xxi; 422 pp. Bibl. 88-240-3747-X.

10552 **Harl, Kenneth W.** Coinage in the Roman economy: 300 B.C. to A.D. 700. 1996, ⇒12,10001. RAJA 101 (1997) 807-808 *(Duncan-Jones, R.P.)*.

10553 **Herbert, K.** Roman imperial coins: Augustus to Hadrian and Antonine selections, 31 BC-AD 180. 1996, ⇒12,10002. RPrudentia 29/2 (1997) 87-91 *(Ehrhardt, C.T.H.R.)*.

10554 *Loffreda, Stanislao* Coins from the synagogue of Capharnaum. Sum. 455. LASBF 47 (1997) 223-244.

10555 **Manfredi, Lorenza-Ilia** Monete puniche: repertorio epigrafico e numismatico delle leggende puniche. Bollettino di numismatica 6: R 1997, Ministero per i Beni Culturali e Ambientali 490 pp. ill.

10556 *Meshorer, Y.* The coinage of Samaria. TEuph 13 (1997) 188.

10557 *Meshorer, Y.* A treasury of Jewish coins from the Persian period to Bar-Kochba. J 1997, Ben-Zvi 332 pp. 80 pl. 965-217-146-8 [JSPE 20,125] H.

10558 *Mildenberg, L.* On the imagery of the Philisto-Arabian coinage— a preview (Pls. I-III). TEuph 13 (1997) 9-16.

10559 *Morawiecki, Lesław* The coins of Masada. Qumran Chronicle 7/1-2 (1997) 65-89.

10560 *Reden, Sitta von* Money and coinage in Ptolemaic Egypt: some preliminary remarks. 21. Papyrologenkongress, 2. 1997, ⇒367. EKramer, B., 1003-1008.

10561 **Troxell, H.A.** Studies in the Macedonian coinage of Alexander the Great. NY 1997, American Numismatic Society 161 pp. 31 pl. $85. 0-89722-261-X [ClR 48,452—Ireland, Stanley].

### T4.2 *Situs effossi*, bulletins; syntheses

10562 **Joffe, Alexander H.** Settlement and society in the Early Bronze Age I and II, southern Levant [Decapolis environs]. Monographs in Mediterranean Archaeology 4: 1993, ⇒11/2,a935. RBiOr 54 (1997) 229-231 *(Van der Steen, Eveline J.)*.

10563 EWexler, Lior; Roshwalb-Hurowitz, Ann Reports and studies of excavations in Judea and Samaria. 'Atiqot 32. J 1997, Israel Antiquities Authority 52*; 207 pp.

### T4.3 **Jerusalem,** *archaeologia* et historia

10564 *Alexander, Philip S.* Jerusalem as the *omphalos* of the world: on the history of a geographical concept. Jdm 46 (1997) 147-158.

10565 **Armstrong, K.** Jerusalén: una ciudad y tres religiones. Barc 1997, Paidós 574 pp. [SalTer 86,261].

10566 **Arnould, Caroline** Les arcs romains de Jérusalem: architecture, décor et urbanisme. NTOA 35: FrS 1997, Univ.-Verl. 319, [48] pp. FS98. 3-7278-1141-2.

10567 *Autané, Maurice* Jésus et Jérusalem. DosB 67 (1997) 12-14.

10568 *Bahat, Dan* Jerusalem—die Hauptstadt von Israel und Juda;

10569  *Bahat, Dan; Hurvitz, Gila* Jerusalem—die Zeit des Ersten Tempels: archäologische Forschungen. Land der Bibel. 1997, ⇒9960. ᴱSeipel, W., 219-230/207-218.

10570  **Barkay, Gabriel** Three First-Temple period burial caves north of Damascus Gate and the date of Jerusalem's northern moat. Sum. 189. Cathedra 83 (1997) 7-26 **H**.

10571  **Baud, Philippe** La "Via Crucis": storia e teologia. R 1997, Città Nuova 111 pp. 88-311-3928-2.

10572  *Belayche, Nicole* Du Mount du Temple au Golgotha: le Capitole de la colonie d'*Aelia Capitolina*. Som., sum. 387. RHR 214 (1997) 387-413.

10573  *Ben Zvi, Ehud* The urban centre of Jerusalem and the development of the literature of the Hebrew Bible. Urbanism. JSOT.S 244: 1997, ⇒265. ᴱAufrecht, W.E., 194-209.

10574  ᴱ**Ben-Arieh, Yehoshua; Davis, Moshe** Jerusalem in the mind of the western world: 1800-1948. With Eyes toward Zion 5: Westport 1997, Praeger xi; 282 pp. $65 [CBQ 59,817].

10575  **Benvenisti, Meron** City of stone: the hidden history of Jerusalem. ᵀ*Nunn, Maxine Kaufman*: Berkeley, CA 1996, University of California viii; 274 pp. 0-520-20521-9.

10576  *Bieberstein, Klaus* Der Tunnel von Jerusalem. WUB 4 (1997) 70-77.

10577  *Bouganim, Ami* Le chantier de Jérusalem;

10578  *Briend, Jacques* De la Jérusalem historique à la Jérusalem mystique. RICP 62 (1997) 79-97/67-77.

10579  **Bux, Nicola; Cardini, Franco** L'anno prossimo a Gerusalemme: la storia, le guerre e le religioni nella città più amata e più contesa. Storia della Chiesa, Saggi 14: CinB 1997, San Paolo 228 pp. Bibl. 88-215-3577-0.

10580  *Cahill, Jane M.* A rejoinder to "Was the Siloam tunnel built by Hezekiah?". BA 60/3 (1997) 184-185.

10581  *Cogan, Mordechai* David's Jerusalem: notes and reflections. 1997, ⇒34. ᴹGᴿᴇᴇɴʙᴇʀɢ M., 193-201.

10582  *Di Segni, Leah* The date of the Beit Ṣafafa inscription again. IEJ 47 (1997) 248-254.

10583  *Eshel, Hanan* Aelia Capitolina: Jerusalem no more. BArR 23/6 (1997) 46-48, 73.

10584  ᴱ**Eshel, Itzak; Prag, Kay** The Iron Age deposits on the southeast hill and isolated burials and cemeteries elsewhere. Excavations by K.M. Kᴇɴʏᴏɴ in Jerusalem 1961-1967, 4. 1995, ⇒11/2,a966; 12,10041. ᴿAJA 101/1 (1997) 170-171 *(Bienkowski, Piotr)*; AfO 44-45 (1997-98) 516-520 *(Weippert, Helga)*.

10585  *Faust, Avraham* The impact of Jerusalem's expansion in the late Iron Age on the forms of rural settlement in its vicinity. Sum. 189. Cathedra 84 (1997) 53-62 **H**.

10586  Gerusalemme: pellegrini, santi e cavalieri nel monoteismo abramico. Mi 1997, La sintesi 239 pp. A cura della CO.RE.IS Italiana. 88-86905-01-7.

10587  *Geva, Hillel* Searching for Roman Jerusalem. BArR 23/6 (1997) 34-45, 72-73.

10588  **Gibson, Shimon; Taylor, Joan E.** Beneath the church of the Holy Sepulchre Jerusalem. 1994, ⇒10,12218*... 12,10047. ᴿOLZ 92 (1997) 705-707 *(Fritz, Volkmar)*.

10589 *Golinkin, David* Jerusalem in Jewish law and custom: a preliminary typology. Jdm 46 (1997) 169-179.

10590 *Grossberg, Asher* Ritual baths in Second Temple period Jerusalem and how they were ritually prepared. Cathedra 83 (1997) 151-168 **H**.

10591 *Gruson, Philippe* Debout! Resplendis... (Isaïe 60);

10592 L'histoire de Jérusalem: de David aux romains;

10593 La vieille ville de Jérusalem. DosB 67 (1997) 8-9/5-7/15-18.

10594 *Henshke, David* הכתתית להלכה חז"ל בין ירושלים: קדושת [The sanctity of Jerusalem: the sages and sectarian *Halakhah*]. Sum. V. Tarb. 67/1 (1997) 5-28.

10595 *Honecker, Martin* Die Krise der Städte und die Stadt Gottes. BZNW 89: 1997, ⇒33. [F]GRAESSER E., 109-122.

10596 *Hoppe, Leslie J.* A refuge for the poor. BiTod 35 (1997) 210-215.

10597 *Hunt, E.D.* Constantine and Jerusalem. JEH 48 (1997) 405-424.

10598 *Jacobson, David M.; Gibson, Shimon* The original form of Barclay's gate. PEQ 129 (1997) 138-149.

10599 *Japhet, Sara* From the king's sanctuary to the chosen city. Jdm 46 (1997) 132-139.

10600 *Kaplony, Andreas* Die fatimidische "Moschee der Wiege Jesu" in Jerusalem. ZDPV 113 (1997) 123-132.

10601 [E]**Körner, Irmela; Paffenholz, Alfred** Jerusalem: Stadt des Friedens: ein Streifzug durch 3000 Jahre. 1996, ⇒12,10063. [R]FrRu 4 (1997) 289-290 *(Krabbe, Dieter)*.

10602 *Krüger, Jürgen* Der Abendmahlssaal in Jerusalem zur Zeit der Kreuzzüge. RQ 92 (1997) 229-247.

10603 *Kühnel, Gustav* Kreuzfahrerideologie und Herrscherikonographie: das Kaiserpaar Helena und Heraklius in der Grabeskirche. ByZ 90 (1997) 366-404.

10604 *Lalor, Brian* The temple mount of Herod the Great at Jerusalem: recent excavations and literary sources. Archaeology and biblical interpretation. 1997, ⇒268. [E]Bartlett, J.R., 95-116.

10605 *Lazarus-Yafeh, Hava* Jerusalem and Mecca. Jdm 46 (1997) 197-205.

10606 *Le Saux, Madeleine* Jérusalem au cœur de la prière. DosB 67 (1997) 10-11.

10607 *Lederman, Yohlanan* Les évêques juifs de Jérusalem. RB 104 (1997) 211-222.

10608 *Levine, Lee I.* Hasmonean Jerusalem: a Jewish city in a Hellenistic orbit. Jdm 46 (1997) 140-146.

10609 *Maïla, Joseph* La place de Jérusalem dans l'Islam. RICP 62 (1997) 99-115.

10610 *Mazar, Eilat* Excavate King David's palace. BArR 23/1 (1997) 50-57, 74.

10611 *Murphy-O'Connor, Jerome* Where was the Capitol in Roman Jerusalem?. BiRe 13/6 (1997) 22-29.

10612 *Muszyński, Henryk* Jerozolima z czasów Dawida w świetle opisów biblijnych i badań archeol ogicznych [Gerusalemme nei tempi di Davide alla luce delle descrizioni bibliche e delle ricerche archeologiche]. Rias. 210. WST 10 (1997) 205-210 **P**.

10613 *Na'aman, Nadav* Cow town or royal capital?: evidence for Iron Age Jerusalem. BArR 23/4 (1997) 43-47, 67.

10614 **Neher-Bernheim, Renée** Jérusalem trois millénaires d'histoire: du roi David à nos jours. Présences du Judaïsmes 20: P 1997, Michel 228 pp. [EeV 107/6,47].

10615 *Nowogórski, Przemysław* Some notes on the problem of the place of Pretorium in Jerusalem (in the context of Christ's case). Sum. 32. Saeculum Christianum 4/2 (1997) 27-32 **P**.

10616 *Pahlitzsch, Johannes* St. Maria Magdalena, St. Thomas und St. Markus: Tradition und Geschichte dreier syrisch-orthodoxer Kirchen in Jerusalem. OrChr 81 (1997) 82-106.

10617 *Perrier, Jacques* Jérusalem, pour le temps et pour l'éternité. Com(F) 22/4 (1997) 40-48 [=RICP 62 (1997) 117-123].

10618 **Pieraccini, Paolo** Gerusalemme, luoghi santi e comunità religiose nella politica internazionale. Pref. *Ferrari, Silvio*: Studi Religiosi: Bologna 1997, EDB xi; 832 pp. L94.000. 88-10-40795-4 [RivBib 45,256].

10619 ᴱ**Poorthuis, Marcel; Safrai, Chana** The centrality of Jerusalem: historical perspectives. 1996, ⇒12,236. ᴿJThS 48 (1997) 170-172 *(Horbury, William)*; CDios 210 (1997) 919-920 *(Gutiérrez, J.)*; CBQ 59 (1997) 611-613 *(Michael, Tony S.L.)*; ThLZ 122 (1997) 1114-1116 *(Otto, Eckart)*.

10620 *Regev, Eyal* More on ritual baths of Jewish groups and sects: on research methods and archaeological evidence: a reply to A. GROSSBERG. Cathedra 83 (1997) 169-176 **H**.

10621 *Reif, Stefan C.* Jerusalem in Jewish liturgy. Jdm 46 (1997) 159-168.

10622 ᴱ**Rosovsky, Nitza** City of the great king: Jerusalem from David to the present. 1996, ⇒12,10082. ᴿJJS 48 (1997) 358-360 *(Rascoff, Samuel J.)*.

10623 **Röwekamp, Georg** Jerusalem: ein Reisebegleiter in die Heilige Stadt von Judentum, Christentum und Islam. FrB 1997, Herder 178 pp. 3-451-26126-X.

10624 **Safdie, Michal Ronnen** The Western Wall. Introd. *Amichai, Yehuda*: Hong Kong 1997, Levin 144 pp. 0-88363-197-0.

10625 *Sanders, E.P.* Jerusalem and its temple in the beginnings of the christian movement. Jdm 46 (1997) 189-196.

10626 *Schwartz, Howard* The quest for Jerusalem. Jdm 46 (1997) 208-217.

10627 *Soupa, Anne* Les deux Jérusalem des chrétiens [Mt 21,1-11; Mk 11,1-10; Lk 19,28-40; John 12,12-19];

10628 La Jérusalem perdue. DosB 67 (1997) 24-26/3-4.

10629 *Steiner, Margreet* Two popular cult sites of ancient Palestine: Cave 1 in Jerusalem and E 207 in Samaria. SJOT 11 (1997) 16-28.

10630 *Sylvestre, Paul* La cupola bella del Risorto. TS(I) [mag.-giu. 1997) 38-41.

10631 **Testa, Emanuele** Le mitiche rocce della salvezza e Gerusalemme SBF.CMi 35: J 1997, Franciscan Printing Press 110 pp. Bibl.

10632 **Trintignac, André** Monter à Jérusalem: une histoire sainte. P 1997, Cerf 447 pp. FF175. 2-204-05502-6 [EstB 55,570].

10633 **Vriezen, Karel J.H.** Die Ausgrabungen unter der Erlöserkirche im Muristan, Jerusalem (1970-1974). Collab. *Carradice, Ian A.; Tchernov, Eitan*: ADPV 19: Wsb 1994, Harrassowitz xviii; 346 pp. DM128. 3-447-03477-7. ᴿRB 104 (1997) 307-309 *(Murphy-O'Connor, J.)*.

10634 **Walker, Peter W.L.** Jesus and the Holy City: New Testament perspectives on Jerusalem. 1996, ⇒12,10091. ᴿScrB 27 (1997) 83-85 *(Campbell, W.S.)*.

10635 *Weinberg, J.* Transmitter and recipient in the process of acculturation: the experience of the Judean citizen-temple-community. TEuph 13 (1997) 91-105.

10636 *Wilken, Robert L.* Jerusalem: the christian holy city. Jdm 46 (1997) 180-188.

## T4.4 Judaea, Negeb; *Situs alphabetice*

10637 **Boragini, Simona,** *(al.)*, Le opere fortificate di Erode il Grande. Verona 1997, Cierre 38 pp. Gruppo di ricerca.

10638 *Gruson, Philippe; Baudry, Marcel* Der Negev;

10639 Judäa und Jerusalem. WUB 4 (1997) 36-39/28-35;

10640 Die Schefela;

10641 Jordantal und Totes Meer. WUB 4 (1997) 24-27/2-7.

10642 **Leonard, Albert** The Jordan valley survey, 1953: some unpublished soundings conducted by James MELLAART. AASOR 50: 1992, ⇒8,e429. ᴿIEJ 47/1-2 (1997) 139-141 *(Garfinkel, Yosef)*; JNES 55/2 (1996) 132-132 *(Joffe, Alexander H.)*.

10643 *Aqaba: Parker, S. Thomas* Preliminary report on the 1994 season of the Roman Aqaba project. BASOR 305 (1997) 19-44.

10644 *'En Boqeq:* **Gichon, Mordechai** 'En Boqeq ,1: Geographie und Geschichte der Oase. 1993, ⇒9,13828; 10,12256. ᴿSyr. 74 (1997) 246-248 *(Dentzer, Jean-Marie)*; JNES 56 (1997) 138-140 *(Harrison, Timothy P.)*.

10645 *'Oded* **Rosen, Steven A.; Avni, Gideon Y.,** *(al.)*, The 'Oded sites: investigations of two early Islamic pastoral camps south of the Ramon Crater. Beer-Sheva 11: Beer-Sheva 1997, Ben-Gurion University vi; (2) 130 pp. Bibl. 965-342-676-1.

10646 *Abu Rish: Magen, I.; Baruch, Y.* Khirbet Abu Rish (Beit 'Anun). Sum. 457. LASBF 47 (1997) 339-358.

10647 *Araba: Smith, Andrew M.; Stevens, Michelle; Niemi, Tina M.* The southeast Araba archaeological survey: a preliminary report of the 1994 season. BASOR 305 (1997) 45-71.

10648 *Beersheba: Coulson, William D.E.; Mook, Margaret S.; Rehard, James W.* Stamped amphora handles from Tel Beersheba. BASOR 306 (1997) 47-62;

10649 *Bunimovitz, S.; Lederman, Z.* A season of excavations at Tel Beth Shemesh: a border town in Judah. Qad. 30/1 (1997) 22-37;

10650 Beth-Shemesh: culture conflict on Judah's frontier. BArR 23/1 (1997) 42-49, 75-77.

10651 *Ekron: Poplutz, Uta* Tel Miqne/Ekron: Geschichte und Kultur einer philistäischen Stadt. BN 87 (1997) 69-99;

10652 *Dothan, Trude* Tel Miqne-Ekron: an Iron Age I Philistine settlement in Canaan. The archaeology of Israel. JSOT.S 237: 1997, ⇒9790. ᴱSilberman, N.A., 96-106.

10653 *Gaza: Shanks, Hershel* Gaza report: nascent Palestinian authority tackles a new dig. BArR 23/2 (1997) 52-53.

10654 *Hamid Tal, Oren* Tel Ḥamid (the lower terrace), 1995, 1996. IEJ 47 (1997) 273-275.

10655   *Kheleifeh*: **Pratico, Gary D.** Nelson GLUECK's 1938-1940 excavations at Tell el-Kheleifeh. 1993, ⇒9,13968... 12,10242. RSyr. 74 (1997) 237-238 *(Braemer, Frank)*.

10656   *Masada*: **Foerster, Gideon** Masada V: the Yigael Yadin excavations 1963-1965: final report: art and architecture. 1995, ⇒11/2,b047; 12,10125. RJSJ 28/1 (1997) 105-110 *(Rutgers, Leonard Victor)*;

10657   *Shanks, Hershel* Masada: the Yigael Yadin excavations 1963-1965: final reports. BArR 23/1 (1997) 58-63;

10658   EHall, John Franklin; Welch, John W. Masada and the world of the New Testament. BYU studies monographs: Provo, Utah 1997, BYU Studies 432 pp. 0-8425-2344-8.

10659   *Mizpah*: *Zorn, Jeffrey R.* An inner and outer gate complex at Tell en-Nasbeh. BASOR 307 (1997) 53-66;

10660   Mizpah: newly discovered stratum reveals Judah's other capital. BArR 23/5 (1997) 28-38, 66.

10661   *Tell es-Sultan*: *Marchetti, Nicolò; Nigro, Lorenzo; Sarie', Issa* First season of excavations of the Italian-Palestinian expedition at Tell es-Sultan/Jericho, April-May 1997. Orient-Express 2 (1997) 35-38.

10662   *Timnah* **Mazar, Amihai** Timnah (Tel Batash) I: stratigraphy and architecture: text/plans and sections. Collab. *Panitz-Cohen, Nava, (al.),*: J 1997, Institute of Archaeology, Hebrew University 2 vols; xiv; 269 pp. 250 phot. 53 fig. 0333-5844 [RB 105,638];

10663   **Kelm, George L.; Mazar, Amihai** Timnah, a biblical city in the Sorek valley. 1995, ⇒11/2,b055; 12,10135. RCBQ 59 (1997) 352-353 *(Jacobs, Paul F.)*.

10664   *Yarmut*: *Miroschedji, Pierre de* Tel Yarmut, 1996. IEJ 47 (1997) 127-136.

10665   *Zora; Eschtaol*: *Lehmann, Gunnar; Niemann, Hermann Michael; Zwickel, Wolfgang* Zora und Eschtaol: ein Nachtrag. UF 29 (1997) 815-816.

## T4.5  Samaria, Sharon

10666   *Gruson, Philippe; Baudry, Marcel* Samarien;

10667   Die Küstenebene. WUB 4 (1997) 8-11/20-23.

10668   EFinkelstein, Israel; Magen, Yitzhak Archaeological survey of the hill country of Benjamin. 1993, ⇒10,12282. TJAOS 117 (1997) 366-367 *(Jacobs, Paul F.)*.

10669   *Finkelstein, Israel, (al.),* Description of sites. Highlands. 1997, ⇒10173. EFinkelstein, I., 131-484.

10670   *Dor*: *Stern, Ephraim* Discoveries at Tel Dor. The archaeology of Israel. JSOT.S 237: 1997, ⇒9790. ESilberman, N., 128-143;

10671   **Stern, Ephraim** Excavations at Dor: final report, areas A and C, vol. IA-B. Qedem Reports 1-2 J 1995, Institute of Archaeology, Hebrew University x; 369; viii; 496 pp. 118 fig. 321 pl. 47 plans. $140. 0793-4289. RAJA 101 (1997) 606-607 *(Berlin, Andrea M.)*;

10672   *Stern, E., (al.),* Tel Dor, 1994-1995: preliminary stratigraphic report. IEJ 47 (1997) 29-56.

10673 **H. Kenes:** *Porat, Leea* — מערות קבורה ומחצבה בחורבת כנס [כרמיאל](Quarry and burial caves at H. Kenes (Karmiel)]. Sum. 15*. ʿAtiqot 33 (1997) 81-88 **H.**

10674 *Jaljuliya: Petersen, Andrew* Jaljuliya: a village on the Cairo-Damascus road. Levant 29 (1997) 95-118.

10675 *Megiddo:* EFeinberg Vamosh, Miriam Megiddo Armageddon. Die israelischen Nationalparks: Deutsch: Ramat Gan 1997, Eretz Ha-Tzvi 31 pp.

10676 *Samaria: Lev-Yadun, Simcha* Flora and climate in southern Samaria: past and present;

10677 *Horowitz, Aharon* Geology and hydrology;

10678 *Finkelstein, Israel; Lederman, Zvi* Introduction;

10679 *Finkelstein, Israel* Geographic units;

10680 Ethno-historical background: land use and demography in recent generations. Highlands. 1997, ⇒10173. EFinkelstein, I., 85-102/73-84/1-8/103-108/109-130;

10681 **Tappy, Ron E.** The archaeology of Israelite Samaria: Early Iron Age through the ninth century BCE. HSS 44: 1992, ⇒8,e500... 12,10161. RJNES 56 (1997) 129-132 *(Joffe, Alexander H.)*;

10682 *Barkai, Ran; Gopher, Avi; Friedman, Erich* Prehistoric occurrences in western Samaria: the 1967-1968 survey. Highlands. 1997, ⇒10173. EFinkelstein, I., 857-881.

10683 *Shiloh:* **Finkelstein, Israel,** *(al.),* Shiloh: the archaeology of a biblical site. 1993, ⇒9,13881; 11/2,b074. RPEQ 129/2 (1997) 168-169 *(Rosenberg, Stephen).*

## т4.6 **Galilaea;** *Golan*

10684 *Aviam, Mordechai* A second-first century B.C.E. fortress and siege complex in eastern Upper Galilee. Archaeology and the Galilee. SFSHJ 143: 1997, ⇒275. EEdwards, D., 97-105.

10685 EBroshi, M. Burial caves of the Roman and Byzantine periods in western Galilee. 162; 19* pp. Sum. Atiqot 33 (1997) **H.**

10686 *Edwards, Douglas R.; McCollough, C. Thomas* Archaeology and the Galilee: an introduction. Archaeology and the Galilee. SFSHJ 143: 1997, ⇒275. EEdwards, D., 1-6.

10687 *Freyne, Seán* Town and country once more: the case of Roman Galilee. Archaeology and the Galilee. SFSHJ 143: 1997, ⇒275. EEdwards, D., 49-56.

10688 *Groh, Dennis E.* The clash between literary and archaeological models of provincial Palestine. Archaeology and the Galilee. SFSHJ 143: 1997, ⇒275. EEdwards, D., 29-37.

10689 **Horsley, Richard A.** Archaeology, history, and society in Galilee. 1996, ⇒12,10170. RBArR 23/4 (1997) 60, 62 *(Meyers, Eric M.).*

10690 *Kealy, Séan P.* Galilee in Jesus' time. PIBA 20 (1997) 81-94.

10691 *Sawicki, Marianne* Spatial management of gender and labor in Greco-Roman Galilee. Archaeology and the Galilee. SFSHJ 143: 1997, ⇒275. EEdwards, D., 7-28.

10692 *Strange, James F.* First century Galilee from archaeology and from the texts. Archaeology and the Galilee. SFSHJ 143: 1997, ⇒275. EEdwards, D., 39-48.

10693   *Anafa:* [E]**Herbert, Sharon C.** Tel Anafa I.1-2: final report on ten years of excavation at a Hellenistic and Roman settlement in northern Israel. Journal of Roman Archaeology Suppl. 10.1.1-2, Kelsey Museum Fieldwork: Ann Arbor 1997, Journal of Roman Archaeology 334 + 153 pp. 148 + 49 fig.; 35 plans; 6 maps; 25 tables. 1047-7594. [R]ZDPV 113 (1997) 140-44 *(Zangenberg, J.)*.

10694   *Asherat: Gorin-Rosen, Yael* כלי זכוכית מקברים באשרת [Glass vessels from burial caves in Asherat]. Sum. 12*. ʿAtiqot 33 (1997) 61-67 **H**;

10695   *Smithline, Howard* שלוש מערות קבורה מהתקופה הרומית באשרת [Three burial cave from the Roman period in Asherat]. Sum. 11*. ʿAtiqot 33 (1997) 47-60 **H**.

10696   *Beth Gan: Liebowitz, Harold* Beth Gan, 1995. IEJ 47 (1997) 117-121.

10697   *Beit Sheʾan:* **Feinberg Vamosh, Miriam** Beit Sheʾan: Hauptstadt der Decapolis. Die israelischen Nationalparks: Ramat Gan 1997, Eretz Ha-Tzvi 31 pp.;

10698   *Mazar, Amihai* The excavations at Tel Beth Shean during the years 1989-94. The archaeology of Israel. JSOT.S 237: 1997, ⇒9780. [E]Silberman, N., 144-164;

10699   **James, Frances W.; McGovern, Patrick E.** The Late Bronze Egyptian garrison at Beth Shan: a study of levels VII and VIII. 1993, 2 vols, ⇒11/2,b086; ⇒12,10176. [R]JAOS 117 (1997) 715-719 *(Mumford, G.D.)*; BiOr 54 (1997) 684-690 *(Bietak, Manfred)*;

10700   **Asher, Ovadiah; Yehudit, Turnheim** 'Peopled' scrolls in Roman architectural decoration in Israel: the Roman theatre at Beth Shean/Scythopolis. 1994, ⇒11/2,b091; 12,10178. [R]RAr (1997/2) 419-420 *(Dentzer-Feydy, Jacqueline)*;

10701   *Mazar, Amihai* Four thousand years of history at Tel Beth-Shean: an account of the renewed excavations. BA 60/2 (1997) 62-76.

10702   *Bethsaida: Arav, Rami; Bernett, Monika* An Egyptian figurine of Pataikos at Bethsaida. IEJ 47 (1997) 198-213;

10703   *Casey, Daniel W.* Bethsaida='house of the fishers'. Holy Land 17 (1997) 154-159.

10704   *Capernaum: Magness, Jodi* The chronology of Capernaum in the early Islamic period. JAOS 117 (1997) 481-486.

10705   *Dan: Geus, C.H.J. de* Dertig jaar opgravingen op Tel Dan, Israël. Phoe. 43 (1997) 138-153.

10706   *Golan:* [⇒10744] **Dar, Shimon** Settlements and cult sites on Mount Hermon, Israel. 1993, ⇒9,13907; 11/2,b111. [R]IEJ 48 (1997) 279-283 *(Maʿoz, Zvi Uri)*.

10707   *Horvat Galil; Nahal Beṣet: Rosen, Arlene Miller* Phytolith evidence for cereal cultivation at Horvat Galil and Naha Beṣet;

10708   *Bar-Yosef Mayer, Daniella E.* The molluscs of Horvat Galil and Nahal Beṣet;

10709   *Liphschitz, Nili* Wood remains from two PPNB sites: Horvat Galil and Nahal Beṣet;

10710   *Gopher, Avi* Horvat Galil—an early PPNB site in the Upper Galilee, Israel. TelAv 24 (1997) 229-36/237-39/223-28/183-222.

10711   *Hazor:* Zarzeki-Peleg, Anabel Hazor, Jokneam and Megiddo in
        the tenth century B.C.E. TelAv 24 (1997) 258-288;
10712   Garfinkel, Yosef; Greenberg, Raphael Area L. Hazor V. 1997,
        ⇒269. [E]Ben-Tor, A., 177-294;
10713   Horowitz, Wayne A combined multiplication table on a prism
        fragment from Hazor. IEJ 47 (1997) 190-197;
10714   Arensburg, Baruch; Belfer-Cohen, Anna Human skeletal remains
        from Hazor Area L.;
10715   Bonfil, Ruhama; Greenberg, Raphael Area A. Hazor V. 1997,
        ⇒269. [E]Ben-Tor, A., 341-343/15-176;
10716   Widell, Magnus The interpretation and reconstruction of the
        double temple at Hazor. SEÅ 62 (1997) 27-56;
10717   Ben-Tor, Amnon The Yigael Yadin Memorial excavations at
        Hazor, 1990-93: aims and preliminary results. The archaeology
        of Israel. JSOT.S 237: 1997, ⇒9780. [E]Silberman, N., 107-127;
10718   Tel Hazor, 1997. IEJ 47 (1997) 261-264;
10719   Mazar, Amihai Area P. Hazor V. 1997, ⇒269. [E]Ben-Tor, A.,
        353-386;
10720   Ben-Tor, Amnon Introduction. Hazor V. 1997, ⇒269. [E]Ben-Tor,
        A., 1-14;
10721   Horwitz, Liora Kolska The animal bone assemblage from the
        Middle Bronze II tomb (T1181, Area L) at Hazor. Hazor V.
        1997, ⇒269. [E]Ben-Tor, A., 344-347.

10722   *Jezreel:* Mitchell, Piers Further evidence of disease in the crusa-
        der period population of Le Petit Gérin (Tel Jezreel);
10723   Na'aman, Nadav Historical and literary notes on the excavation
        of Tel Jezreel;
10724   Moorhead, T.S.N. The late Roman, Byzantine and Umayyad pe-
        riods at Tel Jezreel;
10725   Ussishkin, David; Woodhead, John Excavations at Tel Jezreel
        1994-1996: third preliminary report. TelAv 24 (1997) 169-
        179/122-128/129-166//6-72;
10726   Gophna, Ram; Shlomi, Varda Some notes on early Chalcolithic
        and early Bronze Age material from the sites of 'En Jezreel and
        Tel Jezreel;
10727   Kletter, Raz Clay figurines and scale weights from Tel Jezreel
        TelAv 24 (1997) 73-82/110-121;
10728   Zimhoni, Orna Clues from the enclosure fills: pre-Omride settle-
        ment at Tel Jezreel. Studies. 1997, ⇒10478. 29-56 (=TelAv 24
        (1997) 83-109).

10729   *Kabri:* Stern, Edna J.; Gorin-Rosen, Yael מערות קבורה ליד כברי
        [Burial caves near Kabri]. Afterword Aviam, Mordechai. Appen-
        dix: The significance of the coin of Agrippa II from Cave 3 near
        Kabri (p. 23). Sum. 7*-8* H;
10730   *Kafr Yasif:* Gorin-Rosen, Yael מערת קבורה בכפר יסיף [A burial
        cave at Kafr Yasif]. Sum. 13*. 'Atiqot 33 (1997) 1-22/71-77 H.
10731   Nazareth: Gyürki, László Názáret Jézus idejében [Nazareth in the
        time of Jesus]. Gyermekségtörténet. 1997, ⇒316. Sum., Zsfg.,
        Rias. [E]Benyik, G., 179-185 Hungarian;
10732   Alliata, Eugenio La casa de María en Nazaret. TE 41 (1997) 381-
        391.

10733   *Sepphoris: Fradkin, Arlene* Long-distance trade in the Lower Galilee: new evidence from Sepphoris. Archaeology and the Galilee. SFSHJ 143: 1997, ⇒275. ᴱEdwards, D., 107-116;

10734   *McIver, Robert K.* Jesus and Sepphoris: missing link or negative evidence?. 1997, ⇒83. ᶠSʜᴇᴀ W., 221-232;

10735   *McCollough, C. Thomas; Glazier-McDonald, Beth* Magic and medicine in Byzantine Galilee: a bronze amulet from Sepphoris. Archaeology and the Galilee. SFSHJ 143: 1997, ⇒275. ᴱEdwards, D., 143-149;

10736   *Schuster, Angela M.H.* Ancient Sepphoris: portrait of a cosmopolitan city. Arch. 50/2 (1997) 64-66;

10737   *McCollough, C. Thomas; Edwards, Douglas R.* Transformations of space: the Roman road at Sepphoris. Archaeology and the Galilee. SFSHJ 143: 1997, ⇒275. ᴱEdwards, D., 135-142;

10738   *Rutgers, Leonard V.* Die nieuwste opgravingen in Sepphoris, Galilea. Phoenix 43/1 (1997) 19-36;

10739   *Dessel, J.P.*, (al.), Tell ʿEn Ṣippori, 1996. IEJ 47 (1997) 268-270;

10740   *Weiss, Z.; Netzer, E.* The Hebrew University excavations at Sepphoris. Qad. 30/1 (1997) 2-21;

10741   Architectural development of Sepphoris during the Roman and Byzantine periods. Archaeology and the Galilee. SFSHJ 143: 1997, ⇒275. ᴱEdwards, D., 117-133;

10742   *Beckman, Gary* Tablet fragments from Sepphoris. N.A.B.U. 3 (1997) 81-82;

10743   *Meyers, Eric M.*, (al.), Sepphoris (Ṣippori), 1996. IEJ 47 (1997) 264-268.

10744   *Shaʿar ha-Golan:* [⇒10706] *Garfinkel, Yosef* Shaʿar ha-Golan, 1997. IEJ 47 (1997) 271-273 .

### т4.8 *Transjordania;* (East-) Jordan

10745   *Bikai, Patricia M.; Egan, Virginia* Archaeology in Jordan. AJA 101 (1997) 493-535.

10746   ᴱBisheh, Ghazi; Zaghloul, Muna; Kehrberg, Ina Studies in the history and archaeology of Jordan: department of antiquities, Amman, Hashemite Kingdom of Jordan—Amman, 6: landscape resources and human occupation in Jordan throughout the ages. Studies in the history and archaeology of Jordan: Amman 1997, Dept of Antiquities 432 pp.

10747   *Daoust, Joseph* En Jordanie. EeV 107 (1997) 453-454.

10748   Dicou, Bert Edom, Israel's brother and antagonist: the role of Edom in biblical prophecy and story. JSOT.S 169: 1994, ⇒11/2,b152. ᴿABR 45 (1997) 75-6 *(Wynn-Williams, Damian J.)*.

10749   ᴱGebel, Hans Georg K. The prehistory of Jordan, 2: perspectives from 1997. Studies in early Near Eastern production, susbsistence, and environment 4: B 1997, Ex Oriente iii; 662 pp. 3-9804241-3-8 [NThAR 2000,274].

    Graf, D. Rome and the Arabian frontier ⇒129.

10750   *Harrison, Timothy P.* Shifting patterns of settlement in the highlands of central Jordan during the early Bronze Age. BASOR 306 (1997) 1-37.

10751  *Ji, Chang-Ho C.* The east Jordan valley during Iron Age I;
10752  *Lancaster, William; Lancaster, Fidelity* Jordanian village houses in their contexts: growth, decay and rebuilding. PEQ 129 (1997) 19-37/38-53.
10753  *Mattingly, Gerald L.* A new agenda for research on ancient Moab;
10754  *Miller, Max* Ancient Moab: still largely unknown. BA 60/4 (1997) 214-221/194-204.
10755  [E]*Piccirillo, Michele* Ricerca storico-archeologica in Giordania XVII—1997. LASBF 47 (1997) 463-532.
10756  *Schick, Robert* Southern Jordan in the Fatimid and Seljuq periods. BASOR 305 (1997) 73-85.
10757  *Worschech, Udo* Egypt and Moab;
10758  *Younker, Randall W.* Moabite social structure. BA 60/4 (1997) 229-236/237-248.

10759  ʿ*Aïn ez-Zâra/Callirrhoé:* **Clamer, Christa** Fouilles archéologiques de ʿAïn ez-Zâra/Callirrhoé: villégiature hérodienne. Collab. *Dussart, Odile; Magness, Jodi*: BAH 147: Beyrouth 1997, Institut Français d'Archéologie du Proche-Orient xvi; 187 pp. 105 fig. 36 map. 2-7053-0564-5. [R]RB 104 (1997) 440-441 *(Murphy-O'Connor, J.).*
10760  *Ash-Shorabat; Khirbat Dubab: Bienkowski, Piotr; Adams, Russell; Philpott, R.A.; Sedman, Leonie* Soundings at Ash-Shorabat and Khirbat Dubab in the Wadi Hasa, Jordan: the stratigraphy. Levant 29 (1997) 41-70.
10761  *Dana: Al-Shiyab, Abdel Halim* A palaeoanthropological survey of pleistocene deposits near Dana and Qurayqira, Jordan. TelAv 24 (1997) 240-252.
10762  *Deir ʿAllā: Ibrahim, Moawiyah M.; Van der Kooij, Gerrit* Excavations at Tall Dayr ʿAllā: seasons 1987 and 1994;
10763  *Dhībān: Ji, Chang-Ho C.; ʿAttiyat, Taysir* Archaeological survey of the Dhībān Plateau, 1996: a preliminary report. ADAJ 41 (1997) 95-114/115-128.
10764  *El-Baluʿ; Rabbat-Moab: Worschech, Udo* Ar Moab. ZAW 109 (1997) 246-253 [Isa 15,1].
10765  *Gerasa: Uscatescu, Alexandra; Martín-Bueno, Manuel* The Macellum of Gerasa (Jerash, Jordan): from a market place to an industrial area. BASOR 307 (1997) 67-88.;
10766  *Seigne, Jacques* Les limites orientales et méridionales du territoire de Gerasa. Syr. 74/1 (1997) 121-138.
10767  *Ğawa: Daviau, P.M. Michèle* Tell Jawa: a case study of Ammonite urbanism during Iron Age II. Urbanism. JSOT.S 244: 1997, ⇒265. [E]Aufrecht, W.E., 156-171.
10768  *Ḫirbet eṭ-Ṭannur: Roche, M.-J.* Khirbet et-Tannûr et les contacts entre Édomites et Nabatéens: une nouvelle approche. TEuph 13 (1997) 187.
10769  *Jawa: Younker, Randall W.* Some notes on the identity of Tell Jawa (South), Jordan: Mephaath or Abel Keramim?. 1997, ⇒83. [F]SHEA W., 257-263.
10770  *Johfiyeh: Lamprichs, Roland* Die Umgebung des eisenzeitlichen Tell Johfiyeh: eine archäologische Regionalstudie in Nordjordanien. UF 29 (1997) 435-465.

10771  *Khirbat al-Mudayna: Daviau, P. M. Michèle* Excavations at Mudayna;
10772  Moab's northern border: Khirbat al-Mudayna on the Wadi ath-Thamad. BA 60/4 (1997) 251/222-228.
10773  *Madaba: Harrison, Timothy P.* Investigations of urban life in Madaba, Jordan. BA 60/1 (1997) 53-54.
10774  *Maresha: Kloner, Amos* Underground metropolis: the subterranean world of Maresha. BArR 23/2 (1997) 24-35, 67.
10775  *Netiv Hagdud: Tchernov, Eitan* An early neolithic village in the Jordan Valley II: the fauna of Netiv Hagdud. American School of Prehistoric Research Bulletins 44: CM 1994, Peabody Harvard. $20. 0-87365-548-6. ᴿJAOS 117 (1997) 732-733 *(Bourke, S.J.).*
10776  *Pella: Bourke, Stephen J.* Pre-classical Pella in Jordan: a conspectus of ten years' work (1985-1995). PEQ 129 (1997) 94-115.

10777  *Petra: Wenning, Robert; Kolb, Bernhard; Nehmé, Laila* Vom Zeltlager zur Stadt: profane Architektur in Petra;
10778  *Weber, Thomas; Wenning, Robert* Mehr als ein flüchtiger Eindruck: zur Einführung. Petra antike Felsstadt. 1997, ⇒311. ᴱWeber, T., 56-70/4;
10779  *Wright, G.R.H.* The Khazne at Petra: its nature in the light of its name. Syr. 74/1 (1997) 115-120;
10780  *Shaer, Masy; Aslan, Zaki* Architectural investigation on the building techniques of the Nabataeans with reference to tomb 825. ADAJ 41 (1997) 219-230;
10781  *Schmidt-Colinet, Andreas; Weber, Thomas; Zangenberg, Jürgen* "Arabischer Barock": sepulkrale Kultur in Petra. Petra antike Felsstadt. 1997, ⇒311. ᴱWeber, T., 87-98;
10782  *Parr, Peter J.* 40 Jahre Ausgrabungen in Petra (1929 bis 1969);
10783  *Lindner, Manfred* Petra-Entdecker, Reisende und Forscher;
10784  Neuere Ausgrabungen und Untersuchungen: Ausgrabungen der Naturhistorischen Gesellschaft Nürnberg in Petra;
10785  Ein nabatäisches Klammheiligtum bei Petra. Petra und das Königreich. 1997, ⇒289. ᴱLindner, M., 183-196/9-16/261-270/286-292;
10786  Gut leben in einer unwirtlichen Umwelt: Petra im geographisch-topographischen Umraum. Petra antike Felsstadt. 1997, ⇒311. ᴱWeber, T., 25-37;
10787  Es-Selaᶜ: eine antike Fliehburg 50 km nördlich von Petra;
10788  *Zayadine, Fawzi* Die Felsarchitektur Petras: orientalische Traditionen und hellenistischer Einfluß;
10789  *Lindner, Manfred* Beschreibung der antiken Stadt;
10790  *Künne, Ingrid; Wanke, Margarete* Petra: Landschaft und Pflanzenwelt. Petra und das Königreich. 1997, ⇒289. ᴱLindner, M., 271-285/124-161/17-36/233-256;
10791  *Kolb, Bernhard* Swiss-Liechtenstein excavations at Az-Zanṭūr in Petra 1996, the seventh season. ADAJ 41 (1997) 231-254;
10792  *Khadija, Muhammed Murshed A.* 16 Jahre Feldarchäologie in Petra: 1961-1977. Petra und das Königreich. 1997, ⇒289. ᴱLindner, M., 197-204;
10793  *Joukowsky, Martha Sharp* The 1996 Brown University archaeological excavations at the 'Great' southern temple at Petra. ADAJ 41 (1997) 195-218;

10794   *Gunsam, Elisabeth* Die nördliche Hubta-Wasserleitung in Petra. Petra und das Königreich. 1997, ⇒289. ELindner, M., 319-329;

10795   *Freyberger, Klaus St.; Joukowsky, Martha Sharp* Blattranken, Greifen und Elefanten: sakrale Architektur in Petra;

10796   *Fiema, Zbigniew T.; Koenen, Ludwig; Zayadine, Fawzi* Petra Romana, Byzantina et Islamica: eine Metropole Arabiens nach dem Ende des nabatäischen Reiches;

10797   *Zayadine, Fawzi* Zwischen Siq und ad-Der: ein Rundgang durch Petra. Petra antike Felsstadt. 1997, ⇒311. EWeber, T., 71-86/145-163/38-55;

10798   *Zeitler, John P.* Die Siedlungsabfolge am Fuße des el-Hubta-Massivs von Petra: Siedlungsarchäologische Ergebnisse der Grabungen der Naturhistorischen Gesellschaft Nürnberg. Petra und das Königreich. 1997, ⇒289. ELindner, M., 307-318;

10799   **Amadasi Guzzo, Maria Giulia; Equini Schneider, Eugenia** Petra. Centri e monumenti dell'antichità: Mi 1997, Electa 202 pp. Bibl. 88-435-5748-3;

10800   *Lindner, M., (al.),* An Iron Age (Edomite) occupation of Jabal al-Khubtha (Petra) and other discoveries on the 'Mountain of Treachery and Deceit'. ADAJ 41 (1997) 177-188.

10801   *Safi: Schneider, Tammi J.* New project: Tel Safi, Israel. BA 60/4 (1997) 250.

10802   *Tawilan:* **Bennett, Crystal-M.; Bienkowski, Piotr** Excavations at Tawilan in southern Jordan. British Academy Monographs in Archaeology 8: Oxf 1995, OUP 346 pp. £60. 0-19-727007-7. RLevant 29 (1997) 261-262 *(Bartlett, J.R.);* AfO 44-45 (1997-98) 520-522 *(Weippert, Helga).*

10803   *Umm el-Biyara: Lindner, Manfred* Ein christliches Pilgerzeichen auf Umm el-Biyara;

10804   Die Nordterrasse von Umm el-Biyara. Petra und das Königreich. 1997, ⇒289. ELindner, M., 304-306/293-303.

10805   **Wadi Faynan:** *Barker, G.W.; Creighton, O.H.; Gilbertson, D.D., (al.),* The Wadi Faynan project, southern Jordan: a preliminary report on geomorphology and landscape archaeology. Levant 29 (1997) 19-40.

10806   *Zafon: Tubb, Jonathan N.; Dorrell, Peter G.; Cobbing, Felicity J.* Interim report on the ninth season (1996) of excavations at Tell Es-Saʿidiyeh, Jordan. PEQ 129 (1997) 54-77.

## T5.1 Phoenicia—*Libanus,* Lebanon

10807   **Briquel-Chatonnet, Françoise** Les relations entre les cités de la côte phénicienne et les royaumes d'Israël et de Juda. 1992, ⇒8,e636... 12,10272. RBer. 42 (1995-96) 173-177 *(Semmler, Maria-Eugenia Aubet).*

10808   **Lipiński, Edward** Phoenicia and the Bible. 1991, Proceedings of the conference held at Leuven, 15th-16th March 1990. ⇒7,445... 11/2,b211. RPEQ 129 (1997) 82-84 *(Frendo, Anthony J.).*

10809   *Sader, Hélène* Tell el Burak: an unidentified city of Phoenician Sidon. AOAT 247: 1997, ⇒75. FROELLIG W., 363-376.

T5.2  *Situs mediterranei* **phoenicei et punici**

10810  *Aubet Semmler, María* A Phoenician market place in southern
Spain. AOAT 247: 1997, ⇒75. FROELLIG W., 11-22.
10811  **Katzenstein, H. Jacob** The history of Tyre: from the beginning
of the second millennium B.C.E. until the fall of the Neo-
Babylonian Empire in 539 B.C.E. Beer Sheva ²1997, Ben-Gurion
University xxiii; 373 pp. Bibl. 965-342-677-X.
10812  Phoinikes b Shrdn: i fenici in Sardegna: nuove acquisizioni.
EBernardini, Paolo; D'Oriano, Rubens; Spanu, Pier Giorgio
Oristano 1997, S'Alvure 340; 20 pp.
10813  **Pisano, Giovanna** Nuove ricerche puniche in Sardegna. Studia
punica 11: 1996, ⇒12,10283. RRSO 71 (1997) 273-274 *(Garbini,
Giovanni)*.


T5.4  **Ugarit**—*Ras Šamra*

10814  EAhn, Gregor; Dietrich, Manfred Ugarit-Forschungen 29.
Müns 1997, Ugarit-Verlag vi; 865 pp. 3-927120-68-5.
10815  **Amiet, Pierre** Corpus des cylindres de Ras Shamra-Ougarit II:
sceaux-cylindres en hématite et pierres diverses. 1992, ⇒8,e705.
RAfO 44-45 (1997-98) 505-510 *(Salje, Beate)*.
10816  **Baldacci, Massimo** La scoperta di Ugarit. 1996, ⇒12,10288.
RLASBF 47 (1997) 566-569 *(Pappalardo, Carmelo)*.
10817  *Bordreuil, Pierre* Sources et forêts: à propos de la géographie
physique et humaine de l'Ougarit. Des Sumériens. 1997, ⇒377.
ESérandour, A., 59-66.
10818  **Contenson, Henri de** Préhistoire de Ras Shamra: les sondages
stratigraphiques de 1955 à 1976. 1992, ⇒10,12480*; 12,10293. 2
vols. ROr. 66 (1997) 104-106 *(Frangipane, Marcella)*; BiOr 54
(1997) 197-203 *(Akkermans, Peter M.M.G.)*.
10819  *Dalix, Anne-Sophie* Ougarit au XIIIᵉ siècle av. J.-C.: nouvelles
perspectives historiques. CRAI (1997/3) 819-824.
10820  *Dietrich, Manfried* Die Texte aus Ugarit im Spannungsfeld zwischen Königshaus und Bevölkerung. Religion und Gesellschaft.
AOAT 248: 1997, ⇒235. EAlbertz, R., 75-93.
10821  *Greenstein, Edward L.* Kirta. Ugaritic narrative poetry. 1997,
⇒10833. EParker, S.B., 9-48.
10822  *Heltzer, M.* The *hrš qtn* in Ugarit: the meaning of the term and
the functions of these people. UF 29 (1997) 211-214.
10823  *Huehnergard, John* Notes on Ras Shamra-Ougarit VII. Syr. 74/1
(1997) 213-220.
10824  *Husser, Jean-Marie* À propos du festin "marzihu" à Ugarit: abus
et impasse du comparatisme historique. Le comparatisme. 1997,
⇒346. EBoespflug, F., 157-173.
10825  EKaiser , Otto Texte aus der Umwelt des Alten Testaments: Bd.
3: Weisheitstexte, Mythen und Epen: Lfg. 6: Mythen und Epen
IV. Gü 1997, Gü'er 1090-1369 pp. 3-579-00082-9.
10826  *Kottsieper, Ingo* Indizes und Korrekturen zur "Word-List of the
Cuneiform Alphabetic Texts". UF 29 (1997) 245-383.
10827  *Lewis, Theodore J.* The birth of the gracious gods;

10828  The Rapiuma;
10829  El's divine feast. Ugaritic narrative poetry. 1997, ⇒10833.
       EParker, S.B., 205-214/196-205/193-196.
10830  *Mallet, Joël* Ras Shamra-Ougarit (Syrie): la poterie du Bronze
       moyen (fin du IIIe millénaire av. J.-C. et 1re moitié du second).
       UF 29 (1997) 529-577.
10831  *Marcus, David* The betrothal of Yarikh and Nikkal-Ib. Ugaritic
       narrative poetry. 1997, ⇒10833. EParker, S.B., 215-218.
10832  *Mazzini, Giovanni* The torture of Mot: for a reading of KTU 1.6
       V 30-35. SEL 14 (1997) 25-28.
10833  **EParker, Simon B.** Ugaritic narrative poetry. SBL.Writings
       from the Ancient World 9: Atlanta, GA 1997, Scholars xiii; 265
       pp. Bibl. $35/$15. 0-7885-0336-7/7-5.
10834  *Parker, Simon B.* Aqhat;
10835  Baal fathers a bull;
10836  The binding of a monster;
10837  A birth;
10838  The mare and horon;
10839  The wilderness. Ugaritic narrative poetry. 1997, ⇒10833.
       EParker, S.B., 49-80/181-186/192-193/186-187/219-23/188-191.
10840  **Segert, Stanislav** A basic grammar of the Ugaritic language with
       selected texts and glossary. Berkeley, CA ²1997, University of
       California xxvi; 224 pp. Bibl. 0-520-03999-8.
10841  *Smith, Mark S.* The Baal cycle;
10842  CAT 1.96. Ugaritic narrative poetry. 1997, ⇒10833. EParker,
       S.B., 81-180/224-228.
10843  *Tammuz, Oded* Justice, justice shall you pursue. UF 29 (1997)
       641-653.
10844  *Tropper, Josef* Aktuelle Probleme der ugaritischen Grammatik.
       UF 29 (1997) 669-674;
10845  Bedeutende Neuerscheinungen der Ugaritistik. OLZ 92 (1997)
       455-467;
10846  Beiträge zur ugaritischen Lexikographie. UF 29 (1997) 661-668;
10847  *Tropper, Josef; Vita, Juan-Pablo* Epigraphische Bemerkungen zu
       ausgewählten ugaritischen Wirtschaftstexten. UF 29 (1997) 675-
       681.
10848  *Van Soldt, Wilfred* Studies in the topography of Ugarit (2): the
       borders of Ugarit. UF 29 (1997) 683-703 ⇒12,10313.
10849  **Vita, Juan-Pablo** El ejército de Ugarit. 1995, ⇒11/2,a349.
       RAfO 44-45 (1997-98) 369-376 *(Márquez Rowe, I.)*; OLoP 28
       (1997) 251-252 *(Schoors, A.)*.
10850  *Vita, Juan-Pablo* Remarques épigraphiques à propos de quatre
       textes ougaritiques. UF 29 (1997) 705-707;
10851  Šipti-Baʿalu, un "égyptien" à Ougarit. UF 29 (1997) 709-713.
10852  *Wagner, Andreas* Ugarit—am Schnittpunkt der Interessen: inter-
       disziplinärer Arbeitskreis tagte. JOGU 154 (1997) 22.
10853  *Watson, W.G.E.* New examples of the split couplet in Ugaritic.
       UF 29 (1997) 715-721;
10854  The "split couplet" in Ugaritic verse. SEL 14 (1997) 29-42.
10855  *Wyatt, N.* Ilimilku's ideological programme: Ugaritic royal prop-
       aganda, and a biblical postscript. UF 29 (1997) 775-796.
10856  *Xella, Paolo* La "sagesse" de Baal. AOAT 247: 1997, ⇒75.
       FROELLIG W., 435-446.

10857   **Yon, Marguerite** La cité d'Ougarit sur le tell de Ras Shamra.
        Guides archéologiques de l'Institut Français d'Archéologie du
        Proche-Orient 2: Paris 1997, Recherche sur les Civilisations 190
        pp. Bibl. FF180. 2-86538-263-X.

## τ5.5 Ebla

10858   *Archi, Alfonso* Studies in the Ebla pantheon, II. Or. 66 (1997)
        414-425.
10859   *Astour, Michael C.* The toponyms of Ebla. JAOS 117 (1997)
        332-338;
10860   *Baffi Guardata, Francesca; Baldacci, Massimo; Pomponio, Fran-
        cesco* Eblaite Bibliography IV. SEL 14 (1997) 109-124.
10861   **Baldacci, Massimo** Partially published Eblaite texts. 1992,
        ⇒9,14094. [R]RA 91 (1997) 176-178 *(Bonechi, Marco)*.
10862   *Cagni, Luigi* Rassegna di calendari: Ebla e Mesopotamia. RStB
        9/1 (1997) 35-56.
10863   *Catagnoti, Amalia* Les listes des HÚB.(KI) dans les textes admi-
        nistratifs d'Ebla et l'onomastique de Nagar. Mari 8 (1997) 563-
        596.
10864   *D'Agostino F.; Seminara, S.* Sulla continuità del mondo culturale
        della Siria settentrionale: la "Maš³artum" ad Ebla ed Emar. RA
        91/1 (1997) 1-20.
10865   **D'Agostino, Franco** Testi amministrativi di Ebla, Archivio L.
        2769, 3. 1996, ⇒12,10327. [R]AfO 44-45 (1997-98) 275-276
        *(Archi, Alfonso)*.
10866   [E]**Fronzaroli, Pelio** Miscellanea eblaitica, 4. QuSem 19: F 1997,
        Dipartimento di Linguistica, Università di Firenze 221 pp. [ArOr
        66,169—Segert, Stanislav].
10867   *Fronzaroli, Pelio* Les combats de Hadda dans les textes d'Ébla.
        Mari 8 (1997) 283-290.
10868   *Krebernik, Manfred* Zur Interpretation von ARET 5,24-26.
        AOAT 247: 1997, ⇒AOAT 247: 1997, ⇒75. [F]ROELLIG W.,
        185-192.
10869   **Milano, Lucio** Testi amministrativi: assegnazioni di prodotti ali-
        mentari. ARET 9: 1990, ⇒12,10333. [R]RA 91 (1997) 178-180
        *(Catagnoti, Amalia)*.
10870   [E]**Pettinato, Giovanni** Thesaurus inscriptionum eblaicarum, 1:
        volume A, parte prima (a - ABxAŠ-mí). R 1995, La Sapienza.
        [R]AfO 44-45 (1997-98) 272-275 *(Archi, Alfonso)*.
10871   *Pomponio, Francesco* I rendiconti annuali di uscite di argento e le
        offerte alle divinità nella documentazione di Ebla. Sum. 101.
        [R]AfO 44-45 (1997) 101-107.
10872   **Scandone-Matthiae, Gabriella** Méki/Mekim (d'Ébla) dans
        l'"histoire de Sinouhé"?. Mari 8 (1997) 249-250.
10873   *Tonietti, Maria Vittoria* Le cas de Mekum: continuité ou innova-
        tion dans la tradition éblaïte entre IIIe et IIe millénaires?. Mari 8
        (1997) 225-242.

## τ5.8 Situs effossi Syriae in ordine alphabetico

10874   Aktuelles: Syrien, Libanon, Oman, Jordanien. WUB 6 (1997) 50-
        52.
10875   *Tunca, Önhan* À propos des agglomérations de l'âge du Bronze
        dans le Proche-Orient ancien et ethnoarchéologie. Mari 8 (1997)
        181-187.

10876  *Weiss, Harvey* Archaeology in Syria. AJA 101 (1997) 97-148.

10877  **Abu Hgaira: *Martin, L.; Wartke, R.-B.*** Die Grabungen auf dem Tell Abu Hgaira/NO-Syrien;

10878  **Abu Hafur: *Reiche, A.*** Tell Abu Hafur "East"—neuassyrische Besiedlung in der Umgebung von Hasake (Nord-Ost-Syrien). Assyrien im Wandel. 1997, ⇒379. ᴱWaetzoldt, H., 315-316/355-364.

10879  **Aleppo: *Klengel, Horst*** Die historische Rolle der Stadt Aleppo im vorantiken Syrien;

10880  *Gaube, Heinz* Aleppo zwischen Antike und Anfang des 20. Jahrhunderts. Die orientalische Stadt. 1997, ⇒406. ᴱWilhelm, G., 359-374/375-383.

10881  **Antiochia: *Will, Ernest*** Antioche sur l'Oronte, métropole de l'Asie. Syr. 74/1 (1997) 99-113.

10882  **Arwad: *Briquel-Chatonnet, Françoise*** Arwad et l'empire assyrien. AOAT 247: 1997, ⇒AOAT 247: 1997, ⇒75. ᶠRoᴇʟʟɪɢ W., 57-68.

10883  **Barri: *Pecorella, P.E.*** La missione archeologica italiana a Tell Barri (Siria)—1996. Orient-Express 2 (1997) 45-49.

10884  **Bassit: Courbin, Paul** Fouilles de Bassit: tombes du fer. 1993, ⇒11/2,b312. ᴿSyr. 74 (1997) 239-240 *(Thalmann, Jean-Paul)*.

10885  **Brak: [⇒10926] Oates, David; Oates, Joan; McDonald, Helen** Excavations at Tell Brak, 1: the Mitanni and Old Babylonia periods. McDonald Institute Monographs: L 1997, British School of Archaeology in Iraq xxi; 296 pp. Bibl. £45. 0-9519420-5-0.

10886  **Carkemisch: *Starke, Frank*** Sprachen und Schriften in Karkamis. AOAT 247: 1997, ⇒75. ᶠRoᴇʟʟɪɢ W., 381-395.

10887  **Damascus: *Mentré, Mireille*** Damaskus und Babylon;
10888  *Sack, Dorothée* Damaskus: eine antike Metropole;
10889  *Pouzet, Louis* Von der arabischen Eroberung bis zu Abd-al Qader (von 635 n. Chr. bis 1860);
10890  *Knauf, Ernst Axel* Damaskus im Neuen Testament: zwischen Arabien und Rom;
10891  Damaskus im Alten Testament;
10892  *Bianquis, Thierry* Von der Märchen-Oase zur modernen Metropole;
10893  *Soupa, Anne* Damaskus: Drehschreibe des Orients;
10894  *Sulaimanije, Tekkije* Abseits der markierten Routen;
10895  *Tate, Georges* Von Alexander dem Großen bis zur arabischen Eroberung (von 333 v. Chr. bis 635 n. Chr.);
10896  *Weber, Thomas* Das Land der Damaszener: ein Paradies auf Erden. WUB 3 (1997) 35-6/22-4/30-2/50-1/37-9/6-11/2-5/12-6/28-9/19-21.
10897  *Sack, Dorothée* Die historische Stadt Damaskus: Kontinuität und Wandel der städtebaulichen Strukturen. Die orientalische Stadt. 1997, ⇒406. ᴱWilhelm, G., 385-399;
10898  *Lemaire, André* Die Ursprünge von Damaskus (1500 v. Chr.-333 v. Chr.). WUB 3 (1997) 25-28.

10899  **Jerablus-Tahtani: *Peltenburg, Edgar; Campbell, Stuart; Carter, Stephen; Stephen, Fiona M.K.; Tipping, Richard*** Jerablus-Tahtani, Syria, 1996: preliminary report. Levant 29 (1997) 1-18.

10900   *Knediğ; Chabur: Klengel-Brandt, Evelyn, (al.)*, Vorläufiger Bericht über die Ausgrabungen des Vorderasiatischen Museums auf Tall Knediğ / NO-Syrien. MDOG 129 (1997) 39-87.

10901   *Mari: Maul, Stefan M.* Zwischen Sparmaßnahme und Revolte...: die Aktivitäten des Iasim-Sumû, des šandabakkum von Mari;
10902   *Beyer, Dominique* Deux nouveaux de style syrien provenant de Mari;
10903   *Margueron, Jean-Claude, (al.)*, Mari: rapport préliminaire sur les campagnes de 1990 et 1991;
10904   *Margueron, Jean-Claude; Vitoux, François; Bendakir, Mahmoud* Préserver l'architecture de terre: état des recherches conduites à Mari;
10905   *Durand, Jean-Marie* Études sur les noms propres d'époque amorrite, I: les listes publiées par G. Dossin. Mari 8 (1997) 755-774/463-475/9-70/195-205/597-673.

10906   *Qara Quzaq: Olmo Lete, G. del; Molina Martos, M.* Excavations at Tell Qara Quzaq. Assyrien im Wandel. 1997, ⇒379. ᴱWaetzoldt, H., 325-329.
10907   *Sabi Abyad: Nieuwenhuyse, O.* The prehistoric pottery of Tell Sabi Abyad 1996: an interim report. Orient-Express 2 (1997) 60-61;
10908   *Akkermans, Peter M.M.G.* Excavations at Tell Sabi Abyad, 1996. Orient-Express 2 (1997) 38-40.

10909   **Terqa: Masetti-Rouault, Maria-Grazia** Terqa: rapport préliminaire (1987-1989): chantier F, le sondage F3k1 (1988-1989);
10910   *Ozer, André* Terqa: rapport préliminaire (1987-1989): prospection géomorphologique dans la région de Terqa;
10911   *Rouault, Olivier, (al.)*, Terqa: rapport préliminaire (1987-1989): Chantier F (1987-1989): étude générale;
10912   *Pic, Marielle* Terqa: rapport préliminaire (1987-1989): quelques objets (1988-1989);
10913   *Rouault, Olivier* Terqa: rapport préliminaire (1987-1989): introduction;
10914   Terqa: rapport préliminaire (1987-1989): chantier E (1989);
10915   *Limet, Henri; Tunca, Önhan* Terqa: Rapport préliminaire (1987-1989): chantiers A et M: stratigraphie et constructions (1989). Mari 8 (1997) 89-98/115-24/83-8/144-8/73-82/99-103/104-114.
10916   **Umm el-Marra: Curvers, Hans H.; Schwartz, Glenn M.** Umm el-Marra, a Bronze Age urban center in the Jabbul Plain, western Syria. Sum. 201. AJA 101 (1997) 201-239.

т6.1 **Mesopotamia,** *generalia*

10917   *Gerber, Christoph* Der Beitrag Ninives zur nordmesopotamischen Chronologie. Sum. 226. ᴿAfO 44-45 (1997) 226-235.
10918   **Larsen, Mogens Trolle** The conquest of Assyria: excavations in an antique land 1840-1860. 1996, ⇒12,9272. ᴿPhoenix 43/1 (1997) 55-57 *(Duistermaat, Kim)*.
10919   **Potts, Daniel T.** Mesopotamian civilization: the material foundations. Athlone Publications in Egyptology and Ancient Near

Eastern Studies: L 1997, Athlone xxi; 366 pp. 120 fig. 16 tables. £60. 0-485-93001-3. [R]Antiquity 71 (1997) 782, 784 (Moorey, P.R.S.).

10920 **Potts, Timothy** Mesopotamia and the east: an archaeological and historical study of foreign relations ca. 3400-2000 BC. 1994, ⇒12,10365. [R]Or. 66 (1997) 106-108 (Liverani, Mario); AfO 44-45 (1997-98) 467-468 (Glassner, Jean-Jacques); RA 91 (1997) 173-176 (Tallon, Françoise).

## т6.5 Situs effossi Iraq in ordine alphabetico

*al Rimah:* **Postgate, C.** The excavations at Tell al Rimah: the pottery ⇒10466.

10921 *Assur:* **Fales, F.M.** People and professions in Neo-Assyrian Assur. Assyrien im Wandel. 1997, ⇒379. [E]Waetzoldt, H., 33-40;

10922 *Matthes, Olaf* Zur Vorgeschichte der Ausgrabungen in Assur 1898-1903/05. MDOG 129 (1997) 9-27.

10923 *Babylon:* **Westenholz, Joan Goodnick** Babylon—Ursprung der großen Götter. Land der Bibel. 1997, ⇒9960. [E]Seipel, W., 145-162;

10924 **Schmid, Hansjörg** Der Tempelturm Etemenanki in Babylon. 1995, ⇒11/2,b403. [R]JNES 56 (1997) 287-90 (Biggs, Robert D.);

10925 *Marzahn, Joachim* Babylone dans l'histoire. [T]Préville, Agnès de: MoBi 103 (1997) 60-65.

10926 *Brak:* [⇒10885] **Oates, Joan; Oates, David** An open gate: cities of the fourth millennium BC (Tell Brak 1997). Cambridge Archaeological Journal 7/2 (1997) 287-297.

10927 *Khirbet Khatuniyeh:* **Curtis, John; Green, Anthony** Excavations at Khirbet Khatuniyeh: Saddam Dam report II. L 1997, British Museum Press xii; 120 pp. 65 pl. 69 fig. Arabic sum. £30. 0-7141-1144-9 [Antiquity 72,935—Sinclair, Anthony].

10928 *Lagasch:* **Farber, Gertrud** Von Lagaš nach Tübingen. AOAT 247: 1997, ⇒75. [F]ROELLIG W., 109-114.

10929 *Nimrud:* **Collon, Dominique** Nimrud, die Königsstadt Assyriens. WUB 3 (1997) 57-63;

10930 *Paley, S.M.; Sobolewski, R.P.* The outer façade of the throne room of the northwest palace of Ashurnasirpal II at Nimrud (Kalḫu). Assyrien im Wandel. 1997, ⇒379. [E]Waetzoldt, H., 331-335.

10931 *Ninive:* **Battini, Laura** La localisation des archives du palais sud-ouest de Ninive. RA 90 (1996) 33-40;

10932 *Dalley, S.* The hanging gardens of Babylon at Nineveh. Assyrien im Wandel. 1997, ⇒379. [E]Waetzoldt, H., 19-24;

10933 *Russell, John Malcolm* Ninive. Land der Bibel. 1997, ⇒9960. [E]Seipel, W., 117-128.

10934 *Nippur:* **Cole, Steven William** Nippur in late Assyrian Times, c. 755-612 BC. 1996, ⇒12,10397. [R]Mes. 32 (1997) 348-349 (Liverani, M.); AfO 44-45 (1997-98) 419-424 (Jursa, Michael).

10935 *Nuzi:* **Lacheman, E.R.; Owen, D.I.** Studies on the civilization and culture of Nuzi and the Hurrians, 5. WL 1995, Eisenbrauns ix; 357 pp. 0-931464-67-6. [R]AfO 44-45 (1997-98) 365-368 (Müller, Gerfrid G.W.).

10936    *Rijim: Koliński, R.* The form of the Old Assyrian settlement on Tell Rijim, northern Iraq. Assyrien im Wandel. 1997, ⇒379. ᴱWaetzoldt, H., 295-298.

10937    *Urkiš: Buccellati, Giorgio; Kelly-Buccellati, Marilyn* Urkesh: the first Hurrian capital. BA 60/2 (1997) 77-96.

10938    *Uruk-Warka:* **Lindemeyer, Elke; Martin, Lutz** Kleinfunde im Vorderasiatischen Museum zu Berlin: Steingefäße... Uruk Kleinfunde. 1993, ⇒9,14267. ᴿJAOS 117 (1997) 165-166 *(Dunham, Sally).*

10939    *Ur: Westenholz, Joan Goodnick* Ur—Hauptstadt von Sumer. Land der Bibel. 1997, ⇒9960. ᴱSeipel, W., 21-38.

### ᴛ6.7  Arabia

10940    *Breton, Jean-François, (al.),* Le grand monument de Tamna' (Yémen): architecture et identification. Syr. 74/1 (1997) 33-72.

10941    *Cleziou, S.* Ra's al-Jins: un site archéologique moyen-oriental sur les rives de l'Océan indien. Orient-Express 2 (1997) 49-52.

### ᴛ6.9  Iran, *Persia,* Asia centralis

10942    Archäologische Mitteilungen aus Iran, 27. B 1994. ᴿRA 91 (1997) 90-91 *(Amiet, Pierre).*

10943    *Boucharlat, Rémy* Susa under Achaemenid rule. 1997, ⇒58. ᴹLUKONIN V., 54-67.

10944    *Chevalier, Nicole; Amiet, Pierre; André-Salvini, Béatrice; Demange, F.* L'art perse et le musée du Louvre. MoBi 106 (1997) 55-69.

10945    **Malbran-Labat, Florence** Briques de l'époque paléo-élamite à l'empire néo-élamite: les inscriptions royales de Suse. 1995, ⇒11/2,b483. ᴿOr. 66 (1997) 108-110 *(Koch, Heidemarie).*

10946    *Perrot, Jean; Ladiray, Daniel* Der Palast von Susa. Land der Bibel. 1997, ⇒9960. ᴱSeipel, W., 173-186.

10947    *Sarraf, Mohamed Rahim* Neue architektonische und städtebauliche Funde von Ekbatana-Tepe (Hamadan). AMI 29 (1997) 321-339.

10948    *Tallon, Françoise; Briant, Pierre; André-Salvini, Béatrice; Benoit, Agnès* L'empire perse et le grand roi. MoBi 106 (1997) 34-53.

### ᴛ7.1  Ægyptus, *generalia*

10949    Deutsches Archäologisches Institut. Mitteilungen des Deutschen Archäologischen Instituts, Abt. Kairo. MDAI.K 53: Mainz 1997, Von Zabern 293 pp. 42 pl. 3-8053-1997-5.

10950    ᴱFalck, **Martin von; Lichtwark, Friedericke** Ägypten: Schätze... Kunst und Kultur der Christen am Nil. 1996, ⇒12,10412. ᴿPhoenix 43/1 (1997) 50-55 *(Toorians, Lauran).*

10951    **Gamer-Wallert, Ingrid** Vermerk: Fundort unbekannt: ägyptologische Entdeckungen bei Privatsammlern in und um Stuttgart. Tü

1997, Attempto 320 pp. 97 pl. DM178. 3-89308-255-7 [BiOr 55,418—Haslauer, Elfriede].

10952 **Leclant, Jean; Clerc, Gisèle** Fouilles et travaux en Égypte et au Soudan, 1995-1996. Or. 66 (1997) 222-363.

10953 **Nibbi, Alessandra** Some geographical notes on ancient Egypt: a selection of published papers, 1975-1997. Discussions in Egyptology, Special number 3: Oxf 1997, DE 423 pp. £40. 0-9510704-7-9.

10954 **Osing, Jürgen** Aspects de la culture pharaonique. 1992, ⇒8,g36*. ᴿCÉg 143 (1997) 44-47 *(Derchain, Ph.).*

10955 **Page-Gasser, Madeleine; Wiese, André B.** Ägypten: Augenblicke der Ewigkeit: unbekannte Schätze aus Schweizer Privatbesitz. Mainz 1997, Von Zabern viii; 340 pp. DM98 [EuA 73/4,329].

10956 **Robins, Gay** The art of ancient Egypt. L 1997, British Museum 271 pp. £28.50. 0-7141-0988-6.

10957 **Shaw, Ian; Nicholson, Paul** British Museum dictionary of ancient Egypt. 1995, ⇒11/2,b522. ᴿOr. 66 (1997) 92-94 *(Hofmeier, Thomas).*

т7.2 *Elephantine* Karnak [East Bank]—Thebae [West Bank]

10958 *Darnell, Deborah; Darnell, John* Exploring the 'narrow doors' of the Theban desert. Egyptian Archaeology 10 (1997) 24-26.

10959 *Elephantine: Pilgrim, Cornelius von* The town site on the island of Elephantine. Egyptian Archaeology 10 (1997) 16-18.

10960 *Karnak:* **El-Sharkawy, Ali** Der Amun-Tempel von Karnak: die Funktion der Grossen Säulenhalle, erschlossen aus der Analyse der Dekoration ihrer Innenwände. Wissenschaftliche Schriftenreihe Ägyptologie 1: B 1997, Köster 314 pp. Bibl. 3-89574-290-2.

10961 *Thebes:* ᴱ**Reeves, Carl N.** After Tutʿankhamūn: research and excavation in the royal necropolis at Thebes. 1992, ⇒8,g77... 11/2,b553. ᴿCÉg 143 (1997) 56-65 *(Gabolde, Marc)*;

10962 **Eaton-Krauss, M.** The sarcophagus in the tomb of Tutankhamun. 1993, ⇒9,14362... 12,10424. ᴿAJA 101 (1997) 781 *(Lacovara, Peter)*;

10963 **Barthelmess, Petra** Der Übergang ins Jenseits in den thebanischen Beamtengräbern der Ramessidenzeit. 1992, ⇒8,g83... 12,10422. ᴿCÉg 72 (1997) 70-72 *(Englund, Gertie)*;

10964 **Polz, Daniel** Das Grab des Hui und des Kel: Theben Nr. 54. Archäologische Veröffentlichungen 74: Mainz 1997, Von Zabern 148 pp. Beiträge von *S. Klug* und *H. Kürschner*; Photographien von *D. Johannes*: Deutsches Archéologisches Institut, Abt. Kairo. 3-8053-1856-1.

10965 **Bickel, Susanne** Untersuchungen im Totentempel des Merenptah in Theben III: Tore und andere wiederverwendete Bauteile Amenophis' III. BÄBFA 16: Stu 1997, Steiner 175 pp. Beiträge von *Horst Jaritz* et al. Bibl. DM248. 3-515-06803-1.

T7.3 **Amarna**

10966  **Arnold, Dorothea** Royal women of Amarna: images of beauty in
       ancient Egypt. NY 1997, The Metropolitan Museum of Art xxii;
       169 pp. Bibl. $45. 0-8109-6504-6.
10967  *Cochavi-Rainey, Zipora* Egyptian influence in the Amarna texts.
       UF 29 (1997) 95-114.
10968  **Giles, Frederick J.** The Amarna age: western Asia: with a chap-
       ter by *J. Basil Hennessey* and some translations by *A.B. Knapp*:
       The Australian Centre for Egyptology. Studies 5: Warminster
       1997, Aris & P vii; 467 pp. Bibl. 0-885668-800-2.
10969  **Izre'el, Shlomo** The Amarna scholarly tablets. Cuneiform Mo-
       nographs 9: Groningen 1997, STYX xii; 109 pp. 51 pl. 90-
       72371-83-6.
10970  [E]**Kemp, Barry J.** Amarna Reports VI. 1995, ⇒11/2,b581. [R]BiOr
       54 (1997) 672-676 *(Eaton-Krauss, M.)*.
10971  *Krauss, Rolf* Nefretitis Ende. MDAI.K 53 (1997) 209-219;
10972  Zur Chronologie der Nachfolger Achenatens unter Berücksichti-
       gung der DOG-Funde aus Amarna. MDOG 129 (1997) 225-250.
10973  *Na'aman, Nadav* Looking for the Pharaoh's judgment. RA 90
       (1996) 145-159.
10974  *Shaw, Ian* Achetaton (Tell el-Amarna). Land der Bibel. 1997,
       ⇒9960. [E]Seipel, W., 73-89.
10975  *Tropper, Josef* Kanaanäisches in den Amarnabriefen. Sum. 134.
       AfO 44-45 (1997) 134-145;
10976  Ventiv oder *yaqtula*-Volitiv in den Amarnabriefen aus Syrien-
       Palästina?. AOAT 247: 1997, ⇒75. [F]ROELLIG W., 397-405.

T7.4 **Memphis,** *Saqqara*—**Pyramides,** *Giza* (Cairo)

10977  *Callender, Vivienne G.; Jánosi, Peter* The tomb of Queen Kha-
       merernebty II at Giza: a reassessment. MDAI.K 53 (1997) 1-22.
10978  **Cook, Robin** The horizon of Khufu: the pyramids of Giza and
       the geometry of heaven. 1996, ⇒12,10435. [R]DiscEg 37 (1997)
       119-126 *(Legon, John A.R.)*.
10979  *Davies, Sue; Smith, H.S.* Sacred animal temples at Saqqara. The
       temple in ancient Egypt. 1997, ⇒300. [E]Quirke, S., 112-131.
10980  *El-Sanussi, Ashraf; Jones, Michael* A site of the Maadi culture
       near the Giza pyramids. MDAI.K 53 (1997) 241-253.
10981  **Hastings, Elizabeth Anne** The sculpture from the sacred animal
       necropolis at north Saqqara 1964-76. Introd. *Smith, H.S.*: Exca-
       vation Memoir 61: L 1997, Egypt Exploration Society xxxv; 89
       pp. Bibl. 0-885698-135-4.
10982  *Hawass, Zahi* Tombs of the pyramid builders;
10983  *Hawass, Zahi; Lehner, Mark* Builders of the pyramids. Ar-
       chaeology 50/1 (1997) 39-43/30-38.
10984  **Jánosi, Peter** Österreich vor den Pyramiden: die Grabungen Her-
       mann JUNKERs im Auftrag der Österreichischen Akademie der
       Wissenschaften in Wien bei den grossen Pyramiden in Giza.
       DÖAW.PH 648: Veröffentlichungen der ägyptischen Kommis-
       sion 3: W 1997, Verlag der Österreichischen Akademie der Wis-
       senschaften 101 pp. Bibl. 3-7001-2664-6;

10985 Die Pyramidenanlagen der Königinnen: Untersuchungen zu einem Grabtyup des Alten und Mittleren Reiches. DÖAW 13: W 1996, Verl. der Österr. Akad. der Wissenschaften 194 pp. 86 fig. 17 pl. 3-7001-2207-1 [RdE 50,289—Valloggia, Michel].

10986 *Jeffreys, David* Looking for early dynastic Memphis. Egyptian Archaeology 10 (1997) 9-10.

10987 *Kaiser, Werner* Zu den Granitkammern und ihren Vorgängerbauten unter der Stufenpyramide und im Südgrab von Djoser. MDAI.K 53 (1997) 195-207.

10988 **Kanawati, Naguib; Hassan, A.** The Teti cemetery at Saqqara, 2: the tomb of Ankhmahor. The Australian Centre for Egyptology, Reports 9: Warminster 1997, Aris & P 74 pp. 73 pl. £45/$90. 1-85668-802-9 [BiOr 56,81ss—Drenkhahn, Rosemarie].

10989 *Krauss, Rolf* Chronologie und Pyramidenbau in der 4. Dynastie. Or. 66 (1997) 1-14.

10990 **Lehner, M.** The complete pyramids. 83 ill. L 1997, Thames & H 256 pp. £25. 0-500-05084-8 [Egyptian Archaeology 12,28—Spencer, Jeffrey].

10991 *Malek, Jaromir* The temples at Memphis: problems highlighted by the EES survey. The temple in ancient Egypt. 1997, ⇒300. EQuirke, S., 90-101.

10992 **Martin, Geoffrey T.** The hidden tombs of Memphis: new discoveries from the time of Tutankhamun and Ramesses the Great. 1991, ⇒7,d910; 8,g138. RJNES 56 (1997) 115-118 *(Johnson, W. Raymond)*.

10993 **Parra Ortiz, José Miguel** Historia de las Pirámides de Egipto. M 1997, Complutense x; 541 pp. Bibl. 84-89784-15-9.

10994 **Stadelman, Rainer** Die ägyptischen Pyramiden: vom Ziegelbau zum Weltwunder. Kulturgeschichte der antiken Welt 30: Mainz ³1997, Von Zabern 323 pp. Bibl. 3-8053-1142-7.

### T7.5 Delta Nili

10995 *Leblanc, Christian* The tomb of Ramesses II and remains of his funerary treasure. Egyptian Archaeology 10 (1997) 11-13.

10996 **Traczow, Barbara** The topography of ancient Alexandria. TZych, Iwona: Trav. d. Centre d'Archéolog. méditerr. d. l'Acad. polon. d. Scienc. 32: Wsz 1993, Zaklad Archelogii 358 pp 160 ill. 83-900096-7-6 [BiOr 56,656—Haas, Christopher].

### T7.6 *Alii situs Ægypti* alphabetice

10997 *Abusir: Posener-Kriéger, Paule* News from Abusir. The temple in ancient Egypt. 1997, ⇒300. EQuirke, S., 17-23;

10998 *Verner, Miroslav* Excavations at Abusir: seasons of 1994/95 and 1995/96. ZÄS 124/1 (1997) 71-85.

10999 *Amara:* ESpencer, Patricia Amara West I: the architectural report. Collab. *Shinnie, P.L.; Fraser, F.C.; Parker, H.W.*: Excavation Memoir 63: L 1997, The Egypt Exploration Society xxvi; 240 pp. £90. 0-85698-136-2.

11000 *Bakchias:* EPernigotti, Sergio; Capasso, Mario Bakchias IV: rapporto preliminare della campagna di scavo del 1996. Pisa

1997, Istituti Editoriali e Poligrafici Internazionali 111 pp. num. ill. [CÉg 73,190s—Nachtergael, Georges].

11001   *Beydar:* **ᴱLebeau, Marc; Suleiman, Antoine** Tell Beydar, three seasons of excavations (1992-1994): a preliminary report [Trois campagnes de fouilles à Tell Beydar (1992-1994): rapport préliminaire]. Subartu 3: Turnhout 1997, Brepols (8) 243 pp. 2-503-50584-8.

11002   *Cairo: Jones, Michael* Archaeological discoveries in Doqqi and the course of the Nile at Cairo during the Roman period. MDAI.K 53 (1997) 101-111.

11003   *Dabʃa:* **Bietak, M.** Avaris: the capital of the Hyksos. 1996, ⇒12,10460. Recent excavations at Tell el-Dabʿa. ᴿOLZ 92 (1997) 479-483 *(Luft, Ulrich).*

11004   *Dakhla:* **Henein, Nessim Henry** Poterie et potiers d'Al-Qasr: oasis de Dakhla. Préf. *Montmollin, Daniel de:* BÉt 116: Le Caire 1997, Institut Français d'Archéologie Orientale du Caire xv; 242 pp. Bibl. 2-7247-0202-6.

11005   *Deir el-Medina: Montserrat, Dominic; Meskell, Lynn* Mortuary archaeology and religious landscape at Graeco-Roman Deir el-Medina. Sum. 179. JEA 83 (1997) 179-197.

11006   *el-Faraʿîn:* **Way, Thomas von der** Tell el-Faraʿîn: Buto I: Ergebnisse zum frühen Kontext: Kampagnen der Jahre 1983-1989. Archäologische Veröffentlichungen 83: Mainz 1997, Von Zabern 252 pp. num. ill., pl. DM220. 3-8053-1858-8 [BiOr 55,764ss—Wilkinson, Toby A.H.].

11007   *el-Kantara: Abd el-Maqsoud, Mohamed, (al.),* The Roman Castrum of Tell Abu Sayfi at Qantara;

11008   *Elephantine: Vittmann, Günter* Das demotische Graffito vom Satettempel auf Elephantine;

11009   *Kaiser, Werner, (al.),* Stadt und Tempel von Elephantine, 23/24: Grabungsbericht;

11010   *Farama: El-Taher, Refaad; Grossmann, Peter* Excavation of the circular church at Farama-West. MDAI.K 53 (1997) 221-226/263-281/117-193/255-262.

11011   *Mons Claudianus:* **Peacock, D.P.S.; Maxfield, V.A., (al.),** Mons Claudianus 1987-1993: survey and excavation. DFIFAO 37: Le Caire 1997, Institut Français d'Archéologie Orientale du Caire xi; 366 pp. Bibl. 2-7247-0192-5.

11012   *Naukratis:* **Leonard, Albert, (al.),** Ancient Naukratis: excavations at a Greek emporium in Egypt. AASOR 54: NHv 1997, ASOR xxii; 415 pp. Bibl. 0-7885-0392-8.

11013   *Qurnah:* **Negm, Maged** The tomb of Simut called Kyky: Theban tomb 409 at Qurnah. Modern Egyptology: Warminster 1997, Aris & P xii; 49 pp. 63 pl. 0-85668-698-0.

11014   *Serabit el-khadim :* **Valbelle, Dominique; Bonnet, Charles** Le sanctuaire d'Hathor, maîtresse de la turquoise sérabit el-khadim au Moyen Empire. P 1996, Picard 199 pp. 189 fig. 5 plans. 2-7084-0514-4 [BiOr 56,641—Shaw, Ian].

11015   *Tanis: Brissaud, Philippe* Tanis (Tell San el-Hagar). Land der Bibel. 1997, ⇒9960. ᴱSeipel, W., 93-113.

11016   *Brissaud, Philippe* Tanis, énigmes et histoires. BSFE 138 (1997) 18-35.

11017  *Thebes: Vörös, Gyozo; Pudleiner, Rezso* Preliminary report of the excavations at Thoth Hill, Thebes: the temple of Montuhotep Sankhkara (season 1995-1996). MDAI.K 53 (1997) 283-287.

### T7.7  *Antiquitates Nubiae et alibi;* Egypt outside Egypt

11018  [E]**Fulford, Michael; Tomber, Roberta** Excavations at Sabratha 1948-1951, II/2: the finewares and lamps. 1994, ⇒11/2,b704. [R]AJA 101 (1997) 618-619 *(Slane, Kathleen Warner).*
11019  *Heidorn, Lisa A.* The horses of Kush. JNES 56 (1997) 105-114.
11020  **Shinnie, Peter L.** Ancient Nubia. 1996, ⇒12,10473. [R]DiscEg 37 (1997) 133-141 *(Morkot, Robert)*; CÉg 72 (1997) 78-80 *(Welsby, Derek A.).*

### T7.9  Sinai

11021  **Greenwood, Ned** The Sinai—a physical geography. Austin 1997, University of Texas Press 160 pp. $35/$17 [IJMES 31,688s— Kolars, John].
11022  *Grossmann, Peter* Firan in south Sinai. Egyptian Archaeology 10 (1997) 3-5.
11023  **Schultz, Joseph P.; Spatz, Lois** Sinai and Olympus: a comparative study. 1995, ⇒11/2,b736. [R]ClR 47 (1997) 112-14 *(Bowden, Hugh).*

### T8.1  Anatolia *generalia*

11024  **Ivantchik, Askold I.** Les cimmériens au Proche-Orient. OBO 127: 1993, ⇒10,12862. [R]Journal of Ancient History 223 (1997) 69-85 [R., sum. 85] *(Fedoseev, N.F.).*
11025  [E]**Matthews, Roger J.** Ancient Anatolia: fifty years' work by the British Institute of Archaeology at Ankara. L 1997, The British Institute of Archaeology at Ankara xx; 378 pp. 1-898249-11-3.
11026  [E]**Mikasa, Prince Takahito** Essays on Anatolian archaeology. 1993, ⇒9,358; 12,10483. [R]OLZ 92 (1997) 65-68 *(Börker-Klähn, Jutta)*;
11027  Essays on ancient Anatolia and its surrounding civilizations. Bulletin of the Middle Eastern Culture Center in Japan 8: Wsb 1995, Harrassowitz vi; 243 pp. [R]OLZ 92 (1997) 65-68 *(Börker-Klähn, Jutta)*; BiOr 54 (1997) 767-769 *(Duistermaat, Kim).*

### T8.2  Boğazköy—*Hethaei,* the Hittites

11028  *Czichon, Rainer M.* Studien zur Regionalgeschichte von Ḫḫĩ-tuša/Boğazköy 1996. MDOG 129 (1997) 89-102.
11029  **Dardano, Paola** L'aneddoto e il racconto in età antico-hittita: la cosiddetta "Cronaca di Palazzo". Introd. *Marazzi, M.*: BRLF 43: R 1997, Il Calamo xvii; 212 pp. 88-85134-44-0.

11030   *González Salazar, Juan Manuel* Apuntes sobre el curso superior del Éufrates y el reino hitita de Anatolia: nuevas vías de investigación. Orient-Express 2 (1997) 62-63.
11031   *Hawkins, David* Die Hethiter und ihr Reich. Land der Bibel. 1997, ⇒9960. ᴱSeipel, W., 63-69.
11032   *Seeher, Jürgen* Die Ausgrabungen in Boğazköy-Ḫattuša 1996. AA (1997) 317-341.
11033   *Yakar, Jak* Hattusa-Bogazköy: Aspekte hethitischer Architektur. Land der Bibel. 1997, ⇒9960. ᴱSeipel, W., 53-62.

### т8.3  Ephesus; Pergamum

11034   **Friesen, Steven J.** Twice Neokoros: Ephesus, Asia and the cult of the Flavian imperial family. RGRW 116: 1993, ⇒9,14567; 10,12892*. ᴿTJT 13/2 (1997) 272-273 *(Harland, Philip A.)*.
11035   **Günther, Matthias** Die Frühgeschichte des Christentums in Ephesus. ARGU 1: 1995, ⇒11/2,b785. ᴿBZ 41 (1997) 142-145 *(Roloff, Jürgen)*; Salm. 44 (1997) 115-120 *(Trevijano, Ramón)*.
11036   **Hueber, Friedmund** Ephesos: gebaute Geschichte. Contrib. *Erdemgil, Selahattin; Büyükkolanci, Mustafa*: Zaberns Bildbände zur Archäologie: Mainz 1997, Von Zabern 111 pp. Bibl. 3-8053-1814-6.
11037   ᴱ**Koester, Helmut** Ephesos metropolis of Asia: an interdisciplinary approach to its archaeology, religion, and culture. HThS 41: 1995, ⇒11/2,b789. ᴿSalm. 44 (1997) 120-124 *(Trevijano, Ramón)*; JEarlyC 5 (1997) 456-457 *(Norris, Frederick W.)*; CBQ 59 (1997) 807-809 *(Kraabel, A.T.)*.
11038   **Thiessen, Werner** Christen in Ephesus: die historische und theologische Situation in vorpaulinischer und paulinischer Zeit und zur Zeit der Apostelgeschichte und der Pastoralbriefe. Diss., ᴰ*Berger, Klaus*: TANZ 12: 1995, ⇒11/2,b795. ᴿSalm. 44 (1997) 109-115 *(Trevijano, Ramón)*; RB 104 (1997) 454-456 *(Murphy-O'Connor, J.)*; BZ 41 (1997) 142-145 *(Roloff, Jürgen)*.

### т8.6  *Situs Anatoliae*—Turkey sites; Urartu

11039   *Gates, Marie-Henriette* Archaeology in Turkey. AJA 101 (1997) 241-305.
11040   **Marksteiner, Thomas** Die befestigte Siedlung von Limyra: Studien zur vorrömischen Wehrarchitektur und Siedlungsentwicklung in Lykien unter besonderer Berücksichtigung der klassischen Periode. Forschungen aus Limyra 1: W 1997, Phoibos 202, 132 pp. 3-901232-09-5.
11041   *Ruggieri, Vincenzo; Giordano, Franco; Zäh, Alexander* La penisola di Alicarnasso in età bizantina, 1. OCP 63 (1997) 119-161.
11042   **Vandeput, Lutgarde** The architectural decoration in Roman Asia Minor: Sagalassos: a case study. Studies in Eastern Mediterranean Archaeology 1: Lv 1997, Brepols 353 pp. 2-503-50540-6.

11043   *Röllig, Wolfgang* Ein urartäisches Gürtelblech mit Darstellung einer Löwenjagd. Or. 66 (1997) 213-221.

11044 **Salvini, Mirjo** Geschichte und Kultur der Urartäer. 1995, ⇒11/2,b895. ᴿWO 28 (1997) 203-208 *(Kroll, Stephan)*; BiOr 54 (1997) 734-737 *(Muscarella, Oscar White)*.

## T9.1 Cyprus

11045 *Aupert, Pierre* Amathus during the first Iron Age. BASOR 308 (1997) 19-25.
11046 *Buitron-Oliver, Diana* Kourion: the evidence for the kingdom from the 11th to the 6th century B.C. BASOR 308 (1997) 27-36.
11047 *Buitron-Oliver, Diana; Herscher, Ellen* The city-kingdoms of early Iron Age Cyprus in their eastern Mediterranean context;
11048 *Childs, William A.P.* The Iron Age kingdom of Marion;
11049 *Hadjicosti, Maria* The kingdom of Idalion in the light of new evidence. BASOR 308 (1997) 5-7/37-48/49-63.
ᴱ**Karageorghis, V.** 4000 years of images on Cypriote pottery ⇒397.
11050 **Karageorghis, Vassos** The Cypro-archaic period: large and medium size sculpture. The coroplastic art of ancient Cyrus, 3. Nicosia 1993, Leventis. 9963-560-27-X. ᴿRSFen 25/1 (1997) 115-119 *(Ciafaloni, Davide)*.
11051 **Knapp, A. Bernard** The archaeology of Late Bronze Age Cypriot society: the study of settlement, survey and landscape. Occasional Paper 4: Glasgow 1997, University of Glasgow xiii; 108 pp. £12.50. 0-85261-573-6 [AJA 101,819].
11052 ᴱ**Knapp, A.B.** Near Eastern and Aegean texts from the third to the first millennia BC., 2. 1996, ⇒12,10500. ᴿAJA 101 (1997) 629 *(Palaima, Thomas G.)*.
11053 *Reyes, A. T.* Notes on the Iron Age kingdoms of Cyprus;
11054 *Rupp, David W.* Constructing the Cypriot Iron Age: present praxis, future possibilities;
11055 *Smith, Joanna S.* Preliminary comments on a rural cypro-archaic sanctuary in Polis-Peristeries;
11056 *Yon, Marguerite* Kition in the tenth to fourth centuries B.C. BASOR 308 (1997) 65-68/69-75/77-98/9-17.

## T9.3 *Graecia*, Greece—mainland

11057 **Albers, Gabriele** Spätmykenische Stadtheiligtümer. 1994, ⇒11/2,b960. ᴿAJA 101 (1997) 411-412 *(Hägg, Robin)*.
11058 **Bookidis, Nancy; Stroud, Ronald S.** Corinth 18.3: the sanctuary of Demeter and Kore: topography and architecture. Princeton 1997, American School of Classical Studies at Athens xxiii; 510 pp. 66 pl. 109 fig. 12 plans; $125. 0-87661-183-8 [AJA 103,709s—Price, Susan-Marie Cronkite].
11059 **Harris, Diane** The treasures of the Parthenon and Erechtheion. Oxf Monographs on Classical Archaeology: Oxf 1995, OUP xiv; 306 pp. Diss. 1991 ⇒7,e151. $100. 0-19-814940-9. ᴿAJA 101 (1997) 603-604 *(Lapatin, Kenneth D.S.)*.
11060 *Shelmerdine, Cynthia W.* Review of Aegean prehistory VI: the palatial Bronze Age of the southern and central Greek mainland. AJA 101 (1997) 537-585.

т9.4  Creta

11061  **Marangou-Lerat, Antigone** Le vin et les amphores de Crète: de
l'époque classique à l'époque impériale. EtCret 30: P 1995, De
Boccard 187 pp. 19 fig. 35 pl. FF495. 2-86958-073-8. ᴿAJA 101
(1997) 805-806 *(Harrison, George W.M.).*
ᶠPopham M., Minotaur... the archaeology of Crete ⇒72.

11062  **White, Donald** The extramural sanctuary of Demeter and Perse-
phone at Cyrene, Libya. 1993, ⇒10,12829; 11/2,b708. ᴿJAOS
117 (1997) 723-725 *(Métraux, Guy P.R.)*; AJA 101 (1997) 617-
618 *(Wescoat, Bonna D.).*

т9.6  Urbs Roma

11063  **Catalli, Fiorenzo** Foro Romano e Palatino: Roma. IMMI 42: R
1997, Istituto Poligrafico dello Stato, Libreria dello Stato 143 pp.
88-240-3823-9.

11064  **Coarelli, Filippo** Il Campo Marzio: dalle origini alla fine della
Repubblica. R 1997, Quasar x; 676 pp. Bibl. 88-7140-107-7.

11065  **Felle, Antonio Enrico** Inscriptiones Christianae Urbis Romae,
n.s.: concordantiae verborum, nominum et imaginum: tituli
graeci. Inscriptiones Christianae Italiae, Subsidia 4: Bari 1997,
Edipuglia xxxiv; 449 pp. 88-7228-173-3.

11066  **Iacopi, Irene** Gli scavi sul Colle Palatino: testimonianze e documenti. Mi 1997, Electa 60 pp. 88-435-6330-0.

11067  **Palombi, Domenico** Tra Palatino ed Esquilino: Velia, Carinae,
Fagutal: storia urbana di tre quartieri di Roma antica. RINA.S 1:
R 1997, Istituto Nazionale d'Archeologia e Storia dell'Arte ix;
200 pp. 88-7275-101-2.

11068  ᴱ**Parkins, Helen M.** Roman urbanism: beyond the consumer
city. L 1997, Routledge xvi; 227 pp. 13 fig. 2 tables. £45. 0-
415-11771-2.

11069  *Quesnel, Michel* Rome dans la Bible. MoBi 103 (1997) 14-15.
11070  *Turcan, Robert* L'art et la conversion de Rome. MoBi 103 (1997)
4-14.

11071  *White, L. Michael* Synagogue and society in imperial Ostia: archaeological and epigraphic evidence. HThR 90 (1997) 23-58.

т9.7  Catacumbae; *archaeologia paleocristiana*

11072  **Baruffa, Antonio** Las catacumbas de San Calixto: historia—
arqueología—fe. Città del Vaticano ²1996, LEV [Sal. 62,166—
Ramiro Vázquez, Javier].

11073  **Frend, William H.C.** The archaeology of early christianity.
1996, ⇒12,9476. ᴿJRS 87 (1997) 317-318 *(Taylor, Joan E.)*;
BTB 27 (1997) 117 *(Osiek, Carolyn)*; AThR 79 (1997) 599-600
*(Vivian, Tim)*; CHR 83 (1997) 729-731 *(Finney, Paul Corby)*;
HeyJ 38 (1997) 453-454 *(Painter, K.S.).*

11074  *Guyon, Jean* Le message de salut du premier art chrétien. MoBi
103 (1997) 31-35.

11075 **Pergola, Philippe** Le catacombe romane storia e topografia. Catalogo *Palmira Maria Barbini*: R 1997, Nuova Italia Scientifica 263 pp. 29 phot. L35.000 [ACr 86,157s—Vigorelli, Valerio].

### т9.9 *Roma: imperium occidentale*

11076 **Eschebach, Hans; Eschebach, Lisalotte** Pompeji: vom 7. Jahrhundert v.Chr. bis 79 n.Chr. Arbeiten zur Archäologie: Köln 1995, Böhlau xiv; 213 pp. 74 pl. 65 fig. DM228. 3-412-11594-0. RAJA 101 (1997) 420-421 *(Allison, Penelope M.).*

11077 **Giardina, Andrea** L'Italia romana: storie di un'identità incompiuta. Collezione storica: R 1997, Laterza xv; 442 pp. 88-420-5236-1.

11078 **Migotti, Branka** Evidence for christianity in Roman southern Pannonia (northern Croatia): a catalogue of finds and sites. BAR international series 684: Oxf 1997, Archaeopress v; 117 pp. Bibl. 0-86054-870-8.

## XIX. Geographia biblica

### U1.0 **Geographica**

11079 *Abdul-Amir, S.J.* Assyrian frontier sites on the middle Euphrates: new evidence from the Al-Qadisiya (Haditha) Dam region in the western desert of Iraq. Assyrien im Wandel. 1997, ⇒379. EWaetzoldt, H., 219-221.

11080 *Abraham, K.* ŠuŠan in the Egibi texts from the time of Marduk-naṣir-apli. OLoP 28 (1997) 55-85.

11081 *Gawlikowski, Michel* L'empereur Julien sur les bords de l'Euphrate;

11082 *Groneberg, Brigitte* La toponymie mésopotamienne à élément théophore: un premier sondage;

11083 *Inglebert, Hervé Pars oceani orientalis*: les conceptions de l'Orient dans les oeuvres géographiques de l'Antiquité tardive (300-550);

11084 *Jacob, Christian* Premières géographies: poésie, cartes et périégèse en Grèce (VIIIe-fin du VIe s.). Des Sumériens. 1997, ⇒377. ESérandour, A., 145-155/25-40/177-198/157-176.

11085 *Kark, R.* Land purchase and mapping in a midnineteenth-century Palestinian village. PEQ 129 (1997) 150-161.

11086 *Lemaire, André* D'Édom à l'Idumée et à Rome. Des Sumériens. 1997, ⇒377. ESérandour, A., 81-103.

11087 ELiverani, **Mario** Neo-Assyrian geography. 1995, ⇒11/2,c081. RRA 91 (1997) 95-96 *(Garelli, Paul)*; AfO 44-45 (1997-98) 404-409 *(Fuchs, Andreas).*

11088 **Patton, Mark** Islands in time: island sociogeography amd Mediterranean prehistory. 1996, ⇒12,10545. RAntiquity 71 (1997) 241-242 *(Webster, Gary S.).*

11089   TERomer, Frank E. Pomponius Mela's description of the world.
        AA 1997, Univ. of Michigan Press xi; 165 pp. Bibl. 0-472-
        10773-9.
11090   Villard, Pierre La représentation des paysages de montagne à
        l'époque néo-assyrienne. Des Sumériens. 1997, ⇒377.
        ESérandour, A., 41-58.
11091   Zadok, Ran Syro-Mesopotamian notes. AOAT 247: 1997, ⇒75.
        FROELLIG W., 447-457.


## u1.2 Historia geographiae

11092   Bordreuil, Pierre De David à Alexandre (XIᵉ-IVᵉ s. av. J.-C.):
        une longue histoire commune avec Israël. MoBi 104 (1997) 21-
        27.
11093   Charpin, Dominique Sapîratum, ville du Suhûm. Mari 8 (1997)
        341-366.
11094   EDowley, Tim Atlas Bibel und Geschichte des Christentums.
        Wuppertal 1997, Brockhaus 160 pp. 3-417-24666-0.
11095   Frevel, Christian Das Land der Bibel. Lebendige Welt. 1997,
        ⇒565. EZenger, E., 68-80.
11096   Gophna, Ram The southern coastal troughs as EB I subsistence
        areas. IEJ 47 (1997) 155-161.
11097   Khouri, Rami G., (al.), Les temps préhistoriques (VIᵉ-IIᵉ millé-
        naires): des premiers nomades aux premières cités. MoBi 104
        (1997) 14-19.
11098   Knauf-Belleri, Axel Enquête sur la Transjordanie dans l'Ancien
        Testament. MoBi 104 (1997) 28-32.
11099   Masson, Emilia Continuité géopolitique en Anatolie. Des Sumé-
        riens. 1997, ⇒377. ESérandour, A., 67-79.
11100   Mills, Mary E. The Holy Land: contemporary reflections. ScrB
        27 (1997) 22-31.
11101   Renaud, Bernard La "grande mer" dans l'Ancien Testament: de
        la géographie au symbole. La Bíblia i el Mediterrani. 1997,
        ⇒385. EBorrell, d'Agustí, 75-101.
11102   Röllig, Wolfgang Aspects of the historical geography of nort-
        heastern Syria from Middle Assyrian to Neo-Assyrian times. As-
        syria 1995. 1997, ⇒376. EParpola, S., 281-293.
11103   Villeneuve, François La Jordanie;
11104   (et al.), D'Alexandre à l'Islam (IVᵉ s. av. - VIIᵉ a. ap. J.-C.)
        [Pétra; La Décapole; Madaba; Machéronte; Jérash; Samra]. MoBi
        104 (1997) 4-13/39-55.
11105   Witakowski, Witold L'horizon géographique de l'historiographie
        syriaque: aperçu préliminaire. Des Sumériens. 1997, ⇒377.
        ESérandour, A., 199-209.
11106   Zayadine, Fawzi Traditions bibliques et découvertes archéologi-
        ques [en Jordanie]. MoBi 104 (1997) 33-37.
11107   Zeidler, Jürgen Die Länge der Unterwelt nach ägyptischer Vor-
        stellung. GöMisz 156 (1997) 101-112.


## u1.4 Atlas—maps

11108   Amiran, David H.K. The Madaba mosaic map as a climate indica-
        tor for the sixth century. IEJ 47 (1997) 97-99.
11109   EDowley, T. De atlas van de Bijbel en de geschiedenis van het
        christendom. Heerenveen 1997, Jongbloed 160 pp. ƒ84.50
        [GThT 98,137];

11110    Atlas of the bible and christianity. GR 1997, Baker 160 pp. $30.
         0-8010-2051-4 [ThD 44,352—Heiser, W. Charles].
11111    **Galbiati, Enrico Rodolfo; Aletti, Aldo** Atlas histórico da bíblia
         e do antigo Oriente. 1991, ⇒9,14904. [R]Did(L) 27/2 (1997) 167-
         168 *(Lourenço, João)*.
11112    *Lecoq, Danielle* Die ältesten Karten des Heiligen Landes. WUB 4
         (1997) 53-59.
11113    **Nebenzahl, Kenneth** Atlas zum Heiligen Land: Karten der Terra
         Sancta durch zwei Jahrtausende. Stu 1995, Katholisches Bibel-
         werk 164 pp. [R]ThR 62 (1997) 460-461 *(Perlitt, Lothar)*.
11114    [E]**Rasmussen, Carl G.** Historisch-geografischer Atlas zur Bibel.
         Neuhausen-Stu 1997, Hänssler 256 pp. 3-7751-2632-5.
11115    *Rubin, Rfhav* Validity of early maps of Palestine as geographical-
         historical sources. Discussion with *Syon, Danny* p.184. Cathedra
         83 (1997) 182-183 **H.**
11116    **Thrower, N.J.W.** Maps & civilization: cartography in culture
         and society. 1996, ⇒12,10564. [R]NeoTest. 31 (1997) 413-414
         *(Craffert, Pieter F.)*.
11117    **Tsafrir, Y.; Di Segni, L.; Green, J.** Tabula imperii romani:
         Iudaea-Palestina, Eretz Israel in the Hellenistic, Roman, and By-
         zantine periods. 1994, ⇒10,13231; 11/2,c131. [R]IEJ 48 (1997)
         295-297 *(Meshel, Zeev)*.

## U1.5  *Photographiae;* Guide-books, *Führer;* Onomastica

11118    **Howe, Kathleen Stewart** Revealing the Holy Land: the pho-
         tographic exploration of Palestine. Santa Barbara 1997, Santa
         Barbara Museum of Art 144 pp. $60/30 [BAR 24/3,58—
         Feldman, Steven].

11119    **Padovese, Luigi** Guida alla Siria. Guide: CasM 1994, Piemme
         192 pp. L30.000. 88-384-2183-8. [R]Laur. 38 (1997) 545-546
         *(Martignani, Luigi)*.
11120    **Potin, Jacques** Jesus in his homeland. [T]*Dees, Colette Joly*: Ma-
         ryknoll 1997, Orbis 125 pp. $35. 1-57075-143-9 [ThD 45,85—
         Heiser, W. Charles].
11121    **Staccioli, Romolo Augusto** Guida di Roma antica. BUR 585: Mi
         1997, Biblioteca Universale Rizzoli 499 pp. 88-17-16585-9.
11122    **Tondok, Wil; Tondok, Sigrid** Ägypten individuell: ein Reise-
         handbuch zum Erleben, Erkennen, Verstehen eines phantastischen
         Landes. Reise-Know-how: Hohenthann [12]1997, Reise-Know-
         How-Verl. Hermann 573 pp. 3-89662-470-9.

11123    **Liverani, Mario** Studies on the annals of Ashurnasirpal II,2: to-
         pographical analysis. 1992, ⇒8,g796... 12,10570. [R]WO 28
         (1997) 201-202 *(Kessler, Karlheinz)*.

## U2.1  Geologia; *Hydrographia;* Clima

11124    *Buckland, Paul C.; Dugmore, Andrew J.; Edwards, Kevin J.*
         Bronze Age myths?: volcanic activity and human response in the

Mediterranean and North Atlantic regions. Antiquity 71 (1997) 581-593.

11125 *Nur, Amos; Ron, Hagai* Earthquake!: inspiration for Armageddon. BArR 23/4 (1997) 48-55.

11126 *Briend, Jacques* Wasser—Quelle und Symbol des Lebens. WUB 6 (1997) 61-62.

11127 **Farrington, Andrew** The Roman baths of Lycia: an architectural study. British Institute of Archaeology at Ankara Monograph 20: L 1995, British Institute of Archaeology at Ankara xxv; 176 pp. 91 fig. 111 plans. 2 maps. 19 tables. $47. 1-898248-04-0. ᴿAJA 101 (1997) 615-616 *(Nielsen, Inge)*.

11128 **Hirschfeld, Yizhar,** *(al.)*, The Roman baths of Hammat Gader: final report. J 1997, Israel Exploration Society xv; 488 pp. $90. 965-221-0358 [RB 105,286—Langlamet, F.].

11129 *Lindner, Manfred; Hübl, Hannes* Where Pharao's daughter got her drinking water from: the En Brak conduit to Petra. ZDPV 113 (1997) 61-67.

11130 *Issar, Arie S.; Yakir, Dan* Isotopes from wood buried in the Roman siege ramp of Masada: the Roman period's colder climate. BA 60/2 (1997) 101-106.

11131 *Jasmin, Michaël* Reconstructions paléo-environnementales et changements climatiques durant l'holocène. Orient-Express 2 (1997) 63-64.

11132 *Pilch, John J.* The bible and the weather. BiTod 35 (1997) 171-6.

### ʋ2.5 *Fauna,* animalia

11133 **Birch, Charles; Vischer, Lukas** Living with the animals: the community of God's creatures. Risk Book 77: Genève 1997, World Council of Churches xii; 82 pp. FS11.50. 2-8254-1227-9. ᴿET 109 (1997-98) 97-98 *(Rodd, C.S.)*.

11134 *Briend, Jacques; Quesnel, Michel* L'élevage aux temps bibliques. MoBi 103 (1997) 57-58.

11135 *Daoust, Joseph* L'élevage dans la bible. EeV 107 (1997) 215-216.

11136 **Eaton, John** El círculo de la creación: los animales a la luz de la biblia. ᵀ*Díez, Ramón Alfonso; Carmen Blanco, Ma del*: Los cuatro vientos 5: Bilbao 1996, Desclée de B 151 pp. 84-330-1155-3 [ActBib 34,200—O'Callaghan, J.].

11137 *Eichmann, Ricardo* Ein Hund, ein Schwein, ein Musikant. AOAT 247: 1997, ⇒75. ꟳRoellig W., 97-108.

11138 *Fraikin, Jean* Serpents et dragons dans le bestiaire sacré de Samuel Bochart ou le folklore dans la bible. CISy 86-88 (1997) 97-128.

11139 *Heimpel, Wolfgang* Moroccan locusts in Qaṭṭunan. RA 90 (1996) 101-120.

11140 *Kaltenbrunner, Gerd-Klaus* Geschöpfe des fünften Tages: Adler, Taube und Sperling als Geheimniskünder: zur Symbolik und Theologie des Tiers in der Bibel. Theologisches 27 (1997) 330-336.

11141 **Leitz, Christian** Die Schlangennamen in den ägyptischen und griechischen Giftbüchern. Akad. der Wissenschaften und der Literatur, Abh. der Geistes- und Sozialwissenschaftlichen Kl. 1997,6: Mainz 1997, Akad. der Wissenschaften 166 pp. Bibl. 3-515-07227-6.

11142 **Linzey, Andrew; Cohn-Sherbok, Dan** After Noah: animals and the liberation of theology. L 1997, Mowbray xx; 128 pp. £13. 0-264-67450-2 [RRT 1998/2,91].

11143 *Lion, Brigitte; Michel, Cécile* Criquets et autres insectes à Mari. Mari 8 (1997) 707-724.

11144 **Maspero, Francesco** Bestiario antico: gli animali-simbolo e il loro significato nell'immaginario dei popoli antichi. CasM 1997, Piemme 371 pp. Bibl. 88-384-2955-3.

11145 *Panagiotakopulu, Eva* Archaeoentomology's potential in Near Eastern archaeology. BA 60/1 (1997) 52.

11146 **Park, Doo Hwan** Tiere und Farben in der Offenbarung: eine Untersuchung zur Herkunft, Funktion und theologischer Bedeutung der Tier- und Farbmotive in der Apokalypse des Johannes. Diss. Bethel 1997, DLindemann, A. [RTL 29,587].

11147 *Reed, Stephen A.* Meat eating and the Hebrew bible. FKNIERIM R., 1997, ⇒48. ESun, H., 281-294.

11148 **Sancassano, Maria Lucia** Il serpente e le sue immagini: il motivo del serpente nella poesia greca dall'Iliade all'Odissea. Biblioteca di Athenaeum 36: Como 1997, New Press 205 pp. Bibl.

11149 *Sivers, Fanny de* L'innocence animale en face du monde angélique. Engel und Dämonen. FARG 29: 1997, ⇒343. EAhn, G., 167-169.

11150 *Tiede, Peter* Der Gerechte kennt die Bedürfnisse seiner Tiere: der Mensch und die Haustiere in der Sicht des Alten Testaments. Entschluss 52/3 (1997) 22, 27-29.

11151 *Wilson, Penelope* Slaughtering the crocodile at Edfu and Dendera. The temple in ancient Egypt. 1997, ⇒300. EQuirke, S., 179-203.

## U2.6 *Flora;* plantae biblicae et antiquae

11152 *Cahill, Jane M.* Royal rosettes: fit for a king. BArR 23/5 (1997) 48-57, 68-69.

11153 *Compagnoni, Pia* Trees in the biblical pages. TGarcia, Gabriel. Holy Land 17 (1997) 58-60.

11154 *Gauckler, Konrad* Die kostbarsten Drogen der Alten Welt: Weihrauch, Myrrhe, Balsam. Petra und das Königreich. 1997, ⇒289. ELindner, M., 257-260.

11155 *Hepper, F. Nigel* Figs;

11156 The olive tree and its oil;

11157 The rose of Sharon and lily of the field. Holy Land 17 (1997) 65-68/61-65/69-71.

11158 *Rouillard-Bonraisin, Hedwige* Cent ans de botanique au Proche-Orient ancien. Congress volume 1995. VT.S 66: 1997, ⇒323. EEmerton, J.A., 249-260.

11159 *Soesilo, Daud* Translating the biblical 'barley' into Indonesian [CEV]. PPBT 48 (1997) 245-248.

11160 *Wigoder, Devorah Emmet* A biblical spice rack. BiRe 13/5 (1997) 32-35.

υ2.8 **Agricultura, alimentatio**

11161   **Bagnall, Roger S.** The Kellis agricultural account book (P. Kell.
IV Gr. 96). Oxbow Monograph 92; Dakhleh Oasis Project, Monograph 7: Oxf 1997, Oxbow xi; 253 pp. Bibl. 1-900188-40-6.
11162   **Baker, Elizabeth** Does the bible teach nutrition?. Mukilteo
1997, WinePress 161 pp. 1-579-21035-X [NThAR 2000,31].
11163   **Bresciani, Edda** Food and drink: life resources in ancient Egypt.
ᵀ*Adkins, H.*: Lucca 1997, Fazzi 47 pp. L10.000. 88-7246-277-0.
11164   *Briend, Jacques* Die landwirtschaftlichen Arbeiten in Texten der
Hebräischen Bibel. WUB 5 (1997) 60-61.
11165   **Cauvin, Jacques** Naissance des divinités, naissance de
l'agriculture: la révolution des symboles au Néolithique.
Empreintes: P 1997, CNRS 310 pp. 2-271-05454-0.
11166   ᴱ**Cavarra, Angela Adriana; Manodori, Alberto** Non mangerai
di quel frutto...: l'alimentazione nell'Antico Testamento. R 1997,
Biblioteca Casanatense 95 pp. Bibl. 88-86924-04-6.
11167   *Cebulj, Christian* Von Minze und Kümmel, Knechten und Ver-
waltern: zur Landwirtschaft im Neuen Testament und seiner
Umwelt. Entschluss 52/3 (1997) 30-33.
11168   *Daoust, Joseph* Les travaux agricoles dans la bible. EeV 107
(1997) 119-120.
11169   **Faïz, Mohammed el-** L'agronomie de la Mésopotamie antique:
analyse du 'livre de l'agriculture nabatéenne' de Qûtâmä. 1995,
⇒11/2,c248. ᴿJESHO 40/1 (1997) 117-122 *(Lehmann, Gunnar)*.
11170   *Freidank, Helmut* Noch einmal zum Vorgang *pišerti karuʾe*;
11171   *Liverani, Mario* Lower Mesopotamian fields: south vs. north.
AOAT 247: 1997, ⇒75. ᶠRoELLIG W., 129-143/219-227.
11172   *Penna, Romano* Il vino e le sue metafore nella grecità classica,
nell'Israele antico, e nel Nuovo Testamento. La Bíblia i el Mediterrani. 1997, ⇒385. ᴱBorrell, d'Agustí, 41-73.
11173   *Quesnel, Michel* Die Landwirtschaft in neutestamentlicher Zeit.
WUB 5 (1997) 61-62.
11174   *Ruiz López, Demetria* El vino en el antiguo Oriente bíblico. La
Bíblia i el Mediterrani. 1997, ⇒385. ᴱBorrell, d'Agustí, 373-88.
11175   *Staubli, Thomas* Abel wurde ein Schafhirt, Kain wurde ein Die-
ner des Ackers. Entschluss 52/3 (1997) 18-21.


υ2.9 **Medicina** biblica et antiqua

11176   **Amundsen, Darrel W.** Medicine, society and faith in the ancient
and medieval worlds. 1996, ⇒12,10630. ᴿCIR 47 (1997) 344-346
*(Horden, Peregrine)*.
11177   **Appelboom, Thierry; Bluard, Christine** L'art de guérir: images
de la pensée médicale à travers les temps. Anvers 1997, Fonds
Mercator 222 pp. Bibl. 90-6153-394-5.
11178   **Avalos, Hector I.** Illness and health care in the ancient Near
East: the role of the temple in Greece, Mesopotamia, and Israel.
HSM 54: 1995, ⇒11/2,c408; 12,10631. ᴿBiOr 54 (1997) 406-
410 *(Stol, M.)*; JAOS 117/1 (1997) 169-171 *(Biggs, Robert D.)*;
AJS Review 22/1 (1997) 107-109 *(Noegel, Scott B.)*.

**Flashar, H.** Médicine et morale dans l'antiquité ⇒362.

11179 ᴱ**Garofalo, Ivan** Anonymus Darembergii: de morbis acutis et chroniis. ᵀ*Fuchs, Brian.* Studies in Ancient Medicine 12: Lei 1997, Brill xxx; 375 pp. With commentary. 90-04-10227-2.

11180 **Grandet, Pierre** Le papyrus Harris I (BM 9999). 1994, 2 vols, ⇒10,13490. ᴿJESHO 40 (1997) 295-299 *(Haring, Ben).*

11181 *Haussperger, Martha* Die mesopotamische Medizin und ihre Ärzte aus heutiger Sicht. Zsfg. 196. ZA 87 (1997) 196-218.

11182 **Hogan, Larry P.** Healing in the Second Temple period. NTOA 21: 1992, ⇒8,k59... 10,13492. ᴿEstB 55 (1997) 275-277 *(González García, F.).*

11183 ᴱ**Jacob, Irene: Jacob, Walter** The healing past: pharmaceuticals in the biblical and rabbinic world. 1993, ⇒9,283; 11/2,c458. ᴿJNES 56 (1997) 123-124 *(Biggs, Robert D.).*

11184 ᴱ**Lucas, Ernest** Christian healing: what can we believe?. L 1997, SPCK 202 pp. £13. 1-901443-00-0 [Ethics & Medicine 14,92s— Short, David].

11185 **Mazzini, Innocenzo** La medicina dei greci e dei romani: lettera-tura, lingua, scienza. Guide allo studio della Civiltà Romana 9/3: R 1997, Jouvence 2 vols. L50.000. 88-7801-248-3.

11186 **Métraux, Guy P.R.** Sculptors and physicians in fifth-century Greece: a preliminary study. Montreal 1995, McGill xvi; 154 pp. 15 pl. 4 fig. $40. 0-7735-1231-4. ᴿAJA 101 (1997) 604-605 *(King, Helen).*

11187 **Nunn, John F.** Ancient Egyptian medicine. 1996, ⇒12,10638. ᴿAJA 101 (1997) 405-406 *(Becker, Marshall Joseph)*; JARCE 34 (1997) 271 *(Harer, W. Benson)*; ArOr 65 (1997) 400-401 *(Krejčí, Jaromír).*

11188 **Stol, M.** Epilepsy in Babylonia. Cuneiform Monographs: 1993, ⇒9,15206; 11/2,c497. ᴿOLZ 92/1 (1997) 61-63 *(Freydank, Hel-mit).*

11189 *Wasserman, Nathan* An Old-Babylonian medical text against the kurarum disease. RA 90 (1996) 1-5. Addition. RA 91 (1997) 31-32.

11190 *Zias, J.* Diseases and their treatment in ancient Israel from a pa-laeopathological perspective. Qad. 30/1 (1997) 54-59 **H.**

U3 *Duodecim tribus;* **Israel tribes;** land ideology

11191 **Gafni, Isaiah M.** Land, center and diaspora: Jewish constructs in late antiquity. JSPE.S 21: Shf 1997, Academic 136 pp. £25/$40. 1-85075-644-9.

11192 **Halpern-Amaru, Betsy** Rewriting the bible: land and covenant in post-biblical Jewish literature. 1994, ⇒11/2,6784; 12,8055. ᴿJQR 88 (1997) 89-90 *(Mendels, Doron).*

11193 *Kallai, Zecharia* The twelve-tribe systems of Israel. VT 47 (1997) 53-90.

11194 *Lefebvre, Philippe* Mystère et disparition de Dan: de la Septante à l'Apocalypse. IX Congress IOSCS. SBL.SCSt 45: 1997, ⇒340. ᴱTaylor, B.A., 279-307 [Gn 49,17; 2 Sam 24,6; 1 Kgs 4; 2 Kgs 21,11; Rev 7].

11195  *Long, Burke O.* Scenery of eternity: William Foxwell
ALBRIGHT and notions of "Holy Land". 1997, ⇒29.
<sup>F</sup>GERSTENBERGER E.S., 317-332.
11196  **Neef, Heinz-Dieter** Ephraim. BZAW 238: 1995, ⇒11/2,c518.
<sup>R</sup>ThLZ 122 (1997) 137-139 *(Fritz, Volkmar)*; CBQ 59 (1997)
745-746 *(Hostetter, Edwin C.)*; JBL 116 (1997) 534-536 *(Hauser, Alan J.)*.
11197  **Rusconi, Carlo** Il grande pedagogo: il popolo ebreo nella bibbia.
Collab. *Schönborn, Card. Christoph; Rosen, David*: I libri dello
spirito cristiano, Biblioteca Universale Rizzoli: Mi 1997,
Biblioteca Universale Rizzoli 219 pp. L13.000. 88-17-11138-4.
11198  *Schoen, Ulrich* Jüdische, christliche und islamische Zionismen:
"the land is holy to all three". Dialog der Religionen 7/2 (1997)
191-196.
11199  *Stichel, Rainer* Die Zwölfstämme-Ordnung der Israeliten als
Idealverfassung nach byzantinischen Zeugnissen. Religion und
Gesellschaft. AOAT 248: 1997, ⇒235. <sup>E</sup>Albertz, R., 141-154.
11200  *Vannini, Francesco* Dalla terra promessa alla terra nuova. Som.
887. Presenza Pastorale 67 (1997) 887-909.
11201  **Weinfeld, Moshe** The promise of the land: the inheritance of the
land of Canaan by the Israelites. 1993, ⇒9,15229; 11/2,c521.
<sup>R</sup>JNES 56 (1997) 159-160 *(Knoppers, Gary N.)*.
11202  *Wilcken, John* The biblical promised land and Australian aboriginal peoples. ACR 74/1 (1997) 86-98.

### U4  *Viae,* roads, routes

11203  *Dearman, John Andrew* Roads and settlements in Moab. BA 60/4
(1997) 205-213.
11204  *Holum, Kenneth* Iter principis: Hadrian's imperial tour. BArR
23/6 (1997) 50-51, 76.
11205  *Joannès, Francis* Palmyre et les routes du désert au début du deuxième millénaire av. J.-C. Mari 8 (1997) 393-415.
11206  *Kennedy, David* Romans roads and routes in north-east Jordan.
Levant 29 (1997) 71-93.
11207  *Kessler, Karlheinz* 'Royal roads' and other questions of the Neo-
Assyrian communication system. Assyria 1995. 1997, ⇒376.
<sup>E</sup>Parpola, S., 129-136.
11208  *Mare, W. Harold* Abila and Palmyra: ancient trade and trade
routes from southern Syria into Mesopotamia. Aram 7 (1997)
189-215.
11209  **Mark, Samuel** From Egypt to Mesopotamia: a study of pre-
dynastic trade routes. Studies in nautical archaeology 4: College
Station, Tex 1997, Texas A & M University Press xiii; 181 pp.
Bibl. £25. 0-89096-777-6.
11210  **Pikoulas, Y.A.** Road network and defence from Corinth to Argos
and Arkadia. Athens 1995, Horos xvi; 450 pp. 87 maps; 128 ill.
<sup>R</sup>CIR 47 (1997) 399-400 *(Roy, J.)*.
11211  Das Wrack von Uluburun. WUB 6 (1997) 48-49.

### U5.0  *Ethnographia,* sociologia; servitus

11212  **Assmann, Jan** Das kulturelle Gedächtnis: Schrift, Erinnerung
und politische Identität in frühen Hochkulturen. Mü <sup>2</sup>1997, Beck
344 pp. DM38. 3-406-42375-2 [ThLZ 123,938s—Pöttner, M.].

11213  *Bar-Kochva, Bezalel* Mosaic Judaism and Judaism of the Second Temple period—the Jewish ethnography of Strabo. Sum. v. Tarbiz 66 (1997) 297-336 **H**.

11214  *Blanco, Severiano* La emigración en la biblia. Mision Abierta 5 (1997) 19-26.

11215  **Blaschke, Andreas** Quellen und Kommentare zur Geschichte und Bedeutung der Beschneidung in alt-, zwischen-, neu- und frühneutestamentlicher Zeit. Diss. Heidelberg 1997, <sup>D</sup>*Berger, K.*, 491 pp. [RTL 29,581].

11216  *Blasi, Anthony J.* Sociology of early christianity—by way of introduction. Sociology of Religion 58/4 (1997) 299-303.

11217  *Blenkinsopp, Joseph* The family in First Temple Israel. Families. 1997, ⇒219. <sup>E</sup>Perdue, L.G., 48-103.

11218  **Brisson, Luc** Le sexe incertain: androgynie et hermaphroditisme dans l'antiquité gréco-romaine. Vérité des mythes-sources: P 1997, Belles Lettres 172 pp. Bibl. 2-251-32425-9.

11219  *Carneiro, Robert L.* Eine Theorie zur Entstehung des Staates. Die Entstehung des Königtums. 1997, ⇒308. <sup>E</sup>Sigrist, C., 113-124.

11220  **Carrier, Hervé** Guide pour l'inculturation de l'évangile. Studia Sociali 5: R 1997, Gregorian University Press 384 pp. L40.000. 88-7652-704-4.

11221  <sup>E</sup>**Chalcraft, D.J.** Social-scientific Old Testament criticism: a Sheffield reader. BiSe 47: Shf 1997, Academic 400 pp. £15. 1-85075-813-1.

11222  *Collins, John J.* Marriage, divorce, and family in Second Temple Judaism. Families. 1997, ⇒219. <sup>E</sup>Perdue, L.G., 104-162.

11223  <sup>E</sup>**Cornell, Tim J.; Lomas, Kathryn** Gender and ethnicity in ancient Italy. Accordia Specialist Studies on Italy 6: L 1997, Accordia Research Institute ix; 156 pp. 1-873415-14-1.

11224  **Debergé, Pierre** Enquête sur le pouvoir: approche biblique et théologique. Racines: Montrouge 1997, Nouvelle Cité 205 pp. 2-85313-311-7.

11225  *deSilva, David A.* Investigating honor discourse: guidelines from classical rhetoricians. SBL.SPS 36 (1997) 491-525.

11226  *Dietrich, Walter* Wem das Land gehört: ein Beitrag zur Sozialgeschichte Israels im 6. Jahrhundert v.Chr. 1997, ⇒29. <sup>F</sup>GERSTENBERGER E.S., 350-376.

11227  *Duarte Castillo, Raúl* Israel acuñó su identidad en la época persa. EfMex 15 (1997) 165-176.

11228  *Eberts, Harry W.* Plurality and ethnicity in early christian mission. Sum. 305. Sociology of Religion 58/4 (1997) 305-321.

11229  *Eltrop, Bettina* Kinderarbeit. BiKi 52 (1997) 131-135.

11230  <sup>E</sup>**Fitzgerald, John T.** Greco-Roman perspectives on friendship. SBL Resources for Biblical Study 34: Atlanta, Georgia 1997, Scholars xiii; 330 pp. $45. 0-7885-0272-7.

11231  **Grimm, Veronika E.** From feasting to fasting, the evolution of a sin: attitudes to food in late antiquity. 1996, ⇒12,10684. JEarlyC 5 (1997) 467-468 *(Leyerle, Blake)*; JThS 48 (1997) 662-665 *(Rousseau, Philip)*.

11232  *Guijarro Oporto, Santiago* Datos textuales y arqueológicos sobre la familia en la Galilea del siglo I. La Bíblia i el Mediterrani. 1997, ⇒385. <sup>E</sup>Borrell, d'Agustí, 315-326.

11233  **Harrill, J. Albert** The manumission of slaves in early christianity. HUTh 32: 1995, ⇒11/1,4889; 12,10685. <sup>R</sup>Milltown

Studies 39 (1997) 150-2 *(Byrne, Patrick)*; RB 104 (1997) 465-67 *(Murphy-O'Connor, J.)*; ChH 66 (1997) 548-549 *(Hanson, Craig L.)*; TJT 13 (1997) 276-278 *(Smith, Daniel A.)* [1 Cor 7,21].

11234 *Hesse, Brian; Wapnish, Paula* Can pig remains be used for ethnic diagnosis in the ancient Near East?. The archaeology of Israel. JSOT.S 237: 1997, ⇒9790. ᴱSilberman, N.A., 238-270.

11235 *Horrell, David* Leadership patterns and the development of ideology in early christianity. Sum. 323. Sociology of Religion 58 (1997) 323-341.

11236 **Horsley, Richard A.** Sociology and the Jesus movement. 1989, ⇒7,e673... 10,13611. ᴿVJTR 61 (1997) 640-641 *(Lobo, Jossie)*.

11237 *Horsley, Richard A.* Popular prophetic movements at the time of Jesus: their principal features and social origins. NT backgrounds. 1997 <1986>, ⇒3975. ᴱEvans, C.A., 124-148.

11238 **Ilan, Tal** Jewish women in Greco-Roman Palestine: an inquiry into images and status. TSAJ 44: 1996, ⇒12,10693. ᴿJJS 48/1 (1997) 156-159 *(Schwartz, Joshua)*; AJS Review 22/1 (1997) 114-116 *(Reinhartz, Adele)*; TJT 13 (1997) 259-261 *(Batten, Alicia)*; CBQ 59 (1997) 583-584 *(Love, Stuart L.)*; JBL 116 (1997) 354-357 *(Wegner, Judith Romney)*; BTB 27 (1997) 177 *(Lillie, Betty Jane)*.

11239 **Jones, S.** The archaeology of ethnicity: constructing identities in the past and present. L 1997, Routledge xiv; 180 pp. Bibl. 0-415-14158-3.

11240 **Just, Felix** From Tobit to Bartimaeus, from Qumran to Siloam: the social role of blind people and attitudes toward the blind in New Testament times. Diss. Yale 1997, ᴰMeeks, W.A. [RTL 29,585].

11241 *Kirchschläger, Walter* The generation gap: a biblical perspective. ThD 44 (1997) 243-246 <Diak. 27 (1996) 366-372.

11242 **Konstan, David** Friendship in the classical world. Key Themes in Ancient History: C 1997, CUP xiv; 206 pp. Bibl. 0-521-45998-2.

11243 *Kraus, Wolgang* Zum Begriff der Deszendenz: ein selektiver Überblick. Anthr. 92 (1997) 139-163.

11244 **Krause, Jens-Uwe** Witwen und Waisen im römischen Reich I-IV. 1994-1995, ⇒10,13621; 12,10701. ᴿJAC 40 (1997) 211-217 *(Noethlichs, Karl Leo)*.

11245 *Lluís Font, Pere* Reflexions sobre la inculturació grecoromana del cristianisme. La Bíblia i el Mediterrani. 1997, ⇒385. ᴱBorrell, d'Agustí, 191-204.

11246 **Lüdemann, Gerd** Heretics: the other side of early christianity. 1996, ⇒12,10704. ᴿRRT (1997/1) 27-29 *(Young, Frances M.)*; JEarlyC 5 (1997) 585-586 *(Spoerl, Kelley McCarthy)*.

11247 **Markschies, Christoph** Zwischen den Welten wandern: Strukturen des antiken Christentums. Fischer-Taschenbücher 60101: Fra 1997, Fischer-Taschenbuch-Verl. 284 pp. 3-596-60101-0.

11248 **Matthews, Victor H.; Benjamin, Don C.** Social world of ancient Israel. 1250-587 BCE. 1993, ⇒9,15342... 12,10708. ᴿBZ 41 (1997) 288-290 *(Zapff, Burkard)*.

11249 **McKenzie, Steven L.** All God's children: a biblical critique of racism. LVL 1997, Westminster x; 140 pp. $12. 0-664-25695-3 [ThD 44,371—Heiser, W. Charles].

11250 *Methuen, Charlotte* The "virgin widow": a problematic social role for the early church?. HThR 90 (1997) 285-298.

11251 *Meyers, Carol* The familiy in early Israel. Families. 1997, ⇒219. <sup>E</sup>Perdue, L.G., 1-47.

<sup>E</sup>**Moggi, M.** Schiavi e dipendenti ⇒368.

11252 *Morgan, Lewis H.* Das Eigentum auf der oberen Stufe der Barbarei. Die Entstehung des Königtums. 1997, ⇒308. <sup>E</sup>Sigrist, C., 33-42.

<sup>E</sup>**Moxnes, H.** Constructing early christian families ⇒295.

11253 *Olivier, Johannes P.J.* Restitution as economic redress: the fine print of the Old Babylonian *mešarum*-edict of Ammiṣaduqa. ZAR 3 (1997) 12-25 [Lev 25; Dt 15; Neh 5; Jer 34].

11254 **Ortwein, Gudrun** Status und Statusverzicht im Neuen Testament und seiner Umwelt. Diss. Heidelberg 1997-98, <sup>D</sup>*Theissen, G.*, 300 pp. [RTL 29,587].

11255 *Pearson, Birger A.* Unity and diversity in the early church as a social phenomenon. The emergence. 1997, ⇒154. 169-185.

11256 *Perdue, Leo G.* The household, Old Testament theology, and contemporary hermeneutics;

11257 The Israelite and early Jewish family: summary and conclusions. Families. 1997, ⇒219. <sup>E</sup>Perdue, L.G., 223-257/163-222.

11258 *Rattrey, Robert S.* Landbesitz und -veräußerung bei den Aschanti. Entstehung des Königtums. 1997, ⇒308. <sup>E</sup>Sigrist, C., 25-32.

11259 *Riches, John K.* The social world of Jesus. Gospel interpretation. 1997, ⇒210. <sup>E</sup>Kingsbury, J.D., 283-294.

11260 *Sellnow, Irmgard* Die Errichtung von Zentralgewalten bei einigen südafrikanischen Viehzüchtervölkern;

11261 *Sigrist, Christian* Der antiherrschaftliche Widerstand. Entstehung des Königtums. 1997, ⇒308. <sup>E</sup>Sigrist, C., 93-100/191-192;

11262 Ein Gemeinwesen ohne Obrigkeit: Gedanken zu WELLHAUSENS Akephalie-Paradigma. Religion und Gesellschaft. AOAT 248: 1997, ⇒235. <sup>E</sup>Albertz, R., 133-140;

11263 Das Gleichheitsbewußtsein als Determinante der Akephalie. Entstehung des Königtums. 1997, ⇒308. <sup>E</sup>Sigrist, C., 186-190.

11264 *Smith-Christopher, Daniel L.* Reassessing the historical and sociological impact of the Babylonian exile (597/587-539 BCE). Exile. JSJ.S 56: 1997, ⇒227. <sup>E</sup>Scott, J.M., 7-36.

11265 *Southall, Aidan W.* Zum Begriff des segmentären Staates: das Beispiel der Alur. Entstehung des Königtums. 1997, ⇒308. <sup>E</sup>Sigrist, C., 67-92.

11266 *Sprinkle, Joe M.* Old Testament perspectives on divorce and remarriage. JETS 40 (1997) 529-550.

11267 *Stager, Lawrence; Smith, Patricia* DNA analysis sheds new light on oldest profession at Ashkelon. BArR 23/4 (1997) 16.

11268 *Stähler, Klaus* Der Gärtner als Herrscher. Religion und Gesellschaft. AOAT 248: 1997, ⇒235. <sup>E</sup>Albertz, R., 109-114.

11269 **Stegemann, Ekkehard W. & Wolfgang** Urchristliche Sozialgeschichte: die Anfänge im Judentum und die Christusgemeinde in der mediterranen Welt. 1995, ⇒11/2,c756; 12,10725. <sup>R</sup>ActBib 34 (1997) 208-209 *(Boada, J.)*.

11270 *Stiegler, Stefan* Geöffnete Gemeinschaft: alttestamentliche Anmerkungen zum Thema "Gemeinde und Mitgliedschaft". Zeitschrift für Theologie und Gemeinde 2 (1997) 207-218.

11271 *Tanret, Michel; Dekiere, Luc* Un esclave est vendu. RA 90 (1996) 161-169.

11272 **Theissen, Gerd** Social reality and the early christians. 1992, ⇒8,k258... 12,10727. ᴿSJTh 50 (1997) 509-510 *(Barclay, John)*;

11273 Histoire sociale du christianisme primitif. MoBi 33: 1996, ⇒12,10728. ᴿETR 72 (1997) 139-140 *(Cuvillier, Élian)*; BLE 98 (1997) 77-78 *(Debergé, P.)*; CBFV 36 (1997) 169-174 *(Lanoir, Corinne)*; RHPhR 77 (1997) 241-242 *(Prigent, P.)*; VieCon 69 (1997) 333-334 *(Luciani, Didier)*.

11274 ᴱ**Van Tongerloo, Alois** La fête dans les civilisations orientales [Feasts in the oriental civilisations]. Collab. *Ries, Julien; Cannuyer, Christian*: Acta Orientalia Belgica 10: Bru 1997, Société Belge d'Études Orientales x; 234 pp. Bibl. du *L. Leloir* pp. 6-18.

11275 *Wanamaker, Charles A.* Jesus the ancestor: reading the story of Jesus from an African christian perspective. Scriptura 62 (1997) 281-298.

11276 *Wright, Benjamin G. III* Jewish ritual baths—interpreting the digs and the texts: some issues in the social history of Second Temple Judaism. The archaeology of Israel. JSOT.S 237: 1997, ⇒9790. ᴱSilberman, N.A., 190-214.

11277 **Wudke, Kurt** Von der Sippe zum Staat: aus den Berichten des Alten Testaments zum Werden eines Volkes. Fra 1997, Haag und H 142 pp. 3-86137-614-8 [NThAR 1998,335].

11278 **Zwingenberger, Uta** Dorfkultur der frühen Eisenzeit in Mittelpalästina. Diss. Münster 1997/98, ᴰ*Zenger* [BZ 42,317].

## u5.3 Commercium, oeconomica

11279 **Aberbach, Moshe** Labor, crafts and commerce in ancient Israel. 1994, ⇒11/2,a206; 12,9538. ᴿJAOS 117 (1997) 365-366 *(McNutt, Paula M.)*.

11280 **Badian, Ernst** Zöllner und Sünder: Unternehmer im Dienst der römischen Republik. ᵀ*Will, Wolfgang; Cox, Stephen*: DaWiss 1997, 263 pp. DM58 [BiKi 52/3,142].

11281 **Cline, Eric H.** Sailing the wine-dark sea: international trade and the Late Bronze Age Aegean. 1994, ⇒10,13696; 11/2,c802. ᴿAJA 101 (1997) 399-400 *(Rehak, Paul)*.

11282 **Felber, Heinz** Demotische Ackerpachtverträge der Ptolemäerzeit: Untersuchungen zu Aufbau, Entwicklung und inhaltlichen Aspekten einer Gruppe von demotischen Urkunden. ÄA 58: Wsb 1997, Harrassowitz viii; 243 pp. 3-447-03972-8.

11283 **Gelb, Ignace,** *(al.)*, Earliest land tenure systems in the Near East I-II. 1989-1991, ⇒7,d698; 10,13439. ᴿBSOAS 60 (1997) 542-543 *(Geller, M.J.)*.
ᴱ**Gillis, C.** Trade and production in pre-monetary Greece ⇒392.

11284 *Hopkins, David C.* The weight of the bronze could not be calculated: Solomon and economic reconstruction. The age of Solomon. 1997, ⇒282. ᴱHandy, L.K., 300-311.

11285 *Joannès, Francis; Lemaire, André* Contrats babyloniens d'époque achéménide du bît-abî râm avec une épigraphie araméenne. RA 90 (1996) 41-60.

11286 *Klengel, Horst* Eine altbabylonische Kaufurkunde betreffend Feld von "Stiftsdamen" des Gottes Šamaš in Sippar. AOAT 247: 1997, ⇒75. <sup>F</sup>ROELLIG W., 163-170.

11287 *Michel, C.* À table avec les marchands paléo-assyriens. Assyrien im Wandel. 1997, ⇒379. <sup>E</sup>Waetzoldt, H., 95-113.

11288 *Müller, Gerfrid G.W.* Gedanken zur neuassyrischen "Geldwirtschaft". Assyrien im Wandel. 1997, ⇒379. <sup>E</sup>Waetzoldt, H., 115-121.

11289 **Nissen, Hans J.** Archaic bookkeeping... in the ancient Near East. 1993, ⇒9,15429. <sup>R</sup>JNES 56 (1997) 292-294 *(Nemet-Nejat, K.R.)*.

11290 **Pastor, Jack** Land and economy in ancient Palestine. L 1997, Routledge. $75. 0-415-15960-1 [NEA(BA) 62/1,56s—Harrison, Timothy P.].

11291 **Skaist, Aaron** The Old Babylonian loan contract. 1994, ⇒11/2,c847; 12,10754. <sup>R</sup>Or. 66 (1997) 124 *(Simonetti, Cristina)*; AfO 44-45 (1997-98) 347-349 *(Charpin, Dominique)*.

11292 **Smith, Stuart Tyson** Askut in Nubia: the economics and ideology of Egyptian imperialism in the second millennium BC. 1995, ⇒11/2,c848. <sup>R</sup>Cambridge Archaeological Journal 7/1 (1997): 125-131 *(Kemp, Barry)*; 131-133 *(Trigger, Bruce G.)*; 133-135 *(Postgate, Nicholas)*; 135-137 *(Sinopoli, Carla M.)*; DiscEg 38 (1997) 139-148 *(Taylor, John H.)*; JAR 53 (1997) 491-493 *(Wegner, Joseph W.)*.

11293 *Vargyas, P.* Getreidekursangaben und Preistarife in Assyrien und Babylonien des 2. und 1. Jahrtausends. Assyrien im Wandel. 1997, ⇒379. <sup>E</sup>Waetzoldt, H., 185-190.

11294 *Veenhof, Klaas R.* 'Modern' features in Old Assyrian trade. Sum. 336. JESHO 40 (1997) 336-366.

11295 *Yakar, J.* Anatolian trade with Syro-Mesopotamia prior to the establishment of the Assyrian merchant colonies. Assyrien im Wandel. 1997, ⇒379. <sup>E</sup>Waetzoldt, H., 365-372.

## u5.7 Nomadismus, ecology

11296 **Andrews, Peter Alford** Nomad tent types in the Middle East. Collab. *Centlivres-Demont, M.; Tapper, R.L.* BTAVO.B 74/1.1-2: Wsb 1997, Reichert 2 vols, v. 1: Text; v. 2: Ill. 3-88226-890-5.

11297 *Echlin, Edward P.* Jesus, the hope of creation. Month 30 (1997) 437-441.

11298 **Khazanov, Anatoly M.** Nomads and the outside world. <sup>T</sup>*Crookenden, Julia*: Madison 1994, Univ. of Wisconsin Press lix; 382 pp. $18.50. <sup>R</sup>RStR 23 (1997) 350 *(Saidel, Benjamin Adam)*.

11299 *Van Koppen, Frans* L'expédition à Tilmun et la révolte des bédouins. Mari 8 (1997) 417-429.

## u5.8 Urbanismus

11300 *Alston, Richard; Alston, Robert D.* Urbanism and the urban community in Roman Egypt. Sum. 199. JEA 83 (1997) 199-216.

11301   *Banning, E.B.* Spatial perspectives on early urban development in Mesopotamia. Urbanism. JSOT.S 244: 1997, ⇒265. <sup>E</sup>Aufrecht, W.E., 17-34.

11302   *Clason, A.T.; Buitenhuis, H.* Change and continuity in the animal food resources in Bronze Age towns of the orient. Die orientalische Stadt. 1997, ⇒406. <sup>E</sup>Wilhelm, G., 199-219.

11303   **Cohen, Getzel M.** The Hellenistic settlements in Europe, the islands and Asia Minor. 1996, ⇒12,10764. <sup>R</sup>AJA 101 (1997) 798-799 *(Walbank, F.W.)*.

11304   *Fortin, Michel* Urbanisation et "redistribution" de surplus agricoles en Mésopotamie septentrionale (3000-2500 av. J.-C.). Urbanism. JSOT.S 244: 1997, ⇒265. <sup>E</sup>Aufrecht, W.E., 50-81.

11305   *Frevel, Christian* Die Stadtkultur in Israel und Juda in der Königszeit. Lebendige Welt. 1997, ⇒565. <sup>E</sup>Zenger, E., 94-123.

11306   **Fritz, Volkmar** The city in ancient Israel. BiSe 29: 1995, ⇒11/2,c878. <sup>R</sup>CBQ 59 (1997) 117-118 *(Higginbotham, Carolyn)*.

11307   *Gawlikowski, Michal* The oriental city and the advent of Islam;

11308   *George, A.R.* 'Bond of the lands': Babylon, the cosmic capital;

11309   *Heinz, Marlies* Räumliche Ordnung und Stadtkonzepte bronzezeitlicher Siedlungen am mittleren Euphrat in Syrien. Die orientalische Stadt. 1997, ⇒406. <sup>E</sup>Wilhelm, G., 339-350/125-145/289-305.

11310   **Heinz, Marlies** Der Stadtplan als Spiegel der Gesellschaft: Siedlungsstrukturen in Mesopotamien als Indikator für Formen wirtschaftlicher und gesellschaftlicher Organisation. B 1997, Reimer x; 155; 26 pp. 3-496-02620-0.

11311   *Heinz, Marlies* Wandel und Kontinuität als Konzepte der Stadtarchäologie. Die orientalische Stadt. 1997, ⇒406. <sup>E</sup>Wilhelm, G., 67-71.

11312   *Herr, Larry G.* Urbanism at Tell el-ʿUmeiri during the late Bronze IIB-Iron IA transition. Urbanism. JSOT.S 244: 1997, ⇒265. <sup>E</sup>Aufrecht, W.E., 145-155.

11313   **Herzog, Zeʾev** Archaeology of the city: urban planning in ancient Israel and its social implications. Tel Aviv University, Nadler Institute of Archaeology MS 13: Sydney 1997, Yass xiii; 299 pp. $60. 965-440-006-5.

11314   **Kasher, Aryeh** Jews and Hellenistic cities in Eretz Israel. TSAJ 21: 1990, ⇒7,e832; 11/2,c888. <sup>R</sup>TJT 13/1 (1997) 107-108 *(Kloppenborg, John S.)*.

11315   *Liverani, Mario* Ancient Near Eastern cities and modern ideologies;

11316   *Machule, Dittmar* Wandel, Kontinuität und Bruch: die historische Dimension der orientalischen Stadt im Spiegel aktueller Stadtforschung. Die orientalische Stadt. 1997, ⇒406. <sup>E</sup>Wilhelm, G., 85-107/45-66.

11317   *MacKay, D. Bruce* A view from the outskirts: realignments from modern to postmodern in the archaeological study of urbanism. Urbanism. JSOT.S 244: 1997, ⇒265. <sup>E</sup>Aufrecht, W.E., 278-285.

11318   <sup>E</sup>**Manzanilla, Linda** Emergence and change in early urban societies. Fundamental issues in archaeology: NY 1997, Plenum xv; 301 pp. $49.50. 0-306-45494-7.

11319   *Maul, Stefan M.* Die altorientalische Hauptstadt—Abbild und Nabel der Welt;

11320 *Mazzoni, Stefania* The gate and the city: change and continuity in Syro-Hittite urban ideology;

11321 *Novák, Mirko* Die orientalische Residenzstadt: Funktion, Entwicklung und Form;

11322 *Pfälzner, Peter* Die Erklärung städtischen Wandels;

11323 Wandel und Kontinuität im Urbanisierungsprozeß des 3. Jtsds. v.Chr. in Nordmesopotamien;

11324 *Pollock, Susan* Ökonomische Aspekte der urbanen Entwicklung in der Uruk-Zeit. Die orientalische Stadt. 1997, ⇒406. <sup>E</sup>Wilhelm, G., 109-24/307-38/169-97/73-84/239-265/221-237.

11325 *Redford, Donald B.* The ancient Egyptian "city": figment or reality?;

11326 *Rosen, Arlene Miller* The agricultural base of urbanism in the early Bronze Age;

11327 *Rosen, Steven A.* Craft specialization and the rise of secondary urbanism: a view from the southern Levant. Urbanism. JSOT.S 244: 1997, ⇒265. <sup>E</sup>Aufrecht, W.E., 210-220/92-98/82-91.

11328 *Rösel, Hartmut N.* Zur Bedeutung der Stadt im alttestamentlichen Israel. BN 89 (1997) 22-26.

11329 *Routledge, Bruce* Learning to love the king: urbanism and the state in Iron Age Moab;

11330 *Routledge, Carolyn* Temple as the center in ancient Egyptian urbanism;

11331 *Rupp, David W.* "Metro" Nea Paphos: suburban sprawl in southwestern Cyprus in the Hellenistic and earlier Roman periods;

11332 *Sweet, Ronald F.G.* Writing as a factor in the rise of urbanism. Urbanism. JSOT.S 244: 1997, ⇒265. <sup>E</sup>Aufrecht, W.E., 130-144/221-235/236-262/35-49.

11333 *Tate, Georges* Les villes syriennes aux époques hellénistique, romaine et byzantine. Die orientalische Stadt. 1997, ⇒406. <sup>E</sup>Wilhelm, G., 351-358.

11334 *Tsipopoulou, Metaxia* Palace-centred polities in eastern Crete: neopalatial Petras and its neighbors. Urbanism. JSOT.S 244: 1997, ⇒265. <sup>E</sup>Aufrecht, W.E., 263-277.

11335 **Van de Mieroop, Marc** The ancient Mesopotamian city. Oxf 1997, Clarendon xv; 269 pp. £37.50. 0-19-815062-8.

11336 *Weinfeld, Moshe* Einleitung. Land der Bibel. 1997, ⇒9960. <sup>E</sup>Seipel, W., 15-17,

11337 **Winter, Bruce W.** Seek the welfare of the city: christians as benefactors and citizens. 1994, ⇒11/2,c908; 12,10773. <sup>R</sup>RRT (1997/1) 95-96 *(Capper, Brian)*; RB 104 (1997) 460-462 *(Taylor, Justin)*.

11338 *Wirth, Eugen* Kontinuität und Wandel der orientalischen Stadt: zur Prägung von städtischem Leben und städtischen Institutionen durch jahrtausendealte kulturraumspezifische Handlungsgrammatiken. Die orientalische Stadt. 1997, ⇒406. <sup>E</sup>Wilhelm, G., 1-44.

## υ6 Narrationes peregrinorum et exploratorum; *Loca sancta*

11339 *Bowsher, Julian M.C.* An early nineteenth century account of Jerash and the Decapolis: the records of William John BANKES. Levant 29 (1997) 227-246.

11340   **Cunz, Martin** Die Fahrt des Rabbi NACHMAN von Brazlaw ins Land Israel (1798-1799): Geschichte, Hermeneutik, Texte. Diss. Luzern, ᴰ*Thoma, Clemens*: TSMJ 11: Tü 1997, Mohr xviii; 392 pp. DM198. 3-16-146628-4.
11341   *Dauphin, Claudine* On the pilgrim's way to the holy city of Jerusalem: the Basilica of Dor in Israel. Archaeology and biblical interpretation. 1997, ⇒268. ᴱBartlett, J.R., 145-165.
11342   *Donner, Herbert* Heracleustibus. AOAT 247: 1997, ⇒75. ꟳROELLIG W., 91-96.
11343   *Dunand, Françoise* Lieu sacré païen et lieu sacré chrétien: autour des pèlerinages. Le comparatisme. 1997, ⇒346. ᴱBoespflug, F., 239-253.
11344   **García Martín, Pedro** La cruzada pacífica: la peregrinación a Jerusalén de Don Fadrique Enríquez de RIBERA. Barc 1997, Serbal 160 pp. [Hispania 58,1194s—Bunes Ibarra, M.A. de].
11345   **Külzer, Andreas** Peregrinatio graeca in Terram Sanctam. 1994, ⇒12,10781. ᴿOrthFor 11/1 (1997) 76-83 *(Prinzing, Günter)*; OstKSt 46 (1997) 337-339 *(Garzaniti, Marcello)*.
11346   *Maraval, Pierre* The bible as a guide for early christian pilgrims to the Holy Land. The bible in Greek christian antiquity. 1997 <c.1984>, ⇒177. ᴱᵀBlowers, P.M., 375-388;
11347   Récits des premiers pèlerins chrétiens au Proche-Orient: JEROME et PAULA (385-386). VS 77 (1997) 759-775.
11348   *Miedema, Nine* "Transforming textual material into numbers": een reactie op Josephie BREFELDS A Guidebook for the Jerusalem Pilgrimage in the Late Middle Ages. OGE 71 (1997) 181-92.
11349   *Noonan, Patrick* The boat people: (a pilgrimage to Capernaum [pop. 1500] in the year 28 A.D. Holy Land 17 (1997) 98-100.
11350   *Vikan, Gary* Don't leave home without them: pilgrim eulogiai ensure a safe trip. BArR 23/4 (1997) 56-65.
11351   *Villefranche, Henri de* La bible sur le terrain. VS 77 (1997) 667-671.

υ7  *Crucigeri*—**The Crusades;** *Communitates Terrae Sanctae*

11352   **Johns, C.N.** Pilgrims' Castle ('Atlit), David's Tower (Jerusalem) and Qalʿat ar-Rabad ('Ajlun): three Middle Eastern castles from the time of the crusades. ᴱ*Pringle, Denys;* Pref. *Johns, Adam*: CStS: Aldershot 1997, Ashgate xx; 398 pp. £75. 0-86078-627-7 [RB 105,312].
11353   ᴱ**Phillips, Jonathan** The first crusade: origins and impact. Manchester 1997, Manchester Univ. Press xvi; 202 pp. £40/£15 [IHR 20,149ss—Cowdrey, H.E.J.].
11354   **Riley-Smith, Jonathan Simon Christopher** The first crusaders, 1095-1131. C 1997, CUP vi; 300 pp. $45. 0-521-59005-1 [ThD 45,187—Heiser, W. Charles].

11355   *Barkay, Gabriel* Politics—not religious law—rules ultra-orthodox demonstrators. BArR 23/6 (1997) 56-57, 77.
11356   **Beltrame, Fabio** Palestina ai palestinesi. Pref. *Morace, Sara*: Altrimenti 3: R 1997, Prospettiva 124 pp. 88-8022-024-1.

11357 **Cragg, Kenneth** Palestine: the prize and price of Zion. L 1997, Cassell xviii; 237 pp. £17. 0-304-70075-4 [Theol. 101,218s— Need, Stephen W.].

11358 *Elon, Amos* Politics and archaeology. The archaeology of Israel. JSOT.S 237: 1997, ⇒9790. ᴱSilberman, N.A., 34-47.

11359 *Hage, Wolfgang* Die kirchliche Vielfalt des Christentums im Orient. WUB 3 (1997) 33-34.

11360 **Rösch-Metzler, Wiltrud** Ohne Wasser, ohne Land, ohne Recht: an der Seite der Palästinenser: die israelische Rechtsanwältin Lynda BRAYER. Ostfildern bei Stu 1997, Schwaben 170 pp. 3-7966-0902-3.

11361 *Shavit, Yaacov* Archaeology, political culture, and culture in Israel;

11362 *Silberman, Neil Asher* Structuring the past: Israelis, Palestinians, and the symbolic authority of archaeological monuments. The archaeology of Israel. JSOT.S 237: 1997, ⇒9790. ᴱSilberman, N.A., 48-61/62-81.

## XX. Historia scientiae biblicae

### γ1.0 History of exegesis: General

11363 **Bammel, Caroline P.** Tradition and exegesis in early christian writers. L 1995, Variorum xii; 312 pp. $87.50. ᴿAThR 79 (1997) 604-605 *(Grant, Robert M.).*

11364 *Bauer, Johannes B.* Vexierzitate. Studien zu Bibeltext. 1997 <1984>, ⇒111. 45-59.

11365 ᵀ**Bigel, Jean-Pierre** Lire la Bible à l'école des pères: de JUSTIN martyr à BONAVENTURE. Introd. *Hamman, A.G.*: Annotation de *Marie-Hélène Congourdeau*: CPF 66: Turnhout 1997, Brepols 278 pp. FF90. 2-908587-27-0 [RHPhR 77,251].

11366 *Burton-Christie, Douglas* Oral culture and biblical interpretation in early Egyptian monasticism. StPatr 30: 1997, ⇒351. ᴱLivingstone, E.A., 144-150.

11367 ᴱ**Cipriani, Nello** Gesù, il figlio: testi dei padri della chiesa. I Padri Vivi: R 1997, Città Nuova 140 pp. L16.000. 88-311-2900-7.

11368 *Clark, Elizabeth A.* Reading asceticism: exegetical strategies in the early christian rhetoric of renunciation. Bibl.Interp. 5 (1997) 82-105.

11369 *Di Cristina, Salvatore* Il metodo teologico dei Padri. Laós 4/1 (1997) 43-60.

11370 *Dorner, Stephan* Die Theologie der alttestamentlichen Schriftstellen in der 'Regula Benedicti'. EuA 73 (1997) 19-33.

11371 **Gamble, Harry Y.** Books and readers in the early church. 1995, ⇒11/2,g094; 12,10808. ᴿJRH 21/1 (1997) 112-113 *(Pickering, Stuart R.)*; NT 39 (1997) 301-302 *(Rodgers, Peter R.)*; JBL 116 (1997) 552-553 *(Fox, R.J. Lane)*; CritRR 10 (1997) 15-37 *(Epp, Eldon Jay).*

11372 **Gibert, Pierre** Breve storia dell'esegesi biblica. Giornale di Teologia 238: 199, ⇒12,10809. ᴿGr. 78 (1997) 372-373 *(Marconi, Gilberto)*; CivCatt 148 II (1997) 415-417 *(Scaiola, D.).*

11373  **Hinson, E. Glenn** The church triumphant: a history of christianity up to 1300. 1995, ⇒11/2,g102. RChH 66 (1997) 335-336 (*Noble, Thomas F.X.*).

11374  *Hinson, E. Glenn* Women biblical scholars in the late fourth century: the Aventine Circle. StPatr 30: 1997, ⇒351. ELivingstone, E.A., 319-324.

11375  *La Potterie, Ignace de* Le sens spirituel de l'Écriture [*Lubac, Henri de*]. Sum. 645. Gr. 78 (1997) 627-645.

11376  **Ladner, Gerhart B.** God, cosmos and humankind: the world of early christian symbolism. 1995, ⇒11/2,g112. RJEarlyC 5 (1997) 588-590 (*Finney, Paul Corby*).

11377  **Laporte, Jean** La bible et les origines chrétiennes. 1996, ⇒12,10814. RSR 26 (1997) 359-361 (*Lamirande, Émilien*).

11378  *Le Brun, Jacques* Exégèse herméneutique et logique au XVIIe siècle. XVIIe Siècle 49 (1997) 19-30 [EThL 74,165*].

11379  *Leanza, Sandro* La letteratura esegetica in frammenti: la tradizione catenaria. Aug. 37 (1997) 25-36.

11380  *Maritano, Mario* Ermia e la metensomatosi (Irrisio 3-5). BSRel 125: 1997, FJAVIERRE ORTAS A., 181-204.

11381  *Markschies, Christoph* Altkirchliche Christologie und Neues Testament: Beobachtungen zur Bibelhermeneutik des AMBROSIUS von Mailand. BZNW 86: 1997, ⇒41. FHOFIUS O., 875-905;

11382  Wann endet das 'Konstantinische Zeitalter'?: eine Jenaer Antrittsvorlesung. BZNW 85: 1997, ⇒105. FWICKERT U., 157-188.

11383  *McNamara, Martin* The bible in academe and in ecclesia: Antiochene and early Irish exegesis of Messianic psalms. MillSt 39 (1997) 112-129.

11384  **Nodes, D.J.** Doctrines and exegesis in biblical Latin poetry. 1993, ⇒10,14342; 11/2,g754. RAt. 85/1 (1997) 344-345 (*Jucci, Elio*).

11385  *Paulsen, Henning* Auslegungsgeschichte und Geschichte des Urchristentums—die Überprüfung des Paradigmas <1989>;

11386  Zur Wissenschaft vom Urchristentum und der alten Kirche—ein methodischer Versuch <1977>. Zur Literatur. WUNT 99: 1997, ⇒153. 412-425/365-395.

11387  **Raurell, Frederic** I Cappucini e lo studio della bibbia. R 1997, Istituto Francescano di Spiritualità iv; 489 pp. 84-920074-8-6. RRCatT 22 (1997) 445-446 (*Ricart, Ignasi*).

11388  **Reventlow, Henning Graf** Epochen der Bibelauslegung I-II. 1990-1994, ⇒6,k10... 11/2,g136, g767. ROrdKor 38 (1997) 226-228 (*Heinemann, Franz Karl*); ThRv 93 (1997) 383-384 [Vol. 2] (*Hödl, Ludwig*).

11389  **Rinaldi, Giancarlo** La bibbia dei pagani: 1, quadro storico; 2, testi e documenti. Bo 1997, EDB 2 vols; 428; 654 pp. L47.000 + 59.000 [RdT 39,948].

11390  *Roux, R.* The doctrine of the imitation of Christ in the *Liber Graduum*: between exegetical theory and soteriology. StPatr 30: 1997, ⇒351. ELivingstone, E.A., 259-264.

11391  **Salisbury, Joyce E.** Perpetua's Passion: the death and memory of a young Roman woman. NY 1997, Routledge 228 pp. Bibl. 0-415-91837-5.

11392  ESæbø, **Magne** Hebrew Bible/OT: the history of its interpretation 1:... Middle Ages. 1996, ⇒12,10821. RJThS 48 (1997) 630-

633 *(Lange, N.R.M. de)*; SJOT 11 (1997) 307-310 *(Petersen, Allan Rosengren)*; CBQ 59 (1997) 809-811 *(Cook, Joan E.)*; JBTh 12 (1997) 335-351 *(Schaper, Joachim)*.

11393 Schrama, Martijn Letterlijk en figuurlijk: de uitleg van de heilige Schrift in de patristische traditie. Com(NL) 22 (1997) 434-448 [EThL 74,163*].

11394 Sellin, Gerhard Die Allegorese und die Anfänge der Schriftauslegung. Theologische Probleme. 1997, ⇒223. ᴱReventlow, Henning Graf, 91-132.

11395 Simonetti, Manlio Letteratura in frammenti dei primi tre secoli. Aug. 37 (1997) 5-24.

11396 Sources chrétiennes. Les Pères de l'Église au XXe siècle: histoire—littérature—théologie: "L'aventure des Sources chrétiennes". Patrimoines, Christianisme: P 1997, Cerf 575 pp. 2-204-05498-4.

11397 Studer, Basil Neuerscheinungen zur Exegese der Kirchenväter. ThRv 93 (1997) 91-94.

11398 **Winteler, Victor** Auf den Spuren der Bibel: von Qumran bis CHAGALL. Basel 1995, Brunnen 111 pp. 3-7655-6802-3 [NThAR 2000,2].

11399 Young, Frances The fourth century reaction against allegory. StPatr 30: 1997, ⇒351. ᴱLivingstone, E.A., 120-125.

Y1.4 *Patres apostolici et saeculi II*—First two centuries

11400 Callam, Daniel Bishops and presbyters in the Apostolic Fathers. StPatr 31: 1997, ⇒351. ᴱLivingstone, E.A., 107-111.

11401 Carleton Paget, James The vision of the church in the Apostolic Fathers. 1997, ⇒93. ᶠSᴡᴇᴇᴛ J., 193-206.

11402 Crouzel, Henri The theology of the first three centuries: the school of Alexandria and its fortunes. History of Theology, 1. 1997, ⇒241. ᴱDi Berardino, A., 145-184.

11403 Frend, W.H.C. Christianity in the second century: orthodoxy and diversity. JEH 48 (1997) 302-313.

11404 Grech, Prosper The theology of the first three centuries: the beginnings of christian theology. History of Theology, 1. 1997, ⇒241. ᴱDi Berardino, A., 17-81.

11405 **Günther, Matthias** Einleitung in die Apostolischen Väter. ARGU 4: Fra 1997, Lang xi; 135 pp. 3-631-31242-3.

11406 Noormann, Rolf Himmelsbürger auf Erden: Anmerkungen zum Weltverhältnis und zum "Paulinismus" des Auctor ad Diognetum. BZNW 85: 1997, ⇒105. ᶠWɪᴄᴋᴇʀᴛ U., 199-229.

11407 Olbricht, Thomas H. Exegesis in the second century. Handbook. NTTS 25: 1997, ⇒971. ᴱPorter, S.E., 407-423.

11408 **Orbe, Antonio** La teologia de secoli II e III: il confronto della grande chiesa con lo gnosticismo I-II. 1995, ⇒11/2,g161; 12,10835. ᴿCivCatt 148 IV (1997) 301-304 *(Cremascoli, G.)*.

11409 Osborn, Eric The theology of the first three centuries: the Greco-Roman world: challenge and response. History of Theology, 1. 1997, ⇒241. ᴱDi Berardino, A., 82-118.

11410 Paulsen, Henning Erwägungen zu Acta Apollonii 14-22 <1975>;

11411   Papyrus Oxyrhynchus I.5 und die διαδοχὴ τῶν προφητῶν
        <1979>. Zur Literatur. WUNT 99: 1997, ⇒153. 210-219/162-
        172.
11412   **Ridings, Daniel** The Attic Moses: the dependency theme in some
        early christian writers. SGLG 59: 1995, ⇒11/2,g164; 12,10837.
        ᴿSpec. 72/2 (1997) 558-559 *(Chadwick, Henry)*; At. 85/2 (1997)
        676-679 *(Belloni, Luigi)*.
11413   *Simonetti, Manlio* The theology of the first three centuries: a
        theology without learning. History of Theology, 1. 1997, ⇒241.
        ᴱDi Berardino, A., 185-191.
11414   *Stewart-Sykes, Alistair* Papyrus Oxyrhynchus 5: a prophetic pro-
        test from second century Rome. StPatr 31: 1997, ⇒351.
        ᴱLivingstone, E.A., 196-205.

11415   CLEMENS A: *Harcus, A.R.* They speak to us across the centu-
        ries 1: Clement of Alexandria. ET 108 (1997) 292-295;
11416   *Riutort Mestre, Pere* Bíblia i món clàssic a CLIMENT
        d'Alexandria. La Bíblia i el Mediterrani. 1997, ⇒385. ᴱBorrell,
        d'Agustí, 351-363.
11417   ᴱᵀ**Le Boulluec, Alain** Clemens Alexandrinus: Stromata: les Stro-
        mates: Stromate VII. Introd., texte critique, trad., notes; Bibl.
        SC 428: P 1997, Cerf 351 pp. FF197. 2-204-05828-9;
11418   *Osborn, Eric* The bible and christian morality in CLEMENT of
        Alexandria. The bible in Greek christian antiquity. 1997
        <c.1984>, ⇒177. ᴱᵀBlowers, P.M., 112-130;
11419   *Edsman, Carl-Martin* CLEMENT of Alexandria and Greek
        myths;
11420   *Harding, Sara Fletcher* Christ as greater than Moses in
        CLEMENT of Alexandria's *Stromateis* I-II. StPatr 31: 1997,
        ⇒351. ᴱLivingstone, E.A., 385-388/397-400;

11421   CLEMENS R: *Sánchez Bosch, Jordi* Santiago, Pedro y Pablo en
        las Seudoclementinas. StAns 124: 1997, ⇒57. ꟻLOEHRER M. —
        TRAGAN P., 547-573;
11422   *Pratscher, Wilhelm* Soteriologie und Ethik im Kontext von
        Eschatologie und Schöpfungslehre in 2.Clem 1. BZNW 89: 1997,
        ⇒33. ꟻGRAESSER E., 261-274;
11423   Schriftzitate im 2. Klemensbrief. SNTU.A 22 (1997) 139-159.

11424   DIDACHE: ᴱ**Jefford, Clayton N.** The Didache in context. NT.S
        77: 1995, ⇒10,248... 12,10866. ᴿLouvSt 22 (1997) 93-95 *(Ver-
        heyden, Joseph)*; CBQ 59 (1997) 806-807 *(Finn, Thomas M.)*;
11425   *Bridge, Steven L.* To give or not to give?: deciphering the saying
        of *Didache* 1.6. JEarlyC 5 (1997) 555-568;
11426   *Draper, Jonathan A.* Resurrection and Zechariah 14,5 in the Di-
        dache Apocalypse. JEarlyC 5/2 (1997) 155-179;
11427   *Rordorf, Willy* Die Mahlgebete in Didache Kap. 9-10: ein neuer
        Status quaestionis. VigChr 51 (1997) 229-246.

11428   HERMAS: *Stewart-Sykes, A.* The christology of Hermas and the
        interpretation of the fifth similitude. Aug. 37 (1997) 273-284;
11429   *O'Brien, D.P.* The Cumaean Sibyl as the revelation-bearer in the
        *Shepherd of Hermas*. JEarlyC 5 (1997) 473-496;

11430 **Brox, Norbert** Der Hirt des Hermas. KAV 7: 1991, ⇒7,g46...
10,13978. RJAC 40 (1997) 220-224 *(Hilhorst, A.)*;
11431 **Ayán Calvo, Juan José** Hermas: el pastor. 1995, ⇒11/2,g205;
12,10874. RScrTh 29/1 (1997) 292-293 *(Ramos-Lissón, D.)*; EE
72 (1997) 382-383 *(Raczkiewicz, Marek)*.

11432 IGNATIUS: *Lucca, Claudia* Ignazio di Antiochia e il martirio:
un'analisi de *Romani* 2. Sal. 59 (1997) 621-645;
11433 *Rius-Camps, Josep* L'espistolari d'Ignasi d'Antioquia (VI): tra-
ducció, notes i comentari: carta espúria a Policarp, part de la
cloenda de la primitiva carta d'Ignasi als Efesis. Sum. 45. RCatT
22 (1997) 1-45;
11434 *Lindemann, Andreas* Antwort auf die "Thesen zur Echtheit und
Datierung der sieben Briefe des Ignatius von Antiochien";
11435 *Hübner, Reinhard M.* Thesen zur Echtheit und Datierung der sieben Briefe des Ignatius von Antiochien. ZAC 1 (1997) 185-
194/44-72;
11436 *Paulsen, Henning* Ignatius von Antiochien. Zur Literatur.
WUNT 99: 1997, ⇒153. 141-153;
11437 *Rius-Camps, Josep* El protognosticismo de los docetas en las cartas de IGNACIO, el obispo de Siria *(IEph-ISme ITr)*, y sus cone-
xiones con los evangelios contemporáneos. StPatr 31: 1997,
⇒351. ELivingstone, E.A., 172-195.

11438 IRENAEUS: EMaschio, Giorgio; Bellini, Enzo <ed> Irenaeus
Lugdunensis: Adversus haereses [Contro le eresie: e gli altri
scritti]. Già e non ancora 320: Mi 1997, Jaca 700 pp. Bibl. 88-
16-30320-4;
11439 *Lanne, Emmanuel* Le nom de Jésus-Christ et son invocation chez
saint Irénée de Lyon. Tradition. BEThL 129: 1997 <1975-76>,
⇒142. 69-100;
11440 *Jourjon, Maurice* IRENAEUS's reading of the bible. The bible in
Greek christian antiquity. 1997 <c.1984>, ⇒177. ETBlowers,
P.M., 105-111;
11441 **Grant, Robert M.** Irenaeus of Lyons. The Early Church Fathers:
L 1997, Routledge vi; 214 pp. Bibl. $75. 0-415-11838-7;
11442 **Fantino, Jacques** La théologie d'Irénée: lecture des Écritures en
réponse à l'exégèse gnostique: une approche trinitaire. CFi 180:
1994. RJThS 48 (1997) 241-244 *(Minns, D.)*;
11443 **Donovan, Mary Ann** One right reading?: a guide to Irenaeus.
ColMn 1997, Liturgical x; 197 pp. Bibl. 0-8146-5875-X;
11444 TEBrox, Norbert Irenaeus von Lyon: Adversus haereses: gegen
die Häresien, IV. Fontes christiani 8/4: 1997, Herder 396 pp. 3-
451-22128-4/228-0;
11445 *Wyrwa, Dietmar* Kosmos und Heilsgeschichte bei IRENAEUS
von Lyon. BZNW 85: 1997, ⇒105. FWICKERT U., 443-480;
11446 *(a) Lanne, Emmanuel* L'église de Rome 'a gloriosissimis duobus
apostolis Petro et Paulo Romae fundatae et constituae ecclesiae'
(AH III.3,2). Tradition. BEThL 129: 1997 <1976>, ⇒142.
101-138.
*(b) Raponi, Sante* Cristo Gesù, compimento delle attese
dell'umanità in S. Ireneo di Lione. RVS 51 (1997) 446-465.

11447   JUSTINUS: *Munier, Charles* A propos d'une édition récente des Apologies de Justin. RevSR 71 (1997) 299-309;
11448   *Price, R.M.* Are there 'holy pagans' in JUSTIN Martyr?. StPatr 31: 1997, ⇒351. ELivingstone, E.A., 167-171;
11449   **Misiarczyk, Leszek** Elementi midrashici nel dialogo con Trifone di Giustino martire: l'esegesi messianica di alcune profezie vete-rotestamentarie. R 1997, Pontificia Universitas Lateranensis xliv; 97 pp. Pars diss;
11450   *Merlo, Paolo* Argomenti di teologia fondamentale in San Giustino. BSRel 125: 1997, ⇒45. FJAVIERRE ORTAS A, 143-179;
11451   EMarcovich, Miroslav Iustini martyris dialogus cum Tryphone. PTS 47: B 1997, De Gruyter xv; 339 pp. DM198. 3-11-015-738-1 [Bijdr. 58,359];
11452   *Widdicombe, Peter* JUSTIN Martyr, allegorical interpretation, and the Greek myths [Gal 2,2];
11453   *Pouderon, Bernard* Le contexte polémique du *De resurrectione* attribué à JUSTIN: destinataires et adversaires. StPatr 31: 1997, ⇒351. ELivingstone, E.A., 234-239/143-166;
11454   *Hill, Charles E.* JUSTIN and the New Testament writings. StPatr 30: 1997, ⇒351. ELivingstone, E.A., 42-48;
11455   TBarnard, Leslie William Justin Martyr: the first and second apologies. ACW 56: Mahwah, NJ 1997, Paulist vi; 245 pp. Introd., notes. $30. 0-8091-0472-5. RJEarlyC 5 (1997) 602-603 *(Horner, Timothy J.)*.

11456   POLYCARPUS: TBauer, Johannes B. Die Polykarpbriefe. 1995, ⇒11/2,g238; 12,10887. RJAC 40 (1997) 218-220 *(Löhr, Winrich A.)*;
11457   *Holmes, Michael W.* A note on the text of Polycarp Philippians 11.3. VigChr 51 (1997) 207-210.

## Y1.6 Origenes

11458   *Anatolios, Khaled* Christ, scripture, and the christian story of meaning in ORIGEN. Rés. 77. Gr. 78 (1997) 55-77.
11459   TEAntoniono, Normando Origenes: de oratione: la preghiera. R 1997, Città N 211 pp. 88-311-3138-9.
11460   *Bammel, Ernst* Die Zitate aus den Apokryphen bei ORIGENES <1991>;
11461   Die Zitate in ORIGENES' Schrift wider CELSUS <1987>. Judaica et Paulina. WUNT 91: 1997, ⇒109. 161-167/57-61.
11462   *Borret, Marcel* CELSUS: a pagan perspective on scripture. The bible in Greek christian antiquity. 1997 <c.1984>, ⇒177. ETBlowers, P.M., 259-288.
11463   *Bunge, Gabriel* 'Créé pour être': à propos d'une citation scriptu-raire inaperçue dans le 'Peri Archon' d'ORIGENE (III,5,6). BLE 98 (1997) 21-29 [Wis 1,14].
11464   *Choi, Mihwa* Christianity, magic, and difference: name-calling and resistance between the lines in Contra Celsum. Semeia 79 (1997) 75-92.

11465 **Clark, Elizabeth** The Origenist controversy: the cultural construction of an early christian debate. 1992, ⇒8,k669... 11/2,g243. ᴿSJTh 50/1 (1997) 115-117 *(Cameron, Averil)*.

ᴱ**Cocchini, F.** Il dono e la sua ombra: ricerche sul Peri euches di Origene ⇒349.

11466 *Cocchini, Francesca* La bibbia nel περι ευχης: problematiche storico-esegetiche. Il dono. 1997, ⇒349. ᴱCocchini, F., 97-115.;

11467 La "lettera", il "velo" e l'"ombra": presupposti scritturistici della polemica antigiudaica di Origene. ASEs 14 (1997) 101-119.

11468 ᴱ**Dorival, Gilles; Le Boulluec, Alain** Origeniana Sexta: Origène et la Bible. 1995, ⇒11/2,571; 12,10893. ᴿStPat 44 (1997) 224-226 *(Corsato, Celestino)*; ThLZ 122 (1997) 341-344 *(Ullmann, Wolfgang)*; JEH 48 (1997) 737-739 *(Clark, Elizabeth A.)*; ChH 66 (1997) 540-541 *(Trigg, Joseph W.)*; CDios 210 (1997) 645-647 *(Gutiérrez, J.)*.

11469 *Edwards, M.J.* Precursors of Oʀɪɢᴇɴ's hermeneutic theory. StPatr 29: 1997, ⇒351. ᴱLivingstone, E.A., 232-237.

11470 **Fédou, Michel** La sagesse et le monde: le Christ d'Origène. CJJC: 1995, ⇒11/2,g251; 12,10894. ᴿTS 58 (1997) 156-158 *(Bright, Pamela)*; ASEs 14 (1997) 554-556 *(Pieri, Francesco)*.

11471 *Fernández Eyzaguirre, Samuel* ¡Oh, hombre, quién eres tú, para pedir cuentas a Dios! (Rom 9,20): Orígenes en defensa del método de las *quaestiones et responsiones*. Epimeleia 6 (1997) 155-170 [Rom 9,20].

11472 ᴱ**Geerlings, Wilhelm; König, Hildegard** Origenes: vir ecclesiasticus. Hereditas 9: 1995, Symposium *H.-J. Vogt*. ⇒11/2,539; 12,10895. ᴿZKG 108/2 (1997) 255-256 *(Böhm, Thomas)*.

11473 *Heine, Ronald* Reading the bible with Oʀɪɢᴇɴ. The bible in Greek christian antiquity. 1997 <c.1984>, ⇒177. ᴱᵀBlowers, P.M., 131-148.

11474 **Laporte, Jean** Théologie liturgique de Pʜɪʟᴏɴ d'Alexandrie et d'Origène. 1995, ⇒11/2,6835; 12,8088. ᴿMD 209 (1997) 127-130 *(Wolinski, Joseph)*.

11475 *Lyman, J. Rebecca* The making of a heretic: the life of Oʀɪɢᴇɴ in Epiphanius *Panarion* 64. StPatr 31: 1997, ⇒351. ᴱLivingstone, E.A., 445-451.

11476 *Scognamiglio, Rosario* 'Il santuario che stiamo costruendo è la chiesa...': commento di Origene sulla costruzione del tempio. PaVi 42/6 (1997) 45-48.

11477 *Simonetti, Manlio* The theology of the first three centuries: the east after Oʀɪɢᴇɴ. History of Theology, 1. 1997, ⇒241. ᴱDi Berardino, A., 192-204.

11478 *Vos, Johan S.* Das Agraphon "Seid kundige Geldwechsler!" bei Origenes. NT.S 89: 1997, ⇒7. ᶠBᴀᴀʀᴅᴀ T., 277-302.

## Y1.8 Tertullianus

11479 ᴱ**Braun, René** Tertullien: contre Marcion. SC 365, 368, 399: 1990-1994, 3 vols, ⇒10,14031*; 11/2,g272. ᴿGn. 69 (1997) 602-612 *(Tränkle, Hermann)*.

11480 *Brennecke, Hanns Christof* 'An fidelis ad militiam converti possit'? (Tertullian, *De idolatria* 19,1): frühchristliches Bekenntnis

und Militärdienst im Widerspruch?. BZNW 85: 1997, ⇒105.
FWICKERT U., 45-100.

11481  **Georgeot, J.-M.** Index. De Saint-Marc jusqu'à Tertullien 2/1:
n.p. 1997, n.p. 126 pp.

11482  *Osborn, Eric* Tertullian as philosopher and Roman. BZNW 85:
1997, ⇒105. FWICKERT U., 231-247.

11483  **Osborn, Eric Francis** Tertullian, first theologian of the West. C
1997, CUP xxi; 285 pp. Bibl. £40/$60. 0-521-59035-3.

11484  *Vinzent, Markus* Christ's resurrection: the Pauline basis of
MARCION's teaching. StPatr 31: 1997, ⇒351. ELivingstone,
E.A., 225-233 [Gal 2,02].


ɣ2.0  *Patres graeci*—The Greek Fathers


11485  **Bardy, Gustave** Storia della letteratura cristiana antica greca:
storia letteraria, 'letteratura critica e approfondimenti. EDi Nola,
*Gerardo*: Città del Vaticano 1996, Vaticana 582 pp. Bibl. RMar.
59 (1997) 349-351 *(Maritano, Mario)*.

11486  *Bauer, Johannes B.* Zu den christlichen Gedichten der Anthologia
Graeca. Studien zu Bibeltext. 1997 <1961>, ⇒111. 128-136.

11487  *George, Martin* Vergöttlichung des Menschen": von der platoni-
schen Philosophie zur Soteriologie der griechischen Kirchenväter.
BZNW 85: 1997, ⇒105. FWICKERT U., 115-155.

11488  TGrant, Robert M.; Menzies, Glen W. Joseph's bible notes
(Hypomnestikon). SBL.TT 41/9: 1996, ⇒12,10908. RJThS 48
(1997) 258-261 *(Adler, William)*; BiOr 54 (1997) 195-197 *(Van
der Horst, P.W.)*; ThLZ 122 (1997) 460-462 *(Niebuhr, Karl-
Wilhelm)*.

11489  *Nikolaou, Theodor* Die Rolle der Philosophie in der griechischen
Patristik: einige Grundgedanken. MThZ 48 (1997) 301-312.


11490  BASILIUS Caes.: **Fedwick, Paul Jonathan** The *Homiliae mora-
les, Hexaemeron, De litteris* with additional coverage of the letters. Bibliotheca Basiliana universalis: a study of the manuscript
tradition, translations and editions of the works of Basil of Caesarea. CChr.SG: Turnhout 1996, Brepols 2 vols; lxiv; 1326 pp.
Part one: Manuscripts, part two: Editions, translations. 2-503-5-
520-1/1-2. RRHE 92 (1997) 523-525 *(Gain, B.)*;

11491  EVan Roey, Albert Une homélie inédite contre les Anoméens attri-
buée à saint Basile de Césarée. OLoP 28 (1997) 179-191.

11492  ETThomson, Robert W. The Syriac version of the *Hexaemeron*
by Basil of Caesarea. CSCO 550-551: 1995, ⇒11/1,275.
RMuséon 110/1-2 (1997) 251-254 *(Mathews, E.G.)*;

11493  **Rousseau, Philip** Basil of Caesarea. Transformation of the Classical Heritage 20: 1994, ⇒10,14085... 12,10914. RZKG 108
(1997) 256-260 *(Vinzent, Markus)*; RHE 92 (1997) 520-522
*(Gain, B.)*.


11494  CHRYSOSTOMUS: *Childers, J.W.* CHRYSOSTOM's exegetical
homilies on the New Testament in Syriac translation. StPatr 33:
1997, ⇒351. ELivingstone, E.A., 509-516.

11495 ᵀStébé, Marie-Hélène Joannes Chrysostomus: homiliae: la conversion. CPF 8: P ²1997, Migne 175 pp. Introd., notes *A.G. Hamman.* Bibl. 2-908587-29-7;

11496 **Rau, Eckhard** Von Jesus zu Paulus: Entwicklung und Rezeption der antiochenischen Theologie im Urchristentum. 1994, ⇒10,14092; 12,10918. ᴿJBL 115 (1996) 548-550 *(Donaldson, Terence L.)*;

11497 **Kelly, J.N.D.** Golden Mouth: the story of John Chrysostom, ascetic, preacher, bishop. 1995, ⇒11/2,g337; 12,10917. ᴿAThR 79 (1997) 273-274 *(Vivian, T.)*; ChH 66 (1997) 85-87 *(Mitchell, Margaret M.)*; CHR 83/2 (1997) 296-298 *(Ettlinger, Gerard H.)*; SJTh 50 (1997) 520-522 *(Louth, Andrew).*

11498 *Wylie, Amanda Berry* Musical aesthetics and biblical interpretation in John CHRYSOSTOM. StPatr 32: 1997, ⇒351. ᴱLivingstone, E.A., 386-392.

11499 DIONYSIOS Alexandria: *Tissot, Yves* Le rapt de Denys d'Alexandrie et la chronologie de ses lettres festales. RHPhR 77 (1997) 51-65.

11500 EUSEBIUS Emesenus: **Haar Romeny, Robert B. ter** A Syrian in Greek dress: the use of Greek, Hebrew and Syriac biblical texts in Eusebius of Emesa's Commentary on Genesis. Traditio exegetica graeca 6: Lv 1997, Peeters xii; 484 pp. Bibl. FB2.400. 90-6831-958-2.

11501 GREGORIUS Naz.: **Somers, Véronique** Histoire des collections complètes des discours de Grégoire de Nazianze. PIOL 48: Lv(N) 1997, Institut Orientaliste ix; 712 pp. 90-6831-963-9;

11502 *Norris, Frederick* GREGORY Nazianzen: constructing and constructed by scripture. The bible in Greek christian antiquity. 1997 <c.1984>, ⇒177. ᴱᵀBlowers, P.M., 149-162;

11503 **Demoen, Kristoffel** Pagan and biblical exempla in Gregory Nazianzen: a study in rhetoric and hermeneutica. CChr.LP II: 1996, ⇒12,10926. ᴿVigChr 51 (1997) 329-330 *(Bartelink, G.J.M.)*; ClR 47 (1997) 289-290 *(Tompkins, Ian G.).*

11504 GREGORIUS Nyssa: **Böhm, Thomas** Theoria, Unendlichkeit, Aufstieg: philosophische Implikationen zu *De vita Moysis* von Gregor von Nyssa. SVigChr 35: 1996, ⇒12,10928. ᴿVigChr 51 (1997) 321-323 *(Geljon, A.C.).*

11505 ISIDORUS Pelusiota: ᵀᴱÉvieux, Pierre Isidore de Péluse: lettres: tome I, lettres 1214-1413. SC 422: P 1997, Cerf 555 pp. Bibl. 2-204-05557-3.

11506 (*a*) JOHANNES Philiponos: ᵀᴱScholten, Clemens Johannes Philiponos: de opificio mundi: über die Erschaffung der Welt. FC 23/1-3: FrB 1997, Herder 3 vols. DM142. 3-451-23801-2/2-0/3-9 [Bijdr. 58,358].
(*b*) METHODIUS Olympius: **Patterson, Lloyd George** Methodius of Olympus: divine sovereignty, human freedom, and life in Christ. Wsh 1997, The Catholic University of America Press xiii; 261 pp. Bibl. $60. 0-8132-0875-0.

11507  SEVERIANOS Gabala: ᴱᵀ*Carter, Robert E.* A Greek homily on
       the temptation (CPG 4906) by Severian of Gabala: introduction,
       critical edition and translation. Tr. 52 (1997) 47-71 [Mt 4,1-11].

11508  THEODORETUS Cyrus: **Guinot, Jean-Noël** L'exégèse de Thé-
       odoret de Cyr. ThH 100: 1995, ⇒11/2,g403; 12,10934.
       ᴿOrpheus 18/1 (1997) 256-261 *(Simonetti, Manlio)*; ThPh 72
       (1997) 577-579 *(Sieben, H.J.)*; ThLZ 122 (1997) 922-926 *(Berg-
       jan, Silke-Petra)*; POC 46 (1996) 485-486 *(Ternant, P.)*; REG
       110 (1997) 683-685 *(Pouderon, Bernard)*; EThL 73 (1997) 468-
       471 *(Verheyden, J.)*; Ter. 48 (1997) 849-850 *(Diego Sánchez,
       Manuel)*;
11509  *Guinot, Jean-Noël* THEODORET of Cyrus: bishop and exegete.
       The bible in Greek christian antiquity. 1997 <c.1984>, ⇒177.
       ᴱᵀBlowers, P.M., 163-193;
11510  Les fondements scripturaires de la polémique entre juifs et chré-
       tiens dans les commentaires de Théodoret de Cyr. Sum. 4. ASEs
       14/1 (1997) 153-178.
11511  THEODOROS Mopsuestia: **Efrem, Yildiz** La 'teoria' biblica bat-
       tesimale secondo Mar Teodoros l'Interprete. Diss. extr. Pont.
       Univ. Urbaniana 1997, ᴰ*Federici, Tommaso*, 125 pp.


       Y2.4 **Augustinus**

11512  *Bochet, Isabelle* Le cercle herméneutique dans le *De doctrina
       christiana* d'AUGUSTIN;
11513  *Cameron, Michael* Transfiguration: christology and the roots of
       figurative exegesis in St. AUGUSTINE. StPatr 33: 1997, ⇒351.
       ᴱLivingstone, E.A., 16-21/40-47.
11514  ᴱ**Carrozzi, L.; Pollastri, A.** Sant'Agostino: locuzioni e questioni
       sull'ettateuco: questioni sulla Genesi: questioni su Esodo. Nuova
       Biblioteca Agostiniana, opere esegetiche 11/1: R 1997, Città N
       790 pp. Testo latino dell'edizione Maurina confrontato con il
       *Corpus Christianorum* e con il *Corpus Scriptorum Ecclesiastico-
       rum Latinorum* [REAug 44,367].
11515  *Cutino, Michele* Perlegi totum intentissime atque cautissime (C.
       Acad. 2,2,5): la cautela di Agostino nella lettura delle sacre scrit-
       ture. Helmantica 48 (1997) 365-374 [REAug 44,372].
11516  **Delaroche, Bruno** Saint Augustin lecteur et interprète de Saint
       Paul: dans le *De peccatorum meritis et remissione* (hiver 411-
       412). 1996, ⇒12,10937. ᴿETR 72 (1997) 141-142 *(Pérès,
       Jacques-Noël)*; JEarlyC 5 (1997) 303-305 *(Gorday, Peter J.)*.
11517  **Ferraro, Giuseppe** Lo spirito e Cristo: nel commento al quarto
       vangelo e nel trattato trinitario di Sant'Agostino. Letture bibliche
       9: Città del Vaticano 1997, Libreria Editrice Vaticana 251 pp.
       L39.000. 88-209-2435-8.
11518  **Fiedrowicz, Michael** Könnte ich dich je vergessen, Jerusalem?:
       der Gottesstaat im Spiegel der Psalmendeutung Augustins. Wü
       1997, Augustinus 170 pp.;
11519  Psalmus vox totius Christi: Studien zu Augustins 'Enarrationes in
       Psalmos'. FrB 1997, Herder 490 pp. Diss.-Habil. Bochum 1997.
       3-451-26406-4 [NThAR 1999,3].

11520 <sup>E</sup>**Fuhrer, Therese** Augustin, contra Academicos (vel De Academicis): Bücher 2 und 3. PTS 46: B 1997, De Gruyter x; 532 pp. 3-11-015204-5.

11521 <sup>T</sup>**Gentili, Domenico; Tarulli, Vincenzo,** *collab.*, Sant'Agostino: discorso del Signore sulla Montagna: questioni sui vangeli: diciassette questioni sul vangelo di Matteo: alcune questioni sulla lettera ai Romani: esposizione della lettera ai Galati: inizio dell'esposizione della lettera ai Romani. Nuova Biblioteca Agostiniana, opere esegetiche 10/2: R 1997, Città N 833 pp. Testo latino dell'edizione Maurina confrontato con il *Corpus Christianorum* e con il *Corpus Scriptorum Ecclesiasticorum Latinorum* [REAug 44,364].

11522 *Gillette, Gertrude* The glory of Christ's second coming in AUGUSTINE's *Enarrationes in psalmos.* StPatr 33: 1997, ⇒351. <sup>E</sup>Livingstone, E.A., 88-93.

  <sup>E</sup>*Gorday, P.* Selections from Augustine's propositions... Romans ⇒6354.

11523 *Gori, Franco* La tradizione manoscritta delle *Enarrationes in psalmos graduum* di AGOSTINO: studio preliminare per l'edizione critica. Aug. 37 (1997) 183-228.

11524 *Langa Aguilar, Pedro* La Sagrada Escritura y San Agustín predicador. RelCult 43/1 (1997) 69-89.

11525 *Larrabe, José Luis* El evangelio como ley de gracia según San Agustín. RevAg 38 (1997) 425-457.

11526 **Lössl, Josef** Intellectus gratiae: die erkenntnistheoretische und hermeneutische Dimension der Gnadenlehre Augustinus von Hippo. Leiden 1997, Brill xii; 501 pp. DM245.

11527 <sup>E</sup>**Mayer, Cornelius** Augustinus-Lexikon, 2: Vorspann, Fasc. 1/2: Cor-Deus. Basel 1996, Schwabe xlviii; 320 col. DM78. 3-7965-1007-8 [ThLZ 125,525ss—Zelzer, Michaela].

11528 **Neto, Ricardo Dias** 'Psalterium meum, gaudium meum': a alegria do justo na presença de Deus: doutrina de Santo Agostinho de Hipona nas *Enarrationes in Psalmos.* Excerpt Diss. Gregoriana no. 4390, R 1997, 99 pp. <sup>D</sup>*Pastor, Félix Alejandro.*

11529 **Rist, John M.** Augustine. 1994, ⇒11/2,g473. <sup>R</sup>ABR 45 (1997) 93-95 *(Osborn, Eric).*

11530 *Sahelices Gonzáles, Paulino* Seguir e mitar a Cristo, según San Agustín. RevAg 38 (1997) 631-664.

11531 **Scott, T. Kermit** Augustine: his thought in context. 1995, ⇒11/2,g474. <sup>R</sup>JEarlyC 5 (1997) 454-456 *(Martin, Thomas F.).*

11532 *Stead, Christopher* AUGUSTINE, the Meno and the subconscious mind. BZNW 85: 1997, ⇒105. <sup>F</sup>WICKERT U., 339-345.

11533 **Studer, Basil** The grace of Christ and grace of God in Augustine of Hippo: christocentrism or theocentrism?. <sup>T</sup>*O'Connell, Matthew*: Michael Glazier Book: ColMn 1997, Liturgical 262 pp. £23 [DoLi 48,510s—McCarthy, Thomas].

11534 *Studer, Basil Theologia-Oikonomia:* zu einem traditionellen Thema in AUGUSTIN *De Trinitate.* StAns 124: 1997, ⇒57. <sup>F</sup>LOEHRER M. — TRAGAN P., 575-600.

• 11535 <sup>T</sup>**Taruli, Vincenzo** Sant'Agostino: il consenso degli evangelisti. Opere di Sant'Agostino 10/1, libri, opere esegetiche. Nuova Biblioteca Agostiniana: R 1996, Città N cxxxvi; 546 pp. Testo latino dall'edizione Maurina confrontato con il *CSEL;* introd. *Pio de Luis* [REAug 43,387—Madec, Goulven].

11536 **Weidmann, Clemens** Die handschriftliche Überlieferung der Werke des Heiligen Augustinus: Werkverzeichnis. Collab. *Miskovská, Hana* et al.: DÖAW.PH 645; VKCLK 13-14: W 1997, Verlag der Österreichischen Akademie der Wissenschaften 2 vols. 3-7001-2660-3.

### γ2.5 Hieronymus

11537 *Clausi, Benedetto* Bibbia e polemica negli scritti controversiali di GEROLAMO. .

11538 *Duval, Yves-Marie* GEROLAMO tra TERTULLIANO e ORIGENE. Motivi letterari. 1997, ⇒331. ᴱMoreschini, C., 39-79/107-135.

11539 *Hennings, Ralph* Hieronymus zum Bischofsamt. ZKG 108 (1997) 1-11.

11540 ᴱ**Hilberg, Isidorus** Hieronymus: epistularum pars I (Ep. 1-70)—pars II (Ep. 71-120)—pars III (Ep. 121-154). Collab. *Smolak, Conradus*: CSEL 54-56/1: W ²1996, Verl. der Österr. Akad. der Wissenschaften 798; 515; 368 pp. [REAug 43,390—Touboulic, Anne-Isabelle].

11541 ᴱ**Kamptner, Margit** Hieronymus epistularum indices et addenda. CSEL 56/2: W 1996, Verl. der Österr. Akademie der Wissenschaften 312 pp. [REAug 43,390—Touboulic, Anne-Isabelle].

11542 **Laurence, Patrick** Jérôme et le nouveau modèle feminin: la conversion à la 'vie parfaite'. Coll. EtAug.Antiq. 155: P 1997, Institut des Études Augustiniennes 555 pp. FF362. 2-85121-167-6 [[RBen 109,244—Wankenne, L.].

11543 *Leanza, Sandro* GEROLAMO e la tradizione ebraica;

11544 *Menestrina, Giovanni* Varianti d'autore nel carteggio AGOSTINO-GEROLAMO;

11545 *Moreschini, Claudio* L'utilizzazione di PORFIRIO in GEROLAMO;

11546 *Nazzaro, Antonio V.* Intertestualità biblico-patristica e classica nell'*Epistola* 22 di GEROLAMO. Motivi letterari. 1997, ⇒331. ᴱMoreschini, C., 17-38/223-243/175-195/197-221.

11547 **Pernoud, Régine** Vita di San Girolamo. I triangoli 41: CasM 1997, Piemme 110 pp. L14.000. 88-384-2804-2 [Presenza pastorale 67,862].

11548 *Prinzivalli, Emanuela* 'Sicubi dubitas, hebraeos interroga': Girolamo tra difesa dell'*hebraica veritas* e polemica antigiudaica. Sum. 5. ASEs 14/1 (1997) 179-206.

11549 *Quacquarelli, Antonio* L'uomo e la sua appartenenza alle due città nell'esegesi biblica di GEROLAMO. Motivi letterari. 1997, ⇒331. ᴱMoreschini, C., 159-171.

11550 *Ratti, Stéphane* Jérôme et Nicomaque Flavien: sur les sources de la *Chronique* pour les années 357-364. Hist. 46 (1997) 479-508.

11551 **Reaburn, Mary Ann** Jerome's use of the psalms in his commentary on Daniel. Diss. Melbourne College of Divinity 1997-8, ᴰ*O'Hagan, Angelo* [Sum. Pacifica 11,246].

11552 **Rebenich, Stefan** Hieronymus und sein Kreis. Hist. 72: 1992, ⇒9,16040... 12,10960. ᴿZKG 108 (1997) 260-263 *(Krumeich, Christa)*.

11553 *Rebenich, Stefan* Asceticism, orthodoxy and patronage: JEROME in Constantinople. StPatr 33: 1997, ⇒351. ᴱLivingstone, E.A., 358-377.
11554 *Scourfield, J.H.D.* A note on JEROME's homily on the rich man and Lazarus. JThS 48 (1997) 536-539 [Lk 16,19-31].
11555 ᵀᴱValero, **Juan Bautista** San Jerónimo: epistolario. 1995, ⇒10,14210; 11/2,g525. ᴿTE 41 (1997) 460-462 *(Velasco, A.)*.
11556 *Weingarten, Susan* JEROME and the *Golden Ass*. StPatr 33: 1997, ⇒351. ᴱLivingstone, E.A., 383-389.

### Y2.6 Patres Latini *in ordine alphabetico*

11557 **Dekkers, E.** Clavis patrum latinorum. ³1995, ⇒12,10961. ᴿZKTh 119 (1997) 482-484 *(Kessler, Stephan Ch.)*; EThL 73 (1997) 121-143 *(Verheyden, J.)*.
11558 **Dodel, Franz** Das Sitzen der Wüstenväter: eine Untersuchung anhand der Apophthegmata Patrum. Par. 42: FrB 1997, Universitätsverlag x; 193 pp. Bibl. 3-7278-1110-2.
11559 ᴱᵀ**Fear, A.T.** Lives of the Visigothic Fathers. Translated texts for historians 26: Liverpool 1997, University Press xxxix; 167 pp. Bibl. 0-85323-582-1.

11560 AMBROSIUS M: **Pasini, Cesare** Ambrogio di Milano: azione e pensiero di un vescovo. 1996, ⇒12,10968. ᴿREAug 43/1 (1997) 214-216 *(Pouchet, Jean-Robert)*;
11561 **Ramsey, Boniface** Ambrose. The Early Church Fathers: L 1997, Routledge xi; 238 pp. Bibl. $55. 0-415-11-8425;
11562 *Ravasi, Gianfranco* Sant'Ambrogio: predicatore ed interprete della parola di Dio. Ambrosius 73/2 (1997) 143-147;
11563 **Savon, Hervé** Ambroise de Milan. P 1997, Desclée 382 pp. Bibl. 2-7189-0687-1;
11564 *Peretto, Elio* Testo biblico e sua applicazione nel *De obitu valentiniani* di AMBROGIO. 1997 <1989>, ⇒155. Saggi, 57-528;
11565 *Visonà, Giuseppe* Ambrogio Teodosio Davide: note sull'*Apologia prophetae David* e sull'*Apologia David altera* di sant'Ambrogio. AnScR 2 (1997) 257-299.

11566 CYPRIANUS: ᴱ**Gallicet, Ezio** Epistulae: la chiesa: sui cristiani caduti nella persecuzione: l'unità della chiesa cattolica: lettere scelte. LCPM 26: Mi 1997, Paoline 453 pp. Bibl. 88-315-1416-4;
11567 *Deléani, Simone* Quelques observations sur la syntaxe des titres dans les florilèges scripturaires de saint CYPRIEN. StPatr 31: 1997, ⇒351. ᴱLivingstone, E.A., 281-286;
11568 *Torrance, Iain* They speak to us across the centuries 2, Cyprian. ET 108 (1997) 356-359.

11569 EPHRAEM Syrus: ᵀ**Nin, Manel** Ephraem Syrus: contra haereses: homilia in meretricem: himnes i homilíes. Clàssics del Cristianisme 68: Barc 1997, Proa 230 pp. 84-8256-341-6;
11570 **Griffith, Sidney H.** 'Faith adoring the mystery': reading the bible with St. Ephraem the Syrian. Père Marquette Theology Lec-

ture 28: Milwaukee, Wis. 1997, Marquette University Press v; 62 pp. 0-87462-577-7 [NThAR 1997,289];

11571   **Feghali, Paul** Les origines du monde et de l'homme dans l'oeuvre de saint Éphrem. Antioche Chrétienne: P 1997, Cariscript 311 pp. FF180. 2-87601-253-7 [RTL 29,254—Houdart, Marie-André] [Acts 10,1-11,18].

11572   EUSEBIUS Caes.: ᴱᵀ**Meagher, P.M.**; **Velasco-Delgado, Argimiro** Eusebio de Cesarea: historia eclesiástica. M ²1997, BAC 2 vols; 82 + 690 pp. [EsVe 28,499s—Gómez, Vito T.];

11573   ᵀ**Traverso, Alberto** Eusebius Caesariensis: contra Hieroclem [Eusebio di Cesarea: contro Ierocle]. CTePa 137: R 1997, Città N 124 pp. 88-311-3137-O.

11574   FULGENTIUS Ruspensis: ᵀ**Eno, Robert B.** Fulgentius Ruspensis: opera selecta: selected works [The life of the Blessed Bishop Fulgentius; to Peter on the Faith; on the forgiveness of sins; to Monimus; the letters of Fulgentius]. FaCh 95: Wsh 1997, Cath. Univ. of America Pr. xviii; 583 pp. Bibl. 0-8132-0095-4.

11575   GREGORIUS Elvira: ᵀᴱ**Pascual Torró, Joaquín** Gregorio de Elvira: tratados sobre los libros de las santas escrituras. Fuentes Patrísticas 9: M 1997, Ciudad N 480 pp. Ptas5.000. 84-89651-17-5. ᴿEstAg 32 (1997) 566-567 *(Luis, P. de)*; Salm. 44 (1997) 438-442 *(Trevijano, Ramón)*;

11576   *Tovar Paz, Francisco Javier* La 'inversión del orden' en el *Tractatus in Sacram Scripturam* n.° 16 de Gregorio de Elvira. Emerita 65 (1997) 91-102 [EThL 74,178*].

11577   GREGORIUS M: ᵀ**Fiedrowicz, Michael** Evangelienhomilien. FC 28,1-2: FrB 1997-98, Herder 2 vols. 3-451-;

11578   **Markus, Robert Austin** Gregory the Great and his world. C 1997, CUP xxiii; 241 pp. Bibl. $60/$23. 0-521-58608-9;

11579   **Recchia, Vincenzo** Gregorio Magno papa. 1996, ⇒12,10974. ᴿSal. 59 (1997) 531-541 *(Dal Covolo, Enrico)*;

11580   *Kessler, Stephan Ch.* Die Exegese GREGORs des Großen am Beispiel der *Homiliae in Ezechielem*. StPatr 30: 1997, ⇒351. ᴱLivingstone, E.A., 49-53.

11581   HILARIUS, Pseudo-: *Bauer, Johannes B.* Der Bibletext und seine Interpretation bei Pseudo-Hilarius (Libellus). Studien zu Bibeltext. 1997 <1987>, ⇒111. 73-93.

11582   HILARIUS P: **Ferreira, Manuel Serra** Fé e profecia em Santo Hilário de Poitiers. Diss. ᴰ*Orbe, António*: Fundamenta 13: Lisboa 1995, Univ. Católica Portuguesa 295 pp. ᴿREAug 43/1 (1997) 210-211 *(Milhau, Marc)*.

11583   ISIDORO Leon: **Suárez González, Ana I.** Los códices III.1, III.2, III.3, IV y V: (Biblia, Liber capituli, Misal). Patrimonio Cultural de San Isidoro de León. Bᵢ Serie bibliográfica 2: León 1997, Universidad de León 542 pp. Bibl. 84-7719-595-1.

11584   LEO M: ᴱ**Naldini, Mario** Fra storia e teologia. I sermoni di Leone Magno, 1. Pref. *Ravasi, Gianfranco*: BPat 30: F 1997, Nardini 250 pp. 88-404-2035-5.

MAXIMUS Conf.: <sup>TE</sup>Argárate, P. Tratados espirituales
⇒4669;
<sup>T</sup>Congourdeau, M.-H. L'agonie du Christ ⇒7255.

11585 PACIANUS Barcinonensis: <sup>E</sup>Granado, Carmelo Pacien de Bar-
celone: écrits. <sup>T</sup>Épitalon, Chantal; Lestienne, Michel SC 410:
1995, ⇒11/2,g575. <sup>R</sup>REAug 43/1 (1997) 211-214 (Deléani, Simone).

11586 PAULINUS Nola: Swoboda, Antoni Egzegeza alegoryczna pisma
świętego w Listach Paulina z Noli [L'esegesi allegorica della
sacra scrittura nelle lettere di S. Paolino di Nola]. Riass. 268.
Vox Patrum 17 (1997) 261-268 P. [Ps 102,7-8; Mt 25,1-13].

11587 RUFINUS Aquileiensis: <sup>T</sup>Amidon, Philip R. Rufinus
Aquileiensis: Prologus in libros historiarum Eusebii: continuatio
Eusebii Historiarum; the Church History of Rufinus of Aquileia:
books 10 and 11. NY 1997, OUP xix; 132 pp. Bibl. 0-19-
511031-5.

11588 TYCHONIUS: <sup>E</sup>Leoni, Luisa & Daniela Ticonio: sette regole
per la scrittura. Epifania della Parola 4: Bo 1997, EDB 108 pp.
L21.000. 88-10-40231-6 [RivBib 45,384].

## Y3.0 Medium aevum, generalia

11589 Buc, Philippe L'ambiguité du livre: prince, pouvoir, et peuple
dans les commentaires de la bible au Moyen Age. ThH 95: 1994,
⇒10,14279... 12,10983. <sup>R</sup>JThS 48 (1997) 728-730 (Smith,
Lesley).

11590 Causse, Maurice Les "synoptiques franciscains" et leurs sources.
RHPhR 77 (1997) 273-299.

11591 Gorman, Michael WIGBOD and biblical studies under
CHARLEMAGNE. RBen 107 (1997) 40-76.

11592 Stella, Francesco La poesia carolingia latina a tema biblico.
MeLa Bt 9: 1993, ⇒9,16233. <sup>R</sup>MÄ 103/1 (1997) 117-129
(Meyers, Jean).

## Y3.4 Exegetae mediaevales [Hebraei ⇒K7]

11593 BEATO Liebana: Romero Pose, Eugenio La utilización del Gen
en BEATO de Liebana: el cristocentrismo de la creación. 1997,
⇒76. <sup>M</sup>RUIZ DE LA PENA J., 97-110.

11594 BEDA: Bonner, Gerald Bede—priest and scholar. MillSt 39
(1997) 66-77.

11595 BERNARD Clairvaux: Brigitte, Soeur Gesù e Gesù crocifisso in
San Bernardo. Sum. 339. La Sapienza della Croce 12-13/4-1
(1997-98) 339-351, 17-24;

11596 Bauer, Johannes B. Bibelzitate und Agrapha im mittellateinischen
Schrifttum am Beispiel BERNHARDS von Clairvaux. Studien zu
Bibeltext. 1997 <1992>, ⇒111. 113-127.

11597 BONAVENTURA da Bagnoregio, pseudo-: <sup>E</sup>Joannes de Caulibus; Stallings-Taney, M. Meditaciones vitae Christi. CChr.CM
153: Turnhout 1997, Brepols xxiii, 391 pp. olim S. Bonauenturo
attributae. 2-503-03000-9.

11598 CHRISTIANUS Stavelot: *Peretto, Elio* CRISTIANO di Stavelot: cultura ed esegesi etimologica. 1997 <1985>, ⇒155. Saggi, 321-344.

11599 ERIUGENA: **EVan Riel, Gerd; Steel, Carlos; McEvoy, James** Johannes Scottus Eriugena, the bible and hermeneutics. AMP 1/20: 1996, ⇒12,276. RE pimeleia 6 (1997) 343-348 *(Piemonte, Gustavo A.)*; RThPh 129 (1997) 195-196 *(Borel, Jean)*;

11600 **EContreni, John J.; Ó Néill, Pádraig P.** Joannes Scotus Eriugena: glossae divinae historiae: the biblical glosses of John Scottus Eriugena. Millennio Medievale I/Testi 1: F 1997, SISMEL xxx; 253 pp. L80.000. 88-87027-04-8. RPIBA 20 (1997) 99-107 *(McNamara, Martin)*.

11601 HRABANUS Maurus: **EPerrin, Michel** In honorem sanctae crucis. CChr.CM 100-100A: Turnhout 1997, Brepols 2 vols. 2-503-04001-2.

11602 HUGO St. Vict.: *Zinn, Grover A.* Hugh of St. Victor's *De Scripturis et Scriptoribus Sacris* as an Accessus treatise for the study of the bible. Tr. 52 (1997) 111-134.

11603 HOGO Orléans: *Bauer, Johannes B. Stola* und *tapeta*: zu den Oxforder Gedichten des Primas. Studien zu Bibeltext. 1997 <1982>, ⇒111. 107-112.

11604 ISIDORUS Pelusiota: **TEÉvieux, Pierre** Isidore de Péluse: Lettres I: 1214-1413. SC 422: P 1997, Cerf 555 pp. 2-204-05557-3.

11605 OLIVI Peter of John: **EFlood, David; Gál, Gedeon** Peter of John Olivi on the bible: principia quinque in sacram scripturam: postilla in Isaiam et in 1 ad Corinthios. Text 18: NY 1997, Franciscan Institute 431 pp. 1-57659-128-X [ETR 73,307].

11606 THOMAS Cobham: **EMorenzoni, Franco** Thomas de Chobham: summa de commendatione uirtutum et extirpatione uitiorum. CChr.CM 82B: Turnhout 1997, Brepols xviii; 309 pp. Bibl. 2-503-03825-5.

Y4.1 Luther

11607 **Asendorf, Ulrich** Lectura in Biblia—Luthers Genesisvorlesung (1534-1545). FSÖTh 87: Gö 1997, Vandenhoeck & R 503 pp. DM178. 3-525-56294-2 [LM 38,46—Wilckens, Ulrich].

11608 **Forde, Gerhard O.** On being a theologian of the cross: reflections on Luther's Heidelberg disputation, 1518. GR 1997, Eerdmans 121 pp. $20. [TrinJ 19,238ss—Gramm, Kent].

11609 **Genthe, Hans Jochen** Martin Luther: sein Leben und Denken. Gö 1996, Vandenhoeck & R 343 pp. 3-525-55433-8 [EE 72,561—Alemany, José J.].

11610 **Greschat, Martin; Lottes, Günther** Luther in seiner Zeit: Persönlichkeit und Wirken des Reformators. Stu 1997, Kohlhammer 127 pp. [SCJ 30,227s—Corpis, Duane].

11611 *Jüngel, Eberhard* ... unum aliquid assecutus, omnia assecutus ... zum Verständnis des Verstehens—nach M. Luther, De servo arbitrio (WA 18,605 = BoA 3,100). BZNW 86: 1997, ⇒41. FHOFIUS O., 73-99.

11612 **Kaennel, Lucie** Luther était-il antisémite?. Entrée libre 38: Genève 1997, Labor et F 112 pp. FF55. 2-8309-0869-4 [RTL 29,127].

11613 *Kvam, Kristen E.* 'The sweat of the brow is of many kinds': Luther on the duties of Adam and his sons. CThMi 24 (1997) 44-49 [Gen 3,17-19].

11614 *Lienhard, Marc* Luther est-il "protestant"?: le sacrement chez Luther et dans la tradition luthérienne. RHPhR 77 (1997) 141-64.

11615 *Müller, Hans Martin* 'Evangelium latuit in lege': Luthers Kreuzespredigt als Schlüssel seiner Bibelhermeneutik. BZNW 86: 1997, ⇒41. ᶠHoᴏꜰɪᴜs O., 101-126.

11616 *Sánchez Ramiro, Demetrio* Pecado original y bautismo en el comentario de Lᴜᴛᴇʀᴏ a Romanos. 1997, ⇒76. ᴹRᴜɪᴢ ᴅᴇ ʟᴀ Pᴇɴᴀ J., 245-261.

11617 *Schwier, Helmut* Gepredigtes und gefeiertes Abendmahl: Luthers Abendmahlspredigten im Kontext der Deutschen Messe. WuD 24 (1997) 237-262.

11618 **Thompson, Mark** A sure ground on which to stand: the relation of authority and interpretive method in Luther's approach to scripture. Diss. Oxf 1997, ᴰMcGrath, Alister E. [Abs. TynB 48,373-376].

11619 *Weinrich, Michael* Die Anfechtung des Glaubens: die Spannung zwischen Gewißheit und Erfahrung bei Martin Luther;

11620 *Welker, Michael* Wort und Geist. BZNW 86: 1997, ⇒41. ᶠHoᴏꜰɪᴜs O., 127-158/159-169.

### Y4.3 Exegesis et controversia saeculi XVI

11621 *Diekmannshenke, Hajo* Spontane versus kanonisierte Intertextualität: vom neuen Umgang mit der Bibel in der Reformationszeit. Textbeziehungen. 1997, ⇒287. ᴱKlein, J., 149-166.

11622 ᴱ**Marianne, Ruel Robins** Paroles d'évangile: quatre pamphlets allemands des années 1520. 1996, ⇒12,10996. ᴿRHPhR 77/3 (1997) 366-367 *(Schrenck, G.)*.

11623 **Rambaldi, Susanna Peyronel** Dai Paesi Bassi all'Italia: 'Il Sommario della Sacra Scrittura', un libro proibito nella società del Cinquecento. Studi e Testi per la Storia Religiosa del Cinquecento 8: F 1997, Olschki 429 pp. L88.000 [SCJ 30,595s— Schutte, Ane Jacobson].

11624 **Reventlow, Henning Graf** Renaissance, Reformation, Humanismus. Epochen der Bibelauslegung, 3. Mü 1997, Beck 271 pp. DM68. 3-406-34987-0 [OrdKor 40,367s—Heinemann, F.K.].

11625 *Steinmetz, David C.* Divided by a common past: the reshaping of the christian exegetical tradition in the sixteenth century. Journal of Medieval and Early Modern Studies 27/2 (1997) 245-264.

### Y4.4 Periti aetatis reformatoriae

11626 Aʀɢᴜʟᴀ: **Matheson, Peter** Argula von Grumbach: a woman's voice in the Reformation. 1995, 11/2,k032. ᴿAUSS 35 (1997) 289-290 *(Reeve, Teresa)*.

11627 Cᴀʟᴠɪɴ: **Horton, Michael S.** Calvin and the law-gospel hermeneutic. ProEc 6/1 (1997) 27-42;

11628 **Steinmetz, David C.** Calvin in context. 1995, ⇒12,11004. ᴿSCJ 28/1 (1997) 289-290 *(Klauber, Martin I.)*.

11629 CARLSTADT: TEFurcha, E.J. The essential Carlstadt: fifteen tracts by Andreas Bodenstein von Karlstadt. 1995, ⇒12,11005. RAUSS 35 (1997) 267-270 *(Moon, Jerry)*.

11630 ERASMUS: *Carrington, Laurel* The boundaries between text and reader: Erasmus' approach to reading scripture. Zsfg. 21. ARG 88 (1997) 5-22.

11631 HAEVERNICK: **Ernst, Karsten** Auferstehungsmorgen: Heinrich A. Chr. Hävernick: Erweckung zwischen Reformation, Reaktion und Revolution. Diss. Tü 1995. TVGMS: Giessen 1997, Brunnen xii; 487 pp. 3-7655-9420-2.

11632 MARCUS: **Knoch-Mund, Gaby** Disputationsliteratur als Instrument antijüdischer Polemik: Leben und Werk des Marcus Lombardus, eines Grenzgängers zwischen Judentum und Christentum im Zeitalter des deutschen Humanismus. Bibliotheca Germanica 33: Tü 1997, Francke x; 490 pp. [FrRu 4,287—Niewöhner, F.].

11633 MELANCTHON: EWengert, Timothy J.; Graham, M. Patrick Philip Melanchthon (1497-1560) and the commentary. Shf 1997, Academic 304 pp. $74 [SCJ 30,638s—Zophy, Jonathan W.].

11634 PEDRO de Aragón: *Jericó Bermejo, Ignacio* 'Sacra scriptura et traditiones apostolicae in ecclesia': la problemática sobre el dogma de fe en los comentarios de Pedro de Aragón (1584). RevAg 38 (1997) 899-987.

11635 SADOLETO: **Gesigora, Gerd** Ein humanistischer Psalmenexeget des 16. Jahrhunderts: Jacopo Sadoleto (1477-1547): paradigmatische Studien zur Hermeneutik und Psalmenexegese des 16. Jahrhunderts. EHS.T 556: Fra 1997, Lang 499 pp. 3-631-49361-4.

11636 TYNDALE: *Wansbrough, Henry* William Tyndale—a martyr for the bible?. JSOT.S 153: 1997, ⇒4. FASHTON J., 188-197;

11637 **Daniell, David** William Tyndale: a biography. 1994, ⇒10,14568... 12,11010. RJR 77 (1997) 628-630 *(Thompsett, Fredrica Harris)*.

11638 VALDES: *Pino Tejera Lopez, Maria del* Juan de Valdes y su interpretación de la escritura. Almogaren 21 (1997) 53-87.

Y4.5 *Exegesis post-reformatoria*—**Historical criticism to 1800**

11639 **Bordoli, Roberto** Ragione e Scrittura tra DESCARTES e SPINOZA: saggio sulla 'Philosophia S. Scripturae interpres' di Lodewijk MEYER e della sua recezione. Filosofia e scienza nel '500 e '600, Studi 47. Mi 1997, Angeli 480 pp. L65.000. 88-464-0041-0.

11640 **Breuer, Edward** The limits of enlightenment: Jews, Germans and the eighteenth-century study of Scripture. HJM 7: 1996, ⇒12,11015. RJJS 48/1 (1997) 180-181 *(Sorkin, David)*.

11641 **Harrisville, Roy A.; Sundberg, Walter** The bible in modern culture: theology and historical-critical method from SPINOZA to KAESEMANN. 1995, ⇒11/2,k460; 12,11032. RThLZ 122 (1997) 651-652 *(Merk, Otto)*; JRH 21/1 (1997) 115-117 *(Howard, Thomas A.)*.

Y4.7 **Auctores 1600-1800 alphabetice**

11642 BAYLE: *Doueihi, Milad* Adam critique et historique. Som., sum. 311. RHR 214 (1997) 311-339.

11643  BRENTANO: *Bohlen, Reinhold* Dominikus VON BRENTANO: sein Leben und Wirken. Dominikus VON BRENTANO. 1997, ⇒178. ᴱBohlen, R., 13-43;

11644  *Bohlen, Reinhold* Statt eines Vorworts. 7-11;

11645  *Brentano, Dominik von* Das letzte Wort über die Brentanoische Bibelübersetzung den Freunden der Wahrheit gewidmet von dem Verfasser derselben, Freiburg im Jahr 1793. 253-305;

11646  *Immler, Gerhard* Katholische Aufklärung und Staatskirchentum im geistlichen Fürstentum: Dominikus VON BRENTANO und die geistlichen Behörden der Fürstabtei Kempten. 91-107;

11647  *Stadler, Alois* Die Familie BRENTANO in Rapperswil. 45-82;

11648  *Wolff, Norbert* Bibel und Bibelwissenschaft in der Aufklärungszeit. 205-227;

11649  *Bohlen, Reinhold* Verzeichnis der selbständig erschienenen Schriften des Dominikus VON BRENTANO. 247-251;

11650  *Böck, Franz-Rasso* "Zur aufgehenden Sonne": Aufklärung in der Reichsstadt Kempten. 109-120;

11651  *Stadler, Alois* Die Geistlichen der Familie BRENTANO von Rapperswil als Nutzniesser des Mailändischen Stpendiums und der Brentanischen Stiftung. 83-90;

11652  *Schneider, Bernhard* "Katholische Aufklärung"— Etikettenschwindel, Illusion oder Realität. 229-246.

11653  BUXTORF: *Smend, Rudolf* Der ältere Buxtorf. ThZ 53 (1997) 109-117.

11654  LESSING: *Smend, Rudolf* LESSING als Gestalt der Kirchengeschichte. Bibel, Theologie. KVR 1582: 1997 <1983>, ⇒162. 75-93.

11655  PASCAL: *Groothuis, Douglas* Pascal's biblical omission argument against natural theology. AsbTJ 52 (1997) 17-26.

11656  PIAGGIO: ᴱCapasso, M. Bicentenario della morte di Antonio Piaggio. Papyrologica Lupiensia 5: Galatina (LE) 1997, Congedo 262 pp. [RivBib 47,374ss—Passoni Dell'Acqua, Anna].

11657  RAMBACH: *Stadelmann, Helge* "Schriftgemäßheit" in der pietistischen Hermeneutik Johann Jacob RAMBACHS. TVGMS 424: 1997, ⇒59. ᶠMAIER G., 315-331.

11658  REIMARUS: *Schultze, Harald* Reimarus, Hermann Samuel (1694-1768). TRE 28. 1997, ⇒420. 470-473.

11659  SPINOZA: *Passos, João Décio* ESPINOSA e sua proposta de leitura bíblica. Espaços 5 (1997) 43-60 [EThL 74,165*].

11660  WESLEY: Jones, Scott J. John Wesley's conception and use of scripture. 1995, ⇒11/2,k282. ChH 66 (1997) 373-374 *(English, John C.)*; AUSS 35 (1997) 285-286 *(Whidden, Woodrow W.)*;

11661  Collins, Kenneth J. The scripture way of salvation: the heart of John Wesley's theology. Nv 1997, Abingdon 256 pp. $19. 0-687-00962-6 [RRT 1998/1,89].

## Y5.0 *Saeculum XIX*—Exegesis—19th century

11662  *Montagnes, Bernard* La crise de la Revue biblique en 1898-1899. AFP 67 (1997) 345-379.

11663  Scheuchenpflug, Peter Die katholische Bibelbewegung im frühen 19. Jahrhundert. Diss. Rg 1997, ᴰBaumgartner, K.: STPS

27: Wü 1997, Echter 448 pp. DM56. 3-429-01966-4 [EThL 74,165*].

11664 BAUR: *Elze, Martin* Ottilie WILDERMUTH über Ferdinand Christian BAUR. 1997, ⇒92. FSTUHLMACHER P., 107-111.

11665 DELITZSCH Friedrich: **Lehmann, Reinhard G.** Friedrich Delitzsch und der Bibel—Babel—Streit. OBO 133: 1994, ⇒10,14651; 12,11024. RWZKM 87 (1997) 296-299 *(Leonhard, Clemens)*; AcOr 58 (1997) 201-202 *(Barstad, H.M.)*.

11666 KUENEN: *Smend, Rudolf* Abraham Kuenen (1828-1891): ein Klassiker der Einleitungswissenschaft. BEThL 133: 1997, FBREKELMANS C., 569-586.

11667 OVERBECK: EStauffacher-Schaub, M.; Stegemann, E.W.; Brändle, R. Franz Overbeck: Werke und Nachlaß, 2: Schriften bis 1880. Stu 1994, Metzler ix; 576 pp. [VigChr 54,106—Fitschen, Klaus];

11668 EStauffacher-Schaub, M.; Reibnitz, B. von Franz Overbeck: Werke und Nachlaß, 5: Kirchenlexicon: Texte; ausgewählte Artikel. Stu 1995, Metzler xx; 762 pp. [VigChr 54,106—Fitschen, Klaus];

11669 EReibnitz, B. von Franz Overbeck: Werke und Nachlaß, 6/1: Kirchenlexicon: Materialien; Christentum und Kultur. Stu 1996, Metzler x; 345 pp. [VigChr 54,106—Fitschen, Klaus];

11670 EReibnitz, B. von; Stauffacher-Schaub, M. Franz Overbeck: Werke und Nachlaß, 6/2: Kirchenlexicon: Materialien; Gesamtinventar. Stu 1997, Metzler ix; 388 pp. [VigChr 54,106—Fitschen, Klaus].

11671 SMITH William Robertson: **Bediako, Gillian M.** Primal religion and the bible: William Robertson Smith and his heritage. Diss. Aberdeen, DWalls, A.F.: JSOT.S 246: Shf 1997, Academic 402 pp. Bibl. £45/$74. 0-85075843-3;

11672 EJohnstone, William William Robertson Smith: essays in reassessment. JSOT.S 189: 1995, ⇒11/2,k377; 12,11027. RJSSt 42 (1997) 128-130 *(Houston, Walter J.)*.

11673 WELLHAUSEN: *Smend, Rudolf* Wellhausen in Greifswald. Bibel, Theologie. KVR 1582: 1997 <1981>, ⇒162. 135-165.

11674 WREDE: *Morgan, Robert* Re-reading Wrede. ET 108 (1997) 207-210.

### Y6.0 *Saeculum XX*—20th Century Exegesis

11675 EFabris, Rinaldo La bibbia nell'epoca moderna e contemporanea. La Bibbia nella Storia. 1992, ⇒9,16763. RBeO 39/1 (1997) 61-62 *(Jucci, Elio)*.

11676 Fitzmyer, Joseph A. The Biblical Commission's document *The interpretation of the Bible in the church*: text and commentary. SubBi 18: 1995, ⇒11/2,1424; 12,714. REstB 55/1 (1997) 117-118 *(Huarte, J.)*.

11677 EGourgues, Michel; Laberge, Léo 'De bien des manières': la recherche biblique aux abords du xxie siècle. LeDiv 163: 1995, ⇒11/1,84; 12,182. RETR 72 (1997) 301-302 *(Cuvillier, Élian)*; CBQ 59 (1997) 606-608 *(Forestell, J. Terence)*.

11678 **Lehmkühler, Karsten** Kultus und Theologie: Dogmatik und Exegese in der religionsgeschichtlichen Schule. FSÖTh 76: 1996, ⇒12,11033. RJETh 11 (1997) 241-243 *(Schmid, J.H.)*.

11679 *Van Belle, Gilbert* De faculteit Godgeleerdheid in de K.U. Leuven, 1969-1995: bijbelwetenschap. ANL 39: 1997, ⇒245. EGevers, L., 63-154 [EThL 74,166*].

11680 *Włodarczyk, Stanisław* Powrót do zasad teorii synkatabasis we współczesnej egzegezie katolickiej [De reversione principii condescensionis in hodierna exegesi catholica]. RBL 50 (1997) 113-118 **P**.

11681 ALBRIGHT: *Freedman, David Noel* W.F. ALBRIGHT as historian. Divine Commitment 1. 1997 <1989>, ⇒124. 447-456.

11682 ALTHAUS: **Meiser, Martin** Paul Althaus als Neutestamentler. CThM 15: 1993, ⇒8,m638... 12,11085. RZKG 108 (1997) 433-434 *(Kantzenbach, Friedrich Wilhelm)*.

11683 BARTH: *Keller, Roger R.* Karl Barth's treatment of the Old Testament as expectation. AUSS 35/2 (1997) 165-179;

11684 **Lohmann, Johann Friedrich** Die Rezeption des Neukantianismus im "Römerbrief" und ihre Bedeutung für die weitere Ausarbeitung der Theologie Karl Barths. Diss. Mainz 1995, DHerms: B 1995, De Gruyter 421 pp. DM218. RJETh 11 (1997) 243-246 *(Walldorf, Jochen)*;

11685 **Cunningham, Mary Kathleen** What is theological exegesis?: interpretation and use of scripture in Barth's doctrine of election. 1995, ⇒11/2⇒k756. RAThR 79 (1997) 630-631 *(Malcolm, Lois)*.

11686 BAUMGARTNER: *Smend, Rudolf* Der Exeget und der Dogmatiker—anhand des Briefwechsels zwischen W. BAUMGARTNER und K. BARTH. Bibel, Theologie. KVR 1582: 1997 <1996>, ⇒162. 135-165.

11687 BEA: **Schmidt, Stjepan** Agostino Bea: cardenale dell'ecumenismo e del dialogo. CinB 1996, San Paolo 202 pp. 88-215-3297-6 [EE 72,558—Alemany, José J.].

11688 BULTMANN: *Meding, Wichmann von* Rudolf Bultmanns Widerstand gegen die Mythologisierung der christlichen Verkündigung mit einem Anhang: Bultmanns Vorlesungseinleitung vom 2.5. 1933. ThZ 53 (1997) 195-215;

11689 *Paulsen, Henning* Rudolf BULTMANN 1933. Zur Literatur. WUNT 99: 1997, ⇒153. 468-477;

11690 **Valerio, Karolina de** Altes Testament und Judentum im Frühwerk Rudolf Bultmanns. 1994, ⇒10,14798... 12,11047. RJBL 116 (1997) 132-134 *(Kay, James F.)*;

11691 **Jaspert, Bernd** Sachgemässe Exegese: die Protokolle aus Rudolf Bultmanns neutestamentlichen Seminaren 1921-1951. MThSt 43: 1996, ⇒12,11046. RThLZ 122 (1997) 1023-1026 *(Merk, Otto)*;

11692 **Gagey, Henri-Jérome** Jésus dans la théologie de Bultmann. CJJC 57: 1993, ⇒10,14791; 12,11045. RIrén. 70/1 (1997) 152-153;

11693 *Marucci, Corrado* La teologia della rivelazione in R. Bultmann. 1997, ⇒30. FGIORDANO M, 325-353 [Jer 31,31-34].

11694 CHOMSKY: **Barsky, Robert F.** Noam Chomsky: a life of dissent. CM 1997, MIT Press xi; 237 pp. 0-262-02418-7.

11695 COLENSO: *Mitchell, Gordon* A hermeneutic of intercultural learning: the writings of John Colenso. OTEs 10 (1997) 449-458.

11696 COUROYER: *Puech, Émile* Biographie intellectuelle du R.P.B. Couroyer. CRB 36: 1997, ⇒21. <sup>M</sup>COUROYER B., 9-28.

11697 DALMAN: *Thiel, Winfried* Gustaf Dalman und die Ausgrabugen in Jerusalem: aus der Korrespondenz G. Dalmans mit der Deutschen Orient-Gesellschaft. Jahrbuch des Deutschen Evangelischen Instituts für Altertumswissenschaft des Heiligen Landes 5 (1997) 45-58.

11698 DHORME: *Spycket, Agnès* Les archives d'Édouard Dhorme (1881-1966) à la bibliothèque du Saulchoir à Paris. RB 104 (1997) 5-39.

11699 FREI: **Demson, David E.** Hans Frei and Karl Barth: different ways of reading scripture. GR 1997, Eerdmans xi; 116 pp. $18. 0-8028-4168-6 [ThD 44,358—Heiser, W. Charles].

11700 FRIEDLANDER: *Homolka, Walter* Rabbiner Albert Hoschander Friedlander. 1997, ⇒25. <sup>F</sup>FRIEDLANDER A., 279-280.

11701 GERSTENBERGER: *Childs, Brevard S.* Erhard Gerstenberger: the Yale years. 1997, ⇒29. <sup>F</sup>GERSTENBERGER E.S., 1-5.

11702 GIRARD: <sup>E</sup>**Williams, James G.** The Girard reader. 1996, ⇒12,11053. Month 31 (1997) 114-115 *(Taylor, Simon)*.

11703 GOLDBERG A.: *Schlüter, Margarete; Schäfer, Peter* Arnold Goldberg (1928-1991). Mystik. TSAJ 61: 1997, ⇒128. <sup>E</sup>Schlüter, M., vii-xxiii.

11704 GRELOT: **Grelot, Pierre** Il rinnovamento biblico nel ventesimo secolo: memorie di un protagonista. 1996, ⇒12,11031. <sup>R</sup>LASBF 47 (1997) 617-619 *(Chrupcała, Lesław Daniel)*.

11705 IOANNES PAULUS II: *Chmiel, Jerzy* Homo patiens w biblii, na kanwie nauczania Jana Pawła II [Homo patiens in Sacra Scriptura secundum Ioannem Paulum PP. II]. RBL 50 (1997) 127-132 P.

11706 KNIERIM: *Knierim, Hildegard* Way stations. <sup>F</sup>KNIERIM R: 1997, ⇒48. 1-12.

11707 LAGRANGE: **Montagnes, Bernard** Le père Lagrange, 1855-1938: l'exégèse catholique dans la crise moderniste. 1995, ⇒11/2,k502; 12,11062. <sup>R</sup>Recollectio 20 (1997) 338-39 *(Martínez Cuesta, Ángel)*;

11708 *Montagnes, Bernard* L'amitié Battifol-Lagrange. BLE 98 (1997) 3-20;

11709 Les années d'initiation dominicaine du Père Lagrange ou l'apprentissage de l'humilité (1879-1884). RThom 97 (1997) 355-368;

11710 *Doré, Joseph*: Un spirituel, le père Lagrange. VS 77 (1997) 309-334.

11711 LEIBOWITZ Y: *Sagi, Avi* Contending with modernity: scripture in the thought of Yeshayahu Leibowitz and Joseph Soloveitchik. JR 77 (1997) 421-441.

11712 LOISY: *Miegge, Mario* Ritorno a LOISY: dal punto di vista di un ecumenismo critico. Protest. 52 (1997) 185-187.

11713 LUBAC: **Russo, A.** Henri de Lubac: biographie. <sup>T</sup>*Di Nunzio, A.*: P 1997, Brepols 281 pp. FF119 [NRTh 122,284s—Chantraine, G.].

11714 MATHEW: **Lindsey, William D.** Shailer Mathew's lives of Jesus: the search for a theological foundation for the social gospel. Albany, NY 1997, SUNY Press x; 307 pp. $59.50/$20. 0-7914-3507-5/8-3 [JR 79,304s—Greenfield, Larry L.].

11715 MATTIOLI: **Da Campagnola, Stanislao** Anselmo Mattioli tra studi biblici e biblioteca "Oasis" (1913-1996). Perugia 1997, Frati Minori Cappuccini dell'Umbria 110 pp.

11716 METZGER: **Metzger, Bruce Manning** Reminiscences of an octogenarian. Peabody 1997, Hendrickson xi; 242 pp. $25. 1-56563-264-8 [BiTod 36,135—Senior, Donald].

11717 MOLTMANN-WENDEL: **Moltmann-Wendel, Elisabeth** Autobiography. L 1997, SCM xx; 188 pp. £15. 0-334-02708-X. RET 109 (1997-98) 352 *(Rodd, C.S.)*.

11718 MOWINCKEL: *Hjelde, Sigurd* Sigmund Mowinckels Lehrjahre in Deutschland. ZAW 109 (1997) 589-611.

11719 PIXLEY: **Fricke, Michael** Bibelauslegung in Nicaragua: Jorge Pixley im Spannungsfeld von Befreiungstheologie, historisch-kritischer Exegese und baptistischer Tradition. Diss. Marburg 1997, DGerstenberger, E.S.: Exegese in unserer Zeit 2: Müns 1997, LIT xii; 379 pp. DM58.80. 3-8258-3140-X [ThLZ 123,1200s—Erbele, Dorothea].

11720 RAD, VON: *Smend, Rudolf* Rad, Gerhard von (1901-1971). TRE 28. 1997, ⇒420. 89-91.

11721 RIUS-CAMPS: *Ferrer, Joan* Una lectura nova del llibre més mediterrani del Nou Testament: l'obra exegètica de Josep RIUS-CAMPS sobre els Fets del Apòstols. La Bíblia i el Mediterrani. 1997, ⇒385. EBorrell, d'Agustí, 155-160.

11722 SCHLATTER: **Neuer, Werner** Adolf Schlatter: a biography of Germany's premier biblical theologian. TYarbrough, R.: GR 1996 Baker 229 pp. $11. 0-8010-2069-7. RWThJ 59 (1997) 125-127 *(McCartney, Dan G.)*;

11723 Adolf Schlatter: ein Leben für Theologie und Kirche. 1996, ⇒12,11076. RThRv 93 (1997) 225-227 *(Mußner, Franz)*; WThJ 59/1 (1997) 127-128 *(McCartney, Dan G.)*; TrinJ 18 (1997) 258-262 *(Southwell, Andrew)*.

11724 SCHWEITZER: *Günzler, Claus* Denkende Frömmigkeit und frommes Denken: das 'elementare Denken' als Schnittpunkt von Philosopie und Religion bei Albert Schweitzer. BZNW 89: 1997, ⇒33. FGRAESSER E., 69-84;

11725 **Schweitzer, Albert** Memoirs of childhood and youth. TBergel, Kurt; Bergel, Alice R.: Syracuse 1997, Syracuse Univ. Press vi; 96 pp. $20. 0-8156-0446-7 [ThD 45,91—Heiser, W. Charles];

11726 Conversations sur le Nouveau Testament. 1996, ⇒12,11078. RETR 72/1 (1997) 147-148 *(Gounelle, André)*.

11727 SOARES-PRABHU: *D'Souza, Keith* George M. Soares-Prabhu, S.J.: a theologian for our times. 1997, ⇒89. FSOARES-PRABHU G., 3-35.

11728 SOUCEK: *Pokorný, Petr* In honor of Josef B. Souček. Bibelauslegung. WUNT 100: 1997 <1992>, ⇒970. EPokorný, Petr, 13-23.

11729 VITTORINO: **Raspanti, Giacomo** Mario Vittorino exegeta di S. Paolo. 1996, ⇒12,11082. RASEs 14 (1997) 565-566 *(Pieri, F.)*.

11730 WINSTON D.: *Runia, David T.; Sterling, Gregory E.* David Winston: a bibliography of his publications 1966-1997;

11731 *Sterling, Gregory E.* The path of wisdom: a portrait of David Winston. StPhilo 9 (1997) xvii-xxiii/xi-xvi.

γ6.3 *Influxus Scripturae saeculo XX*—Survey of current outlooks

11732   **Gibellini, Rosino** Panorama de la théologie au XX^e siècle. Théologies. 1994, ⇒10,14872; 11/2,k592. ^RRTL 28 (1997) 544-546 *(Brito, E.)*.
^EHandy, L. The age of Solomon: scholarship at the turn of the millennium ⇒282.
^EPorter, S. Handbook to exegesis of the NT ⇒971.

11733   *Vanhoye, Albert* L'exégèse catholique aujourd'hui. ^TFernandez, *Irène*: Interview. Com(F) 22/6 (1997) 91-103; Com(US) 19,440-451.

γ7.2 *(Acta) Congressuum biblica:* nuntii, rapports, Berichte

11734   *Aulisa, Immacolata* I Salmi nell'esegesi patristica (Trani, 7-12 aprile 1997). VetChr 34 (1997) 367-378.

11735   *Bertolone, Vincenzo* Introduzione al primo Congresso Internazionale—una ricerca interdisciplinare, Istituto di ricerca sul santo Volto di Cristo—Pontificia Università Urbaniana 12 ott. 1997. PalCl 76/8-9 (1997) 615-636.

11736   *Casalini, Nello* Atti della Settimana Biblica Abruzzese 1985-1994. RivBib 45 (1997) 113-116.

11737   *Chmiel, Jerzy* Dawid w biblii: XVII Kongres ACFEB, Lille 1997 [Figures de David à travers la bible: XVIIe Congrès ACFEB, Lille 1997]. RBL 50 (1997) 292-293 **P**.

11738   *Chmiel, Jerzy* 'Nie wypowiedziane przymierze?': Sympozjum biblijne w Innsbrucku (1997) ['Der ungekündigte Bund?': Tagung in Innsbruck (1997)]. RBL 50 (1997) 210-211 **P**.

11739   *Hiebert, Robert J.V.* Report on the 'Symposium über den Septuaginta-Psalter und seine Tochterübersetzungen'. Gö 23-26.7.1997; prog. 26-30. BIOSCS 30 (1997) 25-26.

11740   *Hohnjec, Nikola Colloquium Biblicum Lovaniense* o knjzi propovjednika [1997]. BoSm 67 (1997) 549-550. **Croatian**.

11741   *Iovino, Paolo* L'insegnamento della S. Scrittura: metodi e problemi: Seminario di Studio, Giovedì, 6 febb. 1997. Ho Theológos 15 (1997) 131-142.

11742   *Klauck, Hans-Josef* 51. General Meeting der Studiorum Novi Testamenti Societas vom 6.-10. August 1996 in Straßburg. BZ 41 (1997) 156-158;

11743   Tagung der deutschsprachigen katholischen Neutestamentler in Innsbruck vom 17-21. März 1997. BZ 41 (1997) 315-316.

11744   Komunikat towarzystwa biblijnego w polsce [Nuntium Societatis Biblicae Poloniae]. RBL 50 (1997) 161-162 **P**.

11745   *Matras, Tadeusz* XXXIV Spotkanie biblistów polskich w Radomiu (1996) [De XXXIV conventu biblistarum Poloniae (Radom 1996)]. RBL 50 (1997) 155-159 **P**.

11746   *Minissale, Antonino* Convegno internazionale su Ben Sira. First International Ben Sira Conference. RivBib 45 (1997) 121-125.

11747   *Olsson, Birger* Matteussymposium i Lund 1996: inledning. 1997, ⇒28. ^FGERHARDSSON B., 5-9.

11748   *Pisarek, Stanisław* Pięćdziesiąty pierwszy Kongres Studiorum Novi Testamenti Societatis (SNTS) [51^ème Congrès Studiorum

Novi Testamenti Societatis (SNTS)]. Strasburg (Francja), 6-10 sierpnia 1996 r. AtK 128 (1997) 280-282.

11749 *Schmidt-Sommer, Irmgard* Sechzigste Wiederkehr der Beuroner Bibeltage. EuA 73 (1997) 156-157.
*Schoors, A.* Qohelet in the context of wisdom ⇒3213.

11750 *Shanks, Hershel* New Orleans gumbo: plenty of spice at annual meeting [SBL 1996]. BArR 23/2 (1997) 54-59, 69.

11751 *Schwank, Benedikt* Birmingham 1997: SNTS. EuA 73 (1997) 400-402;

11752 Szeged 1997. Die Person Jesu und die Parabeln, 1-4.9.1997. EuA 73 (1997) 475-476;

11753 Der ungekündigte Bund?: Tagung in Innsbruck vom 17.-21. März 1997. EuA 73 (1997) 228-229.

11754 *Tampellini, Stefano* Septuaginta: libri sacri della diaspora giudaica e dei cristiani. II giornata di studio: *da torah a nómos*; Milano, Università cattolica, 13.5.1997. ASEs 14 (1997) 549-550.

11755 *Turek, Waldemar* V Sympozjum o Św. Pawle (Tars, 28-30 czerwca 1997) [V Conventus de S. Paulo (Tarsus, 28-30 VI 1997)]. Vox Patrum 17 (1997) 581-583.

11756 *Van Belle, Gilbert* Colloque: Studiorum Novi Testamenti Societas. 4-8.8.1997, Birmingham. EThL 73 (1997) 532.

### Y7.8 *(Acta) Congressuum archaeologica:* nuntii

11757 22nd Archaeological Conference in Israel. 31.3-1.4.1996, Tel Aviv Univ.;

11758 23rd Archaeological Congress in Israel. 16-17.4.1997, Jerusalem. IEJ 47 (1997) 136-137/275-277.

11759 The 98th Annual Meeting of the Archaeological Institute of America (1996). Report; abstracts. AJA 101 (1997) 331-393.

11760 *Geva, H.* The Twenty-Third Archaeological Congress in Israel. Conference presentation. Qad. 30/1 (1997) 63-64.

### Y8.0 *Periti;* Scholars, personalia, organizations

11761 *Brockhaus, Ulrich* Dem Jubilar eine persönliche Würdigung. TVGMS 424: 1997, ⇒59. FMA IE R G., 11.

11762 *Caquot, André* Rapport sur l'état et l'activité de l'École Biblique et Archéologique Française de Jérusalem, 1996-1997. CRAI 4 (1997) 1273-1275.

11763 Dank an Gerhard DOP FFE L. BVLI 41 (1997) 23-25.

11764 *Frede, Hermann J.* Un itinerario di ricerca. BVLI 41 (1997) 4-10.
EGevers, L. De faculteit Godgeleerdheid in de K.U. Leuven, 1969-1995 ⇒245.

11765 Internationaler biographischer Index der Religion: Theologen, Prediger, Rabbiner und Ordensleute: World biographical index of religion: theologians, preachers, rabbis and members of a religious order. Mü 1997, Saur 5 vols; lxviii; 2504 pp. öS10.877. 3-598-11299-8 [ZKTh 119,490—Meyer, Hans Bernhard].

11766 *Larkin, Ernest, (al.),* Remembrances of friend, teacher, and colleague;

11767  *Malley, John* The emphasis on the word of God in Carmel during recent years. 1997, ⇒70. ᶠMURPHY R., Master, 57-87/277-282.
11768  **Mrkonjic, Tomislav** Celestin TOMIC, OFMConv.: biobliogra-fija. Zagreb 1997, Provincijalat hrvatskih franjevaca konventualaca 25-67.
11769  ᴱ**Nullens, Patrick** Dicht bij de bijbel: feestbundel ter gelegenheid van het 75-jarig jubileum van het Bijbelinstituut België, 1922-1997. Heverlee 1997, Centrum voor Pastorale Counseling 227 pp. 90-71813-15-0 [EThL 74,159*].
11770  **Rizzardi, Giuseppe** L. MASSIGNON (1883-1962): un profilo dell'orientalista cattolico. Quodlibet 6: 1996, ⇒12,11067. IslChr 23 (1997) 296-297 *(Borrmans, Maurice)*.
11771  *Schreiner, Stefan* L. BAECKS Beitrag zur neutestamentlichen Wissenschaft: das Evangelium als Urkunde der jüdischen Glaubensgeschichte. Orien. 61/2,3 (1997) 20-22, 32-36.
11772  *Stowasser, Martin* Leben und Werk von Magnus LOERER und Pius-Ramon TRAGAN. StAns 124: 1997, ⇒57. ᶠLOEHRER M. — TRAGAN P., 15-22.

## ʏ8.5  *Periti;* in memoriam

11773  Ando, Shiro 1958-1996. ZDMG 147 (1997) 7-9 *(Pistor-Hatam, Anja).*
11774  Bauer, Wolfgang 23.2.1930-14.1.1997. ZDMG 147 (1997) 261-265 *(Schmidt-Glintzer, Helwig).*
11775  Birot, Maurice 8.7.1916-10.5.1993. Mari 8 (1997) 5-6 *(Joannès, Francis).*
11776  Brunner, Elke 11.5.1913-18.2.1997. ZÄS 124/2 (1997) I-III *(Blumenthal, Elke; Hornung, Erik).*
11777  Cagni, Luigi Giovanni 4.3.1929-27.1.1998. AfO 44-45 (1997-98) 579-581 *(Graziani, Simonetta).*
11778  Calmeyer, Peter 5.9.1930-22.11.1995. MDOG 128 (1996) 5-6 *(Hrouda, Barthel).*
11779  Courbin, Paul 1922-1994. Syr. 74 (1997) 221 *(Will, E.).*
11780  Dewailly, Louis-Marie 29.12.1906-17.12.1995. SEÅ 62 (1997) 7-12 *(Riesenfeld, Harald).*
11781  Fischer, Bonifatius 1915-19.4.1997. BIOSCS 30 (1997) 9-10.
11782  Frézouls, Edmond 1925-1995. Syr. 74 (1997) 221-22 *(Will, E.).*
11783  Frede, Hermann Josef 12.9.1922-29.5.1998. BIOSCS 30 (1997) 10-11.
11784  Greenfield, Jonas-Carl 30.10.1926-13.3.1995. REJ 156 (1997) 495-497 *(Laperrousaz, Ernest Marie).*
11785  Jacob, Edmond *Heintz, Jean-Georges* Bibliographie Edmond Jacob [1979-1998]. UF 29 (1997) 199-209.
11786  Kammenhuber, Annelies 19.3.1922-24.12.1995. Or. 66 (1997) 86-88 *(Archi, Alfonso)*; MDOG 128 (1996) 7-9 *(Heinhold-Krahmer, Susanne).*
11787  Kassing, Altfrid Theodor 1924-1.4.1997. BiKi 52/3 (1997) 151 *(Haass, Karl).*
11788  Kirkbride-Helbaek, Diana 1915-13.8.1997. Iraq 59 (1997) iii-iv *(Postgate, J.N.).*
11789  Leanza, Sandro 1940-15.12.1996. ASEs 14/1 (1997) 221-228 *(Barbàra, Maria Antonietta).*

11790 Luke, John Tracy 19.2.1935-11.10.1995. AfO 44-45 (1997-98) 583-584 *(Robertson, John F.)*.
11791 Mannucci, Valerio 10.5.1932-27.2.1995. VivH 8 (1997) 197-201 (bibl. 202-207) *(Marconcini, Benito)*.
11792 Masson, Olivier 3.4.1922-23.2.1997. Sem. 47 (1997) 5-7 *(Sznycer, Maurice)*.
11793 Mazar, Benjamin 28.6.1906-8.9.1995. REJ 156 (1997) 497-498 *(Laperrousaz, Ernest Marie)*.
11794 Mehl, Roger 1912-1997. RHPhR 77 (1997) 129-131 *(Vincent, G.)*.
11795 Mitton, C. Leslie 1907-March 1998. ET 109 (1997-98) 257 *(Rodd, C.S.)*.
11796 Moscati, Sabatino 24.11.1922-8.9.1997. RSO 71 (1997) 263-266 *(Garbini, Giovanni)*; CRAI (1997) 788-789 *(Nicolet, Claude)*; Henoch 19 (1997) 246-248 (+ select bibl.) *(Soggin, J. Alberto)*.
11797 Oberhuber, Karl 31.10.1915-4.1.1997. AfO 44-45 (1997-98) 585-587 *(Schretter, Manfred)*.
11798 Picard, Jean-Claude ob. 1996. Apocrypha 8 (1997) 303-304 *(Geoltrain, Pierre)*.
11799 Porada, Edith 22.12.1912-24.3.1994. AfO 44-45 (1997-98) 587-588 *(Collon, Dominique)*.
11800 Pritchard, James Bennet 1909-1997. BASOR 308 (1997) 1-3 *(Anderson, William P.)*.
11801 Ruiz de la Peña, Juan Luis 1.10.1937-27.9.1996. RET 57 (1997) 7-18 *(Díaz, Carlos)*.
11802 Rusche, Helga 1913-21.9.1996. BZ 41 (1997) 313-314 *(Nützel, Johannes M.)*.
11803 Schottroff, Willy 1931-1997.
11804 Soden, Wolfram von 19.6.1908-6.10.1996. AfO 44-45 (1997-98) 588-594 *(Borger, R.)*; MDOG 129 (1997) 5-7 *(Röllig, Wolfgang)*; ZA 87 (1997) 163-167 *(Edzard, Dietz Otto)*; ZA 87 (1997) 168-180 [Bibl.] *(Perchthaler, Dirk; Gaugler, Nadja)*; WO 28 (1997) 5-6 *(Röllig, Wolfgang)*; ZAH 10 (1997) 1-3 *(Müller, Hans-Peter)*.
11805 Sparks, Hedley ob. 22.11.1996. JThS 48/1 (1997) *(Chadwick, Henry)*.
11806 Stanley, David Michael 17.10.1914-30.12.1996. CBQ 59 (1997) 101.
11807 Teeple, Howard M. 1911-9.1.1997. BR 42 (1997) 5 *(Aune, David E.)*.
11808 Thausing, Gertrud 1905-1997. WZKM 87 (1997) 9-10 *(Bietak, Manfred)*.
11809 Tripathi, Chandrabhal B. 1929-1996. ZDMG 147 (1997) 1-6 *(Bruhn, Klaus)*.
11810 Van Dijk, Johannes Jacobus Adrianus 28.1.1915-14.5.1996. AfO 44-45 (1997-98) 581-583 *(Borger, R.)*; Or. 66 (1997) 89-91 *(Edzard, Dietz Otto)*.
11811 Vögtle, Anton 17.12.1910-17.3.1996. BZ 41 (1997) 154-156 *(Broer, Ingo)*.
11812 Widengren, Geo 1907-1996. SEÅ 62 (1997) 5-6 *(Ringgren, Helmer)*.
11813 Will, Ernest 25.4.1913-24.9.1997. Syr. 74 (1997) 1-2 *(Dentzer, Jean-Marie)*; CRAI (1997) 787-788 *(Nicolet, Claude)*.
11814 Yoder, John Howard 1927-1997.
11815 Zimhoni, Orna 1951-1996. TelAv 24/1 (1997) 3-5 *(Ussishkin, David)*.

# Index Alphabeticus

## Auctorum

Arav R 1447 10702
Archer L 1636
Archi A 10858
$^R$10865 10870
11786
Arendse R 4057
Arens E 643 6335 **K**
5957
Arensburg B 10714
Areta Caes. $^M$5949
Argarate P 1568
$^{TE}$4669
Argula von Grumb.
11626
Ariarajah S 836
Arichea D 6713
Arinze Card. F 7570
Aristoteles $^M$6983
Arjava A 7827
Arkush A $^R$7018
Arlandson J 5216
Armellada B de
$^R$7267 7274
Arminjon B 3064
Armstrong K 1502
1535 6864 6865
10565
Arnal W 4058s 4258
4417s $^E$170 $^R$4458
Arnaldi A 9448
Arnaud D 8192
9712
Arnold C 7455 **D**
10268 10966 **J**
6069
Arnould C 10566
Arranz M $^M$7636
Arregui J 4290
Arslan E 10548
$^E$9466
Arteaga Natividad R
1569 **Manieu A**
$^R$7431
Artés Hernández J
8678
Arthur J 3735
Artola Arbiza A 500
837
Artus O 1147 2217
Artzi P. 6098 9932
Arzt P 2699 8417
Aschim A $^R$8775
Ascione A $^E$30 7278

Ascough R 6235
$^R$7212
Asen B 2365
Asendorf U 11607
$^R$702
Asenjo J $^R$545 3863
5059 6027
Asgeirsson J 9371
Asher O 10700 -
**Greve J** 7856
Ashton J 5659
$^E$5658 $^F$4
Ashworth J 5217
Askani H 1403
Aslan Z 10780
Asnaghi A 7480
Assmann J 1935
2216 9573s 9850ss
11212 $^E$236 $^R$9665
Astour M 9713
10859 $^F$5
Aström P 10177
Asurmendi J 3708
3766
Athanasius A $^M$3284
6754
Atherton M 1074
Athmann P 2617
Atias Y $^M$1345
Atkinson K 8968
Attias J $^E$8689
'Attiyat T 10763
Attridge H $^E$8799
$^R$6196 6751
Aubet Semmler M
10810
Aubigné A d' $^M$1728
Aubin C 4902
Aubrun J 3953
Auffarth C 1659
$^R$9472
Auffret P 2976 2878
2914 2922s 2944
2954 2956 2974
2979 $^M$2953
Aufrecht W 8193
10410 $^E$265
$^R$10428
Augenstein J 5672
Augustinus Hippo
11512-11536 2807
2903 5651 5913
6354 6564 $^M$647

1532 1569 1668
1684 2915 3008
3057 4588 4683
5638 5796 5852
6339 6454 6581
7486 11544
Augustus $^M$9457
Auld A 1936 6866
Aulisa I 11734 $^R$155
4389 9028
Aune D 3357 4060
5923 $^E$6924
$^R$11807
Auneau J 570
Aupert P 11045
Aurenche C 9437
Ausín S 71164033
$^E$314 $^R$3412 3438
5637
Ausloos H 1493
2078 2312
Austad T 7918
Autané M 2873
4061 4544 4826
4923 5032 10567
Auvray P 7999
Auwers J 2769
Auzou G 1890
Avalos H 11178
Avemarie F 8841
8969
Aviam M 10499
10684 10500
Avigad N 10411
Aviram J $^E$384 $^F$6
Avis P $^E$6907
Avishur Y 2770
$^E$1308
Avitabile B 1738
Avni G 10645
Ayad B 8223
Ayán Calvo J 11431
Ayers J 5126
Ayguani M 2918
Aymer M 8679
Ayo N 3086
Ayoun R 1937
$^R$4278
Azar É $^T$8509
Azcárraga Servert M
de 1225

Bernett M 10702
Bernheim G 1940 **P** 6824s
Bernstein M E8 8924 R8784 8799
Berquist J 2390 8975
Berrigan D 3717
Berrouard M 4660
Berry D R2924 **P** 8464
Berschin W E8465
Bersianik L M1122
Bertalot R 5375 7395
Berthoud É 10314
Berti S E9008
Bertolino R 8224 R9650
Bertolone V 10315 11735
Bertrand D 8639
Berzonsky V 4853
Besançon M 4573
Besserman L R2830 **P** 9126
Best E 113 3958 6619 6625 6671 R5014
Betancourt P E399
Bethge H ET9397 R9407
Betlem H R2044
Betlyon J R1
Betori G 612
Bettenzoli G 2125
Betti U F11
Bettiolo P E8574
Betz H 947 5174 6102 R6591 9455 O 1281 8908
Beuchot M 647
Beuken W 3522 E3003 F12
Beutel A 902
Beutler J 5186 5682 5839 R165 4028 5265 5878
Bevans S E820
Bevir M 9807
Bexell G 4616 7062
Bey H von der R7590 7762

Beyer D 10902
Beyerhaus P 7533 7773
Beyerle S 2290
Beyerlin W F2816
Beyers R E8648 T8640
Beyse K R9143
Bezuidenhout L 1020
Bianchi E 2855 5361 7030 7413 **F** 1893 2672 R3237 T4920 U E345
Bianquis T 10892
Bickel S 10965
Bickmann J R6248
Biddle M 3662 R3859 3906 7984 T428 1509
Bieberstein K 2294 2329 10576 S 5281
Bielecki S E50
Biemer G 5497
Bienert W D7842
Bienkowski P 10760 10802 R10138 10457 10584
Bierbrier M 10304s E10504
Bieringer R D6555 E6389 R5665
Bieritz K 4291
Bietak M 11003 R10699 11808
Biffi Card. G 7252
Bigel J T11365
Biggs R R371 6967 10924 11178 11183
Bignardi P 573
Biguzzi B 5964 **G** 5034 5114 5965 R5931 5960
Bij de Vaate A 8081
Bikai P 10745
Bilde P E10004s
Bilezikian G 648
Bilkes L 7714
Bill H R5548
Billington S E9443
Bingemer M R4225

Binger T 9509
Bingham D R9376
Bingöl O 10270 10442
Binz S 838 7205 7534
Biot C 4647
Biran A E6 384
Birch B 3814 **C** 11133
Bird A 6714 R432 **P** 114 809 903 1021- 4 1404 1573 1664s 3360 7859 8152 9510 E175
Birdsall J 4576 4731 R1251 1309 1320
Birnbaum E 8585
Birot M 11775
Bischoff B E1453 M1507
Bisheh G E10746
Bissoli C E176 **G** 2550 R5164
Bivar A R9971
Black C 5035s E5756 R4104 **D** R1255 R6653 **J** 8311
Blackburn B R4715
Blanchard R 649 **Y** 948 4366 5634 R5707
Blanchetière F E4380 9198
Blanco F R1592 **S** 4926 11214
Blandenier J 7587
Blanquet J 4547
Blaschke A 11215
Blasi A 11216 - **Cappellini E** 1941
Blásquez R 4070 4292
Blass F 8349
Blattenberger D 6478
Blau J 8003 8082 **R** R2097
Blaumeister H 2790
Blazen I 6390
Blemmydes N M5782

Bordoli R 11639

Bordoni M 7396

Bordreuil P 6028 8083 8194 8225 10817 11092

Borel J R341 1595 11599

Borg B R10510 M 4075 4076 E4420 M4192

Borgehammar S R5420

Borgen P 3959 5838 6615 8586ss E318

Borger R R11804 11810

Borges de Sousa Á E7117

Borges Hackmann G 7460

Borghi E 8415

Borgonovo G 3005 3054 9720

Bori P 116 E5814

Boring M 4077 9438 R6488

Börker-Klähn J 10271 R11026s

Bormann L E27

Börner-Klein D T2200 9064

Bornkamm G 6072 7120

Boroskaya N 10241

Borrell A 5039 5144 7664 E385

Børresen K E237

Borret M 11462

Borrmans M 4330 R11770

Börschlein W 7064 8155

Borse U 5407

Bosch i Veciana A 1127

Bosch R 2856 V R6251

Boschi B 2021

Boschian-Campaner C 1102

Bosenius B 6523

Bosetti E 1025 2022 2367 6800s

Boshoff P 4078 8391 9200 W R9515

Bosio E 6277

Bosowski A 5166

Bosshard-Nepustil E 3364

Bossman D 4492

Bosson N 2754

Bossuyt P 5504

Botas M 905

Botella V R6947

Botermann H 10095 R6086

Botha J 4367 6385 P 1669 2895 5040 10057 S 7063

Bothe B R9128

Bottecchia Dehò M 8680

Bottéro J 6883 9444

Botterweck G E415s

Botticelli S M4570

Bottier L R2896

Bottini G 5477

Bottino A R7825

Böttrich C 5172 6551 8534s 8550

Boubakeur D 1943

Boucharlat R 10943

Boucherat J E7831

Boud'Hors A T8681

Bouganim A 10577

Boughton L 4855

Bouhot J E6791

Boulnois M 7254

Boune C T4921

Bourguet D D2948 3575 P du 10316

Bourke S 10776 R10775

Bousquet F E238

Bousset W M5331

Bouteneff P R7263

Bouvier B T8682 F T8682

Bouzard W 2817

Bouzek Jan 10134 E360

Bovati P 2088 3678 3858 3863 7065

Bovon F 5220 5261s 5284 5466 6256

E8641

Bowden H R11023 J T1142 1615 3413 6080 6825

Bowe B 6405 R232

Bowersock G 10106

Bowker J E437

Bowley J E8796

Bowman A 9859 R 2382

Bowsher J 11339

Box R 2818

Boxall I 5966

Boyarin D 1128 6212 9065s

Boyd A R6397 G 7104 R 1638 - Taylor C 2704

Boyer F 1944 9860 M 4493 5041 5285

Boyle B 3691

Bozzini I 574

Bracchi R 8389

Brack-Bernsen L 9934

Brackney W 4856s

Bradford R 8473

Bradley K 6684 N E65

Bradshaw C 1355 J 9581 P R4563

Braemer F R10655

Brakeman L 1026

Brambilla F 4972 7281

Brändle R E11667

Brands G E10021

Brandscheidt R 1716

Brandt P 8405 R5262 6199

Branham B E9484

Branick V 6294 R6535

Branigan K 10506

Brant J 654

Brassey P 3529

Brauer B 3365

Braulik G 117 2239- 42 2265 2274 2276 8162 9513 E56

Bräumer H 1878

Braun R 2665 E11479 W 4079

Buckwalter H 5286
Budau A 3963
Budd P 2164
Budde A 950
Bueno de la Fuente E 7208
Bueno E 7284
Buetubela B 7536
Bühlmann W 3068
Buioni M 4929
Buis P 2503
Buitenhuis H 11302
Buitron-Oliver D 11046s
Bulai A 3963
Bull K R4457 5716
Bullmore M 6440
Bultmann L 7716 R M4993 7309 11688-93
Bunge G 11463
Bunimovitz S 10649s
Buono A E7785
Burba K 2061
Burchard C 6139 D6844
Burckhardt J M10179
Burdon C 5967
Burge O T9416
Burgmann H F18
Burkard G TE9583
Burke C 7832
Burkert W 9467 E347
Burnett R R760
Burns C 3122 R3134 J R8975 9528
Burr D 5926
Burrell D 7427 R9110 6876
Burridge R 4023
Burrows M 4618
Burrus V 655
Burton-Christie D 7666 11366 R5761
Buscemi A 6073 M R6257
Busch P 6039
Busey R R7094
Bush F 539 2391 L R1638

Busse U 5683 R4927
Busto Saíz J 2504 6074
Buth R 5378 8393
Butler S 4781 7285 T 1151
Buttrick D D3754
Butzkamm A 10317
Bux N 10579
Buxtorf J M8074 11653
Buzzard A 4260
Buzzetti C 577s 1342 1405 8351 R3616
Bwanali P 6696
Byargeon R 3195
Bynum C 6506
Byrne B 6140 6278 R6084 6302 6358 6704 P R5235 11233
Byrskog S 4495 4637 5003 6315 E28

Caba J 5837
Caballero Arencibia A 1129 Cuesta J 5506
Cabodevilla J 4294
Cachia N 5857
Caesar L R3001
Cagiati A 8977
Cagin M 4295
Cagni L 10862 11777
Cahill J 10580 11152 M E5007 R446 7795
Caillot J 7513
Caird G 7959
Cairus A R2202
Calambrogio L 4612
Calame C 9468
Calduch Benages N 3302 3319s 3343s 3346 6932
Calinescu A E10252
Calise C 7122
Callaghan D 4603 4610 M 4353

Callahan A 6685 9374 J 7537 T 3368
Callam D 11400
Callander J 10184
Callaway P 8849
Callegher B 10549
Callender V 10977
Calloud J 1718 4463
Callu J T10097
Calmeyer P 11778
Calvert K R9461
Calvin 3442 5636 6520 6557 6742 M11627s
Calvo M R1569
Calzolari V 8684s
Cama-Calderón A 7863
Camacho F 4080 5022 5153 7418 R4009
Camarero M 484 5842
Camargo Bartalotti C T4525
Cambe M T8686
Cameron A R11465 M 11513 R 9375
Camery-Hoggatt J 879
Camp C 3163 3181 3321s 7864
Campani G 4331
Campanini S E8119s
Campbell A 2467 D3638 B 6730 C 880s D 6682 8409 R6310 6421 E R99 G R5991 J 8732 8962 S 10899 E10509 W R6189 6285 10634
Campenhausen H von 7588
Campenon C 10450
Camplani A E9862
Campos Dilmo F de 5043
Camprodon J 5811
Camps G 2090
Camus J 6933
Canal J 7786

Cebulj C 4809 11167
Ceccherelli I 8084
Celan P M9189
Celsus M11462
Cenci A 5288
Centini M 4550
Cepeda Salazar A R6004 7852
Cerbelaud D 1670 1719s 5876 9202
Ceresko A 2295 3123 3302 9724 R3149
Cereti G R7802
Cernuda A 4083
Cerrato J 3114
Cha J 3906
Chabane J 8007
Chadwick H R1253 1609 11412 11805 J 8352
Chagall M10296 11398
Chahwan A 2794
Chalcraft D E182 11221
Chalier C 661 1721
Champeaux J 3371
Chance J 5452 R5286
Chaney W R2555
Chang H 6345
Chaniotis A 9469
Chapa J 4033 R164
Chaplin D R10000
Chapman G 7289
Charbonneau-Lassay L 10387
Chardin T de M1692
Chardonnens D 3009
Chareire I 4648
Chariton M6957
Charlap L 9119
Charles F 7627 J 6821
Charles the Bald M1326
Charlesworth J 3556 4084s 4261s 5170 5611 8511 E321 8851s 8896
Charlier P 1947

Charpin D 9725 9937 11093 E371 R8279 8311 9943 11291
Charron R 9399s
Charry E 662
Chasin E 9127
Châtillon J TE1756
Chavalas M 9726 E9727 R9959 10428
Chavel S 3685
Chavero Blanco F R7819
Chebel 1789
Chédozeau B 907
Cheetham D R9205
Cheney E 4967 7866 M 3010
Chenu B 3372
Cheon S 3281
Cherix P 8654 9352s
Chesnutt R 8569
Chester A 6237
Chevalier J 5970 N 10944
Chevalley B 5806
Chialà S 8536
Chiarini P E663
Chiat M R9530
Chica A 580 7540
Chidester D 485
Chierchia G 8475
Chiesa B R8101
Childers J 11494
Childress K T6557
Childs B 664 1155 1879 4381 7961ss 11701 W 11048
Chilton B 183 908 1244 2025 2554 3465 4086s 4089 4263 4296 4591 4782 4804 4861 5150 5209 5805 6885 9203s 9250 E4088
Chinitz J 2477
Chiodi S 2026 9644
Chipman J T161 2089
Chirichigno G 2166
Chirico L De 665

T784
Chisholm R R8103
Chlackalackal S 9411
Chmiel J 993 1104 1284 3323s 11705 11737s
Choi M 11464
Cholakis A 5429
Chomsky N 8476s M11694
Chong K 2129
Chouraqui A 1948ss
Chow J 6407s S 3886
Chrisologus P M7251
Christe Y 5971
Christensen D 508 K 7068 S R5004
Christian M T4217 P E7650
Christiansen E 7011
Christianson E 3225
Christianus S M11598
Chrostowski W 1809 3719 R622 9042
Chrupcała L 5465 5609 R11 980 2167 3357 3980 4271 5315 5885 5965 11704
Chrysostomus 4500 M1503 1536 2350 2863 3437 6689 11494-8
Chu J 2393
Chyutin M 8853
Ciafaloni D R11050
Ciałowicz K 9587 R9710 9915
Cibotto G E4671
Ciccarese M 2992
Cicero M6940
Cidrac C de 5798
Ciervide J R7326
Cifola B 9938
Cilia L 5132 E5008 5079 R5679
Çilingiroğlu A 387
Cimosa M 1285 1757 2755 3872

Erlanger S 9160
Erlemann K 7928
Erniakulathil J 4811
Ernst A E762 J 4592
5265 R4783 5709
6078 K 11631 M
2699 8428
Eschebach H 11076
L 11076
Eschweiler P 10275
Escribano-Alberca I
6910
Eshbaugh H 6558
Eshel E 2989 8805
8848 8854s 8917
M8735 H 2989
8731 8742 8918
10583 I E10584
Eskenazi T 1031
Eslava Glan J 10513
Esler P 6604 E190
Eslinger L 2491
2446 R2236
Espeja J 4303 7965
Espinel M 4673
4865
Essen G 4979
Estep W 4866
Estes D 3189
Estevez Lopez E
3974
Estrada B R435 -
Barbier B 7464
Ettlinger G R11497
Eusebius C 11572
M945 9319 11573
Emesa M1510s
1533 1820 11500
Evagrius P M2823
3238 ·
Evang M 6813 E33
Evans C 183 2453
2490 3469 4089
4102-12 4674
4830 5173 5176
5415 5482 7127
7213 7929 8776
E77 181 191 220
276 299 748s 3975
4088 R164 2271
4273 G 7543 J
1412 K 6939 -
Pritchard E 2433

Evdokimov M 935
R10346
Evenari M 10082
Everly D E72
Évieux P TE11505
11604
Ewert D 4867s
Exum J 812 1032ss
2356 2384 E192
Eynikel E 2246
2632 8399 E1156
Eyre C 9873

Faes de Mottoni B
R1592
Fabb N 8484
Fabiny T 5363
Fàbrega V R3992
5292 6723
Fabris R 1907 5696
6217 6257 7012s
7930 E519 11675
R496 500 5502
5543
Fabry H 7071 8860
E415-8 8743
T1241
Facco M R1115
Facey A 1908 3889
4505
Fackenheim E 9161
Fackre G 6911 7544
Faessler M 3071
Fagan B E277
Fagaras S 7369
Fager J 2198
Fagerberg R6559
Fahd T 3384
Faier Zvi TE3829
Faix W R629
Faïz M el- 11169
Falck M von E10950
Fales F 8234 10921
E2109
Faley R 7014
Falgueras Salinas I
7792
Falk D 8919 R8836
8852
Fallner H E4378
Fallon M 4466 5009
5266

Falsini R 4869 7679
Fanin L 585 3976
8460
Fantham E 278
Fantino J 11442
Fantoli A 1642
Fantoni V 2434
Farber G 10928 W
9652 10417
Farfán Navarro E
5697 5812
Farina M 5364
Farkaš P 6040
Farkasfalvy D 4552
Farmer C 5662 R
679 W E224
Farr C 1327
Farrelly B 7429 M
7441
Farrington A 11127
Farris M 5470 S 884
Farrugia E R19 65
7333
Fasani S 4691
Fassberg S 3304
R2235 8048
Fassetta R T3110
Fatica L 5647
Fattorini G 519
Fatum L 6698 E43
Faul F 7720
Faulstich E 10389
Faust A 10585
Faustus R T7370
Favard-Meeks C
2560 9594 9613
Favaro G 9414
Fayol M E8480
Feagin G 5050
Fear A ET11559
Fechter F R3523
Federici T 4980
D1909 5801 6497
Fedoseev N R11024
Fédou M 7298
11470
Fedwick P 11490
Fee G 6146s 6240
6483 6733
Feghali P 11571
Feiereis K E98
Feigmanis A 9162
Feinberg V 10697

Gugler  W  2618
R2299 2304 9768
Guglielmoni L 5356
Guichard M 9537s
Guidetti V 5774
Guijarro  S  6951
11232
Guillamin J T4653
Guillaume J 3982 P
3045
Guillelmus  a  S.
Theod. 3081
Guillén  Armendáriz
F 4042 **Torralba J**
R3905
Guillerand A 5640
Guillermain  C
R5251
Guillet J 4131 4384
Guinan M 2995
Guinot  J  5799
11508ss
Guitton J 4132
Guksch H 10514
Gulácsi Z 9339
Gulley N 3800
Gultom P 1582
Gundlach  R  9881s
E394s
Gundry  R  4469
5014 5167 R4799 -
**Volf J** 6264 6477
6599 R6299
Gunkel H 1509
Gunn D 1230 1680
2456 E172
Gunneweg A 7172
Gunsam E 10794
Günther  M  11035
11405
Güntner G R10471
Gunton C 1583 7199
7219 E440
Günzler C 11724
Gupta S 10337
Guralnick E 10391
Gurary N 9148
Gurney O R9796
Gustafson  J  7721
M7714
Güterbock  H  131
10420
Guthrie G 6755s

Gutiérrez J R74 529
1170  1348  2591
3914  5265  5657
5704  5865  5872
6751  7622  8385
8956  9488  9769
10619 11468
Güting E R6128
Guttgemanns  E
D4728
Guy L 5471
Guyon J 11074
Gyselen R E10421
Gysens J 9539
Gyürki L 10731

Ha H 6774
Haack S 694
Haacker  K  4678
4937  6079  6355
E422
Haag  E  R3812  **H**
427 7598
Haak R R3455 3925
Haar Romeny R ter
1510  1880  1511
11500
Haas G 7722 **V** 8340
9571
Haase R 2106s R375
W 202
Haass K R11787
Habel N 1762 3636
Habermas G E4701 **J**
M8479
Habermehl P R1694
7665
Habicht C 10017
Habinek T E281
Hachlili  R  10207
10517
Hachmann R E10542
Hackett J 8099
Hackländer N 10278
Hackmann G 7305
Hadad A T3066
Hadas-Lebel M 8019
9750 10066 R185
Haddad B 7911
H a d e r m a n n -
Misguich L 10338
Hadjicosti M 11049

Hadley J 9540s
Haelewyck  J  2487
R3706 8698
Haensch R 10112
Haerinck E 9948
Hafemann  S  6151
6535 6601 E92
Hage  W  11359
R9542
Hagedorn  D  E2996
R2991 U E2996
Hagelia H 1793
Hagen K 6559 6586
Hägg  R  E365  396
9471s         9497
R11057
Haggenmüller  O
1992
Hagner D 4385 4470
4774 7723 E7973
Hahlbrock P T4095
Hahn  E  695  6620
E59  **F**  1165  5983
D10065 F36
Hahne H 6346
Hahnen  P  4338
10244
Haider P E9542
Haight  R  R4812
7311
Haik G 4983
Hainsworth J R2742
Hainthaler  T  7443
E7261
Hainz  J  4634  E46
441
Halbertal M 956
Haldas G 7837
Halder A 6952
Haldimann K 5882
Halevi S 1512
ha-Levi J M1119
Hall J E10018 10658
**R** 9822 **S** E3208
Hallager  B  E10454
**E** E10454
Hallak S 10339
Hallet C 7798
Hallett T T2829
Hallman J 7265
Hallo W 9751 E203
R452
Hallote R R10133

Healy J 814
Heard C 3930
Heath D 1291 **M**
 ᵀ2788
Heaton E 3139
Hebel J ᴹ7948
Hebler M ᴱ247
HeChasid Y 9149
Hecht C 10340
Heck C 1825
Heckel T 4044 **U**
 6105
Hedrick C 4745
 5434
Hefling C ᴿ7231
Hegedüs I ᴱ84
Hegel G 4190
Heger P 2138
Hegstad H 4267
He-Hasid J 9149
Heid S 5919 7599
 ᴿ10371
Heide G 6065
Heidegger M ᴹ1127
 9225
Heidemanns K 848
Heidorn L 11019
Heijkoop H 3395
Heijne C von 1813
Heijst A van ᴱ815
Heil C 3920 6456
 ᴱ4428 **J** 4644 4738
 4768 4806 4841
 5057 5885 ᴿ6278
Heiligenthal R 327
 4133
Heimerdinger J 5558
Heimpel W 2881
 9660 11139
Heine R 2775 11473
 S 7799
Heinemann E ᵀ4276
 **F** ᴿ206 535 565
 11388 **W** 1168
Heinhold-Krahmer S
 ᴿ11786
Heininger B 6197
 6775
Heintz F 5572 **J**
 1169 1795 3396
 11785 ᴰ3850 ᴱ374
Heinz A ᴿ1362 **H**
 7377 **M** 11309ss

ᴱ267
Heiser C ᴱ479
Heither T 4679 9220
 ᵀᴱ6283
Held H 5230
Helderman J 9378
 ᴿ9350
Helewa G 6430
 6537
Heller J 2882 **K**
 1584
Hellholm D 6337
 ᴱ132
Hellström P ᴱ9473
Hellwig M 4134
 4879
Hélou C 5941
Helsper M ᴿ5303
Heltzer M 8088
 10415 10550
 10822 ᴿ1015
 10411 ᴱ23
Heman F ᴹ9168
Hemelsoet B 4813
 5821 5296
Hemer C 5607 8397
Hempel C 8760
 8865 8922 ᴿ8737
 8842
Henaut B 4135
Hendel R 697s 6877
 7934 ᴿ1513 10178
Henderson I 4371 **J**
 4880
Hendren N 7132
Hendrickx H 5393
Hendrix R 10457
Hendry A ᵀ1224
Henein N 11004
Hengel M 134 5427
 5665 6080 6154
 7220 8947s 9306
 9825 ᴰ5702s 7158
 8982 ᴱ1170
Henig M ᴿ10252
Henkin J 9109
Henn W 7549 7580
Henne P 7266
Hennig G 1137
Henning I 589 **-Hess**
 **H** 2643 3581
Hennings R 11539
Henrix H 9167

Henry C 135 6878
Hensell E ᴿ6094
 6527
Henshke D 10594
Hentschel G 2219
 ᴱ144
Henze D ᴱ9221
Hepper F 11155ss
Heras G ᴿ4531 7853
Herb M 10237
Herbert E 8816s
 ᴿ3643 8833 **G**
 ᴹ4355 **K** 10553 **S**
 ᴱ10693
Herbin F 9602
Herbordt S 10422
Hergenröder C 5709
Herman Z 7221
Hermann W ᴿ7190
Hermans C 8487 **T**
 7600
Hermanson E 1417
Hermant D 5297
Hermisson H 699
 3536
Hermosilla M 4938
Herms E 958 6155
 ᴰ11684
Hermsen E ᴿ9623
H e r n á n d e z
 Valenzuela J
 ᴿ7816
Herodotus ᴹ2322
Herr B 2589 **L** 2601
 9754 10458 11312
 **M** ᴱ4380
Herranz M 3983
Herrenschmidt C
 9444
Herrera García R
 ᵀ6909 **O** ᴹ5850 ·
Herrmann C 10423
 **G** 10279 **S** 3637
Herscher E 11047
Herzer J 3706
Herzog C 7110 **H**
 ᴿ10493 **R** ᴱ8468 **Z**
 11313
Hesiod ᴹ2980 3171
 9814
Heß I 996
Hess D 4781 **R** 1052
 1546 2340 7133

Hölzl R $^R$10237
Holzner J 6081
Homerski J 3640 3737 $^D$3411
Homolka W 11700
Honecker M 10595
Hong J 532
Honig B 2398
Honigman S 8994
Honoré J 7306
Hood H 4353 J 9110
Hooker M 136 1358 3985 4137 4571 5016 5058 5110 5343 5776 R 1080
Hoop R de 8176
Hoops M $^R$5611
Hoornaert E 3986
Hope L $^R$2269
Hoping H 1586 $^R$1708
Hopkins D 1548 11284 J 7882s
Hoppe L 10596 $^R$2323 9505 R 4138 6699
Horbury W 7550 8434 $^E$9230 $^R$8085 9292 10619
Horden P $^R$11176
Horn F 5603 $^E$7987 $^R$4005
Horner T $^R$9292 11455
Hornig G 701
Hornung E 9604 $^R$11776 $^T$9603
Horowitz A 10677 W 8277 9661 10015 10713
Horrell D 6461 6467 6812 11235 $^R$6195 6442 6453
Horrocks G 8360
Horsley G 8361 10424 R 3987 6411 10085 10689 11236s $^E$204
Horton M 11628
Horwitz L 10721
Hossfeld F 2803 3230 7174 10145

Hossfeld F $^D$494 2951
Hostetter E 9756 $^R$3119 11196
Hotze G 6156 6525
Houlden J 7551 L $^R$3454
House P 2508
Houston W 2741 $^R$754 1534 11672
Houtman A 9046s C 1881s 2081 2300 2317
Houwink ten Cate P $^F$42
Houziaux A 1549
Hovhanessian V 8696
Howard D 2938 J $^R$7134 R 6491 T $^R$11641 -Brook W 5711
Howe K 11118
Howell J 2409
Howlett D 1081s
Hrabanus M $^M$11601
Hrouda B $^R$11778
Hruby K 8995
Huarte J $^R$6751 11676
Hubaut M 6082
Hubbard D 539 M 1867 R 2410 $^R$2392
Hubeňák F $^R$5954
Huber K $^R$5076
Hübl H 11129
Hubmaier B $^M$4905
Hubmann F 3666 $^R$676
Hübner H 705 4404 6107 7968ss $^R$1170 R 11435 U 2082 5797 10393 $^R$2304 10458
Huddlestun J $^E$124
Hudson A $^R$2830
Hueber F 11036
Huehnergard J 8241 8278s 10823
Huffman D 4139
Huffmon H 3398
Huggett J 4746

Huggins R 6341
Hughes F 6412 G 8435 K 5475 P 1959
Hugo Orléans $^M$11603 S. Vict. $^M$11602 V $^M$1728
Huie-Jolly M 5817s
Huizing K 205 702 6958
Hull E $^T$2789
Hüllstrung W $^R$2582 2827
Human D 703
Hume C 6560 6740
Humphrey E 4140 8570 H 5059 $^R$590
Hünermann P 7307 $^E$4784
Hunger H 284 10027 $^R$8287
Hunt A 6413 E 10597
Hunter A $^R$4495 C 1359
Huntington R 10527
Hunwick A $^E$4141
Hurley R 704
Hurowitz V 3602 8280 9662 10281 $^R$1578 2069 2243 3592 9515
Hurst L $^E$7959
Hurtado L 4142 $^R$64 4452 6146
Hurth E $^R$1113
Hurvitz A 2301 3306 8171 G 10569
Hurwitt J $^R$10386 10397 10405
Husbands M $^R$4339
Husser J 9544 10824
Hussey T 10176
Hutson C 6716 6735
Hutter M 9663 $^R$9571
Hüttner M $^R$10423
Hutton R 2196 7470 $^R$8167 S $^R$5945
Huwyler B 3694 $^E$138 $^R$3625
Huxley M 1625

Jean-Marie M 9546
Jeanrond V $^E$4143
Jebanesan S 9707
Jefford C 7725
$^E$11424
Jeffreys D 10986
Jegher-Bucher V 6554
Jenkins I 10460 $^R$10385
Jenni E 138 1587 2275 2485 2828 2913 2958 3658 4681 8022ss 8100 8138 8141 8143 8145 8154 8166 8175 8187 $^E$428
Jennings E 6633 W 706
Jens W $^E$51
Jensen A 5712 D 5188 H 2479 J 3514 R 10341
Jeppesen K $^R$2893 7011 9714
Jeremias G $^D$4940 J 2939 3399 3819 3859 6880 $^D$3501
Jerick D 1803 2302
Jericó Bermejo I 11634
Jerome (See Hieronymus)
Jerumanis P 5713
Jervell J 5514
Jervis A $^R$190
Jeschke M 4881
Jesnick I 9474
Jetter H 5891
Jewett R 5580 6305
Jeyes U 8281
Ji Chang-Ho C 10210 10519 10751 10763
Jiménez J 4343 $^R$6882 **Hernández** E 3094 L $^E$7774
Jinbachian M 3095
Jinkins M 4939
Joannes de Caulibus $^E$11597
Joannès F 9000 9664 11205 11285 $^E$371 $^R$11775

JOANNES PAULUS II 4307 $^M$11705
Jobes K 2712 3780
Joblin J $^D$5850
Jobling D 1138 2519 $^R$7906
Jobsen A 2676
Jodar E 3506
Joerg U $^E$1378s
Joffe A 10562 $^R$384 9727 10197 10638 10680
Johannes P $^M$1609 11506
Johannsen F 610
Johns C 11352 L $^E$321
Johnson D 5515 E 6356 7308 $^E$6302 $^R$7824 $^E$6157 J 2341 K 2437 5045 L 4144 5516 6284 6828 $^D$5215 $^R$4144 R 3756 6803 $^R$10992 S 9380
Johnston P $^R$9504 R 2054
Johnstone W 2139 2647 $^E$11672 $^R$1936 3134
Joji K 5469
Jolivet I 6306
Jolliffe R $^R$5880 8355 8384
Jolly K 939 P 10443
Jonas H 9309
Joncheray J $^E$248
Jones B 3820 3527 $^R$3839 C 3156 10101 D 3619 6758 7726 G 139 $^R$244 7294 7309 I 4747 J $^R$6265 L 4145 5714 M 10980 11002 P 4748 $^E$285 10116 S 8698 11239 11661 T 4882
Jong C de 3695 S de 3231s
Jonge H de 1173 5158 8517 $^E$7 7936 M de 5204 8566 $^R$8545

Jongeling K 8207
Jonker G 9665 L 1174
Joosse N 1316
Joosten J 1317 2188 2424 8025 8190 $^R$1864
Jördens A $^R$9853
Jordon S 7884
Joseph J 2250
Josephson J 10394
Josephus F $^M$4083 8941 9265 10038-76
Josipovici G 1084
Jossua J 4661
Jost R 2342 $^E$79
Josuttis M 887
Joubert J 1993 S 6861
Joukowsky M 10793 10795
Joulin M 5867
Joüon P 8026
Jourjon M 11440
Jouve P $^M$1126
Joy M $^E$8489
Joyal M $^E$9485
Jucci E $^R$116 1862 11384 11675
Juckel A $^E$6096 $^R$1438
Judah Hahasid $^M$1463
Judge E $^D$6273 8618
Juel D 5061 5136 7407 7640
Juel D $^R$5250
Jullien C & F 9757
Jung C $^M$1139 3041 3043 7289 W 6901
Jüngel E 11611
Jüngling H 3329 $^D$3196 $^E$46
Junker H $^M$10984 R $^R$1654
Junod E $^T$8650 8699
Jürgens B 6043 6595 P 8326
Jurič S $^R$5868 6073
Jursa M 2111 $^R$42 90 10934
Just A 5272 F 11240 $^R$4704 5707

H 5461
Kreitzer L 1056
6431 6621
Krejčí J $^R$11187
Kremer J 6399
Krentz E 6246
Kretzenbacher L
7496
Kreuzer S 2266 2319
Kriechbaum F 6959
Kriegbaum B 7445
Krieger K 4151
5382 10068 $^R$4138
Krimmer H 889
Krinetzki G 2252
Krochmalnik D 9002
Kroeger J $^R$7355
Kroeze J 8030s
Kroll J $^R$9996 S
$^R$11044
Kronsteiner O $^E$1391
Krotkoff G $^F$49
Kruchten J $^R$9921
Kruger H 3604 5484
P 3570
Krüger J 10602 K
8353 R 5303 T
3002 3141 3233s
3272 6960 $^D$1916
$^E$91 $^R$3119
Kruisheer D 1514
Krumeich C $^R$11552
Krupp M $^R$8783
Kruse C 6358 $^R$8403
Kselman J 2897
2900
Kubiak Z 9445
Kucala M 1392
Kuczynski M 2830
Kudasiewicz J 4409
5422 5232 $^F$50
Kuenen A $^M$11666
Kugel J 1477 3142
$^D$831 3291 R
$^M$710
Kügler H 7729 J
4586 5304 5719
5792 $^R$4068 4093
Kugler R 2171 8545
8925 $^R$2163 2289
Kühlmann W $^R$7948
Kuhn H 6445 $^D$7633
Kühne H 10431

Kühnel G 10603
Kuhrt A 9762 $^E$9979
Kühschelm R $^R$4138
6843
Kula M 9231
Kulisz J 4152
Külling H 5600
Kullmann W 1057
Kulmar T 1840
Külzer A 11345
Kümmel W 4153
Kunduru J 4752
Küng H 6162 7557
9232 $^F$51
Kunkel W 10077
Kunnatholy A 5233
Künne I 10790
Kunnumpuram K
$^E$250
Kuntz J 3539
Kuntzmann R 1727
1804
Kunz A 3942
Kupper J 10230
Küppers K 4943
Kurth D 10488
Kurz W 5234 5579
5779 $^R$6759
Kuschel K 1113
1765s 4346 7312s
$^E$51
Kushelevsky R 2292
Kushinir-Stein A
10265
Kustár Z 3444
Kuthirakkattel S
6781
Kutschera F 3235
Kutter P 4958
Kutz K 2997
Kuyt A 9137
Kvalbein H 912
4519 4729 7730
Kvam K 11613
Kwok P 9421
Kysar R 5825

La Porta S 9403
La Potterie I de 851s
1176 4154 4682
5720s 5780 6359
7017 11375

La Rosa G 4155
Laansma J 4733
Laato A 2493 $^R$3831
Labahn A 3540 $^R$188
M $^R$188
Labbens J 4156
Laberge L $^D$4839
$^E$11677 $^R$2256
Laboury D $^R$395
Labuschagne C 2232
2286
Lacambre D 9763
Lacaze G 9607
Lacey D de 7224
Lach J 2831 $^F$52
Lacheman E 10935
Lachièze-Rey M
1644s
LaCocque A 4966
Laconi M 5305
Lacovara P 9891
$^R$10258 10962
La'da Csaba A
$^R$9859
Ladd G 7973
Ladiray D 10946
Ladner G 11376
Laffey A 1588 $^R$179
2705
Laffineur R $^E$397
399
Laffite J 3890
Lafont B 9764 G
7937 S 10231
Lafrenière B 5018
Laga C 3098
Lagarde M $^R$4330
Laghi Card. P 913
Lago L $^R$7965
LaGrand J 4520
$^R$4716
Lagrange J $^M$1656
11707-10
LaHurd C 7731
Laiti G 6033 6048
Lajtar A 8440 $^R$8439
Laks A $^E$8441
Laliberté M 4157
Lalor B 10604
Lamarche P 1292
5019 $^R$409
Lamb R 5190
Lamberg-Karlovsky

Lorenzani M E7001
Lorenzin T 7041
R2778 2816
Loretz O 2253 2971
3494 3508 8168
8201ss 9522s E434
R8270
Loss N 3875
Lossky V M7801
Lössl J 11526 4683
Lottes G E11610
Loube H 10006
Loubser J R7968
Loughlin G 821
R7322
Louis the Pious
M1506
Lourenço J R11111
Louth A R7262s
7381 11497
Louyot Y 1591 1745
Love S R11238
Loza V 2035 2055
2093
Lozachmeur H 8248
10435
Lozares A 1331
Lubac H de 722
M1176 4329 11375
11713
Lubega M 4723
Lubsczyk H 144
Luby E 10185
Lucas E E251
E11184 R 6511
Lucca C 11432
Lucchesi E 8577
8657s
Lucchetti Bingemer
M R7319
Lucci L 7804
Luchetti M 7683
Luciani D 470
R3071 4147 5755
9236 11273 F
2588
Lucianus S 9483
Lucifero di Cagliari
M5639
Lüdemann G 1142
3992 4555 4987
9313 11246 D9302
T9359

Ludlam I 9487
Ludwig M 6845
Luft U 9894 R9614
11003
Lugo Rodríguez R
6792 R5261
Luis Carballada R de
R9079 P de 6609
R3436 11575
T5913 de León
6279
Luisier P R8603
Luke J 11790 K
1203 4441
Lukinovich A 8405
Lukonin V M58
9939
Lull D R6146
Lund J 8140 R1464
O 2874 R 723
Lundager J E507
Lundberg M E8779
Lundbom J 3621
Lundin R 724 E214
Lupas L E1368
Lupieri E 4597
Lusini G R8574
8579
Lust J 1293 3641
3721 3730 3732
3917 7138 R48 61
107 2246 2260
2289 2631 3182
3458 3527 3726
7052
Lustig J E9895
Lustiger Card. Jean
4655
Luter B 7838
Luther M M902 984
1520 1854 2059
2871 2912 3267
4618 4828 5375
6155 6327 6559
6586 11607-11620
Lutterbach H R6263
Luttikhuizen G 9358
Lutzky H 2223
Luvino A 9896
Lux R 3263 3891
D3942 E215 U
4476 4522 7977
Luzenberger A de

R3430
Luzzatto A 3074
8184
Lybaek L 4734
Lyke L 2497
Lyman J 11475
R7601 9340
Lyon D 725
Lyons C E288 W
5567
Lys D 6902

Ma W 7775 E63
Maaijer R R8299
Maartens P 6373
MacAdam H R4919
MacArthur J 540
Macchi J 3656 8956
E2323 R1882 2289
Maccini R 5724
Maccoby H 4836
MacCoy T 6635
MacDonald J 6228
M 7839
MacDonnell J 10348
MacGrath J 5725
5781
Mach M 1844
Machinist P 9952
D2616
Machule D 11316
Macintosh A 3837
Mack B 3993s 4166
M1632
MacKay D 2359
11317 T 5943
Mackensen M 10480
MacKenzie R 1266
5990
MacKeown J 1553
Mackiewicz M 2865
2921
MacLennan H 4353
Macphail R E381
MacQuarrie J 1963
Madany B R4351
Madden P 5823
Madera Vargas I
7684
Maderna-Sieben C
9897

5155   R5178   L
M11632  M  2174
E25 R 994
Mare W 11208
Marello P 9771
Mares F E2761
Margain   J   1691
10435 R8049 8075
Margalith O 9772
Marguerat D 4524
5239  5523  8704
E9236
Margueron J 9673
10215       10287
10903s
Marianne Ruel R
E11622
Marie  Jérôme  Fr.
7043 7316
Marín  Heredia  F
145   545   1423
R917   9768   i
Torner J 998
Marin M 4477
Marinatos N E9497
Marincola J 9832
Marinelli E 10521ss
Maritain J M1124
Maritano  M  11380
R11485
Marius  V  M6581
6626
Marjanen A 7840
Mark S 11209
Markkanen R E290
Markos   Eremites
M1682
Marks  H  1059  R
7139
Markschies C 9315s
11247      11381s
R9529
Marksteiner T 11040
Markus R 11578
Marot C T2756
Marpeck P M4905
Marquardt F 7940
Márques  Rowe  I
R8343      10234
10849
Marrassini P T8705
Marrocu G E216
Marrow S R2550

Marsden     Richard
1332
Marsh  Clive  4168
10350 R4022
Marshall C 5068 D
726  H  915s  4169
5240  5992  6167
D4733 R1447 5329
5555
Martel  G  de  2399
2411s
Martelet   G   1692
1994
Marten-Finnis   S
9180
Martens Elmer 7002
7181
Martensen H 4598
Martian S 3997
Martignani L R4220
5837 6119 11119
Martin A R582 9849
C  T1595  D  6416
6432 F 917s R4144
7200  Fr.  7229  G
1768 10524 10992
J 8608 9994 R5717
8592   L   6360
10877  10938  M
R302 R 6659 E430
R6849  Riego  M
R5918  S  6734  T
6339  6675  7732
R11531  V  9237  -
Bueno M 10765 -
Lunas T E1968
Martínez Borobio E
8250  Camino  J
1596  Cuesta  A
R11707  de  Pisón
R 1593s E D5857
Fraseda  F  7269
González  E  7685
F  8559  Riu  A
T7006  T  T2230
9045
Martini   Card.   C
1180  3642  3998
4170  5308  5335
6200  6725  7643s
7686   7733   L
R9199 R M9091
Martino S de R9571

Martins  Ramos  J
1628   Terra   J
5069ss 5145
Marto A 7473
Martone   C   1294
3308 8771 8821s
8871 R8749 ·8753
T8814
Martyn J 146 1086
3931  5729  6168s
6221  6247  6541
6561      6576-80
6593  6605  6611
6616s 7474
Marucchi A E8470
Marucci   C   7607
11693 R4671
Marx A 1729 2037
8964 C 8633
März C 6846 R4429
Marzahn J 10925
Marzo S T4700
Marzotto D 5524
Mas D 546
Maschio G E11438
Masciarelli M 5373
Masenya  M  3203
7888
Masetti-Rouault  M
9550 10909
Mashiah R 8105
Masini M 2400 5336
7044
Mason R 547 R3925
S 10069 R10068
Maspero F 11144
Masseroni E 7687
Massignon L 1769
M11770
Massini A 584
Massmann L 2194
Masson E 11099 O
11792
Masuch G 8456
Matabaro P 5881
Matand J 6170
Mateos J 5022 7418
Mateo-Seco L 6454
6505 R7349
Matera   F   7734
R6583 7243 7724
Mathes M 1871
Matheson P 11626 S

Moingt J 6883 7271
7319
Moiser J 6667
Moitel P 4572 5111
5495 5830 5896
Mojzes P E7310
Mojola A R7776
Molanus J M10340
Moldovan I 5734
Molenberg C 1519
Molina Martos M
10906
Molinari A 735
8707
Mollenhauer H
T1210 4019
Möller H 2866 K
R2808
Moloney F 4894
5648 5832 5883
D7919
Moltmann J 7320s
7383s E68 F68
M5980 7947 -
Wendel E 11717
Molyneaux B E292
Momigliano A 9008
Monaca E 7647
Monari L 5074 5526
7385
Mondati F 5994
Monferrer Sala J
1823
Monforte J 597
Monfrin F 10353
Monge J T1781
Monloubou L 7045
7941 R1782 2957
4284
Monsabré H 6883
Monshouwer D
5075 5800 R5678
5763
Montagnes B
11707ss 11662
Montagnini F 6642
R6148 6514
Montague G 736
R6672 7231
Montaldi G T872
Montero S 444
Montes M T6871
Montsarrat J & V
855 R2323

Montserrat D 9901
10528 R10510 -
Torrents J 9366
9404 9406 E9365
Montuschi F 6194
Moo D 6285 E920
4000
Mook M 10648
Moon J R11629
Moor J de 1997
3605
Moore A R4422
7872 G 9051 M
2402 R2283 2476
S 1183 4129
E5031 R5029 T
5493 5557
Moores J 6314
Moorey P R10919
Moorhead J 2084 T
10724
Mopsik C 9242
Mora C R10439 Paz
C 856 V R5543
Morag S 8109
Moraglia F E1115
Moral d 8659
Moraleda Molero D
3759
Morandi G 6051s
Morandini S R1766
4275 7332 7873
Morano C 1333
Morard F T8660
8708
Morawiecki L 10559
Moreira O T7342
Moreland J E4253 M
4433
Morello G D10161
Moreno Garcia A
3241s 6343 J
9902s
Morenz L 9775
8331 10292
Morenzoni F E11606
Moreschini C 6115
11545 E331
Morfino M 3100
Morgado L R464
Morgan D R3121
3159 L 11252 R
6286 11674 R7954
7968

Morgen M 4403
5463 5907 E6746
Morgenstern M
R8802
Moriconi B R5700
Morisco G 1116
Moritzen N 9243
Morkot R R11020
Morla Asensio V
150s
Morley J 7559
Morray-Jones C
R3786
Morrice W 4186
R8363
Morris G 3839 L
5649 6562 S R304
Morrison C 2609
E70
Morrone F 4187
Morrow W 2269
R2083
Morschauser S
R8332
Mortley R 9835
Morton A 4026
5948 R R5991
Moscati S 11796
Mosconi L 737 5277
Moscoso Pacheco A
5405
Moses A 4799 S
6913 9182
Mosetto F 5833
Mosis R 9244s R564
Moss A 3184 H
1598
Mossman J E293
Mosso D 4895
Most G E294 E8441
Moster J 3026
Motta A. de Lacerda
R R7299 U R1095
Motyer S 5667 5735
Motz L 9477
Moucarry C 9695
Moulakis A E10034
Moule C 921 R6672
Moulton J 8365
Mounce R 6287
Moussé J 4274
Mouton E 6629
7081 7737 M
10529

Olbricht E 740 **T** 336 1062 11407
Oldenhage T 4757
O'Leary A R446 **S** 6060
Olgiati G T9381
Olivar A R60 7590
Olivares E R7946
Oliver Alcón F R1661
Olivi P M5926 6982 11605
Olivier J P J 2113 11253
Ollenburger B E7183 E10
Olmo Lete G del 8209 10906 E297 9446
Olmsted H 2469
Olofsson S 2763
O'Loughlin F 4899 **T** 1554
Olson D 2209 2224 2256 3659 6042 **R** 6630
Olsson B 11747 E28 333
Olsthoorn M R4957 5199
Olyan S 3786
O'Mahony A E401
Omanson R 2718
Omara R 6497
O'Mara V 4720
Onasch K 10357
Oñate Ojeda J 1041
Ondřejová I E360
O'Neil E 5741 6972 **J** 4193 5476 8546
O'Neill G E4742
Ó Néill P E11600
Onuki T 4376
Oosthuizen M 2270
Opgen-Rhein H J 3904
Oppel D 5137
Oppenheimer Aharon 7142
Orazzo A TE2965
Orbe Antonio 11408 D11582 F71
Orchard B 4559

Orde K vom 2679
Ordon H E50
Ordóñez García J R7826
Oredsson D 9780 R9714
Orel V 1443 1999 2475 3873 8115
Oren E E403 9905
Origenes 2204 2896 5306 6274 6283 M1685 1901 1928 2072 3100 3102 4679 5279 5312 5390 5769 5874 6162 6394 7600 9220 11458-11478
Orlandini G 3645
Orlin E 10124
Orr M R3991
Orsatti M 3174 4587 6692
Ortega Arjonilla E E361 -**Monasterio** M 1886
Orth L T7165 **W** 10025
Ortiz García A T5261
Ortiz Valdivieso P 8116 8370
Ortkemper F 893 8774
Ortlund R 3841
Ortwein G 11254
Osborn E 11418 11482 11409 11483 R11529 **J** 10446 **K** 4990
Osburn C 5528
Osiek C 4194 4991 6452 6973 7843 7897 R62 8464 8570 11073
Osing J 9618 10954
Ossanna T 1001 7813
Osten-Sacken P von der D4011 E8995
Østergaard J 10164
Ostriker A 7898 R1557
Ostrowiecki H 1091

O'Sullivan M R8797
Osuna J 7648
Oswald W 1916
Oswalt J 3590 R3455 3821
O'Toole J R7815 **R** 6230 D6547 R5441
Otranto G 9253
Ott H 741 **M** 10358
Otter-Beaujean A E350
Otto E 1483 2096 2257 7085s R2083 2294 3910 7102 9751 10619
Outtier B 8661 8709
Overall C 4708
Overbeck F M11667-70
Overholt T 6974
Overman J 4195 4525 5529
Overstreet L 3944
Ovid M1334
Owan K 3176
Owczarek S 1484
Owen D 10935 **E** 8824
Owens R R2172
Oxford J R4941
Oyer L 4992
Özen A 4987
Ozer A 10910

**P**able M 742
Pablo Maroto D E3075
Pacianus B M11585
Paciorek A 7272
Pacomio L 626
Paczkowski M 5783 R5814
Padberg L v. 7561 R2555 7533
Padovese L 11119 E5668 6119s
Paffenholz Alfred E10601
Paffenroth K 5311 R5245
Pagazzi G 7330

3450 3824 R5991 6672
Peckham B 8045 D2316
Pecorella P 10883
Pedde F 10505
Peden A 9907
Pedersen O 8291 S 6268 7983
Pedrini A R10521
Pedro de Aragón M11634
Peelman A 7334
Peels H 6886 8170
Peerbolte L 6711
Peers G 10361
Pego Puigbo Armando R1079
Pekáry T R10102
Pelckmans P 1972 R2004
Pelcovitz R TE1465
Pelikan J 861 1555 4352 7814s
Pell B 4353
Peloso S 1117
Pelser G 4993 R6485
Peltenburg E 10899
Pemán J 4312 4952
Pemsel-Maier Sabine 7387
Penchansky D 1699 7984 R2508 2548
Penglase C 8292
Penicaud A 6113
Penn M R4334
Penna R 4047 5744 6174 6311 6324 7236 8899 11172 E335 R4193 6236 6243 8814
Penner T 6849
Penney J 5241 6494
Perani M 1921 9013s E8119s
Perchthaler Dirk R11804
Percy M 4710
Perdue L 219 2482 3190 11256-57 T7185s
Pereira F 5400
Perera R 7335

Pérès J 8663 8711 R7255 11516 T8712
Peretto E 155 925 5312 5381 5390 5401 5592 5745 5793 6361 6680 6975 8664 9364 9382 11564 11598
Perez Alonso M 1349 **Fernández** M 8118 8878 9055 ET2176 R9064
**Gordo A** 6267 **Herrero F** 4526 5242
Pergola P 11075
Perkins P 6622
Perlitt L D3540 R2233 11113
Perlman S 7143
Pernigotti S E11000
Pernot L 9498
Pernoud R 11547
Perrier J 10617
Perrin M E11601 N 3972
Perrin Y R9460
Perrone L 6121 M 10547
Perroni M 5213 7899 E57
Perrot C 4560 R4419 J 10946
Perry J 5081 -Trauthig H T7555
Person R 1223 3894
Pervo R 6976 R5254 6199 8683
Pesce M 4389 6936 9255 R6751 9053
Pesch O 7388
Peschke K 7742
Peskowitz M 9088 10530
Peter R 5023
Péter-Contesse René 1429 8181
Peterlin D 6653
Peterman G 6668
Peters D 5128 7844 F R1765 H 6835 M R2842 T R5987

Petersen A 10674 R11392 D 3410 E207ss R3377 N 5746 W 1320 1444 5844 E7 R6096
Peterson B 6546 E 6250 6289J 6515
Petit F 1521 1922 J R7320 M 8522
Petitdemange Guy 9186
Petraglio R 3336 3351
Petrarca F T2825
Petras D 7693
Petrozzi M 4561
Pettazzoni R 9499
Pettinato G 8211 8293 D10870
Pettorelli J 1700
Pettus R 1430
Pezhumkattil A 3347
Pezzoli-Olgiati Daria 5996 R6039
Pfaff H 3476
Pfälzner Peter 10464 11322s
Pfann S 8825
Pfeffer G 1556
Pfeifer G R6 8881 H R3891 M 7694 10491
Pfeiffer H R10521 M T6263
Pfitzner V 6743
Pfordresher J R824
Philip F T2249
Philippe M 5820 5836 5997 7432
Philips D M4905
Phillips A 7088 R2083 G 1822 7743 J 2867 E11353 P 7476 V 5082
Philo M1299 1495 1498 1575 6273 6985 8584-8618
Philonenko M 4686 6067 8964 9689 10362 D3307
Philostratos M4709
Philpott R 10760

Poo M 9620 R9573

Poorthuis M 7408
E2884 10619

Pope M R2474 2770

Popham M F72

Popkes W 4005
6850

Poplutz U 10651

Popović A 2840

Poppi A R4410

Porada E 11799

Porat Leea 10532
10673 P 8449

Porcedda W T1906

Porcile M 7900

Porebski S 8471

Porphyrios M9298
11545

Porsch F R7994

Portaro S R7579

Porten B 298 R8208

Porter D E628 J
3736 S 336 1063
1191 1194s 3450
4201 4391 6122s
6177 6631 6729
7338 8371 8450
8667 8776 E220s
256 299 748s 971
3975 8494 R6314
W 4356

Porton G 3477 9015
9089

Poscharsky P F73

Posen R 1248

Posener-Kriéger P
2571 10997

Postgate C 10466 N
8294 R11292
11788

Pothier R 4902

Potin J 11120

Pottenstein U von
2060

Potter D 9457

Pöttner M 6437
R4371

Potts D 10919
R9762 T 10920

Pouchet J R11560

Poucouta P 3895
6024 7005

R11508

Poudrier R 6978
7390

Poulin J 599 9257
10165

Poupard Card. Paul
1649

Poupon G T8714

Pouzet L 10889

Poveda P 4688

Powell C 6712 M
4527 5085 5314
E4461 R4799

Power D 4903

Powery E R1297

Poythress V 5999

Pozo Abejón G del
7521

Pozo C R4970 8693

Pozzoli L 4202 4357

Praetorius I R1601

Prag K E10584
R10133

Prakash K 5801

Praśkiewicz S R7719

Prasannabhai Fr.
4904

Pratico G 10655

Prato G 9781ss E337
R151 1879 3003
3218 3310 3333
6934 8093 8903

Pratscher W 11422s
R1140

Prazer J 5384

Precedo M R553 913
3005

Pregeant R 4006

Prendergast T R4600
5483

Preston P 10295 T
2416

Prete B 5480s

Prétot P R7698

Preus J 1196 R 7500

Preuss H 7185s

Préville Agnès de
T10925

Prévost J-P 2781
3412s 5951

Price J R10127 R
833 4412 5244

S 9458

Prickett S 824 E1356

Pridmore J 4203

Prieur A 5315

Prieur J 8668 T8715

Prigent Pierre 4358
10363-64 R5965
9236 11273

Prignaud J T4231

Primavesi A 7006
7901

Pringle Denys 10218
E11352

Prinsloo G 2929 W
2985 3562 R2791

Printz M 629

Prinzing G E1322
R11345

Prinzivalli E 11548

Prior M 1006 5399
E404

Priotto M 115 1924
2041

Pritchard J 11800
M10183

Pritz R 7145

Pröbstl V 1501

Proctor J R6094

Prod'hom S 5277

Propp V M817

Proust M M1105

Prout E 3896

Provan I 2509 R7961
9801

Provera L R8351

Provon I D2836

Pryor J 6979 5807

Pucci M R8419

Pudleiner R 11017

Puech É 4048s 7146
7501 8541 8777
8879s 8951 11696

Puhvel J 6887 8342

Puig A E385 i
Tàrrech A 1007
4775 9016

Puigdollers N 6125

Pui-lan K 750

Pulleyn S 9478

Pummer R 8957
R8959

Punt Jeremy 751

Rosenbaum H 4050
E1253 **M** 3548
R1864
Rosenberg S R10683
Rosenblatt J 2097
R1970 **M** R7871 **N**
1558
Rosenfeld B 2573
Rosenstiehl M 557
Rosenzweig F
M1403 9182
Roshwalb-Hurowitz
A E10563
Rosier B 10368
Rosito M 1702
Rosmini A M1115
1118
Rosner B 6442
E6231 **F** T9123
Rosovsky N E10622
Ross E 4955 10369
**K** 7341
Rossé G 5622
Rossi De Gasperis F
7449 7818 **G**
R1131 1133 **M**
R7044
Rossier F 7052
Rossoni G 2672
Rota Scalabrini P
1927 3145 4772
Roth M 2116 **J** 5248
S 9187 9911 **W**
973
Rothenbusch R 2085
Rothgangel M 630
Rotroff Susan 10468
E366
Rottenecker S 2464
M2465
Rottzoll Dirk 1524
1703 T1523
Rotzetter A 6433
Rouault G M10350
O 10911 10913s
Rouet A 4658
Rouillard-Bonraisin
H 11158
Rouiller G 4801
D5977
Roukema R R6393
6398
Roulin G 9627

Roure D 5152 6008
7565
Rousseau J 1447 **P**
11493 R11231
Rousselle A 7745
9323
Roussin L 10492
Routledge B 11329
C 11330
Rouveret A 10298
Rouwhorst G 7053
Roux C 7092 **J le**
1201 **R** 11390
Rovner J 9092
Röwekamp G 10623
Rowland C 3808
5751 6009 7149 E4
R5952
Rowlett L 2347s
Roy Jamini M10337
R11210
Royalty Robert 6010
R5920
Royse J 8605
Rozman F 7945
Ruager S 6773
Rubenstein J 2152
R9015
Rubin B 7150 **N**
9093 **R** 11115
Rubinstein E F8048
Rubio Pardo J R1751
Rücker H E144
Ruck-Schröder A
2002 4011
Rudberg S E1565
Rudisill K 9360
Rudman D 3248s
3264 3270
Rudolph C 3030 **K**
R9407
Ruether R R7311
7871
Ruffin M 2428
Ruffinatto A 3077
Ruffle J E3
Rufinus A M11587
T6274
Rufus S M5349
Ruggieri V 11041
R3072
Ruggiero I 9459
Rühle I 2526

Ruijgh C J 8497
F8373
Ruiz Aldaz J R7358
**Arenas O** 7342
**Cañamares J**
R575 **de la Peña J**
7946 11801 M76 **J**
3733 6049 **López**
**D** 11174
Rumi M9699
Rumianek R 3504
3731
Rummel S 1559
Rumscheidt M & B
T7908
Runia David 8606-8
11730 E302 R8596
Rüpke Jörg E9449
R9452
Rupp David 11054
11331
Ruppert L D2085
3908
Rupprecht H 8452
Rusche H 11802
Ruschenbusch Eber-
hard R2105
Rusconi C 11197 **R**
E120 3419
Russell C E3453 **D**
1827 **J** 4689 4996
7701 10933 **L**
E7905 **W** 6582
Russo A 11713
Russotto M 755
4659
Rüter M E1667
Rüterswörden U
1604 D9536 R2269
Rutgers L 10127
10738 R10326
10656
Rutledge D 7906
Ruwe A 2189
Ruyter B de 7936
Ruzer S 1605
Ryan G E7649 **J**
5346 6364 R1677
Ryholt K 9912
Ryou D 3925

**S**aadiah G 8012

Scognamiglio R 1928 2072 11476
Scoralick Ruth 2955 3115 3196 3280 R3160
Scott J 4014 5596 6224 6252 8529 8560 6583 9025 E227 R6086 6523 K 11531 T 3549
Scourfield J 11554
Screech M 7505
Scriba A 2003 7244
Scroggs R F82 R552 6416
Scurlock J 9684
Seaford R 5537
Sebastian V 8390
Sebastiani L 5358
Sebott R E46
Seboué B 7348
Seccombe D 5318
Sedaca D 7153
Seddik Y 1975
Sedlmeier F 2982 3725 8151
Sedman L 10760
Sed-Rajna G T9072
Seebaß H 1528-29 2222 R2045 2206 2321
Seeher J 11032
Seelenfreund Morton 8500
Seeley David 4223 R7954
Seeman C R754
Seewann Maria 6375 8414
Segal Alan 1449 10219s E 2721 R E9327
Ségalen J 7651
Segalla G 1277 4051 4224 4529 5625 5787 6806 E1454 R567 1698 4177 4255 4288 5775 5816 5963 5965 6094 6136 7236 7883 8814 T5654
Seger J E99

Segert S 10840 R298 306 8202 8207 8244
Segovia F F 5753 D5714 E228
Segre M 1655
Segundo J 4225
Seibold J 7567
Seidel B 3647 E 9274 J 4776
Seidl T 3104 8055 D2515 2673
Seifert B 3842 E 1010 6984
Seigne J 10766
Seiler J 3105
Seim J 7154 9189 T 7910
Seipel W E9960 10167
Seitz C 3455 D3523 M 764 E87
Seland T 5319
Selander S 4482
Selbach V 1352
Selby G 6441
Selinger R 5606
Sellert W E2104
Sellew P 9386s
Sellin G 1067 11394 E229 305 R6530
Sellnow I 11260
Selman M E7484
Sembrano L 2444 3201
Semff M 10372
Seminara S 8298 9517 10864
Semmler M R10807
Senior D 4483 4530s 4956
Senna P R4007
Seow C 3216 3273 E7094
Sérandour A 8128 E377
Serra A 5340 7820 R9028 i Oller J TR7207
Serraima C R1351 3986
Servais J 7618

Sesboüé B 4226 7245 7349 R6118
Sessner H 10373
Setzer C 7850 9026 9275
Severianos Gabala M11507
Sevilla Jiménez C 3899
Sevin M 602
Sevrin J 5754 9388
Seybold Klaus 2785 2809 2934 E138 2816
Sezer T 10482
Sfar M 9704
Sferco L 4501
Sforno 'Ô 1465
Shae G 5875
Shaer M 10780
Shalev S 10194
Shanks H 8129 8788 9788 9789 10152 10653 10657 11753 E306 339 8787 10151
Shapira A E161 M M8104 8106 8123
Shapiro A 10536 M 1249 S 8789
Sharon M 8315
Sharp C 3693 8886
Shavit Y 11361
Shaw Brent 9462 C 2586 I 10957 10974
Shea W F83
Shead A 3252
Shedinger R 4484
Sheehan W E478
Sheeley Steven 1369 R4006
Shelmerdine Cynthia 11060
Shemesh A 8934 9027
Shenk W E7568
Shepherd J 2844
Sheres I 8935
Sheridan J 5349
Sheriffs D 7095
Sherman A 7779

1977 2065 4392
11653-54 11666
11673 11686
11720 $^R$100 7191
Smet J $^T$2918
Smillie G 6646
Smit J 5486 6459
6462 6472 6474
6509
Smith A 769 6129
10647 **B** 3861 **C**
1806 2381 4532 **D**
4599 $^R$11233 **G**
5187 **H** 2556
10979 **J** 11055 **L**
$^R$11589 **M** 1929
2888 2987 5757
10841 10842
$^F$5756 $^M$9044
$^R$3620 8338 9504
**P** 3593 11267
$^E$8491 **R** $^M$3392
11671-72 $^R$9620
10280 **S** 11292 **T**
5758 **W** 9431 -
**Christopher D**
11264 $^E$232 $^R$2660
8167 8975 9431
Smithline H 10538
10695
Smyth F $^R$9627 9971
Snape S $^R$9927
Sneed M 3253
Snell D 3177 9793
$^R$3196
Snodgrass K 3550
4228 4533 5426
$^R$7231
Snyder G 5759
$^R$6651 **H** 4910
Snyman G 770 2670
$^R$1758
Soards Marion L
$^R$6199 6666
Soares-Prabhu G $^F$89
$^M$11727
Sobolewski R 10930
Sobrino J 7351 7770
$^M$7288
Socrates $^M$4936
Soden W von 8301s
11804 $^R$8268

Söding T 4017 4609
6184s 6232 6721
$^E$47 188
Soesilo D 11159
Soggin A 1530 1610
1631 3657 9794
$^R$297 991 1454
1528 1979 2521
2582s 9784 11796
Sokoloff M $^E$1319
$^R$1438 8233
Solari G 631
Soldano C $^{ET}$3078
Söldner M $^E$10471
Sole L 3236 **S** $^R$1348
Soljačić I 4802
Sollamo R 8374
Sölle D 9278
Söllner P 6012
Soloff R 8161
Solomon A 8130 **N**
$^R$1607
Soloveitchik Joseph
$^M$11711
Solov'ëv V 6915
Somaratna G 9708
Somers V 11501
Sommer B $^R$3901
Song B 6425 **J** 3584
Sonnet J 2258 3079
$^R$3120 3157 3161
Sonô F 9432
Soranzo M 5360
Sorci P 5359
Sorel A 4360
Sorg T 771
Sorkin D $^R$11640
Sorrentino D $^R$7325
**S** $^R$3794
Sörries R $^E$73
Sotomayor M $^R$8638
Souček J 977 1204
4633 6183 6540
6807 6851 $^M$11728
Soukup P 1432 $^E$233
Soulen K 4393 6896
$^R$3454
Souletie J 1162 7947
Soupa A 1855 2786
4361 5760 10627s
10893
Southall A 11265

Southern M 8215 **P**
10104
Southwell A $^R$11723
Souzenelle A de
7912
Søvndal S $^R$1399
Sowers Sidney G
$^R$4941 7629
Spadaro A $^R$4332
Spaeth P $^T$2056
Spalinger A $^R$9857
Spanu P $^E$10812
Sparks H 11805
Spatafora A 6013
Spatz L 11023
Speckman M 5249
Spencer F $^R$6350 **J**
$^E$9915 **P** $^E$10999 **S**
5538 $^R$4950
Sperlich W 9987
Sperling D $^R$2328
Spero S 8501
Sperti L $^R$10526
Speyr A von 3423
6820 6903 7822
Spicq C 432 8375
Spieckermann H 927
1856 7024 7096
Spiegel Y 4958
Spieser C 9632 **J**
10375
Spijkerboer A $^T$6275
Spina F 1828 2421
Spineto N 9433
Spinks Bryan $^R$4905
6791
Spinoza B $^M$1486
11639 11641
11659
Spittler R 7653
Spivey N 10300
10405 $^E$10467
Spoerl K $^R$11246
Sponde J de 2864
Šporčić I 3844
Spottorno V 10073
Spreafico A 1930
3926 8009s
Sprinkle J 11266
Spronk K 3929
Spycket A 11698
$^F$90

Stollberg D 897
Stolper M 8257
Stolz F 8058 9561 $^E$347 $^R$2476
Stone B $^R$9772 **K** 774 7097 **L** 1208 **M** 8567 8887
Stoneman R 10030
Stoof Magdalena $^R$10283 10428
Stordalen T $^R$3001 3010 6954
Stott D $^T$416 **J** 6722
Stow K 9145
Stowasser M 5096 7750 11772
Strabo $^M$9487 11213
Strahm D 7353
Stramare T 4566 $^R$3969 4547
Strand K $^R$6060
Strange J 1780 4233 10692 $^R$2294
Stratton Beverly 3579 7913
Straus J 10129
Strauss M 5250
Stravinsky I $^M$4356
Streck M $^R$8302
Strecker G 1209s 4627 5909 7987 4019 $^E$433
Streete G 775 1043
Strege M 4913
Strelan R 6632
Stricher Joseph 2846 4567-4570 5251 5323ss 5540
Stricker B 9633
Strickert F 2692
Strijdom J 1632
Strijp R 6987
Stringfellow William $^M$881
Strobel A 6744
Strohl J 4914
Stronach D 9963
Strong J 9795 $^R$3710
Stronstad R 5252
Stroobant de S-É J $^R$2810 $^T$2810
Strotmann A 3292
Stroud R 11058

Stroumsa Guy 9434 9500
Strozier C $^E$6063
Strübind K 2157
Strutwolf H $^R$9409
Strydom J 3425
Stuckenbruck Loren 3802 6014 8888 $^{ET}$8829 $^R$2003
Stucky R 10179
Studer B 868 1211-13 11397 11533s $^E$241 $^R$2896
Stüer C $^T$1132
Stuhlmacher P 979 7988 $^E$3582 $^F$92 $^M$701 791
Stuhlman D 3498
Stuhlmueller C $^E$446
Sturm J 9796
Stutschinsky A 633
Stutz P 2847
Stylianopoulos Theodore 776
Suárez González A 11583
Suchocki M 1711
Sudbrack J 9329
Suermann H $^R$1318
Sugden C 7571
Sugirtharajah R 7354 $^E$261
Suhl A $^R$5101
Sulaimanije T 10894
Suleiman A $^E$11001
Sullivan Blair $^T$120 3419 **L** 777 7703
Sulowski J 1613
Sulyok E 5347
Summers R 8376
Summerson H 1370
Sun H $^E$48
Sundberg W 11641
Sundermann W 9349
Sundermeier T $^E$236
Surmar B 3426
Susin L 4316 7704
Susman M 3033
Sutton R $^R$10284
Suzuki Y 2259
Svensson J 5888
Swain S $^E$8426
Swancutt D 5824

Swanson D 8889 **J** 1439 **R** 163 1279 2382 4485
Swarat U 928
Swartley W 5097 5439
Sweder K $^R$4431
Sweek J $^R$2243
Sweeney M 2362 3458 3551 3609 7192 $^R$2246 2640 3401 3925 $^M$2517
Sweet J P M $^F$93 **R** 11332
Sweetland D 5253 $^R$5656
Swetnam J 5788 8377 $^D$6150 6444 $^R$5853
Swidler L $^E$7310
Świerczek E 7093
Swoboda A 11586
Swüste G $^E$6202
Sybertz D 814
Sykes S 3935
Sylvestre P 10630
Symeon M $^M$1310
Synek E 2101
Synnes Martin 6023 6726
Syreeni K 4536
Sys J $^R$3007
Szabó F 4997
Székely J 5413s
Szesnat H 6988
Szidat J $^R$10097
Szlufik-Szczęsna E $^T$4777
Sznycer M 8216 10130 $^R$11792
Szpek H 3034 $^R$1852
Szwarc U 1877

**T**abachnick Stephen 10181
Tábet Miguel Á 9282 $^D$4043
Tabuyo Ortega M 605
Tadmor Hayim 1012 8303 9964
Tafferner A 2370

Tiradritti F $^E$9466

Tissot Yves 11499 $^T$9384

Tite P 6811

Tkacz C 1334

Tobin T 8614

Tobler J 485

Tödt I $^E$1667

Tolbert Mary 5098 $^E$228

Toll C 7424

Tollefson K 2683 6852

Tollington J 3936

Tolmie D 5872

Toloni G 2633s

Tolve-Vincenza Umberto $^T$4691

Tomber R $^E$11018

Tombs D 4201 7338 7360 $^E$221 256

Tomes R 3650

Tomic C $^F$96

Tomlin G 6426

Tomson P 4240 9035 9099 9284

Ton J 7706

Tondok W 11122 **S** 11122

Toni R 5584

Tonietti M 10873

Toperoff S 9058

Torallas T 8615

Tornos A 7165

Török L 9917

Torrance I 11568 **T** 779

Torremans R 10540

Torró J $^T$5027

Tosaus J 1097

Toschi S 2960

Tosello V 5810

Tosi M 9579

Tournay R 8958

Tournier M 2004

Touwen Klaas 4813 5296

Tov E 1239ss 1304 1451 2427 3459 3627 8791 8830 $^E$3624

Tovar Paz F 11576

Tovey D 5762

Towner S 3217

Townsend J $^T$9100 **M** 6837

Trabacchin G 2005 2049

Trabucco G 7507

Tracy S $^E$359

Traczow B 10996

Tragan P 5627 $^F$57

Traherne T $^M$4355

Trapp J 1457

Trask R 8503

Traunecker C 2579 9635

Traverso A $^T$11573

Travis Stephen 559 606

Treanor O 4961

Trebilco P 9036

Trebolle Barrera J 1305 8751ss

Tredici K del $^E$27

Treier D 3856

Trela J 4764

Tremolada P 5485

Trémouille M 9564

Trenchard W 10458

Trevett C 9330

Trevijano Etchevarria R 5544 9389s

Trexler R 4585

Triacca A $^E$355

Trible P 3901

Trigg J $^E$1978

Trigger B 9918

Trimaille M 6126 6623

Trintignac A 10632

Tripathi C 11809

Tripodi A $^E$1115

Tritle L $^E$10031

Trobisch D 980

Trocmé É 4020 5552 6495

Troía P $^E$10249

Troiani L 1306 10032 $^E$8531

Trombatore S 5099

Tromp J 8547 8566 8568

Tronina A 8831

Tropper Joseph 2378 8218s 8316 8486

10844-7 10975s

Troschina N 780

Trott zu Solz H von 9285

Trotter A 6745

Troxell H 10561

Troy L 7916

Troyer K de 2724s 7917

Trublet J $^E$3149

Trudinger P 5453 5804

Trujillo L 4241

Trummer P 6015

Trunk D 4713s

Tsafrir Y 11117

Tschirschnitz Alfred 8063

Tshidibi B 2466

Tsipopoulou Metaxia 11334

Tsuji M 6853

Tsukimoto A 8305

Tsumura D 8064 $^E$1547

Tubach J 9391

Tubb J 10806 **K** $^E$309

Tucci L 1013

Tucker G 3428 3482 7007 $^F$97

Tuckett C M 4396 4439s 4457 $^E$234 5329

Tudor-Craig Pamela 10378

Tuell S 3743

Tullock J 560

Tully M 4242

Tunca Önhan 10875 10915

Tuñi J 4407 5628s

Tuplin C 10033

Turcan R 11070

Turek Waldemar 6203 11755

Turiot C 1214

Turner J $^E$341 **M** 5254 7392 8673s **P** 7751

Twelftree G 4715

Twomey V $^E$681

Tyloch W $^T$8832

Van Staden P 5440
Van Straten F 9482
Van 't Riet P 5763
Van Tilborg S 5766
Van Tongerloo A
E9334 11274
Van Uchelen N 8939
Van Veldhuizen P
5179
Van Walsem René
10541
Van Wieringen A
3595 3512
Van Winkle D 3564
3597ss
Van Wolde E 1531
1615 2405-8 3040
8069 E342
Van Wyk D 7246
Van Zyl H 4414 S
5331
Vana L 9060
Vandenabeele      F
E397
Vandenbroeck Paul
7709
Vandeput L 10222
11042
Vander Stichele C
1017
VanderKam J 1821
8542  8562  8583
8793  8892  8940
E8745 8792
Vandermeersch Pat-
rick 1145
Vandersleyen Claude
9919
VanGemeren Willem
E436
Vanhetloo W 7451
Vanhoozer K 784s
Vanhoye A 871 913
1216  4403  5332
6566  6746  6769
7452 7655s 7710
11733 E6746 6768
Vanni U 7657
Vannier M 2902
Vannini F 11200
Vanoni G 828
Vanstiphout H L J
E8307

Vanstone W 7525
Vanzan P 7772
Vara Donado José
E10074
Vardy P 4031
Vargyas P 11293
Varó F 7404
Vasey M 7098
Vasholz R 7194
Vassiliadis P 6016
Vauchez A D454
Vaux R de 561 8794
Vaydat P 3041
Vaz A dos Santos
1633
Vecchio S 6938
Veenhof K 11294
Veeser A 786
Veijola T E2260
Veilleur J 4999
Velasco-Delgado A
TE11572
Velema W D7714
Veltri G 8966 9118
Venema G 1980
Venetz H 6253 7393
7573
Venit M 10303
Venter P 3791 3798
Ventura M 1123
Ventzke W F10542
Verburg Winfried
4584 6517
Verdeyen P E3081
T3110
Verdon T E10380
Vereecken J E101
Vergani V 929
Vergeer C 4247s
Vergote A 2267
Verheij A 8070
Verhelst Stéphane
7711 8458
Verhey A M7714
Verheyden J 5189
Verhoef E 5418
6693
Vermes Geza 4282s
8795
Vermeylen J 2261
3524 3651 3764
Vernant J 9444
Verner M 10998

Vernet J 7574
Vernieux R 9920
Vernus Pascal 9847
9921s
Verrier J 1069
Verseput D J 6855
6857
Vervenne M 2050
8157 E1888
Vesco J 2905 2964
Vetrali T 6017s
Vetter D 9037
Via D 6917
Vian F TE9501s G
1307 9288
Vianès L 3950
Viau M 7202
Vicent Saera R 2158
Victor U TE9483
Vicuna L 3850
Vidal D E4773 J
T1134 M 4284s S
5630
Vidovic F 6991 M
5159
Vieweger D 10441
Viganò D 4327
Vigée C 607
Vignolo R 5102s
5767
Vikan G 11350
Vikström B 787
Viladrich M 8317
Vilanova E 7712
Vílchez Líndez J
3218
Villanueva M T7307
Villard P 11090
Villefranche H de
11351
Villeneuve F 11103s
E386 10201
Villey A 9350
Vinel F 3255s T3219
Vintinner D 3765
Vinzent M 11484
Viotto P 1124
Virgulin      Stefano
2702 3485
Vironda M E1454
Vischer L 11133
Visentin M 5370
Visicato G 8306

» 11399 **G** 3765 **I**
8075s **N** 6193 **R**
1152 8384 9707s
Younger L [E]203
Younker R 10758
10769
Ysebaert J 7619
Yurco F 2311

**Z**accagnini C 2121
Zadok Ran 9966-67
11091
Zager W 5109 6585
Zaghloul M [E]10746
Zäh A 11041
Zahniser M [E]49
Zahrnt H 4256
Zakovitch Y 2926
3350
Zaleski J 5911 6513
7855 **P** 6496
Zamora J 8199
Zanchettin L [E]4488
Zandee J 9639
Zangenberg J 8959
10781
Zani L 5154
Zanker Paul 9464
10307 [E]407
Zannini P 4581
Zannoni A 4257
Zapff B 3513 3908
Zardoni S 7620
Zaretsky T 7425
Zarras K 3496
Zarzeki-Peleg Ana-

bel 10711
Zauzich K 8338
Zawadzki S 9982
Zayadine F 9570
10788 10796-97
11106
Zdun P 8839
Zehetbauer M 7759
Zehnder M 8135
Zeidler J 11107
Zeilinger F 6522
Zeitler J 10798
Zeller D 4962
Zemánek P 8222
Zemka S 805
Zenger E 566s 608
873 1492 1590
2803 2812 2851s
2981 2986 3447
3511 4400 9294ss
10383 [E]564s 2816
Zeplowitz I 9043
Zerafa P 7103
Zerhusen B 6504
Zervos G 8725
Zerwick M 8385
Zevini Giorgio 5657
5770s 5789
Zevit Z 8960
Zewi T 8077 8137
Zgoll A 9687
Zgorzelski A 832
Zias J 11190
Zibelius-Chen Karo-
la 9928
Ziegler C 10406
10169 [E]10168 **N**

9725
Ziehr W 7509
Ziffer I 10308
Zimhoni O 10478
10728 11815
Zimmermann Hans
[E]663 **J** 7158
Zincone S 3437
Zink J 7659 -
**Sawyer B** 900
5143
Zinn G 11602
Zipes J [E]450
Zipor M 1754
Zivie A 1982 9929s
-Coche C 9592
9640
Zizioulas J [M]7332
Zonhoven L 9931
Zorn J 1220 10546
10659s
Zovkić M 6641
Zschoch H 3267
Zuber H 557
Zuck R 1018 [E]806
3044 7195 7363
Zucker D 3438
Zumstein J 807 5632
5772 5892
Zundel M [M]1692
Zuurmond R 5193
9848
Zwickel W 2544
2582 10156 10665
Zwiep A 5257
Zwingenberger Uta
11278

# Situs

ʾOded 10645
ʿAin Fattir 8458
ʿAïn ez-Zâra/Callir-
rhoé 10759
al Rimah 10466
ʿAqaba 10643
ʿAyin Zakkar 8204
ʿEn Asawir 10477
ʿEn Boqeq 10644
Abu Ḫǧaira 10877

Abu Hafur 10878
Abu Rish (Beit
ʿAnun) 10646
Abusir 2571
10997s
Abydos 10257
Ain Ghazal 10461
Akko 10451
Aleppo 10879s
Alexandria 8710

9874 10013 10303
10996
Amara 10999
Anafa 10693
Antiochia 10881
Araba 10647
Arwad 10882
Ash-Shorabat 10760
Ashdod 9778
Asherat 10186

Naḥal-Beṣet 10707ss
Nami 393
Naukratis 11012
Nazareth 7663
10731s
Netiv-Hagdud 10775
Nimrud 10279
10929s
Nineveh 9963
10932s
Nippur 9683 10934
Nizzana 10476
Nuzi 10189 10935
Oboda 10217
Palmyra 11205
Pella 10776
Persepolis 10006
Petra 289 311 8243
8252 8437 10082
10179 10777-800
11129
Pompei 8464
Qara Quzaq 10906
Qurnah 11013
Ra's al-Jins 10941
Rabbat-Moab 10764
Rijim 10936

Sabi Abyad 10907s
Sabratha 11018
Safi 10801
Sagalassos 10222
11042
Sais 9638
Samaria 2584 2630
10172 10556
10676-82
Saqqara 2556 10979
10981
Sepphoris 10223
10437 10733-43
Serabit el-Ḥadim
2551 9525 9580
11014
Shaʿab 10499
Shechem 2310
Shiloh 10683
Shioukh-Fawqani
8234
Sidon 4780 10502
10809
Sippar 10483
Suleimeh (Hamrin)
10408
Susa 10943 10945s

11080
Šiqmim 10299
Tanis 11015s
Tawilan 10802
Terqa 10419 10465
10473 10909-15
Thebes 10514 10518
10531 10961-5
11017
Timnah-(Tel Batash)
10662s
Troy 10146
Tyre 2043 10811
Umm-el-Biyara
10803s
Umm-el-Marra
10916
Ur 10939
Urkiš 10937
Uruk 9493 9666
9681
Uruk-Warka 10938
Wadi-Faynan 10805
Yarmut 10664
Zafon 10806
Zora 10665

# Voces

**Akkadicae**

adê 2283
*baqaru* 8136
*inūma* 8137
*nābutu* 8138
*naparšudu* 8138
*šimtu* 9670

**Aramaicae**

*ḥmnʾ* 8139
*maṭṭar* 8140
*smr* 8231

**Graecae**

ἀγάπη 8386s
ἀγιωσύνη 1301 8388

αἰών 8389
Ἄλας 8390
ἀποσυνάγωγοσ
8391
ἀρραβών 8392
Ἄρτος 5902
βασιλικός 5815
Βοανηργές 8393
διαθήκη 6613 8394
δοῦλος 8395
δόχα 1301 8388
εἰκών 8396
ἔμπορος 8428
ἕξις 6782
ἐπιούσιος 8397
ἐπίτροπος 8398
καιρός 8399s
καρδιογνώστης 8401
καταλάσσω 6193

κατέχον 6711
κοιλία 6667
κρίσις 6148
κύριος 5508 7247
λαικός 8402
μορφή 8396
νόμος 8403s
Οἶκος; οἰκία 8405
οἰκουμένη 5292
ὁράω 5623
ὅτι 3255
παιδαγωγός 8406
παῖς 8395
παράκλητος 8407
πειρασμός 8408
πίστις 8409-13
πώρωσις 8414
σκεῦος 6706
σορος 5406

# Sacra Scriptura

24: 2472
25: 2472 2496
26: 2471 10048
28: 2430 2473-6
30: 10055
31,1-6: 2451

## 2 Samuel

1,17-27: 2484
1,19: 2451
2,31: 2485
3,33-34: 2486
4,1-12: 2487
5,6-8: 2488s
5,8: 2490
6,1-23: 2488
6: 10049
7: 2491ss 2932 7124
11,2-27: 1020
11: 2494
12,1-12: 1048
12: 2477
13,1-22: 1806 2495 7857
13: 1054 1837 2472 2496
14,5: 8000
14: 2497
15,34: 8000
18,9-33: 2498
18,9: 2499
21,1-14: 2500
21,4-14: 2501
21,15-22: 10050
21: 2475
23,1-7: 2502
23,8-37: 10050
24,6: 11194

## 1 Regum

1-2: 6984
1-11: 2520 2533 7907
3-11: 2519 2523 2527 2530s
3,16-18: 2540
3,16-27: 809

3,16-28: 2541
4,3: 2542
4,7-19: 2543s
4: 11194
6-7: 2575 2580
7,19-8,19: 8818
9,17-18: 2545
10,1-13: 2546s
11-14: 2548
11,1-4: 2522
11,26-40: 10047
11: 2585
12,24: 2585s
12: 2587 10063
13,11-32: 2588
13: 1048 2589
14: 2430 2585
16,32: 2590
17-19: 2594
17,1-22,38: 3408
17: 2593 5584
18: 2605 9503
19,1-18: 2605
20,13: 1996
20: 2430 2514 2604
21: 2477 2613
22,19-25: 2601
22: 2430 2608

## 2 Regum

1,2-10,28: 3408
3: 2514
5,1-19: 2621
5,14-17: 7056
5: 2514 2622s
6,8-7,17: 2514
6,24-7,20: 2624
8,13: 2625
9,1-10,36: 2626 10061
11,1-3: 2627
11: 2628
12,1-22: 10051
16,5-9: 8168
16: 2629
17,21-23: 2630

21,1-18: 2631
21,3-16: 2635
21,11: 11194
21: 2632
22-23: 3690
22: 9840
23,11: 2633s
23,21-23: 2041
23,26-27: 2635
23: 9840
24,3-4: 2635
25,27-30: 9840

## 1 Chronica

1-9: 2665
7,21-24: 2666
11,6: 2489
13-16: 10049
21: 2667
22-2 Chr 9: 2523
25,1-7: 2668
25,4: 2671
27,30: 2671
29,15: 8151

## 2 Chronica

1-9: 2527 2530s 2538
3-4: 2580
10-13: 2548
11,5-12: 2669
14-16: 2670
17,7: 2671
22,11: 2627
24,1-27: 10051
24,26: 2671
26,11-15: 2672
26,11-23: 3670
28,9: 2671
29-31: 2673
35,22: 2430
35,25: 3670

## *Esdras*, **Ezra**

1,1-11: 3670
9,6-7: 2684

## Nehemias

5,1-13: 3685
5,1-19: 2685
5,6-11: 2686
5: 2113 11253
8,10: 6931
9: 1501 2687 7556
10,10-11: 2688
10,36-37: 8034
13,2: 2228
13,23-31: 2689

## Esther

1,11: 2724
2,17: 2724
6,8: 2724
8,1-17: 2725
8,15: 2724

## *1 Machab.*

1,44-51: 3806

## *2 Machab.*

7,13: 7163

## Psalmi

1,3: 3146
1: 2779 2871
2: 2872s 5818 7124
6: 7857
8,3: 2874
8: 137 2875ss
11,5: 8034
13: 2878
16: 2879s
18,2: 2881
22,1: 2882
22,17: 2883
22: 2884s
23: 2886ss
24: 2889
25: 2890
26: 2878
27: 2878
28,6: 2765
29,9: 2891

14,1-10: 3294
16-19: 3295
16,15-17,1:
  3296
17,1-18,4:
  3297
17,4-15: 3293
19,1-9: 3291

*Ecus,* **Sirach**

1,11-30: 3342
1: 3343
2,1-6: 3344
2,1-18: 3345
2: 3346
6,18-37: 3347
17,1-10: 8565
22,27-23,6:
  3349
36,1-22: 3349
37,13-14: 6960
39,12-35: 3262
46,6:  3350
46,13-20: 3351
48,1-49,16:
  3352
50,26: 8958
51,21-35: 3353

**Isaias**

1-11: 3487
1-39: 3480
1,2-9: 3488
1,2: 3489
2,1-5: 3490ss
5,1-7: 3493s
6,1-4: 2563
6,3: 2074 2130
6,9-10: 5129
6: 3501s 10292
7-11: 137
7,1-17:    137
  3503    7912
  8168
7,14:    3504-7
  4542
7,14-17: 137
8,5-10: 3508
8,16-9,6: 3596
8,19-23: 3509
8,23-9,1: 4542

9,5: 3510
11,1-10: 3511
12,1-6: 3512
13: 3513
14,12-15: 3514
14,13: 9523
14,29: 10292
15,1: 10764
22,15-25: 3515
22,22: 4782
24-27: 3516
25,6-8: 3517
25,10: 3518
26,13-27,11:
  3519
26,19: 7163
27,10-11: 3520
28,14-22: 3517
29,1-8: 7912
30,15-35,5:
  1329
30,15: 3521
30: 3522
34-35: 3523
35,5-39,8:
  1329
35,6: 2490
36-39: 3524
40,1-41,20:
  1329s
40,1-11: 3554
40,3-5: 3555
40,3: 3556
40,6-8: 3557
40,19-46,7:
  3558
40,20: 3559
40: 3560
41,26: 3561
41,28: 3561
42,5-9: 3576
42,8: 1996
42,10-12: 3562
43,2: 3563
43,11: 1996
44,1-5: 3564
44,24-45,7:
  3565
44,24-25: 3253
44,26-28: 3566
45,5: 1996
45,7: 3567
45: 4797

46,13-50,3:
  3568s
47,1-3: 3570
47,7: 3571
49,1-6: 3577
49,7-12: 3576
49,14-26: 3572
49-55: 3578
50,1-11: 3573
50,10-11: 3576
51,20: 8149
51,21: 3138
52-53:    3446
  3453 3579
52,7: 1786
52,13-53,12:
  5477
53,1-12: 3580
53,4: 4692
53,9: 8147
53,10: 3581
53,12: 5485
53: 3582s 7096
54,9: 8149
54,11-17: 3517
55,1-5: 3584
55: 3585 5824
56-59: 3596
56,1-7: 5173
56,1-8: 3597
56,5: 3598
56,6: 3599
58,1-2: 3600
58,1-13: 3601
58,10: 3602
58: 3603
59,19: 3604
59:   552  3601
  6884
60,1-22: 3467
60,1-63,6:
  3605
60: 3517 10591
61,1-2: 1786
61,1-3: 3606s
61,6: 2154
61,10-11: 3608
61:  4131  4240
  5404
63,9: 6879
63,15: 6879
65-66: 3609
65,11-16: 1226

    3611
65,16-25: 3610
66,24: 8958

**Jeremias**

1,1-19: 3653s
1:  3397  3655
  7056
2: 3656
3,16: 3657
3,17: 3658
4,5-31: 3659
4,23: 3660
6,25: 3661
7-20: 3662
7,11-15: 5173
7: 7456
8,8-9:    3907
  3948
9,22-23: 3663
10,1-16: 3664
10,12-13: 8838
13,12:    2380
  5075 5800
17,5-8: 2779
17,19-27: 3656
18,1-12: 3665
18,7-10: 3397
18,18-23: 3666
20,3: 3661
20,10: 3661
23,5-6: 3671
23,18-24: 3048
23,25-40: 3667
25,1-29: 3668
25,10: 3669
25,11-12: 3670
25,15-33: 3671
26,36-43: 3672
26: 3397 7456
28,5: 3673
28: 3397
29,10: 3670
30-31: 3674s
30-33: 3676
31,8-9: 3671
31,20: 6879
31,31-34:
  3677-80 9034
  11693
31,31-37: 3681
31,33:    3682

•

5787 5789
1,5-6: 10424
1,7: 5684
1,16: 5790
1,18: 5791s
1,26: 5898
1,29: 5793
1,32: 4602
1,35-51:   5794
    5898
1,45-51: 5795
2,1-11:    2380
    5075    5796-
    5800
2,1-12: 5801
2,3-4: 5745
2,6: 5802
2,10: 5803
2,13-22:   5175
    5804
2,15: 5805
3,25: 5807
3,35: 5715
4,1-41: 5808s
4,5-42: 5810
4,6: 5811
4,14: 5812
4,23-24: 5813s
4,46-53: 5815
4: 739 1822
5,1-47: 5816
5,17-23: 5817
5,17-29: 5818
6,1-14: 5820
6,1-15: 5821
6,15-21: 5822
6,16-21: 5823
6,22-71: 5824
6,25-71: 5825
6,27: 9380
6,37-46:   4730
    6946
6,51-58: 5826
6,54: 5827
6,60-71: 5828
6:   4892   5671
    5829-40
7-8: 484 5841s
7,37-39: 5843
7,53-8,11:
    5844ss
8,2-11: 5847
8,3: 5848

8,12: 5849
8,29: 4131
8,32: 5850
8,39-47: 5851
8,57: 1276
9: 5852s
10,1-18: 5854s
10,11-18: 5856
10,11: 5857
10,27-29: 5715
10,34: 5733
10,40-11,54:
    5858s
11,25-27: 5860
11,35: 4249
11,54: 5861
11: 5862 10247
12,12-19: 4826
    10627
12,31: 5863
12,38: 5733
13-17:     5646
    5870s 5878
13,1-17,26:
    5872
13,1-5: 5873
13,1-20: 9439
13,2-11: 5874
13,3: 5715
13,9: 5875
13,26: 5876
13,31-16,33:
    5877
13: 5879s
14,27: 5881
15: 5882
16: 5882
17,1-26: 5883
17: 5884
18-21: 5885
18,9: 5886
18,28-19,16:
    5887
18,39: 5803
18: 5888
19,16-30: 5889
19,24: 5733
19,25-27: 5892
19,26-27: 5745
19,28-30: 5893
19,28: 5894
19,30: 5895
19: 5888

20-21: 5896
20,1-18: 5897s
20,21: 7056
20,23: 5899
20,24-29: 5900
20,29: 5901
20,31: 5684
21,1-14: 5823
21,9: 5902
21,15-17: 5903
21,15-19: 5904
21,25: 5905
21: 5906

**Actus Apostol.**

1,8: 5232 5557
1,14: 7783
1,15-26: 5558
1,18-19: 1385
1,21: 5513
1,24: 8401
2,1-13:    2148
    5559
2,1-47: 5560
2,6: 2148
2,14-40: 5561
2,14-41: 5250
2:   5562   6504
    7456
3,1-10: 5563
3: 5564
4: 5564
4,25: 10258
4,30: 10334
5,1-11: 5565
5,12: 10334
5,29: 5566
5,38-39: 5567
6,1: 5553
6,2-4: 6803
6,7: 6803
6,8-7,60: 5319
6: 5568
7,2-17: 5569
7: 5570s
8,5-25: 5572s
8,26-40: 5574
8,26: 5575
9,1-19: 5576
9,3-7: 5537
9,10-16: 5577
9,26-30: 5544

9: 5578
10-11: 5579
10,1-11,18:
    11571
11,27-30: 5544
12,25: 5544
13-14: 5585
13,4-12: 5586
13,16-41: 5250
13,16-52: 5587
13,32-33: 5304
13,48-14,20:
    5588
14,7-20: 5589
14: 5496 5590
15,1-21: 5591
15,1-29: 5592
15,1-35: 5544
15,8: 8401
15,16-18: 5593
15,20: 6029
15,29: 6029
15,41-16,10:
    5594
15: 5595s
16,11: 8397
16,26: 5537
17,16-34: 5594
    5597-00
17,18: 5601
17,22-34: 5602
17,32: 5601
18,18-22: 5603
18: 5604s
19,23-40: 5606
21,15-26: 5595
21,15-27: 5603
21,15-36: 5319
23,12-15: 5319
23,24-26:
    5607s
28,17-31: 5609
28,30-31: 5610

**Ad Romanos**

1-8: 6314
1,1-7: 6315
1,14: 6225
1,16-3,31:
    6316
1,16: 6317
1,17: 3931

Finito di stampare
nel mese di gennaio 2001

presso la tipografia
"Giovanni Olivieri" di E. Montefoschi
00187 Roma - Via dell'Archetto, 10,11,12

ISBN 88-7653-614-0

W
1577